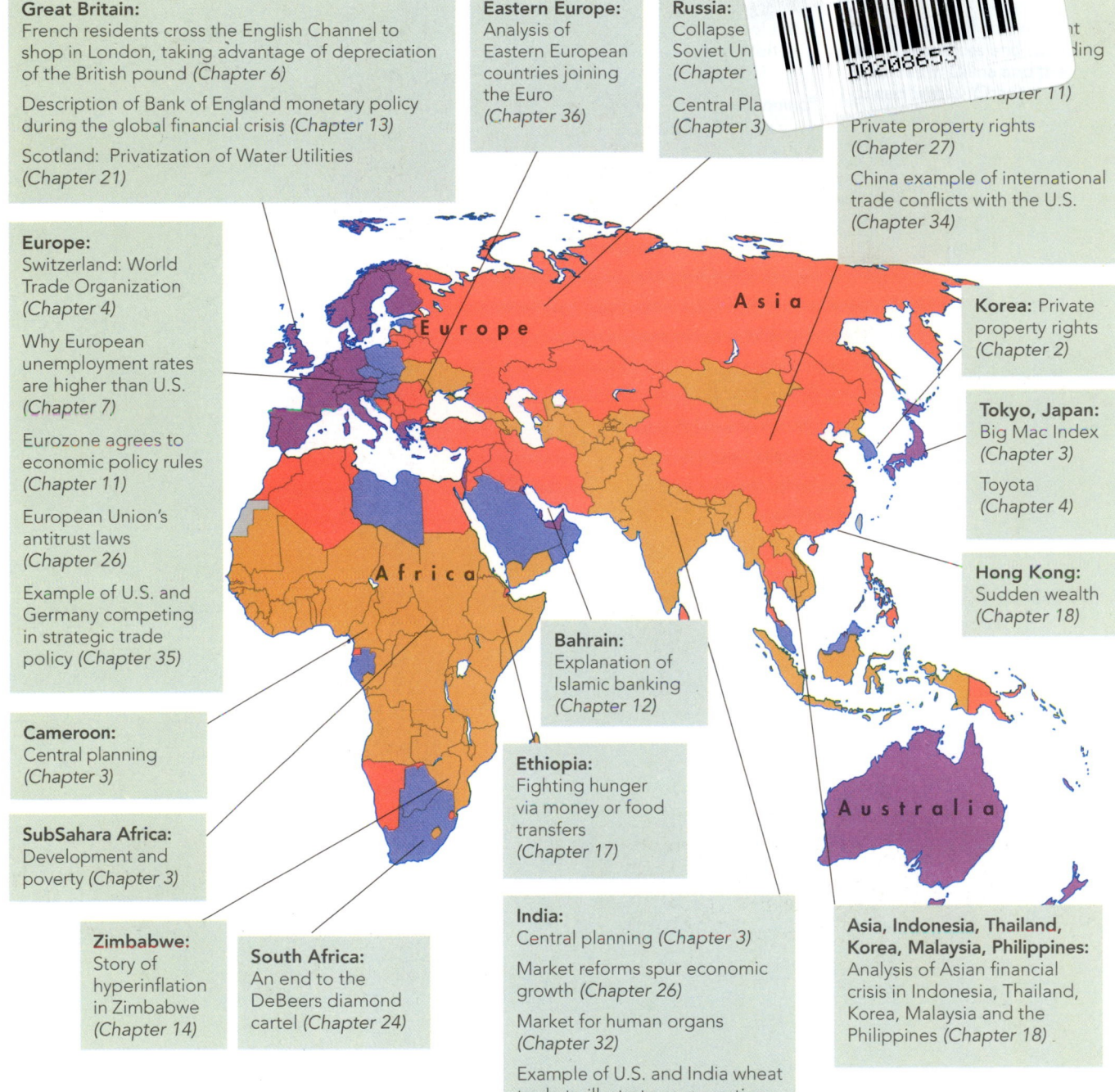

Great Britain:
French residents cross the English Channel to shop in London, taking advantage of depreciation of the British pound *(Chapter 6)*

Description of Bank of England monetary policy during the global financial crisis *(Chapter 13)*

Scotland: Privatization of Water Utilities *(Chapter 21)*

Europe:
Switzerland: World Trade Organization *(Chapter 4)*

Why European unemployment rates are higher than U.S. *(Chapter 7)*

Eurozone agrees to economic policy rules *(Chapter 11)*

European Union's antitrust laws *(Chapter 26)*

Example of U.S. and Germany competing in strategic trade policy *(Chapter 35)*

Cameroon:
Central planning *(Chapter 3)*

SubSahara Africa:
Development and poverty *(Chapter 3)*

Zimbabwe:
Story of hyperinflation in Zimbabwe *(Chapter 14)*

South Africa:
An end to the DeBeers diamond cartel *(Chapter 24)*

Eastern Europe:
Analysis of Eastern European countries joining the Euro *(Chapter 36)*

Russia:
Collapse ... Soviet Un... *(Chapter ...)*

Central Pla... *(Chapter 3)*

... ...ding *(Chapter 11)*

Private property rights *(Chapter 27)*

China example of international trade conflicts with the U.S. *(Chapter 34)*

Korea: Private property rights *(Chapter 2)*

Tokyo, Japan:
Big Mac Index *(Chapter 3)*

Toyota *(Chapter 4)*

Hong Kong:
Sudden wealth *(Chapter 18)*

Bahrain:
Explanation of Islamic banking *(Chapter 12)*

Ethiopia:
Fighting hunger via money or food transfers *(Chapter 17)*

India:
Central planning *(Chapter 3)*

Market reforms spur economic growth *(Chapter 26)*

Market for human organs *(Chapter 32)*

Example of U.S. and India wheat trade to illustrate comparative advantage *(Chapter 34)*

Asia, Indonesia, Thailand, Korea, Malaysia, Philippines:
Analysis of Asian financial crisis in Indonesia, Thailand, Korea, Malaysia and the Philippines *(Chapter 18)*

WILLIAM BOYES • MICHAEL MELVIN

WILLIAM BOYES • MICHAEL MELVIN

economics
NINTH EDITION

Economic understanding in a Global Context...
no borders, no boundaries!

Boyes and Melvin's *Economics, 9e* introduces students to the latest thinking of today's economists on important economic phenomena while equipping them with a solid global understanding of economic principles. With this edition's reader-friendly approach, carefully integrated learning features, memorable examples, and unique global emphasis, you can clearly illustrate the connections between key economic principles and today's actual business practices.

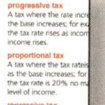

Updated Economic Insight boxes emphasize the relevance of concepts to current events. These new features highlight some of today's most current events to focus on the relevance and real-world applications of the concepts in the chapter.

New and updated Economically Speaking and Commentary features highlight the economic impact of today's most important events. Recent newspaper and magazine articles in this edition's updated and new Economically Speaking and Commentary features present economic causes and consequences of important world events.

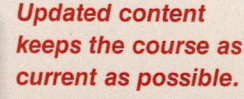

Updated content keeps the course as current as possible.

Updated examples throughout the text, extensive revisions to the chapter on elasticity, further development of the debate on government economic intervention, and a new discussion of the Economic Freedom Index keep this course up-to-date with current developments. You'll also find additional material on game theory, updated information on health care costs, and a detailed examination of income distribution.

Economic understanding in a Global Context

... no borders, no boundaries!

Economics CourseMate

Economics CourseMate brings course concepts to life with interactive learning, study, and exam-preparation tools that support the printed textbook. Watch student comprehension soar as your class works with the printed textbook and the text-specific website. Economics CourseMate goes beyond the book to deliver what you need!

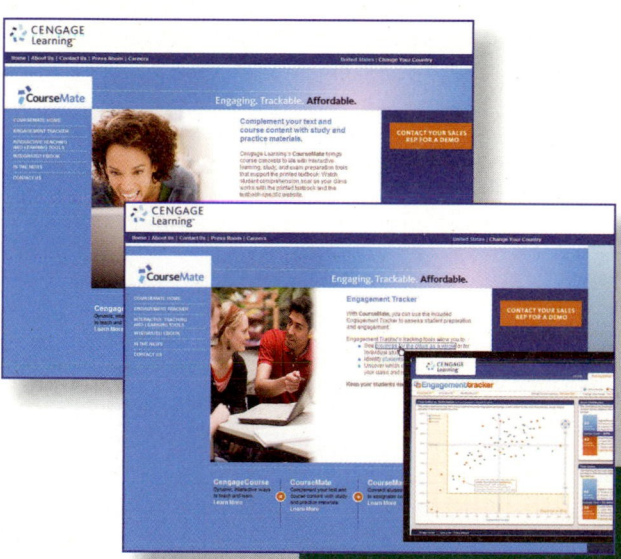

CourseMate

Engagement Tracker

How do you know your students have read the material or viewed the resources you've assigned? Engagement Tracker assesses student preparation and engagement. Use the tracking tools to see progress for the class as a whole or for individual students. Identify students at risk early in the course. Uncover which concepts are most difficult for your class. Monitor time on task. Keep your students engaged.

Interactive Teaching and Learning Tools

Economics CourseMate provides interactive teaching and learning tools including:

- Quizzes
- Flashcards
- Graphing Tutorials
- Videos
- News, Debates, and Data

Interactive eBook

In addition to interactive teaching and learning tools, Economics CourseMate includes an interactive eBook. Students can take notes, highlight, search and interact with embedded media specific to their book. Go to **login.cengage.com** to access these resources within CourseMate.

*Learn more at **www.cengage.com/coursemate**.*

Global Economic Watch

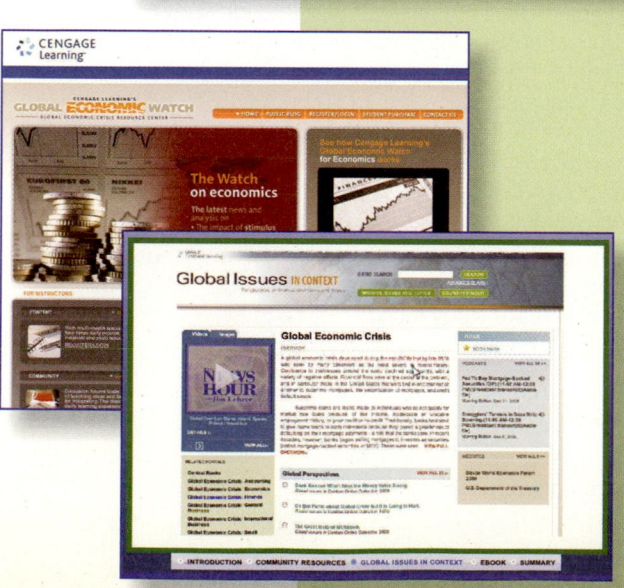

CENGAGE LEARNING'S
GLOBAL ECONOMIC WATCH
GLOBAL ECONOMIC CRISIS RESOURCE CENTER

The Watch, a groundbreaking resource, stimulates discussion and understanding of the global downturn.

- A content-rich blog of breaking news, expert analysis, and commentary—updated multiple times daily.
- A powerful real-time database of hundreds of relevant and vetted journal, newspaper, and periodical articles, videos, and podcasts—updated four times every day.
- A thorough overview and timeline of events leading up to the global economic crisis.
- Discussion and testing content, PowerPoint slides on key topics, sample syllabi, and other teaching resources.

*For more information, visit **www.cengage.com/thewatch**.*

Economic understanding in a Global Context ... no borders, no boundaries!

ADDITIONAL OPTIONS FOR *ECONOMICS, 9E*

CenageNOW

This robust, online course management and learning system gives instructors the tools they need and students the practice they need to be successful. For instructors, it includes resources organized around lecturing, creating assignments, grading, quizzing, and tracking student progress and performance. Students can use a Personalized Study diagnostic tool to determine areas that need more study focus. Built-in technology tools help students master concepts as well as prepare for exams.

www.cengage.com/coursemaster

WebTutor

WebTutor is an online teaching and learning system that provides text-specific media assets, quizzing, weblinks, discussion topics, interactive games and exercises, and more to supplement the classroom experience and ensure that students leave with the resources they need to succeed in today's business world.

Tomlinson Videos

This dynamic online multimedia video lecture series provides students with instructional assistance in economic concepts 24/7. Students can watch these brief video segments as often as they wish to prepare for class, review topics or study for exams.

Cenagebrain.com

On CengageBrain.com students will be able to save up to 60% on their course materials through our full spectrum of options. Students will have the option to rent their textbooks, purchase print textbooks, e-textbooks, or individual e-chapters and audio books all for substantial savings over average retail prices. CengageBrain.com also includes access to Cengage Learning's broad range of homework and study tools, and features a selection of free content. Students can:

- Study in less time to get the grade they want... using online resources such as chapter quizzing, flashcards, and interactive study tools.
- Prepare for tests anywhere, anytime.
- Practice, review, and master course concepts... using printed guides and manuals that work hand-in-hand with each chapter of this textbook.

www.cengagebrain.com

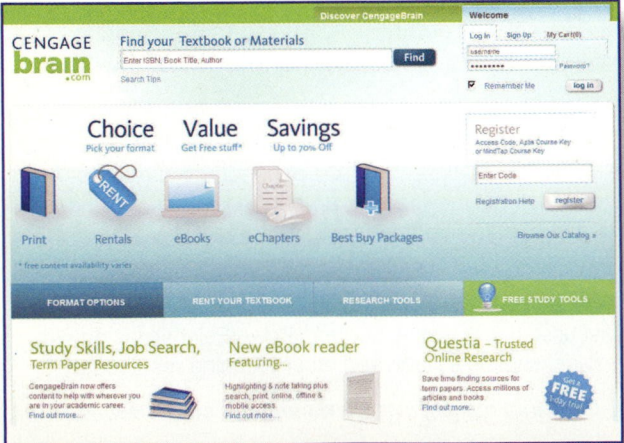

economics

NINTH EDITION

WILLIAM BOYES

Arizona State University

MICHAEL MELVIN

Arizona State University and BlackRock

SOUTH-WESTERN
CENGAGE Learning·

Australia · Brazil · Japan · Korea · Mexico · Singapore · Spain · United Kingdom · United States

SOUTH-WESTERN
CENGAGE Learning®

Economics, Ninth Edition
William Boyes, Michael Melvin

Vice President of Editorial, Business: Jack W. Calhoun

Publisher: Joe Sabatino

Acquisitions Editor: Steve Scoble

Developmental Editor: Clara Goosman

Editorial Assistant: Allyn Bissmeyer

Sr. Marketing Manager: John Carey

Sr. Content Project Manager: Tamborah Moore

Media Editor: Anita Verma

Manufacturing Planner: Kevin Kluck

Marketing Communications Manager: Sarah Greber

Marketing Coordinator: Betty Jung

Production Service: Cenveo/Cadmus

Sr. Art Director: Michelle Kunkler

Cover and Internal Designer: Chris Miller

Cover Image: © Maciej Frolow/Getty Images, Inc.

Rights Acquisitions Specialist text and images: Amber Hosea

Text permissions researcher: Vinodh Ramachandran/PMG

Image permissions researcher: Scott Rosen/ Bill Smith Group

For product information and technology assistance, contact us at
Cengage Learning Customer & Sales Support, 1-800-354-9706

For permission to use material from this text or product, submit all requests online at **www.cengage.com/permissions**
Further permissions questions can be emailed to
permissionrequest@cengage.com

Exam*View*® is a registered trademark of eInstruction Corp. **Windows** is a registered trademark of the Microsoft Corporation used herein under license. Macintosh and Power Macintosh are registered trademarks of Apple Computer, Inc.

Cengage Learning WebTutor™ is a trademark of Cengage Learning.

Library of Congress Control Number: 2011943695

ISBN-13: 978-1-111-82613-0
ISBN-10: 1-111-82613-7

South-Western Cengage Learning
5191 Natorp Boulevard
Mason, OH 45040
USA

Cengage Learning products are represented in Canada by Nelson Education, Ltd.

For your course and learning solutions, visit **www.cengage.com**
Purchase any of our products at your local college store or at our preferred online store **www.cengagebrain.com**

To Melissa, Katie, and Lindsey –W. B.
To Bettina, Jason, Jeremy, Anna, and Sonia –M. M.

brief contents

contents

Part Two

MACROECONOMIC BASICS

CHAPTER 5

National Income Accounting 93

Part Four
PRODUCT MARKET BASICS

suggested outlines for one-term courses*

* Chapter numbers represent *Economics, 9th ed.* For *Macroeconomics, 9th ed.,* and *Microeconomics, 9th ed.,* see the conversion chart in the Brief Contents section.

preface

In the first edition of *Economics*, we integrated a global perspective with traditional economic principles to give students a framework to understand the globally developing economic world. Events since then have made this approach even more imperative. In the 1990s, the Soviet Union disintegrated and newly independent nations emerged. Much of Latin America was turning toward free markets and away from government controls. But by 2005, several of these nations were turning back—away from free markets. Hugo Chavez and Evo Morales were guiding Venezuela and Bolivia away from free markets and toward government-run and controlled economies. Vladimir Putin was driving Russia toward more government control. Other events were making the world seem very small: North Korea was testing nuclear weapons, Somalia was embroiled in a civil war, terrorism was prevalent in nations around the world, and much of Africa remained mired in poverty. In 2007, the interconnectedness of nations was once again highlighted when the world fell into a recession created by the housing collapse in the United States. When economic growth returned in the summer of 2009, it was slow and unemployment remained high. In 2011 the European Union and the eurozone are facing severe challenges as Greece, Portugal, Spain, Italy, and Ireland face debt burdens that some believe will not be repaid.

Students and instructors have embraced the idea that the economies of countries are interrelated and that this should be made clear in the study of economics. *Economics* gives students the tools they need to make connections between the economic principles they learn and the now-global world they live in.

In this edition, we continue to refine and improve the text as a teaching and learning instrument while expanding its international base by updating and adding examples related to global economics.

Changes in the Ninth Edition

The ninth edition of *Economics* has been thoroughly updated and refined, taking into account the events of 2008–2011. A detailed account of all the additions, deletions, and modifications can be found in the Transition Guide in the *Instructor's Resource Manual* (found on the instructor's site at www.cengage.com/economics/boyes and also on the Instructor's Resource CD).

Revised Macroeconomic Coverage

The focus of this new edition has been to ensure that the information and discussion faithfully represent the latest thinking of economists on important macroeconomic phenomena. To this end, many small additions and revisions appear throughout. Larger changes of note include: many applications to the recent financial crisis and associated recession appear throughout the macro section; in Chapter 11, potential solutions to the debt crisis in the eurozone are addressed; Chapter 13 now includes a discussion of a recent Federal Reserve policymaking meeting where inflation worries were deemphasized and avoiding slower growth and recession were primary concerns; Chapter 14 contains a new example of the hyperinflation in Zimbabwe—the worst in recent times; Chapter 16 has a new example of cross-country differences in broadband usage to illustrate differences in levels of development; Chapter 35 has a new example of U.S. sugar quotas to illustrate why U.S. sugar prices are higher than the rest of the world; and Chapter 36 uses the crisis in the eurozone as a lesson in how a currency union requires harmonious macro policies among member countries to survive.

The macroeconomic chapters have all been updated to include the latest available economic statistics. In many chapters, numerical examples have been revised to provide greater clarity in the graphical presentations, and many of the Economically Speaking boxes and commentaries have been revised or replaced with more current examples of economic activity around the world.

Revised Microeconomic Coverage

The principal objective of the microeconomic material is to enable students to see the forest while wandering around in the trees; to learn the fundamentals while seeing their applicability to current events. Changes in the ninth edition have been made to further that objective. The debate about whether governments should intervene in economies is further developed in Chapters 26 and 27. Additionally, in Chapter 12 a discussion of the Economic Freedom Index has been added. In Chapter 25, the discussion of kinked demand curve has been eliminated and additional game theory material has been included. Chapter 32 on aging and health care has been updated and a discussion of why health care costs continue rising is included. In addition, a market for human organs is discussed. In Chapter 33, a detailed examination of income distribution has been included. In every chapter examples have been updated and global applications provided.

Successful Features Retained from the Eighth Edition

In addition to the considerable updating and revising we've done for the ninth edition, there are several features preserved from the previous edition that we think instructors will find interesting.

Enhanced Student Relevance

With all of the demands on today's students, it's no wonder that they resist spending time on a subject unless they see how the material relates to them and how they will benefit from mastering it. We incorporate features throughout the text that show economics as the relevant and necessary subject we know it to be.

Real-World Examples Students are rarely intrigued by unknown manufacturers or service companies. Our text talks about people and firms that students recognize. We describe business decisions made by McDonald's and Wal-Mart, and by the local video store or café. We discuss standards of living around the world, comparing the poverty of sub-Saharan Africa to the wealth of the industrial nations. We discuss policies applied to real-world economic issues. We talk about political, environmental, and other social issues. These examples grab students' interest. Reviewers have repeatedly praised the use of novel examples to convey economic concepts.

Economic Insight Boxes These brief boxes use contemporary material from current periodicals and journals to illustrate or extend the discussion in the chapter. By reserving interesting but more technical sidelights for boxes, we lessen the likelihood that students will be confused or distracted by issues that are not critical to understanding the chapter. By including excerpts from articles, we help students move from theory to real-world examples. And by including plenty of contemporary issues, we guarantee that students will see how economics relates to their own lives.

Economically Speaking Boxes The objective of the principles course is to teach students how to translate to the real world the predictions that come out of economic models, and to translate real-world events into an economic model in order to analyze and understand what lies behind the events. The Economically Speaking boxes present students with examples of this kind of analysis. Students read an article at the end of each chapter. The commentary that follows shows how the facts and events in the article translate into a specific economic model or idea, thereby demonstrating the relevance of the theory. Nearly two-thirds of the articles and commentaries are new to the ninth edition, and cover such current events as U.S. trade with China, the collapse of consumer confidence during the financial crisis, illegal immigration, Venezuela's redistribution of wealth, high gasoline prices, the impact of the government's bailout of large companies, the true effects of "fair trade" coffee, and the change in India's permit raj.

Global Business Insight Boxes These boxes link business events and developments around the world to the economic concepts discussed in the main text of the chapters. Topics include such basic micro- and macroeconomic issues as global competition, resource pricing, and foreign exchange.

An Effective and Proven System of Teaching and Learning Aids

This text is designed to make teaching easier by enhancing student learning. Tested pedagogy motivates students, emphasizes clarity, reinforces relationships, simplifies review, and fosters critical thinking. And, as we have discovered from reviewer and user feedback, this pedagogy works.

In-Text Referencing System Sections are numbered for easy reference and to reinforce hierarchies of ideas. Numbered section heads serve as an outline of the chapter, allowing instructors flexibility in assigning reading and making it easy for students to find topics to review. Each item in the key terms list and summary at the end of the chapter refers students back to the appropriate section number.

The section numbering system appears throughout the Boyes and Melvin ancillary package; *Study Guides* and *Instructor's Resource Manual* are both organized according to the same system.

Fundamental Questions These questions help to organize the chapter and highlight those issues that are critical to understanding. Each fundamental question also appears in the margin next to the related text discussion and, with brief answers, in the chapter summaries. A fuller discussion of and answer to each of these questions may be found in the *Study Guides* that are available as supplements to this text. The fundamental questions also serve as one of several criteria used to categorize questions in the *Test Banks*.

Preview This motivating lead-in sets the stage for the chapter. Much more so than a road map, it helps students identify real-world issues that relate to the concepts that will be presented.

Recaps Briefly listing the main points covered, a recap appears at the end of each major section within a chapter. Students are able to quickly review what they have just read before going on to the next section.

Summary The summary at the end of each chapter is organized along two dimensions. The primary organizational device is the list of fundamental questions. A brief synopsis of the discussion that helps students to answer those questions is arranged by section below each of the questions. Students are encouraged to create their own links among topics as they keep in mind the connections between the big picture and the details that make it up.

Comments Found in the text margins, these comments highlight especially important concepts, point out common mistakes, and warn students of common pitfalls. They alert students to parts of the discussion that they should read with particular care.

Key Terms Key terms appear in bold type in the text. They also appear with their definition in the margin and are listed at the end of the chapter for easy review. All key terms are included in the Glossary at the end of the text.

Friendly Appearance

Economics can be intimidating; this is why we've tried to keep *Economics 9th edition* looking friendly and inviting. The one-column design and ample white space in this text provide an accessible backdrop. More than 300 figures rely on well-developed pedagogy and consistent use of color to reinforce understanding. Striking colors were chosen to enhance readability and provide visual interest. Specific curves were assigned specific colors, and families of curves were assigned related colors.

Annotations on the art point out areas of particular concern or importance. Students can see exactly which part of a graph illustrates a shortage or a surplus, a change in consumption, or a consumer surplus. Tables that provide data from which graphs are plotted are paired with their graphs. Where appropriate, color is used to show correlations between the art and the table, and captions clearly explain what is shown in the figures and link them to the text discussion.

The color photographs not only provide visual images but make the text appealing. These vibrant photos tell stories as well as illustrate concepts, and lengthy captions explain what is in the photos, again drawing connections between the images and the text discussion.

Thoroughly International Coverage

Students understand that they live in a global economy; they can hardly shop, watch the news, or read a newspaper without stumbling upon this basic fact. International examples are presented in every chapter but are not merely added on, as is the case with many other texts. By introducing international effects on demand and supply in Chapter 3 and then describing in a nontechnical manner the basics of the foreign exchange market and the balance of payments in Chapter 6, we are able to incorporate the international sector into the economic models and applications wherever appropriate thereafter. Because the international content is incorporated from the beginning, students develop a far more realistic picture of the national economy; as a result, they don't have to alter their thinking to allow for international factors later on. The three chapters that focus on international topics at the end of the text allow those instructors who desire to delve much more deeply into international issues to do so.

The global applicability of economics is emphasized by *using traditional economic concepts to explain international economic events and using international events to illustrate economic concepts that have traditionally been illustrated with domestic examples.* Instructors need not know the international institutions in order to introduce international examples, since the topics through which they are addressed are familiar; for example, price ceilings, price discrimination, expenditures on resources, marginal productivity theory, and others.

Uniquely international elements of the macroeconomic coverage in the text include:

- The treatment of the international sector as an economic participant and the inclusion of net exports as early as Chapter 4
- The early description of the foreign exchange market and the balance of payments in Chapter 6
- International elements in the development of aggregate demand and supply
- An entire chapter devoted to globalization

Uniquely international elements of the microeconomic coverage in the text include:

- The treatment of the international sector as an economic participant and the inclusion of net exports as early as Chapter 4
- Extensive analyses of the effects of trade barriers, tariffs, and quotas
- An examination of strategic trade
- An examination of dumping as a special case of price discrimination
- The identification of problems faced by multinational firms
- A comparison of behavior, results, and institutions among nations with respect to consumption, production, firm size, government policies toward business, labor markets, health care, income distribution, environmental policy, and other issues

Modern Macroeconomic Organization and Content

Macroeconomics is changing and textbooks must reflect that change. We begin with the basics: GDP, unemployment, and inflation. These are the ongoing concerns of any economy, for they have a significant influence on how people feel. These are the issues that don't go away. In addition to these core topics is an easy-to-understand, descriptive introduction to the foreign exchange market and the balance of payments. We provide a critical alternative for those instructors who believe that it is no longer reasonable to relegate this material to the final chapters, where coverage may be rushed.

Armed with these basics, students are ready to delve into the richness of macroeconomic thought. Macro models and approaches have evolved over the years, and they continue to invite exciting theoretical and policy debates. The majority of the instructors we asked voiced frustration with the challenge of pulling this rich and varied material together in class, and stressed that a coherent picture of the aggregate demand and supply model was critical. We have structured the macro portion to allow for many teaching preferences while ensuring a clear delineation of the aggregate demand/aggregate supply (*AD/AS*) model.

To help instructors successfully present a single coherent model, we present aggregate demand and aggregate supply first in Chapter 8, immediately following the chapter on inflation and unemployment. This sequence allows for a smooth transition from business cycle fluctuations to *AD/AS*. The Keynesian income and expenditures model is presented in full in Chapters 9 and 10 as the fixed-price version of the *AD/AS* model (with a horizontal aggregate supply curve). Those who want to use the *AD/AS* model exclusively will have no problem moving from the Chapter 8 presentation to the fiscal policy material in Chapter 11. The policy chapters rely on the *AD/AS* model for analysis.

The macroeconomic policy chapters begin with a thorough presentation of fiscal policy, money and banking, and monetary policy, with international elements included. Chapter 14 covers contemporary policy issues, and various schools of thought are treated in Chapter 15, when students are ready to appreciate the differences between and can benefit from a discussion of the new Keynesian and new classical models as well as their precursors.

Part Five, "Product Markets," brings together the concepts and issues presented in the core macro chapters to explain how economies grow and what factors encourage or discourage growth. Most of the world's population live in poor countries. Growth and development are critical to those people. The material in these chapters also addresses issues of importance to industrial countries, such as the determinants of productivity growth and the benefits and costs of globalization.

Part Eight, "Issues in International Trade and Finance," provides a thorough discussion of world trade, international trade restrictions, and exchange rates and links between countries.

Modern Microeconomic Organization and Content

Instructors often face a quandary when teaching microeconomic material. They want students to understand the basic theories of economics and the powerful intuition that thinking like an economist can provide, but they also want to enlist students' attention with real-life, current issues. In the ninth edition of *Microeconomics,* theory is never far away from applications. One of the primary lessons of microeconomics is captured in Bastiat's "Broken Window Fallacy." When it seems that some policy or some action will solve a certain problem, what we often do is focus on that problem and fail to examine the unseen—what is the possible effect of the policy? Will the policy solve the problem but actually create greater problems? For instance, students may think that a ban of some behavior might be beneficial but they fail to see that the ban may harm others more than help those it is supposed to help. In this text we ensure that students can see why environmental issues such as pollution and the razing of rain forests occur but we also teach about the costs and benefits of various proposed solutions to these problems. Students can see why incomes are unequal within a country and among countries and can learn about the costs and benefits of attempting to reduce inequality. Students can see why collusion occurs among competing firms and what the costs and benefits are of minimizing such behavior through antitrust action or regulation.

Part Four presents basic concepts such as elasticity, consumer behavior, and costs of production. Parts Five and Six both begin with overview chapters (Chapter 22 on profit maximization and Chapter 28 on resource markets). These overviews give students a chance to look at the big picture before delving into details they often find confusing. Chapter 22, for instance, gives students an intuitive overview of market structures before they explore each type of structure in more detail in succeeding chapters. Chapter 22 lightens the load that the more detailed chapters have to bear, easing students into the market-structure material. Traditional topics are covered in the separate market structure chapters, Chapters 23 to 25, but the coverage is also modern, including such topics as strategic behavior, price discrimination, nonprice competition, and the economics of information. Having fought their way first through the cost curves and then the market structures, students often complain that they do not see the relevance of that material to real-world situations. The intuitive overview chapter alleviates some of that frustration.

A Complete Teaching and Learning Package

In today's market no book is complete without a full complement of ancillaries. Those instructors who face huge lecture classes find good PowerPoint slides and a large variety of reliable test questions to be critical instructional tools. Those who teach online in distance or hybrid courses need reliable course management systems with built-in assignments and resource materials. Other instructors want plenty of options available to their students for review, application, and remediation. All of these needs are addressed in the Boyes and Melvin supplements package. And to foster the development of consistent teaching and study strategies, the ancillaries pick up pedagogical features of the text—such as the fundamental questions—wherever appropriate.

Support for Instructors

Instructor's Resource Manual (IRM)

Patricia Diane Nipper has produced a manual that will streamline preparation for both new and experienced faculty. Preliminary sections cover class administration, alternative syllabi, and an introduction to the use of cooperative learning in teaching the principles of economics.

The *IRM* also contains a detailed chapter-by-chapter review of all the changes made in the ninth edition. This Transition Guide should help instructors more easily move from the use of the eighth edition to this new edition.

Each chapter of the *IRM* contains an overview that describes the content and unique features of the chapter and the objectives that students will need to master in order to succeed with later chapters; the chapter's fundamental questions and key terms; a lecture outline with teaching strategies—general techniques and guidelines, essay topics, and other hints to enliven classes; opportunities for discussion; answers to every end-of-chapter exercise; answers to *Study Guide* homework questions; and active learning exercises.

Testing Materials

Printed Test Banks Two separate *Test Banks* for *Macroeconomics* and *Microeconomics,* edited and revised by Mike Ryan of Gainsville State College and Chin-Chyuan Tai of Averett University, are available with this edition of *Economics.* In all, more than 4,000 test items, approximately 20 percent of which are new to this edition, provide a wealth of material for classroom testing. Features include:

- Multiple choice, true/false, and essay questions in every chapter
- Questions new to this edition marked for easy identification
- An increased number of analytical, applied, and graphical questions
- The identification of all test items according to topic, question type (factual, interpretive, or applied), level of difficulty, and applicable fundamental question

ExamView

This testing software contains all of the questions in the printed test bank. This program is an easy-to-use test creation software compatible with Microsoft Windows. Instructors can add or edit questions, instructions, and answers; and select questions by previewing them on the screen, selecting them randomly, or selecting them by number. Instructors can also create and administer quizzes online, whether over the Internet, a local area network (LAN), or a wide area network (WAN). The ExamView testing software is available on the Instructor's Resource CD.

Instructor Online Resources

The Boyes and Melvin ninth edition provides a rich store of teaching resources for instructors online at www.cengage.com/economics/boyes. Instructors will need to sign up at the site for a username and password to get onto the password-protected parts of the site. This site includes a variety of support materials to help you organize, plan, and deliver your lectures; assign and grade homework; and stay up-to-date with current economics news. Here you'll find a thoroughly updated set of multimedia PowerPoint slides covering key points in each chapter, with graphs, charts, and photos. An online version of the *Instructor's Resource Manual* contains solutions to end-of-chapter exercises and discussion questions.

Aplia Online Learning Platform

Founded in 2000 by economist and professor Paul Romer in an effort to improve his own economics courses at Stanford, Aplia is the leading online learning platform for economics. Aplia provides a rich online experience that gets students involved and gives instructors the tools and support they need. The integrated Aplia courses offered for Boyes and Melvin include math review/tutorials, news analyses, and online homework assignments correlated to the relevant Boyes and Melvin text. In addition, a digital version of the text is embedded in the course to make it easy for students to access the text when completing assignments. Instructors should consult their South-Western/Cengage Learning sales representative for more information on how to use Aplia with this text.

Support for Students

Student Online Resources

The student companion website, located at www.cengagebrain.com, lets students continue their learning at their own pace with practice quizzes, chapter summaries, online exercises, and flashcards, among other online resources.

Acknowledgments

Writing a text of this scope is a challenge that requires the expertise and efforts of many. We are grateful to our friends and colleagues who have so generously given their time, creativity, and insight to help us create a text that best meets the needs of today's students.

We'd especially like to thank the many reviewers of *Economics* listed on the following pages who weighed in on key issues throughout the development of each edition. Their comments have proved invaluable in revising this text. Unsolicited feedback from current users has also been greatly appreciated.

We would also like to thank Patricia Diane Nipper of Southside Virginia Community College for her work on the ninth and previous editions of the *Instructor's Resource Manual.* Thanks also to Chin-Chyuan Tai of Averett University and Mike Ryan of Gainsville State College for their intensive work on the *Test Banks,* and for their attention to the accuracy of the text. Carol Conces of UC Berkeley provided excellent research assistance in revising the 9th edition.

We want to thank the many people at South-Western/Cengage Learning who devoted countless hours to making this text the best it could be, including Steve Scoble, Clara Goosman, Tamborah Moore at Cengage Learning, and Rachitra Suresh Kumar of Cenveo.

Finally, we wish to thank our families and friends. The inspiration they provided through the conception and development of this book cannot be measured but certainly was essential.

Our students at Arizona State University continue to help us improve the text through each edition; their many questions have given us invaluable insight into how best to present this intriguing subject. It is our hope that this textbook will bring a clear understanding of economic thought to many other students as well. We welcome any feedback for improvements.

W. B. M. M.

Reviewers

Okechukwu Dennis Anyamele
Jackson State University—Jackson, MS

David Black
University of Toledo—Toledo, OH

Gary Bogner
Baker College-Muskegon—Muskegon, MI

Rick Boulware
University of South Carolina—Beaufort Beaufort, SC

Bradley Braun
University of Central Florida—Orlando, FL

William S. Brewer
Genesee Community College—Batavia, NY

Gregory Brown
Martin Community College—Williamston, NC

Kristin Carrico
Umpqua Community College—Roseburg, OR

Jill L. Caviglia
Salisbury State University—Salisbury, MD

Mitch Charkiewicz
Central Connecticut State University—New Britain, CT

Kenny Christianson
Binghamton University—Binghamton, NY

Mike Cohick
Collin County Community—College Plano, TX

Valerie A. Collins
Colorado Mountain College—Glenwood Springs, CO

Wilfrid W. Csaplar, Jr.
Southside Virginia Community College—Keysville, VA

Bob Cunningham
Alma College—Alma, MI

Steven R. Cunningham
University of Connecticut—Storrs, CT

Stephen B. Davis
Valley City State University—Valley City, ND

Lynne Pierson Doti
Chapman University—Orange, CA

Raymond J. Egan
WA (Retired, formerly at Pierce College),—Lakewood, WA

Martha Field
Greenfield Community College—Greenfield, MA

Fred Fisher
Colorado Mountain College—Glenwood Springs, CO

Davis Folsom
University of South Carolina, Beaufort—Beaufort, SC

Kaya V. P. Ford
Northern Virginia Community College—Alexandria, VA

Bradley Garton
Laramie County Community College—Laramie, Wyoming

Omer Gokcekus
North Carolina Central University—Durham, NC

R. W. Hafer
Southern Illinois University—Edwardsville, IL

Michael Harsh
Randolph-Macon College—Ashland, VA

Arleen Hoag
Owens Community College—Toledo, OH

Calvin Hoy
County College of Morris—Randolph, NJ

Miren Ivankovic
Southern Wesleyan University—Central, SC

James Johnson
Black Hawk College—Moline, IL

Jeff Keil
J. Sargeant Reynolds Community College—Richmond, VA

Donna Kish-Goodling
Muhlenberg College—Allentown, PA

Ali Kutan
Southern Illinois University—Edwardsville, IL

Nikiforos Laopodis
Villa Julie College—Stevenson, MD

John D. Lathrop
New Mexico Junior College—Hobbs, NM

Paul Lockard
Black Hawk College—Moline, IL

Glenna Lunday
Western Oklahoma State College—Altus, OK

Leslie Manns
Doane College—Crete, NE

Dan Marburger
Arkansas State University—Jonesboro, AR

Buddy Miller
Carteret Community College—Morehead City, NC

Stan Mitchell
McLennan Community College—Waco, TX

Charles Okeke
Community College of Southern Nevada—Las Vegas, NV

Robert Payne
Baker College—Port Huron, MI

John C. Pharr
Cedar Valley College—Lancaster, TX

Dick Risinit
Reading Area Community College—Reading, PA

Rose M. Rubin
University of Memphis—Memphis, TN

Robert S. Rycroft
Mary Washington College—Fredericksburg, VA

Charles Saccardo
Bentley College—Waltham, MA

Charles Sackrey
Bucknell University—Lewisburg, PA

Rolando Santos
Lakeland Community College—Kirkland, OH

Karen Rapp Schultes
University of Michigan—Dearborn, MI

Gerald Scott
Florida Atlantic University—Boca Raton, FL

J. Richard Sealscott
Northwest State Community College—Archbold, OH

Steve Seteroff
Chapman University College—Silverdale, WA

James R. Shemwell
Mississippi County Community College—Blytheville, AR

Richard Skolnik
SUNY-Oswego—Oswego, NY

Scott F. Smith

University at Albany, State University of New York—Albany, NY

Thom Smith
Hill College—Hillsboro, TX

John Somers
Portland Community College,—Sylvania Portland, OR

John P. Speir Jr.
The University of Hartford—West Hartford, CT

John J. Spitzer
State University of New York College at Brockport—Brockport, NY

Chin-Chyuan Tai
Averett University—Danville, VA

Rob Verner
Ursuline College—Pepper Pike, OH

Michele T. Villinski
DePauw University—Greencastle, IN

Larry Waldman
University of New Mexico—Albuquerque, NM

Mark E. Wohar
University of Nebraska—Omaha, NE

Edward M. Wolfe
Piedmont College—Athens, GA

Darrel A. Young
University of Texas—Austin, TX

Girma Zelleke
Kutztown University—Kutztown, PA

Boyes/Melvin Advisory Board

Peter Allan
Victor Valley College—Victorville, CA

Warren Bilotta
Louisiana State University—Alexandria, LA

Julie Derrick
Brevard Community College—Cocoa, FL

David Eaton
Murray State University—Murray, KY

Jafar Geranssayeh
Palomar Community College—San Marcos, CA

Lisa Grobar
California State University—Long Beach, CA

Jeff Keele
Porterville College—Porterville, CA

Vani Kotcherlakota
University of Nebraska—Kearney, NE

Vince Marra
University of Delaware—Newark, DE

Gretchen Mester
Anne Arundel Community College—Arnold, MD

Kenneth M. Parzych
Eastern Connecticut State University—Willimantic, CA

Lea Templer
College of the Canyons—Santa Clarita, CA

Hal Wendling
Heartland Community College—Normal, IL

Sourushe Zandvakili
University of Cincinnati—Cincinnati, OH

CHAPTER 1

Economics: The World around You

© MACIEJ FROLOW/GETTY IMAGES, INC

© PIXINITY/SHUTTERSTOCK.COM; LOGO: © FROXX/SHUTTERSTOCK

FUNDAMENTAL QUESTIONS

1 Why study economics?

2 What is economics?

3 What is the economic way of thinking?

Americans today are more educated than ever before. Today, about 31 percent of Americans aged 25 or older hold a college (bachelor's or associate's) degree, whereas 20 years ago, only 19 percent of Americans held a similar degree. Nearly 15.5 million Americans (5 percent of the population) are currently attending college, and over 50 percent of Americans aged 18 to 22 are currently enrolled in a degree program.

Why do people go to college? College has not gotten any cheaper—indeed, tuition and other costs associated with college have risen much more rapidly than average income. Perhaps it is because college is more valuable today than it was in the past. In the 1990s, technological change and increased international trade placed a premium on a college education; more and more jobs required the skills acquired in college. As a result, the wage disparity between college-educated and non-college-educated workers rose fairly rapidly in the 1990s. Those with a college degree could expect to make about 45 percent more than those without a college degree. Since 2001, however, this differential has actually declined. Outsourcing of skilled jobs to China and India may be part of the explanation, and a larger increase in the number of college-educated people than the increase in the jobs requiring college skills may have kept wages from rising. The number of college-trained workers in the United States has grown by 32 percent over the past 10 years, compared with only an 8 percent rise for all other education levels. Still, even though the differential has been declining, college-educated people earn nearly twice as much as people without college degrees over their lifetimes. But college-educated people also often have large student loans they must repay. The net differential depends on what people major in and how long they take to finish their education.

Why are you attending college? Perhaps you've never really given it a great deal of thought—your family always just assumed that college was a necessary step after high school; perhaps you analyzed the situation and decided that college was better than the alternatives. Whichever approach you took, you were practicing economics. You were examining alternatives and making choices. This is what economics is about.

Why do the citizens of different countries have different standards of living? Why is the difference between rich and poor much greater in emerging nations than it is in the industrial nations? Answers to questions like these emerge in your study of economics. In this photo, a shantytown is shown next to new, modern apartment buildings and other structures.

1. Why Study Economics?

1 Why study economics?

Why are you studying economics? Is it because you are required to, because you have an interest in it, because you are looking for a well-paying job, or because you want to do something to help others? All of these are valid reasons. The college degree is important to your future living standards; economics is a fascinating subject, as you will see; an economics degree can lead to a good job; and understanding economics can help policymakers, charities, and individuals think about better ways to help the unfortunate.

1.a. The Value of a Degree

What is the difference between a high school diploma and a medical degree? About $3.2 million (U.S.), says the U.S. Census Bureau. Someone whose education does not go beyond high school and who works full time can expect to earn about $1.2 million between the ages of 25 and 64. Graduating from college and earning an advanced degree translate into much higher lifetime earnings: an estimated $4.4 million for doctors, lawyers, and others with professional degrees; $2.5 million for those with a master's degree; and $2.1 million for college graduates.

Putting money into a four-year college education turns out to be a better financial investment than putting the same money into the stock market, even before the 2006–2009 stock-market collapse. The rate of return on the money spent to earn a bachelor's degree is 12 percent per year, compared with the long-run average annual return on stocks of 7 percent.

In the 1970s, when the information age was young, kids from poorer, less educated families were catching up to kids from more affluent families when it came to earning college degrees. But now the gap between rich and poor is widening. Students in the poorest quarter of the population have an 8.6 percent chance of getting a college degree, whereas students in the top quarter have a 74.9 percent chance. The difference between being college-educated and not extends to more than just income. Divorce rates for college grads are plummeting, but they are not for everyone else. The divorce rate for high school grads is now twice as high as that of college grads. High school grads are twice as likely to smoke as college grads, they are much less likely to exercise, and they are likely to live shorter and less healthy lives.

Once you choose to go to college, how do you choose what to study? A bachelor's degree in economics prepares you for a career in any number of occupations—in business, finance, banking, the nonprofit sector, journalism, international relations, education, or government. Graduates find positions at investment banking companies and public utilities, in real estate and international relations, in government and private organizations. An economics degree is also excellent preparation for graduate study—in law, finance, business, economics, government, public administration, environmental studies, health-care administration, labor relations, urban planning, diplomacy, and other fields.

1.b. What Is Economics?

Economists are concerned with why the world is what it is—it is the study of human behavior. In 1990, the Soviet Union collapsed, setting countries free throughout Eastern Europe and Asia, because of economics. The nations of Latin America are struggling with progress and development because of economics. It is estimated that somewhere between 11 and 20 million people live in the United States illegally, and they do so because of economics. In 2011, many of the nations of the Mideast underwent turmoil as dictators were thrown out. This also stems from economics, and, in fact, every issue in the news today concerns economics. It is a broad, fascinating field of study that deals with every aspect of life.

Economics is often counterintuitive. In fact, economics is probably best defined as the study of *unintended consequences*. When you study economics, you learn that there are costs to everything—there is no free lunch. This is the logic of economics that those who have not studied economics may fail to understand. To give you an idea of how economics is often counterintuitive, consider the story known as "The Broken Window Fallacy," introduced in 1850 by French economist Frédéric Bastiat. A baker had a beautiful front window that allowed him to show off his delights. One day, a punk kid heaved a rock through the window, shattering it. The baker and several local business owners ran out through their doors and began crying about the demise of society and the harm such hooligans do. Then, one man said, "Wait, think about it. This young man actually helped us out. By breaking the window, he made the baker hire a glazier to replace the window. That creates a job for the glazier who then spends his income and this helps others." Bastiat notes that this ignores what you don't see. You see the broken window and the glazier's job, but you don't see what would have happened had the window not been shattered. The baker might have purchased a new pair of boots, thereby creating a job for the boot maker. As a result of the broken window, the boot maker is made worse off. Economics attempts to focus on the unseen as well as the seen; it is for this reason that economics often seems counterintuitive.

Your study of economics will be interesting and challenging. It will challenge some beliefs that you now hold. It will also help you build skills that will be of value to you in your life and in whatever occupation you choose.

2. The Definition of Economics

2 What is economics?

What is economics? It is the study of how *scarcity* and *unlimited wants* lead to certain predictable human behaviors. People have unlimited wants—they always want more goods and services than they have or can purchase with their incomes; they want more time; they want more love, or health care, or chocolate cake, or coffee. Whether they are wealthy or poor, what they have is never enough. Since people do not have everything they want, they have to make choices. The choices they make and the manner in which these choices are made explain much of why the real world is what it is.

2.a. Scarcity

Scarcity is the reason the study of economics exists—without scarcity, there would be no need to worry about who gets what. Everyone would have everything that he or she wants. **Scarcity** of something means that there is not enough of that item to satisfy everyone who wants it. Any item that costs something is scarce. If it were not scarce, it would be free, and you could have as much as you wanted without paying for it. Anything with a price on it is called an **economic good**. An economic good refers to *goods and services*—where goods are physical products, such as books or food, and services are nonphysical products, such as haircuts or golf lessons.

2.a.1. Free Goods, Economic Bads, and Resources
If there is enough of an item to satisfy wants, even at a zero price, the item is said to be a **free good**. It is difficult to think of examples of free goods. At one time people referred to air as free, but with air pollution control devices and other costly activities directed toward the maintenance of air quality standards, *clean* air, at least, is not a free good.

An **economic bad** is anything that you would pay to get rid of. It is not so hard to think of examples of bads: pollution, garbage, and disease fit the description.

Some goods are used to produce other goods. For instance, to make chocolate chip cookies, we need flour, sugar, chocolate chips, butter, our own labor, and an oven. To distinguish between the ingredients of a good and the good itself, we call the ingredients **resources**. (Resources are also called **factors of production** and **inputs**; the terms are interchangeable.) The ingredients of the cookies are the resources, and the cookies are the goods.

Economists have classified resources into three broad categories: land, labor, and capital.

scarcity
The shortage that exists when less of something is available than is wanted at a zero price.

economic good
Any item that is scarce.

free good
A good for which there is no scarcity.

economic bad
Any item for which we would pay to have less.

resources, factors of production or **inputs**
Goods used to produce other goods, i.e., land, labor, and capital.

1. **Land** includes all natural resources, such as minerals, timber, and water, as well as the land itself.
2. **Labor** refers to the physical and intellectual services of people, including the training, education, and abilities of the individuals in a society.
3. **Capital** refers to products such as machinery and equipment that are used in production. You will often hear the term *capital* used to describe the financial backing for some project or the stocks and bonds used to finance some business. This common usage is not incorrect, but it should be distinguished from the physical entity—the machinery and equipment and the buildings, warehouses, and factories. Thus we refer to stocks and bonds as *financial capital* and to the physical entity as capital.

People obtain income by selling their resources or the use of their resources. Owners of land receive *rent*; people who provide labor services are paid *wages*; and owners of capital receive *interest*.

The income that resource owners acquire from selling the use of their resources provides them with the ability to buy goods and services. Producers use the money received from selling their goods to pay for the resource services.

2.b. Choices

Scarcity means that people have to make choices. People don't have everything they want, and they do not have the time or the money to purchase everything they want. When people choose some things, they have to give up, or forgo, other things. *Economics is the study of how people choose to use their scarce resources to attempt to satisfy their unlimited wants.*

2.c. Rational Self-Interest

Rational self-interest is the term that economists use to describe how people make choices. It means that people will make the choices that, at the time and with the information they have at their disposal, will give them the greatest amount of satisfaction, make them the happiest, or provide them the greatest comfort.

You are probably reading this book because you chose to attend college. Many of the people in your age group chose not to attend college. All of you made rational choices based on what you perceived to have been in your best interest. How could it be in your best interest to do one thing and in another person's best interest to do exactly the opposite? Each person has unique goals and attitudes and faces different costs. Although your weighing of the alternatives came down on the side of attending college, other people weighed similar alternatives and came down on the side of not attending college. Both decisions were rational because in both cases the individual compared alternatives and selected the option that the *individual* thought was in his or her best interest.

It is important to note that rational self-interest depends on the information at hand and the individual's perception of what is in his or her best interest. Even though the probability of death in an accident is nearly 20 percent less if seat belts are worn, many people choose not to use them. Are these people rational? The answer is yes. Perhaps they do not want their clothes wrinkled, or perhaps seat belts are just too inconvenient, or perhaps they think the odds of getting in an accident are just too small to worry about. Whatever the reason, these people are choosing the option that at the time gives them the greatest satisfaction. *This is rational self-interest.* Economists sometimes use the term *bounded rationality* to emphasize the point that people do not have perfect knowledge or perfect insight. In this book we simply use the term *rational* to refer to the comparison of costs and benefits.

land
All natural resources, such as minerals, timber, and water, as well as the land itself.

labor
The physical and intellectual services of people, including the training, education, and abilities of the individuals in a society.

capital
Products such as machinery and equipment that are used in production.

rational self-interest
The means by which people choose the options that give them the greatest amount of satisfaction.

Economists think that most of the time most human beings are weighing alternatives, looking at costs and benefits, and making decisions in a way that they believe makes them better off. This is not to say that economists look upon human beings as androids who lack feelings and are only able to carry out complex calculations like a computer. Rather, economists believe that people's feelings and attitudes enter into their comparisons of alternatives and help determine how people decide that something is in their best interest.

Human beings are self-interested, *not selfish*. Selfish has a negative connotation, saying that people have a concern only for themselves. People do contribute to charitable organizations and help others; people do make individual sacrifices because those sacrifices benefit their families or people that they care about; soldiers do risk their lives to defend their country. All these acts are made in the name of rational self-interest.

RECAP

1. Scarcity exists when people want more of an item than exists at a zero price.

2. Goods are produced with resources (also called factors of production and inputs). Economists have classified resources into three categories: land, labor, and capital.

3. Choices have to be made because of scarcity. People cannot have or do everything that they desire all the time.

4. People make choices in a manner known as rational self-interest; people make the choices that, at the time and with the information they have at their disposal, will give them the greatest satisfaction.

3. The Economic Approach

3 What is the economic way of thinking?

Economists often refer to the "economic approach" or to "economic thinking." By this, they mean that the principles of scarcity and rational self-interest are used in a specific way to search out answers to questions about the real world.

3.a. Positive and Normative Analysis

positive analysis
Analysis of what is.

In applying the principles of economics to questions about the real world, it is important to avoid imposing your opinions or value judgments on others. Analysis that does not impose the value judgments of one individual on the decisions of others is called **positive analysis**. If you demonstrate that unemployment in the automobile industry in the United States rises when people purchase cars produced in other countries instead of cars produced in the United States, you are undertaking positive analysis.

normative analysis
Analysis of what ought to be.

However, if you claim that there ought to be a law to stop people from buying foreign-made cars, you are imposing your value judgments on the decisions and desires of others. That is not positive analysis. It is, instead, **normative analysis**. *Normative means "what ought to be"; positive means "what is."* If you demonstrate that the probability of death in an automobile accident is 20 percent higher if seat belts are not worn, you are using positive analysis. If you argue that there should be a law requiring seat belts to be worn, you are using normative analysis.

3.b. Common Mistakes

Conclusions based on opinion or value judgments do not advance one's understanding of events.

Why are so many items sold for $2.99 rather than $3? Most people attribute this practice to ignorance on the part of others: "People look at the first number and round to it—they see $2.99 but think $2." Although this reasoning may be correct, no one admits to such behavior when asked. A common error in the attempt to understand human behavior is

© froxx/Shutterstock

to argue that other people do not understand something or are stupid. Instead of relying on rational self-interest to explain human behavior, ignorance or stupidity is called on.

Another common mistake in economic analysis, called the **fallacy of composition**, is the error of attributing what applies in the case of one to the case of many. If one person in a theater realizes that a fire has broken out and races to the exit, that one person is better off. If we assume that a thousand people in a crowded theater would be better off if they all behaved exactly like the single individual, we would be committing the mistake known as the fallacy of composition. For example, you reach an intersection just as the light switches to yellow. You reason that you can make it into the intersection before the light turns red. However, others reason the same way. Many people enter the intersection with the yellow light; it turns red, and traffic in the intersection is congested. The traffic going the other way can't move. You correctly reasoned that you alone could enter the intersection on the yellow light and then move on through. But it would be a fallacy of composition to assume that many drivers could enter the intersection and pass on through before the intersection is congested.

The mistaken interpretation of **association as causation** occurs when unrelated or coincidental events that occur at about the same time are believed to have a cause-and-effect relationship. For example, the result of the football Super Bowl game is sometimes said to predict how the stock market will perform. According to this "theory," if the NFC team wins, the stock market will rise in the new year, but if the AFC team wins, the market will fall. This bit of folklore is a clear example of confusion between causation and association. Simply because two events seem to occur together does not mean that one causes the other. Clearly, a football game cannot cause the stock market to rise or fall. For another example, on Gobbler's Knob, Punxsutawney, Pennsylvania, at 7:27 A.M. on February 2, Punxsutawney Phil saw his shadow. Six more weeks of winter followed. However, whether the sun was or was not hidden behind a cloud at 7:27 A.M. on February 2 had nothing to do with causing a shortened or extended winter. Groundhog Day is the celebration of the mistake of attributing association as causation.

3.c. Microeconomics and Macroeconomics

Economics is the study of how people choose to allocate their scarce resources among their unlimited wants and involves the application of certain principles—scarcity, choice, and rational self-interest—in a consistent manner. The study of economics is usually separated into two general areas, *microeconomics* and *macroeconomics*. **Microeconomics** is the study of economics at the level of the individual economic entity: the individual firm, the individual consumer, and the individual worker. In **macroeconomics**, rather than analyzing the behavior of an individual consumer, we look at the sum of the behaviors of all consumers together, which is called the consumer sector or household sector. Similarly, instead of examining the behavior of an individual firm, in macroeconomics we examine the sum of the behaviors of all firms, called the business sector.

Topics such as whether the president's stimulus plan is working, whether government debt is beneficial or not, whether the Federal Reserve (the central bank of the United States) should control interest rates or the money supply, and whether the Federal Reserve has been too loose or too tight with its policies, as well as the effect of changing exchange rates on the economy, are discussed in macroeconomics. How a firm manages during a recession, whether to raise or lower prices, whether to alter the brand or the advertising, whether people will purchase slightly less or significantly less gasoline as gas prices rise, and the effect on firms and employees of increased government regulations are generally microeconomic topics. Remember that the focus in microeconomics is the individual—the individual firm, employee, customer, government official, and so forth—while the focus in macroeconomics is on the entire consumer sector, business sector, government sector, and global sector.

fallacy of composition
The mistaken assumption that what applies in the case of one applies to the case of many.

association as causation
The mistaken assumption that because two events seem to occur together, one causes the other.

microeconomics
The study of economics at the level of the individual.

macroeconomics
The study of the economy as a whole.

RECAP

1. The objective of economics is to understand why the real world is the way it is.

2. Positive analysis refers to what is, while normative analysis refers to what ought to be.

3. Assuming that others are ignorant, the fallacy of composition, and interpreting association as causa-tion are three commonly made errors in economic analysis.

4. The study of economics is typically divided into two parts, macroeconomics and microeconomics.

SUMMARY

1. **Why study economics?**

   - The study of economics may be the road to a better job and will add skills that have value to you in your life and in your occupation. *§1*

   - Economics is interesting; it might be called the study of unintended consequences. *§1.b*

2. **What is economics?**

   - The resources that go into the production of goods are land, labor, and capital. *§2.a.1*

   - Economics is the study of how people choose to allocate scarce resources to satisfy their unlimited wants. *§2.b*

   - Scarcity is universal; it applies to anything people would like more of than is available at a zero price. Because of scarcity, choices must be made, and these choices are made in a way that is in the decision maker's rational self-interest. *§2.a, 2.b, 2.c*

   - People make choices that, at the time and with the information at hand, will give them the greatest satisfaction. *§2.c*

3. **What is the economic way of thinking?**

   - Positive analysis is analysis of what is; normative analysis is analysis of what ought to be. *§3.a*

   - Assuming that others are ignorant, the fallacy of composition, and interpreting association as causation are three commonly made errors in economic analysis. *§3.b*

   - The study of economics is typically divided into two parts, macroeconomics and microeconomics. *§3.c*

KEY TERMS

association as causation, 7	free good, 4	normative analysis, 6
capital, 5	inputs, 4	positive analysis, 6
economic bad, 4	labor, 5	rational self-interest, 5
economic good, 4	land, 5	resources, 4
factors of production, 4	macroeconomics, 7	scarcity, 4
fallacy of composition, 7	microeconomics, 7	

EXERCISES

1. Which of the following are economic goods? Explain why each is or is not an economic good.
   a. steaks
   b. houses
   c. cars
   d. garbage
   e. T-shirts

2. Many people go to a medical doctor every time they are ill; others never visit a doctor. Explain how

human behavior could include such opposite behaviors.

3. Erin has purchased a $35 ticket to a Dave Matthews concert. She is invited to a send-off party for a friend who is moving to another part of the country. The party is scheduled for the same day as the concert. If she had known about the party before she bought the concert ticket, she would have chosen to attend the party. Will Erin choose to attend the concert? Explain.

4. It is well documented in scientific research that smoking is harmful to health. Smokers have higher incidences of coronary disease, cancer, and other catastrophic illnesses. Knowing this, about 30 percent of young people begin smoking, and about 20 percent of the U.S. population smokes. Are the people who choose to smoke irrational? What do you think of the argument that we should ban smoking in order to protect these people from themselves?

5. Indicate whether each of the following statements is true or false. If the statement is false, change it to make it true.
   a. Positive analysis imposes the value judgments of one individual on the decisions of others.
   b. Rational self-interest is the same thing as selfishness.
   c. An economic good is scarce if it has a positive price.
   d. An economic bad is an item that has a positive price.
   e. A resource is an ingredient used to make factors of production.

6. Are the following statements normative or positive? If a statement is normative, change it to a positive statement.
   a. The government should provide free tuition to all college students.
   b. An effective way to increase the skills of the workforce is to provide free tuition to all college students.
   c. The government must provide job training if we are to compete with other countries.

7. If people behave in ways that they believe are in their best self-interest, how would you explain the following?
   a. Mother Teresa devoted her entire life to living in the worst slums of Asia, providing aid to others.
   b. Bernie Madoff created a scheme whereby people gave him billions of dollars to invest that he simply kept for himself.
   c. Pat Tillman gave up millions of dollars when he chose to enlist in the military following the 9/11 attack on the United States rather than play professional football.

8. Use economics to explain why men's and women's restrooms tend to be located near each other in airports and other public buildings.

9. Use the Broken Window Fallacy to explain what the "seen" and "unseen" effects of the government's decision to subsidize "green jobs" might be.

10. Use economics to explain why people leave tips (a) at a restaurant they visit often and (b) at a restaurant they visit only once.

11. Use economics to explain why people contribute to charities.

12. Use economics to explain this statement: "Increasing the speed limit has, to some degree, compromised highway safety on interstate roads but enhanced safety on non-interstate roads."

13. Apply the Broken Window Fallacy to the argument that an earthquake in Haiti is beneficial in the sense that reconstruction will create jobs and income.

You can find further practice tests in the Online Quiz at **www.cengage.com/economics/boyes**.

WOMEN STILL LAG BEHIND MEN IN PAY

Northeast Mississippi Daily Journal (Tupelo) May 15, 2011

I usually don't get riled up when it comes to so-called feminist causes. But when it comes to equal pay for men and women, I do.

The country "celebrated" Equal Pay Day on April 12. The day symbolizes how far into 2011 women had to work to earn what men did in 2010. That's nearly 3 and a half additional months.

In Mississippi, on average, a woman working full time is paid $28,506 per year, while a man working full time is paid $37,528 annually, according to research from the National Partnership for Women & Families. That's a gap of $9,022. Nationally, full-time working women are paid $10,622 less than men.

If the wage gap were eliminated, Mississippi's working women would have enough money for any of the following:

- 79 more weeks of food.
- Nine more months of mortgage and utilities payments.
- 14 more months of rent.
- Two more years of family health insurance premiums.
- More than 2,000 gallons of gas.

Because of the gender gap, women need to work more than 11 extra years to earn as much as men before retirement, according to *The Washington Post*.

Today, women are paid about 77 cents for every $1 a man earns. The pay drops for black women to 61 cents and Latinas to 52 cents. On top of that, women with children are paid 2.5 percent less than women without children. Yet, men with children get paid 2.1 percent more than men without children, according to a Government Accountability Office study. Unless things change, women won't come close to being paid the same amount as men until 2058—when today's high school students are preparing for retirement.

People argue that men get paid more because they enter into higher-paying jobs. The facts don't support that point of view. The National Association of Colleges and Employees last week released data showing that female graduates from the Class of 2010 are making 17 percent less than their male counterparts. Even when salary is adjusted by major, men come out ahead in most cases. A noticeable exception was engineering, where women made more because they are rare and command a premium.

But NACE said being a rarity isn't a guarantee of a higher salary. Women earning degrees in computer science are also scarce—representing about 18 percent of degrees—but averaged $52,531 in starting salary, while men earned $56,227. And in education—a field that is dominated by women—NACE data also showed that the female grads are getting cheated.

Women account for nearly 80 percent of education graduates, but their starting salary averaged $29,092. The men? $39,849.

So employers, as you get ready to hire a new crop of college graduates, do your part to help close the gender gap. We women work our tails off and we deserve to get paid the same amount as the men do.

Source: Carlie Kollath, Northeast Mississippi Daily Journal, Tupelo, May 15, 2011 Sunday.

According to the article, the pay gap between men and women is very large and narrowing very slowly. How could choice and costs and benefits explain such a gap? Economics is the study of human behavior, so it ought to be able to explain why people would choose one occupation over another or choose one college major over another. Do women choose occupations that pay less than occupations men choose because women want to have families or to enjoy other aspects of life, whereas men devote themselves to work, define themselves in terms of their work? If so, this could explain the differential in pay.

Economists argue that decisions are the result of comparing costs and benefits. In this article, two major decisions are not discussed but are implied: going to college and selecting a major. The first decision compares the future income and quality of living that a college degree will offer with the costs of obtaining that college degree. What you major in determines your value to a firm or the skills you have to pursue graduate study or other careers. What is the cost of the degree? It is the expense of college—what many students take out loans to pay. It is also the forgone income—that is, the income that you would have earned had you not gone to college. Someone who takes four or five years to complete college has paid tuition, purchased books and materials, and paid for room and board over those years. Those costs range from a bare minimum of $20,000 to well over $100,000. You may have worked part time while you were attending college, but if you had not been attending college, you could have worked full time. The difference for the years of college would have been about $50,000. Thus, the cost of college could have been $150,000 or more. But the cost of a major also includes the opportunity costs of the time devoted to completing the program. It is more costly to get an engineering degree than an education degree because the engineering program is difficult: The time commitment above and beyond the education major is significant. Women who major in education make 60 percent of what female engineers make in their first year of work. But far more women still choose education over engineering. Why would they do this? For some, the idea that at some stage in their career, they will choose to leave the labor force and have children means they will want a career that enables them to leave and perhaps return later, when the children are in school. A highly scientific field where knowledge changes rapidly would be a poor choice since leaving for a few years would mean it is virtually impossible to come back into the profession; the knowledge one had at the time of leaving the workforce would be obsolete within a few years. Selecting education makes a lot of sense for the women expecting to have and raise a family. They can return to education without having lost knowledge. They can work the same hours as their children are in school, thus being able to take care of young children.

Selecting a major involves a comparison of costs and benefits. Different majors mean different amounts of future income. If the choice of major were only a matter of comparisons of future income, there would be fewer art history majors and elementary-school teachers but more engineers and medical doctors. But income is not the only thing that enters into one's benefit calculations. Interest in the subject, living styles, amount of leisure time, and other aspects of life enter into one's choice of a college major. Every college student tends to select the major that fits with the life style they hope to have—the major that yields the greatest net benefits to each individual.

If salary differentials between men and women are due to choice of college major and occupation, why then would one say "Even when salary is adjusted by major, men come out ahead in most cases"? Moreover, why would women make more in engineering and less in computer science than men? Both are scientific fields, and in both fields women constitute only about 18 percent of the profession. Does knowledge change more rapidly in computer science than in engineering? If so, could that explain the difference between the pay gap between men and women in the two fields? Using the principles of economics, see if you can come up with a possible explanation.

Working with Graphs

According to the old saying, one picture is worth a thousand words. If that maxim is correct, and, in addition, if producing a thousand words takes more time and effort than producing one picture, it is no wonder that economists rely so extensively on pictures. The pictures that economists use to explain concepts are called *graphs*. The purpose of this appendix is to explain how graphs are constructed and how to interpret them.

1. Reading Graphs

The three kinds of graphs used by economists are shown in Figures 1, 2, and 3. Figure 1 is a *line graph*. It is the most commonly used type of graph in economics. Figure 2 is a *bar graph*. It is probably used more often in popular magazines than any other kind of graph. Figure 3 is a *pie graph* or *pie chart*. Although it is less popular than bar and line graphs, the pie graph appears often enough that you need to be familiar with it.

1.a. Relationships between Variables

Figure 1 is a line graph showing the ratio of the median income of people who have completed four or more years of college to the median income of those who have completed just four years of high school. The line shows the value of a college education in terms of the additional income earned relative to the income earned without a college degree on a year-to-year basis. You can see that the premium for completing college rose from the mid-1970s until 2001 and has declined slightly since.

Figure 2 is a bar graph indicating the unemployment rate by educational attainment. The blue refers to high school dropouts, the red refers to those with four years of high school, and the green refers to those with four or more years of college. One set of bars is presented for males and one set for females. The bars are arranged in order, with the highest incidence of unemployment depicted first, the next highest second, and the lowest third. This arrangement is made only for ease in reading and interpretation. The bars could be arranged in any order. The graph illustrates that unemployment strikes those with less education more than it does those with more education.

Figure 3 is a pie chart showing the percentage of the U.S. population completing various numbers of years of schooling. Unlike line and bar graphs, a pie chart is not actually a picture of a relationship between two variables. Instead, the pie represents the whole, 100 percent of the U.S. population, and the pieces of the pie represent parts of the whole—the percentage of the population completing one to four years of elementary school only, five to seven years of elementary school, and so on, up to four or more years of college.

Because a pie chart does not show the relationship between variables, it is not as useful for explaining economic concepts as line and bar graphs. Line graphs are used more often than bar graphs to explain economic concepts.

FIGURE 1 Ratio of Median Incomes of College-to-High School-Educated Workers

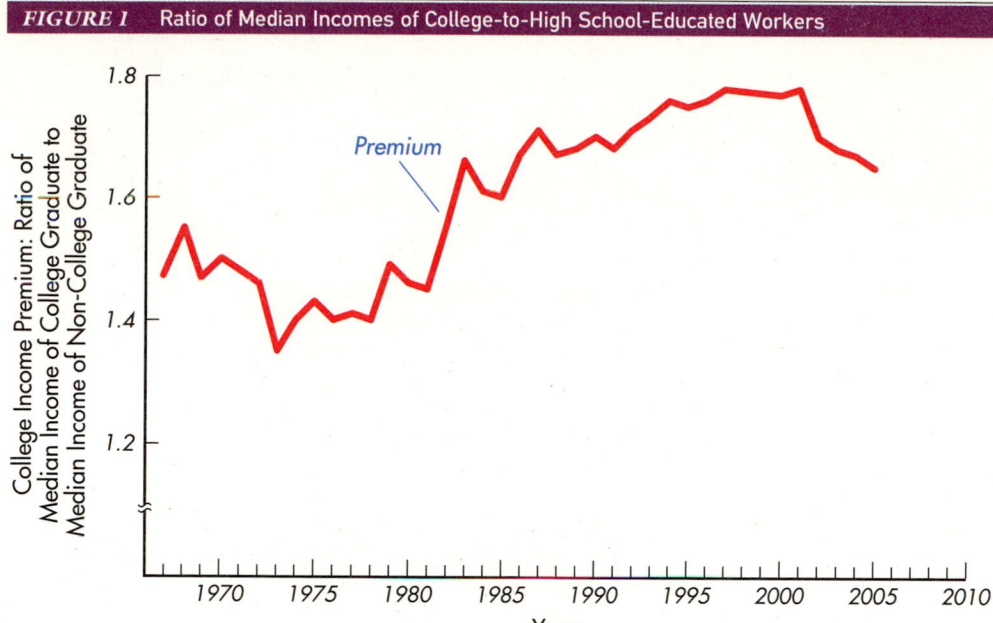

Figure 1 is a line graph showing the ratio of the median income of people who have completed four or more years of college to the median income of those who have completed four years of high school. The line shows the income premium for educational attainment, or the value of a college education in terms of income, from year to year. The rise in the line since about 1979 shows that the premium for completing college has risen.

Source: U.S. Statistical Abstract, 2005. *U.S. Census Bureau;* www.census.gov.

FIGURE 2 Unemployment and Education

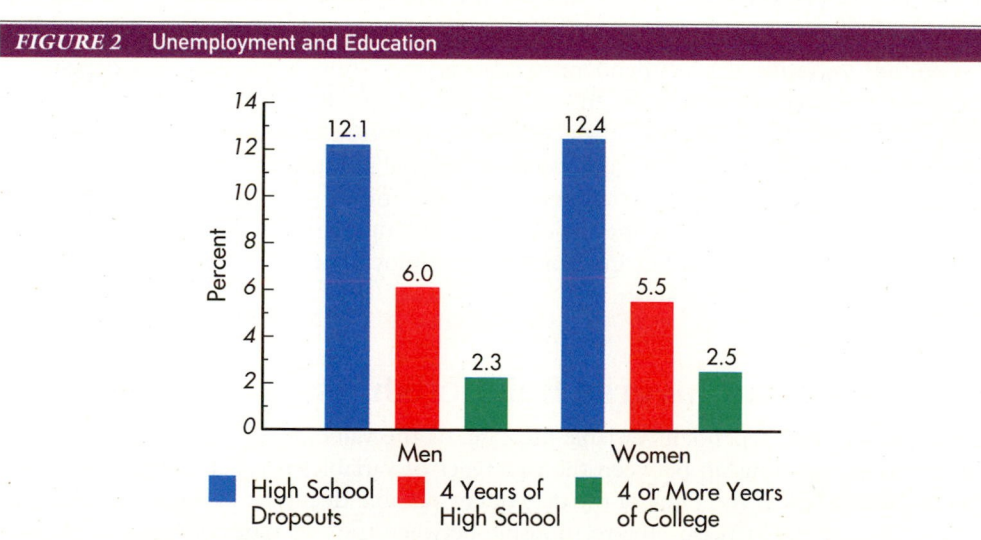

Figure 2 is a bar graph indicating the unemployment rate by educational attainment. The blue refers to high school dropouts, the red refers to those with four years of high school, and the green refers to those with four or more years of college. One set of bars is presented for males and one set for females. The bars are arranged in order, with the highest incidence of unemployment shown first, the next highest second, and the lowest third. This arrangement is made only for ease in reading and interpretation. The bars could be arranged in any order.

Source: *U.S. Census Bureau;* www.census.gov/population.

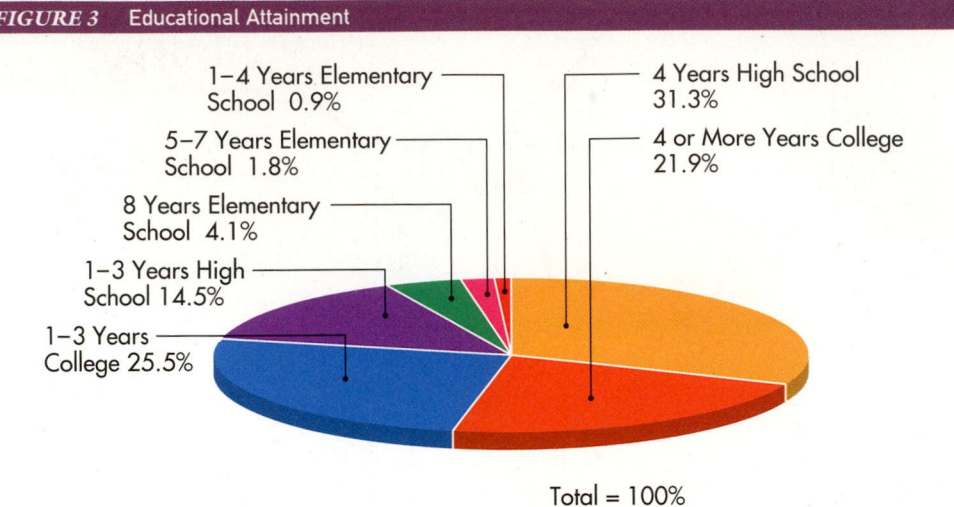

FIGURE 3   Educational Attainment

1–4 Years Elementary School 0.9%

5–7 Years Elementary School 1.8%

8 Years Elementary School 4.1%

1–3 Years High School 14.5%

1–3 Years College 25.5%

4 Years High School 31.3%

4 or More Years College 21.9%

Total = 100%

Figure 3 is a pie chart showing the percentage of the U.S. population completing various years of schooling. Unlike line and bar graphs, a pie chart is not actually a picture of a relationship between two variables. Instead, the pie represents the whole, 100 percent of the U.S. population in this case, and the pieces of the pie represent parts of the whole—the percentage of the population completing one to four years of elementary school only, five to seven years of elementary school, and so on, up to four or more years of college.

Source: *U.S. Census Bureau, 2009*; www.census.gov/population.

1.b. Independent and Dependent Variables

independent variable
A variable whose value does not depend on the values of other variables.

Most line and bar graphs involve just two variables, an **independent variable** and a **dependent variable**. An independent variable is one whose value does not depend on the values of other variables; a dependent variable, on the other hand, is one whose value does depend on the values of other variables. The value of the dependent variable is determined after the value of the independent variable is determined.

dependent variable
A variable whose value depends on the value of the independent variable.

In Figure 2, the *independent* variable is the educational status of the man or woman, and the *dependent* variable is the incidence of unemployment (the percentage of the group that is unemployed). The incidence of unemployment depends on the educational attainment of the man or woman.

1.c. Direct and Inverse Relationships

direct, or **positive**, **relationship**
The relationship that exists when the values of related variables move in the same direction.

If the value of the dependent variable increases as the value of the independent variable increases, the relationship between the two types of variables is called a **direct**, or **positive**, **relationship**. If the value of the dependent variable decreases as the value of the independent variable increases, the relationship between the two types of variables is called an **inverse**, or **negative**, **relationship**.

inverse, or **negative**, **relationship**
The relationship that exists when the values of related variables move in opposite directions.

In Figure 2, unemployment and educational attainment are inversely, or negatively, related: As people acquire more education, they become less likely to be unemployed.

2. Constructing a Graph

Let's now construct a graph. We will begin with a consideration of the horizontal and vertical axes, or lines, and then we will put the axes together. We are going to construct a *straight-line curve*. This sounds contradictory, but it is common terminology. Economists often refer to the demand or supply *curve*, and that curve may be a straight line.

2.a. The Axes

It is important to understand how the *axes* (the horizontal and vertical lines) are used and what they measure. Let's begin with the horizontal axis, the line running across the page. Notice in Figure 4(a) that the line is divided into equal segments. Each point on the line represents a quantity, or the value of the variable being measured. For example, each segment could represent one year or 10,000 pounds of diamonds or some other value. Whatever is measured, the value increases from left to right, beginning with negative values, going on to zero, which is called the *origin*, and then moving on to positive numbers.

A number line in the vertical direction can be constructed as well, and this is also shown in Figure 4(a). Zero is the origin, and the numbers increase from bottom to top. Like the horizontal axis, the vertical axis is divided into equal segments; the distance between 0 and 10 is the same as the distance between 0 and −10, the distance between 10 and 20, and so on.

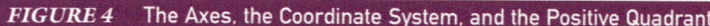

FIGURE 4   The Axes, the Coordinate System, and the Positive Quadrant

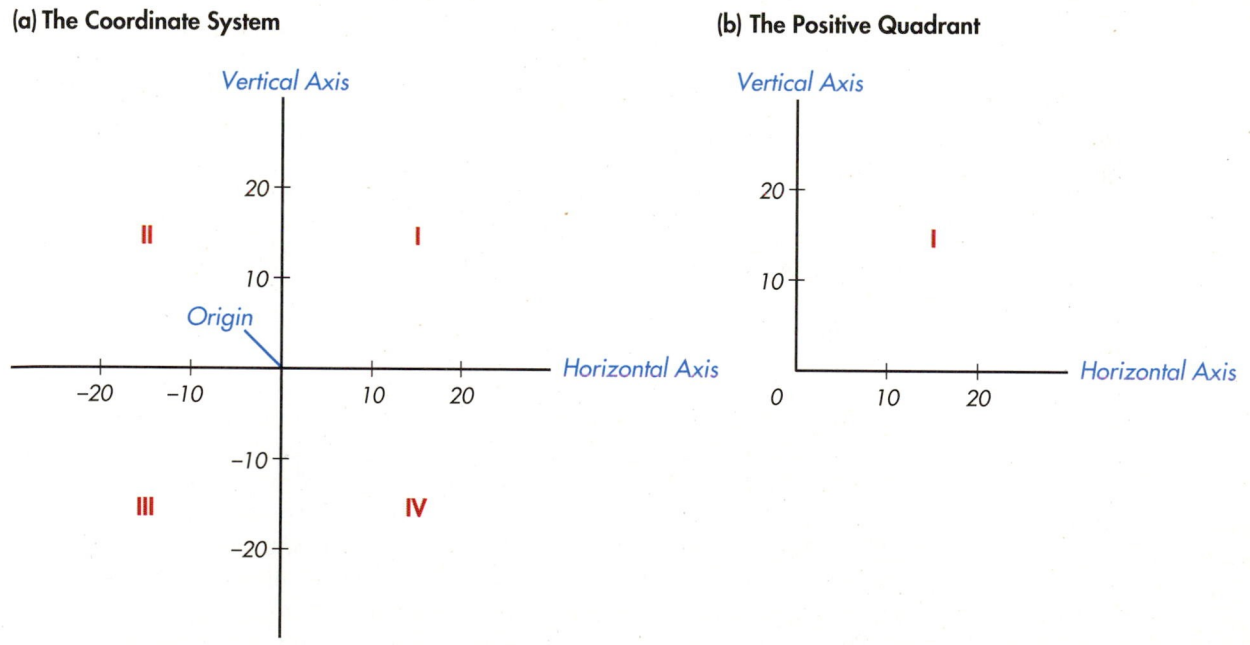

Figure 4(a) shows the vertical and horizontal axes. The horizontal axis has an origin, measured as zero, in the middle. Negative numbers are to the left of zero, and positive numbers are to the right. The vertical axis also has an origin in the middle. Positive numbers are above the origin, and negative numbers are below. The horizontal and vertical axes together show the entire coordinate system. Positive numbers are in quadrant I, negative numbers in quadrant III, and combinations of negative and positive numbers in quadrants II and IV. Figure 4(b) shows only the positive quadrant. Because most economic data are positive, often only the upper right quadrant, the positive quadrant, of the coordinate system is used.

In most cases, the variable measured along the horizontal axis is the independent variable. This isn't always true in economics, however. Economists often measure the independent variable on the vertical axis. Do not assume that the variable on the horizontal axis is independent and the variable on the vertical axis is dependent.

Putting the horizontal and vertical lines together lets us express relationships between two variables graphically. The axes cross, or intersect, at their origins, as shown in Figure 4(a). From the common origin, movements to the right and up, in the area—called a quadrant—marked I, are combinations of positive numbers; movements to the left and down, in quadrant III, are combinations of negative numbers; movements to the right and down, in quadrant IV, are negative values on the vertical axis and positive values on the horizontal axis; and movements to the left and up, in quadrant II, are positive values on the vertical axis and negative values on the horizontal axis.

Economic data are typically positive numbers: the unemployment rate, the inflation rate, the price of something, the quantity of something produced or sold, and so on. Because economic data are usually positive numbers, the only part of the coordinate system that usually comes into play in economics is the upper right portion, quadrant I. That is why economists may simply sketch a vertical line down to the origin and then extend a horizontal line out to the right, as shown in Figure 4(b). Once in a while, economic data are negative—for instance, profit is negative when costs exceed revenues. When data are negative, quadrants II, III, and IV of the coordinate system may be used.

2.b. Constructing a Graph from a Table

Now that you are familiar with the axes—that is, the coordinate system—you are ready to construct a graph using the data in the table in Figure 5. The table lists a series of possible price levels for a T-shirt and the corresponding number of T-shirts that people choose to purchase. The data are only hypothetical; they are not drawn from actual cases.

The information given in the table is graphed in Figure 5. We begin by marking off and labeling the axes. The vertical axis is the list of possible price levels. We begin at zero and move up the axis in equal increments of $10. The horizontal axis is the number of T-shirts sold. We begin at zero and move along the axis in equal increments of 1,000 T-shirts. According to the information presented in the table, if the price is higher than $100, no one buys a T-shirt. The combination of $100 and 0 T-shirts is point A on the graph. To plot this point, find the quantity zero on the horizontal axis (it is at the origin), and then move up the vertical axis from zero to a price level of $100. (Note that we have measured the units in the table and on the graph in thousands.) At a price of $90, there are 1,000 T-shirts purchased. To plot the combination of $90 and 1,000 T-shirts, find 1,000 units on the horizontal axis and then measure up from there to a price of $90. This is point B. Point C represents a price of $80 and 2,000 T-shirts. Point D represents a price of $70 and 3,000 T-shirts. Each combination of price and T-shirts purchased listed in the table is plotted in Figure 5.

The final step in constructing a line graph is to connect the points that are plotted. When the points are connected, the straight line slanting downward from left to right in Figure 5 is obtained. It shows the relationship between the price of T-shirts and the number of T-shirts purchased.

FIGURE 5   Constructing a Line Graph

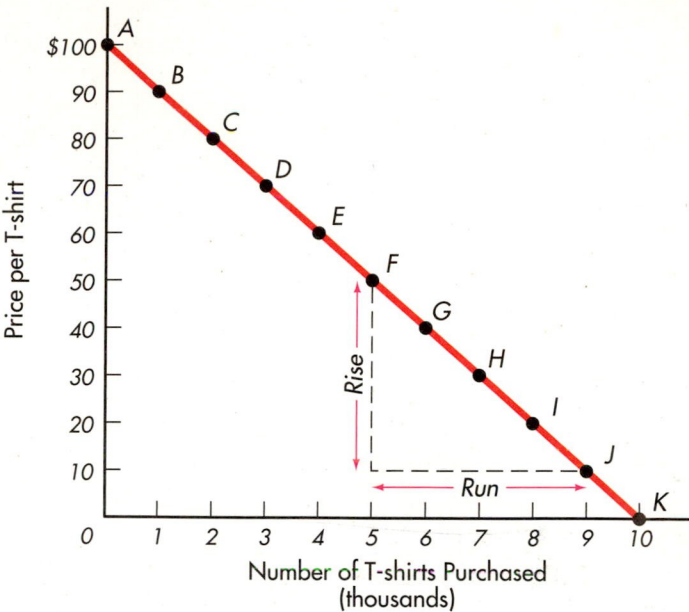

Point	Price per T-shirt	Number of T-shirts
A	$100	0
B	90	1,000
C	80	2,000
D	70	3,000
E	60	4,000
F	50	5,000
G	40	6,000
H	30	7,000
I	20	8,000
J	10	9,000
K	0	10,000

The information given in the table is plotted or graphed. The vertical axis measures price per T-shirt. The horizontal axis measures the number of T-shirts in thousands. We begin at zero in each case and then go up (if the vertical axis) or out (if the horizontal axis) in equal amounts. The vertical axis goes from $0 to $10 to $20 and so on, while the horizontal axis goes from 0 to 1,000 to 2,000 and so on. Each point is plotted. For instance, point A is a price of $100 and a number of T-shirts of 0. This is found by going to 0 on the horizontal axis and then up to $100 on the vertical axis. Point B is a price of $90 and a number of 1,000. Once the points are plotted, a line connecting the points is drawn.

2.c. Interpreting Points on a Graph

Let's use Figure 5 to demonstrate how points on a graph may be interpreted. Suppose the current price of a T-shirt is $30. Are you able to tell how many T-shirts are being purchased at this price? By tracing that price level from the vertical axis over to the curve and then down to the horizontal axis, you find that 7,000 T-shirts are being purchased. You can also find what happens to the number purchased if the price falls from $30 to $10. By tracing from the price of $10 horizontally to the curve and then down to the horizontal axis, you discover that 9,000 T-shirts are purchased. Thus, according to the graph, a decrease in the price from $30 to $10 results in 2,000 more T-shirts being purchased.

2.d. Shifts of Curves

Graphs can be used to illustrate the effects of a change in a variable that is not represented on the graph. For instance, the curve drawn in Figure 5 shows the relationship between the price of T-shirts and the number of T-shirts purchased. When this curve was drawn, the only two variables that were allowed to change were the price and the number of T-shirts. However, it is likely that people's incomes determine their reaction to the price of T-shirts as well. An increase in income would enable people to purchase more T-shirts. Thus, at every price, more T-shirts would be purchased. How would this be represented? As an outward shift of the curve, from points A, B, C, and so on to A', B', C', and so on, as shown in Figure 6.

Following the shift of the curve, we can see that more T-shirts are purchased at each price than was the case prior to the income increase. For instance, at a price of $20, the

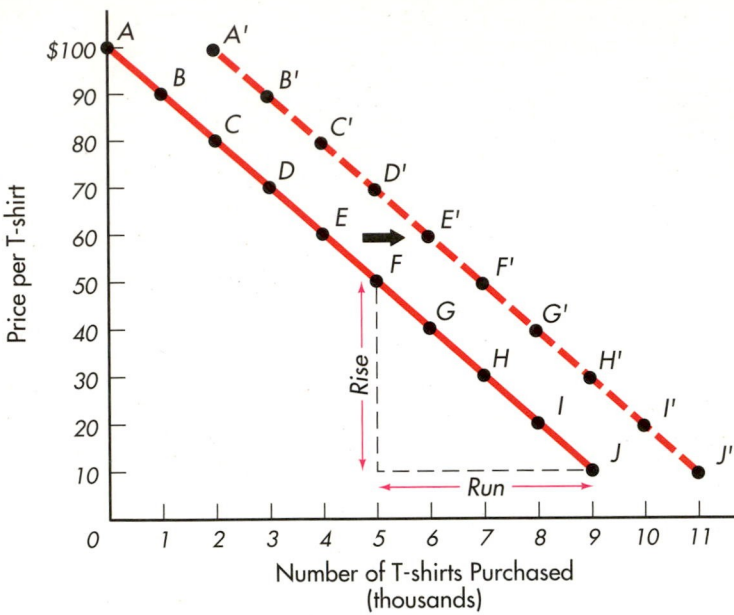

FIGURE 6   Shift of Curve

An increase in income allows more people to purchase T-shirts at each price. At a price of $80, for instance, 4,000 T-shirts are purchased instead of 2,000.

© 2013 Cengage Learning

increased income allows 10,000 T-shirts to be purchased rather than 8,000. The important point to note is that if some variable that influences the relationship shown in a curve or line graph changes, then *the entire curve or line changes—that is, it shifts.*

3. Slope

A curve may represent an inverse, or negative, relationship or a direct, or positive, relationship. The slope of the curve reveals the kind of relationship that exists between two variables.

3.a. Positive and Negative Slopes

slope
The steepness of a curve, measured as the ratio of the rise to the run.

The **slope** of a curve is its steepness, the rate at which the value of a variable measured on the vertical axis changes with respect to a given change in the value of the variable measured on the horizontal axis. If the value of a variable measured on one axis goes up when the value of the variable measured on the other axis goes down, the variables have an inverse (or negative) relationship. If the values of the variables rise or fall together, the variables have a direct (or positive) relationship. Inverse relationships are represented by curves that run downward from left to right; direct relationships are represented by curves that run upward from left to right.

Slope is calculated by measuring the amount by which the variable on the vertical axis changes and dividing that figure by the amount by which the variable on the horizontal axis changes. The vertical change is called the *rise*, and the horizontal change is called the *run*. Slope is referred to as the *rise over the run*:

$$\text{Slope} = \frac{\text{rise}}{\text{run}}$$

The slope of any inverse relationship is negative. The slope of any direct relationship is positive.

Let's calculate the slope of the curve in Figure 5. Price (P) is measured on the vertical axis, and the quantity of T-shirts purchased (Q) is measured on the horizontal axis. The rise is the change in price (ΔP), the change in the value of the variable measured on the vertical axis. The run is the change in the quantity of T-shirts purchased (ΔQ), the change in the value of the variable measured on the horizontal axis. (The symbol Δ means "change in"—it is the Greek letter delta—so ΔP means "change in P" and ΔQ means "change in Q".) Remember that slope equals the rise over the run. Thus, the equation for the slope of the straight-line curve running downward from left to right in Figure 5 is

$$\frac{\Delta P}{\Delta Q}$$

As the price (P) declines, the number of T-shirts purchased (Q) increases. The rise is negative, and the run is positive. Thus, the slope is a negative value. The slope is the same anywhere along a straight line. Thus, it does not matter where we calculate the changes along the vertical and horizontal axes. For instance, from 0 to 10,000 on the horizontal axis—a run of 10,000—the vertical change, the rise, is a negative $100 (from $100 down to $0). Thus, the rise over the run is −100/10,000, or −.01. Similarly, from 5,000 to 9,000 in the horizontal direction, the corresponding rise is $50 to $10, so that the rise over the run is −40/4,000 or −.01.

Remember that direct, or positive, relationships between variables are represented by lines that run upward from left to right. Figure 7 is a graph showing the number of

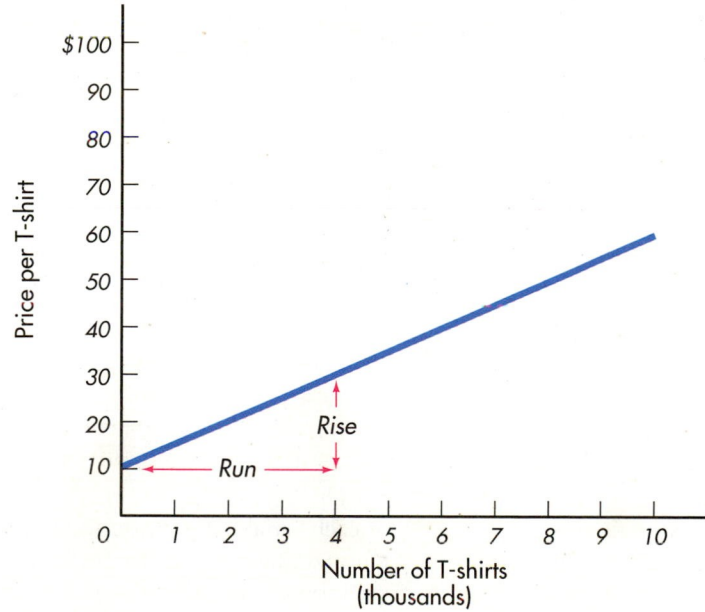

FIGURE 7 T-Shirts Offered for Sale at Each Price

Figure 7 is a graph showing the number of T-shirts offered for sale at various prices. The line shows that as price rises so does the number of T-shirts offered for sale. At a price of $10, no shirts are offered. At a price of $20, 2,000 shirts are offered for sale. At a price of $30, 4,000 shirts are offered for sale, and so on. The rise over the run is 20/4,000 = .005.

T-shirts that producers offer for sale at various price levels. The curve represents the relationship between the two variables, the number of T-shirts offered for sale and price. It shows that as price rises, so does the number of T-shirts offered for sale. The slope of the curve is positive. The change in the rise (the vertical direction) that comes with an increase in the run (the horizontal direction) is positive. Because the graph is a straight line, you can measure the rise and run using any two points along the curve and the slope will be the same. We find the slope by calculating the rise that accompanies the run. Moving from 0 to 4,000 T-shirts gives us a run of 4,000. Looking at the curve, we see that the corresponding rise is $20. Thus, the rise over the run is 20/4,000, or .005.

SUMMARY

- There are three commonly used types of graphs: the line graph, the bar graph, and the pie chart. §1.*a*

- An independent variable is a variable whose value does not depend on the values of other variables. The values of a dependent variable do depend on the values of other variables. §1.*b*

- A direct, or positive, relationship occurs when the value of the dependent variable increases as the value of the independent variable increases. An indirect, or negative, relationship occurs when the value of the dependent variable decreases as the value of the independent variable increases. §1.*c*

- Most economic data are positive numbers, and so only the upper right quadrant of the coordinate system is often used in economics. §2.*a*

- A curve shifts when a variable that affects the dependent variable and is not measured on the axes changes. §2.*d*

- The slope of a curve is the rise over the run: the change in the variable measured on the vertical axis over the corresponding change in the variable measured on the horizontal axis. §3.*a*

- The slope of a straight-line curve is the same at all points along the curve. §3.*a*

KEY TERMS

EXERCISES

1. Listed in the following table are two sets of figures: the total quantity of Mexican pesos (new pesos) in circulation (the total amount of Mexican money available) and the peso price of a U.S. dollar (how many pesos are needed to purchase one U.S. dollar). Values are given for the years 1990–2009 for each variable.

   a. Plot each variable by measuring time (years) on the horizontal axis and, in the first graph, pesos in circulation on the vertical axis and, in the second graph, peso price of a dollar on the vertical axis.
   b. Plot the combinations of variables by measuring pesos in circulation on the horizontal axis and peso prices of a dollar on the vertical axis.

c. In each of the graphs in parts a and b, what are the dependent and independent variables?

d. In each of the graphs in parts a and b, indicate whether the relationship between the dependent and independent variables is direct or inverse.

Year	Pesos in Circulation (billions)	Peso Price of a U.S. Dollar
1990	19.6	2.8126
1991	27.0	3.0184
1992	36.2	3.0949
1993	42.0	3.1156
1994	47.2	3.3751
1995	56.9	6.4194
1996	66.8	7.5994
1997	84.0	8.5850
1998	109.0	9.9680
1999	131.0	9.4270
2000	188.8	9.6420
2001	209.0	9.2850
2002	225.0	9.5270
2003	264.0	10.9000
2004	303.0	11.4000
2005	340.0	10.4750
2006	380.0	10.87
2007	450.0	10.86
2008	495.0	13.53
2009	578.0	13.76

2. Plot the data listed in the table below.

a. Use price as the vertical axis and quantity as the horizontal axis and plot the first two columns.

b. Show what quantity is sold when the price is $550.

c. Directly below the graph in part a, plot the data in columns 2 and 3. Use total revenue as the vertical axis and quantity as the horizontal axis.

d. What is total revenue when the price is $550? Will total revenue increase or decrease when the price is lowered?

Price	Quantity Sold	Total Revenue
$1,000	200	200,000
900	400	360,000
800	600	480,000
700	800	560,000
600	1,000	600,000
500	1,200	600,000
400	1,400	560,000
300	1,600	480,000
200	1,800	360,000
100	2,000	200,000

CHAPTER 2

Choice, Opportunity Costs, and Specialization

© MACIEJ FROLOW/GETTY IMAGES, INC

© IOFOTO/DREAMSTIME.COM; LOGO: © FROXX/SHUTTERSTOCK

FUNDAMENTAL QUESTIONS

1 What are opportunity costs? Are they part of the economic way of thinking?

2 What is a production possibilities curve?

3 Why does specialization occur?

4 What are the benefits of trade?

n the previous chapter, we learned that scarcity forces people to make choices. A choice means that you select one thing instead of selecting others. What you don't select is the cost of the choice you make. The old saying that "there is no free lunch" means that every choice requires that something be given up or sacrificed. In this chapter, we discuss how costs affect the behavior of individuals, firms, and societies as a whole.

1. Opportunity Costs

A choice is simply a comparison of alternatives: to attend class or not to attend class, to purchase a double latte mocha with whipped cream or to buy songs from iTunes, to purchase a new car or to keep the old one. When one option is chosen, the benefits of the alternatives are forgone. When you choose to purchase the double latte mocha for $4, you don't have that $4 to spend on anything else. *Economists refer to the forgone opportunities or forgone benefits of the next best alternative as* **opportunity costs**. Opportunity costs are the highest-valued alternative that must be forgone when a choice is made. If you bought four iTunes items instead of buying the latte, then we say the opportunity cost of the latte is the benefit you don't enjoy from the iTunes purchases.

The concept of cost is often more than the dollars and cents you shell out at the cash register. Buying used books saves money but often increases frustration and may affect your grades. The book might be missing pages, unreadable in spots, or out of date. The full cost of the book is the price you paid for the used copy plus the frustration of having an incomplete book. An attorney in Scottsdale, Arizona, is paid $325 an hour to write contracts. The attorney loves Ralph Lauren dress shirts and can get them for $100 at Nordstrom in Scottsdale or, when they are available, for $50 at the outlet mall in Casa Grande. He likes to purchase just one or two shirts at a time and usually buys them at Nordstrom, taking 15 minutes out of his lunch time to go to the store. Is this smart? Well, he figures he could spend two hours driving to Casa Grande and back and save $50 per shirt. But this also means he is not writing contracts and charging $325 per hour during those two hours. The real cost of the $50 saved on a single shirt in Casa Grande is the amount that the attorney would give up in income, $325 per hour less the $50 savings on each shirt, plus the cost of the additional gas used.

When economists refer to costs, it is opportunity costs they are measuring. The cost of anything is what must be given up to get that item. Every human activity responds to costs in one way or another. When the cost of something falls, that something becomes more attractive to us, all else being the same. For instance, when the cost of text messaging phone service dropped, more of us signed up for the service. Conversely, when the cost of something rises, and all else remains unchanged, we tend to use less of it. When photo radar machines were placed on the freeways in Arizona, the cost of speeding went up because the likelihood of getting caught speeding dramatically increased. As a result, the amount of speeding dropped—average speeds went from 78 to 65 virtually overnight.

1.a. Trade-offs

Life is a continuous sequence of decisions, and every single decision involves choosing one thing over another or trading off something for something else. A **trade-off** means a sacrifice—giving up one good or activity in order to obtain some other good or activity. Each term you must decide whether or not to register for college. You could work full time and not attend college, attend college and not work, or work part time and attend college. The time you devote to college will decrease as you devote more time to work. You trade off hours spent at work for hours spent in college; in other words, you compare the benefits you think you will get from going to college this term with the costs of college this term.

1.b. The Production Possibilities Curve

Trade-offs can be illustrated in a graph known as the **production possibilities curve (PPC)**. The production possibilities curve shows all possible combinations of quantities of goods and services that can be produced when the existing resources are used *fully and efficiently*. Figure 1 shows a production possibilities curve (based on information in the table in Figure 1) for the production of defense goods and services and nondefense

1 What are opportunity costs? Are they part of the economic way of thinking?

opportunity cost
The highest-valued alternative that must be forgone when a choice is made.

trade-off
The giving up of one good or activity in order to obtain some other good or activity.

2 What is a production possibilities curve?

production possibilities curve (PPC)
A graphical representation showing all possible combinations of quantities of goods and services that can be produced using the existing resources fully and efficiently.

ECONOMIC INSIGHT

A Tricky Question on Opportunity Costs

A few years ago, a problem similar to the following was given to economists at their annual convention. Only a small percentage came up with the right answer.

You have won a free ticket for a concert by a popular performer we will call A (the ticket has no resale value). Another performer you also like, B, is putting on a concert at the same time and that is your next-best alternative activity (and vice versa). A ticket for B's concert is $40. On any given day, you would be willing to pay up to $50 for B's ticket. You decide to attend A's concert. Based on this information, what is your opportunity cost of going to A's concert?

a) $40
b) $50
c) $0
d) $10
e) $60

You chose to go to the free concert, so you value that ticket at least equal to how much you value a ticket to B's concert. You would have been willing to pay $50 for B's concert but would have had to pay $40, so the net benefit you would have received is $10. It is this you give up to attend A's concert.

FIGURE 1   The Production Possibilities Curve

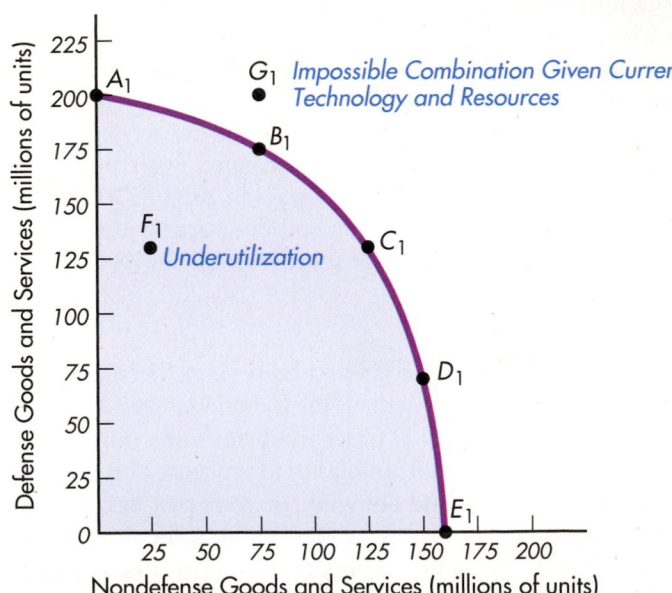

With a limited amount of resources, only certain combinations of defense and nondefense goods and services can be produced. The maximum amounts that can be produced, given various tradeoffs, are represented by points A_1 through E_1. Point F_1 lies inside the curve and represents the underutilization of resources. More of one type of goods could be produced without producing less of the other, or more of both types could be produced. Point G_1 represents an impossible combination. There are insufficient resources to produce quantities lying beyond the curve.

goods and services by a nation. Defense goods and services include guns, ships, bombs, personnel, and so forth that are used for national defense. Nondefense goods and services include education, housing, health care, and food that are not used for national defense. All societies allocate their scarce resources in order to produce some combination of defense and nondefense goods and services. Because resources are scarce, a nation cannot produce as much of everything as it wants. When it produces more health care, it cannot produce as much education or automobiles; when it devotes more of its resources to the military area, fewer resources are available to devote to health care.

In Figure 1, units of defense goods and services are measured on the vertical axis, and units of nondefense goods and services are measured on the horizontal axis. If all resources are allocated to producing defense goods and services, then 200 million units can be produced, but there will be no production of nondefense goods and services. The combination of 200 million units of defense goods and services and 0 units of nondefense goods and services is point A_1, a point on the vertical axis. At 175 million units of defense goods and services, 75 million units of nondefense goods and services can be produced (point B_1). Point C_1 represents 125 million units of nondefense goods and services and 130 million units of defense goods. Point D_1 represents 150 million units of nondefense goods and services and 70 million units of defense goods and services. Point E_1, a point on the horizontal axis, shows the combination of no production of defense goods and services and 160 million units of nondefense goods and services.

1.b.1. Points Inside the Production Possibilities Curve
Suppose a nation produces 130 million units of defense goods and services and 25 million units of nondefense goods and services. That combination, Point F_1 in Figure 1, lies inside the production possibilities curve. A point lying inside the production possibilities curve indicates that resources are not being fully or efficiently used. If the existing workforce is employed only 20 hours per week, it is not being fully used. If two workers are used when one would be sufficient—say, two people in each Domino's Pizza delivery car—then resources are not being used efficiently. If there are resources available for use, society can move from point F_1 to a point on the PPC, such as point C_1. The move would gain 100 million units of nondefense goods and services with no loss of defense goods and services.

During recessions, unemployment rises and other resources are not fully and efficiently used. A point inside a nation's PPC could represent recession. This would be represented as a point inside the PPC, such as F_1. Should the economy expand, and resources become more fully and efficiently used, this would be represented as a move out from a point such as F_1 to a point on the PPC, such as point C_1.

1.b.2. Points Outside the Production Possibilities Curve
Point G_1 in Figure 1 represents the production of 200 million units of defense goods and services and 75 million units of nondefense goods and services. Point G_1, however, represents the use of more resources than are available—it lies outside the production possibilities curve. Unless more resources can be obtained and/or the quality of resources improved (for example, through technological change) so that the nation can produce more with the same quantity of resources, there is no way that the society can currently produce 200 million units of defense goods and services and 75 million units of nondefense goods.

1.b.3. Shifts of the Production Possibilities Curve
If a nation obtains more resources or if the existing resources become more efficient, then the PPC shifts outward. Suppose a country discovers new sources of oil within its borders and is able to

FIGURE 2   A Shift of the Production Possibilities Curve

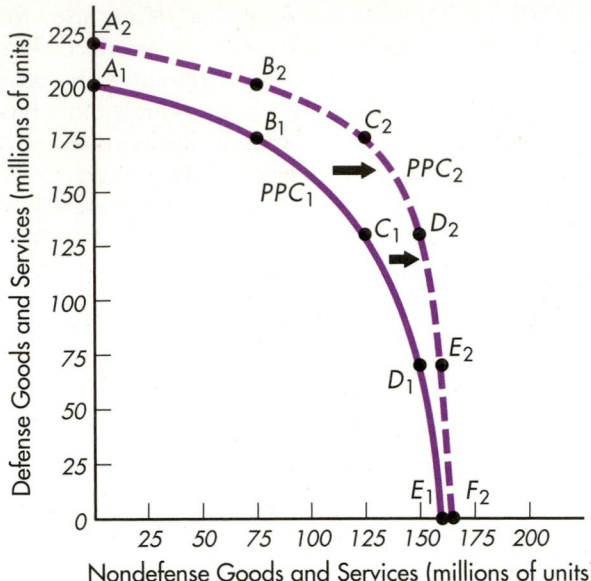

Whenever everything else is not constant, the curve shifts. In this case, an increase in the quantity of a resource enables the society to produce more of both types of goods. The curve shifts out, away from the origin.

greatly increase its production of oil. Greater oil supplies would enable the country to increase production of all types of goods and services.

Figure 2 shows the production possibilities curve before (PPC_1) and after (PPC_2) the discovery of oil. PPC_1 is based on the data given in Figure 1. PPC_2 is based on the data given in Figure 2, which shows the increase in production of goods and services that result from the increase in oil supplies. The first combination of goods and services on PPC_2, point A_2, is 220 million units of defense goods and 0 units of nondefense goods. The second point, B_2, is a combination of 200 million units of defense goods and 75 million units of nondefense goods. C_2 through F_2 are the combinations shown in Figure 2. Connecting these points yields the bowed-out curve PPC_2. Because of the availability of new supplies of oil, the nation is able to increase production of all goods, as shown by the *shift* from PPC_1 to PPC_2. A comparison of the two curves shows that more goods and services for both defense and nondefense are possible along PPC_2 than along PPC_1.

The outward shift of the PPC can be the result of an increase in the quantity of resources, but it also can occur because the quality of resources improves. Economists call an increase in the quality of resources an increase in the productivity of resources. Consider a technological breakthrough that improves the speed with which data are transmitted. Following this breakthrough, it might require fewer people and machines to do the same amount of work, and it might take less time to produce the same quantity and quality of goods. Each quality improvement in resources is illustrated as an outward shift of the PPC.

RECAP

1. Opportunity costs are the benefits that are forgone as a result of a choice. When you choose one thing, you must give up—forgo—others.

2. The production possibilities curve (PPC) illustrates the concept of opportunity cost. Each point on the PPC means that every other point is a forgone opportunity.

3. The PPC represents all combinations of goods and services that can be produced using limited resources efficiently to their full capabilities.

4. Points inside the PPC represent the underutilization, unemployment, or inefficient use of resources—more goods and services could be produced by using the limited resources more fully or efficiently.

5. Points outside the PPC represent combinations of goods and services that are unattainable given the limitation of resources.

6. If more resources are obtained or a technological change or innovation occurs, the PPC shifts out.

2. Specialization and Trade

The PPC illustrates the idea of scarcity—there are limits; combinations outside of the curve are not attainable with current resources and technology; choices have to be made—it is not possible to satisfy unlimited wants. The PPC also illustrates the idea of costs—no matter which combination of goods and services a society chooses to produce, other combinations of goods and services are sacrificed.

 3 Why does specialization occur?

2.a. Marginal Cost

As the production of some types of goods is increased, some other types of goods and services cannot be produced. According to the graph in Figure 1, we see that moving from point A_1 to point B_1 on the PPC means increasing nondefense production from 0 to 75 million units and decreasing defense production from 200 million to 175 million units. Thus, the marginal cost of 75 million units of nondefense is 25 million units of defense. The incremental amount of defense given up with each increase in the production of nondefense goods is known as the **marginal cost** or **marginal opportunity cost**. *Marginal* means "change" or "incremental," so marginal cost is the incremental amount of one good or service that must be given up to obtain one additional unit of another good or service.

Each move along the PPC means giving up some defense goods to get some more nondefense goods. Each additional nondefense good produced requires giving up an increasing number of defense goods. The marginal cost increases with each successive increase of nondefense production. In other words, all other things being equal, it gets more and more costly to produce nondefense goods the more nondefense goods you have.

Marginal cost increases because of specialization. The first resources transferred from defense to nondefense production are those that are least specialized in the production of defense goods. Switching these resources is less costly (less has to be given up) than switching the specialists. Shifting an accountant who can do accounting in either defense- or nondefense-related industries equally well would not cause a big change in defense production. However, shifting a rocket scientist, who is not very useful in producing nondefense goods, would make a big difference. Marginal is a very useful concept in economics. It means incremental or next unit or last unit. Economists often say economic thinking is marginal, by which they mean that it is the incremental or additional that determines behavior, not the total. When the next cookie is not as enjoyable to purchase and eat as is whatever else I might do with that money, I choose not to purchase the cookie.

marginal cost or **marginal opportunity cost**
The amount of one good or service that must be given up to obtain one additional unit of another good or service, no matter how many units are being produced.

© froxx/Shutterstock

4 What are the benefits of trade?

> *Individuals, firms, and nations select the option with the lowest opportunity costs.*

2.b. Specialize Where Opportunity Costs Are Lowest

If we have a choice, we should devote our time and efforts to those activities in which we are relatively better than others. In other words, we should specialize in those activities that require us to give up the smallest amount of other things relative to others. A plumber does plumbing and leaves teaching to the teachers. The teacher teaches and leaves electrical work to the electrician. A country such as Grenada specializes in spice production and leaves manufacturing to other countries.

2.b.1. Trade
If we focus on one thing, how do we get the other things that we want? The answer is that we trade or exchange goods and services. The teacher teaches, earns a salary, and hires a plumber to fix the sinks. This is called voluntary trade or voluntary exchange. The teacher is trading money to the plumber for the plumber's services. The teacher is trading her time to the students and getting money in return.

By specializing in the activities in which opportunity costs are lowest and then trading, everyone will end up with more than if everyone tried to produce everything. This is the **gains from trade**. Consider two students, Josh and Elena, who are sharing an apartment. Neither can cook, so they just order out a lot. But cleaning and laundry are other matters. Cleaning means vacuuming, dusting, mopping, and washing windows. A load of laundry consists of the wash, the drying, and the folding. If Josh and Elena both devote 10 hours to cleaning, each can clean 10 rooms. If they spend all their time and effort on laundry, Josh is able to complete 5 loads while Elena can do 10 loads.

gains from trade
The difference between what can be produced and consumed without specialization and trade and with specialization and trade.

	Elena		Josh	
	Cleaning	Laundry	Cleaning	Laundry
All resources devoted:				
To Cleaning	0	10	0	5
To Laundry	10	0	10	0

Since Elena is better at cleaning and just as good at laundry, why should she want to work with Josh? The answer depends on relative costs. What does it cost Elena to do 1 load of laundry? She has to not clean 1 room. So, it costs her 1 room of cleaning to do 1 load of laundry. Josh can do 2 loads of laundry in the time he can clean just 1 room. So, it costs Josh just 1/2 of a clean room to do 1 load of laundry. Josh is *relatively* better at doing laundry—he can do it for lower costs than can Elena. He has a comparative advantage in laundry. **Comparative advantage** refers to a comparison of opportunity costs—do you have lower costs of carrying out some activity than someone else? If so, you have a comparative advantage.

Who is relatively better at cleaning? It costs Josh 2 loads of laundry to clean 1 room and it costs Elena 1 load of laundry to clean 1 room. So Elena is relatively more efficient at cleaning. She has a comparative advantage in cleaning.

If Elena specializes in cleaning and Josh in laundry, and then they trade, they will both be better off. To see this, let's begin where there is no trade and Josh and Elena each spends half their time and effort on cleaning and half on laundry. By spending half her time on cleaning, Elena can clean 5 rooms, whereas Josh can only clean 2.5 by spending half his time on cleaning. They each can do 5 loads of laundry if they devote half their time to laundry.

comparative advantage
The ability to produce a good or service at a lower opportunity cost than someone else.

	Elena		Josh	
	Cleaning	Laundry	Cleaning	Laundry
All resources devoted:				
To Cleaning	0	10	0	5
To Laundry	10	0	10	0
No Specialization	5	5	5	2.5

Now, let's assume that they specialize according to comparative advantage and then trade at a rate of 1 clean room for 1 completed load of laundry. Elena cleans 10 rooms. To get 5 loads of laundry, she needs to trade 5 cleaned rooms. She ends up the same as if she did not specialize. Josh, on the other hand, specializes by completing 10 loads of laundry. He can get 5 cleaned rooms for 5 loads of laundry, and he ends up 2.5 cleaned rooms better than if he had not traded.

	Elena		Josh	
	Cleaning	Laundry	Cleaning	Laundry
Specialization and trade at ratio of 2:1	5	5	5	5

Notice that there are gains from trade. There are 2.5 more clean rooms as a result of specialization and trade. In this case, the gains all went to Josh because the trading price, 1 to 1, was the same as Elena's personal opportunity cost ratio. Let's now change the trading price so that Elena gets the gains. Let's assume that they specialize and trade at a ratio of 2 loads of laundry for 1 clean room, Josh's personal opportunity cost ratio. In this case, Elena trades 2.5 cleaned rooms to get 5 loads of laundry. She is the one who gains this time:

	Elena		Josh	
	Cleaning	Laundry	Cleaning	Laundry
Specialization and trade at ratio of 2:1	5	7.5	5	2.5

In each of the two examples, just one party gained. This is because the trades took place first at Elena's opportunity cost ratio and then at Josh's opportunity cost ratio. In reality, people won't trade voluntarily unless they gain. Elena and Josh would work out how many cleaned rooms to trade for a load of laundry so that they both gained something.

Specialization and trade enable individuals, firms, and nations to acquire combinations of goods that lie beyond their own resource capabilities. Voluntary, free trade results in more being created—more income being generated, that is—and higher standards of living are being created because everything is produced at the lowest possible cost.

When you buy something, you are trading—you are exchanging money for some item. Similarly, when you sell something, you are trading—exchanging some item for money. Imagine your world without trade. A good start would be to put yourself in the place of Tom Hanks's character in the movie *Cast Away*. If you've seen the movie, you can remember the scene where he was able to rub two sticks together to create fire. From then on, he had some light at night and some means for cooking food. But until then, he went to sleep when it became dark and he woke up in a small, drafty tent-house that he had put together. So here you are in Hanks's place. All alone, you would get clothes only by utilizing items that you had found. You might be able to create some tea or coffee from something you had grown and eat something that you had caught or raised, but you would spend all your waking hours just trying to survive. An attempt to create a fishing net or some other tool would mean not gathering food that was available. Compare that type of existence to what you have today, and you are measuring the cumulative gains from trade. Society would have remained hunter-gatherers had it not been for trade.

2.c. Comparative Advantage

We have seen that the choice of which area or activity to specialize in is made on the basis of opportunity costs. Economists refer to the ability of one person or nation to do something with a lower opportunity cost than another as comparative advantage.

ECONOMIC INSIGHT

Comparative Advantage

(Salute Science for This One: Women Are Better at Ironing)

"According to a new study, women proved themselves innate domestic goddesses in a series of household tasks—threading a needle, making a bed, and ironing—beating their male counterparts in three-minute trials for each activity. But men, ever-handy specimens they are, fared better at reading maps, changing a tire, and pitching a tent. The study was carried out by research analysts MindLab International and featured more than 1,200 adults. It found clear divisions in what men and women could complete in just three minutes from a selection of various tasks. Women could iron two shirts far more adeptly in the time limit. Overall they excelled in those jobs which needed speedy hand-to-eye co-ordination and verbal reasoning, such as threading six needles or winning an argument with logic. Men, in contrast, did better at those jobs which needed what researchers call spatial awareness, such as map reading, understanding self assembly instructions, and putting up a tent."

Many readers of the blog were upset that this seemed to demean women, that they are destined to stay home and do home chores—remain barefoot and pregnant. According to the study, women have an absolute advantage in ironing, but it does not mean that they have a comparative advantage. Men can change tires better than women, and women can iron better than men. Women have both an absolute and a comparative advantage in ironing, and men have both an absolute and comparative advantage at changing tires. But suppose women can iron 10 shirts in the same time they can change 2 tires while men can iron 10 shirts in the same time they can change 1 tire. In this case the opportunity cost of ironing 1 shirt is .02 tires for women and .01 for men. Men have a comparative advantage in ironing. So it is comparative advantage that determines specialization, not absolute advantage.

Source: Lauren Bans, Slate.com XX Factor. Tuesday, March 16, 2010.

Mexico has a comparative advantage in low-skilled, low-wage workers relative to the United States. Free trade means that Mexico should specialize in those activities requiring low-skilled, low-wage workers. However, Mexico's government has intervened in the country's economy to such an extent that resources cannot flow to where their value is highest. As a result, many of the labor resources have to leave Mexico in order to be able to earn a living.

Comparative advantage applies to every case of trade or exchange. This sometimes seems counterintuitive. Shouldn't countries that have lots of natural resources and a skilled labor force do everything themselves? The answer is no. Even though the United States has many more natural resources and a much larger and better-educated population than Grenada, Grenada has a comparative advantage in producing spices. The United States could produce more of everything than Grenada, but the opportunity cost of producing spices is higher in the United States than it is in Grenada. Both Grenada and the United States gain by having Grenada specialize in spice production and trade with the United States.

If you go around the world and look at what goods and services are traded, you can usually identify the comparative advantage. Some trade occurs simply because a country has more of something. Saudi Arabia trades oil because it has more than anyone else. But countries don't have to have more of something for there to be gains from trade. They simply have to do something at a lower cost than another country. For instance, most developing nations have a comparative advantage in activities that use unskilled labor. Unskilled labor is much less expensive in Mexico, China, India, Pakistan, Bangladesh, and many other countries than in the United States. So gains from trade occur when these countries do things that use unskilled labor and then trade with the United States for foodstuffs or high-technology goods. The United States is sending many unskilled speaking jobs, such as telephone call agents, to India because Indians speak English and their wages are low.

Trade is not based solely on wage differences. Most trade in the world occurs between industrial or developed nations rather than between a developed and a less-developed nation. Each of the nations has comparative advantages in some goods and services. Germany might have a comparative advantage in engineering automobiles, Denmark in producing Havarti cheese, France in wine, Switzerland in banking, and so on. Each country gains by specializing according to comparative advantage and then trading.

2.d. Private Property Rights

> *Individuals specialize in the activity in which their opportunity costs are lowest.*

Each of us will specialize in some activity, earn income, and then trade our output (or income) for other goods and services that we want. Specialization and trade ensure that we are better off than we would be if we did everything ourselves. *Specialization according to comparative advantage followed by trade allows everyone to acquire more of the goods they want.* But, for trade to occur, we must have confidence that we own what we create, and that what we own cannot be taken away. **Private property rights** are necessary for trade to occur. If I order a pizza to be delivered by Papa John's to my house, but anyone can come over and eat it when it arrives, I won't have an incentive to order any pizzas. If I can live in a house, but I can't own it, I have no incentive to take care of it. Private property rights refer to the right of ownership, and it requires a legal system of laws and courts and police to ensure ownership. If someone steals my car, someone will be penalized, since stealing a car is against the law. And if someone mugs me, takes my wallet, and leaves me bleeding on the sidewalk, that is theft of person and property and is also against the law. I have ownership rights to my body, to my assets, and to the things I have bought.

private property right
The right of ownership.

If no one owns something, no one has the incentive to take care of it. An example is presented in the Land Titling in Argentina case discussed in the following Economics Insight box. Consider the fish in the ocean. No one owns the fish, and hence, no one has the incentive to protect them, raise them, and ensure that future generations of fish exist. Someone has to own an item for someone to care for it. Also, it is *private* property rights that count, not *public* property rights. If no one owns something, no one takes care of it. But equally, if everyone owns something, no one has an incentive to take care of it. In the former Soviet Union, the government owned virtually everything. No one had an incentive to take care of anything. As a result, housing was decrepit and dingy, industries were inefficient and run down, chemicals were dumped in the rivers and on the land, the air was polluted, and, in general, standards of living were very low.

RECAP

1. Marginal cost is the incremental amount of one good or service that must be given up to obtain one additional unit of another good or service.

2. The rule of specialization is: specialize where the opportunity cost is lowest.

3. Comparative advantage exists whenever one person (firm, nation) can do something with lower opportunity costs than some other individual (firm, nation) can.

4. Specialization and trade enable individuals, firms, and nations to get more than they could without specialization and trade. This is called *gains from trade*.

5. Private property rights are necessary for voluntary trade to develop. Private property rights refer to the laws, courts, and police required to enforce the prohibition of theft and murder.

ECONOMIC INSIGHT

The Importance of Private Property Rights

There are many real-life cases showing the importance of property rights in the behavior and standards of living of people. In Korea, those who have lived under private property rights and economic freedom (South Korea) have flourished economically relative to those grinding out tough lives under a despotic regime that allows no freedom and no private property (North Korea). Korea was occupied by Japan from 1905 until it was divided into two countries following World War II. North Korea retained a strong version of communism and totalitarianism, while South Korea slowly moved in the direction of private property rights and, eventually, political democracy. The differences in economic growth and changes in standards of living during the past 30 years are astounding. North Korea is mired in poverty, unable to feed its population. The economy is in such shambles that more than 2 million people have starved to death and more than 60 percent of the children are malnourished. South Koreans enjoy a standard of living far higher than that of North Korea.

In Buenos Aires, Argentina, a group of squatters organized by a Catholic chapel took over some vacant land as their residences.[1] Some of the squatters were able to obtain property rights while others were not. After about 20 years, the differences between the lives of those with property rights and those without were substantial. Those with property rights invested in their properties, while those without property rights did not. The result was that there is a significant difference in housing quality between the owned and unowned properties. The owned properties were upgraded, expanded, and improved. The unowned properties were run-down, crumbling shanties. The really amazing thing, though, is that those with ownership behaved so differently than those without ownership: They had fewer children and

the children acquired more education and had better health. Why does a title make a difference?

The problem with a lack of property rights or a system in which property rights are not secure and established is that people cannot use the property for collateral or cannot expect to get anything back if they invest in the property.

In the 1930s, the Finns and Estonians enjoyed a similar standard of living. The two countries are virtually neighbors. Their languages share a common linguistic root, they are culturally similar, and they share many values. In 2000, the average Finn earned two and a half times to more than seven times what the average Estonian earned. Fifty years of Communist rule surely had something to do with the gap in incomes that opened between the two countries. In the past, substantial differences existed between the standard of living in East and West Germany—two countries with essentially the same resources, education, culture, language, religion, history, and geography. Despite its own recent economic miracle, China's real per-capita GDP in 2000 was still just under \$4,000. Taiwan's is over \$17,000, more than four times China's.[2] In each of these comparisons, culture, language, and traditions are the same. Outcomes are markedly different. The countries with private property rights grew richer; the others faltered or went backwards.

---

[1] See the study by Sebastian Galiani and Ernesto Schargrodsky, "Property Rights for the Poor: Effects of Land Titling," Coase Institute Working Paper, August 9, 2005, for a complete discussion of this and other issues related to the Argentine case.

[2] Gerald P. O'Driscoll Jr. and Lee Hoskins, "Property Rights: The Key to Economic Development," Policy Analysis No. 482, Cato Institute, August 7, 2003.

SUMMARY

1. **What are opportunity costs? Are they part of the economic way of thinking?**

   - Opportunity costs are the forgone opportunities of the next best alternative. Choice means both gaining something and giving up something. When you choose one option, you forgo all others. The benefits of the next best alternative are the opportunity costs of your choice. *§1*

2. **What is a production possibilities curve?**

   - A production possibilities curve (PPC) represents the trade-offs involved in the allocation of scarce resources. It shows the maximum quantity of goods and services that can be produced using limited resources to the fullest extent possible. *§1.b*

3. **Why does specialization occur?**

   - Comparative advantage accounts for specialization. We specialize in the activities in which we have the lowest opportunity costs, that is, in which we have a comparative advantage. *§2.c*

4. **What are the benefits of trade?**

   - Voluntary trade enables people to get more than they could get by doing everything themselves. The amount they get by specializing and trading is called gains from trade. *§2.b.1*

- Specialization and trade enable those involved to acquire more than they could if they did not specialize and engage in trade. *§2.c*

- Private property rights are necessary for voluntary trade to occur. Private property rights refer to the legal system that ensures that people own their persons and their property. Others cannot steal that property or harm that person. *§2.d*

KEY TERMS

comparative advantage, 28
gains from trade, 28
marginal cost, 27

marginal opportunity cost, 27
opportunity costs, 23
private property rights, 31

production possibilities curve (PPC), 23
trade-off, 23

EXERCISES

1. In most political campaigns, candidates promise more than they can deliver. In the United States, both Democrats and Republicans promise better health care, a better environment, only minor reductions in defense, better education, an improved system of roads, bridges, sewer systems, water systems, and so on. What economic concept do candidates ignore?

2. Janine is an accountant who makes $30,000 a year. Robert is a college student who makes $8,000 a year. All other things being equal, who is more likely to stand in a long line to get a concert ticket? Explain.

3. In 2009, President Barack Obama and Congress enacted a budget that included increases in spending for the war in Iraq and national defense, as well as huge increases in welfare programs, education, and many other programs. The budget expenditures exceeded the revenues by over a trillion dollars. The argument was that "we need these things," and therefore there is no limit to what the government should provide. Is there a limit? What concept is ignored by those politicians who claim that there is no limit to what the government should provide?

4. The following numbers measure the trade-off between grades and income:

Total Hours	Hours Studying	GPA	Hours Working	Income
60	30	2.0	30	$150
60	10	1.0	50	$250
60	0	0.0	60	$300

   a. Calculate the opportunity cost of an increase in the number of hours spent studying in order to earn a 3.0 grade point average (GPA) rather than a 2.0 GPA. (Assume linear relationships.)
   b. Is the opportunity cost the same for a move from a 0.0 GPA to a 1.0 GPA as it is for a move from a 1.0 GPA to a 2.0 GPA?
   c. What is the opportunity cost of an increase in income from $100 to $150?

5. Suppose a second individual has the following trade-offs between income and grades:

Total Hours	Hours Studying	GPA	Hours Working	Income
60	50	4.0	10	$ 60
60	40	3.0	20	$120
60	20	2.0	40	$240
60	10	1.0	50	$300
60	0	0.0	60	$360

a. Define comparative advantage.
b. Does either individual (the one in exercise 4 or the one in exercise 5) have a comparative advantage in both activities?
c. Who should specialize in studying and who should specialize in working?

6. A doctor earns $250,000 per year, while a professor earns $40,000. They play tennis against each other each Saturday morning, each giving up a morning of relaxing, reading the paper, and playing with their children. They could each decide to work a few extra hours on Saturday and earn more income. But they choose to play tennis or to relax around the house. Are their opportunity costs of playing tennis different?

7. Plot the PPC of a nation given by the following data.

Combination	Health Care	All Other Goods
A	0	100
B	25	90
C	50	70
D	75	40
E	100	0

a. Calculate the marginal opportunity cost of each combination.
b. What is the opportunity cost of combination C?
c. Suppose a second nation has the following data. Plot the PPC, and then determine which nation has the comparative advantage in which activity. Show whether the two nations can gain from specialization and trade.

Combination	Health Care	All Other Goods
A	0	50
B	20	40
C	40	25
D	60	5
E	65	0

8. A doctor earns $200 per hour, a plumber $40 per hour, and a professor $20 per hour. Everything else the same, which one will devote more hours to negotiating the price of a new car? Explain.

9. Perhaps you've heard of the old saying, "There is no such thing as a free lunch." What does it mean? If someone invites you to a lunch and offers to pay for it, is it free to you?

10. You have waited 30 minutes in a line for the Star Tours ride at Disneyland. You see a sign that says, "From this point on, your wait is 45 minutes." You must decide whether to remain in the line or to move elsewhere. On what basis do you make the decision? Do the 30 minutes you've already stood in line come into play?

11. A university is deciding between two meal plans. One plan charges a fixed fee of $600 per semester and allows students to eat as much as they want. The other plan charges a fee based on the quantity of food consumed. Under which plan will students eat the most?

12. Evaluate this statement: "You are a natural athlete, an attractive person who learns easily and communicates well. Clearly, you can do everything better than your friends and acquaintances. As a result, the term *specialization* has no meaning for you. Specialization would cost you rather than benefit you."

13. During China's Cultural Revolution in the late 1960s and early 1970s, highly educated people were forced to move to farms and work in the fields. Some were common laborers for eight or more years. What does this policy say about specialization and the PPC? Would you predict that the policy would lead to an increase in output?

14. In elementary school and through middle school, most students have the same teacher throughout the day and for the entire school year. Then, beginning in high school, different subjects are taught by different teachers. In college, the same subject is often taught at different levels—freshman, sophomore, junior-senior, or graduate—by different faculty. Is education taking advantage of specialization only from high school on? Comment on the differences between elementary school and college and the use of specialization.

15. The top officials in the federal government and high-ranking officers of large corporations often have chauffeurs to drive them around the city or from meeting to meeting. Is this simply one of the perquisites of their position, or is the use of chauffeurs justifiable on the basis of comparative advantage?

16. In Botswana, Zimbabwe, and South Africa, individuals can own and farm elephants. In other African countries, the elephants are put on large reserves. Explain why the elephant population in Botswana, Zimbabwe, and South Africa has risen, whereas that in the rest of Africa has fallen.

You can find further practice tests in the Online Quiz at **www.cengage.com/economics/boyes**.

FLAT OWNERS TAKE TO BARRICADES AS CHÁVEZ SEIZES PRIVATE ASSETS

The Times (London), November 12, 2010

Hugo Chávez is speeding up his seizure of assets before newly elected opposition members of parliament take their seats in January.

The President of Venezuela is now trying to address a housing shortage by grabbing control of private residential apartment blocks.

The left-wing leader has redoubled efforts to extend state control over the economy after a major electoral setback in September in which opposition parties wiped out the two-thirds majority that he needs to overturn existing legislation. Since then, 26 companies have been effectively nationalised, including Owens-Illinois, the U.S. glassmaker; Sidetur, a steelmaker; five milk distributors; and Venezuela's largest agricultural supplier.

President Chávez has been forced to defend himself against accusations that he has no respect for individual property after seizing six residential apartment blocks and the "temporary occupation" of a further eight in cities including Caracas.

He has justified the expropriation of the properties by arguing that the construction companies that built them had either left the flats unfinished or had been badly delayed in completing them. He said that the moves represented an "act of justice," and accused construction and property companies of organised crime, arguing that by charging homebuyers high rates of interest on unfinished apartments, they were guilty of fraud.

At the weekend, residents of one complex that has been seized issued a statement insisting that the construction company had not reneged on its obligations.

"We strongly reject the expropriation measure," they said. Residents of the largely middle-class blocks have hastily implemented security to keep officials out, organising round-the-clock surveillance and putting sirens at entrances.

Critics, including Venezuela's largest business chamber, said that the measure would scare off investment and put at risk the construction this year of 52,000 homes by private companies. Venezuela faces a record housing shortage of 2 million homes.

Julio Borges, the opposition politician, accused Mr. Chávez of trampling over private-property rights and steering Venezuela towards Cuba-style communism. Mr. Borges told a news conference on Sunday that Venezuelans did not want to live in a "country of slaves, where the Government is the owner of everything and the people aren't owners of anything."

The Government compensates owners for loss of property, but companies whose assets have been seized say that payment is slow and often very low.

HANNAH STRANGE

Source: © Hannah Strange, NI Syndication Limited, November 12, 2010.

Commentary

There is a story that goes something like this: Everybody, Somebody, Anybody, and Nobody were faced with an important task. Everybody was sure that Somebody would do it. Anybody could have done it, but Nobody did it. Somebody got angry about that because it was Everybody's job. Everybody thought Anybody could do it. But Nobody realized that Everybody wouldn't do it. The end result was that Everybody blamed Somebody when Nobody did what Anybody could have done.

The story points out that if you own something, you have an incentive to take care of it. When no one owns something or when everyone owns something, no one has an incentive to take care of it. That is what private property rights are all about: They ensure individual ownership, thereby providing incentive to care for what is owned. When all housing in China's major cities was owned by the government, the houses and apartments were not taken care of. But, as soon as China allowed some private ownership of apartments, the improvements were amazing—clean and lighted hallways, and other improvements in the buildings. Similarly, in the low- to no income projects of the large cities in the eastern United States, where apartments are owned by the government, the poor have no incentive to ensure that the housing is cared for. But when the projects are sold to private owners, the apartments are improved and cared for.

The PPC shows combinations of two goods, services, or activities that people can devote their resources to producing. Points along the curve are all possible combinations of two goods that can be produced using an individual's resources fully and efficiently. If you can own what you create, you have an incentive to produce somewhere along the PPC. But, if you don't own what you create, why should you worry about whether you are using resources efficiently or fully? You will operate at a point inside the PPC, such as point A. You will produce less than you are capable of producing. Because you will produce less, you will have no incentive to specialize and trade—you don't own what you produce, so you don't care whether it is in accordance with comparative advantage. There is nothing to trade because you own nothing.

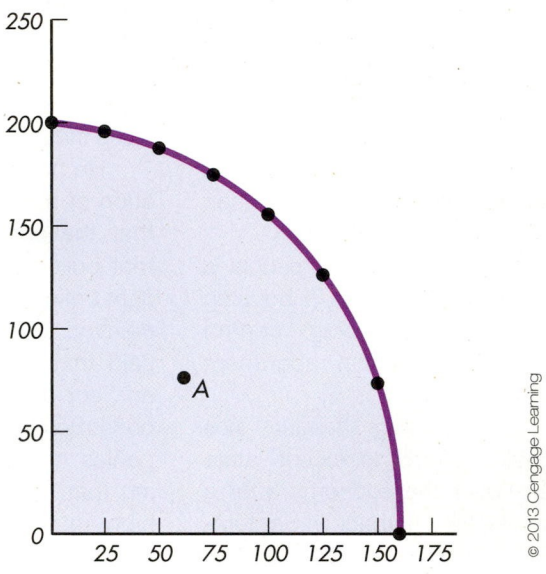

In Venezuela, the problem is that the poor own nothing. Over 75 percent of the population in most Latin American nations do not hold title to the property on which their houses rest or the fields in which they labor. Without ownership, there is no incentive to improve the property. It is no different for the apartment owners—when they do not own their property, they have no incentive to take care of it. Why should any private apartment owner in Venezuela invest in the property, maintain it, or even improve it? The direction in which Chavez is taking Venezuela is the direction in which Castro took Cuba, Mao took China, and Lenin, Stalin, and others took Russia. The result is a shrinking PPC and a reduction in standards of living.

CHAPTER 3

Markets, Demand and Supply, and the Price System

© OLGA CHERNETSKAYA & LEONID YASTREMSKY/SHUTTERSTOCK.COM;
LOGO: © FROXX/SHUTTERSTOCK.COM

© MACIEJ FROLOW/GETTY IMAGES, INC

 **FUNDAMENTAL QUESTIONS**

1 How do we decide who gets the scarce goods and resources?

2 What is demand?

3 What is supply?

4 How is price determined by demand and supply?

5 What causes price to change?

6 What happens when price is not allowed to change with market forces?

People (and firms and nations) can get more if they specialize in certain activities and then trade with one another to acquire the goods and services that they desire than they can if they do everything themselves. This is what we described in the previous chapter as gains from trade. But how does everyone get together to trade? Who decides who specializes in what, and who determines who gets what?

In some countries, the government decides who gets what and what is produced. In India until the mid-1990s, in the Soviet Union from 1917 until 1989, in China at least until 1980, and in Cuba, Venezuela, and Cameroon and other African nations today, a few government officials dictate what is produced, by whom it is produced, where it is produced, what price it sells at, and who may buy it.

In most developed or industrial nations, government officials dictate what, how, for whom, and at what price a few things are produced, but for most goods and services, private individuals decide. When you walk into your local Starbucks to get a tall coffee, do you wonder who told the people working there to work there, or who told the coffee growers to send their coffee beans to this particular Starbucks, or who told the bakery to provide this Starbucks with croissants? Probably not. Most of us take all these things for granted. Yet, it is a remarkable phenomenon—we get what we want, when we want it, and where we want it. How does this work? It is the market process; no one dictates what is produced, how it is produced, the price at which it sells, or who buys it. All this occurs through the self-interested behavior of individuals interacting in a **market**.

The term *market* refers to the interaction of buyers and sellers. A market may be a specific location, such as the supermarket, or it may be the exchange of particular

A market arises when buyers and sellers exchange a well-defined good or service. In the case of a supermarket like this one, buyers purchase groceries and household items. The market occurs in a building at a specific location.

market
A place or service that enables buyers and sellers to exchange goods and services.

In the case of the flower market, shoppers can examine the day's assortment and make their choices. This flower market does not occur at a specific location nor in a fixed building.

goods or services at many different locations, such as the foreign exchange market. A market makes possible the exchange of goods and services. It may be a formally organized exchange, such as the New York Stock Exchange, or it may be loosely organized, like the market for used bicycles or automobiles. A market may be confined to one location, as in the case of a supermarket, or it may encompass a city, a state, a country, or the entire world, such as the market for foreign exchange.

In this chapter, we discuss the allocation of goods and services—how it is determined what is produced and who gets what.

1. Allocation Systems

 1 How do we decide who gets the scarce goods and resources?

An allocation system is the process of determining who gets the goods and services and who doesn't. There are many different allocation systems that we might use. One is to have someone, say the government, determine who gets what, as in Cuba or Cameroon. Another is to have a first-come, first-served system, where those who arrive first get the goods and services. A third is to have a lottery, with the lucky winners getting the goods and services. A fourth is the market or price system, where those with the incomes are able to buy the goods and services. Which is best? Take the quiz on the next page, and then we'll discuss allocation systems some more.

1.a. Fairness

How did you respond to the four questions in each scenario? If you are like most people, you believe that the price on the bottles of water ought to be raised and that the first patients showing up at the doctor's office ought to get service. Very few believe that the price or the market ought to be used to allocate important items like health care. Most claim that the price system is not fair. Yet none of the allocation approaches is "fair" if fairness means that everyone gets what he or she wants. In every case, someone gets the good or service and someone does not. This is what scarcity is all about—there is not enough to go around. With the market system, it is those without income or wealth who must do without. Is this fair? No. Under the first-come, first-served system, it is those who arrive later who do without. This isn't fair either, since those who are slow, old, disabled, or otherwise not first to arrive won't get the goods and services. Under the government scheme, it is those who are not in favor or those who do not match up with the government's rules who do without. In the former Soviet Union, Cuba, Cameroon, and other government-run countries, it is the government officials who get most of the goods and services through what we call corruption, graft, and bribes. And, with a random procedure, it is those who do not have the lucky ticket or the correct number who are left out.

None of these allocation systems is fair in the sense that no one gets left out. Scarcity means that someone gets left out. Only if your measure of fair is equal opportunity is the lottery system fair. When everything is allocated by lottery, everyone has an equal chance of winning. But otherwise, life is not fair.

Allocation Quiz

I. At a sightseeing point reachable only after a strenuous hike, a firm has established a stand where bottled water is sold. The water, carried in by the employees of the firm, is sold to thirsty hikers in six-ounce bottles. The price is $1 per bottle. Typically, only 100 bottles of the water are sold each day. On a particularly hot day, however, 200 hikers each want to buy at least one bottle of water. Indicate what you think of each of the following means of distributing the water to the hikers by responding to each allocation approach with one of the following five responses:

a. Agree completely
b. Agree with slight reservation
c. Disagree
d. Strongly disagree
e. Totally unacceptable

1. Increasing the price until the quantity of bottles of water that hikers are willing and able to purchase exactly equals the number of bottles available for sale
2. Selling the water for $1 per bottle on a first-come, first-served basis
3. Having the local authority (government) buy the water for $1 per bottle and distribute it according to its own judgment
4. Selling the water for $1 per bottle following a random selection procedure or lottery

II. A physician has been providing medical services at a fee of $100 per patient and typically sees 30 patients per day. One day the flu bug has been so vicious that the number of patients attempting to visit the physician exceeds 60. Indicate what you think of each of the following means of distributing the physician's services to the sick patients by responding with one of the following five responses:

a. Agree completely
b. Agree with slight reservation
c. Disagree
d. Strongly disagree
e. Totally unacceptable

1. Raising the price until the number of patients the doctor sees is exactly equal to the number of patients who are willing and able to pay the doctor's fee
2. Selling the services for $100 per patient on a first-come, first-served basis
3. Having the local authority (government) pay the physician $100 per patient and choose who is to receive the services according to its own judgment
4. Selling the physician's services for $100 per patient following a random selection procedure or lottery

1.b. Incentives

Since each allocation mechanism is unfair, how do we decide which to use? One way might be by the incentives that each creates. Do the incentives lead to behavior that will improve things, increase supplies, and raise standards of living?

With the first-come, first-served allocation scheme, the incentive is to be first. You have no reason to improve the quality of your products or to increase the value of your resources. There is no incentive to increase the amounts of goods and services supplied. Why would anyone produce when all everyone wants is to be first? As a result, with a first-come, first-served allocation system, growth will not occur, and standards of living will not rise. A society based *solely* on first-come, first-served would die a quick death.

A government scheme provides an incentive either to be a member of government and thus help determine the allocation rules or to do exactly what the government orders you to do. There are no incentives to improve production and efficiency or to increase the quantities supplied, and thus there is no reason for the economy to grow. This type of system is a failure, as evidenced by the Soviet Union, Mao Tse-Tung's China, Cuba, and socialist systems in Latin America and Africa and in virtually every poor country in the world.

The random allocation system incentivizes you to do nothing—you simply hope that manna from heaven falls on you.

With the market system, the incentive is to acquire purchasing ability—to obtain income and wealth. This means that you must provide goods that have high value to others and provide resources that have high value to producers—to enhance your worth as an employee by acquiring education or training, and to enhance the value of the resources you own.

Very importantly, the market system also provides incentives for quantities of scarce goods to increase. In the case of the water stand in Scenario I, if the price of the water increases and the owner of the water stand is earning significant profits, others may carry or truck water to the top of the hill and sell it to thirsty hikers; the amount of water available thus increases. In the case of the doctor in Scenario II, other doctors may think that opening an office near the first might be a way to earn more; the amount of physician services available increases. Since the market system creates the incentive for the amount supplied to increase, economies grow and expand, and standards of living improve. The market system also ensures that resources are allocated to where they are most highly valued. If the price of an item rises, consumers may switch to another item, or another good or service, that can serve about the same purpose. When consumers switch, production of the alternative good rises, and thus the resources used in its production must increase as well. As a result, resources are reallocated from lower-valued uses to higher-valued uses.

1.c. The Market Process: Arbitrage

When the Mazda Miata was introduced in the United States in 1990, the little sports roadster was an especially desired product in southern California. As shown in Figure 1, the suggested retail price was $13,996, the price at which it was selling in Detroit. In Los Angeles, the purchase price was nearly $25,000. Several entrepreneurs recognized the profit potential in the $10,000 price differential and sent hundreds of students to Detroit to pick up Miatas and drive them back to Los Angeles. Within a reasonably short time, the price differential between Detroit and Los Angeles was reduced. The increased sales in Detroit drove the price there up, while the increased number of Miatas being sold in Los Angeles reduced the price there. The price differential continued to decline until it was less than the cost of shipping the cars from Detroit to Los Angeles. This story of the Mazda Miata illustrates how markets work to allocate scarce goods, services, and resources. A product is purchased where its price is low and sold where its price is high. As a result, resources devoted to that product flow to where they have the highest value. The same type of situation occurred with the introduction of the Mini Cooper in 2001. The car was selling for much more in California than in New York and Chicago, so people purchased the cars in Chicago or New York and had the cars shipped to California.

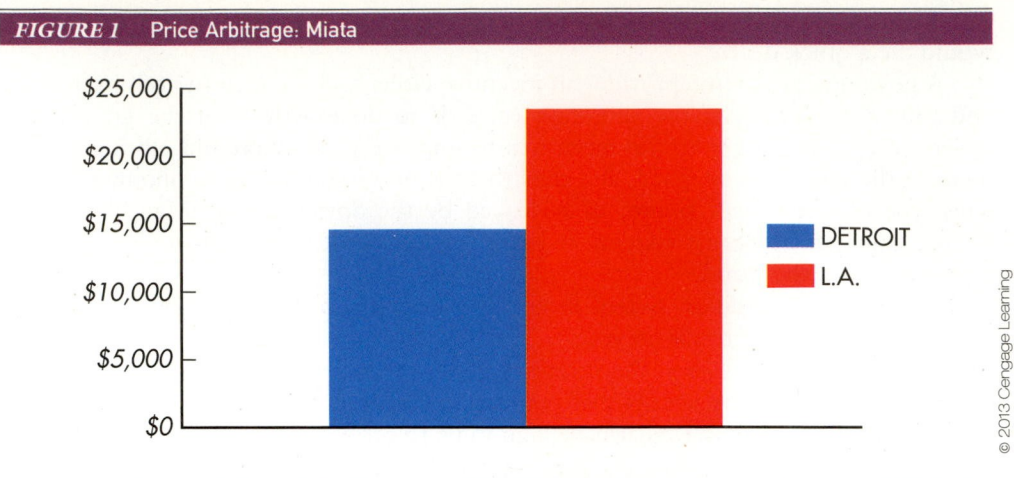

FIGURE 1   Price Arbitrage: Miata

© 2013 Cengage Learning

Suppose an electronics firm is inefficient, its employees are surly, and its products are not displayed well. To attempt to earn a profit, the firm charges more than the efficiently run firm down the street. Where do customers go? Obviously, they seek out the best deal and go to the more efficient firm. The more efficient store has to get more supplies, hire more employees, acquire more space, and so on. The inefficient store lays off employees, sells used equipment, and gets rid of its inventory. The resources thus go from where they were not as highly valued to where they are most highly valued.

Why does the market process work? For a very simple reason: People are looking for the best deal—the highest-quality products at the lowest prices. So when an opportunity for a "best deal" arises, people respond to it by purchasing where the price is low and selling where the price is high.

As long as the market is free to change, it will ensure that resources are allocated to where they have the highest value and people get what they want at the lowest price. But what happens if something interferes with the market process? Each year *The Economist* magazine[1] publishes its Big Mac Index. This index lists the price of a Big Mac in many different countries. Adjusting for different currencies, one year the index looked something like Figure 2.

What do you bright entrepreneurs see? That's right—an arbitrage opportunity: You could load up a Boeing 747 with Big Macs in Phoenix and fly to Tokyo and sell the Big Macs for a nice profit. The larger supply in Tokyo would reduce the Tokyo price, and the greater demand in Phoenix would raise the price there. Why does that not happen? Part of the reason might be that the food is not portable; it deteriorates in the airplane. Another reason is that regulations would not allow it: Japan would not allow someone to simply land on the tarmac and beginning selling Big Macs out of a cargo hold. Arbitrage in the movement of Big Macs does not take place because regulations interfere with the market process. So, when something interferes with the market process, resources do not go to where they are most highly valued, and consumers don't get what they want at the lowest prices.

[1] http://www.economist.com/markets/indicators/displaystory.cfm?story_id=12991434, accessed January 22, 2009.

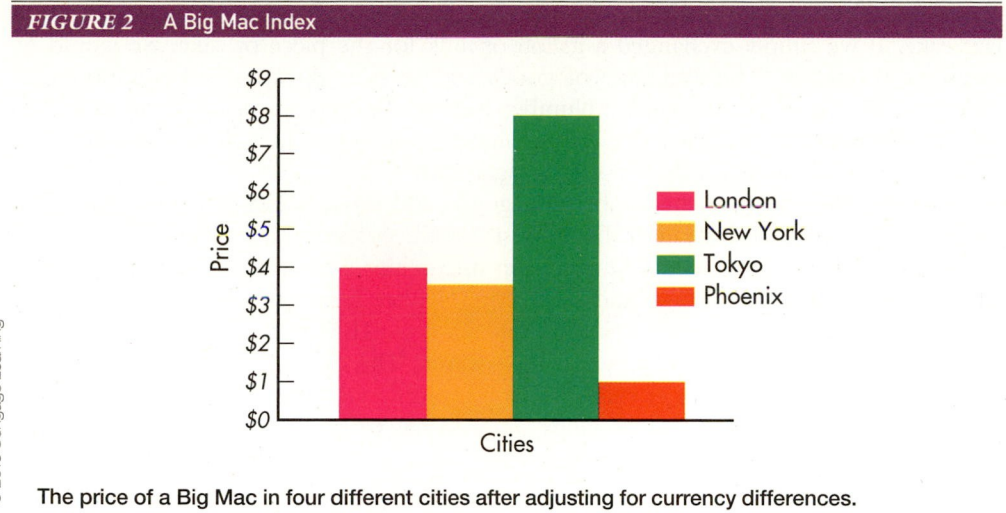

FIGURE 2   A Big Mac Index

The price of a Big Mac in four different cities after adjusting for currency differences.

© 2013 Cengage Learning

RECAP

1. Scarce goods and resources can be allocated in many different ways. Four common approaches are first-come, first-served; prices; government; and random.

2. No allocation mechanism is fair in the sense that everyone gets everything they want. This would defy the idea of scarcity. Some people will get the goods and resources and others will not.

3. The incentives each allocation system creates is a fundamental reason that markets are selected to do the allocation. Only a market system creates the incentives that lead to increasing standards of living.

2. Markets and Money

The market process refers to the way that scarce goods and services are allocated through the individual actions of buyers and sellers. The price adjusts to the actions of buyers and sellers so as to ensure that resources are used where they have the highest value—the price of the Miata in Los Angeles declines as more Miatas end up in Los Angeles. The price measures the opportunity cost—how much has to be given up in order to get something else. If you pay a dollar for a cup of coffee, then the opportunity cost of that coffee is everything else that dollar could have been used to buy. In most cases, when you buy something you exchange money for that something. There are cases where you actually exchange one good for another—you might mow someone's lawn in exchange for them taking care of your house while you are on vacation. Every market exchange is not necessarily a monetary exchange.

2.a. Barter and Money Exchanges

The purpose of markets is to facilitate the exchange of goods and services between buyers and sellers. In some cases, money changes hands; in others, only goods and services are exchanged. Recall from the previous chapter that the cost (price) of something is what must be given up to acquire a unit of that something. If the price of a gallon of milk is $2, then the cost of that gallon of milk is whatever would have been purchased with that $2. Suppose that the $2 would have been used to purchase one piece of

barter
The direct exchange of goods and services without the use of money.

chocolate cake. Then we could say that the cost of a gallon of milk is one piece of chocolate cake. If we simply exchanged a gallon of milk for the piece of cake, we would be engaging in **barter**. The exchange of goods and services directly, without money, is called barter. Barter occurs when a plumber fixes a leaky pipe for a lawyer in exchange for the lawyer's work on a will or when a Chinese citizen provides fresh vegetables to a U.S. visitor in exchange for a pack of U.S. cigarettes.

Most markets involve money because goods and services can be exchanged more easily with money than without it. Economists say the costs of transacting are lower with money than without it. When IBM purchases microchips from Yakamoto of Japan, IBM and Yakamoto don't exchange goods directly. Neither firm may have what the other wants. Barter requires a **double coincidence of wants**: IBM must have what Yakamoto wants, and Yakamoto must have what IBM wants. The difficulty of finding a double coincidence of wants for barter transactions is typically very high. Using money makes trading easier. To obtain the microchips, all IBM has to do is provide dollars to Yakamoto. Yakamoto is willing to accept the money, since it can spend that money to obtain the goods that it wants.

double coincidence of wants
The situation that exists when A has what B wants and B has what A wants.

RECAP

1. Barter refers to exchanges made without the use of money.

2. Money makes it easier and less expensive to exchange goods and services.

3. Demand

2 What is demand?

A market consists of demand and supply—buyers and sellers. To understand how a price level is determined and why a price rises or falls, it is necessary to know how demand and supply function. We begin by considering demand alone, then supply, and then we put the two together. Before we begin, we discuss some economic terminology that is often confusing.

Economists distinguish between the terms **demand** and **quantity demanded**. When they refer to the *quantity demanded*, they are talking about the amount of a product that people are willing and able to purchase at a *specific* price. When they refer to *demand*, they are talking about the amount that people would be willing and able to purchase at *every possible* price. Demand is the quantities demanded at every price. Thus, the statement that "the demand for U.S. white wine rose following an increase in the price of French white wine" means that at each price for U.S. white wine, more people were willing and able to purchase U.S. white wine. They switched from the French wine to the U.S. wine. And the statement that "the quantity demanded of white wine fell as the price of white wine rose" means that people were willing and able to purchase less white wine because the price of the wine rose.

demand
The amount of a product that people are willing and able to purchase at each possible price during a given period of time, everything else held constant.

quantity demanded
The amount of a product that people are willing and able to purchase at a specific price.

3.a. The Law of Demand

law of demand
The quantity of a well-defined good or service that people are willing and able to purchase during a particular period of time decreases as the price of that good or service rises and increases as the price falls, everything else held constant.

Consumers and merchants know that if you lower the price of a good or service without altering its quality or quantity, people will beat a path to your doorway. This simple truth is referred to as the **law of demand**.

According to the law of demand, people purchase more of something when the price of that item falls. More formally, the law of demand states that the quantity of some item that people are willing and able to purchase during a particular period of time decreases as the price rises, and vice versa.

The more formal definition of the law of demand can be broken down into five phrases:

1. The quantity of a well-defined good or service that
2. people are willing and able to purchase
3. during a particular period of time
4. decreases as the price of that good or service rises and increases as the price falls,
5. everything else held constant.

The first phrase ensures that we are referring to the same item, that we are not mixing different goods. A watch is a commodity that is defined and distinguished from other goods by several characteristics: quality, color, and design of the watch face, to name a few. The law of demand applies to a well-defined good, in this case, a watch. If one of the characteristics should change, the good would no longer be well defined—in fact, it would be a different good. A Rolex watch is different from a Timex watch; Polo brand golf shirts are different goods from a generic brand golf shirts; Mercedes-Benz automobiles are different goods from Saturn automobiles.

The second phrase indicates that not only must people *want* to purchase some good, but they must be *able* to purchase that good in order for their wants to be counted as part of demand. For example, Sue would love to buy a membership in the Paradise Valley Country Club, but because the membership costs $35,000, she is not able to purchase the membership. Though she is willing, she is not able. At a price of $5,000, however, she is willing and able to purchase the membership.

The third phrase points out that the demand for any good is defined for a specific period of time. Without reference to a time period, a demand relationship would not make any sense. For instance, the statement that "at a price of $3 per Happy Meal, 13 million Happy Meals are demanded" provides no useful information. Are the 13 million meals sold in one week or one year? Think of demand as a rate of purchase at each possible price over a period of time—2 per month, 1 per day, and so on.

The fourth phrase points out that price and quantity demanded move in opposite directions; that is, as the price rises, the quantity demanded falls, and as the price falls, the quantity demanded rises.

Demand is a measure of the relationship between the price and quantity demanded of a particular good or service when the determinants of demand do not change. The **determinants of demand** are income, tastes, prices of related goods and services, expectations, and the number of buyers. If any one of these items changes, demand changes. The final phrase, everything else held constant, ensures that the determinants of demand do not change. We are focusing on the relationship between price and quantity demanded—everything else held constant.

determinants of demand
Factors other than the price of the good that influence demand—income, tastes, prices of related goods and services, expectations, and number of buyers.

3.b. The Demand Schedule

A **demand schedule** is a table or list of prices and the corresponding quantities demanded for a particular good or service. Consider the demand for access time to online games. Console games made their debut in the 1970s, but it has been in the first decade of this century in which the growth of online games or interactive console games has really exploded. There are different formats and ways to download games and access networks, but let us deal with a simple setting wherein you can purchase access to a network featuring games such as World of Warcraft on a weekly basis. The table in Figure 3 is a demand schedule for hours of access to the games. It shows the number of hours per week that a consumer named Bob would be willing and able to buy at each price during a month, everything else held constant. As the price of the access time gets higher relative to the prices of other goods, Bob would be willing and able to purchase fewer access hours.

demand schedule
A table or list of prices and the corresponding quantities demanded for a particular good or service.

FIGURE 3   Bob's Demand Schedule and Demand Curve for Hours of Access per Week

Combination	Price per Hour (constant quality units)	Quantity Demanded per Week (constant quality units)
A	$5	10
B	$4	20
C	$3	30
D	$2	40
E	$1	50

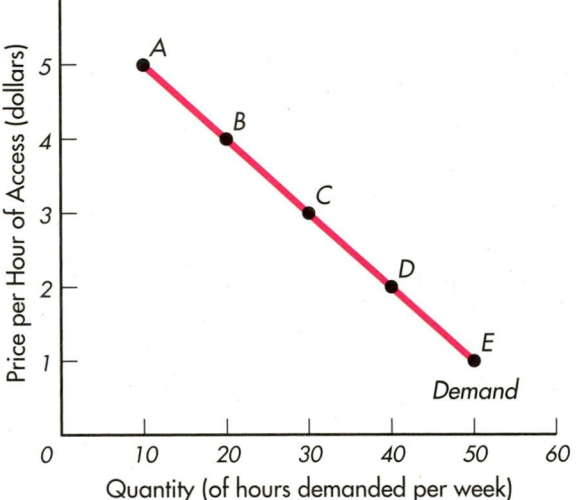

The number of hours of access to online games that Bob is willing and able to buy at each price during the week is listed in the table, or the demand schedule. The demand curve is derived from the combinations given in the demand schedule. The price-quantity combination of $5 per hour and 10 hours is point *A*. The combination of $4 per hour and 20 hours is point *B*. Each combination is plotted, and the points are connected to form the demand curve.

© 2013 Cengage Learning

At a price of $5 per hour, Bob indicates that he will purchase only 10 hours during the week. At a price of $4, Bob tells us that he will purchase 20 hours during the week. As the price drops from $5 to $4 to $3 to $2 and to $1, Bob is willing and able to purchase more access time. At a price of $1, Bob would purchase 50 hours of access for the week.

3.c. The Demand Curve

demand curve
A graph of a demand schedule that measures price on the vertical axis and quantity demanded on the horizontal axis.

A **demand curve** is a graph of the demand schedule. The demand curve shown in Figure 3 is plotted from the information given in the demand schedule. The price per hour of access time (price per unit) is measured on the vertical axis, and the number of hours of access per week (quantity per unit of time) is measured on the horizontal axis. The demand curve slopes downward because of the inverse relationship between the price and the quantity that Bob is willing and able to purchase. Point *A* in Figure 3 corresponds to combination *A* in the table: a price of $5 and 10 hours per week demanded.

Similarly, points *B*, *C*, *D*, and *E* in Figure 3 represent the corresponding combinations in the table. The line connecting these points is Bob's demand curve for hours of access to a network game.

All demand curves slope down because of the law of demand: As price falls, quantity demanded increases. The demand curves for bread, electricity, automobiles, colleges, labor services, health care, and any other good or service you can think of slope down. You might be saying to yourself, "That's not true. When the price of some rock concerts goes up, more people want to attend the concert. As the ticket price goes up, going to the concert becomes more prestigious, and the quantity demanded actually rises." To avoid confusion in such circumstances, we say "everything else held constant." With this statement, we are assuming that tastes don't change and that, therefore, the goods *cannot* become more prestigious as the price changes. Similarly, we do not allow the quality or the brand name of a product to change as we define the demand schedule or demand curve. We concentrate on the one quality or the one brand; so when we say that the price of a good has risen, we are talking about a good that is identical at all prices.

3.d. From Individual Demand Curves to a Market Curve

Bob's demand curve for hours of access to a network game is plotted in Figure 3. Unless Bob is the only person who plays the game, his demand curve is not the total or market demand curve. Market demand is derived by adding up the quantities that everyone is willing and able to purchase at each price—the sum of all individual demands. The market demand curve is the horizontal sum of all individual demand curves of all consumers in the market. The table in Figure 4 lists the demand schedules of three individuals, Bob, Maria, and Liu. If these three were the only consumers in the market, then the market demand would be the sum of their individual demands, shown as the last column of the table.

Bob's, Maria's, and Liu's demand schedules are plotted as individual demand curves in Figure 4(a). In Figure 4(b), their individual demand curves have been added together to obtain the market demand curve for hours of access per week to a network game. (Notice that we add in a horizontal direction—that is, we add the quantities at each price, not the prices at each quantity.) At a price of $5, we add the quantity that Bob would be willing and able to buy, 10, to the quantity that Maria would be willing and able buy, 5, to the quantity that Liu would be willing and able buy, 15, to get the market quantity demanded of 30. At a price of $4, we add the quantities that each of the consumers is willing and able to buy to get the total quantity demanded of 48. At all prices, then, we add the quantities demanded by each individual consumer to get the total, or market quantity, demanded.

3.e. Changes in Demand and Changes in Quantity Demanded

When one of the determinants of demand—income, tastes, prices of related goods, expectations, or number of buyers—is allowed to change, the demand for a good or service changes as well. What does it mean to say that demand changes? Demand is the entire demand schedule, or demand curve. When we say that demand changes, we are referring to a change in the quantities demanded at each and every price.

For example, if Bob's income rises, then he is willing and able to purchase more access time for the network game. At each and every price, the number of hours of access time that Bob is willing and able to buy each week rises. An increase in demand is expressed by a rightward shift of the demand curve, such as shown in Figure 5(a) in the move from D_1 to D_2. Conversely, if Bob's income declined, then he would be willing

When speaking of the demand curve or demand schedule, we are using constant-quality units. The quality of a good does not change as the price changes along a demand curve.

A change in demand is represented by a shift of the demand curve.

FIGURE 4   The Market Demand Schedule and Demand Curve

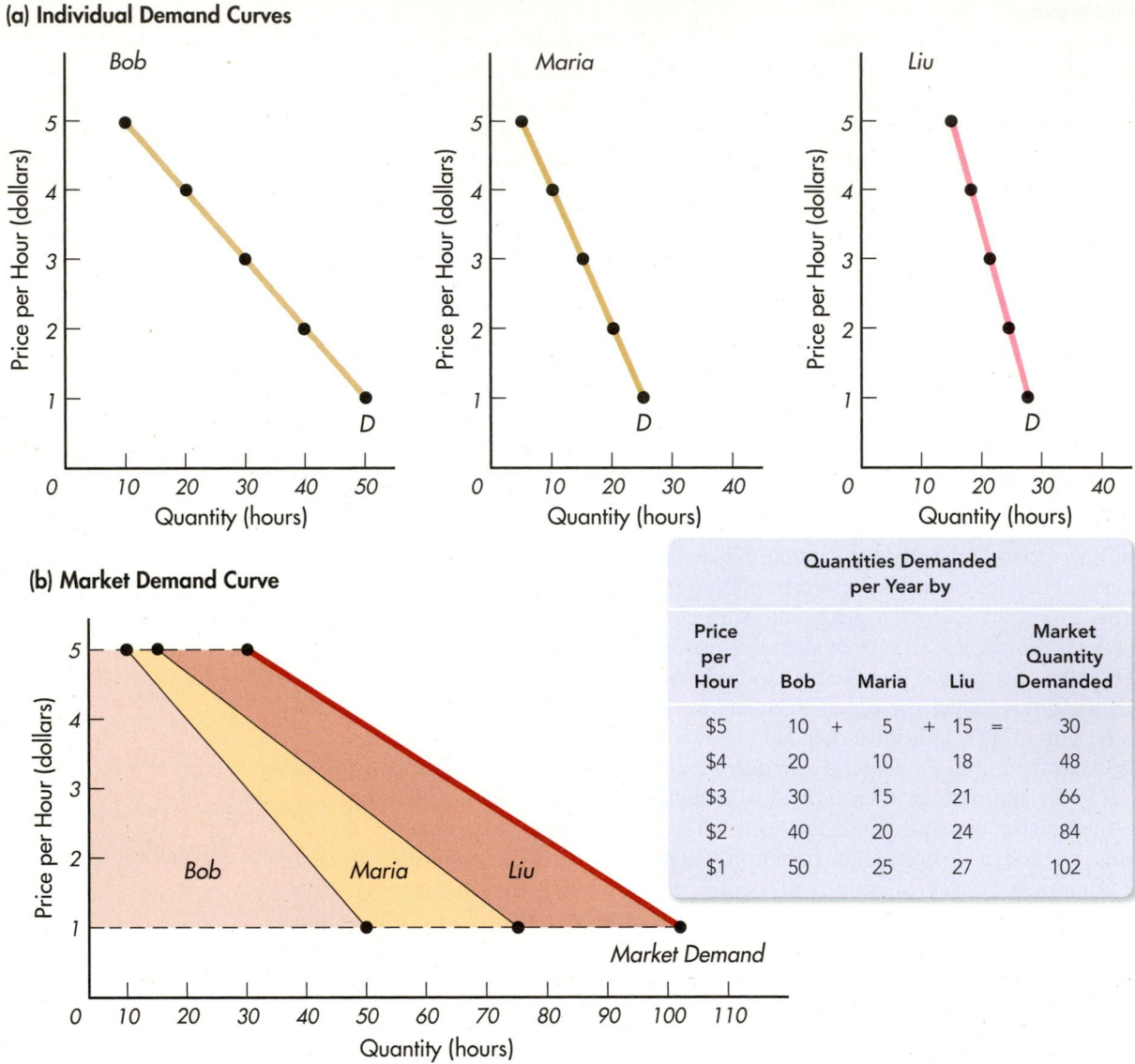

(a) Individual Demand Curves

Price per Hour				Market
Price per Hour	Bob	Maria	Liu	Market Quantity Demanded
$5	10 +	5 +	15 =	30
$4	20	10	18	48
$3	30	15	21	66
$2	40	20	24	84
$1	50	25	27	102

The market is defined to consist of three individuals: Bob, Maria, and Liu. Their demand schedules are listed in the table and plotted as the individual demand curves shown in Figure 4(a). By adding the quantities that each demands at every price, we obtain the market demand curve shown in Figure 4(b). At a price of $1, we add Bob's quantity demanded of 50 to Maria's quantity demanded of 25 to Liu's quantity demanded of 27 to obtain the market quantity demanded of 102. At a price of $2, we add Bob's 40 to Maria's 20 to Liu's 24 to obtain the market quantity demanded of 84. To obtain the market demand curve, for every price we sum the quantities demanded by each market participant.

and able to purchase less access time. This decrease in demand is expressed as a leftward shift of the demand curve, as shown in Figure 5(b) in the move from D_1 to D_2.

When the price of a good or service is the only factor that changes, the quantity demanded changes, but the demand curve does not shift. Instead, as the price of the access time is decreased (increased), everything else held constant, the quantity that people are willing and able to purchase increases (decreases). This change is merely a

> *A change in quantity demanded is represented by a movement along one demand curve.*

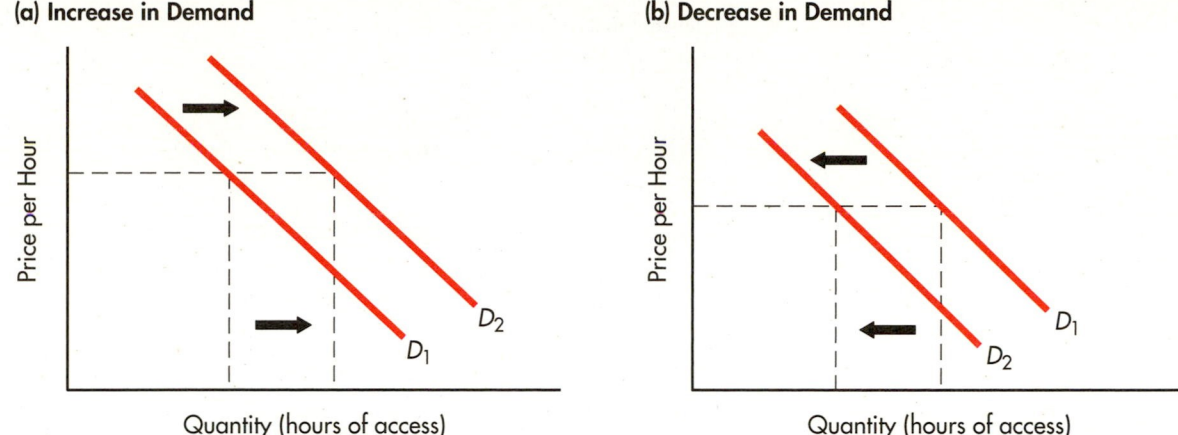

FIGURE 5   An Increase and a Decrease in Demand

(a) Increase in Demand

(b) Decrease in Demand

In Figure 5(a), an increase in demand occurs due to an increase in income. The consumer is willing and able to purchase more at *every price*. This change is expressed as a rightward shift of the demand curve from D_1 to D_2. Figure 5(b) shows a decrease in demand due to a decrease in income. The consumer is willing to purchase less at *every price*. This is illustrated as a leftward shift of demand from D_1 to D_2.

movement from one point on the demand curve to another point on the same demand curve, not a shift of the demand curve. A *change in the quantity demanded* is the phrase that economists use to describe the change in the quantities of a particular good or service that people are willing and able to purchase as the price of that good or service changes. A change in the quantity demanded, from point *A* to point *B* on the demand curve, is shown in Figure 6(b). Compare this to a change in demand illustrated by the shift of the entire curve as shown in Figure 6(a).

The demand curve shifts when income, tastes, prices of related goods, expectations, or the number of buyers changes. Let's consider how each of these determinants of demand affects the demand curve.

3.e.1. Income

The demand for any good or service depends on income. For most goods and services, the higher someone's income is, with everything else the same, the more that person can purchase at any given price. These are called **normal goods**. The increase in Bob's income causes his demand to increase. This change is shown in Figure 6(a) by the shift to the right from the curve labeled D_1 to the curve labeled D_2. Increased income means a greater ability to purchase goods and services. At every price, more hours of access time are demanded along curve D_2 than along curve D_1; this is an increase in demand.

For some goods and services, however, the amount demanded declines as income rises, everything else the same. The reason could be that these are goods or services that people use only when their incomes are declining—such as bankruptcy services. In addition, people might not like the good or service as well as they like a more expensive good or service, so when their income rises, they purchase the more expensive items. These types of items are called **inferior goods**.

3.e.2. Tastes

The demand for any good or service depends on individuals' tastes and preferences. When the iPod came out in 2000, it became an instant success. The Sony Walkman lost market share and essentially disappeared. Tastes changed toward the more mobile iPod and, more importantly, toward the more powerful iPod. Thousands of

normal goods
Goods for which demand increases as income increases.

inferior goods
Goods for which demand decreases as income increases.

FIGURE 6   A Change in Demand and a Change in the Quantity Demanded

Price per Hour	Quantities Demanded per Week	
	Before	After
$5	10	15
$4	20	25
$3	30	35
$2	40	45
$1	50	55

(a) Change in Demand

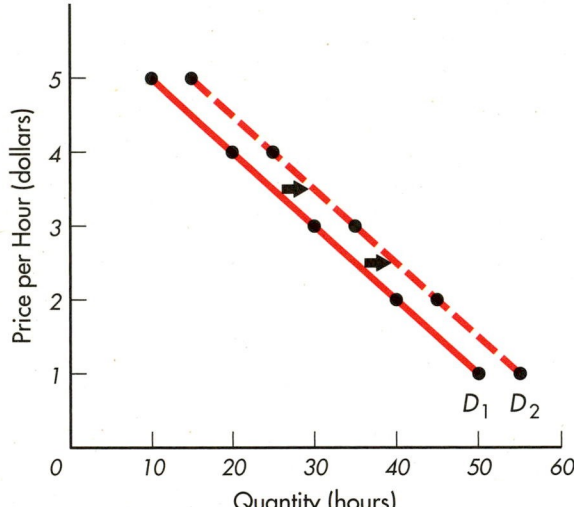

(b) Change in Quantity Demanded

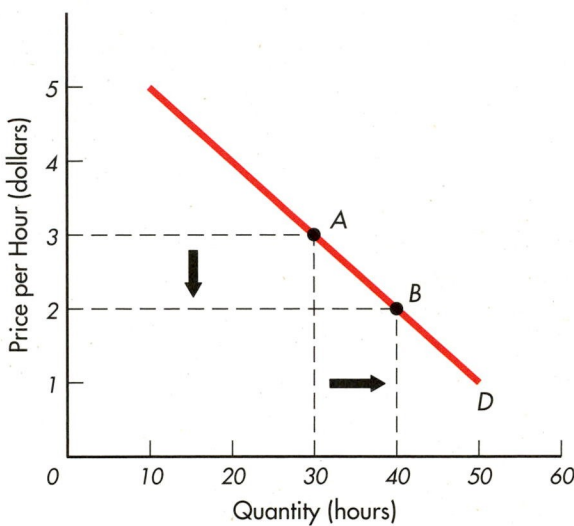

According to the table, Bob's demand for access time has increased by 5 hours at each price. In Figure 6(a), this change is shown as a shift of the demand curve from D_1 to D_2. Figure 6(b) shows a change in the quantity demanded. The change in quantity demanded is an increase in the quantity that consumers are willing and able to purchase at a lower price. It is shown as a movement along the demand curve from point *A* to point *B*.

songs could be stored on an iPod, while the Walkman was constrained by the size of the CD. The iPhone incorporates the iPod into a mobile phone, and it too has been a huge success. Consumers no longer demand the old fixed-line phones but instead want more capabilities in their mobile phones and MP3 devices; their tastes have changed.

3.e.3. Prices of Related Goods and Services

Goods and services may be related in two ways. **Substitute goods** can be used in place of each other, so that as the cost of one rises, everything else the same, people will buy more of the other. Bread and crackers, BMWs and Acuras, movie downloads and theater movies, universities and community colleges, electricity and natural gas, and time used to access network games and time used for other activities are, more or less, pairs of substitutes. As the price of entertainment venues rises, everything else held constant, the demand for access time for network games will rise; the demand curve for access time will shift to the right.

substitute goods
Goods that can be used in place of each other; as the price of one rises, the demand for the other rises.

Complementary goods are goods that are used together, and so as the price of one rises, everything else the same, consumers buy less of it but also buy less of the complementary good. Bread and margarine, beer and peanuts, cameras and film, shoes and socks, CDs and CD players, a computer or game board and access to network games, and iPods and iTunes are examples of pairs of complementary goods. As the price of a machine on which to play network games rises, people purchase less access time to those network games. The demand curve for a complementary good shifts to the left when the price of the related good increases.

complementary goods
Goods that are used together; as the price of one rises, the demand for the other falls.

3.e.4. Expectations
Expectations about future events can have an effect on demand today. People make purchases today because they expect their income level to be a certain amount in the future, or because they expect the price of certain items to be higher in the future. You might buy running shoes today if you expect the price of those shoes to be higher tomorrow. You might buy your airline ticket home now rather than wait until semester break if you expect the price to be higher next month.

3.e.5. Number of Buyers
Market demand consists of the sum of the demands of all individuals. The more individuals there are with income to spend, the greater the market demand is likely to be. For example, the populations of Florida and Arizona are much larger during the winter than they are during the summer. The demand for any particular good or service in Arizona and Florida rises (the demand curve shifts to the right) during the winter and falls (the demand curve shifts to the left) during the summer.

RECAP

1. According to the law of demand, as the price of any good or service rises (falls), the quantity demanded of that good or service falls (rises), during a specific period of time, everything else held constant.

2. A demand schedule is a listing of the quantity demanded at each price.

3. The demand curve is a downward-sloping line plotted using the values in the demand schedule.

4. Market demand is the sum of all individual demands.

5. Demand changes when one of the determinants of demand changes. A demand change is illustrated as a shift of the demand curve.

6. The determinants of demand are income, tastes, prices of related goods and services, expectations, and number of buyers.

7. The quantity demanded changes when the price of the good or service changes. This is a change from one point on the demand curve to another point on the same demand curve.

4. Supply

Why do students get discounts at movie theaters? Demand *and* supply. Why do restaurants offer early bird specials? Demand *and* supply. Why is the price of hotel accommodations in Phoenix higher in the winter than in the summer? Demand *and* supply. Why is the price of beef higher in Japan than in the United States? Demand *and* supply. Both demand and supply determine price; neither demand nor supply alone determines price. We just discussed demand; we now discuss supply.

 3 What is supply?

supply
The amount of a good or service that producers are willing and able to offer for sale at each possible price during a period of time, everything else held constant.

4.a. The Law of Supply

Just as demand is the relation between the price and the quantity demanded of a good or service, supply is the relation between the price and the quantity supplied. **Supply** is the amount of the good or service that producers are willing and able to offer for sale at each possible price during a period of time, everything else held constant. **Quantity supplied** is

quantity supplied
The amount that sellers are willing and able to offer at a given price during a particular period of time, everything else held constant.

law of supply
The quantity of a well-defined good or service that producers are willing and able to offer for sale during a particular period of time increases as the price of the good or service increases and decreases as the price decreases, everything else held constant.

the amount of the good or service that producers are willing and able to offer for sale at a *specific* price during a period of time, everything else held constant. According to the **law of supply**, as the price of a good or service rises, the quantity supplied rises, and vice versa.

The formal statement of the law of supply consists of five phrases:

1. The quantity of a well-defined good or service that
2. producers are willing and able to offer for sale
3. during a particular period of time
4. increases as the price of the good or service increases and decreases as the price decreases,
5. everything else held constant.

The first phrase is the same as the first phrase in the law of demand. The second phrase indicates that producers must not only *want* to offer the product for sale but be *able* to offer the product. The third phrase points out that the quantities producers will offer for sale depend on the period of time being considered. The fourth phrase points out that more will be supplied at higher than at lower prices. The final phrase ensures that the **determinants of supply** do not change. The determinants of supply are those factors other than the price of the good or service that influence the willingness and ability of producers to offer their goods and services for sale—the prices of resources used to produce the product, technology and productivity, expectations of producers, the number of producers in the market, and the prices of related goods and services. If any one of these should change, supply changes.

determinants of supply
Factors other than the price of the good that influence supply—prices of resources, technology and productivity, expectations of producers, number of producers, and the prices of related goods and services.

4.b. The Supply Schedule and Supply Curve

A **supply schedule** is a table or list of the prices and the corresponding quantities supplied of a good or service. The table in Figure 7 presents a single firm's supply schedule for access to network games. (We will assume that three firms offer access to the same network games.) The schedule lists the quantities that each firm is willing and able to supply at each price, everything else held constant. As the price increases, the firm is willing and able to offer more access time to the network games.

supply schedule
A table or list of prices and the corresponding quantities supplied of a particular good or service.

FIGURE 7   Aber's Supply Schedule and Supply Curve of Access Time to Network Games

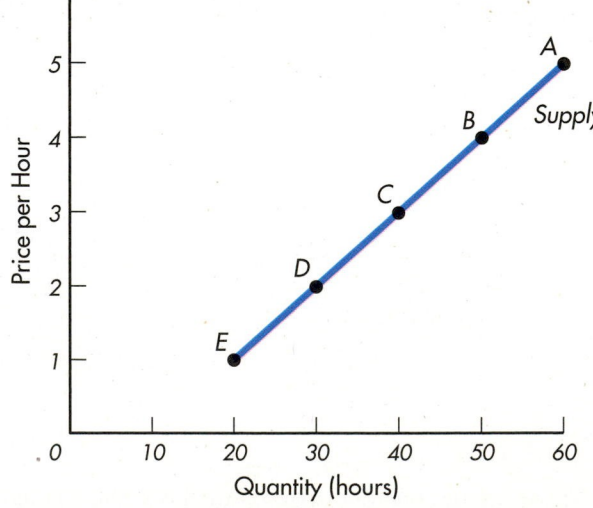

Combination	Price per Hour (constant quality units)	Quantity Supplied per Week (constant quality units)
A	$5	60
B	$4	50
C	$3	40
D	$2	30
E	$1	20

The quantity that Aber is willing and able to offer for sale at each price is listed in the supply schedule and shown on the supply curve. At point *A*, the price is $5 per hour and the quantity supplied is 60 hours. The combination of $4 per hour and 50 hours is point *B*. Each price-quantity combination is plotted, and the points are connected to form the supply curve.

A **supply curve** is a graph of the supply schedule. Figure 7 shows Aber's supply curve of access time to the network games. The price and quantity combinations given in the supply schedule correspond to the points on the curve. For instance, combination A in the table corresponds to point A on the curve; combination B in the table corresponds to point B on the curve, and so on for each price-quantity combination.

The supply curve slopes upward. This means that a supplier is willing and able to offer more for sale at higher prices than it is at lower prices. This should make sense—if prices rise, everything else held constant, the supplier will earn more profits. Higher profits create the incentive for the supplier to offer more for sale.

> **supply curve**
> A graph of a supply schedule that measures price on the vertical axis and quantity supplied on the horizontal axis.

4.c. From Individual Supply Curves to the Market Supply

To derive market supply, the quantities that each producer supplies at each price are added together, just as the quantities demanded by each consumer are added together to get market demand. The table in Figure 8 lists the supply schedules of three firms that sell access to network games: Aber, Broadband, and Courage. The supply schedules are plotted in Figure 8(a). Then in Figure 8(b) the individual supply curves have been added together (in a horizontal direction) to obtain the market supply curve. At a price of $5, the quantity supplied by Aber is 60, the quantity supplied by Broadband is 30, and the quantity supplied by Courage is 12. This means a total quantity supplied in the market of 102. At a price of $4, the quantities supplied are 50, 25, and 9, for a total market quantity supplied of 84. The market supply schedule is the last column in the table. The graph of the price and quantity combinations listed in this column is the market supply curve. The market supply curve slopes up because each of the individual supply curves has a positive slope. The market supply curve tells us that the quantity supplied in the market increases as the price rises.

4.d. Changes in Supply and Changes in Quantity Supplied

> *A change in the quantity supplied is a movement along the supply curve. A change in the supply is a shift of the supply curve.*

When we draw the supply curve, we allow only the price and quantity supplied of the good or service that we are discussing to change. Everything else that might affect supply is assumed not to change. If any of the determinants of supply—the prices of resources used to produce the product, technology and productivity, expectations of producers, the number of producers in the market, and the prices of related goods and services—changes, the supply schedule changes and the supply curve shifts.

4.d.1. Prices of Resources
If labor costs rise, higher prices will be necessary to induce each store to offer as many hours of access as it did before the cost of the resource rose. The higher cost of resources causes a decrease in supply, meaning a leftward shift of the supply curve, from S_1 to S_2 in Figure 9(a). Compare point B on curve S_2 with point A on curve S_1. Both points correspond to a price of $3, but along curve S_1, sellers are willing to offer 66 hours of access time, whereas curve S_2 indicates that sellers will offer only 57 hours of access time.

4.d.2. Technology and Productivity
If resources are used more efficiently in the production of a good or service, more of that good or service can be supplied for the same cost, or the original quantity supplied can be produced for a lower cost. As a result, the supply curve shifts to the right, as in Figure 9(b).

The move from horse-drawn plows to tractors or from mainframe computers to personal computers meant that each worker was able to produce more. The increase in

FIGURE 8   The Market Supply Schedule and Curve of Access Time to Network Games

Price per Hour	Quantities Supplied per Year by			Market Quantity Supplied
	Aber	Broadband	Courage	
$5	60 +	30 +	12 =	102
$4	50	25	9	84
$3	40	20	6	66
$2	30	15	3	48
$1	20	10	0	30

(a) Individual Supply Curves

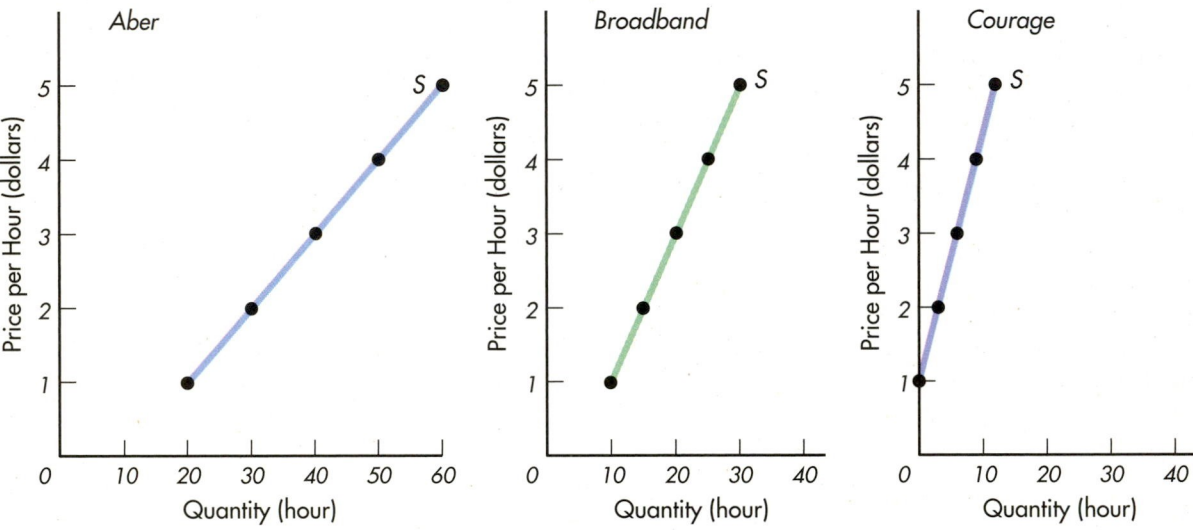

(b) Market Supply Curve

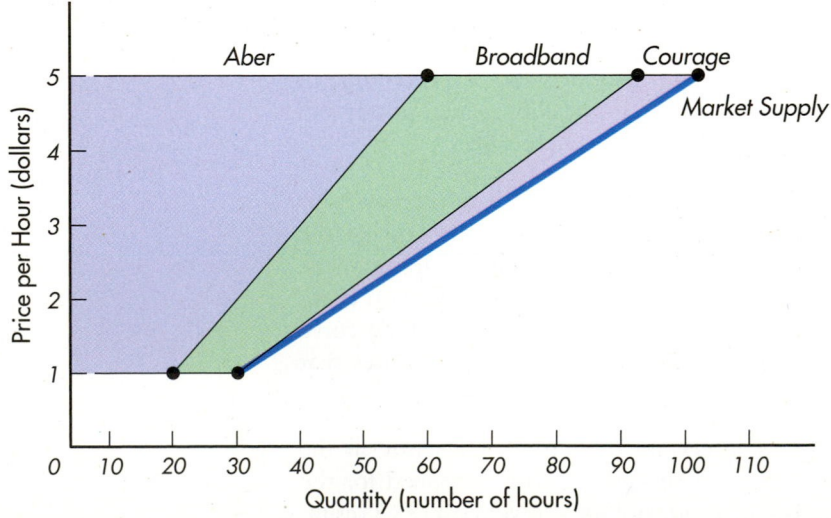

The market supply is derived by summing the quantities that each supplier is willing and able to offer for sale at each price. In this example, there are three producers: The supply schedules of each are listed in the table and plotted as the individual supply curves shown in Figure 8(a). By adding the quantities supplied at each price, we obtain the market supply curve shown in Figure 8(b). For instance, at a price of $5, Aber offers 60 units, Broadband 30 units, and Courage 12 units, for a market supply quantity of 102. The market supply curve reflects the quantities that each producer is able and willing to supply at each price.

FIGURE 9   A Shift of the Supply Curve

(a) Decrease in Supply

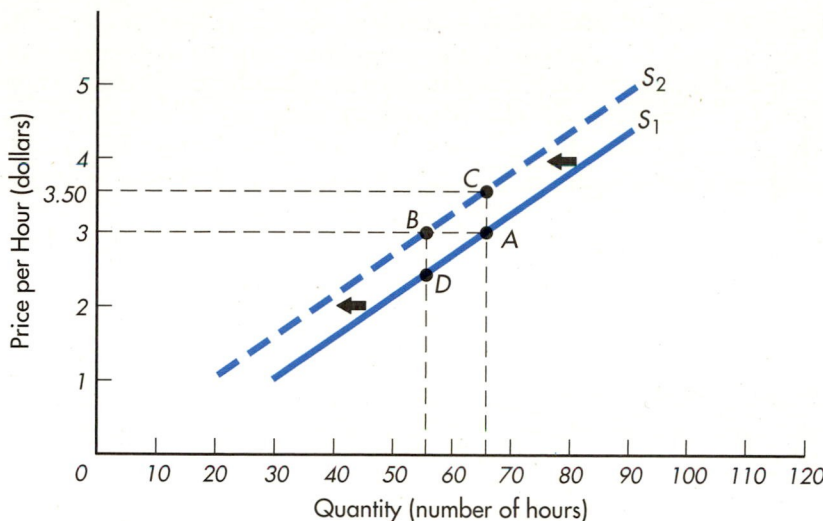

(b) Increase in Supply

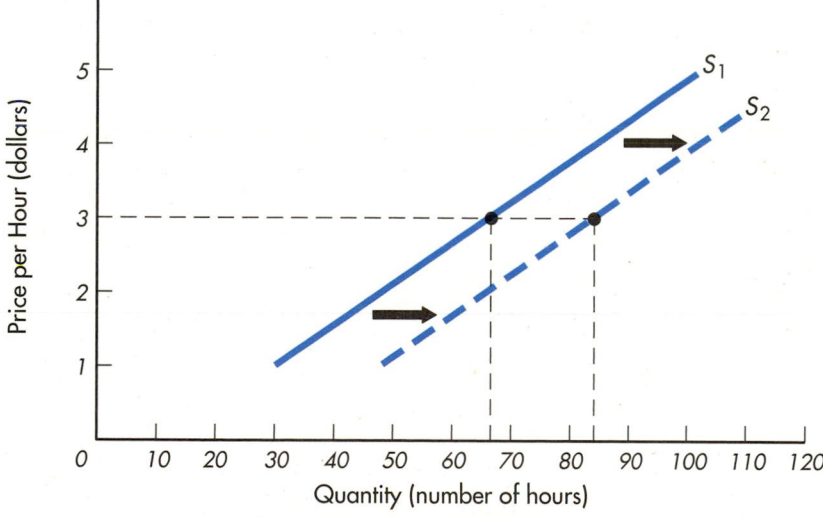

Figure 9(a) shows a decrease in supply and the shift of the supply curve to the left, from S_1 to S_2. The decrease is caused by a change in one of the determinants of access time to network games—an increase in the price of labor. Because of the increased price of labor, producers are willing and able to offer fewer access hours at each price than they were before the cost of labor rose. Supply curve S_2 shows that at a price of $3 per hour of access, suppliers will offer 57 hours. That is 9 hours less than the 66 hours at $3 per access hour indicated by supply curve S_1. Conversely, to offer a given quantity, producers must receive a higher price per access hour than they previously were getting: $3.50 per hour for 66 hours (on supply curve S_2) instead of $3 per hour (on supply curve S_1). Figure 9(b) shows an increase in supply. A technological improvement or an increase in productivity causes the supply curve to shift to the right, from S_1 to S_2. At each price, a higher quantity is offered for sale. At a price of $3, 66 hours were offered, but with the shift of the supply curve, the quantity of hours for sale at $3 apiece increases to 84. Conversely, producers can reduce prices for a given quantity—for example, charging $2 per hour for 66 hours.

productivity
The quantity of output produced per unit of resource.

output produced by each unit of a resource is called a *productivity increase*. **Productivity** is defined as the quantity of output produced per unit of resource. Improvements in technology cause productivity increases, which lead to an increase in supply.

4.d.3. Expectations of Suppliers

Sellers may choose to alter the quantity offered for sale today because of a change in expectations regarding the determinants of supply. A supply curve illustrates the quantities that suppliers are willing and able to supply at every possible price. If suppliers expect that something is going to occur to resource supplies or the cost of resources, then they may alter the quantities that they are willing and able to supply at every possible price. The key point is that the supply curve will shift if producers expect something to occur that will alter their anticipated profits at every possible price, not just a change in one price. For instance, the expectation that demand will decline in the future does not lead to a shift of the supply curve; it leads instead to a decline in quantity supplied, because the new demand curve (the expected lower demand) would intersect the supply curve at a lower price and a smaller output level.

4.d.4. Number of Suppliers

When more people decide to supply a good or service, the market supply increases. More is offered for sale at each and every price, causing a rightward shift of the supply curve.

4.d.5. Prices of Related Goods or Services

The opportunity cost of producing and selling any good or service is the forgone opportunity to produce any other good or service. If the price of an alternative good changes, then the opportunity cost of producing a particular good changes. This could cause the supply curve to change. For instance, if McDonald's can offer hamburgers or salads with equal ease, an increase in the price of salads could lead the manager to offer more salads and fewer hamburgers. The supply curve of salads would shift to the right, and the supply curve of hamburgers would shift to the left.

A *change in supply* occurs when the quantity supplied at each and every price changes or there is a shift in the supply curve—like the shift from S_1 to S_2 in Figure 10(a). A change in one of the determinants of supply brings about a change in supply.

When only the price changes, a greater or smaller quantity is supplied. This is shown as a movement along the supply curve, not as a shift of the curve. A change in price is said to cause a *change in the quantity supplied*. An increase in quantity supplied is shown in the move from point *A* to point *B* on the supply curve of Figure 10(b).

RECAP

1. According to the law of supply, the quantity supplied of any good or service is directly related to the price of the good or service during a specific period of time, everything else held constant.

2. Market supply is found by adding together the quantities supplied at each price by every producer in the market.

3. Supply changes if the prices of relevant resources change, if technology or productivity changes, if producers' expectations change, if the number of producers changes, or if the prices of related goods and services change.

4. Changes in supply are reflected in shifts of the supply curve. Changes in the quantity supplied are reflected in movements along the supply curve.

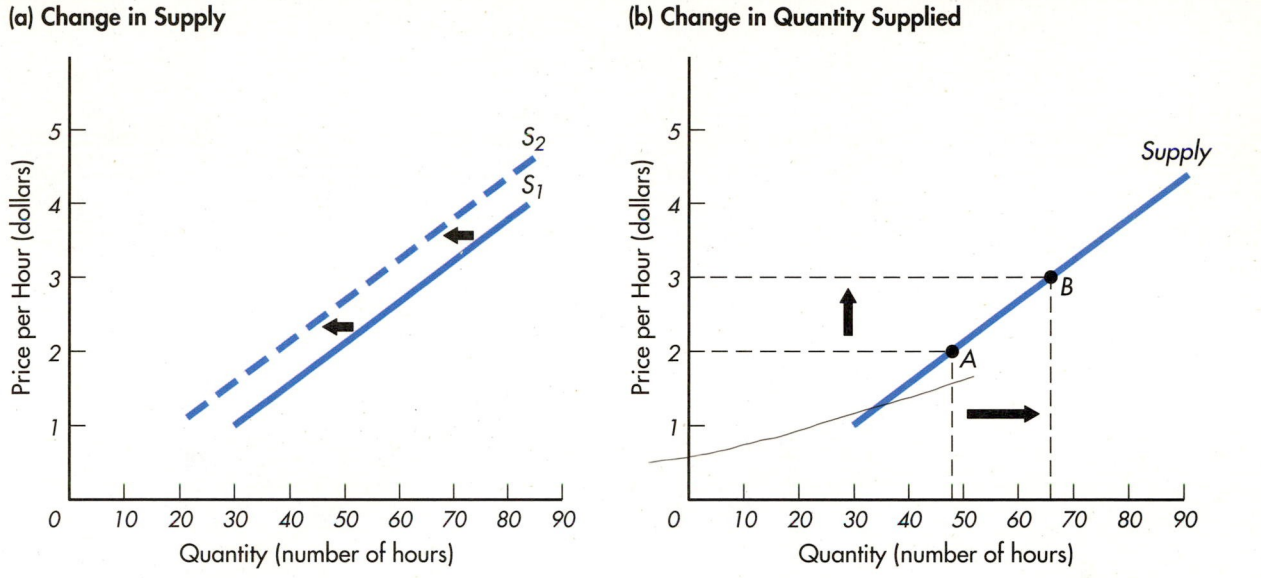

FIGURE 10   A Change in Supply and a Change in the Quantity Supplied

(a) Change in Supply

(b) Change in Quantity Supplied

In Figure 10(a), the quantities that producers are willing and able to offer for sale at every price decrease, causing a leftward shift of the supply curve from S_1 to S_2. In Figure 10(b), the quantities that producers are willing and able to offer for sale increase, because of an increase in the price of the good, causing a movement along the supply curve from point *A* to point *B*.

5. Equilibrium: Putting Demand and Supply Together

 4 How is price determined by demand and supply?

The demand curve shows the quantity of a good or service that buyers are willing and able to purchase at each price. The supply curve shows the quantity that producers are willing and able to offer for sale at each price. Only where the two curves intersect is the quantity supplied equal to the quantity demanded. This intersection is the point of **equilibrium**. Equilibrium is a pedagogical device; that is, it is used for teaching or educational purposes. In reality, demand and supply are changing all the time so that the market process is always working; there is not really a static, constant equilibrium price and quantity. Nevertheless, because prices and quantities are always moving toward an equilibrium, the concept is well worth considering. And in our analyses and discussions, we will focus on an equilibrium point in order to illustrate the effects of some change in either demand or supply.

equilibrium
The price and quantity at which quantity demanded and quantity supplied are equal.

5.a. Determination of Equilibrium

Figure 11 brings together the market demand and market supply curves for access hours to network games. The supply and demand schedules are listed in the table, and the curves are plotted in the graph in Figure 11. Notice that the curves intersect at only one point, labeled *e*, a price of $3 and a quantity of 66. The intersection point is the equilibrium price, the only price at which the quantity demanded and quantity supplied are the same. You can see that at any other price, the quantity demanded and quantity supplied are not the same. This is called **disequilibrium**.

disequilibrium
Prices at which quantity demanded and quantity supplied are not equal at a particular price.

FIGURE 11   Equilibrium

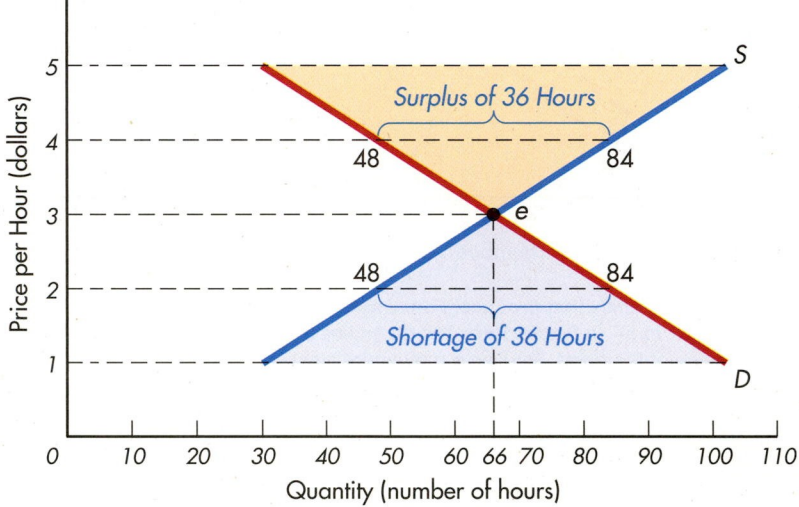

Price per Hour	Quantity Demanded per Week	Quantity Supplied per Week	Status
$5	30	102	Surplus of 72
$4	48	84	Surplus of 36
$3	66	66	Equilibrium
$2	84	48	Shortage of 36
$1	102	30	Shortage of 72

Equilibrium is established at the point where the quantity that suppliers are willing and able to offer for sale is the same as the quantity that buyers are willing and able to purchase. Here, equilibrium occurs at the price of $3 per hour and a quantity of 66 hours per week. It is shown as point e, at the intersection of the demand and supply curves. At prices above $3, the quantity supplied is greater than the quantity demanded, and the result is a surplus. At prices below $3, the quantity supplied is less than the quantity demanded, and the result is a shortage. The area shaded tan shows all prices at which there is a surplus—where quantity supplied is greater than the quantity demanded. The amount of the surplus is measured in a horizontal direction at each price. The area shaded blue represents all prices at which a shortage exists—where the quantity demanded is greater than the quantity supplied. The amount of the shortage is measured in a horizontal direction at each price.

© 2013 Cengage Learning

surplus
A quantity supplied that is larger than the quantity demanded at a given price; it occurs whenever the price is greater than the equilibrium price.

shortage
A quantity supplied that is smaller than the quantity demanded at a given price; it occurs whenever the price is less than the equilibrium price.

Whenever the price is greater than the equilibrium price, a **surplus** arises. For example, at $4, the quantity of hours of access demanded is 48, and the quantity supplied is 84. Thus, at $4 per hour, there is a surplus of 36 hours—that is, 36 hours supplied are not purchased. Conversely, whenever the price is below the equilibrium price, the quantity demanded is greater than the quantity supplied, and there is a **shortage**. For instance, if the price is $2 per hour of access, consumers will want and be able to pay for more hours of access than are available. As shown in the table in Figure 11, the quantity demanded at a price of $2 is 84, but the quantity supplied is only 48. There is a shortage of 36 hours of access at the price of $2.

Neither a surplus nor a shortage will exist for long if the price of the product is free to change. Suppliers who are stuck with hours of access not being purchased will lower the price and reduce the quantities they are offering for sale in order to eliminate a surplus. Conversely, suppliers who cannot supply enough hours to meet demand and who have consumers on hold or losing connection will raise the price to eliminate a shortage. Surpluses lead to decreases in the price and the quantity supplied and increases in the quantity demanded. Shortages lead to increases in the price and the quantity supplied and decreases in the quantity demanded.

A shortage exists only when the quantity that people are willing and able to purchase at a particular price is more than the quantity supplied *at that price*. Scarcity occurs when more is wanted at a zero price than is available.

5.b. Changes in the Equilibrium Price: Demand Shifts

 5 What causes price to change?

Equilibrium is the combination of price and quantity at which the quantities demanded and supplied are the same. Once an equilibrium is achieved, there is no incentive for suppliers or consumers to move away from it. An equilibrium price changes only when demand and/or supply changes—that is, when the determinants of demand or the determinants of supply change.

Let's consider a change in demand and what it means for the equilibrium price. Suppose that experiments on rats show that playing network games causes brain damage. As a result, a large segment of the human population decides not to purchase access time to the games. Suppliers experience a decrease in the number of customers willing and able to pay for access, as shown in Figure 12 by a leftward shift of the demand curve, from curve D_1 to curve D_2.

Once the demand curve has shifted, the original equilibrium price of $3 per hour of access per week at point e_1 is no longer equilibrium. At a price of $3, the quantity supplied is still 66, but the quantity demanded has declined to 48 (look at the demand curve D_2 at a price of $3). There is, therefore, a surplus of 18 hours of access time per week at the price of $3.

FIGURE 12 The Effects of a Shift of the Demand Curve

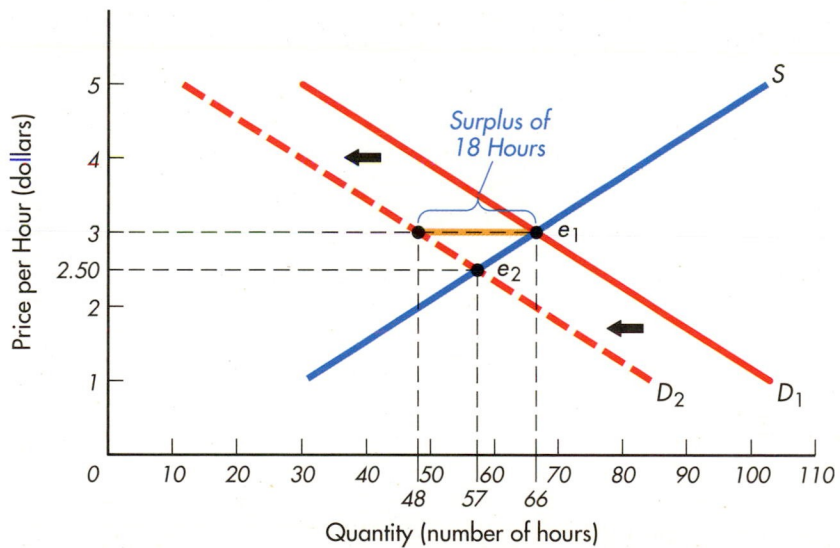

The initial equilibrium price ($3 per hour of access time) and quantity (66 hours of access time) are established at point e_1, where the initial demand and supply curves intersect. A change in the tastes for access hours to the network games causes demand to decrease, and the demand curve shifts to the left. At $3 per hour of access, the initial quantity supplied, 66 hours, is now greater than the quantity demanded, 48 hours. The surplus of 18 hours causes suppliers to reduce the amount of hours of access offered and to lower the price. The market reaches a new equilibrium, at point e_2, $2.50 per hour and 57 hours per week.

With a surplus comes downward pressure on the price. This downward pressure occurs because producers acquire fewer hours of access for purchase and reduce the price in an attempt to sell those hours not being used. Suppliers continue reducing the price and the quantity available until consumers purchase all the hours that the sellers have available, or until a new equilibrium is established. That new equilibrium occurs at point e_2 with a price of $2.50 and a quantity of 57.

The decrease in demand is represented by the leftward shift of the demand curve. A decrease in demand results in a lower equilibrium price and a lower equilibrium quantity as long as there is no change in supply. Conversely, an increase in demand would be represented as a rightward shift of the demand curve and would result in a higher equilibrium price and a higher equilibrium quantity as long as there is no change in supply.

5.c. Changes in the Equilibrium Price: Supply Shifts

The equilibrium price and quantity may be altered by a change in supply as well. If the price of relevant resources, technology and productivity, the expectations of suppliers, the number of suppliers, or the prices of related products change, supply changes.

Let's consider an example. Suppose a tax is imposed on all Internet access and that this tax increases the cost for the network game suppliers to provide access time. This is represented by a leftward shift of the supply curve in Figure 13.

The leftward shift of the supply curve, from curve S_1 to curve S_2, leads to a new equilibrium price and quantity. At the original equilibrium price of $3 at point e_1, 66 hours of access are supplied. After the shift in the supply curve, 48 hours are supplied at a price of $3 per hour, and there is a shortage of 18 hours per week. The shortage puts upward pressure on price. As the price rises, consumers decrease the quantities that they are willing and able to purchase, and suppliers increase the quantities that they are willing and able to supply. Eventually, a new equilibrium price and quantity is established at $3.50 and 57 hours of access each week at point e_2.

FIGURE 13   The Effects of a Shift of the Supply Curve

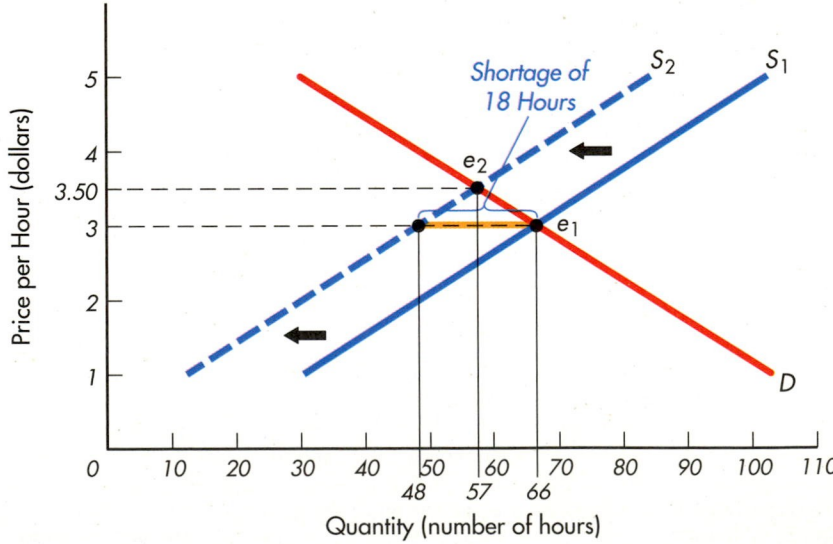

The initial equilibrium price and quantity are $3 and 66 hours, at point e_1. When the Internet tax is imposed, suppliers' costs have risen, and so they are willing and able to offer fewer hours for sale at each price. The result is a leftward (upward) shift of the supply curve, from S_1 to S_2. At the old price of $3, the quantity demanded is still 66, but the quantity supplied falls to 48. The shortage is 18 hours of access time. The shortage leads to a new equilibrium, e_2, the intersection between curves S_2 and D, which is $3.50 per hour of access time and 57 hours of access time.

The decrease in supply is represented by the leftward shift of the supply curve. A decrease in supply with no change in demand results in a higher price and a lower quantity. Conversely, an increase in supply would be represented as a rightward shift of the supply curve. An increase in supply with no change in demand would result in a lower price and a higher quantity.

5.d. Market Adjustment and Market Interference

We have examined a hypothetical (imaginary) market for access time to network games in order to represent what goes on in real markets. We have established that the price of a good or service is defined by an equilibrium between demand and supply. We noted that an equilibrium could be disturbed by a change in demand, a change in supply, or simultaneous changes in demand and supply. The important point of this discussion is to demonstrate that when they are not in equilibrium, the price and the quantities demanded and/or supplied change and move toward an equilibrium. The market is always attempting to reach equilibrium.

Looking at last year's sweaters piled up on the sale racks, waiting over an hour for a table at a restaurant, or hearing that 5 or 6 percent of people who are willing and able to work are unemployed may make you wonder whether equilibrium is ever established. In fact, it is not uncommon to observe situations in which quantities demanded and quantities supplied are not equal. But this observation does not cast doubt on the usefulness of the equilibrium concept. Even if not all markets clear, or reach equilibrium, all the time, we can be reasonably assured that market forces are operating so that the market is moving toward an equilibrium. When you see the store having a sale, you know that the market is moving toward equilibrium. When you hear that the price of something is rising because so many people are buying it, you know that the market is moving toward equilibrium. Sometimes the market is not allowed to move toward equilibrium, as discussed in the following section.

5.d.1. Market Interference: Price Ceilings and Price Floors

A **price floor** is a situation in which the price is not allowed to decrease below a certain level. Consider Figure 14, representing the market for sugar. The equilibrium price of sugar is $.10 a pound, but because the government has set a price floor of $.20 a pound, as shown by the solid yellow line, the price is not allowed to move to its equilibrium level. A surplus of 250,000 pounds of sugar results from the price floor. Sugar growers produce 1 million pounds of sugar, and consumers purchase 750,000 pounds of sugar.

We saw previously that whenever the price is above the equilibrium price, a surplus arises and begins to force the price to decline. The price floor interferes with the functioning of the market; a surplus exists because the government will not allow the price to drop. The sugar surplus builds up as each week more sugar is produced than is consumed.

What would occur if the government had set the price floor at $.09 a pound? Since at $.09 a pound a shortage of sugar would result, the price would rise. A price floor keeps the price only from falling, not from rising. So the price rises to its equilibrium level of $.10. Only if the price floor is set above the equilibrium price is it an effective price floor.

A **price ceiling** is the situation in which a price is not allowed to rise to its equilibrium level. Los Angeles, San Francisco, and New York are among more than 125 U.S. cities that have some type of *rent controls*. The New York City rent control law places a ceiling on the rents that landlords can charge for apartments. Figure 15 is a demand and supply graph representing the market for apartments in New York. The equilibrium price is $3,000 a month. The government has set a price of $1,500 a month as the maximum that can be charged. The price ceiling is shown by the solid yellow line. At the rent control price of $1,500 per month, 3,000 apartments are available, but consumers want 6,000 apartments. There is a shortage of 3,000 apartments.

6 What happens when price is not allowed to change with market forces?

price floor
A situation in which the price is not allowed to decrease below a certain level.

price ceiling
A situation in which the price is not allowed to rise above a certain level.

© froxx/Shutterstock.com

FIGURE 14   A Price Floor

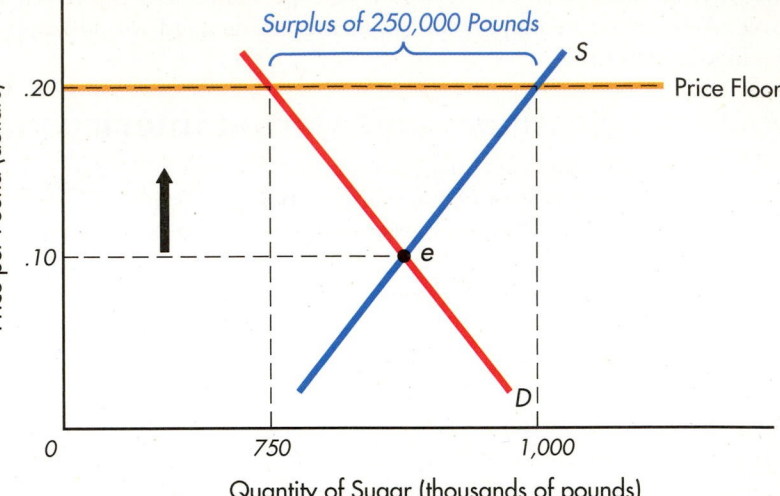

The equilibrium price of sugar is $.10 a pound, but because the government has set a price floor of $.20 a pound, as shown by the solid yellow line, the price is not allowed to move to its equilibrium level. A surplus of 250,000 pounds of sugar results from the price floor. Sugar growers produce 1 million pounds of sugar, and consumers purchase 750,000 pounds of sugar.

FIGURE 15   Rent Controls

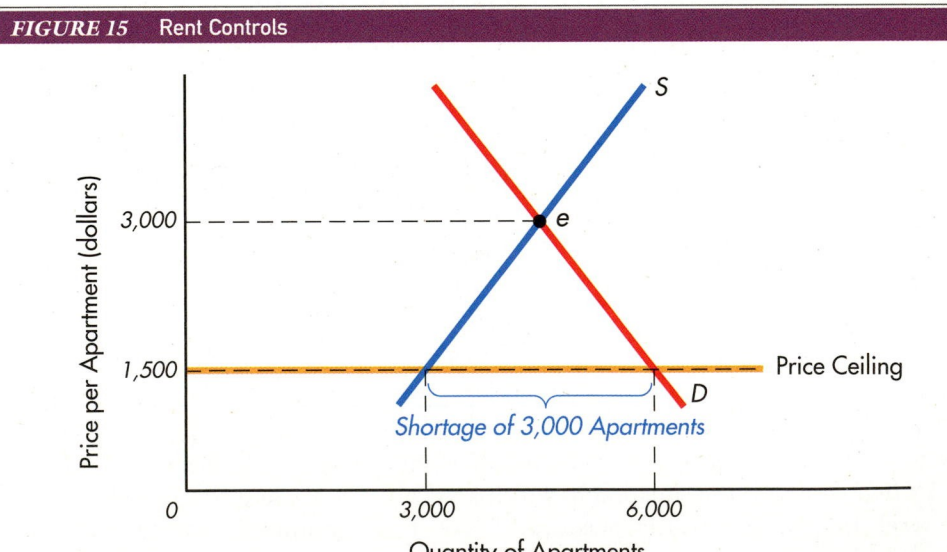

A demand and supply graph representing the market for apartments in New York City is shown. The equilibrium price is $3,000 a month. The government has set a price of $1,500 a month. The government's price ceiling is shown by the solid yellow line. At the government's price, 3,000 apartments are available but consumers want 6,000. There is a shortage of 3,000 apartments.

The shortage means that not everyone who is willing and able to rent an apartment will be able to. Since the price is not allowed to ration the apartments, something else will have to. It may be that those who are willing and able to stand in line the longest get the apartments. Perhaps bribing an important official might be the way to get an apartment. Perhaps relatives of officials or important citizens will get the apartments. Whenever a price ceiling exists, a shortage results, and some rationing device other than price will arise.

Had the government set the rent control price at $4,000 per month, the price ceiling would not have had an effect. Since the equilibrium is $3,000 a month, the price would not have risen to $4,000. Only if the price ceiling is below the equilibrium price will it be an effective price ceiling.

Price ceilings are not uncommon in the United States or in other economies. China had a severe housing shortage for 30 years because the price of housing was kept below equilibrium. Faced with unhappy citizens and realizing the cause of the shortage, officials began to lift the restrictions on housing prices in 1985. The shortage has diminished. In the former Soviet Union, prices for all goods and services were defined by the government. For most consumer items, the price was set below equilibrium, and shortages existed. The long lines of people waiting to purchase food or clothing were the result of the price ceilings on all goods and services. In the United States, price ceilings on all goods and services have been imposed at times. During World War I and World War II, and during the Nixon administration of the early 1970s, wage and price controls were imposed. These were price ceilings on all goods and services. As a result of the ceilings, people were unable to purchase many of the products they desired. The Organization of Petroleum Exporting Countries (OPEC) restricted the quantity of oil in the early 1970s and drove its price up considerably. The U.S. government responded by placing a price ceiling on gasoline. The result was long lines at gas stations because of shortages of gasoline.

Price floors are quite common in economies as well. The agricultural policies of most of the developed nations are founded on price floors—the government guarantees that the price of an agricultural product will not fall below some level. Price floors result in surpluses, and this has been the case with agricultural products as well. The surpluses in agricultural products in the United States have resulted in cases where dairy farmers have dumped milk in rivers, where grain was given to other nations at taxpayer expense, and where citrus ranchers have picked and then discarded thousands of tons of citrus, all to reduce huge surpluses.

When price ceilings or price floors do not allow a market to reach equilibrium, shortages or surpluses will result. Since the price is not allowed to allocate the goods or services, another allocation mechanism will—first-come, first-served; government; or lottery.

5.e. Market Adjustment: Watch the Price of Eggs

During the 1990s, country after country turned from government-run economies to market economies. In Latin America, in Eastern Europe and Russia, in China, and in India, former socialist or dictatorial nations sought to free their stagnant and collapsing economies from government control. In these countries, government price controls were lifted, and people were allowed to buy and sell what they wanted. The leaders of the reforms were often told by their economic advisers, "Watch the price of eggs. If the price rises and more eggs are offered for sale, and then the price falls, it is a sign that markets are working."

So, when the price control was lifted, prices shot upward, frightening both the leaders and the individual people. But, within hours of the lifting of price controls, markets arose in which eggs, other produce, and some clothing items appeared. Shortages disappeared. Why? What was occurring?

Why did the advisers focus on eggs and not the heavy industries like shipbuilding, oil refining, or power generation? They focused on eggs because the market for eggs would be the quickest to emerge. Once they were free to do so, local farmers would bring their eggs to the city to sell; it doesn't take long to produce eggs. As the price of eggs rose, more eggs would be brought to market. Items such as ships, airplanes, tractors, and so forth would not increase in supply nearly as rapidly as would eggs; it would take years for these items to be produced.

The market for eggs is depicted in Figure 16. The government-controlled price is P_G. The price ceiling meant shortages, as the quantity demanded is larger than the quantity supplied. When the price ceiling is lifted, the price immediately shoots up to P_D, but the quantity supplied does not change. Eventually, the high price leads to increasing quantities of eggs being supplied. Quite rapidly, in the case of eggs, the price drops to the equilibrium.

The adjustment process took much more time in the heavy industries. Once the price controls on items like gasoline, electricity, or industrial products were lifted, the price shot up, but the quantities supplied could not increase for quite some time. As a result, prices remained very high for months or years, until suppliers could begin offering more gasoline, electricity, ships, airplanes, and tractors. To the citizens, it seemed as if the markets were not working because the higher price did not bring forth increased quantities supplied.

Years, not days, were necessary for a complete transition from government-run to market-based economies in those countries where heavy industry was a large part of the economy, such as Poland.[2] In Russia, the transition to a market economy has not fully occurred. In countries that were primarily agricultural, such as China, the transition has occurred more rapidly.

FIGURE 16   Ending Price Controls

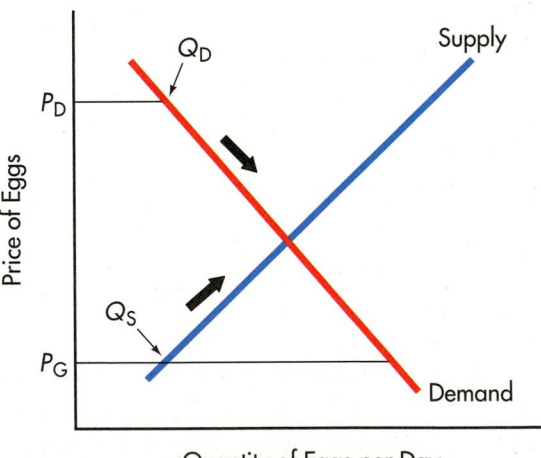

The controlled price is at P_G. When price controls are lifted, price immediately shoots up to P_D because the quantity supplied does not immediately change. Eventually, the quantity that is supplied rises, and as it rises, the price is driven to the equilibrium level.

© 2013 Cengage Learning

---

[2] The video *Commanding Heights*, based on the book of the same name by Daniel Yergin and Joseph Stanislaus, provides a vivid portrayal of the transition from government to market economies during the 1990s.

RECAP

1. Equilibrium occurs when the quantity demanded and the quantity supplied are equal: It is the price-quantity combination where the demand and supply curves intersect.

2. A price that is above the equilibrium price creates a surplus. Producers are willing and able to offer more for sale than buyers are willing and able to purchase.

3. A price that is below the equilibrium price leads to a shortage, because buyers are willing and able to purchase more than producers are willing and able to offer for sale.

4. When demand changes, price and quantity change in the same direction—both rise as demand increases, and both fall as demand decreases.

5. When supply changes, price and quantity change, but not in the same direction. When supply increases, price falls and quantity rises. When supply decreases, price rises and quantity falls.

6. When both demand and supply change, the direction of the change in price and quantity depends on the relative sizes of the changes of demand and supply.

7. A price floor is a situation in which a price is set above the equilibrium price. This creates a surplus.

8. A price ceiling is a case in which a price is set below the equilibrium price. This creates a shortage.

9. When a price ceiling is lifted, the market will adjust. The speed of adjustment of the quantity supplied and prices depends on how rapidly resources can be altered, goods and services produced, and supplies brought to market.

SUMMARY

1. **How do we decide who gets the scarce goods and resources?**

   - An allocation system is a way to determine who gets the scarce goods and resources. Allocation schemes include lottery; government; market; and first-come, first-served. *§1*

   - The advantage of a market system over other allocation schemes is the incentive created by the market system. *§1.b*

2. **What is demand?**

   - Demand is the quantities that buyers are willing and able to buy at alternative prices. *§3*

   - The quantity demanded is a specific amount at one price. *§3*

   - The law of demand states that as the price of a well-defined commodity rises (falls), the quantity demanded during a given period of time will fall (rise), everything else held constant. *§3.a*

   - Demand will change when one of the determinants of demand changes, that is, when income,

   tastes, prices of related goods and services, expectations, or number of buyers changes. A demand change is illustrated as a shift of the demand curve. *§3.e*

3. **What is supply?**

   - Supply is the quantities that sellers will offer for sale at alternative prices. *§4.a*

   - The quantity supplied is the amount that sellers offer for sale at one price. *§4.a*

   - The law of supply states that as the price of a well-defined commodity rises (falls), the quantity supplied during a given period of time will rise (fall), everything else held constant. *§4.a*

   - Supply changes when one of the determinants of supply changes, that is, when prices of resources, technology and productivity, expectations of producers, the number of producers, or the prices of related goods or services change. A supply change is illustrated as a shift of the supply curve. *§4.d*

4. **How is price determined by demand and supply?**

   - Together, demand and supply determine the equilibrium price and quantity. §5

5. **What causes price to change?**

   - A price that is above equilibrium creates a surplus, which leads to a lower price. A price that is below equilibrium creates a shortage, which leads to a higher price. §5.a

   - A change in demand or a change in supply (a shift of either curve) will cause the equilibrium price and quantity to change. §5.b, 5.c

6. **What happens when price is not allowed to change with market forces?**

   - Markets are not always in equilibrium, but when not, surpluses or shortages arise and force the price to move them toward equilibrium. §5.d

   - A price floor is a situation in which a price is not allowed to decrease below a certain level—it is set above the equilibrium price. This creates a surplus. A price ceiling is a case in which a price is not allowed to rise—it is set below the equilibrium price. This creates a shortage. §5.d

KEY TERMS

barter, 44
complementary goods, 51
demand, 44
demand curve, 46
demand schedule, 45
determinants of demand, 45
determinants of supply, 52
disequilibrium, 57
double coincidence of wants, 44

equilibrium, 57
inferior goods, 49
law of demand, 44
law of supply, 52
market, 38
normal goods, 49
price ceiling, 61
price floor, 61
productivity, 56

quantity demanded, 44
quantity supplied, 51
shortage, 58
substitute goods, 50
supply, 51
supply curve, 53
supply schedule, 52
surplus, 58

EXERCISES

1. Illustrate each of the following events using a demand and supply diagram for bananas.
   a. Reports surface that imported bananas are infected with a deadly virus.
   b. Consumers' incomes drop.
   c. The price of bananas rises.
   d. The price of oranges falls.
   e. Consumers expect the price of bananas to decrease in the future.

2. Answer true or false, and if the statement is false, change it to make it true. Illustrate your answers on a demand and supply graph.
   a. An increase in demand is represented by a movement up the demand curve.
   b. An increase in supply is represented by a movement up the supply curve.
   c. An increase in demand without any changes in supply will cause the price to rise.
   d. An increase in supply without any changes in demand will cause the price to rise.

3. Using the following schedule, define the equilibrium price and quantity. Describe the situation at a price of $10. What will occur? Describe the situation at a price of $2. What will occur?

Price	Quantity Demanded	Quantity Supplied
$1	500	100
$2	400	120
$3	350	150
$4	320	200
$5	300	300
$6	275	410
$7	260	500
$8	230	650
$9	200	800
$10	150	975

4. Suppose the government imposed a minimum price of $7 in the schedule of exercise 3. What would occur? Illustrate.

5. In exercise 3, indicate what the price would have to be to represent an effective price ceiling. Point out the surplus or shortage that results. Illustrate a price floor and provide an example of a price floor.

6. A common feature of skiing is waiting in lift lines. Does the existence of lift lines mean that the price is not working to allocate the scarce resource? If so, what should be done about it?

7. Why don't we observe barter systems as often as we observe the use of currency?

8. A severe drought in California has resulted in a nearly 30 percent reduction in the quantity of citrus grown and produced in California. Explain what effect this event might have on the Florida citrus market.

9. The prices of the Ralph Lauren Polo line of clothing are considerably higher than those of comparable-quality lines. Yet this line sells more than a J. C. Penney brand line of clothing. Does this violate the law of demand?

10. In December, the price of Christmas trees rises and the quantity of trees sold rises. Is this a violation of the law of demand?

11. In recent years, the price of artificial Christmas trees has fallen while the quality has risen. What impact has this event had on the price of cut Christmas trees?

12. Many restaurants don't take reservations. You simply arrive and wait your turn. If you arrive at 7:30 in the evening, you have at least an hour wait. Notwithstanding that fact, a few people arrive, speak quietly with the maître d', hand him some money, and are promptly seated. At some restaurants that do take reservations, there is a month wait for a Saturday evening, three weeks for a Friday evening, two weeks for Tuesday through Thursday, and virtually no wait for Sunday or Monday evening. How do you explain these events using demand and supply?

13. Evaluate the following statement: "The demand for U.S. oranges has increased because the quantity of U.S. oranges demanded in Japan has risen."

14. In December 1992, the federal government began requiring that all foods display information about fat content and other ingredients on food packages. The displays had to be verified by independent laboratories. The price of an evaluation of a food product could run as much as $20,000. What impact do you think this law had on the market for meat?

15. Draw a PPC. Which combination shown by the PPC will be produced? How is this combination determined? Does the combination that is produced depend on how goods and services are allocated?

16. The price of oil increased to more than $100 per barrel following the turmoil in the Mideast in 2011. Illustrate, using a market for oil, why the price rose.

17. Using exercise 16, illustrate what would have occurred had a price ceiling on oil of $80 per barrel existed.

You can find further practice tests in the Online Quiz at **www.cengage.com/economics/boyes**.

THE WRONG ANSWER FOR HIGH GAS PRICES

The Baltimore Sun, September 8, 2005

Washington—When Rudyard Kipling said it was a great virtue "if you can keep your head when all about you are losing theirs and blaming it on you," he was not thinking of Sen. Maria Cantwell, a Democrat from Washington. This week, as gasoline prices remained above $3 a gallon, she proposed giving the president the power to tell retailers what they can charge at the pump.

A lot of people grew anxious seeing long lines forming the week before last, as motorists rushed to fill their tanks in the aftermath of Hurricane Katrina. But Ms. Cantwell apparently enjoyed the sight well enough that she'd like to make those lines a permanent feature of the landscape. If so, she has the right approach. The government does many things badly, but one thing it knows how to do is create shortages through the vigorous use of price controls.

That's what it did in the oil market in 1979–80, under President Jimmy Carter. He was replaced by Ronald Reagan, who lifted price caps on gas and thus not only banished shortages but brought about an era of low prices.

Ms. Cantwell thinks oil companies have manipulated the energy market to gouge consumers, though she is awaiting evidence to support that theory. "I just don't have the document to prove it," she declared. Her suspicions were roused when she noticed that prices climbed in Seattle—though most of its oil comes from Alaska, which was not hit by a hurricane.

Maybe no one has told Ms. Cantwell that oil trades in an international market, and that when companies and consumers in the South can't get fuel from their usual sources, they will buy it from other ones, even if they have to go as far as Prudhoe Bay.

If prices rose in Dallas and didn't rise in Seattle, oil producers would have a big incentive to ship all their supplies to Texas—leaving Washingtonians to pay nothing for nothing. When a freeze damages Florida's orange juice crop, does Ms. Cantwell think only Floridians feel the pain?

Sen. Byron Dorgan, a Democrat from North Dakota, meanwhile, was outraged by the thought of giant oil companies making money merely for supplying the nation's energy needs. He claimed they will reap $80 billion in "windfall profits" and wants the government to confiscate a large share of that sum through a special federal tax.

But the prospect of occasional "windfall" profits is one reason corporations are willing to risk their money drilling wells that may turn out to be drier than Alan Greenspan's reading list. Take them away, and investors may decide they'd rather speculate in real estate.

It's hard to see why oil companies shouldn't make a lot of money when the commodity they provide is suddenly in short supply. After all, they are vulnerable to weak profits or even losses during times of glut. Back when Americans were enjoying abundant cheap gasoline, the joke was that the surest way to make a small fortune in the oil industry was to start with a large fortune.

Oil companies are also subject to the whims of nature. No one is holding a charity fundraiser for the business people whose rigs and refineries were smashed by Katrina. No one will come to their aid if prices drop by half.

Besides, high prices serve two essential functions: encouraging production and fostering conservation. Spurred by the lure of windfall profits, oil companies will move heaven and earth to get more gasoline to consumers. Shocked by the tab when they fill up a 5,600-pound SUV, motorists will look for opportunities to leave the Suburban at home. They may even commit a sin not covered by the Ten Commandments: Coveting their neighbor's Prius.

Controlling prices, by contrast, would have exactly the opposite effect: telling consumers they should waste fuel to their hearts' content and telling producers to leave the black stuff in the ground. When events in the world conspire to make oil dear, there is nothing to be gained from masking that fact. We can ignore reality, but reality won't ignore us.

STEVE CHAPMAN

Dictating the retail price that companies can sell gasoline at is nothing more than a price ceiling. In the figure below left, the ceiling price of P_m is less than the equilibrium price P_1. This price ceiling creates a shortage: At the controlled price P_m, the quantity of gasoline demanded is Q_d, while the quantity supplied is only Q_s. The difference, $Q_d - Q_s$, is the quantity of gasoline that consumers would be willing and able to buy but can't because there is none available. What does a shortage in gasoline look like? It is long lines at gas pumps. It is people stranded because they have run out of gas.

How is this shortage resolved? Since price cannot be used to resolve the shortage, something else will. Common replacements for price are first-come, first-served and corruption.

First-come, first-served is what we typically see. Long lines form at gas stations. People "top off" their tanks, driving into a station whenever they see an opening in order to keep their gas tanks full. One result is many more people at pumps than would otherwise be the case. Another is that some gas stations close because they can't obtain supplies.

Crude oil, the main source of gasoline, is traded in a global market. If prices rise in one part of the world but are not allowed to rise in others, the crude oil will be shipped to where its return is highest. As the article notes, "If prices rose in Dallas and didn't rise in Seattle, oil producers would have a big incentive to ship all their supplies to Texas—leaving Washingtonians to pay nothing for nothing. When a freeze damages Florida's orange juice crop, does Ms. Cantwell think only Floridians feel the pain?" If the United States limited gasoline prices to

$2 per gallon and other parts of the world allowed the price to rise to $4 per gallon, the oil would be shipped to where it could be refined and a profit made from selling gasoline. In short, price ceilings lead to shortages. Even if the oil was not shipped around the world, why would anyone invest millions of dollars in drilling for oil when they would not make a profit? As the commentary notes, controlling prices tells producers to leave the black stuff in the ground. Refineries would be shut down, and no new spending on oil wells and facilities would occur. Over time, the supply of gasoline would decline even further, shown as the move from S_1 to S_2 in the figure below on the right. This would create larger shortages.

In the Soviet Union, China, Cuba, India, and other nations that imposed price controls on many goods and services for a long period of time, first-come, first-served allocation was replaced with graft and corruption. If you bribed the right official, you could get some bread or milk. If you paid off the manager, you could find other items that you needed. Corruption leads to a collapse of civilization—standards of living decline.

As noted in the chapter, allocation schemes other than price do not create incentives for improvement or increases in standards of living. What incentive does the first-come, first served system create? Just to be first. All you do is stand in lines. Nothing more is produced, and no alternatives to gasoline are ever discovered. In contrast, if price is not controlled, it rises to equilibrium, the quantity supplied rises, and the quantity demanded falls. The higher price brings out entrepreneurs seeking profits. These entrepreneurs will discover more efficient ways to transport people and alternative energy sources to oil and gasoline.

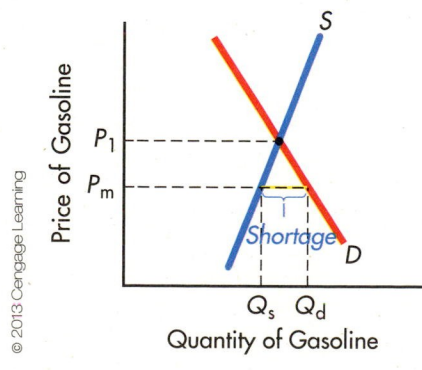

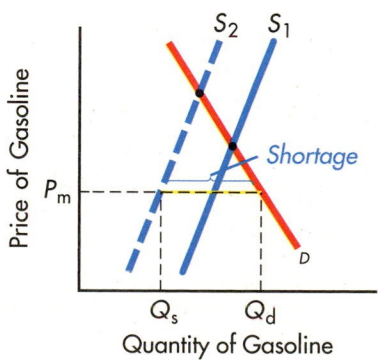

CHAPTER 4

The Market System and the Private and Public Sectors

© MACIEJ FROLOW/GETTY IMAGES, INC

© CULTURA CREATIVE/ALAMY; LOGO: © FROXX/SHUTTERSTOCK.COM

FUNDAMENTAL QUESTIONS

1. In a market system, who decides what goods and services are produced and how they are produced, and who obtains the goods and services that are produced?

2. What is a household, and what is household income and spending?

3. What is a business firm, and what is business spending?

4. How does the international sector affect the economy?

5. What is the public sector? What is public sector spending?

6. How do the private and public sectors interact?

You decide to buy a new Toyota, so you go to a Toyota dealer and exchange money for the car. The Toyota dealer has rented land and buildings and hired workers in order to make cars available to you and other members of the public. The employees earn incomes paid by the Toyota dealer and then use those incomes to buy food from the grocery store. This transaction generates revenue for the grocery store, which hires workers and pays them incomes that they then use to buy groceries and Toyotas.

The story is complicated by the fact that your Toyota may have been manufactured in Japan and then shipped to the United States before it was sold by the local Toyota dealer. Your purchase of the Toyota creates revenue for both the local dealer and the manufacturer, which pays autoworkers to assemble the cars. When you buy your Toyota, you pay a sales tax, which the government uses to support its expenditures on police, fire protection, national defense, the legal system, and other services. In short, many people in different areas of the economy are involved in what seems to be a single transaction.

We begin this chapter by examining the interaction of buyers and sellers in a market system. We then look at the main sectors of an economy—households, firms, the international, and the government—to determine how they interact.

1. The Market System

As we learned in Chapter 2, the production possibilities curve (PPC) represents all possible combinations of goods and services that a society can produce if its resources are used fully and efficiently. Which combination, that is, which point on the PPC, will society choose? In a price or market system, the answer is given by demand and supply. Consumers demonstrate what they are willing and able to pay for by buying different goods and services. If a business is to succeed, it must supply what people want at a price that people can afford.

 1 In a market system, who decides what goods and services are produced and how they are produced, and who obtains the goods and services that are produced?

1.a. Consumer Sovereignty

Tablet sales are dominating laptop computer sales, which exceed sales of desktop PCs. Smartphones have taken over from mobile phones. A smartphone can take care of all of your handheld computing and communication needs in a single, small package. The first smartphone was called Simon; it was designed by IBM in 1992. Smartphone adoption in the U.S. initially lagged that of other developed areas, such as Japan or Europe, but the North American market expanded considerably beginning in 2008.

In the 1990s, people wanted mobile devices to carry out those daily tasks. The Blackberry, iPod, and other devices served various functions. By emphasizing convenience and flexibility, Nokia, Sharp, Fujitsu, and RIM grabbed a big share of the smartphone market worldwide, and Apple did well in North America. While these and a few manufacturers became successful, the star of the story is not these companies. It is the consumer. In a market system, if consumers are willing and able to pay for more powerful and flexible phones, more such phones appear. If consumers are willing and able to pay for a small phone that takes pictures and entertains you and does other tasks, such a phone will be available.

Why does the consumer have such power? The name of the game for business is profit, and the only way a business can make a profit is by satisfying consumer wants. Consumers, not politicians or business firms, ultimately determine what is to be produced. An entrepreneur or firm may introduce a new product—such as the iPod—something consumers had not thought about prior to its introduction, but once the product is introduced, the consumers determine whether that product will continue to be produced. A firm that produces something that no consumers want will not remain in business very long. **Consumer sovereignty**—the authority of consumers to determine what is produced through their purchases of goods and services—dictates what goods and services will be produced. Firms and inventors come up with new products, but if consumers are not willing and able to purchase these products, the products will not exist for long.

consumer sovereignty
The authority of consumers to determine what is produced through their purchases of goods and services.

1.b. Profit and the Allocation of Resources

When a good or service seems to have the potential to generate a profit, some entrepreneur will put together the resources needed to offer that good or service for sale. If the potential profit turns into a loss, the entrepreneur may stop buying resources and turn to some other occupation or project. The resources used in the losing operation will then be available for use in an activity where they are more highly valued.

To illustrate how resources get allocated in the market system, let's look at the market for PDAs and smartphones. The PDA was introduced in the market several years before the smartphone. Figure 1 shows a change in demand for PDAs. The initial demand curve, D_1, and supply curve, S, are shown in Figure 1(a). With these demand and supply curves, the equilibrium price (P_1) is $80, and the equilibrium quantity (Q_1) is 100 thousand units per year. At this price-quantity combination, the number of PDAs demanded equals the number of PDAs offered for sale; equilibrium is reached, so we say that the market clears (there is no shortage or surplus).

The second part of the figure shows what happened when consumer tastes changed; people preferred to have a smartphone rather than just a PDA. This change in tastes caused the demand for PDAs to decline; illustrated by a leftward shift of the demand curve, from D_1 to D_2, in Figure 1(b). The demand curve shifted to the left because fewer PDAs were demanded at each price. Consumer tastes, not the price of PDAs, changed first. (A price change would have led to a change in the quantity demanded and would be represented by a move *along* demand curve D_1.) The change in tastes caused a change in demand and a leftward shift of the demand curve. The shift from D_1 to D_2 created a new equilibrium point. The equilibrium price (P_2) decreased to $60, and the equilibrium quantity (Q_2) decreased to 80 (thousand) units.

While the market for PDAs was changing, so was the market for smartphones. Figure 2(a) shows the original demand for the smartphone and its original price of $500. Figure 2(b) shows a rightward shift of the demand curve, from D_1 to D_2, representing the increased demand for smartphones. This demand change resulted in a higher market-clearing price for smartphones, from $500 to $600.

The changing profit potential of the two markets induced existing firms to switch from PDAs to smartphones and for new firms to offer smartphones from the start. Nokia dominated the smartphone market, but Apple, which at first did not offer smartphones, had to play catch up and begin offering its own smartphone. It did so with its iPhone.

As demand fell for the PDA, the market-clearing price of PDAs fell (from $80 to $60 in Figure 1[b]), and the quantity of PDAs sold also declined (from 100 to 80). The decreased demand led to a lower price, which meant that many PDA firms saw declining profits. In the smartphone business, the opposite occurred. As the demand for smartphones rose, the market-clearing price rose (from $500 to $600 in Figure 2[b]); the number of smartphones sold also rose (from 50 to 60 thousand). The increased demand, higher price, and resulting higher profit induced firms to increase production.

Why did the production of smartphones increase while the production of PDAs declined? Not because of a government decree. Not because of the desires of the business sector, especially the owners of the smartphone manufacturers. The consumer—*consumer sovereignty*—made all this happen. Businesses that failed to respond to consumer desires and failed to provide the desired good at the lowest price failed to survive.

1.c. Creative Destruction

After demand shifted to smartphones, the resources that had been used in the production of PDAs were available for use elsewhere. Some former employees were able to get jobs in the smartphone industry. Some of the equipment used in manufacturing PDAs was purchased by the smartphone firms; some of the components that previously would

FIGURE 1 A Demand Change in the Market for PDAs

(a) PDA Market

(b) The Effect of a Change in Tastes on PDA Market

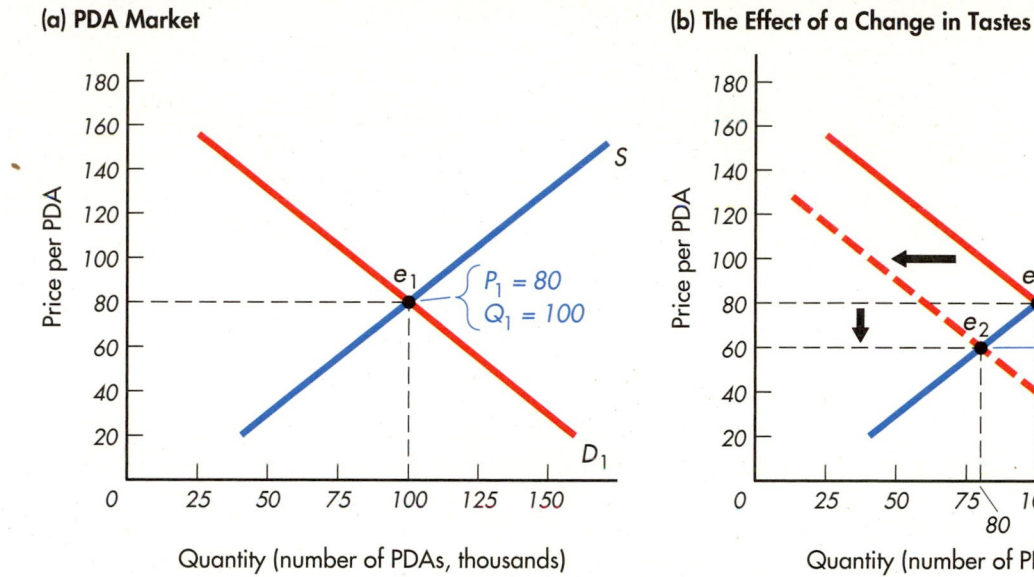

In Figure 1(a), the initial market-clearing price (P_1) and market-clearing quantity (Q_1) are shown. In Figure 1(b), the market-clearing price and quantity change from P_1 and Q_1 to P_2 and Q_2 as the demand curve shifts to the left because of a change in tastes. The result of decreased demand is a lower price and a lower quantity produced.

FIGURE 2 A Demand Change in the Market for Smartphones

(a) Smartphone Market

(b) The Effect of a Change in Tastes in Smartphone Market

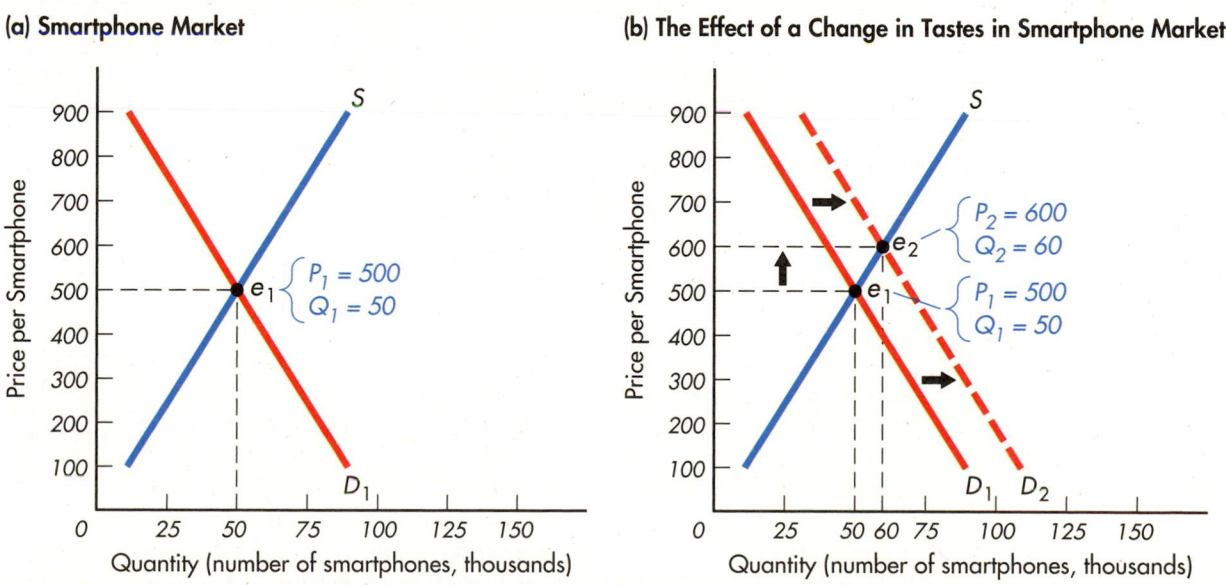

In Figure 2(a), the initial market-clearing price (P_1) and quantity (Q_1) are shown. In Figure 2(b), the demand for smartphones increases, thus driving up the market-clearing price (P_2) and quantity (Q_2) as the demand curve shifts to the right, from D_1 to D_2.

have gone to the PDAs were used in the smartphones. Although some former employees of the PDA business became employed in the smartphone business, others had to find entirely new positions in totally different businesses. Some of the equipment used to manufacture PDAs was sold as scrap; other equipment was sold to other manufacturers. In other words, the resources moved from an activity where their value was relatively low to an activity where they were more highly valued. No one commanded the resources to move. They moved because they could earn more in some other activity.

This same story applies in case after case after case. The Sony Walkman was replaced by Apple's iPod, and the early iPod is now contained in the iPhone. The process of new products and new firms replacing existing products and firms is called *creative destruction*. This is what the market process is all about—creating new ideas, new products, and new ways of doing things, and replacing the obsolete, costly, and inefficient. Every year *Forbes* magazine publishes a list of the 100 largest companies in terms of sales. In 1987, *Forbes* compared that year's list to the 100 largest firms in 1917. Only 39 of the 1917 group remained in 1987. Of the 39 that remained in business, 18 had managed to stay in the top 100. Of the 18 that stayed in the top 100, only 2 had performed better than the market average—Kodak and GE. Both of these have since fallen, barely surviving. This seems an amazing change, but the pace of change has only quickened since 1987. Fewer than 25 percent of today's major corporations will continue to exist in 25 years.

In 1900, over 60 percent of the U.S. workforce was employed in agriculture. Today, less than 3 percent are employed in agriculture. Yet the U.S. produces far more agriculture today than it did in 1900. The technology used in agriculture so increased the productivity on farms that only 3 percent of the workforce is needed. Since 57 percent of the workforce that was in agriculture in 1900 is not today, where did workers go? Since they were no longer needed in agriculture, people received training in high technology or many other fields that had a greater value for them than working on the farm would have. In a sense, jobs on the farm were destroyed, but they were destroyed by the creation of new jobs in technology or services.

Firms produce the goods and services and use the resources that enable them to generate the highest profits. If one firm does this better than others, then that firm earns a greater profit than others. Seeing that success, other firms copy or mimic the first firm. If a firm cannot be as profitable as the others, it will eventually go out of business or move to another line of business where it can be successful. In the process of firms always seeking to lower their costs and make higher profits, society finds that the goods and services that buyers want are produced in the least costly manner. Not only do consumers get the goods and services that they want and will pay for, but they get these products at the lowest possible price.

1.d. The Determination of Income

Consumer demands dictate what is produced, and the search for profit defines how goods and services are produced. For whom are the goods and services produced; that is, who gets the goods and services? As we discussed in Chapter 3, in a price or market system, those who have the ability to pay for the products get the products. Your income determines your ability to pay, but where does income come from? A person's income is obtained by selling the services of the resources that person owns.

In reality, households own all resources. Everyone owns his or her own labor; some households also own land, and many also own firms or portions of firms. When a household owns shares of stock, it owns a portion of the firm whose shares it owns. Many households own shares of stock either as direct investments or as part of their retirement fund. The firm you or your parents work for might provide a 401(k) or some other retirement plan. A portion of these plans typically own shares of stock. All firms, whether private firms or firms traded through stock markets, are owned by households in some way. Thus, if a firm acquires equipment, buildings, land, and natural resources, it is actually households that ultimately own those things. If a firm were taken apart and its parts sold off, households would end up with the money.

Typically we think of our income as what we are paid for our labor services. But you may also receive income from the shares of stock that you own (dividends and appreciation) and the various savings accounts that you own (interest). You may receive rent from being a landlord or from allowing a firm to use the services of your land. You may get profits from a business that you started.

RECAP

1. In a market system, consumers are sovereign and decide by means of their purchases what goods and services will be produced.

2. In a market system, firms decide how to produce the goods and services that consumers want. In order to earn maximum profits, firms use the least-cost combinations of resources.

3. Income and prices determine who gets what in a market system. Income is determined by the ownership of resources.

2. The Private Sector

Buyers and sellers of goods and services and resource owners are linked together in an economy. For every dollar someone spends, someone else receives a dollar as income. In the remainder of this chapter, we learn more about the linkages among the sectors of the economy. We classify the buyers and the resource owners into the household sector; the sellers or business firms are the business sector; households and firms in other countries, who may also be buyers and sellers of this country's goods and services, are the international sector. These three sectors—households, business firms, and the international firms and consumers—constitute the **private sector** of the economy. The private sector refers to any part of the economy that is not part of government. The **public sector** refers to the government, government spending and taxing, and government sponsored and run entities. The relative sizes of private and public sectors vary from economy to economy. The market economies tend to have smaller public sectors relative to the total economy than do the more socialist or centrally planned economies.

private sector
Households, businesses, and the international sector.

public sector
The government.

2.a. Households

A **household** consists of one or more persons who occupy a unit of housing. The unit of housing may be a house, an apartment, or even a single room, as long as it constitutes separate living quarters. A household may consist of related family members, like a father, mother, and children, or it may comprise unrelated individuals, like three college students sharing an apartment. The person in whose name the house or apartment is owned or rented is called the householder.

Household spending is called **consumption**. Householders consume housing, transportation, food, entertainment, and other goods and services. Household spending (also called consumer spending) per year in the United States is shown in Figure 3, along with household income. The pattern is generally one of steady increase, but you can see that from the second quarter 2008 to the second quarter 2010, real household expenditures actually declined. (A quarter refers to three months.) This was a

2 What is a household, and what is household income and spending?

household
One or more persons who occupy a unit of housing.

consumption
Household spending.

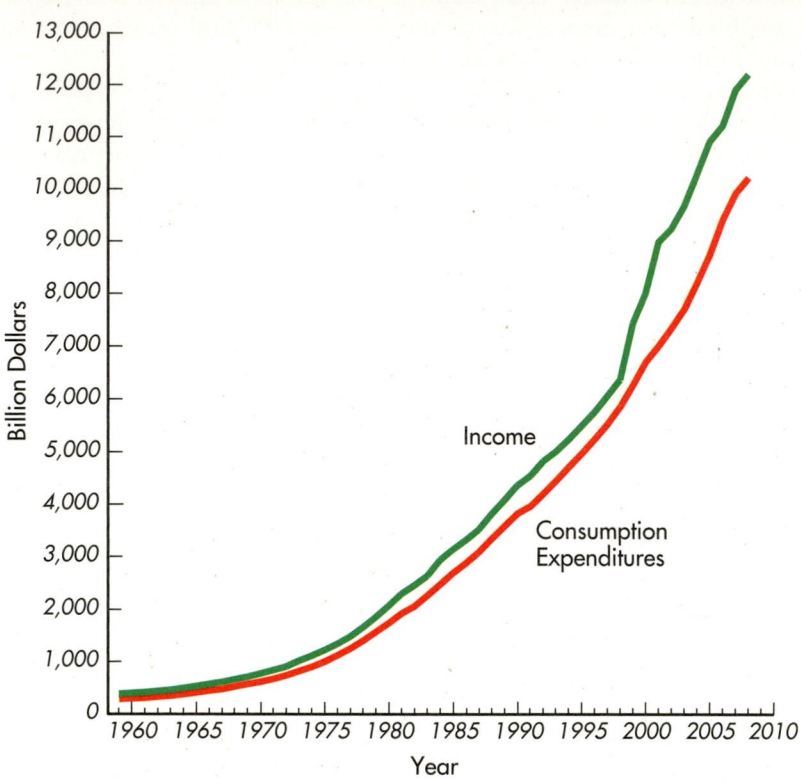

FIGURE 3   Household Spending and Income

Source: U.S. Department of Commerce, Bureau of Economic Analysis; www.census.gov.

 3 What is a business firm, and what is business spending?

business firm
A business organization controlled by a single management.

sole proprietorship
A business owned by one person who receives all the profits and is responsible for all the debts incurred by the business.

partnership
A business with two or more owners who share the firm's profits and losses.

corporation
A legal entity owned by shareholders whose liability for the firm's losses is limited to the value of the stock they own.

period of financial crisis and recession. Spending by the household sector is the largest component—constituting about 70 percent of total spending in the economy.

2.b. Business Firms

A **business firm** is a business organization controlled by a single management. The firm's business may be conducted at more than one location. The terms *company*, *enterprise*, and *business* are used interchangeably with *firm*.

Firms are organized as sole proprietorships, partnerships, or corporations. A **sole proprietorship** is a business owned by one person. This type of firm may be a one-person operation or a large enterprise with many employees. In either case, the owner receives all the profits and is responsible for all the debts incurred by the business.

A **partnership** is a business owned by two or more partners who share both the profits of the business and responsibility for the firm's losses. The partners can be individuals, estates, or other businesses.

A **corporation** is a business whose identity in the eyes of the law is distinct from the identity of its owners. State law allows the formation of corporations. A corporation is an economic entity that, like a person, can own property and borrow money in its own name. The owners of a corporation are shareholders. The corporation has limited liability, which means that if a corporation cannot pay its debts, creditors cannot seek payment from the shareholders' personal wealth. The shareholders' liability is limited to the value of the stock they own.

Many firms are global in their operations, even though they may have been founded and may be owned by residents of a single country. Firms typically first enter the international market by selling products to foreign countries. As revenues from these sales increase, the firms realize advantages by locating subsidiaries in foreign countries. Companies seek the location where taxes and regulations are the lowest and, of course, where profit potential is highest. A **multinational business** is a firm that owns and operates producing units in foreign countries. The best-known U.S. corporations are multinational firms. Ford, IBM, PepsiCo, and McDonald's all own operating units in many different countries. Ford Motor Company, for instance, is the parent firm of sales organizations and assembly plants located around the world.

Expenditures by business firms for capital goods—machines, tools, and buildings—that will be used to produce goods and services are called **investments**. Notice that the meaning of investment here is different from the everyday meaning, "a financial transaction such as buying bonds or stocks." In economics, the term *investment* refers to business spending for capital goods.

Investment spending declined from 2007–2010; businesses had reduced expenditures on capital goods in 2007–2009 because sales had declined and the outlook for future sales was not very good. Investment is equal to roughly one-fourth of consumption, or household spending, but fluctuates a great deal more than consumption. Investment spending between 1959 and 2011 is shown in Figure 4. Compare Figures 3 and 4

multinational business
A firm that owns and operates producing units in foreign countries.

investment
Spending on capital goods to be used in producing goods and services.

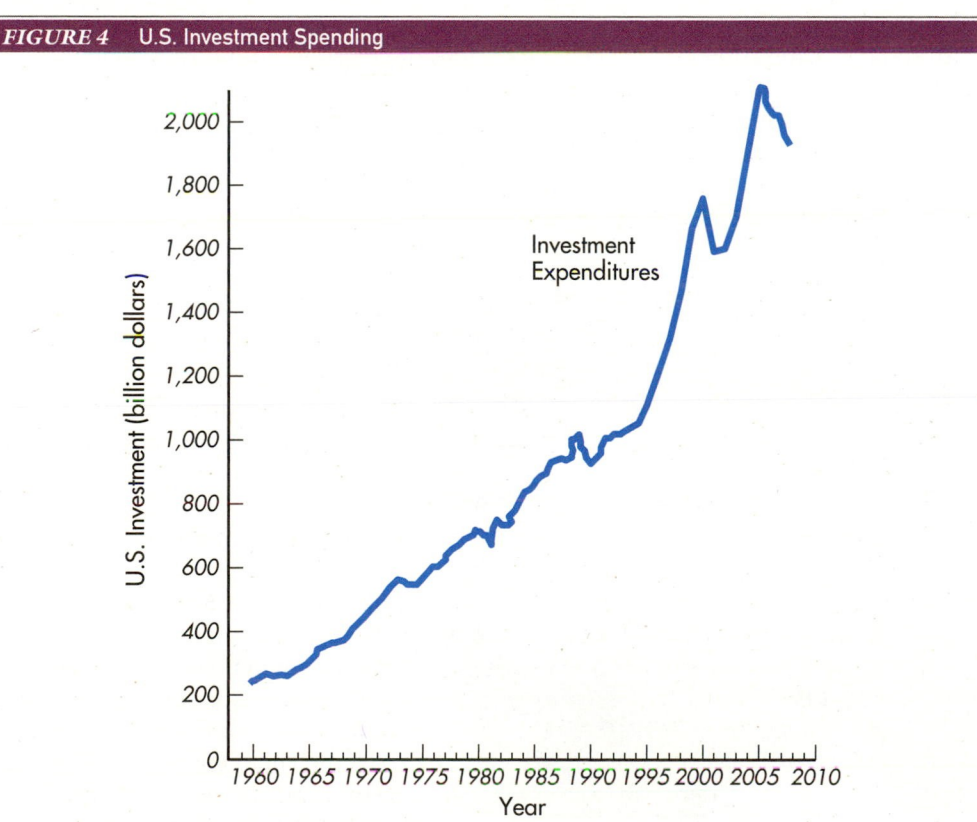

FIGURE 4   U.S. Investment Spending

Business expenditures on capital goods have been increasing erratically since 1959.

Source: *Economic Report of the President, 2010.*

and notice how much investment fluctuates relative to consumption. Consumption normally rises at a fairly steady rate.

2.c. The International Sector

4 How does the international sector affect the economy?

Economic conditions in the United States affect conditions throughout the world, and conditions in other parts of the world have a significant effect on economic conditions in the United States.

The nations of the world may be divided into two categories: industrial countries and developing countries. (Developing countries are often referred to as emerging markets or LDCs, less-developed countries.) Developing countries greatly outnumber industrial countries (see Figure 5). The World Bank (an international organization that makes loans to developing countries) groups countries according to per capita income (income per person). Low-income economies are those with per capita incomes of less than $1,000. Middle-income economies have per capita annual incomes of $1,000–$10,000. High-income economies—oil exporters and industrial market economies—are distinguished from the middle-income economies and have per capita incomes of greater than $10,000. Some countries are not members of the World Bank and so are not categorized, and information about a few small countries is so limited that the World Bank is unable to classify them.

It is readily apparent from Figure 5 that low-income economies are heavily concentrated in Africa and Asia. An important question in economics is: *Why?* Why are some countries rich and others poor? Why are poor countries concentrated in Africa and Asia with some in Latin America? These are questions discussed in both microeconomics and macroeconomics.

The World Bank uses per capita income to classify 23 countries as "industrial market economies." They are listed in the bar chart in Figure 6. The 23 countries listed in Figure 6 are among the wealthiest countries in the world. Not appearing on the list are the high-income oil-exporting nations like Libya, Saudi Arabia, Kuwait, and the United Arab Emirates. The World Bank considers those countries to be "still developing."

The economies of the industrial nations are highly interdependent. As conditions change in one country, business firms and individuals may shift large sums of money between countries. As funds flow from one country to another, economic conditions in one country spread to other countries. As a result, the major economic powers like the United States, the European Monetary Union, Japan, and China are forced to pay close attention to each other's economic policies.

The United States tends to buy primary products such as agricultural produce and minerals from

"The best and brightest are leaving." Statements like this are heard in many nations throughout the world. The best trained and most innovative people in many countries find their opportunities greater in the United States. As a result, they leave their countries to gain citizenship in the United States. But it is not easy for people to move from one country to another. The flow of goods and services among nations—international trade—occurs more readily than does the flow of workers.

ECONOMIC INSIGHT

The Successful Entrepreneur
(Sometimes It's Better to Be Lucky Than Good)

Entrepreneurs do not always develop an abstract idea into reality when starting a new firm. Sometimes people stumble onto a good thing by accident and then are clever enough and willing to take the necessary risk to turn their lucky find into a commercial success.

In 1875, a Philadelphia pharmacist on his honeymoon tasted tea made from an innkeeper's old family recipe. The tea, made from 16 wild roots and berries, was so delicious that the pharmacist asked the innkeeper's wife for the recipe. When he returned to his pharmacy, he created a solid concentrate of the drink that could be sold for home consumption.

The pharmacist was Charles Hires, a devout Quaker, who intended to sell "Hires Herb Tea" to hard-drinking Pennsylvania coal miners as a nonalcoholic alternative to beer and whiskey. A friend of Hires suggested that miners would not drink anything called "tea" and recommended that he call his drink "root beer."

The initial response to Hires Root Beer was so enthusiastic that Hires soon began nationwide distribution. The yellow box of root beer extract became a familiar sight in homes and drugstore fountains across the United States. By 1895, Hires, who started with a $3,000 loan, was operating a business valued at half a million dollars (a lot of money in 1895) and bottling ready-to-drink root beer across the country.

Hires, of course, is not the only entrepreneur who was clever enough to turn a lucky discovery into a business success. In 1894, in Battle Creek, Michigan, a sanitarium handyman named Will Kellogg was helping his older brother prepare wheat meal to serve to patients in the sanitarium's dining room. The two men would boil wheat dough and then run it through rollers to produce thin sheets of meal. One day they left a batch of the dough out overnight. The next day, when the dough was run through the rollers, it broke up into flakes instead of forming a sheet.

By letting the dough stand overnight, the Kellogg's had allowed moisture to be distributed evenly to each individual wheat berry. When the dough went through the rollers, the berries formed separate flakes instead of binding together. The Kellogg's toasted the wheat flakes and served them to the patients. They were an immediate success. In fact, the brothers had to start a mailorder flaked-cereal business because patients wanted flaked cereal for their households.

Kellogg saw the market potential of the discovery and started his own cereal company (his brother refused to join him in the business). He was a great promoter who used innovations like four-color magazine ads and free-sample promotions. In New York City, he offered a free box of corn flakes to every woman who winked at her grocer on a specified day. The promotion was considered risqué, but Kellogg's sales in New York increased from two railroad cars of cereal a month to one car a day.

Will Kellogg, a poorly paid sanitarium worker in his mid-forties, became a daring entrepreneur after his mistake with wheat flour led to the discovery of a way to produce flaked cereal. He became one of the richest men in America because of his entrepreneurial ability.

Source: From FUCINI. ENTREPRENEURS. © 1985 Gale, a part of Cengage Learning, Inc. Reproduced by permission. www.cengage.com/permissions.

---

the developing countries and manufactured products from the industrial nations. Products that a country buys from another country are called **imports**. Products that a country sells to another country are called **exports**. The United States tends to sell, or *export*, manufactured goods to all countries. There is a myth that the United States no longer has a manufacturing sector—that it has all been sent to China or other less-developed nations. But that is not true. While there are fewer jobs in manufacturing than in the past, the total manufacturing output has increased virtually every year. In addition, the United States is the largest producer and exporter of grains and other agricultural output in the world. The efficiency of U.S. farming relative to farming in much of the rest of the world gives the United States a comparative advantage in many agricultural products.

Economic activity of the United States with the rest of the world includes U.S. spending on foreign goods and foreign spending on U.S. goods. Figure 7 shows how U.S.

imports
Products that a country buys from other countries.

exports
Products that a country sells to other countries.

FIGURE 5　World Economic Development

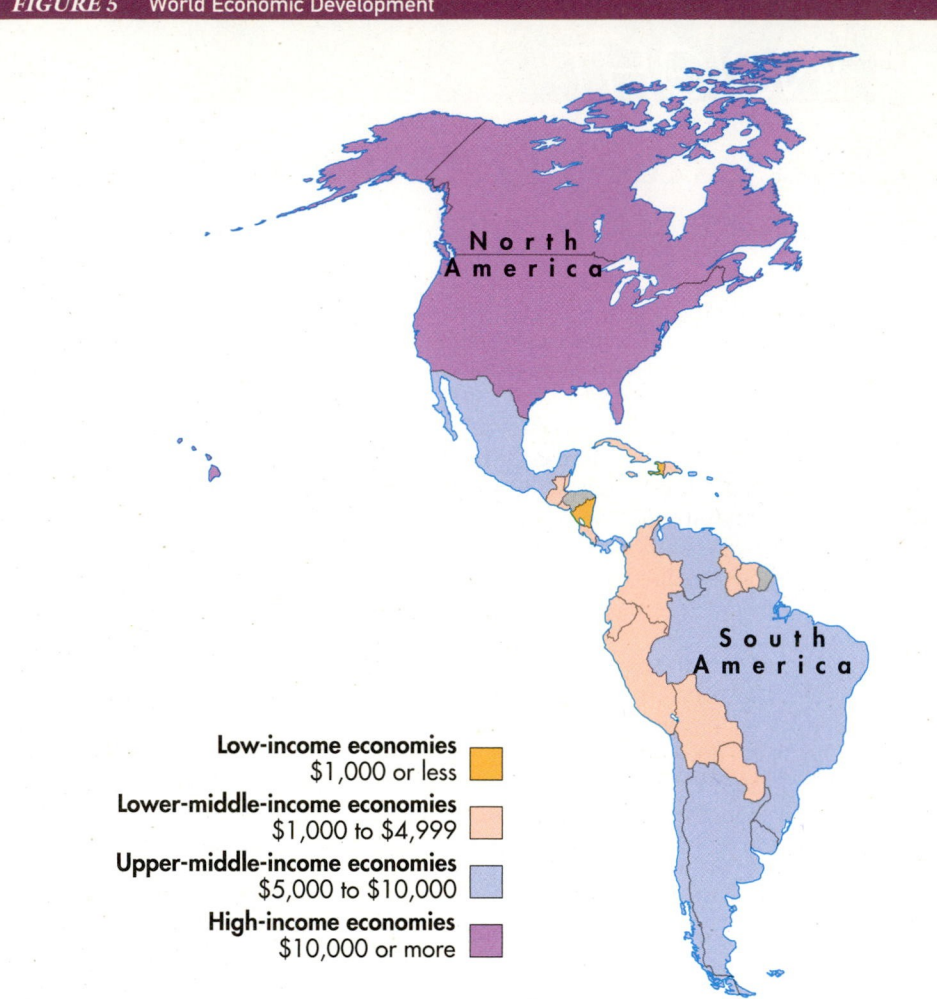

Low-income economies
$1,000 or less

Lower-middle-income economies
$1,000 to $4,999

Upper-middle-income economies
$5,000 to $10,000

High-income economies
$10,000 or more

The colors on the map identify low-income, middle-income, and high-income economies. Countries have been placed in each group on the basis of GNP per capita and, in some instances, other distinguishing economic characteristics.

Source: World Bank; http://nebula.worldbank.org/website/GNIwdi/viewer.htm.

trade surplus
The situation that exists when imports are less than exports.

trade deficit
The situation that exists when imports exceed exports.

net exports
The difference between the value of exports and the value of imports.

exports and imports are spread over different countries. Notice that the largest trading partners with the United States are Canada, Mexico, China, and Western Europe.

When exports exceed imports, a **trade surplus** exists. When imports exceed exports, a **trade deficit** exists. The term **net exports** refers to the difference between the value of exports and the value of imports: Net exports equals exports minus imports. Figure 8 traces U.S. net exports over time. Positive net exports represent trade surpluses; negative net exports represent trade deficits. The trade deficits (indicated by negative net exports) starting in the 1980s were unprecedented. Reasons for this pattern of international trade are discussed in later chapters.

FIGURE 6   The Industrial Market Economies

The bar chart lists some of the wealthiest countries in the world in terms of income per person.

Source: World Bank, *World Development Report, 2009*; http://siteresources.worldbank.org/DATASTATISTICS/Resources/GNOPC.pdf.

RECAP

1. A household consists of one or more persons who occupy a unit of housing.

2. Household spending is called consumption.

3. Business firms may be organized as sole proprietorships, partnerships, or corporations.

4. Business investment spending fluctuates widely over time.

5. The majority of U.S. trade is with the industrial market economies.

FIGURE 7   Direction of U.S. Trade

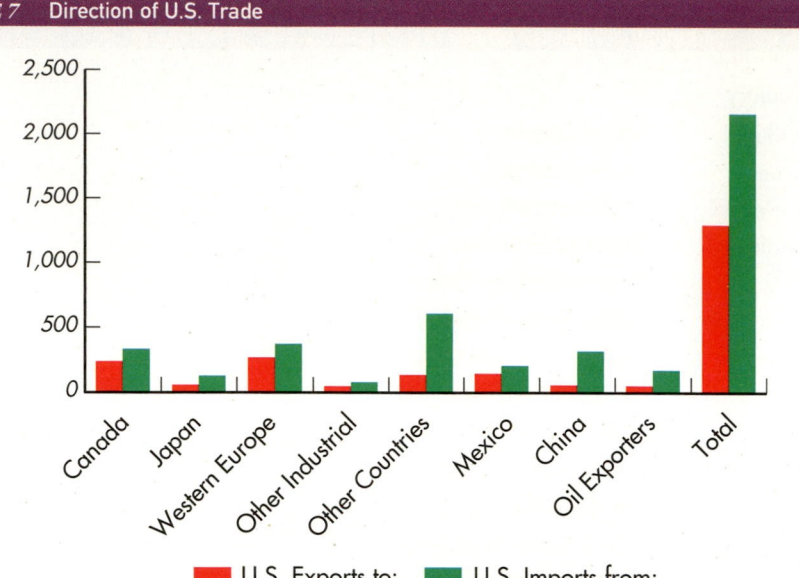

This chart shows that a trade deficit exists for the United States, since U.S. imports greatly exceed U.S. exports. The chart also shows that the largest trading partners with the U.S. are Western Europe, Japan, Canada, Mexico, and China.

Source: *Economic Report of the President, 2010*; www.census.gov/foreign-trade/Press-Release/current_press_release/exh14a.xls.

FIGURE 8   U.S. Net Exports

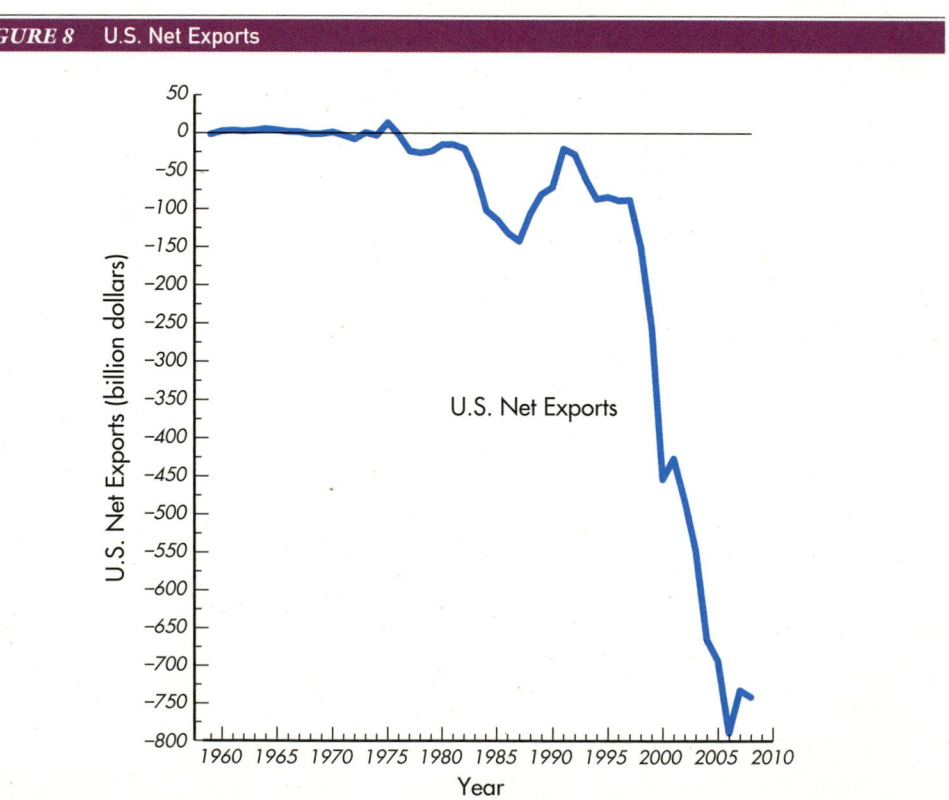

Prior to the late 1960s, the United States generally exported more than it imported and had a trade surplus. Since 1976, net exports have been negative, and the United States has had a trade deficit.

Source: *Economic Report of the President, 2010*: www.gpoaccess.gov/eop/2010/B103.xls.

The United States Capitol is where the Senate and House of Representatives meet. The Capitol represents the public sector—government. Thomas Jefferson insisted the legislative building be called the "Capitol" rather than "Congress House." He thought "Capitol" represented the shining city on a hill. The word *capitol* comes from Latin, meaning city on a hill.

3. The Public Sector

 5 What is the public sector? What is public sector spending?

When we refer to the public sector, it is government that we are talking about, either federal, state, or local government. In the United States, government's influence is extensive. From conception to death, individuals are affected by the activities of the government. Many mothers receive prenatal care through government programs. We are born in hospitals that are subsidized or run by the government. We are delivered by doctors who received training in subsidized colleges. Our births are recorded on certificates filed with the government. Ninety percent of students attend public schools as opposed to private schools. Many people live in housing that is directly subsidized by the government or have mortgages that are insured by the government. Most people, at one time or another, put savings into accounts that are insured by the government. Virtually all of us, at some time in our lives, receive money from the government—from student loan programs, unemployment compensation, disability insurance, social security, or Medicare. We drive on government roads, recreate on government lands, and fish in government waters.

3.a. Growth of Government

Government in the United States exists at the federal, state, and local levels. The nation was founded as a "republic," meaning that government is divided between the federal level and state and local levels. Local government includes county, regional, and municipal units. Economic discussions tend to focus on the federal government because national economic policy is set at that level. Nevertheless, each level affects us through its taxing and spending decisions and its laws regulating behavior. In the beginning of the United States, the federal government was a small player. States had the power—called states' rights—because the country's founders believed that government closest to

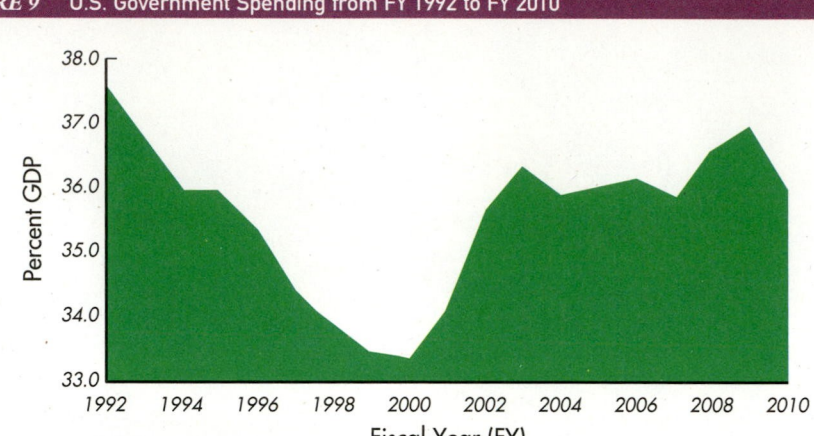

FIGURE 9   U.S. Government Spending from FY 1992 to FY 2010

Total government spending—federal, state, and local divided by gross domestic product (GDP)—the total spending of all sectors in the economy.

Source: www.usgovernmentspending.com.

the people could be constrained better than a federal government. But virtually upon founding, people began to demand more federal government and less states' rights.

According to virtually any measure, total government in the United States has been a growth industry since 1930. The number of people employed by the local, state, and federal governments combined grew from 3 million in 1930 to more than 18 million today; there are now more people employed in government than in manufacturing. Annual expenditures by the federal government rose from $3 billion in 1930 to nearly $4 trillion today. In 1929, government spending constituted less than 2.5 percent of total spending in the economy. Today it is around 30 percent, as shown in Figure 9. The number of rules and regulations created by the government is so large that it is measured by the number of telephone book-sized pages needed just to list them, and that number is more than 70,000.

6   How do the private and public sectors interact?

transfer payments
Income transferred by the government from a citizen who is earning income to another citizen.

3.b. Government Spending

Federal, state, and local government spending for goods and services is shown in Figure 10. Spending on goods and services by all levels of government combined is larger than investment spending but much smaller than consumption.

In addition to purchasing goods and services, government also takes money from some taxpayers and transfers it to others. Such **transfer payments** are a part of total government expenditures, so the total government budget is much larger than just the expenditures for goods and services. In 2011, total expenditures of federal, state, and local government for goods and services were about $5.5 trillion. In this same year, transfer payments made by all levels of government were about $2 trillion.

The magnitude of federal government spending relative to federal government revenue from taxes has become an important issue in recent years. Figure 11 shows that the federal budget was roughly balanced until the early 1970s. The budget is a measure of spending and revenue. A balanced budget occurs when federal spending is approximately equal to federal revenue. This was the case through the 1950s and 1960s.

FIGURE 10 Federal, State, and Local Government Expenditures for Goods and Services

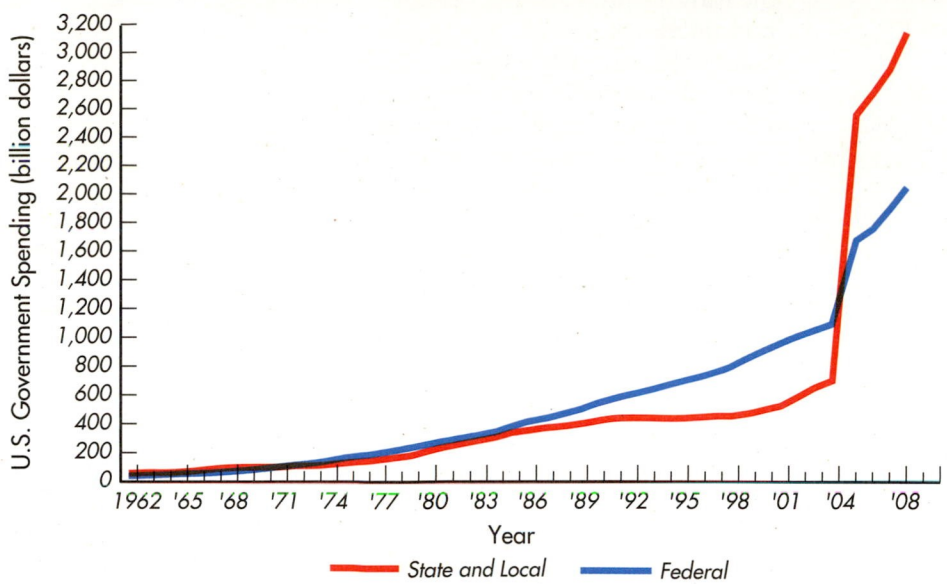

Government spending at federal and at state and local levels rose steadily from the 1960s until about 1980. Then state and local spending rose more quickly than federal spending until 2003. Since then, federal spending has increased at a very rapid pace.

Source: Data are from the *Economic Report of the President, 2010.*

FIGURE 11 U.S. Federal Budget Deficits

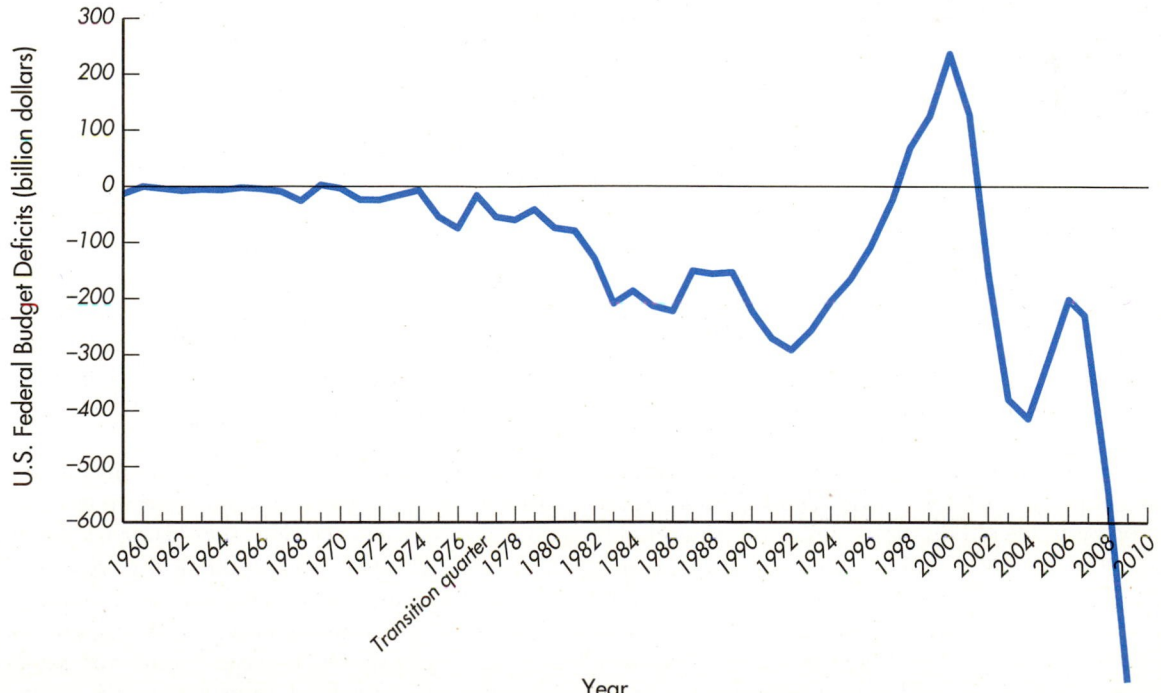

The budget deficit is equal to the excess of government spending over tax revenue. If taxes are greater than government spending, a budget surplus (shown as a positive number) exists.

Source: Data are from the *Economic Report of the President, 2010.*

budget surplus
The excess that results when government spending is less than tax revenue.

budget deficit
The shortage that results when government spending is greater than tax revenue.

If federal government spending is less than tax revenue, a **budget surplus** exists. By the early 1980s, federal government spending was much larger than revenue, so a large **budget deficit** existed. The federal budget deficit grew very rapidly to about $290 billion by the early 1990s before beginning to drop and turning to surplus by 1998. After four years of surpluses, a deficit was again realized in 2002, and the deficit has grown since then. It exploded in 2008–2011, leading to record levels of debt. Debt is the accumulation of deficits; each deficit adds to the debt. The total debt of the U.S. federal government exceeds $14 trillion.

RECAP

1. The public sector refers to government.

2. Government spending is larger than investment spending but much smaller than consumption spending.

3. When government spending exceeds tax revenue, a budget deficit exists. When government spending is less than tax revenue, a budget surplus exists.

4. Linking the Sectors

Now that we have an idea of the size and structure of each of the private sectors—households, businesses, international—and the public sector—government—let's see how the sectors are connected.

4.a. Households and the Rest of the Economy

Households own all the basic resources, or factors of production, in the economy. Household members own land and provide labor, and they are the stockholders, proprietors, and partners who own business firms. Businesses, governments, and foreign businesses employ the services of resources in order to produce goods and services. Households receive wages and benefits for their services.

What do households do with the income they receive? They spend most of it, they pay taxes, and they save some. When households save, they do so in different ways. The most common way is to deposit their savings in **financial intermediaries** such as banks and credit unions. They may also put money into pension funds, through what are called 401k funds or IRAs. These funds may be stocks and bonds, as well as cash. Financial intermediaries (banks, credit unions, etc.) use the deposits from savers to make loans to borrowers. Households borrow money to purchase homes, cars, and other items. Businesses borrow money to purchase machines, equipment, and buildings, and to hire labor. The money that is saved by households thus reenters the economy in the form of business spending.

financial intermediaries
Institutions that accept deposits from savers and make loans to borrowers.

circular flow diagram
A model showing the flow of output and income from one sector of the economy to another.

Some economists like to illustrate how the sectors of the economy are connected by what is called "the circular flow diagram." The **circular flow diagram** pictured in Figure 12 shows the household and business sectors only. Households provide resources and services to firms for wages and benefits. This is shown by the flow of resource services, a blue arrow running from households to firms and government, and payments for these services, a yellow arrow from firms to households. Households may spend part of their income and save part of it. The spending is shown as the payments for goods and services, a yellow arrow from the household sector to the business sector, and the flow of those goods and services from the business sector to the household sector is shown by the blue arrow. Household savings is shown as the orange arrow running from the

FIGURE 12   The Circular Flow: Households, Firms, Government, and Foreign Countries

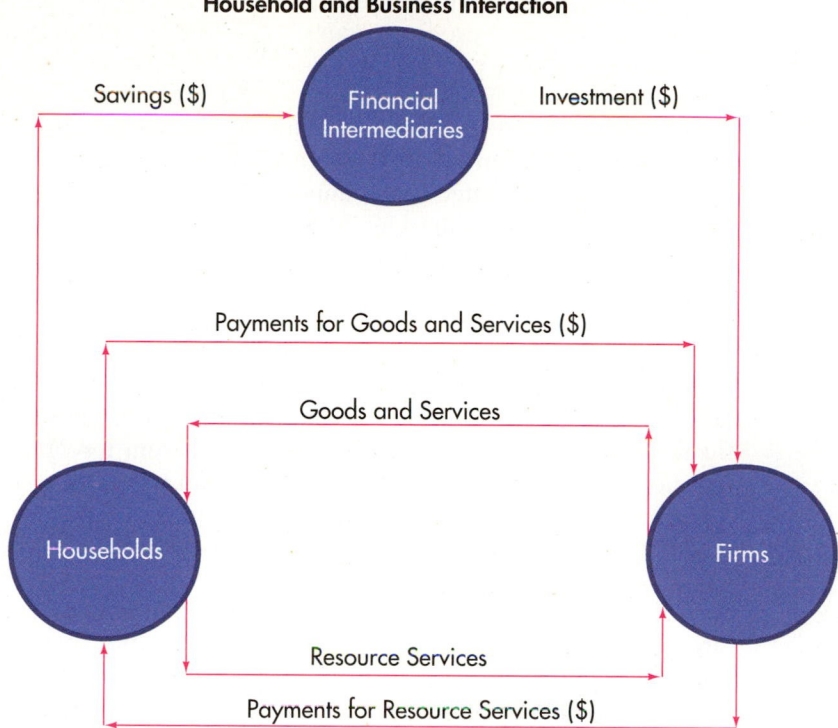

Firms and governments hire resources from households. The payments for these resources represent household income. Households spend their income for goods and services produced by the firms. Household spending represents revenue for firms. Households save some of their income and pay taxes to the government. The amounts saved reenters the circular flow as investment spending. Financial intermediaries like banks take in the savings of households and then lend this money to business firms for investment spending. The diagram assumes that households and government are not directly engaged in international trade.

© 2013 Cengage Learning

household sector to financial intermediaries. These intermediaries provide loans to households and businesses. The borrowing by businesses is shown by the orange arrow running from the financial intermediaries to firms (for simplification we don't draw the arrow running from intermediaries to households). Firms use the loans to invest—purchase equipment, buildings, and resources.

4.b. Government

The government sector buys goods and services from businesses and hires labor from households. The government uses the resource services and goods and services to carry out its many activities. The government's revenues are primarily the taxes that households and firms pay, and expenditures by government include defense and nondefense items and activities.

4.c. The International Sector

Foreign countries also affect and are affected by the household, business, and government sectors of the home country. We typically buy a foreign-made product from a local business firm rather than directly from the foreign producer. For instance, glancing at products in retail stores, we can see "Made in China" or "Made in Mexico" on many of the products. Yet you purchase these from U.S. firms using dollars. The business firm purchases the items from the foreign countries. Even in some "Made in America" products you are purchasing foreign products and services. For instance, when you purchase an iPod, you are purchasing a product that has parts from Japan, the Philippines, Taiwan, and China, as well as the United States. This makes it difficult to accurately measure the relative values of goods and services purchased and sold from one country to another. About 30 to 40 percent of the iPod's price is actually counted as an import (purchase of a Chinese good by the United States) from China to the United States. Nevertheless, we attempt to provide some measures of the extent of trade among nations with exports (sales) and imports (purchases).

As mentioned previously, net exports is the difference between exports of goods from one country and imports of goods by that country. Net exports of the home country may be either positive (a trade surplus) or negative (a trade deficit). When net exports are positive, there is a net flow of goods from the firms of the home country to foreign countries and a net flow of money from foreign countries to the firms of the home country. When net exports are negative, the opposite occurs. A trade deficit involves net flows of goods from foreign countries to the firms of the home country and net money flows from the domestic firms to the foreign countries. As an example, the United States has been a negative net exporter with China so that Chinese goods flowed to the United States while U.S. dollars flowed to China. If exports and imports are equal, net exports are zero because the value of exports is offset by the value of imports.

Adding the foreign sector to the circular flow diagram would produce a very complicated diagram with arrows running to and from each of the sectors, often through financial intermediaries. The point of the circular flow diagram is to illustrate that the various sectors of the economy are interconnected. What goes on in one sector affects what occurs in other sectors. For instance, when the government increases taxes on the business sector, the business sector might reduce employment and purchases of resources from the private sector. When the government increases its deficit (increases spending more than revenue), it might have to finance that debt by selling bonds to the financial intermediaries. This could reduce the amount of money the intermediaries have to lend to households and businesses. If households suddenly start saving more, then the funds available for firm investment are increased and, at the same time, household spending is reduced so that business sales of goods and services decline. Should the home country place a tax on foreign goods and services, households and businesses would reduce spending on foreign goods and increase spending on domestic goods, or those not subject to the higher tax. This could lead to retaliation by other countries, thereby reducing the home country's sales to foreign businesses and households, or it could lead to higher prices domestically. As we will learn throughout our study of the economy, the sectors are interrelated and economies throughout the world are interconnected.

RECAP

1. The private sector refers to the household, business, and nongovernmental international sectors.

2. The public sector refers to government.

SUMMARY

1. **In a market system, who decides what goods and services are produced and how they are produced, and who obtains the goods and services that are produced?**

   - In a market system, consumers are sovereign and decide by means of their purchases what goods and services will be produced. *§1.a*

   - In a market system, firms decide how to produce the goods and services that consumers want. In order to earn maximum profits, firms use the least-cost combinations of resources. *§1.c*

   - Income and prices determine who gets what in a market system. Income is determined by the ownership of resources. *§1.d*

2. **What is a household, and what is household income and spending?**

   - A household consists of one or more persons who occupy a unit of housing. *§2.a*

   - Household spending is called consumption and is the largest component of spending in the economy. *§2.a*

3. **What is a business firm, and what is business spending?**

   - A business firm is a business organization controlled by a single management. *§2.b*

   - Businesses may be organized as sole proprietorships, partnerships, or corporations. *§2.b*

   - Business investment spending—the expenditure by business firms for capital goods—fluctuates a great deal over time. *§2.b*

4. **How does the international sector affect the economy?**

   - The international trade of the United States occurs predominantly with the other industrial economies. *§2.c*

   - Exports are products sold to the rest of the world. Imports are products bought from the rest of the world. *§2.c*

   - Exports minus imports equal net exports. Positive net exports mean that exports are greater than imports and a trade surplus exists. Negative net exports mean that imports exceed exports and a trade deficit exists. *§2.c*

5. **What is the public sector? What is public sector spending?**

   - The public sector refers to government, all levels of government–federal, state, and local. *§3*

   - When a government spends more than it receives in taxes, the government runs a deficit; when it receives more than it spends, it runs a surplus. *§3.b*

6. **How do the private and public sectors interact?**

   - Government interacts with both households and firms. Households get government services and pay taxes; they provide resource services and receive income. Firms sell goods and services to government and receive income. *§4.b*

KEY TERMS

budget deficit, 86	exports, 79	partnership, 76
budget surplus, 86	financial intermediaries, 86	private sector, 75
business firm, 76	household, 75	public sector, 75
circular flow diagram, 86	imports, 79	sole proprietorship, 76
consumer sovereignty, 71	investment, 77	trade deficit, 80
consumption, 75	multinational business, 77	trade surplus, 80
corporation, 76	net exports, 80	transfer payments, 84

EXERCISES

1. What is consumer sovereignty? What does it have to do with determining what goods and services are produced? Who determines how goods and services are produced? Who receives the goods and services in a market system?

2. Is a family a household? Is a household a family?

3. Which sector (households, business, or international) spends the most? Which sector spends the least? Which sector has the most volatility of spending?

4. What does it mean if net exports are negative?

5. Total spending in the economy is equal to consumption plus investment plus government spending plus net exports. If households want to save and thus do not use all of their income for consumption, what will happen to total spending? Because total spending in the economy is equal to total income and output, what will happen to the output of goods and services if households want to save more?

6. People sometimes argue that imports should be limited by government policy. Suppose a government quota on the quantity of imports causes net exports to rise. Explain why total expenditures and national output may rise after the quota is imposed. Who is likely to benefit from the quota? Who will be hurt?

7. Explain the effects of a decision by the household sector to increase saving.

8. Suppose there are three countries in the world. Country A exports $11 million worth of goods to country B and $5 million worth of goods to country C; country B exports $3 million worth of goods to country A and $6 million worth of goods to country C; and country C exports $4 million worth of goods to country A and $1 million worth of goods to country B.
   a. What are the net exports of countries A, B, and C?
   b. Which country is running a trade deficit? A trade surplus?

9. List the four sectors of the economy along with the type of spending associated with each sector. Order the types of spending in terms of magnitude, and give an example of each kind of spending.

10. Using the interconnection between sectors of the economy, illustrate the effects of imposing an increase in taxes on the household sector.

11. Explain how the government can run budget deficits—that is, spend more than it receives in tax revenue.

12. What is the ratio of government spending to GDP? What is the ratio of payments on the debt (interest payments) to GDP? (You may find this at http://www.gpoaccess.gov/eop/tables11.html.)

13. See if you can find the ratio of debt to GDP for several developed nations. Who has the highest ratio?

You can find further practice tests in the Online Quiz at **www.cengage.com/economics/boyes**.

IMPACT OF BAILOUTS

The Globe and Mail (Canada), January 28, 2009

Geneva

Government bailouts of banks and the auto sector could trigger trade disputes over their impact on competition, the head of the World Trade Organization said yesterday. In a report to the WTO's 153 member states, director-general Pascal Lamy said state aid packages meant to stave off financial crises need to be implemented so they do not violate global trade rules or discriminate against foreign companies.

"Nothing can be said, for the time being, about the likely trade impact of these measures, many of which are still lacking publicly announced details," Mr. Lamy said, suggesting the market effects of cash infusions, guarantees and other bailout steps will become clearer with time.

"It must be recognized that some of the measures at least, which, in most cases, constitute some form of state aid or subsidy, may eventually have negative spillover effects on other markets or introduce distortions to competition between financial institutions," he said.

The WTO's dispute settlement body arbitrates disagreements between governments about tariffs, subsidies and other barriers that are seen to create an uneven playing field.

Some of the biggest WTO disputes to date have centered on the European Union's rules on banana imports, state aid for aircraft makers, and European bans on genetically modified foods. And auto industry aid packages in Canada, Germany, France, Australia, Argentina, South Korea, China and elsewhere all could lead to WTO complaints.

Efforts to infuse liquidity and remove toxic assets from big banks in the United States and Europe also could lead to WTO litigation if they disrupt the availability of funds or give domestic banks an unfair advantage, Mr. Lamy's report said.

Several countries have imposed trade-restricting policies since the onset of the financial crisis in September, 2008, the report said.

Laura MacInnis

A government bailout is the government's transfer of money to a particular company or industry. The bailouts of auto manufacturing companies and banks means that the government is using tax revenues or running a deficit to provide the money to auto companies and banks either as a loan or a subsidy. Why would the director-general of the World Trade Organization (WTO), Pascal Lamy, state that "the aid packages meant to stave off financial crises need to be implemented so they do not violate global trade rules or discriminate against foreign companies"?

How could bailouts lead to trade restrictions? If an aid package from the U.S. government to the U.S. auto manufacturers—Ford, GM, and Chrysler—did not also provide aid to other auto manufacturers who produce in the United States, such as Toyota, BMW, and Honda, then it would provide an advantage to the U.S. auto makers compared to the foreign auto makers. Since the cost of manufacturing a car by Ford, GM, and Chrysler in the United States is about 25% more than the cost of manufacturing a car by the foreign auto companies due to pay and benefits provided workers, the foreign auto producers have an advantage. They can offer the same quality car at a lower price than the U.S. companies can. Now, what occurs if the U.S. government offers billions of dollars in aid to the U.S. auto companies? The aid enables the U.S. companies to offer their products for lower prices than the foreign auto companies. Now the foreign auto companies are at a disadvantage. How can they offset the disadvantage? Their government could provide aid to them or, conversely, could penalize the U.S. government by imposing barriers on the sale of U.S. goods into their country.

The WTO is the World Trade Organization and is the body that deals with trade disputes among countries. The article notes how the WTO has been attempting to ensure that the bailouts and aid packages governments are providing industries do not serve to affect trade. But, as the WTO report notes, several trade restrictions have come about due to the bailouts.

CHAPTER 5

National Income Accounting

© MACIEJ FROLOW/GETTY IMAGES, INC

The Korean economy grew at an average rate of 4.9 percent per year from 2000 to 2007. This compares with an average rate of 1.9 percent per year for the United States over the same period. Still, the U.S. economy is much larger than the Korean economy—in fact, it is larger than the economies of the 50 largest developing countries combined. The size of an economy cannot be compared across countries without common standards of measurement. National income accounting provides these standards. Economists use this system to evaluate the economic condition of a country and to compare conditions across time and across countries.

A national economy is a complex arrangement of many different buyers and sellers—households, businesses, and government units—and of their interactions with the rest of the world. To assess the economic health of a country or to

FUNDAMENTAL QUESTIONS

1 How is the total output of an economy measured?

2 Who produces the nation's goods and services?

3 Who purchases the goods and services produced?

4 Who receives the income from the production of goods and services?

5 What is the difference between nominal and real GDP?

6 What is a price index?

compare the performance of an economy from year to year, economists must be able to measure national output and real GDP. Without these data, policymakers cannot evaluate their economic policies. For instance, in the United States, real GDP fell in 1980, 1981, and 1982, and again in 1990–1991, 2001, and 2008–2009. This drop in real GDP was accompanied by widespread job losses and a general decline in the economic health of the country. As this information became known, political and economic debate centered on economic policies, on what should be done to stimulate the economy. Without real GDP statistics, policymakers would not have known that there were problems, let alone how to go about fixing them.

1. Measures of Output and Income

1 How is the total output of an economy measured?

national income accounting
The framework that summarizes and categorizes productive activity in an economy over a specific period of time, typically a year.

In this chapter, we discuss gross domestic product (GDP), real GDP, and other measures of national productive activity by making use of the **national income accounting** system used by all countries. National income accounting provides a framework for discussing macroeconomics. Figure 1 reproduces the circular flow diagram you saw in Chapter 4. The lines connecting the various sectors of the economy represent flows of goods and services and of money expenditures (income). National income accounting is the process of counting the value of the flows between sectors and then summing them to find the total value of the economic activity in an economy. National income accounting fills in the dollar values in the circular flow.

National income accounting measures the output of an entire economy as well as the flows between sectors. It summarizes the level of production in an economy over a specific period of time, typically a year. In practice, the process *estimates* the amount of activity that occurs. It is beyond the capability of government officials to count every transaction that takes place in a modern economy. Still, national income accounting generates useful and fairly accurate measures of economic activity in most countries, especially wealthy industrial countries that have comprehensive accounting systems.

1.a. Gross Domestic Product

The most common measure of a nation's output is GDP.

Modern economies produce an amazing variety of goods and services. To measure an economy's total production, economists combine the quantities of oranges, golf balls, automobiles, and all the other goods and services produced into a single measure of output. Of course, simply adding up the number of things produced—the number of oranges, golf balls, and automobiles—does not reveal the *value* of what is being produced. If a nation produces 1 million more oranges and 1 million fewer automobiles this year than it did last year, the total number of things produced remains the same. But because automobiles are much more valuable than oranges, the value of the nation's output has dropped substantially. Prices reflect the value of goods and services in the market, so economists use the money value of things to create a measure of total output, a measure that is more meaningful than the sum of the units produced.

gross domestic product (GDP)
The market value of all final goods and services produced in a year within a country.

The most common measure of a nation's output is gross domestic product. **Gross domestic product (GDP)** is the market value of all final goods and services produced in a year within a country's borders. A closer look at three parts of this definition—*market value*, *final goods and services*, and *produced in a year*—will make clear what the GDP does and does not include.

FIGURE 1 The Circular Flow: Households, Firms, Government, and Foreign Countries

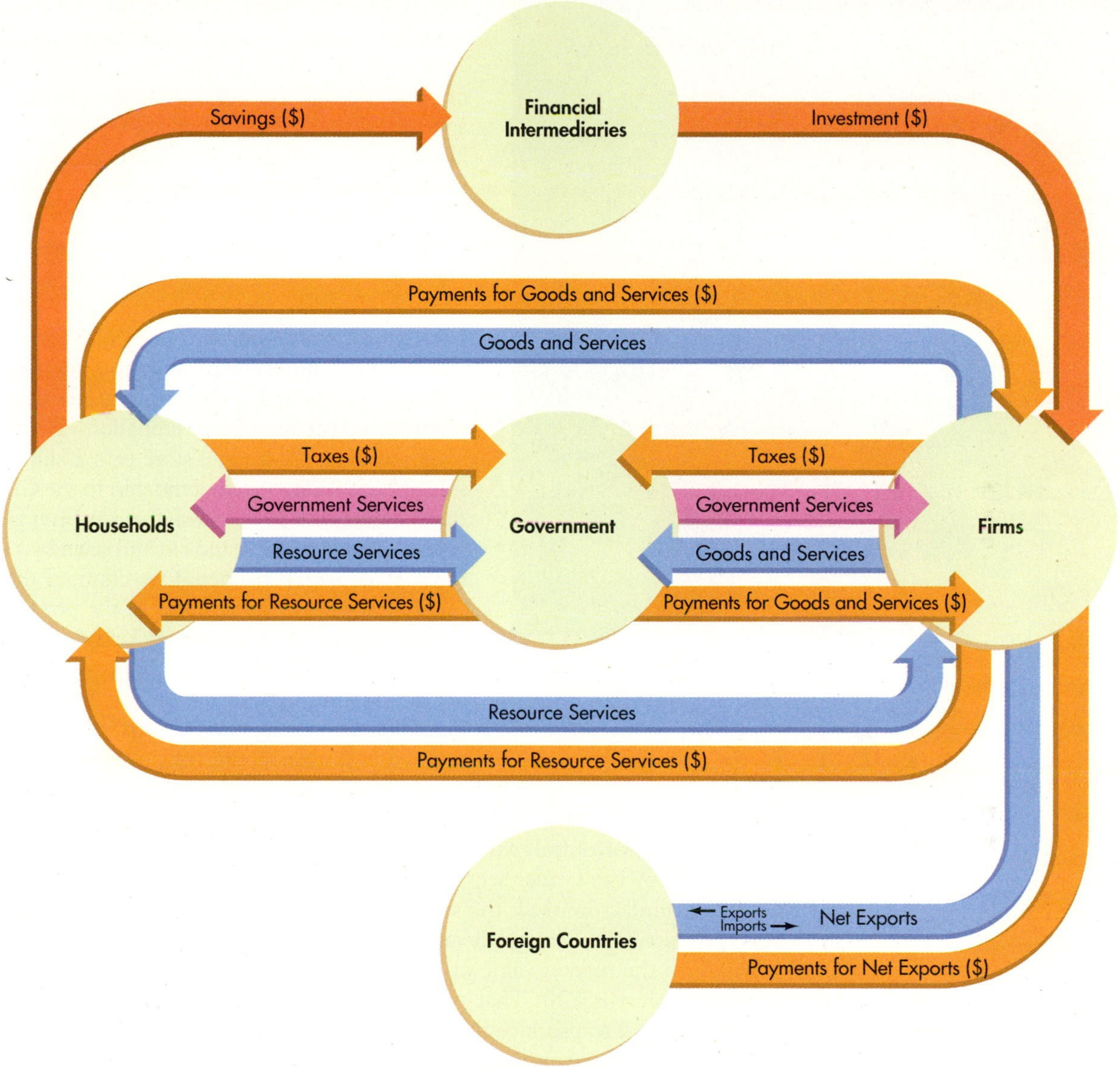

The value of national output equals expenditures plus income. If the domestic economy has positive net exports (a trade surplus), goods and services flow out of the domestic firms toward the foreign countries and money payments flow from the foreign countries to the domestic firms. If the domestic economy has negative net exports (a trade deficit), just the reverse is true.

Market Value The *market value* of final goods and services is their value at market price. The process of determining market value is straightforward when prices are known and transactions are observable. However, there are cases in which prices are not known and transactions are not observable. For instance, illegal drug transactions are not reported to the government, which means that they are not included in GDP statistics. In fact, almost any activity that is not traded in a market is not included. For example, production that takes place in households, such as home-makers' services, is not counted, nor are unreported barter and cash transactions. For instance, if a lawyer has a sick dog and a

All final goods and services produced in a year are counted in the GDP. For instance, the value of a horseback excursion through the Grand Canyon is part of the national output of the United States. The value of the trip would be equal to the amount that travelers would have to pay the guide company in order to take the trip. This price would reflect the value of the personnel, equipment, and food provided by the guide company.

© Tony Gervis/Getty Images

intermediate good
A good that is used as an input in the production of final goods and services.

value added
The difference between the value of output and the value of the intermediate goods used in the production of that output.

veterinarian needs some legal advice, by trading services and not reporting the activity to the tax authorities, each can avoid taxation on the income that would have been reported had they sold their services to each other. If the value of a transaction is not recorded as taxable income, it generally does not appear in the GDP. There are some exceptions, however. Contributions to GDP are estimated for *in-kind wages*, such as nonmonetary compensation like room and board. GDP values also are assigned to the output consumed by a producer—for example, the home consumption of crops by a farmer.

Final Goods and Services   The second part of the definition of GDP limits the measure to *final goods and services*, the goods and services that are available to the ultimate consumer. This limitation avoids double counting. Suppose a retail store sells a shirt to a consumer for $20. The value of the shirt in the GDP is $20. But the shirt is made of cotton that has been grown by a farmer, woven at a mill, and cut and sewn by a manufacturer. What would happen if we counted the value of the shirt at each of these stages of the production process? We would overstate the market value of the shirt.

Intermediate goods are goods that are used in the production of a final product. For instance, the ingredients for a meal are intermediate goods to a restaurant. Similarly, the cotton and the cloth are intermediate goods in the production of the shirt. The stages of production of the $20 shirt are shown in Figure 2. The value-of-output axis measures the value of the product at each stage. The cotton produced by the farmer sells for $1. The cloth woven by the textile mill sells for $5. The shirt manufacturer sells the shirt wholesale to the retail store for $12. The retail store sells the shirt—the final good—to the ultimate consumer for $20. Remember that GDP is based on the market value of final goods and services. In our example, the market value of the shirt is $20. That price already includes the value of the intermediate goods that were used to produce the shirt. If we added to it the value of output at every stage of production, we would be counting the value of the intermediate goods twice, and we would be overstating the GDP.

It is possible to compute GDP by computing the **value added** at each stage of production. Value added is the difference between the value of output and the value of the intermediate goods used in the production of that output. In Figure 2, the value added by each stage of production is listed at the right. The farmer adds $1 to the value of the shirt. The mill takes the cotton worth $1 and produces cloth worth $5, adding $4 to the value of the shirt. The manufacturer uses $5 worth of cloth to produce a shirt that it sells for $12, so the manufacturer adds $7 to the shirt's value. Finally, the retail store adds $8 to the value of the shirt: It pays the manufacturer $12 for the shirt and sells it to the consumer for $20. The sum of the value added at each stage of production is $20. The total value added, then, is equal to the market value of the final product.

Economists can thus compute GDP using two methods. The final goods and services method uses the market value of the final good or service; the value-added method uses the value added at each stage of production. Both methods count the value of

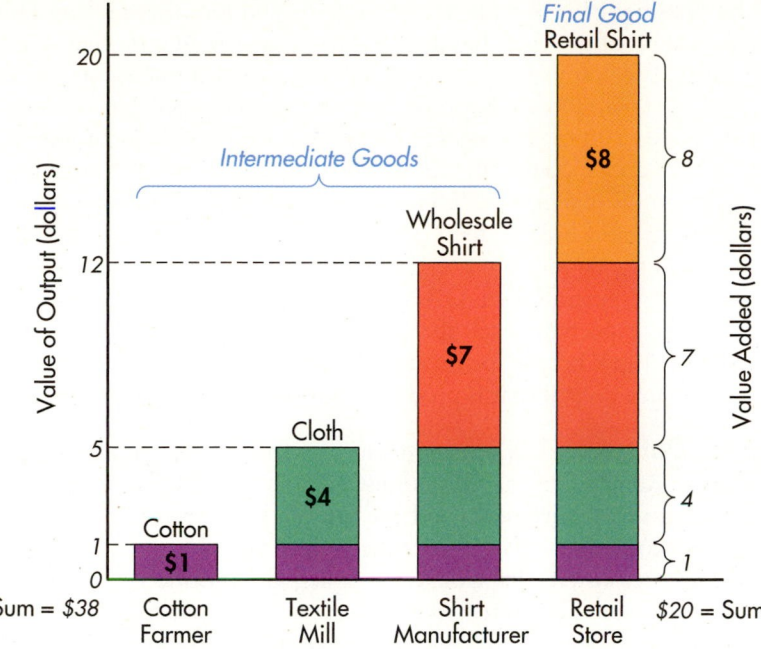

FIGURE 2   Stages of Production and Value Added in Shirt Manufacturing

A cotton farmer sells cotton to a textile mill for $1, adding $1 to the value of the final shirt. The textile mill sells cloth to a shirt manufacturer for $5, adding $4 to the value of the final shirt. The manufacturer sells the shirt wholesale to the retail store for $12, adding $7 to the value of the final shirt. The retail store sells the final shirt to a consumer for $20, adding $8 to the value of the final shirt. The sum of the prices received at each stage of production equals $38, which is greater than the price of the final shirt. The sum of the value added at each stage of production equals $20, which equals the market value of the shirt.

© 2013 Cengage Learning

intermediate goods only once. This is an important distinction: GDP is not based on the market value of *all* goods and services, but on the market value of all *final* goods and services.

Produced in a Year GDP measures the value of the output *produced in a year*. The value of goods produced last year is counted in last year's GDP; the value of goods produced this year is counted in this year's GDP. The year of production, not the year of sale, determines the allocation to GDP. Although the value of last year's goods is not counted in this year's GDP, the value of services involved in the sale is. This year's GDP does not include the value of a house built last year, but it does include the value of the real estate broker's fee; it does not include the value of a used car, but it does include the income earned by the used-car dealer in the sale of that car.

To determine the value of goods produced in a year but not sold in that year, economists calculate changes in inventory. **Inventory** is a firm's stock of unsold goods. If a shirt that is produced this year remains on the retail store's shelf at the end of the year, it increases the value of the store's inventory. A $20 shirt increases that value by $20. Changes in inventory allow economists to count goods in the year in which they are produced, whether or not they are sold.

Changes in inventory can be planned or unplanned. A store may want a cushion above expected sales (*planned inventory changes*), or it may not be able to sell all the goods that it expected to sell when it placed the order (*unplanned inventory changes*).

inventory
The stock of unsold goods held by a firm.

For instance, suppose Jeremy owns a surfboard shop, and he always wants to keep 10 more surfboards than he expects to sell. He does this so that in case business is surprisingly good, he does not have to turn away customers and lose those sales to his competitors. At the beginning of the year, Jeremy has 10 surfboards, and he then builds as many new boards during the year as he expects to sell. He *plans* on having an inventory at the end of the year of 10 surfboards. Suppose Jeremy expects to sell 100 surfboards during the year, so he builds 100 new boards. If business is surprisingly poor and he sells only 80 surfboards, how do we count the 20 new boards that he made but did not sell? We count the change in his inventory. He started the year with 10 surfboards and ends the year with 20 more unsold boards, for a year-end inventory of 30. The change in inventory of 20 (equal to the ending inventory of 30 minus the starting inventory of 10) represents output that is counted in GDP. In Jeremy's case, the inventory change is unplanned, since he expected to sell the 20 extra surfboards that he has in his shop at the end of the year. But whether the inventory change is planned or unplanned, changes in inventory will count output that is produced but not sold in a given year.

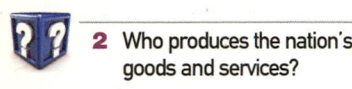

2 Who produces the nation's goods and services?

1.a.1. GDP as Output The GDP is a measure of the market value of a nation's total output in a year. Remember that economists divide the economy into four sectors: households, businesses, government, and the international sector. Figure 1 shows how the total value of economic activity equals the sum of the output produced in each sector. Figure 3 indicates where the U.S. GDP is actually produced.[1] Since GDP counts the output produced in the United States, U.S. GDP is produced in business firms, households, and government located within the boundaries of the United States.

Not unexpectedly in a capitalist country, privately owned businesses account for the largest percentage of output: In the United States, 75 percent of the GDP is produced by private firms. Government produces 12 percent of the GDP, and households produce 12 percent. Figure 3 defines GDP in terms of output: GDP is the value of final goods and services produced in a year by domestic households, businesses, and government units. Even if some of the firms producing in the United States are foreign owned, the output that they produce in the United State is counted in the U.S. GDP.

> GDP is the value of final goods and services produced by domestic households, businesses, and government.

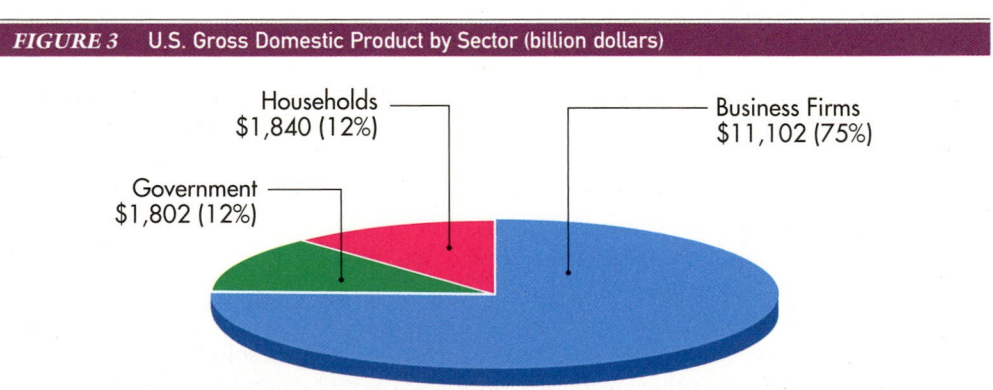

FIGURE 3   U.S. Gross Domestic Product by Sector (billion dollars)

Households
$1,840 (12%)

Business Firms
$11,102 (75%)

Government
$1,802 (12%)

Business firms produce 75 percent of the U.S. GDP. Government produces 12 percent; households, 12 percent.

Source: *Bureau of Economic Analysis; www.bea.gov.*

---

[1] Due to rounding, percentages and dollar amounts in Figures 3 to 5 will not add exactly to the totals given.

1.a.2. GDP as Expenditures

The circular flow diagram in Figure 1 shows not only the output of goods and services from each sector but also the payments for goods and services. Here we look at GDP in terms of what each sector pays for the goods and services that it purchases.

The dollar value of total expenditures—the sum of the amount that each sector spends on final goods and services—equals the dollar value of output. In Chapter 4, you learned that household spending is called *consumption*. Households spend their income on goods and services to be consumed. Business spending is called *investment*. Investment is spending on capital goods that will be used to produce other goods and services. The other two components of total spending are *government spending* and *net exports*. Net exports are the value of *exports* (goods and services sold to the rest of the world) minus the value of *imports* (goods and services bought from the rest of the world).

$$GDP = consumption + investment + government\ spending + net\ exports$$

Or, in the shorter form commonly used by economists,

$$GDP = C + I + G + X$$

where X is net exports.

Figure 4 shows the U.S. GDP in terms of total expenditures. Consumption, or household spending, accounts for 70 percent of national expenditures. Government spending represents 21 percent of expenditures, and business investment represents 13 percent. Net exports are negative (−4 percent), which means that imports exceeded exports. To determine total national expenditures on domestic output, the value of imports, or spending on foreign output, is subtracted from total expenditures.

1.a.3. GDP as Income

The total value of output can be calculated by adding up the expenditures of each sector. And because one sector's expenditures are another's income, the total value of output can also be computed by adding up the income of all sectors.

Business firms use factors of production to produce goods and services. Remember that the income earned by factors of production is classified as wages, interest, rent, and profits. *Wages* are payments to labor, including fringe benefits, social security contributions, and retirement payments. *Interest* is the net interest paid by businesses to households plus the net interest received from foreigners (the interest that they pay us minus

3 Who purchases the goods and services produced?

$GDP = C + I + G + X$

4 Who receives the income from the production of goods and services?

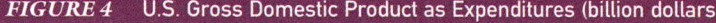

FIGURE 4 U.S. Gross Domestic Product as Expenditures (billion dollars)

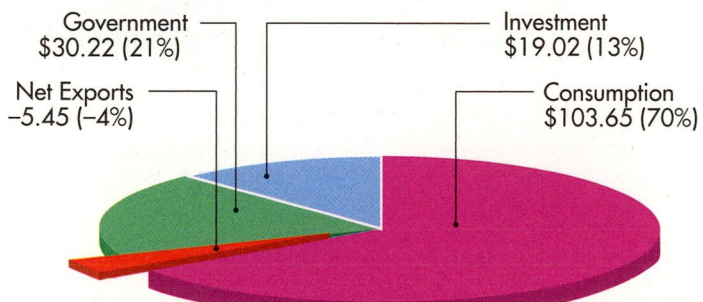

Government
$30.22 (21%)

Investment
$19.02 (13%)

Net Exports
−5.45 (−4%)

Consumption
$103.65 (70%)

Consumption by households accounts for 70 percent of the GDP, followed by government spending at 21 percent, investment by business firms at 13 percent, and net exports at −4 percent.

Source: Bureau of Economic Analysis, third quarter 2010, www.bea.gov.

the interest that we pay them). *Rent* is income earned from selling the use of real property (houses, shops, and farms). Finally, *profits* are the sum of corporate profits plus proprietors' income (income from sole proprietorships and partnerships).

Figure 5 shows the U.S. GDP in terms of income. Notice that wages account for 55 percent of the GDP. Interest and profits account for 6 and 9 percent of the GDP, respectively. Proprietors' income accounts for 7 percent. Rent (2 percent) is very small in comparison. *Net factor income from abroad* is income received from U.S.-owned resources located in other countries minus income paid to foreign-owned resources located in the United States. Since U.S. GDP refers only to income earned within U.S. borders, we must add income payments from the rest of the world and subtract income payments to the rest of the world to arrive at GDP (1 percent).

Figure 5 also includes two income categories that we have not discussed: capital consumption allowance and indirect business taxes. **Capital consumption allowance** is not a money payment to a factor of production; it is the estimated value of capital goods used up or worn out in production plus the value of accidental damage to capital goods. The value of accidental damage is relatively small, so it is common to hear economists refer to capital consumption allowance as **depreciation**. Machines and other capital goods wear out over time. The reduction in the value of the capital stock as a result of its being used up or worn out over time is called depreciation. A depreciating capital good loses value each year of its useful life until its value is zero.

Even though capital consumption allowance does not represent income received by a factor of production, it must be accounted for in GDP as income. If it were not, the value of GDP measured as output would be higher than the value of GDP measured as income. Depreciation is a kind of resource payment, part of the total payment to the owners of capital. All of the income categories—wages, interest, rent, profits, and capital consumption allowance—are expenses incurred in the production of output.

capital consumption allowance
The estimated value of depreciation plus the value of accidental damage to capital stock.

depreciation
A reduction in the value of capital goods over time as a result of their use in production.

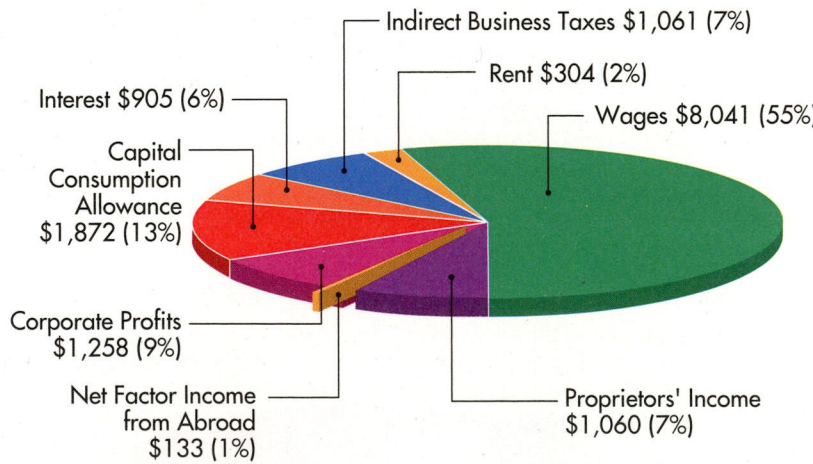

FIGURE 5   U.S. Gross Domestic Product as Income Received (billion dollars)

Indirect Business Taxes $1,061 (7%)
Rent $304 (2%)
Interest $905 (6%)
Wages $8,041 (55%)
Capital Consumption Allowance $1,872 (13%)
Corporate Profits $1,258 (9%)
Net Factor Income from Abroad $133 (1%)
Proprietors' Income $1,060 (7%)

The largest component of income is wages, at 55 percent of the GDP. Profits represent 9 percent; interest, 6 percent; proprietors' income, 7 percent; and rent, 2 percent. Capital consumption allowance (13 percent) and indirect business taxes (7 percent) are not income received but still must be added; net factor income from abroad must be added (1 percent). (Note: Percentages do not always equal 100 percent.)

Source: *Bureau of Economic Analysis, third quarter 2010,* www.bea.gov.

The last item in Figure 5 is indirect business taxes. **Indirect business taxes**, like capital consumption allowance, are not payments to a factor of production. They are taxes collected by businesses that then are turned over to the government. Both excise taxes and sales taxes are forms of indirect business taxes.

For example, suppose a motel room in Florida costs $80 a night, but a consumer would be charged $90. The motel receives $80 of that $90 as the value of the service sold; the other $10 is an excise tax. The motel cannot keep the $10; it must turn it over to the state government. (In effect, the motel is acting as the government's tax collector.) The consumer spends $90; the motel earns $80. To balance expenditures and income, we have to allocate the $10 difference to indirect business taxes.

To summarize, GDP measured as income includes the four payments to the factors of production: wages, interest, rent, and profits. These income items represent expenses incurred in the production of GDP. From these we must subtract net factor income from abroad and then add two nonincome items—capital consumption allowance and indirect business taxes—to find real GDP.

GDP = wages + interest + rent + profits − net factor income from abroad + capital consumption allowance + indirect business taxes

The GDP is the total value of output produced in a year, the total value of expenditures made to purchase that output, and the total value of income received by the factors of production. Because all three are measures of the same thing—GDP—all must be equal.

1.b. Other Measures of Output and Income

GDP is the most commonly used measure of a nation's output, but it is not the only measure. Economists rely on a number of other measures as well in analyzing the performance of components of an economy.

1.b.1. Gross National Product Gross national product (GNP) equals GDP plus receipts of factor income from the rest of the world minus payments of factor income to the rest of the world. If we add to GDP the value of income earned by U.S. residents from factors of production located outside the United States and subtract the value of income earned by foreign residents from factors of production located inside the United States, we have a measure of the value of output produced by U.S.-owned resources—GNP.

Figure 6 shows the national income accounts in the United States. The figure begins with the GDP and then shows the calculations necessary to obtain the GNP and other measures of national output. In 2010, the U.S. GNP was $14,933.6 billion.

1.b.2. Net National Product Net national product (NNP) equals GNP minus capital consumption allowance. The NNP measures the value of goods and services produced in a year less the value of capital goods that became obsolete or were used up during the year. Because NNP includes only net additions to a nation's capital, it is a better measure of the expansion or contraction of current output than is GNP. Remember how we defined GDP in terms of expenditures in section 1.a.2:

GDP = consumption + investment + government spending + net exports

The investment measure in GDP (and GNP) is called **gross investment**. Gross investment is total investment, which includes investment expenditures required to replace capital goods consumed in current production. The NNP does not include investment expenditures required to replace worn-out capital goods; it includes only net investment. **Net investment** is equal to gross investment minus capital consumption allowance. Net investment measures business spending over and above that required to replace worn-out capital goods.

---

indirect business tax
A tax that is collected by businesses for a government agency.

> The GDP as income is equal to the sum of wages, interest, rent, and profits, less net factor income from abroad, plus capital consumption allowance and indirect business taxes.

gross national product (GNP)
Gross domestic product plus receipts of factor income from the rest of the world minus payments of factor income to the rest of the world.

net national product (NNP)
Gross national product minus capital consumption allowance.

gross investment
Total investment, including investment expenditures required to replace capital goods consumed in current production.

net investment
Gross investment minus capital consumption allowance.

FIGURE 6   U.S. National Income Accounts, 2010 (billion dollars)

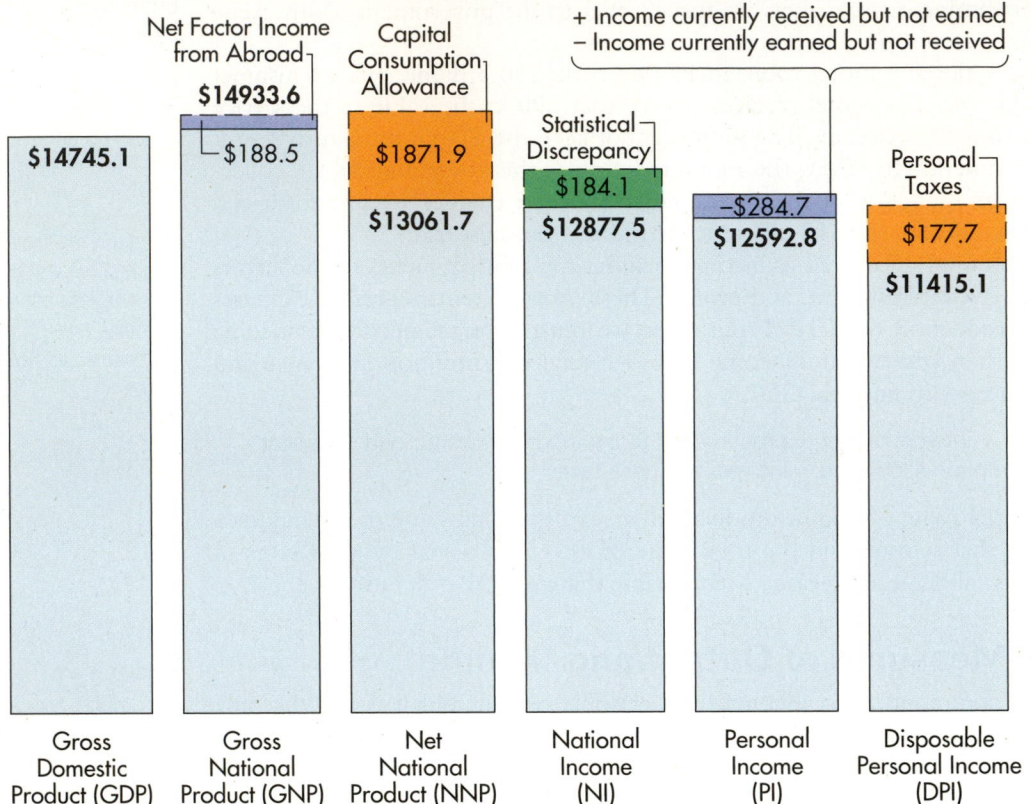

Gross domestic product plus receipts of factor income from the rest of the world minus payments of factor income to the rest of the world equals gross national product. Gross national product minus capital consumption allowance equals net national product. Net national product minus statistical discrepancy equals national income. National income plus income currently received but not earned (transfer payments, personal interest, dividend income) minus income currently earned but not received (retained corporate profits, net interest, social security taxes) equals personal income. Personal income minus personal taxes equals disposable personal income.

Source: Data from *U.S. Bureau of Economic Analysis.*

Figure 6 shows that in 2010 the U.S. NNP was $13,061.7 billion. This means that the U.S. economy produced over $13 trillion worth of goods and services above those required to replace capital stock that had depreciated. Over $1 trillion in capital was "worn out" in 2010.

national income (NI)
Net national product plus or minus statistical discrepancy.

1.b.3. National Income National income (NI) equals the NNP plus or minus a small adjustment called "statistical discrepancy." The NI captures the costs of the factors of production used in producing output. Remember that GDP includes a nonincome expense item: capital consumption allowance (section 1.a.3). Subtracting this plus the statistical discrepancy from the GDP leaves the income payments that actually go to resources.

Because the NNP equals the GNP minus capital consumption allowance, we can subtract the statistical discrepancy from the NNP to find NI, as shown in Figure 6. This measure helps economists analyze how the costs of (or payments received by) resources change.

personal income (PI)
National income plus income currently received but not earned, minus income currently earned but not received.

1.b.4. Personal Income Personal income (PI) is national income adjusted for income that is received but not earned in the current year and income that is earned but not received in the current year. Social security and welfare benefits are examples of income that is received but not earned in the current year. As you learned in Chapter 4, these are called **transfer payments**. Transfer payments represent income transferred from one citizen who is earning income to another citizen, who may not be. The government transfers income by taxing one group of citizens and using the tax payments to fund the income for another group. An example of income that is currently earned but not received is profits that are retained by a corporation to finance current needs rather than paid out to stockholders. Another is social security (FICA) taxes, which are deducted from workers' paychecks.

transfer payment
Income transferred by the government from a citizen who is earning income to another citizen.

1.b.5. Disposable Personal Income
Disposable personal income (DPI) equals personal income minus personal taxes—income taxes, excise and real estate taxes on personal property, and other personal taxes. DPI is the income that individuals have at their disposal for spending or saving. The sum of consumption spending plus saving must equal disposable personal income.

disposable personal income (DPI)
Personal income minus personal taxes.

RECAP

1. Gross domestic product (GDP) is the market value of all final goods and services produced in an economy in a year.

2. The GDP can be calculated by summing the market value of all final goods and services produced in a year, by summing the value added at each stage of production, by adding total expenditures on goods and services (GDP = consumption + investment + government spending + net exports), and by using the total income earned in the production of goods and services (GDP = wages + interest + rent + profits), subtracting net factor income from abroad, and adding depreciation and indirect business taxes.

3. Other measures of output and income include gross national product (GNP), net national product (NNP), national income (NI), personal income (PI), and disposable personal income (DPI).

National Income Accounts

GDP = consumption + investment + government spending + net exports

GNP = GDP + receipts of factor income from the rest of the world − payments of factor income to the rest of the world

NNP = GNP − capital consumption allowance

NI = NNP − statistical discrepancy

PI = NI − income earned but not received + income received but not earned

DPI = PI − personal taxes

---

2. Nominal and Real Measures

The GDP is the market value of all final goods and services produced within a country in a year. Value is measured in money terms, so the U.S. GDP is reported in dollars, the German GDP in euro, the Mexican GDP in pesos, and so on. Market value is the product of two elements: the money price and the quantity produced.

 5 What is the difference between nominal and real GDP?

2.a. Nominal and Real GDP

Nominal GDP measures output in terms of its current dollar value. **Real GDP** is adjusted for changing price levels. In 1980, the U.S. GDP was $2,790 billion; in 2010, it was $14,745 billion—an increase of 428 percent. Does this mean that the United States produced 428 percent more goods and services in 2010 than it did in 1980? If the numbers reported are for nominal GDP, we cannot be sure. Nominal GDP cannot tell us whether the economy produced more goods and services, because nominal GDP changes both when prices change *and* when quantity changes.

nominal GDP
A measure of national output based on the current prices of goods and services.

real GDP
A measure of the quantity of final goods and services produced, obtained by eliminating the influence of price changes from the nominal GDP statistics.

Real GDP measures output in constant prices. This allows economists to identify the changes in the actual production of final goods and services: Real GDP measures the quantity of goods and services produced after eliminating the influence of price changes contained in nominal GDP. In 1980, real GDP in the United States was $5,161.7 billion; in 2010, it was $11,696 billion, an increase of just 127 percent. A large part of the 428 percent increase in nominal GDP reflects increased prices, not increased output.

Because we prefer more goods and services to higher prices, it is better to have nominal GDP rise because of higher output than because of higher prices. We want nominal GDP to increase as a result of an increase in real GDP.

Consider a simple example that illustrates the difference between nominal GDP and real GDP. Suppose a hypothetical economy produces just three goods: oranges, coconuts, and pizzas. The dollar value of output in three different years is listed in Figure 7.

As shown in Figure 7, in year 1, 100 oranges were produced at $.50 per orange, 300 coconuts at $1 per coconut, and 2,000 pizzas at $8 per pizza. The total dollar value of output in year 1 is $16,350. In year 2, prices remain constant at the year 1 values, but the quantity of each good has increased by 10 percent. The dollar value of output in year 2 is $17,985, 10 percent higher than the value of output in year 1. In year 3, the quantity of each good is back at the year 1 level, but prices have increased by 10 percent. Oranges now cost $.55, coconuts $1.10, and pizzas $8.80. The dollar value of output in year 3 is $17,985.

Notice that the dollar value of output ($17,985) in years 2 and 3 is 10 percent higher than the dollar value in year 1. But there is a difference here. In year 2, the increase in output is due entirely to an increase in the production of the three goods. In year 3, the increase is due entirely to an increase in the prices of the goods.

Because prices did not change between years 1 and 2, the increase in nominal GDP is entirely accounted for by an increase in real output, or real GDP. In years 1 and 3, the actual quantities produced did not change, which means that real GDP was constant; only nominal GDP was higher, a product only of higher prices.

Figure 8 plots the growth rate of real GDP for several of the industrial countries. One can see in the figure that the countries show somewhat different patterns of real GDP growth over time. For instance, over the period beginning in the mid-1990s, real GDP grew at a slower pace in Japan than in the other countries. Most of the countries had fairly fast rates of GDP growth in the late 1990s, only to experience a falling growth rate in the early 2000s followed by a pickup in growth, and then the most recent downturn associated with the global recession.

2.b. Price Indexes

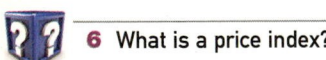 **6** What is a price index?

The total dollar value of output or income is equal to price multiplied by the quantity of goods and services produced:

$$\text{Dollar value of output} = \text{price} \times \text{quantity}$$

By dividing the dollar value of output by price, you can determine the quantity of goods and services produced:

$$\text{Quantity} = \frac{\text{dollar value of output}}{\text{price}}$$

price index
A measure of the average price level in an economy.

In macroeconomics, a **price index** is a measure of the average level of prices in an economy; it shows how prices, on average, have changed. Prices of individual goods can rise and fall relative to one another, but a price index shows the general trend in prices across the economy.

FIGURE 7   Prices and Quantities in a Hypothetical Economy

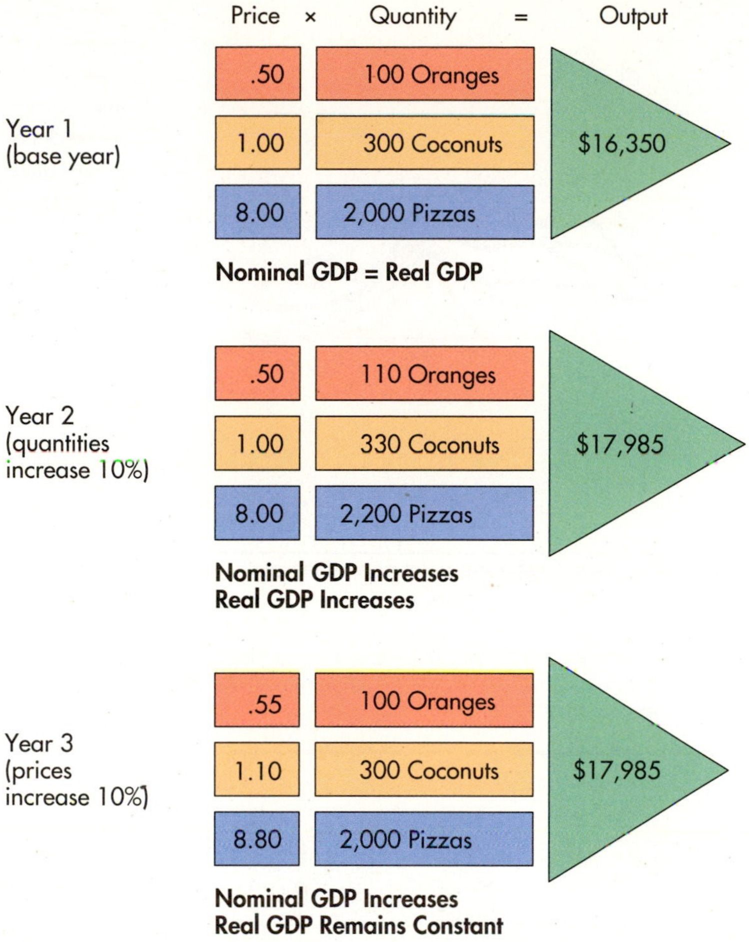

In year 1, total output was $16,350. In year 2, prices remained constant but quantities produced increased by 10 percent, resulting in a higher output of $17,985. With prices constant, we can say that both nominal GDP and real GDP increased from year 1 to year 2. In year 3, quantities produced returned to the year 1 level but prices increased by 10 percent, resulting in the same increased output as in year 2, $17,985. Production has not changed from year 1 to year 3, however, so although nominal GDP has increased, real GDP has remained constant.

© 2013 Cengage Learning

2.b.1. Base Year The example in Figure 7 provides a simple introduction to price indexes. The first step is to pick a **base year**, the year against which other years are measured. Any year can serve as the base year. Suppose we pick year 1 in Figure 7. The value of the price index in year 1, the base year, is defined to be 100. This simply means that prices in year 1 are 100 percent of prices in year 1 (100 percent of 1 is 1). In the example, year 2 prices are equal to year 1 prices, so the price index is equal to 100 in year 2 as well. In year 3, every price has risen 10 percent relative to the base-year (year 1) prices, so the price index is 10 percent higher in year 3, or 110. The value of the price index in any particular year indicates how prices have changed relative to the base year. A value of 110 indicates that prices are 110 percent of base-year prices, or that the average price level has increased 10 percent.

base year
The year against which other years are measured.

The value of the price index in any particular year indicates how prices have changed relative to the base year.

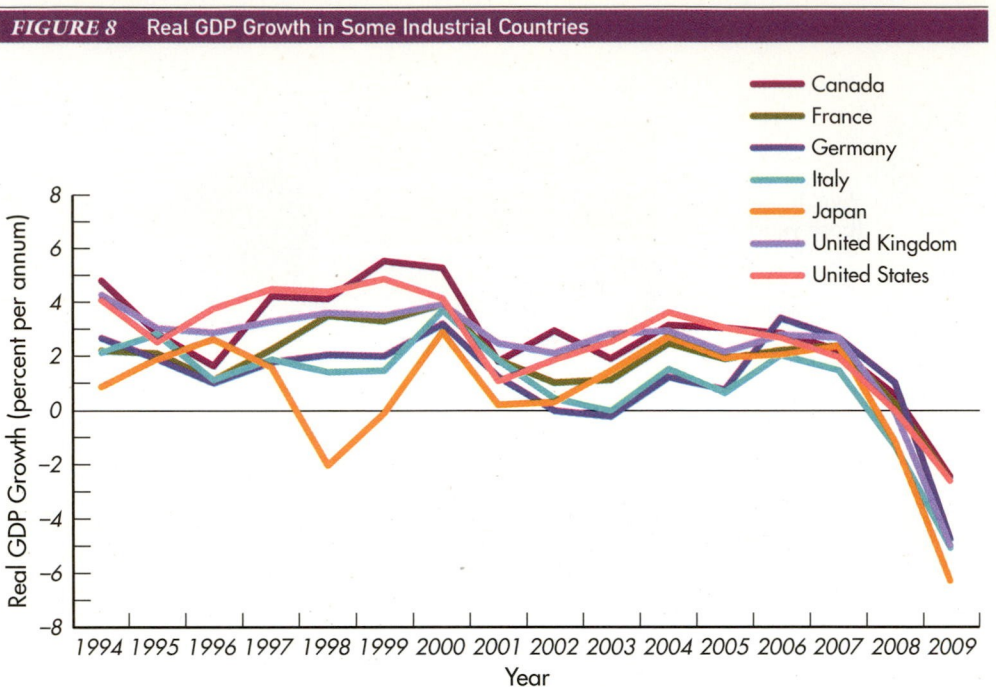

FIGURE 8   Real GDP Growth in Some Industrial Countries

Real GDP grew at a fast pace in the late 1990s in most countries depicted in the figure, only to fall dramatically in 2001 and 2002. Japan has experienced slower growth of real GDP over this period than the other countries.

© 2013 Cengage Learning

Price index in any year = 100 ± percentage change in prices from the base year

2.b.2. Types of Price Indexes

The price of a single good is easy to determine. But how do economists determine a single measure of the prices of the millions of goods and services produced in an economy? They have constructed price indexes to measure the price level; there are several different price indexes used to measure the price level in any economy. Not all prices rise or fall at the same time or by the same amount. This is why there are several measures of the price level in an economy.

The price index that is used to estimate constant-dollar real GDP is the **GDP price index (GDPPI)**, a measure of prices across the economy that reflects all of the categories of goods and services included in GDP. The GDP price index is a very broad measure. Economists use other price indexes to analyze how prices in more specific categories of goods and services change.

Probably the best-known price index is the **consumer price index (CPI)**. The CPI measures the average price of consumer goods and services that a typical household purchases. (See Economic Insight "The Consumer Price Index.") The CPI is a narrower measure than the GDPPI because it includes fewer items. However, because of the relevance of consumer prices to the standard of living, news reports on price changes in the economy typically focus on consumer price changes. In addition, labor contracts sometimes include provisions that raise wages as the CPI goes up. Social security payments also are tied to increases in the CPI. These increases are called **cost-of-living adjustments (COLAs)**

GDP price index (GDPPI)
A broad measure of the prices of goods and services included in the gross domestic product.

consumer price index (CPI)
A measure of the average price of goods and services purchased by the typical household.

cost-of-living adjustment (COLA)
An increase in wages that is designed to match increases in the prices of items purchased by the typical household.

ECONOMIC INSIGHT

The Consumer Price Index

The CPI is calculated by the Department of Labor using price surveys taken in 87 U.S. cities. Although the CPI often is called a *cost-of-living index*, it is not. The CPI represents the cost of a fixed market basket of goods purchased by a hypothetical household, not a real one.

In fact, no household consumes the exact market basket used to estimate the CPI. As relative prices change, households alter their spending patterns. But the CPI market basket changes only every two years. This is due in part to the high cost of surveying the public to determine spending patterns. Then, too, individual households have different tastes and spend different portions of their budgets on the various components of household spending (housing,

food, clothing, transportation, medical care, and so on). Only a household that spends exactly the same portion of its income on each item counted in the CPI would find the CPI representative of its cost of living.

The Department of Labor surveys spending in eight major areas. The figure shows these areas and the percentage of the typical household budget devoted to each area. If you kept track of your spending over the course of several months, you probably would find that you spend much more than the typical household on some items and much less on others. In other words, the CPI is not a very good measure of *your* cost of living.

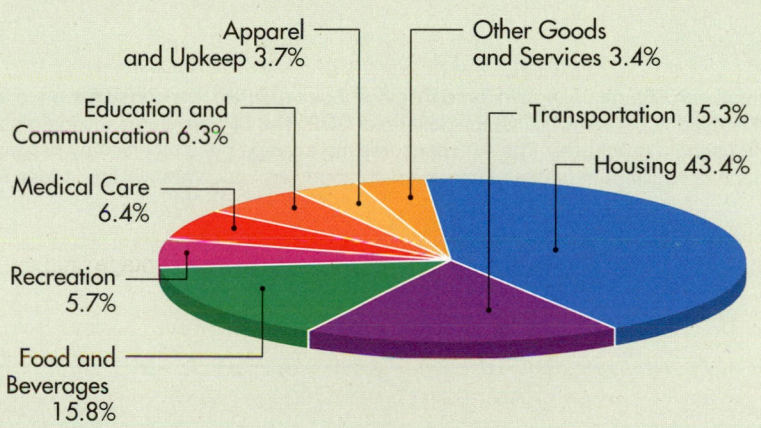

Apparel and Upkeep 3.7%
Education and Communication 6.3%
Medical Care 6.4%
Recreation 5.7%
Food and Beverages 15.8%
Other Goods and Services 3.4%
Transportation 15.3%
Housing 43.4%

Source: Data from *Bureau of Labor Statistics.*

because they are supposed to keep nominal income rising along with the cost of items purchased by the typical household.

The **producer price index (PPI)** measures average prices received by producers. At one time this price index was known as the *wholesale price index (WPI)*. Because the PPI measures price changes at an earlier stage of production than the CPI, it can indicate a coming change in the CPI. If producer input costs are rising, we can expect the price of goods produced to go up as well.

Figure 9 illustrates how the three different measures of prices have changed over time. Notice that the PPI is more volatile than the GDPPI or the CPI. This is because there are smaller fluctuations in the equilibrium prices of final goods than in those of intermediate goods.

producer price index (PPI)
A measure of average prices received by producers.

FIGURE 9   The GDP Price Index, the CPI, and the PPI

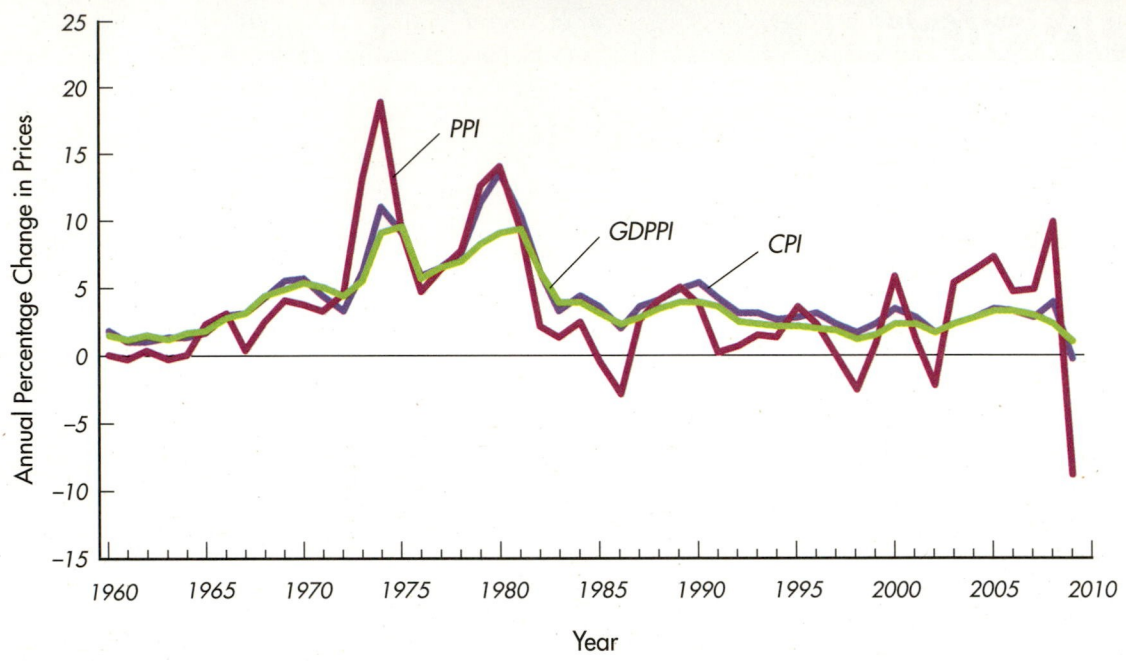

The graph plots the annual percentage change in the GDP price index (GDPPI), the consumer price index (CPI), and the producer price index (PPI). The GDPPI is used to construct constant-dollar real GDP. The CPI measures the average price of consumer goods and services that a typical household purchases. The PPI measures the average price received by producers; it is the most variable of the three because fluctuations in equilibrium prices of intermediate goods are much greater than those for final goods.

Source: www.bls.gov and www.bea.gov.

RECAP

1. Nominal GDP is measured using current dollars.

2. Real GDP measures output with price effects removed.

3. The GDP price index, the consumer price index, and the producer price index are all measures of the level of prices in an economy.

3. Flows of Income and Expenditures

GDP is both a measure of total expenditures on final goods and services and a measure of the total income earned in the production of those goods and services. The idea that total expenditures equal total income is clearly illustrated in Figure 1.

The figure links the four sectors of the economy: households, firms, government, and foreign countries. The arrows between the sectors indicate the direction of the flows. Gold arrows with dollar signs represent money flows; blue green arrows without dollar signs represent flows of real goods and services. The money flows are both income and expenditures. For instance, household expenditures for goods and services from business firms are represented by the gold arrow at the top of the diagram. Household income from firms is represented by the gold arrow flowing from firms to households at the bottom of the diagram. Because one sector's expenditures are another sector's income, the total expenditures on goods and services must be the same as the total income from selling goods and services, and those must both be equal to the total value of the goods and services produced.

RECAP

1. Total spending on final goods and services equals the total income received from producing those goods and services.

2. The circular flow model shows that one sector's expenditures become the income of other sectors.

SUMMARY

1. How is the total output of an economy measured?

- National income accounting is the system that economists use to measure both the output of an economy and the flows between sectors of that economy. *§1*

- Gross domestic product (GDP) is the market value of all final goods and services produced in a year in a country. *§1.a*

- GDP also equals the value added at each stage of production. *§1.a*

2. Who produces the nation's goods and services?

- GDP as output equals the sum of the output of households, business firms, and government within the country. Business firms produce 75 percent of the U.S. GDP. *§1.a.1*

3. Who purchases the goods and services produced?

- The GDP as expenditures equals the sum of consumption plus investment plus government spending plus net exports. In the United States, consumption accounts for roughly two-thirds of total expenditures. *§1.a.2*

4. Who receives the income from the production of goods and services?

- The GDP as income equals the sum of wages, interest, rent, profits, proprietors' income, capital consumption allowance, and indirect business taxes less net factor income from abroad. Wages account for about 60 percent of the total. *§1.a.3*

- Capital consumption allowance is the estimated value of depreciation plus the value of accidental damage to capital stock. *§1.a.3*

- Other measures of national output include gross national product (GNP), net national product (NNP), national income (NI), personal income (PI), and disposable personal income (DPI). *§1.b*

5. What is the difference between nominal and real GDP?

- Nominal GDP measures output in terms of its current dollar value, including the effects of price changes; real GDP measures output after eliminating the effects of price changes. *§2.a*

6. What is a price index?

- A price index is a measure of the average level of prices across an economy. *§2.b*

- The GDP price index is a measure of the prices of all the goods and services included in the GDP. *§2.b.2*

- The consumer price index (CPI) measures the average price of goods and services consumed by the typical household. *§2.b.2*

- The producer price index (PPI) measures average prices received by producers (wholesale prices). *§2.b.2*

- Total expenditures on final goods and services equal total income. *§3*

KEY TERMS

base year, 105

capital consumption
  allowance, 100

consumer price index (CPI), 106

cost-of-living adjustments
  (COLAs), 106

depreciation, 100

disposable personal income
  (DPI), 103

GDP price index (GDPPI), 106

gross domestic product (GDP), 94

gross investment, 101

gross national product (GNP), 101

indirect business taxes, 101

intermediate good, 96

inventory, 97

national income (NI), 102

national income accounting, 94

net investment, 101

net national product (NNP), 101

nominal GDP, 103

personal income (PI), 102

price index, 104

producer price index (PPI), 107

real GDP, 103

transfer payments, 103

value added, 96

EXERCISES

1. The following table lists the stages in the production of a personal computer. What is the value of the computer in GDP?

Stage	Value Added
Components manufacture	$ 100
Assembly	$ 250
Wholesaler	$ 500
Retailer	$2,500

2. What is the difference between GDP and each of the following?
   a. Gross national product
   b. Net national product
   c. National income
   d. Personal income
   e. Disposable personal income

3.

	Year 1		Year 2	
	Quantity	Price	Quantity	Price
Oranges	100	$5	150	$5
Pears	100	$3	75	$4

   a. What is the growth rate of constant-dollar real GDP using year 1 as the base year?
   b. What is the growth rate of constant-dollar real GDP using year 2 as the base year?

4. Why do total expenditures on final goods and services equal total income in the economy?

5. Why don't we measure national output by simply counting the total number of goods and services produced each year?

6. Why isn't the CPI a useful measure of *your* cost of living?

Use the following national income accounting information to answer exercises 7–11:

Consumption	$400
Imports	$ 10
Net investment	$ 20
Government purchases	$100
Exports	$ 20
Capital consumption allowance	$ 20
Statistical discrepancy	$ 5
Receipts of factor income from the rest of the world	$ 12
Payments of factor income to the rest of the world	$ 10

7. What is the GDP for this economy?
8. What is the GNP for this economy?
9. What is the NNP for this economy?
10. What is the national income for this economy?
11. What is the gross investment in this economy?
12. Indirect business taxes and capital consumption allowance are not income, yet they are included in the calculation of GDP as income received. Why do we add these two nonincome components to the other components of income (like wages, rent, interest, profits, and net factor income from abroad) to find GDP?
13. Why has nominal GDP increased faster than real GDP in the United States over time? What would it mean if an economy had real GDP increasing faster than nominal GDP?

14. We usually discuss GDP in terms of what is included in the definition. What is *not* included in GDP? Why are these things excluded?

15. If a surfboard is produced this year but not sold until next year, how is it counted in this year's GDP and not next year's?

You can find further practice tests in the Online Quiz at **www.cengage.com/economics/boyes**.

HIDING IN THE SHADOWS: THE GROWTH OF THE UNDERGROUND ECONOMY

International Monetary Fund, March 2002

A factory worker has a second job driving an unlicensed taxi at night; a plumber fixes a broken water pipe for a client, gets paid in cash, but doesn't declare his earnings to the tax collector; a drug dealer brokers a sale with a prospective customer on a street corner. These are all examples of the underground or shadow economy—activities, both legal and illegal, that add up to trillions of dollars a year that take place "off the books," out of the gaze of taxmen and government statisticians.

Although crime and shadow economic activities have long been a fact of life—and are now increasing around the world—almost all societies try to control their growth, because a prospering shadow economy makes official statistics (on unemployment, official labor force, income, consumption) unreliable. Policies and programs that are framed on the basis of unreliable statistics may be inappropriate and self-defeating....

Also called the underground, informal, or parallel economy, the shadow economy includes not only illegal activities but also unreported income from the production of legal goods and services, either from monetary or barter transactions. Hence, the shadow economy comprises all economic activities that would generally be taxable were they reported to the tax authorities.

TABLE 1 Shadow Economy as Percent of Official GDP, 1988–2000

Country Group	Percent of GDP
Developing	35–44
Transition	21–30
OECD	14–16

The ranges reflect the different estimation methods used by different sources.

Estimating the size of the shadow economy is difficult. After all, people engaged in underground activities do their best to avoid detection. But policymakers and government administrators need information about how many people are active in the shadow economy, how often underground activities occur, and the size of these activities so that they can make appropriate decisions on resource allocation.

Table 1 shows average estimates for the three main country groups—developing countries, transition economies, and 21 advanced economies, the last all members of the Organization for Economic Cooperation and Development (OECD). The comparisons among countries remain somewhat crude because they are based on different estimation methods.

Countries with relatively low tax rates, fewer laws and regulations, and a well-established rule of law tend to have smaller shadow economies.

Macroeconomic and microeconomic modeling studies based on data for several countries suggest that the major driving forces behind the size and growth of the shadow economy are an increasing burden of tax and social security payments, combined with rising restrictions in the official labor market. Wage rates in the official economy also play a role....

Shadow economies tend to be smaller in countries where government institutions are strong and efficient. Indeed, some studies have found that it is not higher taxes per se that increase the size of the shadow economy, but ineffectual and discretionary application of the tax system and regulations by governments.

Source: Friedrich Schneider with Dominik Enste, *Hiding in the Shadows: The Growth of the Underground Economy, Economic Issues,* No. 30, International Monetary Fund, March 2002.

In this chapter, we learned about different measures of macroeconomic performance. It is important to have accurate measures in order to formulate appropriate policy. Bad data on economic performance could result in policymakers attempting to fix problems that don't really exist or failing to address problems that have not been identified. However, it is not easy to measure the performance of an economy. This article indicates a particular type of problem that exists in every economy: the underground economy.

The presence of a large and active underground economy means that the official GDP figure is missing much of the economic activity that occurs. As indicated in the article, this is more than just illegal activity, like dealing in illicit drugs. Perfectly legal activities that are conducted "off the books" are also missed in the official GDP accounting. So if a carpenter performs work for someone, is paid in cash, and never reports the transaction as income to be taxed, this activity is part of the underground economy. Although the carpenter was engaged in productive activity, it will not be counted, and so the official GDP measure will underestimate the true amount of production undertaken in a year.

This article serves as a reminder that, although government officials may do the best job they can of counting economic activity, they will never be able to count everything. As shown in Table 1 of the article, the problems are worse for developing countries and those countries that are in transition from socialism than for the industrial countries (referred to as OECD countries in the table). Yet even in the industrial countries, it is estimated that between 14 and 16 percent of GDP takes place in the underground economy.

CHAPTER 6

An Introduction to the Foreign Exchange Market and the Balance of Payments

FUNDAMENTAL QUESTIONS

1 How do individuals of one nation trade money with individuals of another nation?

2 How do changes in exchange rates affect international trade?

3 How do nations record their transactions with the rest of the world?

n Chapter 5, you learned that gross domestic product equals the sum of consumption, investment, government spending, and net exports (GDP = C + I + G + X). Net exports (X) are one key measure of a nation's transactions with other countries, a principal link between a nation's GDP and developments in the rest of the world. In this chapter, we extend the macroeconomic accounting framework to include more detail on a nation's international transactions. This extension is known as balance of payments accounting.

International transactions have grown rapidly in recent years as the economies of the world have become increasingly interrelated. Improvements in transportation and communication, and global markets for goods and services, have created a community of world economies. Products made in one country are sold in the world market, where they compete against products from other nations. Europeans purchase stocks listed on the New York Stock Exchange; Americans purchase bonds issued in Japan.

Different countries use different monies. When goods and services are exchanged across international borders, national monies also are traded. To make buying and selling decisions in the global marketplace, people must be able to compare prices across countries, to compare prices quoted in Japanese yen with those quoted in Mexican pesos. This chapter begins with a look at how national monies are priced and traded in the foreign exchange market.

1. The Foreign Exchange Market

Foreign exchange is foreign money, including paper money and bank deposits like checking accounts, that is denominated in foreign currency. When someone with U.S. dollars wants to trade those dollars for Japanese yen, the trade takes place in the **foreign exchange market**, a global market in which people trade one currency for another. Many financial markets are located in a specific geographic location. For instance, the New York Stock Exchange is a specific location in New York City where stocks are bought and sold. The Commodity Exchange is a specific location in New York City where contracts to deliver agricultural and metal commodities are bought and sold. The foreign exchange market is not in a single geographic location, however. Trading occurs all over the world, electronically and by telephone. Most of the activity involves large banks in New York, London, and other financial centers. A foreign exchange trader at Citigroup in New York can buy or sell currencies with a trader at Barclays Bank in London by calling the other trader on the telephone or exchanging computer messages.

Only tourism and a few other transactions in the foreign exchange market involve an actual movement of currency. The great majority of transactions involve the buying and selling of bank deposits denominated in foreign currency. A bank deposit can be a checking account that a firm or individual writes checks against to make payments to others, or it can be an interest-earning savings account with no check-writing privileges. Currency notes, like dollar bills, are used in a relatively small fraction of transactions. When a large corporation or a government buys foreign currency, it buys a bank deposit denominated in the foreign currency. Still, all exchanges in the market require that monies have a price.

1.a. Exchange Rates

An **exchange rate** is the price of one country's money in terms of another country's money. Exchange rates are needed to compare prices quoted in two different currencies. Suppose a shirt that has been manufactured in Canada sells for 20 U.S. dollars in Seattle, Washington, and for 25 Canadian dollars in Vancouver, British Columbia. Where would you get the better buy? Unless you know the exchange rate between U.S. and Canadian dollars, you can't tell. The exchange rate allows you to convert the foreign currency price into its domestic currency equivalent, which then can be compared to the domestic price.

Table 1 lists exchange rates for December 21, 2010. The rates are quoted in U.S. dollars per unit of foreign currency in the second column, and in units of foreign currency per U.S. dollar in the last column. For instance, the Canadian dollar was selling for $.9416,

1 How do individuals of one nation trade money with individuals of another nation?

foreign exchange
Currency and bank deposits that are denominated in foreign money.

foreign exchange market
A global market in which people trade one currency for another.

exchange rate
The price of one country's money in terms of another country's money.

Because different countries use different currencies, international business requires the exchange of monies in the foreign exchange market.

or about 94 U.S. cents. The same day, the U.S. dollar was selling for 1.062 Canadian dollars (1 U.S. dollar would buy 1.062 Canadian dollars).

If you know the price of a currency in U.S. dollars, you can find the price of the U.S. dollar in that currency by taking the reciprocal. To find the reciprocal of a number, write it as a fraction and then turn the fraction upside down. Let's say that 1 British pound sells for 2 U.S. dollars. In fraction form, 2 is 2/1. The reciprocal of 2/1 is 1/2, or .5. So 1 U.S. dollar sells for .5 British pound. The table shows that the actual dollar price of the pound on December 21, 2010, was 1.5385. The *reciprocal exchange rate*—the number of pounds per dollar—is .650 (1/1.5385), which was the pound price of 1 dollar that day.

Let's go back to comparing the price of the Canadian shirt in Seattle and in Vancouver. The International Standards Organization (ISO) symbol for the U.S. dollar is USD. The symbol for the Canadian dollar is CAD. (Table 2 lists the symbols for a

TABLE 1	Exchange Rates, December 21, 2010	
Country	**U.S.$ per Currency**	**Currency per U.S.$**
Argentina (peso)	0.2537	3.941
Australia (dollar)	0.8873	1.127
Britain (pound)	1.5385	0.650
Canada (dollar)	0.9416	1.062
China (renminbi)	0.1469	6.807
Israel (shekel)	0.2622	3.814
Japan (yen)	0.0118	84.390
Mexico (peso)	0.0757	13.207
New Zealand (dollar)	0.6978	1.433
Russia (ruble)	0.0324	30.842
Singapore (dollar)	0.7375	1.356
Switzerland (franc)	0.9814	1.019
EU (euro)	1.2674	0.789

Note: The second column lists U.S. dollars per unit of foreign currency, or how much one unit of foreign currency is worth in U.S. dollars. On this day, you could get about 94 U.S. cents for 1 Canadian dollar. The third column lists units of foreign currency per U.S. dollar, or how much 1 U.S. dollar is worth in foreign currency. On the same day, you could get about 1.06 Canadian dollars for 1 U.S. dollar.

GLOBAL BUSINESS *INSIGHT*

Active Trading Around the World

It is often said that the foreign exchange market never closes, since trading can take place in different parts of the world as time passes. However, people in each region tend to work certain normal business hours, and so each major foreign exchange trading location has fairly regular hours during which active trading occurs. The figure below shows the normal hours of active trading in each major trading region. The times are in *Greenwich Mean Time*, or *GMT*, which is the time in London. For instance, we see that active trading in London opens at 0800. This is 8 A.M. in London. Active trading stops in London at 1600, which is 4 P.M. in London. (In many parts of the world, a 24-hour clock registers time from 0000 to 1200 in the morning, where 1200 is noon. Then in the afternoon, time starts to count up from 1200. So 1 P.M. is 1300, 2 P.M. is 1400, and so on.)

The figure shows trading in New York as opening at 1200, or noon in London. Eastern time in the United States is 5 hours behind London time (as seen by the −5 for that region of the world at the bottom of the figure), so that when it is noon in London, it is 5 hours earlier, or 7 A.M., in New York. Note that active trading in London closes at 1600 and active trading in New York opens at 1200, so London and New York trading overlap for 4 hours each day. Similarly, the figure shows that trading in New York also overlaps with trading in Frankfurt, Germany. However, there is no overlap of trading in North America with trading in Asia, as Asian trading centers open after trading has ended in North America and close before trading begins in North America. There is a short overlap of Asian trading with European trading. This figure reminds us that the world of foreign exchange trading, and that of business in general, tends to be conducted during regular business hours in each region.

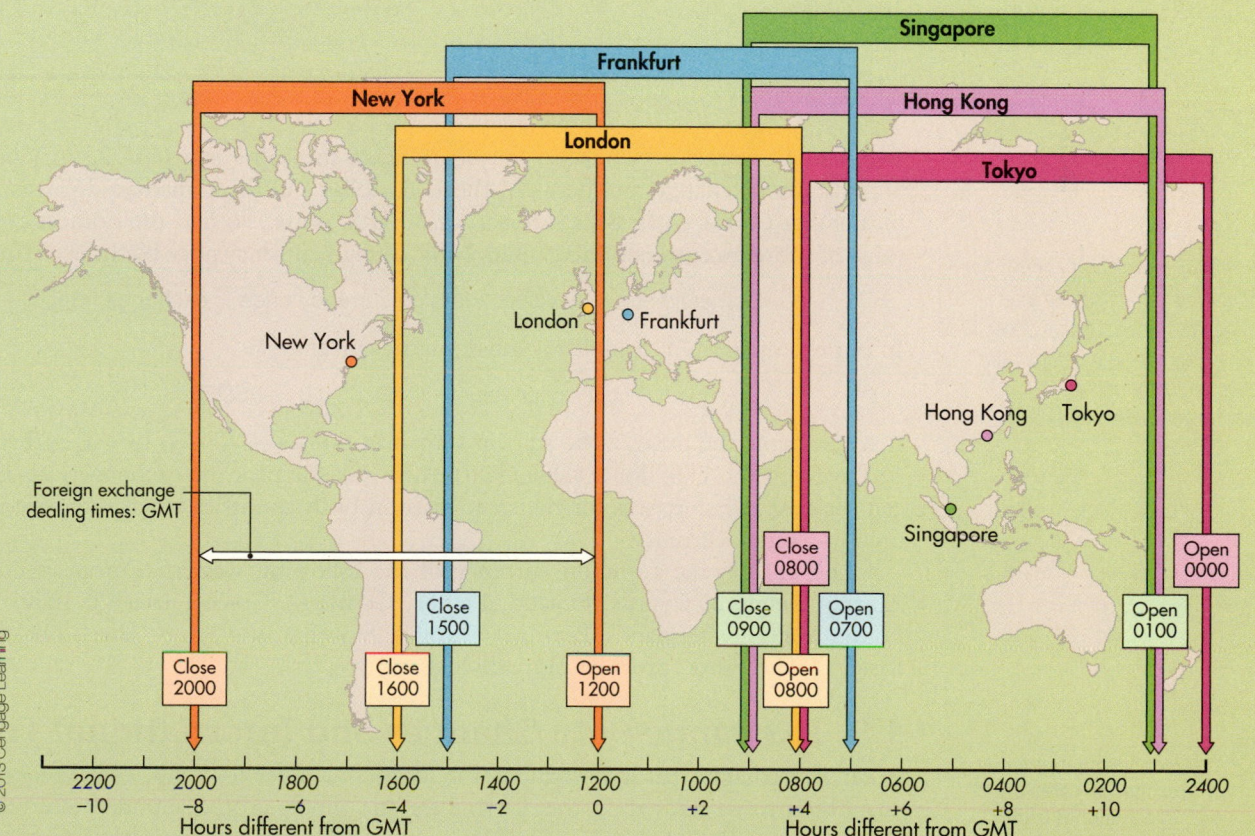

TABLE 2	International Currency Symbols, Selected Countries	
Country	**Currency**	**ISO Symbol**
Australia	Dollar	AUD
Canada	Dollar	CAD
China	Yuan	CNY
Denmark	Krone	DKK
India	Rupee	INR
Iran	Rial	IRR
Japan	Yen	JPY
Kuwait	Dinar	KWD
Mexico	Peso	MXN
Norway	Krone	NOK
Russia	Ruble	RUB
Saudi Arabia	Riyal	SAR
Singapore	Dollar	SGD
South Africa	Rand	ZAR
Sweden	Krona	SEK
Switzerland	Franc	CHF
United Kingdom	Pound	GBP
United States	Dollar	USD
Venezuela	Bolivar	VEB
European Union	Euro	EUR

number of currencies.) The shirt sells for USD20 in Seattle and CAD25 in Vancouver. Suppose the exchange rate between the U.S. dollar and the Canadian dollar is .8. This means that CAD1 costs .8 U.S. dollar, or 80 U.S. cents. To find the domestic currency value of a foreign currency price, multiply the foreign currency price by the exchange rate:

$$\text{Domestic currency value} = \text{foreign currency price} \times \text{exchange rate}$$

In our example, the U.S. dollar is the domestic currency:

$$\text{U.S. dollar value} = \text{CAD25} \times .8 = \text{USD20}$$

> *Find the reciprocal of a number by writing it as a fraction and then turning the fraction upside down. In other words, make the numerator the denominator and the denominator the numerator.*

If we multiply the price of the shirt in Canadian dollars (CAD25) by the exchange rate (.8), we find the U.S. dollar value ($20). After adjusting for the exchange rate, then, we can see that the shirt sells for the same price in both countries when the price is measured in a single currency.

The euro is the common currency of the following western European countries: Austria, Belgium, Cyprus, Finland, France, Germany, Greece, Ireland, Italy, Luxembourg, Malta, Netherlands, Portugal, Slovakia, Slovenia, and Spain. The Global Business Insight "The Euro" provides more discussion.

1.b. Exchange Rate Changes and International Trade

2 How do changes in exchange rates affect international trade?

Because exchange rates determine the domestic currency value of foreign goods, changes in those rates affect the demand for and supply of goods traded internationally. Suppose the price of the shirt in Seattle and in Vancouver remains the same, but the

GLOBAL BUSINESS
INSIGHT

The Euro

The euro began trading in January 1999 and for more than three years circulated jointly with the national currencies of the original 12 countries that adopted the euro. The former currencies of these countries are the Austrian schilling, Belgian franc, Finnish markka, French franc, German mark, Greek drachma, Irish pound, Italian lira, Luxembourg franc, Netherlands guilder, Portuguese escudo, and Spanish peseta. Prior to the beginning of the euro, the value of each of the "legacy currencies" of the euro area was fixed in terms of the euro. For instance, 1 euro was equal to 40.3399 Belgian francs or 1.95583 German marks. In February 2002, the former monies of each of the euroarea countries were withdrawn from circulation, and now only the euro is used in the 12-country area. Since that time, the following countries have joined the euroarea and replaced their domestic currencies with the euro: Estonia, Cyprus, Malta, Slovenia, and Slovakia.

Euro coins are available in the following denominations: 1, 2, 5, 10, 20, and 50 cents and 1 and 2 euro. One side of each coin has an image that is common in all euro-land countries. The other side has a design that is individualized for each country. For instance, a 2-euro coin has a common side with a big number 2 placed over a map of Europe. But the reverse side differs across countries. In Germany, the 2-euro coin has an eagle surrounded by a ring of stars, while in Spain, the 2-euro coin has a portrait of the Spanish king, Carlos I. However, even though each country can issue its own coins, the coins are all usable in any euro-land country. You could receive French coins in Paris and then spend them in Rome. Euro currency or banknotes are available in the following denominations: 5, 10, 20, 50, 100, 200, and 500 euros. The paper money is identical in all countries.

---

exchange rate changes from .8 to .9 U.S. dollar per Canadian dollar. What happens? The U.S. dollar price of the shirt in Vancouver increases. At the new rate, the shirt that sells for CAD25 in Vancouver costs a U.S. buyer USD22.50 (CAD25 × .9).

A rise in the value of a currency is called *appreciation*. In our example, as the exchange rate moves from USD.8 = CAD1 to USD.9 = CAD1, the Canadian dollar appreciates against the U.S. dollar. As a country's currency appreciates, international demand for its products falls, other things equal.

Suppose the exchange rate in our example moves from USD.8 = CAD1 to USD.7 = CAD1. Now the shirt that sells for CAD25 in Vancouver costs a U.S. buyer USD17.50 (CAD25 × .7). In this case, the Canadian dollar has *depreciated* in value relative to the U.S. dollar. As a country's currency depreciates, its goods sell for lower prices in other countries and the demand for its products increases, other things equal.

When the Canadian dollar is appreciating against the U.S. dollar, the U.S. dollar must be depreciating against the Canadian dollar. For instance, when the exchange rate between the U.S. dollar and the Canadian dollar moves from USD.8 = CAD1 to USD.9 = CAD1, the reciprocal exchange rate—the rate between the Canadian dollar and the U.S. dollar—moves from CAD1.25 = USD1 (1/.8 = 1.25) to CAD1.11 = USD1 (1/.9 = 1.11). At the same time that Canadian goods are becoming more expensive to U.S. buyers, U.S. goods are becoming cheaper to Canadian buyers.

In later chapters we look more closely at how changes in exchange rates affect international trade and at how governments use exchange rates to change their net exports.

> A currency appreciates in value when its value rises in relation to another currency.

> A currency depreciates in value when its value falls in relation to another currency.

1. The foreign exchange market is a global market in which foreign money, largely bank deposits, is bought and sold.

2. An exchange rate is the price of one money in terms of another.

3. Foreign demand for domestic goods decreases as the domestic currency appreciates and increases as the domestic currency depreciates.

2. The Balance of Payments

3 How do nations record their transactions with the rest of the world?

balance of payments
A record of a country's trade in goods, services, and financial assets with the rest of the world.

The U.S. economy does not operate in a vacuum. It affects and is affected by the economies of other nations. This point is brought home to Americans when newspaper headlines announce a large trade deficit and politicians denounce foreign countries for running trade surpluses against the United States. In such times, it seems as if everywhere there is talk of the balance of payments.

The **balance of payments** is a record of a country's trade in goods, services, and financial assets with the rest of the world. This record is divided into categories, or accounts, that summarize the nation's international economic transactions. For example, one category measures transactions in merchandise; another measures transactions involving financial assets (bank deposits, bonds, stocks, loans). Balance of payments data are reported quarterly for most developed countries.

Once we understand the various definitions of the balance of payments, there remains the issue of why we should care. One important reason is that balance of payments issues are often hot political topics. One cannot make sense of the political debate without an understanding of balance of payments basics. For instance, the United States is said to have a large deficit in its merchandise trade with the rest of the world. Is this bad? Some politicians will argue that a large trade deficit calls for government action, as it is harmful for a nation to buy more from than it sells to the rest of the world. The economics of the balance of payments allows us to judge the value of such arguments. Some policymakers, labor leaders, and business people will argue that it is bad if a country has a trade deficit with another single country. For instance, if the United States has a trade deficit with Japan, it is common to hear calls for policy aimed at eliminating this *bilateral* trade deficit. Once again, an understanding of the economics of the trade deficit allows a proper evaluation of calls for policies aimed at eliminating bilateral trade imbalances. We will encounter references to policy issues related to the balance of payments in later chapters.

2.a. Accounting for International Transactions

double-entry bookkeeping
A system of accounting in which every transaction is recorded in at least two accounts.

The balance of payments is an accounting statement known as a balance sheet. A balance sheet is based on **double-entry bookkeeping**, a system in which every transaction is recorded in at least two accounts. We do not need to know the details of accounting rules to understand the balance of payments. We can simply think of transactions bringing money into a country as being positive numbers that are recorded as *credits* and transactions taking money out of a country as being negative numbers that are recorded as *debits*. Double-entry bookkeeping requires that the debit and credit entries for any transaction must balance. Suppose a U.S. tractor manufacturer sells a $50,000 tractor to a resident of France. This transaction would have a positive effect on the U.S. balance of trade in merchandise. If a U.S. resident bought a $500 bicycle from a Japanese firm, this would have a negative effect on the U.S. balance of trade in merchandise. Of course, people buy and sell things other than merchandise. The classification of international transactions into major accounts is now considered.

2.b. Balance of Payments Accounts

The balance of payments uses several different accounts to classify transactions (see Table 3). The **current account** is the sum of the balances in the merchandise, services, income, and unilateral transfers accounts.

Merchandise This account records all transactions involving goods. The exports of goods by the United States are merchandise credits, bringing money into the United States; its imports of foreign goods are merchandise debits, taking money out of the United States. When exports (or credits) exceed imports (or debits), the merchandise account shows a **surplus**. When imports exceed exports, the account shows a **deficit**. The balance in the merchandise account is frequently referred to as the **balance of trade**.

In the third quarter of 2010, the merchandise account in the U.S. balance of payments showed a deficit of $171,157 million. This means that the merchandise credits created by U.S. exports were $171,157 million less than the merchandise debits created by U.S. imports. In other words, the United States bought more goods from other nations than it sold to them.

Services This account measures trade involving services. It includes travel and tourism, royalties, transportation costs, and insurance premiums. In Table 3, the balance on the services account was a $36,761 million surplus.

Income Both investment income and employee compensation are included here. The income earned from investments in foreign countries is a credit; the income paid on foreign-owned investments in the United States is a debit. Investment income is the return on a special kind of service: It is the value of services provided by capital in foreign countries. Compensation earned by U.S. workers abroad is a credit. Compensation earned by foreign workers in the United States is a debit. In Table 3, there is a surplus of $41,055 million in the income account.

Unilateral Transfers In a unilateral transfer, one party gives something but gets nothing in return. Gifts and retirement pensions are forms of unilateral transfers.

current account
The sum of the merchandise, services, income, and unilateral transfers accounts in the balance of payments.

surplus
In a balance of payments account, the amount by which credits exceed debits.

deficit
In a balance of payments account, the amount by which debits exceed credits.

balance of trade
The balance in the merchandise account in a nation's balance of payments.

TABLE 3	Simplified U.S. Balance of Payments, 2010 Third Quarter (million dollars)
Account	**Net Balance**
Merchandise	–$171,157
Services	$ 36,761
Income	$ 41,055
Unilateral transfers	–$ 33,886
Current account	–$127,227
Financial account	$181,620
Statistical discrepancy	–$ 54,385

Source: Data from *Bureau of Economic Analysis.*

For instance, if a farmworker in El Centro, California, sends money to his family in Guaymas, Mexico, this is a unilateral transfer from the United States to Mexico. In Table 3, the unilateral transfers balance is a deficit of $33,886 million.

The current account is a useful measure of international transactions because it contains all of the activities involving goods and services. In the third quarter of 2010, the current account showed a deficit of $127,227 million. This means that U.S. imports of merchandise, services, investment income, and unilateral transfers were $127,227 million greater than exports of these items.

financial account
The record in the balance of payments of the flow of financial assets into and out of a country.

If we draw a line in the balance of payments under the current account, then all entries below the line relate to financing the movement of merchandise, services, investment income, and unilateral transfers into and out of the country. The **financial account** is where trade involving financial assets and international investment is recorded. Credits to the financial account reflect foreign purchases of U.S. financial assets or real property like land and buildings, and debits reflect U.S. purchases of foreign financial assets and real property. In Table 3, the U.S. financial account showed a surplus of $181,620 million.

The *statistical discrepancy* account, the last account listed in Table 3, could be called *omissions and errors*. The government cannot accurately measure all transactions that take place. Some international shipments of goods and services go uncounted or are miscounted, as do some international flows of financial assets. The statistical discrepancy account is used to correct for these omissions and errors. In Table 3, measured credits were less than measured debits, so the statistical discrepancy was $54,385 million.

Over all of the balance of payments accounts, the sum of credits must equal the sum of debits. The bottom line—the *net balance*—must be zero. It cannot show a surplus or a deficit. When people talk about a surplus or a deficit in the balance of payments, they are actually talking about a surplus or a deficit in one of the balance of payments accounts. The balance of payments itself, by definition, is always in balance, a function of double-entry bookkeeping.

2.c. The Current Account and the Financial Account

The current account reflects the movement of goods and services into and out of a country. The financial account reflects the flow of financial assets into and out of a country. In Table 3, the current account shows a deficit balance of $127,227 million. Remember that the balance of payments must *balance*. If there is a deficit in the current account, there must be a surplus in the financial account that exactly offsets that deficit.

What is important here is not the bookkeeping process, the concept that the balance of payments must balance, but rather the meaning of deficits and surpluses in the current and financial accounts. These deficits and surpluses tell us whether a country is a net borrower from or lender to the rest of the world. A deficit in the current account means that a country is running a net surplus in its financial account, and it signals that a country is a net borrower from the rest of the world. A country that is running a current account deficit must borrow from abroad an amount sufficient to finance that deficit. A financial account surplus is achieved by selling more bonds and other debts of the domestic country to the rest of the world than the country buys from the rest of the world.

In Chapter 5, we learned that the value of a nation's output, GDP, is equal to the sum of consumption, investment, government spending, and net exports, or $GDP = C + I + G + X$. We could rewrite this equation in terms of X as $X = GDP - C - I - G$. The X in total spending is net exports involving trade in goods and services. As can be seen in Table 3, this is the largest component of the current account. Thus, a country that is running a current account deficit will have a negative X. Since $X = GDP - C - I - G$, one can see that negative net exports or a current account deficit is consistent with domestic spending being in excess of domestic production. A country that is running a current

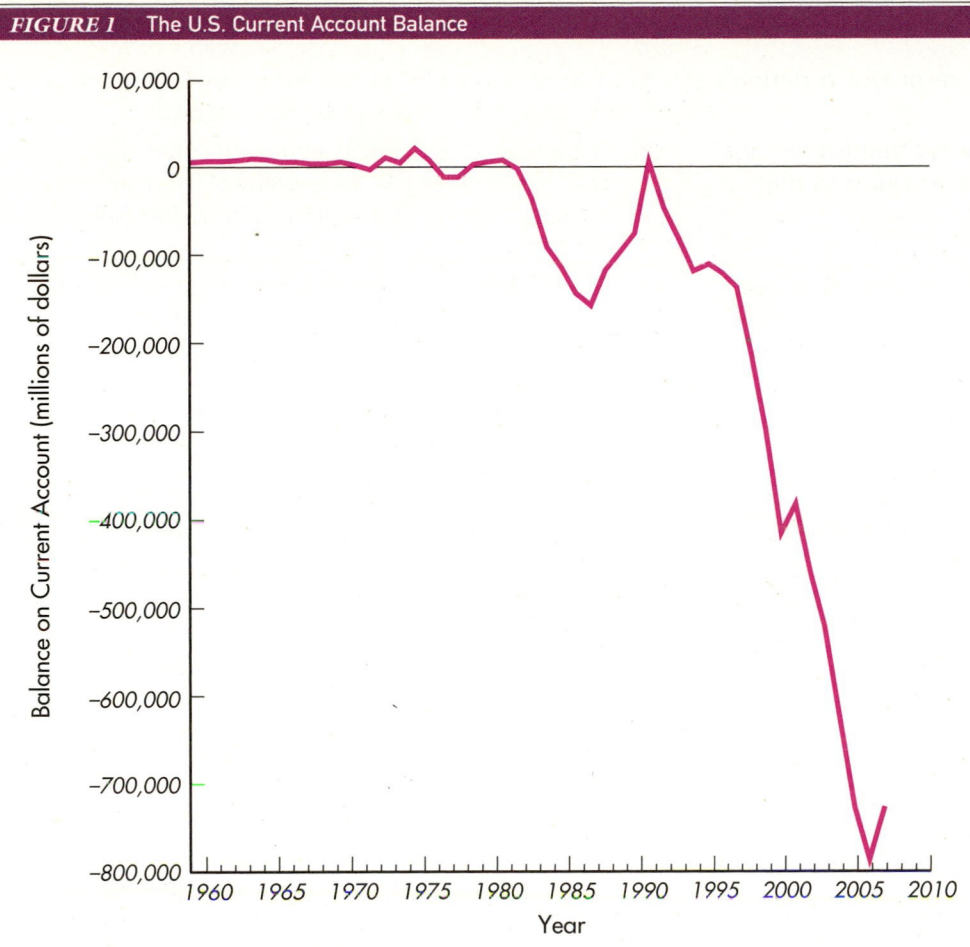

FIGURE 1   The U.S. Current Account Balance

The current account of the balance of payments is the sum of the balances in the merchandise, services, income, and unilateral transfers accounts. The United States experienced very large current account deficits in the 1980s and again more recently.

Source: Bureau of Economic Analysis.

account deficit is spending more than it produces. Such a country must borrow to cover this difference between production and spending.

Figure 1 shows the annual current account balance in the United States. The United States experienced large current account deficits in the 1980s and then again from the mid-1990s to the present. These deficits indicate that the United States consumed more than it produced. This means that the United States sold financial assets to and borrowed large amounts of money from foreign residents to finance its current account deficits. This large amount of foreign borrowing made the United States the largest debtor in the world. A *net debtor* owes more to the rest of the world than it is owed; a *net creditor* is owed more than it owes. The United States was an international net creditor from the end of World War I until the mid-1980s. The country financed its large current account deficits in the 1980s by borrowing from the rest of the world. As a result of this accumulated borrowing, in 1985 the United States became an international net debtor for the first time in almost 70 years. Since that time, the net debtor status of the United States has grown steadily.

RECAP

1. The balance of payments is a record of a nation's international transactions.

2. Double-entry bookkeeping requires that every transaction be entered in at least two accounts so that credits and debits are balanced.

3. In the balance of payments, credits record activities that represent payments into the country, and debits record activities that represent payments out of the country.

4. The current account is the sum of the balances in the merchandise, services, income, and unilateral transfers accounts.

5. A surplus exists when credits exceed debits; a deficit exists when credits are less than debits.

6. The financial account is where the transactions necessary to finance the movement of merchandise, services, income, and unilateral transfers into and out of the country are recorded.

7. The net balance in the balance of payments must be zero.

SUMMARY

1. **How do individuals of one nation trade money with individuals of another nation?**

   - Foreign exchange is currency and bank deposits that are denominated in foreign currency. §1

   - The foreign exchange market is a global market in which people trade one currency for another. §1

   - Exchange rates, the price of one country's money in terms of another country's money, are necessary to compare prices quoted in different currencies. §1.a

   - The value of a good in a domestic currency equals the foreign currency price times the exchange rate. §1.a

2. **How do changes in exchange rates affect international trade?**

   - When a domestic currency appreciates, domestic goods become more expensive to foreigners, and foreign goods become cheaper to domestic residents. §1.b

   - When a domestic currency depreciates, domestic goods become cheaper to foreigners, and foreign goods become more expensive to domestic residents. §1.b

3. **How do nations record their transactions with the rest of the world?**

   - The balance of payments is a record of a nation's transactions with the rest of the world. §2

   - The balance of payments is based on double-entry bookkeeping. §2.a

   - Credits record activities that bring payments into a country; debits record activities that take payments out of a country. §2.a

   - The current account is the sum of the balances in the merchandise, services, income, and unilateral transfers accounts. §2.b

   - In a balance of payments account, a surplus is the amount by which credits exceed debits, and a deficit is the amount by which debits exceed credits. §2.b

   - The financial account reflects the transactions necessary to finance the movement of merchandise, services, income, and unilateral transfers into and out of the country. §2.b

   - The net balance in the balance of payments must be zero. §2.b

   - A deficit in the current account must be offset by a surplus in the financial account. §2.c

   - A country that shows a deficit in its current account (or a surplus in its financial account) is a net borrower. §2.c

KEY TERMS

balance of payments, 120
balance of trade, 121
current account, 121
deficit, 121

double-entry bookkeeping, 120
exchange rate, 115
financial account, 122
foreign exchange, 115

foreign exchange market, 115
surplus, 121

EXERCISES

1. What is the price of 1 U.S. dollar in terms of each of the following currencies, given the following exchange rates?
   a. 1 euro = $1.41
   b. 1 Chinese yuan = $.15
   c. 1 Israeli shekel = $.28
   d. 1 Kuwaiti dinar = $3.60
2. A bicycle manufactured in the United States costs $200. Using the exchange rates listed in Table 1, what would the bicycle cost in each of the following countries?
   a. Argentina
   b. Britain
   c. Canada
3. The U.S. dollar price of a Swedish krona changes from $.1572 to $.1730.
   a. Has the dollar depreciated or appreciated against the krona?
   b. Has the krona appreciated or depreciated against the dollar?

Use the information in the following table on Mexico's 2007 international transactions to answer exercises 4–6 (the amounts are the U.S. dollar values in millions):

Merchandise exports	$271,594
Merchandise imports	$281,649
Services exports	$ 17,512
Services imports	$ 23,784
Income receipts	$ 7,972
Income payments	$ 26,036
Unilateral transfers	$ 24,197

4. What is the balance of trade?
5. What is the current account?
6. Did Mexico become a larger international net debtor during 2007?

7. How reasonable is it for every country to follow policies aimed at increasing net exports?
8. How did the United States become the world's largest debtor nation in the 1980s?
9. If the U.S. dollar appreciated against the Japanese yen, what would you expect to happen to U.S. net exports to Japan?
10. Suppose the U.S. dollar price of a British pound is $1.50; the dollar price of a euro is $1; a hotel room in London, England, costs 120 British pounds; and a comparable hotel room in Hanover, Germany, costs 200 euro.
    a. Which hotel room is cheaper for a U.S. tourist?
    b. What is the exchange rate between the euro and the British pound?
11. Many residents of the United States send money to relatives living in other countries. For instance, a Salvadoran farmworker who is temporarily working in San Diego, California, sends money back to his family in El Salvador. How are such transactions recorded in the balance of payments? Are they debits or credits?
12. Suppose the U.S. dollar price of the Canadian dollar is $.75. How many Canadian dollars will it take to buy a set of dishes selling for $60 in Detroit, Michigan?
13. Why is it true that if the dollar depreciates against the yen, the yen must appreciate against the dollar?
14. Why does the balance of payments contain an account called "statistical discrepancy"?
15. Use the national income identity $GDP = C + I + G + X$ to explain what a current account deficit (negative net exports) means in terms of domestic spending, production, and borrowing.

You can find further practice tests in the Online Quiz at **www.cengage.com/economics/boyes**.

FRENCH CROSS CHANNEL TO BUY CHANEL IN LONDON

London Evening Standard, March 23, 2009

Channel-hopping shoppers are taking advantage of the weak pound and flocking to London to snap up famous French brands, retailers said today.

Chanel, Chloe and Louis Vuitton goods are proving most popular with the French shoppers, according to Selfridges.

The department store, which has a flagship shop in Oxford Street, said trade from France soared by 70 per cent in January and February compared with the same months last year. The trend held for shoppers from other countries using the euro, with trade growing by more than 40 per cent.

The pound's weakness means European customers can make big savings on purchases such as designers handbags, with a Chanel quilted leather bag costing the equivalent of £1,780 in Paris available at Selfridges for £1,525.

Euro shoppers are also snapping up British brands, with sales of Vivienne Westwood handbags up more than 50 per cent this year.

Selfridges' buying director, Anne Pitcher, said: "European customers have clearly resolved not to give up on life's uplifting luxuries and are coming to London to get them at the best possible price."

MARK BLUNDEN

Source: From www.thisisLondon.co.uk/ standard, March 23, 2009.

hy were French shoppers traveling to London to shop? The article says that it has to do with a weak British pound. There are two elements involved in determining the price of an internationally traded good: the price in terms of the home currency of the country in which the good is produced and the exchange rate. With constant pound prices of goods in London, if the British pound depreciates in value against the euro, British goods will become cheaper to French buyers, as emphasized in the article.

If one examines how the euro value of a pound has changed in recent times, it is easy to see how the price of goods in London has changed for French residents. In early 2007, 1 pound was worth about 1.50 euros. But by early 2009, a pound was only worth about 1.05 euros. So if the prices of goods and services in London did not change at all, the prices of London goods to French shoppers fell by about a third. A luxury purse that sells for 1,000 pounds in London would have cost a French shopper about 1,500 euros in 2007 but fell in price to about 1,050 euros by 2009.

This brief article reminds us of how interdependent countries are. The story of the increase in French shoppers in London in 2009 is a good example of how the exchange rate between currencies is one of the key variables linking countries together.

CHAPTER 7

Unemployment and Inflation

© MACIEJ FROLOW/GETTY IMAGES, INC

MARK RALSTON/AFP/GETTY IMAGES; LOGO: © FROXX/SHUTTERSTOCK.COM

FUNDAMENTAL QUESTIONS

1 What is a business cycle?

2 How is the unemployment rate defined and measured?

3 What is the cost of unemployed resources?

4 What is inflation?

5 Why is inflation a problem?

I f you were graduating from college today, what would your job prospects be? In 1932, they would have been bleak. A large number of people were out of work (about one in four workers), and a large number of firms had laid off workers or gone out of business. At any given time, job opportunities depend, not only on the individual's ability and experience, but also on the current state of the economy.

Economies follow cycles of activity: Periods of expansion, in which output and employment increase, are followed by periods of contraction, in which output and employment decrease. For instance, during the expansionary period of the 1990s and 2000, only 4 percent of U.S. workers had no job by 2000. But during the period of contraction of 1981–1982, 9.5 percent of U.S. workers had no job. When the economy is growing, the demand for goods and services tends to increase. To produce those goods and services, firms hire more workers. Economic expansion also has an impact on inflation: As the demand for goods and services goes up, the prices of those goods and services also tend to rise. By 2000, following several years of economic growth, consumer prices in the United States were rising by about 3 percent a year. During periods of contraction, when more people are out of work, demand for goods and services tends to fall, and there is less pressure for rising prices. During the period of the Great Depression in the 1930s in the United States, consumer prices fell by more than 5 percent in 1933. Both price increases and the fraction of workers without jobs are affected by business cycles in fairly regular ways. But their effects on individual standards of living, income, and purchasing power are much less predictable.

Why do certain events move in tandem? What are the links between unemployment and inflation? What causes the business cycle to behave as it does? What effect does government activity have on the business cycle—and on unemployment and inflation? Who is harmed by rising unemployment and inflation? Who benefits? Macroeconomics attempts to answer all of these questions.

1. Business Cycles

In this chapter, we describe the business cycle and examine measures of unemployment and inflation. We talk about the ways in which the business cycle, unemployment, and inflation are related. And we describe their effects on the participants in the economy.

The most widely used measure of a nation's output is gross domestic product (GDP). When we examine the value of real GDP over time, we find periods in which it rises and other periods in which it falls.

1 What is a business cycle?

1.a. Definitions

This pattern—real GDP rising, then falling—is called a **business cycle**. The pattern occurs over and over again, but as Figure 1 shows, the pattern over time is anything but regular. Historically, the duration of business cycles and the rate at which real GDP rises or falls (indicated by the steepness of the line in Figure 1) vary considerably.

Looking at Figure 1, it is clear that the U.S. economy has experienced up-and-down swings in the years since 1959. Still, real GDP has grown at an average rate of approximately 3 percent per year over the long run. While it is important to recognize that periods of economic growth, or prosperity, are followed by periods of contraction, or **recession**, it is also important to recognize the presence of long-term economic growth despite the presence of periodic recessions. In the long run, the economy produces more goods and services. The long-run growth in the economy depends on the growth in productive resources, like land, labor, and capital, along with technological advance. Technological change increases the productivity of resources so that output increases even with a fixed amount of inputs.

Figure 2 shows how real GDP behaves over a hypothetical business cycle and identifies the stages of the cycle. The vertical axis on the graph measures the level of real GDP; the horizontal axis measures time in years. In year 1, real GDP is growing; the economy is in the *expansion* phase, or *boom* period, of the business cycle. Growth

business cycle
Fluctuations in the economy between growth (expressed in rising real GDP) and stagnation (expressed in falling real GDP).

recession
A period in which real GDP falls.

As real income falls, living standards go down. This 1937 photo of a Depression-era breadline indicates the paradox of the world's richest nation, as emphasized on the billboard in the background, having to offer public support to feed able-bodied workers who were out of work due to the severity of the business cycle downturn.

continues until the *peak* is reached, in year 2. Real GDP begins to fall during the *contraction* phase of the cycle, which continues until year 4. The *trough* marks the end of the contraction and the start of a new expansion. Even though the economy is subject to periodic ups and downs, real GDP, the measure of a nation's output, has risen over the long term, as illustrated by the upward-sloping line labeled *Trend*.

If an economy is growing over time, why do economists worry about business cycles? Economists try to understand the causes of business cycles so that they can learn how to moderate or avoid recessions and their harmful effects on standards of living.

1.b. Historical Record

The official dating of recessions in the United States is the responsibility of the National Bureau of Economic Research (NBER), an independent research organization. The NBER has identified the shaded areas in the graph in Figure 1 as recessions and the unshaded areas as expansions. Recessions are periods between cyclical peaks and the troughs that follow them. Expansions are periods between cyclical troughs and the peaks that follow them. There have been 14 recessions since 1929. The most severe was the period between 1929 and 1933, called the Great Depression. During this period, national output fell by 25 percent. A **depression** is a prolonged period of severe economic contraction. The fact that people speak of "the Depression" when they talk about the recession that began in 1929 indicates the severity of that contraction relative to others in recent experience. There was widespread suffering during the Depression. Many people were jobless and homeless, and many firms went bankrupt.

The NBER defines a recession as "a period of significant decline in total output, income, employment, and trade, usually lasting from six months to a year, and marked

depression
A severe, prolonged economic contraction.

FIGURE 1   U.S. Real GDP

Peaks	Troughs
April 1960	February 1961
December 1969	November 1970
November 1973	March 1975
January 1980	July 1980
July 1981	November 1982
July 1990	March 1991
March 2001	November 2001
December 2007	June 2009

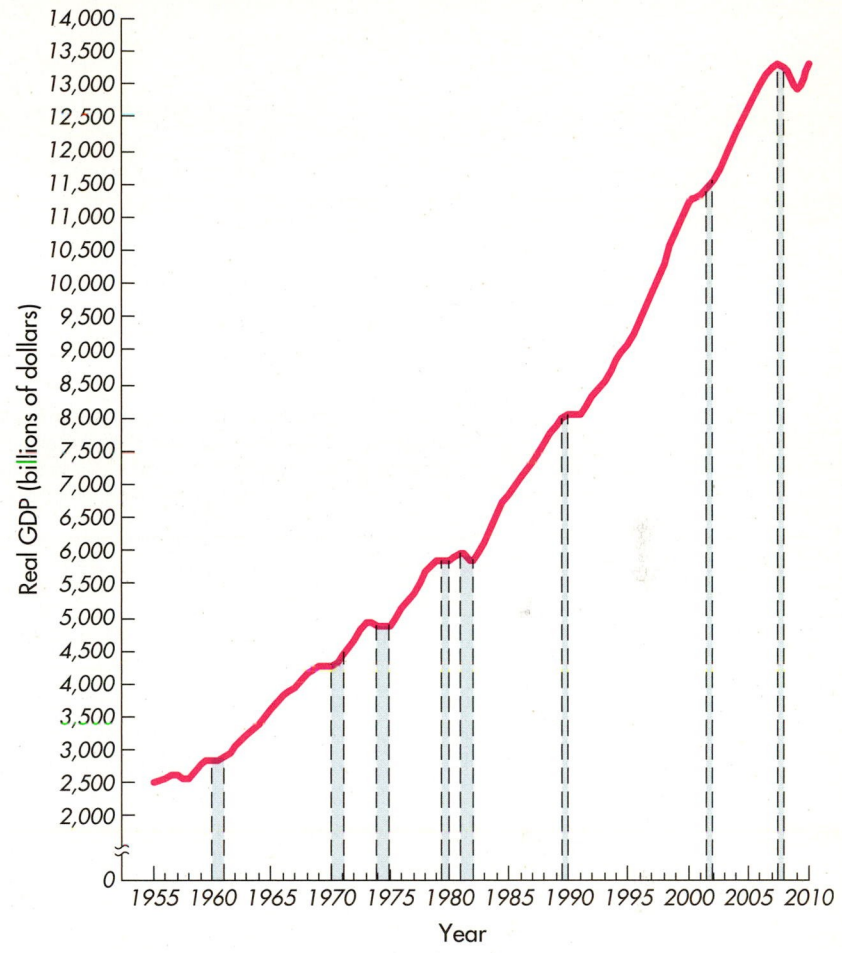

The shaded areas represent periods of economic contraction (recession). The table lists the dates of business cycle peaks and troughs. The peak dates indicate when contractions began; the trough dates, when expansions began.

Source: Data from *Bureau of Economic Analysis*; www.bea.gov/bea/an/nipaguid.pdf.

by widespread contractions in many sectors of the economy." People sometimes say that a recession is defined by two consecutive quarters of declining real GDP. This informal idea of what constitutes a recession seems to be consistent with the past recessions experienced by the United States, as every recession through the 1990s has had at least two quarters of falling real GDP. However, this is not the official definition of a recession. The business cycle dating committee of the NBER generally focuses on monthly data. Close attention is paid to the following monthly data series: employment, real personal income less transfer payments, the volume of sales of the manufacturing and wholesale–retail sectors adjusted for price changes, and industrial production. The focus is not on real GDP, because it is measured only quarterly and does not permit the identification of the month in which business-cycle turning points occur.

On November 28, 2008, the NBER Business Cycle Dating Committee met and determined that December 2007 was the most recent business-cycle peak. It always

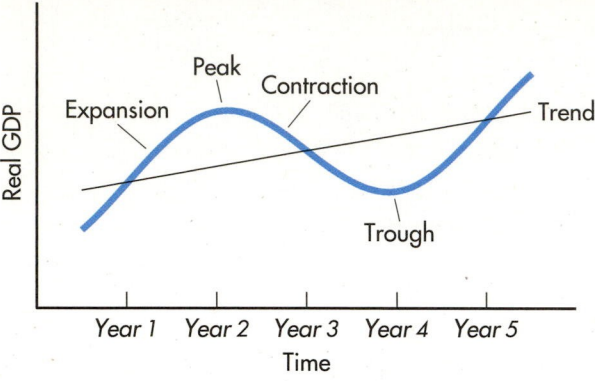

FIGURE 2   The Business Cycle

The business cycle contains four phases: the expansion (boom), when real GDP is increasing; the peak, which marks the end of an expansion and the beginning of a contraction; the contraction (recession), when real GDP is falling; and the trough, which marks the end of a contraction and the beginning of an expansion.

© 2013 Cengage Learning

takes some time for the committee that dates business cycles to have enough evidence to be convinced that the data have identified the turning point in the business cycle. For instance, in determining the end of the previous recession, it wasn't until July 17, 2003, that the NBER announced the recession had ended in November 2001. It took more than 1.5 years to identify the trough that marked the end of the prior recent recession. On September 19, 2010, the NBER determined that a trough in business activity occurred in the U.S. economy in June 2009, marking the end of the recession that had begun in December 2007.

1.c. Indicators

We have been talking about the business cycle in terms of real GDP. There are a number of other variables that move in a fairly regular manner over the business cycle. These variables are classified into three categories—leading indicators, coincident indicators, and lagging indicators—depending on whether they move up or down before, at the same time as, or following a change in real GDP (see Table 1).

Leading indicators generally change before real GDP changes. As a result, economists use them to forecast changes in output. Looking at Table 1, it is easy to see how some of these leading indicators could be used to forecast future output. For instance, new building permits signal new construction. If the number of new permits issued goes up, economists can expect the amount of new construction to increase. Similarly, if manufacturers receive more new orders, economists can expect more goods to be produced.

Leading indicators are not infallible, however. The link between them and future output can be tenuous. For example, leading indicators may fall one month and then rise the next, although real output rises steadily. Economists want to see several consecutive months of a new direction in the leading indicators before forecasting a change in output. Short-run movements in the indicators can be very misleading.

Coincident indicators are economic variables that tend to change at the same time as real output changes. For example, as real output increases, economists expect to see employment and sales rise. The coincident indicators listed in Table 1 have demonstrated a strong tendency over time to change along with changes in real GDP.

leading indicator
A variable that changes real output changes.

coincident indicator
A variable that changes as the as real output changes.

TABLE 1	Indicators of the Business Cycle
Leading Indicators	
Average workweek	New building permits
Unemployment claims	Delivery times of goods
Manufacturers' new orders	Interest rate spread
Stock prices	Money supply
New plant and equipment orders	Consumer expectations
Coincident Indicators	**Lagging Indicators**
Payroll employment	Labor cost per unit of output
Industrial production	Inventories to sales ratio
Personal income	Unemployment duration
Manufacturing and trade sales	Consumer credit to personal income ratio
	Outstanding commercial loans
	Prime interest rate
	Inflation rate for services

© 2013 Cengage Learning

The final group of variables listed in Table 1, **lagging indicators**, do not change in value until after the value of real GDP has changed. For instance, as output increases, jobs are created and more workers are hired. It makes sense, then, to expect the duration of unemployment (the average length of time that workers are unemployed) to fall. The duration of unemployment is a lagging indicator. Similarly, the inflation rate for services (which measures how prices for things like dry cleaners, veterinarians, and other services change) tends to change after real GDP changes. Lagging indicators are used along with leading and coincident indicators to identify the peaks and troughs in business cycles.

lagging indicator
A variable that changes after real output changes.

RECAP

1. The business cycle is a recurring pattern of rising and falling real GDP.

2. Although all economies move through periods of expansion and contraction, the duration of the periods of expansion and recession varies.

3. Real GDP is not the only variable affected by business cycles; leading, lagging, and coincident indicators also show the effects of economic expansion and contraction.

2. Unemployment

Recurring periods of prosperity and recession are reflected in the nation's labor markets. In fact, this is what makes understanding the business cycle so important. If business cycles signified only a little more or a little less profit for businesses, governments would not be so anxious to forecast or to control their swings. It is the human costs of lost jobs and incomes—the inability to maintain standards of living—that make an understanding of business cycles and of the factors that affect unemployment so important.

 2 How is the unemployment rate defined and measured?

© froxx/Shutterstock.com

2.a. Definition and Measurement

unemployment rate
The percentage of the labor force that is not working.

The **unemployment rate** is the percentage of the labor force that is not working. The rate is calculated by dividing the number of people who are unemployed by the number of people in the labor force:

$$\text{Unemployment rate} = \frac{\text{number unemployed}}{\text{number in labor force}}$$

This ratio seems simple enough, but there are several subtle issues at work here. First, the unemployment rate does not measure the percentage of the total population that is not working; it measures the percentage of the *labor force* that is not working. Who is in the labor force? Obviously, everybody who is employed is part of the labor force. But only some of those who are not currently employed are counted in the labor force.

You are in the labor force if you are working or actively seeking work.

The Bureau of Labor Statistics of the Department of Labor compiles labor data each month based on an extensive survey of U.S. households. All U.S. residents are potential members of the labor force. The Labor Department arrives at the size of the actual labor force by using this formula:

Labor force = all U.S. residents minus residents under 16 years of age minus institutionalized adults minus adults not looking for work

So the labor force includes those adults (an adult being someone 16 or older) who are currently employed or actively seeking work. It is relatively simple to see to it that children and institutionalized adults (e.g., those in prison or in long-term care facilities) are not counted in the labor force. It is more difficult to identify and accurately measure adults who are not actively looking for work.

A person is actively seeking work if he or she is available to work, has looked for work in the past four weeks, is waiting for a recall after being laid off, or is starting a job within 30 days. Those who are not working and who meet these criteria are considered unemployed.

Agricultural harvests, like this one in Mexico, create seasonal fluctuations in the employment of labor. During the harvest period, workers are hired to help out. When the harvest has ended, many of these workers will be temporarily unemployed until the next crop requires their labor.

© Richard Thornton/Shutterstock.com

2.b. Interpreting the Unemployment Rate

Is the unemployment rate an accurate measure? The fact that the rate does not include those who are not actively looking for work is not necessarily a failing. Many people who are not actively looking for work—homemakers, older citizens, and students, for example—have made a decision not to work—to do housework, to retire, or to stay in school. These people rightly are not counted among the unemployed.

discouraged workers
Workers who have stopped looking for work because they believe that no one will offer them a job.

But there are people missing from the unemployment statistics who are not working and are not looking for work yet would take a job if one were offered. **Discouraged workers** have looked for work in the past year but have given up looking for work because they believe that no one will hire them. These individuals are ignored by the official unemployment rate, even though they are able to work and may have spent a long time looking for work. Estimates of the number of discouraged workers indicate that, in November 2010, 2.5 million people were not counted in the labor force yet claimed that they were available for work. Of this group, 52 percent, or 1.3 million people, were considered to be discouraged workers. It is clear that the reported unemployment rate underestimates the true burden of unemployment in the economy because it ignores discouraged workers.

Discouraged workers are one source of hidden unemployment; underemployment is another. **Underemployment** is the underutilization of workers, employing them in tasks that do not fully utilize their productive potential; this includes part-time workers who would prefer full-time employment. Even if every worker has a job, substantial underemployment leaves the economy producing less than its potential GDP.

underemployment
The employment of workers in jobs that do not utilize their productive potential.

The effect of discouraged workers and underemployment is to produce an unemployment rate that *understates* actual unemployment. In contrast, the effect of the *underground economy* is to produce a rate that *overstates* actual unemployment. A sizable number of the officially unemployed are actually working. The unemployed construction worker who plays in a band at night may not report that activity because he or she wants to avoid paying taxes on his or her earnings as a musician. This person is officially unemployed but has a source of income. Many officially unemployed individuals have an alternative source of income. This means that official statistics overstate the true magnitude of unemployment. The larger the underground economy, the greater this overstatement.

Activity in the underground economy is not included in official statistics.

We have identified two factors, discouraged workers and underemployment, that cause the official unemployment rate to underestimate true unemployment. Another factor, the underground economy, causes the official rate to overestimate the true rate of unemployment. There is no reason to expect these factors to cancel one another out, and there is no way to know for sure which is most important. The point is to remember what the official data on unemployment do and do not measure.

2.c. Types of Unemployment

Economists have identified four basic types of unemployment:

Seasonal unemployment A product of regular, recurring changes in the hiring needs of certain industries on a monthly or seasonal basis

Frictional unemployment A product of the short-term movement of workers between jobs and of first-time job seekers

Structural unemployment A product of technological change and other changes in the structure of the economy

Cyclical unemployment A product of business-cycle fluctuations

Frictional and structural unemployment are always present in a dynamic economy.

In certain industries, labor needs fluctuate throughout the year. When local crops are harvested, farms need lots of workers; the rest of the year, they do not. (Migrant farmworkers move from one region to another, following the harvests, to avoid seasonal unemployment.) Ski resort towns like Park City, Utah, are booming during the ski season, when employment peaks, but need fewer workers during the rest of the year. In the nation as a whole, the Christmas season is a time of peak employment and low unemployment rates. To avoid confusing seasonal fluctuations in unemployment with other sources of unemployment, unemployment data are seasonally adjusted.

Frictional and structural unemployment exist in any dynamic economy. For individual workers, frictional unemployment is short term in nature. Workers quit one job and soon find another; students graduate and soon find a job. This kind of unemployment cannot be eliminated in a free society. In fact, it is a sign of efficiency in an economy when workers try to increase their income or improve their working conditions by leaving one job for another. Frictional unemployment is often called *search unemployment* because workers take time to search for a job after quitting a job or leaving school.

Frictional unemployment is short term; structural unemployment, on the other hand, can be long term. Workers who are displaced by technological change (assembly line workers who have been replaced by machines, for example) or by a permanent reduction in the demand for an industry's output (cigar makers who have been laid off because of a decrease in demand for tobacco) may not have the necessary skills to maintain their level of income in another industry. Rather than accept a much lower salary, these workers tend to prolong their job search. Eventually they either adjust their expectations to the realities of the job market or enter the pool of discouraged workers.

Structural unemployment is very difficult for those who are unemployed. But for society as a whole, the technological advances that cause structural unemployment raise living standards by giving consumers a greater variety of goods at lower cost.

> *Cyclical unemployment is a product of recession.*

Cyclical unemployment is a result of the business cycle. When a recession occurs, cyclical unemployment increases, and when growth occurs, cyclical unemployment decreases. It is also a primary focus of macroeconomic policy. Economists believe that a greater understanding of business cycles and their causes may enable them to find ways to smooth out those cycles and swings in unemployment. Much of the analysis in future chapters is related to macroeconomic policy aimed at minimizing business-cycle fluctuations. In addition to macroeconomic policy aimed at moderating cyclical unemployment, other policy measures—for example, job training and counseling—are being used to reduce frictional and structural unemployment.

2.d. Costs of Unemployment

3 What is the cost of unemployed resources?

The cost of unemployment is more than the obvious loss of income and status suffered by the individual who is not working. In a broader sense, society as a whole loses when resources are unemployed. Unemployed workers produce no output. So an economy with unemployment will operate inside its production possibilities curve rather than on the curve. Economists measure this lost output in terms of the *GDP gap*:

$$\text{GDP gap} = \text{potential real GDP} - \text{actual real GDP}$$

potential real GDP
The output produced at the natural rate of unemployment.

natural rate of unemployment
The unemployment rate that would exist in the absence of cyclical unemployment.

Potential real GDP is the level of output produced when nonlabor resources are fully utilized and unemployment is at its natural rate. The **natural rate of unemployment** is the unemployment rate that would exist in the absence of cyclical unemployment, so it includes seasonal, frictional, and structural unemployment. The natural rate of unemployment is not fixed; it can change over time. For instance, some economists believe that the natural rate of unemployment has risen in recent decades, a product of the influx of baby boomers and women into the labor force. As more workers move into the labor force (begin looking for jobs), frictional unemployment increases, raising the natural rate of unemployment. The natural rate of unemployment is sometimes called the "nonaccelerating inflation rate of unemployment," or NAIRU. The idea is that there would be upward pressure on wages and prices in a tight labor market in which the unemployment rate fell below the NAIRU. We will see macroeconomic models of this phenomenon in later chapters.

Potential real GDP measures what we are capable of producing at the natural rate of unemployment. If we compute potential real GDP and then subtract actual real GDP, we have a measure of the output lost as a result of unemployment, or the cost of unemployment.

The GDP gap in the United States from 1975 to 2010 is shown in Figure 3. The gap widens during recessions and narrows during expansions. As the gap widens (as the output that is not produced increases), there are fewer goods and services available, and living standards are lower than they would be at the natural rate of unemployment.

FIGURE 3 The GDP Gap

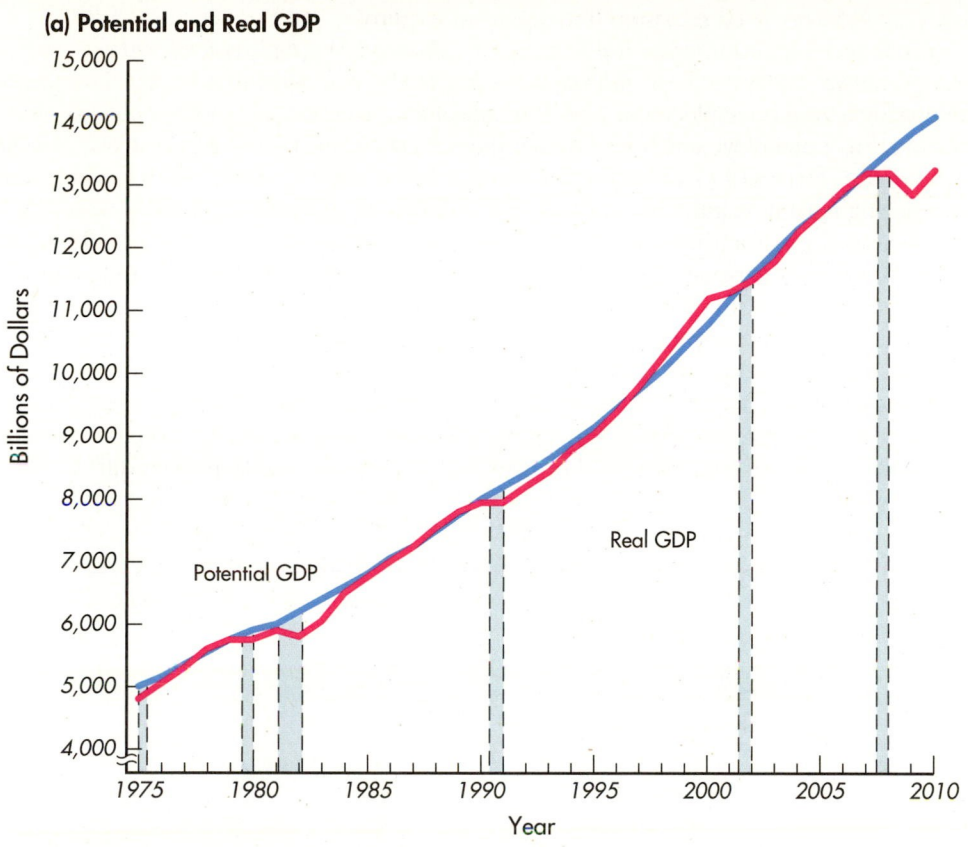

(a) Potential and Real GDP

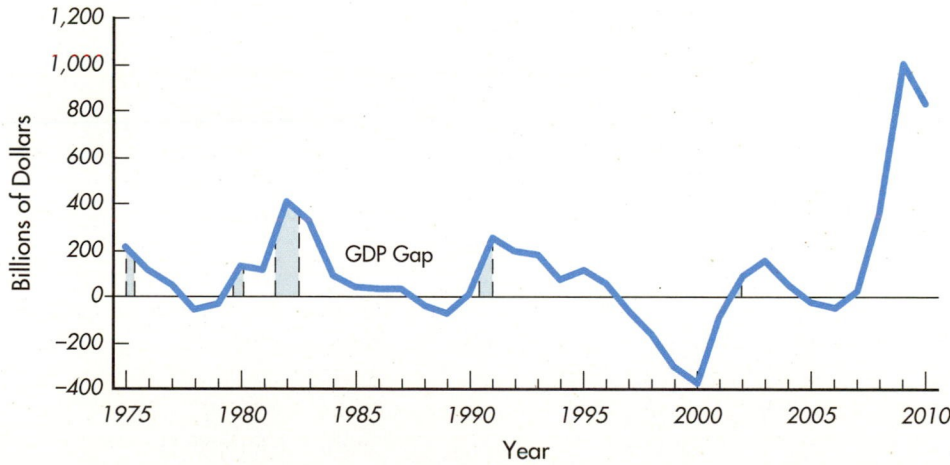

(b) A Graph of the GDP Gap

The GDP gap is the difference between what the economy can produce at the natural rate of unemployment (potential GDP) and actual output (actual GDP). When the unemployment rate is higher than the natural rate, actual GDP is less than potential GDP. The gap between potential and actual real GDP is a cost associated with unemployment. Recession years are shaded to highlight how the gap widens around recessions.

Figure 3(b) is a graph of the gap between potential and real GDP, taken from Figure 3(a). During the strong expansion of the late 1990s, and more recently before the financial crisis and associated recession, the gap went to zero.

Until recently, economists used the term *full employment* instead of *natural rate of unemployment*. Today the term *full employment* is rarely used because it may be interpreted as implying a zero unemployment rate. If frictional and structural unemployment are always present, zero unemployment is impossible; there must always be unemployed resources in an economy. *Natural rate of unemployment* describes the labor market when the economy is producing what it realistically can produce in the absence of cyclical unemployment.

What is the natural rate of unemployment in the United States? In the 1950s and 1960s, economists generally agreed on 4 percent. By the 1970s, the agreed-upon rate had gone up to 5 percent. In the early 1980s, many economists placed the natural rate of unemployment in the United States at 6 to 7 percent. By the late 1980s, some had revised their thinking, placing the rate back at 5 percent. In the late 1990s, one could have said that 4 percent was correct. In fact, economists do not know exactly what the natural rate of unemployment is. It varies over time within a range from around 4 percent to around 7 percent. It will also vary across countries, as labor markets and macroeconomic policies differ.

> Because frictional and structural unemployment are always present, the term full employment *is* misleading. Today economists use the term natural rate of unemployment *instead.*

2.e. The Record of Unemployment

Unemployment rates in the United States from 1960 to 2009 are listed in Table 2. Over this period, the unemployment rate for all workers reached a low of 3.5 percent in 1969

TABLE 2   Unemployment Rates in the United States

| | Unemployment Rate, Civilian Workers[1] | | | | | | | |
| | By Gender | | | | By Race | | | |
Year	All Civilian Workers	Males	Females	Both Sexes 16-19 Years	White	Black or African American	Asian (NSA)	Hispanic or Latino
1960	5.5	5.4	5.9	14.7	5.0	—	—	—
1961	6.7	6.4	7.2	16.8	6.0	—	—	—
1962	5.5	5.2	6.2	14.7	4.9	—	—	—
1963	5.7	5.2	6.5	17.2	5.0	—	—	—
1964	5.2	4.6	6.2	16.2	4.6	—	—	—
1965	4.5	4.0	5.5	14.8	4.1	—	—	—
1966	3.8	3.2	4.8	12.8	3.4	—	—	—
1967	3.8	3.1	5.2	12.9	3.4	—	—	—
1968	3.6	2.9	4.8	12.7	3.2	—	—	—
1969	3.5	2.8	4.7	12.2	3.1	—	—	—
1970	4.9	4.4	5.9	15.3	4.5	—	—	—
1971	5.9	5.3	6.9	16.9	5.4	—	—	—
1972	5.6	5.0	6.6	16.2	5.1	10.4	—	—
1973	4.9	4.2	6.0	14.5	4.3	9.4	—	7.5
1974	5.6	4.9	6.7	16.0	5.0	10.5	—	8.1
1975	8.5	7.9	9.3	19.9	7.8	14.8	—	12.2
1976	7.7	7.1	8.6	19.0	7.0	14.0	—	11.5
1977	7.1	6.3	8.2	17.8	6.2	14.0	—	10.1
1978	6.1	5.3	7.2	16.4	5.2	12.8	—	9.1
1979	5.8	5.1	6.8	16.1	5.1	12.3	—	8.3

1980	7.1	6.9	7.4	17.8	6.3	14.3	—	10.1
1981	7.6	7.4	7.9	19.6	6.7	15.6	—	10.4
1982	9.7	9.9	9.4	23.2	8.6	18.9	—	13.8
1983	9.6	9.9	9.2	22.4	8.4	19.5	—	13.7
1984	7.5	7.4	7.6	18.9	6.5	15.9	—	10.7
1985	7.2	7.0	7.4	18.6	6.2	15.1	—	10.5
1986	7.0	6.9	7.1	18.3	6.0	14.5	—	10.6
1987	6.2	6.2	6.2	16.9	5.3	13.0	—	8.8
1988	5.5	5.5	5.6	15.3	4.7	11.7	—	8.2
1989	5.3	5.2	5.4	15.0	4.5	11.4	—	8.0
1990	5.6	5.7	5.5	15.5	4.8	11.4	—	8.2
1991	6.8	7.2	6.4	18.7	6.1	12.5	—	10.0
1992	7.5	7.9	7.0	20.1	6.6	14.2	—	11.6
1993	6.9	7.2	6.6	19.0	6.1	13.0	—	10.8
1994	6.1	6.2	6.0	17.6	5.3	11.5	—	9.9
1995	5.6	5.6	5.6	17.3	4.9	10.4	—	9.3
1996	5.4	5.4	5.4	16.7	4.7	10.5	—	8.9
1997	4.9	4.9	5.0	16.0	4.2	10.0	—	7.7
1998	4.5	4.4	4.6	14.6	3.9	8.9	—	7.2
1999	4.2	4.1	4.3	13.9	3.7	8.0	—	6.4
2000	4.0	3.9	4.1	13.1	3.5	7.6	3.6	5.7
2001	4.7	4.8	4.7	14.7	4.2	8.6	4.5	6.6
2002	5.8	5.9	5.6	16.5	5.1	10.2	5.9	7.5
2003	6.0	6.3	5.7	17.5	5.2	10.8	6.0	7.7
2004	5.5	5.6	5.4	17.0	4.8	10.4	4.4	7.0
2005	5.1	5.1	5.1	16.6	4.4	10.0	4.0	6.0
2006	4.6	4.6	4.6	15.4	4.0	8.9	3.0	5.2
2007	4.6	4.7	4.5	15.7	4.1	8.3	3.2	5.6
2008	5.8	6.1	5.4	18.7	5.5	11.4	4.1	7.6
2009	9.3	10.3	8.1	24.3	9.4	17.5	7.9	12.5

[1]Unemployed as a percentage of the civilian labor force in the group specified.
Source: *Bureau of Labor Statistics*; http://data.bls.gov/.

and a high of 9.7 percent in 1982. The table shows some general trends in the incidence of unemployment across different demographic groups:

Teenagers have the highest unemployment rates in the economy. This makes sense because teenagers are the least-skilled segment of the labor force.

Whites have lower unemployment rates than nonwhites. Discrimination plays a role here. To the extent that discrimination extends beyond hiring practices and job opportunities for minority workers to the education that is necessary to prepare students to enter the work force, minority workers will have fewer opportunities for employment. The quality of education provided in many schools with large minority populations may not be as good as that provided in schools with large white populations. Equal opportunity programs and legislation are aimed at rectifying this inequality.

Although exact comparisons across countries are difficult to make because different countries measure unemployment in different ways, it is interesting to look at the reported unemployment rates of different countries. Table 3 lists unemployment rates for seven major industrial nations. The rates have been adjusted to match the U.S. definition of unemployment as closely as possible.

TABLE 3	Unemployment Rates in Major Industrial Countries						
	Civilian Unemployment Rate (percent)						
Year	United States	Canada	Japan	France	Germany	Italy	United Kingdom
1980	7.1	7.3	2.0	6.5	2.8	4.4	6.9
1981	7.6	7.3	2.2	7.6	4.0	4.9	9.7
1982	9.7	10.7	2.4	8.3	5.6	5.4	10.8
1983	9.6	11.6	2.7	8.6	6.9	5.9	11.5
1984	7.5	10.9	2.8	10.0	7.1	5.9	11.8
1985	7.2	10.2	2.7	10.5	7.2	6.0	11.4
1986	7.0	9.3	2.8	10.6	6.6	7.5	11.4
1987	6.2	8.4	2.9	10.8	6.3	7.9	10.5
1988	5.5	7.4	2.5	10.3	6.3	7.9	8.6
1989	5.3	7.1	2.3	9.6	5.7	7.8	7.3
1990	5.6	7.7	2.1	8.6	5.0	7.0	7.1
1991	6.8	9.8	2.1	9.1	5.6	6.9	9.5
1992	7.5	10.6	2.2	10.0	6.7	7.3	10.2
1993	6.9	10.8	2.5	11.3	8.0	9.8	10.4
1994	6.1	9.6	2.9	11.9	8.5	10.7	9.5
1995	5.6	8.6	3.2	11.3	8.2	11.3	8.7
1996	5.4	8.8	3.4	11.8	9.0	11.3	8.1
1997	4.9	8.4	3.4	11.7	9.9	11.4	7.0
1998	4.5	7.7	4.1	11.2	9.3	11.5	6.3
1999	4.2	7.0	4.7	10.5	8.5	11.0	6.0
2000	4.0	6.1	4.8	9.1	7.8	10.2	5.5
2001	4.7	6.5	5.1	8.4	7.9	9.2	5.1
2002	5.8	7.0	5.4	8.8	8.6	8.7	5.2
2003	6.0	6.9	5.3	9.2	9.3	8.5	5.0
2004	5.5	6.4	4.8	9.6	10.3	8.1	4.8
2005	5.1	6.0	4.5	9.6	11.2	7.8	4.9
2006	4.6	5.5	4.2	9.5	10.4	6.9	5.5
2007	4.6	5.3	3.9	8.6	8.7	6.2	5.4
2008	5.8	5.3	4.0	7.5	7.5	6.8	5.7
2009	9.3	7.3	4.8	9.1	7.8	7.9	7.7
2010	9.6	7.2*	4.8*	9.3*	7.4*	8.4*	7.9*

* Data based on first three quarters of 2010 only.
Source: *Economic Report of the President, 2010.*

GLOBAL BUSINESS INSIGHT

High Unemployment in Europe

The data in Table 3 indicate that European countries tend to have higher unemployment rates than other industrial countries. This is not true for all European countries, but it is certainly true for the biggest: France, Germany, Italy, and Spain. One factor that contributes to the higher unemployment rates in these countries is government policy with regard to the labor market. Countries that have policies that encourage unemployment should be expected to have more unemployed workers. In a recent speech, a British scholar gave his analysis of why Europe has such high unemployment. One story he told illustrates how government policy aimed at protecting citizens against unemployment can create the very unemployment that is the focus of its concern. In Italy, laws require parents to support their adult children who do not work, even if the children are entirely capable of working. The story goes as follows:

> The Italian Court of Cessation ruled that a professor at Naples University, separated from his family, must continue to pay his 30-year-old son €775 per month until he can find himself suitable employment. This despite the fact that the son owns a house and possesses an investment trust fund worth €450,000. The judges said that an adult son who refused work that did not reflect his training, abilities and personal interests could not be held to blame. In particular the judges said, "You cannot blame a young person, particularly from a well-off family, who refuses a job that does not fit his aspirations." By contrast, under UK law, a separated father would only have to support his children until they completed full-time education. (Nickell, 2002)

The government requirement that parents support unemployed adult children encourages those children to remain unemployed.

Among men of prime working age (age 25–54), there are more who are inactive and not participating in the labor force than there are who are unemployed. The majority of these men are receiving benefits from the government, claiming disability or illness. In the 1970s, there were many fewer disabled or ill workers as a fraction of the population. But as social benefits were increased and the eligibility rules were relaxed, the number of people claiming to suffer from such problems increased also. The unfortunate truth of human nature is that when you provide better support for those who truly need help, there will be more and more who do not truly need it, yet claim a need. The experience of Denmark is instructive in this regard. Denmark has generous unemployment benefits. But in the 1990s, Danish eligibility requirements were tightened, creating greater incentives for the unemployed to look for work. Danish unemployment rates fell dramatically as a result.

Yet another factor contributing to higher unemployment rates in some countries is restrictions on the ability of firms to terminate workers and the requirement that firms pay high separation costs to workers whom they do fire. The more difficult it is for firms to adjust their labor force in the face of economic fluctuations, the less likely firms are to hire new workers. If you own a business and your sales increase, you are likely to hire extra employees to meet the increased demand for your product. However, you cannot be sure that your sales will be permanently higher, so you would be very conservative about hiring new workers if you would have to pay terminated workers a large amount of money if your sales fell and you needed to lay off some of your employees. Such labor market rigidities, aimed at protecting workers from losing their jobs, create incentives against hiring, so that those who would like to work cannot get hired.

The lesson from large European countries is that government policies aimed at protecting workers from unemployment may create a bigger unemployment problem. Thus, the costs imposed on the economy in the form of taxes and reduced labor market flexibility may exceed the benefits to those who keep their jobs or receive unemployment compensation because of the programs.

Source: Stephen Nickell, "A Picture of European Unemployment: Success and Failure," speech given to CESifo Conference in Munich, December 2002, and Lars Ljungqvist and Thomas Sargent, "The European Unemployment Dilemma," *Journal of Political Economy*, 1998.

Knowing their limitations, we can still identify some important trends from the data in Table 3. In the early 1980s, both U.S. and European unemployment rates increased substantially. But in the mid-1980s, when U.S. unemployment began to fall, European unemployment remained high. The issue of high unemployment rates in Europe has become a major topic of discussion at international summit meetings and is addressed in the Global Business Insight "High Unemployment in Europe." The inflexibility of labor markets in Europe is a factor that makes the European economies more prone to slow growth. Japanese unemployment rates, like those in Europe, were much lower than U.S. and Canadian rates in the 1980s. However, by the late 1990s, Japanese rates began to approach those of the United States.

RECAP

1. The unemployment rate is the number of people unemployed as a percentage of the labor force.

2. To be in the labor force, one must either have or be looking for a job.

3. Through its failure to include discouraged workers and the output lost because of underemployment, the unemployment rate understates real unemployment in the United States.

4. Through its failure to include activity in the underground economy, the U.S. unemployment rate overstates actual unemployment.

5. Unemployment data are adjusted to eliminate seasonal fluctuations.

6. Frictional and structural unemployment are always present in a dynamic economy.

7. Cyclical unemployment is a product of recession; it can be moderated by controlling the period of contraction in the business cycle.

8. Economists measure the cost of unemployment in terms of lost output.

9. Unemployment data show that women generally have higher unemployment rates than men, that teenagers have the highest unemployment rates in the economy, and that blacks and other minority groups have higher unemployment rates than whites.

3. Inflation

4 What is inflation?

inflation
A sustained rise in the average level of prices.

Inflation is a sustained rise in the average level of prices. Notice the word *sustained*. Inflation does not mean a short-term increase in prices; it means that prices are rising over a prolonged period of time. Inflation is measured by the percentage change in price level. The inflation rate in the United States was –0.36 percent in 2009. This means that, on average, the level of prices declined slightly over the year. Low inflation, or perhaps even deflation, is what one typically expects during a recession when spending falls.

3.a. Absolute versus Relative Price Changes

5 Why is inflation a problem?

In the modern economy, over any given period, some prices rise faster than others. To evaluate the rate of inflation in a country, then, economists must know what is happening to prices on average. Here it is important to distinguish between *absolute* and *relative* price changes.

Let's look at an example using the prices of fish and beef:

	Year 1	Year 2
1 pound of fish	$1	$2
1 pound of beef	$2	$4

In year 1, beef is twice as expensive as fish. This is the price of beef *relative* to the price of fish. In year 2, beef is still twice as expensive as fish. The relative prices have not changed between years 1 and 2. What has changed? The prices of both beef and fish

© froxx/Shutterstock.com

have doubled. The *absolute* levels of all prices have gone up, but because they have increased by the same percentage, the relative prices are unchanged.

Inflation measures changes in absolute prices. In our example, all prices doubled, so the inflation rate is 100 percent. There was a 100 percent increase in the prices of beef and fish. In reality, inflation does not take place evenly throughout the economy. Prices of some goods rise faster than others, which means that relative prices are changing at the same time that absolute prices are rising. The measured inflation rate records the *average* change in absolute prices.

3.b. Effects of Inflation

To understand the effects of inflation, you have to understand what happens to the value of money in an inflationary period. The real value of money is what it can buy, its *purchasing power*:

> The purchasing power of a dollar is the amount of goods and services it can buy.

$$\text{Real value of } \$1 = \frac{\$1}{\text{price level}}$$

The higher the price level, the lower the real value (or *purchasing power*) of the dollar. For instance, suppose an economy had only one good—milk. If a glass of milk sold for $.50, then $1 would buy two glasses of milk. If the price of milk rose to $1, then a dollar would buy only one glass of milk. The purchasing power, or real value, of money falls as prices rise.

Table 4 lists the real value of the dollar in selected years from 1946 to 2010. The price level in each year is measured relative to the average level of prices over the 1982–1984 period. For instance, the 1946 value, 0.195, means that prices in 1946 were, on average, only 19.5 percent of prices in the 1982–1984 period. Notice that as prices go up, the purchasing power of the dollar falls. In 1946, a dollar bought five times as much as it bought in the early 1980s. The value 5.13 means that one could buy 5.13 times as many goods and services with a dollar in 1946 as one could buy in 1982–1984.

Prices have risen steadily in recent decades. By 2010, they had risen to more than 100 percent above the average level of prices in the 1982–1984 period. Consequently, the purchasing power of a 2010 dollar was lower. In 2010, $1 bought just 46 percent of the goods and services that one could buy with a dollar in 1982–1984.

If prices and nominal income rise by the same percentage, it might seem that inflation is not a problem. It doesn't matter if it takes twice as many dollars to buy fish and beef now than it did before if we have twice as many dollars of income available to buy the products. Obviously, inflation is very much a problem when a household's nominal income rises at a slower rate than prices. Inflation hurts those households whose income does not keep up with the prices of the goods they buy.

In the 1970s, the rate of inflation in the United States rose to near-record levels. Many workers believed that their incomes were lagging behind the rate of inflation, so they negotiated cost-of-living raises in their wage contracts. The typical cost-of living raise ties salary to changes in the consumer price index. If the CPI rises 8 percent during a year, workers receive an 8 percent raise plus compensation for experience or productivity increases. As the U.S. rate of inflation fell during the 1980s, concern about cost-of-living raises subsided as well.

It is important to distinguish between expected and unexpected inflation. *Unexpectedly high inflation* redistributes income away from those who receive fixed incomes (like creditors who receive debt repayments of a fixed amount of dollars per month) and toward those who make fixed expenditures (like debtors who make fixed debt repayments per month). For example, consider a simple loan agreement:

> Unexpectedly high inflation redistributes income away from those who receive fixed incomes and toward those who make fixed expenditures.

TABLE 4	The Real Value of a Dollar	
Year	**Average Price Level[1]**	**Purchasing Power Power of a Dollar[2]**
1946	0.195	5.13
1950	0.241	4.15
1954	0.269	3.72
1958	0.289	3.46
1962	0.302	3.31
1966	0.324	3.09
1970	0.388	2.58
1974	0.493	2.03
1978	0.652	1.53
1982	0.965	1.04
1986	1.096	0.91
1990	1.307	0.77
1994	1.482	0.67
1998	1.63	0.61
2002	1.809	0.55
2006	2.016	0.50
2008	2.153	0.46
2009	2.145	0.47
2010	2.181	0.46

[1]Measured by the consumer price index as given at http://www.bls.gov/cpi/.
[2]Found by taking the reciprocal of the consumer price index (1/CPI).

Maria borrows $100 from Ali, promising to repay the loan in one year at 10 percent interest. One year from now, Maria will pay Ali $110—principal of $100 plus interest of $10 (10 percent of $100, or $10).

When Maria and Ali agree to the terms of the loan, they do so with some expected rate of inflation in mind. Suppose they both expect 5 percent inflation over the year. In other words, they expect that one year from now, it will take 5 percent more money to buy goods than it does now. Ali will need $105 to buy what $100 buys today. Because Ali will receive $110 for the principal and interest on the loan, he will gain purchasing power. However, if the inflation rate over the year turns out to be surprisingly high—say, 15 percent—then Ali will need $115 to buy what $100 buys today. He will lose purchasing power if he makes a loan at a 10 percent rate of interest.

nominal interest rate
The observed interest rate in the market.

real interest rate
The nominal interest rate minus the rate of inflation.

Economists distinguish between nominal and real interest rates when analyzing economic behavior. The **nominal interest rate** is the observed interest rate in the market and includes the effect of inflation. The **real interest rate** is the nominal interest rate minus the rate of inflation:

Real interest rate = nominal interest rate − rate of inflation

Real interest rates are lower than expected when inflation is higher than expected.

If Ali charges Maria a 10 percent nominal interest rate and the inflation rate is 5 percent, the real interest rate is 5 percent (10% − 5% = 5%). This means that Ali will earn a positive real return from the loan. However, if the inflation rate is 10 percent, the real return from a nominal interest rate of 10 percent is zero (10% – 10% = 0). The interest that Ali will receive from the loan will just compensate him for the rise in prices; he will not realize an increase in purchasing power. If the inflation rate is higher than the nominal interest rate, then the real interest rate is negative—the lender will lose purchasing power by making the loan.

Now you can see how unexpected inflation redistributes income. Borrowers and creditors agree to loan terms based on what they *expect* the rate of inflation to be over the period of the loan. If the *actual* rate of inflation turns out to be different from what was expected, then the real interest rate paid by the borrower and received by the lender will be different from what was expected. If Ali and Maria both expect a 5 percent inflation rate and agree to a 10 percent nominal interest rate for the loan, then they both expect a real interest rate of 5 percent (10% – 5% = 5%) to be paid on the loan. If the actual inflation rate turns out to be greater than 5 percent, then the real interest rate will be less than expected. Maria will get to borrow Ali's money at a lower real cost than she expected, and Ali will earn a lower real return than he expected. Unexpectedly high inflation hurts creditors and benefits borrowers because it lowers real interest rates.

Figure 4 shows the real interest rates on U.S. Treasury bills from 1970 through 2010. You can see a pronounced pattern in the graph. In the late 1970s, there was a period of negative real interest rates, followed by high positive real rates in the 1980s. The evidence suggests that nominal interest rates did not rise fast enough in the 1970s to offset high inflation. This was a time of severe strain for many creditors, including savings and loan associations and banks. These firms had lent funds at fixed nominal rates of interest. When those rates of interest turned out to be lower than the rate of inflation, the

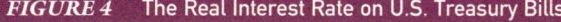

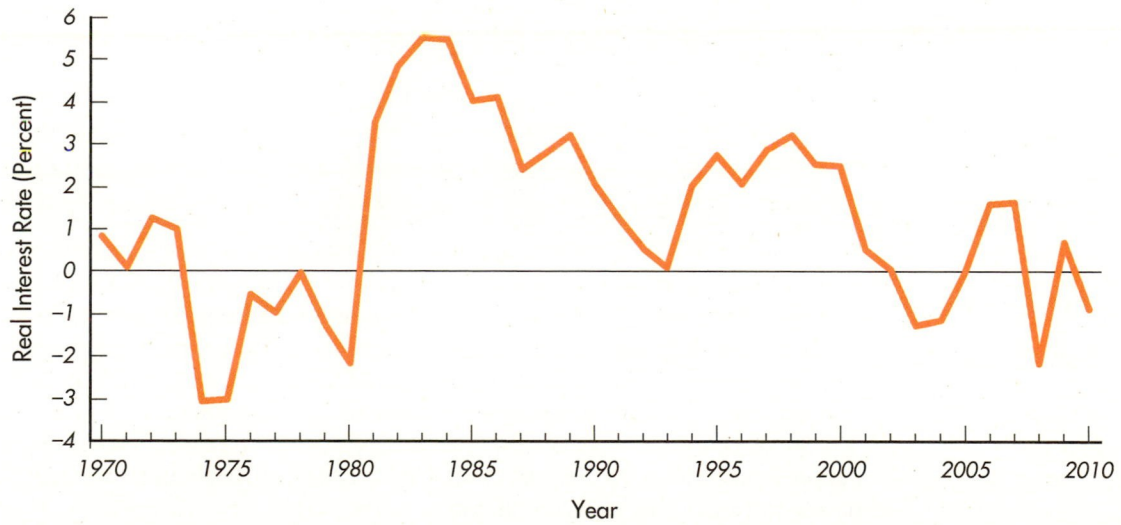

FIGURE 4   The Real Interest Rate on U.S. Treasury Bills

The real interest rate is the difference between the nominal interest rate (the interest rate actually observed) and the rate of inflation over the life of the bond. The figure shows the real interest rate in June and December for each year. For instance, in the first observation, for June 1970, a six-month Treasury bill paid the holder 6.91 percent interest. This is the nominal rate of interest. To find the real rate of interest on the bond, we subtract the rate of inflation that existed over the six months of the bond's life (June to December 1970), which was 5.17 percent. The difference between the nominal interest rate (6.91 percent) and the rate of inflation (5.17 percent) is the real interest rate, 1.74 percent. Notice that real interest rates were negative during most of the 1970s and then turned highly positive (by historical standards) in the early 1980s.

financial institutions suffered significant losses. In the early 1980s, the inflation rate dropped sharply. Because nominal interest rates did not drop nearly as fast as the rate of inflation, real interest rates were high. In this period, many debtors were hurt by the high costs of borrowing to finance business or household expenditures.

Unexpected inflation affects more than the two parties to a loan. Any contract calling for fixed payments over some long-term period changes in value as the rate of inflation changes. For instance, a long-term contract that provides union members with 5 percent raises each year for five years gives the workers more purchasing power if inflation is low than if it is high. Similarly, a contract to sell a product at a fixed price over a long-term period will change in value as inflation changes. Suppose a lumber company promises to supply a builder with lumber at a fixed price for a two-year period. If the rate of inflation in one year turns out to be higher than expected, the lumber company will end up selling the lumber for less profit than it had planned. Inflation raises the lumber company's costs. Usually the company would raise its prices to compensate for the higher costs. Because the company contracted to sell its goods to the builder at a fixed price, however, the builder benefits at the lumber company's expense. Again, unexpectedly high inflation redistributes real income or purchasing power away from those receiving fixed payments to those making fixed payments.

One response to the effects of unexpected inflation is to allow prices, wages, or interest rates to vary with the rate of inflation. Labor unions sometimes negotiate cost-of-living adjustments as part of new wage contracts. Financial institutions offer variable interest rates on home mortgages to reflect current market conditions. Any contract can be written to adjust dollar amounts over time as the rate of inflation changes.

3.c. Types of Inflation

Economists often classify inflation according to the source of the inflationary pressure. The most straightforward method defines inflation in terms of pressure from the demand side of the market or the supply side of the market:

> *Demand-pull inflation* Increases in total spending that are not offset by increases in the supply of goods and services and so cause the average level of prices to rise

> *Cost-push inflation* Increases in production costs that cause firms to raise prices to avoid losses

Sometimes inflation is blamed on "too many dollars chasing too few goods." This is a roundabout way of saying that the inflation stems from demand pressures. Because demand-pull inflation is a product of increased spending, it is more likely to occur in an economy that is producing at maximum capacity. If resources are fully employed, it may not be possible in the short run to increase output to meet increased demand. The result: Existing goods and services are rationed by rising prices.

Some economists claim that the rising prices in the late 1960s were a product of demand-pull inflation. They believe that increased government spending for the Vietnam War caused the level of U.S. prices to rise.

Cost-push inflation can occur in any economy, whatever its output. If prices go up because the costs of resources are rising, the rate of inflation can go up regardless of demand. For example, some economists argue that the inflation in the United States in the 1970s was largely the result of rising oil prices. This means that decreases in the oil supply (a shift to the left in the supply curve) brought about higher oil prices. Because oil is so important in the production of many goods, higher oil prices led to increases in prices throughout the economy. Cost-push inflation stems from changes in the supply side of the market.

Cost-push inflation is sometimes attributed to profit-push or wage-push pressures. *Profit-push pressures* are created by suppliers who want to increase their profit margins by raising prices faster than their costs increase. *Wage-push pressures* are created by labor unions and workers who are able to increase their wages faster than their productivity. There have been times when "greedy" businesses and unions have been blamed for periods of inflation in the United States. The problem with these "theories" is that people have always wanted to improve their economic status and always will. In this sense, people have always been greedy. But inflation has not always been a problem. Were people less greedy in the early 1980s, when inflation was low, than they were in the late 1970s, when inflation was high? Obviously, we have to look for other reasons to explain inflation. We discuss some of those reasons in later chapters.

3.d. The Inflationary Record

Many of our students, having always lived with inflation, are surprised to learn that it is a relatively new problem for the United States. From 1789, when the U.S. Constitution was ratified, until 1940, there was no particular trend in the general price level. At times prices rose, and at times they fell. The average level of prices in 1940 was approximately the same as it was in the late eighteenth century.

Since 1940, prices in the United States have gone up markedly. The price level today is eight times what it was in 1940. But the rate of growth has varied.

Annual rates of inflation for several industrial and developing nations in 2009 are shown in Table 5. Look at the diversity across countries: Rates range from deflations of −1.4 percent in Japan to 13.4 percent inflation in high-inflation nations like Zambia.

Hyperinflation is an extremely high rate of inflation. In most cases, hyperinflation eventually makes a country's currency worthless and leads to the introduction of a new money. Argentina experienced hyperinflation in the 1980s. People had to carry large stacks of currency for small purchases. Cash registers and calculators ran out of digits as prices reached ridiculously high levels. After years of high inflation, Argentina replaced the old peso with the peso Argentino in June 1983. The government set the value of 1 peso Argentino equal to 10,000 old pesos (striking four zeros from all prices). A product that had sold for 10,000 old pesos before the reform sold for 1 new peso after. But Argentina did not follow up its monetary reform with a noninflationary change in economic policy. In 1984 and 1985, the inflation rate exceeded 600 percent each year. As a result, in June 1985, the government again introduced a new currency, the austral, setting its value at 1,000 pesos Argentino. However, the economic policy associated with the introduction of the austral lowered the inflation rate only temporarily. By 1988, the inflation rate was over 300 percent, and in 1989 the inflation rate was over 3,000 percent. The rapid rise in prices associated with the austral resulted in the introduction of yet another currency, again named the peso Argentino, in January 1992, with a value equal to 10,000 australes. This new peso was fixed at a value of 1 peso per 1 U.S. dollar, and this exchange rate lasted for about 10 years because of reasonably stable inflation in Argentina. In late 2001, Argentina experienced another financial crisis brought on by large government budget deficits; the fixed rate of exchange between the peso and the dollar ended, but the peso remained the currency of Argentina.

The most dramatic hyperinflation in recent years, and one of the most dramatic ever, occurred in Zimbabwe in 2007–2008. Although the government was not forthcoming about inflation data, research[1] indicates that the price index rose from a value of

hyperinflation
An extremely high rate of inflation.

[1] Steve H. Hanke, "R.I.P. Zimbabwe Dollar," www.cato.org/zimbabwe.

Country Selected Industrial	Inflation Rate (percent)
Canada	0.3
Germany	0.3
Italy	0.8
Japan	−1.4
United Kingdom	−0.6
United States	−0.4
Selected Developing	
Botswana	8.0
Brazil	4.9
Egypt	11.8
Hong Kong, China	0.6
India	10.9
Israel	3.3
Mexico	5.3
Philippines	3.2
Poland	3.8
South Africa	7.1
Tajikistan	6.4
Zambia	13.4

TABLE 5 Rates of Inflation for Selected Countries, 2009

Source: Data are average annual percentage changes in the GDP price index as reported by the World Bank; http://databank.worldbank.org/.

1.00 in January 2007 to 853,000,000,000,000,000,000,000,000 by mid-November 2008, when the price level was doubling every 24 hours. As prices rose, the government issued larger and larger units of paper money as people had to carry huge stacks of old currency to buy anything. A 100 trillion Zimbabwe dollar bill was issued in January 2009. Then in the same month, the government sanctioned the use of U.S. dollars as a substitute currency in Zimbabwe as the local currency had become essentially worthless.

Table 6 provides data on the other recent cases of hyperinflation. The Zimbabwe episode lasted 26 months until the U.S. dollar was sanctioned as a substitute currency. The hyperinflation episodes in Table 6 range in duration from only 3 months in Turkmenistan, when prices rose by 291 percent, to 58 months in Nicaragua, when prices rose an astounding 11,895,866,143 percent. Hyperinflation is often associated with crises that lead to new governments, new economic policies, and new monies that replace the essentially worthless old money.

In later chapters, we will see how high rates of inflation generally are caused by rapid growth of the money supply. When a central government wants to spend more than it is capable of funding through taxation or borrowing, it simply issues money to finance its budget deficit. As the money supply increases faster than the demand to hold it, spending increases and prices go up.

TABLE 6	Recent Hyperinflations		
Country	Dates	Months Duration	Cumulative Inflation (percent)
Angola	Dec. 94–Jun. 96	19	62,445
Argentina	May 89–Mar. 90	11	15,167
Armenia	Oct. 93–Dec. 94	15	34,158
Azerbaijan	Dec. 92–Dec. 94	25	41,742
Bolivia	Apr. 84–Sep. 85	18	97,282
Brazil	Dec. 89–Mar. 90	4	693
Congo, Dem. Rep.	Nov. 93–Sep. 94	11	69,502
Georgia	Sep. 93–Sep. 94	13	76,219
Nicaragua	Jun. 86–Mar. 91	58	11,895,866,143
Serbia	Feb. 93–Jan. 94	12	156,312,790
Tajikistan	Aug. 93–Dec. 93	9	3,636
Turkmenistan	Nov. 95–Jan. 96	3	291
Ukraine	Apr. 91–Nov. 94	44	1,864,715

Source: Stanley Fischer, Ratna Sahay, and Carlos A. Vegh, "Modern Hyper- and High Inflations," *Journal of Economic Literature*, September 2002, pp. 837–880.

RECAP

1. Inflation is a sustained rise in the average level of prices.

2. The higher the price level, the lower the real value (purchasing power) of money.

3. Unexpectedly high inflation redistributes income away from those who receive fixed-dollar payments (like creditors) and toward those who make fixed-dollar payments (like debtors).

4. The real interest rate is the nominal interest rate minus the rate of inflation.

5. Demand-pull inflation is a product of increased spending; cost-push inflation reflects increased production costs.

6. Hyperinflation is a very high rate of inflation that often results in the introduction of a new currency.

SUMMARY

1. **What is a business cycle?**

- Business cycles are recurring changes in real GDP, in which expansion is followed by contraction. *§1.a*

- The four stages of the business cycle are expansion (boom), peak, contraction (recession), and trough. *§1.a*

- Leading, coincident, and lagging indicators are variables that change in relation to changes in output. *§1.c*

2. **How is the unemployment rate defined and measured?**

- The unemployment rate is the percentage of the labor force that is not working. *§2.a*

- To be in the U.S. labor force, an individual must be working or actively seeking work. *§2.a*

- Unemployment can be classified as seasonal, frictional, structural, or cyclical. *§2.c*

- Frictional and structural unemployment are always present in a dynamic economy; cyclical unemployment is a product of recession. *§2.c*

3. What is the cost of unemployed resources?

- The GDP gap measures the output lost because of unemployment. *§2.d*

4. What is inflation?

- Inflation is a sustained rise in the average level of prices. *§3*

- The higher the level of prices, the lower the purchasing power of money. *§3.b*

5. Why is inflation a problem?

- Inflation becomes a problem when income rises at a slower rate than prices. *§3.b*

- Unexpectedly high inflation hurts those who receive fixed-dollar payments (like creditors) and benefits those who make fixed-dollar payments (like debtors). *§3.b*

- Inflation can stem from demand-pull or cost-push pressures. *§3.c*

- Hyperinflation—an extremely high rate of inflation—can force a country to introduce a new currency. *§3.d*

KEY TERMS

business cycle, 129
coincident indicator, 132
depression, 130
discouraged workers, 134
hyperinflation, 147

inflation, 142
lagging indicator, 133
leading indicator, 132
natural rate of unemployment, 136
nominal interest rate, 144

potential real GDP, 136
real interest rate, 144
recession, 129
underemployment, 135
unemployment rate, 134

EXERCISES

1. What is the labor force? Do you believe that the U.S. government's definition of the labor force is a good one—that it includes all the people it should include? Explain your answer.
2. List the reasons why the official unemployment rate may not reflect the true social burden of unemployment. Explain whether the official numbers overstate or understate *true* unemployment in light of each reason you discuss.
3. Suppose you are able-bodied and intelligent, but lazy. You'd rather sit home and watch television than work, even though you know you could find an acceptable job if you looked.
   a. Are you officially unemployed?
   b. Are you a discouraged worker?
4. Can government do anything to reduce the number of people in the following categories? If so, what?
   a. Frictionally unemployed
   b. Structurally unemployed
   c. Cyclically unemployed
5. Does the GDP gap measure all of the costs of unemployment? Why or why not?
6. Why do teenagers have the highest unemployment rate in the economy?
7. Suppose you are currently earning $15 an hour. If the inflation rate over the current year is 10 percent and your firm provides a cost-of-living raise based on the rate of inflation, what would you expect to earn after your raise? If the cost-of-living raise is always granted on the basis of the past year's inflation, is your nominal income really keeping up with the cost of living?
8. Write an equation that defines the real interest rate. Use the equation to explain why unexpectedly high inflation redistributes income from creditors to debtors.
9. Many home mortgages in recent years have been made with variable interest rates. Typically, the interest rate is adjusted once a year on the basis of current interest rates on government bonds. How do variable interest rate loans protect creditors from the effects of unexpected inflation?
10. The word *cycle* suggests a regular, recurring pattern of activity. Is there a regular pattern to the business cycle? Support your answer by examining the duration (number of months) of each expansion and contraction in Figure 1.

11. Using the list of leading indicators in Table 1, write a brief paragraph explaining why each variable changes before real output changes. In other words, provide an economic reason why each indicator is expected to lead the business cycle.

12. Suppose 500 people were surveyed, and of those 500, 450 were working full time. Of the 50 not working, 10 were full-time college students, 18 were retired, 5 were under 16 years of age, 7 had stopped looking for work because they believed there were no jobs for them, and 10 were actively looking for work.
    a. How many of the 500 surveyed are in the labor force?
    b. What is the unemployment rate among the 500 surveyed people?

13. Consider the following price information:

	Year 1	Year 2
Cup of coffee	$ .50	$1.00
Glass of milk	$1.00	$2.00

    a. Based on the information given, what was the inflation rate between year 1 and year 2?
    b. What happened to the price of coffee relative to that of milk between year 1 and year 2?

14. Use a supply and demand diagram to illustrate:
    a. Cost-push inflation caused by a labor union successfully negotiating for a higher wage.
    b. Demand-pull inflation caused by an increase in demand for domestic products from foreign buyers.

15. During the Bolivian hyperinflation in the 1980s, Bolivians used U.S. dollars as a substitute for the domestic currency (the peso) for many transactions. Explain how the value of money is affected by hyperinflation and the incentives to use a low-inflation currency like the dollar as a substitute for a high-inflation currency like the Bolivian peso.

16. Suppose the government raises the benefits available to unemployed workers and then discovers that the number of unemployed workers has increased substantially, although there has been no other change in the economy. How can government policies aimed at helping the unemployed actually create more unemployment?

17. Toward the end of the recent recession, the economy was characterized by a "jobless recovery"—output and hours worked were rising, but employment was not. Explain what may have been happening.

You can find further practice tests in the Online Quiz at **www.cengage.com/economics/boyes**.

OLDER WORKERS AND THE RECESSION

San Diego Union-Tribune, December 8, 2008

Last week's triple dose of grim employment news stirred memories of the early 1980s. Made official on Monday, the current recession has already outlasted any downturn since 1982.... Friday's sock to the solar plexus? The economy lost 533,000 jobs last month, the largest monthly decline since 1974.

It gets worse. For older workers, this recession is unprecedented. Last month, 298,000 Americans ages 65 and older were unemployed, 50 percent more than when the recession began a year ago.

During previous downturns, relatively few older Americans were counted as unemployed. Although many lost their jobs, they generally retired instead of looking for work. During the severe 1981–82 recession, seniors' unemployment rate grew by just 0.8 percentage points—only about one-fourth the increase for prime-age workers (25 to 54).

Today, however, seniors are nearly as likely as their juniors to join unemployment lines, because pink-slipped seniors can no longer afford to put their feet up. Shrinking Social Security benefits, traditional pension plans, and 401(k) balances combine with soaring health care costs to force them to keep pounding the pavement.

Rising medical expenses, which consume 15 percent of older people's budgets, can also jinx retirement. And only one in three large private employers offers retiree health benefits to supplement Medicare, compared with two in three in the 1980s. Meanwhile, Medicare's new drug benefit has barely dented seniors' out-of-pocket spending.

Whipsawed by these trends, it's no surprise that three in 10 Americans ages 65 to 69 were working or jobhunting in 2007, up from two in 10 in 1982. Paychecks provided nearly one-fifth of this group's income in 2006.

The stock market shed about half its value over the past 14 months, destroying $2.8 trillion in 401(k) and individual retirement accounts and intensifying pressure on seniors to work. Older Americans have been hit hardest because those 50 and older hold nearly three-quarters of these assets. (During the 1981–82 recession, the S&P 500 index fell by only 6 percent.)

California should do more to help. Other states already train career center staff on the special challenges older workers face, certify employers friendly to mature workers, develop the entrepreneurial skills of older dislocated workers, and create Web sites for older job-seekers.

It's also time for a federal stimulus package committing billions of dollars to rebuilding our crumbling infrastructure. That's a sure way to create jobs, some of them for seniors.

Budgets are tight. But investing in getting willing-and-able seniors back to work would boost the nation's output, spur spending, get the economy back on track and ease the recession's toll on our oldest workers, most of whom have done their bit for their families and the economy for decades.

RICHARD W. JOHNSON,
THE URBAN INSTITUTE

The article says that the recession in 2008 had created many more unemployed older workers than in prior recessions. Partly, this is because people retired at earlier ages in past decades but now, due to longer life expectancy as well as delayed and smaller retirement benefits, older workers remain in the labor force seeking jobs. Should we expect older workers to have an easier or tougher time finding a job than younger workers? What does economics have to say about why older workers might find it harder to find new jobs than younger workers? The answer lies in the type of knowledge that workers possess that may make them attractive to certain employers.

Many newly unemployed workers have worked for many years and have earned higher salaries than they can expect to earn in other jobs. This, of course, is the problem. If they could simply find another job that offered them comparable pay, they would not be so devastated by the prospect of losing their jobs. This raises an interesting question: If someone is highly valued at one firm and paid accordingly, why isn't that person as valuable to other companies who could now hire her or him? In fact, laid-off workers with successful job histories at one firm are often unable to meet entry-level requirements at other jobs.

We can better understand the causes of the plight of many laid-off industrial workers if we consider the determinants of people's wages. Economic theory suggests that people's wages are tied to the amount they contribute to their firm, which implies that people's wages increase with their skills. We can think of two broad categories of skills:

general skills that make people valuable to any firm, and more specialized skills that make people valuable to certain firms. Examples of general skills include welding, bookkeeping, and an ability to manage people. Skills that are useful to only one firm are those that are specifically tied to the product or structure of that firm. Specific knowledge of this second type is not transferable to other firms.

People who work in a particular firm for an extended period learn both general skills that make them valuable to any similar company and specific skills that make them valuable to their company only. Experienced workers who are seeking new jobs must possess or else learn general skills that make them attractive in an economy with rapid technological change.

The distinction between general and firm-specific skills suggests why the workers who are least likely to benefit from retraining are those within a few years of retirement. Older workers who must undergo on-the-job training will not be able to use their new firm-specific skills for as many years as younger workers will. It is not worthwhile for firms to hire and train workers who are near retirement.

Structural change is an integral part of a dynamic, growing economy. Dislocations are probably inevitable when large-scale structural change occurs, and these dislocations benefit some people while hurting others. Although retraining helps mitigate some of the effects of the upheaval that accompanies structural change, unfortunately it cannot solve all the problems that arise. For the economy as a whole, such change is necessary. Unfortunately, some people are always harmed when the economy undergoes structural change.

CHAPTER 8

Macroeconomic Equilibrium: Aggregate Demand and Supply

❓❓ FUNDAMENTAL QUESTIONS

1 What factors affect aggregate demand?

2 What causes the aggregate demand curve to shift?

3 What factors affect aggregate supply?

4 Why does the short-run aggregate supply curve become steeper as real GDP increases?

5 Why is the long-run aggregate supply curve vertical?

6 What causes the aggregate supply curve to shift?

7 What determines the equilibrium price level and real GDP?

Total output and income in the United States have grown over time. Each generation has experienced a higher standard of living than the previous generation. Yet, as we learned in the chapter titled "Unemployment and Inflation," economic growth has not been steady. Economies go through periods of expansion followed by periods of contraction or recession, and such business cycles have major impacts on people's lives, incomes, and living standards.

Economic stagnation and recession throw many, often those who are already relatively poor, out of their jobs and into real poverty. Economic growth increases the number of jobs and draws people out of poverty and into the mainstream of economic progress. To understand why economies grow and why they go through cycles, we must discover why firms decide to produce more or less and why buyers decide to buy more or less. The approach we take is similar to the approach we followed in the first five chapters of the text, using demand and supply curves. In the chapter titled "Markets, Demand and Supply, and the Price System" and the chapter titled "The Market System and the Private and Public Sectors," we derived demand and supply curves and used them to examine questions involving the equilibrium price and quantities demanded and supplied of a single good or service. This simple yet powerful microeconomic technique of analysis has a macroeconomic counterpart: aggregate demand and aggregate supply, which are used to determine an equilibrium price level and quantity of goods and services produced for the *entire economy*. In this chapter we shall use aggregate demand and supply curves to illustrate the causes of business cycles and economic growth.

1. Aggregate Demand, Aggregate Supply, and Business Cycles

What causes economic growth and business cycles? We can provide some answers to this important question using aggregate demand (AD) and aggregate supply (AS) curves. Suppose we represent the economy with a simple demand and supply diagram, as shown in Figure 1. Aggregate demand represents the total spending in the economy at alternative price levels. Aggregate supply represents the total output of the economy at alternative price levels. To understand the causes of business cycles and inflation, we must understand how aggregate demand and aggregate supply cause the equilibrium price level and real GDP, the nation's output of goods and services, to change. The intersection between the AD and AS curves defines the equilibrium level of real GDP and level of prices. The equilibrium price level is P_e, and the equilibrium level of real GDP is Y_e. This price and output level represents the level of prices and output for some particular period of time, say 2010. Once that equilibrium is established, there is no tendency for prices and output to change until changes occur in either the aggregate demand curve or the aggregate supply curve. Let's first consider a change in aggregate demand and then look at a change in aggregate supply.

1.a. Aggregate Demand and Business Cycles

An increase in aggregate demand is illustrated by a shift of the AD curve to the right, like the shift from AD_1 to AD_2 in Figure 2. This represents a situation in which buyers are buying more at every price level. The shift causes the equilibrium level of real GDP to rise from Y_{e1} to Y_{e2}, illustrating the expansionary phase of the business cycle. As output rises, unemployment decreases. The increase in aggregate demand also leads to a higher price level, as shown by the change in the price level from P_{e1} to P_{e2}. The increase in the price level represents an example of **demand-pull inflation**, which is inflation caused by increasing demand for output.

demand-pull inflation
Inflation caused by increasing demand for output.

If aggregate demand falls, like the shift from AD_1 to AD_3, then there is a lower equilibrium level of real GDP, Y_{e3}. In this case, buyers are buying *less* at every price level. The drop in real GDP caused by lower demand would represent an economic slowdown or a recession when output falls and unemployment rises.

Technology advance shifts the aggregate supply curve outward and increases output. An example of a technological advance that has increased efficiency in the airline industry is the self check-in kiosk. This allows the airlines to lower costs, as customers do not require an airline employee for assistance.

1.b. Aggregate Supply and Business Cycles

Changes in aggregate supply can also cause business cycles. Figure 3 illustrates what happens when aggregate supply changes. An increase in aggregate supply is illustrated by the shift from AS_1 to AS_2, leading to an increase in the equilibrium level of real GDP from Y_{e1} to Y_{e2}. An increase in aggregate supply comes about when firms produce more at every price level. Such an increase could result from an improvement in technology or a decrease in the costs of production.

If aggregate supply decreases, as in the shift from AS_1 to AS_3, then the equilibrium level of real GDP would fall to Y_{e3} and the equilibrium price level would increase from P_{e1} to P_{e3}. A decrease in aggregate supply could be caused by higher production costs that lead producers to raise their prices. This is an example of **cost-push inflation**—where the price level rises as a result of increased costs of production and the associated decrease in aggregate supply.

cost-push inflation

Inflation caused by rising costs of production.

FIGURE 1   Aggregate Demand and Aggregate Supply Equilibrium

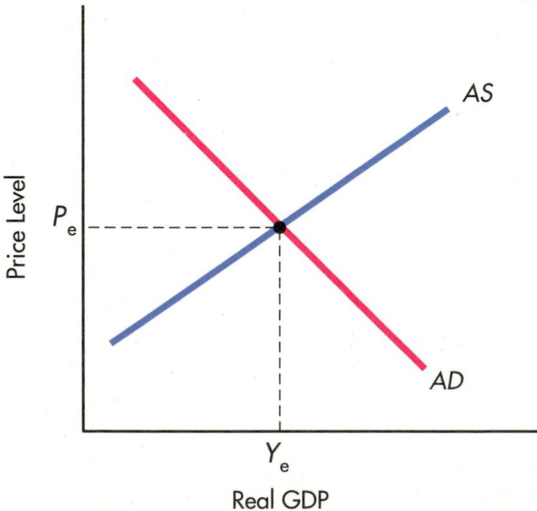

The equilibrium price level and real GDP are determined by the intersection of the *AD* and *AS* curves.

FIGURE 2   Effects of a Change in Aggregate Demand

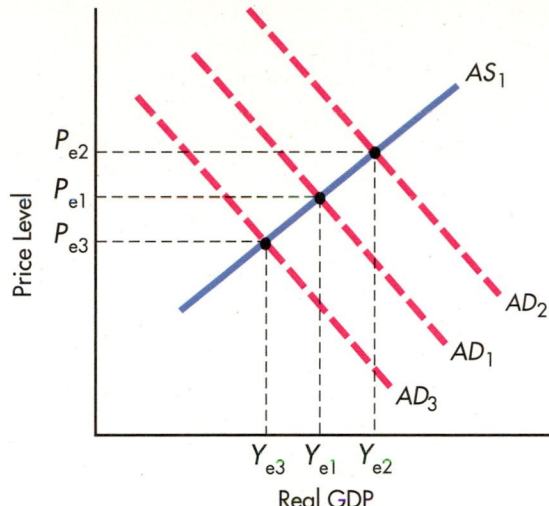

If aggregate demand increases from AD_1 to AD_2, the equilibrium price level increases to P_{e2} and the equilibrium level of real GDP rises to Y_{e2}. If aggregate demand decreases from AD_1 to AD_3, the equilibrium price level falls to P_{e3} and the equilibrium level of real GDP drops to Y_{e3}.

FIGURE 3   Effects of a Change in Aggregate Supply

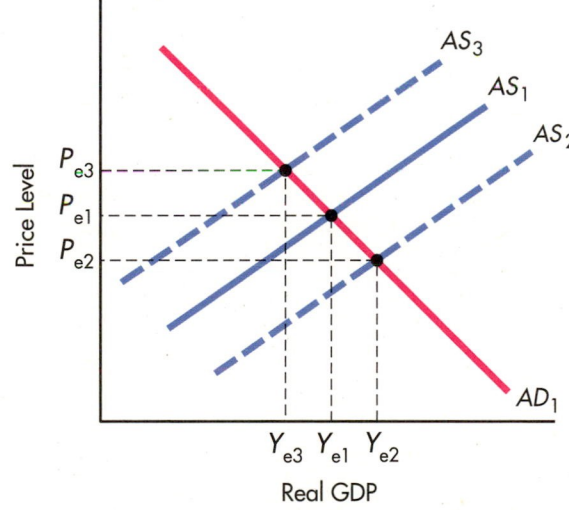

If aggregate supply increases from AS_1 to AS_2, the equilibrium price level falls from P_{e1} to P_{e2} and the equilibrium level of real GDP rises to Y_{e2}. If aggregate supply decreases from AS_1 to AS_3, the equilibrium price level rises to P_{e3} and the equilibrium level of real GDP falls to Y_{e3}.

1.c. A Look Ahead

Business cycles result from changes in aggregate demand, from changes in aggregate supply, and from changes in both *AD* and *AS*. The degree to which real GDP declines during a recession or increases during an expansion depends on the amount by which the *AD* and/or *AS* curves shift. The degree to which an expansion produces output growth or increased inflation depends on the shapes of the *AD* and *AS* curves. We need to consider why the curves have the shapes they do, and what causes them to shift.

The comparison we made earlier, between aggregate demand, aggregate supply, and their microeconomic counterparts, the supply and demand curves, is only superficial. As we examine the aggregate demand and supply curves, you will see that the reasons underlying the shapes and movements of *AD* and *AS* are in fact quite different from those explaining the shapes and movements of the supply and demand curves.

RECAP

1. Aggregate demand (*AD*) represents the total spending in the economy at alternative price levels.

2. Aggregate supply (*AS*) represents the total output of the economy at alternative price levels.

3. The intersection between the *AD* and *AS* curves defines the equilibrium level of real GDP and the level of prices.

4. Business cycles result from changes in *AD* and/or *AS*.

2. Factors That Influence Aggregate Demand

1 What factors affect aggregate demand?

Aggregate demand is the relation between aggregate expenditures, or total spending, and the price level. Aggregate expenditures are the sum of the expenditures of each sector of the economy: households (consumption), business firms (investment), government, and the rest of the world (net exports). Each sector of the economy has different reasons for spending; for instance, household spending depends heavily on household income, whereas business spending depends on the profits that businesses expect to earn. Because each sector of the economy has a different reason for the amount of spending it undertakes, aggregate spending depends on all of these reasons. To understand aggregate demand, therefore, requires that we look at the factors that influence the expenditures of each sector of the economy.

2.a. Consumption

How much households spend depends on their income, their wealth, expectations about future prices and incomes, demographics like the age distribution of the population, and taxes.

- Income: If current income rises, households purchase more goods and services.
- Wealth: Wealth is different from income. It is the value of the assets owned by a household, including homes, cars, bank deposits, stocks, and bonds. An increase in household wealth will increase consumption.
- Expectations: Expectations regarding future changes in income or wealth can affect consumption today. If households expect a recession and worry about job loss, consumption tends to fall. On the other hand, if households become more optimistic regarding future increases in income and wealth, consumption rises today.
- Demographics: Demographic change can affect consumption in several different ways. Population growth is generally associated with higher consumption for an economy. Younger households and older households generally consume more and save less than middle-aged households. Therefore, as the age distribution of a nation changes, so will consumption.

- Taxes: Higher taxes will lower the disposable income of households and decrease consumption, while lower taxes will raise disposable income and increase consumption. Government policy may change taxes and thereby bring about a change in consumption.

2.b. Investment

Investment is business spending on capital goods and inventories. In general, investment depends on the expected profitability of such spending, so any factor that could affect profitability will be a determinant of investment. Factors affecting the expected profitability of business projects include the interest rate, technology, the cost of capital goods, and capacity utilization.

- Interest rate: Investment is negatively related to the interest rate. The interest rate is the cost of borrowed funds. The greater the cost of borrowing, other things being equal, the fewer the investment projects that offer sufficient profit to be undertaken. As the interest rate falls, investment is stimulated, as the cost of financing the investment is lowered.
- Technology: New production technology stimulates investment spending, as firms are forced to adopt new production methods to stay competitive.
- Cost of capital goods: If machines and equipment purchased by firms rise in price, then the higher costs associated with investment will lower profitability, and investment will fall.
- Capacity utilization: The more excess capacity (unused capital goods) there is available, the more firms can expand production without purchasing new capital goods, and the lower investment will be. As firms approach full capacity, more investment spending will be required to expand output further.

2.c. Government Spending

Government spending may be set by government authorities independent of current income or other determinants of aggregate expenditures.

2.d. Net Exports

Net exports are equal to exports minus imports. We assume that exports are determined by conditions in the rest of the world, such as foreign income, tastes, prices, exchange rates, and government policy. Imports are determined by similar domestic factors.

- Income: As domestic income rises and consumption rises, some of this consumption includes goods produced in other countries. Therefore, as domestic income rises, imports rise and net exports fall. Similarly, as foreign income rises, foreign residents buy more domestic goods, and net exports rise.
- Prices: Other things being equal, higher (lower) foreign prices make domestic goods relatively cheaper (more expensive) and increase (decrease) net exports. Higher (lower) domestic prices make domestic goods relatively more expensive (cheaper) and decrease (increase) net exports.
- Exchange rates: Other things being equal, a depreciation of the domestic currency on the foreign exchange market will make domestic goods cheaper to foreign buyers and make foreign goods more expensive to domestic buyers, so that net exports will rise. An appreciation of the domestic currency will have just the opposite effects.
- Government policy: Net exports may fall if foreign governments restrict the entry of domestic goods into their countries, reducing domestic exports. If the domestic government restricts imports into the domestic economy, net exports may rise.

2.e. Aggregate Expenditures

You can see how aggregate expenditures, the sum of all spending on U.S. goods and services, must depend on prices, income, and all of the other determinants discussed in the previous sections. As with the demand curve for a specific good or service, we want to classify the factors that influence spending into the price and the nonprice determinants for the aggregate demand curves. The components of aggregate expenditures that change as the price level changes will lead to movements along the aggregate demand curve—changes in quantity demanded—whereas changes in aggregate expenditures caused by nonprice effects will cause shifts of the aggregate demand curve—changes in aggregate demand. In the following section, we look first at the price effects, or movements along an aggregate demand curve. Following that discussion, we focus on the nonprice determinants of aggregate demand.

RECAP

1. Aggregate expenditures are the sum of consumption, investment, government spending, and net exports.

2. Consumption depends on household income, wealth, expectations, demographics, and taxation.

3. Investment depends on the interest rate, technology, the cost of capital goods, and capacity utilization.

4. Government spending is determined independent of current income.

5. Net exports depend on foreign and domestic incomes, prices, government policies, and exchange rates.

3. The Aggregate Demand Curve

When we examined the demand curves in Chapter 3, we divided our study into two parts: the movement along the curve—changes in quantity demanded—and the shifts of the curve—changes in demand. We take the same approach here in examining aggregate demand. We first look at the movements along the aggregate demand curve caused by changes in the price level. We then turn to the nonprice determinants of aggregate demand that cause shifts in the curve.

3.a. Why the Aggregate Demand Curve Slopes Downward

Aggregate demand curves are downward sloping just like the demand curves for individual goods that were shown in Chapter 3, although for different reasons. Along the demand curve for an individual good, the price of that good changes while the prices of all other goods remain constant. This means that the good in question becomes relatively more or less expensive compared to all other goods in the economy. Consumers tend to substitute a less expensive good for a more expensive good. The effect of this substitution is an inverse relationship between price and quantity demanded. As the price of a good rises, the quantity demanded falls. For the economy as a whole, however, it is not a substitution of a less expensive good for a more expensive good that causes the demand curve to slope down. Instead, the aggregate quantity demanded, or total spending, will change as the price level changes as a result of the wealth effect, the interest rate effect, and the international trade effect of a price-level change on aggregate expenditures. We will discuss each of these effects in turn.

3.a.1. The Wealth Effect

Individuals and businesses own money, stocks, bonds, and other financial assets. The purchasing power of these assets is the quantity of goods and services for which the assets can be exchanged. When the level of prices falls, the purchasing power of these assets increases, allowing households and businesses to purchase more. When prices go up, the purchasing power of financial assets falls, causing households and businesses to spend less. This is the **wealth effect** (sometimes called the *real-balance effect*) of a price change: a change in the real value of wealth that causes spending to change when the level of prices changes. *Real values* are values that have been adjusted for price-level changes. Here *real value* means "purchasing power." When the price level changes, the purchasing power of financial assets also changes. When prices rise, the real value of assets and wealth falls, and aggregate expenditures tend to fall. When prices fall, the real value of assets and wealth rises, and aggregate expenditures tend to rise.

wealth effect
A change in the real value of wealth that causes spending to change when the level of prices changes.

3.a.2. The Interest Rate Effect

When the price level rises, the purchasing power of each dollar falls, which means that more money is required to buy any particular quantity of goods and services (see Figure 4). Suppose that a family of three needs $100 each week to buy food. If the price level doubles, the same quantity of food costs $200. The household must have twice as much money to buy the same amount of food. Conversely, when prices fall, the family needs less money to buy food because the purchasing power of each dollar is greater.

FIGURE 4   The Interest Rate Effect of Price-Level Changes on Aggregate Expenditures

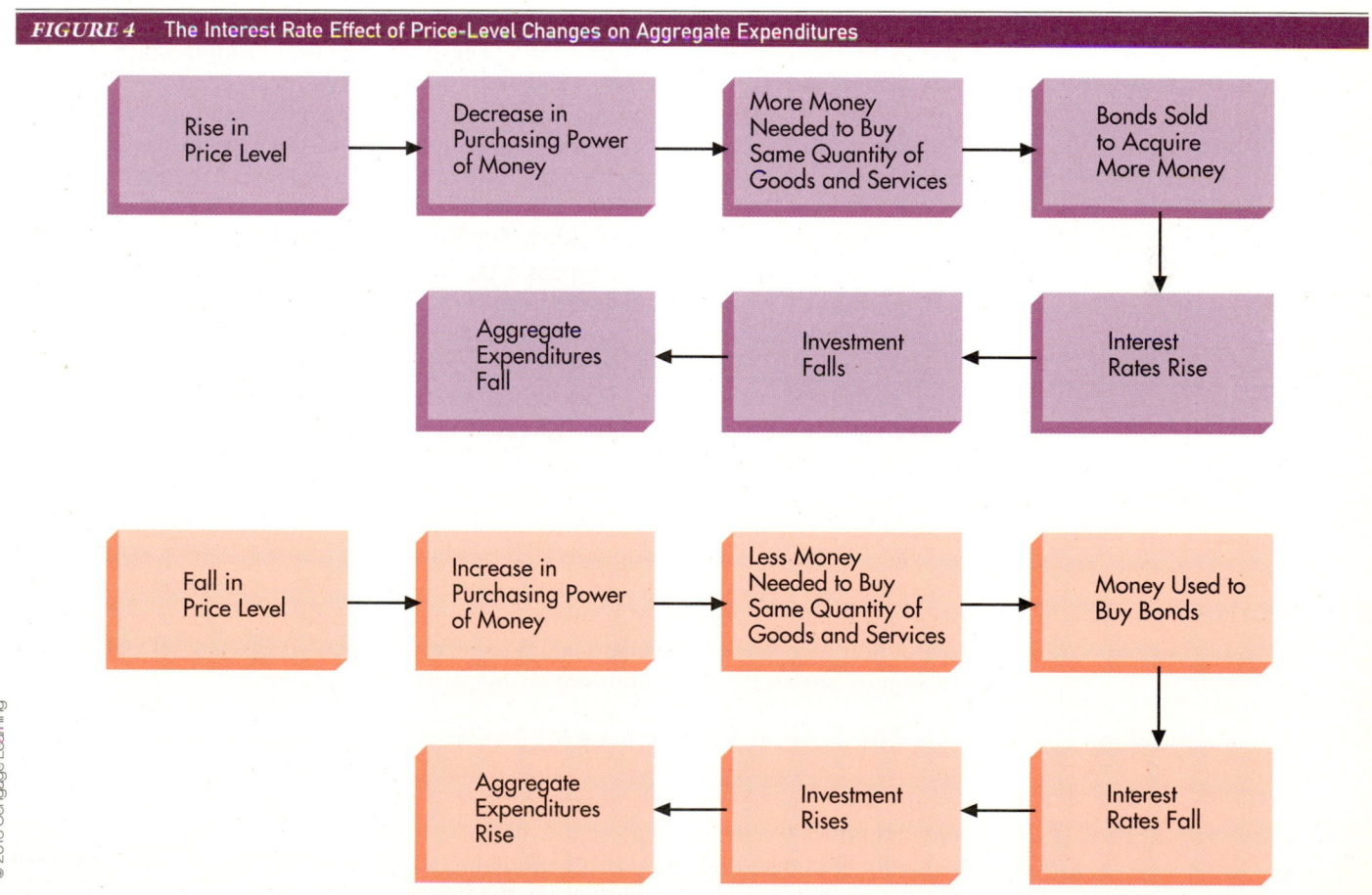

© 2013 Cengage Learning

When the price level changes, the purchasing power of financial assets changes.

When prices go up, people need more money. So they sell their other financial assets, such as bonds, to get that money. The increase in the supply of bonds lowers bond prices and raises interest rates. Since bonds typically pay fixed-dollar interest payments each year, as the price of a bond varies, the interest rate (or yield) will change. For instance, suppose you pay $1,000 for a bond that pays $100 a year in interest. The interest rate on this bond is found by dividing the annual interest payment by the bond price, or $100/$1,000 = 10 percent. If the price of the bond falls to $900, then the interest rate is equal to the annual interest payment (which remains fixed at $100 for the life of the bond) divided by the new price of $900: $100/$900 = 11 percent. When bond prices fall, interest rates rise, and when bond prices rise, interest rates fall.

If people want more money and they sell some of their bond holdings to raise the money, bond prices will fall and interest rates will rise. The rise in interest rates is necessary to sell the larger quantity of bonds, but it causes investment expenditures to fall, which causes aggregate expenditures to fall.

When prices fall, people need less money to purchase the same quantity of goods. So they use their money holdings to buy bonds and other financial assets. The increased demand for bonds increases bond prices and causes interest rates to fall. Lower interest rates increase investment expenditures, thereby pushing aggregate expenditures up.

interest rate effect
A change in interest rates that causes investment and therefore aggregate expenditures to change as the level of prices changes.

Figure 4 shows the **interest rate effect**, the relationship among the price level, interest rates, and aggregate expenditures. As the price level rises, interest rates rise and aggregate expenditures fall. As the price level falls, interest rates fall and aggregate expenditures rise.

3.a.3. The International Trade Effect

The third channel through which a price-level change affects the quantity of goods and services demanded is called the **international trade effect**. A change in the level of domestic prices can cause net exports to change. If domestic prices rise while foreign prices and the foreign exchange rate remain constant, domestic goods become more expensive in relation to foreign goods.

international trade effect
A change in aggregate expenditures resulting from a change in the domestic price level that changes the price of domestic goods relative to that of foreign goods.

Suppose the United States sells oranges to Japan. If the oranges sell for $1 per pound and the yen-dollar exchange rate is 100 yen = $1, a pound of U.S. oranges costs a Japanese buyer 100 yen. What happens if the level of prices in the United States goes up 10 percent? All prices, including the price of oranges, increase 10 percent. Oranges in the United States sell for $1.10 a pound after the price increase. If the exchange rate is still 100 yen = $1, a pound of oranges now costs the Japanese buyer 110 yen (100 × 1.10). If the prices of oranges from other countries do not change, some Japanese buyers may buy oranges from those countries instead of from the United States. The increase in the level of U.S. prices makes U.S. goods more expensive relative to foreign goods and causes U.S. net exports to fall; a decrease in the level of U.S. prices makes U.S. goods cheaper in relation to foreign goods, which increases U.S. net exports.

When the price of domestic goods increases in relation to the price of foreign goods, net exports fall, causing aggregate expenditures to fall. When the price of domestic goods falls in relation to the price of foreign goods, net exports rise, causing aggregate expenditures to rise. The international trade effect of a change in the level of domestic prices causes aggregate expenditures to change in the opposite direction.

aggregate demand curve
A curve that shows the different equilibrium levels of expenditures on domestic output at different levels of prices.

3.a.4. The Sum of the Price-Level Effects

The **aggregate demand curve** (*AD*) shows how the equilibrium level of expenditures for the economy's output changes as the price level changes. In other words, the curve shows the amount that people spend at different price levels.

Figure 5 displays the typical shape of the *AD* curve. The price level is plotted on the vertical axis, and real GDP is plotted on the horizontal axis. Suppose that initially the economy is at point *A*, with prices at P_0. At this point, spending equals $500. If prices

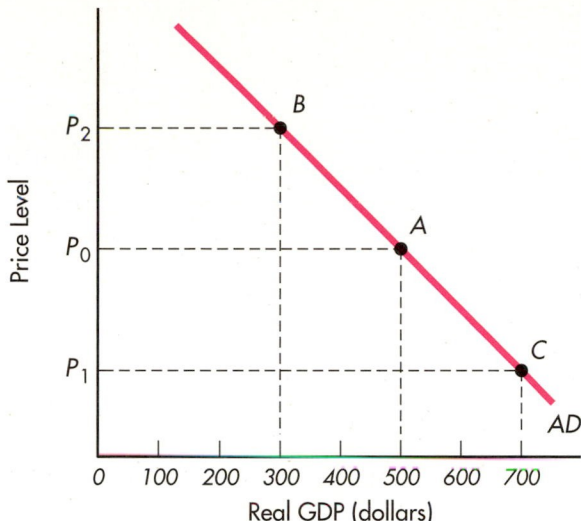

FIGURE 5   The Aggregate Demand Curve

The aggregate demand curve (*AD*) shows the level of expenditures at different price levels. At price level P_0, expenditures are $500; at P_1, they are $700; and at P_2, they are $300.

fall to P_1, expenditures equal $700 and the economy is at point *C*. If prices rise from P_0 to P_2, expenditures equal $300 at point *B*.

Because aggregate expenditures increase when the price level decreases and decrease when the price level increases, the aggregate demand curve slopes down. The aggregate demand curve is drawn with the price level for the *entire economy* on the vertical axis. A price-level change here means that, on average, *all prices in the economy change*; there is no relative price change among domestic goods. The negative slope of the aggregate demand curve is a product of the wealth effect, the interest rate effect, and the international trade effect.

A lower domestic price level increases consumption (the wealth effect), investment (the interest rate effect), and net exports (the international trade effect). As the price level drops, aggregate expenditures rise.

A higher domestic price level reduces consumption (the wealth effect), investment (the interest rate effect), and net exports (the international trade effect). As prices rise, aggregate expenditures fall. These price effects are summarized in Figure 6.

3.b. Changes in Aggregate Demand: Nonprice Determinants

The aggregate demand curve shows the level of aggregate expenditures at alternative price levels. We draw the curve by varying the price level and finding out what the resulting total expenditures are, holding all other things constant. As those "other things"— the nonprice determinants of aggregate demand—change, the aggregate demand curve shifts. The nonprice determinants of aggregate demand include all of the factors covered in the discussion of the components of expenditures—income, wealth, demographics, expectations, taxes, the interest rate (interest rates can change for reasons other than price-level changes), the cost of capital goods, capacity utilization, foreign income and price levels, exchange rates, and government policy. A change in any one of these can cause the *AD* curve to shift. In the discussions that follow, we will focus particularly on

 2 What causes the aggregate demand curve to shift?

FIGURE 6   Why the Aggregate Demand Curve Slopes Downward

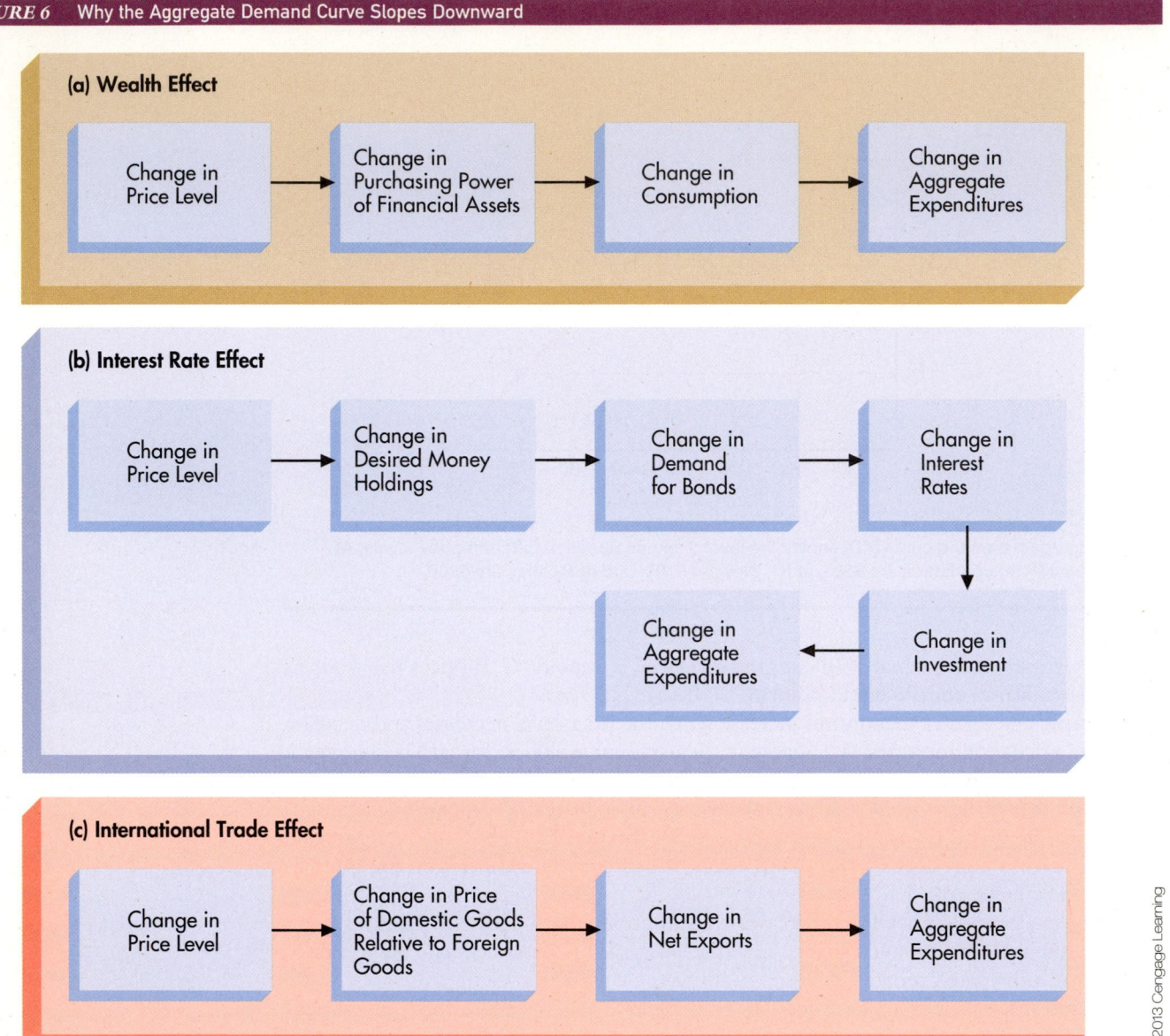

© 2013 Cengage Learning

the effects of expectations, foreign income, and price levels; we will also mention government policy, which will be examined in detail in the chapter titled "Fiscal Policy." Figure 7 summarizes these effects, which are discussed next.

3.b.1. Expectations

Consumption and business spending are affected by expectations. Consumption is sensitive to people's expectations of future income, prices, and wealth. For example, when people expect the economy to do well in the future, they increase their consumption today at every price level. This is reflected in a shift of the aggregate demand curve to the right, from AD_0 to AD_1, as shown in Figure 8. When aggregate demand increases, aggregate expenditures increase at every price level.

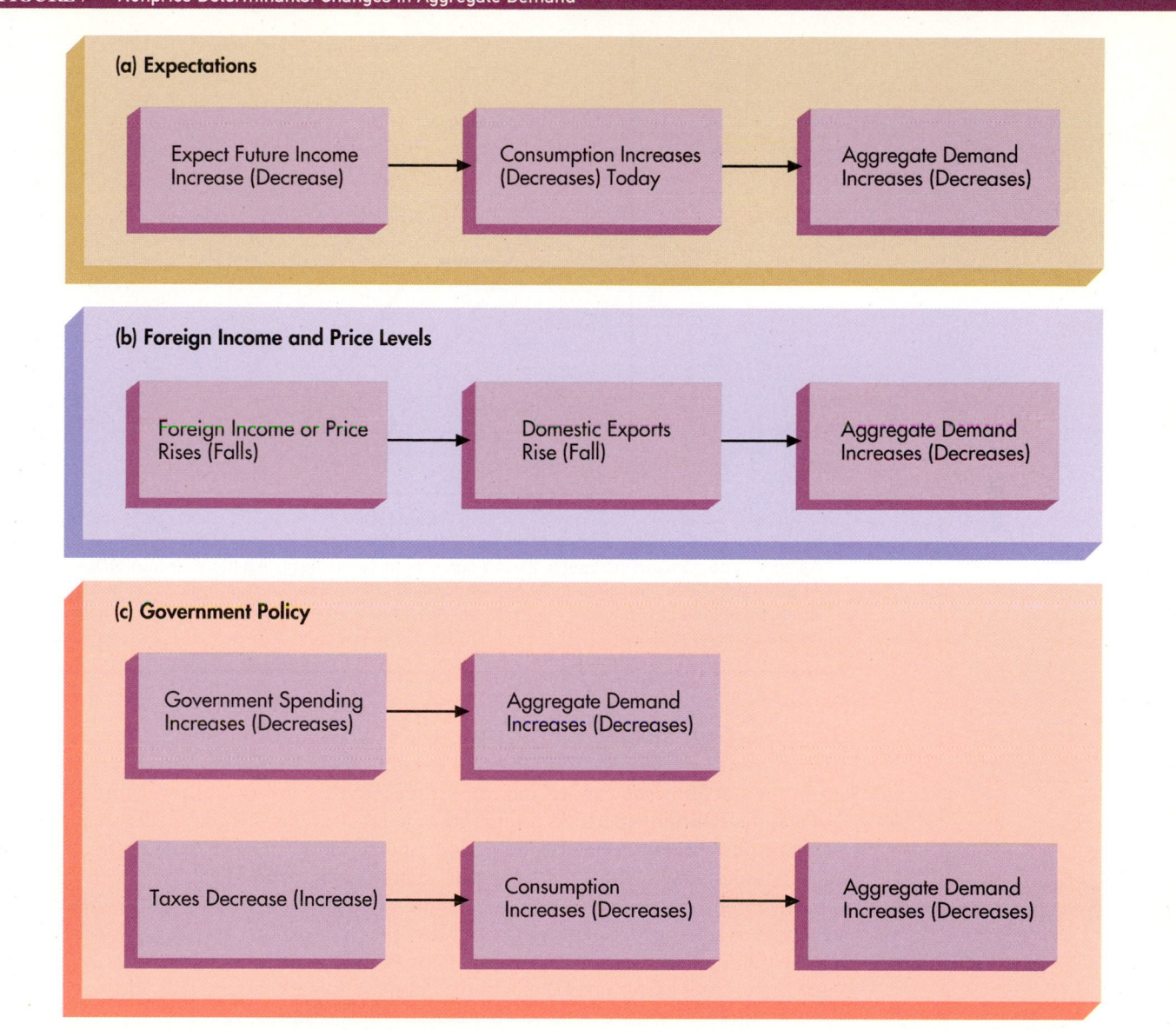

FIGURE 7   Nonprice Determinants: Changes in Aggregate Demand

(a) Expectations

Expect Future Income Increase (Decrease) → Consumption Increases (Decreases) Today → Aggregate Demand Increases (Decreases)

(b) Foreign Income and Price Levels

Foreign Income or Price Rises (Falls) → Domestic Exports Rise (Fall) → Aggregate Demand Increases (Decreases)

(c) Government Policy

Government Spending Increases (Decreases) → Aggregate Demand Increases (Decreases)

Taxes Decrease (Increase) → Consumption Increases (Decreases) → Aggregate Demand Increases (Decreases)

© 2013 Cengage Learning

On the other hand, if people expect a recession in the near future, they tend to reduce their consumption and increase their saving in order to protect themselves against a greater likelihood of losing a job or a forced cutback in hours worked. As consumption drops, aggregate demand decreases. The AD curve shifts to the left, from AD_0 to AD_2. At every price level along AD_2, planned expenditures are less than they are along AD_0.

Expectations also play an important role in investment decisions. Before undertaking a particular project, businesses forecast the likely revenues and costs associated with that project. When the profit outlook is good—say, a tax cut is on the horizon—investment and therefore aggregate demand increase. When profits are expected to fall, investment and aggregate demand decrease.

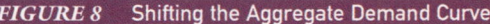

FIGURE 8 Shifting the Aggregate Demand Curve

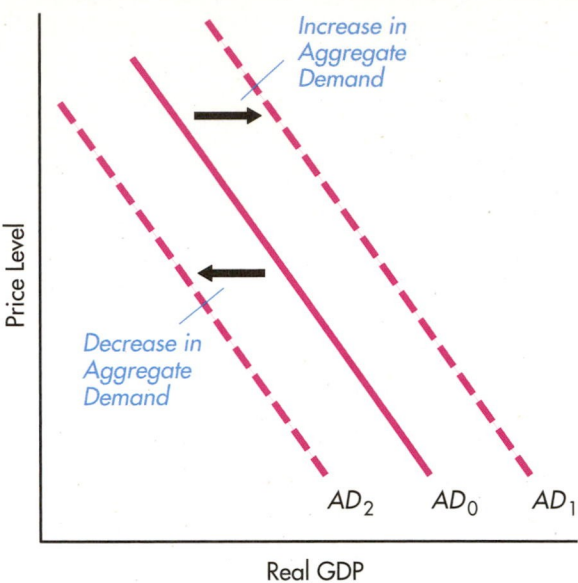

As aggregate demand increases, the *AD* curve shifts to the right, like the shift from AD_0 to AD_1. At every price level, the quantity of output demanded increases. As aggregate demand falls, the *AD* curve shifts to the left, like the shift from AD_0 to AD_2. At every price level, the quantity of output demanded falls.

© 2013 Cengage Learning

3.b.2. Foreign Income and Price Levels

When foreign income increases, so does foreign spending. Some of this increased spending is for goods produced in the domestic economy. As domestic exports increase, aggregate demand rises. Lower foreign income has just the opposite effect. As foreign income falls, foreign spending falls, including foreign spending on the exports of the domestic economy. Lower foreign income, then, causes domestic net exports and domestic aggregate demand to fall.

Higher foreign income increases net exports and aggregate demand; lower foreign income reduces net exports and aggregate demand.

If foreign prices rise in relation to domestic prices, domestic goods become less expensive relative to foreign goods, and domestic net exports increase. This means that aggregate demand rises, or the aggregate demand curve shifts right, as the level of foreign prices rises. Conversely, when the level of foreign prices falls, domestic goods become more expensive relative to foreign goods, causing domestic net exports and aggregate demand to fall.

Changes in the level of foreign prices change domestic net exports and aggregate demand in the same direction.

Let's go back to the market for oranges. Suppose U.S. growers compete with Brazilian growers for the Japanese orange market. If the level of prices in Brazil rises while the level of prices in the United States remains stable, the price of Brazilian oranges to the Japanese buyer rises in relation to the price of U.S. oranges. What happens? Exports of U.S. oranges to Japan should rise, while exports of Brazilian oranges to Japan should fall.[1]

3.b.3. Government Policy

One of the goals of macroeconomic policy is to achieve economic growth without inflation. For GDP to increase, either *AD* or *AS* would have to change. Government economic policy can cause the aggregate demand curve to shift. An increase in government spending or a decrease in taxes will increase aggregate

---

[1] This assumes no change in exchange rates. If the Brazilian currency were to depreciate in value as Brazilian prices rose, then the cheaper exchange rate would at least partially offset the higher price and reduce the impact of the price change on exports.

demand; a decrease in government spending or an increase in taxes will decrease aggregate demand. We devote an entire chapter to fiscal policy, an examination of the effect of taxes and government spending on aggregate demand. In another chapter, on monetary policy, we describe how changes in the money supply can cause the aggregate demand curve to shift.

RECAP

1. The aggregate demand curve shows the level of aggregate expenditures at different price levels.

2. Aggregate expenditures are the sum of consumption, investment, government spending, and net exports.

3. The wealth effect, the interest rate effect, and the international trade effect are three reasons why the

aggregate demand curve slopes down. These effects explain movements along a given *AD* curve.

4. The aggregate demand curve shifts with changes in the nonprice determinants of aggregate demand: expectations, foreign income and price levels, and government policy.

4. Aggregate Supply

The **aggregate supply curve** shows the quantity of real GDP produced at different price levels. The aggregate supply curve (*AS*) looks like the supply curve for an individual good, but, as with aggregate demand and the microeconomic demand curve, different factors are at work. The positive relationship between price and quantity supplied of an individual good is based on the change in the price of that good relative to the prices of all other goods. As the price of a single good rises relative to the prices of other goods, sellers are willing to offer more of the good for sale. With aggregate supply, on the other hand, we are analyzing how the amount of all goods and services produced changes as the level of prices changes. The direct relationship between prices and national output is explained by the effect of changing prices on profits, not by relative price changes.

 3 What factors affect aggregate supply?

aggregate supply curve
A curve that shows the amount of real GDP produced at different price levels.

4.a. Why the Aggregate Supply Curve Slopes Upward

Along the aggregate supply curve, everything is held fixed except the price level and the output. The price level is the price of output. The prices of resources—that is, the costs of production (wages, rent, and interest)—are assumed to be constant, at least for a short time following a change in the price level.

If the price level rises while the costs of production remain fixed, business profits go up. As profits rise, firms are willing to produce more output. As the price level rises, then, the quantity of output that firms are willing to supply increases. The result is the positively sloped aggregate supply curve shown in Figure 9.

As the price level rises from P_0 to P_1 in Figure 9, real GDP increases from \$300 to \$500. The higher the price level, the higher are profits, everything else held constant, and the greater is the quantity of output produced in the economy. Conversely, as the price level falls, the quantity of output produced falls.

4.b. Short-Run versus Long-Run Aggregate Supply

The curve in Figure 9 is a *short-run* aggregate supply curve because the costs of production are held constant. Although production costs may not rise immediately when the

FIGURE 9   Aggregate Supply

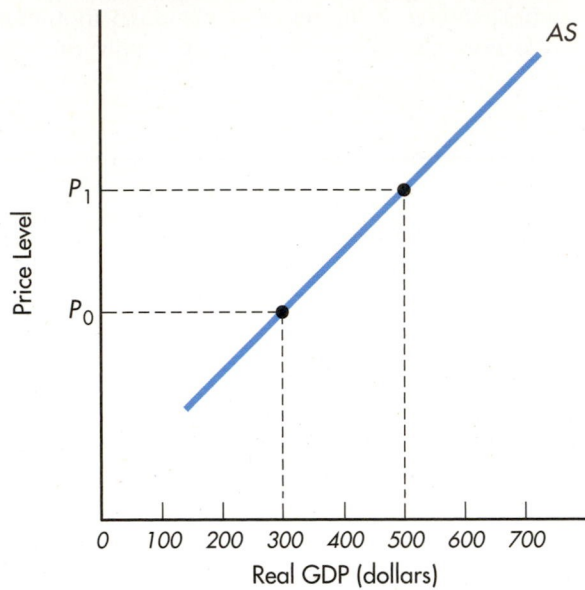

The aggregate supply curve shows the amount of real GDP produced at different price levels. The *AS* curve slopes up, indicating that the higher the price level, the greater the quantity of output produced.

price level rises, eventually they will. Labor will demand higher wages to compensate for the higher cost of living; suppliers will charge more for materials. The positive slope of the *AS* curve, then, is a short-run phenomenon. How short is the short run? It is the period of time over which production costs remain constant. (In the long run, all costs change or are variable.) For the economy as a whole, the short run can be months or, at most, a few years.

4 Why does the short-run aggregate supply curve become steeper as real GDP increases?

4.b.1. Short-Run Aggregate Supply Curve

Figure 9 represents the general shape of the short-run aggregate supply curve. In Figure 10, you see a more realistic version of the same curve—its steepness varies. The steepness of the aggregate supply curve depends on the ability and willingness of producers to respond to price-level changes in the short run. Figure 10 shows the typical shape of the short-run aggregate supply curve.

Notice that as the level of real GDP increases in Figure 10, the *AS* curve becomes steeper. This is because each increase in output requires firms to hire more and more resources, until eventually full capacity is reached in some areas of the economy, resources are fully employed, and some firms reach maximum output. At this point, increases in the price level bring about smaller and smaller increases in output from firms as a whole. The short-run aggregate supply curve becomes increasingly steep as the economy approaches maximum output.

5 Why is the long-run aggregate supply curve vertical?

4.b.2. Long-Run Aggregate Supply Curve

Aggregate supply in the short run is different from aggregate supply in the long run (see Figure 11). That difference stems from the fact that, in the long run, quantities and costs of resources are not fixed. Over time, contracts expire, and wages and other resource costs adjust to current conditions. The increased flexibility of resource costs in the long run has costs rising and falling with

FIGURE 10   The Shape of the Short-Run Aggregate Supply Curve

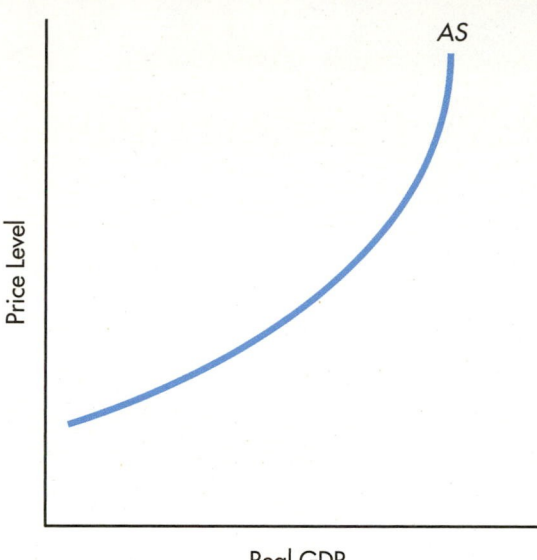

The upward-sloping aggregate supply curve occurs when the price level must rise to induce further increases in output. The curve gets steeper as real GDP increases, since the closer the economy comes to the capacity level of output, the less output will rise in response to higher prices as more and more firms reach their maximum level of output in the short run.

FIGURE 11   The Shape of the Long-Run Aggregate Supply Curve

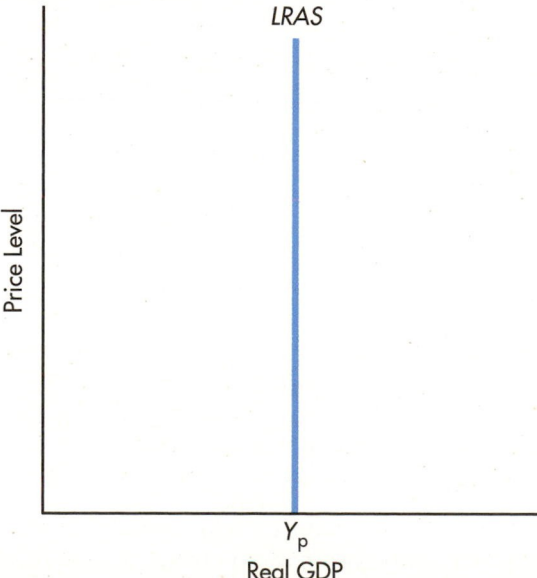

In the long run, the *AS* curve is a vertical line at the potential level of real GDP, which indicates that there is no relationship between price-level changes and the quantity of output produced.

© 2013 Cengage Learning

ECONOMIC INSIGHT

How Lack of Information in the Short Run Affects Wages in the Long Run

Workers do not have perfect information. In other words, they do not know everything that occurs. This lack of information includes information about the price level. If workers form incorrect expectations regarding the price level in the short run, they may be willing to work for a different wage in the short run than in the long run. For example, if workers thought that the inflation rate would be 3 percent over the next year, they would want a smaller wage raise than if they believed that the inflation rate would be 6 percent. If, in fact, they base their wage negotiations on 3 percent inflation and accept a wage based on that inflation rate, but it turns out that the price level has increased by 6 percent, workers will then seek higher wages. In the long run, wages will reflect price-level changes.

If it cost nothing to obtain information, everyone who was interested would always know the current economic conditions. However, since there are costs of obtaining and understanding information about the economy, people will make mistakes in the short run. Both managers and employees make mistakes as a result of lack of information. Such mistakes are not caused by stupidity but by ignorance—ignorance of future as well as current economic conditions. In the long run, mistakes about the price level are recognized, and wages adjust to the known price level.

We now have two reasons why wages will be more flexible in the long run than in the short run: long-term contracts and lack of information in the short run. The same arguments could be made for other resources as well. For these two reasons, the short-run aggregate supply curve is generally upward sloping because resource prices are relatively fixed in the short run.

---

the price level and changes the shape of the aggregate supply curve. Lack of information about economic conditions in the short run also contributes to the inflexibility of resource prices as compared to the long run. The Economic Insight "How Lack of Information in the Short Run Affects Wages in the Long Run" shows why this is true for labor, as well as for other resources.

long-run aggregate supply curve (LRAS)
A vertical line at the potential level of real GDP.

The **long-run aggregate supply curve (*LRAS*)** is viewed by most economists as being a vertical line at the potential level of real GDP or output (Y_p), as shown in Figure 11. Remember that the potential level of real GDP is the income level that is produced in the absence of any cyclical unemployment, or when the natural rate of unemployment exists. In the long run, wages and other resource costs fully adjust to price changes. The short-run *AS* curve slopes upward because we assume that the costs of production, particularly wages, do not change to offset changing prices. In the short run, then, higher prices increase producers' profits and stimulate production. In the long run, however, because the costs of production adjust completely to the change in prices, neither profits nor production increases. What we find here are higher wages and other costs of production to match the higher level of prices.

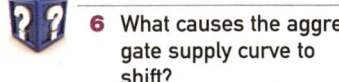

6 What causes the aggregate supply curve to shift?

4.c. Changes in Aggregate Supply: Nonprice Determinants

The aggregate supply curve is drawn with everything but the price level and real GDP held constant. There are several things that can change and cause the aggregate supply curve to shift. The shift from AS_0 to AS_1 in Figure 12 represents an increase in aggregate supply. The AS_1 curve lies to the right of AS_0, which means that at every price level, production is higher on AS_1 than on AS_0. The shift from AS_0 to AS_2 represents a decrease in aggregate supply. The AS_2 curve lies to the left of AS_0, which means that at every

FIGURE 12   Changes in Aggregate Supply

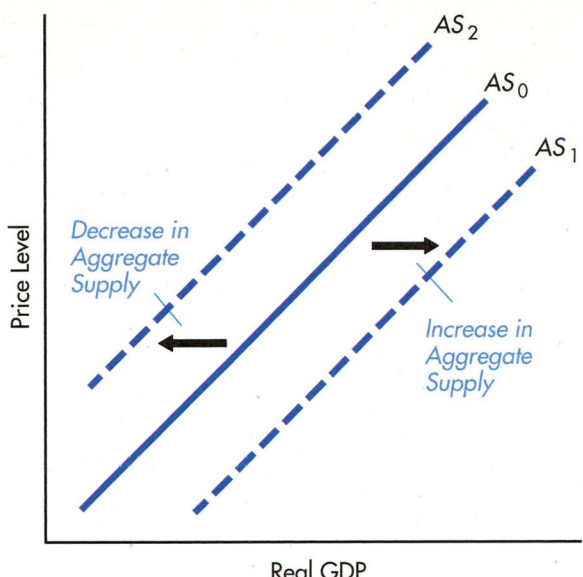

The aggregate supply curve shifts with changes in resource prices, technology, and expectations. When aggregate supply increases, the curve shifts to the right, like the shift from AS_0 to AS_1, so that at every price level more is being produced. When aggregate supply falls, the curve shifts to the left, like the shift from AS_0 to AS_2, so that at every price level less is being produced.

price level, production along AS_2 is less than that along AS_0. The nonprice determinants of aggregate supply are resource prices, technology, and expectations. Figure 13 summarizes the nonprice determinants of aggregate supply, discussed in detail next.

4.c.1. Resource Prices
When the price of output changes, the costs of production do not change immediately. At first, then, a change in profits induces a change in production. Costs eventually change in response to the change in prices and production, and when they do, the aggregate supply curve shifts. When the cost of resources—labor, capital goods, and materials—falls, the aggregate supply curve shifts to the right, from AS_0 to AS_1 in Figure 12. This means that firms are willing to produce more output at any given price level. When the cost of resources goes up, profits fall and the aggregate supply curve shifts to the left, from AS_0 to AS_2. Here, at any given level of price, firms produce less output.

Remember that the vertical axis of the aggregate supply graph represents the price level for all goods and services produced in the economy. Only those changes in resource prices that raise the costs of production across the economy have an impact on the aggregate supply curve. For example, oil is an important raw material. If a new source of oil is discovered, the price of oil falls and aggregate supply increases. However, if oil-exporting countries restrict oil supplies and the price of oil increases substantially, aggregate supply decreases, a situation that occurred in the 1970s when OPEC reduced the supply of oil (see the Global Business Insight "Oil and Aggregate Supply"). If the price of only one minor resource were to change, then aggregate supply would be unlikely to change. For instance, if the price of land in Las Cruces, New Mexico, increased, we would not expect the U.S. aggregate supply curve to be affected.

FIGURE 13   Determinants of Aggregate Supply Shift the AS Curve

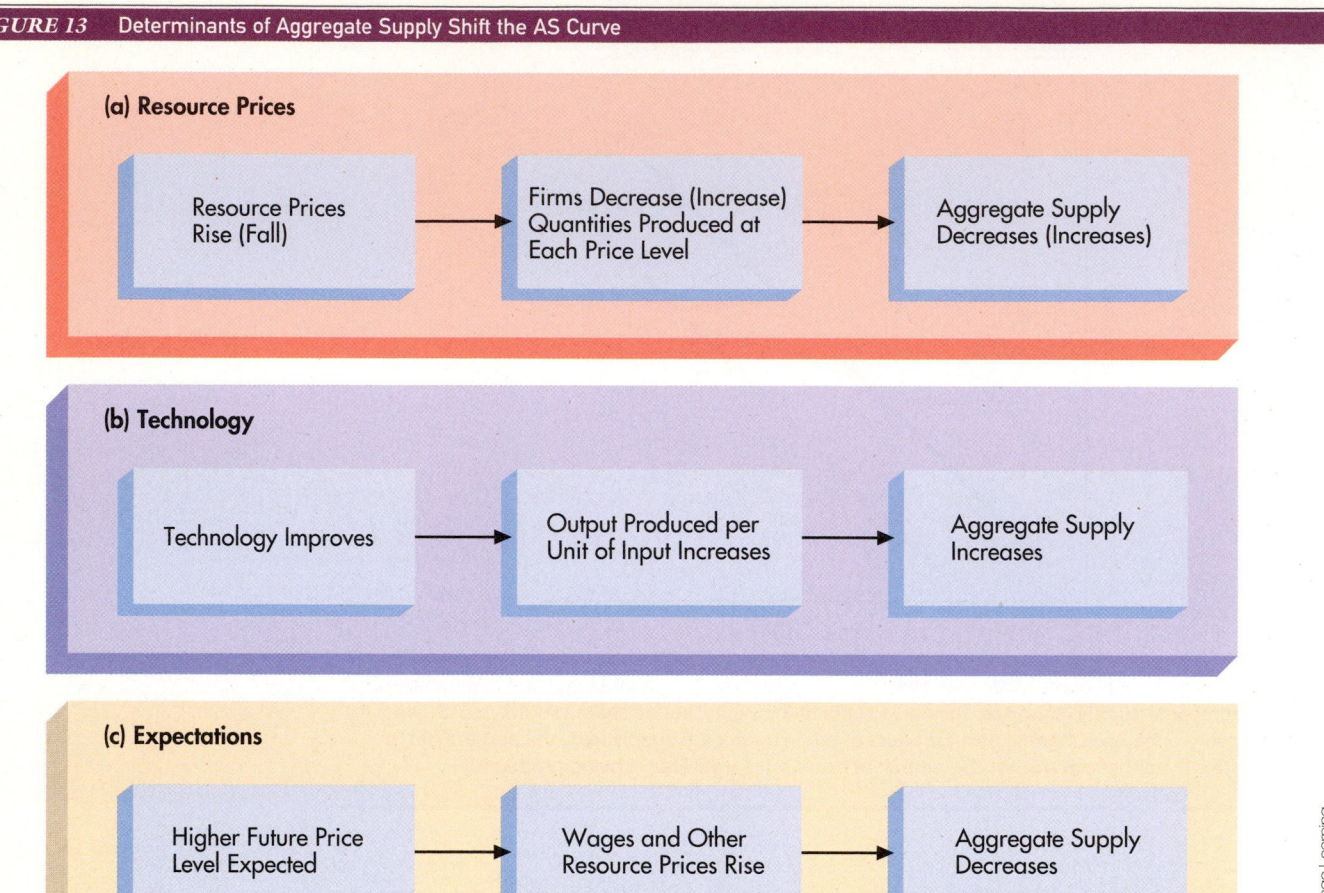

© 2013 Cengage Learning

4.c.2. Technology

Technological innovations allow businesses to increase the productivity of their existing resources. As new technology is adopted, the amount of output that can be produced by each unit of input increases, moving the aggregate supply curve to the right. For example, personal computers and word-processing software have allowed secretaries to produce much more output in a day than typewriters allowed.

4.c.3. Expectations

To understand how expectations can affect aggregate supply, consider the case of labor contracts. Manufacturing workers typically contract for a nominal wage based on what they and their employers expect the future level of prices to be. Because wages typically are set for at least a year, any unexpected increase in the price level during the year lowers real wages. Firms receive higher prices for their output, but the cost of labor stays the same. So profits and production go up.

If wages rise in anticipation of higher prices but prices do not go up, the cost of labor rises. Higher real wages caused by expectations of higher prices reduce current profits and production, moving the aggregate supply curve to the left. Other things being equal, anticipated higher prices cause aggregate supply to decrease; conversely, anticipated lower prices cause aggregate supply to increase. In this sense, expectations of price-level changes that shift aggregate supply actually bring about price-level changes.

GLOBAL BUSINESS INSIGHT

Oil and Aggregate Supply

It seems that every few years there are big fluctuations in oil prices that lead to much talk about high oil prices leading to a fall in GDP for oil-importing countries. What is the link between oil prices and real GDP? A look back to recent history helps develop our understanding of this link.

In 1973 and 1974, and again in 1979 and 1980, the Organization of Petroleum Exporting Countries (OPEC) reduced the supply of oil, driving the price of oil up dramatically. For example, the price of Saudi Arabian crude oil more than tripled between 1973 and 1974, and more than doubled between 1979 and 1980. Researchers estimate that the rapid jump in oil prices reduced output by 17 percent in Japan, by 7 percent in the United States, and by 1.9 percent in Germany.[*]

Oil is an important resource in many industries. When the price of oil increases as a result of restricted oil output, aggregate supply falls. You can see this in the graph shown at the right. When the price of oil goes up, the aggregate supply curve falls from AS_1 to AS_2. When aggregate supply falls, the equilibrium level of real GDP (the intersection of the AS curve and the AD curve) falls from Y_1 to Y_2.

Higher oil prices caused by restricted oil output would decrease not only short-run aggregate supply and current equilibrium real GDP, as shown in the graph, but also potential equilibrium income at the natural rate of unemployment. Unless other factors change to contribute to economic growth, the higher resource (oil) price reduces the productive capacity of the economy.

There is evidence that fluctuations in oil prices have less effect on the economy today than they did in the past.[†] The amount of energy that goes into producing a dollar of GDP has declined over time so that oil plays a less important role in determining aggregate supply today than in the 1970s and earlier. This means that any given change in oil prices today will be associated with smaller shifts in the AS curve than in earlier decades.

While we have focused on the AS curve and oil prices, more recently the AD curve has entered the discussion. Unlike earlier episodes, where oil price rises were the result of restricting the supply of oil, in the mid-2000s, the price of oil was being driven higher by rising demand—particularly from China and the United States.[‡] The recession of 2008

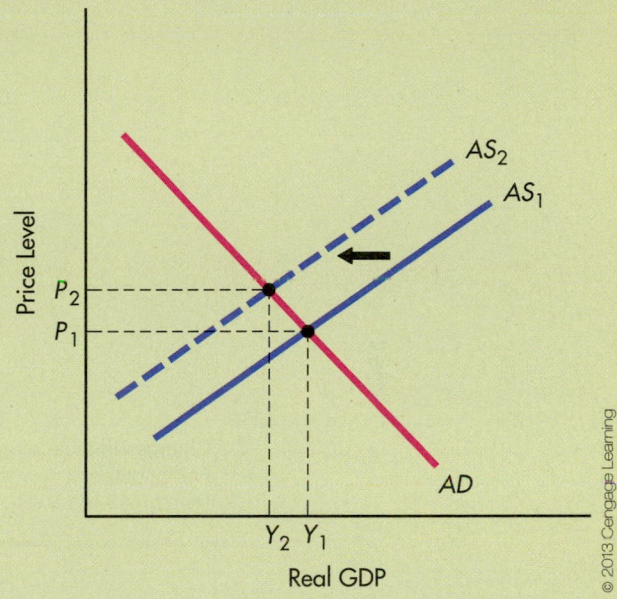

showed that oil prices can drop just as dramatically due to demand shifts as in the earlier supply-driven episodes once supply increased. As spending fell during the recession, oil prices fell sharply from over $140 per barrel in July 2008 to $90 by September and reached a low of less than $40 in January 2009. As the economy grew out of the recession, prices reached $88 per barrel by December 2010.

[*]These estimates were taken from Robert H. Rasche and John A. Tatom, "Energy Price Shocks, Aggregate Supply, and Monetary Policy: The Theory and the International Evidence," *Carnegie-Rochester Conference Series on Public Policy*, Vol. 14, eds. Karl Brunner and Allan H. Meltzer (North-Holland, 1981), pp. 9–93.

[†]See Stephen P. A. Brown and Mine K. Yücel, "Oil Prices and the Economy," Federal Reserve Bank of Dallas, *Southwest Economy*, July–August 2000.

[‡]See Christopher J. Neely, "Will Oil Prices Choke Growth," Federal Reserve Bank of St. Louis, *International Economic Trends*, July 2004.

FIGURE 14   Shifting the Long-Run Aggregate Supply Curve

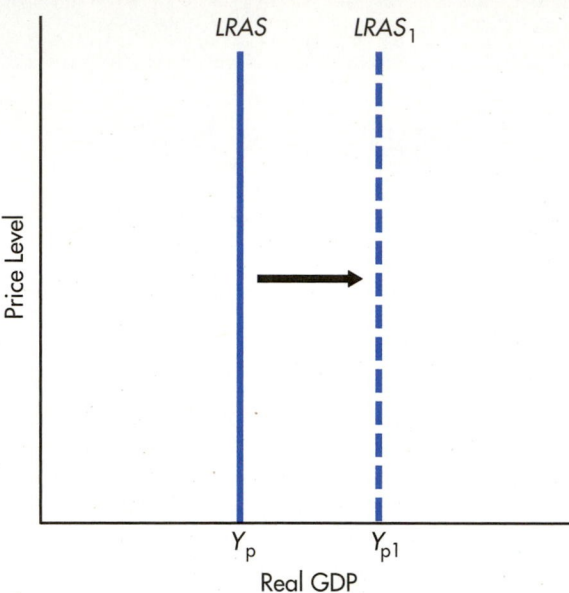

Changes in technology and the availability and quality of resources can shift the *LRAS* curve. For instance, a new technology that increases productivity would move the curve to the right, from *LRAS* to *LRAS₁*.

© 2013 Cengage Learning

4.c.4. Economic Growth: Long-Run Aggregate Supply Shifts
The vertical long-run aggregate supply curve, as shown in Figure 11, does not mean that the economy is forever fixed at the current level of potential real gross domestic product. Over time, as new technologies are developed and the quantity and quality of resources increase, potential output also increases, shifting both the short- and the long-run aggregate supply curves to the right. Figure 14 shows long-run economic growth by the shift in the aggregate supply curve from *LRAS* to *LRAS₁*. The movement of the long-run aggregate supply curve to the right reflects the increase in potential real GDP from Y_p to Y_{p1}. Even though the price level has no effect on the level of output in the long run, changes in the determinants of the supply of real output in the economy do.

RECAP

1. The aggregate supply curve shows the quantity of output (real GDP) produced at different price levels.

2. The aggregate supply curve slopes up because, everything else held constant, higher prices increase producers' profits, creating an incentive to increase output.

3. The aggregate supply curve shifts with changes in resource prices, technology, and expectations. These are nonprice determinants of aggregate supply.

4. The short-run aggregate supply curve is upward sloping, showing that increases in production are accompanied by higher prices.

5. The long-run aggregate supply curve is vertical at potential real GDP because, eventually, wages and the costs of other resources adjust fully to price-level changes.

5. Aggregate Demand and Supply Equilibrium

Now that we have defined the aggregate demand and aggregate supply curves separately, we can put them together to determine the equilibrium price level and real GDP.

© froxx/Shutterstock.com

7 What determines the equilibrium price level and real GDP?

5.a. Short-Run Equilibrium

Figure 15 shows the level of equilibrium in a hypothetical economy. Initially, the economy is in equilibrium at point 1, where *AD* and *AS* intersect. At this point, the equilibrium price level is P_1, and the equilibrium real GDP is $500. At price level P_1, the amount of output demanded is equal to the amount supplied. Suppose aggregate demand increases from AD_1 to AD_2. In the short run, aggregate supply does not change, so the new equilibrium is at the intersection of the new aggregate demand curve, AD_2, and the same aggregate supply curve, AS_1, at point 2. The new equilibrium price level is P_2, and the new equilibrium real GDP is $600. Note that in the short run, the equilibrium point on the short-run aggregate supply curve can lie to the right of the long-run aggregate supply curve (*LRAS*). This is because the *LRAS* represents the potential level of real GDP, not the capacity level. It is possible to produce more than the potential level of real GDP in the short run if the unemployment rate falls below the natural rate of unemployment.

FIGURE 15	Aggregate Demand and Supply Equilibrium

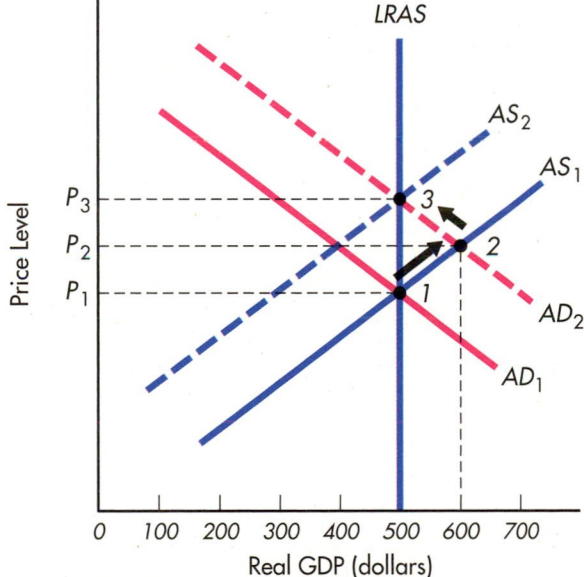

The equilibrium price level and real GDP is at the intersection of the *AD* and *AS* curves. Initially, equilibrium occurs at point *1*, where the AD_1 and AS_1 curves intersect. Here the price level is P_1 and real GDP is $500. If aggregate demand increases, moving from AD_1 to AD_2, in the short run there is a new equilibrium at point *2*, where AD_2 intersects AS_1. The price level rises to P_2, and the equilibrium level of real GDP increases to $600. Over time, as wages and the costs of other resources rise in response to higher prices, aggregate supply falls, moving AS_1 to AS_2. Final equilibrium occurs at point *3*, where the AS_2 curve intersects the AD_2 curve. The price level rises to P_3, but the equilibrium level of real GDP returns to its initial level, $500. In the long run, there is no relationship between prices and the equilibrium level of real GDP because the costs of resources adjust to changes in the level of prices.

© 2013 Cengage Learning

5.b. Long-Run Equilibrium

An increase in aggregate demand increases real GDP only temporarily.

Point 2 is not a permanent equilibrium because aggregate supply decreases to AS_2 once the costs of production rise in response to higher prices. Final equilibrium is at point 3, where the price level is P_3 and real GDP is $500. Notice that equilibrium real GDP here is the same as the initial equilibrium at point 1. Points 1 and 3 both lie along the long-run aggregate supply curve (*LRAS*). The initial shock to or change in the economy was an increase in aggregate demand. The change in aggregate expenditures initially led to higher output and higher prices. Over time, however, as resource costs rise and profit falls, output falls back to its original value.

We are not saying that the level of output never changes. The long-run aggregate supply curve shifts as technology changes and new supplies of resources are obtained. But the output change that results from a change in aggregate demand is a temporary, or short-run, phenomenon. The price level eventually adjusts, and output eventually returns to the potential level.

RECAP

1. The equilibrium price level and real GDP are at the point where the aggregate demand and aggregate supply curves intersect.

2. In the short run, a shift in aggregate demand establishes a temporary equilibrium along the short-run aggregate supply curve.

3. In the long run, the short-run aggregate supply curve shifts so that changes in aggregate demand affect only the price level, not the equilibrium level of output or real GDP.

SUMMARY

1. **What factors affect aggregate demand?**

   - Aggregate demand is the relation between aggregate expenditures and the price level. *§2*

   - Aggregate demand is the sum of consumption, investment, government spending, and net exports at alternative price levels. *§2.a, 2.b, 2.c, 2.d*

   - Aggregate expenditures change with changes in the price level because of the wealth effect, the interest rate effect, and the international trade effect. These cause a movement along the AD curve. *§3.a*

2. **What causes the aggregate demand curve to shift?**

   - The aggregate demand (*AD*) curve shows the level of expenditures for real GDP at different price levels. *§3.a.4*

   - Because expenditures and prices move in opposite directions, the *AD* curve is negatively sloped. *§3.a.4*

   - The nonprice determinants of aggregate demand include expectations, foreign income and price levels, and government policy. *§3.b*

3. **What factors affect aggregate supply?**

   - The aggregate supply curve shows the quantity of real GDP produced at different price levels. *§4*

   - Movements along the *AS* curve are caused by changes in price. Shifts in the curve are caused by the determinants of AS. *§4.c*

4. **Why does the short-run aggregate supply curve become steeper as real GDP increases?**

   - As real GDP rises and the economy pushes closer to capacity output, the level of prices must rise to induce increased production. *§4.b.1*

5. **Why is the long-run aggregate supply curve vertical?**

   • The long-run aggregate supply curve is a vertical line at the potential level of real GDP. The shape of the curve indicates that higher prices have no effect on output when an economy is producing at potential real GDP. *§4.b.2*

6. **What causes the aggregate supply curve to shift?**

   • The nonprice determinants of aggregate supply are resource prices, technology, and expectations. *§4.c.1, 4.c.2, 4.c.3*

7. **What determines the equilibrium price level and real GDP?**

   • The equilibrium price level and real GDP are at the intersection of the aggregate demand and aggregate supply curves. *§5.a*

   • In the short run, a shift in aggregate demand establishes a new, but temporary, equilibrium along the short-run aggregate supply curve. *§5.a*

   • In the long run, the short-run aggregate supply curve shifts so that changes in aggregate demand determine the price level but not the equilibrium level of output or real GDP. *§5.b*

KEY TERMS

aggregate demand curve, 162
aggregate supply curve, 167
cost-push inflation, 156

demand-pull inflation, 155
interest rate effect, 162
international trade effect, 162

long-run aggregate supply curve
   (LRAS), 170
wealth effect, 161

EXERCISES

1. How is the aggregate demand curve different from the demand curve for a single good, like hamburgers?
2. Why does the aggregate demand curve slope downward? Give real-world examples of the three effects that explain the slope of the curve.
3. How does an increase in foreign income affect domestic aggregate expenditures and demand? Draw a diagram to illustrate your answer.
4. How does a decrease in foreign price levels affect domestic aggregate expenditures and demand? Draw a diagram to illustrate your answer.
5. How is the aggregate supply curve different from the supply curve for a single good, like pizza?
6. There are several determinants of aggregate supply that can cause the aggregate supply curve to shift.
   a. Describe those determinants and give an example of a change in each.
   b. Draw and label an aggregate supply diagram that illustrates the effect of the change in each determinant.
7. Draw a short-run aggregate supply curve that gets steeper as real GDP rises.
   a. Explain why the curve has this shape.
   b. Now draw a long-run aggregate supply curve that intersects a short-run AS curve. What is the

relationship between short-run AS and long-run AS?

8. Draw and carefully label an aggregate demand and supply diagram with initial equilibrium at P_0 and Y_0.
   a. Using the diagram, explain what happens when aggregate demand falls.
   b. How is the short run different from the long run?
9. Draw an aggregate demand and supply diagram for Japan. In the diagram, show how each of the following affects aggregate demand and supply.
   a. The U.S. gross domestic product falls.
   b. The level of prices in Korea falls.
   c. Labor receives a large wage increase.
   d. Economists predict higher prices next year.
10. If the long-run aggregate supply curve gives the level of potential real GDP, how can the short-run aggregate supply curve ever lie to the right of the long-run aggregate supply curve?
11. What will happen to the equilibrium price level and real GDP if:
   a. Aggregate demand and aggregate supply both increase?
   b. Aggregate demand increases and aggregate supply decreases?

   c. Aggregate demand and aggregate supply both decrease?

   d. Aggregate demand decreases and aggregate supply increases?

12. During the Great Depression, the U.S. economy experienced a falling price level and declining real GDP. Using an aggregate demand and aggregate supply diagram, illustrate and explain how this could occur.

13. Suppose aggregate demand increases, causing an increase in real GDP but no change in the price level. Using an aggregate demand and aggregate supply diagram, illustrate and explain how this could occur.

14. Suppose aggregate demand increases, causing an increase in the price level but no change in real GDP. Using an aggregate demand and aggregate supply diagram, illustrate and explain how this could occur.

15. Use an aggregate demand and aggregate supply diagram to illustrate and explain how each of the following will affect the equilibrium price level and real GDP:

   a. Consumers expect a recession.

   b. Foreign income rises.

   c. Foreign price levels fall.

   d. Government spending increases.

   e. Workers expect higher future inflation and negotiate higher wages now.

   f. Technological improvements increase productivity.

16. In the boom years of the late 1990s, it was often said that rapidly increasing stock prices were responsible for much of the rapid growth of real GDP. Explain how this could be true, using aggregate demand and aggregate supply analysis.

17. Suppose you read in the newspaper that rising oil prices would contribute to a global recession. Use aggregate demand and supply analysis to explain how high oil prices could reduce real GDP.

18. Find an article in today's news that could indicate a shift in aggregate supply and/or demand, and draw corresponding aggregate supply and demand curves.

You can find further practice tests in the Online Quiz at **www.cengage.com/economics/boyes**.

THE CONFERENCE BOARD CONSUMER CONFIDENCE INDEX PLUMMETS FURTHER IN FEBRUARY

The Conference Board, February 24, 2009

The Conference Board Consumer Confidence Index, which had decreased moderately in January, declined in February, reaching yet another all-time low. The Index now stands at 25.0 (1985 = 100), down from 37.4 in January. The Present Situation Index declined to 21.2 from 29.7 last month. The Expectations Index decreased to 27.5 from 42.5 in January.

The Consumer Confidence Survey is based on a representative sample of 5,000 U.S. households....

Says Lynn Franco, Director of The Conference Board Consumer Research Center: "The Consumer Confidence Index, which was relatively flat in January, reached yet another all-time low in February (Index began in 1967). The decline in the Present Situation Index, driven by worsening business conditions and a rapidly deteriorating job market, suggests that overall economic conditions have weakened even further this quarter. Looking ahead, increasing concerns about business conditions, employment and earnings have further sapped confidence and driven expectations to their lowest level ever. In addition, inflation expectations, which had been easing over the past several months, have moderately picked up. All in all, not only do consumers feel overall economic conditions have grown more dire, but just as disconcerting, they anticipate no improvement in conditions over the next six months."

Consumers' appraisal of overall current conditions, which was already bleak, worsened further. Those claiming business conditions are "bad" rose to 51.1 percent from 47.9 percent, while those saying business conditions are "good" edged up to 6.8 percent from 6.5 percent last month. Consumers' assessment of the labor market turned considerably more pessimistic in February. Those saying jobs are "hard to get" increased to 47.8 percent from 41.1 percent in January, while those stating jobs are "plentiful" fell to 4.4 percent from 7.1 percent.

Consumers' short-term outlook turned significantly more negative this month. Consumers anticipating business conditions will worsen over the next six months increased to 40.5 percent from 31.1 percent, while those expecting conditions to improve declined to 8.7 percent from 12.8 percent in January.

The employment outlook was also much grimmer. The percentage of consumers expecting fewer jobs in the months ahead increased to 47.3 percent from 36.9 percent, while those expecting more jobs declined to 7.1 percent from 9.1 percent. The proportion of consumers expecting an increase in their incomes declined to 7.6 percent from 10.3 percent.

Why would a business firm want to receive reports regarding consumer confidence in the U.S. economy? The answer lies in the role of expectations as a determinant of consumption spending and therefore aggregate demand. If households are confident that incomes will rise and prosperous times are ahead, they are much more likely to spend more than if they expect a recession. By monitoring consumer confidence in the economy, we can better understand consumer spending. Since consumption accounts for about two-thirds of GDP, changes in household spending can play a big role in business-cycle fluctuations.

In terms of aggregate demand and supply analysis, if households are more optimistic about the economy's performance, then the aggregate demand curve should shift to the right, like the shift from AD_0 to AD_1 in the accompanying figure. This would increase the equilibrium level of real GDP from Y_0 to Y_1. If households are less optimistic about the economy's performance, then the aggregate demand curve should shift to the left, like the shift from AD_0 to AD_2. This would decrease the equilibrium level of real GDP from Y_0 to Y_2.

Because of the implications of shifts in consumer confidence for business-cycle fluctuations, government officials, along with businesspeople, watch the consumer confidence measures to maintain a sense of what is happening in the typical household. The two best-known surveys, the University of Michigan and Conference Board surveys, ask questions like: "Six months from now, do you think business conditions will be better, the same, or worse?" and "Would you say that you are better off or worse off financially than you were a year ago?" The answers to these questions and others are used as inputs in constructing an index of consumer confidence so that the press typically reports only how the overall index changes rather than the responses to any particular question.

Although the popular consumer confidence indexes fluctuate up and down every month, researchers have found that the monthly fluctuations are not very useful in predicting consumption or GDP. However, major shifts in the indexes or several months of rising or falling indexes may provide an early signal of forthcoming changes in consumption and GDP.

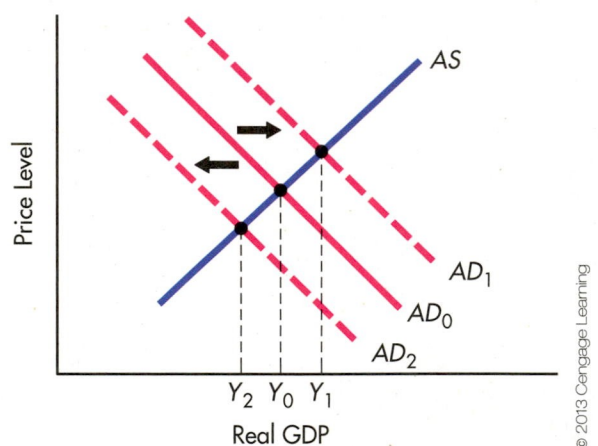

© 2013 Cengage Learning

CHAPTER 9

Aggregate Expenditures

© MACIEJ FROLOW/GETTY IMAGES, INC

© DMITRIJS DMITRIJEVS/SHUTTERSTOCK.COM; LOGO: FROXX/SHUTTERSTOCK.COM

FUNDAMENTAL QUESTIONS

1 How are consumption and saving related?

2 What are the determinants of consumption?

3 What are the determinants of investment?

4 What are the determinants of government spending?

5 What are the determinants of net exports?

6 What is the aggregate expenditures function?

To understand why real GDP, unemployment, and inflation rise and fall over time, we must know what causes the aggregate demand and aggregate supply curves to shift. We cannot understand why the U.S. economy has experienced 11 recessions since 1945 or why, in the 1990s and 2000s, we witnessed the longest peacetime business-cycle expansion in modern times unless we understand why the *AD* and *AS* curves shift. In this chapter, we examine in more detail the demand side of the economy.

In the chapter titled "Macroeconomic Equilibrium: Aggregate Demand and Supply," we discussed how the price level affects aggregate expenditures through the interest rate, international trade, and wealth effects. This chapter examines the nonprice determinants of spending and shifts in aggregate demand in greater detail and assumes that the price level is fixed. This assumption means that the aggregate supply

FIGURE 1   The Fixed-Price Keynesian Model

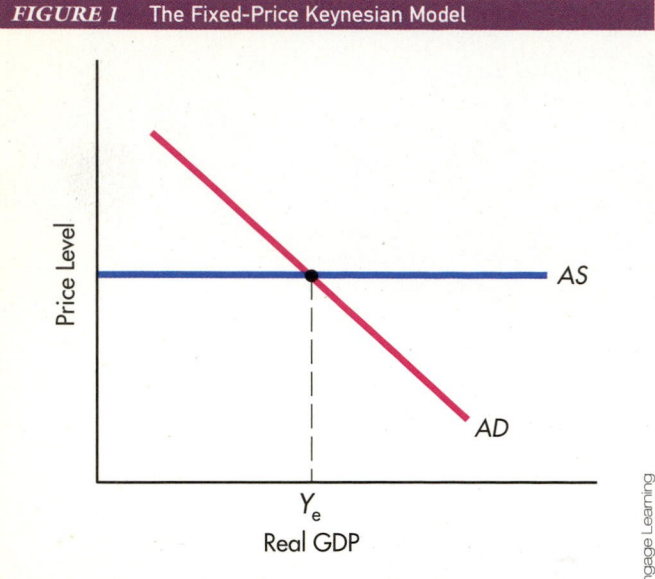

The Keynesian assumption that the price level is fixed requires a horizontal aggregate supply curve. In this case, aggregate demand will determine the equilibrium level of real GDP.

exist. Firms can hire from this pool of unemployed labor and increase their output at no extra cost and without any pressure on the price level. It is not surprising that Keynes would rely on such a model at a time when he was surrounded by mass unemployment. He was more interested in the determination of income and output than in the problem of inflation.

With a horizontal *AS* curve, as shown in Figure 1, the location of the *AD* curve will determine the equilibrium level of real GDP, Y_e. If we understand what determines aggregate demand—consumption, investment, government spending, and net exports—we will understand what determines real GDP.

We begin our detailed examination of aggregate expenditures by discussing consumption, which accounts for approximately 70 percent of total expenditures in the U.S. economy. We then look at investment (16 percent of total expenditures), government spending (19 percent of total expenditures), and net exports (−5 percent of total expenditures).

curve is a horizontal line at the fixed-price level. This approach was used by John Maynard Keynes, who analyzed the macro economy during the Great Depression.

A fixed-price level, as shown in Figure 1, suggests a situation in which unemployment and excess capacity

1. Consumption and Saving

1 How are consumption and saving related?

Households can do three things with their income: They can spend it for the consumption of goods and services, they can save it, or they can pay taxes with it. Disposable income is what is left after taxes have been paid. It is the sum of consumption and saving:

$$\text{Disposable income} = \text{consumption} + \text{saving}$$

or

$$Yd = C + S$$

Disposable income is the income that households actually have available for spending after taxes. Whatever disposable income is not spent is saved.

Why are we talking about saving, which is not a component of total spending, in a chapter that sets out to discuss the components of total spending? Saving is simply "not consuming"; it is impossible to separate the incentives to save from the incentives to consume.

1.a. Saving and Savings

Before we go on, it is necessary to understand the difference between *saving* and *savings*. *Saving* occurs over a unit of time—a week, a month, a year. For instance, you might save $10 a week or $40 a month. Saving is a *flow* concept. *Savings* are an amount accumulated at a particular point in time—today, December 31, or your 65th birthday. For example, you might have savings of $2,500 on December 31. Savings are a *stock* concept.

Like saving, GDP and its components are flow concepts. They are measured by the year or quarter of the year. Consumption, investment, government spending, and net exports are also flows. Each of them is an amount spent over a period of time.

Consumption spending is the largest component of aggregate expenditures. Households in Chichicastenango, Guatemala, come to the produce market shown here to purchase food. Their expenditures on food will be counted in the consumption and the GDP of Guatemala. If the households decide to save less and spend more, then, other things being equal, the higher consumption will raise the GDP of Guatemala.

1.b. The Consumption and Saving Functions

The primary determinant of the level of consumption over any given period is the level of disposable income. The higher the disposable income, the more households are willing and able to spend. This relationship between disposable income and consumption is called the **consumption function**. Figure 2 contains the consumption function for the United States over the long-run period from 1990 to 2009. For each year in this period, the values of disposable income and consumption are plotted in the figure. Note that Figure 2 also contains a 45-degree line. (A 45-degree line makes a graph easier to read because every point on the line represents the same value on both axes.) This line splits the area of the figure in half and shows all points at which the value of disposable income and the value of consumption are equal. Since the actual consumption function lies below the 45-degree line, it can be seen that consumption is less than disposable income—but not much less.

The consumption function in Figure 2 is a long-run consumption function. In the short run, like this year, the relationship between consumption and disposable income may be much flatter than that shown in Figure 2. We now turn to a deeper analysis of the consumption function to better understand this important relationship.

To focus on the relationship between income and consumption, we draw a new graph, Figure 3, with income on the horizontal axis and consumption on the vertical axis. Figure 3(a) shows a hypothetical consumption function. In this economy, when disposable income is zero, consumption is $30. As disposable income rises, consumption rises. For instance, when disposable income is $100, consumption is $100.

We use C to represent consumption and Yd to represent disposable income. The line labeled C in Figure 3(a) is the consumption function: It represents the relationship between disposable income and consumption. The other line in the figure creates a 45-degree angle with either axis. In Figure 3(a), as in Figure 2, the 45-degree line shows all the points where consumption equals disposable income.

> *Saving occurs over a unit of time; it is a flow concept.*

> *Savings are an amount accumulated at a point in time; they are a stock concept.*

consumption function
The relationship between disposable income and consumption.

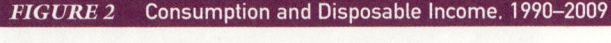

FIGURE 2   Consumption and Disposable Income, 1990–2009

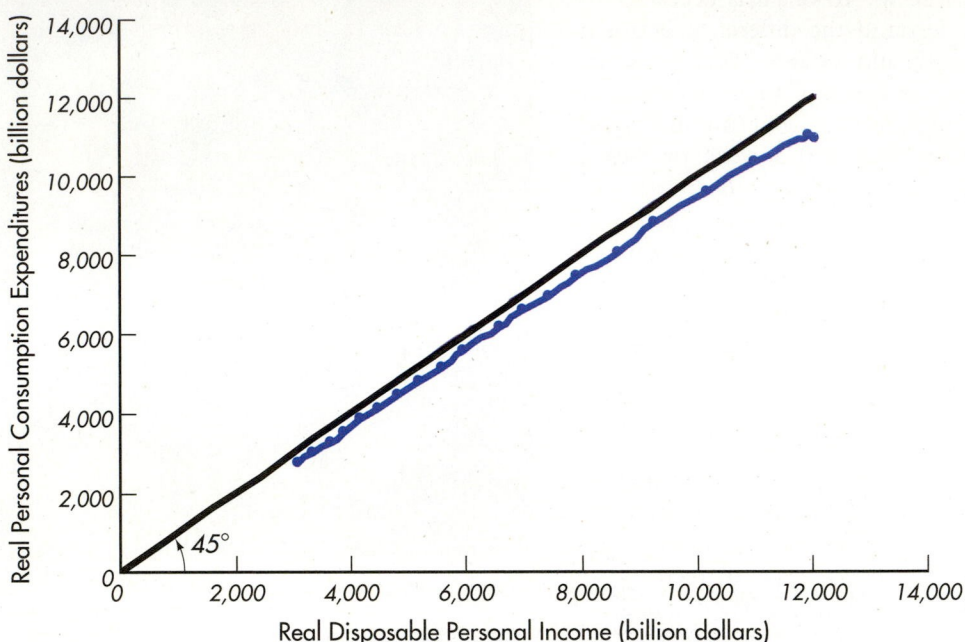

The figure shows the long-run consumption function for the United States. The 45-degree line shows all points at which consumption and disposable income are equal. Note that the actual consumption function lies only slightly below the 45-degree line. This indicates that consumption is less than disposable income—but not much less.

Source: www.bea.gov.

The level of disposable income at which all disposable income is being spent occurs at the point where the consumption function (line C) crosses the 45-degree line. In the graph, C equals Yd when disposable income is $100. Consumers save a fraction of any disposable income above $100. You can see this in the graph. Saving occurs at any level of disposable income at which the consumption function lies below the 45-degree line (at which consumption is less than disposable income). The amount of saving is measured by the vertical distance between the 45-degree line and the consumption function. If disposable income is $600, consumption is $450 and saving is $150.

The **saving function** is the relationship between disposable income and saving. Figure 3(b) plots the saving function (S). When the level of disposable income is at $100, consumption equals disposable income, so saving is zero. As disposable income increases beyond $100, saving goes up. In Figure 3(a), saving is the vertical distance between the 45-degree line and the consumption function. In Figure 3(b), we can read the level of saving directly from the saving function.

Notice that at relatively low levels of disposable income, consumption exceeds disposable income. How can consumption be greater than disposable income? When a household spends more than it earns in income, the household must finance the spending above income by borrowing or using savings. This is called **dissaving**. In Figure 3(a), dissaving occurs at levels of disposable income between $0 and $100, where the consumption function lies above the 45-degree line. Dissaving, like saving, is measured

saving function
The relationship between disposable income and saving.

dissaving
Spending financed by borrowing or using savings.

FIGURE 3 Disposable Income Consumption and Saving in a Hypothetical Economy

Disposable Income (Yd)	Consumption (C)	Saving (S)
$0	$30	− $30
$100	$100	$0
$200	$170	$30
$300	$240	$60
$400	$310	$90
$500	$380	$120
$600	$450	$150
$700	$570	$180

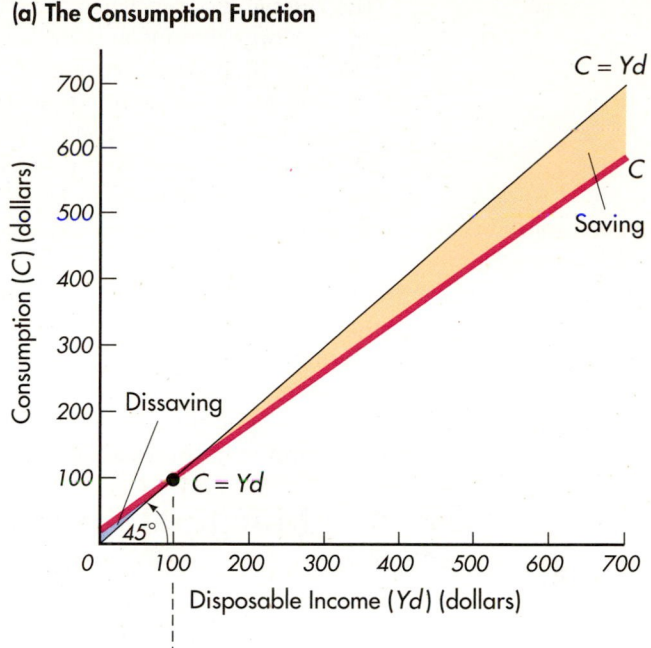

(a) The Consumption Function

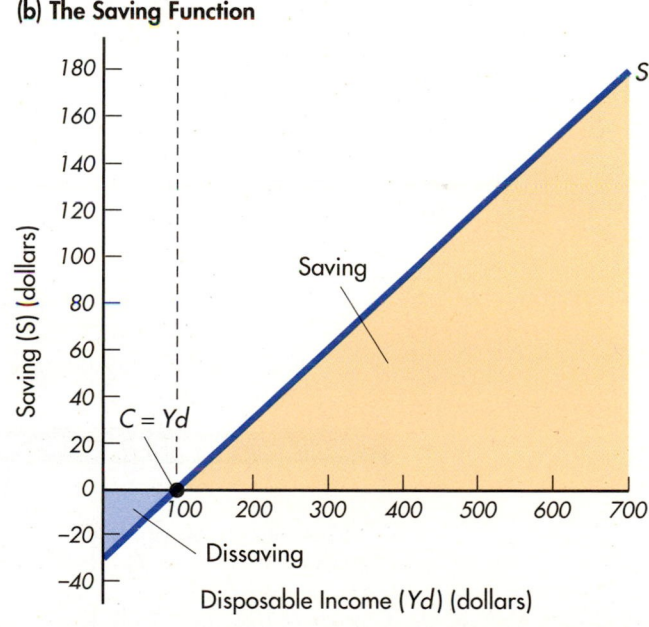

(b) The Saving Function

Figure 3(a) shows that consumption is a positive function of disposable income: It goes up as disposable income rises. The line labeled $C = Yd$ forms a 45-degree angle at the origin. It shows all points where consumption equals disposable income. The point at which the consumption function (line C) crosses the 45-degree line—where disposable income measures $100—is the point at which consumption equals disposable income. At lower levels of disposable income, consumption is greater than disposable income; at higher levels, consumption is less than disposable income. Figure 3(b) shows the saving function. Saving equals disposable income minus consumption. When consumption equals disposable income, saving is 0. At higher levels of disposable income, we find positive saving; at lower levels, we find negative saving, or dissaving.

by the vertical distance between the 45-degree line and the consumption function, but dissaving occurs when the consumption function lies *above* the 45-degree line. In Figure 3(b), dissaving occurs when the saving function (line S) lies below the disposable income axis, at disposable income levels between $0 and $100. For example, when disposable income is $0, dissaving (negative saving) is −$30.

Both the consumption function and the saving function have positive slopes: As disposable income rises, consumption and saving increase. Consumption and saving, then, are positive functions of disposable income. Notice that when disposable income equals zero, consumption is still positive.

autonomous consumption
Consumption that is independent of income.

There is a level of consumption, called **autonomous consumption**, that does not depend on income. (*Autonomous* here means "independent of income.") In Figure 3(a), consumption equals $30 when disposable income equals $0. This $30 is autonomous consumption; it does not depend on income but will vary with the nonincome determinants of consumption that will soon be introduced. The intercept of the consumption function (the value of C when Yd equals $0) measures the amount of autonomous consumption. The intercept in Figure 3(a) is $30, which means that autonomous consumption in this example is $30.

1.c. Marginal Propensity to Consume and Save

Total consumption equals autonomous consumption plus the spending that depends on income. As disposable income rises, consumption rises. This relationship between *change* in disposable income and *change* in consumption is the **marginal propensity to consume (MPC)**. The *MPC* measures change in consumption as a proportion of the change in disposable income.

marginal propensity to consume (*MPC*)
The change in consumption as a proportion of the change in disposable income.

$$MPC = \frac{\text{change in consumption}}{\text{change in disposable income}}$$

In Table 1, columns 1 and 2 list the consumption function data used in Figure 3. The marginal propensity to consume is shown in column 4. In our example, each time that disposable income changes by $100, consumption changes by $70. This means that consumers spend 70 percent of any extra income that they receive.

$$MPC = \frac{\$70}{\$100}$$
$$= .70$$

TABLE 1	Marginal Propensity to Consume and to Save			
Disposable Income (*Yd*)	Consumption (*C*)	Saving (*S*)	Marginal Propensity to Consume (*MPC*)	Marginal Propensity to Save (*MPS*)
$ 0	$ 30	−$ 30	—	—
$100	$100	$ 0	.70	.30
$200	$170	$ 30	.70	.30
$300	$240	$ 60	.70	.30
$400	$310	$ 90	.70	.30
$500	$380	$120	.70	.30
$600	$450	$150	.70	.30
$700	$520	$180	.70	.30

The *MPC* tells us what fractional change in income is used for consumption. The **marginal propensity to save (*MPS*)** defines the relationship between change in saving and change in disposable income. It is the change in saving divided by the change in disposable income:

$$MPC = \frac{\text{change in consumption}}{\text{change in disposable income}}$$

The *MPS* in Table 1 is a constant 30 percent at all levels of income. Each time that disposable income changes by $100, saving changes by $30:

$$MPC = \frac{\$70}{\$100}$$
$$= .30$$

The *MPC* and the *MPS* will always be constant at all levels of disposable income in our examples.

Because disposable income will be either consumed or saved, the marginal propensity to consume plus the marginal propensity to save must total 1:

$$MPC + MPS = 1$$

The percentage of additional income that is not consumed must be saved. If consumers spend 70 percent of any extra income, they save 30 percent of that income.

The *MPC* and the *MPS* determine the rate of consumption and saving as disposable income changes. The *MPC* is the slope of the consumption function; the *MPS* is the slope of the saving function. Remember that the slope of a line measures the change along the vertical axis that corresponds to a change along the horizontal axis, the rise over the run (see the Appendix to Chapter 1). In the case of the consumption function, the slope is the change in consumption (the change on the vertical axis) divided by the change in disposable income (the change on the horizontal axis):

$$\text{Slope of consumption function} = \frac{\text{change in consumption}}{\text{change in disposable income}}$$
$$= MPC$$

The higher the *MPC*, the greater the fraction of any additional disposable income that consumers will spend. At an *MPC* of .70, consumers spend 70 percent of any change in disposable income; at an *MPC* of .85, consumers want to spend 85 percent of any change in disposable income. The size of the *MPC* shows up graphically as the steepness of the consumption function. The consumption function with an *MPC* of .85 is a steeper line than the one drawn in Figure 3(a). In general, the steeper the consumption function, the larger the *MPC*. If the *MPC* is less than .70, the consumption function will be flatter than the one in the figure.

The slope of the saving function is the *MPS*:

$$\text{Slope of consumption function} = \frac{\text{change in saving}}{\text{change in disposable income}}$$
$$= MPS$$

In general, the steeper the saving function, the greater the slope and the greater the *MPS*.

Figure 4(a) shows three consumption functions. Since all three consumption functions have the same intercept, autonomous consumption is the same for all. But each consumption function in Figure 4(a) has a different slope. Line C_1 has an *MPC* of .70. A larger *MPC*, .80, produces a steeper consumption function (line C_2). A smaller *MPC*,

marginal propensity to save (*MPS*)
The change in saving as a proportion of the change in disposable income.

The slope of the consumption function is the same as the MPC; the slope of the saving function is the same as the MPS.

FIGURE 4 Marginal Propensity to Consume and Save

(a) Three Consumption Functions

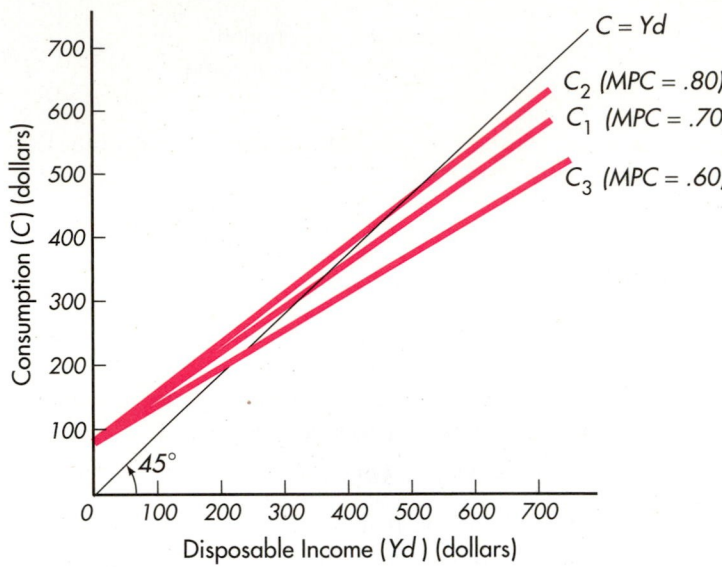

(b) Three Saving Functions

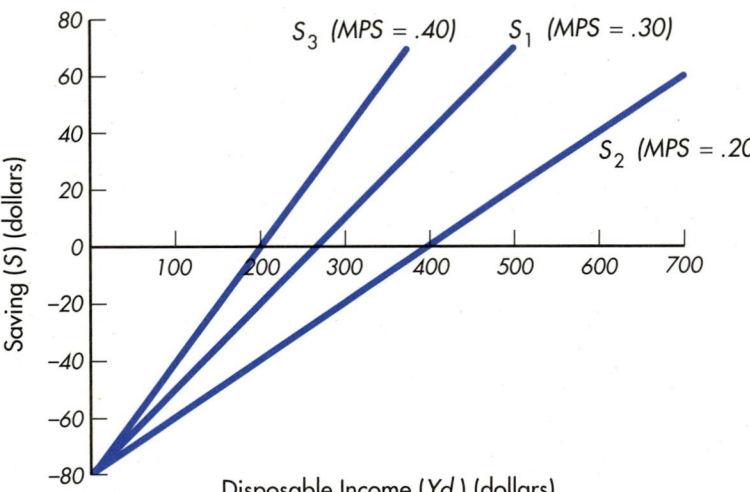

The *MPC* is the slope of the consumption function. The greater the *MPC*, the steeper the consumption function. The *MPS* is the slope of the saving function. The greater the *MPS*, the steeper the saving function. Because the sum of the *MPC* and the *MPS* is 1, the greater the *MPC*, the smaller the *MPS*. The steeper the consumption function, then, the flatter the saving function.

.60, produces a flatter consumption function (line C_3). The saving functions that correspond to these consumption functions are shown in Figure 4(b). Function S_1, with an *MPS* of .30, corresponds to consumption function C_1, with an *MPC* of .70 (remember: *MPS* = 1 − *MPC*). Function S_2 corresponds to C_2, and S_3 corresponds to C_3. The higher the *MPC* (the steeper the consumption function), the lower the *MPS* (the flatter the saving function). If people spend a greater fraction of extra income, they save a smaller fraction.

1.d. Average Propensity to Consume and Save

Suppose our interest is not in the proportion of change in disposable income that is consumed or saved, but in the proportion of disposable income that is consumed or saved. For this, we must know the average propensity to consume and the average propensity to save.

The **average propensity to consume (APC)** is the proportion of disposable income that is spent for consumption:

$$APC = consumption/disposable\ income$$

or

$$APS = \frac{C}{Yd}$$

The **average propensity to save (APS)** is the proportion of disposable income that is saved:

$$APC = \frac{saving}{disposable\ income}$$

or

$$APS = \frac{S}{Yd}$$

Table 2 uses the consumption and saving data plotted in Figure 3. The APC and APS are shown in columns 4 and 5. When disposable income is $100, consumption is also $100, so the ratio of consumption to disposable income (C/Yd) equals 1 ($100/$100). At this point, saving equals $0, so the ratio of saving to disposable income (S/Yd) also equals $0 ($0/$100). We really do not have to compute the APS because we already know the APC. There are only two things that can be done with disposable income: spend it or save it. The percentage of income spent plus the percentage saved must add up to 100 percent of disposable income. This means that

$$APC + APS = 1$$

If the APC equals 1, then the APS must equal 0.

average propensity to consume (APC)
The proportion of disposable income spent for consumption.

average propensity to save (APS)
The proportion of disposable income saved.

TABLE 2	Average Propensity to Consume and to Save			
Disposable Income (Yd)	Consumption (C)	Saving (S)	Average Propensity to Consume (APC)	Average Propensity to Save (APS)
$ 0	$ 30	$ 30	—	—
$100	$100	$ 0	1	0
$200	$170	$ 30	.85	.15
$300	$240	$ 60	.80	.20
$400	$310	$ 90	.78	.22
$500	$380	$120	.76	.24
$600	$450	$150	.75	.25
$700	$520	$180	.74	.26

© 2013 Cengage Learning

When disposable income equals $600, consumption equals $450, so the *APC* equals .75 ($450/$600) and the *APS* equals .25 ($150/$600). As always, the *APC* plus the *APS* equals 1. If households are spending 75 percent of their disposable income, they must be saving 25 percent.

Notice in Table 2 that the *APC* falls as disposable income rises. This is because households spend only part of any change in income. In Figure 3(a), the consumption function rises more slowly than the 45-degree line. (Remember that consumption equals disposable income along the 45-degree line.) The consumption function tells us, then, that consumption rises as disposable income rises, but not by as much as disposable income rises. Because households spend a smaller fraction of disposable income as that income rises, they must be saving a larger fraction. You can see this in Table 2, where the *APS* rises as disposable income rises. At low levels of income, the *APS* is negative, a product of dissaving (we are dividing negative saving by disposable income). As disposable income rises, saving rises as a percentage of disposable income; this means that the *APS* is increasing.

1.e. Determinants of Consumption

2 What are the determinants of consumption?

Disposable income is an important determinant of household spending. But disposable income is not the only factor that influences consumption. Wealth, expectations, demographics, and taxation (taxation effects will be considered in the chapter titled "Fiscal Policy") are other determinants of consumption.

1.e.1. Disposable Income
Household income is the primary determinant of consumption, which is why the consumption function is drawn with disposable income on the horizontal axis. Household income is usually measured as current disposable income. By *current* we mean income that is received in the current period—the current period could be today, this month, this year, or whatever period we are discussing. Past income and future income certainly can affect household spending, but they do so through household wealth or expectations, not through income. Disposable income is after-tax income.

The two-dimensional graphs we have been using relate consumption only to current disposable income. A change in consumption caused by a change in disposable income is shown by *movement along* the consumption function. The effects of other variables are shown by *shifting* the intercept of the consumption function up and down as the values of these other variables change. All variables *except* disposable income change *autonomous* consumption.

Changes in taxes will affect disposable income. *If we assume that there are no taxes, then Yd equals Y, and consumption (and other expenditures) may be drawn as a function of real GDP rather than disposable income.* The chapter titled "Fiscal Policy" is devoted to an analysis of government fiscal policy, including taxation. As a result, we put off our discussion of tax effects until then; this allows us to simplify our analysis of aggregate expenditures. The discussion of the components of aggregate expenditures in the remainder of this chapter and in later chapters will be related graphically to pretax real GDP rather than to disposable income.

1.e.2. Wealth
Wealth is the value of all the assets owned by a household. Wealth is a stock variable; it includes homes, cars, checking and savings accounts, and stocks and bonds, as well as the value of income expected in the future. As household wealth increases, households have more resources available for spending, so consumption increases at every level of real GDP. You can see this in Figure 5(a) as a shift of the

wealth
The value of all assets owned by a household.

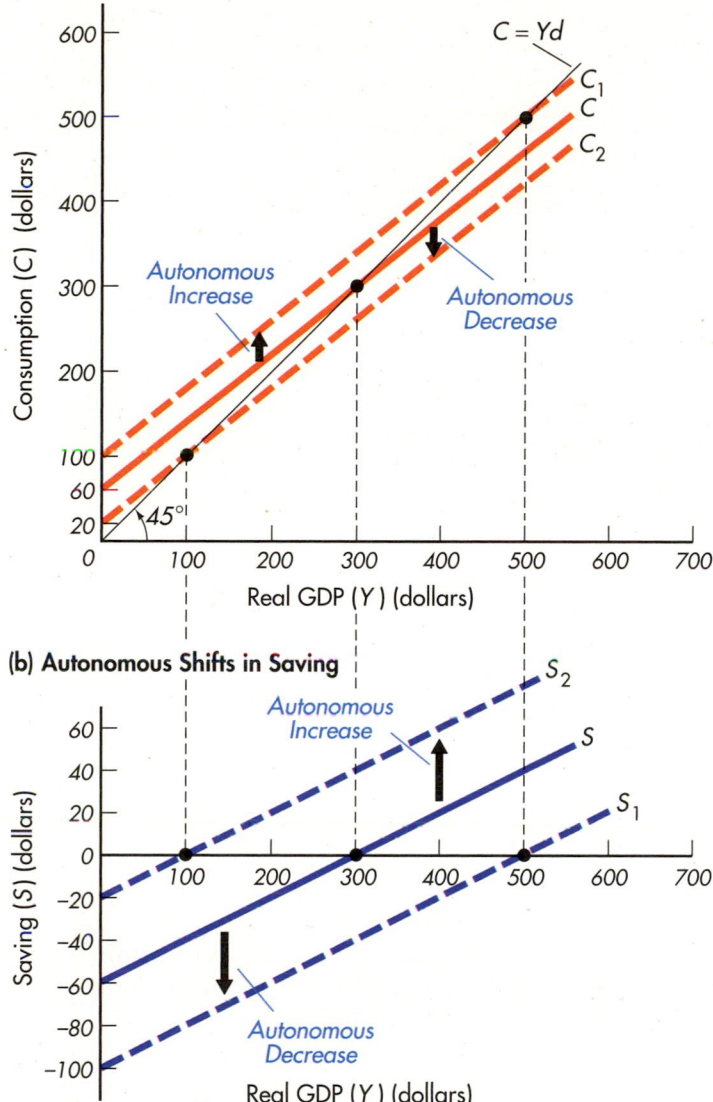

FIGURE 5   Autonomous Shifts in Consumption and in Saving

(a) Autonomous Shifts in Consumption

(b) Autonomous Shifts in Saving

Autonomous consumption is the amount of consumption that exists when real GDP is 0. It is the intercept of the consumption function. The shift from C to C_1 is an autonomous increase in consumption of \$40; it moves the intercept of the consumption function from \$60 to \$100. The shift from C to C_2 is an autonomous decrease in consumption of \$40; it moves the intercept of the consumption function from \$60 to \$20. Autonomous saving is the amount of saving that exists when real GDP is 0. This is the intercept of the saving function. The shift from S to S_1 is an autonomous decrease in saving of \$40; it moves the intercept of the saving function from −\$60 to −\$100. The shift from S to S_2 is an autonomous increase in saving of \$40; it moves the intercept of the saving function from −\$60 to −\$20. Because disposable income minus consumption equals saving, an autonomous increase in consumption is associated with an autonomous decrease in saving, and an autonomous decrease in consumption is associated with an autonomous increase in saving.

consumption function from C to C_1. The autonomous increase in consumption shifts the intercept of the consumption function from $60 to $100, so consumption increases by $40 at every level of real GDP. If households spend more of their current income as their wealth increases, they save less. You can see this as the downward shift of the saving function in Figure 5(b), from S to S_1. The higher level of wealth has households more willing to dissave at each income level than before. Dissaving now occurs at any level of income below $500. During the long expansionary period of the 1990s, stock price increases made many households much wealthier and stimulated consumption.

A decrease in wealth has just the opposite effect. For instance, during the 2008 recession, property values in most areas of the United States declined. Household wealth declined as the value of real estate fell, and spending fell as a result. Here you would see an autonomous drop in consumption, like the shift from C to C_2, and an autonomous increase in saving, like the shift from S to S_2. Now at every level of real GDP, households spend $40 less than before and save $40 more. The intercept of the consumption function is $20, not $60, and the intercept of the saving function is −$20, not −$60. The new consumption function parallels the old one; the curves are the same vertical distance apart at every level of income. So consumption is $40 lower at every level of income. Similarly, the saving functions are parallel because saving is $40 greater at every level of real GDP along S_2 compared to S.

1.e.3. Expectations

Another important determinant of consumption is consumer expectations about future income, prices, and wealth. When consumers expect a recession, when they are worried about losing their jobs or facing cutbacks in hours worked, they tend to spend less and save more. This means an autonomous decrease in consumption and increase in saving, like the shift from C to C_2 and from S to S_2 in Figure 5. Conversely, when consumers are optimistic, we find an autonomous increase in consumption and decrease in saving, like the shift from C to C_1 and from S to S_1 in Figure 5.

Expectations are subjective opinions; they are difficult to observe and measure. This creates problems for economists trying to analyze the effect of expectations on consumption. The Conference Board surveys households to construct its *Consumer Confidence Index*, a measure of consumer opinion regarding the outlook for the economy. Economists follow the index in order to predict how consumer spending will change. Since consumption is the largest component of GDP, changes in consumption have important implications for business cycles.

Clearly the Consumer Confidence Index is not always a reliable indicator of expansion or recession. Still, economists' increasing use of this and other measures to better understand fluctuations in consumption underscores the importance of consumer expectations in the economy (see the Economic Insight "Permanent Income, Life Cycles, and Consumption").

1.e.4. Demographics

Other things being equal, economists expect the level of consumption to rise with increases in population. The focus here is on both the number of people in the economy and the composition of that population. The size of the population affects the position of the consumption function; the age of the population affects the slope of the consumption function. The greater the size of the population, other things equal, the higher the intercept of the consumption function. With regard to the effect of age composition on the economy, young households typically are accumulating durable consumer goods (refrigerators, washing machines, automobiles); they have higher *MPCs* than older households.

ECONOMIC INSIGHT

Permanent Income, Life Cycles, and Consumption

Studies of the consumption function over a long period of time find a function like the one labeled C_L in the graph, as we saw earlier in Figure 2. This function has a marginal propensity to consume of .90 and an intercept of 0. Consumption functions studied over a shorter period of time have lower MPCs and positive intercepts, like the function C_S in the graph, with an MPC of .60. How do we reconcile these two functions?

Economists offer two related explanations for the difference between long-run and short-run consumption behavior: the permanent income hypothesis and the life-cycle hypothesis. The fundamental idea is that people consume on the basis of their idea of what their long-run or permanent level of income is. A substantial increase in income this month does not affect consumption much in the short run unless it is perceived as a permanent increase.

Let's use point 1 on the graph as our starting point. Here disposable income is $50,000 and consumption is $45,000. Now suppose household income rises to $60,000. Initially consumption increases by 60 percent, the short-run MPC. The household moves from point 1 to point 2 along the short-run consumption function (C_S). The short-run consumption function has a lower MPC than the long-run consumption function because households do not completely adjust their spending and saving habits with short-run fluctuations in income. Once the household is convinced that $60,000 is a permanent level of income, it moves from point 2 to point 3 along the long-run consumption function. At point 3, consumption has increased by 90 percent, the long-run MPC. In the long run, households adjust fully to changes in income; in the short run, a fluctuation in income does not cause as large a fluctuation in consumption.

When income falls below the permanent income level, the household is willing to dissave or borrow to support its normal level of consumption. When income rises above the permanent income level, the household saves at a higher rate than the long-run MPS. The lower MPC in the short run works to smooth out consumption in the long run. The household does not adjust current consumption with every up and down movement in household income.

To maintain a steady rate of consumption over time, households follow a pattern of saving over the life cycle. Saving is low when current income is low relative to permanent income (during school years, periods of unemployment, or retirement). Saving is high when current income is high relative to the lifetime average, typically during middle age.

In the long run, households adjust fully to changes in income. In the short run, in order to smooth consumption over time, they do not. This explains both the difference between the long-run and short-run consumption functions and the stability of consumption over time.

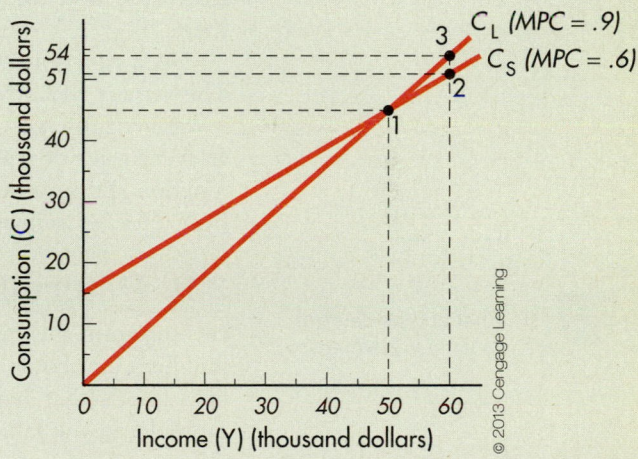

RECAP

1. It is impossible to separate incentives to save from incentives to consume.

2. Saving is a flow variable; savings is a stock variable.

3. Dissaving is spending financed by borrowing or using savings.

4. The marginal propensity to consume measures change in consumption as a proportion of change in disposable income.

5. The marginal propensity to save measures change in saving as a proportion of change in disposable income.

6. The *MPC* plus the *MPS* must equal 1.

7. Change in the *MPC* changes the slope of the consumption function; change in the *MPS* changes the slope of the saving function.

8. The average propensity to consume measures that portion of disposable income spent for consumption.

9. The average propensity to save measures that portion of disposable income saved.

10. The sum of the *APC* and the *APS* must equal 1.

11. The determinants of consumption include income, wealth, expectations, demographics, and taxation.

12. A change in consumption caused by a change in disposable income is shown by movement along the consumption function.

13. Changes in wealth, expectations, or population change autonomous consumption, which is shown as a shift of the consumption function.

2. Investment

Investment is business spending on capital goods and inventories. It is the most variable component of total spending. In this section of the chapter, we take a look at the determinants of investment and see why investment changes so much over the business cycle.

2.a. Autonomous Investment

In order to simplify our analysis of real GDP in the next chapter, we assume that investment is autonomous, that it is independent of current real GDP. This does not mean that we assume that investment is fixed at a constant amount. There are several factors that cause investment to change, but we assume that current real GDP is not one of them.

As a function of real GDP, autonomous investment is drawn as a horizontal line. This means that investment remains constant as real GDP changes. In Figure 6, the investment function (the horizontal line labeled I) indicates that investment equals $50 at every level of real GDP. As the determinants of investment change, the investment function shifts autonomously. As investment increases, the function shifts upward (e.g., from I to I_1); as investment decreases, the function shifts downward (from I to I_2).

2.b. Determinants of Investment

3 What are the determinants of investment?

Investment is business spending on capital goods and inventories. Capital goods are the buildings and equipment that businesses need to produce their products. Inventories are final goods that have not been sold. Inventories can be planned or unplanned. For example, in the fall, a retail department store wants to have enough sizes and styles of the new clothing lines to attract customers. Without a good-sized inventory, sales will suffer. The goods it buys are *planned* inventory, based on expected sales. But come February, the store wants to have as few fall clothes left unsold as possible. Goods that have not been sold at this stage are *unplanned* inventory. They are a sign that sales were not as good as expected and that too much was purchased last year.

Both types of inventories—planned and unplanned—are called investment. But only planned investment—capital purchases plus planned inventories—is combined with planned consumer, government, and foreign-sector spending to determine the equilibrium level of aggregate expenditures, as we will see in the next chapter. Unplanned investment and unwanted inventories do not affect the equilibrium. They are simply the leftovers of what has recently gone on in the economy. What economists are interested in are the determinants of planned investment.

FIGURE 6   Investment as a Function of Income

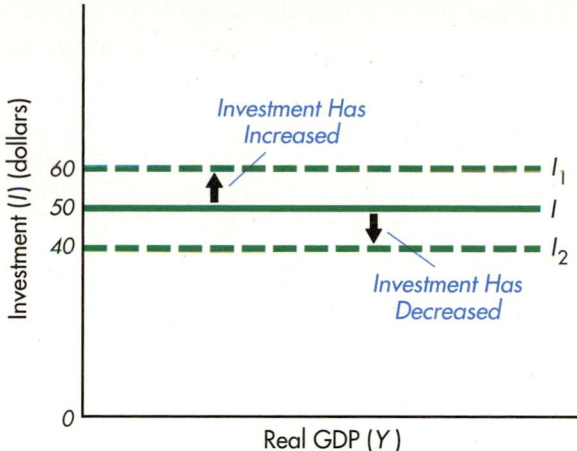

Investment is assumed to be autonomous. Because it is independent of current real GDP, it is drawn as a horizontal line. An autonomous increase in investment shifts the function upward, from I to I_1. An increase could be the product of lower interest rates, optimism in business about future sales and revenues, technological change, an investment tax credit that lowers the cost of capital goods, or a need to expand capacity because of a lack of available productive resources. An autonomous decrease in investment moves the function down, from I to I_2. The same factors that cause investment to rise can also cause it to fall when they move in the opposite direction.

2.b.1. The Interest Rate

Business investment is made in the hopes of earning profits. The greater the expected profit, the greater the investment. A primary determinant of whether an investment opportunity will be profitable is the rate of interest. The interest rate is the cost of borrowed funds. Much of business spending is financed by borrowing. As the rate of interest goes up, fewer investment projects offer enough profit to warrant undertaking them. In other words, the higher the interest rate, the lower the rate of investment. As the interest rate falls, opportunities for greater profits increase and investment rises.

Let's look at a simple example. A firm can acquire a machine for $100 that will yield $120 in output. Whether the firm is willing to undertake the investment depends on whether it will earn a sufficient return on its investment. The return on an investment is the profit from the investment divided by its cost.

If the firm has to borrow $100 to make the investment, it will have to pay interest to the lender. Suppose the lender charges 10 percent interest. The firm will have to pay 10 percent of $100, or $10, interest. This raises the cost of the investment to $110, the $100 cost of the machine plus the $10 interest. The firm's return on the investment is 9 percent:

$$\text{Return on investment} = (\$120 - \$110)/\$110$$
$$= .09$$

As the interest rate rises, the firm's cost of borrowing also rises, and the return on investment falls. When the interest rate is 20 percent, the firm must pay $20 in interest, so the total cost of the investment is $120. Here the return is 0 ([$120 − $120]/$120). The higher interest rate reduces the return on the investment and discourages investment spending.

As the interest rate falls, the firm's cost of borrowing falls and the return on the investment rises. If the interest rate is 5 percent, the firm must pay $5 in interest. The total cost of the investment is $105, and the return is 14 percent ([$120 − $105]/$105). The lower interest rate increases the return on the investment and encourages investment spending.

2.b.2. Profit Expectations

Firms undertake investment in the expectation of earning a profit. Obviously, they cannot know exactly how much profit they will earn. So they use forecasts of revenues and costs to decide on an appropriate level of investment. It is their *expected* rate of return that actually determines their level of investment.

Many factors affect expectations of profit and, therefore, change the level of investment. Among them are new firms entering the market; political change; new laws, taxes, or subsidies from government; and the overall economic health of the country or the world as measured by gross domestic product.

2.b.3. Other Determinants of Investment

Everything that might affect a firm's expected rate of return determines its level of investment. But three factors—technological change, the cost of capital goods, and capacity utilization—warrant special attention.

Technological Change Technological change is often a driving force behind new investment. New products or processes can be crucial to remaining competitive in an industry. The computer industry, for example, is driven by technological change. As faster and larger-capacity memory chips are developed, computer manufacturers must utilize them in order to stay competitive.

The impact of technology on investment spending is not new. For example, the invention of the cotton gin stimulated investment spending in the early 1800s, and the introduction of the gasoline-powered tractor in 1905 created an agricultural investment boom in the early 1900s. More recently, the development of integrated circuits stimulated investment spending in the electronics industry.

One measure of the importance of technology is the commitment to research and development. Data on spending for research and development across countries are listed in Table 3. The data indicate that rich countries tend to spend a greater percentage of GDP on research and development, rely less on government financing of research and development, and have a greater fraction of the workforce employed in research positions.

A commitment to research and development is a sign of the technological progress that marks the industrial nations. The industrial nations are the countries in which new technology generally originates. New technology developed in any country tends to stimulate investment spending across all nations, as firms in similar industries are forced to adopt new production methods to keep up with their competition.

Cost of Capital Goods The cost of capital goods also affects investment spending. As capital goods become more expensive, the rate of return on investment in them drops and the amount of investment falls. One factor that can cause the cost of capital goods to change sharply is government tax policy. The U.S. government has enacted and then removed investment tax credits several times in the past. These credits allow firms to deduct part of the cost of investment from their tax bill. When the cost of investment drops, investment increases. When the cost of investment increases, the level of investment falls.

Capacity Utilization If its existing capital stock is being used heavily, a firm has an incentive to buy more. But if much of its capital stock is standing idle, the firm has little incentive to increase that stock. Economists sometimes refer to the productive capacity of the economy as the amount of output that can be produced by businesses. In fact, the

TABLE 3	Research and Development Expenditures as a Percentage of GDP, 2008		
	% of GDP	% Government Financed	Researchers per 1,000 Workers
Australia	1.8	44.4	8.4
Canada	2.0	34.5	7.8
Finland	3.5	25.7	16.6
France	2.1	38.4	8.2
Germany	2.5	31.1	7.2
Italy	1.1	50.8	3.4
Japan	3.3	17.7	11.0
Mexico	0.5	59.1	1.2
Poland	0.6	62.7	4.5
Turkey	0.8	50.6	1.9
United Kingdom	1.8	31.3	5.9
United States	2.6	31.2	9.7

Source: Data from *OECD Factbook*, OECD, 2008.

Federal Reserve constructs a measure of capacity utilization that indicates how close the economy is to capacity output.

Figure 7 plots the rate of capacity utilization in the U.S. economy. Between 1975 and 2010, U.S. industry operated at a high rate of 85 percent of capacity in 1979 and at a low rate of 73.9 percent of capacity in the recession year of 1982. We never expect to see 100 percent of capacity utilized for the same reasons that we never expect to see zero unemployment. There are always capital goods that are temporarily unused, just as there is frictional unemployment of labor, and there are always capital goods that are obsolete because of technological change, similar to the case of structural unemployment of labor.

When the economy is utilizing its capacity at a high rate, there is pressure to increase the production of capital goods and expand productive capacity. When capacity utilization is low—when factories and machines are sitting idle—investment tends to fall.

2.c. Volatility

We said that investment is the most variable component of total spending. What role do the determinants of investment play in that volatility?

Interest rates fluctuate widely. They are much more variable than income. Interest rates are a very important determinant of investment. Clearly, the fact that they are so variable contributes to the variability of investment.

Expectations are subjective judgments about the future. Expectations can and often do change suddenly with new information. A rumor of a technological breakthrough, a speech by the president or a powerful member of Congress, even a revised weather forecast can cause firms to reexamine their thinking about the expected profitability of an investment. In developing economies, the protection of private property rights can have a large impact on investment spending. If a business expects a change in government policy to increase the likelihood of the government's expropriating its property, obviously it is not going to undertake new investments. Conversely, if a firm believes that the government will protect private property and encourage the accumulation of wealth,

FIGURE 7   Capacity Utilization Rates for Total U.S. Industry

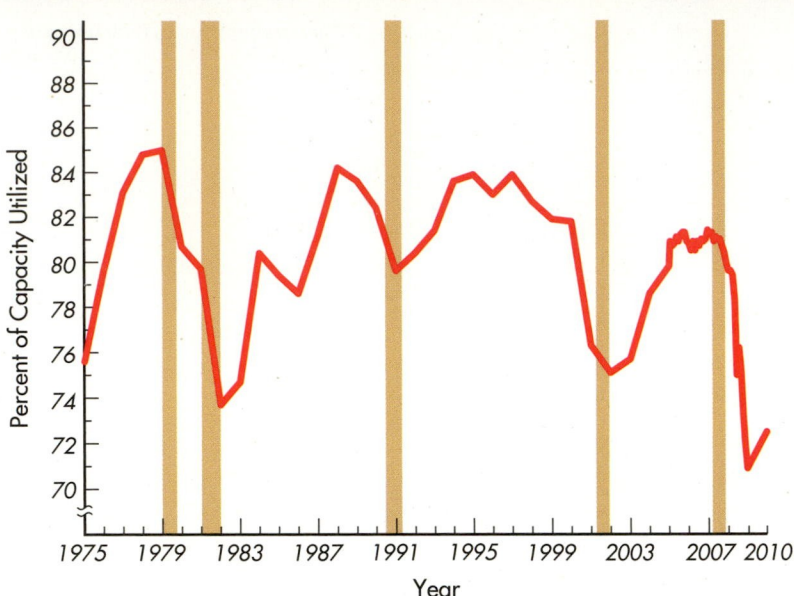

The Federal Reserve estimates the rate at which capacity is utilized in U.S. industry. The higher the rate, the greater the pressure for investment to expand productive capacity. Shaded areas represent recessions.

© 2013 Cengage Learning

it will increase its investment spending. The fact that expectations are subject to large and frequent swings contributes to the volatility of investment.

Technological change proceeds very unevenly, making it difficult to forecast. Historically we find large increases in investment when a new technology is first developed and decreases in investment once the new technology is in place. This causes investment to move up and down unevenly through time.

Changes in tax policy occur infrequently, but they can create large incentives to invest or not to invest. Tax laws in the United States have swung back and forth on whether to offer an investment tax credit. A credit was first introduced in 1962. It was repealed in 1969, then readopted in 1971, and later revised in 1975, 1976, and 1981. In 1986, the investment tax credit was repealed again. Each of these changes had an impact on the cost of capital goods and contributed to the volatility of investment.

Finally, investment generally rises and falls with the rate of capacity utilization over the business cycle. As capacity utilization rises, some firms must add more factories and machines in order to continue increasing their output and avoid reaching their maximum output level. As capacity utilization fluctuates, so will investment.

RECAP

1. As a function of real GDP, autonomous investment is drawn as a horizontal line.

2. The primary determinants of investment are the interest rate and profit expectations. Technological change, the cost of capital goods, and the rate of capacity utilization have an enormous impact on those expectations.

3. Investment fluctuates widely over the business cycle because the determinants of investment are so variable.

3. Government Spending

Government spending on goods and services is the second largest component of aggregate expenditures in the United States. In later chapters, we examine the behavior of government in detail. Here we focus on how the government sector fits into the aggregate expenditures–income relationship. We assume that government spending is set by government authorities at whatever level they choose, independent of current income. In other words, we assume that government spending, like investment, is autonomous.

Figure 8 depicts government expenditures as a function of real GDP. The function, labeled G, is a horizontal line. If government officials increase government expenditures, the function shifts upward, parallel to the original curve, by an amount equal to the increase in expenditures (for example, from G to G_1). If government expenditures are reduced, the function shifts downward by an amount equal to the drop in expenditures (for example, from G to G_2).

 4 What are the determinants of government spending?

4. Net Exports

The last component of aggregate expenditures is net exports, or spending by the international sector. Net exports equal a country's exports of goods and services (what it sells to the rest of the world) minus its imports of goods and services (what it buys from the rest of the world). When net exports are positive, there is a surplus in the merchandise and services accounts. When net exports are negative, there is a deficit. The United States has had a net exports deficit since 1975. This is a relatively new phenomenon; the country had run surpluses throughout the post–World War II era until that time.

 5 What are the determinants of net exports?

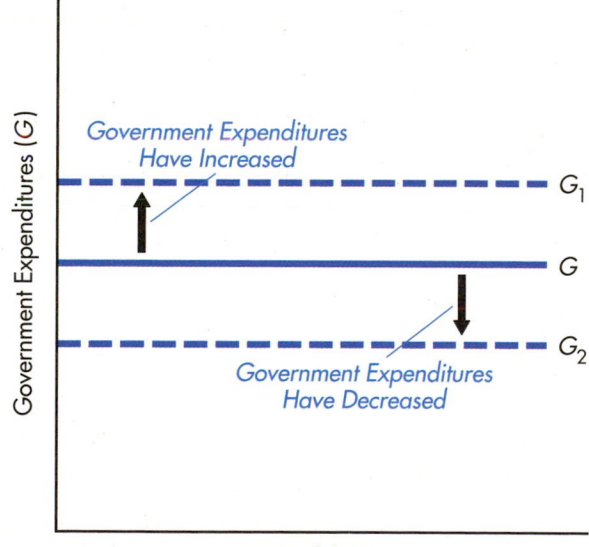

FIGURE 8   Government Expenditures as a Function of Real GDP

Government spending is assumed to be autonomous and set by government policy. The government spending function is the horizontal line labeled G. Autonomous increases in government spending move the function upward (for example, from G to G_1); decreases move the function downward (for example, from G to G_2).

4.a. Exports

We assume that exports are autonomous. There are many factors that determine the actual value of exports, among them foreign income, tastes, prices, government trade restrictions, and exchange rates. But we assume that exports are not affected by current domestic income. You see this in the second column of Table 4, where exports are $50 at each level of real GDP.

As foreign income increases, foreign consumption rises—including consumption of goods produced in other countries—so domestic exports increase at every level of domestic real GDP. Decreases in foreign income lower domestic exports at every level of domestic real GDP. Similarly, changes in tastes or government restrictions on international trade or exchange rates can cause the level of exports to shift autonomously. When tastes favor domestic goods, exports go up. When tastes change, exports go down. When foreign governments impose restrictions on international trade, domestic exports fall. When restrictions are lowered, exports rise. Finally, as discussed in the chapter titled "An Introduction to the Foreign Exchange Market and the Balance of Payments," when the domestic currency depreciates on the foreign exchange market, making domestic goods cheaper in foreign countries, exports rise. When the domestic currency appreciates on the foreign exchange market, making domestic goods more expensive in foreign countries, exports fall.

4.b. Imports

Domestic purchases from the rest of the world (imports) are also determined by tastes, trade restrictions, and exchange rates. Here domestic income plays a role, too. The greater domestic real GDP, the greater domestic imports. The import data in Table 4 show imports increasing with real GDP. When real GDP is 0, autonomous imports equal $0. As real GDP increases, imports increase.

marginal propensity to import (MPI)
The change in imports as a proportion of the change in income.

We measure the sensitivity of changes in imports to changes in real GDP by the marginal propensity to import. The **marginal propensity to import (MPI)** is the proportion of any extra income spent on imports:

$$MPI = \frac{\text{change in import}}{\text{change in income}}$$

In Table 4, the *MPI* is .10, or 10 percent. Every time income changes by $100, imports change by $10.

How do other factors—tastes, government trade restrictions, and exchange rates—affect imports? When domestic tastes favor foreign goods, imports rise. When they do not, imports fall. When the domestic government tightens restrictions on international trade,

TABLE 4	Hypothetical Export and Import Schedule		
Real GDP	**Exports**	**Imports**	**Net Exports**
$ 0	$50	$ 0	$50
$100	$50	$10	$40
$200	$50	$20	$30
$300	$50	$30	$20
$400	$50	$40	$10
$500	$50	$50	$ 0
$600	$50	$60	−$10
$700	$50	$70	−$20

FIGURE 9   Net Exports as a Function of Real GDP

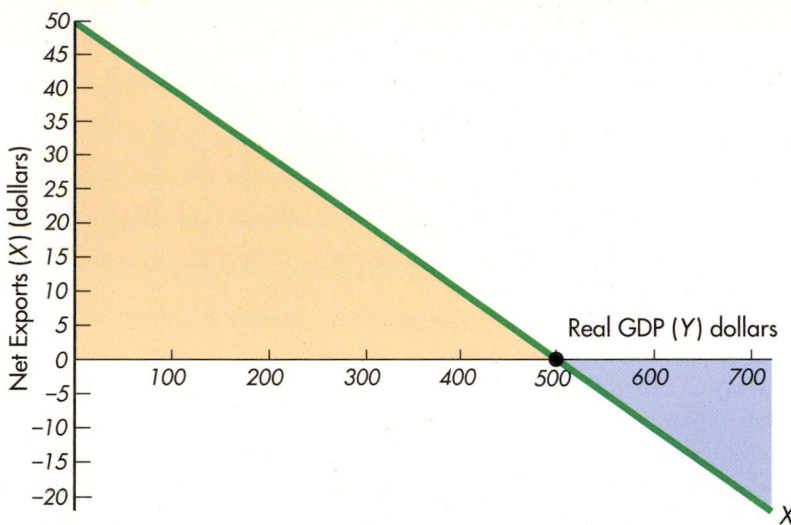

The net exports function is the downward-sloping line labeled *X*. Because exports are autonomous and imports increase with income, net exports fall as domestic real GDP rises. Notice that net exports can be positive or negative.

© 2013 Cengage Learning

imports fall. When those restrictions are loosened, imports rise. Finally, when the domestic currency depreciates on the foreign exchange market, making foreign goods more expensive to domestic residents, imports fall. And when the domestic currency appreciates on the foreign exchange market, lowering the price of foreign goods, imports rise.

4.c. The Net Export Function

In our hypothetical economy in Table 4, net exports are listed in the last column. They are the difference between exports and imports. Because imports rise with domestic income, the higher that income is, the lower net exports are.

The net exports function, labeled *X*, is shown in Figure 9. The downward slope of the function (given by the *MPI*) indicates that net exports fall as real GDP increases. Net exports are the only component of aggregate expenditures that can take on a negative value (saving can be negative, but it is not part of spending). Negative net exports mean that the domestic economy is importing more than it exports. The net exports function shifts with changes in foreign income, prices, tastes, government trade restrictions, and exchange rates. For example, as foreign income increases, domestic exports increase and the net exports function shifts upward.

The higher domestic income is, the lower net exports are.

RECAP

1. Net exports equal a country's exports minus its imports.

2. Exports are determined by foreign income, tastes, government trade restrictions, and exchange rates; they are independent of domestic real GDP.

3. Imports are a positive function of domestic real GDP; they also depend on tastes, domestic government trade restrictions, and exchange rates.

4. The marginal propensity to import measures the change in imports as a proportion of the change in domestic income.

5. Net exports fall as domestic real GDP rises.

5. The Aggregate Expenditures Function

The aggregate, or total, expenditures function is the sum of the individual functions for each component of planned spending. Aggregate expenditures (AE) equal consumption (C), plus investment (I), plus government spending (G), plus net exports (X):

$$AE = C + I + G + X$$

5.a. Aggregate Expenditures Table and Function

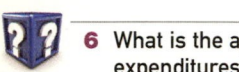

6 What is the aggregate expenditures function?

The table in Figure 10 lists aggregate expenditures data for a hypothetical economy. Real GDP is in the first column; the individual components of aggregate expenditures are in columns 2 through 5. Aggregate expenditures, listed in column 6, are the sum of the components at each level of income.

The aggregate expenditures function (AE) can be derived graphically by summing the individual expenditure functions (Figure 10) in a vertical direction. We begin with the consumption function (C) and then add autonomous investment, $50, to the consumption function at every level of income to arrive at the $C + I$ function. To this we add constant government spending, $70, at every level of income to find the $C + I + G$ function. Finally, we add the net exports function to find $C + I + G + X$, or the AE function.

Notice that the C, $C + I$, and $C + I + G$ functions are all parallel. They all have the same slope, which is determined by the MPC. This is because I and G are autonomous. The AE function has a smaller slope than the other functions because the slope of the net exports function is negative. By adding the X function to the $C + I + G$ function, we are decreasing the slope of the AE function; the $C + I + G + X$ function has a smaller, flatter slope than the $C + I + G$ function.

The X function increases spending for levels of real GDP below $500 and decreases spending for levels of real GDP above $500. At $500, net exports equal 0 (see column 5). Because domestic imports increase as domestic income increases, net exports fall as income rises. At incomes above $500, net exports are negative, so aggregate expenditures are less than $C + I + G$.

5.b. The Next Step

Though we have also been using *aggregate demand* to refer to total spending, you can see from Figure 10 that the aggregate expenditures line slopes up, whereas the aggregate demand curve you saw in Figure 1 slopes down. In the next chapter, we will explore the formal relationship between these two related concepts when we go about determining the equilibrium level of real GDP using the AE function.

The concept of macroeconomic equilibrium points out the key role that aggregate expenditures play in determining output and income. As you will see, the equilibrium level of real GDP is that level toward which the economy automatically tends to move. Once that equilibrium is established, there is no tendency for real GDP to change unless a change in autonomous expenditures occurs. If aggregate expenditures rise, then the equilibrium level of real GDP rises. If aggregate expenditures fall, then the equilibrium level of real GDP falls. Such shifts in the AE function are associated with shifts in C, I, G, or X.

FIGURE 10   The Aggregate Expenditures Function

(1) Y	(2) C	(3) I	(4) G	(5) X	(6) AE
$0	$30	$50	$70	$50	$200
$100	$100	$50	$70	$40	$260
$200	$170	$50	$70	$30	$320
$300	$240	$50	$70	$20	$380
$400	$310	$50	$70	$10	$440
$500	$380	$50	$70	$0	$500
$600	$450	$50	$70	−$10	$560
$700	$520	$50	$70	−$20	$620

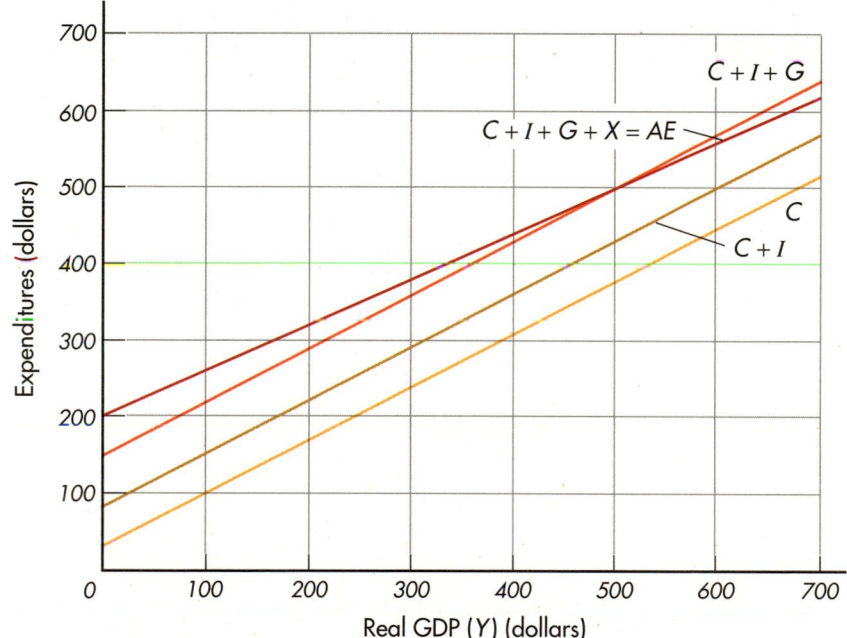

To find the aggregate expenditures function, we begin with the consumption function (labeled C) and add the investment function (I) to create the $C + I$ function. We then add the government spending function (G) to find the $C + I + G$ function. Notice that the C, $C + I$, and $C + I + G$ functions are all parallel. They have the same slope because investment and government spending are assumed to be autonomous. Because I and G do not change with income, the slopes of the $C + I$ and $C + I + G$ functions are equal to the slope of the consumption function (the MPC). Net exports are added to the $C + I + G$ function to find the aggregate expenditures function, $C + I + G + X$. The aggregate expenditures function has a smaller slope than the other functions because the slope of the net exports function is negative.

RECAP

1. Aggregate expenditures are the sum of planned consumption, planned investment, planned government spending, and planned net exports at every level of real GDP.

2. Assuming that I and G are autonomous, the C, $C + I$, and $C + I + G$ functions are parallel lines.

3. Net exports increase aggregate expenditures at relatively low levels of domestic real GDP and decrease aggregate expenditures at relatively high levels of domestic real GDP.

SUMMARY

1. How are consumption and saving related?

- Consumption and saving are the components of disposable income; they are determined by the same variables. $1

- Dissaving occurs when consumption exceeds income. $1.b

- The marginal propensity to consume (MPC) is change in consumption divided by change in disposable income; the marginal propensity to save (MPS) is change in saving divided by change in disposable income. $1.c

- The average propensity to consume (APC) is consumption divided by disposable income; the average propensity to save (APS) is saving divided by disposable income. $1.d

2. What are the determinants of consumption?

- The determinants of consumption are income, wealth, expectations, demographics, and taxation. $1.e

3. What are the determinants of investment?

- Investment is assumed to be autonomous, independent of current income. $2.a

- The determinants of investment are the interest rate, profit expectations, technological change, the cost of capital goods, and the rate at which capacity is utilized. $2.b

- Firms use the expected return on investment to determine the expected profitability of an investment project. $2.b.1

- Investment is highly variable over the business cycle because the determinants of investment are themselves so variable. $2.c

4. What are the determinants of government spending?

- Government spending is set by government authorities at whatever level they choose. $3

5. What are the determinants of net exports?

- Net exports are the difference between what a country exports and what it imports; both exports and imports are a product of foreign or domestic income, tastes, foreign and domestic government trade restrictions, and exchange rates. $4.a, 4.b

- Because imports rise with domestic income, the higher that income is, the lower net exports are. $4.c

6. What is the aggregate expenditures function?

- The aggregate expenditures function is the sum of the individual functions for each component of spending. $5

- The slope of the aggregate expenditures function is flatter than that of the consumption function because it includes the net exports function, which has a negative slope. $5.a

KEY TERMS

autonomous consumption, 186
average propensity to consume
   (APC), 189
average propensity to save
   (APS), 189
consumption function, 183

dissaving, 184
marginal propensity to consume
   (MPC), 186
marginal propensity to import
   (MPI), 200

marginal propensity to save
   (MPS), 187
saving function, 184
wealth, 190

EXERCISES

1. Why do we study the consumption and saving functions together?
2. Explain the difference between a flow variable and a stock variable. Classify each of the following as a stock or a flow: income, wealth, saving, savings, consumption, investment, government expenditures, net exports, GDP.
3. Fill in the blanks in the following table:

Income	Consumption	Saving	MPC	MPS	APC	APS
$1,000	$ 400					.60
$2,000	$ 900	$1,100				
$3,000	$1,400			.50		
$4,000		$2,100				

4. Why is consumption so much more stable over the business cycle than investment? In formulating your answer, discuss household behavior as well as business behavior.
5. Assuming investment is autonomous, draw an investment function with income on the horizontal axis. Show how the function shifts if:
   a. The interest rate falls.
   b. An investment tax credit is repealed by Congress.
   c. A new president is expected to be a strong advocate of pro-business policies.
   d. There is a great deal of excess capacity in the economy.
6. Use the following table to answer these questions:

Y	C	I	G	X
$ 500	$500	$10	$20	$60
$ 600	$590	$10	$20	$40
$ 700	$680	$10	$20	$20
$ 800	$770	$10	$20	$ 0
$ 900	$860	$10	$20	– $20
$1,000	$950	$10	$20	– $40

   a. What is the MPC?
   b. What is the MPS?
   c. What is the MPI?
   d. What is the level of aggregate expenditures at each level of income?
   e. Graph the aggregate expenditures function.
7. Based on the table in exercise 6, what is the linear equation for each of the following functions?
   a. Consumption
   b. Investment
   c. Net exports
   d. Aggregate expenditures
8. Is the AE function the same thing as a demand curve? Why or why not?
9. What is the level of saving if:
   a. Disposable income is $500 and consumption is $450?
   b. Disposable income is $1,200 and the APS is .9?
   c. The MPC equals .9, disposable income rises from $800 to $900, and saving is originally $120 when income equals $800?
10. What is the marginal propensity to consume if:
   a. Consumption increases by $75 when disposable income rises by $100?
   b. Consumption falls by $50 when disposable income falls by $100?
   c. Saving equals $20 when disposable income equals $100 and saving equals $40 when disposable income equals $300?
11. How can the APC fall as income rises if the MPC is constant?
12. Why would economies with older populations tend to have consumption functions with greater slopes?
13. Draw a diagram and illustrate the effects of the following on the net exports function for the United States:

a. The French government imposes restrictions on French imports of U.S. goods.

b. The U.S. national income rises.

c. Foreign income falls.

d. The dollar depreciates on the foreign exchange market.

14. Why is the slope of the $C + I + G$ function different from the slope of the $C + I + G + X$ function?

15. Suppose the consumption function is $C = \$200 + 0.8Y$.

a. What is the amount of autonomous consumption?

b. What is the marginal propensity to consume?

c. What would consumption equal when real GDP equals $1,000?

16. Explain why the consumption function is flatter in the short run than in the long run. Draw a diagram to illustrate your answer.

You can find further practice tests in the Online Quiz at **www.cengage.com/economics/boyes**.

© MACIEJ FROLOW/GETTY IMAGES, INC

2009 TRADE GAP IS $380.7 BILLION

Bureau of Economic Analysis, February 10, 2010

The U.S. goods and services deficit decreased in 2009, according to the U.S. Bureau of Economic Analysis and the U.S. Census Bureau. The deficit decreased from $695.9 billion in 2008 to $380.7 billion in 2009, as imports decreased more than exports. As a percentage of U.S. gross domestic product, the goods and services deficit was 2.7 percent in 2009, down from 4.8 percent in 2008.

Exports

Exports of goods and services decreased $273.5 billion in 2009 to $1,553.1 billion. Goods exports decreased $231.4 billion, and services exports decreased $42.1 billion.

- The largest decreases in goods exports were in *industrial supplies and materials* ($91.7 billion); *capital goods* ($67.3 billion); and *automotive vehicles, parts, and engines* ($39.8 billion).

- The largest decreases in services exports were in *travel* ($15.7 billion); *other transportation* ($14.0 billion), which includes freight and port services; and *royalties and license fees* ($8.2 billion).

Imports

Imports of goods and services decreased $588.8 billion in 2009 to $1,933.7 billion. Goods imports decreased $554.7 billion and services imports decreased $34.1 billion.

- The largest decreases in goods imports were in *industrial supplies and materials* ($318.4 billion); *capital goods* ($84.5 billion); and *automotive vehicles, parts, and engines* ($73.8 billion).

- The largest decreases in services imports were in *other transportation* ($17.9 billion), *travel* ($7.1 billion), and *passenger fares* ($7.1 billion).

Goods by Geographic Area

- The goods deficit with Canada decreased from $78.3 billion in 2008 to $20.2 billion in 2009. Exports decreased $56.5 billion to $204.7 billion, while imports decreased $114.6 billion to $224.9 billion.

- The goods deficit with China decreased from $268.0 billion in 2008 to $226.8 billion in 2009. Exports decreased $0.2 billion to $69.6 billion, while imports decreased $41.4 billion to $296.4 billion.

- The goods deficit with the European Union decreased from $95.8 billion in 2008 to $60.5 billion in 2009. Exports decreased $51.0 billion to $220.8 billion, while imports decreased $86.3 billion to $281.3 billion.

Source: U.S. Department of Commerce.

Commentary

In this chapter, we saw how net exports contribute to aggregate expenditures. Merchandise exports bring money from the rest of the world, and higher net exports mean greater aggregate expenditures. Merchandise imports involve outflows of money to foreign countries, and lower net exports mean lower aggregate expenditures.

We saw in the chapter that higher domestic real GDP leads to higher imports and lower net exports. This article points out that the U.S. net export deficit fell in 2008, a year of recession. As U.S. incomes fell, U.S. demand for foreign goods fell and the deficit with the rest of the world shrank. However, in a time of falling incomes, international trade deficits become more politically sensitive than in good times. Because of the effect of net exports on aggregate expenditures, we often hear arguments for policies aimed at increasing exports and decreasing imports. Domestic residents are often resentful of foreign producers and blame foreign competitors for job losses in the home country. However, we must consider the circumstances and then ask if a policy aimed at increasing the national trade surplus (or decreasing the deficit) is really desirable.

Since one country's export is another's import, it is impossible for everyone to have a surplus—on a worldwide basis, the total value of exports equals the total value of imports. If someone must always have a trade deficit when others have trade surpluses, is it necessarily true that surpluses are good and deficits bad so that one country is benefiting at another's expense? In a sense, imports should be preferred to exports, since exports represent goods that are no longer available for domestic consumption and will be consumed by foreign importers. In later chapters you will learn that the benefits of free international trade include more efficient production and increased consumption. Furthermore, if trade among nations is voluntary, it is difficult to argue that deficit countries are harmed while surplus countries benefit from trade.

In general, it is not obvious whether a country is better or worse off running merchandise surpluses rather than deficits. Consider the following simple example of a world with two countries, R and P. Country R is a rich creditor country that is growing rapidly and has a net exports deficit. Country P is a poor debtor country that is growing slowly and has positive net exports. Should we prefer living conditions in P to living conditions in R based solely on the knowledge that P has a net exports surplus and R has a net exports deficit? Although this is indeed a simplistic example, there are real-world analogues of rich creditor countries with international trade deficits and poor debtor nations with international trade surpluses. The point is that you cannot analyze the balance of payments apart from other economic considerations. Deficits are not inherently bad, nor are surpluses necessarily good.

An Algebraic Model of Aggregate Expenditures

Aggregate expenditures (AE) equal consumption (C) plus investment (I) plus government spending (G) plus net exports (X). If we can develop an equation for each component of spending, we can put them together in a single model.

Consumption The consumption function can be written in general form as

$$C = C^a + cYd$$

where C^a is autonomous consumption and c is the *MPC*. The consumption function for the data in the chapter titled "Aggregate Expenditures" is

$$C = \$30 + .70Yd$$

as shown in Figure 1.

Saving The corresponding saving function is

$$S = -\$30 + .30Yd$$

as illustrated in Figure 2.

FIGURE 1   The Consumption Function

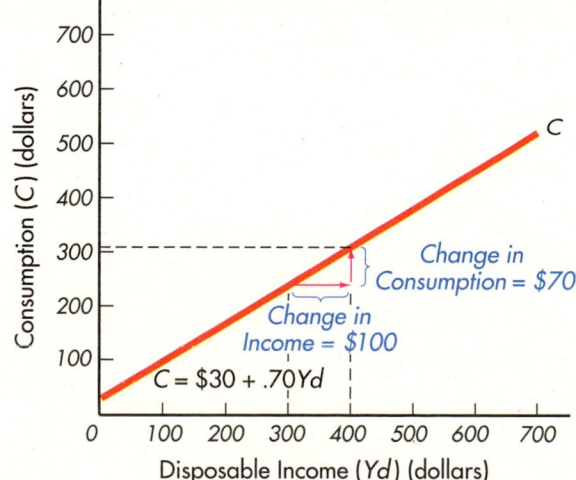

FIGURE 2   The Saving Function

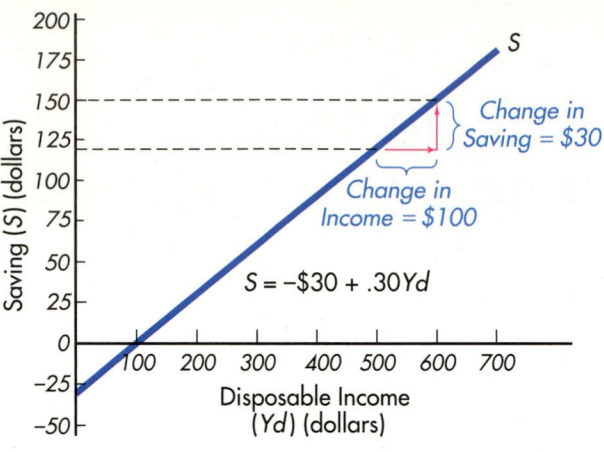

Investment Investment is autonomous at I^a, which is equal to $50.

Government Spending Government spending is autonomous at G^a, which is equal to $70.

Net Exports Exports are autonomous at EX^a and are equal to $50. Imports are given by the function

$$IM = IM^a = imY$$

where *im* is the *MPI*. Here, then,

$$IM = \$0 + .10Y$$

Net exports equal exports minus imports, or

$$X = \$50 - \$0 - .10Y$$
$$= \$50 - .10Y$$

as shown in Figure 3.

Aggregate Expenditures Summing the functions for the four components (and ignoring taxes, so that Yd equals Y) gives

$$AE = C^a + cY + I^a + G^a + EX^a - IM^a - imY$$
$$= \$30 + .70Y + \$50 + \$70 + \$50 - \$0 - .10Y$$
$$= \$200 + .60Y$$

as shown in Figure 4.

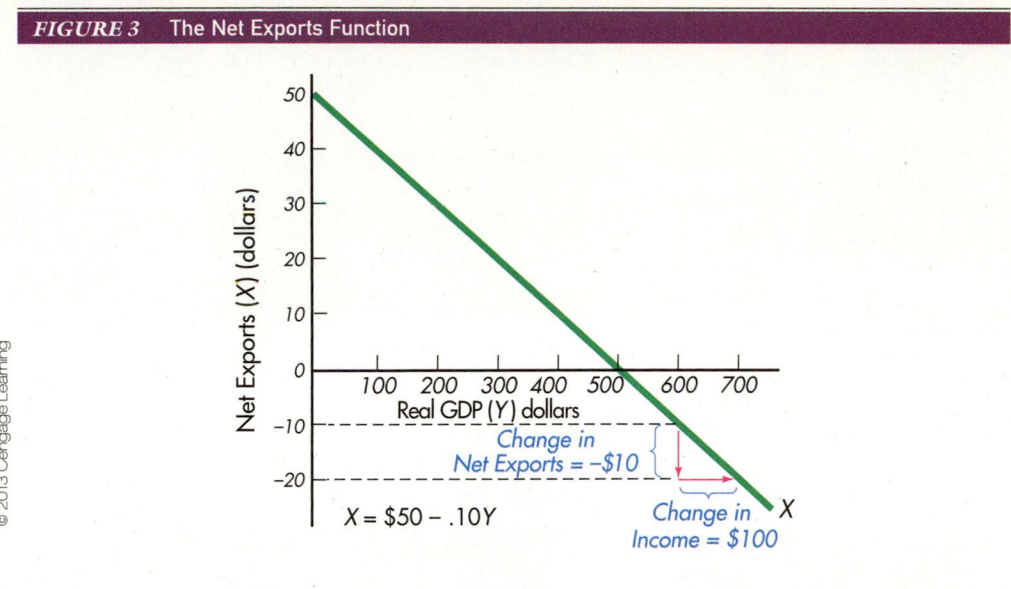

FIGURE 3   The Net Exports Function

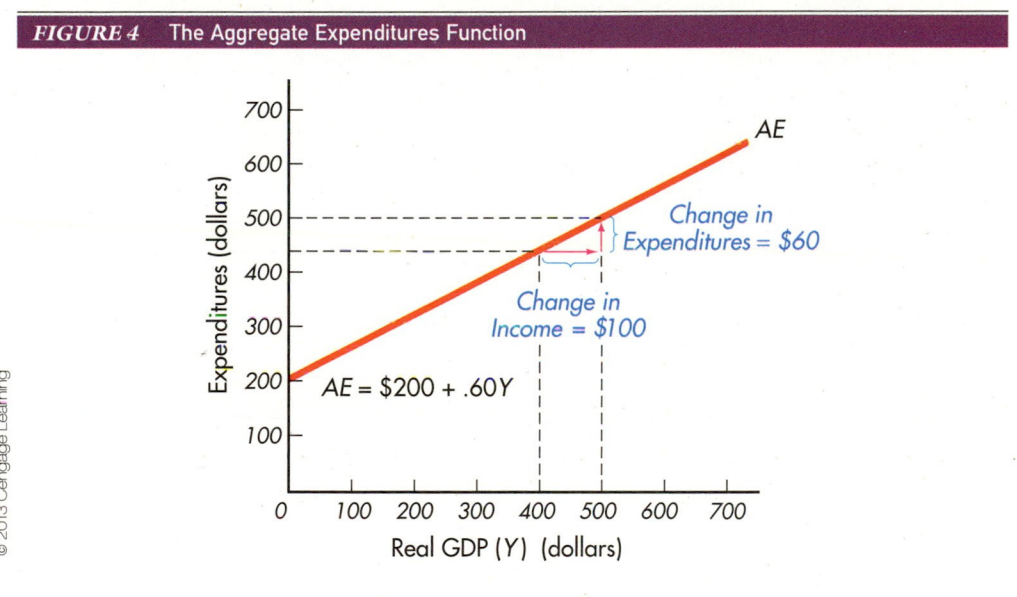

FIGURE 4   The Aggregate Expenditures Function

In the Appendix to Chapter 10, we use the algebraic model of aggregate expenditures presented here to solve for the equilibrium level of real GDP.

Income and Expenditures Equilibrium

© MACIEJ FROLOW/GETTY IMAGES, INC

FUNDAMENTAL QUESTIONS

1 What does equilibrium mean in macroeconomics?

2 How do aggregate expenditures affect income, or real GDP?

3 What are the leakages from and injections into spending?

4 Why does equilibrium real GDP change by a multiple of a change in autonomous expenditures?

5 What is the spending multiplier?

6 What is the relationship between the GDP gap and the recessionary gap?

7 How does international trade affect the size of the spending multiplier?

8 Why does the aggregate expenditures curve shift with changes in the price level?

© SAM DCRUZ/SHUTTERSTOCK.COM; LOGO: © FROXX/SHUTTERSTOCK.COM

What determines the level of income and expenditures, or real GDP? In the chapter titled "Macroeconomic Equilibrium: Aggregate Demand and Supply," we used aggregate demand and aggregate supply to answer this question. Then, in the chapter titled "Aggregate Expenditures," we developed the components of aggregate expenditures in more detail to provide the foundation for an additional approach to answering the question "What determines the level of real GDP?" If you know the answer to this question, you are well on your way to understanding business cycles. Sometimes real GDP is growing and jobs are relatively easy to find; at other times real GDP is falling and large numbers of people are out of work. Macroeconomists use several models to analyze the causes of business cycles. Underlying all of these models is the concept of macroeconomic equilibrium.

Equilibrium here means what it did when we talked about supply and demand: a point of balance, a point from which there is no tendency to move. In macroeconomics, equilibrium is the level of income and expenditures that the economy tends to move toward and remain at until autonomous spending changes.

Economists have not always agreed on how an economy reaches equilibrium or on the forces that move an economy from one equilibrium to another. This last issue formed the basis of economic debate during the Great Depression of the 1930s. Before the 1930s, economists generally believed that the economy was always at or moving toward an equilibrium consistent with a high level of employed resources. The British economist John Maynard Keynes did not agree. He believed that an economy can come to rest at a level of real GDP that is too low to provide employment for all those who desire it. He also believed that certain actions are necessary to ensure that the economy rises to a level of real GDP consistent with a high level of employment. In particular, Keynes argued that government must intervene in the economy in a big way (see the Economic Insight "John Maynard Keynes").

To understand the debate that began during the 1930s and continues on various fronts today, it is necessary to understand the Keynesian view of how equilibrium real GDP is determined. This is our focus here. We have seen in the chapter titled "Macroeconomic Equilibrium: Aggregate Demand and Supply" that the aggregate demand and supply model of macroeconomic equilibrium allows the price level to fluctuate as the equilibrium level of real GDP changes. The Keynesian income-expenditures model assumes that the price level is fixed. It emphasizes aggregate expenditures without explicitly considering the supply side of the economy. This is why we considered the components of spending in detail in the chapter titled "Aggregate Expenditures"—to provide a foundation for the analysis in this chapter. The Keynesian model may be viewed as a special fixed-price case of the aggregate demand and aggregate supply model. In later chapters, we examine the relationship between equilibrium and the level of employed resources and the effect of government policy on both of these elements.

1. Equilibrium Income and Expenditures

Equilibrium is a point from which there is no tendency to move. People do not change their behavior when everything is consistent with what they expect. However, when plans and reality do not match, people adjust their behavior to make them match. Determining a nation's equilibrium level of income and expenditures is the process of defining the level of income and expenditures at which plans and reality are the same.

1.a. Expenditures and Income

We use the aggregate expenditures function described at the end of the chapter titled "Aggregate Expenditures" to demonstrate how equilibrium is determined. Keep in mind that the aggregate expenditures function represents *planned* expenditures at

1 What does equilibrium mean in macroeconomics?

2 How do aggregate expenditures affect income, or real GDP?

ECONOMIC INSIGHT

John Maynard Keynes

John Maynard Keynes (pronounced "canes") is considered by many to be the greatest economist of the twentieth century. His major work, *The General Theory of Employment, Interest, and Money*, had a profound impact on macroeconomics, both in thought and policy. Keynes was born in Cambridge, England, on June 5, 1883. He studied economics at Cambridge University, where he became a lecturer in economics in 1908. During World War I, Keynes worked for the British treasury. At the end of the war, he was the treasury's representative at the Versailles Peace Conference. He resigned from the British delegation at the conference to protest the harsh terms being imposed on the defeated countries. His resignation and the publication of *Economic Consequences of the Peace* (1919) made him an international celebrity.

In 1936, Keynes published *The General Theory*. It was a time of world recession (it has been estimated that around one-quarter of the U.S. labor force was unemployed at the height of the Depression), and policymakers were searching for ways to explain the persistent unemployment. In the book, Keynes suggested that an economy could be at equilibrium at less than potential GDP. More important, he argued that government policy could be altered to end recession. His analysis emphasized aggregate expenditures. If private expenditures were not sufficient to create equilibrium at potential GDP, government expenditures could be increased to stimulate income and output. This was a startling concept. Most economists of the time believed that government should not take an active role in the economy. With his *General Theory*, Keynes started a "revolution" in macroeconomics.

different levels of income, or real GDP. We focus on planned expenditures because they represent the amount that households, firms, government, and the foreign sector expect to spend.

Net exports equal exports minus imports. These papayas being washed in Tapapulcha, Mexico, will be shipped to the United States. Once sold to a U.S. importer, the papayas represent Mexican exports and contribute to increased GDP in Mexico by means of higher net exports.

Actual expenditures always equal income and output because they reflect changes in inventories. That is, inventories automatically raise or lower investment expenditures so that actual spending equals income, which equals output, which equals real GDP. However, aggregate expenditures (which are planned spending) may not equal real GDP. What happens when planned spending and real GDP are not equal?

When planned spending on goods and services *exceeds* the current value of output, the production of goods and services increases. Because output equals income, the level of real GDP also increases. This is the situation for all income levels below $500 in Figure 1. At these levels, total spending is greater than real GDP, which means that more goods and services are being purchased than are being produced.

FIGURE 1 The Equilibrium Level of Real GDP

(1) Real GDP (Y)	(2) Consumption (C)	(3) Investment (I)	(4) Government Spending (G)	(5) Net Exports (X)	(6) Aggregate Expenditures (AE)	(7) Unplanned Change in Inventories	(8) Change in Real GDP
$0	$30	$50	$70	$50	$200	−$200	Increase
$100	$100	$50	$70	$40	$260	−$160	Increase
$200	$170	$50	$70	$30	$320	−$120	Increase
$300	$240	$50	$70	$20	$380	−$80	Increase
$400	$310	$50	$70	$10	$440	−$40	Increase
$500	$380	$50	$70	$0	$500	$0	No change
$600	$450	$50	$70	−$10	$560	$40	Decrease
$700	$520	$50	$70	−$20	$620	$80	Decrease

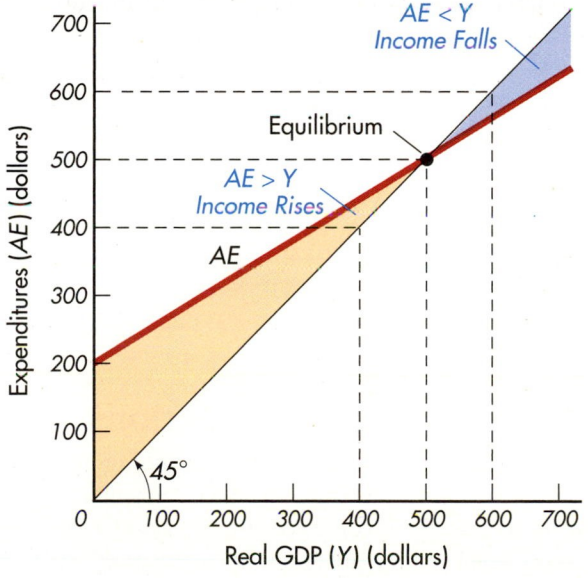

Macroeconomic equilibrium occurs where aggregate expenditures (AE) equal real GDP (Y). In the graph it is the point where the AE line crosses the 45-degree line, where expenditures and real GDP both equal $500. When aggregate expenditures exceed real GDP (as they do at a real GDP level of $400, for example), real GDP rises to the equilibrium level. When aggregate expenditures are less than real GDP (as they are at a real GDP level of $600, for example), real GDP falls back to the equilibrium level.

The only way this can happen is for goods produced in the past to be sold. When planned spending is greater than real GDP, business inventories fall. This change in inventories offsets the excess of planned expenditures over real GDP, so that actual expenditures (including the unplanned change in inventories) equal real GDP. You can see this in column 7 of the table in Figure 1, where the change in inventories offsets the excess of aggregate expenditures over real GDP (the difference between columns 6 and 1).

What happens when inventories fall? As inventories fall, manufacturers increase production to meet the demand for products. The increased production raises the level of real GDP. *When aggregate expenditures exceed real GDP, real GDP rises.*

When aggregate expenditures exceed real GDP, real GDP rises.

At real GDP levels above $500 in the table, aggregate expenditures are less than income. As a result, inventories are accumulating above planned levels—more goods and services are being produced than are being purchased. As inventories rise, businesses begin to reduce the quantity of output they produce. The unplanned increase in inventories is counted as a form of investment spending so that actual expenditures equal real GDP. For example, when real GDP is $600, aggregate expenditures are only $560. The $40 of goods that are produced but not sold are measured as inventory investment. The $560 of aggregate expenditures plus the $40 of unplanned inventories equal $600, the level of real GDP. As inventories increase, firms cut production; this causes real GDP to fall. *When aggregate expenditures are less than real GDP, real GDP falls.*

When aggregate expenditures are less than real GDP, real GDP falls.

There is only one level of real GDP in the table in Figure 1 at which real GDP does not change. When real GDP is $500, aggregate expenditures equal $500. The equilibrium level of real GDP (or output) is that point at which aggregate expenditures equal real GDP (or output).

The equilibrium level of real GDP is where aggregate expenditures equal real GDP.

When aggregate expenditures equal real GDP, planned spending equals the output produced and the income generated from producing that output. As long as planned spending is consistent with real GDP, real GDP does not change. But if planned spending is higher or lower than real GDP, real GDP does change. Equilibrium is that point at which planned spending and real GDP are equal.

The graph in Figure 1 illustrates equilibrium. The 45-degree line shows all possible points where aggregate expenditures (measured on the vertical axis) equal real GDP (measured on the horizontal axis). The equilibrium level of real GDP, then, is simply the point where the aggregate expenditures line (*AE*) crosses the 45-degree line. In the figure, equilibrium occurs where real GDP and expenditures are $500.

When the *AE* curve lies above the 45-degree line—for example, at a real GDP level of $400—aggregate expenditures are greater than real GDP. What happens? Real GDP rises to the equilibrium level, where it tends to stay. When the *AE* curve lies below the 45-degree line—at a real GDP level of $600, for example—aggregate expenditures are less than real GDP; this pushes real GDP down. Once real GDP falls to the equilibrium level ($500 in our example), it tends to stay there.

1.b. Leakages and Injections

3 What are the leakages from and injections into spending?

Equilibrium can be determined by using aggregate expenditures and real GDP, which represents income. Another way to determine equilibrium involves leakages from and injections into the income stream, the circular flow of income and expenditures.

Leakages reduce autonomous aggregate expenditures. There are three leakages in the stream from domestic income to spending: saving, taxes, and imports.

Saving, taxes, and imports are leakages that reduce autonomous aggregate expenditures.

- The more households save, the less they spend. An increase in autonomous saving means a decrease in autonomous consumption, which could cause the equilibrium level of real GDP to fall (see the Economic Insight "The Paradox of Thrift").
- Taxes are an involuntary reduction in consumption. The government transfers income away from households. Higher taxes lower autonomous consumption, in the process lowering autonomous aggregate expenditures and the equilibrium level of real GDP.
- Imports are expenditures for foreign goods and services. They reduce expenditures on domestic goods and services. An autonomous increase in imports reduces net exports, causing autonomous aggregate expenditures and the equilibrium level of real GDP to fall.

For equilibrium to occur, these leakages must be offset by corresponding *injections* of spending into the domestic economy through investment, government spending, and exports.

Investment, government spending, and exports are injections that increase autonomous aggregate expenditures.

- Household saving generates funds that businesses can borrow and spend for investment purposes.

ECONOMIC INSIGHT

The Paradox of Thrift

People generally believe that saving is good and more saving is better. However, if every family increased its saving, the result could be less income for the economy as a whole. In fact, increased saving could actually lower savings for all households.

An increase in saving may provide an example of the *paradox of thrift*. A *paradox* is a true proposition that seems to contradict common beliefs. We believe that we will be better off if we increase our saving, but in the aggregate, increased saving could cause the economy to be worse off. The paradox of thrift is a *fallacy of composition*: the assumption that what is true of a part is true of the whole. It often is unsafe to generalize from what is true at the micro level to what is true at the macro level.

The graph illustrates the effect of higher saving. Initial equilibrium occurs where the $S_1 + T + IM$ curve intersects the $I + G + EX$ curve, at an income of $500. Suppose

saving increases by $20 at every level of income. The $S_1 + T + IM$ curve shifts up to the $S_2 + T + IM$ curve. A new equilibrium is established at an income level of $400. The higher rate of saving causes equilibrium income to fall by $100.

Notice that the graph is drawn with a constant $I + G + EX$ line. If investment increases along with saving, equilibrium income will not necessarily fall. In fact, because saving is necessary before there can be any investment, we would expect a greater demand for investment funds to induce higher saving. If increased saving is used to fund investment expenditures, the economy should grow over time to higher and higher levels of income. Only if the increased saving is not injected back into the economy is there a paradox of thrift. The fact that governments do not discourage saving suggests that the paradox of thrift generally is not a real-world problem.

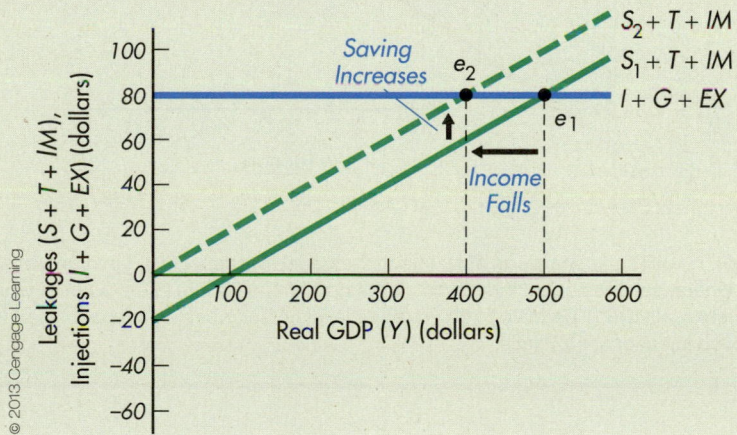

- The taxes collected by government are used to finance government purchases of goods and services.
- Exports bring foreign expenditures into the domestic economy.

There is no reason to expect that each injection will match its corresponding leakage—that investment will equal saving, that government spending will equal taxes, or that exports will equal imports. But for equilibrium to occur, total injections must equal total leakages.

Figure 2 shows how leakages and injections determine the equilibrium level of real GDP. Column 5 of the table lists the total leakages from aggregate expenditures: saving (S) plus taxes (T) plus imports (IM). Saving and imports both increase when real GDP increases. We assume that there are no taxes, so the total amount of leakages ($S + T + IM$) increases as real GDP increases.

> The equilibrium level of real GDP occurs where leakages equal injections.

FIGURE 2   Leakages, Injections, and Equilibrium Income

(1) Real GDP (Y)	(2) Saving (S)	(3) Taxes (T)	(4) Imports (IM)	(5) Leakages (S + T + IM)	(6) Investment (I)	(7) Government Spending (G)	(8) Exports (EX)	(9) Injections (I + G + EX)	(10) Change in Real GDP
$0	$30	$0	$0	−$30	$50	$70	$50	$170	Increase
$100	$0	$0	$10	$10	$50	$70	$50	$170	Increase
$200	$30	$0	$20	$50	$50	$70	$50	$170	Increase
$300	$60	$0	$30	$90	$50	$70	$50	$170	Increase
$400	$90	$0	$40	$130	$50	$70	$50	$170	Increase
$500	$120	$0	$50	$170	$50	$70	$50	$170	No change
$600	$150	$0	$60	$210	$50	$70	$50	$170	Decrease
$700	$180	$0	$70	$250	$50	$70	$50	$170	Decrease

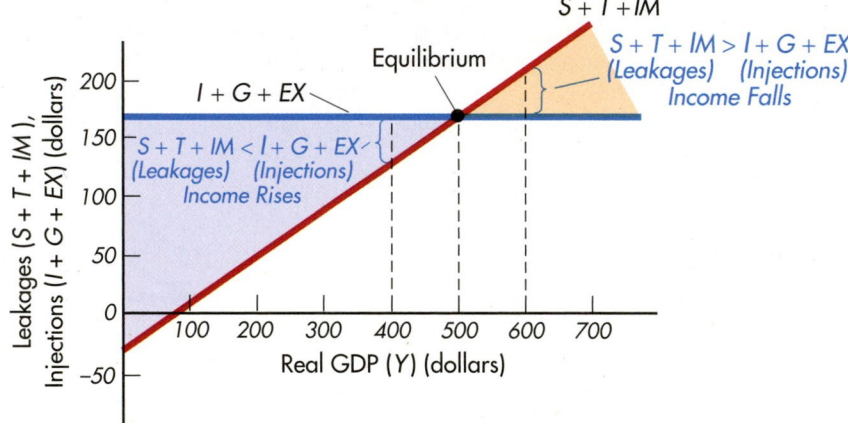

Leakages equal saving (S), taxes (T), and imports (IM). Injections equal investment (I), government spending (G), and exports (EX). Equilibrium is that point where leakages equal injections. In the graph, equilibrium is the point at which the S + T + IM curve intersects the I + G + EX curve, where real GDP (Y) equals $500. At lower levels of income, injections exceed leakages, so Y rises. At higher levels of income, leakages exceed injections, so Y falls.

Column 9 lists the injections at alternative income levels. Because investment (I), government spending (G), and exports (EX) are all autonomous, total injections (I + G + EX) are constant at all levels of real GDP.

To determine the equilibrium level of real GDP, we compare leakages with injections. When injections exceed leakages, planned spending is greater than current income or output, so real GDP rises. In the table in Figure 2, this occurs for levels of real GDP under $500, so real GDP increases if it is under $500 (see the last column). When leakages exceed injections, planned spending is less than current real GDP, so real GDP falls. In Figure 2, at all levels of real GDP above $500, real GDP falls. Only when leakages equal injections is the equilibrium level of real GDP established. When real GDP equals $500, both leakages and injections equal $170, so there is no pressure for real GDP to change. The equilibrium level of real GDP occurs where leakages (S + T + IM) equal injections (I + G + EX).

Figure 2 shows the interaction of leakages and injections graphically. The equilibrium point is where the S + T + IM and I + G + EX curves intersect, at a real GDP level of $500. At higher levels of real GDP, leakages are greater than injections (the $S + T + IM$ curve lies above the $I + G + EX$ curve). When leakages are greater than injections, real GDP falls to the equilibrium point. At lower levels of income, injections are greater than leakages (the $I + G + EX$ curve lies above the $S + T + IM$ curve). Here real GDP rises until it reaches $500. Only at $500 is there no pressure for real GDP to change.

If you compare Figures 1 and 2, you can see that it does not matter whether we use aggregate expenditures or leakages and injections—the equilibrium level of real GDP is the same.

RECAP

1. Equilibrium is a point from which there is no tendency to move.

2. When aggregate expenditures exceed real GDP, real GDP rises.

3. When aggregate expenditures are less than real GDP, real GDP falls.

4. Saving, taxes, and imports are leakages of planned spending from domestic aggregate expenditures.

5. Investment, government spending, and exports are injections of planned spending into domestic aggregate expenditures.

6. Equilibrium occurs at the level of real GDP at which aggregate expenditures equal real GDP, and leakages equal injections.

---

2. Changes in Equilibrium Income and Expenditures

Equilibrium is a point from which there is no tendency to move. But in fact, the equilibrium level of real GDP does move. In the last section, we described how aggregate expenditures push real GDP, representing the economy's income and output, up or down toward their level of equilibrium. Here we examine how changes in autonomous expenditures affect equilibrium. This becomes very important in understanding macroeconomic policy, the kinds of things that government can do to control the business cycle.

 4 Why does equilibrium real GDP change by a multiple of a change in autonomous expenditures?

2.a. The Spending Multiplier

Remember that equilibrium is that point where aggregate expenditures equal real GDP. If we increase autonomous expenditures, then we raise the equilibrium level of real GDP—but by how much? It seems logical to expect a one-to-one ratio: If autonomous spending increases by a dollar, equilibrium real GDP should increase by a dollar. Actually, equilibrium real GDP increases by *more* than a dollar. The change in autonomous expenditures is *multiplied* into a larger change in the equilibrium level of real GDP.

 5 What is the spending multiplier?

In the chapter titled "National Income Accounting," we used a circular flow diagram to show the relationship of expenditures to income. In that diagram, we saw how one sector's expenditures become another sector's income. This concept helps explain the effect of a change in autonomous expenditures on the equilibrium level of income or real GDP. If A's autonomous spending increases, then B's income rises. Then B spends part of that income in the domestic economy (the rest is saved or used to buy foreign goods), generating new income for C. In turn, C spends part of that income in the domestic economy, generating new income for D. And the rounds of increased spending and income continue. All of this is the product of A's initial autonomous increase in

Any change in autonomous expenditures is multiplied into a larger change in equilibrium real GDP.

© froxx/Shutterstock.com

© froxx/Shutterstock.com

spending. And each round of increased spending and income affects the equilibrium level of income, or real GDP.

Let's look at an example, using Table 1. Suppose government spending goes up $20 to improve public parks. What happens to the equilibrium level of income? The autonomous increase in government spending increases the income of park employees by $20. As the income of the park employees increases, so does their consumption. For example, let's say they spend more money on hamburgers. In the process, they are increasing the income of the hamburger producers, who in turn increase their consumption.

Table 1 shows how a single change in spending generates further changes. Round 1 is the initial increase in government spending to improve public parks. That $20 expenditure increases the income of park employees by $20 (column 1). As income increases, those components of aggregate expenditures that depend on current income—consumption and net exports—also increase by some fraction of the $20.

Consumption changes by the marginal propensity to consume multiplied by the change in income; imports change by the marginal propensity to import multiplied by the change in income. To find the total effect of the initial change in spending, we must know the fraction of any change in income that is spent in the domestic economy. In the hypothetical economy we have been using, the *MPC* is .70 and the *MPI* is .10. This means that for each $1 of new income, consumption rises by $.70 and imports rise by $.10. Spending on *domestic* goods and services, then, rises by $.60. Because consumption is spending on domestic goods and services, and imports are spending on foreign goods and services, the percentage of a change in income that is spent domestically is the difference between the *MPC* and the *MPI*. If the *MPC* equals .70 and the *MPI*

TABLE 1	The Spending Multiplier Effect			
	(1) Change in Income	**(2)** Change in Domestic Expenditures	**(3)** Change in Saving	**(4)** Change in Imports
Round 1	$20.00	$12.00	$ 6.00	$2.00
Round 2	12.00	7.20	3.60	1.20
Round 3	7.20	4.32	2.16	0.72
Round 4	4.32	2.59	1.30	0.43
	⋮	⋮	⋮	⋮
Totals	$50.00	$30.00	$15.00	$5.00

Column 2 = column 1 × (*MPC* − *MPI*)

Column 3 = column 1 × *MPS*

Column 4 = column 1 × *MPI*

$$\text{Multiplier} = \frac{1}{MPS + MPI}$$
$$= \frac{1}{(.30 + .10)}$$
$$= \frac{1}{.40}$$
$$= 2.50$$

equals .10, then 60 percent of any change in domestic income ($MPC - MPI = .60$) is spent on domestic goods and services.

In round 1 of Table 1, the initial increase in income of $20 induces an increase in spending on domestic goods and services of $12 (.60 × $20). Out of the $20, $6 is saved, because the marginal propensity to save is .30 ($1 - MPC$). The other $2 is spent on imports ($MPI = .10$). The park employees receive $20 more income. They spend $12 on hamburgers at a local restaurant, they save $6, and they spend $2 on imported coffee.

Only $12 of the workers' new income is spent on goods produced in the domestic economy, hamburgers. That $12 becomes income to the restaurant's employees and owner. When their income increases by $12, they spend 60 percent of that income ($7.20) on domestic goods (round 2, column 2). The rest of the income is saved or spent on imports.

Each time income increases, expenditures increase. But the increase is smaller and smaller in each new round of spending. Why? Because 30 percent of each change in income is saved and another 10 percent is spent on imports. These are leakages out of the income stream. This means that just 60 percent of the change in income is spent and passed on to others in the domestic economy as income in the next round.

To find the total effect of the initial change in spending of $20, we could keep on computing the change in income and spending round after round, and then sum the total of all rounds. The change in income and spending never reaches zero, but it becomes infinitely small.

Fortunately, we do not have to compute the increases in spending round by round to find the total increase. If we know the percentage of additional income that "leaks" from domestic consumption at each round, we can determine the total change in income, or real GDP, by finding its reciprocal. This measure is called the **spending multiplier**. The leakages are that portion of the change in income that is saved (the MPS) and that proportion of the change in income that is spent on imports (the MPI).

$$\text{Multiplier} = \frac{1}{\text{leakages}}$$
$$= \frac{1}{MPS + MPI}$$

When the MPS is .30 and the MPI is .10, the multiplier equals 2.5 (1/.4). An initial change in expenditures of $20 results in a total change in real GDP of $50, 2.5 times the original change in expenditures. The greater the leakages, the smaller the multiplier. When the MPS equals .35 and the MPI equals .15, the multiplier equals 2 (1/.50). The multiplier is smaller here because less new income is being spent in the domestic economy. The more people save, the smaller the expansionary effect on income of a change in spending. And the more people spend on imports, the smaller the expansionary effect on income of a change in spending. Notice that the multiplier would be larger in a *closed economy*, an economy that does not trade with the rest of the world. In that economy, because the MPI equals zero, the spending multiplier is simply equal to the reciprocal of the MPS.

2.b. The Spending Multiplier and Equilibrium

The spending multiplier is an extremely useful concept. It allows us to calculate how a change in autonomous expenditures affects real GDP. To better understand how changes in spending can bring about changes in equilibrium income, or real GDP, let's modify the example we used in Figure 1. In the table in Figure 3, we have increased government spending to $110. The autonomous increase in government spending raises aggregate expenditures by $40 at every level of income. Aggregate expenditures now equal real GDP at $600. The increase in government spending of $40 yields an increase in equilibrium real GDP of $100.

> *The percentage of a change in income that is spent domestically is the difference between the MPC and the MPI.*

spending multiplier
A measure of the change in equilibrium income or real GDP produced by a change in autonomous expenditures.

 6 What is the relationship between the GDP gap and the recessionary gap?

The graph in Figure 3 illustrates the multiplier effect and shows the change in equilibrium income when spending increases by $40. The original aggregate expenditures curve, AE_1, intersects the 45-degree line at a real GDP level of $500. A spending increase of $40 at every level of real GDP creates a new aggregate expenditures curve, AE_2, which lies $40 above the original curve. The curve AE_2 is parallel to AE_1 because the increase is in autonomous spending. The new curve, AE_2, intersects the 45-degree line at an income of $600.

In the chapter titled "Unemployment and Inflation," we introduced the concept of the natural rate of unemployment—the unemployment rate that exists in the absence of cyclical

FIGURE 3   A Change in Equilibrium Expenditures and Income

(1) Real GDP (Y)	(2) Consumption (C)	(3) Investment (I)	(4) Government Spending (G)	(5) Net Exports (X)	(6) Aggregate Expenditures (AE)	(7) Unplanned Change in Inventories	(8) Change in Real GDP
$0	$30	$50	$110	$50	$240	−$240	Increase
$100	$100	$50	$110	$40	$300	−$200	Increase
$200	$170	$50	$110	$30	$360	−$160	Increase
$300	$240	$50	$110	$20	$440	−$120	Increase
$400	$310	$50	$110	$10	$480	−$80	Increase
$500	$380	$50	$110	$0	$540	−$40	Increase
$600	$450	$50	$110	−$10	$600	$0	No Change
$700	$520	$50	$110	−$20	$660	$40	Decrease

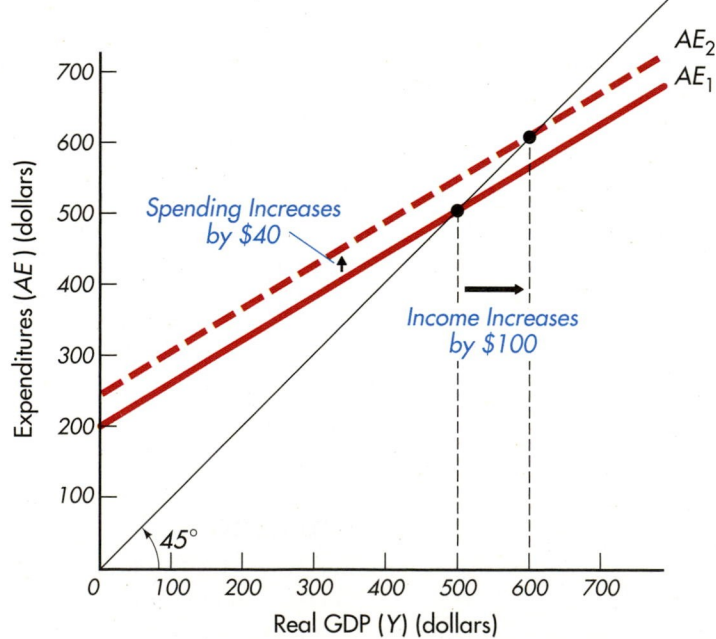

A change in aggregate expenditures (AE) causes a change in equilibrium real GDP (Y). Initially equilibrium is $500, the point at which the AE_1 curve intersects the 45-degree line. If autonomous expenditures increase by $40, the aggregate expenditures curve shifts up to AE_2. The new curve intersects the 45-degree line at a new equilibrium level of real GDP, $600. An increase in autonomous expenditures of $40, then, causes equilibrium real GDP to increase by $100.

unemployment. When the economy operates at the natural rate of unemployment, the corresponding level of output (and income) is called potential real GDP. However, equilibrium does not necessarily occur at potential real GDP. Equilibrium occurs at any level of real GDP at which planned expenditures equal real GDP. Suppose that equilibrium real GDP is not at the level of potential real GDP and that government policymakers make the achievement of potential real GDP an important goal. In this case, government policy is addressed toward closing the *GDP gap*, the difference between potential real GDP and actual real GDP. The nature of that policy depends on the value of the multiplier.

If we know the size of the GDP gap and we know the size of the spending multiplier, we can determine by how much spending needs to change in order to yield equilibrium at potential real GDP. Remember that the GDP gap equals potential real GDP minus actual real GDP:

$$\text{GDP gap} = \text{potential real GDP} - \text{actual real GDP}$$

When real GDP is less than potential real GDP, the GDP gap is the amount by which GDP must rise to reach its potential. Suppose potential real GDP is \$500, but the economy is in equilibrium at \$300. The GDP must rise by \$200 to reach potential real GDP. How much must spending rise? If we know the size of the spending multiplier, we simply divide the spending multiplier into the GDP gap to determine how much spending must rise to achieve equilibrium at potential real GDP. This required change in spending is called the **recessionary gap**:

$$\text{Recessionary gap} = \frac{\text{GDP gap}}{\text{spending multiplier}}$$

Figure 4 shows an economy in which equilibrium real GDP (Y_e) is less than potential real GDP (Y_p). The difference between the two—the GDP gap—is \$200. It is the *horizontal* distance between equilibrium real GDP and potential real GDP. The amount by which spending must rise in order for real GDP to reach a new equilibrium level of \$500 is measured by the recessionary gap. The recessionary gap is the *vertical* distance between the aggregate expenditures curve and the 45-degree line at the potential real GDP level.

The recessionary gap in Figure 4 is \$80:

$$\text{Recessionary gap} = \frac{\$200}{2.5}$$
$$= \$80$$

With a spending multiplier of 2.5, if aggregate expenditures rise by \$80, equilibrium income rises by the \$200 necessary to close the GDP gap. Government policy may be addressed to closing the gap, as an increase in government expenditures of \$80 would move the economy to the potential level of real GDP in this example.

2.c. Real-World Complications

Our definition of the spending multiplier,

$$\frac{1}{MPS + MPI}$$

is a simplification of reality. Often other factors besides the *MPS* and *MPI* determine the actual multiplier in an economy. If prices rise when spending increases, the spending multiplier will not be as large as shown here. Also, taxes (which are ignored until the chapter titled "Fiscal Policy") will reduce the size of the multiplier. Another factor is the treatment of imports. We have assumed that whatever is spent on imports is permanently lost to the domestic economy. For a country whose imports are a small fraction of the exports of its trading partners, this is a realistic assumption. But for a country whose

7 How does international trade affect the size of the spending multiplier?

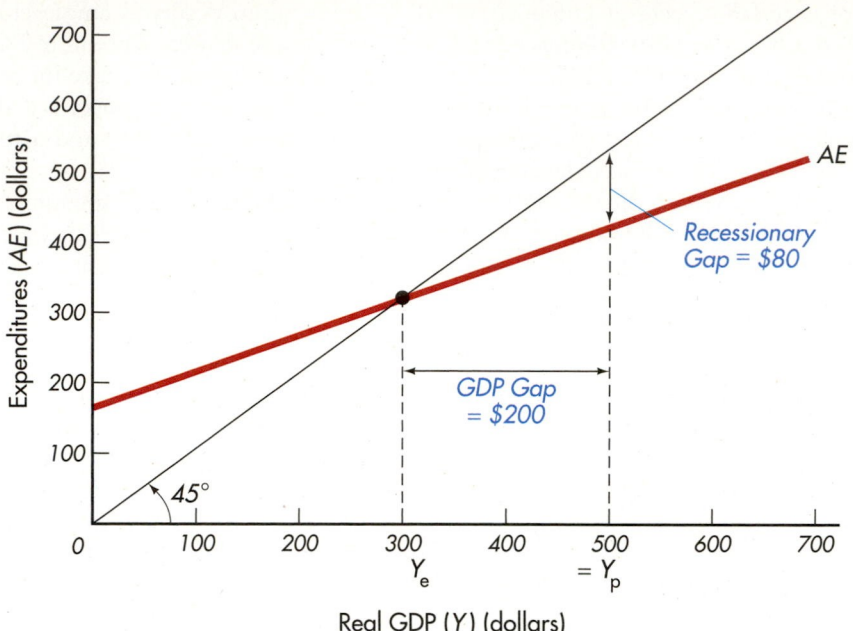

FIGURE 4   The GDP Gap and the Recessionary Gap

In the graph, the GDP gap is $200, the difference between potential real GDP (Y_p) of $500 and equilibrium real GDP (Y_e) of $300. The GDP gap tells us that equilibrium real GDP must rise by $200 to reach equilibrium at the potential level of real GDP. The recessionary gap indicates the amount that autonomous expenditures must rise to close the GDP gap. The recessionary gap is the vertical distance between the 45-degree line and the *AE* curve at the potential level of real GDP, or $80. If autonomous expenditures are increased by $80, the *AE* curve will move up, intersecting with the 45-degree line at $500.

© 2013 Cengage Learning

imports are very important in determining the volume of exports of the rest of the world, this simple spending multiplier understates the true multiplier effect. To see why, let's examine how U.S. imports affect income in the rest of the world.

2.c.1. Foreign Repercussions of Domestic Imports
When a resident of the United States buys goods from another country, that purchase becomes income to foreign residents. If Mike in Miami buys coral jewelry from Victor in the Dominican Republic, Mike's purchase increases Victor's income. So the import of jewelry into the United States increases income in the Dominican Republic.

Imports purchased by one country can have a large effect on the level of income in other countries. For instance, Canada and Mexico are very dependent on sales to the United States, since about 80 percent of their exports go to the United States. South Africa, on the other hand, sells about 5 percent of its total exports to U.S. buyers. If U.S. imports from South Africa doubled, the effect on total South African exports and income would be small. But if imports from Canada or Mexico doubled, the effect on those countries' exports and income would be substantial.

Imports into the United States play a key role in determining the real GDP of the major U.S. trading partners. This is important because foreign income is a determinant of U.S. exports. As that income rises, U.S. exports rise (see the chapter titled "Aggregate Expenditures"). That is, foreign imports increase with foreign income, and some of those imports come from the United States. And, of course, when foreign spending on U.S. goods increases, national income in the United States rises.

The simple spending multiplier understates the true multiplier effects of increases in autonomous expenditures because of the foreign repercussions of domestic spending. Some spending on imports comes back to the domestic economy in the form of exports. This means that the chain of spending can be different from that assumed in the simple spending multiplier. Figure 5 illustrates the difference.

Figure 5(a) shows the sequence of spending when there are no foreign repercussions from domestic imports. In this case, domestic spending rises, which causes domestic income, or real GDP, to rise. Higher domestic real GDP leads to increased spending on imports as well as further increases in domestic spending, which induce further increases in real GDP, and so on, as the multiplier process works itself out. Notice, however, that the imports are simply a leakage from the spending stream.

FIGURE 5   The Sequence of Expenditures

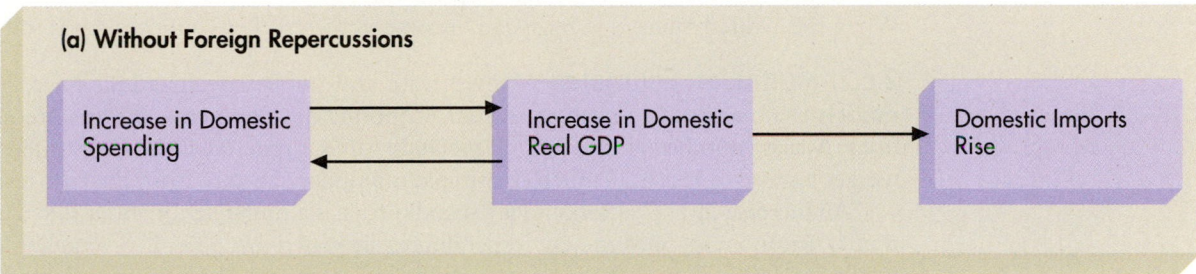

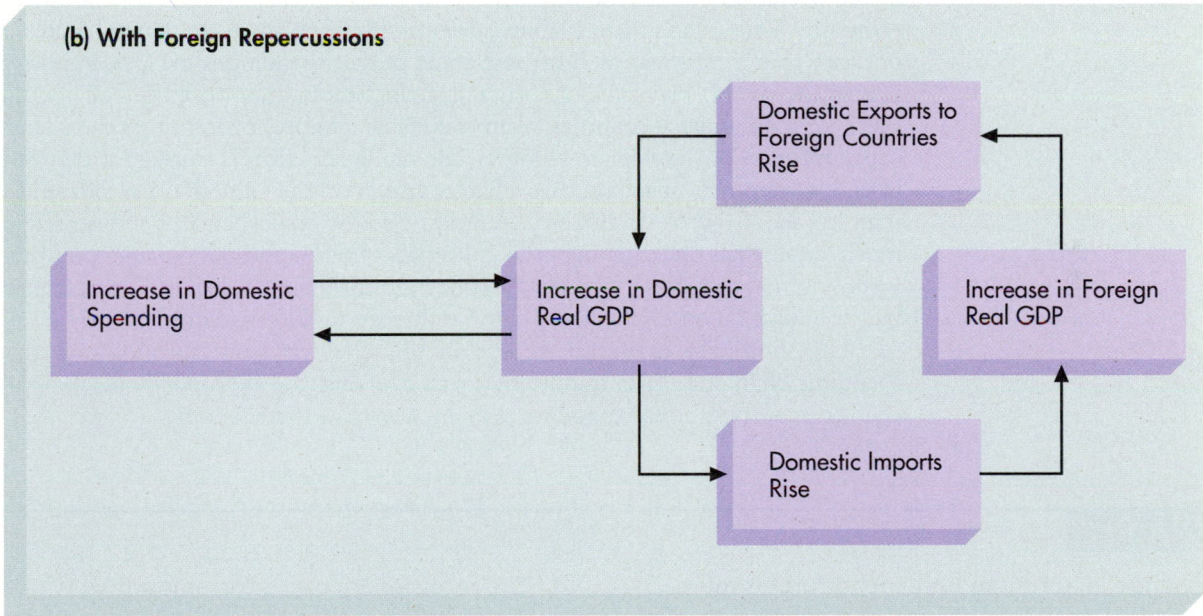

If there are no foreign repercussions from changes in domestic income or real GDP, the simple spending multiplier holds. Increases in domestic spending increase domestic income or real GDP, which causes domestic spending—including spending on foreign goods—to rise further. Here higher expenditures on domestic imports do not have any effect on domestic exports to foreign countries.

If there are foreign repercussions from changes in domestic real GDP, the simple spending multiplier underestimates the actual effect of a change in autonomous expenditures on the equilibrium level of real GDP. As Figure 5(b) shows, increases in domestic spending increase domestic income, or real GDP, which causes domestic spending—including spending on foreign goods—to rise further. Here higher spending on foreign goods causes foreign real GDP to rise, and with it, spending on domestic exports. Higher domestic exports stimulate domestic real GDP further. The actual multiplier effect of an increase in domestic spending, then, is larger than it is when domestic imports have no effect on domestic exports.

In Figure 5(b), the sequence of expenditures includes the foreign repercussions of domestic imports. As before, increases in domestic spending cause domestic income, or real GDP, to rise; this, in turn, leads to more domestic spending as well as greater domestic imports. Now, however, the greater imports increase foreign income, or real GDP, which increases foreign imports of goods produced in the domestic economy. As domestic exports rise, domestic real GDP rises. This is a more realistic view of how spending and income interact to create interdependencies among nations.

The diagrams in Figure 5 show why the multiplier effect is higher with foreign repercussions than without. Rather than complicate the multiplier definition, we continue to use the simple spending multiplier. But remember that (holding prices constant and ignoring taxes) our definition underestimates the true magnitude of the multiplier's effects in open economies. In fact, the foreign repercussions of domestic imports help explain the similarity in business cycles across countries. When the United States is booming, the economies of other countries that depend on exports to the U.S. market also boom. When the United States is in recession, income in these other countries tends to fall.

2.c.2. Multiplier Estimates

Many private and public organizations have developed models that are used to analyze current economic developments and to forecast future ones. A large number of these models include foreign repercussions. From these models, we get a sense of just how much the simple multiplier can vary from the true multiplier.

An increase in U.S. autonomous expenditures has a multiplier of about 0.8. This means that if autonomous government expenditures increased by $25, U.S. equilibrium GDP would be $20 higher after one year. A multiplier less than 1 suggests important "leakages" in the operation of the economy. One such leakage stems from the openness of the U.S. economy. Thus, when there is an expansionary fiscal policy in the United States, the GDP of other countries is increased because some of that spending is on U.S. imports from the rest of the world. Estimates of spending multipliers indicate that the equilibrium level of GDP for the industrial countries taken as a whole increases by 0.4 times the change in U.S. expenditures. For developing countries, the multiplier effect is smaller, at 0.1. So increases in U.S. government spending have a bigger impact on the GDP of other industrial countries than on the GDP of developing countries. Because trade between industrial countries is much larger than the trade between industrial countries and developing countries, it is not surprising that increases in spending in one industrial country, like the United States, have a bigger impact on other industrial countries than on developing countries.

The multiplier examples we use in this chapter show autonomous government spending changing. It is important to realize that the multiplier effects apply to any change in autonomous expenditures in any sector of the economy.

RECAP

1. Any change in autonomous expenditures is multiplied into a larger change in the equilibrium level of real GDP.

2. The multiplier measures the change in equilibrium real GDP produced by a change in autonomous spending.

3. The multiplier equals

$$\frac{1}{\text{Leakages}} = \frac{1}{MPS + MPI}$$

4. The recessionary gap is the amount by which spending must increase in order to achieve equilibrium at potential real GDP. Graphically, it is measured by the vertical distance between the 45-degree line and the aggregate expenditures curve at potential real GDP.

5. The true spending multiplier may differ from the simple spending multiplier (1/[*MPS* + *MPI*]) because of the foreign repercussions of domestic spending. Price changes and taxes cause the simple spending multiplier to overestimate the true multiplier.

3. Aggregate Expenditures and Aggregate Demand

The approach to macroeconomic equilibrium presented in this chapter focuses on aggregate expenditures and income. It is called the *Keynesian model*. This model of the economy can be very useful in explaining some real-world events, but it suffers from a serious drawback: It assumes that the supply of goods and services in the economy always adjusts to aggregate expenditures, that there is no need for price changes. The Keynesian model is a *fixed-price model*.

In the real world, we find that shortages of goods and services are often met by rising prices, not just increased production. We also find that when supply increases in the face of relatively constant demand, prices may fall. In other words, prices as well as production adjust to differences between demand and supply. We introduced price as a component of macroeconomic equilibrium in Chapter 8 in the aggregate demand and supply model. You may recall that aggregate expenditures represent demand when the price level is constant. This can be demonstrated by using the income and expenditures approach developed in this chapter to derive the aggregate demand curve that was introduced in Chapter 8.

3.a. Aggregate Expenditures and Changing Price Levels

As discussed in Chapter 8, the *AE* curve will shift with changes in the price level because of the wealth effect, the interest rate effect, and the international trade effect. Wealth is one of the nonincome determinants of consumption. Households hold part of their wealth in financial assets like money and bonds. As the price level falls, the purchasing power of money rises and aggregate expenditures increase. As the price level rises, the purchasing power of money falls and aggregate expenditures fall.

The interest rate is a determinant of investment spending. As the price level changes, interest rates may change as households and business firms change their demand for money. The change in interest rates will then affect investment spending. For instance, when the price level rises, more money is needed to buy any given quantity of goods and services. To acquire more money, households and firms sell their nonmonetary financial assets, like bonds. The increased supply of bonds will tend to raise interest rates to attract buyers. The higher interest rates will tend to lower investment spending and aggregate expenditures. Conversely, a lower price level will tend to be associated with lower interest rates, greater investment spending, and greater aggregate expenditures.

Net exports may change, causing aggregate expenditures to change, when the domestic price level changes. If domestic prices rise while foreign prices and the exchange rate are constant, then domestic goods become more expensive relative to foreign goods, and net exports and aggregate expenditures tend to fall. If domestic prices fall while foreign prices and the exchange rate are constant, then domestic goods become cheaper relative to foreign goods, and net exports and aggregate expenditures tend to rise.

8 Why does the aggregate expenditures curve shift with changes in the price level?

3.b. Deriving the Aggregate Demand Curve

The aggregate demand curve (*AD*) shows how the equilibrium level of expenditures changes as the price level changes. In other words, the curve shows the amount that people spend at different price levels. Let's use the example in Figure 6 to show how aggregate demand is derived from the shifting aggregate expenditures curve (*AE*).

FIGURE 6   Aggregate Expenditures and Aggregate Demand

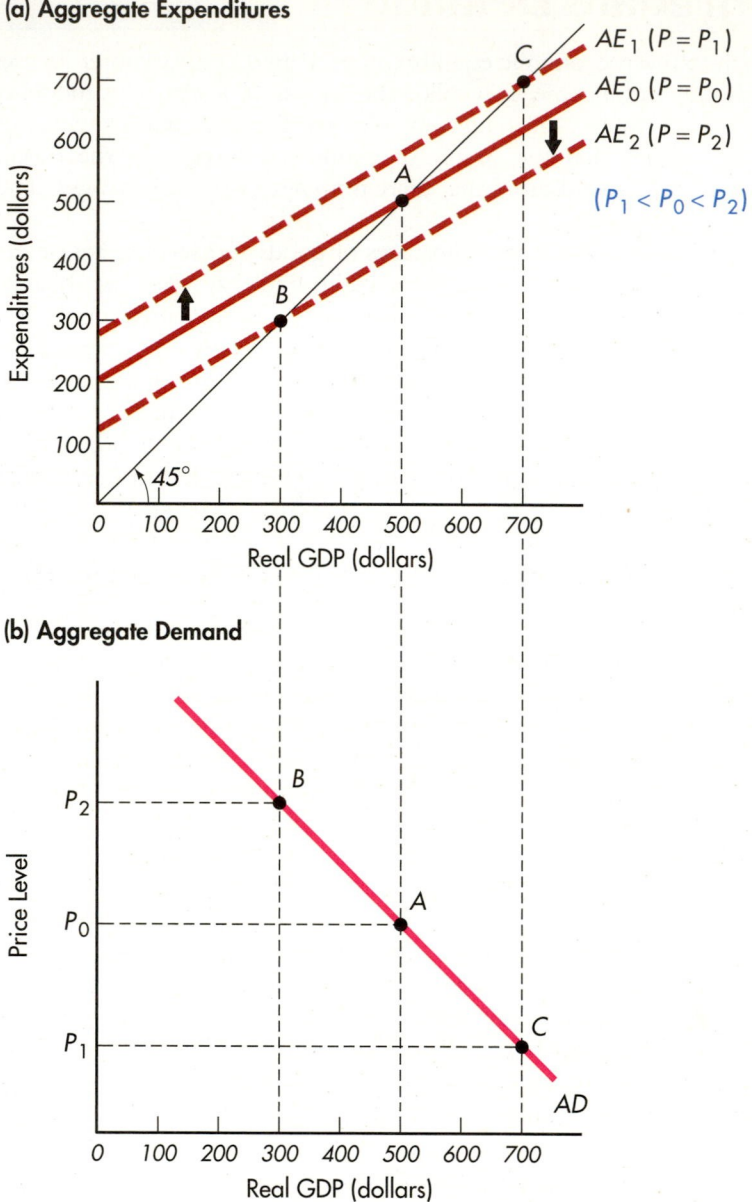

Figure 6(a) shows how changes in the price level cause the *AE* curve to shift. The initial curve, *AE*$_0$, is drawn at the initial level of prices, *P*$_0$. On this curve, the equilibrium level of aggregate expenditures (where expenditures equal real GDP) is $500. If the price level falls to *P*$_1$, autonomous expenditures increase, shifting the curve up to *AE*$_1$, and moving the equilibrium level of aggregate expenditures to $700. If the price level rises to *P*$_2$, autonomous expenditures fall, shifting the curve down to *AE*$_2$ and moving the equilibrium level of aggregate expenditures to $300. The aggregate demand curve (*AD*) in Figure 6(b) is derived from the aggregate expenditures curves. The *AD* curve shows the equilibrium level of aggregate expenditures at different price levels. At price level *P*$_0$, equilibrium aggregate expenditures are $500; at *P*$_1$, they are $700; and at *P*$_2$, they are $300.

The aggregate demand curve is derived from the AE curve. Figure 6(a) shows three AE curves, each drawn for a different price level. Suppose that the initial equilibrium occurs at point A on curve AE_0 with prices at P_0. At this point, equilibrium real GDP and expenditures are \$500. If prices fall to P_1, the AE curve shifts up to AE_1. Here equilibrium is at point C, where real GDP equals \$700. If prices rise from P_0 to P_2, the AE curve falls to AE_2. Here equilibrium is at point B, where real GDP equals \$300.

In Figure 6(b), price level is plotted on the vertical axis and real GDP is plotted on the horizontal axis. A price-level change here means that, on average, all prices in the economy change. The negative slope of the aggregate demand curve results from the effect of changing prices on wealth, interest rates, and international trade. If you move vertically down from points A, B, and C in Figure 6(a), you find corresponding points along the aggregate demand curve in Figure 6(b). The AD curve shows all of the combinations of price levels and corresponding equilibrium levels of real GDP and aggregate expenditures.

3.c. A Fixed-Price *AD–AS* Model

The Keynesian model of fixed-price equilibrium may be considered a special case of the aggregate demand and aggregate supply equilibrium. We can define a horizontal segment of the aggregate supply curve as the Keynesian region of the curve. This represents an economy with substantial unemployment and excess capacity, so that real GDP and output may be increased without pressure on the price level. Figure 7 illustrates this case.

In Figure 7, the aggregate supply curve is horizontal at price level P_e. Throughout the range of the AS curve, the price level is fixed. Suppose aggregate expenditures increase for some reason other than a price-level change. For instance, consumers could expect their future incomes to rise, so they increase consumption now; or business firms could expect sales to rise in the future, so they increase investment spending now; or government spending rises to improve the national highway system; or foreign prices

---

FIGURE 7 A Fixed-Price *AD–AS* Model

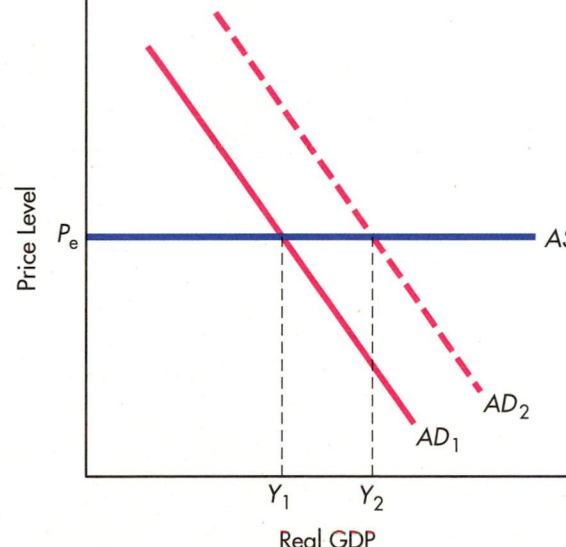

If the *AS* curve is horizontal, then shifts in the *AD* curve will have no effect on the equilibrium level of prices but will change the equilibrium level of real GDP.

rise, and so net exports increase. If aggregate expenditures rise as a result of something other than a domestic price-level change, then the aggregate demand curve shifts to the right, like the shift from AD_1 to AD_2 in Figure 7. This increase in AD causes real GDP to rise to Y_2, yet the price level remains fixed at P_e.

Because the fixed-price model of macroeconomic equilibrium requires a horizontal AS curve, many economists believe that this model is too restrictive and not representative of the modern economy. As a result, we will generally see the AD–AS model using upward-sloping AS curves so that price as well as real GDP fluctuates with shifts in aggregate demand.

> The Keynesian model is a fixed-price model.

RECAP

1. As the price level rises (falls), aggregate expenditures fall (rise).

2. Aggregate demand is the equilibrium level of aggregate expenditures at alternative price levels.

3. The Keynesian fixed-price model is represented by a horizontal aggregate supply curve.

SUMMARY

1. **What does equilibrium mean in macroeconomics?**

   - Macroeconomic equilibrium is the point at which aggregate expenditures equal real GDP. *§1.a*

2. **How do aggregate expenditures affect income, or real GDP?**

   - When aggregate expenditures exceed income, or real GDP, real GDP rises; when they are less than real GDP, real GDP falls. *§1.a*

3. **What are the leakages from and injections into spending?**

   - Leakages are saving, taxes, and imports; injections are investment, government spending, and exports. *§1.b*

   - Equilibrium real GDP occurs where leakages equal injections. *§1.b*

4. **Why does equilibrium real GDP change by a multiple of a change in autonomous expenditures?**

   - The effect of a change in autonomous spending is multiplied by a spiral of increased spending and income. *§2.a*

5. **What is the spending multiplier?**

   - The spending multiplier equals the reciprocal of the sum of the *MPS* and the *MPI*. *§2.a*

6. **What is the relationship between the GDP gap and the recessionary gap?**

   - The recessionary gap is the amount by which autonomous expenditures must change to eliminate the GDP gap and reach potential GDP. *§2.b*

7. **How does international trade affect the size of the spending multiplier?**

   - The actual spending multiplier may be larger than the reciprocal of the sum of the *MPS* and the *MPI* because of the foreign repercussions of changes in domestic spending. *§2.c.1*

8. **Why does the aggregate expenditures curve shift with changes in the price level?**

   - The *AE* curve shifts with changes in the price level because of the wealth effect, the interest rate effect, and the international trade effect. *§3.a*

   - The Keynesian model of fixed-price equilibrium is a special case of the *AD* and *AS* equilibrium. *§3.c*

KEY TERMS

recessionary gap, 223   spending multiplier, 221

EXERCISES

1. Explain the role of inventories in keeping actual expenditures equal to real GDP.
2. Rework Figure 1 assuming a closed economy (net exports equal zero at all levels of income). What is the equilibrium level of real GDP? What is the spending multiplier?
3. Draw a graph representing a hypothetical economy. Carefully label the two axes, the $S + T + IM$ curve, the $I + G + EX$ curve, and the equilibrium level of real GDP. Illustrate the effect of an increase in the level of autonomous saving.
4. Given the following information, what is the spending multiplier in each case?
   a. $MPC = .90$, $MPI = .10$
   b. $MPC = .90$, $MPI = .20$
   c. $MPC = .80$, $MPI = .30$
   d. $MPC = .90$, $MPI = 0$
5. Draw a graph representing a hypothetical economy in a recession. Carefully label the two axes, the 45-degree line, the AE curve, and the equilibrium level of real GDP. Indicate and label the GDP gap and the recessionary gap.
6. Explain the effect of foreign repercussions on the value of the spending multiplier.
7. Suppose the MPC is .80, the MPI is .10, and the income tax rate is 15 percent. What is the multiplier in this economy?

   Use the information in the following table to do exercises 8–15:

Y	C	I	G	X
$100	$120	$20	$30	$10
$300	$300	$20	$30	−$10
$500	$480	$20	$30	−$30
$700	$660	$20	$30	−$50

8. What is the MPC?
9. What is the MPI?
10. What is the MPS?
11. What is the multiplier?
12. What is the equilibrium level of real GDP?
13. What is the value of autonomous consumption?
14. If government spending increases by $15, what is the new equilibrium level of real GDP?
15. What are the equations for the consumption, net exports, and aggregate expenditures functions?
16. Derive the aggregate demand curve from an aggregate expenditures diagram. Explain how aggregate demand relates to aggregate expenditures.
17. In the chapter titled "Macroeconomic Equilibrium: Aggregate Demand and Supply," the aggregate supply (AS) curve was upward sloping. Now, in this chapter, we have a flat AS curve. What are the implications for equilibrium real GDP if AD shifts by some amount and the AS curve is perfectly flat in one economy and upward sloping in another?
18. Why should the business cycles of Canada and Mexico be much like the U.S. business cycle, while those of South Africa and Turkey may differ from the U.S. pattern of economic expansion and contraction?

You can find further practice tests in the Online Quiz at **www.cengage.com/economics/boyes**.

Economically Speaking

Results: North Americans Are Better Off after 14 Years of NAFTA

The North American Free Trade Agreement (NAFTA) revolutionized trade and investment in North America, helping to unlock our region's economic potential.... NAFTA has helped to stimulate economic growth and create higher-paying jobs across North America. It has also paved the way for greater market competition and enhanced choice and purchasing power for North American consumers, families, farmers, and businesses.

Furthermore, NAFTA has provided North American businesses with better access to materials, technologies, investment capital, and talent available across North America. This has helped make our businesses more competitive, both within North America and around the world. With rapidly growing economies in Asia and South America challenging North America's competitiveness, NAFTA remains key to sustained growth and prosperity in the region.

NAFTA has proven that trade liberalization plays an important role in promoting transparency, economic growth, and legal certainty. In the face of increased global competition, Canada, the United States, and Mexico will work to strengthen the competitiveness of the North American region by continuing to pursue trade within the NAFTA region....

Did you know?

- Since NAFTA came into effect, trade among the NAFTA partners has more than tripled, reaching US$946.1 billion in 2008. Over that period, Canada–U.S. trade has more than doubled, while trade between Mexico and the U.S. has quadrupled. (C$ figure = $1.0 trillion).
- Today, the NAFTA partners exchange about US$2.6 billion in goods on a daily basis with each other. That's about US$108 million per hour. (C$ figures = $2.8 billion and $115 million).

Source: http://www.naftanow.org/results.

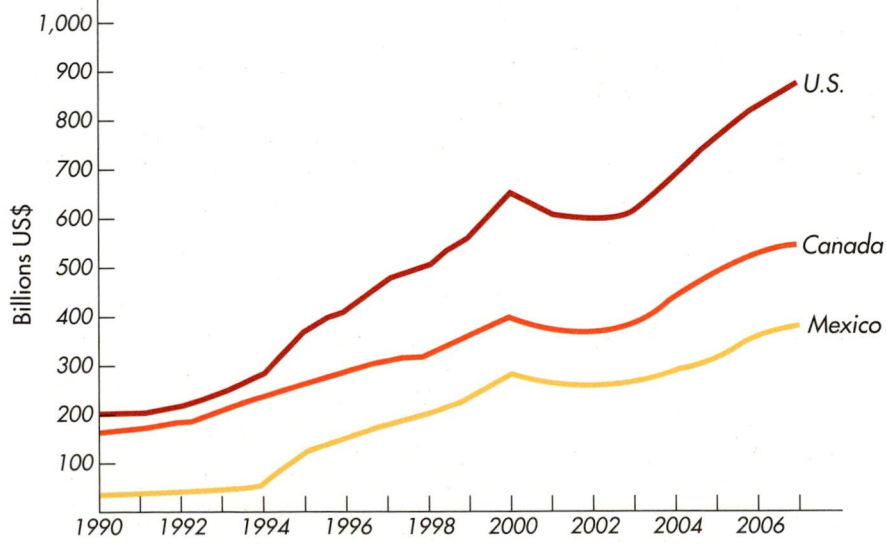

Trade with NAFTA Partners

Chart showing climbing trade in US$ 1993–2007; Canada–U.S., Canada–Mexico, U.S.–Mexico.

Source: U.S. Department of Commerce (Bureau of Census); Canada: Statistics Canada; Mexico: Secretary of Economy.

This article reemphasizes a main point made in this chapter: Countries are linked internationally, and so aggregate expenditure shifts in one country will have an impact on other nations. When other countries, like Mexico, sell goods to the United States, those exports increase Mexican GDP, since net exports is one of the components of GDP. Remembering that net exports increase with a country's GDP, we should expect net exports to vary over the business cycle. Since U.S. imports vary with U.S. GDP, slower growth in the United States tends to reduce U.S. imports, leading to lower GDP in the countries that export to the United States. Conversely, when the U.S. economy is booming, U.S. imports from Mexico will rise and stimulate GDP growth in Mexico.

The article discusses how the economies of the United States and Mexico have become more highly synchronized. As the U.S. experiences business-cycle fluctuations, these fluctuations tend to be matched in Mexico.

The United States had a recession in 2008. Did the economies of the major trading partners of the United States have recessions around this time? There was a recession in Canada that roughly coincided with the U.S. recession. However, in Europe, real GDP continued to grow for a while following the onset of the U.S. recession. This reflects the fact that the Canadian economy is much more integrated with that of the United States than European economies.

We should also expect Mexico to be greatly affected by U.S. business cycles, since about 85 percent of Mexican exports go to the United States. Australia, South Africa, Sweden, and Turkey are likely to have business cycles that are more independent of U.S. influences, since their exports to the United States as a share of their total exports are less than 10 percent.

The international links between countries should grow over time as restrictions on international trade are removed and transportation and communication costs continue to fall. The future may be one in which national business cycles are increasingly interdependent, and such interdependencies will have to be given greater emphasis in national policymaking.

An Algebraic Model of Income and Expenditures Equilibrium

Continuing the example we began in the Appendix to Chapter 9, if we know the equation for each component of aggregate expenditures (AE), we can solve for the equilibrium level of real GDP (Y) for the economy represented in Figure 1 of the chapter:

$$C = \$30 + .70Y$$
$$I = \$50$$
$$G = \$70$$
$$X = \$50 - .10Y$$

Summing these components, we can find the aggregate expenditures function:

$$AE = \$30 + .70Y + \$50 + \$70 + \$50 - .10Y = \$200 + .60Y$$

Given the AE function, we can solve for the equilibrium level of Y, where:

$$Y = AE$$
$$Y = \$200 + .60Y$$
$$Y - .60Y = \$200$$
$$.40Y = \$200$$
$$.40Y/.40 = \$200/.40$$
$$Y = \$500$$

The Spending Multiplier It is also possible to solve for the spending multiplier algebraically. We start by writing the general equations for each function, where C^a, I^a, G^a, EX^a, and IM^a represent autonomous consumption, investment, government spending, exports, and imports, respectively, and where c represents the MPC and im represents the MPI:

$$C = C^a + cY$$
$$I = I^a$$
$$G = G^a$$
$$X = EX^a - IM^a - imY$$

Now we sum the individual equations for the components of aggregate expenditures to get the aggregate expenditures function:

$$AE = C + I + G + X$$
$$= C^a + cY + I^a + G^a + EX^a + IM^a + imY$$
$$= (C^a + I^a + EX^a + IM^a) + cY + imY$$

We know that aggregate expenditures equal income. So

$$Y = (C^a + I^a + G^a + EX^a + IM^a) + cY + imY$$

Solving for Y, we first gather all of the terms involving Y on the left side of the equation:

$$Y[1 - (c - im)] + C^a + I^a + G^a + EX^a - IM^a$$

Next, we divide each side of the equation by $[1 - (c - im)]$ to get an equation for Y:

$$Y = \frac{1}{1 - (c - im)}C^a + I^a + G^a + EX^a - IM^a$$

A change in autonomous expenditures causes Y to change by

$$\frac{1}{1 - (c - im)}$$

times the change in expenditures. Because c is the *MPC* and *im* is the *MPI*, the multiplier can be written

$$\frac{1}{1 - (MPC - MPI)}$$

or, since $1 - MPC = MPS$, then $1 - (MPC + MPI) = MPS + MPI$, and the spending multiplier equals

$$\frac{1}{(MPC - MPI)}$$

CHAPTER 11

Fiscal Policy

© MACIEJ FROLOW/GETTY IMAGES, INC

© SOLARIA/SHUTTERSTOCK.COM; LOGO: © FROXX/SHUTTERSTOCK.COM

FUNDAMENTAL QUESTIONS

1 How can fiscal policy eliminate a GDP gap?

2 How has U.S. fiscal policy changed over time?

3 What are the effects of budget deficits?

4 How does fiscal policy differ across countries?

Macroeconomics plays a key role in national politics. When Jimmy Carter ran for the presidency against Gerald Ford in 1976, he created a "misery index" to measure the state of the economy. The index was the sum of the inflation rate and the unemployment rate, and Carter showed that it had risen during Ford's term in office. When Ronald Reagan challenged Carter in 1980, he used the misery index to show that inflation and unemployment had gone up during the Carter years as well. The implication is that presidents are responsible for the condition of the economy. If the inflation rate or the unemployment rate is relatively high coming into an election year, an incumbent president is open to criticism by opponents. For instance, many people believe that George Bush was defeated by Bill Clinton in 1992 because of the recession that began in 1990—a recession that was not announced as having ended in March 1991 until after the

Fiscal policy includes government spending on the provision of goods and services as well as infrastructure. In this photo, workers create mud bricks in the desert. The bricks will be used in infrastructure construction projects. Such activities are often provided by government and funded by taxpayers.

election. Clinton's 1992 campaign made economic growth a focus of its attacks on Bush, and his 1996 campaign emphasized the strength of the economy.

In 1996, a healthy economy helped Clinton defeat Bob Dole. And in the election of 2004, Bush supporters made economic growth a major focal point of their campaign against Kerry. More recently, Barack Obama's successful campaign for president had economic issues as a leading concern with the U.S. recession beginning in 2008. This was more than just campaign rhetoric, however. By law the government *is* responsible for the macroeconomic health of the nation. The Employment Act of 1946 states:

It is the continuing policy and responsibility of the Federal Government to use all practical means consistent with its needs and obligations and other essential considerations of national policy to coordinate and utilize all its plans, functions, and resources for the purpose of creating and maintaining, in a manner calculated to foster and promote free competitive enterprise and the general welfare conditions under which there will be afforded useful employment opportunities, including self-employment for those able, willing, and seeking to work, and to promote maximum employment, production, and purchasing power.

Fiscal policy is one tool that government uses to guide the economy along an expansionary path. In this chapter, we examine the role of fiscal policy—government spending and taxation—in determining the equilibrium level of income. Then we review the budget process and the history of fiscal policy in the United States. Finally, we describe the difference in fiscal policy between industrial and developing countries.

1. Fiscal Policy and Aggregate Demand

1 How can fiscal policy eliminate a GDP gap?

The GDP gap is the difference between potential real GDP and the equilibrium level of real GDP. If the government wants to close the GDP gap so that the equilibrium level of real GDP reaches its potential, it must use fiscal policy to alter aggregate expenditures and cause the aggregate demand curve to shift.

Fiscal policy is the government's policy with respect to spending and taxation. Since aggregate demand includes consumption, investment, net exports, and government spending, government spending on goods and services has a direct effect on the level of aggregate demand. Taxes affect aggregate demand indirectly by changing the disposable income of households, which alters consumption.

1.a. Shifting the Aggregate Demand Curve

By varying the level of government spending, policymakers can affect the level of real GDP.

Changes in government spending and taxes shift the aggregate demand curve. Remember that the aggregate demand curve represents combinations of equilibrium aggregate expenditures and alternative price levels. An increase in government spending or a decrease in taxes raises the level of expenditures at every level of prices and moves the aggregate demand curve to the right.

Figure 1 shows the increase in aggregate demand that would result from an increase in government spending or a decrease in taxes. Only if the aggregate supply curve is horizontal do prices remain fixed as aggregate demand increases. In Figure 1(a), equilibrium occurs along the horizontal segment (the Keynesian region) of the *AS* curve. If government spending increases and the price level remains constant, aggregate demand shifts from *AD* to *AD*$_1$; it increases by the horizontal distance from point *A* to point *B*. Once aggregate demand shifts, the *AD*$_1$ and *AS* curves intersect at potential real GDP, Y_p.

But Figure 1(a) is not realistic. The *AS* curve is not likely to be horizontal all the way to the level of potential real GDP; it should begin sloping up well before Y_p. And once the economy reaches the capacity level of output, the *AS* curve should become a vertical line, as shown in Figure 1(b).

If the *AS* curve slopes up before reaching the potential real GDP level, as it does in Figure 1(b), expenditures have to go up by more than the amount suggested in Figure 1(a) for the economy to reach Y_p. Why? Because when prices rise, the effect of spending on real GDP is reduced. This effect is shown in Figure 1(b). To increase the equilibrium level of real GDP from Y_e to Y_p, aggregate demand must shift by the amount from point *A* to point *C*, a larger increase than that shown in Figure 1(a), where the price level is fixed.

1.b. Multiplier Effects

Changes in government spending may have an effect on real GDP that is a multiple of the original change in government spending; a $1 change in government spending may increase real GDP by more than $1. This is because the original $1 of expenditure is spent over and over again in the economy as it passes from person to person. The government spending multiplier measures the multiple by which an increase in government spending increases real GDP. Similarly, a change in taxes may have an effect on real GDP that is a multiple of the original change in taxes. (The appendix to this chapter provides an algebraic analysis of the government spending and tax multipliers.)

If the price level rises as real GDP increases, the multiplier effects of any given change in aggregate expenditures are smaller than they would be if the price level remained constant.

If the price level rises as real GDP increases, the multiplier effects of any given change in aggregate demand are smaller than they would be if the price level remained constant. In addition to changes in the price level modifying the effect of government spending and taxes on real GDP, there are other factors that affect how much real GDP will change following a change in government spending. One such factor is how the government pays for, or finances, its spending.

FIGURE 1   Eliminating the Recessionary Gap: Higher Prices Mean Greater Spending

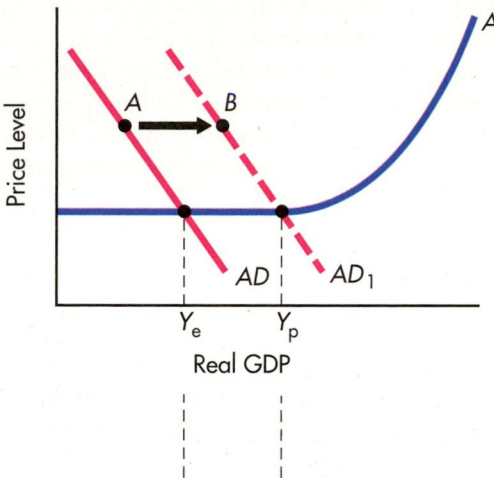

**(a) Aggregate Demand and Supply
(constant prices in Keynesian range of *AS* curve)**

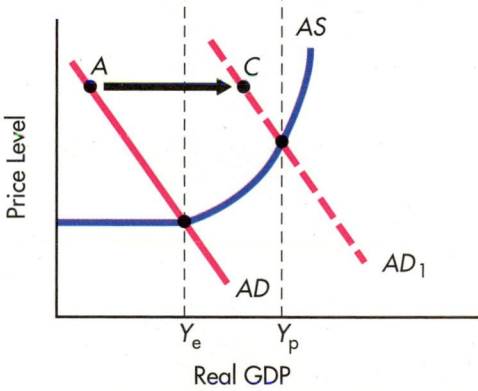

**(b) Aggregate Demand and Supply
(rising prices in intermediate range of *AS* curve)**

When aggregate demand increases from *AD* to AD_1 in Figure 1(a), equilibrium real GDP increases by the full amount of the shift in demand. This is because the aggregate supply curve is horizontal over the area of the shift in aggregate demand. In Figure 1(b), in order for equilibrium real GDP to rise from Y_e to Y_p, aggregate demand must shift by more than it does in Figure 1(a). In reality, the aggregate supply curve begins to slope up before potential real GDP (Y_p) is reached, as shown in Figure 1(b) of the figure.

Government spending must be financed by some combination of taxing, borrowing, and creating money:

$$\text{Government spending} = \text{taxes} + \text{change in government debt} \\ + \text{change in government-issued money}$$

In the chapter titled "Monetary Policy," we discuss the effect of financing government spending by creating money. As you will see, this source of government financing is relied on heavily in some developing countries. Here we talk about the financing problem that is relevant for industrial countries: how taxes and government debt can modify the expansionary effect of government spending on national income.

1.c. Government Spending Financed by Tax Increases

Suppose that government spending rises by $100 billion and that this expenditure is financed by a tax increase of $100 billion. Such a "balanced-budget" change in fiscal policy will cause equilibrium real GDP to rise. This is because government spending increases aggregate expenditures directly, but higher taxes lower aggregate expenditures indirectly through consumption spending. For instance, if taxes increase by $100, consumers will not cut their spending by $100, but will cut it by some fraction, say 9/10, of the increase. If consumers spend 90 percent of a change in their disposable income, then a tax increase of $100 would lower consumption by $90. So the net effect of raising government spending and taxes by the same amount is an increase in aggregate demand, illustrated in Figure 2 as the shift from AD to AD_1. However, it may be incorrect to assume that the only thing that changes is aggregate demand. An increase in taxes may also affect aggregate supply.

Aggregate supply measures the output that producers offer for sale at different levels of prices. When taxes go up, workers have less incentive to work because their after-tax income is lower. The cost of taking a day off or extending a vacation for a few extra days is less than it is when taxes are lower and after-tax income is higher. When taxes go up, then, output can fall, causing the aggregate supply curve to shift to the left. Such supply-side effects of taxes have been emphasized by the so-called supply-side economists, as discussed in the Economic Insight "Supply-Side Economics and the Laffer Curve."

Figure 2 shows the possible effects of an increase in government spending financed by taxes. The economy is initially in equilibrium at point A, with prices at P_1 and real GDP at Y_1. The increase in government spending shifts the aggregate demand curve from AD to AD_1. If this were the only change, the economy would be in equilibrium at

FIGURE 2　The Effect of Taxation on Aggregate Supply

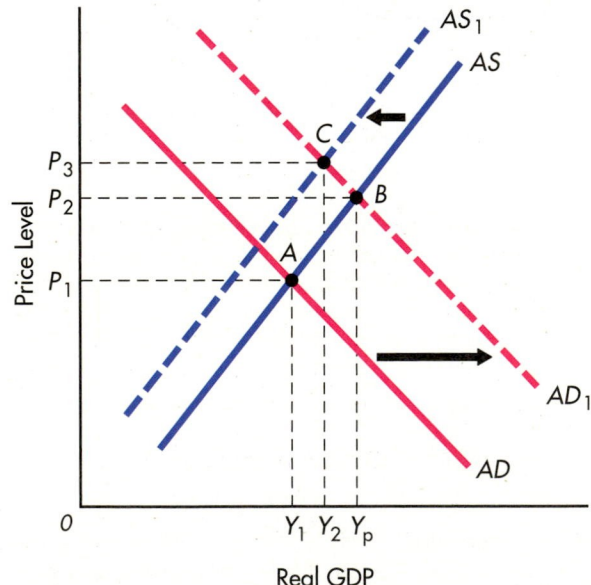

An increase in government spending shifts the aggregate demand curve from AD to AD_1, moving equilibrium from point A to point B and equilibrium real GDP from Y_1 to Y_p. If higher taxes reduce the incentive to work, aggregate supply could fall from AS to AS_1, moving equilibrium to point C and equilibrium real GDP to Y_2, a level below potential real GDP.

© 2013 Cengage Learning

ECONOMIC INSIGHT

Supply-Side Economics and the Laffer Curve

The large budget deficits incurred by the U.S. government in the 1980s were in part a product of lower tax rates engineered by the Reagan administration. President Reagan's economic team took office in January 1981 hoping that lower taxes would stimulate the supply of goods and services to a level that would raise tax revenues, even though tax rates as a percentage of income had been cut. These arguments were repeated in 1995 by members of Congress pushing for tax-rate cuts. This emphasis on greater incentives to produce created by lower taxes has come to be known as *supply-side economics*.

The most widely publicized element of supply-side economics was the *Laffer curve*. The curve is drawn with the tax rate on the vertical axis and tax revenue on the horizontal axis. When the rate of taxation is zero, there is no tax revenue. As the tax rate increases, tax revenue increases up to a point. The assumption here is that there is some rate of taxation that is so high that it discourages productive activity. Once this rate is reached, tax revenue begins to fall as the rate of taxation goes up. In the graph, tax revenue is maximized at R_{max} with a tax rate of t percent. Any increase in the rate of taxation above t percent produces lower tax revenues. In the extreme case—a 100 percent tax rate—no one is willing to work because the government taxes away all income.

Critics of the supply-side tax cuts proposed by the Reagan administration argued that lower taxes would increase the budget deficit. Supply-side advocates insisted that if the United States were in the backward-bending region of the

Laffer curve (above t percent in the graph), tax cuts would actually raise, not lower, tax revenue. The evidence following the tax cuts indicates that the tax cuts did, however, contribute to a larger budget deficit, implying that the United States was not on the backward-bending portion of the Laffer curve.

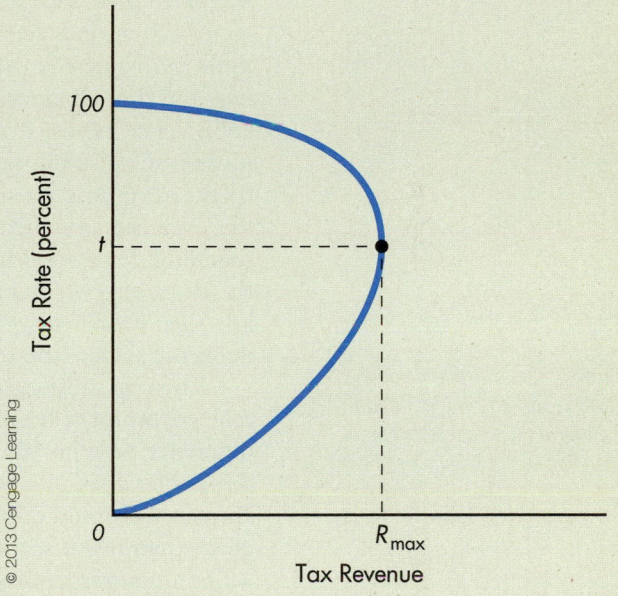

point *B*. But if the increase in taxes reduces output, the aggregate supply curve moves back from AS to AS_1, and output does not expand all the way to Y_p. The decrease in aggregate supply creates a new equilibrium at point *C*. Here real GDP is at Y_2 (less than Y_p), and the price level is P_3 (higher than P_2).

The standard analysis of government spending and taxation assumes that aggregate supply is not affected by the change in fiscal policy, leading us to expect a greater change in real GDP than may actually occur. If tax changes do affect aggregate supply, the expansionary effects of government spending financed by tax increases are moderated. The actual magnitude of this effect is the subject of debate among economists. Most argue that the evidence in the United States indicates that tax increases have a fairly small effect on aggregate supply.

1.d. Government Spending Financed by Borrowing

The standard multiplier analysis of government spending does not differentiate among the different methods of financing that spending. Yet you just saw how taxation can offset at least part of the expansionary effect of higher government spending. Borrowing to finance government spending can also limit the increase in aggregate demand.

A government borrows funds by selling bonds to the public. These bonds represent debt that must be repaid at a future date. Debt is, in a way, a kind of substitute for current taxes. Instead of increasing current taxes to finance higher spending, the government borrows the savings of households and businesses. Of course, the debt will mature and have to be repaid. This means that taxes will have to be higher in the future in order to provide the government with the funds to pay off the debt.

Current government borrowing, then, implies higher future taxes. This can limit the expansionary effect of increased government spending. If households and businesses take higher future taxes into account, they tend to save more today so that they will be able to pay those taxes in the future. And as saving today increases, consumption today falls.

The idea that current government borrowing can reduce current nongovernment expenditures was suggested originally by the early nineteenth-century English economist David Ricardo. Ricardo recognized that government borrowing could function like increased current taxes, reducing current household and business expenditures. *Ricardian equivalence* is the principle that government-spending activities financed by taxation and those financed by borrowing have the same effect on the economy. If Ricardian equivalence holds, it doesn't matter whether the government raises taxes or borrows more to finance increased spending. The effect is the same: Private-sector spending falls by the same amount today, and this drop in private spending will at least partially offset the expansionary effect of government spending on real GDP. Just how much private spending drops (and how far to the left the aggregate demand curve shifts) depends on the degree to which current saving increases in response to expected higher taxes. The less that people respond to the future tax liabilities arising from current government debt, the smaller the reduction in private spending.

There is substantial disagreement among economists over the extent to which current government borrowing acts like an increase in taxes. Some argue that it makes no difference whether the government raises current taxes or borrows. Others insist that the public does not base current spending on future tax liabilities. If the first group is correct, we would expect government spending financed by borrowing to have a smaller effect than if the second group is correct. Research on this issue continues, with most economists questioning the relevance of Ricardian equivalence and a small but influential group arguing its importance.

> *Ricardian equivalence holds if taxation and government borrowing both have the same effect on spending in the private sector.*

1.e. Crowding Out

crowding out
A drop in consumption or investment spending caused by government spending.

Expansionary fiscal policy can crowd out private-sector spending; that is, an increase in government spending can reduce consumption and investment. **Crowding out** is usually discussed in the context of government spending financed by borrowing rather than by taxes. We have just seen how future taxes can cause consumption to fall today, but investment can also be affected. Increases in government borrowing drive up interest rates. As interest rates go up, investment falls. This sort of indirect crowding out works through the bond market. The U.S government borrows by selling Treasury bonds or bills. Because the government is not a profit-making institution, it does not have to earn a profitable return on the money it raises by selling bonds. A corporation does, however. When interest rates rise, fewer corporations offer new bonds to raise investment funds because the cost of repaying the bond debt may exceed the rate of return on the investment.

Crowding out, like Ricardian equivalence, is important in principle, but economists have never demonstrated conclusively that its effects can substantially alter spending in the private sector. Still, you should be aware of the possibility in order to understand the potential shortcomings of changes in government spending and taxation.

RECAP

1. Fiscal policy refers to government spending and taxation.

2. By increasing spending or cutting taxes, a government can close the GDP gap.

3. If government spending and taxes increase by the same amount, equilibrium real GDP rises.

4. If a tax increase affects aggregate supply, then a balanced-budget change in fiscal policy will have a smaller expansionary effect on equilibrium real GDP than otherwise.

5. Current government borrowing reduces current spending in the private sector if people increase current saving in order to pay future tax liabilities.

6. Ricardian equivalence holds when taxation and government borrowing have the same effect on current spending in the private sector.

7. Increased government borrowing can crowd private borrowers out of the bond market so that investment falls.

2. Fiscal Policy in the United States

2 How has U.S. fiscal policy changed over time?

Our discussion of fiscal policy assumes that this policy is made at the federal level. In the modern economy, this is a reasonable assumption. This was not the case before the 1930s, however. Before the Depression, the federal government limited its activities largely to national defense and foreign policy and left other areas of government policy to the individual states. With the growth in the importance of the federal government in fiscal policy has come a growth in the role of the federal budget process.

When one is talking about the federal budget, the monetary amounts of the various categories of expenditures are so huge that they are often difficult to comprehend. But if you were to divide up the annual budget by the number of individual taxpayers, you'd come up with an average individual statement that might make more sense, as shown in the Economic Insight "The Taxpayer's Federal Government Credit Card Statement."

The federal budget is determined as much by politics as by economics. Politicians respond to different groups of voters by supporting different government programs, regardless of the needed fiscal policy. It is the political response to constituents that tends to drive up federal budget deficits (the difference between government expenditures and tax revenues), not the need for expansionary fiscal policy. As a result, deficits have become commonplace.

2.a. The Historical Record

The U.S. government has grown dramatically since the early part of the century. Figure 3 shows federal revenues and expenditures over time. Note that expenditures were lower than revenues in the 1998–2001 period. Figure 4 places the growth of government in perspective by plotting U.S. government spending as a percentage of gross domestic product over time. Before the Great Depression, federal spending was approximately 3 percent of the GDP; by the end of the Depression, it had risen to about 10 percent. The ratio of spending to GDP reached its peak during World War II, when federal spending hit 44 percent of the GDP. After the war, the ratio fell dramatically and then slowly increased to a peak of about 24 percent in 1983. In recent years, the ratio has been around 20 percent.

Fiscal policy has two components: discretionary fiscal policy and automatic stabilizers. **Discretionary fiscal policy** refers to changes in government spending and taxation that are aimed at achieving a policy goal. **Automatic stabilizers** are elements of fiscal policy that automatically change in value as national income changes. Figures 3 and 4 suggest that government spending is dominated by growth over time. But there is

discretionary fiscal policy
Changes in government spending and taxation that are aimed at achieving a policy goal.

automatic stabilizer
An element of fiscal policy that changes automatically as national income changes.

© froxx/Shutterstock.com

ECONOMIC INSIGHT

The Taxpayer's Federal Government Credit Card Statement

Suppose the U.S. government's expenditures and revenues were accounted for annually to each individual income taxpayer like a credit card statement. For 2011, the statement would look like the accompanying table.

Statement for 2011 Budget Year	
Previous balance	$42,508.48
New purchases	
Defense	$ 5,178.58
Social Security	$ 5,166.76
Medicare	$ 3,844.68
Medicaid	$ 1,913.89
Other	$ 9,078.98
Total Spending	$25,182.93
Payments received	
Individual income and social security taxes	$ 9,672.49
Corporate income taxes	$ 2,569.03
Other	$ 9,069.70
Total payments	$21,311.23
Finance charge	$ 2,101.32
New balance due	$48,988.89

© 2013 Cengage Learning

no indication here of discretionary changes in fiscal policy, changes in government spending and taxation that are aimed at meeting specific policy goals. Perhaps a better way to evaluate the fiscal policy record is in terms of the budget deficit. Government expenditures can rise, but the effect on aggregate demand could be offset by a simultaneous increase in taxes so that there is no expansionary effect on the equilibrium level of national income. By looking at the deficit, we see the combined spending and tax policy results, which are missing if only government expenditures are considered.

Figure 5 illustrates the pattern of the U.S. federal deficit and the deficit as a percentage of GDP over time. Figure 5(a) shows that the United States ran close to a balanced budget for much of the 1950s and 1960s. There were large deficits associated with financing World War II, and then large deficits resulting from fiscal policy decisions in recent decades. However, from 1998 to 2001, the first surpluses since 1969 were recorded. Figure 5(b) shows that the deficit as a percentage of GDP was much larger during World War II than it was in the 1980s and 1990s.

Historically, aside from wartime, budget deficits increase the most during recessions. When real GDP falls, tax revenues go down, and government spending on unemployment and welfare benefits goes up. These are examples of automatic stabilizers in action. As income falls, taxes fall and personal benefit payments rise to partially offset the effect of the drop in income. The rapid growth of the deficit in the 1980s involved more than the recessions in 1980 and 1982, however. The economy grew rapidly after the 1982 recession ended, but so did the fiscal deficit. The increase in the deficit was the product of a rapid increase in government spending to fund new programs and enlarge existing programs while taxes were held constant. In the late 1990s, the deficit decreased. This

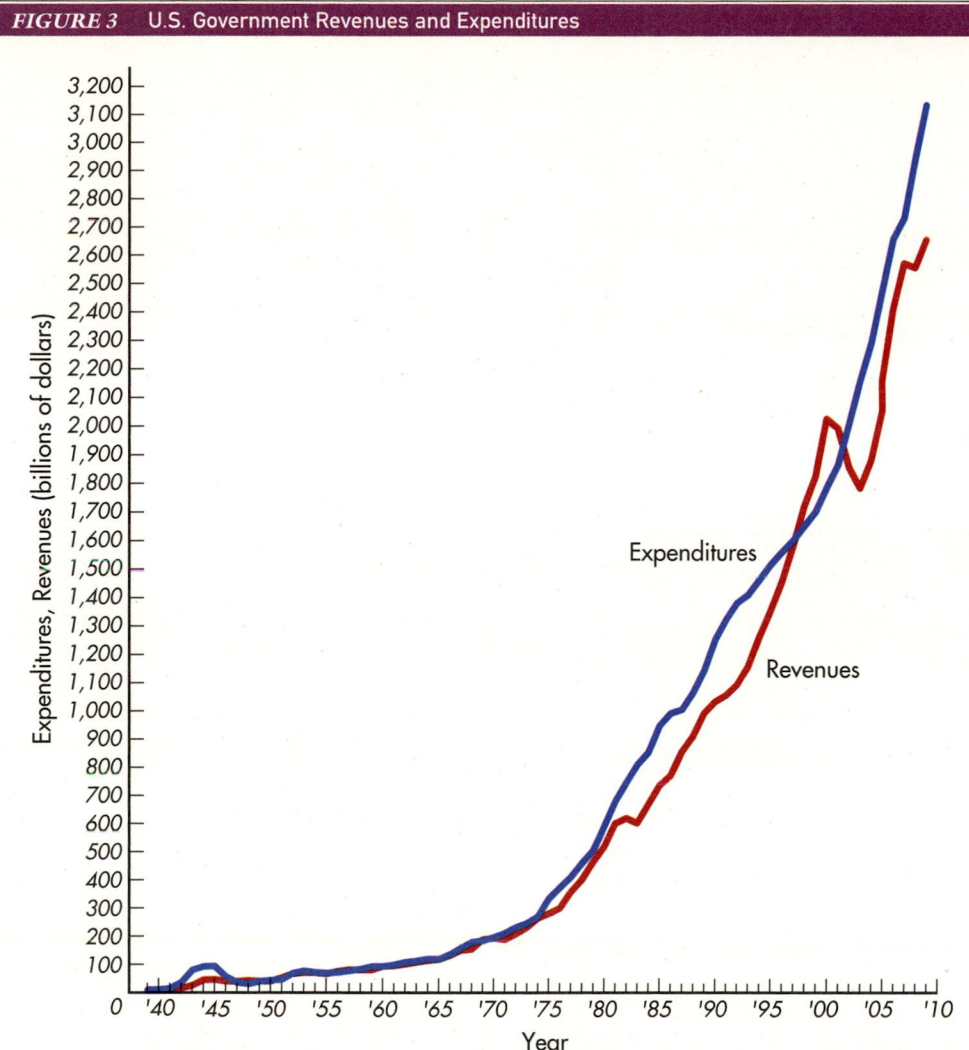

FIGURE 3 U.S. Government Revenues and Expenditures

Revenues are total revenues of the U.S. government in each fiscal year. Expenditures are total spending of the U.S. government in each fiscal year. The difference between the two curves equals the U.S. budget deficit (when expenditures exceed revenues) or surplus (when revenues exceed expenditures).

Source: Data are drawn from *Economic Report of the President, 2010.*

was the result of surprisingly large tax revenue gains, generated by strong economic growth, combined with only moderate government spending increases. The deficit is unlikely to fall significantly in the next few years, however, as government spending for defense and homeland security rises.

2.b. Deficits and the National Debt

The large federal deficits of the 1980s and 1990s led many observers to question whether a deficit can harm the economy. Figure 5 shows how the fiscal deficit has changed over time. One major implication of a large deficit is the resulting increase in the national debt, the total stock of government bonds outstanding. Table 1 lists data

3 What are the effects of budget deficits?

FIGURE 4   U.S. Government Expenditures as a Percentage of Gross Domestic Product

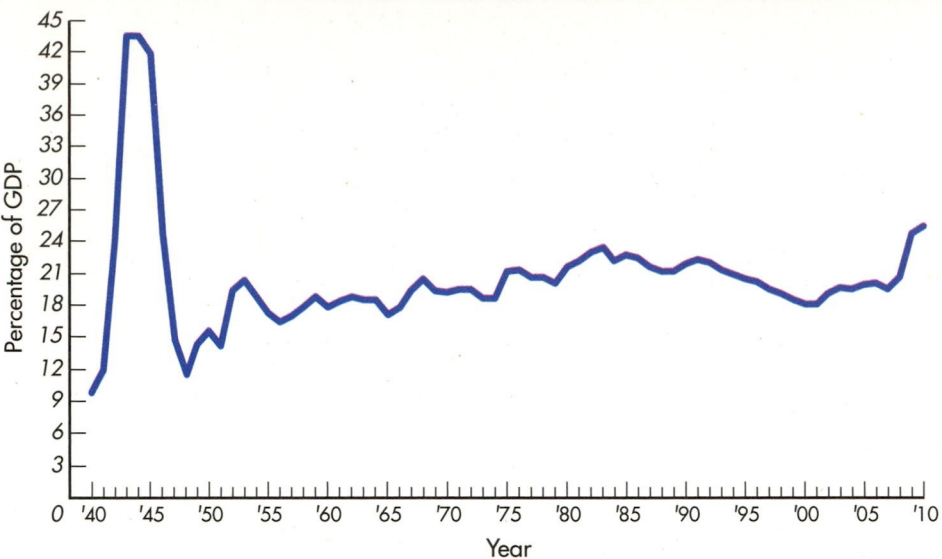

U.S. federal government spending as a percentage of the GDP reached a high of 44 percent in 1943 and 1944. Discounting wartime spending and cutbacks after the war, you can see the upward trend in U.S. government spending, which constituted a larger and larger share of the GDP until the early 1980s.

FIGURE 5   The U.S. Deficit

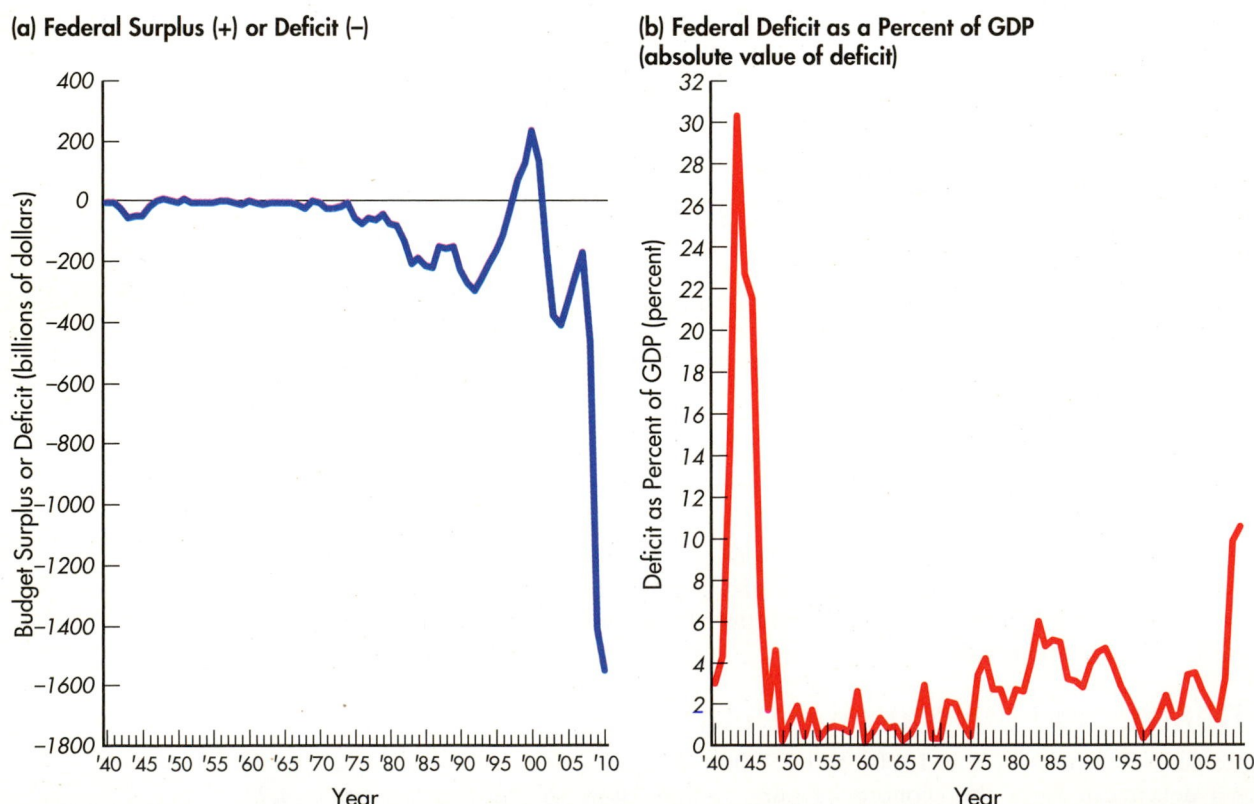

As Figure 5(a) shows, since 1940 the U.S. government has rarely shown a surplus. For much of the 1950s and 1960s, the United States was close to a balanced budget. Figure 5(b) shows the federal deficit as a percentage of GDP. The deficits during the 1950s and 1960s generally were small. The early 1980s were a time of rapid growth in the federal budget deficit, and this is reflected in the growth of the deficit as a percentage of GDP.

on the debt of the United States. Notice that the total debt doubled between 1981 ($994.8 billion) and 1986 ($2,120.6 billion), and then doubled again between 1986 and 1993. Column 3 shows debt as a percentage of GDP. In the late 1990s, the debt was falling as a percentage of GDP. During World War II, the debt was greater than the GDP for five years. Despite the talk of "unprecedented" federal deficits in the 1980s and 1990s, clearly the ratio of the debt to GDP was by no means unprecedented.

We have not yet answered the question of whether deficits are bad. To do so, we have to consider their potential effects.

TABLE 1	Debt of the U.S. Government (Dollar Amounts in Billions)			
(1) Year	(2) Total Debt	(3) Debt/GDP (percent)	(4) Net Interest	(5) Interest/Government Spending (percent)
1958	$ 279.7	63	$ 5.6	6.8
1960	$ 290.5	57	$ 6.9	7.5
1962	$ 302.9	55	$ 6.9	6.5
1964	$ 316.1	50	$ 8.2	6.9
1966	$ 328.5	44	$ 9.4	7.0
1968	$ 368.7	43	$ 11.1	6.2
1970	$ 380.9	39	$ 14.4	7.4
1972	$ 435.9	38	$ 15.5	6.7
1974	$ 483.9	34	$ 21.4	8.0
1976	$ 629.0	37	$ 26.7	7.3
1978	$ 776.6	36	$ 35.4	7.9
1980	$ 909.1	34	$ 52.5	9.1
1981	$ 994.8	34	$ 68.8	10.5
1982	$ 1,137.3	36	$ 85.0	11.6
1983	$ 1,371.7	41	$ 89.8	11.2
1984	$ 1,564.7	42	$111.1	13.2
1985	$ 1,817.5	46	$129.5	13.6
1986	$ 2,120.6	50	$136.0	13.7
1987	$ 2,396.1	53	$138.7	13.8
1988	$ 2,601.3	54	$151.8	14.3
1989	$ 2,868.0	55	$169.3	14.8
1990	$ 3,206.6	56	$184.2	14.7
1991	$ 3,598.5	61	$194.5	14.7
1992	$ 4,002.1	65	$199.4	14.4
1993	$ 4,351.4	67	$198.8	14.1
1994	$ 4,643.7	66	$203.0	13.9
1995	$ 4,921.0	66	$232.2	15.3
1996	$ 5,181.9	66	$241.1	15.5
1997	$ 5,369.7	65	$244.0	15.2
1998	$ 5,478.7	63	$241.2	14.6
1999	$ 5,606.1	57	$229.7	13.5

(Continued)

TABLE 1	Debt of the U.S. Government (Dollar Amounts in Billions) (Continued)			
(1) Year	(2) Total Debt	(3) Debt/GDP (percent)	(4) Net Interest	(5) Interest/Government Spending (percent)
2000	$ 5,628.7	57	$222.9	12.5
2001	$ 5,769.9	57	$206.2	11.1
2002	$ 6,198.4	59	$171.0	8.5
2003	$ 6,760.0	63	$153.1	7.1
2004	$ 7,354.7	64	$160.2	7.0
2005	$ 7,905.3	64	$184.0	7.4
2006	$ 8,451.4	64	$226.6	8.5
2007	$ 8,950.7	65	$237.1	8.7
2008	$ 9,623.4	67	$248.9	8.4
2009	$10,438.4	70	$228.0	7.3
2010	$13,528.8	93	$186.9	5.7
2011	$15,476.2	102	$206.7	5.4

© 2013 Cengage Learning

2.b.1. Deficits, Interest Rates, and Investment

Because government deficits mean government borrowing and debt, many economists argue that deficits raise interest rates as lenders require a higher interest rate to induce them to hold more government debt. Increased government borrowing raises interest rates; this, in turn, can depress investment. (Remember that as interest rates rise, the rate of return on investment drops, along with the incentive to invest.) What happens when government borrowing crowds out private investment? Lower investment means fewer capital goods in the future. So deficits lower the level of output in the economy, both today and in the future. In this sense, deficits are potentially bad.

2.b.2. Deficits and International Trade

If government deficits raise real interest rates (the nominal interest rate minus the expected inflation rate), they also may have an effect on international trade. A higher real return on U.S. securities makes those securities more attractive to foreign investors. As the foreign demand for U.S. securities increases, so does the demand for U.S. dollars in exchange for Japanese yen, British pounds, and other foreign currencies. As the demand for dollars increases, the dollar *appreciates* in value on the foreign exchange market. This means that the dollar becomes more expensive to foreigners, while foreign currency becomes cheaper to U.S. residents. This kind of change in the exchange rate encourages U.S. residents to buy more foreign goods and encourages foreign residents to buy fewer U.S. goods. Ultimately, then, as deficits and government debt increase, U.S. net exports tend to fall. Such foreign trade effects are another potentially bad effect of deficits.

Through their effects on investment, deficits can lower the level of output in the economy.

2.b.3. Interest Payments on the National Debt

The national debt is the stock of government bonds outstanding. It is the product of past and current budget deficits. As the size of the debt increases, the amount of interest that must be paid on the debt tends to rise. Column 4 of Table 1 lists the amount of interest paid on the debt; column 5 lists the interest as a percentage of government expenditures. The numbers in both columns have risen steadily over time and only recently started to drop.

The increase in the interest cost of the national debt is an aspect of fiscal deficits that worries some people. However, to the extent that U.S. citizens hold government bonds, we owe the debt to ourselves. The tax liability of funding the interest payments is offset by the interest income that bondholders earn. In this case there is no net change in national wealth when the national debt changes.

Of course, we do not owe the national debt just to ourselves. The United States is the world's largest national financial market, and many U.S. securities, including government bonds, are held by foreign residents. Today, foreign holdings of the U.S. national debt amount to about 28 percent of the outstanding debt. Because the tax liability for paying the interest on the debt falls on U.S. taxpayers, the greater the payments made to foreigners, the lower the wealth of U.S. residents, other things being equal.

Other things are not equal, however. To understand the real impact of foreign holdings on the economy, we have to evaluate what the economy would have been like if the debt had not been sold to foreign investors. If the foreign savings placed in U.S. bonds allowed the United States to increase investment and its productive capacity beyond what would have been possible in the absence of foreign lending, then the country could very well be better off for having sold government bonds to foreigners. The presence of foreign funds may keep interest rates lower than they would otherwise be, preventing the substantial crowding out associated with an increase in the national debt.

So while deficits are potentially bad as a result of the crowding out of investment, larger trade deficits with the rest of the world, and greater interest costs of the debt, we cannot generally say that all deficits are bad. It depends on what benefit the deficit provides. If the deficit spending allowed for greater productivity than would have occurred otherwise, the benefits may outweigh the costs. The financial crisis of 2008 provides a great example: Fiscal policy around the world involved governments increasing spending dramatically so that budget deficits increased substantially. However, the thinking was that the cost of not having government stimulate the economy would have been a much worse recession with many more people unemployed and incomes falling even more, so that the benefits of the deficits were widely thought to outweigh the costs.

2.c. Automatic Stabilizers

We have largely been talking about discretionary fiscal policy, the changes in government spending and taxing that policymakers make consciously. *Automatic stabilizers* are the elements of fiscal policy that change automatically as income changes. Automatic stabilizers partially offset changes in income: As income falls, automatic stabilizers increase spending; as income rises, automatic stabilizers decrease spending. Any program that responds to fluctuations in the business cycle in a way that moderates the effect of those fluctuations is an automatic stabilizer. Examples are progressive income taxes and transfer payments.

In our examples of tax changes, we have been using *lump-sum taxes*—taxes that are a flat dollar amount regardless of income. However, income taxes are determined as a percentage of income. In the United States, the federal income tax is a **progressive tax**: As income rises, so does the rate of taxation. A person with a very low income pays no income tax, while a person with a high income can pay more than a third of that income in taxes. Countries use different rates of taxation on income. Taxes can be regressive (the tax rate falls as income rises) or proportional (the tax rate is constant as income rises) as well as progressive. But most countries, including the United States, use a progressive tax, with the percentage of income paid as taxes rising as taxable income rises.

progressive tax
A tax whose rate rises as income rises.

Progressive income taxes act as an automatic stabilizer. As income falls, so does the average tax rate. Suppose a household earning $60,000 must pay 30 percent of its income ($18,000) in taxes, leaving 70 percent of its income ($42,000) for spending. If that household's income drops to $40,000 and the tax rate falls to 25 percent, the household has 75 percent of its income ($30,000) available for spending. But if the tax rate is 30 percent at all levels of income, the household earning $40,000 would have only 70 percent of its income ($28,000) to spend. By allowing a greater percentage of earned income to be spent, progressive taxes help offset the effect of lower income on spending.

All industrial countries have progressive federal income tax systems. For instance, the tax rate in Japan starts at 5 percent for low-income households and rises to a maximum of 40 percent for high-income households. In the United States, individual

transfer payment
A payment to one person that is funded by taxing others.

income tax rates start at 10 percent and rise to a maximum of 35 percent. In the U.K. tax system, rates rise from 10 percent to 50 percent, while tax rates in Germany rise from 15 to 45 percent and those in France, from 5.5 to 40 percent.

A **transfer payment** is a payment to one person that is funded by taxing others. Food stamps, welfare benefits, and unemployment benefits are all government transfer payments: Current taxpayers provide the funds to pay those who qualify for the programs. Transfer payments that use income to establish eligibility act as automatic stabilizers. In a recession, as income falls, more people qualify for food stamps or welfare benefits, raising the level of transfer payments.

Unemployment insurance is also an automatic stabilizer. As unemployment rises, more workers receive unemployment benefits. Unemployment benefits tend to rise in a recession and fall during an expansion. This countercyclical pattern of benefit payments offsets the effect of business-cycle fluctuations on consumption.

RECAP

1. Fiscal policy in the United States is a product of the budget process.

2. Federal spending in the United States has grown rapidly over time, from just 3 percent of GDP before the Great Depression to about 20 percent of GDP today.

3. Government budget deficits can hurt the economy through their effect on interest rates and private

investment, net exports, and the tax burden on current and future taxpayers.

4. Automatic stabilizers are government programs that are already in place and that respond automatically to fluctuations in the business cycle, moderating the effect of those fluctuations.

4 How does fiscal policy differ across countries?

3. Fiscal Policy in Different Countries

A country's fiscal policy reflects its philosophy toward government spending and taxation. In this section we present comparative data that demonstrate the variety of fiscal policies in the world.

3.a. Government Spending

Our discussion up to this point has centered on U.S. fiscal policy. But fiscal policy and the role of government in the economy can be very different across countries. Government has played an increasingly larger role in the major industrial countries over time. Table 2 shows how government spending has gone up as a percentage of output in five industrial nations. In every case, government spending accounted for a larger percentage of output in 2008 than it did 100 years earlier. For instance, in 1880, government spending was only 6 percent of the GNP in Sweden. By 1929 it had risen to 8 percent, and by 2008, to 26 percent.

Historically, in industrial countries, the growth of government spending has been matched by growth in revenues. But in the 1960s, government spending began to grow faster than revenues, creating increasingly larger debtor nations.

> Government spending has grown over time as a fraction of GNP in all industrial countries.

Developing countries have not shown the uniform growth in government spending found in industrial countries. In fact, in some developing countries (e.g., Chile, the Dominican Republic, and Peru), government spending is a smaller percentage of GDP today than it was 20 years ago. And we find a greater variation in the role of government in developing countries.

TABLE 2	Share of Government Spending in GNP in Selected Industrial Countries. 1880. 1929. and 2008 (Percent)				
Year	France	Germany	Sweden	United Kingdom	United States
1880	15	10[1]	6	10	8
1929	19	31	8	24	10
2008	23	18	26	21	16

[1]1881

Source: Data are drawn from World Bank, *World Development Report 1996* and *2006* and OECD.StatExtracts.

One important difference between the typical developed country and the typical developing country is that government plays a larger role in investment spending in the developing country. One reason for this difference is that state-owned enterprises account for a larger percentage of economic activity in developing countries than they do in developed countries. Also, developing countries usually rely more on government rather than the private sector to build their infrastructure—schools, roads, hospitals—than do developed countries.

How a government spends its money is a function of its income. Here we find differences not only between industrial and developing countries, but also among developing countries. Figure 6 reports central government spending for the United States, an industrial country, and a large developing country, China.

This figure clearly illustrates the relative importance of social welfare spending in industrial and developing countries. Although standards of living are lowest in the poorest countries, these countries do not have the resources to spend on social services (education, health, housing, social security, welfare). The United States spends 43 percent of

FIGURE 6   Central Government Spending by Functional Category

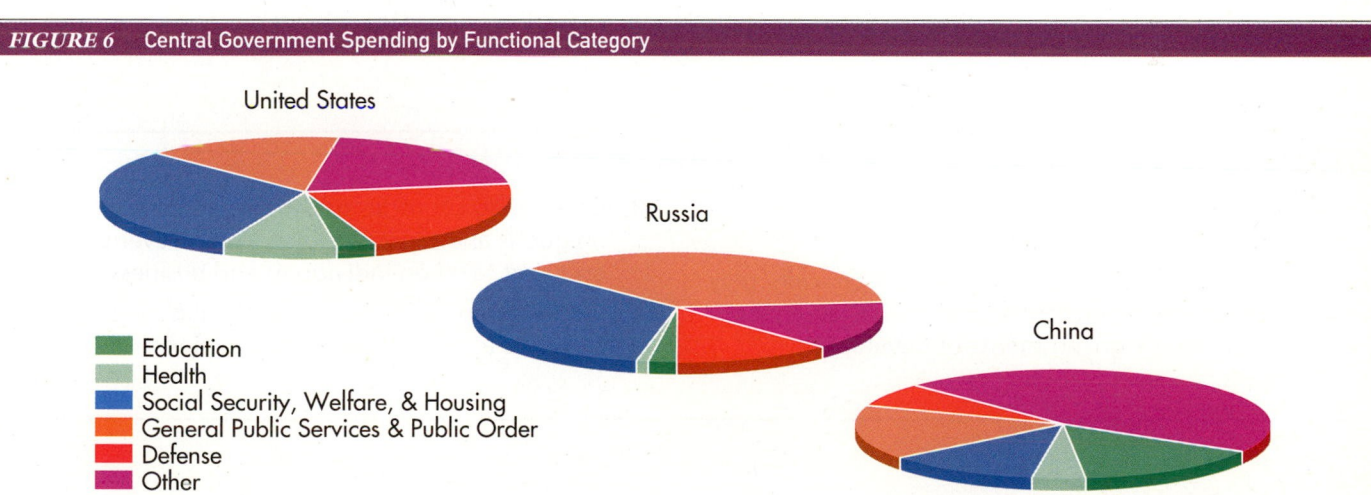

The charts show the pattern of government spending in an industrial country, the United States, and a low-income developing country, China. Social programs (education, health, and social security) account for 43 percent of federal government expenditures in the United States, but only 31 percent in China.

Source: Data are drawn from International Monetary Fund, *Government Finance Statistics Yearbook, 2008.*

its budget on social security, health, and education programs. China spends 31 percent of its budget on these programs, and that is substantially more than most developing countries.

3.b. Taxation

There are two different types of taxes: *direct taxes* (on individuals and firms) and *indirect taxes* (on goods and services). Figure 7 compares the importance of different sources of central government tax revenue for an industrial country, the United States, and a developing country, China. The most obvious difference is that personal income taxes are much more important in industrial countries than in developing countries. Why? Because personal taxes are hard to collect in agricultural nations, where a large percentage of household production is for personal consumption. Taxes on businesses are easier to collect and thus are more important in developing countries.

That industrial countries are better able to afford social programs is reflected in the great disparity in social security taxes between industrial countries and developing countries. With so many workers living near the subsistence level in the poorest countries, their governments simply cannot tax workers for retirement and health security programs.

Figure 7 also shows that taxes on international trade are very important in developing countries. Because goods arriving or leaving a country must pass through customs inspection, export and import taxes are relatively easy to collect compared to income taxes. In general, developing countries depend more on indirect taxes on goods and services than do developed countries.

value-added tax (VAT)
A general sales tax collected at each stage of production.

Figure 7 lists "Goods and Services" taxes. Of these, 65 percent are **value-added taxes (VATs)** for industrial countries, while 61 percent of developing country commodity taxes come from value-added taxes. A value-added tax is an indirect tax imposed on each sale at each stage of production. Each seller from the first stage of production on collects the VAT from the buyer, then deducts any VATs it has paid in buying its inputs. The difference is remitted to the government. From time to time, Congress has debated the merits of a VAT in the United States, but it has never approved this kind of tax. The Global Business Insight "Value-Added Tax" provides further discussion.

RECAP

1. Over time, government spending has become more important in industrial countries.

2. Governments in developing countries typically play a larger role in investment spending in their economies than do the governments of developed countries.

3. Developing countries depend more on indirect taxes on goods and services as a source of revenue than on direct taxes on individuals and businesses.

4. Value-added taxes are general sales taxes that are collected at every stage of production.

FIGURE 7 Central Government Tax Composition by Income Group

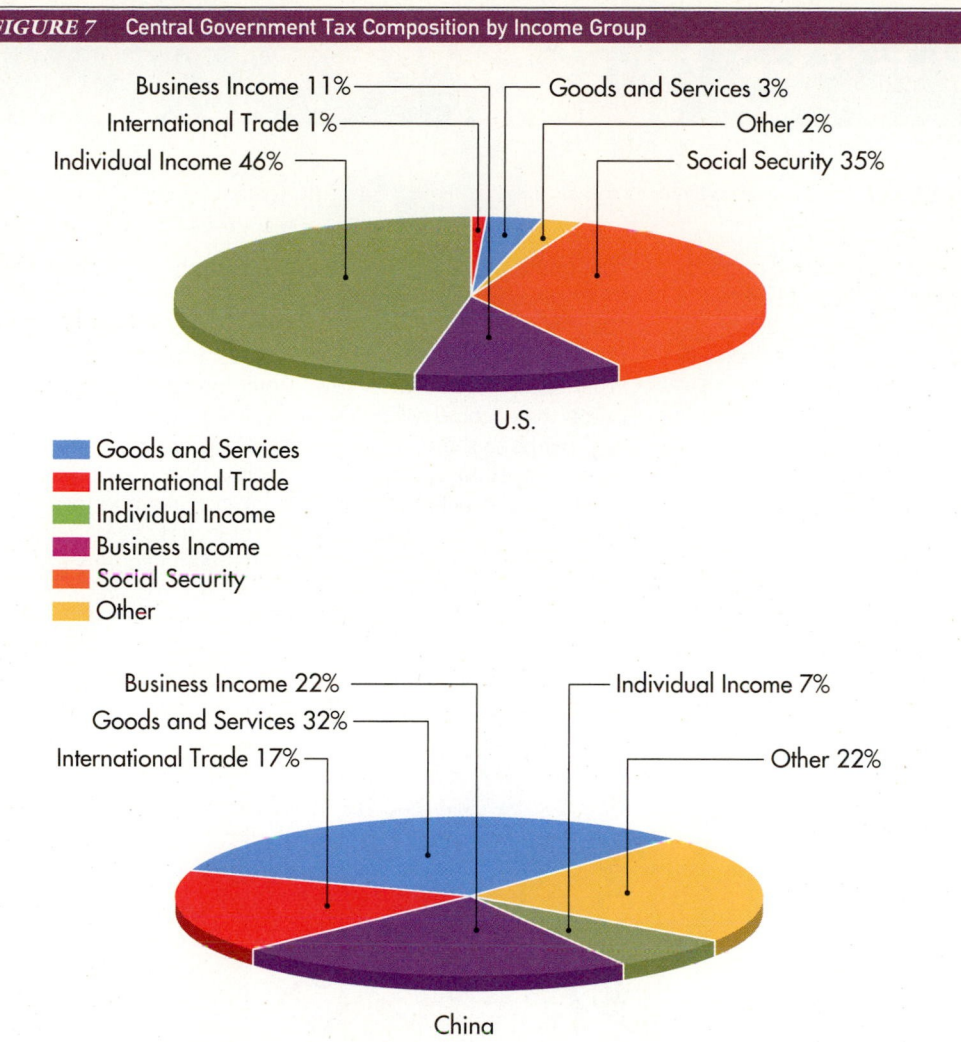

Business Income 11%
International Trade 1%
Individual Income 46%
Goods and Services 3%
Other 2%
Social Security 35%

U.S.

Goods and Services
International Trade
Individual Income
Business Income
Social Security
Other

Business Income 22%
Goods and Services 32%
International Trade 17%
Individual Income 7%
Other 22%

China

When we group countries by income level, the importance of different sources of tax revenue is obvious. Domestic income taxes account for 46 percent of government revenue in the United States and just 7 percent in China. Business income taxes are more important in developing countries like China. Social security taxes are a major source of government revenue in industrial countries; they are less important in developing countries, which cannot afford social programs. International trade taxes represent just 1 percent of tax revenues in industrial countries like the United States; in China, 17 percent of tax revenue comes from international trade taxes, and developing countries rely heavily on these taxes. (Note: Percentages do not total 100 because of rounding.)

Source: Data are drawn from *Government Finance Statistics, 2008.*

GLOBAL BUSINESS INSIGHT

Value-Added Tax

A value-added tax (VAT) is a tax levied on all sales of goods and services at each stage of production. As implied by the name, the tax applies only to the value added at each stage, and so a firm that pays value-added taxes will pay tax only on the value that it added to the good or service that it sells. If a firm sells melons at a fruit stand, the VAT it pays is based on the difference between the cost the firm paid for the melons and the sales price it charges to its customers who buy the fruit. Of course, the customers bear the cost of the VAT, as it is built into the price they must pay.

As the accompanying map indicates, VATs are very popular around the world. Many countries adopted VATs in the 1990s. It is clear that more countries use VATs than do not. Such a tax has its advantages. One important consideration is that a VAT is a tax on consumption. Anyone who buys goods and services will contribute to the government's VAT revenue. Thus, VATs are very powerful revenue generators. Those individuals who evade income taxes and pay less than their legal obligation will not escape the VAT. For instance, a criminal who earns income illegally and pays no tax on that income will be taxed on all legal goods and services that he or she purchases. In this sense, there is a certain attractiveness to taxing consumption rather than income. But a VAT also acts as a regressive tax in that a poor person would tend to pay a higher fraction of income as VAT than a rich person. It is important to realize that no country relies strictly on a VAT for government revenue. VATs are part of an overall government tax policy that attempts to incorporate fairness along with a need to raise sufficient revenue to finance public expenditures.

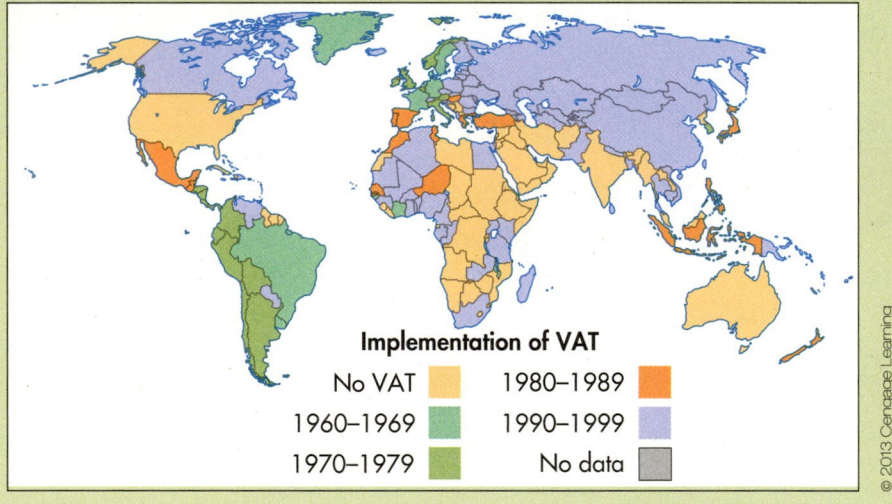

Implementation of VAT

No VAT		1980–1989	
1960–1969		1990–1999	
1970–1979		No data	

© 2013 Cengage Learning

Source: International Monetary Fund, VATs are Appropriate for Wide Range of Economies, but Certain Preconditions are Vital for Success, IMF Survey, Volume 29, Number 9, May 2000. Reprinted with permission of the International Monetary Fund.

SUMMARY

1. How can fiscal policy eliminate a GDP gap?

- A GDP gap can be closed by increasing government spending or by cutting taxes. *§1*

- Government spending affects aggregate expenditures directly; taxes affect aggregate expenditures indirectly through their effect on consumption. *§1*

- Aggregate expenditures must rise to bring equilibrium real GDP up to potential real GDP to eliminate the GDP gap. *§1*

- An increase in government spending that is matched by an increase in taxes raises equilibrium spending and real GDP. *§1.c*

- If the public expects to pay higher taxes as a result of government borrowing, then the expansionary effects of government deficits may be reduced. *§1.d*

- Government borrowing can crowd out private spending by raising interest rates and reducing investments. *§1.e*

2. How has U.S. fiscal policy changed over time?

- Federal government spending in the United States has increased from just 3 percent of the GDP before the Great Depression to around 20 percent of the GDP today. *§2.a*

- Fiscal policy has two components: discretionary fiscal policy and automatic stabilizers. *§2.c*

3. What are the effects of budget deficits?

- Budget deficits, through their effects on interest rates, international trade, and the national debt, can reduce investment, output, net exports, and national wealth. *§2.b*

- Progressive taxes and transfer payments are automatic stabilizers, elements of fiscal policy that change automatically as national income changes. *§2.c*

4. How does fiscal policy differ across countries?

- Industrial countries spend a much larger percentage of their government budget for social programs than developing countries do. *§3.a*

- Industrial countries depend more on direct taxes and less on indirect taxes than developing countries do. *§3.b*

KEY TERMS

automatic stabilizer, 243
crowding out, 242

discretionary fiscal policy, 243
progressive tax, 249

transfer payment, 250
value-added tax (VAT), 252

EXERCISES

1. What is the role of aggregate demand in eliminating the GDP gap? How does the slope of the AS curve affect the fiscal policy actions necessary to eliminate the GDP gap?
2. What is the "government budget constraint"? In other words, what are the sources of financing government spending?
3. In what ways are government deficits harmful to the economy?
4. Define and give three examples of automatic stabilizers.
5. Briefly describe the major differences between fiscal policy in industrial countries and that in developing countries.
6. Why will real GDP tend to rise when government spending and taxes rise by the same amount?
7. How can a larger government fiscal deficit cause a larger international trade deficit?
8. Why do government budget deficits grow during recessions?

9. Taxes can be progressive, regressive, or proportional. Define each, and briefly offer an argument for why income taxes are usually progressive.
10. What is a value-added tax (VAT), and what is an advantage of such a tax relative to an income tax?

    The following exercises are based on the appendix to this chapter.

    Answer exercises 11–14 on the basis of the following information. Assume that equilibrium real GDP is $800 billion, potential real GDP is $900 billion, the *MPC* is .80, and the *MPI* is .40.
11. What is the size of the GDP gap?
12. How much must government spending increase to eliminate the GDP gap?
13. How much must taxes fall to eliminate the GDP gap?
14. If government spending and taxes both change by the same amount, how much must they change to eliminate the recessionary gap?

15. Suppose the *MPC* is .90 and the *MPI* is .10. If government expenditures go up $100 billion while taxes fall $10 billion, what happens to the equilibrium level of real GDP?

    Use the following equations for exercises 16–18.

$$C = \$100 + .8Y$$
$$I = \$200$$
$$G = \$250$$
$$X = \$100 - .2Y$$

16. What is the equilibrium level of real GDP?
17. What is the new equilibrium level of real GDP if government spending increases by $150?

18. What is the new equilibrium level of real GDP if government spending and taxes both increase by $150?
19. Make a graph showing the spending and tax revenue of your state government for as many years as you can find (use the government of your home country if you are not from the United States). What trends do you notice? What spending categories make up the largest share of the state budget? What are the largest sources of revenue?

You can find further practice tests in the Online Quiz at **www.cengage.com/economics/boyes**.

AGREEMENT REACHED ON EURO PACT: EU PRESIDENT

The Times of India Online, March 2011

BRUSSELS: European Union president Herman Van Rompuy announced on Friday via Twitter that the 17 eurozone nations had reached agreement on a pact to coordinate economic policy more centrally.

"We have an agreement on the pact for the euro," said Van Rompuy, who was tasked with piloting through proposals put to a summit to bolster the eurozone's defences against a persistent and damaging debt crisis.

His Twitter site was later amended to say it was "an agreement in principle" with "other elements of the package" still being discussed.

All aspects of economic policy are covered in the pact with the aim of ensuring greater policy coordination so that the eurozone economies prove more competitive and better able to manage their public finances.

If that is achieved, then the debt crisis can be controlled and resolved, avoiding the need for further costly bailouts after Greece and Ireland had to be rescued last year.

The agreement will need to be endorsed at a March 24–25 summit of all 27 EU states.

A draft of the 'Pact for the Euro,' as seen earlier by AFP, sets out four areas for closer cooperation—competitiveness, employment, sustainable public finances and reinforcing financial stability.

Individual states will be responsible for specific measures, but all are supposed to work towards these same goals.

The objective is "to achieve a new quality of economic policy coordination in the euro area, improve competitiveness, thereby leading to a higher degree of convergence," the document states.

The logic is that if eurozone states have the same goals and obey the same rules, then the huge debt burdens and public deficits straining public finances and threatening the euro will ultimately be brought under control.

Eurozone leaders are also looking at how they can bolster the eurozone debt rescue system set up after the Greek bailout last May.

The three-year European Financial Stability Facility is worth notionally 440 billion euros ($610 billion) but in practice it can only provide half that amount. Making its full capacity available is still an issue.

Its 2013 replacement, the permanent European Stability Mechanism, will have double the firepower but there are difficult debates over its ultimate size and powers, especially whether it will be able to buy up eurozone government debt.

Commentary

Government budget deficits are a global concern. While we usually think in terms of internal political and economic pressures on a nation to keep its government budget from generating large and unsustainable deficits, the article discusses the case of the European Union (EU), where member countries face multinational pressure to comply with the EU *stability pact*. When the euro was in the planning stage, it was decided that every country that wanted to use the euro as its currency would have to have a stable, sustainable fiscal policy. The EU created the stability pact to explicitly state the limits on national governments' flexibility with regard to debt and deficits. The stability pact requires all euroland countries to maintain budget deficits of less than 3 percent of GDP and government debt of less than 60 percent of GDP. Crises in Greece and Ireland drew increased attention to the interconnectedness of Eurozone economies. In 2010, The Van Rompuy report and legislative initiatives by the European Commission addressed areas for improvement in economic governance:

- Greater focus on public debt levels and satisfactory path of debt reduction
- Effective enforcement through sanctions, including deposits, and tighter voting rules
- Better regulation to enforce reliable and timely statistics
- Surveillance mechanisms for excessive macroeconomic imbalances

For the countries that share the same currency, the euro, it makes sense that they maintain similar fiscal policies in order to maintain a stable value for the euro against external currencies like the dollar. However, should other countries that have their own national money, like the United States or Japan, worry about maintaining a small deficit?

You may have heard arguments concerning the effects of a budget deficit that proceed by means of an analogy between the government's budget and a family's budget. Just as a family cannot spend more than it earns, so the argument goes, the government cannot follow this practice without bringing itself to ruin. The problem with this analogy is that the government has the ability to raise money through taxes and bond sales, options that are not open to a family.

A more appropriate analogy is to compare the government's budget to that of a large corporation. Large corporations run persistent deficits that are never paid back. Instead, when corporate debt comes due, the corporations "roll over" their debt by selling new debt. They are able to do this because they use their debt to finance investment that enables them to increase their worth. To the extent that the government is investing in projects like road repairs and building the nation's infrastructure, it is increasing the productive capacity of the economy, which widens the tax base and increases potential future tax receipts.

There are, of course, legitimate problems associated with a budget deficit. The government has two options if it cannot pay for its expenditures with tax receipts. One method of financing the budget deficit is by creating money. This is an unattractive option because it leads to inflation. Another method is to borrow funds by selling government bonds. A problem with this option is that the government must compete with private investment for scarce loanable funds. Unless saving increases at the same time, interest rates rise and government borrowing crowds out private investment. This results in a lower capital stock and diminished prospects for future economic growth.

So while the euroland countries face pressure, and potential fines, from the European Union if they exceed the limits of the stability pact, there are pressures from financial markets on all countries. The financial markets punish those countries that have excessive budget deficits. A country with big budget deficits will find its interest rates rising as investors buying the bonds sold by a country that borrows ever larger amounts of money will demand a higher and higher return. Those countries that resort to printing money to finance a budget deficit end up with higher and higher inflation rates. Such a policy has brought down more than one government in the past. Good government, as measured by careful management of the budget, is rewarded with good economic conditions (other things equal) and political survival.

An Algebraic Examination of the Balanced-Budget Change in Fiscal Policy

What would happen if government spending and taxes went up by the same amount?

We can analyze such a change by expanding the analysis begun in the appendix to Chapter 10.

The spending multiplier is the simple multiplier defined in Chapter 10:

$$\text{Spending muliplier} = \frac{1}{MPS + MPI}$$

In the Chapter 10 example, because the MPS equals .30 and the MPI equals .10, the spending multiplier equals 2.5:

$$\text{Spending muliplier} = \frac{1}{MPS + MPI} = \frac{1}{.30 + .10}$$
$$= \frac{1}{.40} = 2.5$$

When government spending increases by \$20, the equilibrium level of real GDP increases by 2.5 times \$20, or \$50.

We also can define a tax multiplier, a measure of the effect of a change in taxes on equilibrium real GDP. Because a percentage of any change in income is saved and spent on imports, we know that a tax cut increases expenditures by less than the amount of the cut. The percentage of the tax cut that actually is spent is the marginal propensity to consume ($MPC - MPI$). If consumers save 30 percent of any extra income, they spend 70 percent, the MPC. But the domestic economy does not realize 70 percent of the extra income because 10 percent of the extra income is spent on imports. The percentage of any extra income that actually is spent at home is the MPC minus the MPI. In our example, 60 percent ($.70 - .10$) of any extra income is spent in the domestic economy.

With this information, we can define the tax multiplier like this:

$$\text{Tax multiplier} = -(MPC - MPI)\frac{1}{MPS + MPI}$$

In our example, the tax multiplier is -1.5:

$$\text{Tax multiplier} = -(.70 - .10)\frac{1}{.30 + .10}$$
$$= -(.60)(2.5) = -1.5$$

A tax cut increases equilibrium real GDP by 1.5 times the amount of the cut. Notice that the tax multiplier is always a *negative* number because a change in taxes moves income and expenditures in the opposite direction. Higher taxes lower income and expenditures; lower taxes raise income and expenditures.

Now that we have reviewed the spending and tax multipliers, we can examine the effect of a balanced-budget change in fiscal policy, where government spending and taxes change by the same amount. To simplify the analysis, we assume that taxes are lump-sum taxes (taxpayers must pay a certain amount of dollars as tax) rather than income taxes (where the tax rises with income). We can use the algebraic model presented in the appendix to Chapter 10 to illustrate the effect of a balanced-budget change in government spending. Here are the model equations:

$$C = \$30 - .70Y$$
$$I = \$50$$
$$G = \$70$$
$$X = \$50 - .10Y$$

Solving for the equilibrium level of Y (as we did in the appendix to Chapter 10), Y equals $500, where Y equals aggregate expenditures.

Now suppose that G increases by $10 and that this increase is funded by taxes of $10. The increase in G changes autonomous government spending to $80. The increase in taxes affects the levels of C and X. The new model equations are:

$$C = \$30 + .70(Y - \$10) = \$23 + .70Y$$
$$X = \$50 - .10(Y - \$10) = \$51 - .10Y$$

Using the new G, C, and X functions, we can find the new equilibrium level of real GDP by setting Y equal to AE ($C + I + G + X$):

$$Y = C + I + G + X$$
$$Y = \$23 + .70Y + \$50 + \$80 + \$51 - .10Y$$
$$Y = \$204 + .60Y$$
$$Y - .60Y = \$204$$
$$.40Y = \$204$$
$$Y = \$510$$

Increasing government spending and taxes by $10 each raises the equilibrium level of real GDP by $10. A balanced-budget increase in G increases Y by the change in G. If government spending and taxes both fall by the same amount, then real GDP will also fall by an amount equal to the change in government spending and taxes.

CHAPTER 12

Money and Banking

© MACIEJ FROLOW/GETTY IMAGES, INC

U p to this point, we have been talking about aggregate expenditures, aggregate demand and supply, and fiscal policy without explicitly discussing money. Yet money is used by every sector of the economy in all nations and plays a crucial role in every economy. In this chapter, we discuss what money is, how the quantity of money is determined, and the role of banks in determining this quantity. In the next chapter, we examine the role of money in the aggregate demand and supply model.

As you will see in the next two chapters, the quantity of money has a major impact on interest rates, inflation, and the amount of spending in the economy. Thus, money is important for macroeconomic policymaking, and government officials use both monetary and fiscal policy to influence the equilibrium level of real GDP and prices.

FUNDAMENTAL QUESTIONS

1 What is money?

2 How is the U.S. money supply defined?

3 How do countries pay for international transactions?

4 Why are banks considered intermediaries?

5 How does international banking differ from domestic banking?

6 How do banks create money?

Banks and the banking system also play key roles, both at home and abroad, in the determination of the amount of money in circulation and the movement of money between nations. After we define money and its functions, we look at the banking system. We begin with banking in the United States, and then discuss international banking. Someone once joked that banks follow the rule of 3-6-3: They borrow at 3 percent interest, lend at 6 percent interest, and close at 3 P.M. If those days ever existed, clearly they no longer do today. The banking industry in the United States and the rest of the world has undergone tremendous change in recent years. New technology and government deregulation are allowing banks to respond to changing economic conditions in ways that were unthinkable only a few years ago, and these changes have had dramatic effects on the economy.

1. What Is Money?

 1 What is money?

money
Anything that is generally acceptable to sellers in exchange for goods and services.

liquid asset
An asset that can easily be exchanged for goods and services.

Money is anything that is generally acceptable to sellers in exchange for goods and services. The cash in your wallet can be used to buy groceries or a movie ticket. You simply present your cash to the cashier, who readily accepts it. If you wanted to use your car to buy groceries or a movie ticket, the exchange would be more complicated. You would probably have to sell the car before you could use it to buy other goods and services. Cars are seldom exchanged directly for goods and services (except for other cars). Because cars are not a generally acceptable means of paying for other goods and services, we don't consider them to be money. Money is the most liquid asset. A **liquid asset** is an asset that can easily be exchanged for goods and services. Cash is a liquid asset; a car is not. How liquid must an asset be before we consider it money? To answer this question, we must first consider the functions of money.

1.a. Functions of Money

Money serves four basic functions: It is a *medium of exchange*, a *unit of account*, a *store of value*, and a *standard of deferred payment*. Not all monies serve all of these functions equally well, as will be apparent in the following discussion. But to be money, an item must perform enough of these functions to induce people to use it.

1.a.1. Medium of Exchange
Money is a medium of exchange; it is given in exchange for goods and services. Sellers willingly accept money as payment for the products and services that they produce. Without money, we would have to resort to *barter*, the direct exchange of goods and services for other goods and services.

For a barter system to work, there must be a *double coincidence of wants*. Suppose Bill is a carpenter and Jane is a plumber. In a monetary economy, when Bill needs plumbing repairs in his home, he simply pays Jane for the repairs, using money. Because everyone wants money, money is an acceptable means of payment. In a barter economy, Bill must offer his services as a carpenter in exchange for Jane's work. If Jane does not want any carpentry work done, Bill and Jane cannot enter into a mutually beneficial transaction. Bill has to find a person who can do what he wants and who also wants what he can do—there must be a double coincidence of wants.

The example of Bill and Jane illustrates the fact that barter is a lot less efficient than using money. This means that the cost of a transaction in a barter economy is higher than the cost of a transaction in a monetary economy.

The use of money as a medium of exchange lowers transaction costs.

© froxx/Shutterstock.com

The people of Yap Island highly value, and thus accept as their medium of exchange, giant stones. In most cultures, however, money must be *portable* in order to be an effective medium of exchange—a property that the stone money of Yap Island clearly lacks. Another important property of money is *divisibility*. Money must be measurable in both small units (for low-value goods and services) and large units (for high-value goods and services). Yap stone money is not divisible, so it is not a good medium of exchange for the majority of goods that are bought and sold.

1.a.2. Unit of Account

Money is a unit of account: We price goods and services in terms of money. This common unit of measurement allows us to compare relative values easily. If whole-wheat bread sells for a dollar a loaf and white bread sells for 50 cents, we know that whole-wheat bread is twice as expensive as white bread.

Using money as a unit of account is efficient. It reduces the costs of gathering information on what things are worth. The use of money as a unit of account lowers information costs relative to barter. In a barter economy, people constantly have to evaluate the worth of the goods and services being offered. When money prices are placed on goods and services, their relative value is obvious.

> *The use of money as a unit of account lowers information costs.*

1.a.3. Store of Value

Money functions as a store of value or purchasing power. If you are paid today, you do not have to hurry out to spend your money. It will still have value next week or next month. Some monies retain their value better than others. In colonial New England, both fish and furs served as money. But because fish does not store as well as furs, its usefulness as a store of value was limited. An important property of a money is its *durability*, its ability to retain its value over time.

Inflation plays a major role in determining the effectiveness of a money as a store of value. The higher the rate of inflation, the faster the purchasing power of money falls. In high-inflation countries, workers spend their pay as fast as possible because the purchasing power of their money is falling rapidly. It makes no sense to hold on to a money that is quickly losing value. In countries where the domestic money does not serve as a good store of value, it ceases to fulfill this function of money, and people begin to use something else as money, like the currency of another nation. For instance, U.S. dollars have long been a favorite store of value in Latin American countries that have experienced high inflation. This phenomenon—**currency substitution**—has been documented in Argentina, Bolivia, Mexico, and other countries during times of high inflation.

currency substitution
The use of foreign money as a substitute for domestic money when the domestic economy has a high rate of inflation.

1.a.4. Standard of Deferred Payment

Finally, money is a standard of deferred payment. Debt obligations are written in terms of money values. If you have a credit card bill that is due in 30 days, the value you owe is stated in monetary units—for example, dollars in the United States and yen in Japan. We use money values to state amounts of debt, and we use money to pay our debts.

We should make a distinction here between money and credit. Money is what we use to pay for goods and services. **Credit** is available savings that are lent to borrowers to spend. If you use your Visa or MasterCard to buy a shirt, you are not buying the shirt with your money. You are taking out a loan from the bank that issued the credit card in order to buy the shirt. Credit and money are different. Money is an asset, something you own. Credit is *debt*, something you owe.

 2 How is the U.S. money supply defined?

credit
Available savings that are lent to borrowers to spend.

1.b. The U.S. Money Supply

The quantity of money that is available for spending is an important determinant of many key macroeconomic variables, since changes in the money supply affect interest rates, inflation, and other indicators of economic health. When economists measure the money supply, they measure spendable assets. Identifying those assets, however, can be difficult. Although it would seem that *all* bank deposits are money, some bank deposits are held for spending, while others are held for saving. In defining the money supply, then, economists must differentiate among assets on the basis of their liquidity and the likelihood of their being used for spending.

The problem of distinguishing among assets has produced more than one definition of the money supply. Today in the United States, the Federal Reserve uses M1 and M2.[1] Economists and policymakers use both definitions to evaluate the availability of funds for spending. Although economists have tried to identify a single measure that best influences the business cycle and changes in interest rates and inflation, research indicates that different definitions work better to explain changes in macroeconomic variables at different times.

1.b.1. M1 Money Supply

M1 money supply
The financial assets that are the most liquid.

transactions account
A checking account at a bank or other financial institution that can be drawn on to make payments.

The narrowest and most liquid measure of the money supply is the **M1 money supply**, or financial assets that are immediately available for spending. This definition emphasizes the use of money as a medium of exchange. The M1 money supply consists of currency held by the nonbank public, traveler's checks, demand deposits, and other checkable deposits. Demand deposits and other checkable deposits are **transactions accounts**; they can be used to make direct payments to a third party.

Surveys find that families use their checking account for about 30 percent of purchases. Cash transactions account for about 44 percent of purchases.

The components of the M1 money supply are used for about 74 percent of family purchases. This is one reason why the M1 money supply may be a useful variable in formulating macroeconomic policy.

- *Currency* includes coins and paper money in circulation (in the hands of the public). In 2010, currency represented 50 percent of the M1 money supply. A common misconception about currency today is that it is backed by gold or silver. This is not true. There is nothing backing the U.S. dollar except the confidence of the public. This kind of monetary system is called a *fiduciary monetary system*. *Fiduciary* comes from the Latin *fiducia*, which means "trust." Our monetary system is based on trust. As long as we believe that our money is an acceptable form of payment for goods and services, the system works. It is not necessary for money to be backed by any precious object. As long as people believe that a money has value, it will serve as money.

The United States has not always operated under a fiduciary monetary system. At one time, the U.S. government issued gold and silver coins and paper money that could be exchanged for silver. In 1967, Congress authorized the U.S. Treasury to stop redeeming "silver certificate" paper money for silver. Coins with an intrinsic value are known as *commodity money*; they have value as a commodity in addition to their face value. The problem with commodity money is that as the value of the commodity increases, the money stops being circulated. People hoard coins when their commodity value exceeds their face value. For example, no one would take an old $20 gold piece to the grocery store to buy $20 worth of groceries because the gold is worth much more than $20 today.

The tendency to hoard money when its commodity value increases is called *Gresham's Law*. Thomas Gresham was a successful businessman and financial adviser to Queen Elizabeth I. He insisted that if two coins have the same face value but different intrinsic values—perhaps one coin is silver and the other brass—the cheaper coin will be used in exchange, while the more expensive coin will be hoarded. People sometimes state Gresham's Law as "bad money drives out good money," meaning that the money

---

[1] Until March 2006, the Federal Reserve also published a broader measure of the money supply known as M3.

with the low commodity value will be used in exchange, while the money with the high commodity value will be driven out of hand-to-hand use and be hoarded.[2]

- *Traveler's checks.* Outstanding U.S. dollar–denominated traveler's checks issued by nonbank institutions are counted as part of the M1 money supply. There are several nonbank issuers, among them American Express and Cook's. (Traveler's checks issued by banks are included in demand deposits. When a bank issues its own traveler's checks, it deposits the amount paid by the purchaser in a special account that is used to redeem the checks. Because this amount is counted as part of demand deposits, it is not counted again as part of outstanding traveler's checks.) Traveler's checks account for less than 1 percent of the M1 money supply.

- *Demand deposits.* Demand deposits are checking account deposits at a commercial bank. These deposits pay no interest. They are called *demand deposits* because the bank must pay the amount of the check immediately upon the demand of the depositor. Demand deposits accounted for 28 percent of the M1 money supply in 2010.

- *Other checkable deposits.* Until the 1980s, demand deposits were the only kind of checking account. Today there are many different kinds of checking accounts, known as *other checkable deposits (OCDs)*. These OCDs are accounts at financial institutions that pay interest and also give the depositor check-writing privileges. Among the OCDs included in the M1 money supply are the following:

  - *Negotiable orders of withdrawal (NOW) accounts* are interest-bearing checking accounts offered by savings and loan institutions.

  - *Automatic transfer system (ATS) accounts* are accounts at commercial banks that combine an interest-bearing savings account with a non-interest-bearing checking account. The depositor keeps a small balance in the checking account; any time the checking account balance is overdrawn, funds are automatically transferred from the savings account.

  - *Credit union share draft accounts* are interest-bearing checking accounts that credit unions offer their members.

  - *Demand deposits at mutual savings banks* are checking account deposits at non-profit savings and loan organizations. Any profits after operating expenses have been paid may be distributed to depositors.

> According to Gresham's Law, bad money drives out good money.

1.b.2. M2 Money Supply

The components of the M1 money supply are the most liquid assets, the assets that are most likely to be used for transactions. The **M2 money supply** is a broader definition of the money supply that includes assets in somewhat less liquid forms. The M2 money supply includes the M1 money supply plus savings deposits, small-denomination time deposits, and balances in retail money market mutual funds.

> **M2 money supply**
> M1 plus less liquid assets.

- *Savings deposits* are accounts at banks and savings and loan associations that earn interest but offer no check-writing privileges.

- *Small-denomination time deposits* are often called *certificates of deposit*. Funds in these accounts must be deposited for a specified period of time. (Small means less than $100,000.)

- *Retail money market mutual fund balances* combine the *deposits of many* individuals and invest them in government Treasury bills and other short-term securities. Many money market mutual funds grant check-writing privileges but limit the size and number of checks.

  Figure 1 summarizes the two definitions of the money supply.

---

[2] Actually, Gresham was not the first to recognize that bad money drives out good money. A fourteenth-century French theologian, Nicholas Oresme, made the same argument in his book *A Treatise on the Origin, Nature, Law, and Alterations of Money*, written almost 200 years before Gresham was born.

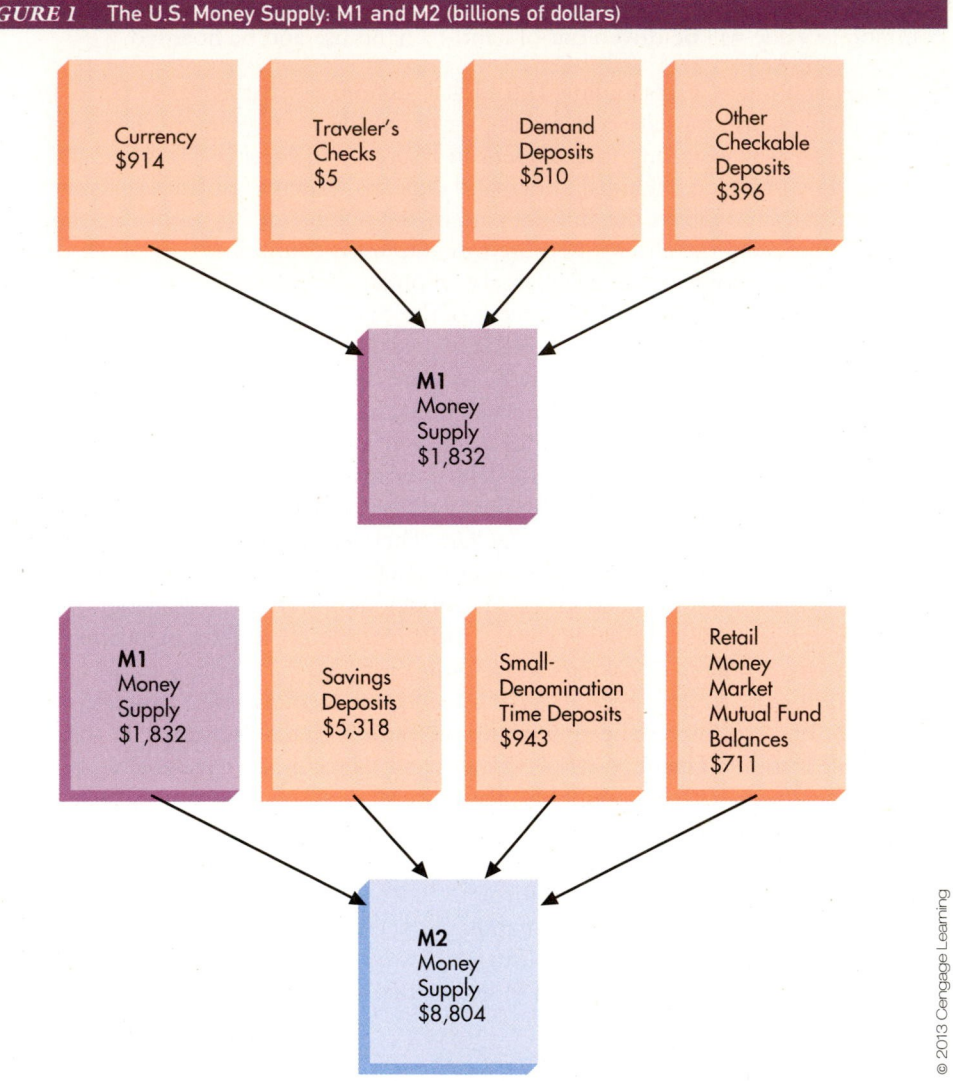

FIGURE 1   The U.S. Money Supply: M1 and M2 (billions of dollars)

© 2013 Cengage Learning

1.c. Global Money

3 How do countries pay for international transactions?

So far we have discussed the money supply in a domestic context. Just as the United States uses dollars as its domestic money, every nation has its own monetary unit of account. Japan has the yen, Mexico the peso, Canada the Canadian dollar, and so on. Since each nation uses a different money, how do countries pay for transactions that involve residents of other countries? As you saw in the chapter titled "An Introduction to the Foreign Exchange Market and the Balance of Payments," the foreign exchange market links national monies together so that transactions can be made across national borders. If Sears in the United States buys a home entertainment system from Sony in Japan, Sears can exchange dollars for yen in order to pay Sony in yen. The exchange rate between the dollar and the yen determines how many dollars are needed to purchase the required number of yen. For instance, if Sony wants 1,000,000 yen for the system and the exchange rate is ¥100 = $1, Sears needs $10,000 (1,000,000/100) to buy the yen.

Sales contracts between developed countries usually are written (invoiced) in the national currency of the exporter. To complete the transaction, the importer buys the exporter's currency on the foreign exchange market. Trade between developing and developed nations typically is invoiced in the currency of the developed country, whether the developed country is the exporter or the importer, because the currency of the developed country is usually more stable and more widely traded on the foreign exchange market than the currency of the developing country. As a result, the currencies of the major developed countries tend to dominate the international medium-of-exchange and unit-of-account functions of money.

1.c.1. International Reserve Currencies

Governments hold monies as a temporary store of value until money is needed to settle international debts. At one time, gold was the primary **international reserve asset**, an asset used to settle debts between governments. Although gold still serves as an international reserve asset, its role is unimportant relative to that of currencies. Today national currencies function as international reserves. The currencies that are held for this purpose are called **international reserve currencies**.

Table 1 shows the importance of the major international reserve currencies over time. In the mid-1970s, the U.S. dollar made up almost 80 percent of international reserve holdings. By 1990, its share had fallen to less than 50 percent, but that share has risen again recently.

Prior to the euro, there was an artificial currency in Europe, the **European currency unit (ECU)**. The industrial nations of western Europe used ECUs to settle debts between them. The ECU was a **composite currency**; its value was an average of the values of several different national currencies: the Austrian schilling, the Belgian franc, the Danish krone, the Finnish markka, the French franc, the German mark, the Greek drachma, the Irish pound, the Italian lira, the Luxembourg franc, the Netherlands guilder, the Spanish peseta, and the Portuguese escudo (the U.K. pound was withdrawn from the system in September 1992).

The ECU was not an actual money but an accounting entry that was transferred between two parties. It was a step along the way to a new actual money, the *euro*, which replaced the ECU and circulates throughout the member countries as a real European money.

Another composite currency used in international financial transactions is the **special drawing right (SDR)**. The value of the SDR is an average of the values of the currencies of the major industrial countries: the U.S. dollar, the euro, the Japanese yen, and the U.K. pound. This currency was created in 1970 by the International Monetary Fund, an international organization that oversees the monetary relationships among

> The currencies of the major developed countries tend to dominate the international medium-of-exchange and unit of-account functions of money.

international reserve asset
An asset used to settle debts between governments.

international reserve currency
A currency held by a government to settle international debts.

European currency unit (ECU)
A unit of account formerly used by Western European nations as their official reserve asset.

composite currency
An artificial unit of account that is an average of the values of several national currencies.

special drawing right (SDR)
A composite currency whose value is the average of the values of the U.S. dollar, the euro, the Japanese yen, and the U.K. pound.

TABLE 1	International Reserve Currencies (Percentage Shares of National Currencies in Total Official Holdings of Foreign Exchange)									
Year	U.S. Dollar	Pound Sterling	Deutsche Mark	French Franc	Japanese Yen	Swiss Franc	Netherlands Guilder	Euro	ECU	Unspecified Currencies
1976	78.8	1.0	8.7	1.5	1.9	2.1	0.8	—	—	5.2
1980	56.6	2.5	12.8	1.5	3.7	2.8	1.1	—	16.4	2.7
1990	47.8	2.8	16.5	2.2	7.7	1.2	1.0	—	9.7	11.1
2000	70.5	2.8	—	—	6.3	0.3	—	18.8	—	1.4
2004	65.9	3.3	—	—	3.9	0.2	—	24.9	—	1.9
2008	64.0	4.0	—	—	3.3	0.1	—	26.5	—	2.0

Source: Data are drawn from International Monetary Fund, *Annual Report*, various issues.

countries. The SDRs are an international reserve asset; they are used to settle international debts by transferring governments' accounts held at the International Monetary Fund. We discuss the role of the International Monetary Fund in later chapters.

Prior to the actual introduction of the euro, there was much discussion about its potential popularity as a reserve currency. In fact, some analysts were asserting that we should expect the euro to replace the U.S. dollar as the world's dominant currency. As Table 1 shows, the euro is now the second most popular reserve currency, but it has a much lower share of reserve currency use than the dollar does. The dominant world currency evolves over time as business firms and individuals find one currency more useful than another. Prior to the dominance of the dollar, the British pound was the world's most important reserve currency. As the U.S. economy grew in importance and U.S. financial markets developed to the huge size they now are, the growing use of the dollar emerged naturally as a result of the large volume of financial transactions involving the United States. Perhaps over time, the euro will someday replace the dollar as the world's dominant money.

RECAP

1. Money is the most liquid asset.

2. Money serves as a medium of exchange, a unit of account, a store of value, and a standard of deferred payment.

3. The use of money lowers transaction and information costs relative to barter.

4. To be used as money, an asset should be portable, divisible, and durable.

5. The M1 money supply is the most liquid definition of money and equals the sum of currency, traveler's checks, demand deposits, and other checkable deposits.

6. The M2 money supply equals the sum of the M1 money supply, savings deposits, small-denomination time deposits, and retail money market mutual fund balances.

7. International reserve currencies are held by governments to settle international debts.

8. Composite currencies have their value determined as an average of the values of several national currencies.

2. Banking

Commercial banks are financial institutions that offer deposits on which checks can be written. In the United States and most other countries, commercial banks are privately owned. *Thrift institutions* are financial institutions that historically offered just savings accounts, not checking accounts. Savings and loan associations, credit unions, and mutual savings banks are all thrift institutions. Prior to 1980, the differences between commercial banks and thrift institutions were much greater than they are today. For example, only commercial banks could offer checking accounts, and those accounts earned no interest. The law also regulated maximum interest rates. In 1980, Congress passed the Depository Institutions Deregulation and Monetary Control Act, in part to stimulate competition among financial institutions. Now thrift institutions and even brokerage houses offer many of the same services as commercial banks. In 1999, Congress passed the Gramm-Leach-Bliley Act, which allowed commercial banks to expand their business into other areas of finance, including insurance and selling securities. This permitted greater integration of financial products under one umbrella known as a financial holding company. During the financial crisis of 2008, some of these large banks suffered dramatically as a result of aggressive risk-taking in financial products that turned out to be unsuccessful.

2.a. Financial Intermediaries

Both commercial banks and thrift institutions are *financial intermediaries*, middlemen between savers and borrowers. Banks accept deposits from individuals and firms, then use those deposits to make loans to individuals and firms. The borrowers are likely to be different individuals or firms from the depositors, although it is not uncommon for a household or business to be both a depositor and a borrower at the same institution. Of course, depositors and borrowers have very different interests. For instance, depositors typically prefer short-term deposits; they don't want to tie up their money for a long time. Borrowers, on the other hand, usually want more time for repayment. Banks typically package short-term deposits into longer-term loans. To function as intermediaries, banks must serve the interests of both depositors and borrowers.

A bank is willing to serve as an intermediary because it hopes to earn a profit from this activity. It pays a lower interest rate on deposits than it charges on loans; the difference is a source of profit for the bank. Islamic banks are prohibited by holy law from charging interest on loans; thus, they use a different system for making a profit (see the Global Business Insight "Islamic Banking").

 4 Why are banks considered intermediaries?

2.b. U.S. Banking

2.b.1. Current Structure
If you add together all the pieces of the bar graph in Figure 2, you see that there were 109,711 depository institution offices operating in the United States in 2009. Roughly 89 percent of these offices were operated by banks and 11 percent by savings institutions.

Historically, U.S. banks were allowed to operate in just one state. In some states, banks could operate in only one location. This is known as *unit banking*. Today there are still many unit banks, but these are typically small community banks.

FIGURE 2   U.S. Depository Institutions

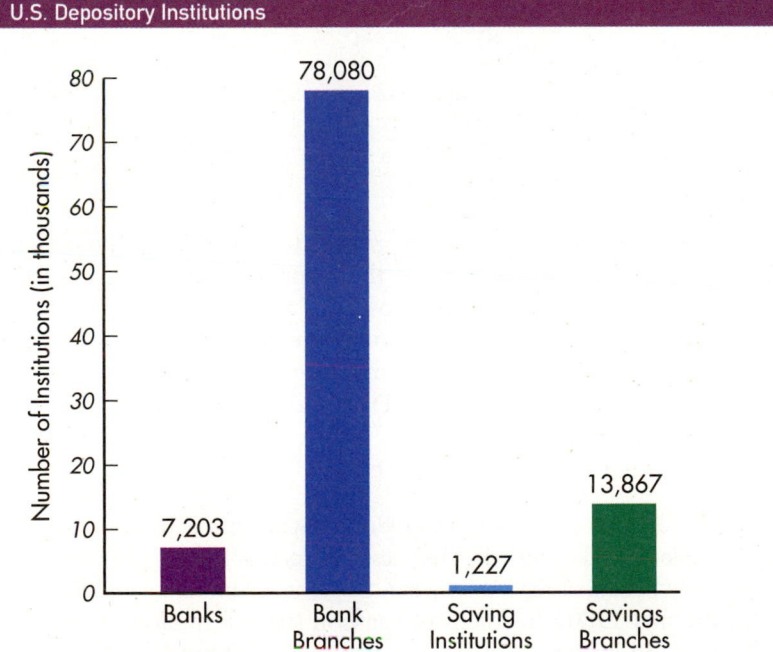

There are many more banks and bank branches than there are savings institutions and savings branches.

Source: Data are drawn from *Federal Deposit Insurance Corporation, Statistics on Banking;* www.fdic.gov.

GLOBAL BUSINESS INSIGHT

Islamic Banking

According to the Muslim holy book, the Koran, Islamic law prohibits interest charges on loans. Banks that operate under Islamic law still act as intermediaries between borrowers and lenders. However, they do not charge interest on loans or pay interest on deposits. Instead, they take a predetermined percentage of the borrowing firm's profits until the loan is repaid, then share those profits with depositors.

Since the mid-1970s, over a hundred Islamic banks have opened, most of them in Arab nations. Deposits in these banks have grown rapidly. In fact, in some banks, deposits have grown faster than good loan opportunities, forcing the banks to refuse new deposits until their loan portfolio could grow to match the available deposits. One bank in Bahrain claimed that over 60 percent of deposits during its first two years in operation were made by people who had never made a bank deposit before. In addition to profit-sharing deposits, Islamic banks typically offer checking accounts, traveler's checks, and trade-related services on a fee basis.

Because the growth of deposits has usually exceeded the growth of local investment opportunities, Islamic banks have been lending money to traditional banks to fund investments that satisfy the moral and commercial needs of both, such as lending to private firms. These funds cannot be used to invest in interest-bearing securities or in firms that deal in alcohol, pork, gambling, or arms. The growth of mutually profitable investment opportunities suggests that Islamic banks are meeting both the dictates of Muslim depositors and the profitability requirements of modern banking.

The potential for expansion and profitability of Islamic financial services has led major banks to create units dedicated to providing Islamic banking services. In addition, there are stock mutual funds that screen firms for compliance with Islamic law before buying their stock. For instance, since most financial institutions earn and pay large amounts of interest, such firms would tend to be excluded from an Islamic mutual fund.

The most popular instrument for financing Islamic investments is *murabaha*. This is essentially cost-plus financing, where the financial institution purchases goods or services for a client and then, over time, is repaid an amount that equals the original cost plus an additional amount of profit. Such an arrangement is even used for financing mortgages on property in the United States. A financial institution will buy a property and then charge a client rent until the rent payments equal the purchase price plus some profit. After the full payment is received, the title to the property is passed to the client.

Sources: Peter Koh, "The Shari'ah Alternative," *Euromoney* (October 2002). A good source of additional information is found on the website www.failaka .com.

Over time, legal barriers have been reduced so that today almost all states permit entry to banks located out of state. In the future, banking is likely to be done on a national rather than a local scale. The growth of automated teller machines (ATMs) is a big step in this direction. The ATM networks give bank customers access to services over a much wider geographic area than any single bank's branches cover. These international networks allow a bank customer from Dallas to withdraw cash in Seattle, Zurich, or almost anywhere in the world. Today more than one-fourth of ATM transactions occur at banks that are not the customer's own bank.

2.b.2. Bank Failures Banking in the United States has had a colorful history of booms and panics. Banking is like any other business. Banks that are poorly managed can fail; banks that are properly managed tend to prosper. Regional economic conditions are also very important. In the mid-1980s, hundreds of banks in states with large oil industries, like Texas and Oklahoma, and in farming states, like Kansas and Nebraska, could not collect many of their loans as a result of falling oil and agricultural prices. Those states that were heavily dependent on the oil industry and on farming had significantly more banks fail than did other states. The problem was not so much bad management as it was a matter of unexpectedly bad business conditions. The lesson here is simple: Commercial banks, like other profit-making enterprises, are not exempt from failure.

At one time, a bank panic could close a bank. A bank panic occurs when depositors, fearing that a bank will close, rush to withdraw their funds. Banks keep only a fraction of their deposits on reserve, so bank panics often resulted in bank closings as depositors tried to withdraw more money than the banks had on hand on a given day. In the United States today, this is no longer true. The **Federal Deposit Insurance Corporation (FDIC)** was created in 1933. The FDIC is a federal agency that insures bank deposits in commercial banks so that depositors do not lose their deposits if a bank fails. FDIC insurance covers depositors against losses up to $250,000 in a bank account. Figure 3 shows the number of failed banks and the number without deposit insurance. In the 1930s, many of the banks that failed were not insured by the FDIC. In this environment, it made sense for depositors to worry about losing their money. In the 1980s, the number of bank failures increased dramatically, but none of the failed banks were uninsured. Deposits in those banks were protected by the federal government. Even though large banks have failed in recent times, the depositors have not lost their deposits.

Figure 3 shows a rise in the number of bank failures associated with the financial crisis of 2008 (which actually began in 2007). We see that from 0 bank failures in 2006, there were 3 in 2007, 30 in 2008, and 90 by September 2009. The financial crisis resulted in many banks experiencing large losses on loans due to businesses and households who were unable to repay their debts.

Deposit insurance exists today in most of the world's countries. Africa is the only continent where deposit insurance is not found widely. Looking at the countries that are neighbors of the United States, Canada insures deposits up to 100,000 Canadian dollars (worth about 100,980 U.S. dollars at the time this text was revised), while Mexico insures deposits up to 1,567,000 pesos (worth about 129,000 U.S. dollars at the time this text was revised).

> *A bank panic occurs when depositors become frightened and rush to withdraw their funds.*

Federal Deposit Insurance Corporation (FDIC)
A federal agency that insures deposits in commercial banks.

FIGURE 3   Number of Failed and Uninsured Banks

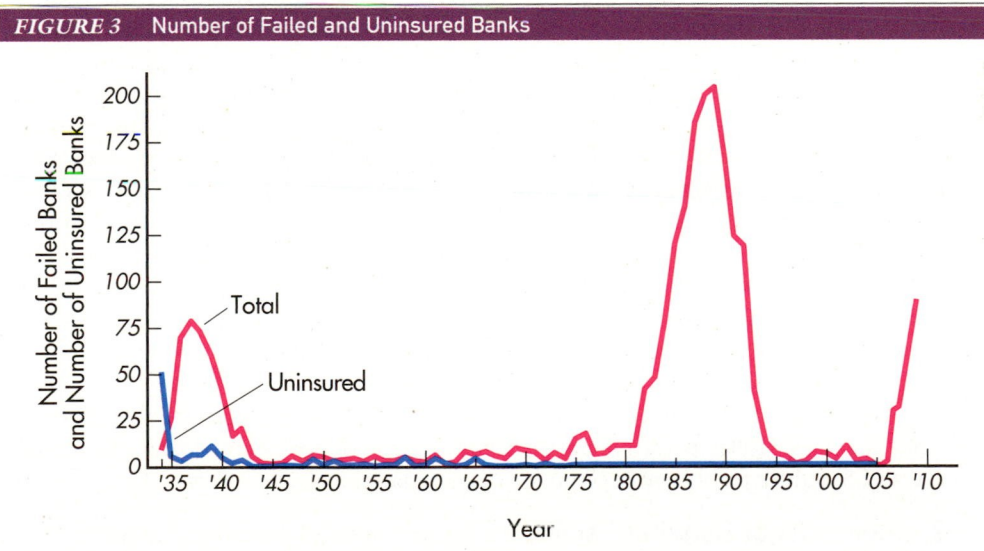

The number of banks that went out of business in the 1980s was the highest it had been since the Depression. Unlike the banks that failed in the 1930s, however, the banks that closed in the 1980s were covered by deposit insurance, so depositors did not lose their money.

Source: Data are from *Federal Deposit Insurance Corporation, Statistics on Banking;* www.fdic.gov.

5 How does international banking differ from domestic banking?

Eurocurrency market or **offshore banking**
The market for deposits and loans generally denominated in a currency other than the currency of the country in which the transaction occurs.

2.c. International Banking

Large banks today are truly transnational enterprises. International banks, like domestic banks, act as financial intermediaries, but they operate in a different legal environment. The laws regulating domestic banking in each nation are typically very restrictive, yet many nations allow international banking to operate largely unregulated. Because they are not hampered by regulations, international banks typically can offer depositors and borrowers better terms than could be negotiated at a domestic bank.

2.c.1. Eurocurrency Market
Because of the competitive interest rates offered on loans and deposits, there is a large market for deposits and loans at international banks. For instance, a bank in London, Tokyo, or the Bahamas may accept deposits and make loans denominated in U.S. dollars. The international deposit and loan market often is called the **Eurocurrency market**, or **offshore banking**. In the Eurocurrency market, the currency used in a banking transaction generally is not the domestic currency of the country in which the bank is located. (The prefix "Euro-" is misleading here. Although the market originated in Europe, today it is global and operates with different foreign currencies; it is in no way limited to European currencies or European banks.) There are deposits and loans in Eurodollars, Euroyen, Euroeuro, and any other major currency.

In those countries that allow offshore banking, we find two sets of banking rules: restrictive regulations for banking in the domestic market, and little or no regulation for offshore banking activities. Domestic banks are required to hold reserves against deposits and to carry deposit insurance, and they often face government-mandated credit or interest rate restrictions. The Eurocurrency market operates with few or no costly restrictions, and international banks generally pay lower taxes than domestic banks. Because offshore banks operate with lower costs, they are able to offer their customers better terms than domestic banks can.

Offshore banks are able to offer a higher rate on dollar deposits and a lower rate on dollar loans than their domestic competitors. Without these differences, the Eurodollar market probably would not exist because Eurodollar transactions are riskier than domestic transactions in the United States as a result of the lack of government regulation and deposit insurance.

There are always risks involved in international banking. Funds are subject to control by both the country in which the bank is located and the country in whose currency the deposit or loan is denominated. Suppose a Canadian firm wants to withdraw funds from a U.S. dollar–denominated bank deposit in Hong Kong. This transaction is subject to control in Hong Kong. For example, the government may not allow foreign exchange to leave the country freely. It is also subject to U.S. control. If the United States reduces its outflow of dollars, for instance, the Hong Kong bank may have difficulty paying the Canadian firm with U.S. dollars.

The Eurocurrency market exists for all of the major international currencies, but the value of activity in Eurodollars dwarfs the rest. Eurodollars account for about 60 percent of deposit and loan activity in the Eurocurrency market. This emphasizes the important role that the U.S. dollar plays in global finance. Even deposits and loans that do not involve a U.S. lender or borrower often are denominated in U.S. dollars.

2.c.2. International Banking Facilities
The term *offshore banking* is somewhat misleading in the United States today. Prior to December 1981, U.S. banks were forced to process international deposits and loans through their offshore branches. Many of the branches in places like the Cayman Islands and the Bahamas were little more than "shells," small offices with a telephone. Yet these branches allowed U.S. banks to avoid the reserve requirements and interest rate regulations that restricted domestic banking activities.

In December 1981, the Federal Reserve Board legalized **international banking facilities (IBFs)**, allowing domestic banks to take part in international banking on U.S. soil. The IBFs are not physical entities; they are bookkeeping systems set up in existing bank offices to record international banking transactions. The IBFs can receive deposits from and make loans to nonresidents of the United States and the restrictions that apply to other IBFs. These deposits and loans must be kept separate from other transactions because IBFs are not subject to the reserve requirements, interest rate regulations, or FDIC deposit insurance premiums that apply to domestic U.S. banking. The goal of permitting IBFs was to allow banking offices in the United States to compete with offshore banks without having to use offshore banking offices.

international banking facility (IBF)
A division of a U.S. bank that is allowed to receive deposits from and make loans to nonresidents of the United States without the restrictions that apply to domestic U.S. banks.

2.d. Informal Financial Markets in Developing Countries

In many developing countries, a sizable portion of the population has no access to formal financial institutions like banks. In these cases, it is common for informal financial markets to develop. Such markets may take many different forms. Sometimes they take the form of an individual making small loans to local residents. Sometimes groups of individuals form a self-help group where they pool their resources to provide loans to each other. To give some idea of the nature of these sorts of arrangements, a few common types are reviewed here.

A common form of informal financial arrangement is rotating savings and associations, or **ROSCAs**. These tend to go by different names in different countries, such as *tandas* in Mexico, *susu* in Ghana, *hui* in China, and *chits* in India. ROSCAs are like savings clubs; members contribute money every week or month into a common fund, and then each month one member of the group receives the full amount contributed by everyone. This usually operates for a cycle of as many months as there are members in the group. For instance, if there are 12 members in the group contributing $10 a month, then a cycle would last 12 months, and each month a different member of the group would receive the $120 available. Thus the ROSCA is a vehicle for saving in which only the last member of the group to receive the funds has saved over the full 12-month period before having the use of $120. The determination of who receives the funds in which month is typically made by a random drawing at the beginning of the cycle. So a ROSCA is a means of saving that allows all but one member in each cycle to receive funds faster than the members could save on their own.

ROSCA
A rotating savings and credit association popular in developing countries.

The informal market in many countries is dominated by individual lenders, who tend to specialize in a local area and make loans primarily for the acquisition of seeds, fertilizer, or mechanical equipment needed by farmers. Surveys in China indicate that about two-thirds of farm loans to poor rural households are made by informal lenders. Such informal lenders are distinct from friends and relatives, who can also be important in lending to poor households. The interest rate charged by informal lenders is typically significantly higher than that charged by banks or government lending institutions. The higher interest rates may reflect the higher risk associated with the borrower, who may have no collateral (goods or possessions that can be transferred to the lender if the borrower does not repay).

Informal loans among friends or relatives are typically one-time loans for purposes like financing weddings or home construction. If your cousin lends you money today in your time of need, then you are expected to lend to him at some later time if he has a need. Repeat loans, like those to a farmer in advance of the harvest each year, tend to be made by individuals who are unrelated to the borrower and are in the business of providing such financing.

A form of informal financial market that gained much publicity after the September 11, 2001, terrorist attacks on New York City's World Trade Center is the **hawala** network. In much of the developing world with heavy Muslim populations, people can send

hawala
An international informal financial market used by Muslims.

money all over the world using the hawala network. Let's say that a Pakistani immigrant who is working as a taxi driver in New York wants to send money to a relative in a remote village of Pakistan. He can go to a hawala agent and give the money to the agent, who writes down the destination location and the amount of money to be sent. The agent then gives the taxi driver a code number and the location of an agent in Pakistan, which the driver passes along to his relative. The agent in the United States then calls a counterpart agent in Pakistan and informs that person of the amount of money and the code number. The Pakistani agent will pay the money to whoever walks in his door with the right code number. Since no records of the name or address of either the source of the money or the recipient are kept, it is easy to see how such a network can be an effective source of financing for terrorist activities. For this reason, the hawala network was a source of much investigation following the 2001 terrorist attacks in the United States. Of course, such a network serves many more than just terrorists, and it is an important part of the informal financial market operating in many countries. For poor people without bank accounts, such informal markets allow some access to financial services.

RECAP

1. The Depository Institutions Deregulation and Monetary Control Act (1980) eliminated many of the differences between commercial banks and thrift institutions.

2. Banks are financial intermediaries.

3. The deregulation act also eliminated many of the differences between national and state banks.

4. Since the FDIC insures bank deposits in commercial banks, bank panics are no longer a threat to the banking system.

5. The international deposit and loan market is called the Eurocurrency market or offshore banking.

6. With the legalization of international banking facilities in 1981, the Federal Reserve allowed international banking activities on U.S. soil.

7. Informal financial markets play an important role in developing countries.

3. Banks and the Money Supply

Banks create money by lending money. They take deposits, then lend a portion of those deposits in order to earn interest income. The portion of their deposits that banks keep on hand is a *reserve* to meet the demand for withdrawals. In a **fractional reserve banking system**, banks keep less than 100 percent of their deposits as reserves. If all banks hold 10 percent of their deposits as a reserve, for example, then 90 percent of their deposits are available for loans. When they loan these deposits, money is created.

fractional reserve banking system

A system in which banks keep less than 100 percent of their deposits available for withdrawal.

6 How do banks create money?

3.a. Deposits and Loans

Figure 4 shows a simple balance sheet for First National Bank. A *balance sheet* is a financial statement that records a firm's assets (what the firm owns) and liabilities (what the firm owes). The bank has cash assets ($100,000) and loan assets ($900,000). The deposits placed in the bank ($1,000,000) are a liability (they are an asset of the depositors).[3] Total assets always equal total liabilities on a balance sheet.

Banks keep a percentage of their deposits on reserve. In the United States, the reserve requirement is set by the Federal Reserve Board (which will be discussed in detail

---

[3] In our simplified balance sheet, we assume that there is no net worth, or owner's equity. Net worth is the value of the owner's claim on the firm (the owner's equity) and is found as the difference between the value of assets and the value of nonequity liabilities.

FIGURE 4 First National Bank Balance Sheet, Initial Position

First National Bank

Assets		Liabilities	
Cash	$ 100,000	Deposits	$1,000,000
Loans	900,000		
Total	$1,000,000	Total	$1,000,000

$$\text{Total reserves} = \$100,000$$
$$\text{Required reserves} = 0.1(\$1,000,000) = \$100,000$$
$$\text{Excess reserves} = 0$$

The bank has cash totaling $100,000 and loans totaling $900,000, for total assets of $1,000,000. Deposits of $1,000,000 make up its total liabilities. With a reserve requirement of 10 percent, the bank must hold required reserves of 10 percent of its deposits, or $100,000. Because the bank is holding cash of $100,000, its total reserves equal its required reserves. Because it has no excess reserves, the bank cannot make new loans.

© 2013 Cengage Learning

in the next chapter). Banks can keep more than the minimum reserve if they choose. Let's assume that the reserve requirement is set at 10 percent and that banks always hold actual reserves equal to 10 percent of deposits. With deposits of $1,000,000, the bank must keep $100,000 (0.1 × $1,000,000) in cash reserves held in its vault. This $100,000 is the bank's **required reserves**, as the Federal Reserve requires the banks to keep 10 percent of deposits on reserve. This is exactly what First National Bank has on hand in Figure 4. Any cash held in excess of $100,000 would represent **excess reserves**. Excess reserves can be loaned by the bank. A bank is *loaned up* when it has zero excess reserves. Because its total reserves equal its required reserves, First National Bank has no excess reserves and is loaned up. The bank cannot make any new loans.

What happens if the bank receives a new deposit of $100,000? Figure 5 shows the bank's balance sheet right after the deposit is made. Its cash reserves are now $200,000, and its deposits are now $1,100,000. With the additional deposit, the bank's total reserves equal $200,000. Its required reserves are $110,000 (0.1 × $1,100,000). So its excess reserves are $90,000 ($200,000 − $110,000). Since a bank can lend its excess reserves, First National Bank can loan an additional $90,000.

Suppose the bank lends someone $90,000 by depositing $90,000 in the borrower's First National account. At the time the loan is made, the money supply increases by the amount of the loan, $90,000. By making the loan, the bank has increased the money supply. But this is not the end of the story. The borrower spends the $90,000, and it winds up being deposited in the Second National Bank.

Figure 6 shows the balance sheets of both banks after the loan has been made and the money has been spent and deposited at Second National Bank. First National Bank now has loans of $990,000 and no excess reserves (the required reserves of $110,000 equal total reserves). So First National Bank can make no more loans until a new deposit is made. However, Second National Bank has a new deposit of $90,000 (to simplify the analysis, we assume that this is the first transaction at Second National Bank). Its required reserves are 10 percent of $90,000, or $9,000. With total reserves of $90,000, Second National Bank has excess reserves of $81,000. It can make loans up to $81,000.

required reserves
The cash reserves (a percentage of deposits) that a bank must keep on hand or on deposit with the Federal Reserve.

excess reserves
The cash reserves beyond those required, which can be loaned.

FIGURE 5   First National Bank Balance Sheet after $100,000 Deposit

First National Bank

Assets		Liabilities	
Cash	$ 200,000	Deposits	$1,100,000
Loans	900,000		
Total	$1,1000,000	Total	$1,100,000

Total reserves = $200,000
Required reserves = 0.1($1,000,000) = $110,000
Excess reserves = $90,000

A $100,000 deposit increases the bank's cash reserves to $200,000 and its deposits to $1,100,000. The bank must hold 10 percent of deposits, or $110,000, on reserve. The difference between total reserves ($200,000) and required reserves ($110,000) is excess reserves ($90,000). The bank now has $90,000 available for lending.

© 2013 Cengage Learning

Notice what has happened to the banks' deposits as a result of the initial $100,000 deposit in First National Bank. Deposits at First National Bank have increased by $100,000. Second National Bank has a new deposit of $90,000, and the loans it makes will increase the money supply even more. Table 2 shows how the initial deposit of $100,000 is multiplied through the banking system. Each time a new loan is made, the money is spent and redeposited in the banking system. But each bank keeps 10 percent of the deposit on reserve, lending only 90 percent. So the amount of money loaned decreases by 10 percent each time it goes through another bank. If we carried the calculations out, you would see that the total increase in deposits associated with the initial $100,000 deposit is $1,000,000. Required reserves would increase by $100,000, and new loans would increase by $900,000.

3.b. Deposit Expansion Multiplier

deposit expansion multiplier
The reciprocal of the reserve requirement.

Rather than calculate the excess reserves at each bank, as we did in Table 2, we can use a simple formula to find the maximum increase in deposits given a new deposit. The **deposit expansion multiplier** equals the reciprocal of the reserve requirement:

$$\text{Deposite expansion multiplier} = \frac{1}{\text{reserve requirement}}$$

In our example, the reserve requirement is 10 percent, or 0.1. So the deposit expansion multiplier equals 1/0.1, or 10. An initial increase in deposits of $100,000 expands deposits in the banking system by 10 times $100,000, or $1,000,000. This is because the new $100,000 deposit creates $90,000 in excess reserves and 10 × $90,000 = $900,000, which when added to the initial deposit of $100,000 equals $1,000,000. The maximum increase in deposits is found by multiplying the deposit expansion multiplier by the amount of the new deposit.

FIGURE 6   Balance Sheets after a $90,000 Loan Made by First National Bank Is Spent and Deposited at Second National Bank

First National Bank

Assets		Liabilities	
Cash	$ 110,000	Deposits	$1,100,000
Loans	990,000		
Total	$1,100,000	Total	$1,100,000

$$\text{Total reserves} = \$110,000$$
$$\text{Required reserves} = 0.1(\$1,100,000) - \$110,000$$
$$\text{Excess reserves} = 0$$

Second National Bank

Assets		Liabilities	
Cash	$90,000	Deposits	$90,000
Total	$90,000	Total	$90,000

$$\text{Total reserves} = \$90,000$$
$$\text{Required reserves} = 0.1(\$90,000) = \$9,000$$
$$\text{Excess reserves} = \$81,000$$

Once First National Bank makes the $90,000 loan, its cash reserves fall to $110,000 and its loans increase to $990,000. At this point, the bank's total reserves ($110,000) equal its required reserves (10 percent of deposits). Because it has no excess reserves, the bank cannot make new loans. Second National Bank receives a deposit of $90,000. It must hold 10 percent, or $9,000, on reserve. Its excess reserves equal total reserves ($90,000) minus required reserves ($9,000), or $81,000. Second National Bank can make a maximum loan of $81,000.

TABLE 2   The Effect on Bank Deposits of an Initial Bank Deposit of $100,000

Bank	New Deposit	Required Reserves	Excess Reserves (new loans)
First National	$ 100,000	$ 10,000	$ 90,000
Second National	90,000	9,000	81,000
Third National	81,000	8,100	72,900
Fourth National	72,900	7,290	65,610
Fifth National	65,610	6,561	59,049
Sixth National	59,049	5,905	53,144
…	…	…	…
Total	$1,000,000	$100,000	$900,000

With no new deposits, the banking system can increase the money supply only by the multiplier times excess reserves:

Deposit expansion multiplier × excess reserves = maximum increase in deposits

The deposit expansion multiplier indicates the *maximum* possible change in total deposits when a new deposit is made. For the effect to be that large, all excess reserves must be loaned out, and all of the money that is deposited must stay in the banking system.

If banks hold more reserves than the minimum required, they lend a smaller fraction of any new deposits, and this reduces the effect of the deposit expansion multiplier. For instance, if the reserve requirement is 10 percent, we know that the deposit expansion multiplier is 10. If a bank chooses to hold 20 percent of its deposits on reserve, the deposit expansion multiplier is only 5 (1/.20).

If money (currency and coin) is withdrawn from the banking system and kept as cash, deposits and bank reserves are smaller, and there is less money to loan out. This *currency drain*—removal of money—reduces the deposit expansion multiplier. The greater the currency drain, the smaller the multiplier. There is always some currency drain, as people carry currency to pay for day-to-day transactions. However, during historical periods of bank panic, where people lost confidence in banks, large currency withdrawals contributed to declines in the money supply.

> *A single bank increases the money supply by lending its excess reserves; the banking system increases the money supply by the deposit expansion multiplier times the excess reserves of the system.*

Remember that the deposit expansion multiplier measures the *maximum* expansion of the money supply by the banking system. Any single bank can lend only its excess reserves, but the whole banking system can expand the money supply by a multiple of the initial excess reserves. Thus, the banking system as a whole can increase the money supply by the deposit expansion multiplier times the excess reserves of the system. The initial bank is limited to its initial loan; the banking system generates loan after loan based on that initial loan. A new deposit can increase the money supply by the deposit expansion multiplier times the new deposit.

In the next chapter, we discuss how changes in the reserve requirement affect the money supply and the economy. This area of policymaking is controlled by the Federal Reserve.

RECAP

1. The fractional reserve banking system allows banks to expand the money supply by making loans.

2. Banks must keep a fraction of their deposits on reserve; their excess reserves are available for lending.

3. The deposit expansion multiplier measures the maximum increase in the money supply given a new deposit; it is the reciprocal of the reserve requirement.

4. A single bank increases the money supply by lending its excess reserves.

5. The banking system can increase the money supply by the deposit expansion multiplier times the excess reserves in the banking system.

SUMMARY

1. **What is money?**

   - Money is anything that is generally acceptable to sellers in exchange for goods and services. *§1*

   - Money serves as a medium of exchange, a unit of account, a store of value, and a standard of deferred payment. *§1.a*

   - Money, because it is more efficient than barter, lowers transaction costs. *§1.a.1*

   - Money should be portable, divisible, and durable. *§1.a.1, 1.a.3*

2. **How is the U.S. money supply defined?**

   - There are two definitions of money based on its liquidity. *§1.b*

- The M1 money supply equals the sum of currency plus traveler's checks plus demand deposits plus other checkable deposits. §1.b.1

- The M2 money supply equals the M1 money supply plus savings deposits, small-denomination time deposits, and retail money market mutual fund balances. §1.b.2

3. How do countries pay for international transactions?

- Using the foreign exchange market, governments (along with individuals and firms) are able to convert national currencies to pay for trade. §1.c

- The U.S. dollar is the world's major international reserve currency. §1.c.1

- The European currency unit (ECU) was a composite currency whose value was an average of the values of several western European currencies. §1.c.1

4. Why are banks considered intermediaries?

- Banks serve as middlemen between savers and borrowers. §2.a

5. How does international banking differ from domestic banking?

- Domestic banking in most nations is strictly regulated; international banking is not. §2.c

- The Eurocurrency market is the international deposit and loan market. §2.c.1

- International banking facilities (IBFs) allow U.S. domestic banks to carry on international banking activities on U.S. soil. §2.c.2

- Informal financial markets are important in developing countries. §2.d

6. How do banks create money?

- Banks can make loans up to the amount of their excess reserves, their total reserves minus their required reserves. §3.a

- The deposit expansion multiplier is the reciprocal of the reserve requirement. §3.b

- A single bank expands the money supply by lending its excess reserves. §3.b

- The banking system can increase the money supply by the deposit expansion multiplier times the excess reserves in the system. §3

KEY TERMS

composite currency, 267
credit, 263
currency substitution, 263
deposit expansion multiplier, 276
eurocurrency market, or offshore banking, 272
european currency unit (ECU), 267
excess reserves, 275

federal deposit insurance corporation (FDIC), 271
fractional reserve banking system, 274
hawala, 273
international banking facility (IBF), 273
international reserve asset, 267
international reserve currency, 267

liquid asset, 262
M1 money supply, 264
M2 money supply, 265
money, 262
required reserves, 275
ROSCA, 273
special drawing right (SDR), 267
transactions accounts, 264

EXERCISES

1. Describe the four functions of money, using the U.S. dollar to provide an example of how dollars serve each function.
2. During World War II, cigarettes were used as money in prisoner of war camps. Considering the attributes that a good money should possess,

why would cigarettes emerge as money among prisoners?
3. What is a financial intermediary? Give an example of how your bank or credit union serves as a financial intermediary between you and the rest of the economy.

4. What is the Eurocurrency market, and how is banking in the Eurocurrency market different from domestic banking?
5. What are IBFs? Why do you think they were legalized?
6. First Bank has cash reserves of $200,000, loans of $800,000, and deposits of $1,000,000.
   a. Prepare a balance sheet for the bank.
   b. If the bank maintains a reserve requirement of 15 percent, what is the largest loan it can make?
   c. What is the maximum amount by which the money supply can be increased as a result of First Bank's new loan?
   d. If the reserve requirement is reduced to 12 percent, how much larger of a loan can the bank make? How much more can the money supply be increased?
7. Yesterday Bank A had no excess reserves. Today it received a new deposit of $4,000.
   a. If the bank maintains a reserve requirement of 2 percent, what is the maximum loan that Bank A can make?
   b. What is the maximum amount by which the money supply can be increased as a result of Bank A's new loan?
8. "M2 is a better definition of the money supply than M1." Agree or disagree with this statement. In your argument, clearly state the criteria on which you are basing your decision.
9. The deposit expansion multiplier measures the maximum possible expansion of the money supply in the banking system. What factors could cause the actual expansion of the money supply to differ from that given by the deposit expansion multiplier?

10. What is liquidity? Rank the following assets in order of their liquidity: $10 bill, personal check for $20, savings account with $400 in it, stereo, car, house, traveler's check.

Use the following table on the components of money in a hypothetical economy to do exercises 11 and 12.

Money Component	Amount
Traveler's checks	$ 100
Currency	$2,000
Small-denomination time deposits	$3,500
Savings deposits	$6,000
Demand deposits	$5,000
Other checkable deposits	$9,000
Retail money market mutual funds	$7,500

11. What is the value of M1 in the above table?
12. What is the value of M2 in the above table?
13. The deposit expansion multiplier has been defined as the reciprocal of the reserve requirement. Suppose that banks must hold 10 percent of their deposits in reserve. However, banks also lose 10 percent of their deposits through cash drains out of the banking system.
    a. What would the deposit expansion multiplier be if there were no cash drain?
    b. With the cash drain, what is the value of the deposit expansion multiplier?

You can find further practice tests in the Online Quiz at **www.cengage.com/economics/boyes**.

INTERNATIONAL DEMAND FOR THE DOLLAR

Because of its relative stability and near-universal recognition and acceptance, USD function as both a store of value and a medium of exchange when other stable or convenient assets (for example, national currencies) are not available. Thus, during times of economic or political crisis, a stable and familiar currency, such as USD, often is sought as a portable and liquid hedge against possible devaluation. Similarly, USD are a popular medium of exchange in regional or cross-border trade when credit markets are undeveloped or banks are underdeveloped or unreliable.

U.S. currency in the form of banknotes (paper currency) in circulation outside the U.S. Treasury and the Federal Reserve System was about $759 billion by the end of 2005. Current estimates indicate that the proportion of U.S. currency held abroad is as much as 60 percent of the amount in circulation, or roughly $450 billion. The accompanying table shows the total amount of U.S. banknotes in circulation as well as the share attributed to the $100 denomination. In value terms, the share of USD held as $100s has increased from around 21 percent at the end of 1965 to nearly 72 percent at the end of 2005. In addition, the share of $100 notes estimated to be held outside the United States has also increased. As shown in the right-hand column of the table, the share of $100 notes held outside the United States rose sharply over the period from 1975 to 1995 and then remained relatively stable at around two-thirds of all $100 notes since 1999.

The international circulation of U.S. currency in Europe expanded after World War I in the wake of the hyperinflation induced by the obligations arising from the Treaty of Versailles. At that time, U.S. currency was viewed favorably because the United States was still on the gold standard, while Great Britain, whose currency was the leading alternative to U.S. currency, remained off the gold standard until May 1925. Other countries, such as Panama, adopted U.S. currency as their official currency. In the past two decades, the international usage of U.S. banknotes expanded largely because of two events: the breakup of the Soviet Union and episodes of high and volatile inflation in Latin America.

During a period of instability, the magnitude of the inflows of U.S. banknotes depends on a country's experience with U.S. currency in the past and its economic circumstances. In particular, demand for USD appears to depend on two factors. The first factor is the ability of people to purchase U.S. banknotes, and the second factor is their confidence in the domestic banking system. The less confidence people have that the value of their bank holdings will be protected, the more likely they are to want to hold U.S. banknotes. Similarly, the more developed the banking system, the more likely it is that people will have a wide variety of options for saving and for making transactions.

Because many holders of U.S. currency view it as a form of insurance against future instability, they are reluctant to alter their usage patterns for USD during periods of economic stability by either shifting out of U.S. banknotes or by switching to another currency, such as the euro. Since the introduction of euro banknotes in the beginning of 2002, it appeared that demand for USD waned somewhat in countries in and near the eurozone. However, responses to International Currency Awareness Program (ICAP) team inquiries indicated that USD holders have moved to holding euros in addition to, rather than instead of, USD. It is likely that underlying patterns of U.S. currency usage will change slowly in countries that already use USD. In countries that do not now use USD to a significant degree, it is difficult to predict if and when a crisis prompting demand for a second currency might develop.

Source: U.S. Treasury Dept., The Use and Counterfeiting of U.S. Currency Abroad, Part 3, Section 1.3, 2006. http://www.federalreserve.gov/boarddocs/rptcongress/counterfeit/counterfeit2006.pdf.

				(4)	(5)
TABLE 3			**U.S. Banknotes in Circulation, $100s in Circulation, and $100s Held Abroad (Billions of Dollars, Except as Noted, at Year-Ends)**		
Year	**(1)** **Total**	**(2)** **$100s**	**(3)** **Share of $100s in** **Total (percent)**	**Estimates of $100s** **Held Abroad,** **Wholesale**	**Estimates of Share of** **$100s Held Abroad** **Wholesale (percent)**
1965	38.0	8.1	21.4	3.9	48.3
1970	50.8	12.1	23.8	5.7	47.5
1975	77.6	23.1	29.8	10.0	43.2
1980	124.8	49.3	39.5	23.8	48.4
1985	182.0	81.2	44.6	45.8	56.4
1990	268.2	140.2	52.3	85.7	61.1
1995	401.5	241.5	60.2	169.2	70.1
1999	601.2	386.2	64.2	254.6	65.9
2000	563.9	377.7	67.0	256.0	67.7
2001	611.7	421.0	68.8	279.8	66.4
2002	654.8	458.7	70.1	301.3	65.7
2003	690.2	487.8	70.7	317.9	65.2
2004	719.9	516.7	71.8	332.7	64.4
2005	758.8	545.0	71.8	352.0	64.6
2010	914.1	684.8	74.9	389.8	56.9

Source: Columns 1 and 2: *Treasury Bulletin,* various issues, Table USCC-2. Figures include vault cash but exclude coin. Column 4: Federal Reserve Board Flow of Funds Accounts (Z.1. Statistical Release, Table L. 204, line 22).

There is considerable evidence that U.S. dollars are held in large amounts in many developing countries. Residents of these countries hold dollars because their domestic inflation rate is (or has been) very high, and by holding dollars, they can avoid the rapid erosion of purchasing power that is associated with holding the domestic currency. This "dollarization" of a country begins with people's holding dollars rather than domestic currency as savings (the store-of-value function of money). But if high inflation continues, dollars, rather than domestic currency, come to be used in day-to-day transactions as the medium of exchange. In the late 1980s, as the Polish economy became heavily dollarized, a common joke in Poland was: "What do America and Poland have in common? In America, you can buy everything for dollars and nothing for zlotys [the Polish currency]. In Poland, it is exactly the same." In 2009, one could have made the same comment about Zimbabwe, where the economy was officially dollarized after hyperinflation that eventually led to the issue of a 100 trillion Zimbabwe dollar bill. These were soon selling on eBay for less than 1 U.S. dollar each.

One implication of the demand for dollars in developing countries is that dollar currency leaves the United States. This currency drain will affect the size of the deposit expansion multiplier. In the chapter, the deposit expansion multiplier was defined as

$$\text{Deposit expansion multiplier} = \frac{1}{\text{reserve requirement}}$$

This definition was based on the assumption that when a bank receives a deposit, all of the deposit will be loaned except for the fraction that the bank is required to keep as the legal reserve requirement set by the Federal Reserve. With a currency drain, some of the deposit is withdrawn from the banking system as cash. As a result, the deposit expansion multiplier is now

$$\text{Deposit expansion multiplier} = \frac{1}{\text{reserve requirement} + \text{currency drain}}$$

For instance, if the reserve requirement equals 10 percent, our original definition of the deposit expansion multiplier would provide a multiplier equal to $1/.10 = 10$. But if people withdraw 10 percent of their deposits as cash, then the 10 percent currency drain is added to the 10 percent reserve requirement to yield a deposit expansion multiplier of $1/.20 = 5$. So the larger the currency drain, the smaller the money-creating potential of the banking system.

An additional interesting aspect of the foreign demand for dollars is the *seigniorage*, or revenue earned by the government from creating money. If it costs about 7 cents to print a dollar bill, but the exchange value is a dollar's worth of goods and services, then the government earns about 93 cents for each dollar put into circulation. If foreigners hold U.S. currency, then the government earns a profit from providing a stable-valued dollar that people want to hold. However, we should not overestimate the value of this in terms of the U.S. government budget. Even if all the new currency issued by the U.S. government flowed out to the rest of the world, the seigniorage earned by the United States over the past decade would have averaged less than 1.7 percent of federal government revenue. Given the relatively insignificant revenue earned from seigniorage, it is not surprising that U.S. policy with regard to the dollarization of developing countries has largely been one of disinterest.

CHAPTER 13

Monetary Policy

© MACIEJ FROLOW/GETTY IMAGES, INC

© VVP/DREAMSTIME LLC; LOGO: © FROXX/SHUTTERSTOCK.COM

FUNDAMENTAL QUESTIONS

1 What does the Federal Reserve do?

2 How is monetary policy set?

3 What are the tools of monetary policy?

4 What role do central banks play in the foreign exchange market?

5 What are the determinants of the demand for money?

6 How does monetary policy affect the equilibrium level of real GDP?

In the previous chapter, we saw how banks "create" money by making loans. However, that money must get into the system to begin with. Most of us never think about how money enters the economy. All we worry about is having money available when we need it. But there is a government body that controls the U.S. money supply, and in this chapter we will learn about this agency—the Federal Reserve System and the Board of Governors that oversees monetary policy.

The amount of money that is available for spending by individuals or businesses affects prices, interest rates, foreign exchange rates, and the level of income in the economy. Thus, having control of the money supply gives the Federal Reserve powerful influence over these important economic variables. As we learned in the chapter titled "Fiscal Policy," the control of government spending and taxes is one of two ways by which government can change the equilibrium level of real GDP.

Monetary policy as carried out by the Federal Reserve is the other mechanism through which attempts are made to manage the economy. In this chapter we will also explore the tools of monetary policy and see how changes in the money supply affect the equilibrium level of real GDP.

1. The Federal Reserve System

1 What does the Federal Reserve do?

© froxx/Shutterstock.com

The Federal Reserve is the central bank of the United States. A *central bank* performs several functions: accepting deposits from and making loans to commercial banks, acting as a banker for the federal government, and controlling the money supply. We discuss these functions in greater detail later on, but first we look at the structure of the Federal Reserve System, or the Fed.

1.a. Structure of the Fed

Congress created the Federal Reserve System in 1913, through the Federal Reserve Act. Bank panics and failures had convinced lawmakers that the United States needed an agency that could control the money supply and make loans to commercial banks when those banks found themselves without sufficient reserves. Because Americans tended to distrust large banking interests, Congress called for a decentralized central bank. The Federal Reserve System divides the nation into 12 districts, each with its own Federal Reserve Bank (Figure 1).

1.a.1. Board of Governors
Although Congress created a decentralized system so that each district bank would represent the special interests of its own region, in practice the Fed is much more centralized than its creators intended. Monetary policy is largely set by the Board of Governors in Washington, D.C. This board is made up of seven members, who are appointed by the president and confirmed by the Senate.

The most visible and powerful member of the board is the chairman. In fact, the chairman of the Board of Governors has been called *the second most powerful person in the United States.* This individual serves as a leader and spokesperson for the board and typically exercises more authority in determining the course of monetary policy than do the other governors.

The chairman is appointed by the president to a four-year term. In recent years, most chairmen have been reappointed to one or more additional terms (Table 1). The governors serve 14-year terms, with the terms staggered so that a new position comes up for appointment every two years. This system allows continuity in the policy-making process and is intended to place the board above politics. Congress created the Fed as an independent agency: Monetary policy is supposed to be formulated independent of Congress and the president. Of course, this is impossible in practice because the president appoints and the Senate approves the members of the board. But because the governors serve 14-year terms, they outlast the president who appointed them.

1.a.2. District Banks
Each of the Fed's 12 district banks is formally directed by a nine-person board of directors. Three directors represent commercial banks in the district, and three represent nonbanking business interests. These six individuals are elected by the Federal Reserve System member banks in the district. The three remaining directors are appointed by the Fed's Board of Governors. District bank directors are not involved in the day-to-day operations of the district banks, but they meet regularly to oversee bank operations. They also choose the president of the bank. The president,

FIGURE 1   The Federal Reserve System

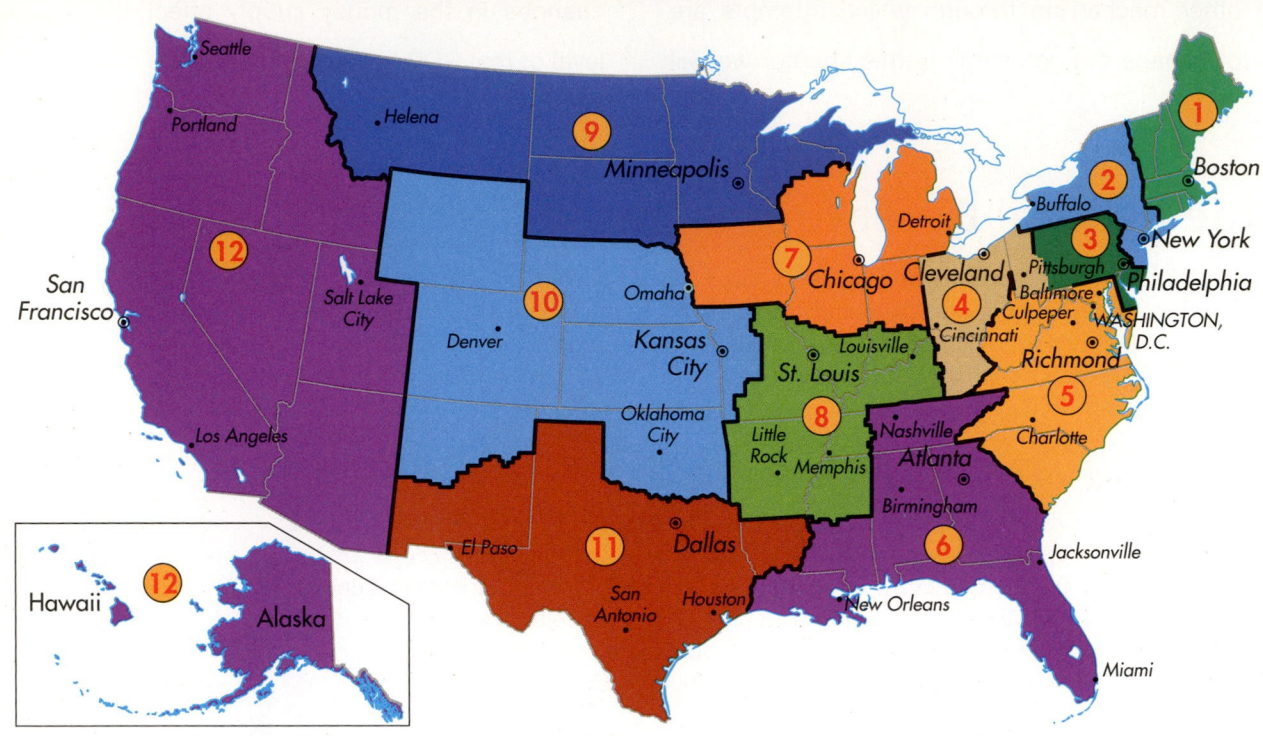

The Federal Reserve System divides the country into 12 districts. Each district has its own Federal Reserve bank, headquarters for Fed operations in that district. For example, the first district bank is in Boston; the twelfth is in San Francisco. There are also branch banks in Los Angeles, Miami, and other cities.

Source: Federal Reserve Bulletin.

TABLE 1   Recent Chairmen of the Federal Reserve Board

Name	Age at Appointment	Term Began	Term Ended	Years of Tenure
William McChesney Martin	44	4/2/51	1/31/70	18.8
Arthur Burns	65	1/31/70	2/1/78	8.0
G. William Miller	52	3/8/78	8/6/79	1.4
Paul Volcker	51	8/6/79	8/5/87	8.0
Alan Greenspan	61	8/11/87	1/31/06	18.4
Ben Bernanke	52	2/1/06		

Federal Open Market Committee (FOMC)
The official policy-making body of the Federal Reserve System.

who is in charge of operations, participates in monetary policy making with the Board of Governors in Washington, D.C.

1.a.3. The Federal Open Market Committee The **Federal Open Market Committee (FOMC)** is the official policy-making body of the Federal Reserve System. The committee is made up of the seven members of the Board of Governors plus five of

© AP Photo/Kevin Wolf

The chairman of the Federal Reserve Board of Governors is sometimes referred to as the second most powerful person in the United States. At the time this book was written, Ben Bernanke was the Fed chairman. His leadership of the Fed has important implications for money and credit conditions in the United States.

the 12 district bank presidents. All of the district bank presidents except the president of the Federal Reserve Bank of New York take turns serving on the FOMC. Because the New York Fed actually carries out monetary policy, that bank's president is always on the committee. In section 2 we talk more about the FOMC's role and the tactics it uses.

1.b. Functions of the Fed

The Federal Reserve System offers banking services to the banking community and the U.S. Treasury and supervises the nation's banking system. The Fed also regulates the U.S. money supply.

1.b.1. Banking Services and Supervision
The Fed provides several basic services to the banking community: It supplies currency to banks, holds their reserves, and clears checks. The Fed supplies U.S. currency (Federal Reserve notes) to the banking community through its 12 district banks. (See the Economic Insight "What's on a 20-Dollar Bill?")

Commercial banks in each district also hold reserves in the form of deposits at their district bank. In addition, the Fed makes loans to banks. In this sense, the Fed is a *banker's bank*. And the Fed clears checks, transferring funds to the banks where checks are deposited from the banks on which the checks are drawn.

The Fed also supervises the nation's banks, ensuring that they operate in a sound and prudent manner. And it acts as the banker for the U.S. government, selling U.S. government securities for the U.S. Treasury.

1.b.2. Controlling the Money Supply
All of the functions that the Federal Reserve carries out are important, but none is more important than managing the nation's money supply. Before 1913, when the Fed was created, the money supply did not change to meet fluctuations in the demand for money. These fluctuations can stem from changes in income or from seasonal patterns of demand. For example, every year during the

ECONOMIC
INSIGHT

What's on a 20-Dollar Bill?

The figure shows both sides of a 20-dollar bill. We've numbered several elements for identification.

1. Watermark

A watermark, created during the paper-making process, depicts the same historical figure as the portrait. It is visible from both sides when the bill is held up to a light.

2. Security thread

An embedded polymer strip, positioned in a unique spot for each denomination, guards against counterfeiting. The thread itself, which is visible when the bill is held up to a bright light, contains microprinting—the letters *USA*, the denomination of the bill, and a flag. When viewed under ultraviolet light, the thread glows a distinctive color for each denomination.

3. Color-shifting ink

The ink used in the numeral in the lower right-hand corner on the front of the bill looks green when viewed straight on but copper when viewed at an angle.

4. Serial number

No two notes of the same kind, denomination, and series have the same serial number. This fact can be important in detecting counterfeit notes, as many counterfeiters make large batches of a particular note with the same number.

Notes are numbered in lots of 100 million. Each lot has a different suffix letter, beginning with *A* and following in alphabetical order through *Z*, omitting *O* because of its similarity to the numerical zero.

Serial numbers consist of two prefix letters, eight numerals, and a one-letter suffix. The first letter of the prefix designates the series. The second letter of the prefix designates the Federal Reserve Bank to which the note was issued, with *A* designating the first district, or the Boston Fed, and *L*, the twelfth letter in the alphabet, designating the twelfth district, or the San Francisco Fed.

5. "In God We Trust"

Secretary of the Treasury Salmon P. Chase first authorized the use of "In God We Trust" on U.S. money on the 2-cent coin in 1864. In 1955, Congress mandated the use of this phrase on all currency and coins.

Sources: Federal Reserve Bank of Atlanta and Bureau of Engraving and Printing.

Christmas season, the demand for currency rises because people carry more money to buy gifts. During the holiday season, the Fed increases the supply of currency to meet the demand for cash withdrawals from banks. After the holiday season, the demand for currency drops and the public deposits currency in banks, which then return the currency to the Fed.

The Fed controls the money supply to achieve the policy goals set by the FOMC. It does this largely through its ability to influence bank reserves and the money creating power of commercial banks that we talked about in the chapter titled "Money and Banking."

RECAP

1. As the central bank of the United States, the Federal Reserve accepts deposits from and makes loans to commercial banks, acts as a banker for the federal government, and controls the money supply.

2. The Federal Reserve System is made up of the Board of Governors in Washington, D.C., and 12 district banks.

3. The most visible and powerful member of the Board of Governors is the chairman.

4. The governors are appointed by the president and confirmed by the Senate to serve 14-year terms.

5. Monetary policy is made by the Federal Open Market Committee, whose members include the seven governors and five of the 12 district bank presidents.

6. The Fed provides currency, holds reserves, clears checks, and supervises commercial banks.

7. The most important function that the Fed performs is controlling the U.S. money supply.

2. Implementing Monetary Policy

 2 How is monetary policy set?

Changes in the amount of money in an economy affect the inflation rate, the interest rate, and the equilibrium level of national income. Throughout history, incorrect monetary policy has made currencies worthless and toppled governments. This is why controlling the money supply is so important.

2.a. Policy Goals

The ultimate goal of monetary policy is much like that of fiscal policy: economic growth with stable prices. *Economic growth* means greater output; *stable prices* mean a low, steady rate of inflation.

The objective of monetary policy is economic growth with stable prices.

2.a.1. Intermediate Targets The Fed does not control GDP or the price level directly. Instead, it controls the money supply, which in turn affects GDP and the level of prices. The money supply, or the growth of the money supply, is an **intermediate target**, an objective that helps the Fed achieve its ultimate policy objective—economic growth with stable prices.

intermediate target
An objective used to achieve some ultimate policy goal.

Using the growth of the money supply as an intermediate target assumes that there is a fairly stable relationship between changes in the money supply and changes in income and prices. The bases for this assumption are the equation of exchange and the quantity theory of money. The **equation of exchange** is a definition that relates the quantity of money to nominal GDP:

equation of exchange
An equation that relates the quantity of money to nominal GDP.

$$MV = PQ$$

where:

$$M = \text{quantity of money}$$
$$V = \text{velocity of money}$$
$$P = \text{price level}$$
$$Q = \text{the quantity of output, like real income or real GDP}$$

This equation is true by definition: Money times the velocity of money will always be equal to nominal GDP.

In the chapter titled "Money and Banking," we said that there are two definitions of the money supply: M1 and M2. The **velocity of money** is the average number of times each dollar is spent on final goods and services in a year. If P is the price level and Q is real GDP (the quantity of goods and services produced in the economy), then PQ equals nominal GDP. If

$$MV = PQ$$

then

$$V = \frac{PQ}{M}$$

velocity of money
The average number of times each dollar is spent on final goods and services in a year.

Suppose the price level is 2 and real GDP is $500; PQ, or nominal GDP, is $1,000. If the money supply is $200, then velocity is 5 ($1,000/$200). A velocity of 5 means that each dollar must be spent an average of 5 times during the year if a money supply of $200 is going to support the purchase of $1,000 worth of new goods and services.

The **quantity theory of money** uses the equation of exchange to relate changes in the money supply to changes in prices and output. If the money supply (M) increases and velocity (V) is constant, then nominal GDP (PQ) must increase. If the economy is operating at maximum capacity (producing at the maximum level of Q), an increase in M causes an increase in P. And if there is substantial unemployment, so that Q can increase, the increase in M may mean a higher price level (P) as well as higher real GDP (Q).

quantity theory of money
The theory that, with constant velocity, changes in the quantity of money change nominal GDP.

The Fed attempts to set money growth targets that are consistent with rising output and low inflation. In terms of the quantity theory of money, the Fed wants to increase M at a rate that supports steadily rising Q with slow and steady increases in P. The assumption that there is a reasonably stable relationship among M, P, and Q is what motivates the Fed to use money supply growth rates as an intermediate target to achieve its ultimate goal—higher Q with slow increases in P.

Of course, other central banks may have different goals. An example of a central bank that pursues inflation targeting is given in the Global Business Insight "The European Central Bank."

The FOMC used to set explicit ranges for money growth targets; however, in 2000 it stopped doing so. Although it no longer publicly announces a range for money growth, the FOMC still monitors the money supply growth rates. This shift away from announced targets reflects the belief that in recent years, money growth has become an unreliable indicator of monetary conditions as a result of unpredictable changes in velocity.

From the late 1950s to the mid-1970s, the velocity of the M1 money supply grew at a steady pace, from 3.5 in 1959 to 5.5 in 1975. Knowing that V was growing at a steady pace, the Fed was able to set a target growth rate for the M1 money supply and be confident that this would produce a fairly predictable growth in nominal GDP. But when velocity is not constant, there can be problems with using money growth rates as an intermediate target. This is exactly what happened starting in the late 1970s. Figure 2 plots the velocity of the M1 and M2 money supplies from 1959. Although the M2 velocity continued to indicate a stable pattern of growth, M1 velocity behaved erratically. With the breakdown of the relationship between the M1 money supply and GDP,

GLOBAL BUSINESS INSIGHT

The European Central Bank

The European Central Bank (ECB) began operations on June 1, 1998, in Frankfurt, Germany, and now conducts monetary policy for the euro-area countries. The national central banks like the Bank of Italy and the German Bundesbank are still operating and perform many of the functions that they had prior to the ECB, such as bank regulation and supervision and facilitating payments systems in each nation. In some sense, they are like the regional banks of the Federal Reserve System in the United States. Monetary policy for the euro area is conducted by the ECB in Frankfurt, just as monetary policy for the United States is conducted by the Federal Reserve in Washington, D.C. Yet the national central banks of the euro area play an important role in their respective countries. The entire network of national central banks and the ECB is called the European System of Central Banks. Monetary policy for the euro area

is determined by the *Governing Council* of the ECB. This council is composed of the heads of the national central banks of the euro-area countries plus the members of the ECB *Executive Board*. The board is made up of the ECB president and vice president and four others chosen by the heads of the governments of the euro-area nations.

The ECB pursues a primary goal of price stability, defined as an inflation rate of less than 2 percent per year. Subject to the achievement of this primary goal, additional issues, such as economic growth, may be addressed. A benefit of a stated policy goal is that people can more easily form expectations of future ECB policy. This builds public confidence in the central bank and allows for greater stability than if the public were always trying to guess what the central bank really cares about and how policy will be changed as market conditions change.

the Fed shifted its emphasis from the M1 money supply, concentrating instead on achieving targeted growth in the M2 money supply. More recently, the velocity of M2 has also become less predictable.

Economists are still debating the reason for the fluctuations in velocity. Some argue that new deposits and innovations in banking have led to fluctuations in the money held as traditional demand deposits, with bank customers switching to different types of financial assets. These unpredictable changes in financial asset holdings affect the various money supplies and their velocities.

In addition to its interest in money growth, the Fed monitors other key variables that are used to indicate the future course of the economy. These include commodity prices, interest rates, and foreign exchange rates. The Fed may not set formal targets for all of them, but it considers them in setting policy. At the time of this edition, the FOMC had an explicit target for the *federal funds rate* of interest—the interest rate that banks pay for borrowing overnight from other banks. We will discuss this interest rate in more detail in the next section.

2.a.2. Inflation Targeting
Some countries have moved away from pursuing intermediate targets like money growth rates and have instead focused on an ultimate goal: a low inflation rate. In part, these countries realize that using monetary policy to support economic growth, low unemployment, and also low inflation has often resulted in an inflationary bias. The public generally likes to see policies supporting faster economic growth, like lower interest rates, whereas fighting inflation may mean unpopular higher interest rates and slower growth. Thus, a central bank may find it politically attractive to stimulate the economy, meaning that inflation takes a secondary position. In addition, if the central bank always considers multiple goals like low unemployment and low inflation, the public may not be able to understand the central bank's decision-making process easily, with the result that there is great uncertainty regarding monetary policy, and

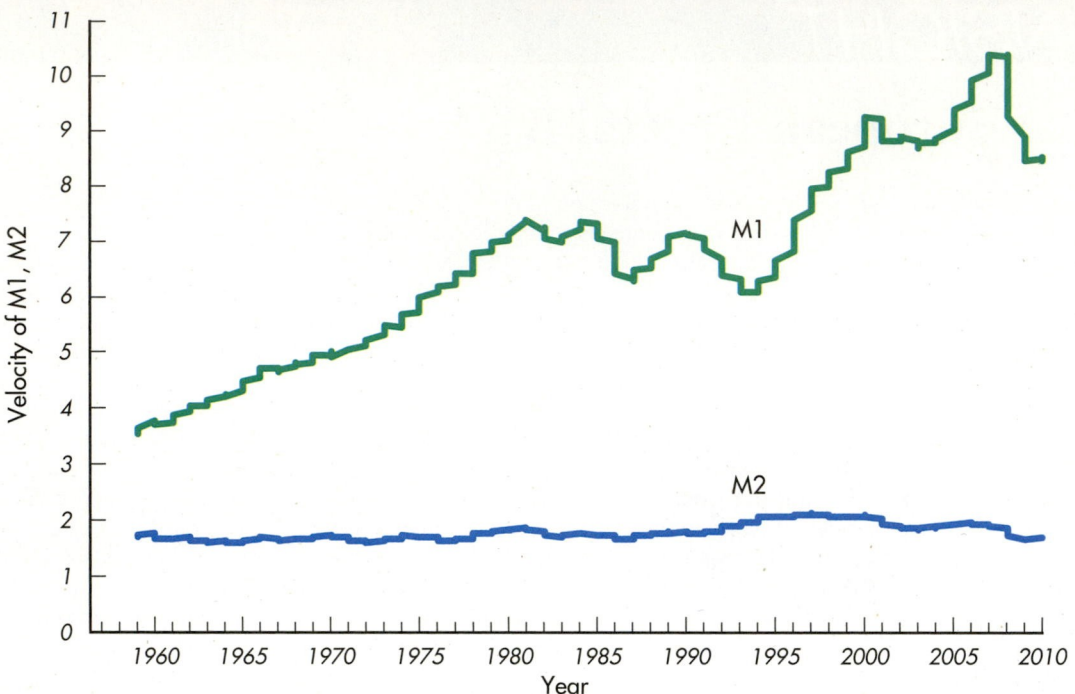

FIGURE 2   Velocity of the M1 and M2 Money Supplies

The velocity of money is the ratio of nominal GDP to the money supply. The narrower the definition of money, the higher its velocity. So M1, the narrowest definition, has a higher velocity than M2. In recent years, the velocity of M1 has been much less stable than the velocity of the broader money definitions.

business firms and households have more difficulty making economic plans for the future. Commitment to a target inflation rate greatly reduces that uncertainty.

Inflation targeting has been adopted in several countries, including New Zealand, Canada, the United Kingdom, Australia, Switzerland, Chile, Korea, South Africa, and Europe (by the European Central Bank). It is important to realize that in order to use inflation targeting, a central bank must be independent from fiscal policy. It is not enough to announce a target for the inflation rate. The central bank must not be in the position of having to help finance government spending. Only with this independence can a central bank truly have a credible inflation target.

2.b. Operating Procedures

FOMC directive
Instructions issued by the FOMC to the Federal Reserve Bank of New York to implement monetary policy.

federal funds rate
The interest rate that a bank charges when it lends excess reserves to another bank.

The FOMC sets federal funds rate targets and then implements them through the Federal Reserve Bank of New York. The mechanism for translating policy into action is an **FOMC directive**. At the conclusion of each FOMC meeting, a policy statement is issued to the public that indicates the contents of the directive. The statement and associated directive outline the conduct of monetary policy over the six-week period until the FOMC meets again to reconsider its targets and specify policy tools.

Figure 3 contains the statement issued by the FOMC meeting of April 27, 2011. The FOMC directed the bond traders at the Federal Reserve Bank of New York to buy or sell government bonds as needed to keep the **federal funds rate**, or the interest rate that one bank charges another for overnight lending, between 0 and 0.25 percent. If the rate starts to rise above 0.25 percent, then the New York Fed will buy bonds from bond

FIGURE 3   FOMC Directive and Policy Statement

FEDERAL RESERVE press release

Release Date: April 27, 2011

For immediate release

Information received since the Federal Open Market Committee met in March indicates that the economic recovery is proceeding at a moderate pace and overall conditions in the labor market are improving gradually. Household spending and business investment in equipment and software continue to expand. However, investment in nonresidential structures is still weak, and the housing sector continues to be depressed. Commodity prices have risen significantly since last summer, and concerns about global supplies of crude oil have contributed to a further increase in oil prices since the Committee met in March. Inflation has picked up in recent months, but longer-term inflation expectations have remained stable and measures of underlying inflation are still subdued.

Consistent with its statutory mandate, the Committee seeks to foster maximum employment and price stability. The unemployment rate remains elevated, and measures of underlying inflation continue to be somewhat low, relative to levels that the Committee judges to be consistent, over the longer run, with its dual mandate. Increases in the prices of energy and other commodities have pushed up inflation in recent months. The Committee expects these effects to be transitory, but it will pay close attention to the evolution of inflation and inflation expectations. The Committee continues to anticipate a gradual return to higher levels of resource utilization in a context of price stability.

To promote a stronger pace of economic recovery and to help ensure that inflation, over time, is at levels consistent with its mandate, the Committee decided today to continue expanding its holdings of securities as announced in November. In particular, the Committee is maintaining its existing policy of reinvesting principal payments from its securities holdings and will complete purchases of $600 billion of longer-term Treasury securities by the end of the current quarter. The Committee will regularly review the size and composition of its securities holdings in light of incoming information and is prepared to adjust those holdings as needed to best foster maximum employment and price stability.

The Committee will maintain the target range for the federal funds rate at 0 to 1/4 percent and continues to anticipate that economic conditions, including low rates of resource utilization, subdued inflation trends, and stable inflation expectations, are likely to warrant exceptionally low levels for the federal funds rate for an extended period.

The Committee will continue to monitor the economic outlook and financial developments and will employ its policy tools as necessary to support the economic recovery and to help ensure that inflation, over time, is at levels consistent with its mandate.

Voting for the FOMC monetary policy action were: Ben S. Bernanke, Chairman; William C. Dudley, Vice Chairman; Elizabeth A. Duke; Charles L. Evans; Richard W. Fisher; Narayana Kocherlakota; Charles I. Plosser; Sarah Bloom Raskin; Daniel K. Tarullo; and Janet L. Yellen.

The FOMC always issues a directive to guide the conduct of monetary policy between meetings. In addition, a press statement at the conclusion of the meeting indicates the committee's view regarding the likely course of policy in the near future and offers guidance as to the contents of the directive. At the meeting that took place on April 29, 2009, the policy statement shown here was issued.

dealers. The dealers are paid with funds drawn on the Federal Reserve, which are then deposited in the dealers' accounts in commercial banks. This will inject money into the banking system. It will increase bank excess reserves, giving the banks more money to lend; as a result, the cost of these funds, the federal funds rate, will fall. Due to the financial crisis, the lower bound on interest rates was set at zero. The FOMC was intent on stimulating the economy to help end the recession. In normal times, the lower bound is set at some positive interest rate. If the rate drops below that rate, then the New York Fed will sell bonds to bond dealers. The dealers pay for the bonds with funds drawn on commercial banks. This drains money from the banking system. Bank excess reserves will fall, and since banks will have less money to lend, the cost of these funds, the federal funds rate, will rise. So the actual federal funds rate fluctuates around the target rate set by the FOMC directive.

In Figure 3, the policy statement issued at the conclusion of the meeting held on April 27, 2011 is given. A key part of this statement is the phrase: "Information received since the Federal Open Market Committee met in March indicates that the economic recovery is proceeding at a moderate pace...." Then in the next paragraph the statement says, "The unemployment rate remains elevated and measures of underlying inflation continue to be somewhat low..." Thus, the Fed saw the economy growing slowly and in need of support for continuing growth. The goals are stable prices and economic growth. If the view was balanced, this would indicate that the FOMC did not clearly see either mounting inflation pressures or recession pressures. However, the concern over a weak economy in the wake of the financial crisis led the FOMC to maintain the historically low interest rate target for federal funds between 0 and 0.25 percent. Going forward, as there are more signs of recovery well under way, we would expect the FOMC to raise the target interest rate to ensure that spending does not rise too quickly and contribute to inflation.

3 What are the tools of monetary policy?

2.b.1. Tools of Monetary Policy The Fed controls the money supply and interest rates by changing bank reserves. There are three tools that the Fed can use to change reserves: the *reserve requirement*, the *discount rate*, and *open market operations*. In the last chapter, you saw that banks can expand the money supply by a multiple of their excess reserves—the deposit expansion multiplier, the reciprocal of the reserve requirement.

Reserve Requirement The Fed requires banks to hold a fraction of their transaction deposits as reserves. This fraction is the reserve requirement. *Transaction deposits* are checking accounts and other deposits that can be used to pay third parties. Large banks hold a greater percentage of deposits in reserve than small banks do (the reserve requirement increases from 0 for the first $10.7 million of deposits to 3 percent for deposits from $10.7 to $58.8 million, and then to 10 percent for deposits in excess of $58.8 million).

Remember from the chapter titled "Money and Banking" that required reserves are the dollar amount of reserves that a bank must hold to meet its reserve requirement. There are two ways in which required reserves may be held: vault cash at the bank or a deposit in the Fed. The sum of a bank's *vault cash* (coin and currency in the bank's vault) and its deposit in the Fed is called its **legal reserves**. When legal reserves equal required reserves, the bank has no excess reserves and can make no new loans. When legal reserves exceed required reserves, the bank has excess reserves available for lending.

legal reserves
The cash a bank holds in its vault plus its deposit in the Fed.

As bank excess reserves change, the lending and money-creating potential of the banking system changes. One way in which the Fed can alter excess reserves is by changing the reserve requirement. If it lowers the reserve requirement, a portion of what was previously required reserves becomes excess reserves, which can be used to make loans and expand the money supply. A lower reserve requirement also increases the deposit expansion multiplier. By raising the reserve requirement, the Fed reduces the money-creating potential of the banking system and tends to reduce the money supply. A higher reserve requirement also lowers the deposit expansion multiplier.

Consider the example in Table 2. If First National Bank's balance sheet shows vault cash of $100,000 and a deposit in the Fed of $200,000, the bank has legal reserves of $300,000. The amount of money that the bank can lend is determined by its excess reserves. Excess reserves (ER) equal legal reserves (LR) minus required reserves (RR):

$$ER = LR - RR$$

TABLE 2   The Effect of a Change in the Reserve Requirement

Balance Sheet of First National Bank

Assets		Liabilities	
Vault cash	$ 100,000	Deposits	$1,000,000
Deposits in Fed	200,000		
Loans	700,000		
Total	$1,000,000	Total	$1,000,000

Legal reserves (LR) equal vault cash plus the deposit in the Fed, or $300,000:

$$LR = \$100,000 + \$200,000$$
$$= \$300,000$$

Excess reserves (ER) equal legal reserves minus required reserves (RR):

$$ER = LR - RR$$

Required reserves equal the reserve requirement (r) times deposits (D):

$$RR = rD$$

If the reserve requirement is 10 percent:

$$RR = (.10)(\$1,000,000)$$
$$= \$100,000$$
$$ER = \$300,000 = \$100,000$$
$$= \$200,000$$

First National Bank can make a maximum loan of $200,000.

The banking system can expand the money supply by the deposit expansion multiplier ($1/r$) times the excess reserves of the bank, or $2,000,000:

$$(1/.10)(\$200,000) = 10(\$200,000)$$
$$= \$2,000,000$$

If the reserve requirement is 20 percent:

$$RR = (.20)(\$1,000,000)$$
$$= \$200,000$$
$$ER = \$300,000 - \$200,000$$
$$= \$100,000$$

First National Bank can make a maximum loan of $100,000.

The banking system can expand the money supply by the deposit expansion multiplier ($1/r$) times the excess reserves of the bank, or $500,000:

$$(1/.20)(\$100,000) = 5(\$100,000)$$
$$= \$500,000$$

If the reserve requirement (r) is 10 percent (.10), the bank must keep 10 percent of its deposits (D) as required reserves:

$$RR = rD$$
$$= .10(\$1,000,000)$$
$$= \$100,000$$

In this case, the bank has excess reserves of $200,000 ($300,000 – $100,000). The bank can make a maximum loan of $200,000. The banking system can expand the money supply by the deposit expansion multiplier ($1/r$) times the excess reserves of the bank, or $2,000,000 ($1/.10 \times \$200,000$).

If the reserve requirement goes up to 20 percent (.20), required reserves are now 20 percent of $1,000,000, or $200,000. Excess reserves are now $100,000, which is the maximum loan that the bank can make. The banking system can expand the money supply by $500,000:

$$\frac{1}{.20}(\$100,000) = 5(\$100,00)$$
$$= \$500,000$$

By raising the reserve requirement, the Fed can reduce the money-creating potential of the banking system and the money supply. And by lowering the reserve requirement, the Fed can increase the money-creating potential of the banking system and the money supply.

Discount Rate If a bank needs more reserves in order to make new loans, it typically borrows from other banks in the federal funds market. The market is called the *federal funds market* because the funds are being loaned from one commercial bank's excess reserves on deposit with the Federal Reserve to another commercial bank's deposit account at the Fed. For instance, if First National Bank has excess reserves of $1 million, it can lend the excess to Second National Bank. When a bank borrows in the federal funds market, it pays a rate of interest called the federal funds rate.

discount rate
The interest rate that the Fed charges commercial banks when they borrow from it.

At times, however, banks borrow directly from the Fed. The **discount rate** is the rate of interest that the Fed charges banks. (In other countries, the rate of interest the central bank charges commercial banks is often called the *bank rate*.) Another way in which the Fed controls the level of bank reserves and the money supply is by changing the discount rate.

When the Fed raises the discount rate, it raises the cost of borrowing reserves, reducing the amount of reserves borrowed. Lower levels of reserves limit bank lending and the expansion of the money supply. When the Fed lowers the discount rate, it lowers the cost of borrowing reserves, increasing the amount of borrowing. As bank reserves increase, so do loans and the money supply.

There are actually two different discount rates, both set above the federal funds target rate. The rate on *primary credit* is for loans made to banks that are in good financial condition. At the time this edition was revised, the interest rate on primary credit was set at .5 percent. In addition to the discount rate for primary credit loans, there is another discount rate for *secondary credit*. This rate is for banks that are having financial difficulties. At the time of this edition, the secondary credit rate was set at 1 percent. Loans made at these discount rates are for very short terms, typically overnight.

open market operations
The buying and selling of government and federal agency bonds by the Fed to control bank reserves, the federal funds rate, and the money supply.

Open Market Operations The major tool of monetary policy is the Fed's **open market operations**, the buying and selling of U.S. government and federal agency bonds. Suppose the FOMC wants to increase bank reserves to lower the federal funds rate. The committee issues a directive to the bond-trading desk at the Federal Reserve Bank of New York to change the federal funds rate to a lower level. In order to accomplish this, the Fed buys bonds, with the results described earlier. If the higher reserves that result lead to increased bank lending to the public, then the new loans in turn expand the money supply through the deposit expansion multiplier process.

If the Fed wants to increase the federal funds rate, it sells bonds. As a result, the money supply decreases through the deposit expansion multiplier process.

To lower the federal funds rate and increase the money supply, the Fed buys U.S. government bonds. To increase the federal funds rate and decrease the money supply, it sells U.S. government bonds.

Its open market operations allow the Fed to control the federal funds rate and the money supply. To lower the federal funds rate and increase the money supply, the Fed buys U.S. government bonds. To raise the federal funds rate and decrease the money supply, it sells U.S. government bonds. The effect of selling these bonds, however, varies, depending on whether there are excess reserves in the banking system. If there are excess reserves, the money supply does not necessarily decrease when the Fed sells bonds. The open market sale may simply reduce the level of excess reserves, reducing the rate at which the money supply increases.

TABLE 3	The Effect of an Open Market Operation		
Balance Sheet of First National Bank			
Assets		**Liabilities**	
Vault cash	$ 100,000	Deposits	$1,000,000
Deposits in Fed	200,000		
Loans	700,000		
Total	$1,000,000	Total	$1,000,000

Initially, legal reserves (LR) equal vault cash plus the deposit in the Fed, or $300,000:

$$LR = \$100,000 + \$200,000$$
$$= \$300,000$$

If the reserve requirement (r) is 20 percent (.20), required reserves (RR) equal $200,000:

$$.20(\$1,000,000) = \$200,000$$

Excess reserves (ER), then, equal $100,000 ($300,000 − $200,000). The bank can make a maximum loan of $100,000. The banking system can expand the money supply by the deposit expansion multiplier (1/r) times the excess reserves of the bank, or $500,000:

$$(1/.20)(\$100,000) = 5(\$100,000)$$
$$= \$500,000$$

Open market purchase:

The Fed purchases $100,000 worth of bonds from a dealer, who deposits the $100,000 in an account at First National. At this point the bank has legal reserves of $400,000, required reserves of $220,000, and excess reserves of $180,000. It can make a maximum loan of $180,000, which can expand the money supply by $900,000 [(1/.20)($180,000)].

Open market sale:

The Fed sells $100,000 worth of bonds to a dealer, who pays with a check drawn on an account at First National. At this point, the bank has legal reserves of $200,000, required reserves of $180,000 (its deposits now equal $900,000), and excess reserves of $20,000. It can make a maximum loan of $20,000, which can expand the money supply by $100,000 [(1/.20)($20,000)].

Table 3 shows how open market operations change bank reserves and illustrates the money-creating power of the banking system. First National Bank's initial balance sheet shows excess reserves of $100,000 with a 20 percent reserve requirement.

Therefore, the bank can make a maximum loan of $100,000. On the basis of the bank's reserve position, the banking system can increase the money supply by a maximum of $500,000.

If the Fed purchases $100,000 worth of bonds from a private dealer, who deposits the $100,000 in an account at First National Bank, the excess reserves of First National Bank increase to $180,000. These reserves can generate a maximum increase in the money supply of $900,000. The open market purchase increases the excess reserves of the banking system, stimulating the growth of money and, eventually, nominal GDP.

What happens when an open market sale takes place? If the Fed sells $100,000 worth of bonds to a private bond dealer, the dealer pays for the bonds using a check drawn on First National Bank. First National's deposits drop from $1,000,000 to $900,000, and its legal reserves drop from $300,000 to $200,000. With excess reserves of $20,000, the banking system can increase the money supply by only $100,000. The open market sale reduces the money-creating potential of the banking system from $500,000 initially to $100,000.

Quantitative Easing What if a central bank has moved its target interest rate near to zero so that interest rates cannot fall further? If the central bank wants additional stimulus for the economy it can employ a policy known as **quantitative easing**. Quantitative easing is a policy of buying financial assets in order to ease credit conditions and make loans more readily available to the public. These financial assets can be government bonds, private corporate bonds, or any other financial asset the central bank chooses. The idea is to flood the economy with money to try to stimulate spending and provide a boost to GDP growth.

The Bank of Japan employed quantitative easing from March 2001 to March 2006 as the policy interest rate was set at zero, yet the economy was in recession with deflation. During the financial crisis of 2008, several central banks, including the Federal Reserve and the Bank of England, employed quantitative easing by cutting interest rates almost to zero, and still the recession continued. In November 2010, the Fed announced plans to buy six hundred billion dollars in government bonds in a second round of quantitative easing. Once the economy starts to recover, the additional purchases of assets ends, and the central bank raises interest rates to avoid inflation creation by overstimulating the economy.

2.b.2. FOMC Directives

When it sets monetary policy, the FOMC begins with its *ultimate goal*: economic growth at stable prices. It defines that goal in terms of GDP and inflation. Then it works backwards to identify its *intermediate target*, the rate at which the money supply must grow to achieve the wanted growth in GDP. Then it must decide how to achieve its intermediate target. In Figure 4, as is usually the case in real life, the Fed uses open market operations. But to know whether it should buy or sell bonds, the FOMC must have some indication of whether the money supply is growing too fast or too slowly. The committee relies on a *short-run operating target* for this information. The short-run target indicates how the money supply should change. Both the quantity of excess reserves in the banking system and the federal funds rate can serve as short-run operating targets.

The FOMC carries out its policies through directives to the bond-trading desk at the Federal Reserve Bank of New York. The directives specify a short-run operating target that the trading desk must use in its day-to-day operations. In recent years, the target has been the federal funds rate.

FIGURE 4   Monetary Policy: Tools, Targets, and Goals

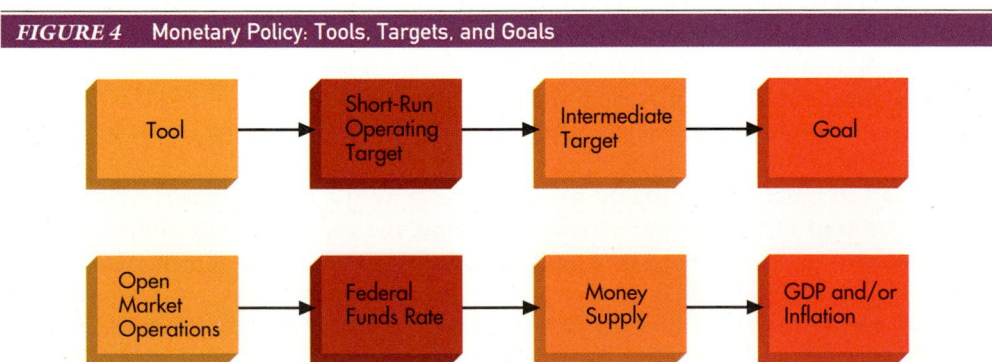

The Fed primarily uses open market operations to implement monetary policy. The decision to buy or sell bonds is based on a short-run operating target, like the federal funds rate. The short-run operating target is set to achieve an intermediate target, a certain level of money supply. The intermediate target is set to achieve the ultimate goal, a certain level of gross domestic product and/or inflation.

2.c. Foreign Exchange Market Intervention

In the mid-1980s, conditions in the foreign exchange market took on a high priority in FOMC directives. There was concern that the value of the dollar in relation to other currencies was contributing to a large U.S. international trade deficit. Furthermore, the governments of the major industrial countries had decided to work together to maintain more stable exchange rates. This meant that the Federal Reserve and the central banks of the other developed countries had to devote more attention to maintaining exchange rates within a certain target band of values. Although more recently exchange rates have had less of a role in FOMC meetings, it is still important to understand how central banks may intervene to change exchange rates. Other central banks have made exchange rates a focus of their policy. For example, in 2009 the Swiss National Bank announced that the Swiss franc had appreciated in value too much and that this was "an inappropriate tightening of monetary conditions." As a result, the bank sold Swiss francs in the foreign exchange market and stated that they stood ready to do this to ensure that the currency would not appreciate further.

2.c.1. Mechanics of Intervention
Foreign exchange market intervention is the buying and selling of foreign exchange by a central bank in order to move exchange rates up or down. We can use a simple supply and demand diagram to illustrate the role of intervention. Figure 5 shows the U.S. dollar–Japanese yen exchange market. The demand curve is the demand for dollars produced by the demand for U.S. goods and financial assets. The supply curve is the supply of dollars generated by U.S. residents'

4 What role do central banks play in the foreign exchange market?

foreign exchange market intervention
The buying and selling of currencies by a central bank to achieve a specified exchange rate.

FIGURE 5   The Dollar–Yen Foreign Exchange Market

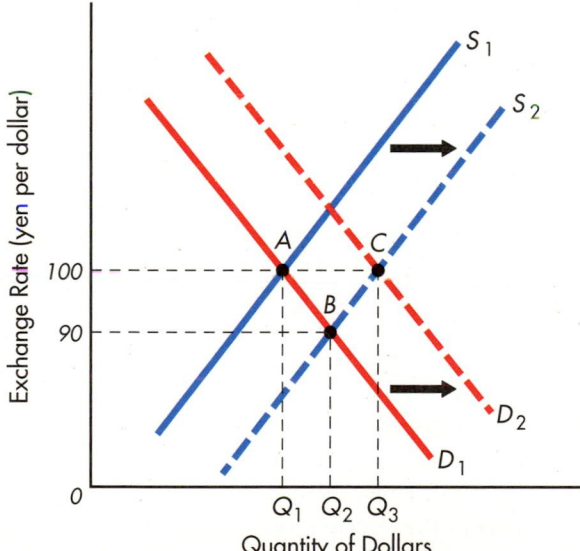

The demand is the demand for dollars arising out of the Japanese demand for U.S. goods and services. The supply is the supply of dollars arising out of the U.S. demand for Japanese goods and services. Initially, the equilibrium exchange rate is at the intersection of the demand curve (D_1) and the supply curve (S_1), at point A where the exchange rate is ¥100 = $1. An increase in the U.S. demand for Japanese goods increases S_1 to S_2 and pushes the equilibrium exchange rate down to point B, where ¥90 = $1. If the Fed's target exchange rate is ¥100 = $1, the Fed must intervene and buy dollars in the foreign exchange market. This increases demand to D_2 and raises the equilibrium exchange rate to point C, where ¥100 = $1.

demand for the products and financial assets of other countries. Here, the supply of dollars to the dollar–yen market comes from the U.S. demand to buy Japanese products.

The initial equilibrium exchange rate is at point *A*, where the demand curve (D_1) and the supply curve (S_1) intersect. At point *A*, the exchange rate is ¥100 = $1, and Q_1 dollars are exchanged for yen. Suppose that over time, U.S. residents buy more from Japan than Japanese residents buy from the United States. As the supply of dollars increases in relation to the demand for dollars, equilibrium shifts to point *B*. At point *B*, Q_2 dollars are exchanged at a rate of ¥90 = $1. The dollar has *depreciated* against the yen, or, conversely, the yen has *appreciated* against the dollar.

When the dollar depreciates, U.S. goods are cheaper to Japanese buyers (it takes fewer yen to buy each dollar). The depreciated dollar stimulates U.S. exports to Japan. It also raises the price of Japanese goods to U.S. buyers, reducing U.S. imports from Japan. Rather than allowing exchange rates to change, with the subsequent changes in trade, central banks often seek to maintain fixed exchange rates because of international agreements or desired trade in goods or financial assets.

Suppose the Fed sets a target range for the dollar at a minimum exchange rate of ¥100 = $1. If the exchange rate falls below the minimum, the Fed must intervene in the foreign exchange market to increase the value of the dollar. In Figure 5, you can see that the only way to increase the dollar's value is to increase the demand for dollars. The Fed intervenes in the foreign exchange market by buying dollars in exchange for yen. It uses its holdings of Japanese yen to purchase $Q_3 - Q_1$ dollars, shifting the demand curve to D_2. Now equilibrium is at point *C*, where Q_3 dollars are exchanged at the rate of ¥100 = $1.

The kind of intervention shown in Figure 5 is only temporary because the Fed has a limited supply of yen. Under another intervention plan, the Bank of Japan would support the ¥100 = $1 exchange rate by using yen to buy dollars. The Bank of Japan could carry on this kind of policy indefinitely because it has the power to create yen. A third alternative is *coordinated intervention*, in which both the Fed and the Bank of Japan sell yen in exchange for dollars to support the minimum yen–dollar exchange rate. Following the Japanese earthquake in March 2011, there was a coordinated intervention involving the Bank of Japan, the Fed, and central banks of other developed economies aimed at lowering the value of the yen to make Japanese products cheaper to the rest of the world.

> *Coordinated intervention involves more than one central bank in attempts to shift the equilibrium exchange rate.*

2.c.2. Effects of Intervention
Intervention can be used to shift the demand and supply for currency and thereby change the exchange rate. Foreign exchange market intervention also has effects on the money supply. If the Federal Reserve wanted to increase the dollar price of the euro, it would create dollars to purchase euros. Thus, when foreign exchange market intervention involves the use of domestic currency to buy foreign currency, it increases the domestic money supply. The expansionary effect of this intervention can be offset by a domestic open market operation in a process called **sterilization**. If the Fed creates dollars to buy euros, for example, it increases the money supply, as we have just seen. To reduce the money supply, the Fed can direct an open market bond sale. The bond sale sterilizes the effect of the intervention on the domestic money supply.

sterilization
The use of domestic open market operations to offset the effects of a foreign exchange market intervention on the domestic money supply.

RECAP

1. The ultimate goal of monetary policy is economic growth with stable prices.

2. The Fed controls GDP indirectly, through its control of the money supply.

3. The equation of exchange ($MV = PQ$) relates the quantity of money to nominal GDP.

4. The quantity theory of money states that with constant velocity, changes in the quantity of money change nominal GDP.

5. Every six weeks, the Federal Open Market Committee issues a directive to the Federal Reserve Bank of New York that defines the FOMC's monetary targets and policy tools.

6. The Fed controls the nation's money supply by changing bank excess reserves.

7. The tools of monetary policy are reserve requirements, the discount rate, and open market operations.

8. The money supply tends to increase (decrease) as the reserve requirement falls (rises), the discount rate falls (rises), and the Fed buys (sells) bonds.

9. If the policy interest rate is lowered near zero, quantitative easing can be used to further stimulate the economy.

10. Each FOMC directive defines its short-run operating target in terms of the federal funds rate.

11. Foreign exchange market intervention is the buying and selling of foreign exchange by a central bank to achieve a targeted exchange rate.

12. Sterilization is the use of domestic open market operations to offset the money supply effects of foreign exchange market intervention.

3. Monetary Policy and Equilibrium Income

To see how changes in the money supply affect the equilibrium level of real GDP, we incorporate monetary policy into the aggregate demand and supply model. The first step in understanding monetary policy is understanding the demand for money. If you know what determines money demand, you can see how monetary policy is used to shift aggregate demand and change the equilibrium level of real GDP.

 5 What are the determinants of the demand for money?

3.a. Money Demand

Why do you hold money? What does it do for you? What determines how much money you will hold? These questions are addressed in this section. Wanting to hold more money is not the same as wanting more income. You can decide to carry more cash or keep more dollars in your checking account even though your income has not changed. The quantity of dollars that you want to hold is your demand for money. By summing the quantity of money demanded by each individual, we can find the money demand for the entire economy. Once we understand what determines money demand, we can put that demand together with the money supply and examine how money influences the interest rate and the equilibrium level of income.

In the chapter titled "Money and Banking," we discussed the functions of money—that is, what money is used for. People use money as a unit of account, a medium of exchange, a store of value, and a standard of deferred payment. These last functions help explain the demand for money.

People use money for transactions, to buy goods and services. The **transactions demand for money** is a demand to hold money in order to spend it on goods and services. Holding money in your pocket or checking account is a demand for money. Spending money is not demanding it; by spending it, you are getting rid of it.

transactions demand for money
The demand to hold money to buy goods and services.

If your boss paid you the same instant that you wanted to buy something, the timing of your receipts and expenditures would match perfectly. You would not have to hold money for transactions. But because receipts typically occur much less often than expenditures, money is necessary to cover transactions between paychecks.

People also hold money to take care of emergencies. The **precautionary demand for money** exists because emergencies happen. People never know when an unexpected expense will crop up or when actual expenditures will exceed planned expenditures. So they hold money as a precaution.

precautionary demand for money
The demand for money to cover unplanned transactions or emergencies.

speculative demand for money
The demand for money created by uncertainty about the value of other assets.

Finally, there is a **speculative demand for money**, a demand created by uncertainty about the value of other assets. This demand exists because money is the most liquid store of value. If you want to buy a stock, but you believe the price is going to fall in the next few days, you hold the money until you are ready to buy the stock.

The speculative demand for money is not necessarily tied to a particular use of funds. People hold money because they expect the price of any asset to fall. Holding money is less risky than buying the asset today if the price of the asset seems likely to fall. For example, suppose you buy and sell fine art. The price of art fluctuates over time. You try to buy when prices are low and sell when prices are high. If you expect prices to fall in the short term, you hold money rather than art until the prices do fall. Then you use money to buy art for resale when the prices go up again.

3.a.1. The Money Demand Function
If you understand why people hold money, you can understand what changes the amount of money that they hold. As you've just seen, people hold money in order to (1) carry out transactions (transactions demand), (2) be prepared for emergencies (precautionary demand), and (3) speculate on purchases of various assets (speculative demand). The interest rate and nominal income (income measured in current dollars) influence how much money people hold in order to carry out these three activities.

The interest rate is the opportunity cost of holding money.

The Interest Rate   There is an inverse relationship between the interest rate and the quantity of money demanded (see Figure 6). The interest rate is the *opportunity cost* of holding money. If you bury one thousand dollar bills in your backyard, that currency is earning no interest—you are forgoing the interest. At a low interest rate, the cost of the forgone interest is small. At a higher interest rate, however, the cost of holding wealth in

---

FIGURE 6   The Money Demand Function

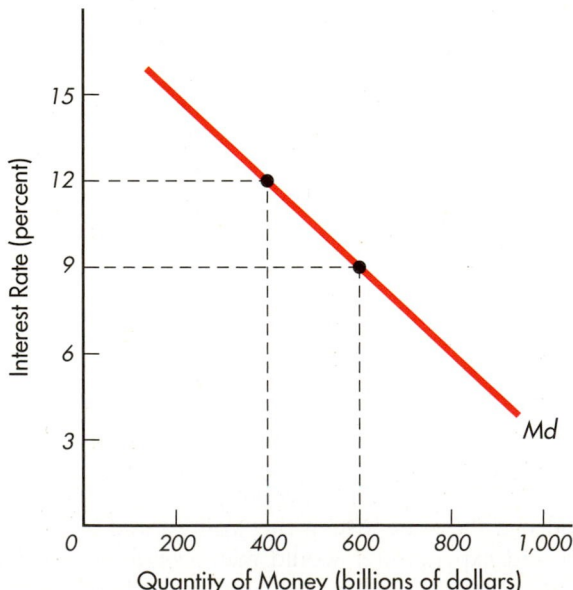

Money demand (*Md*) is a negative function of the rate of interest. The interest rate is the opportunity cost of holding money. The higher the interest rate, the lower the quantity of money demanded. At an interest rate of 9 percent, the quantity of money demanded is $600 billion. At an interest rate of 12 percent, the quantity of money demanded falls to $400 billion.

the form of money means giving up more interest. The higher the rate of interest, the greater the interest forgone by holding money, so the less money held. The costs of holding money limit the amount of money held.

Some components of the money supply pay interest to the depositor. Here the opportunity cost of holding money is the difference between the interest rate on a bond or some other nonmonetary asset and the interest rate on money. If a bond pays 9 percent interest a year and a bank deposit pays 5 percent, the opportunity cost of holding the deposit is 4 percent.

Figure 6 shows a money demand function, where the demand for money depends on the interest rate. The downward slope of the money demand curve (Md) shows the inverse relation between the interest rate and the quantity of money demanded. For instance, at an interest rate of 12 percent, the quantity of money demanded is $400 billion. If the interest rate falls to 9 percent, the quantity of money demanded increases to $600 billion.

Nominal Income The demand for money also depends on nominal income. Money demand varies directly with nominal income because as income increases, more transactions are carried out and more money is required for those transactions.

The transactions demand for money rises with nominal income.

The greater nominal income is, the greater the demand for money. This is true whether the increase in nominal income is a product of a higher price level or an increase in real income. Both generate a greater dollar volume of transactions. If the prices of all goods increase, then more money must be used to purchase goods and services. And as real income increases, more goods and services are being produced and sold and living standards rise; this means that more money is being demanded to execute the higher level of transactions.

A change in nominal income changes the demand for money at any given interest rate. Figure 7 shows the effect of changes in nominal income on the money demand curve. If income rises from Y_0 to Y_1, money demand increases from Md to Md_1. If income falls from Y_0 to Y_2, money demand falls from Md to Md_2. When the money demand function shifts from Md to Md_1, the quantity of money demanded at an interest rate of 9 percent increases from $600 billion to $800 billion.

When the money demand function shifts from Md to Md_2, the quantity of money demanded at 9 percent interest falls from $600 billion to $400 billion.

3.a.2. The Money Supply Function
The Federal Reserve is responsible for setting the money supply. The fact that the Fed can choose the money supply means that the money supply function is independent of the current interest rate and income. Figure 8 illustrates the money supply function (Ms). In the figure, the money supply is $600 billion at all interest rate levels. If the Fed increases the money supply, the vertical money supply function shifts to the right. If the Fed decreases the money supply, the function shifts to the left.

3.a.3. Equilibrium in the Money Market
To find the equilibrium interest rate and quantity of money, we have to combine the money demand and money supply functions in one diagram. Figure 9 graphs equilibrium in the money market. Equilibrium, point e, is at the intersection of the money demand and money supply functions. In the figure, the equilibrium interest rate is 9 percent, and the quantity of money is $600 billion.

What forces work to ensure that the economy tends toward the equilibrium rate of interest? Let's look at Figure 9 again to understand what happens if the interest rate is not at equilibrium. If the interest rate falls below 9 percent, there will be an excess demand for money. People will want more money than the Fed is supplying. But because the supply of money does not change, the demand for more money just forces the interest rate to rise. How? Suppose people try to increase their money holdings by

FIGURE 7   The Effect of a Change in Income on Money Demand

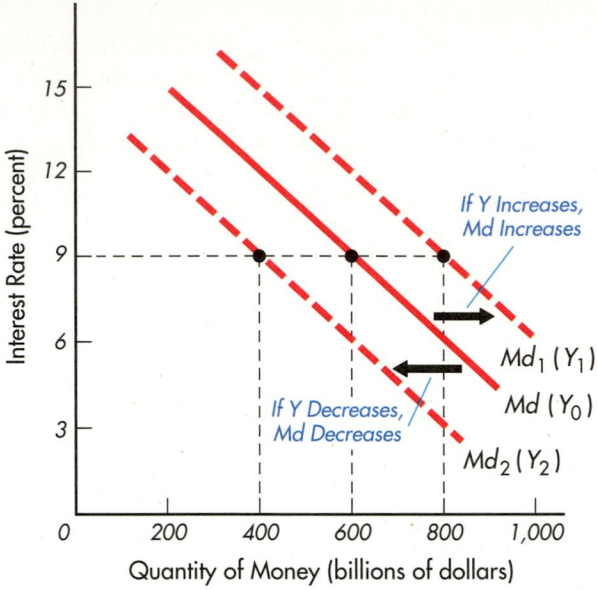

A change in real GDP, whatever the interest rate, shifts the money demand curve. Initially real GDP is Y_0; the money demand curve at that level of income is Md. At an interest rate of 9 percent, the quantity of money demanded is $600 billion. If income increases to Y_1, the money demand shifts to Md_1. Here $800 billion is demanded at 9 percent. If income falls to Y_2, the money demand curve falls to Md_2, where $400 billion is demanded at 9 percent.

FIGURE 8   The Money Supply Function

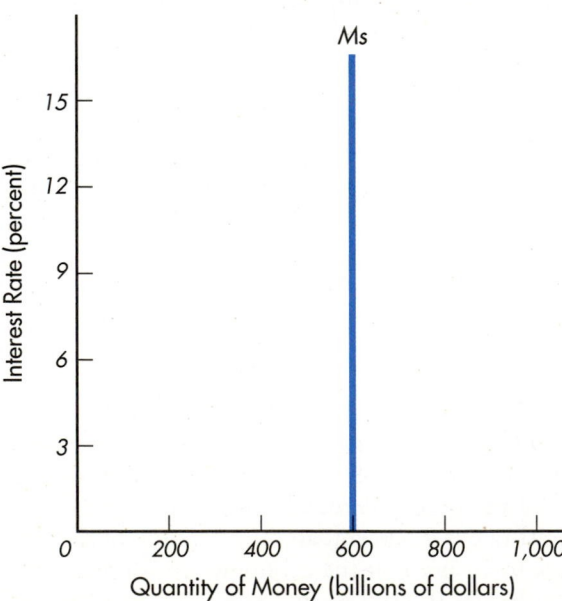

The money supply function (Ms) is a vertical line. This indicates that the Fed can choose any money supply it wants, independent of the interest rate (and real GDP). In the figure, the money supply is set at $600 billion at all interest rates. The Fed can increase or decrease the money supply, shifting the curve to the right or left, but the curve remains vertical.

© 2013 Cengage Learning

FIGURE 9   Equilibrium in the Money Market

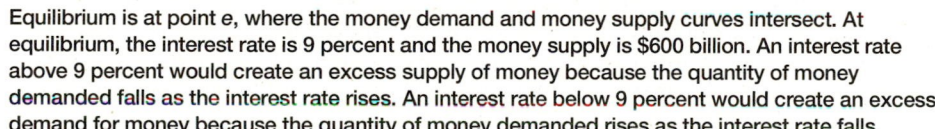

Equilibrium is at point *e*, where the money demand and money supply curves intersect. At equilibrium, the interest rate is 9 percent and the money supply is $600 billion. An interest rate above 9 percent would create an excess supply of money because the quantity of money demanded falls as the interest rate rises. An interest rate below 9 percent would create an excess demand for money because the quantity of money demanded rises as the interest rate falls.

converting bonds and other nonmonetary assets into money. As bonds and other non-monetary assets are sold for money, the interest rate goes up.

To understand the connection between the rate of interest and buying and selling bonds, you must realize that the current interest rate (yield) on a bond is determined by the bond price:

$$\text{Current interest rate} = \frac{\text{annual interest payment}}{\text{bond price}}$$

The numerator, the annual interest payment, is fixed for the life of the bond. The denominator, the bond price, fluctuates with supply and demand. As the bond price changes, the interest rate changes.

Suppose a bond pays $100 a year in interest and sells for $1,000. The interest rate is 10 percent ($100/$1,000). If the supply of bonds increases because people want to convert bonds to money, the price of bonds falls. Suppose the price drops to $800. At that price, the interest rate equals 12.5 percent ($100/$800). This is the mechanism by which an excess demand for money changes the interest rate. As the interest rate goes up, the excess demand for money disappears.

Just the opposite occurs at interest rates above equilibrium. In Figure 9, any rate of interest above 9 percent creates an excess supply of money. Now people are holding more of their wealth in the form of money than they would like. What happens? They want to convert some of their money balances into nonmonetary assets, like bonds. As the demand for bonds rises, bond prices increase. And as bond prices go up, interest rates fall. This drop in interest rates restores equilibrium in the money market.

3.b. Money and Equilibrium Income

6 How does monetary policy affect the equilibrium level of real GDP?

Now we are ready to relate monetary policy to the equilibrium level of real GDP. We use Figure 10 to show how a change in the money supply affects real GDP. In Figure 10(a), as the money supply increases from Ms_1 to Ms_2, the equilibrium rate of interest falls from i_1 to i_2.

Remember that investment (business spending on capital goods) declines as the rate of interest increases. The interest rate is the cost of borrowed funds. As the interest rate rises, the return on investment falls, and with it the level of investment. As the interest rate falls, the return on investment rises, and with it the level of investment. In Figure 10(a), the interest rate falls. In Figure 10(b), you can see the effect of the lower interest rate on investment spending. As the interest rate falls from i_1 to i_2, investment increases from I_1 to I_2. Figure 10(c) is the aggregate demand and supply equilibrium diagram. When investment spending increases, aggregate expenditures are higher at every price level, so the aggregate demand curve shifts to the right, from AD_1 to AD_2. The increase in aggregate demand increases equilibrium income from Y_1 to Y_2.

How does monetary policy affect equilibrium income? As the money supply increases, the equilibrium interest rate falls. As the interest rate falls, the equilibrium level of investment rises. Increased investment increases aggregate demand and equilibrium income. A decrease in the money supply works in reverse: As the interest rate rises, investment falls; as investment falls, aggregate demand and equilibrium income go down.

An excess supply of (demand for) money can increase (decrease) consumption as well as investment.

The mechanism we have just described is an oversimplification because the only element of aggregate expenditures that changes in this model is investment. But an excess demand for or supply of money involves more than simply selling or buying bonds. An excess supply of money probably would be reflected in increased consumption as well. If households are holding more money than they want to hold, they buy not only bonds but also goods and services, so that consumption increases. If they are holding less money than they want to hold, they will both sell bonds and consume less. So the effect of monetary policy on aggregate demand is a product of a change in both investment and consumption. We discuss this in the chapter titled "Macroeconomic Policy: Trade-offs, Expectations, Credibility, and Sources of Business Cycles," where we also examine the important role that expected policy changes can play.

FIGURE 10   Monetary Policy and Equilibrium Income

(a) Money Supply Increases and Interest Rate Falls

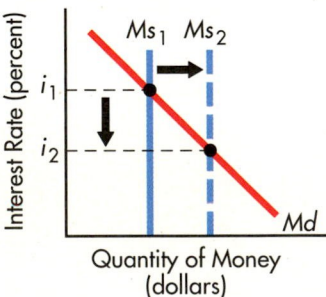

(b) Investment Spending Increases

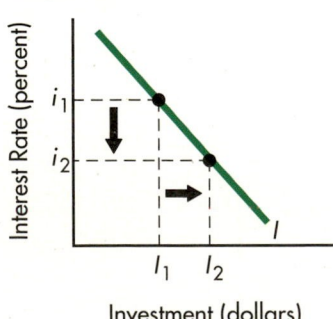

(c) Aggregate Demand and Equilibrium Income Increase

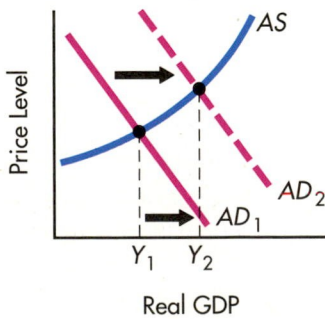

The three diagrams show the sequence of events by which a change in the money supply affects the equilibrium level of real GDP. In Figure 10(a), the money supply increases, lowering the equilibrium interest rate. In Figure 10(b), the lower interest rate pushes the level of investment up. In Figure 10(c), the increase in investment increases aggregate demand and equilibrium real GDP.

RECAP

1. The transactions demand for money is a demand to hold money to buy goods and services.

2. The precautionary demand for money exists because not all expenditures can be planned.

3. The speculative demand for money is created by uncertainty about the value of other assets.

4. There is an inverse relationship between the interest rate and the quantity of money demanded.

5. The greater the nominal income, the greater the demand for money.

6. Because the Federal Reserve sets the money supply, the money supply function is independent of the interest rate and nominal income.

7. The current yield on a bond equals the annual interest payment divided by the price of the bond.

8. An increase in the money supply lowers the interest rate; this raises the level of investment, and this in turn increases aggregate demand and equilibrium income. A decrease in the money supply works in reverse.

SUMMARY

1. **What does the Federal Reserve do?**

   - The Federal Reserve is the central bank of the United States. *§1*

   - The Federal Reserve System is operated by 12 district banks and a Board of Governors in Washington, D.C. *§1.a*

   - The Fed services and supervises the banking system, acts as the banker for the U.S. Treasury, and controls the money supply. *§1.b*

2. **How is monetary policy set?**

   - The Fed controls nominal GDP indirectly by controlling the quantity of money in the nation's economy. *§2.a.1*

   - The Fed uses the growth of the money supply as an intermediate target to help it achieve its ultimate goal—economic growth with stable prices. *§2.a.1*

   - Some countries have adopted inflation targeting to guide their monetary policy. *§2.a.2*

3. **What are the tools of monetary policy?**

   - The three tools of monetary policy are the reserve requirement, the discount rate, and open market operations. *§2.b.1*

   - The Fed buys bonds to increase the money supply and sells bonds to decrease the money supply. *§2.b.1*

   - If the policy interest rate is near zero, a central bank may use quantitative easing to further stimulate the economy and buy financial assets to flood the market with money. *§2.b.1*

   - The Federal Open Market Committee (FOMC) issues directives to the Federal Reserve Bank of New York outlining the conduct of monetary policy. *§2.b.2*

4. **What role do central banks play in the foreign exchange market?**

   - Central banks intervene in the foreign exchange market when it is necessary to maintain a targeted exchange rate. *§2.c*

5. **What are the determinants of the demand for money?**

   - The demand for money stems from the need to buy goods and services, to prepare for emergencies, and to retain a store of value. *§3.a*

   - There is an inverse relationship between the quantity of money demanded and the interest rate. *§3.a.1*

   - The greater the nominal income, the greater the demand for money. *§3.a.1*

   - Because the Fed sets the money supply, the money supply function is independent of the interest rate and real GDP. *§3.a.2*

6. How does monetary policy affect the equilibrium level of real GDP?

- By altering the money supply, the Fed changes the interest rate and the level of investment, shifting aggregate demand and the equilibrium level of real GDP. §3.b

KEY TERMS

discount rate, 296
equation of exchange, 289
federal funds rate, 292
federal open market committee (FOMC), 286
FOMC directive, 292
foreign exchange market intervention, 299

intermediate target, 289
legal reserves, 294
open market operations, 296
precautionary demand for money, 301
quantitative easing, 298
quantity theory of money, 290

speculative demand for money, 302
sterilization, 300
transactions demand for money, 301
velocity of money, 290

EXERCISES

1. The Federal Reserve System divides the nation into 12 districts.
   a. List the 12 cities in which the district banks are located.
   b. Which Federal Reserve district do you live in?
2. Briefly describe the functions that the Fed performs for the banking community. In what sense is the Fed a banker's bank?
3. Draw a graph showing equilibrium in the money market. Carefully label all curves and axes, and explain why the curves have the slopes that they do.
4. Using the graph you prepared for exercise 3, illustrate and explain what happens when the Fed increases the money supply.
5. When the Fed decreases the money supply, the equilibrium level of income changes. Illustrate and explain how.
6. Describe the quantity theory of money, defining each variable. Explain how changes in the money supply can affect real GDP and the price level. Under what circumstances could an increase in the money supply have *no* effect on nominal GDP?
7. There are several tools that the Fed uses to implement monetary policy.
   a. Briefly describe these tools.
   b. Explain how the Fed would use each tool in order to increase the money supply.
   c. Suppose the federal funds rate equals zero. Does that mean the Fed can do nothing more to stimulate the economy? Explain your answer.

8. First Bank has total deposits of $2,000,000 and legal reserves of $220,000.
   a. If the reserve requirement is 10 percent, what is the maximum loan that First Bank can make, and what is the maximum increase in the money supply based on First Bank's reserve position?
   b. If the reserve requirement is changed to 5 percent, how much can First Bank lend, and by how much can the money supply be expanded?
9. Suppose you are a member of the FOMC and the U.S. economy is entering a recession. Write a directive to the New York Fed about the conduct of monetary policy over the next two months. Your directive should address a target for the rate of growth of the M_2 money supply, the federal funds rate, the rate of inflation, and the foreign exchange value of the dollar versus the Japanese yen and euro. You may refer to the Board of Governors website, www.federalreserve.gov/monetarypolicy, for examples, since this site posts FOMC directives.
10. Suppose the Fed has a target range for the yen–dollar exchange rate. How would it keep the exchange rate within the target range if free market forces push the exchange rate out of the range? Use a graph to help explain your answer.
11. Why do you demand money? What determines how much money you keep in your pocket, purse, or bank accounts?
12. What is the current yield on a bond? Why do interest rates change when bond prices change?

13. If the Fed increases the money supply, what will happen to each of the following (other things being equal)?
    a. Interest rates
    b. Money demand
    c. Investment spending
    d. Aggregate demand
    e. The equilibrium level of national income

14. It is sometimes said that the Federal Reserve System is a nonpolitical agency. In what sense is this true? Why might you doubt that politics have no effect on Fed decisions?

15. Suppose the banking system has vault cash of $1,000, deposits at the Fed of $2,000, and demand deposits of $10,000.

a. If the reserve requirement is 20 percent, what is the maximum potential increase in the money supply, given the banks' reserve position?

b. If the Fed now purchases $100 worth of government bonds from private bond dealers, what are the excess reserves of the banking system? (Assume that the bond dealers deposit the $100 in demand deposits.) How much can the banking system increase the money supply, given the new reserve position?

16. What does ECB stand for? Where is the ECB located? In what way is central banking in the euro-area countries similar to the Federal Reserve System?

You can find further practice tests in the Online Quiz at **www.cengage.com/economics/boyes**.

BANK OF ENGLAND MAINTAINS BANK RATE AT 0.5 PERCENT AND INCREASES SIZE OF ASSET PURCHASE PROGRAM BY £50 BILLION TO £125 BILLION

May 7, 2009

The Bank of England's Monetary Policy Committee today voted to maintain the official Bank Rate paid on commercial bank reserves at 0.5%. The Committee also voted to continue with its programme of asset purchases financed by the issuance of central bank reserves and to increase its size by £50 billion to a total of £125 billion.

The world economy remains in deep recession. Output has continued to contract and international trade has fallen precipitously. The global banking and financial system remains fragile despite further significant intervention by the authorities. In the United Kingdom, GDP fell sharply in the first quarter of 2009. But surveys at home and abroad show promising signs that the pace of decline has begun to moderate. . . .

The Committee noted that the outlook for economic activity was dominated by two countervailing forces. The process of adjustment in train in the U.K. economy, as private saving rises and banks restructure their balance sheets, combined with weak global demand, will continue to act as a significant drag on economic activity. But pushing in the opposite direction, there is considerable economic stimulus stemming from the easing in monetary and fiscal policy, at home and abroad, the substantial depreciation in sterling, past falls in commodity prices, and actions by authorities internationally to improve the availability of credit. That stimulus should in due course lead to a recovery in economic growth, bringing inflation back towards the 2% target. But

the timing and strength of that recovery is highly uncertain.

In the light of that outlook and in order to keep CPI inflation on track to meet the 2% inflation target over the medium term, the Committee judged that maintaining Bank Rate at 0.5% was appropriate. The Committee also agreed to continue with its programme of purchases of government and corporate debt financed by the issuance of central bank reserves and to increase its size by £50 billion to a total of £125 billion. The Committee expected that it would take another three months to complete that programme, and it will keep the scale of the programme under review.

Source: News Release, The Bank of England. http://www.bankofengland.co.uk/publications/news/2009/037.htm

Like the Board of Governors of the Federal Reserve System sets U.S. monetary policy, the Monetary Policy Committee (MPC) of the Bank of England sets U.K. monetary policy. If a monetary policymaker believes that economic growth is too slow and inflation is not likely to increase, then it tries to increase aggregate demand by increasing money growth. As we learned in this chapter, when the Fed increases the money supply, interest rates fall, aggregate demand rises, and real GDP growth increases. The same holds for other central banks.

The article says that the MPC left its bank rate at 0.5 percent at the meeting of May 7, 2009. The U.K. Bank Rate is the equivalent of the federal funds rate in the United States. It is the key target for monetary policy. The article goes on to describe the uncertainty facing the MPC in May 2009. The financial crisis had resulted in a global recession where GDP was falling along with inflation. The MPC recognized this but also mentioned that "the pace of decline had begun to moderate" and policy was very expansionary so that one should expect economic conditions to improve going forward. However, the MPC statement also says that "the timing and strength of that recovery is highly uncertain."

It is important to realize that policymakers do not have very much information at the time when they must make policy decisions. For instance, the consumer price index is available only with a one-month lag, so our knowledge of inflation is always running a month behind the actual economy. The GDP is even worse. The GDP data are available only quarterly, and we do not find out about GDP until well after a quarter ends, and even then substantial revisions to the numbers often occur many months after the quarter. The point is simply that the Federal Reserve, the MPC, and other policymaking institutions must formulate policy today on the basis of less than complete knowledge of the *current* situation, and the policy must be addressed to a best guess of the *future* situation. It is like trying to drive a car looking only in the rearview mirror. You can see where you have been, but you must make decisions about where you will go next without knowing exactly where you are currently.

For these reasons, policymakers often find themselves the target of critics who dispute their current and future outlook on inflation and other key economic variables. Central banks want to act in advance of rising inflation or slowing GDP growth to avoid a bad economic outcome. However, even central banks cannot always clearly determine the state of the economy and, consequently, the best course of action.

CHAPTER 14

Macroeconomic Policy: Tradeoffs, Expectations, Credibility, and Sources of Business Cycles

© MACIEJ FROLOW/GETTY IMAGES, INC

FUNDAMENTAL QUESTIONS

1 Is there a tradeoff between inflation and the unemployment rate?

2 How does the tradeoff between inflation and the unemployment rate vary from the short to the long run?

3 What is the relationship between unexpected inflation and the unemployment rate?

4 How are macroeconomic expectations formed?

5 What makes government policies credible?

6 Are business cycles related to political elections?

7 How do real shocks to the economy affect business cycles?

8 How is inflationary monetary policy related to government fiscal policy?

Macroeconomics is a dynamic discipline. Monetary and fiscal policies change over time. And so does our understanding of those policies. Economists debate the nature of business cycles—what causes them and what, if anything, government can do about them. Some economists argue that policies that lower the unemployment rate tend to raise the rate of inflation. Others insist that only unexpected inflation can influence real GDP and employment. If the latter economists are right, does government always have to surprise the public in order to improve economic conditions?

Some economists claim that politicians manipulate the business cycle to increase their chances of reelection. If they are right, we should expect economic growth just before national elections. But what happens after the elections? What are the long-term effects of political business cycles? Because of these issues, the material in this chapter should be considered somewhat controversial. In the chapter titled "Macroeconomic Viewpoints: New Keynesian, Monetarist, and New Classical," we will examine the controversies in more detail, and it will be more apparent where the sources of controversy lie.

© David Falconer/National Archives

Those who were around in the 1970s can remember the long lines and shortages at gas stations and the rapid increase in the price of oil that resulted from the oil embargo imposed by the Organization of Petroleum Exporting Countries. There was another effect of the oil price shock—the aggregate supply curve in the United States and other oil-importing nations shifted to the left, lowering the equilibrium level of real GDP while raising the price level. Such real sources of business cycles can explain why national output can rise or fall in the absence of any discretionary government macroeconomic policy.

1. The Phillips Curve

In 1958, a New Zealand economist, A. W. Phillips, published a study of the relationship between the unemployment rate and the rate of change in wages in England. He found that, over the period from 1826 to 1957, there had been an inverse relationship between the unemployment rate and the rate of change in wages: The unemployment rate fell in years when there were relatively large increases in wages and rose in years when wages increased relatively little. Phillips's study started other economists searching for similar relationships in other countries. In those subsequent studies, it became common to substitute the rate of inflation for the rate of change in wages.

Early studies in the United States found an inverse relationship between inflation and the unemployment rate. The graph that illustrates this relationship is called a **Phillips curve**. Figure 1 shows a Phillips curve for the United States in the 1960s. Over this period, lower inflation rates were associated with higher unemployment rates, as shown by the downward-sloping curve.

The slope of the curve in Figure 1 depicts an inverse relationship between the rate of inflation and the unemployment rate: As the inflation rate falls, the unemployment rate rises. In 1969, the inflation rate was relatively high, at 5.5 percent, while the

Phillips curve
A graph that illustrates the relationship between inflation and the unemployment rate.

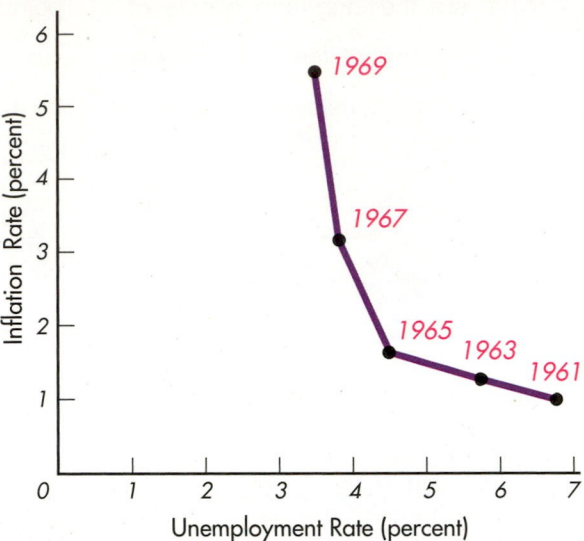

FIGURE 1   A Phillips Curve, United States, 1961–1969

In the 1960s, as the rate of inflation rose, the unemployment rate fell. This inverse relationship suggests a tradeoff between the rate of inflation and the unemployment rate.

unemployment rate was relatively low, at 3.5 percent. In 1967, an inflation rate of 3.1 percent was consistent with an unemployment rate of 3.8 percent; and in 1961, 1 percent inflation occurred with 6.7 percent unemployment.

The downward-sloping Phillips curve seems to indicate that there is a tradeoff between unemployment and inflation. A country can have a lower unemployment rate by accepting higher inflation, or a lower rate of inflation by accepting higher unemployment. Certainly this was the case in the United States in the 1960s. But is the curve depicted in Figure 1 representative of the tradeoff over long periods of time?

1 Is there a tradeoff between inflation and the unemployment rate?

1.a. An Inflation–Unemployment Tradeoff?

Figure 2 shows unemployment and inflation rates in the United States for several years from 1955 to 2010. The points in the figure do not lie along a downward-sloping curve like the one shown in Figure 1. For example, in 1955, the unemployment rate was 4.4 percent and the inflation rate was −0.4 percent. In 1960, the unemployment rate was 5.5 percent and the inflation rate was 1.7 percent. Both the unemployment rate and the inflation rate had increased since 1955. Moving through time, you can see that the inflation rate tended to increase along with the unemployment rate through the 1960s and 1970s. By 1980, the unemployment rate was 7.1 percent and the inflation rate was 13.5 percent.

The scattered points in Figure 2 show no evidence of a tradeoff between unemployment and inflation. A downward-sloping Phillips curve does not seem to exist over the long term.

2 How does the tradeoff between inflation and the unemployment rate vary from the short to the long run?

1.b. Short-Run versus Long-Run Tradeoffs

Most economists believe that the downward-sloping Phillips curve and the tradeoff between inflation and unemployment that it implies are short-term phenomena. Think of a series of Phillips curves, one for each of the points in Figure 2. From 1955 to 1980, the curves shifted out to the right. In the early 1980s, they shifted in to the left.

Figure 3 shows a series of Phillips curves that could account for the data in Figure 2. At any point in time, a downward-sloping Phillips curve indicates a tradeoff between

FIGURE 2   Unemployment and Inflation in the United States, 1955–2010

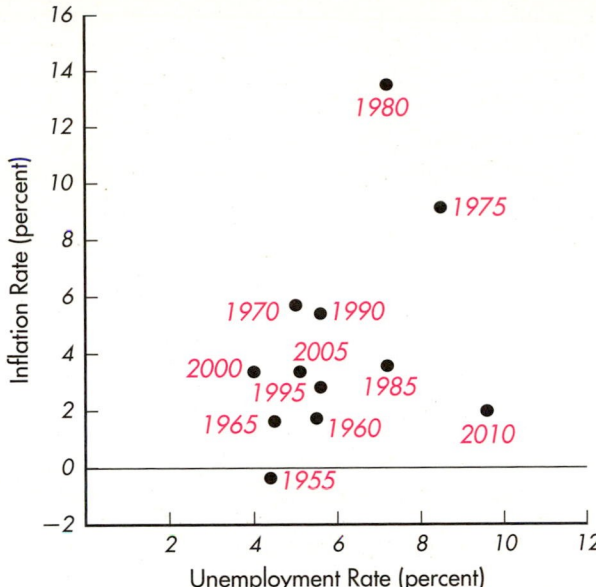

The data on inflation and unemployment rates in the United States between 1955 and 2010 show no particular relationship between inflation and unemployment over the long run. There is no evidence here of a downward-sloping Phillips curve.

FIGURE 3   The Shifting Phillips Curve

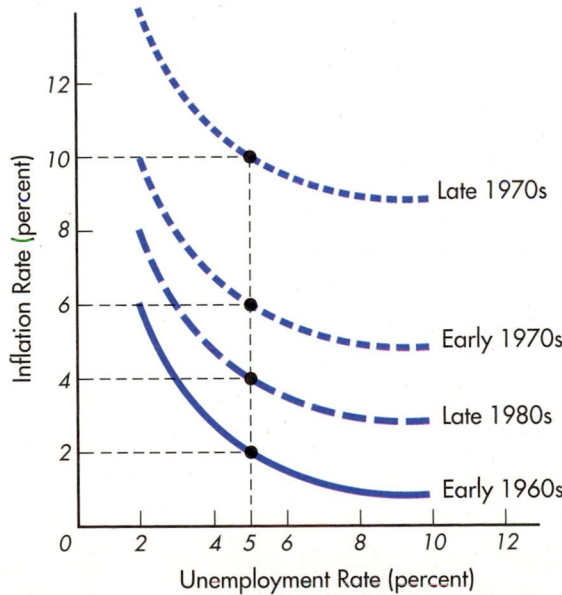

We can reconcile the long-run data on unemployment and inflation with the downward-sloping Phillips curve by using a series of Phillips curves. (In effect, we treat the long run as a series of short-run curves.) The Phillips curve for the early 1960s shows 5 percent unemployment and 2 percent inflation. Over time, the short-run curve shifted out to the right. The early 1970s curve shows 5 percent unemployment and 6 percent inflation. And the short-run curve for the late 1970s shows 5 percent unemployment and 10 percent inflation. In the early 1980s, the short-run Phillips curve began to shift down toward the origin. By the late 1980s, 5 percent unemployment was consistent with 4 percent inflation.

inflation and unemployment. Many economists believe that this kind of tradeoff is just a short-term phenomenon. Over time, the Phillips curve shifts so that the short-run trade-off between inflation and unemployment disappears in the long run.

On the early 1960s curve in Figure 3, 5 percent unemployment is consistent with 2 percent inflation. By the early 1970s, the curve had shifted up. Here 5 percent unemployment is associated with 6 percent inflation. On the late 1970s curve, 5 percent unemployment is consistent with 10 percent inflation. For more than two decades, the tradeoff between inflation and unemployment worsened as the Phillips curves shifted up, so that higher and higher inflation rates were associated with any given level of unemployment. Then in the 1980s, the tradeoff seemed to improve as the Phillips curve shifted down. On the late 1980s curve, 5 percent unemployment is consistent with 4 percent inflation.

> *The data indicate that the Phillips curve may have shifted out in the 1960s and 1970s and shifted in during the 1980s.*

The Phillips curves in Figure 3 represent changes that took place over time in the United States. We cannot be sure of the actual shape of a Phillips curve at any time, but an outward shift of the curve in the 1960s and 1970s and an inward shift during the 1980s are consistent with the data. Later in this chapter, we describe how changing government policy and the public's expectations about that policy may have shifted aggregate demand and aggregate supply and produced these shifts in the Phillips curves.

1.b.1. In the Short Run

Figure 4 uses the aggregate demand and supply analysis we developed in the chapter titled "Macroeconomic Equilibrium: Aggregate Demand and Supply" to explain the Phillips curve. Initially the economy is operating at point 1 in both diagrams. In Figure 4(a), the aggregate demand curve (AD_1) and the aggregate supply curve (AS_1) intersect at price level P_1 and real GDP level Y_p, the level of potential real GDP. Remember that potential real GDP is the level of income and output generated at the natural rate of unemployment, the unemployment rate that exists in the absence of cyclical unemployment. In Figure 4(b), point 1 lies on Phillips curve I, where the inflation rate is 3 percent and the unemployment rate is 5 percent. We assume that the 5 percent unemployment rate at the level of potential real GDP is the natural rate of unemployment (U_n). A discussion of the natural rate of unemployment and its determinants is given in the Economic Insight, "The Natural Rate of Unemployment."

What happens when aggregate demand goes up from AD_1 to AD_2? A new equilibrium is established along the short-run aggregate supply curve (AS_1) at point 2. Here the price level (P_2) is higher, as is the level of real GDP (Y_2). In part (b), the increase in price and income is reflected in the movement along Phillips curve I to point 2. At point 2, the inflation rate is 6 percent and the unemployment rate is 3 percent. The increase in expenditures raises the inflation rate and lowers the unemployment rate (because national output has surpassed potential output).

Notice that there appears to be a tradeoff between inflation and unemployment on Phillips curve I. The increase in spending increases output and stimulates employment so that the unemployment rate falls. And the higher spending pushes the rate of inflation up. But this tradeoff is only temporary. Point 2 in both diagrams is only a short-run equilibrium.

1.b.2. In the Long Run

As we discussed in the chapter titled "Macroeconomic Equilibrium: Aggregate Demand and Supply," the short-run aggregate supply curve shifts over time as production costs rise in response to higher prices. Once the aggregate supply curve shifts to AS_2, long-run equilibrium occurs at point 3, where AS_2 intersects AD_2. Here, the price level is P_3 and real GDP returns to its potential level, Y_p.

The shift in aggregate supply lowers real GDP. As income falls, the unemployment rate goes up. The decrease in aggregate supply is reflected in the movement from point 2 on Phillips curve I to point 3 on Phillips curve II. As real GDP returns to its potential

FIGURE 4 Aggregate Demand and Supply and the Phillips Curve

(a) Aggregate Demand and Supply

(b) Phillips Curve

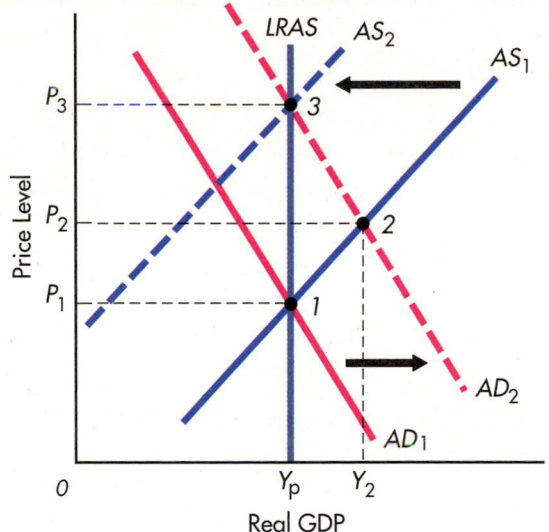

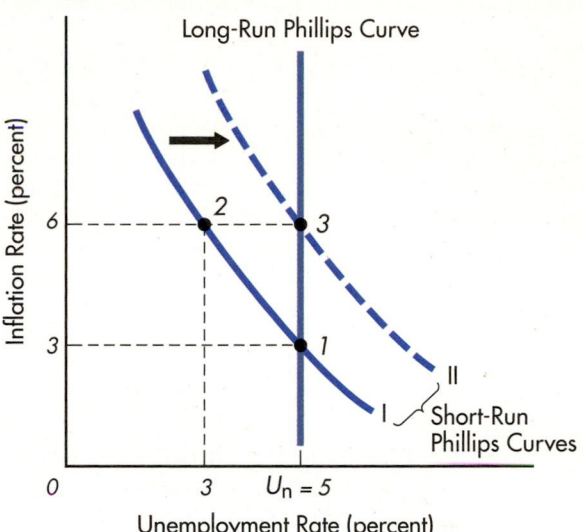

The movement from point 1 to point 2 to point 3 traces the adjustment of the economy to an increase in aggregate demand. Point 1 is initial equilibrium in both diagrams. At this point, potential real GDP is Y_p and the price level is P_1 in the aggregate demand and supply diagram, and the inflation rate is 3 percent with an unemployment rate of 5 percent (the natural rate) along short-run curve I in the Phillips curve diagram.

If the aggregate demand curve shifts from AD_1 to AD_2, equilibrium real GDP goes up to Y_2 and the price level rises to P_2 in the aggregate demand and supply diagram. The increase in aggregate demand pushes the inflation rate up to 6 percent and the unemployment rate down to 3 percent along Phillips curve I. The movement from point 1 to point 2 along the curve indicates a tradeoff between inflation and the unemployment rate.

Over time, the *AS* curve shifts in response to rising production costs at the higher rate of inflation. Along AS_2, equilibrium is at point 3, where real GDP falls back to Y_p and the price level rises to P_3. As we move from point 2 to point 3 in Figure 4(b), we shift to short-run Phillips curve II. Here the inflation rate remains high (at 6 percent), while the unemployment rate goes back up to 5 percent, the rate consistent with production at Y_p. In the long run, then, there is no tradeoff between inflation and unemployment. The vertical long-run aggregate supply curve at the potential level of real GDP is associated with the vertical long-run Phillips curve at the natural rate of unemployment.

level (Y_p), unemployment returns to the natural rate (U_n), 5 percent. In the long run, as the economy adjusts to an increase in aggregate demand and expectations adjust to the new inflation rate, there is a period in which real GDP falls and the price level rises.

Over time, there is no relationship between the price level and the level of real GDP. You can see this in the aggregate demand and supply diagram. Points 1 and 3 both lie along the long-run aggregate supply curve (*LRAS*) at potential real GDP. The *LRAS* curve has its analogue in the long-run Phillips curve, a vertical line at the natural rate of unemployment. Points 1 and 3 both lie along this curve.

> *The long-run Phillips curve is a vertical line at the natural rate of unemployment.*

RECAP

1. The Phillips curve shows an inverse relationship between inflation and unemployment.

2. The downward slope of the Phillips curve indicates a tradeoff between inflation and unemployment.

3. Over the long run, that tradeoff disappears.

4. The long-run Phillips curve is a vertical line at the natural rate of unemployment, analogous to the long-run aggregate supply curve at potential real GDP.

ECONOMIC INSIGHT

The Natural Rate of Unemployment

The natural rate of unemployment is defined as the unemployment rate that exists in the absence of cyclical unemployment. As we discussed in the chapter titled "Unemployment and Inflation," the natural rate of unemployment reflects the normal amount of frictional unemployment (people who are temporarily between jobs), structural unemployment (people who have lost jobs because of technological change), and seasonal unemployment (people who have lost jobs because the jobs are available only at certain times of the year). What factors determine the normal amount of frictional and structural unemployment?

One of the most important factors is demographic change. As the age, gender, and racial makeup of the labor force changes, the natural rate of unemployment also changes. For instance, when the baby boom generation entered the labor force, the natural rate of unemployment increased because new workers typically have the highest unemployment rates. Between 1956 and 1979, the proportion of young adults (ages 16 to 24) in the labor force increased, increasing the natural rate of unemployment. Since 1980, the average age of U.S. workers has been rising. As workers age, employers can more easily evaluate a worker's ability based upon that worker's job history. In addition, younger workers are more likely to have difficulty finding a good job match for their skills and so are likely to have higher frictional unemployment, whereas older workers are more likely to have a long-term job with a single employer. As the labor force ages, therefore, we should expect the natural rate of unemployment to fall.

In addition to the composition of the labor force, several other factors affect the natural rate of unemployment:

- In the early 1990s, structural changes in the economy, such as the shift from manufacturing to service jobs and the downsizing and restructuring of firms throughout the economy, contributed to a higher natural rate of unemployment. Related to these structural changes is a decline in the demand for low-skilled workers, so that rising unemployment is overwhelmingly concentrated among workers with limited education and skills.

- Increases in the legal minimum wage tend to raise the natural rate of unemployment. When the government mandates that employers pay some workers a higher wage than a freely competitive labor market would pay, fewer workers are employed.

- The more generous the unemployment benefits, the higher the natural rate of unemployment. Increased benefits reduce the cost of being out of work and allow unemployed workers to take their time finding a new job. For these reasons, we observe higher natural rates of unemployment in European countries, where unemployed workers receive higher benefits.

- Income taxes can also affect the natural rate of unemployment. Higher taxes mean that workers keep less of their earned income and so have less incentive to work.

The effect of these factors on the unemployment rate is complex, so it is difficult to state exactly what the natural rate of unemployment is. But as these factors change over time, the natural rate of unemployment also changes.

One last thing: It is not clear that minimizing the natural rate of unemployment is a universal goal. Minimum wages, unemployment benefits, and taxes have other important implications besides their effect on the natural rate of unemployment. We cannot expect these variables to be set solely in terms of their effect on unemployment.

2. The Role of Expectations

The data and analysis in the previous section indicate that there is no long-run tradeoff between inflation and unemployment. But they do not explain the movement of the Phillips curve in the 1960s, 1970s, and 1980s. To understand why the short-run curve shifts, you must understand the role that unexpected inflation plays in the economy.

2.a. Expected versus Unexpected Inflation

Figure 5 shows two short-run Phillips curves like those in Figure 4. Each curve is drawn for a particular expected rate of inflation. Curve I shows the tradeoff between inflation and unemployment when the inflation rate is expected to be 3 percent. If the actual rate of inflation (measured along the vertical axis) is 3 percent, the economy is operating at point 1, with an unemployment rate of 5 percent (the natural rate). If the inflation rate unexpectedly increases to 6 percent, the economy moves from point 1 to point 2 along Phillips curve I. Obviously, unexpected inflation can affect the unemployment rate. There are three factors at work here: wage expectations, inventory fluctuations, and wage contracts.

3 What is the relationship between unexpected inflation and the unemployment rate?

2.a.1. Wage Expectations and Unemployment
Unemployed workers who are looking for a job choose a **reservation wage**, the minimum wage that they are willing to accept. They continue to look for work until they receive an offer that equals or exceeds their reservation wage.

Wages are not the only factor that workers take into consideration before accepting a job offer. A firm that offers good working conditions and fringe benefits can pay a lower wage than a firm that does not offer these advantages. But other things being equal, workers choose higher wages over lower wages. We simplify our analysis here by assuming that the only variable that affects the unemployed worker who is looking for a job is the reservation wage.

The link between unexpected inflation and the unemployment rate stems from the fact that wage offers are surprisingly high when the rate of inflation is surprisingly high. An unexpected increase in inflation means that prices are higher than anticipated, as are nominal income and wages. If aggregate demand increases unexpectedly, then prices,

reservation wage
The minimum wage that a worker is willing to accept.

FIGURE 5 Expectations and the Phillips Curve

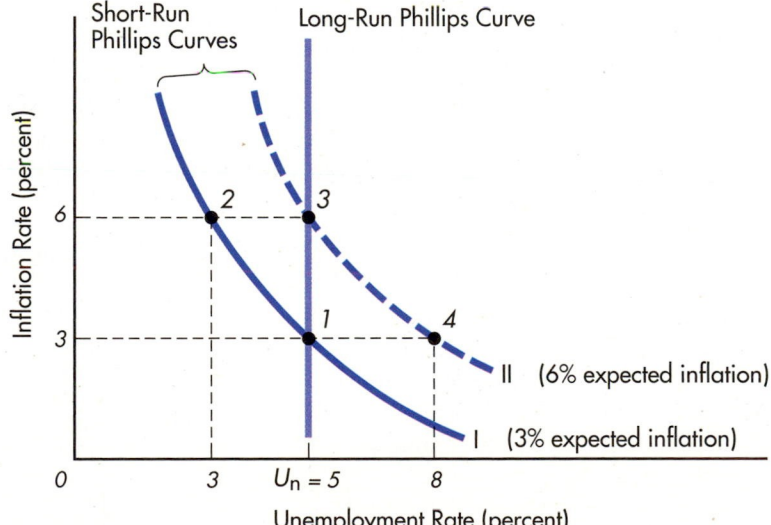

Short-run Phillips curve I shows the tradeoff between inflation and the unemployment rate as long as people expect 3 percent inflation. When the actual rate of inflation is 3 percent, the rate of unemployment (U_n) is 5 percent (point 1). Short-run Phillips curve II shows the tradeoff as long as people expect 6 percent inflation. When the actual rate of inflation is 6 percent, the unemployment rate is 5 percent (point 3).

output, employment, and wages go up. Unemployed workers with a constant reservation wage find it easier to obtain a satisfactory wage offer during a period when wages are rising faster than the workers expected. This means that more unemployed workers find jobs, and they find those jobs more quickly than they do in a period when the rate of inflation is expected. So the unemployment rate falls during a period of unexpectedly high inflation (Figure 6).

Consider an example. Suppose an accountant named Jason determines that he must find a job that pays at least $105 a day. Jason's reservation wage is $105. Furthermore, Jason expects prices and wages to be fairly stable across the economy; he expects no inflation. Jason looks for a job and finds that the jobs he qualifies for are offering wages of only $100 a day. Because his job offers are all paying less than his reservation wage, he keeps on looking. Let's say that aggregate demand rises unexpectedly. Firms increase production and raise prices. To hire more workers, they increase the wages they offer. Suppose wages go up 5 percent. Now the jobs that Jason qualifies for are offering 5 percent higher wages, $105 a day instead of $100 a day. At this higher wage rate, Jason quickly accepts a job and starts working. This example explains why the move from point 1 to point 2 in Figure 5 occurs.

The short-run Phillips curve assumes a constant *expected* rate of inflation. It also assumes that every unemployed worker who is looking for a job has a constant reservation wage. When inflation rises unexpectedly, then, wages rise faster than expected and the unemployment rate falls. The element of surprise is critical here. If the increase in inflation is *expected*, unemployed workers who are looking for a job will revise their reservation wage to match the expected change in the level of prices. If reservation wages go up with the rate of inflation, there is no tradeoff between inflation and the unemployment rate. Higher inflation is associated with the original unemployment rate.

> *If the reservation wage goes up with the rate of inflation, there is no tradeoff between inflation and the unemployment rate.*

Let's go back to Jason, the accountant who wants a job that pays $105 a day. Previously we said that if wages increased to $105 because of an unexpected increase in aggregate demand, he would quickly find an acceptable job. However, if Jason knows that the price level is going to go up 5 percent, then he knows that a wage increase from $100 to $105 is not a real wage increase because he will need $105 in order to buy what $100 would buy before. The *nominal wage* is the number of dollars earned; the *real wage* is the purchasing power of those dollars. If the nominal wage increases 5 percent at the same time that prices have gone up 5 percent, it takes 5 percent more money to buy the same goods and services. The real wage has not changed. What happens? Jason revises his reservation wage to account for the higher price level. If he wants a 5 percent

---

FIGURE 6   Inflation, Unemployment, and Wage Expectations

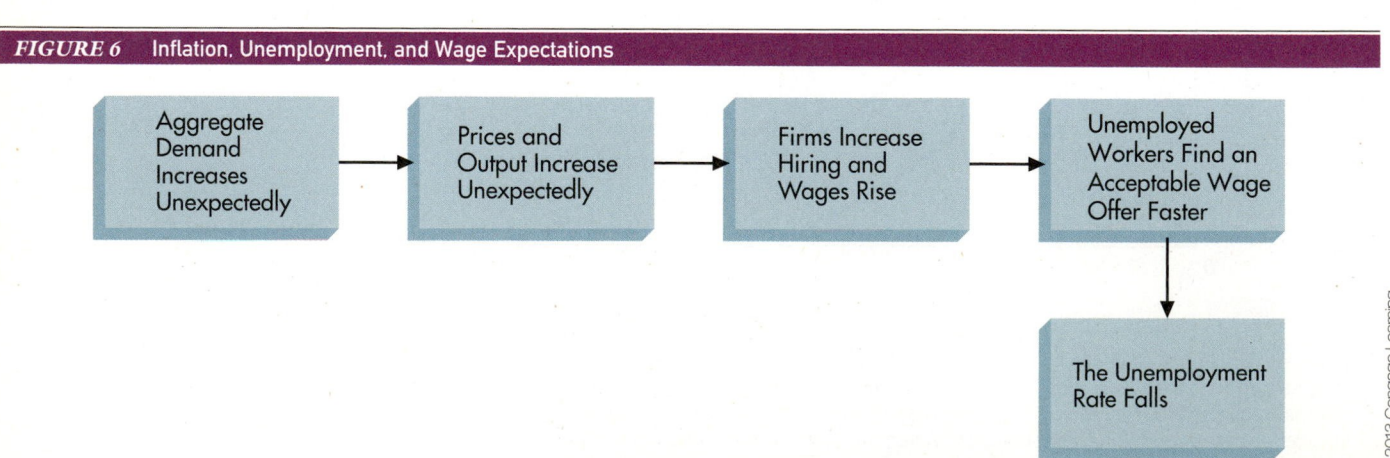

© 2013 Cengage Learning

higher real wage, his reservation wage goes up to $110.25 (5 percent more than $105). Now if employers offer him $105, he refuses and keeps searching.

In Figure 5, an expected increase in inflation moves us from point 1 on curve I to point 3 on curve II. When increased inflation is expected, the reservation wage reflects the higher rate of inflation, and there is no tradeoff between inflation and the unemployment rate. Instead, the economy moves along the long-run Phillips curve, with unemployment at its natural rate. The clockwise movement from point 1 to point 2 to point 3 is the pattern that follows an unexpected increase in aggregate demand.

What if the inflation rate is lower than expected? Here we find a reservation wage that reflects higher expected inflation. This means that those people who are looking for jobs are going to have a difficult time finding acceptable wage offers, the number of unemployed workers is going to increase, and the unemployment rate is going to rise. This sequence is shown in Figure 5 as the economy moves from point 3 to point 4. When the actual inflation rate is 6 percent and the expected inflation rate is also 6 percent, the economy is operating at the natural rate of unemployment. When the inflation rate falls to 3 percent but workers still expect 6 percent inflation, the unemployment rate rises (at point 4 along curve II). Eventually, if the inflation rate remains at 3 percent, workers adjust their expectations to the lower rate and the economy moves to point 1 on curve I. The short-run effect of unexpected *disinflation* is rising unemployment. Over time, the short-run increase in the unemployment rate is eliminated.

As long as the actual rate of inflation equals the expected rate, the economy remains at the natural rate of unemployment. The tradeoff between inflation and the unemployment rate comes from unexpected inflation.

> *As long as the actual rate of inflation equals the expected rate, the economy operates at the natural rate of unemployment.*

2.a.2. Inventory Fluctuations and Unemployment
Businesses hold inventories based on what they expect their sales to be. When aggregate demand is greater than expected, inventories fall below the targeted levels. To restore inventories to the levels wanted, production is increased. Increased production leads to increased employment. If aggregate demand is lower than expected, inventories rise above the targeted levels. To reduce inventories, production is cut back and workers are laid off from their jobs until sales have lowered the unwanted inventories. Once production increases, employment rises again.

Inventory, production, and employment all play a part in the Phillips curve analysis (Figure 7). Expected sales and inventory levels are based on an expected level of aggregate demand. If aggregate demand is greater than expected, inventories fall and prices of the remaining goods in stock rise. With the unexpected increase in inflation, the unemployment rate falls as businesses hire more workers to increase output to offset falling inventories. This sequence represents movement along a short-run Phillips curve because there is a tradeoff between inflation and the unemployment rate. We find the same tradeoff if aggregate demand is lower than expected. Here inventories increase and prices are lower than anticipated. With the unexpected decrease in inflation, the unemployment rate goes up as workers are laid off to reduce output until inventory levels fall.

> *When aggregate demand is higher than expected, inventories are lower than expected and prices are higher than expected, so the unemployment rate falls. When aggregate demand is lower than expected, inventories are higher than expected and prices are lower than expected, so the unemployment rate rises.*

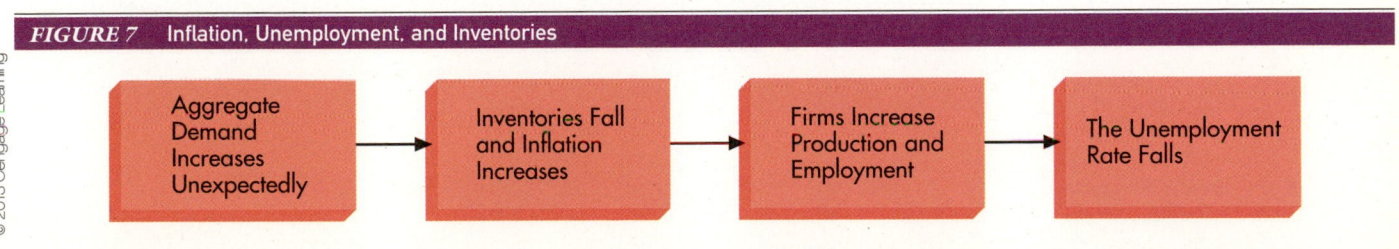

FIGURE 7   Inflation, Unemployment, and Inventories

Aggregate Demand Increases Unexpectedly → Inventories Fall and Inflation Increases → Firms Increase Production and Employment → The Unemployment Rate Falls

© 2013 Cengage Learning

2.a.3. Wage Contracts and Unemployment

Another factor that explains the short-run tradeoff between inflation and unemployment is labor contracts that fix wages for an extended period of time. When an existing contract expires, management must renegotiate with labor. A firm that is facing lower demand for its products may negotiate lower wages in order to keep as many workers employed as before. If the demand for a firm's products falls while a wage contract is in force, the firm must maintain wages; this means that it is going to have to lay off workers.

For example, a pizza restaurant with $1,000 a day in revenues employs 4 workers at $40 a day each. The firm's total labor costs are $160 a day. Suppose revenues fall to $500 a day. If the firm wants to cut its labor costs in half, to $80, it has two choices: It can maintain wages at $40 a day and lay off 2 workers, or it can lower wages to $20 a day and keep all 4 workers. If the restaurant has a contract with the employees that sets wages at $40 a day, it must lay off 2 workers.

If demand increases while a wage contract is in force, a business hires more workers at the fixed wage. Once the contract expires, the firm's workers will negotiate higher wages, to reflect the increased demand. For instance, suppose prices in the economy, including the price of pizzas, go up 10 percent. If the pizza restaurant can raise its prices 10 percent and sell as many pizzas as before (because the price of every other food also has gone up 10 percent), its daily revenues increase from $1,000 to $1,100. If the restaurant has a labor contract that fixes wages at $40 a day, its profits are going to go up, reflecting the higher price of pizzas. With its increased profits, the restaurant may be willing to hire more workers. Once the labor contract expires, the workers ask for a 10 percent wage increase to match the price level increase. If wages go up to $44 a day (10 percent higher than $40), the firm cannot hire more workers because wages have gone up in proportion to the increase in prices. If the costs of doing business rise at the same rate as prices, both profits and employment remain the same.

In the national economy, wage contracts are staggered; they expire at different times. Only 30 to 40 percent of all contracts expire each year across the entire economy. As economic conditions change, firms with expiring wage contracts can adjust *wages* to those conditions, whereas firms with existing contracts must adjust *employment* to those conditions.

How do long-term wage contracts tie in with the Phillips curve analysis? The expected rate of inflation is based on expected aggregate demand and is reflected in the wage that is agreed on in the contract. When the actual rate of inflation equals the expected rate, businesses retain the same number of workers that they had planned on when they signed the contract. For the economy overall, when actual and expected inflation rates are the same, the economy is operating at the natural rate of unemployment. That is, businesses are not hiring new workers because of an unexpected increase in aggregate demand, and they are not laying off workers because of an unexpected decrease in aggregate demand.

When aggregate demand is higher than expected, those firms with unexpired wage contracts hire more workers at the fixed wage, reducing unemployment (Figure 8).

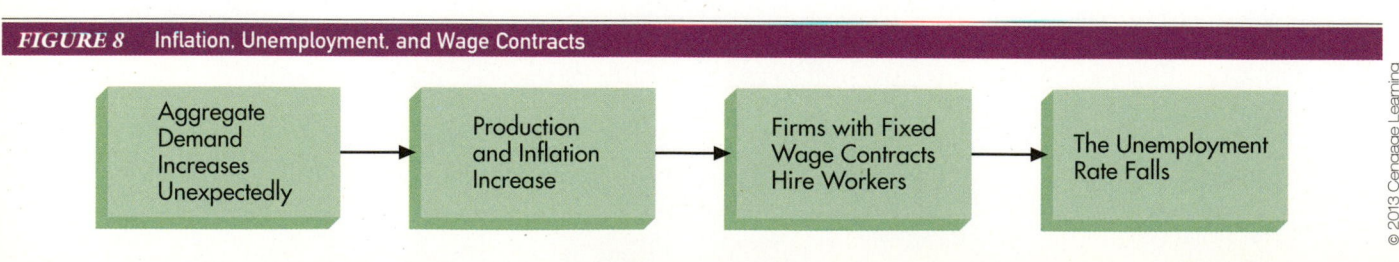

FIGURE 8   Inflation. Unemployment. and Wage Contracts

Aggregate Demand Increases Unexpectedly → Production and Inflation Increase → Firms with Fixed Wage Contracts Hire Workers → The Unemployment Rate Falls

© 2013 Cengage Learning

ECONOMIC INSIGHT

Why Wages Don't Fall During Recessions

A look at macroeconomic data across countries reveals that, when economies experience recessions, unemployment rates rise, but wages fall very little, if at all. If we think of a supply and demand diagram for labor, we would think that as demand for labor falls in a recession, both the equilibrium quantity of labor and the equilibrium price, the wage rate, would fall. We do see the quantity effect, as workers lose their jobs and the unemployment rate rises. Why don't we see wages falling also?

The text discusses long-term labor contracts as one reason why wages may be relatively inflexible over time. Beyond the presence of contracts, recent research points to human behavior as a contributing factor. Surveys of firms and workers indicate that worker morale is a major reason why wages are not reduced during recessions. Workers would view a wage cut as an indication that the firm does not value their work as much, and they might, therefore, suffer lower morale, with the result being lower effort.

When some workers are laid off, those workers suffer from the job loss, but they are no longer at the firm and thus cannot harm morale and work effort. Only in cases where the very survival of the firm is clearly at stake do wage cuts appear to be acceptable to workers.

So wages are "sticky downwards" because this promotes good worker effort and ensures that workers and firms share the same goals of efficient production and profit maximization. Rather than keep all workers when demand falls by paying lower wages to all, it may be better for the firm to lay off some workers and keep paying the remaining employees the same wage as before.

Sources: Truman F. Bewley, *Why Wages Don't Fall During a Recession* (Cambridge: Harvard University Press, 1999), and Peter Howitt, "Looking Inside the Labor Market: A Review Article," *Journal of Economic Literature*, March 2002.

Those firms with expiring contracts have to offer higher wages in order to maintain the existing level of employment at the new demand condition. When aggregate demand is lower than expected, those firms with unexpired contracts have to lay off workers because they cannot lower the wage, while those firms with expiring contracts negotiate lower wages in order to keep their workers.

If wages were always flexible, unexpected changes in aggregate demand might be reflected largely in *wage* rather than *employment* adjustments. Wage contracts force businesses to adjust employment when aggregate demand changes unexpectedly. The Economic Insight "Why Wages Don't Fall During Recessions" addresses this issue further.

> *Wage contracts force businesses to adjust employment rather than wages in response to an unexpected change in aggregate demand.*

2.b. Forming Expectations

Expectations play a key role in explaining the short-run Phillips curve, the tradeoff between inflation and the unemployment rate. How are these expectations formed?

 4 How are macroeconomic expectations formed?

2.b.1. Adaptive Expectations
Expectations can be formed solely on the basis of experience. **Adaptive expectations** are expectations that are determined by what has happened in the recent past.

People learn from their experiences. For example, suppose the inflation rate has been 3 percent for the past few years. Based on past experience, then, people expect the inflation rate in the future to remain at 3 percent. If the Federal Reserve increases the growth of the money supply to a rate that produces 6 percent inflation, the public will be surprised by the higher rate of inflation. This unexpected inflation creates a short-run tradeoff between inflation and the unemployment rate along a short-run Phillips curve. Over time, if the inflation rate remains at 6 percent, the public will learn that the 3 percent rate is too low and will adapt its expectations to the actual, higher inflation rate.

adaptive expectation
An expectation formed on the basis of information collected in the past.

Once public expectations have adapted to the new rate of inflation, the economy returns to the natural rate of unemployment along the long-run Phillips curve.

2.b.2. Rational Expectations

rational expectation
An expectation that is formed using all available relevant information.

Many economists believe that adaptive expectations are too narrow. If people look only at past information, they are ignoring what could be important information in the current period. **Rational expectations** are based on all available relevant information.

We are not saying that people have to know everything in order to form expectations. Rational expectations require only that people consider all the information that they believe to be relevant. This information includes their past experience, but also what is currently happening and what they expect to happen in the future. For instance, in forming expectations about inflation, people consider rates in the recent past, current policy, and anticipated shifts in aggregate demand and supply that could affect the future rate of inflation.

If the inflation rate has been 3 percent over the past few years, adaptive expectations suggest that the future inflation rate will be 3 percent. No other information is considered. Rational expectations are based on more than the historical rate. Suppose the Fed announces a new policy that everyone believes will increase inflation in the future. With rational expectations, the effect of this announcement will be considered. Thus, when the actual rate of inflation turns out to be more than 3 percent, there is no short-run tradeoff between inflation and the unemployment rate. The economy moves directly along the long-run Phillips curve to the higher inflation rate, while unemployment remains at the natural rate.

RECAP

1. Wage expectations, inventory fluctuations, and wage contracts help explain the short-run tradeoff between inflation and the unemployment rate.

2. The reservation wage is the minimum wage that a worker is willing to accept.

3. Because wage expectations reflect expected inflation, when the inflation rate is surprisingly high, unemployed workers find jobs faster and the unemployment rate falls.

4. Unexpected increases in aggregate demand lower inventories and raise prices. To increase output (to replenish shrinking inventories), businesses hire more workers, which reduces the unemployment rate.

5. When aggregate demand is higher than expected, those businesses with wage contracts hire more workers at the fixed wage, lowering unemployment.

6. If wages were always flexible, unexpected changes in aggregate demand would be reflected in wage adjustments rather than employment adjustments.

7. Adaptive expectations are formed on the basis of information about the past.

8. Rational expectations are formed using all available relevant information.

3. Credibility and Time Inconsistency

The rate of inflation is a product of growth in the money supply. That growth is controlled by the country's central bank. If the Federal Reserve follows a policy of rapidly increasing the money supply, one consequence is rapid inflation. If it follows a policy of slow growth, it keeps inflation down.

To help the public predict the future course of monetary policy, Congress passed the Federal Reserve Reform Act (1977) and the Full Employment and Balanced Growth

Act (1978). The Full Employment Act requires that the chairman of the Board of Governors of the Federal Reserve System testify before Congress semiannually about the Fed's targets for money growth, along with other policy plans.

Of course, the Fed's plans are only plans. There is no requirement that the central bank actually follow the plans it announces to Congress. During the course of the year, the Fed may decide that a new policy is necessary in light of economic developments. Changing conditions mean that plans can be **time inconsistent**. A plan is time inconsistent when it is changed over time in response to changed conditions.

time inconsistent
A characteristic of a policy or plan that changes over time in response to changing conditions.

3.a. The Policymaker's Problem

Time inconsistency gives the Fed a credibility problem and the public the problem of guessing where monetary policy and the inflation rate are actually heading. Figure 9 shows an example of how announced monetary policy can turn out to be time inconsistent. The Fed, like all central banks, always announces that it plans to follow a low-money-growth policy to promote a low rate of inflation. (It is unlikely that a central bank would ever state that it intends to follow an inflationary monetary policy.) Yet we know that the world is often characterized by higher rates of inflation. Because the actual inflation rate often ends up being higher than the intended inflation rate, low-inflation plans often are time inconsistent.

In Figure 9, labor contracts are signed following the central bank's announcement. The contracts call for either low-wage increases or high-wage increases. If everyone believes that the money supply is going to grow at the announced low rate, then the low-wage contracts are signed. However, if there is reason to believe that the announced policy is time inconsistent, the high-wage contracts are signed.

Over time, the central bank either follows the announced low-money-growth policy or implements a high-money-growth policy. If the low-wage contract is in force and the central bank follows the low-money-growth policy, the actual inflation rate will match the low rate that people expected, and the unemployment rate will equal the natural rate. If the central bank follows a high-money-growth policy, the rate of inflation will be higher than expected, and the unemployment rate will fall below the natural rate.

If the high-wage contract is in force and the low-money-growth policy is followed, the inflation rate will be lower than expected, and the unemployment rate will exceed the natural rate. If the high-money-growth policy is followed, the inflation rate will be as expected, and the unemployment will be at the natural rate.

Look at what happens to unemployment. Regardless of which labor contract is signed, if the central bank wants to keep unemployment as low as possible, it must deviate from its announced plan. The plan turns out to be time inconsistent. Because the public knows that unemployment, like the rate of inflation, is a factor in the Fed's policy-making, the central bank's announced plan is not credible.

3.b. Credibility

If the public does not believe the low-money-growth plans of the central bank, high-wage contracts will always be signed, and the central bank will always have to follow a high-money-growth policy to maintain the natural rate of unemployment. This cycle creates an economy in which high inflation persists year after year. If the central bank always followed its announced plan of low money growth and low inflation, the public would believe the plan, low-wage contracts would always be signed, and the natural rate of unemployment would exist at the low rate of inflation. In either case, high or low inflation, if the inflation rate is at the expected level, the unemployment rate does not change. If the central bank eliminates the goal of reducing unemployment below the natural rate, the problem of inflation disappears. However, the public must be convinced

 5 What makes government policies credible?

FIGURE 9   Time Inconsistency: An Example

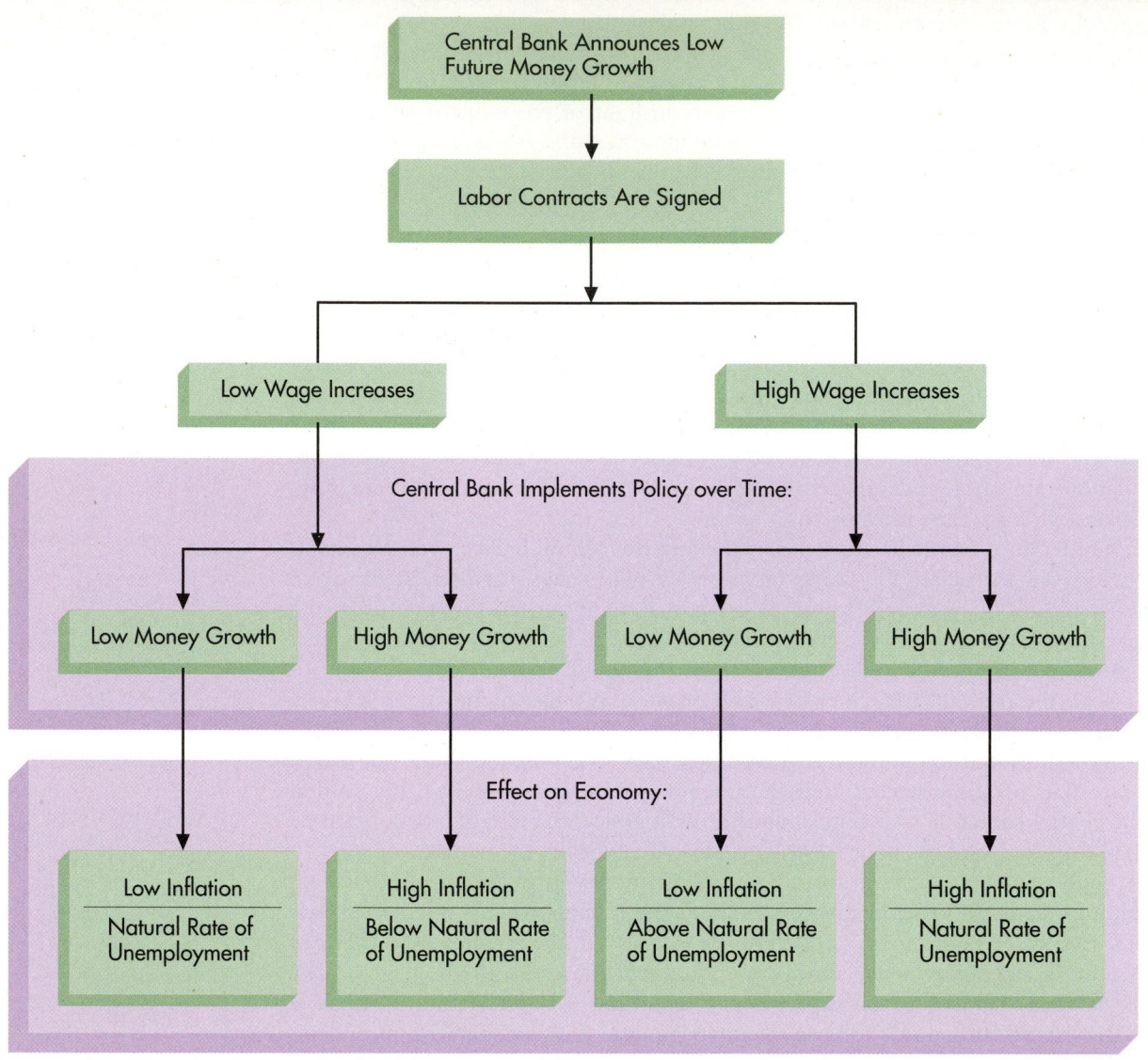

Regardless of which labor contract is signed, the central bank achieves the lowest unemployment rate by following the high-money-growth policy—the opposite of its announced policy.

that the central bank intends to pursue low money growth in the long run, avoiding the temptation to reduce the unemployment rate in the short run.

How does the central bank achieve credibility? One way is to fix the growth rate of the money supply by law. Congress could pass a law requiring that the Fed maintain a growth rate of, say, 3 to 5 percent a year. There would be problems in defining the money supply, but this kind of law would give the Fed's policies credibility.

In the past decade, central banks around the world have increasingly turned to inflation targeting as a manner of achieving credibility. By establishing a publicly announced target for inflation, the public can anticipate what policy will be by knowing whether the inflation rate is above or below the target. For instance, some banks target a particular inflation rate—for example, the Bank of England targets a rate of 2 percent. Other banks target a range for inflation—for example, the European Central Bank's target of near or below 2 percent, as well as the Bank of Canada's 1–3 percent. The Federal Reserve does not announce an official inflation target, but it is believed by many that an inflation rate in the range of 1–2 percent is implicit in Fed policy.

A key for establishing credibility is to create incentives for monetary authorities to take a long-term view of monetary policy. In the long run, the economy is better off if policymakers do not try to exploit the short-run tradeoff between inflation and the unemployment rate. The central bank can achieve a lower rate of inflation at the natural rate of unemployment by avoiding unexpected increases in the rate at which money and inflation grow.

Reputation is a key factor here. If the central bank considers the effects of its actual policy on public expectations, it will find it easier to achieve low inflation by establishing a reputation for low-inflation policies. A central bank with a reputation for time-consistent plans will find that labor contracts will call for low-wage increases because people believe that the bank is going to follow its announced plans and generate a low rate of inflation. In other words, by maintaining a reputation for following through on its announced policy, the Fed can earn the public confidence necessary to produce a low rate of inflation in the long run.

RECAP

1. A plan is time inconsistent when it changes over time in response to changing conditions.

2. If the public believes that an announced policy is time inconsistent, policymakers have a credibility problem that can limit the success of their plans.

3. Credibility can be achieved by fixing the growth rate of the money supply by law or by creating incentives for policymakers to follow through on their announced plans.

4. Sources of Business Cycles

In the chapter titled "Fiscal Policy," we examined the effect of fiscal policy on the equilibrium level of real GDP. Changes in government spending and taxes can expand or contract the economy. In the chapter titled "Monetary Policy," we described how monetary policy affects the equilibrium level of real GDP. Changes in the money supply can also produce booms and recessions. In addition to the policy-induced sources of business cycles covered in earlier chapters, there are other sources of economic fluctuations that economists have studied. One is the election campaign of incumbent politicians; when a business cycle results from this action, it is called a *political business cycle*. Macroeconomic policy may be used to promote the reelection of incumbent politicians. We also examine another source of business cycles that is not related to discretionary policy actions, the *real business cycle*.

4.a. The Political Business Cycle

If a short-run tradeoff exists between inflation and unemployment, an incumbent administration could stimulate the economy just before an election to lower the unemployment rate, making voters happy and increasing the probability of reelection. Of course, after the election, the long-run adjustment to the expansionary policy would lead to higher inflation and move unemployment back to the natural rate.

Figure 10 illustrates the pattern. Before the election, the economy is initially at point 1 in Figure 10(a) and Figure 10(b). The incumbent administration stimulates the

 6 Are business cycles related to political elections?

FIGURE 10   The Political Business Cycle

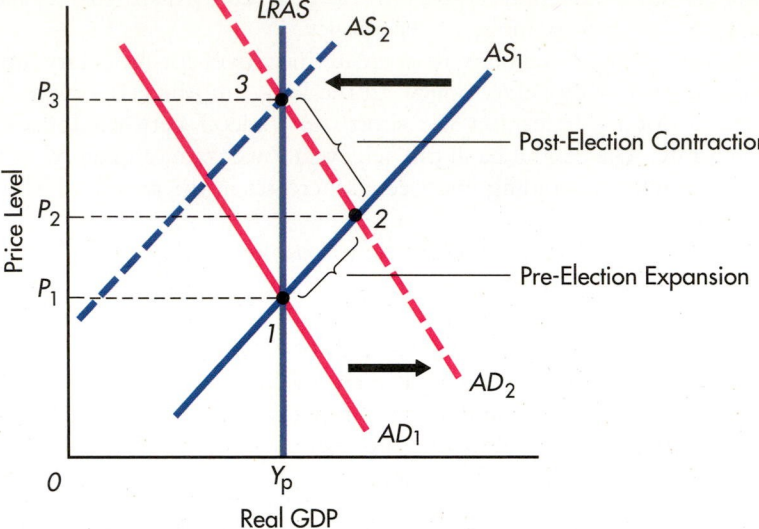

(a) Aggregate Demand and Supply

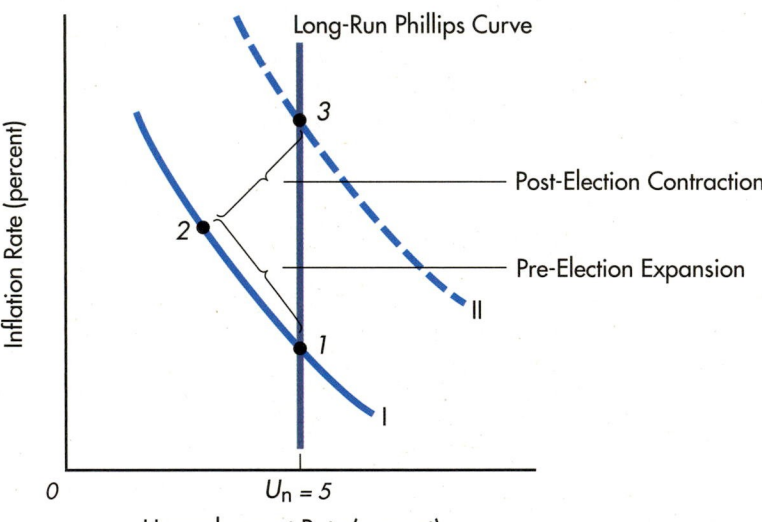

(b) Phillips Curve

Before the election, the government stimulates the economy, unexpectedly increasing aggregate demand. The economy moves from point 1 to point 2, pushing equilibrium real GDP above Y_p (Figure 10[a]) and the unemployment rate below U_n (Figure 10[b]). The incumbent politicians hope that rising incomes and lower unemployment will translate into votes. After the election comes adjustment to the higher aggregate demand, as the economy moves from point 2 to point 3. The aggregate supply curve shifts to the left, and equilibrium real GDP falls back to Y_p. Unemployment goes back up to U_n, and the rate of inflation rises.

© 2013 Cengage Learning

economy by increasing government spending or increasing the growth of the money supply. Aggregate demand shifts from AD_1 to AD_2 in Figure 10(a). In the short run, the increase in aggregate demand is unexpected, so the economy moves along the initial aggregate supply curve (AS_1) to point 2. This movement is reflected in Figure 10(b) of the figure, in the movement from point 1 to point 2 along short-run Phillips curve I. The pre-election expansionary policy increases real GDP and lowers the unemployment rate. Once the public adjusts its expectations to the higher inflation rate, the economy experiences a recession. Real GDP falls back to its potential level (Y_p), and the unemployment rate goes back up to the natural rate (U_n), as shown by the movement from point 2 to point 3 in both parts of the figure.

An unexpected increase in government spending or money growth temporarily stimulates the economy. If an election comes during the period of expansion, higher incomes and lower unemployment may increase support for the incumbent administration. The long-run adjustment back to potential real GDP and the natural rate of unemployment comes after the election.

Economists do not agree on whether a political business cycle exists in the United States. But they do agree that an effort to exploit the short-run tradeoff between inflation and the unemployment rate would shift the short-run Phillips curve out, as shown in Figure 10(b).

The evidence for a political business cycle is not clear. If government macroeconomic policy is designed to stimulate the economy before elections and to bear the costs of rising unemployment and inflation after elections, we should see recessions regularly following national elections. Table 1 lists the presidential elections since 1948 along with the recessions that followed them. In six cases, a recession occurred the year after an election. A recession began before President Kennedy's election, and there was no recession during the Johnson, second Reagan, and Clinton administrations. Of course, just because recessions do not follow every election does not guarantee that some business cycles have not stemmed from political manipulation. If a short-run Phillips curve exists, the potential for a political business cycle exists as long as the public does not expect the government to stimulate the economy before elections.

TABLE 1	Presidential Elections and U.S. Recessions, 1948–2009
Presidential Election (Winner)	**Next Recession**
November 1948 (Truman)	November 1948–October 1949
November 1952 (Eisenhower)	June 1953–May 1954
November 1956 (Eisenhower)	June 1957–April 1958
November 1960 (Kennedy)	April 1960–February 1961
November 1964 (Johnson)	
November 1968 (Nixon)	October 1969–November 1970
November 1972 (Nixon)	December 1973–March 1975
November 1976 (Carter)	January 1980–July 1980
November 1980 (Reagan)	May 1981–November 1982
November 1984 (Reagan)	
November 1988 (G. H. W. Bush)	July 1990–March 1991
November 1992 (Clinton)	
November 1996 (Clinton)	
November 2000 (G. W. Bush)	March 2001–November 2001
November 2004 (G. W. Bush)	December 2007—June 2009
November 2008 (Obama)	

7 How do real shocks to the economy affect business cycles?

shock
An unexpected change in a variable.

4.b. Real Business Cycles

In recent years, economists have paid increasing attention to real **shocks**—unexpected changes—to the economy as a source of business cycles. Many believe that it is not only fiscal or monetary policy that triggers expansion or contraction in the economy, but also technological change, change in tastes, labor strikes, weather, war, terrorism, or other real changes. A real business cycle is one that is generated by a change in one of those real variables.

Interest in the real business cycle was stimulated by the oil price shocks in the early 1970s and the important role they played in triggering the recession of 1973–1975. At that time, many economists were focusing on the role of unexpected changes in monetary policy in generating business cycles. They argued that these kinds of policy changes (changes in a nominal variable, the money supply) were responsible for the shifts in aggregate demand that led to expansions and contractions. When OPEC raised oil prices, it caused major shifts in aggregate supply. Higher oil prices in 1973 and 1974, and in 1979 and 1980, reduced aggregate supply, pushing the equilibrium level of real GDP down. Lower oil prices in 1986 raised aggregate supply and equilibrium real GDP.

An economy-wide real shock, like a substantial change in the price of oil, can affect output and employment across all sectors of the economy. Even an industry-specific shock can generate a recession or expansion in the entire economy if the industry produces a product used by a substantial number of other industries. For example, a labor strike in the steel industry would have major recessionary implications for the economy as a whole. If the output of steel fell, the price of steel would be bid up by all the industries that use steel as an input. This would shift the short-run aggregate supply curve to the left, as shown in Figure 11(a), and would move equilibrium real GDP from Y_1 down to Y_2.

Real shocks can also have expansionary effects on the economy. Suppose that the weather is particularly good one year, so that harvests are surprisingly large. What

Extreme weather can be a source of real business-cycle fluctuations. Hurricane Katrina destroyed some of the capital stock of the nation along the Gulf Coast and was associated with a temporary reduction in output.

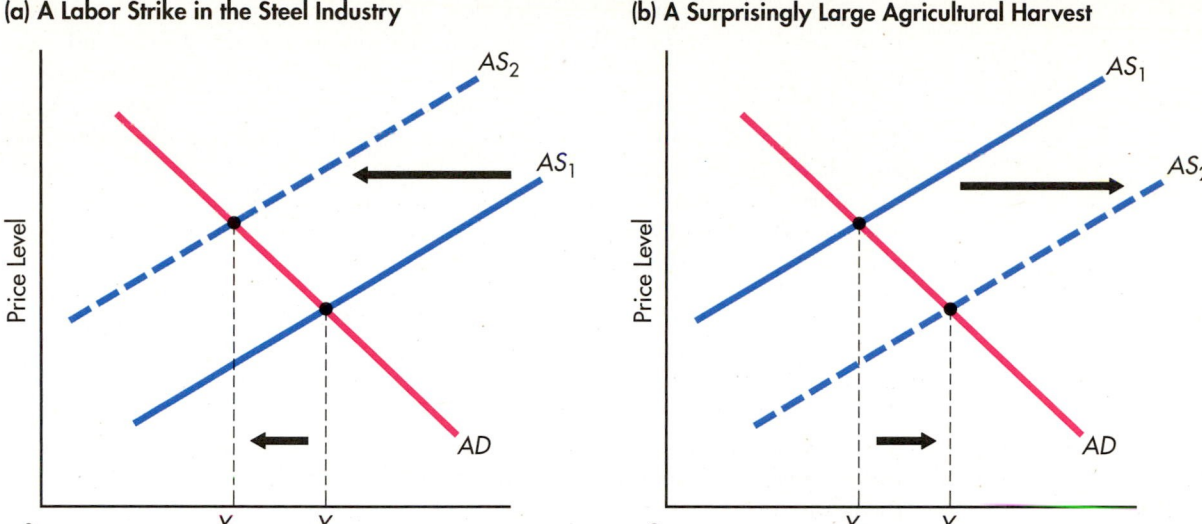

FIGURE 11 The Impact of Real Shocks on Equilibrium Real GDP

A labor strike in a key industry can shift the aggregate supply curve to the left, like the shift from AS_1 to AS_2. This pushes equilibrium real GDP down from Y_1 to Y_2.

If good weather leads to a banner harvest, the aggregate supply curve shifts to the right, like the shift from AS_1 to AS_2, raising equilibrium real GDP from Y_1 to Y_2.

happens? The price of food, cotton, and other agricultural output tends to fall, and the short-run aggregate supply curve shifts to the right, as shown in Figure 11(b), raising equilibrium real GDP from Y_1 to Y_2.

Real business cycles explain why national output can expand or contract in the absence of a discretionary macroeconomic policy that would shift aggregate demand. To fully understand business cycles, we must consider both policy-induced changes in real GDP, as covered in the chapters titled "Fiscal Policy" and "Monetary Policy," and real shocks that occur independent of government actions.

> *A business cycle can be the product of discretionary government policy or of real shocks that occur independent of government actions.*

4.c. Output Volatility

Since the mid-1980s, U.S. output growth had become noticeably less volatile prior to the financial crisis and the associated global recession that began in 2007. Some economists have referred to this period of relatively low variability of real GDP growth as the "Great Moderation." The global recession beginning in 2007 ended this "moderation" in the volatility of real GDP. Why was output growth so stable prior to this most recent recession, and what should determine how volatile real GDP is? Several factors, which are also important determinants of output volatility, may have contributed to the moderation of real GDP prior to 2007.

4.c.1. Better Inventory Management
Research suggests that at least part of the dampening of real GDP growth fluctuations is due to advances in inventory management techniques, made possible by improvements in information technology and communications. Inventories do not fluctuate as much as they used to, because firms are now able to order what they want to hold in inventory with relatively short lags for delivery. This means that they can hold less inventory and respond to changes in sales as

needed. In the past, inventory management was aimed at managing with longer delivery times, and so firms tended to hold larger inventories than they expected to need in order to avoid being caught short if sales were greater than expected. In this earlier environment, if sales were lower than expected, then orders for new goods, and consequently production, dropped dramatically in order to allow inventories to be reduced over time to match the lower level of sales. If sales were much higher than expected, inventories dropped to very low levels until firms could restock to catch up with sales. Today, firms are able to receive shipments of new inventory with a much shorter delay; "just in time" inventory management allows firms to adjust inventories to changing business conditions quickly. This has helped level out both inventories and overall production of goods and has contributed to lower real output volatility.

4.c.2. Changes in Financial Markets

Prior to the early 1980s, the maximum rate of interest that U.S. banks could pay on deposits was limited by a Federal Reserve regulation known as *Regulation Q*. Thus, when interest rates rose above what banks could pay, people would withdraw money from banks and seek higher interest rates elsewhere. This forced banks to reduce their lending on things like home mortgages. As a result, investment in residential housing was much more volatile during the era prior to the removal of the ceiling on interest rates. In addition to changes in financial market regulations, which contribute to less output volatility, more and better financial products have become available to help people smooth their consumption across fluctuations in income. The greater availability of financial products for saving and borrowing has resulted in less variability in consumer spending over time, which in turn contributes to less variability in real output.

The financial crisis beginning in 2007 revealed that some financial products and lending practices, which had been developed during the good times in the earlier part of the decade, created excessive borrowing and risk taking. This tendency was sharply reversed during the financial crisis: Banks dramatically reduced credit availability, cut lending, and tightened credit policies in an attempt to improve the quality of their loans. Financial innovation can help business firms and households smooth consumption against income fluctuations and reduce volatility. However, prudent regulation of financial institutions and adequate controls on lending practices are necessary to avoid financial crises that lead to greater volatility.

4.c.3. Improved Macroeconomic Policy

The belief in a tradeoff between inflation and unemployment, as suggested by the Phillips curve of the 1960s in Figure 1, led policymakers to try to exploit this tradeoff. Their attempts to stimulate the economy resulted in higher inflation, and when they tightened policy to restrain inflation, real output contracted. In the 1980s, it was generally acknowledged that such a tradeoff was probably not easily exploitable, if it was exploitable at all. This realization led to more stable macroeconomic policy, which contributed to less variability in real output.

4.c.4. Good Luck

The real-business-cycle approach emphasizes real shocks to the economy as an important catalyst of business-cycle fluctuations. From the mid-1980s, real economic shocks tended to be less severe than in earlier times. For instance, the oil price shocks of the 1970s were much more destabilizing than more recent oil price shocks. In addition, shifts in productivity were much more pronounced in earlier decades than during the last 20 years. If good luck with regard to the size and impact of real shocks was important in explaining the Great Moderation, such luck does not continue forever: It is not surprising that, eventually, the variability of real output growth increased in 2007–2009.

It is important to realize that there is disagreement among economists as to the causes of the reduction in the variability of real output growth that occurred prior to the financial crisis. It is also possible that all the explanations offered are not independent, and that each has been partly affected by the others. For instance, if monetary policy has become better over time and has contributed to low and stable inflation, then even major real economic shocks should not lead to big changes in inflation, which means that the effects of the shocks could be more moderate than in earlier times. Only time will tell whether the reduction in the growth of real output volatility is a permanent or a temporary economic phenomenon.

RECAP

1. The political business cycle is a short-term expansion stimulated by an administration before an election to earn votes. After the election comes the long-term adjustment (rising unemployment and inflation).

2. A real business cycle is an expansion and contraction caused by a change in tastes or technology, strikes, weather, or other real factors.

3. Prior to the recent financial crisis, the growth rate of real output was much less volatile in the 1980s and 1990s than in earlier decades. Reasons given include better inventory management, development of financial markets, better macroeconomic policy, and smaller real shocks.

5. The Link between Monetary and Fiscal Policies

In earlier chapters, we described how monetary and fiscal policies determine the equilibrium level of prices and national income. In our discussions, we have talked about monetary policy and fiscal policy individually. Here we consider the relationship between them.

In some countries, monetary and fiscal policies are carried out by a single central authority. Even in the United States, where the Federal Reserve was created as an independent agency, monetary policy and fiscal policy are always related. The actions of the central bank have an impact on the proper role of fiscal policy, and the actions of fiscal policymakers have an impact on the proper role of monetary policy.

For example, suppose the central bank follows a monetary policy that raises interest rates. That policy raises the interest cost of new government debt, in the process increasing government expenditures. On the other hand, a fiscal policy that generates large fiscal deficits could contribute to higher interest rates. If the central bank has targeted an interest rate that lies below the current rate, the central bank could be drawn into an expansionary monetary policy. This interdependence of monetary and fiscal policy is important to policymakers, and also to businesspeople and others who seek to understand current economic developments.

5.a. The Government Budget Constraint

The *government budget constraint* clarifies the relationship between monetary and fiscal policies:

$$G = T + B + \Delta M$$

where:

G = government spending

T = tax revenue

B = government borrowing

ΔM = change in the money supply[1]

The government budget constraint always holds because there are only three ways for the government to finance its spending: by taxing, by borrowing, and by creating money.

8 How is inflationary monetary policy related to government fiscal policy?

---

[1] The M in the government budget constraint is government-issued money (usually called base money or high-powered money). It is easiest to think of this kind of money as currency, although in practice base money includes more than currency.

We can rewrite the government budget constraint with the change in M on the left-hand side of the equation:

$$\Delta M = (G - T) - B$$

In this form, you can see that the change in government-issued money equals the government fiscal deficit $(G - T)$ minus borrowing. This equation is always true. A government that has the ability to borrow at reasonable costs will not have the incentive to create rapid money growth and the consequent inflation that results in order to finance its budget deficit.

5.b. Monetary Reforms

In the United States and other industrial nations, monetary and fiscal policies are conducted by separate, independent agencies. Fiscal authorities (Congress and the president in the United States) cannot impose monetary policy on the central bank. But in some developing countries, monetary and fiscal policies are controlled by a central political authority. Here monetary policy is often an extension of fiscal policy. Fiscal policy can impose an inflationary burden on monetary policy. If a country is running a large fiscal deficit and much of this deficit cannot be financed by government borrowing, monetary authorities must create money to finance the deficit.

Creating money to finance fiscal deficits has produced very rapid rates of inflation in several countries. As prices reach astronomical levels, currency with very large face values must be issued. For instance, when Bolivia faced a sharp drop in the availability of willing lenders in the mid-1980s, the government began to create money to finance its fiscal deficit. As the money supply increased in relation to the output of goods and services, prices rose. In 1985, the government was creating money so fast that the rate of inflation reached 8,170 percent. Lunch in a La Paz hotel could cost 10 million Bolivian pesos. You can imagine the problem of counting money and recording money values with cash registers and calculators. As the rate of inflation increased, Bolivians had to carry stacks of currency to pay for goods and services. Eventually the government issued a 1 million peso note, then 5 million and 10 million peso notes.

This extremely high inflation, or hyperinflation, ended when a new government introduced its economic program in August 1985. The program reduced government spending dramatically, which slowed the growth of the fiscal deficit. At the same time, a monetary reform was introduced. A **monetary reform** is a new monetary policy that includes the introduction of a new monetary unit. The central bank of Bolivia announced that it would restrict money creation and introduced a new currency, the boliviano, in January 1987. It set 1 boliviano equal to 1 million Bolivian pesos.

monetary reform
A new monetary policy that includes the introduction of a new monetary unit.

The new monetary unit, the boliviano, did not lower prices; it lowered the units in which prices were quoted. Lunch now cost 10 bolivianos instead of 10 million pesos. More important, the rate of inflation dropped abruptly.

Did the new unit of currency end the hyperinflation? No. The rate of inflation dropped because the new fiscal policy controls introduced by the government relieved the pressure on the central bank to create money in order to finance government spending. Remember the government budget constraint: The only way to reduce the amount of money being created is to reduce the fiscal deficit $(G - T)$ minus borrowing (B). Once fiscal policy is under control, monetary reform is possible. If a government introduces a new monetary unit without changing its fiscal policy, the new monetary unit by itself has no lasting effect on the rate of inflation.

The introduction of a new monetary unit without a change in fiscal policy has no lasting effect on the rate of inflation.

The most dramatic hyperinflation in recent years, and one of the most dramatic ever, occurred in Zimbabwe in 2007–2008. While the government was not forthcoming about inflation data, research[2] indicates that the price index rose from a value of 1.00 in

[2] Steve H. Hanke, "R.I.P. Zimbabwe Dollar," www.cato.org/Zimbabwe

January 2007 to 853,000,000,000,000,000,000,000 by mid-November 2008, when the price level was doubling every 24 hours. As prices rose, the government issued larger and larger units of paper money as people had to carry huge stacks of old currency to buy anything. A 100 trillion Zimbabwe dollar bill was issued in January 2009. Then in the same month, the government sanctioned the use of U.S. dollars as a substitute currency in Zimbabwe as the local currency had become essentially worthless.

Table 2 lists monetary reforms enacted in recent years. Argentina had a monetary reform in June 1983. Yet by June 1985, another reform was needed. The inflationary problems that Argentina faced could not be solved just by issuing a new unit of currency. Fiscal reform also was needed, and none was made. In any circumstances involving inflationary monetary policy, monetary reform by itself is not enough. It must be coupled with a reduction in the fiscal deficit or an increase in government borrowing to produce a permanent change in the rate of inflation.

TABLE 2	Recent Monetary Reforms			
Country	**Old Currency**	**New Currency**	**Date of Change**	**Change**
Angola	Readjusted kwanza	Kwanza	December 1999	1 kwanza = 1,000,000 readjusted kwanza
Argentina	Peso	Peso argentino	June 1983	1 peso argentine = 10,000 pesos
	Peso argentino	Austral	June 1985	1 austra = 1,000 pesos argentino
	Austral	Peso argentino	January 1992	1 peso argentino = 10,000 australes
Bolivia	Peso	Boliviano	January 1987	1 boliviano = 1,000,000 pesos
Brazil	Cruzeiro	Cruzado	February 1986	1 cruzado = 1,000 cruzeiros
	Cruzado	New cruzado	January 1989	1 new cruzado = 1,000,000 cruzados
	New cruzado	Cruzeiro	March 1990	1 cruzeiro = 1 new cruzado
	Cruzeiro	Real	July 1994	1 real = 2,700 cruzeiros
Chile	Peso	Escudo	January 1969	1 escudo = 1,000 pesos
	Escudo	Peso	September 1975	1 peso = 1,000 escudos
Congo, D.R.	New Zaire	Congolese franc	June 1998	1 Congolese franc = 100,000 new Zaire
Georgia	Kuponi	Lari	September 1995	1 lari = 1,000,000 kuponi
Israel	Pound	Shekel	February 1980	1 shekel = 10 pounds
	Old shekel	New shekel	September 1985	1 new shekel = 1,000 old shekels
Mexico	Peso	New peso	January 1993	1 new peso = 1,000 pesos
Peru	Sol	Inti	February 1985	1 inti = 1,000 soles
	Inti	New Sol	July 1991	1 new sol = 1,000,000 intis
Poland	Zloty	New zloty	January 1995	1 new zloty = 10,000 zlotys
Russia	Ruble	New ruble	January 1998	1 new ruble = 1,000 rubles
Turkey	Lira	New Lira	January 2005	1 new lira = 1,000,000 lira
Ukraine	Karbovanets	Hryvnia	September 1996	1 hryvnia = 100,000 karbovanets
Uruguay	Old peso	New peso	July 1975	1 new peso = 1,000 old pesos
Yugoslavia	Dinar	New dinar	January 1994	1 new dinar = 13,000,000 dinars

Monetary policy is tied to fiscal policy through the government budget constraint. Although money creation is not an important source of deficit financing in developed countries, it has been and still is a significant source of revenue for developing countries, where taxes are difficult to collect and borrowing is limited.

RECAP

1. The government budget constraint ($G = T + B + \Delta M$) defines the relationship between fiscal and monetary policies.

2. The implications of fiscal policy for the growth of the money supply can be seen by rewriting the government budget constraint this way:

$$\Delta M = (G - T) - B$$

3. A monetary reform is a new monetary policy that includes the introduction of a new unit of currency.

4. A government can end an inflationary monetary policy only with a fiscal reform that lowers the fiscal deficit ($G - T$) minus borrowing (B).

SUMMARY

1. **Is there a tradeoff between inflation and the unemployment rate?**

   - The Phillips curve shows the relationship between inflation and the unemployment rate. §1

2. **How does the tradeoff between inflation and the unemployment rate vary from the short to the long run?**

   - In the long run, there is no tradeoff between inflation and the unemployment rate. §1.b

   - The long-run Phillips curve is a vertical line at the natural rate of unemployment. §1.b.2

3. **What is the relationship between unexpected inflation and the unemployment rate?**

   - Unexpected inflation can affect the unemployment rate through wage expectations, inventory fluctuations, and wage contracts. §2.a, 2.a.1, 2.a.2, 2.a.3

4. **How are macroeconomic expectations formed?**

   - Adaptive expectations are formed on the basis of past experience; rational expectations are formed on the basis of all available relevant information. §2.b.1, 2.b.2

5. **What makes government policies credible?**

   - A policy is credible only if it is time consistent. §3.b

6. **Are business cycles related to political elections?**

   - A political business cycle is created by politicians who want to improve their chances of reelection by stimulating the economy just before an election. §4.a

7. **How do real shocks to the economy affect business cycles?**

   - Real business cycles are the product of an unexpected change in technology, weather, or some other real variable. §4.b

8. **How is inflationary monetary policy related to government fiscal policy?**

   - The government budget constraint defines the relationship between monetary and fiscal policies. §5.a

   - When government-issued money is used to finance fiscal deficits, inflationary monetary policy can be a product of fiscal policy. §5.b

KEY TERMS

adaptive expectation, 323

monetary reform, 334

phillips curve, 313

rational expectation, 324

reservation wage, 319

shock, 330

time inconsistent, 325

EXERCISES

1. What is the difference between the short-run Phillips curve and the long-run Phillips curve? Use an aggregate supply and demand diagram to explain why there is a difference between them.
2. Give two reasons why there may be a short-run tradeoff between unexpected inflation and the unemployment rate.
3. "Unexpected increases in the money supply cause clockwise movements in the Phillips curve diagram; unexpected decreases in the money supply cause counterclockwise movements in the Phillips curve diagram." Evaluate this statement, using a graph to illustrate your answer.
4. Economists have identified two kinds of macroeconomic expectations.
   a. Define them.
   b. What are the implications for macroeconomic policy of these two forms of expectations?
5. Write down the government budget constraint and explain how it can be used to understand the relationship between fiscal and monetary policies.
6. Using the government budget constraint, explain:
   a. Why some countries experience hyperinflation.
   b. How fiscal policy must change in order to implement a noninflationary monetary policy.
7. Parents, like governments, establish credibility by seeing to it that their "policies" (the rules that they outline for their children) are time consistent. Analyze the potential for time consistency of these rules:
   a. If you don't eat the squash, you'll go to bed 30 minutes early tonight!
   b. If you get any grades below a C, you won't be allowed to watch television on school nights!
   c. If you don't go to my alma mater, I won't pay for your college education!
   d. If you marry that disgusting person, I'll disinherit you!
8. Suppose an economy has witnessed an 8 percent rate of growth in its money supply and prices over the last few years. How do you think the public will respond to an announced plan to increase the money supply by 4 percent over the next year if:
   a. The central bank has a reputation for always meeting its announced policy goals.
   b. The central bank rarely does what it says it will do.
9. What are the implications for the timing of business cycle fluctuations over the years if all business cycles are:
   a. Manipulated by incumbent administrations.
   b. A product of real shocks to the economy.
10. Suppose the Federal Reserve System were abolished and Congress assumed responsibility for monetary policy along with fiscal policy. What potential harm to the economy could result from such a change?
11. Suppose tax revenues equal $100 billion, government spending equals $130 billion, and the government borrows $25 billion. How much do you expect the money supply to increase, given the government budget constraint?
12. If the government budget deficit equals $240 billion and the money supply increases by $100 billion, how much must the government borrow?
13. Discuss how each of the following sources of real business cycles would affect the economy.
   a. Farmers go on strike for six months.
   b. Oil prices fall substantially.
   c. Particularly favorable weather increases agricultural output nationwide.
14. Using an aggregate demand and aggregate supply diagram, illustrate and explain how a political business cycle is created.
15. Use a Phillips curve diagram to illustrate and explain how a political business cycle is created.
16. What is the natural rate of unemployment? What can cause it to change over time?
17. Many developing countries have experienced high money growth rates and, consequently, high inflation. Use the government budget constraint to explain how a poor country that wants to increase

government spending can get into an inflationary situation.

18. What factors should affect the variability of the growth rate of real output? Which do you think could provide for more stability going forward, and which are likely to be less important?

19. Starting in 2011, the Federal Reserve chairman will participate in a quarterly press conference as part of a new strategy to increase communication with the public. Discuss the rationale behind such policy in light of expectations, expected versus unexpected inflation, and credibility.

You can find further practice tests in the Online Quiz at **www.cengage.com/economics/boyes**.

TESTIMONY OF CHAIRMAN BEN S. BERNANKE BEFORE THE JOINT ECONOMIC COMMITTEE, U.S. CONGRESS, WASHINGTON, D.C.

The Economic Outlook, May 5, 2009

Chair Maloney, Vice Chairman Schumer, Ranking Members Brownback and Brady, and other members of the Committee, I am pleased to be here today to offer my views on recent economic developments, the outlook for the economy, and current conditions in financial markets.

Recent Economic Developments

The U.S. economy has contracted sharply since last autumn, with real gross domestic product (GDP) having dropped at an annual rate of more than 6 percent in the fourth quarter of 2008 and the first quarter of this year. Among the enormous costs of the downturn is the loss of some 5 million payroll jobs over the past 15 months. The most recent information on the labor market—the number of new and continuing claims for unemployment insurance through late April—suggests that we are likely to see further sizable job losses and increased unemployment in coming months.

However, the recent data also suggest that the pace of contraction may be slowing, and they include some tentative signs that final demand, especially demand by households, may be stabilizing. Consumer spending, which dropped sharply in the second half of last year, grew in the first quarter. In coming months, households' spending power will be boosted by the fiscal stimulus program, and we have seen some improvement in consumer sentiment. Nonetheless, a number of factors are likely to continue to weigh on consumer spending, among them the weak labor market and the declines in equity and housing wealth that households have experienced over the past two years. In addition, credit conditions for consumers remain tight....

As economic activity weakened during the second half of 2008 and prices of energy and other commodities began to fall rapidly, inflationary pressures diminished appreciably. Weakness in demand and reduced cost pressures have continued to keep inflation low so far this year.... Core PCE inflation (prices excluding food and energy) dropped below an annual rate of 1 percent in the final quarter of 2008, when retailers and auto dealers marked down their prices significantly. In the first quarter of this year, core consumer price inflation moved back up, but to a still-low annual rate of 1.5 percent.

The Economic Outlook

We continue to expect economic activity to bottom out, then to turn up later this year. Key elements of this forecast are our assessments that the housing market is beginning to stabilize and that the sharp inventory liquidation that has been in progress will slow over the next few quarters. Final demand should also be supported by fiscal and monetary stimulus. An important caveat is that our forecast assumes continuing gradual repair of the financial system; a relapse in financial conditions would be a significant drag on economic activity and could cause the incipient recovery to stall.... Even after a recovery gets under way, the rate of growth of real economic activity is likely to remain below its longer-run potential for a while, implying that the current slack in resource utilization will increase further. We expect that the recovery will only gradually gain momentum and that economic slack will diminish slowly. In particular, businesses are likely to be cautious about hiring, implying that the unemployment rate could remain high for a time, even after economic growth resumes.

In this environment, we anticipate that inflation will remain low.

Indeed, given the sizable margin of slack in resource utilization and diminished cost pressures from oil and other commodities, inflation is likely to move down some over the next year relative to its pace in 2008. However, inflation expectations, as measured by various household and business surveys, appear to have remained relatively stable, which should limit further declines in inflation. . . .

Macroeconomic policy in the United States is determined by Congress, the presidential administration, and the Federal Reserve. Twice a year, the chairman of the Federal Reserve Board must testify before Congress on Fed monetary policy. The article reports an appearance in 2009 by Federal Reserve Chairman Ben Bernanke, which highlights some of the issues raised in this chapter.

The U.S. economy was in the deepest recession since the 1930s at the time of Bernanke's testimony. Unemployment was rising and inflation was low due to weak demand for goods and services. The issue of government credibility was highlighted by Bernanke's statement, "Inflation expectations, as measured by various household and business surveys, appear to have remained relatively stable, which should limit further declines in inflation." In other words, the Fed predicted that the United States would not experience a serious deflation from the recession because the public believed that inflation would remain low but positive due to Fed policies.

Bernanke highlighted the source of business cycles, saying, "Credit conditions for consumers remain tight." This condition is consistent with a recession associated with a financial crisis and a sharp reduction in borrowing by business firms and households. In addition, the "improvement in consumer sentiment" was expected to lead to increased spending by households and stimulate the economy. However, the wealth destruction associated with a large drop in housing prices would need to be overcome to see a return to normalcy. The most valuable asset for most households is the home. When home values dropped dramatically, household wealth dropped dramatically as well. Much of the government's policy during the crisis was aimed at stimulating the housing market and making home mortgage lending more affordable.

Of course, there is no guarantee that government policy aimed at minimizing business-cycle fluctuations will be successful. Since the policy is set today, yet is aimed at bettering economic conditions in the future, there is always the possibility that an activist policy will aggravate business-cycle fluctuations rather than moderate them. For instance, suppose the Fed lowers the federal funds rate today because of a belief that the economy needs to be stimulated in order to increase spending. If the economy is already starting to improve without the Fed's intervention (perhaps because of some earlier Fed action), the new stimulus may cause spending to grow too much and generate inflation that otherwise would not have occurred. Economic policy making is always done with some degree of uncertainty. Although policymakers such as Ben Bernanke may support policy changes aimed at growing the economy with low inflation, there is always a chance that their policies will have unintended consequences.

CHAPTER 15

Macroeconomic Viewpoints: New Keynesian, Monetarist, and New Classical

FUNDAMENTAL QUESTIONS

1 What do Keynesian economists believe about macroeconomic policy?

2 What role do monetarists believe the government should play in the economy?

3 What is new classical economics?

4 How do theories of economics change over time?

Economists do not all agree on macroeconomic policy. Sometimes disagreements are due to normative differences, or differences in personal values, regarding what the truly pressing needs are that should be addressed. Other disagreements are based on different views of how the economy operates and what determines the equilibrium level of real GDP.

It would be very easy to classify economists, to call them liberals or conservatives, for example. But an economist who believes that the government should not intervene in social decisions (abortion, censorship) may favor an active role for government in economic decisions (trade protection, unemployment insurance, welfare benefits). Another economist may support an active role for government in regulating the social behavior of individuals, yet believe that government should allow free markets to operate without interference.

In this chapter, an overview of important differences among schools of macroeconomic thought is presented. Most economists probably do not align themselves solely with any one theory of macroeconomics, choosing instead to incorporate pieces of various schools of thought. But the three approaches we discuss in this chapter—Keynesian, monetarist, and new classical—have had enormous impact on macroeconomic thinking and policy. Economic thinking has evolved over time as economists develop new economic theories to fit the realities of a changing world.

1. Keynesian Economics

Keynesian macroeconomics (named after the English economist John Maynard Keynes) dominated the economics profession from the 1940s through the 1960s. Some economists today refer to themselves as "new Keynesians." The common thread that pervades Keynesian economics is an emphasis on the inflexibility of wages and prices. This leads many Keynesians to recommend an activist government macroeconomic policy aimed at achieving a satisfactory rate of economic growth.

1 What do Keynesian economists believe about macroeconomic policy?

1.a. The Keynesian Model

Keynesian economics grew out of the Great Depression, when inflation was not a problem but output was falling. As a result, the Keynesian model of macroeconomic equilibrium assumes that prices are constant and that changes in aggregate expenditures determine equilibrium real GDP. In an aggregate demand and supply analysis, the simple Keynesian model looks like the graph in Figure 1. The aggregate supply curve is a horizontal line at a fixed level of prices, P_1. Changes in aggregate demand, such as from AD_1 to AD_2, cause changes in real GDP with no change in the price level.

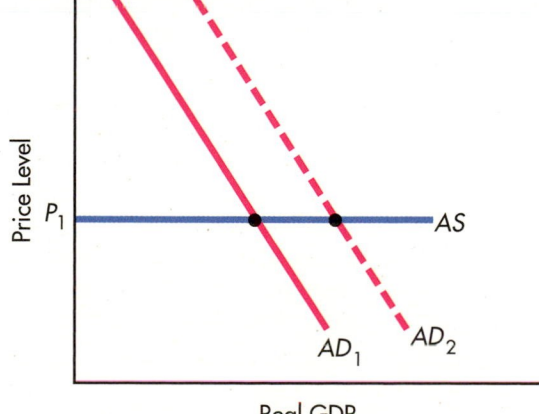

FIGURE 1 The Fixed-Price Keynesian Model

In the simple Keynesian model, prices are fixed at P_1 by the horizontal aggregate supply curve, so that changes in aggregate demand determine equilibrium real GDP.

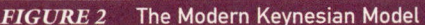

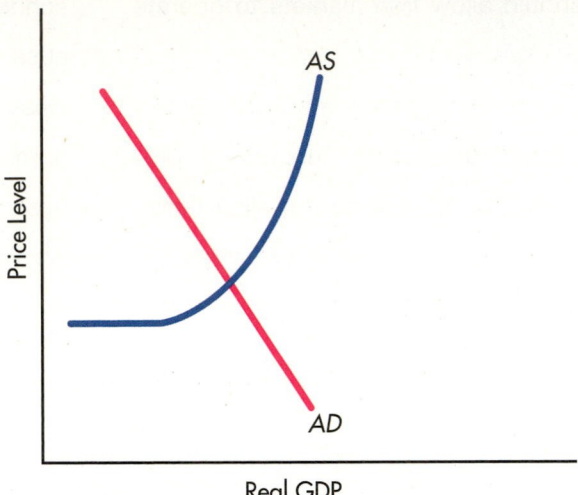

FIGURE 2   The Modern Keynesian Model

Modern Keynesians typically believe that the aggregate supply curve is horizontal only at relatively low levels of real GDP. As real GDP increases, more and more industries reach their capacity level of output, and the aggregate supply curve becomes positively sloped.

© 2013 Cengage Learning

Figure 1 reflects the traditional Keynesian emphasis on aggregate demand as a determinant of equilibrium real GDP. But no economist today would argue that the aggregate supply curve is always horizontal at every level of real GDP. More representative of Keynesian economics today is the aggregate supply curve shown in Figure 2. At low levels of real GDP, the curve is flat. In this region (the Keynesian region), increases in aggregate demand are associated with increases in output, but not with increases in prices. This flat region of the aggregate supply curve reflects the Keynesian belief that inflation is not a problem when unemployment is high. As the level of real GDP increases, and more and more industries reach their capacity level of output, the aggregate supply curve becomes positively sloped.

The economic theories that John Maynard Keynes proposed in the 1930s have given way to new theories. Today **Keynesian economics** focuses on the role the government plays in stabilizing the economy by managing aggregate demand. *New Keynesians* believe that wages and prices are not flexible in the short run. They use their analysis of business behavior to explain the Keynesian region on the aggregate supply curve of Figure 2. They believe that the economy is not always in equilibrium. For instance, if the demand for labor falls, we would expect the equilibrium price of labor (the wage) to fall and, because fewer people want to work at a lower wage, the number of people employed to fall. New Keynesians argue that wages do not tend to fall, because firms choose to lay off workers rather than decrease wages. Businesses retain high wages for their remaining employees in order to maintain morale and productivity. As a result, wages are quite rigid. This wage rigidity is reflected in price rigidity in goods markets, according to new Keynesian economics.

1.b. The Policymakers' Role

Keynesians believe that the government must take an active role in the economy to restore equilibrium. Traditional Keynesians identified the private sector as an important

Keynesian economics
A school of thought that emphasizes the role government plays in stabilizing the economy by managing aggregate demand.

New Keynesian macroeconomists argue that wages and prices are not flexible in the short run.

source of shifts in aggregate demand. For example, they argued that investment is susceptible to sudden changes. If business spending falls, the argument continued, monetary and fiscal policies should be used to stimulate spending and offset the drop in business spending. Government intervention is necessary to offset private-sector shifts in aggregate demand and avoid recession. And if private spending increases, creating inflationary pressure, then monetary and fiscal policies should restrain spending, again to offset private-sector shifts in aggregate demand.

New Keynesian macroeconomics does not focus on fluctuations in aggregate demand as the primary source of the problems facing policymakers. Keynesian economists realize that aggregate supply shocks can be substantial. But whatever the source of the instability—aggregate demand or aggregate supply—they emphasize active government policy to return the economy to equilibrium.

RECAP

1. Keynesian economists today reject the simple fixed-price model in favor of a model in which the aggregate supply curve is relatively flat at low levels of real GDP and slopes upward as real GDP approaches its potential level.

2. Keynesians believe that the tendency for the economy to experience disequilibrium in labor and goods markets requires the government to intervene in the economy.

2. Monetarist Economics

The Keynesian view dominated macroeconomics in the 1940s, the 1950s, and most of the 1960s. In the late 1960s and the 1970s, Keynesian economics faced a challenge from **monetarist economics**, a school of thought that emphasizes the role that changes in the money supply play in determining equilibrium real GDP and prices. The leading monetarist, Milton Friedman, had been developing monetarist theory since the 1940s, but it took several decades for his ideas to become popular. In part, the shift was a product of the forcefulness of Friedman's arguments, but the relatively poor macroeconomic performance of the United States in the 1970s probably contributed to a growing disenchantment with Keynesian economics, creating an environment that was ripe for new ideas. The Economic Insight "Milton Friedman" describes how Friedman's monetarist theories became popular.

monetarist economics
A school of thought that emphasizes the role changes in the money supply play in determining equilibrium real GDP and price level.

2.a. The Monetarist Model

Monetarists focus on the role of the money supply in determining the equilibrium level of real GDP and prices. In the chapter titled "Monetary Policy," we discussed monetary policy and equilibrium income. We showed that monetary policy is linked to changes in the equilibrium level of real GDP through changes in investment (and consumption). Keynesians traditionally assumed that monetary policy affects aggregate demand by changing the interest rate and, consequently, investment spending. Monetarists believe that changes in the money supply have broad effects on expenditures through both investment and consumption. An increase in the money supply pushes aggregate demand up by increasing both business and household spending and raises the equilibrium level of real GDP. A decrease in the money supply does the opposite.

Monetarists believe that changes in monetary policy (or fiscal policy, for that matter) have only a short-term effect on real GDP. In the long run, they expect real GDP to be at a level consistent with the natural rate of unemployment. As a result, the long-run

ECONOMIC INSIGHT

Milton Friedman

Milton Friedman is widely considered to be the father of monetarism. Born in 1912 in New York City, Friedman spent most of his career at the University of Chicago. Early in his professional life, he recognized the importance of developing economics as an empirical science—that is, using data to test the applicability of economic theory.

In 1957, Friedman published *A Theory of the Consumption Function*. In this book, he discussed the importance of *permanent income*, rather than current income, in understanding consumer spending. His analysis of consumption won widespread acclaim, an acclaim that would be a long time coming for his work relating monetary policy to real output and prices.

In the 1950s, Keynesian theory dominated economics. Most macroeconomists believed that the supply of money in the economy was of little importance. In 1963, with the publication of *A Monetary History of the United States, 1867–1960* (coauthored with Anna Schwartz of the National Bureau of Economic Research), Friedman focused attention on the monetarist argument. Still, Keynesian economics dominated scholarly and policy debate.

In the late 1960s and early 1970s, the rate of inflation and the rate of unemployment increased simultaneously. This was a situation that Keynesian economics could not explain. The timing was right for a new theory of macroeconomic behavior, and monetarism, with Milton Friedman as its most influential advocate, grew in popularity. The new stature of monetarism was clearly visible in 1979, when the Fed adopted a monetarist approach to targeting the money supply.

In 1976, Milton Friedman was awarded the Nobel Prize for economics. By this time he had become a public figure. He wrote a column for *Newsweek* from 1966 to 1984, and in 1980 developed a popular public television series, *Free to Choose*, based on his book of the same title. Through the popular media, Friedman became the most effective and well-known supporter of free markets in the United States and much of the rest of the world until his death in 2006. Many would argue that only Keynes has had as much influence on scholarly literature and public policy in economics as Milton Friedman.

> *Monetarists believe that accelerating inflation is a product of efforts to increase real GDP through expansionary monetary policy.*

effect of a change in the money supply is fully reflected in a change in the price level. Attempts to exploit the short-run effects of expansionary monetary policy produce an inflationary spiral, in which the level of GDP increases temporarily, then falls back to the potential level while prices rise. This is the rightward shift of the Phillips curve that we described in the chapter titled "Macroeconomic Policy: Tradeoffs, Expectations, Credibility, and Sources of Business Cycles."

2.b. The Policymakers' Role

2 What role do monetarists believe the government should play in the economy?

Unlike Keynesian economists, monetarists do not believe that the economy is subject to a disequilibrium that must be offset by government action. Most monetarists believe that the economy tends toward equilibrium at the level of potential real GDP. Their faith in the free market (price) system leads them to favor minimal government intervention.

Monetarists often argue that government policy heightens the effects of the business cycle. This is especially true of monetary policy. To prove their point, monetarists link changes in the growth of the money supply to business-cycle fluctuations. Specifically, they suggest that periods of relatively fast money growth are followed by booms and inflation, whereas periods of relatively slow money growth are followed by recessions. The link between money growth, real GDP, and inflation has not been as visible in recent years as it was in the 1970s–1990s. The Federal Reserve used to formulate policy in terms of money growth targets, but stopped doing that a few years ago. This was a sign that the link between money growth, inflation, and real output was not a strong as it used to be. Sometimes there seem to be closer relationships than at other times. This makes it difficult to predict the effect of a particular change in monetary policy on prices or real GDP. In addition, a number of other variables influence GDP.

Monetarists favor nonactivist government policy because they believe that the government's attempts to make the economy better off by aiming monetary and fiscal policies at low inflation and low unemployment often make things worse. Why? Because economic policy, which is very powerful, operates with a long and variable lag. First, policymakers have to recognize that a problem exists. This is the *recognition lag*. Then they must formulate an appropriate policy. This is the *reaction lag*. Then the effects of the policy must work through the economy. This is the *effect lag*.

When the Federal Reserve changes the rate of growth of the money supply, real GDP and inflation do not change immediately. In fact, studies show that as much as two years can pass between a change in policy and the effect of that change on real GDP. This means that when policymakers institute a change targeted at a particular level of real GDP or rate of inflation, the effect of the policy is not felt for a long time. And it is possible that the economy could be facing an entirely different set of problems in a year or two from those that policymakers are addressing today. But today's policy will still have effects next year, and those effects may aggravate next year's problems.

Because of the long and variable lag in the effect of fiscal and monetary policies, monetarists argue that policymakers should set policy according to rules that do not change from month to month or even year to year. What kinds of rules? A fiscal policy rule might be to balance the budget annually; a monetary policy rule might be to require that the money supply grow at a fixed rate over time or that the central bank commit to following an inflation target. These kinds of rules restrict policymakers from formulating discretionary policy. Monetarists believe that when discretionary shifts in policy are reduced, economic growth is steadier than it is when government consciously sets out to achieve full employment and low inflation.

> *Economic policy operates with a long and variable lag.*

RECAP

1. Monetarists emphasize the role that changes in the money supply play in determining equilibrium real GDP and the level of prices.

2. Monetarists do not believe that the economy is subject to disequilibrium in the labor and goods markets or that government should take an active role in the economy.

3. Because economic policy operates with a long and variable lag, attempts by government to stabilize the economy may, in fact, make matters worse.

4. Monetarists believe that formal rules, rather than the discretion of policymakers, should govern economic policymaking.

3. New Classical Economics

In the 1970s, an alternative to Keynesian and monetarist economics was developed: new classical economics. But before we discuss the new classical theory, let's look at the old one.

Classical economics is the theory that was popular before Keynes changed the face of economics in the 1930s. According to classical economics, real GDP is determined by aggregate supply, while the equilibrium price level is determined by aggregate demand. Figure 3, the classical aggregate demand and supply diagram, shows the classical economist's view of the world. The vertical aggregate supply curve means that the equilibrium level of output (income) is a product only of the determinants of aggregate

classical economics
A school of thought that assumes that real GDP is determined by aggregate supply, while the equilibrium price level is determined by aggregate demand.

FIGURE 3   The Classical Model

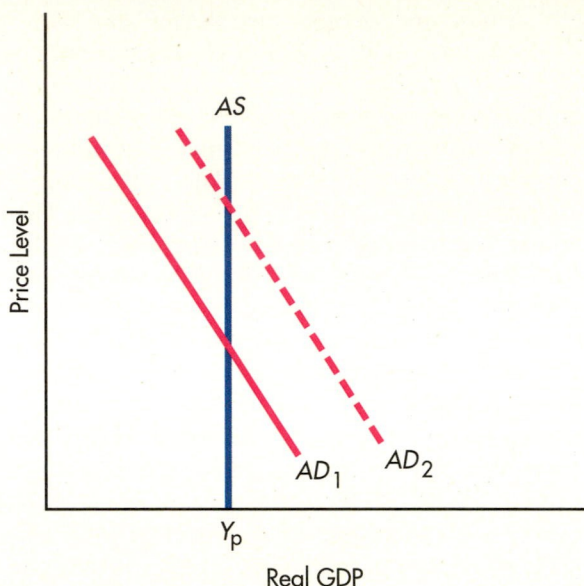

The vertical aggregate supply curve indicates that equilibrium real GDP is determined strictly by the determinants of aggregate supply.

supply: the price of resources, technology, and expectations (see the chapter titled "Macroeconomic Equilibrium: Aggregate Demand and Supply").

If the aggregate supply curve is vertical, then changes in aggregate demand, such as from AD_1 to AD_2, change only the price level; they do not affect the equilibrium level of output. Classical economics assumes that prices and wages are perfectly flexible. This rules out contracts that fix prices or wages for periods of time. It also rules out the possibility that people are not aware of all prices and wages. They know when prices have gone up and ask for wage increases to compensate.

Both Keynesians and monetarists would argue that information about the economy, including prices and wages, is not perfect. When workers and businesses negotiate wages, they may not know what current prices are, and they certainly do not know what future prices will be. Furthermore, many labor contracts fix wages for long periods of time. This means that wages are not flexible; they cannot adjust immediately to new price levels.

3.a. The New Classical Model

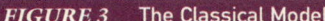

3 What is new classical economics?

new classical economics
A school of thought that holds that changes in real GDP are a product of unexpected changes in the level of prices.

New classical economics was a response to the problems of meeting economic policy goals in the 1970s. New classical economists questioned some of the assumptions on which Keynesian economics was based. For instance, new classical economists believe wages are flexible, while both traditional Keynesian and new Keynesian economists assume that wages can be fixed in the short run.

New classical economics does not assume that people know everything that is happening, as the old theory did. People make mistakes because their expectations of prices or some other critical variable are different from the future reality. New classical economists emphasize rational expectations. As defined in the chapter titled "Macroeconomic Policy: Tradeoffs, Expectations, Credibility, and Sources of Business Cycles," *rational expectations* are based on all available relevant information. This was a new way of thinking about expectations. Earlier theories assumed that people formed adaptive expectations—that their expectations were based only on their past experience. With rational expectations, people learn not only from their past experience, but also from any other information that helps them predict the future.

Suppose the chairman of the Federal Reserve Board announces a new monetary policy. Price-level expectations that are formed rationally take this announcement into consideration; those that are formed adaptively do not. It is much easier for policymakers to make unexpected changes in policy if expectations are formed adaptively rather than rationally.

Another element of new classical economics is the belief that markets are in equilibrium. Keynesian economics argues that disequilibrium in markets demands government intervention. For instance, Keynesian economists define a recession as a disequilibrium in the labor market—a surplus of labor—that requires expansionary government policy. New classical economists believe that because real wages are lower during a recession, people are more willing to substitute nonlabor activities (going back to school, early retirement, work at home, or leisure) for work. As the economy recovers and wages go up, people substitute away from nonlabor activities toward more working hours. The substitution of labor for leisure and leisure for labor, over time, suggests that much of observed unemployment is voluntary in the sense that those who are unemployed choose not to take a job at a wage below their reservation wage (see the chapter titled "Macroeconomic Policy: Tradeoffs, Expectations, Credibility, and Sources of Business Cycles").

3.b. The Policymakers' Role

New classical economics emphasizes expectations. Its basic tenet is that changes in monetary policy can change the equilibrium level of real GDP only if those changes are *unexpected*. Fiscal policy can change equilibrium real GDP only if it *unexpectedly* changes the level of prices or one of the determinants of aggregate supply.

Figure 4 (which is the same as Figure 4 in the chapter titled "Macroeconomic Policy: Tradeoffs, Expectations, Credibility, and Sources of Business Cycles") illustrates the new classical view of the effect of an unexpected increase in the money supply. Suppose initially the expected rate of inflation is 3 percent and the actual rate of inflation is also 3 percent. The economy is operating at point 1 in Figure 4(b), the Phillips curve diagram, with unemployment at 5 percent, which is assumed to be the natural rate of unemployment. At the natural rate of unemployment, the economy is producing the potential level of real GDP (Y_p) at price level P_1. If the central bank unexpectedly increases the money supply, pushing the inflation rate up from 3 percent to 6 percent, the economy moves from point 1 to point 2 along short-run Phillips curve I, which is based on 3 percent expected inflation. The unemployment rate is now 3 percent, which is less than the natural rate. In part (a), real GDP rises above potential income to Y_2.

Over time, people come to expect 6 percent inflation. They adjust to the higher inflation rate, and the economy moves back to the natural rate of unemployment. At the expected rate of inflation, 6 percent, the economy is operating at point 3 on short-run Phillips curve II. As the expected rate of inflation increases from 3 percent to 6 percent, workers negotiate higher wages and the aggregate supply curve shifts to the left, from AS_1 to AS_2. A new equilibrium exists at point 3 in the aggregate demand and supply diagram, and real GDP drops back to its potential level.

The analysis changes dramatically if the change in the money supply is expected. Now the economy moves not from point 1 to point 2 to point 3 but from point 1 directly to point 3. This is because the shift from point 1 to point 2 is temporary, based on unexpected inflation. If the inflation is expected, the economy is on short-run Phillips curve II, where inflation is 6 percent, unemployment is at the natural rate, and real GDP is at the potential level.

FIGURE 4   New Classical Economics

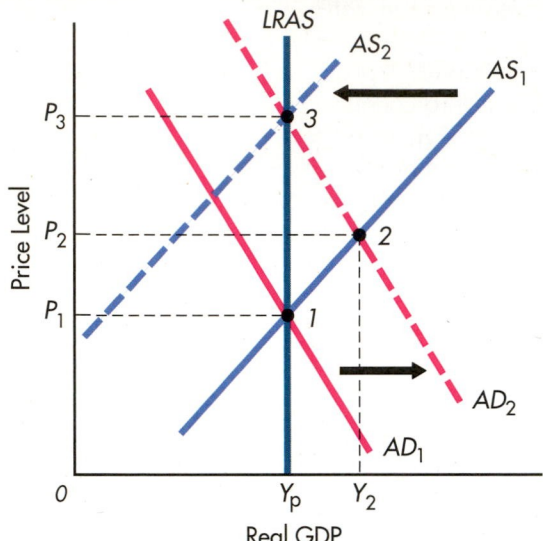

(a) Aggregate Demand and Supply

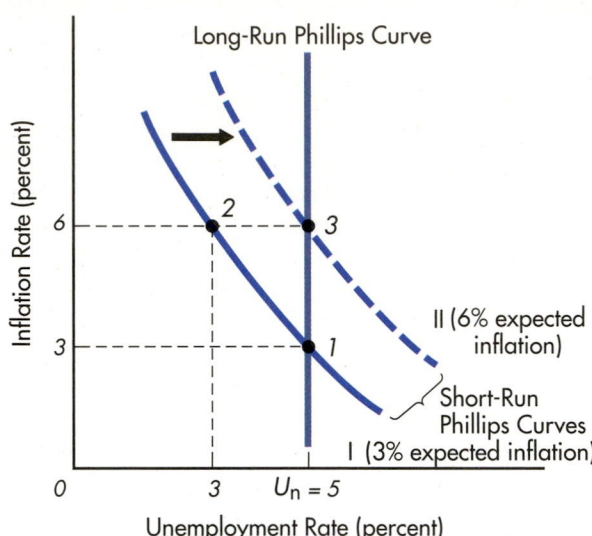

(b) Phillips Curve

New classical economists believe that government-induced shifts in aggregate demand affect real GDP only if they are unexpected. In Figure 4(a), the economy initially is operating at point 1, with real GDP at Y_p, the potential level. An unexpected increase in aggregate demand shifts the economy to point 2, where both real GDP (Y_2) and prices (P_2) are higher. Over time, as sellers adjust to higher prices and costs of doing business, aggregate supply shifts from AS_1 to AS_2. This shift moves the economy to point 3. Here GDP is back at the potential level, and prices are even higher. In the long run, an increase in aggregate demand does not increase output. The long-run aggregate supply curve (LRAS) is a vertical line at the potential level of real GDP. In Figure 4(b), if the expected rate of inflation is 3 percent and actual inflation is 3 percent, the economy is operating at point 1, at the natural rate of unemployment (U_n). If aggregate demand increases, there is an unexpected increase in inflation from 3 percent to 6 percent. This moves the economy from point 1 to point 2 along short-run Phillips curve I. Here the unemployment rate is 3 percent. As people learn to expect 6 percent inflation, they adjust to the higher rate and the economy moves back to the natural rate of unemployment, at point 3. If the increase in inflation is expected, then the economy moves directly from point 1 to point 3 with no temporary decrease in the unemployment rate.

> *New classical economists believe that wages and prices are flexible and that people form expectations rationally, so that only unexpected changes in the price level can affect real GDP.*

The lesson of new classical economics for policymakers is that managing aggregate demand has an effect on real GDP only if change is unexpected. Any predictable policy simply affects prices. As a result, new classical economists argue that monetary and fiscal policies should be aimed at maintaining a low, stable rate of inflation and should not attempt to alter real national output and unemployment. This brings new classical economists close to the monetarists, who would choose policy rules over discretionary policy.

RECAP

1. New classical economics holds that wages are flexible and that expectations are formed rationally, so that only unexpected changes in prices have an effect on real GDP.

2. New classical economists believe that markets are always in equilibrium.

3. According to new classical economic theory, any predictable macroeconomic policy has an effect only on prices.

4. New classical economists argue that monetary and fiscal policies should try to achieve a low, stable rate of inflation rather than changes in real GDP or unemployment.

4. Comparison and Influence

The three theories of macroeconomics we have been talking about are often treated as though they are different in every way. Yet at times they overlap and even share conclusions. Moreover, as we mentioned at the beginning of the chapter, it is an oversimplification to categorize economists by a single school of thought. Many if not most economists do not classify themselves by economic theory. Typically they take elements of each, so that their approach to macroeconomics is more a synthesis of the various theories than strict adherence to any one theory.

Macroeconomic theories have developed over time in response to the economy's performance and the shortcomings of existing theories. Keynesian economics became popular in the 1930s because classical economics did not explain or help resolve the Great Depression. Monetarist economics offered an explanation for rising unemployment and rising inflation in the United States in the 1960s and 1970s. New classical economics suggested an alternative explanation for rising unemployment and inflation that the static Phillips curve analysis used by traditional Keynesians could not explain. Each of these theories, then, was developed or became popular because an existing theory did not answer pressing new questions.

All of these theories have influenced government policy. A by-product of Keynes's work in the 1930s was the wide acceptance and practice of activist government fiscal policy. Monetarist influence was dramatically apparent in the change in monetary policy announced by the Federal Reserve in 1979. Monetarists had criticized the Fed's policy of targeting interest rates. They argued that money-growth targets would stabilize income and prices. In October 1979, Chairman Paul Volcker announced that the Fed would concentrate more on achieving money-growth targets and less on controlling interest rates. This change in policy reflected the Fed's concern over rising inflation and the belief that the monetarists were right, that a low rate of money growth would bring about a low rate of inflation. The new policy led to an abrupt drop in the rate of inflation, from more than 13 percent in 1979 to less than 4 percent in 1982.

The new classical economists' emphasis on expectations calls for more information from policymakers to allow private citizens to incorporate government plans into their outlook for the future. The Federal Reserve Reform Act (1977) and the Full Employment and Balanced Growth Act (1978) require the Board of Governors to report to Congress semiannually on its goals and money targets for the next 12 months. New classical economists also believe that only credible government policies can affect expectations. In the last chapter we discussed the time consistency of plans. For plans to be credible, to influence private expectations, they must be time consistent.

Table 1 summarizes the three approaches to macroeconomics, describing the major source of problems facing policymakers and the proper role of government policy according to each view. Only Keynesian economics supports an active role for government; the other two theories suggest that government should not intervene in the economy.

The government policy response to the financial crisis that began in 2007 incorporated ideas from the different approaches to macroeconomics. There was a huge increase in government spending financed by borrowing, a very Keynesian approach to stimulating aggregate demand. There was also an emphasis on shaping expectations of the public that fiscal and monetary policy were addressing declining incomes and output, as well as falling prices. If the public believes that their incomes are only temporarily depressed, they will spend more now. If the public believes that deflation will be avoided, they will be more willing to spend rather than hold on to their cash (money rises in value as prices fall), and they will not write contracts that build in expectations of falling prices and wages and further contribute to such price and wage declines. Finally, central banks

4 How do theories of economics change over time?

TABLE 1	Major Approaches to Macroeconomic Policy	
Approach	**Major Source of Problems**	**Proper Role for Government**
New Keynesian	Disequilibrium in private labor and goods markets	To actively manage monetary and fiscal policies to restore equilibrium
Monetarist	Government's discretionary policies that increase and decrease aggregate demand	To follow fixed rules for money growth and minimize fiscal policy shocks
New classical	Government's attempt to manipulate aggregate demand, even though government policies have effect on real GDP only if unexpected	To follow predictable monetary and fiscal policies for long-run stability

© 2013 Cengage Learning

around the world greatly increased the supply of money to support credit availability and spending by business firms and households. In fact, the global policy response to the financial crisis was unprecedented—which serves to emphasize the macroeconomic lessons learned by economists and government policymakers from past history and macroeconomic theory.

RECAP

1. Different economic theories developed over time as changing economic conditions pointed out the shortcomings of existing theories.

2. Keynesian, monetarist, and new classical economics have each influenced macroeconomic policy.

3. Only Keynesian economists believe that government should actively intervene to stabilize the economy.

SUMMARY

- Economists do not all agree on the determinants of economic equilibrium or the appropriate role of government policy. *Preview*

1. **What do Keynesian economists believe about macroeconomic policy?**

   - Keynesian economists believe that the government should take an active role in stabilizing the economy by managing aggregate demand. *§1.a, 1.b*

2. **What role do monetarists believe the government should play in the economy?**

   - Monetarists do not believe that the economy is subject to serious disequilibrium, which means that they favor minimal government intervention in the economy. *§2.b*

- Monetarists believe that a government that takes an active role in the economy may do more harm than good because economic policy operates with a long and variable lag. *§2.b*

3. **What is new classical economics?**

   - New classical economics holds that only unexpected changes in policy can influence real GDP, so that government policy should target a low, stable rate of inflation. *§3.b*

4. **How do theories of economics change over time?**

   - New economic theories are a response to changing economic conditions that reveal the shortcomings of existing theories. *§4*

KEY TERMS

classical economics, 347

keynesian economics, 344

monetarist economics, 345

new classical economics, 348

EXERCISES

1. What is the difference between traditional Keynesian and new Keynesian economics?

2. Why does monetary policy operate with a long and variable lag? Give an example to illustrate your explanation.

3. What is the difference between old classical and new classical economics?

4. Draw an aggregate demand and supply diagram for each theory of macroeconomics. Use the diagrams to explain how the government can influence equilibrium real GDP and prices.

5. What, if any, similarities are there among the theories of economics discussed in this chapter regarding the use of fiscal and monetary policies to stimulate real GDP?

6. If unexpected increases in the growth rate of the money supply can increase real GDP, why doesn't the Fed follow a policy of unexpectedly increasing the money supply to increase the growth of real GDP?

7. "The popular macroeconomic theories have evolved over time as economic conditions have changed to reveal shortcomings of existing theory." Evaluate this quote in terms of the emergence of the three theories discussed in this chapter.

8. Has the recent financial crisis and recession supported or discredited any of the macroeconomic theories discussed in this chapter? If it was a result of excessive credit creation associated with central banks keeping interest rates too low for too long, what might you answer?

9. Do sticky wages seem realistic? If you wanted to research the stickiness of wages, how might you design your study?

For exercises 10–17, tell which school of thought would most likely be associated with the following quotes:

10. "Changes in prices and wages are too slow to support the new classical assumption of persistent macroeconomic equilibrium."

11. "The best monetary policy is to keep the money supply growing at a slow and steady rate."

12. "Frictional unemployment is a result of workers voluntarily substituting leisure for labor when wages fall."

13. "A change in the money supply will affect GDP after a long and variable lag, so it is difficult to predict the effects of money on output."

14. "Government policymakers should use fiscal policy to adjust aggregate demand in response to aggregate supply shocks."

15. "The economy is subject to recurring disequilibrium in labor and goods markets, so government can serve a useful function of helping the economy adjust to equilibrium."

16. "Since the aggregate supply curve is horizontal, aggregate demand will determine the equilibrium level of real GDP."

17. "If everyone believed that the monetary authority was going to cut the inflation rate from 6 percent to 3 percent, such a reduction in inflation could be achieved without any significant increase in unemployment."

You can find further practice tests in the Online Quiz at **www.cengage.com/economics/boyes**.

THE GHOSTS OF CHRISTMAS PAST HAUNT ECONOMISTS

Africa News, January 10, 2003

Financial crises have come back because policymakers fail to learn earlier lessons. In Charles Dickens' great novel, *A Christmas Carol*, the soulless businessman Ebenezer Scrooge is tormented by a visit from the Spirit of Christmas Past. Today, economists are similarly troubled by unwanted ghosts, as they ponder the reappearance of economic ills long thought buried and dead.

From Stephen Roach at Morgan Stanley to Paul Krugman at Princeton, to the governors of the US Federal Reserve and the senior staff at the European Central Bank, to almost everyone in Japan, economists all over the world are worrying about deflation. Their thoughts retrace the economic thinking of more than 50 years ago, a time when economists concluded that the thing to do with deflation was to avoid it like the plague.

Back in 1933 Irving Fisher—Milton Friedman's predecessor atop the US's monetarist school of economists—announced that governments could prevent deep depressions by avoiding deflation. Deflation—a steady, continuing decline in prices—gave businesses and consumers powerful incentives to cut spending and hoard cash.

It reduced the ability of businesses and banks to service their debt, and might trigger a chain of big bankruptcies that would destroy confidence in the financial system, providing further incentives to hoard. Such strong incentives to hoard rather than spend can keep demand low and falling, and unemployment high and rising, for a much longer time than even the most laissez-faire-oriented politician or economist had ever dared contemplate. Hence the Keynesian solution: use monetary policy (lower interest rates) and fiscal policy (expanded government spending and reduced taxes) to keep the economy from ever approaching the precipice where deflation becomes possible.

But if this is an issue solved more than 50 years ago, why is it haunting us now? Why is this menace a matter of grave concern in Japan today, and a threat worth worrying about in the US? . . .

The truth is that economic policymakers are juggling sets of potential disasters, exchanging the one that appears most threatening for a threat that seems more distant.

In the US, the Bush administration is sceptical of the stimulative power of monetary policy and wants bigger fiscal deficits to reduce unemployment, hoping that the future dangers posed by persistent deficits—low investment, slow growth, loss of confidence, uncontrolled inflation and exchange rate depreciation—can be finessed, or will not become visible until after the Bush team leaves office.

In Europe, the European Central Bank believes the danger of uncontrolled inflation following a loss of public confidence in its commitment to low inflation outweighs the costs of European unemployment that is far too high. . . .

The ghosts of economics' past return because the lessons of the present are always oversold. Politicians and policymakers advance their approach to economics as the One True Doctrine. What they are doing, however, is dealing with the biggest problem of the moment, but at the price of removing institutions and policies that policymakers before them had put into place to control problems they felt to be the most pressing.

Ebenezer Scrooge's nocturnal visitors were able to convince him of the errors of his ways. Let us hope today's economists also learn the lessons of their unwanted ghosts.

J. Bradford Delong

Source: Excerpt from *The Ghosts of Christmas Past Haunt Economists.* January 10, 2003 by J. Bradford Delong p. 36. © Project Syndicate, January 10, 2003.

Macroeconomics has always been a lively field, filled with controversy over the proper approach to modeling the economy, the correct interpretation of experience, and the role that government policy can and should play. Indeed, debate in macroeconomics is as old as the field itself. The views of John Maynard Keynes, the founder of macroeconomics, were challenged by his colleague at Cambridge University, Arthur Pigou. This debate focused on the importance of the "real balance effect," whereby a fall in the price level raises real money balances (or the purchasing power of the money supply), increases wealth, and thus increases consumption. Like most debates in macroeconomics, this was more than an ivory tower exercise, since the real balance effect provides a channel by which the economy can bring itself out of a slump without government intervention.

The article indicates that, in early 2003, the issue of falling prices was back again as a policy concern. The Japanese economy had experienced deflation in recent years, and some were worried that the United States could also move from low inflation to deflation. In the global recession that started in 2007, there were renewed fears of deflation, so this issue does not go away. The author claims that economists knew long ago that deflation could be avoided by expansionary fiscal and monetary policies. A monetarist-type solution would be central bank targeting of inflation. In the early 2000s, some economists were suggesting that this is what the central bank of Japan should do: Set an inflation target and aim monetary policy solely at the achievement of such a target. A Keynesian-type solution would be to increase government spending and/or reduce taxes. The Bush administration in the United States was proposing a Keynesian approach, with tax cuts to stimulate the U.S. economy. The European Central Bank was utilizing a monetarist approach of inflation targeting to achieve public confidence in its commitment to low inflation. Both of these policies may avoid deflation. However, we can never be sure of the effects of a tax cut on important variables like unemployment, interest rates, and real GDP, and the inflation target achieves only the inflation goal and may have undesirable consequences for unemployment and real GDP growth. In short, there is no magic economic solution that always provides the best mix of macroeconomic outcomes. This is a major reason for the debates that have raged in macroeconomics.

The debate between the Keynesians and the monetarists dominated the macroeconomic discourse of the 1950s and 1960s. During this period, those who identified themselves as Keynesians gave primacy to the role of fiscal policy and to the issue of unemployment; these economists had great faith in the ability of the government to fine-tune the economy through the proper application of policy, thereby ensuring stability and growth. Keynesians of this vintage also believed that changes in the money supply had little effect on the economy. In contrast, monetarists were very concerned about inflation, which they believed to be a purely monetary phenomenon. These economists also doubted that active government intervention could stabilize the economy, for they believed that policy operated only with long and variable lags.

Although outside observers may view the debate within macroeconomics as evidence of confusion, a more accurate appraisal is that the debate is a healthy intellectual response to a world in which few things are certain and much is unknown—and perhaps unknowable. The differences seen between schools of thought mask the fact that there is a great deal of consensus about a number of issues in macroeconomics. This consensus is a product of lessons learned from past debates. In a similar fashion, the controversies of today will yield tomorrow's consensus, and our knowledge of the real workings of the economy will grow.

CHAPTER 16

Economic Growth

© MACIEJ FROLOW/GETTY IMAGES, INC

FUNDAMENTAL QUESTIONS

1 What is economic growth?

2 How are economic growth rates determined?

3 What is productivity?

4 What explains productivity changes?

SERGIY TROFIMOV/ISTOCKPHOTO; LOGO: © FROXX/SHUTTERSTOCK.COM

Modern economies tend to raise living standards for the population generation after generation. This is economic growth. However, this was not always the case. Prior to the seventeenth century, economic activity involved a constant struggle to avoid starvation. Only in recent centuries has the idea of living standards being improved within a generation become common. Economist Angus Maddison has estimated that GDP grew at about a rate of 1.0 percent per year between the years 500 and 1500. Yet, since population growth was about the same at 1.0 percent per year, there was no increase in GDP per capita. He estimates that between 1500 and 1700, growth of per capita GDP increased to 1.0 percent per year, and between 1700 and 1820, it increased to about 1.6 percent per year, not too different from recent growth rates for the major industrial countries. Understanding why and how economic growth happens is a very important part of macroeconomics.

Although much of macroeconomics is aimed at understanding business cycles—recurring periods of prosperity and recession—the fact is that, over the long run, most economies do grow wealthier. The long-run trend of real GDP in the United States and most other

countries is positive. Yet the rate at which real GDP grows is very different across countries. Why? What factors cause economies to grow and living standards to rise?

In this chapter we focus on the long-term picture. We begin by defining economic growth and discussing its importance. Then we examine the determinants of economic growth to understand what accounts for the different rates of growth across countries.

1. Defining Economic Growth

What do we mean by economic growth? Economists use two measures of growth—real GDP and per capita real GDP—to compare how economies grow over time.

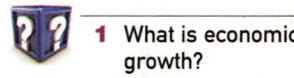

1 What is economic growth?

1.a. Real GDP

Basically, **economic growth** is an increase in real GDP. As more goods and services are produced, the real GDP increases and people are able to consume more.

economic growth
An increase in real GDP.

To calculate the percentage change in real GDP over a year, we simply divide the change in GDP by the value of GDP at the beginning of the year, and then multiply the quotient by 100. For instance, the real GDP of Singapore was approximately 77,260 million Singapore dollars in the third quarter of 2010 and approximately 68,693 million in the third quarter of 2009. This was near the end of the global recession, and the economy grew at a rate of 12.5 percent over that year:

$$\text{Percentage change in real GDP} = (\text{change over year/beginning value}) \times 100$$
$$= [(77{,}260 - 68{,}693)/68{,}693] \times 100$$
$$= 12.5\%$$

1.a.1. Compound Growth From 2000 to 2007, the industrial countries of the world showed an average annual growth rate of real GDP of 2.5 percent. Over the same period, the average annual growth rate of real GDP for developing countries was 6.5 percent. The difference between a growth rate of 2.5 percent and one of 6.5 percent may not seem substantial, but in fact it is. Growth is compounded over time. This means that any given rate of growth is applied every year to a growing base of real GDP, so any difference is magnified over time.

Figure 1 shows the effects of compounding growth rates. The upper line in the figure represents the path of real GDP if the economy grows at a rate of 6.5 percent a year. The lower line shows real GDP growing at a rate of 2.5 percent a year.

Suppose that in each case the economy originally is producing a real GDP of $1 billion. After five years, there is some difference: a GDP of $1.13 billion at 2.5 percent growth versus $1.34 at 6.5 percent growth. However, the effect of compounding becomes more visible over long periods of time. After 40 years, the difference between 2.5 and 6.5 percent growth, a seemingly small difference, represents a substantial

> *Small changes in rates of growth produce big changes in real GDP over a period of many years.*

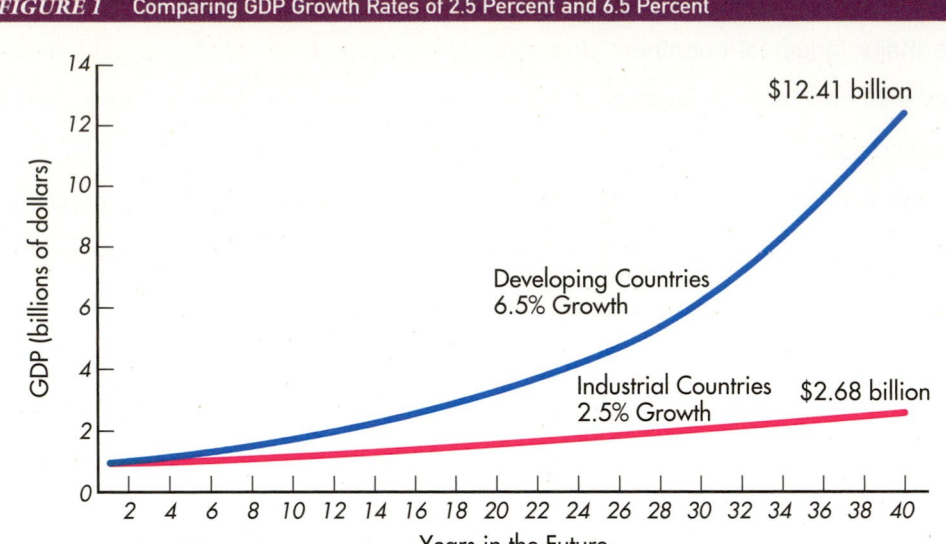

FIGURE 1   Comparing GDP Growth Rates of 2.5 Percent and 6.5 Percent

Between 2000 and 2007, real GDP in the industrial countries grew at an average annual rate of 2.5 percent, while real GDP in developing countries grew at an average annual rate of 6.5 percent. The difference seems small, but the graph shows how even a small difference is compounded over time, producing a substantial difference in real GDP.

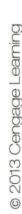

difference in output: A 2.5 percent rate of growth yields an output of $2.68 billion; at 6.5 percent, output is $12.41 billion. After 40 years, the level of output is approximately six times larger at the higher growth rate.

1.a.2. The Rule of 72
Compound growth explains why countries are so concerned about maintaining positive high rates of growth. If growth is maintained at a constant rate, we can estimate the number of years required for output to double by using the **rule of 72**. If we divide 72 by the growth rate, we find the approximate time that it takes for any value to double.

Suppose you deposit $100 in a bank account that pays a constant 6 percent annual interest. If you allow the interest to accumulate over time, the amount of money in the account grows at a rate of 6 percent. At this rate of interest, the rule of 72 tells us that your account will have a value of approximately $200 (double its initial value) after 12 years:

$$\frac{72}{6} = 12$$

The interest rate gives the rate of growth of the amount deposited if earned interest is allowed to accumulate in the account. If the interest rate is 3 percent, the amount will double in 24 (72/3) years. The rule of 72 applies to any value. If real GDP is growing at a rate of 6 percent a year, then real GDP doubles every 12 years. At a 3 percent annual rate, real GDP doubles every 24 years.

Table 1 lists the average annual rate of growth of GDP between 2000 and 2010 and the approximate doubling times for six countries. The countries listed have growth

rule of 72
The number of years required for an amount to double in value is 72 divided by the annual rate of growth.

TABLE 1	GDP Growth Rates and Doubling Times	
Country	Average Annual Growth Rate (percent)*	Approximate Doubling Time (years)
China	10.5	7
South Korea	5.3	14
Bangladesh	5.4	13
Australia	3.2	22
United States	2.5	29
Japan	0.9	76

*Average annual growth rates from 1990 to 2010.
Source: IMF, World Economic Outlook Database, January 2010.

rates ranging from a high of 10.5 percent in China to a low of 0.9 percent in Japan. If these growth rates are maintained over time, it would take just 7 years for the GDP in China to double and 76 years for the GDP in Japan to double.

1.b. Per Capita Real GDP

We've defined economic growth as an increase in real GDP. But if growth is supposed to be associated with higher standards of living, our definition may be misleading. A country could show positive growth in real GDP, but if the population is growing at an even higher rate, output per person can actually fall. Economists, therefore, often adjust the growth rate of output for changes in population. **Per capita real GDP** is real GDP divided by the population. If we define economic growth as rising per capita real GDP, then growth requires a nation's output of goods and services to increase faster than its population.

Per capita GDP is often used as an indicator of economic development. In 2007, African countries had an average per capita GDP of $2,413, while the countries of the euro-zone had an average of $33,296. Although there are great differences in the levels of per capita GDP, the difference in per capita real GDP growth between low-income developing and industrial countries is much smaller than the difference in real GDP growth. The difference in growth rates between the level of output and per capita output points out the danger of just looking at real GDP as an indicator of change in the economic well-being of the citizens in developing countries. Population growth rates are considerably higher in developing countries than they are in industrial countries, so real GDP must grow at a faster rate in developing countries than it does in industrial countries just to maintain a similar growth rate in per capita real GDP. Figure 2 depicts how per capita income differs around the world. The map shows how poverty is concentrated around the world and found largely in Africa and parts of Asia.

per capita real GDP
Real GDP divided by the population.

Economic growth is sometimes defined as an increase in per capita real GDP.

1.c. The Problems with Definitions of Growth

Economic growth is considered to be good because it allows people to have a higher standard of living, to have more material goods. But an increase in real GDP or per capita real GDP does not tell us whether the average citizen is better off. One problem is

FIGURE 2   Differences in Per Capita Income Around the World

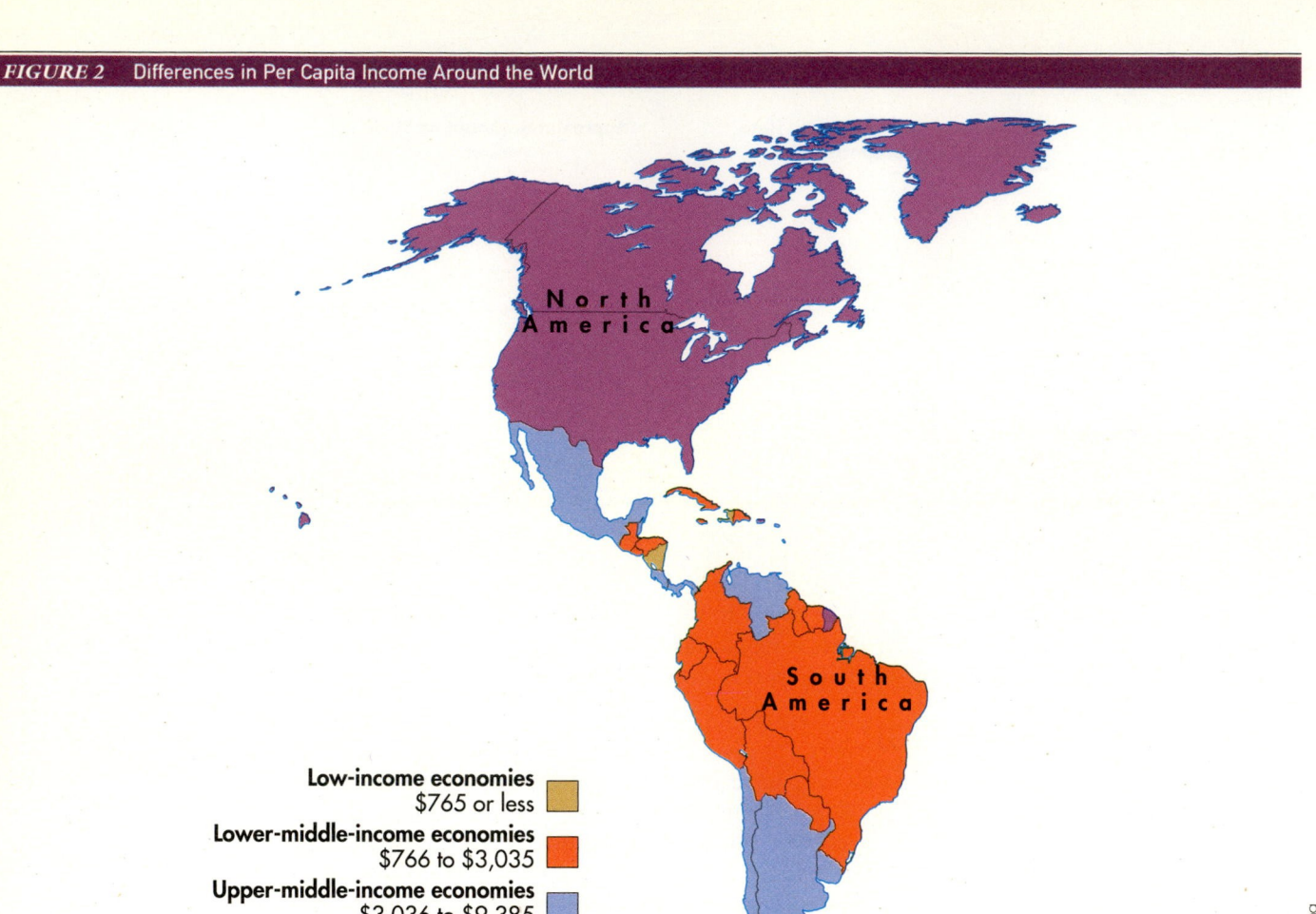

Low-income economies
$765 or less

Lower-middle-income economies
$766 to $3,035

Upper-middle-income economies
$3,036 to $9,385

High-income economies
$9,386 or more

No data

The map shows how concentrated poverty is in Africa and parts of Asia.

> *Per capita real GDP is a questionable indicator of the typical citizen's standard of living or quality of life.*

that these measures say nothing about how income is distributed. The national economy may be growing, yet the poor may be staying poor while the rich get richer.

The lesson here is simple: Economic growth may benefit some groups more than others. And it is entirely possible that, despite national economic growth, some groups can be worse off than they were before. Clearly, neither per capita real GDP nor real GDP accurately measures the standard of living for all of a nation's citizens.

Another reason that real GDP and per capita real GDP are misleading is that neither says anything about the quality of life. People have nonmonetary needs—they care about personal freedom, the environment, and their leisure time. If a rising per capita GDP goes hand in hand with a repressive political regime or a rapidly deteriorating environmental quality, people are not going to feel better off. By the same token, a country could have no economic growth, yet reduce the hours worked each week. More leisure time could make workers feel better off, even though per capita GDP has not changed.

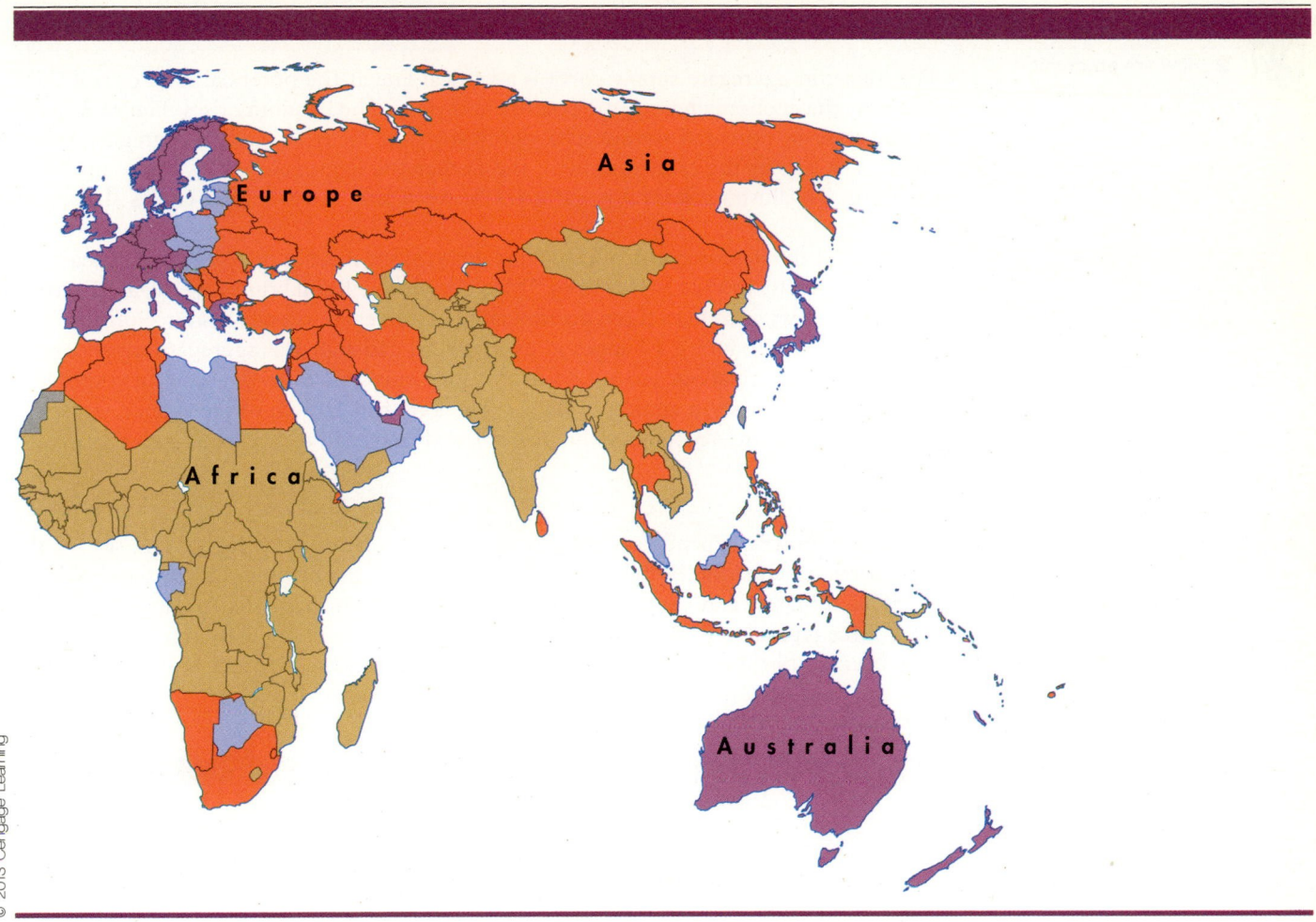

Once again, be careful in interpreting per capita GDP. Don't allow it to represent more than it does. Per capita GDP is simply a measure of the output produced divided by the population. It is a useful measure of economic activity in a country, but it is a questionable measure of the typical citizen's standard of living or quality of life.

RECAP

1. Economic growth is an increase in real GDP.

2. Because growth is compounded over time, small differences in rates of growth are magnified over time.

3. For any constant rate of growth, the time required for real GDP to double is 72 divided by the annual growth rate.

4. Per capita real GDP is real GDP divided by the population.

5. Per capita real GDP says nothing about the distribution of income in a country or the nonmonetary quality of life.

2. The Determinants of Growth

2 How are economic growth rates determined?

The long-run aggregate supply curve is a vertical line at the potential level of real GDP (Y_{p1}). As the economy grows, the potential output of the economy rises. Figure 3 shows the increase in potential output as a rightward shift in the long-run aggregate supply curve. The higher the rate of growth, the farther the aggregate supply curve moves to the right. To illustrate several years' growth, we would show several curves shifting to the right.

> Economic growth raises the potential level of real GDP, shifting the long-run aggregate supply curve to the right.

To find the determinants of economic growth, we must turn to the determinants of aggregate supply. In the chapter titled "Macroeconomic Equilibrium: Aggregate Demand and Supply," we identified three determinants of aggregate supply: resource prices, technology, and expectations. Changes in expectations can shift the aggregate supply curve, but changing expectations are not a basis for long-run growth in the sense of continuous rightward movements in aggregate supply. The long-run growth of the economy rests on growth in productive resources (labor, capital, and land) and technological advances.

2.a. Labor

Economic growth depends on the size and quality of the labor force. The size of the labor force is a function of the size of the working-age population (16 years and older in the United States) and the percentage of that population that is in the labor force. The labor force typically grows more rapidly in developing countries than in industrial countries because birthrates are higher in developing countries. Figure 4 shows the annual

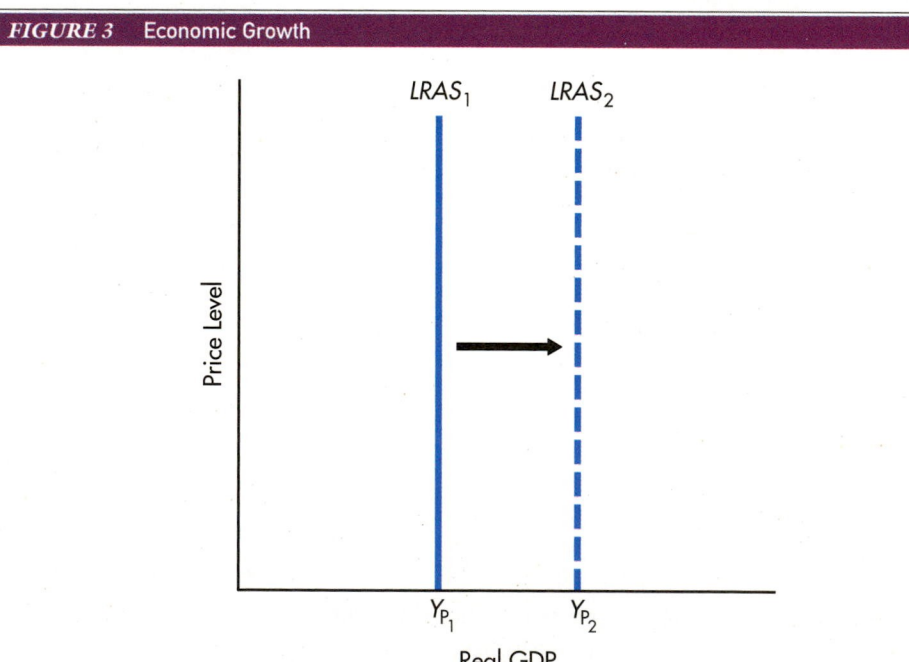

FIGURE 3   Economic Growth

As the economy grows, the long-run aggregate supply curve shifts to the right. This represents an increase in the potential level of real GDP.

growth rates of the population for low-income, middle-income, and high-income countries. Between 1995 and 2010, the population grew at an average annual rate of 1.5 percent in low-income countries, 1.2 percent in middle-income countries, and 0.4 percent in high-income countries.

Based solely on growth in the labor force, it would seem that poor countries are growing faster than rich countries. But the size of the labor force is not all that matters; changes in productivity can compensate for lower growth in the labor force, as we discuss in section 3.

The U.S. labor force has changed considerably in recent decades. The most notable event of the post–World War II period was the baby boom. The children born between the late 1940s and the early 1960s made up more than a third of the total U.S. population in the early 1960s and have significantly altered the age structure of the population. In 1950, 41 percent of the population was 24 years old or younger, and 59 percent was 25 years old or older. By 1970, 46 percent of the population was in the younger group, with 54 percent in the older group. By 1990, this bulge in the age distribution had moved to where about 36 percent of the U.S. population was 24 years or younger. Over time, the bulge will move to older ranges of the population. By 2000, 35 percent of the population was 24 years or younger, with 65 percent 25 years or older.

The initial pressure of the baby boom fell on school systems, which were faced with rapidly expanding enrollments. Over time, as these children aged and entered the labor market, they had a large impact on potential output. The U.S. labor force grew at an average rate of about 2.5 percent a year in the 1970s, approximately twice the rate of growth experienced in the 1950s. The growth of the labor force slowed in the 1980s and 1990s as the baby boom population aged. On the basis of the size of the labor force,

VikramRaghuvanshi/istockphoto.com

Developing countries are playing an increasing role in the "outsourcing" of labor for firms in the industrial world. Here, workers in Bangalore, India, process data for 24/7 customers.

FIGURE 4 Average Annual Population Growth in Low-, Middle-, and High-Income Countries (percent)

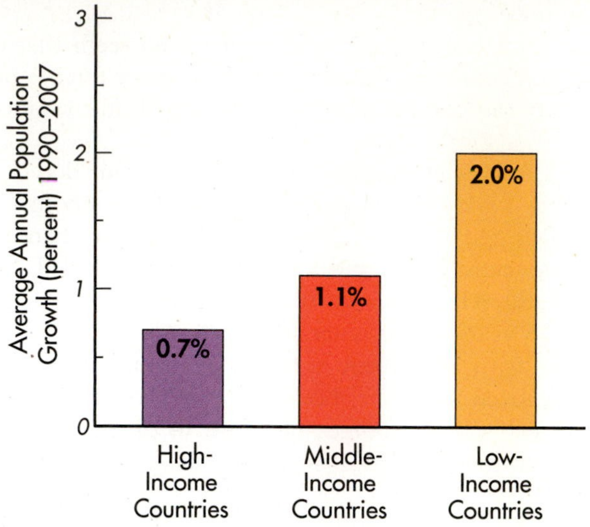

Population growth rates across countries vary considerably. Generally, population grows at a much higher rate in developing countries.

Source: Data are from World Bank; http://devdata.worldbank.org/hnpstats/query/default.html.

the 1970s should have been a time of greater economic growth than the 1950s and 1960s or the 1980s and 1990s. It was not. More important than the size of the labor force is its productivity.

2.b. Capital

Labor is combined with capital to produce goods and services. A rapidly growing labor force by itself is no guarantee of economic growth. Workers need machines, tools, and factories in order to work. If a country has lots of workers but few machines, then the typical worker cannot be very productive. Capital is a critical resource in growing economies.

The ability of a country to invest in capital goods is tied to its ability to save. A lack of current saving can be offset by borrowing, but the availability of borrowing is limited by the prospects for future saving. Debt incurred today must be repaid by not consuming all output in the future. If lenders believe that a nation is going to consume all of its output in the future, they will not make loans today.

The lower the standard of living in a country, the harder it is to forgo current consumption in order to save. It is difficult for a population that is living at or near subsistence level to do without current consumption. This in large part explains the low level of saving in the poorest countries.

2.c. Land

Land surface, water, forests, minerals, and other natural resources are called *land*. Land can be combined with labor and capital to produce goods and services. Abundant natural resources can contribute to economic growth, but natural resources alone do not

ECONOMIC *INSIGHT*

Technological Advance: The Change in the Price of Light

A particularly striking example of the role of technological change is provided by the change in the labor cost of providing light. An economist, William Nordhaus, estimated the effects of technological change on the labor cost of providing lighting. Light can be measured in *lumen hours*, where a lumen is the amount of light provided by one candle. Nordhaus estimated the number of hours of work required to produce 1,000 lumen-hours of light. His estimates of the cost of providing 1,000 lumen hours of light are shown in the accompanying table.

Time	Light Source	Labor Price
500,000 BC	Open fire	58 hours
1750 BC	Babylonian lamp	41.5 hours
1800	Tallow candle	5.4 hours
1900	Filament lamp	0.2 hour
1990	Filament lamp	0.0006 hour

The choice of light is appropriate as the desirable service provided by light, illumination, is essentially unchanged over time. What has changed dramatically is the manner in which light is produced and the cost of producing it. The example shows not only how changing technology has increased the productivity of light production, but also how the pace of technological advance has quickened in recent times. The faster technology progresses, the faster the cost of production falls.

Impeded by low levels of education and limited funds for research and development, the developing countries lag behind the industrial countries in developing and implementing new technology. Typically these countries follow the lead of the industrial world, adopting new technology developed in that world once it is affordable and feasible, given their capital and labor resources. In the next chapter we discuss the role of foreign aid, including technological assistance, in promoting economic growth in developing countries.

*William Nordhaus, "Do Real-Output and Real-Wage Measures Capture Reality? The History of Lighting Suggests Not," in The Economics of New Goods, ed. Timothy Bresnahan and Robert Gordon (Chicago: University of Chicago Press, 1997).

generate growth. Several developing countries, such as Argentina and Brazil, are relatively rich in natural resources but have not been very successful in exploiting these resources to produce goods and services. Japan, on the other hand, has relatively few natural resources but showed dramatic economic growth until a recession in the late 1990s. The experience of Japan makes it clear that abundant natural resources are not a necessary condition for economic growth.

> *Abundant natural resources are not a necessary condition for economic growth.*

2.d. Technology

A key determinant of economic growth is **technology**, or ways of combining resources to produce goods and services. New management techniques, scientific discoveries, and other innovations improve technology. Technological advances allow the production of more output from a given amount of resources. This means that technological progress accelerates economic growth for any given rate of growth in the labor force and the capital stock. A particularly dramatic example of technological change is provided in the Economic Insight "Technological Advance: The Change in the Price of Light."

Technological change depends on the scientific community. The more educated a population, the greater its potential for technological advances. Industrial countries have better-educated populations than developing countries do. Education gives industrial

technology
Ways of combining resources to produce output.

> *Technological advances allow the production of more output from a given amount of resources.*

countries a substantial advantage over developing countries in creating and implementing innovations. In addition, the richest industrial countries traditionally have spent 2 to 3 percent of their GNP on research and development, an investment that developing countries cannot afford. The greater the funding for research and development, the greater the likelihood of technological advances.

RECAP

1. Economic growth raises the potential level of real GDP, shifting the long-run aggregate supply curve to the right.

2. The long-run growth of the economy is a product of growth in labor, capital, and natural resources and advances in technology.

3. The size of the labor force is determined by the working-age population and the percentage of that population that is in the labor force.

4. The post–World War II baby boom created a bulge in the age distribution of the U.S. population.

5. Growth in capital stock is tied to current and future saving.

6. Abundant natural resources contribute to economic growth but are not essential to that growth.

7. Technology is the way in which resources are combined to produce output.

8. Hampered by low levels of education and limited financial resources, developing countries lag behind the industrial nations in developing and implementing new technology.

3. Productivity

3 What is productivity?

total factor productivity (*TFP*)
The ratio of the economy's output to its stock of labor and capital.

In the last section, we described how output depends on resource inputs like labor and capital. One way to assess the contribution that a resource makes to output is its productivity. *Productivity* is the ratio of the output produced to the amount of input. We can measure the productivity of a single resource—say, labor or capital—or the overall productivity of all resources. **Total factor productivity (*TFP*)** is the term that economists use to describe the overall productivity of an economy. It is the ratio of the economy's output to its stock of labor and capital.

3.a. Productivity and Economic Growth

Economic growth depends on both the growth of resources and technological progress. Advances in technology allow resources to be more productive. If the quantity of resources is growing and each resource is more productive, then output grows even faster than the quantity of resources. Economic growth, then, is the sum of the growth rate of total factor productivity and the growth rate of resources:

Economic growth = growth rate of *TFP* + growth rate of resources

The amount by which output grows because the labor force is growing depends on how much labor contributes to the production of output. Similarly, the amount by which output grows because capital is growing depends on how much capital contributes to the production of output. To relate the growth of labor and capital to the growth of output (we assume no change in natural resources), the growth of labor and the growth of capital must be multiplied by their relative contributions to the production of output. The most straightforward way to measure those contributions is to use the share of real GDP received by each resource. For instance, in the United States, labor receives about 70 percent (.70) of real GDP and capital receives about 30 percent (.30). So we can determine the growth of output by using this formula:

$$\%\Delta Y = \%\Delta TFP + .70(\%\Delta L) + .30(\%\Delta K)$$

where

$$\%\Delta = \text{percentage change in}$$
$$Y = \text{real GDP}$$
$$TFP = \text{total factor productivity}$$
$$L = \text{size of the labor force}$$
$$K = \text{capital stock}$$

The equation shows how economic growth depends on changes in productivity ($\%\Delta TFP$) as well as changes in resources ($\%\Delta L$ and $\%\Delta K$). Even if labor (L) and capital stock (K) are constant, technological innovation will generate economic growth through changes in total factor productivity (TFP).

For example, suppose TFP is growing at a rate of 2 percent a year. Then, even with labor and capital stock held constant, the economy grows at a rate of 2 percent a year. If labor and capital stock also grow at a rate of 2 percent a year, output grows by the sum of the growth rates of all three components (TFP, .70 times labor growth, and .30 times the capital stock growth), or 4 percent.

How do we account for differences in growth rates across countries? Because almost all countries have experienced growth in the labor force, percentage increases in labor forces have generally supported economic growth. But growth in the capital stock has been steadier in the industrial countries than in the developing countries, so differences in capital growth rates may explain some of the differences in economic growth across countries. Yet differences in resource growth rates alone cannot explain the major differences we find across countries. In recent years, those differences seem to be related to productivity.

3.b. Determinants of Productivity

Productivity in the United States has fluctuated considerably in recent years. From 1948 to 1965, TFP grew at an annual average rate of 2.02 percent. In the 1970s, TFP growth averaged 0.7 percent per year; in the 1980s, 0.6 percent; and by the late 1990s, 1 percent. If the pre-1965 rate of growth had been maintained, output in the United States would be an estimated 39 percent higher today than it actually is. What caused this dramatic change in productivity—first down in the 1970s and 1980s, and then up in the 1990s? More generally, what determines the productivity changes for any country?

Several factors determine productivity growth. They include the quality of the labor force, technological innovations, energy prices, and a shift from manufacturing to service industries.

 4 What explains productivity changes?

3.b.1. Labor Quality
Labor productivity is measured as output per hour of labor. Figure 5 shows how the productivity of labor in the United States and four other countries changed between 1979 and 2009. We see that Korea generally has had the fastest rate of labor productivity growth and Canada the lowest over this time period. Although changes in the productivity of labor can stem from technological innovation and changes in the capital stock, they can also come from changes in the quality of labor. These changes may be a product of the level and quality of education, demographic change, and changing attitudes toward work.

Education Level The average level of education in the world has gone up over time. Table 2 lists three measures of education level for the United States.

The first measure, median school years completed, increased from 8.6 years in 1940 to 12.9 years in 2000. From 1940 to 2009, the percentage of adults with at least a high

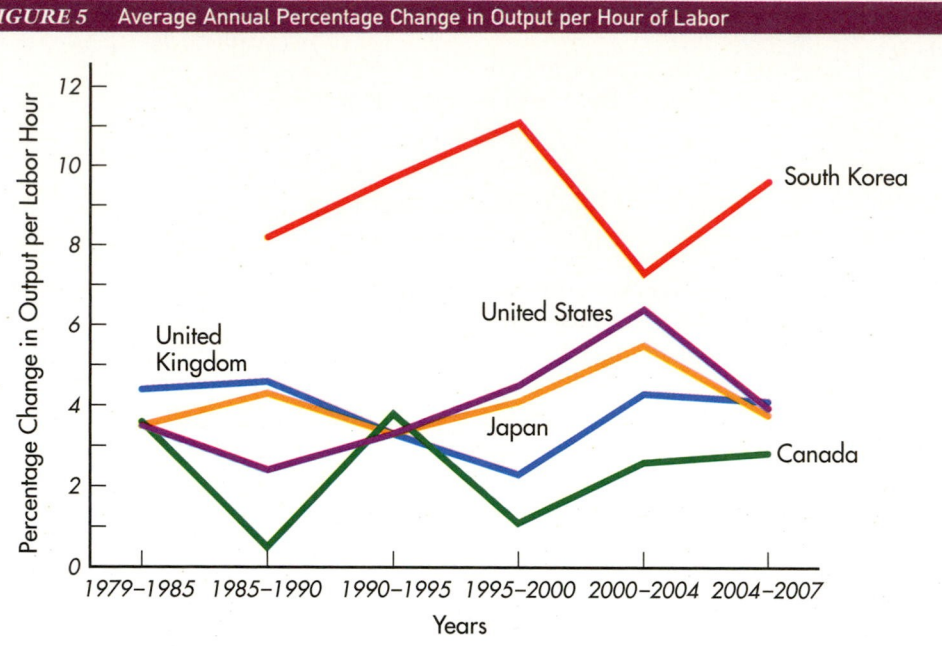

FIGURE 5 Average Annual Percentage Change in Output per Hour of Labor

Output per labor hour is a measure of productivity.

Source: Data from *Bureau of Labor Statistics*; www.bls.gov/fls/home/htm.

school education rose from more than 24 percent to 86.7 percent, and the percentage of those with a college education rose from less than 5 percent to 29.5 percent. The figures seem to indicate that the level of education supports increases in U.S. productivity.

Demographic Change Changes in the size and composition of the population have an impact on the labor market. As the baby boom generation entered the labor force in the late 1960s and early 1970s, a large pool of inexperienced, unskilled workers was created. The average quality of the labor force may have fallen at this time, as reflected in some large drops in output per hour of labor. In the 1980s, the baby boom segment of the labor force had more experience, skills, and education, thus pushing the quality of the labor force up.

Another important demographic change that has affected the quality of the labor force is the participation rates of women. As more and more women entered the labor

TABLE 2   The Average Level of Education, United States, 1940–2009*

	1940	1950	1960	1970	1980	1990	2000	2009
Median school years completed	8.6	9.3	10.6	12.1	12.5	12.7	12.9	N/A
People with at least a high school education (percent)	24.5	34.3	41.1	52.3	66.5	75.2	84.1	86.7
People with at least four years of college (percent)	4.6	6.2	7.7	10.7	16.2	20.3	25.6	29.5

*People 25 years of age and over.
Source: U.S. Census Bureau; http://www.census.gov/hhes/socdemo/education/data/cps/2009/tables.html.

force in the 1980s, the pool of untrained workers increased, probably reducing the average quality of labor. Over time, as female participation rates have stabilized, the average quality of labor should rise as the skills and experience of female workers rise.

Finally, immigration can play a role in labor force quality. For instance, the 1970s and 1980s saw a change in the pattern of U.S. immigration. Although many highly skilled professionals immigrate to the United States as part of the "brain drain" from developing countries, recent immigrants, both legal and illegal, have generally added to the supply of unskilled labor and reduced the average quality of the labor force.

3.b.2. Technological Innovation

New technology alters total factor productivity. Innovations increase productivity, so when productivity falls, it is natural to look at technological developments to see whether they are a factor in the change. The pace of technological innovation is difficult to measure. Expenditures on research and development are related to the discovery of new knowledge, but actual changes in technology do not proceed as evenly as those expenditures. We expect a long lag between funding and operating a laboratory and the discovery of useful technology. Still, a decline in spending on research and development may indicate less of a commitment to increasing productivity.

The most notable technological innovation in recent decades has been the widespread availability of cheaper and faster computers. The information technology (IT) revolution has played an important role in enhancing productivity.

One may think of the purchase of computer hardware or software as investment. The capital stock increases with such purchases. However, researchers have also found that there are increases in total factor productivity associated with the development and spread of information technology. Such gains have not been realized by all countries. Poor countries lag far behind the rich in the implementation of IT. Table 3 provides data on the number of broadband users per 100 people in selected countries in 2011. Clearly, the productivity-enhancing benefits of IT have been realized in countries like South Korea, Hong Kong, the Netherlands, and the other countries at the top of the table, where the number of broadband users per 100 people is 24.66, 23.35, and 23.34, respectively.

However, in developing countries, the benefits of IT innovations are not being fully exploited as a result of poverty and lack of skills. In Table 3, the lowest level of broadband use is 0.06 in India. However, in poorer countries that are not listed in the table, the level of usage is even less. This indicates an inability to implement IT widely across the economy. IT is just one example of how productivity may differ across countries as a result of differing uses of modern technology.

3.b.3. Other Factors

We have seen how changing labor quality and technological innovation are related to changes in productivity. Other reasons have been offered to explain the changes in productivity across countries and over time. We examine three of them: the cost of energy, the shift from a manufacturing to a service-oriented economy, and the development of financial markets.

Energy Prices In 1973, 1974, and 1979, OPEC succeeded in raising the price of oil substantially. The timing of the dramatic increase in oil prices coincided with a drop in productivity growth in the United States. U.S. output per labor hour actually fell in 1974 and 1979. Higher energy prices resulting from restricted oil output should directly decrease aggregate supply because energy is an important input across industries. As the price of energy increases, the costs of production rise and aggregate supply decreases.

Higher energy prices can affect productivity through their impact on the capital stock. As energy prices go up, energy-inefficient capital goods become obsolete. Like any other decline in the value of the capital stock, this change reduces economic growth.

TABLE 3	Broadband Users per 100 People	
Rank	**Country**	**Broadband Users per 100 People**
1	South Korea	24.66
2	Hong Kong	23.35
3	Netherlands	23.34
4	Denmark	22.55
5	Switzerland	20.7
6	Canada	19.3
7	Norway	19.25
8	Finland	19.2
9	Sweden	18.68
10	Taiwan	18.41
11	Israel	18.24
12	Belgium	17.92
13	Japan	16.41
14	France	14.72
15	United Kingdom	14.66
16	United States	13.82
17	Austria	13.05
18	Australia	11.77
19	Portugal	10.87
19	Spain	10.87
21	Germany	10.2
22	Italy	10.16
23	Chile	4.1
24	Poland	3.52
25	China	2.68
26	Argentina	1.75
27	Turkey	1.62
28	Brazil	1.56
29	Russia	0.99
30	Mexico	0.88
31	India	0.06

Source: http://www.nationmaster.com/graph/int_bro_acc-internet-broadband-access, 2011.

Standard measures of capital stock do not account for energy obsolescence, so they suggest that total factor productivity fell in the 1970s. However, if the stock of usable capital actually did go down, it was the growth rate of capital, not *TFP*, that fell.

Manufacturing versus Services   In recent decades, the industrial economies have seen a shift away from manufacturing toward services. Some economists believe that productivity grows more slowly in service industries than in manufacturing because of the less capital-intensive nature of providing services. Therefore, the movement into services reduces the overall growth rate of the economy.

Although a greater emphasis on service industries may explain a drop in productivity, we must be careful with this kind of generalization. It is more difficult to measure changes in the quality of services than changes in the quality of goods. If prices in an industry rise with no change in the quantity of output, it makes sense to conclude that the real level of output in the industry has fallen. However, if prices have gone up because the quality of the service has increased, then output actually has changed. Suppose a hotel remodels its rooms. In effect, it is improving the quality of its service. Increased prices here would reflect this change in output.

Service industries—fast-food restaurants, airlines, hotels, banks—are not all alike. One way in which service firms compete is on the basis of the quality of service that they provide. Because productivity is measured by the amount of output per unit of input, if we don't adjust for quality changes, we may underestimate the amount of output and so underestimate the productivity of the industry. The issue of productivity measurement in the service industries is an important topic of discussion among economists today.

Financial Market Development   The evidence across countries suggests that economic growth is related to the development of financial markets. For any given amount of labor and capital, the more developed an economy's financial markets are, the more efficient should be the allocation of resources and, therefore, the greater the productivity. A nation may have a high rate of saving and investment and a sizable capital stock, but the key to efficient production is the allocation of resources to their best use.

Financial markets facilitate the allocation of resources. This occurs through the following mechanisms:

- Financial institutions act as intermediaries between savers and borrowers and screen borrowers so that the best projects are more likely to be funded.
- Financial institutions monitor the behavior of borrowers to ensure that the borrowed funds are used as intended.
- Financial institutions lower the risk of providing funds for investment purposes, as they provide loans to different individuals and firms, and through this diversification of loans reduce the likelihood of suffering a catastrophic loss. If one borrower defaults on a loan, the financial institution does not fail as it still has many other loans that are being repaid. This is a far different situation from the one that an individual making a single large loan may face. If you lend a large amount of your wealth to a single borrower and that borrower defaults on the loan, your living standard may be at great risk. Because of the "risk sharing" that takes place in financial institutions, the cost of borrowed funds, the interest rate, will be lower than in an environment in which there is no such pooling of loan risks.
- The more developed the financial sector of an economy, the more types of financing alternatives there are for funding investment. For instance, the typical poor country has a banking sector and a very limited stock market, if any at all. Firms in such a country must rely on bank loans. The governments in such countries often determine where banks are allowed to lend based on political considerations. As economies develop, the financial sector evolves so that alternatives to bank financing come into being. Firms in economies with well-developed financial markets can raise funds by selling shares of ownership in the stock market, by issuing debt in the form of bonds to nonbank lenders, or by borrowing from banks. The more developed a country's financial markets, the more efficient the funding sources for borrowers and the more productive the economy.

3.c. Growth and Development

Economic growth depends on the growth of productivity and resources. Productivity grows unevenly, and its rate of growth is reflected in economic growth. Although the labor force seems to grow faster in developing countries than in industrial countries, lower rates of saving have limited the growth of the capital stock in developing countries. Without capital, workers cannot be very productive. This means that the relatively high rate of growth in the labor force in the developing world does not translate into a high rate of economic growth. We use this information on economic growth in the chapter titled "Development Economics" to explain and analyze the strategies used by developing countries to stimulate output and increase standards of living.

RECAP

1. Productivity is the ratio of the output produced to the amount of input.

2. Total factor productivity is the nation's real GDP (output) divided by its stock of labor and capital.

3. Economic growth is the sum of the growth rate of total factor productivity and the growth rate of resources (labor and capital).

4. Changes in productivity may be explained by the quality of the labor force, technological innovations, energy prices, a shift from manufacturing to service industries, and financial market development.

SUMMARY

1. **What is economic growth?**

- Economic growth is an increase in real GDP. *§1.a*

- Economic growth is compounded over time. *§1.a.1*

- Per capita real GDP is real GDP divided by the population. *§1.b*

- The definitions of economic growth are misleading because they do not indicate anything about the distribution of income or the quality of life. *§1.c*

2. **How are economic growth rates determined?**

- The growth of the economy is tied to the growth of productive resources and technological advances. *§2*

- Because their populations tend to grow more rapidly, developing countries typically experience faster growth in the labor force than do industrial countries. *§2.a*

- The inability to save limits the growth of the capital stock in developing countries. *§2.b*

- Abundant natural resources are not necessary for rapid economic growth. *§2.c*

- Technology defines the ways in which resources can be combined to produce goods and services. *§2.d*

3. **What is productivity?**

- Productivity is the ratio of the output produced to the amount of input. *§3*

- Total factor productivity is the overall productivity of an economy. *§3*

- The percentage change in real GDP equals the percentage change in total factor productivity plus the percentage changes in labor and capital multiplied by the share of GDP taken by labor and capital. *§3.a*

4. **What explains productivity changes?**

- Productivity changes with changes in the quality of the labor force, technological innovations, changes in energy prices, a shift from manufacturing to service industries, and financial market development. *§3.b*

KEY TERMS

economic growth, 357   rule of 72, 358   total factor productivity
per capita real GDP, 359   technology, 365   (*TFP*), 366

EXERCISES

1. Why is the growth of per capita real GDP a better measure of economic growth than the growth of real GDP?

2. What is the level of output after four years if initial output equals $1,000 and the economy grows at a rate of 8 percent a year?

3. Use the data in the following table to determine the average annual growth rate for each country in terms of real GDP growth and per capita real GDP growth (real GDP is in billions of U.S. dollars, and population is in millions of people). Which country grew at the faster rate?

	1999		2001	
Country	**Real GDP**	**Population**	**Real GDP**	**Population**
Morocco	108.0	30.1	112.0	31.2
Australia	416.2	19.2	528.0	19.5

4. Suppose labor's share of GDP is 70 percent and capital's is 30 percent, real GDP is growing at a rate of 4 percent a year, the labor force is growing at 2 percent, and the capital stock is growing at 3 percent. What is the growth rate of total factor productivity?

5. Suppose labor's share of GDP is 70 percent and capital's is 30 percent, total factor productivity is growing at an annual rate of 2 percent, the labor force is growing at a rate of 1 percent, and the capital stock is growing at a rate of 4 percent. What is the annual growth rate of real GDP?

6. Discuss possible reasons for the slowdown in U.S. productivity growth that occurred in the 1970s and 1980s, and relate each reason to the equation for economic growth. Does the growth of *TFP* or of resources change?

7. How did the post–World War II baby boom affect the growth of the U.S. labor force? What effect is this baby boom likely to have on the future U.S. labor force?

8. How do developing and industrial countries differ in their use of technological change, labor, capital, and natural resources to produce economic growth? Why do these differences exist?

9. How would an aging population affect economic growth?

10. If real GDP for China was 10,312 billion yuan at the end of 2002 and 9,593 billion yuan at the end of 2001, what is the annual rate of growth of the Chinese economy?

11. If Botswana's economy grew at a rate of 1 percent during 2006 and real GDP at the beginning of the year was 44 billion pula, then what is real GDP at the end of the year?

12. Suppose a country has a real GDP equal to $1 billion today. If this economy grows at a rate of 4 percent a year, what will be the value of real GDP after five years?

13. Is the following statement true or false? Explain your answer. "Abundant natural resources are a necessary condition for economic growth."

14. What is the difference between total factor productivity and the productivity of labor? Why do you suppose that people often measure a nation's productivity using labor productivity only?

15. How would each of the following affect productivity in the United States?
    a. The quality of education in high schools increases.
    b. A cutback in oil production by oil-exporting nations raises oil prices.
    c. A large number of unskilled immigrant laborers move into the country.

16. How does the development of financial markets enhance the productivity of a country?

You can find further practice tests in the Online Quiz at **www.cengage.com/economics/boyes**.

RIDING A SURGE OF TECHNOLOGY

Federal Reserve Bank of Dallas 2003 Annual Report

Because productivity determines how well we live, Americans want to know how they're doing. In an economy as large and diverse as ours, it's a Herculean task to calculate a productivity number that sums up the efforts of 130 million workers, employed in millions of establishments that produce more than $11 trillion in output. The Bureau of Labor Statistics (BLS) does the best it can in producing quarterly estimates of output per hour, derived largely from surveys of businesses.

BLS data show that U.S. productivity has grown steadily over the long haul, with output per hour rising an average 2.3 percent annually since 1870. A few percentage points a year might not sound like much, but this historical rate doubles per capita income every three decades or so.

The productivity path has been choppy due to business-cycle upturns and slowdowns as well as longer-term economic trends. From 1950 to 1973, for example, output per hour rose a healthy 2.7 percent annually. Over the next 22 years, productivity sank below its long-term trend, rising just 1.5 percent a year. The slowdown remains something of a mystery, although some economists suggest that early investments in computers and information technology didn't provide a big enough payoff.

Productivity broke out of its two-decade doldrums in the mid-1990s as computers, scanners, the Internet and other innovations finally reached critical mass in America's workplaces. Average annual productivity gains have surged at 3.2 percent since 1995.

The revival shows every sign of continuing. The economy emerged from the 2001 recession with productivity growth well above the average of the seven significant business cycles since 1960. In the first 11 quarters after employment peaked, productivity jumped 13 percent, compared with the historical norm of 8 percent. In another break with the past, the gains spread beyond manufacturing, the traditional productivity leader, and into the whole economy, including retailing and services.

Productivity's postrecession surge has been strong enough to spark controversy. The labor market has languished, with no net job creation two years into the recovery. Some see productivity as a millstone that allows companies to expand without hiring more workers. But viewing productivity as a drag on employment is myopic. Americans don't face a choice between having work and working a better way. Higher productivity raises incomes and profits, which fuels demand, boosts investment and puts more people to work, usually at new jobs.

We could dismantle our factory robots and farm equipment with the idea of hiring lots of busy hands to build cars and till the soil. We could junk our backhoes and dig ditches with shovels. Doing so would be absurd. We'd immediately see that renouncing productivity would do us great harm. Prices would be higher, wages lower and the economy smaller. Work would be harder. Living standards would be dragged backward in time, sacrificed to the false god of more jobs.

Rather than shunning productivity, we should embrace it and move forward. As the economic recovery continues, the United States may not be able to sustain the same pace of productivity growth it has the past two years. Even with a slowdown, the nation will likely build on recent years' strong productivity growth, rather than relapse into the post-1973 slump.

The bullish case for future productivity centers on the technologies that have made U.S. workplaces more efficient in recent years. The microchip revolution still has plenty of kick left in it. And as world markets integrate, we should add to our productivity gains from trade.

Further out, new generations of world-shaking technologies will impact the way we work. Take nanotechnology, the science of rearranging atoms and molecules. It promises to create new materials that are stronger, lighter and more flexible and substances with perfect insulating, lubricating and conducting properties. Biotechnology will emerge, too, as a potent force for progress.

When combined with America's entrepreneurial bent and open markets, the inventory of cutting-edge technologies should deliver rapid productivity growth for years. Healthy gains in output per hour may restore the luster of the New Economy, a concept tarnished by the dotcom implosion. The New Economy carries a powerful policy implication: With stronger productivity, the economy can grow faster without fueling inflation.

Measuring a nation's productivity has never been an easy task. As the article says, it is "a Herculean task to calculate a productivity number that sums up the efforts of 130 million workers, employed in millions of establishments that produce more than $11 trillion in output." Since business and government policy makers make important decisions on the basis of the economic data provided by government, accurate measurement is crucial.

An example of the controversy related to the measurement problems is the issue of the "New Economy." As mentioned at the end of the article, the New Economy means that, with strong increases in productivity, the economy can grow faster without higher inflation. This is a world in which technological advances in computers and information technology are driving increased productivity and output.

To estimate the contribution of computers to growth, one can modify the growth equation presented in section 3.a of this chapter to allow computers to be treated apart from the rest of the capital stock:

$$\%\Delta Y = \%\Delta TFP + .70(\%\Delta L) + .29(\%\Delta K) + .01(\%\Delta COMP)$$

Note that this equation has computers accounting for 1 percent of the real GDP, and other capital for 29 percent.

The growth equation with computers treated separately from the rest of the capital stock allows us to estimate the effect of computers on growth (the product of their GDP share, .01, and the percentage change in the stock of computers).

A study conducted by Dale Jorgensen, Mun Ho, and Kevin Stiroh* estimated that a little less than half of the change in *TFP* over the period 1995–2003 can be explained by IT, compared with less than .10 over the earlier period 1959–1973. The U.S. evidence thus indicates a clear role for IT in increasing *TFP*.

The article points out that productivity advances allow higher living standards and create new jobs. Countries that develop and employ new technology will have faster economic growth, less poverty, and less inflation than they would otherwise.

---

* Dale W. Jorgensen, Mun S. Ho, and Kevin J. Stiroh, "Will the U.S. Productivity Resurgency Continue?" Federal Reserve Bank of New York, *Current Issues in Economics and Finance,* December 2004.

Development Economics

AP PHOTO/FARAH ABDI WARSAMEH; LOGO: © FROXX/SHUTTERSTOCK.COM

FUNDAMENTAL QUESTIONS

1 How is poverty measured?

2 Why are some countries poorer than others?

3 What strategies can a nation use to increase its economic growth?

4 How are savings in one nation used to speed development in other nations?

There is an enormous difference between the standards of living in the poorest and the richest countries in the world. In Botswana, the average life expectancy at birth is 61 years, 17 years less than in the United States. In Cambodia, only an estimated 65 percent of the population has access to safe water. In Ghana, 30 percent of the population exists on less than $1.25 per day. And in Chad, only 35 percent of women and 53 percent of men between 15 and 24 years of age can read.

The plight of developing countries is our focus in this chapter. We begin by discussing the extent of poverty and how it is measured across countries. Then we turn to the reasons why developing countries are poor and look at strategies for stimulating growth and development. The reasons for poverty are many, and the remedies often are rooted more in politics than in economics. Still, economics has much to say about how to improve the living standards of the world's poorest citizens.

1. The Developing World

Three-fourths of the world's population lives in developing countries. These countries are often called *less-developed countries (LDCs)*.

The common link among developing countries is low per capita GNP or GDP, which implies a relatively low standard of living for the typical citizen. In other respects, the developing countries are a diverse group, with their cultures, their politics, and even their geography varying enormously. Although we have used GDP throughout the text as the popular measure of a nation's output, in this chapter we frequently refer to GNP, as this is the measure used by the World Bank in classifying countries in terms of stage of development.

The developing countries are located primarily in South and East Asia, Africa, the Middle East, and Latin America (Figure 1). The total population of developing countries is over 5.6 billion people. Of this population, 23 percent live in China and 20 percent live in India. The next largest concentration of people is in Indonesia (4 percent), followed by Brazil, Pakistan, Bangladesh, and Nigeria. Except for Latin America, where 74 percent of the population lives in cities, most Third World citizens live in rural areas and are largely dependent on agriculture.

1.a. Measuring Poverty

1 How is poverty measured?

Poverty typically is defined in absolute terms.

Poverty is not easy to measure. Typically, poverty is defined in an *absolute* sense: A family is poor if its income falls below a certain level. For example, the poverty level for a family of four in the United States in 2010 was an income of $22,050. The World Bank uses per capita GNP of $995 or less as its criterion for a low-income country. The countries in gold in Figure 1 meet this absolute definition of poverty.

Poverty is also a *relative* concept. A family's income in relation to the incomes of other families in the country or region is important in determining whether that family feels poor. The poverty level in the United States would represent a substantial increase in the living standard of most of the people in the world. Yet a poor family in the United States does not feel less poor because it has more money than poor families in other countries. In a nation where the median income of a family of four is more than $65,000, a family with an income of $20,000 clearly feels poorer.

Because poverty is also a relative concept, using a particular level of income to distinguish the poor from the not poor is often controversial. Besides the obvious problem of where to draw the poverty line, there is the more difficult problem of comparing poverty across countries with different currencies, customs, and living arrangements. Also, data are often limited and difficult to obtain because many of the poor in developing countries live in isolated areas. This makes it difficult to draw a comprehensive picture of the typical poor household in the Third World.

FIGURE 1   The World by Stage of Development

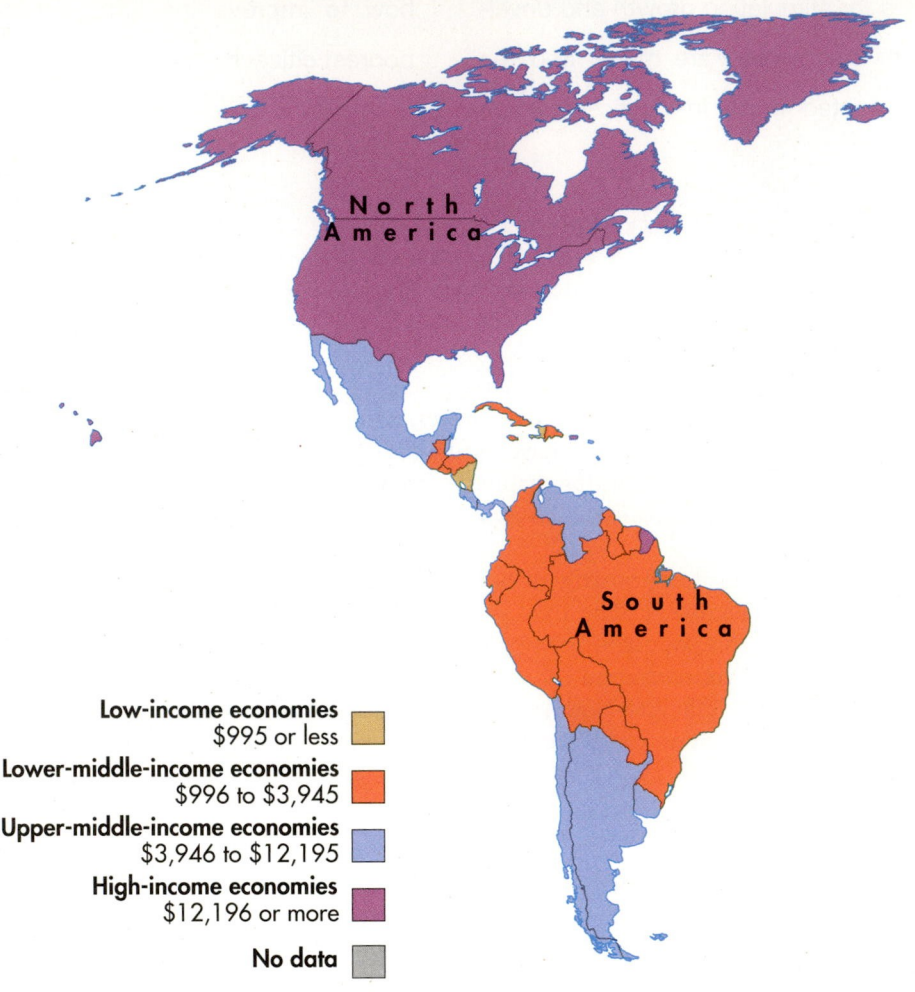

Low-income economies
$995 or less

Lower-middle-income economies
$996 to $3,945

Upper-middle-income economies
$3,946 to $12,195

High-income economies
$12,196 or more

No data

The map of the world is colored to show each country's income level as measured by per capita GNP.
Source: World Bank, http://go.worldbank.org/7EIAD6CKOO.

1.b. Basic Human Needs

> *Basic human needs are a minimal level of caloric intake, health care, clothing, and shelter.*

Some economists and other social scientists, recognizing the limitations of an absolute definition of poverty (like the per capita GNP measure that is most commonly used), suggest using indicators of how well basic human needs are being met. Although they disagree on the exact definition of *basic human needs*, the general idea is to set minimal levels of caloric intake, health care, clothing, and shelter.

Another alternative to per capita GNP is a physical *quality-of-life index* to evaluate living standards. One approach uses life expectancy, infant mortality, and literacy as indicators—a very narrow definition that ignores elements like justice, personal freedom, environmental quality, and employment opportunities. Nonetheless, these three indicators are, at least in theory, measures of social progress that allow meaningful comparisons across countries, whatever their social or political orientation.

Table 1 lists per capita GNP and indicators of human development for selected countries. The countries are listed in order of per capita GNP, beginning with the

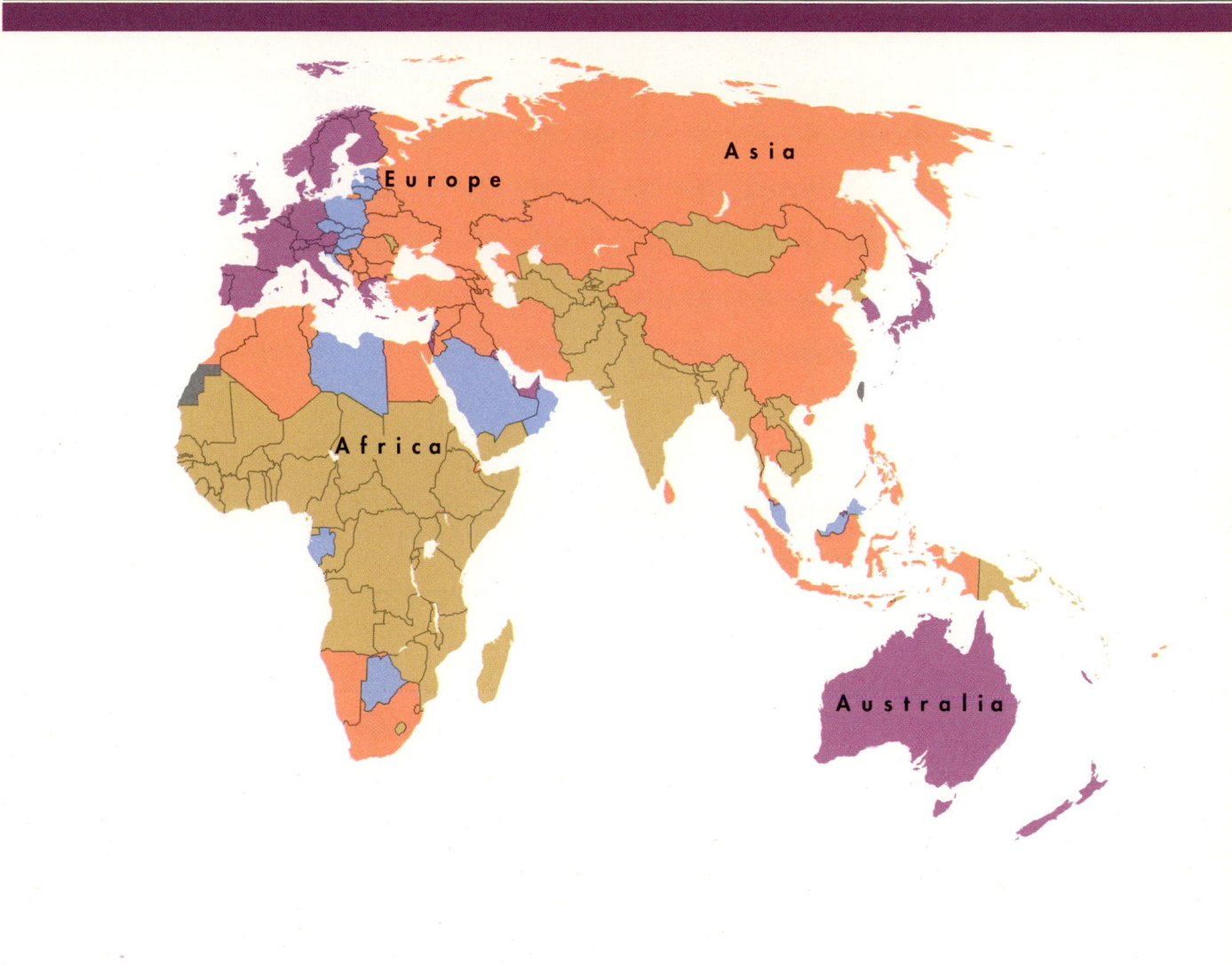

smallest. Generally there is a strong positive relationship between per capita GNP and the other measures. But there are cases where higher per capita GNP does not mean higher quality of life. For instance, Namibia has a higher per capita GNP than China or the Philippines, but life expectancy and literacy are lower in Namibia than in the other two countries. Remember the limitations of per capita output: It is not a measure of everyone's standard of living in a particular country. However, as the table shows, it is a fairly reliable indicator of differences in living standards across countries. Ethiopia has the lowest per capita GNP and is clearly one of the world's poorest nations. Usually, as per capita GNP increases, living standards increase as well.

Per capita GNP and quality-of-life measures are not the only ways to determine a country's level of economic development—we could consider the number of households with running water, televisions, or any other good that varies with living standards. Recognizing that there is no perfect measure of economic development, economists and other social scientists often use several indicators to assess economic progress.

TABLE 1	Quality-of-Life Measures, Selected Countries		
Country	Per Capita GNP*	Life Expectancy at Birth (years)	Female Literacy Rate[†]
Ethiopia	$ 220	53	28%
Bangladesh	$ 470	64	73%
India	$ 950	65	77%
Philippines	$ 1,620	72	95%
China	$ 2,370	73	99%
El Salvador	$ 2,850	72	94%
Namibia	$ 3,450	53	94%
Turkey	$ 8,030	72	94%
Mexico	$ 9,400	75	98%
Greece	$25,740	80	99%
United States	$46,040	78	100%

*2008 data measured in terms of U.S. dollars.
†Percentage of the female population 15 years or older that is literate.
Source: World Bank, http://web.worldbank.org.

RECAP

1. Usually poverty is defined in an absolute sense as a specific level of family income or per capita GNP or GDP.

2. Within a country or region, poverty is a relative concept.

3. Human development indexes based on indicators of basic human needs incorporate nonmonetary measures of well-being that are an alternative to per capita GDP for measuring economic development.

2. Obstacles to Growth

2 Why are some countries poorer than others?

Every country is unique. Each nation's history, both political and cultural, helps economists understand why a particular nation has not developed and what policies offer the best hope for its development. Generally the factors that impede development are political or social. The political factors include a lack of administrative skills, instability, corruption, and the ability of special interest groups to block changes in economic policy. The social obstacles include a lack of entrepreneurs and rapid population growth.

2.a. Political Obstacles

2.a.1. Lack of Administrative Skills
Government support is essential to economic development. Whether support means allowing private enterprise to flourish and develop or actively managing the allocation of resources, a poorly organized or corrupt government can present an obstacle to economic growth. Some developing countries have suffered from well-meaning but inept government management. This is most obvious in countries with a long history of colonization. For example, when the

Democratic Republic of the Congo won independence from Belgium, few of its native citizens were college educated. Moreover, Belgians had run most of the important government offices. Independence brought a large group of inexperienced and unskilled workers to important positions of power. At first there was a period of "learning by doing."

2.a.2. Political Instability and Risk

One of the most important functions that a government performs in stimulating economic growth is providing a political environment that encourages saving and investment. People do not want to do business in an economy that has been weakened by wars, demonstrations, or uncertainty. For instance, since becoming an independent nation in 1825, Bolivia has had more than 150 changes in government. This kind of instability forces citizens to take a short-run view of the economy. Long-term planning is impossible when people do not know what the attitudes and policies of the government that is going to be in power next year or even next month will be.

The key issue here is *property rights*. A country that guarantees the right of private property encourages private investment and development. Where ownership rights may be changed by revolution or political decree, there is little incentive for private investment and development. People will not start new businesses or build new factories if they believe that a change in government or a change in the political will of the current government could result in the confiscation of their property.

> A country must be able to guarantee the rights of private property if it is going to create an environment that encourages private investment.

This confiscation is called **expropriation**. Countries with a history of expropriating foreign-owned property without compensating the owners (paying them the property's market value) have difficulty encouraging foreign investment. An example is Uganda. In 1973, a successful revolution by Idi Amin was followed by the expropriation of over 500 foreign-owned (mostly British) firms. Foreign and domestic investment in Uganda fell dramatically as a result.

expropriation
The government seizure of assets, typically without adequate compensation to the owners.

The loss of foreign investment is particularly important in developing countries. In the chapter titled "Economic Growth," we pointed out that developing countries suffer from a lack of saving. If domestic residents are not able to save because they are living at or below subsistence level, foreign saving is a crucial source of investment. Without that investment, the economies of developing countries cannot grow.

2.a.3. Corruption

Corrupt practices by government officials have long reduced economic growth. Payment of money or gifts in order to receive a government service or benefit is quite widespread in many countries. Research shows that there is a definite negative relationship between the level of corruption in a country and both investment and growth.

Research also shows that corruption thrives in countries where government regulations create distortions between the economic outcomes that would exist with free markets and the actual outcomes. For instance, a country where government permission is required in order to buy or sell foreign currency will have a thriving black market in foreign exchange, and the black market exchange rate of a U.S. dollar will cost much more domestic currency than the official rate offered by the government. This distortion allows government officials an opportunity for personal gain by providing access to the official rate.

Generally speaking, the more competitive a country's markets are, the fewer the opportunities for corruption. So policies aimed at reducing corruption typically involve reducing the discretion that public officials have in granting benefits or imposing costs on others. This may include greater transparency of government practices and the introduction of merit-based competition for government employment.

Corruption reduces growth most directly through government investment in projects with low productivity. The evidence indicates that corrupt governments spend more on capital goods than governments that are less corrupt, but that the investment projects of corrupt governments probably reduce the productivity of the country. In addition, those countries in which corrupt governments engage in large amounts of capital expenditures have relatively small amounts of private investment. Since private investment is aimed at earning a profit, such investment tends to increase the productivity of a nation. Private firms do not undertake risky projects unless they expect to earn a profit. It is possible, however, that a corrupt government may award large construction projects in order to receive financial rewards from the contractors that are hired. The projects chosen may turn out to be inefficient uses of government funds that retard economic growth rather than increase it.

2.a.4. Good Economics as Bad Politics

Every Third World politician wants to maximize economic growth, all things being equal. But all things are rarely equal. Political pressures may force a government to work toward more immediate objectives than economic growth.

For example, maximizing growth may mean reducing the size of government in order to lower taxes and increase investment. However, in many developing countries, the strongest supporters of the political leaders are those working for the current government. Obviously, it's not good political strategy to fire those workers. So the government remains overstaffed and inefficient, and the potential for economic growth falls.

The governments in developing countries often subsidize purchases of food and other basic necessities. Rather than artificially lower some food prices, it is better to move toward free market pricing of food, energy, and other items to better reflect relative scarcity and then give subsidies to the poor to enable them to buy an adequate diet.

In 1977, the Egyptian government lowered its food subsidies in order to use those funds for development. What happened? There was widespread rioting that ended only when the government reinstituted the subsidies. In 1989, Venezuela lowered government subsidies of public transportation and petroleum products. Public transit fares went up 30 percent, to the equivalent of 7 U.S. cents, and gasoline prices went from 16 to 26 cents a gallon. (One official said that the prices were raised "from the cheapest in the world to the cheapest in the world."[1]) The resulting rioting in Caracas led to 50 deaths, over 500 injuries, and more than 1,000 arrests. Lowering government expenditures and reducing the role of government in the economy can be both politically and physically dangerous.

What we are saying here is that seemingly good economics can make for bad politics. Because any change in policy aimed at increasing growth is going to hurt some group in the short run, there always is opposition to change. Often the continued rule of the existing regime depends on not alienating a certain group. Only a government that is stabilized by military force (a dictatorship), popular support (a democracy), or party support (a Communist or socialist country) has the power to implement needed economic change. A government that lacks this power is handicapped by political constraints in its efforts to stimulate economic growth.

The Global Business Insight "Economic Development in the Americas" points out how history plays a role in shaping the institutions and economic framework in which development takes place. The more rapid development of Canada and the United States than of Latin America may be traced back to colonial times and the institutions that evolved from the conditions that existed then.

---

[1] See "Venezuela Rumblings: Riots and Debt Crisis," *New York Times*, March 2, 1989, p. A13.

GLOBAL BUSINESS
INSIGHT

Economic Development in the Americas

It is not well known that, at one time, the United States and Canada were not the richest countries in North and South America. The accompanying table shows how per capita GDP relative to that of the United States has changed over time for several countries.

Per Capita GDP Relative to the United States (percent)

County	1700	1800	1900	2000
Argentina	—	102	52	36
Barbados	150	—	—	44
Brazil	—	50	10	22
Chile	—	46	38	28
Cuba	167	112	—	—
Mexico	89	50	35	26
Peru	—	41	20	14
U.S. Real GDP per capita (1985 dollars)	550	807	3,859	34,260

One can see that some of what were then European colonies, such as Barbados and Cuba, were much richer in 1700 than the group of colonies in North America that eventually became the United States. Others, like Mexico, were about as rich as the colonies that became the United States. In 1800, Argentina was slightly richer than the United States, as was Cuba. But by 1900, per capita GDP had risen much faster in the United States than in these other countries. What happened?

As we have learned, abundant natural resources are not sufficient to ensure economic growth. The industrialization that occurred in the United States in the early 1800s was not duplicated in the Latin American countries. This became a point of divergence for the growth rates of the United States and Latin America. Researchers have suggested that an important difference contributing to the differential rates of development was the provision of government policies, including laws and institutions, in the United States and Canada that encouraged widespread participation in economic development.* Through investment in human capital via education and skills training, workers could experience upward mobility. By saving and investing, individual entrepreneurs could turn small businesses into large, successful enterprises.

In Latin America, institutions developed that blocked opportunities for economic advancement for a large portion of the population. The agriculture and mining industries of Latin America were conducted on a relatively large scale so that there were few entrepreneurs and managers and many poor workers. Even after slavery was ended and these countries achieved their independence from their European colonizers, the institutions of Latin American countries worked against individual investment in human capital and upward mobility. The class of individual entrepreneurs found in Canada and the United States did not emerge in Latin America. The upwardly mobile workers of Canada and the United States provided the opportunities for mass-market consumer goods that drove the industrialization process. But in Latin America, such mass markets of consumers with income to spend did not emerge.

Most poor countries may be characterized as having a small number of very rich individuals and a large number of very poor people. The members of the rich elite want to maintain their position and so support institutions that restrict the opportunities for advancement of the masses of poor people. So the initial development of an environment with a few rich and many poor was carried forward through time. In this way we can see the importance of institutions and government policies for charting a path of high growth and rapid development or low growth and relative stagnation.

---

*Drawn from World Bank, *World Development Report*, 2003, and Stanley L. Engerman and Kenneth L. Sokoloff, "Factor Endowments, Institutions, and Differential Paths of Growth among New World Economies: A View from Economic Historians of the United States," in Stephen H. Haber, ed., *How Latin America Fell Behind: Essays in the Economic Histories of Brazil and Mexico, 1800–1914* (Stanford, CA: Stanford University Press, 1997).

2.b. Social Obstacles

Cultural traditions and attitudes can work against economic development. In traditional societies, children follow in their parents' footsteps. If your father is a carpenter, there is a good chance that you will be a carpenter. Moreover, production is carried out in the same way generation after generation. For an economy to grow, it must be willing to change.

2.b.1. Lack of Entrepreneurs

A society that answers the questions *What to produce?*, *How to produce?*, and *For whom to produce?* by doing things as they were done by the previous generation lacks a key ingredient for economic growth: entrepreneurs. Entrepreneurs are risk takers; they bring innovation and new technology into use. Understanding why some societies are better at producing entrepreneurs than others may help explain why some nations have remained poor, while others have grown rapidly.

One theory is that entrepreneurs often come from *blocked minorities.* Some individuals in the traditional society are blocked from holding prestigious jobs or political office because of discrimination. This discrimination can be based on race, religion, or immigrant status. Because discrimination keeps them from the best traditional occupations, these minority groups can achieve wealth and status only through entrepreneurship. The Chinese in Southeast Asia, the Jews in Europe, and the Indians in Africa were all blocked minorities, forced to turn to entrepreneurship to advance themselves.

In developing countries, entrepreneurship tends to be concentrated among immigrants who have skills and experience that do not exist in poor countries. Many leaders of industry in Latin America, for example, are Italian, German, Arab, or Basque immigrants or the descendants of immigrants; they are not part of the dominant Spanish or native Indian population. The success of these immigrants is less a product of their being discriminated against than of their expertise in commerce. They know the foreign suppliers of goods. They have business skills that are lacking in developing regions. And they have the traditions—among them, the work ethic—and training instilled in their home country.

Motivation also plays a role in the level of entrepreneurship that exists in developing countries. In some societies, traditional values may be an obstacle to development because they do not encourage high achievement. A good example is provided by the tribal culture in sub-Saharan Africa. In this tribal culture, economic success does not result in upward social mobility if the success is obtained outside of the tribe. Instead, it could result in the person being shunned by the rest of the tribe. So incentives work against individual saving and investment or entrepreneurship. The social pressure is to share communally any riches that one obtains and not to rise above the group in any important way. In this sort of environment, development is hindered by the lack of incentives for wealth accumulation and risk taking.

Societies in which the culture supports individual achievement produce more entrepreneurs. It is difficult to identify the specific values in a society that account for a lack of motivation. In the past, researchers have pointed to factors that are not always valid across different societies. For instance, at one time many argued that the Protestant work ethic was responsible for the large number of entrepreneurs in the industrial world. According to this argument, some religions are more supportive of the accumulation of wealth than others. Today this argument is difficult to make because we find economic development in nations with vastly different cultures and religions.

2.b.2. Rapid Population Growth

Remember that per capita real GNP is real GNP divided by the population. Although labor is a factor of production, and labor force growth may increase output, when population rises faster than GNP, the standard of living of the average citizen does not improve. One very real problem for many developing countries is the growth of their populations. With the exception of China and India (where population growth is controlled), population growth in the developing countries is proceeding at a pace that will double the Third World population every 25 years. In large part, the rate at which the population of the Third World is growing is a product of lower death rates. Death rates have fallen, but birthrates have not.

Entrepreneurs are more likely to develop among minority groups that have been blocked from traditional high-paying jobs.

Immigrants provide a pool of entrepreneurs who have skills and knowledge that often are lacking in the developing country.

Social scientists do not all agree on the effects of population growth on development. A growing labor force can serve as an important factor in increasing growth. But those who believe that population growth has a negative effect cite three reasons:

Capital shallowing. Rapid population growth may reduce the amount of capital per worker, lowering the productivity of labor.

Age dependency. Rapid population growth produces a large number of dependent children, whose consumption requirements lower the ability of the economy to save.

Investment diversion. Rapid population growth shifts government expenditures from the country's infrastructure (roads, communication systems) to education and health care.

Population growth may have had a negative effect on development in many countries, but the magnitude of this effect is difficult to assess. And in some cases, population growth probably has stimulated development. For instance, the fact that children consume goods and services and thus lower the ability of a nation to save ignores the fact that the children grow up and become productive adults. Furthermore, any diversion of investment from infrastructure to education and health care is not necessarily a loss, as education and health care will build up the productivity of the labor force. The harmful effect of population growth should be most pronounced in countries where usable land and water are relatively scarce. Although generalizations about acceptable levels of population growth do not fit all circumstances, the World Bank has stated that population growth rates above 2 percent a year act as a brake on economic development.

The GNP can grow steadily year after year, but if the population grows at a faster rate, the standard of living of the average individual falls. The simple answer to reducing population growth seems to be education: programs that teach methods of birth control and family planning. But reducing birthrates is not simply a matter of education. People have to choose to limit the size of their families. It must be socially acceptable and economically advantageous for families to use birth control, and for many families it is neither.

Remember that what is good for society as a whole may not be good for the individual. Children are a source of labor in rural families and a support for parents in their old age. How many children are enough? That depends on the expected infant mortality rate. Although infant mortality rates in developing countries have fallen in recent years, they are still quite high relative to those in the developed countries. Families still tend to follow tradition and so keep having lots of children.

RECAP

1. In some countries, especially those that once were colonies, economic growth has been slow because government officials lack the necessary skills.

2. Countries that are unable to protect private property rights have difficulty attracting investors.

3. Expropriation is the seizure of assets by a government without adequate compensation.

4. Government corruption reduces investment and growth.

5. Often government officials know the right economic policies to follow but are constrained by political considerations from implementing those policies.

6. Immigrants are often the entrepreneurs in developing countries.

7. Rapid population growth may slow development because of the effects of capital shallowing, age dependency, and investment diversion.

3. Development Strategies

3 What strategies can a nation use to increase its economic growth?

Different countries follow different strategies to stimulate economic development. There are two basic types of development strategies: inward oriented and outward oriented.

3.a. Inward-Oriented Strategies

The typical developing country has a comparative advantage over other countries in the production of certain primary products. Having a comparative advantage means that a country has the lowest opportunity cost of producing a good. (We talked about comparative advantage in the chapter titled "Choice, Opportunity Costs, and Specialization.") A **primary product** is a product in the first stage of production, which often serves as an input in the production of some other good. Agricultural produce and minerals are examples of primary products. In the absence of a conscious government policy that directs production, we expect countries to concentrate on the production of that thing in which they have a comparative advantage. For example, we expect Cuba to focus on sugar production, Colombia to focus on coffee production, and the Ivory Coast to focus on cocoa production, with each country selling the output of its primary product to the rest of the world.

Today many developing countries have shifted their resources away from producing primary products for export. Inward-oriented development strategies focus on production for the domestic market rather than exports of goods and services. For these countries, development means industrialization. The objective of this kind of inward-oriented strategy is **import substitution**, or replacing imported manufactured goods with domestic goods.

Import-substitution policies dominate the strategies of the developing world. The basic idea is to identify domestic markets that are being supplied in large part by imports. Those markets that require a level of technology that is available to the domestic economy are candidates for import substitution. Industrialization goes hand in hand with tariffs or quotas on imports that protect the newly developing domestic industry from its more efficient foreign competition. As a result, production and international trade are not based solely on comparative advantages but are affected primarily by these countries' import-substitution policy activities.

Because the domestic industry can survive only through protection from foreign competition, with import-substitution policies, the price of the domestically produced goods is typically higher than that of the imported goods. In addition, the quality of the domestically produced goods may not be as high (at least at first) as the quality of the imported goods. Ideally, as the industry grows and becomes more experienced, price and quality become competitive with those of foreign goods. Once this happens, the import barriers are no longer needed, and the domestic industry may even become an export industry. Unfortunately, this ideal is seldom realized. The Third World is full of inefficient manufacturing companies that are unlikely ever to improve enough to be able to survive without protection from foreign competitors.

3.b. Outward-Oriented Strategies

The inward-oriented strategy of developing domestic industry to supply domestic markets is the most popular development strategy, but it is not the only one. Beginning in the 1960s, a small group of countries (notably South Korea, Hong Kong, Singapore, and Taiwan) chose to focus on the growth of exports. These countries started to follow an outward-oriented strategy, utilizing their most abundant resource to produce those products that they could produce better than others.

The abundant resource in these countries is labor, and the goods they produce are labor-intensive products. This kind of outward-oriented policy is called **export substitution**. These countries use labor to produce manufactured goods for export rather than agricultural products for domestic use.

primary product
A product in the first stage of production, which often serves as an input in the production of another product.

import substitution
The substitution of domestically produced manufactured goods for imported manufactured goods.

export substitution
The use of resources to produce manufactured products for export rather than agricultural products for the domestic market.

Foreign firms in developing countries can utilize technology, which depends in part on having a supply of engineers and technical personnel in the country. India has a large number of technical personnel, and much outsourcing is done there by U.S. firms.

Outward-oriented development strategies are based on efficient, low-cost production. Their success depends on being able to compete effectively with producers in the rest of the world. Most governments using this strategy attempt to stimulate exports. This can mean subsidizing domestic producers to produce goods for export rather than for domestic consumption. International competition is often more intense than the competition at home—producers face stiffer price competition, higher quality standards, and greater marketing expertise in the global marketplace. This means that domestic producers may have to be induced to compete internationally. Inducements can take the form of government assistance in international marketing, tax reductions, low-interest-rate loans, or cash payments.

Another inducement of sorts is to make domestic sales less attractive. This means implementing policies that are just the opposite of import substitution. The government reduces or eliminates domestic tariffs that keep domestic price levels above international levels. As profits from domestic sales fall, domestic industry turns to producing goods for export.

3.c. Comparing Strategies

Import-substitution policies are enacted by countries that believe that industrialization is the key to economic development. In the 1950s and 1960s, economists argued that specializing in the production and export of primary products does not encourage the rapid growth rates that developing countries are looking for. This argument—the *deteriorating-terms-of-trade argument*—was based on the assumption that the real value of primary products would fall over time. If the prices of primary products fall in relation to the prices of manufactured products, then countries that export primary products and import manufactured goods find the cost of manufactured goods rising in terms of the primary products required to buy them. The amount of exports that must be exchanged for some quantity of imports is often called the **terms of trade**.

The deteriorating-terms-of-trade argument in the 1950s and 1960s led policymakers in developing countries to fear that the terms of trade would become

terms of trade
The amount of an exported good that must be given up to obtain an imported good.

increasingly unfavorable. One product of that fear was the choice of an inward-oriented strategy, a focus on domestic industrialization rather than production for export.

At the root of the pessimism about the export of primary products was the belief that technological change would slow the growth of demand for primary products over time. That theory ignored the fact that if the supply of natural resources is fixed, those resources could become more valuable over time, even if demand for them grows slowly or not at all. And even if the real value of primary products does fall over time, this does not necessarily mean that an inward-oriented policy is required. Critics of inward-oriented policies argue that nations should exploit their comparative advantage—that resources should be free to move to their highest valued use. And they argue that market-driven resource allocation is unlikely to occur in an inward-oriented economy where government has imposed restrictions aimed at maximizing the rate of growth of industrial output.

Other economists believe that developing countries have unique problems that call for active government intervention and regulation of economic activity. These economists often favor inward-oriented strategies. They focus on the structure of developing countries in terms of uneven industrial development. Some countries have modern manufacturing industries paying relatively high wages that operate alongside traditional agricultural industries paying low wages. A single economy with industries at very different levels of development is called a **dual economy**. Some insist that, in a dual economy, the markets for goods and resources do not work well. If resources could move freely between industries, then wages would not differ by the huge amounts that are observed in certain developing countries. These economists support active government direction of the economy in countries where markets are not functioning well, believing that resources in these countries are unlikely to move freely to their highest valued use if free markets are allowed.

The growth rates of the outward-oriented economies are significantly higher than those of the inward-oriented economies. The success of the outward-oriented economies is likely to continue in light of a strong increase in saving in those economies. In 1963, domestic saving as a fraction of GDP was only 13 percent in the strongly outward-oriented economies. After more than two decades of economic growth driven by export-promotion policies, the rate of saving in these countries had increased to 31.4 percent of GDP. This high rate of saving increases investment expenditures, which increase the productivity of labor, further stimulating the growth of per capita real GDP.

Why are outward-oriented strategies more successful than inward-oriented strategies? The primary advantage of an outward orientation is the efficient utilization of resources. Import-substitution policies do not allocate resources on the basis of cost minimization. In addition, an outward-oriented strategy allows the economy to grow beyond the scale of the domestic market. Foreign demand creates additional markets for exports, beyond the domestic market.

dual economy
An economy in which two sectors (typically manufacturing and agriculture) show very different levels of development.

The growth rates of outward-oriented economies are significantly higher than those of inward-oriented economies.

RECAP

1. Inward-oriented strategies concentrate on building a domestic industrial sector.

2. Outward-oriented strategies utilize a country's comparative advantage in exporting.

3. The deteriorating-terms-of-trade argument has been used to justify import substitution policies.

4. Evidence indicates that outward-oriented policies have been more successful than inward-oriented policies at generating economic growth.

4. Foreign Investment and Aid

Developing countries rely on savings in the rest of the world to finance much of their investment needs. Foreign savings may come from industrial countries in many different ways. In this section we describe the ways in which savings are transferred from industrial to developing countries and the benefits of foreign investment and aid to developing countries.

4 How are savings in one nation used to speed development in other nations?

4.a. Foreign Savings Flows

Poor countries that are unable to save enough to invest in capital stock must rely on the savings of other countries to help them develop economically. Foreign savings come from both private sources and official government sources.

Private sources of foreign savings can take the form of direct investment, portfolio investment, commercial bank loans, and trade credit. **Foreign direct investment** is the purchase of a physical operating unit, like a factory, or an ownership position in a foreign country that gives the domestic firm making the investment ownership of more than 10 percent of the foreign firm. This is different from **portfolio investment**, which is the purchase of securities, like stocks and bonds. In the case of direct investment, the foreign investor may actually operate the business. Portfolio investment helps finance a business, but host-country managers operate the firm; foreign investors simply hold pieces of paper that represent a share of the ownership or the debt of the firm. **Commercial bank loans** are loans made at market rates of interest to either foreign governments or business firms. These loans are often made by a *bank syndicate*, a group of several banks, to share the risk associated with lending to a single country. Finally, exporting firms and commercial banks offer **trade credit**, allowing importers a period of time before the payment for the goods or services purchased is due. Extension of trade credit usually involves payment in 30 days (or some other term) after the goods are received.

The relative importance of direct investment and bank lending have changed over time. In 1970, direct investment in developing countries was greater than bank loans. By the late 1970s and early 1980s, however, bank loans far exceeded direct investment. Bank lending gives the borrowing country greater flexibility in deciding how to use funds. Direct investment carries with it an element of foreign control over domestic resources. Nationalist sentiment combined with the fear of exploitation by foreign owners and managers led many developing countries to pass laws restricting direct investment. By the early 1990s, however, as more nations were emphasizing the development of free markets, direct investment was again growing in importance as a source of funds for developing countries, and by the late 1990s it was these countries' most important source of funds.

foreign direct investment
The purchase of a physical operating unit or more than 10 percent ownership of a firm in a foreign country.

portfolio investment
The purchase of securities.

commercial bank loan
A bank loan at market rates of interest, often involving a bank syndicate.

trade credit
Allowing an importer a period of time before it must pay for goods or services purchased.

4.b. Benefits of Foreign Investment

Not all developing countries discourage foreign direct investment. In fact, many countries have benefited from foreign investment. Those benefits fall into three categories: new jobs, new technology, and foreign exchange earnings.

4.b.1. New Jobs
Foreign investment should stimulate growth and create new jobs in developing countries. But the number of new jobs created directly by foreign investment is often limited by the nature of the industries in which foreign investment is allowed.

Usually foreign investment is invited in capital-intensive industries, like chemicals or mineral extraction. Because capital goods are expensive and often require advanced technology to operate, foreign firms can build a capital-intensive industry faster than the developing country can. One product of this emphasis on capital-intensive industries is that foreign investment often has little effect on employment in developing countries. A $500 million oil refinery may employ just a few hundred workers, yet the creation of

Many countries have benefited from foreign investment, which can stimulate growth and create new jobs. McDonald's is one such investor, and in China, it has well over 900 restaurants with more than 60,000 employees.

these few hundred jobs, along with other expenditures by the refinery, will stimulate domestic income by raising incomes across the economy.

4.b.2. Technology Transfer

In the chapter titled "Economic Growth," we said that economic growth depends on the growth of resources and technological change. Most expenditures on research and development are made in the major industrial countries. These are also the countries that develop most of the innovations that make production more efficient. For a Third World country with limited scientific resources, the industrial nations are a critical source of information, technology, and expertise.

The ability of foreign firms to utilize modern technology in a developing country depends in part on having a supply of engineers and technical personnel in the host country. India and Mexico have a fairly large number of technical personnel, which means that new technology can be adapted relatively quickly. On the other hand, countries in which a large fraction of the population has less than an elementary-level education must train workers and then keep those workers from migrating to industrial countries, where their salaries are likely to be much higher.

4.b.3. Foreign Exchange Earnings

Developing countries expect foreign investment to improve their balance of payments. The assumption is that multinational firms located inside the developing country will increase exports and thus generate greater foreign currency earnings that can be used for imports or for repaying foreign debt. But this scenario does not unfold if the foreign investment is used to produce goods primarily for domestic consumption. In fact, the presence of a foreign firm can create a larger deficit in the balance of payments if the firm sends profits back to its industrial country headquarters from the developing country and the value of those profits exceeds the value of the foreign exchange earned by exports.

foreign aid
Gifts or low-cost loans made to developing countries from official sources.

4.c. Foreign Aid

Official foreign savings are usually available as either outright gifts or low-interest-rate loans. These funds are called **foreign aid**. Large countries, like the United States, provide much more funding in terms of the dollar value of aid than do small countries. However, some small countries—for example, the Netherlands and Norway—commit a much larger percentage of their GNP to foreign aid.

Foreign aid can take the form of cash grants or transfers of goods or technology, with nothing given in return by the developing country. Often foreign aid is used to reward political allies, particularly when those allies hold a strategic military location. Examples of this politically inspired aid are the former Soviet support of Cuba and U.S. support of Turkey.

Foreign aid that flows from one country to another is called **bilateral aid**. Governments typically have an agency that coordinates and plans foreign aid programs and expenditures. The U.S. Agency for International Development (USAID) performs these functions in the United States. Most of the time, bilateral aid is project-oriented, given to fund a specific project (such as an educational facility or an irrigation project).

bilateral aid
Foreign aid that flows from one country to another.

Food makes up a substantial portion of bilateral aid. After a bad harvest or a natural disaster (drought in the Sudan, floods in Bangladesh), major food-producing nations help feed the hungry. Egypt and Bangladesh were the leading recipients of food aid during the late 1980s. In the early 1990s, attention shifted to Somalia. The major recipients of food aid change over time, as nature and political events combine to change the pattern of hunger and need in the world.

The economics of food aid illustrates a major problem with many kinds of charity. Aid is intended to help those who need it without interfering with domestic production. But when food flows into a developing country, food prices tend to fall, pushing farm income down and discouraging local production. Ideally, food aid should go to the very poor, who are less likely to have the income necessary to purchase domestic production anyway.

Foreign aid does not flow directly from the donors to the needy. It goes through the government of the recipient country. Here we find another problem: the inefficient and sometimes corrupt bureaucracies in recipient nations. There have been cases where recipient governments have sold products that were intended for free distribution to the poor. In other cases, food aid was not distributed because the recipient government had created the conditions leading to starvation. The U.S. intervention in Somalia in 1993 was aimed at helping food aid reach the starving population. In still other cases, a well-intentioned recipient government simply did not have the resources to distribute the aid, so the products ended up largely going to waste. One response to these problems is to rely on voluntary agencies to distribute aid. Another is to rely on multilateral agencies.

Multilateral aid is provided by international organizations that are supported by many nations. The largest and most important multilateral aid institution is the World Bank. The World Bank makes loans to developing countries at below-market rates of interest and oversees projects in developing countries that it has funded. As an international organization, the World Bank is not controlled by any single country. This allows the organization to advise and help developing countries in a nonpolitical way that is usually not possible with bilateral aid.

multilateral aid
Aid provided by international organizations that are supported by many nations.

RECAP

1. Private sources of foreign savings include direct investment, portfolio investment, commercial bank loans, and trade credit.

2. Developing countries can benefit from foreign investment through new jobs, the transfer of technology, and foreign exchange earnings.

3. Foreign aid involves gifts or low-cost loans that are made available to developing countries by official sources.

4. Foreign aid can be provided bilaterally or multilaterally.

SUMMARY

1. **How is poverty measured?**

    - Poverty usually is defined in an absolute sense as the minimum income needed to purchase a minimal standard of living and is measured by per capita GNP or GDP. *§1.a*

    - Some economists and social scientists use a quality-of-life index to evaluate standards of living. *§1.b*

2. **Why are some countries poorer than others?**

    - Both political obstacles (lack of skilled officials, instability, corruption, and constraints imposed by special interest groups) and social obstacles (cultural attitudes that discourage entrepreneurial activity and encourage rapid population growth) limit economic growth in developing countries. *§2.a, 2.b*

3. **What strategies can a nation use to increase its economic growth?**

    - Inward-oriented development strategies focus on developing a domestic manufacturing sector to produce goods that can substitute for imported manufactured goods. *§3.a*

    - Outward-oriented development strategies focus on producing manufactured goods for export. *§3.b*

    - The growth rates of outward-oriented economies are significantly higher than those of inward-oriented economies. *§3.c*

4. **How are savings in one nation used to speed development in other nations?**

    - Private sources of foreign savings include direct investment, portfolio investment, commercial bank loans, and trade credit. *§4.a*

    - Foreign investment in developing countries can increase their economic growth by creating jobs, transferring modern technology, and stimulating exports to increase foreign exchange earnings. *§4.b*

    - Official gifts or low-cost loans made to developing countries by official sources are called foreign aid. *§4.c*

    - Foreign aid can be distributed bilaterally or multilaterally. *§4.c*

KEY TERMS

bilateral aid, 391
commercial bank loan, 389
dual economy, 388
export substitution, 386
expropriation, 381

foreign aid, 390
foreign direct investment, 389
import substitution, 386
multilateral aid, 391
portfolio investment, 389

primary product, 386
terms of trade, 387
trade credit, 389

EXERCISES

1. What are basic human needs? Can you list additional needs besides those considered in the chapter?
2. Per capita GNP or GDP is used as an absolute measure of poverty.
    a. What are some criticisms of using per capita GNP as a measure of standard of living?
    b. Do any of these criticisms also apply to a quality-of-life index?
3. In many developing countries, there are economists and politicians who were educated in industrial countries. These individuals know what policies would maximize the growth of their countries, but they do not implement them. Why not?

4. Suppose you are a benevolent dictator who can impose any policy you choose in your country. If your goal is to accelerate economic development, how would you respond to the following problems?
    a. Foreign firms are afraid to invest in your country because your predecessor expropriated many foreign-owned factories.
    b. There are few entrepreneurs in the country.
    c. The dominant domestic religion teaches that the accumulation of wealth is sinful.
    d. It is customary for families to have at least six children.

5. What effect does population growth have on economic development?

6. Why have most developing countries followed inward-oriented development strategies?

7. Why is an outward-oriented development strategy likely to allocate resources more efficiently than an inward-oriented strategy?

8. Who benefits from an import-substitution strategy? Who is harmed?

9. If poverty is a relative concept, why don't we define it in relative terms?

10. "The poor will always be with us." Does this statement have different meanings depending on whether poverty is interpreted as an absolute or a relative concept?

11. How do traditional societies answer the questions *What to produce?*, *How to produce?*, and *For whom to produce?*

12. What are the most important sources of foreign savings for developing countries? Why don't developing countries save more so that they don't have to rely on foreign savings for investment?

13. Private foreign investment and foreign aid are sources of savings to developing countries. Yet each has been controversial at times. What are the potential negative effects of private foreign investment and foreign aid for developing countries?

14. Why do immigrants often play an important role in developing the economies of poor nations? What role did immigrants play in developing the economy of the early United States?

15. How does a nation go about instituting a policy of import substitution? What is a likely result of such a policy?

16. In what ways might development harm the environment? In what ways might development be beneficial for the environment?

17. Search online for information about microfinance in developing countries. What are the potential benefits? What criticism has it received?

You can find further practice tests in the Online Quiz at **www.cengage.com/economics/boyes**.

DOES INTERNATIONAL FOOD AID HARM THE POOR?

The delivery of food aid to developing countries seems like an uncontroversial policy—a straightforward effort that helps the poor and underscores the generosity of donor nations. Yet economists have long debated the merits of food aid. By increasing the local supply of food, such aid may depress prices and thus undercut the income of rural farmers in the recipient nations, for example; it also may discourage local production. And, since the poor often are concentrated in rural areas, food aid in fact may disproportionately hurt the poor.

NBER researchers James Levinsohn and Margaret McMillan tackle this debate in "Does Food Aid Harm the Poor? Household Evidence from Ethiopia."* The impact of lower food prices on the poor, they reason, hinges on whether poor households tend to be net buyers or net sellers of food. The authors seek to answer this question by examining consumption and expenditures survey data from both urban and rural households in Ethiopia. They focus on Ethiopia because it receives more food aid than almost any other nation in the world, but also because it is widely recognized that raising the productivity and profitability of small-scale Ethiopian farmers is essential to reducing poverty in the country.

Food aid can take several forms, but some portion of all types of food aid (including emergency relief aid) is eventually sold in local markets and thus competes with domestic producers. Therefore, food aid will benefit Ethiopia's net food buyers and hurt its net food sellers. To carry out their study, Levinsohn and McMillan merge data from two nationally representative surveys and create a data set of 8,212 urban and 8,308 rural Ethiopian households.

Since wheat is the only cereal imported in the form of food aid, it is the 12 percent of rural households that report income from wheat that stand to gain most from price increases and lose most from price declines.

The authors classify households as either net buyers of wheat (if they buy more than they sell) or net sellers. To determine the poverty impact of food aid, they also classify the households by expenditure per capita and assess whether the poor households are net buyers or sellers of food. Finally, they estimate the magnitude of the price changes caused by food aid and hence the welfare effects of an increase in the price of food.

Levinsohn and McMillan offer several conclusions. First, net buyers of wheat are poorer than net sellers of wheat in Ethiopia. Indeed, roughly 85 percent of the poorest households are net buyers of wheat. Second, there are more buyers of wheat in Ethiopia than sellers of wheat at all levels of income—an important result because it means that at all levels of living standards, more households benefit from food aid (and the subsequent reduction in wheat prices) than are hurt by it. Third, the proportion of net sellers is increasing in living standards, and fourth, poorer households (in rural and in urban areas) benefit proportionately more from a drop in the price of wheat. "In light of this evidence," the authors conclude, "it appears that households at all levels of income benefit from food aid and that—somewhat surprisingly—the benefits go disproportionately to the poorest households."

Levinsohn and McMillan estimate that, in the absence of food aid, the price of wheat in Ethiopia would be $295 per metric ton, compared to an actual price of $193 per metric ton. . . .

CARLOS LOZADA

---

* "Does International Food Aid Harm the Poor?" NBER Working Paper 11048, http://www.nber.org/digest/mar05/w11048.html.

Hunger is a serious global problem that has long commanded economists' attention. One approach to reducing hunger in poor countries has been shipments of food from rich countries. Yet simply delivering free food to countries suffering from famine may not be the best solution.

Famines do not necessarily imply a shortage of food. Instead, famines sometimes represent shortfalls in the purchasing power of the poorest sectors of society. In many cases, grants of income are a better means of alleviating famines than grants of food.

We can understand this argument using demand and supply analysis. In the following two diagrams, we represent the demand for food and the supply of food in a famine-stricken country that is receiving aid. In each diagram, the demand curve D_1 intersects the supply curve S_1 at an equilibrium quantity of food Q_1, which represents a subsistence level of food consumption. The equilibrium depicted in each graph is one in which, in the absence of aid, a famine would occur.

The first graph illustrates the effects of providing aid in the form of food. The food aid increases the available supply of food, which is shown by an outward shift of the supply curve to S_2. The effect of this aid is to increase the equilibrium quantity of food (Q_2) and lower the equilibrium price (P_2). The lower price of food will adversely affect the income of domestic producers. Domestic producers will thus attempt to grow other crops or to search for sources of income other than growing food if they cannot receive enough money for their produce. As the amount of domestic food production falls, the country becomes more dependent on imports of food. In the article, we are told that wheat prices would have been about $100 a ton (or $\frac{1}{3}$) higher if Ethiopia had not received shipments of free wheat to help alleviate hunger. Such higher wheat prices would have surely resulted in more farmers growing wheat.

The second graph illustrates the effect of income aid for the famine-stricken country. The aid is depicted by a shift in the demand curve to D_2. As with food aid, this relief allows consumption to rise to a point above the subsistence level. The effects of this aid on domestic food producers, however, are quite different. The price of food rises, and thus domestic food producers are not hurt by the aid package. As a result, aid in the form of income does not cause disincentives for production. An increase in domestic food production also serves to make a country less dependent on food imports.

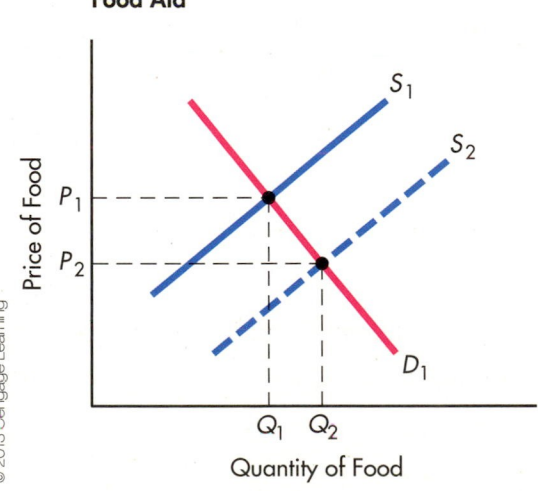

Food Aid

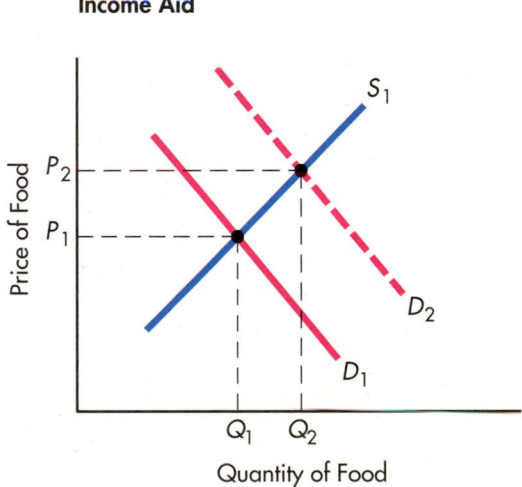

Income Aid

CHAPTER 18

Globalization

© MACIEJ FROLOW/GETTY IMAGES, INC

© BARTLOMIEJ K. KWIECISZEWSKI/SHUTTERSTOCK; LOGO: © FROXX/SHUTTERSTOCK.COM

FUNDAMENTAL QUESTIONS

1. What is globalization?

2. What are the arguments against globalization?

3. What are the arguments in support of globalization?

4. How has globalization affected economic growth and poverty?

5. Can recent financial crises be linked to globalization?

I n every chapter, we have discussed the international aspects of the topics covered. However, we have not yet considered the implications of closer links between economies internationally. The so-called *globalization* of the world's economies has become an issue that is rich in controversy. Thousands have gathered to protest globalization in Washington, D.C., and Seattle in the United States; in Johannesburg, South Africa; in Davos, Switzerland; and in many other places. This chapter will provide an introduction to the potential costs and benefits of globalization and offer an analysis of the historical record regarding the effects of globalization.

It is important to recognize that the debate over globalization continues and that it has political and social as well as economic dimensions. Intelligent people disagree about the impact of globalization on rich as well as poor countries. The reader should keep in mind that the issue is unsettled, and much can change in the coming years.

1. The Meaning of Globalization

Globalization is characterized by an increased cross-border flow of trade in goods, services, and financial assets, along with an increased international mobility of technology, information, and individuals. As globalization progresses, countries become less isolated so that we can think more in terms of a global economy and its implications for individuals and nations.

1 What is globalization?

1.a. Globalization Is Neither New nor Widespread

Globalization is not new. The forces that drive globalization have existed as long as humans have been around. Everyone has a natural desire to improve his or her well-being, so interest in trade has always existed. As we learned in earlier chapters, trade based on comparative advantage raises living standards. Even primitive societies engaged in trade so that their living standards would be higher than would otherwise have been possible. As circumstances permitted a greater range of travel, trade with more remote regions became possible. International trade is not a new phenomenon. World trade as a fraction of world GDP was about the same at the end of the nineteenth century as it is today. However, between World War I and World War II, the value of international trade plummeted. Then, in the postwar era, international trade rose substantially. Thus, the view that the growth of world trade is something new is true only in the shortsighted view of the world since the 1950s.

Globalization is not yet a truly global phenomenon. Some countries have remained largely closed to the rest of the world. These are mostly the world's poorest countries. If a government follows policies that work against economic integration with other countries, international trade and investment will not materialize. Former U.N. Secretary General Kofi Annan stated, "The main losers in today's very unequal world are not those that are too exposed to globalization, but those who have been left out." Yet, as we shall see, globalization is controversial, as not everyone benefits and some groups are made worse off than they were when they were more shielded from integration with the rest of the world.

The movement of people across international borders is greatly limited by government policies. There was much more immigration in the nineteenth and early twentieth centuries than there is at the present time. Barriers to immigration are high today, and workers generally cannot move freely from country to country. This was not always the case. In 1900, 14 percent of the U.S. population was born in a foreign country. Today that number is 12 percent. However, there are some multinational agreements that permit international movements of workers. An important example is the European Union (EU). Within the EU, there is free mobility of labor. Of course, this does not mean that there are widespread relocations of workers from, say, Germany to Italy. Family, language, and customs tie people to particular areas, so that the fact that people have the right to move does not mean that large numbers of them will actually do so. This is analogous to workers in the United States, who have the right to move anywhere in the country but many of whom choose to stay in a particular area because they have personal ties to that area.

1.b. The Role of Technological Change

The pace of globalization has been driven by technological change. International trade and the movement of people are facilitated by falling transportation costs. It is estimated that the real cost of ocean freight transport fell by 70 percent between 1920 and 1990.

International communication is enhanced by reductions in the cost of communications. Measured in terms of the value of a U.S. dollar in the year 2000, a three-minute telephone call from New York to London cost $60.42 in 1960 and $.40 in 2000. Now such a call can be made for free using Voice over Internet Protocol (VoIP) technology. The reduction in communication costs has made possible global interactions that were at best a dream just a few decades ago.

The development of fast, modern computers allows information to be processed at speeds that were unimaginable just a generation ago. As a result, technology is shared more efficiently, so that management of business operations can extend more easily to far-flung locations, and complex transactions can be completed in a fraction of the time that was once required. Technological progress in the computer industry is truly amazing. A computer that would sell for $1,000 today would have cost $1,869,004 in 1960.

The fact that globalization has progressed at an uneven rate over time is due to the uneven pace of technological change, in addition to important events, such as war, that disrupt relationships among nations.

1.c. Measuring Globalization

There are many alternatives for measuring how globalized the world and individual nations are. One useful ranking is provided by the KOF Swiss Economic Institute. It ranks countries in terms of three broad categories:

> *Economic globalization*: long-distance flows of goods, capital, and services as well as information and perceptions that accompany market exchanges;
>
> *Social globalization*: spread of ideas, information, images, and people;
>
> *Political globalization*: diffusion of government policies (measured by things like number of embassies in a country, membership in international organizations, participation in U.N. peace missions, and similar concepts).

Table 1 shows the rankings for several countries. Note that poor countries tend to be missing from the top rank of globalized countries. These countries have few foreign workers and relatively low amounts of international communications and contact. They also have relatively low levels of Internet use, as a large segment of the population does not have access to computers or the training to use computers in daily life.

The more globalized an economy, the greater its links with the rest of the world. The aftermath of the terrorist attacks in the United States on September 11, 2001, showed how measures of globalization may be affected by important events. World trade fell after the attacks, as did global foreign direct investment. International travel and tourism dropped in 2002 for the first time since 1945. However, political engagement increased as a result of multinational efforts aimed at combating terrorism. The number of countries participating in U.N. peacekeeping missions increased. The volume of international telephone calls increased substantially. The increase in telephone use may have been partly due to the drop in international travel. If people choose not to travel for personal or business reasons because of safety concerns, they may be more likely to have telephone conversations with the parties they otherwise would have visited in person. In addition, the number of Internet users grew 22 percent in 2002, with China alone adding 11 million new users. So major events like the terrorist attacks of September 11, 2001, may suppress some measures of globalization while increasing others. This serves as a good reminder to take a broad view when measuring globalization rather than narrowly focusing on one or two measures.

TABLE 1	Globalization Rankings							
Country	Index of Globalization	Country	Economic Globalization	Country	Social Globalization	Country	Political Globalization
Belgium	92.95	Singapore	97.48	Switzerland	94.94	France	98.44
Austria	92.51	Ireland	93.93	Austria	92.77	Italy	98.17
Netherlands	91.9	Luxembourg	93.57	Canada	90.73	Belgium	98.14
Switzerland	90.55	Netherlands	92.4	Belgium	90.61	Austria	96.85
Sweden	89.75	Malta	92.26	Netherlands	88.99	Sweden	96.27
Denmark	89.68	Belgium	91.94	Denmark	88.01	Spain	96.14
Canada	88.24	Estonia	91.66	United Kingdom	87.05	Netherlands	95.77
Portugal	87.54	Hungary	90.45	Germany	85.97	Switzerland	95.09
Finland	87.31	Sweden	89.42	Sweden	85.95	Poland	94.63
Hungary	87.00	Austria	89.33	France	85.84	Canada	94.4
Ireland	86.92	Bahrain	89.32	Portugal	85.59	Portugal	94.36
Czech Republic	86.87	Denmark	88.58	Norway	85.3	Germany	94.21
France	86.18	Czech Republic	88.43	Finland	84.89	Denmark	93.96
Luxembourg	85.84	Cyprus	87.77	Slovak Republic	83.9	United States	93.85
Spain	85.71	Finland	87.33	Czech Republic	83.54	Egypt, Arab Rep.	93.39
Slovak Republic	85.07	Slovak Republic	87.25	Australia	82.96	Argentina	93.38
Singapore	84.58	Chile	87.14	Spain	82.52	Greece	93.11
Germany	84.16	Israel	85.15	Luxembourg	81.6	Turkey	93.11
Australia	83.82	Portugal	85.03	Hungary	80.79	Brazil	92.95
Norway	83.53	Bulgaria	84.1	Liechtenstein	80.11	India	92.69

Source: *KOF Index of Globalization*; http://globalization.kof.ethz.ch/static/pdf/rankings_2010.pdf.

RECAP

1. Globalization is characterized by an increased flow of trade in goods, services, and financial assets across national borders, along with increased international mobility of technology, information, and individuals.

2. The process of globalization is not new, but it accelerated after World War II.

3. Technological advances play an important role in determining the pace of globalization.

4. Measuring globalization involves measurement of the international movements of goods, services, financial assets, people, ideas, and technology.

2. Globalization Controversy

Globalization has stimulated much controversy in recent years. Massive demonstrations have been held to coincide with meetings of the World Trade Organization (WTO), the International Monetary Fund (IMF), the World Bank, and other gatherings of government and business leaders dealing with the process of developing international trade and investment. The two sides see globalization in a very different light. On one

2 What are the arguments against globalization?

side are the critics of globalization, who believe that free international trade in goods and financial assets does more harm than good. On the other side are the supporters of free international trade, who believe that globalization holds the key to increasing the living standards of all the world's people. We will review the arguments on both sides.

2.a. Arguments Against Globalization

Critics of globalization view it as a vehicle for enriching corporate elites, to the detriment of poor people and the environment. In this view, the major international organizations are tools of corporations, whose aim is to increase corporate profits at the expense of people and the environment. Rather than being a democratic system in which the majority of people are involved in economic decision making, globalization is seen by critics as a force that reduces the influence of people at the local level, with power being taken by the global elites, represented by rich corporations and their government supporters. A few specific criticisms associated with the antiglobalization movement follow.

2.a.1. "Fair," Not "Free," Trade
Critics argue that free trade agreements put people out of jobs. When goods are produced by the lowest-cost producer, people working in that industry in less competitive countries will no longer be employed. If foreign competition were limited, then these jobs would be saved. In addition, free trade may encourage governments to participate in a **"race to the bottom,"** with environmental safeguards and workers' rights being ignored in order to attract the investment and jobs that come from a concentration of production based upon comparative advantage. International trade agreements are seen as roadblocks to democratic decision making at the local level, as they transfer power away from local authorities to multinational authorities.

"race to the bottom"
The argument that, with globalization, countries compete for international investment by offering low or no environmental regulations or labor standards.

2.a.2. International Organizations Serve Only the Interests of Corporations
An example of this argument is the assertion that the WTO is a tool of corporations, and that international trade agreements negotiated and enforced through the WTO are used to generate corporate profits against the interests of the citizens of the world. The Global Business Insight "The World Trade Organization" provides background information on the nature of this organization and its duties. International organizations like the WTO are used as platforms for instituting rules for international trade. Thus, an individual who is against free international trade would also be critical of organizations whose aim is the promotion of free trade. The WTO, the IMF, and the World Bank are viewed as undemocratic organizations that have assumed powers over economic decision making that rightly belong to local authorities.

2.a.3. Globalization Occurs at the Cost of Environmental Quality
As stated earlier, critics of globalization fear a "race to the bottom," in which governments block costly regulations related to environmental quality in order to provide a cheaper location for large global firms seeking manufacturing facilities. If the rich countries impose costly regulations on manufacturers, then these firms will shift production to poor countries that are willing to trade environmental degradation for jobs and higher incomes. Related to this issue is World Bank financing for resource extraction projects, such as mining or oil and gas extraction. Such projects are seen as benefiting the corporations that receive contracts for work related to the projects, while environmental destruction is a little-considered by-product. World Bank funding for large dams is also seen as harmful, as these projects frequently involve the relocation of large numbers of poor people, who lose what modest living arrangements they had.

GLOBAL BUSINESS INSIGHT

The World Trade Organization

The World Trade Organization (WTO) is an international organization with 153 member countries, established in 1995 and headquartered in Geneva, Switzerland. The job of the WTO is to provide a venue for negotiating international trade agreements and then to enforce these global rules of international trade. The WTO trade agreements are negotiated and signed by a large majority of the world's nations. These agreements are contracts covering the proper conduct of international trade. An important role of the WTO is the settlement of trade disputes between countries. An example of such a dispute involved bananas and the European Union (EU). The EU restricted banana imports to bananas from only a few countries that were former European colonies. As a result, the price paid for bananas in European markets was about twice the price of bananas in the United States. The world's largest banana companies, Dole, Chiquita, and Del Monte, headquartered in the United States, complained that they were being harmed because their bananas, which came from other countries in Central and South America, were excluded from the EU system, which favored a few former colonies. The WTO ruled that the EU restrictions on banana imports were harmful and against the rules of trade to which all nations had agreed. This is but one example of the role of the WTO in promoting fair and free international trade.

2.a.4. Globalization Encourages Harmful Labor Practices
This argument is based upon a belief that multinational corporations will locate where wages are cheapest and workers' rights weakest. In these settings, on-the-job safety is ignored, and workers who are injured or ill are likely to be dismissed without any compensation. Furthermore, critics believe that globalization may result in the worst employment practices, such as child labor or prisoner labor. If such practices are allowed in poor countries, then the industrial countries will suffer follow-on effects as workers in rich countries lose their jobs to workers in countries where there are no worker protection regulations, no minimum wages, and no retirement plans, and where employers must pay nothing more than the minimum necessary to attract an employee.

2.b. Arguments in Favor of Globalization

Globalization's supporters believe that free trade and international investment result in an increase in living standards in all countries. Of course, some individuals and firms are harmed by the globalization process. Those industries that exist in a country only as a result of protection from foreign competitors will suffer when that country's markets are opened to the rest of the world. Yet the few who suffer are small in number relative to the many who benefit from the advantages that globalization provides. This section will consider each of the criticisms mentioned in the prior section and present the alternative view of those who support globalization.

 3 What are the arguments in support of globalization?

2.b.1. Free Trade Helps Developing Countries
As just discussed, opening markets to free trade will usually harm some individuals and firms. But supporters of globalization believe that the benefits of globalization for all consumers greatly outweigh the costs of providing a social safety net for those who lose their jobs as a result of opening markets to global competitors. Developing countries have much to gain from free trade. Restrictions on trade in rich countries are often aimed at the products that poor countries can produce most efficiently. For instance, textile imports are restricted by the

United States, and this harms many developing countries that could provide clothing and fabrics to the United States at a lower cost than U.S. producers can. The European Union restricts imports of agricultural products in order to increase the incomes of European farmers. If such restrictions were lifted, incomes in poor countries would rise substantially. Supporters of globalization believe that free trade agreements administered by the WTO can offer great benefits to poor countries.

2.b.2. International Organizations Represent Governments and People

Supporters of globalization argue that international organizations offer all countries a platform for expressing their dissatisfaction with economic and social conditions and provide a mechanism for change. Without organizations like the IMF, World Bank, United Nations, and WTO, there would be no opportunities for representatives of all nations to come together to discuss needed changes in the global economy. These organizations also provide for transfers of funds from rich to poor countries that would not occur in an ongoing manner in the absence of such organizations. International organizations are funded by governments, not corporations. Representatives of the government of each member nation participate in the decision making at each organization. This suggests that if international organizations have followed unwise policies, the most effective path for change would be putting political pressure on national governments to support policies that open markets for the goods of poor countries as well as rich countries.

2.b.3. The Connection between Globalization and Environmental Harm Is Weak

Supporters of globalization argue that there is no evidence of a "race to the bottom" in which multinational firms move production to countries with lax environmental standards. Looking at the globalization rankings in Table 1, the countries at the top of the list tend to have more stringent environmental regulations than do less open economies. Figure 1 plots a country's globalization score against a ranking of environmental quality, where the country's environmental performance is determined by its rankings in terms of the quality of its air and water, its protection of land, and its impact on climate change through carbon dioxide emissions. The figure plots data for those countries ranked in the top 30 and bottom 30 on the environmental quality scale that also have globalization rankings. The higher the number for a country, the better its environmental ranking or the greater its globalization. Figure 1 indicates that, in general, the more globalized the country, the better its environmental quality. For instance, Switzerland has the highest ranking in terms of environmental quality, and it is also the most globalized economy. Niger is the lowest ranked in environmental quality and is also ranked low in terms of globalization. The scatter of the countries plotted in Figure 1 suggests that an upward-sloping line would represent the relationship between globalization and environmental quality well.

In addition, there are many cases of environmental degradation associated with countries that are closed to economic relations with the rest of the world. The governments of the former Communist countries of Eastern Europe displayed the greatest disregard of the

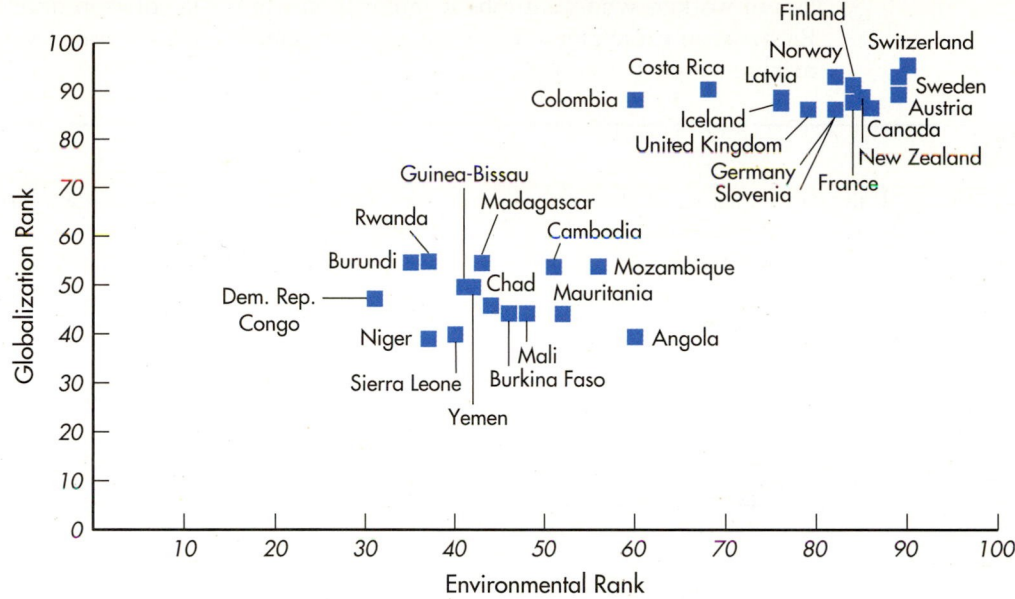

FIGURE 1   Globalization and Environmental Quality

Source: Globalization data are drawn from *KOF Index of Globalization;* http://www.kof.ethz.ch/globalization. Environmental quality rankings are from the "Environmental Performance Index" from www.yale.edu/epi.

environment of any group of nations in modern times. As these nations globalize as part of the transition away from socialism, they are attracting foreign direct investment from rich countries, which has transferred cleaner technology to Eastern Europe and improved environmental quality.

One of the major assumptions made by critics of globalization is that multinational firms will locate production units in developing countries, employ local resources, and then sell the products in the rich countries. This may be typical of certain industries, such as the production of shoes or clothing. However, increasingly, multinational firms' production is aimed at supplying local markets. The U.S. Department of Commerce found that more than 60 percent of the production of U.S. firms' subsidiaries in developing countries was sold in the local market where the production occurred. A look at the global firms that have raced to invest in China indicates that the prospect of selling to the massive Chinese market is the attraction for much of this investment. In this situation, governments do not need to offer a lack of environmental standards in order to attract multinational firms.

2.b.4. Does Globalization Encourage Harmful Labor Practices? Supporters of globalization argue that there is no evidence of a "race to the bottom" in labor standards. In fact, multinational firms tend to pay higher wages than local firms and tend to provide greater benefits for workers than existed in the country prior to globalization. At a basic level, if a worker freely accepts employment, that worker must be better off than he or she would be with the next best alternative. So even though wages in, for instance, Vietnam may be much lower than those in western Europe or North America, this is not evidence that workers are being exploited. The local wages across the Vietnamese economy are lower than those in, say, France or Canada. The workers who

accept employment at a factory in Vietnam operated by a multinational firm prefer such work to working in agriculture at much lower wages. It is common to find long waiting lists of workers who want jobs at multinational firms' factories in developing countries. Rather than exploitation, this suggests that globalization is raising living standards and making people better off.

RECAP

1. Arguments against globalization include a concern that free trade is harmful to people, that international organizations serve only the interests of corporations, and that there is a "race to the bottom," with countries offering lax regulation of environmental quality and labor standards in order to offer multinational firms better opportunities for profit.

2. Supporters of globalization argue that trade based on comparative advantage raises living standards

everywhere; that international organizations are funded by governments, not corporations, and provide a formal mechanism for all governments to be represented and to push for change; and that environmental quality and welfare of workers actually improve with globalization.

3. Globalization, Economic Growth, and Incomes

4 How has globalization affected economic growth and poverty?

Asian tigers
Hong Kong, Korea, Singapore, and Taiwan, countries that globalized in the 1960s and 1970s and experienced fast economic growth.

NICs
Newly industrialized countries.

The increased integration of the world's economies has been associated with economic growth and reduction of poverty in most countries. The so-called **Asian tigers**—Hong Kong, Korea, Singapore, and Taiwan—underwent the process of opening their economies in the 1960s and 1970s and experienced rapid growth and dramatic increases in their living standards. Nowadays, these countries are sometimes referred to as "newly industrialized countries," or **NICs**. More recently, several other countries have been through the globalization process. Figure 2 shows the NICs and the post-1980 globalizers. The 24 post-1980 globalizers are spread around the world. One World Bank study tracked the performance of all of these countries over time to measure how globalization has affected them.[1] The major conclusions of the study are as follows:

- *Economic growth has increased with globalization.* Average growth of per capita GDP increased from 1.4 percent per year in the 1960s to 2.9 percent in the 1970s to 3.5 percent in the 1980s to 5.0 percent in the 1990s. At the same time that these countries were increasing their growth rates, average annual per capita GDP growth in the rich countries fell from 4.7 percent in the 1960s to 2.2 percent in the 1990s. What makes this even more dramatic is the fact that nonglobalizing developing countries had average annual growth rates of only 1.4 percent during the 1990s.

- *Income inequality has not increased.* The benefits of increased economic growth are widely shared in globalizing countries. An important exception to this finding is China, where income inequality has increased. However, government policies in China that resulted in moving to free markets from socialism while restricting internal migration may have played a much bigger role in causing changes in the Chinese income distribution than globalization did.

---

[1] David Dollar and Aart Kraay, "Trade, Growth, and Poverty," *World Bank Policy Research Department Working Paper No. 2615*, 2001. For additional evidence and discussion, see "Globalization: Threat or Opportunity," *IMF Issues Brief*, January 2002, and the articles on the IMF Web site: http://www.imf.org/external/np/exr/key/global.htm.

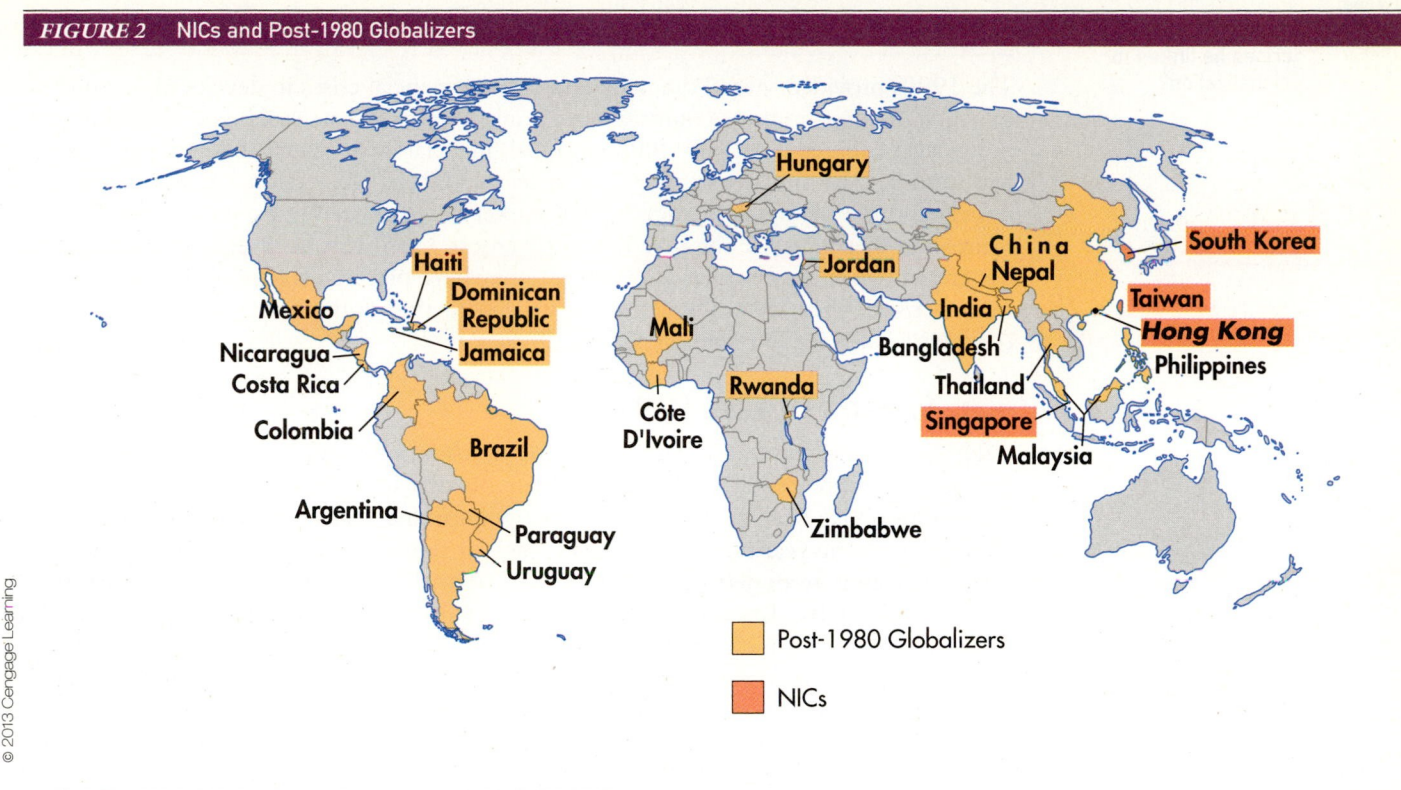

FIGURE 2   NICs and Post-1980 Globalizers

Legend:
- Post-1980 Globalizers
- NICs

Countries labeled on map: Hungary, Haiti, Dominican Republic, Jamaica, Mexico, Nicaragua, Costa Rica, Colombia, Brazil, Argentina, Paraguay, Uruguay, Mali, Côte D'Ivoire, Rwanda, Zimbabwe, Jordan, China, Nepal, India, Bangladesh, Thailand, Singapore, Malaysia, South Korea, Taiwan, Hong Kong, Philippines

© 2013 Cengage Learning

- *The gap between rich countries and globalized developing countries has shrunk.* Some of the countries listed in Figure 2 were among the poorest countries in the world 25 years ago. The higher growth rates experienced by these countries have allowed them to gain ground on the rich countries.
- *Poverty has been reduced.* The fraction of the very poor, those who live on less than $1 per day, declined in the newly globalized economies. For instance, between the 1980s and the 1990s, the fraction of the population living on less than $1 per day fell from 43 percent to 36 percent in Bangladesh, from 20 percent to 15 percent in China, and from 13 percent to 10 percent in Costa Rica.

The evidence from around the world indicates that the real losers in the globalization of the world economy are those countries that have not participated. They tend to be mired in a low-growth path, with enduring poverty and none of the benefits that globalization has conferred.

RECAP

1. Some studies have shown that globalization increases economic growth without increasing income inequality within nations.

2. Some studies have shown that globalization narrows the income gap between rich and poor nations and reduces poverty.

5 Can recent financial crises be linked to globalization?

4. Financial Crises and Globalization

The 1990s provided several dramatic episodes of financial crises in developing countries, in which investors in these countries were punished with substantial losses and local businesses also suffered. In 2007–2008, a global financial crisis struck the developed countries and led to the worst recession since the Great Depression of the 1930s. To understand the nature of the developing market crises of the 1990s, we will first look at some data that illustrate the severity of the crises. Then we will analyze the reasons for the crises. It will be seen that globalization may have played a contributing role in these recent crises. Then we will extend the analysis to the global crisis of 2007–2008 and consider what role globalization played.

4.a. Crises of the 1990s

Table 2 provides summary data on some key economic indicators for countries that underwent severe crises. Crises occurred in Mexico in 1994–1995 and in Southeast Asia—Indonesia, Korea, Malaysia, the Philippines, and Thailand—in 1997. The table shows that in the year prior to the crises, each of these countries except Malaysia owed substantial short-term debt to foreigners. Short-term debt is debt that is due in less than one year. The table lists short-term debt as a fraction of reserves. International reserves were discussed in the chapter titled "Money and Banking," where it was stated that these are assets that countries hold that can be used to settle international payments. The primary international reserve asset is foreign currency, mainly U.S. dollars. So except for Malaysia, all the countries affected by these crises owed more short-term debt to foreigners than the value of their international reserves.

Table 2 also shows that bank loans were a sizable fraction of GDP in all the crisis countries except Mexico. This becomes a problem when business turns bad. If the incomes of individuals and business firms are falling, then they will be less able to repay their loans to banks. As a result, the banks are also in trouble, and the result may be an economic crisis.

In each country, the stock market dropped dramatically. This is seen in Table 2 as the percentage change in stock prices over the first six months following the onset of the crisis. Stock prices dropped by an amount ranging from 26 percent in Korea to 57 percent in Malaysia. Investors in each country lost huge amounts of wealth as a result of the rapid drop in the values of local firms.

TABLE 2	Economic Conditions in Crisis Countries			
Country	**Short-Term External Debt/Reserves (year)**	**Bank Loans/GDP (year)**	**Stock Market Returns (%)**	**Exchange Rate (month/year)**
Mexico	230% (1993)	24% (1993)	−29%	3.88 (12/94); 6.71 (3/95)
Indonesia	226% (1996)	55% (1996)	−40%	2,368 (1/97); 9,743 (1/98)
Korea	300% (1996)	59% (1996)	−26%	850 (1/97); 1,694 (1/98)
Malaysia	42% (1996)	93% (1996)	−57%	2.49 (1/97); 4.38 (1/98)
Philippines	126% (1996)	49% (1996)	−29%	26.3 (1/97); 42.7 (1/98)
Thailand	103% (1996)	99% (1996)	−30%	25.7 (1/97); 52.6 (1/98)

Source: Data on short-term debt/reserves and bank loans/GDP come from Steven B. Kamin, "The Current International Financial Crisis: How Much Is New?" *Journal of International Money and Finance*, August 1999. Stock market returns and exchange rates are drawn from Yahoo! Finance, yahoo.com. Stock market returns are calculated for the six-month period following the onset of the crisis in each country. Exchange rates are the price of local currency per 1 U.S. dollar.

Finally, Table 2 shows that the exchange rate against the U.S. dollar dropped substantially in each country. Exchange rates played a particularly large role in these financial crises and pointed out a vulnerability of small developing countries to globalization in terms of international capital flows.

4.b. Exchange Rates and Financial Crises

Each of the countries in Table 2 had a fixed exchange rate prior to the crisis period. The chapter titled "Monetary Policy" included a discussion of how central banks must intervene in the foreign exchange market to maintain a fixed exchange rate. Here we can apply the same analysis to understand how a fixed exchange rate may contribute to financial crises. Figure 3 illustrates the situation for Mexico. The demand in this figure is the demand for dollars arising out of the Mexican demand for U.S. goods, services, and financial assets. The supply is the supply of dollars arising out of the U.S. demand for Mexican goods, services, and financial assets. Initially, the equilibrium is located at point A, where the exchange rate is 4 pesos per dollar and $10 billion are traded for pesos each

FIGURE 3 Foreign Exchange Market Intervention with a Fixed Exchange Rate

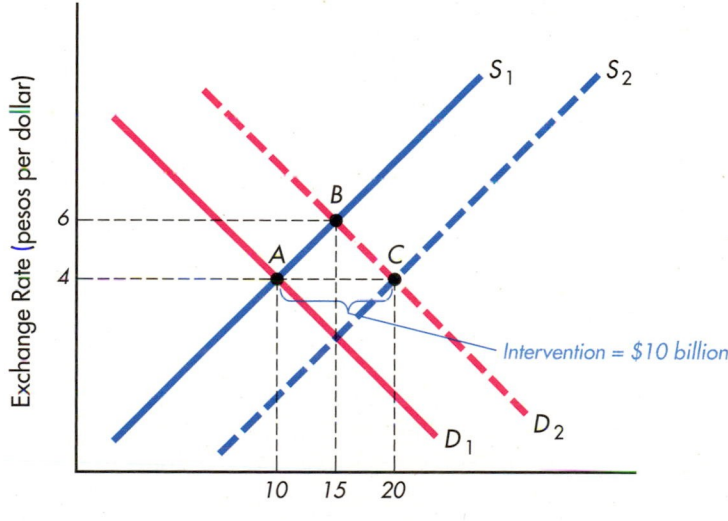

The demand is the demand for dollars arising out of the Mexican demand for U.S. goods, services, and financial assets. The supply is the supply of dollars arising out of the U.S. demand for Mexican goods, services, and financial assets. Initially, the equilibrium is located at point A, where the exchange rate is 4 pesos per dollar and $10 billion are traded for pesos each day. If there is concern that Mexican financial assets will fall in value, then investors will start to sell peso-denominated assets and then will sell their pesos for dollars in order to buy dollar-denominated assets. This shifts the demand curve for dollars from D_1 to D_2. The new equilibrium would then be at point B, with a depreciated peso exchange rate of 6 pesos per dollar and $15 billion per day being traded. To maintain a fixed exchange rate of 4 pesos per dollar and avoid private traders' shifting the equilibrium to point B, the central bank (Banco de Mexico) must intervene in the foreign exchange market, selling dollars equal to the private market demand for dollars in excess of the amount that would yield an equilibrium at point A. In the figure, we see that the new equilibrium with central bank intervention is a point C where the central bank is selling $10 billion per day ($20–$10 billion) in order to maintain the exchange rate at 4 pesos per dollar.

day. If there is concern that Mexican financial assets will fall in value, then investors will start to sell peso-denominated assets; they will then sell their pesos for dollars in order to buy dollar-denominated assets. This shifts the demand curve for dollars from D_1 to D_2. The new equilibrium would be at point B, with a depreciated peso exchange rate of 6 pesos per dollar and $15 billion per day being traded. To maintain a fixed exchange rate of 4 pesos per dollar and keep the private traders from shifting the equilibrium to point B, the central bank (Banco de Mexico) must intervene in the foreign exchange market by selling an amount of dollars equal to the excess of the private market demand for dollars over the amount that would yield equilibrium at point A. In the figure, we see that the new equilibrium with central bank intervention is at point C, where the central bank is selling $10 billion per day ($20–$10 billion) in order to maintain the exchange rate at 4 pesos per dollar.

If the shift in private investors' demand from D_1 to D_2 is not a temporary phenomenon, then this creates a problem for Banco de Mexico: It has a limited supply of international reserves, including U.S. dollars. The intervention to support the fixed exchange rate involves selling dollars and buying pesos. Eventually Banco de Mexico will exhaust its supply of dollars, and it will then be forced to devalue the currency, letting the exchange rate adjust to the free market equilibrium of 6 pesos per dollar. Once speculators realize that the central bank is losing a substantial fraction of its international reserves, a **speculative attack** may occur. This is the term given to a situation in which private speculators start selling even more pesos for dollars, expecting that the central bank will be forced to devalue the currency. If a speculator sells pesos and buys dollars for a price of 4 pesos per dollar, and then the peso is devalued to 6 pesos per dollar, that speculator can turn around and sell the dollars for pesos, receiving $6 - 4 = 2$ pesos in profit for each dollar invested in the speculative activity. Of course, once a speculative attack occurs, the demand for dollars shifts out even further, and the central bank will have to spend even more of its international reserves to defend the fixed exchange rate.

Each of the international financial crises of the 1980s and 1990s involved a fixed exchange rate. In each case, once it became clear that the domestic currency was overvalued relative to its true free market value, speculative attacks occurred, and the central bank lost a sizable amount of its international reserves. With floating or flexible exchange rates, the exchange rate changes every day with the free market forces of supply and demand, so that countries are not forced to intervene and spend their international reserves to maintain a fixed exchange rate. In this situation, a speculative attack cannot occur.

Once the currency has been devalued, it is common for some local business firms to be driven into bankruptcy as a result of the effect of the devaluation on the value of their debt. This is because much borrowing is done in U.S. dollars. In Thailand, for instance, prior to the crisis of 1997, the Thai government had repeatedly stated that under no circumstances would it ever change the fixed exchange rate. Business firms, believing that the exchange rate between the Thai baht and the U.S. dollar would not change, borrowed in U.S. dollars, expecting that the dollars they borrowed and the dollars they would have to repay would be worth the same amount of baht. Imagine a firm that had a debt of $1 million. Prior to the financial crisis that started in the summer of 1997, the exchange rate was about 25 baht to 1 U.S. dollar. At this exchange rate, it would cost 25 million baht to repay $1 million. By January 1998, the exchange rate was about 52 baht per dollar. Thus, the firm would find that the baht price of repaying $1 million had risen to 52 million baht. The cost of repaying the dollar loan had more than doubled as a result of the currency devaluation. Because of such exchange rate changes, the financial crises of the 1990s had devastating effects on local businesses in each country. As business firms in these countries lost value, foreign investors who had invested in these firms also suffered large losses. The 1990s financial crises imposed huge costs on the global economy.

speculative attack
A situation in which private investors sell domestic currency and buy foreign currency, betting that the domestic currency will be devalued.

4.c. What Caused the Crises?

The prior section showed how a fixed exchange rate could contribute to a crisis. The crises of the 1990s taught economists some lessons regarding exchange rates and other factors that increased countries' vulnerability to crises. Considerable resources have been devoted to understanding the nature and causes of financial crises in hopes of avoiding future crises and forecasting those crises that do occur. Forecasting is always difficult in economics, and it is safe to say that there will always be surprises that no economic forecaster anticipates. Yet there are certain variables that are so obviously related to past crises that they may serve as warning indicators of potential future crises. The list includes the following:

- *Fixed exchange rates.* All of the countries involved in recent crises, including Mexico in 1993–1994, the southeast Asian countries in 1997, and Argentina in 2002, had fixed exchange rates prior to the onset of the crisis. Generally, these countries' macroeconomic policies were inconsistent with the maintenance of the fixed exchange rate, and when large devaluations ultimately occurred, domestic residents holding loans denominated in foreign currency suffered huge losses.

- *Falling international reserves.* The maintenance of fixed exchange rates may not be a problem. One way to tell if the exchange rate is no longer an equilibrium rate is to monitor the country's international reserve holdings (largely the foreign currency held by the central bank and the treasury). If the stock of international reserves is falling steadily over time, that is a good indicator that the fixed-exchange-rate regime is under pressure and that there is likely to be a devaluation.

- *Lack of transparency.* Many countries in which there is a financial crisis suffer from a lack of transparency in government activities and a lack of public disclosure of business conditions. Investors need to know the financial situation of firms in order to make informed investment decisions. If accounting rules allow firms to hide the financial impact of actions that would harm investors, then investors may not be able to adequately judge when the risk of investing in a firm rises. In such cases, a financial crisis may come as a surprise to all but the insiders in a troubled firm. Similarly, if the government does not disclose its international reserve position in a timely and informative manner, investors may be taken by surprise when a devaluation occurs. The lack of good information on government and business activities serves as a warning sign of potential future problems.

This short list of warning signs provides an indication of the sorts of variables that an international investor must consider when evaluating the risks of investing in a foreign country. This list is also useful to international organizations like the International Monetary Fund when monitoring countries and advising them on recommended changes in policy.

So far we have not explicitly considered how globalization may contribute to crises. The analysis of Figure 3 provides a hint. If there is free trading in a country's currency and the country has globalized financial markets, so that foreign investors trade domestic financial assets, there is a greater likelihood of a crisis than in a country that is not globalized. The money that comes into the developing country from foreign investors can also flow back out. This points out an additional factor to be considered:

- *Short-term international investment.* The greater the amount of short-term money invested in a country, the greater the potential for a crisis if investors lose confidence in that country. So if foreigners buy large amounts of domestic stocks, bonds, or other financial assets, they can turn around and sell these assets quickly. These asset sales will depress the value of the country's financial markets, and as foreigners sell local currency for foreign currency, like U.S. dollars, the local currency will also fall in value. Too much short-term foreign investment may serve as another warning sign for a financial crisis.

Of course, a country can always avoid financial crises by not globalizing—keeping its domestic markets closed to foreigners. However, such a policy costs more than it is worth. As discussed earlier in this chapter, globalization has paid off by providing faster economic growth and reductions in poverty. To avoid globalization in order to avoid financial crises is to remain in poverty as the rest of the world grows richer. We should think of globalization and financial crises in these terms: A closed economy can follow very bad economic policies for a long time, and the rest of the world will have no influence in bringing about change for the better. A country with a globalized economy will be punished for bad economic policy as foreign investors move money out of the country, contributing to financial market crises in that country. It is not globalization that brings about the crisis. Instead, globalization allows the rest of the world to respond to bad economic policies in a way that highlights the bad policies and imposes costs on the country for following such policies. In this sense, globalization acts to discipline countries. A country with a sound economic policy and good investment opportunities is rewarded with large flows of savings from the rest of the world to lower the cost of developing the local economy.

4.d. The Global Financial Crisis of 2007–2008

While the crises of the 1980s and 1990s were concentrated in developing countries, the global crisis that began in 2007 was concentrated in the developed countries. In fact, the crisis was initially referred to as the "sub-prime crisis," a reference to the fact that defaults on high-risk mortgage loans in the United States were the first wave of the crisis. These were mortgages offered to customers with inadequate income or poor credit histories, but the institutions that made the loans sold the mortgages to others and the true risk associated with the loans was not well understood. How did bad loans on U.S. mortgages translate into a global crisis? These mortgages were originally made by banks in the United States, but they were then packaged into bundles containing a large number of such mortgages, and these bundles, called "securitized mortgages," were then sold to other investors. The globalization of financial markets played a major role. In recent years, there has been more and more international investment, which includes investments by European banks in U.S. mortgages. So when the U.S. borrowers began to default in large numbers, not only were U.S. financial institutions incurring losses on the mortgages, but so were financial institutions in Europe. So the crisis that began in the U.S. home mortgage industry was transmitted across international borders.

The financial crisis of 2007–2008 illustrated how important the integration of international financial markets could be in contributing to the spread of financial problems from one country to another. The answer is not less international investment, but better regulation of financial institutions to ensure prudent risk taking exists in the future. We want investment to flow where it is most productive, and this means that money should flow across international borders to find the best opportunities. There was much more than just international investment in U.S. mortgages, and when the crisis began, such investment was cut back dramatically as financial institutions tried to reduce their losses.

Once losses were sustained by financial institutions, they began to cut back their lending in other areas. This is referred to as *deleveraging*—reducing exposure to risk associated with investments. The deleveraging of financial institutions led to the financial crisis sometimes being referred to as the *credit crisis*, as credit was restricted and more difficult to obtain. Not only were banks less willing to lend to their household and business customers, they were also less willing to lend to other banks as they were not sure whether other banks would be able to repay loans. As lending was reduced, spending by households and business firms fell, and a global recession resulted. Of course, as jobs were lost and incomes fell, the recession resulted in more loan defaults as more and more households and businesses were unable to repay their debts.

TABLE 3	Estimates of Loan Losses Suffered by Financial Institutions, 2007–2010 (in Billions of U.S. Dollars)				
	Outstanding Insurer Loan Values	Bank Losses	Insurer Losses	Other Losses	Percent Loss
U.S.					
Residential mortgages	5,117	206	22	204	8.4%
Commercial mortgages	1,913	116	9	62	9.8%
Consumer loans	1,914	169	14	89	14.2%
Corporate loans	1,895	61	5	32	5.2%
Municipal	2,669	50	4	26	3.0%
Total loans	*13,508*	*602*	*54*	*413*	*7.9%*
Europe					
Residential mortgages	4,632	119	10	63	4.1%
Commercial mortgages	2,137	65	5	34	4.9%
Consumer loans	2,467	109	9	58	7.1%
Corporate loans	11,523	258	21	137	3.6%
Total loans	*20,759*	*551*	*45*	*292*	*4.3%*
Japan					
Consumer loans	3,230	58	3	3	2.0%
Corporate loans	3,339	60	3	3	2.0%
Total loans	*6,569*	*118*	*6*	*6*	*2.0%*

© 2013 Cengage Learning

Table 3 provides measures of the magnitude of the losses suffered by financial institutions due to the crisis. The table reports data for the United States, Europe, and Japan, and shows total loans outstanding and losses sustained by banks, insurance companies, and other firms for loans of different types. For the United States, we see that more than 14 percent of the value of consumer loans will not be repaid and almost 8 percent of the total value of all loans will not be repaid. The numbers are a bit better for Europe and Japan, with a little more than 4 percent of loans unpaid in Europe and only 2 percent in Japan. One can see that the crisis hit U.S. financial institutions the worst, while Japanese institutions were not very exposed to the crisis.

RECAP

1. The 1990s saw financial crises in Mexico, Indonesia, Korea, Malaysia, the Philippines, and Thailand.

2. Fixed exchange rates encouraged speculative attacks and ultimate devaluations of the currencies of the countries involved in the 1990 crises.

3. Exchange-rate devaluations raised the cost of debts that were denominated in foreign currency and imposed large losses on debtor firms.

4. Factors contributing to the 1990s financial crises included fixed exchange rates, falling international reserves, a lack of transparency to investors, and a high level of short-term international investment.

5. Globalization works to discipline countries that follow bad economic policies as foreign investors reduce their investments in those countries. Countries that follow good economic policies are rewarded with greater access to the savings of the rest of the world to help finance growth and development.

6. The financial crisis of 2007–2008 was global and began in the developed countries.

7. The global financial crisis pointed out the need for better regulation of financial institutions to ensure prudent lending and credit management policies.

8. The globalization of financial markets with associated international investment facilitated the trans-mission of financial shocks from one country to another so that a debt crisis originating in one country affects other countries that have invested in those assets.

SUMMARY

1. **What is globalization?**

   - Globalization involves an increased cross-border flow of trade in goods, services, and financial assets, along with increased international mobility of technology, information, and individuals. *§1*

   - The process of globalization has always existed because of its potential to raise living standards. *§1.a*

   - The rapid pace of globalization in recent decades has been made possible by technological advances. *§1.b*

2. **What are the arguments against globalization?**

   - Free trade increases corporate profits but harms people. *§2.a.1*

   - International organizations and the agreements they are associated with serve corporate interests and harm people. *§2.a.2*

   - Globalization occurs at the cost of environmental quality. *§2.a.3*

   - Globalization encourages harmful labor practices. *§2.a.4*

3. **What are the arguments in support of globalization?**

   - Those who lose their jobs to more efficient producers in other countries will be harmed, but the benefits to all consumers far outweigh the losses of those firms and workers that are harmed by globalization. *§2.b.1*

   - International organizations are funded by governments, not firms, and such organizations serve the interests of all nations in that they provide a setting where grievances must be heard and policy changes can be implemented. *§2.b.2*

   - Globalization has not resulted in a "race to the bottom," in which labor practices suffer and environmental decay results. *§2.b.3, 2.b.4*

4. **How has globalization affected economic growth and poverty?**

   - Globalizers have faster economic growth and less poverty than nonglobalizers. *§3*

5. **Can recent financial crises be linked to globalization?**

   - Globalization allows for international financial flows that punish countries that follow bad economic policy. *§4.c*

KEY TERMS

EXERCISES

1. What is globalization?
2. Comment on the following statement: "Globalization is an event of the post-1980s. Prior to this time, we never had to worry about globalization and its effects."
3. Write a script for two speakers arguing about globalization and its effects. Give each speaker a name, and then write a script for a debate between the two. The debate should be no longer than two pages, double-spaced. Each speaker should make a few key points, and the other speaker should offer a reply to each point the first speaker makes.
4. Why has the pace of globalization quickened since the 1950s?
5. If you wanted to compare countries on the basis of how globalized they are, how could you construct some numerical measures that would allow a cross-country comparison?
6. What are the major arguments against globalization?
7. What are the major arguments in favor of globalization?
8. What is the difference between "fair" and "free" trade?
9. What is the WTO? Where is it located, and what does it do?
10. Suppose we find that multinational firms are paying much lower wages in some poor countries than they would have to pay in the United States. Would this be sufficient evidence that these firms are exploiting the workers in the poor countries? Why or why not?
11. How can globalization reduce poverty? What does the evidence suggest about globalization and poverty?
12. There were several major international financial crises in the 1990s. What role did globalization play in these crises?
13. Using a supply and demand diagram, explain how central banks maintain a fixed exchange rate. What can cause an end to the fixed-exchange-rate regime?
14. Using a supply and demand diagram, explain how speculative attacks occur in the foreign exchange market.
15. If you were employed by a major international bank to forecast the likelihood of a financial crisis, what key variables would you want to monitor for the countries you are studying? Why would you want to monitor these variables?
16. What was the role of globalization in the global financial crisis of 2007–2008?
17. What is the role of technology in globalization? Explain several ways that the Internet has increased the pace of globalization and several ways that it has decreased the pace of globalization.
18. Have there been any "setbacks" to globalization?

You can find further practice tests in the Online Quiz at **www.cengage.com/economics/boyes**.

RESHAPING THE GLOBAL ECONOMY

The Economic and Financial Crisis Marks the End (for Now) of a Rapid Expansion of Globalization

The economic and financial turmoil engulfing the world marks the first crisis of the current era of globalization. Considerable country experience has been accumulated on financial crises in individual countries or regions—which policymakers can use to design remedial policies. But there has not been a world financial crisis in most people's living memory. And the experience of the 1930s is frightening because governments at that time proved unable to preserve economic integration and develop cooperative responses.

Even before this crisis, globalization was already being challenged. Despite exceptionally favorable global economic conditions, not everyone bought into the benefits of global free trade and movement of capital and jobs. Although economists, corporations, and some politicians were supportive, critics argued that globalization favored capital rather than labor and the wealthy rather than the poor.

Now the crisis and the national responses to it have started to reshape the global economy and shift the balance between the political and economic forces at play in the process of globalization. The drivers of the recent globalization wave—open markets, the global supply chain, globally integrated companies, and private ownership—are being undermined, and the spirit of protectionism has reemerged. And once-footloose global companies are returning to their national roots.

Globalization: Reshaping or Unmaking?

. . . To start with, *public participation in the private sector has increased significantly in the past few months*. . . . Of the 50 largest banks in the United States and the European Union, 23 and 15, respectively, have received public capital injections; that is, banks representing respectively 76 and 40 percent of pre-crisis market capitalization depend today on taxpayers. Other sectors, such as the automobile and insurance industries, have also received public assistance. Whatever the governments' intention, public support is bound to affect the behavior of once-footloose global firms.

Second, *this crisis challenges globally integrated companies*. Economic integration in the past quarter century has been driven largely by companies' search for cost cutting and talent. Yet globally integrated companies were first put to the test early on in the crisis, with the collapse of banks that acted across international borders. Once-mighty transnational institutions were suddenly at pains to identify which government would support them. . . .

Public aid risks turning global companies into national champions. . . .

Third, *national responses to the crisis can lead to economic and financial fragmentation*. There is initial evidence that, as governments ask banks to continue lending to domestic customers, credit is being rationed disproportionately in foreign markets. This was what happened recently when the Dutch government asked ING Bank to expand domestic lending while reducing its overall balance sheet. Because companies in emerging and less developed economies depend largely on foreign credit, this leaves them especially vulnerable to financial protectionism. Furthermore, government aid—driven by a legitimate concern with jobs—often, implicitly at least, shows preferences for the local economy. The French bias toward domestic employment in its auto industry's plan, the U.S. "Buy American" provision in the stimulus bill, and U.K. Prime Minister Gordon Brown's now infamous "British jobs for British workers" slogan are but a few examples.

Last but not least, *despite the G-20's commitment last November not to increase tariffs, these have gone up since the start of the crisis in several countries, from India and China to Ecuador and Argentina*. This follows a similar move one year ago when export restraints were introduced as countries tried to isolate domestic consumers from increasing international food prices.

It is hard to say whether these changes are merely short-term reactions to a major shock or amount to new and worrisome trends. At the very least, the balance between political and economic forces has been significantly altered. Because political support for globalization was at best shallow while the global economy was in a buoyant state, this suggests the pendulum is now swinging in the opposite direction. Against this background, two lessons from history are worth keeping in mind. One, dismantling protections takes time. It took several decades for many of the trade barriers erected during the interwar period to be brought down. Second, even if a significant part of the progress in liberalizing trade in recent times has been institutionalized and strong reversals à la 1930s are not likely, the downward spiral of protectionism acts fast.

Taken together, these risks pose a significant challenge for global integration. This is true also at the regional level. Economic divergence is rising within Europe, and cooperation within East Asia has been limited to say the least, in spite of the violent shock affecting the region.

Jean Pisani-Ferry and Indhira Santos

Source: Excerpts from "Reshaping the Global Economy," *Finance and Development*, International Monetary Fund, March 2009.

Commentary

This chapter has discussed the benefits and costs of globalization and documented the extent to which globalization has progressed. As pointed out in this article, the global financial crisis has halted the process of globalization. One point made in the article is that political support for globalization has always been mixed and it has been business firms that have led the drive for integration across national borders. The current reversal of globalization has important implications for productivity and living standards going forward.

In a globalized world, competition punishes the relatively unproductive or high-cost producers and rewards the relatively more productive or lower-cost producers. This means that in the industrial countries of Western Europe, North America, and Asia, foreign competition will put some domestic firms out of business, and some workers will lose their jobs. These workers typically do not find new jobs that pay as well as their old jobs. As a result, in the face of increasing competition from foreign firms, a natural response from those who are threatened is to fight change. This typically is reflected in calls by labor unions and firms that are losing money for trade restrictions on foreign goods so that the local firms and workers can keep their jobs. Some of the international demonstrations against globalization have been supported by labor unions from rich countries. Their goal is to slow or even stop the globalization process in order to protect jobs in the rich countries. This is one reason why officials in poor countries complain that so far the globalization process has not resulted in the large gains that could be realized if the rich countries truly opened their markets to the products that the developing countries produce best.

The rich countries are slow to open their markets to the poor countries because of political pressure at home to protect the workers and firms that would be displaced by the foreign competitors. Of course, the cost of such protection is lower living standards for all consumers in the country. The data presented in the chapter suggest that those countries that have not globalized have become poorer as the rest of the world has become richer. If the reversal of globalization that has occurred with the global financial crisis continues in the post-crisis period, some will benefit (typically relatively high-cost producers who can only exist if protected by government trade restrictions), but the majority of households should expect to pay a price in terms of a lower standard of living.

CHAPTER 19

Elasticity: Demand and Supply

© MACIEJ FROLOW/GETTY IMAGES, INC

JAMES STEIDL/SHUTTERSTOCK.COM; LOGO: © FROXX/SHUTTERSTOCK.COM

WORLD PREMIERE NOW SHOWING

FUNDAMENTAL QUESTIONS

1 How do we measure how much consumers alter their purchases in response to a price change?

2 What determines whether consumers alter their purchases a little or a lot in response to a price change?

3 How do we measure how much changes in the determinants of demand affect consumer purchases?

4 How do we measure how much sellers respond to a price change?

Let's begin by trying to gain some perspective on what we have been doing and what we will be doing in the next few chapters. In the first four chapters of this book, we defined economics, opportunity costs, and the "economic way of thinking." The economic way of thinking is to recognize that people are self-interested and as a result do those things that they expect will make them most satisfied or happiest. We say that people compare the costs and benefits of some activity, but it is the incremental, the additional costs and benefits, the change in costs and benefits, or what economists call the marginal costs and marginal benefits, that are important. It is the next minute, the next day, the next dollar, the next month's income that matter in people's decisions.

Economists describe behavior by saying that people compare marginal benefits and marginal costs. If the marginal benefits of some activity are larger than the marginal costs, then people do that activity. If the marginal benefits are less than the marginal costs, then people do not do that activity. One of the things people do is trade or exchange. But, as we discovered, they trade only if they believe that the trade will make them better off. This is what the gains from trade are all about; all parties to a trade can gain and have to think they will gain, or else they will not trade.

The interaction of traders—of buyers and sellers—is represented by a market, that is, by demand and supply. Within a market, demand and supply determine the market price—the price at which buyers and sellers agree to trade.

In the first few chapters, we examined how markets work to allocate scarce goods, services, and resources.

We need to do more, however, if we are to understand why the world is what it is. We have to have a more in-depth understanding of demand and supply. We begin that process here. In this and the following chapter, we examine demand. We delve into the incentives and motivations of consumers. We begin in this chapter with an examination of the responsiveness of consumers and suppliers to changes in the determinants of demand and supply. This is called **elasticity**. By definition, elasticity is *the measure of the responsiveness of quantity demanded or quantity supplied to a change in price or some other important variable.* By "responsiveness" we mean "how much quantity demanded or quantity supplied changes with respect to a change in something else."

elasticity
The responsiveness of quantity demanded or quantity supplied to a change in one of the determinants of demand and/or supply.

1   How do we measure how much consumers alter their purchases in response to a price change?

1. The Price Elasticity of Demand

The manager of a local movie theater raised the price from $9.50 to $10 per movie in order to pay for a new sound system that he had installed. He knew that the higher price would lower ticket sales, but he expected to more than make this up with the higher ticket price. He found that not only had ticket sales declined, but his revenue had fallen as well. Where had the manager gone wrong? The error he made was not knowing what the price elasticity of demand was.

1.a. The Definition of Price Elasticity

The price elasticity of demand is a measure of the magnitude by which consumers alter the quantity of some product that they purchase in response to a change in the price of that product. The more price-elastic demand is, the more responsive consumers are to a price change—that is, the more they will adjust their purchases of a product when the price of that product changes. Conversely, the less price-elastic demand is, the less responsive consumers are to a price change.

price elasticity of demand
The percentage change in the quantity demanded of a product divided by the percentage change in the price of that product.

The **price elasticity of demand**, e_d, is the percentage change in the quantity demanded of a product divided by the percentage change in the price of that product

$$e_d = \frac{\%\Delta Q^D}{\%\Delta P}$$

Notice that whenever P falls, Q^D rises, and when P rises Q^D falls. This means the price elasticity of demand is always negative.[1]

---

[1] Price elasticity is always negative since price and quantity demanded are inversely related. Economists often therefore refer to the absolute value of the price elasticity of demand; in other words, just ignore the negative sign. In this case: 1 is unit elastic, 0 to 1 is inelastic, and 1 to infinity is elastic.

- When price elasticity is between zero and −1, we say that demand is *inelastic*.
- When price elasticity is between −1 and −∞, we say that demand is *elastic*.
- When price elasticity is −1, we say that demand is *unit-elastic*.

1.b. Demand Curve Shapes and Elasticity

A **perfectly elastic demand curve** is a horizontal line that shows that consumers are willing and able to purchase any quantity at the single prevailing price but will switch to another seller at the flip of a switch. In Figure 1(a), a perfectly elastic demand curve represents the demand for the wheat harvested by a single farmer in Canada. The Canadian farmer is only one small producer of wheat, and because he is just one among many, he is unable to charge a price that differs from the price of wheat in the rest of the world. If this farmer's wheat is even slightly more expensive than wheat elsewhere, consumers will buy the wheat produced by other farmers in Canada and the rest of the world and leave this now slightly higher priced farmer without any business.

A **perfectly inelastic demand curve** is a vertical line, illustrating the idea that consumers cannot or will not change the quantity of a good they purchase when the price of the product is changed. Perhaps insulin to a diabetic is a reasonably vivid example of a good whose demand is perfectly inelastic. Of course, this behavior holds only over a certain price range. Eventually, the price would get so high that even a diabetic would be forced to decrease the quantity demanded. Figure 1(b) shows a perfectly inelastic demand curve.

In between the two extreme shapes of demand curves are the demand curves for most products. Figure 1(c) shows two downward-sloping straight-line demand curves, D_1 and D_2. The first demand curve, the steeper one, D_1, represents a more inelastic demand. The flatter curve, D_2, is more elastic. So we could use D_1 to represent the monthly demand for gasoline; it says that even if the price rises by quite a bit, the quantity of gasoline demanded declines by only a small amount. We could use the more

perfectly elastic demand curve
A horizontal demand curve indicating that consumers can and will purchase all they want at one price.

perfectly inelastic demand curve
A vertical demand curve indicating that there is no change in the quantity demanded as the price changes.

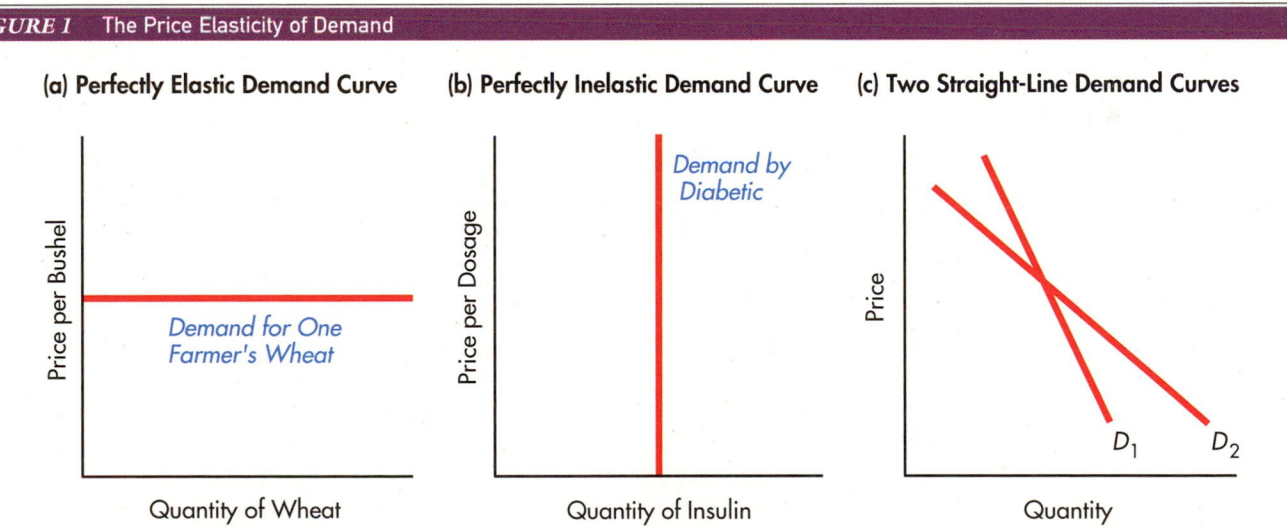

FIGURE 1	The Price Elasticity of Demand

(a) Perfectly Elastic Demand Curve   **(b) Perfectly Inelastic Demand Curve**   **(c) Two Straight-Line Demand Curves**

Demand for One Farmer's Wheat — Price per Bushel / Quantity of Wheat

Demand by Diabetic — Price per Dosage / Quantity of Insulin

D_1 D_2 — Price / Quantity

Figure 1(a), a perfectly elastic demand curve, represents the demand for one farmer's wheat. Because there are so many other suppliers, buyers purchase wheat from the least expensive source. If this farmer's wheat is priced ever so slightly above other farmers' wheat, buyers will switch to another source. Also, because this farmer is just one small producer in a huge market, he can sell everything he wants at the market price. Figure 1(b), a perfectly inelastic demand curve, represents the demand for insulin by a diabetic. A certain quantity is necessary to satisfy the need regardless of the price. Figure 1(c) shows two straight-line demand curves, D_1 and D_2. These demand curves are neither perfectly elastic nor perfectly inelastic.

elastic demand curve, D_2, to represent the demand for gasoline at a single station; it would say that as the price of gasoline at the corner Shell station increases, consumers decide to go to the Chevron station down the street instead of buying at the now more expensive Shell station.

1.b.1. Price Elasticity Changes along a Straight-Line Demand Curve While

we describe an entire demand curve as being more or less elastic than some other curve, we also note that the price elasticity of demand changes as we move up or down a straight-line demand curve. The price elasticity becomes more inelastic as we move down the curve. When we say that an entire demand curve is more elastic than another, such as D_2 compared to D_1, we are just saying that at every single price, D_2 is more elastic than D_1.

> *Demand is price-elastic at the top of the demand curve and inelastic at the bottom.*

All downward-sloping straight-line demand curves are divided into three parts by the price elasticity of demand: the *elastic region*, the *unit-elastic point*, and the *inelastic region*. The demand is elastic from the top of the curve to the unit-elastic point. At all prices below the unit-elastic point, demand is inelastic.

1.c. The Price Elasticity of Demand Is Defined in Percentage Terms

The price elasticity of demand is the *percentage* change in the quantity demanded divided by the *percentage* change in the price. By measuring the price elasticity of demand in terms of percentage changes, economists are able to compare the way consumers respond to changes in the prices of different products. For instance, the change in sales caused by a 1 percent increase in the price of gasoline (measured in gallons) can be compared to the change in sales caused by a 1 percent change in the price of a Big Gulp. Percentage changes ensure that we are comparing apples to apples, not apples to oranges. What sense could be made of a comparison between the effects on quantity demanded of a $1 rise in the price of college tuition, from $10,000 to $10,001, and a $1 rise in the price of a Big Mac, from $4 to $5? But the consumer's reaction to a 1 percent change in tuition could be compared to the consumer's reaction to a 1 percent change in the price of a Big Mac.

In section 1.b, it was pointed out that the price elasticity changes along a straight line demand curve. This is because elasticities are measured in percentage terms. Along a straight-line demand curve, equal dollar changes in price mean equal unit changes in quantity. For instance, if price changes by $1 in Figure 2, quantity demanded changes by 20 units; if price changes from $1 to $2, quantity demanded falls from 200 to 180; if price changes from $2 to $3, quantity demanded falls from 180 to 160; and so on. Each $1 change in price means a 20-unit change in quantity demanded. But those same amounts (constant amounts of $1 and 20 units) do not translate into constant percentage changes.

A $1 change at the top of the demand curve is a significantly different percentage change from a $1 change at the bottom of the demand curve. A $1 change from $10 is a 10 percent change, but a $1 change from $2 is a 50 percent change. Thus, as we move down the demand curve from higher to lower prices, a given dollar change becomes a larger and larger percentage change in price. The opposite is true of quantity changes. As we move downward along the demand curve, the same change in quantity becomes a smaller and smaller percentage change. A 10-unit change from 20 is a 50 percent change, while a 10-unit change from 200 is a 5 percent change. As we move down the straight-line demand curve—thus increasing quantity and reducing price—the percentage change in quantity demanded declines and the percentage change in price increases.

FIGURE 2   The Price Elasticity of Demand Varies along a Straight-Line Demand Curve

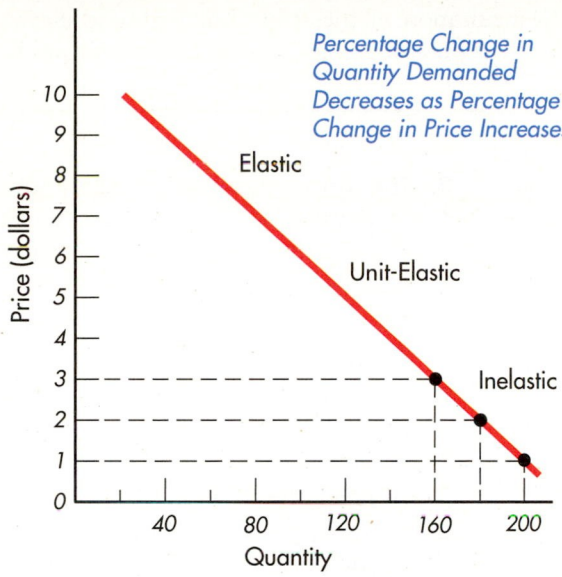

Percentage Change in Quantity Demanded Decreases as Percentage Change in Price Increases

As we move down the demand curve, the price elasticity varies from elastic to unit-elastic to inelastic.

© 2013 Cengage Learning

1.d. Determinants of the Price Elasticity of Demand

The degree to which the demand is price-inelastic or price-elastic depends on the following factors, which differ among products and among consumers:

- How many substitutes there are
- How well a substitute can replace the good or service under consideration
- The importance of the product in the consumer's total budget
- The time period under consideration

 2 What determines whether consumers alter their purchases a little or a lot in response to a price change?

The more substitutes there are for a product, the greater the price elasticity of demand. If you can buy something else when the price of an item goes up and be just as well off, then your demand is elastic. For instance, whether you buy gasoline at one station or another might depend on which one of them charges a penny more a gallon; if so, your demand for gas at a single station is very elastic. In contrast, diabetics have no substitute for insulin, so their demand for insulin is inelastic.

The greater the portion of the consumer's budget that a good constitutes, the more elastic is the demand for the good. Because a new car and an overseas vacation are quite expensive, even a small percentage change in their prices can represent a significant portion of a household's income. As a result, a 1 percent increase in price may cause many households to delay the purchase of a car or a vacation. Coffee, on the other hand, accounts for such a small portion of a household's total weekly expenditures that a large percentage increase in the price of coffee will probably have little effect on the quantity of coffee purchased. The demand for vacations is most likely quite a bit more elastic than the demand for coffee.

The longer the time period under consideration, the more elastic is the demand for any product. The demand for most goods and services will have a lower price elasticity over a shorter time period and will be more price-elastic over a longer span of time. For instance, the demand for gasoline is very inelastic over a period of a month. No good substitutes are available in so brief a period. Over a 10-year period, however, the demand for gasoline is much more elastic. The additional time allows consumers to alter their behavior to make better use of gasoline and to find substitutes for gasoline.

RECAP

1. The price elasticity of demand is a measure of the degree to which consumers will alter the quantities of a product that they purchase in response to changes in the price of that product. The price elasticity of demand is the percentage change in the quantity demanded divided by the corresponding percentage change in the price.

2. When the price elasticity of demand lies between -1 and $-\infty$, demand is said to be *elastic*. When the price elasticity of demand is equal to -1, demand is said to be *unit-elastic*. When the price elasticity of demand lies between -1 and 0, demand is said to be *inelastic*.

3. The price elasticity of demand depends on how readily and easily consumers can switch their purchases from one product to another.

4. Everything else held constant, the greater the number of close substitutes, the greater the price elasticity of demand.

5. Everything else held constant, the greater the proportion of a householder's budget that a good constitutes, the greater the householder's price elasticity of demand for that good.

6. Everything else held constant, the longer the time period under consideration, the greater the price elasticity of demand.

2. Other Demand Elasticities

A price change leads to a movement along the demand curve. When something that affects demand, other than price, changes, the demand curve shifts. How far the demand curve shifts is measured by elasticity—the elasticity of the variable whose value changes. As we saw in Chapter 3, "Markets, Demand and Supply, and the Price System," demand is determined by income, prices of related goods, expectations, tastes, number of buyers, and international effects. A change in any one of these "determinants of demand" will cause the demand curve to shift, and a measure of elasticity exists for each. The *income elasticity of demand* is calculated by comparing the same price on two demand curves that are different only because income is different. This is illustrated in Figure 3. It is the percentage change in quantity demanded caused by a given percentage change in income. The *cross-price elasticity of demand* measures the percentage change in quantity demanded caused by a given percentage change in the price of a related good. The *advertising elasticity of demand* measures the percentage change in quantity demanded caused by a given percentage change in advertising expenditures (change in tastes), and so on. Each elasticity is calculated by dividing the percentage change in quantity demand by the percentage change in the variable under consideration. Figure 3 would illustrate each of the elasticities noted here by altering which determinant of demand causes the curve to shift.

 3 How do we measure how much changes in the determinants of demand affect consumer purchases?

2.a. The Cross-Price Elasticity of Demand

cross-price elasticity of demand
The percentage change in the quantity demanded for one good divided by the percentage change in the price of a related good, everything else held constant.

The **cross-price elasticity of demand** measures the degree to which goods are substitutes or complements (for a discussion of substitutes and complements, see Chapter 3). The cross-price elasticity of demand is defined as the percentage change in the quantity demanded of one good divided by the percentage change in the price of a related good, everything else held constant.

© froxx/Shutterstock.com

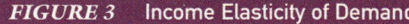

FIGURE 3 Income Elasticity of Demand

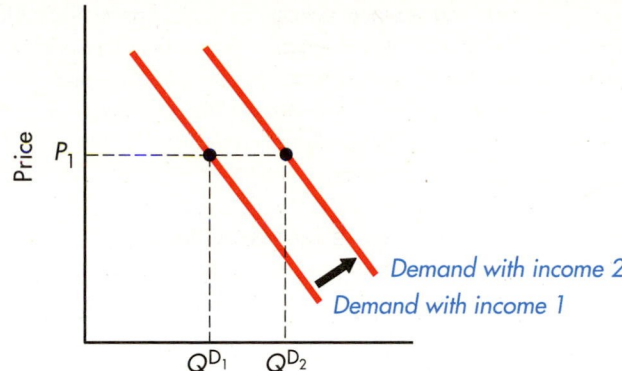

When income rises, demand shifts out. (Similarly, when the other determinants of demand change, the demand curve shifts.) The distance demand shifts at a given price is measured by the income elasticity of demand.

When the cross-price elasticity of demand is positive, the goods are substitutes; when the cross-price elasticity of demand is negative, the goods are complements. If a 1 percent *increase* in the price of a movie ticket leads to a 5 percent *increase* in the quantity of movies that are downloaded off the Internet, movies at the theater and downloaded movies are substitutes. If a 1 percent rise in the price of a movie ticket leads to a 5 percent *drop* in the quantity of popcorn consumed, movies and popcorn are complements.

2.b. The Income Elasticity of Demand

The income elasticity of demand measures the magnitude of consumer responsiveness to income changes. The **income elasticity of demand** is defined as the percentage change in the quantity demanded for a product divided by the percentage change in income, everything else held constant.

Goods whose income elasticity of demand is greater than zero are **normal goods**. Products that are often called necessities have lower income elasticities than products known as luxuries. Gas, electricity, health-oriented drugs, and physicians' services might be considered necessities. Their income elasticities are about 0.4 or 0.5. On the other hand, people tend to view dental services, automobiles, and private education as luxury goods. Their elasticities are 1.5 to 2.0.

When the income elasticity of demand for a good is negative, the good is called an **inferior good**. Some people claim that potatoes, rice, and beans are inferior goods because people who have very low levels of income eat large quantities of these goods but give up those items and begin eating fruit, fish, and higher-quality meats as their incomes rise. Smoking seems to be an inferior good—as income rises, people smoke less.

Clean air, on the other hand, is a **luxury good**. As incomes rise, people are willing to pay to have cleaner air. Air pollution is a problem throughout the world, but air pollution in the poorest nations is much worse than that in the wealthiest nations. Air pollution in India, much of Africa, and China is so bad that associated health problems are epidemic. Isn't it logical that if these nations improved their air, they would improve the condition of their populations considerably, which would contribute to economic growth? It does seem logical, but the problem is that because they have little income, these nations would have to forgo other important things in order to devote resources to cleaning the air. And taking resources away from other areas of the economy, such as

income elasticity of demand
The percentage change in the demand for a good divided by the percentage change in income, everything else held constant.

normal goods
Goods for which the income elasticity of demand is positive.

> Note that the sign of cross-price and income elasticities of demand are not always negative or positive.

inferior goods
Goods for which the income elasticity of demand is negative.

luxury goods
Goods for which the income elasticity of demand is a large positive number.

A woman compares the features of new phones. The quantity of mobile phones purchased as income rises is positive; the income elasticity of demand for mobile phones is positive. Not only is it positive, but it is larger than 1, indicating that as income rises by 10 percent, the quantity of phones purchased rises by more than 10 percent.

point elasticity
Price elasticity of demand measured at a single point on the demand curve.

arc elasticity
Price elasticity of demand measured over a range of prices and quantities along the demand curve.

health care, could lead to more serious health problems than are caused by the pollution. It turns out that a nation will not begin devoting resources to cleaning its air until its per capita income is above $15,000 per year, and a nation with over $15,000 in income per year per person is considered to be a rich nation. The greater a nation's per capita income, the more likely it is that it can reduce air pollution. Air pollution *reduction* is a luxury good—as income rises, a lot more of pollution reduction is demanded.

2.c. Calculating Elasticity

Price elasticity can be calculated in one of two ways, the **point elasticity** and the **arc elasticity**. The interpretation of the two is essentially the same—a measure of the responsiveness of consumers to a price change. The difference is that the point elasticity applies to a single price, while the arc elasticity applies to a price range. The point elasticity is a measure of the sensitivity of consumers to a very small price change from a particular price. The arc elasticity is a measure of the sensitivity of consumers to a larger price change—a range from one price to another.

The calculation of elasticity involves finding the percentage change. The formula for figuring out the percentage change in something, say X, is as follows:

$$\frac{(X_2 - X_1)}{X_1}$$

For example, if X increased from 1.00 to 1.25, we would have:

$$\frac{(1.25 - 1.00)}{1.00}$$

or 25%.

2.c.1. Point Elasticity The price elasticity is, therefore, just the ratio of two percentage changes:

$$\frac{\% \text{ Change in } Q}{\% \text{ Change in } P} = \frac{(Q_2 - Q_1)/Q_1}{(P_2 - P_1)/P_1}$$

This can be written in a simpler form by performing a slight modification (invert the denominator and multiply):

$$\frac{(Q_2 - Q_1)}{(P_2 - P_1)} \left[\frac{P_1}{Q_1}\right]$$

Part 1 in this formula is the change in quantity divided by the change in price.

$$\frac{(Q_2 - Q_1)}{(P_2 - P_1)}$$

which can be written as:

$$\frac{\Delta Q}{\Delta P}$$

Part 2 is the initial price divided by the initial quantity.

$$\frac{P_1}{Q_1}$$

Thus, the point price elasticity of demand is $[\Delta Q / \Delta P] * [P/Q]$.

What does the point elasticity look like graphically? Remember that when we graph demand and supply, price (P) is always on the vertical axis, and quantity (Q) is always on the horizontal axis. This means that Part 1 of the elasticity formula is the inverse of the slope of the demand curve. The slope is the rise/run or $[\Delta P/\Delta Q]$. Part 1 of the price elasticity formula is run/rise or $[\Delta Q/\Delta P]$. If the demand curve is a straight line, the slope is a constant number. For instance, if the equation has the form $P = aQ + B$, Part 1 is $1/a$.

Part 2 is (P_1/Q_1). There is *one* price and *one* quantity in this second part; a single *point* on the curve. Part 2 will change as we move along the demand curve. If we start at a low price and high quantity (remember, the law of demand states that price and quantity are inversely related), then P/Q is a small number. As we move up the demand curve, P/Q gets larger (as we go up the demand curve, P increases and Q decreases).

Since Part 1 is constant (the inverse of the slope), and Part 2 is a variable that gets larger as we move up the demand curve, demand gets more elastic as we move up the demand curve.

2.c.2. Arc Elasticity

The difference between the two formulas, arc and point, is the base. In the point elasticity formula, the initial price and quantity, P_1 and Q_1, are used as the base rather than the average or midpoint over the entire price and quantity range. The arc elasticity is calculated in the following way:

$$\frac{[Q_2 - Q_1]/[Q_2 + Q_1]/2}{[P_2 - P_1]/[P_2 + P_1]/2}$$

Notice that $[Q_2 + Q_1]/2$ is the average quantity and $[P_2 + P_1]/2$ is the average price over the price range from P_1 to P_2. So the arc elasticity formula is simply the change in quantity divided by the change in price multiplied by the ratio of the average price to the average quantity.

$$[\Delta Q/\Delta P] \ [\text{average } P/\text{average } Q]$$

As an example, suppose that at a price of \$6 per ticket, the average moviegoer demands 2 tickets per month, and at a price of \$4 per ticket, the average moviegoer purchases 6 tickets per month. Calculate the price elasticity of demand using the arc and the point elasticity. First, the arc elasticity. The change in quantity demanded is $(Q_2 - Q_1) = 6 - 2 = 4$. *The percentage change* is the change divided by the base. The base is the average of the two quantities: $(Q_1 + Q_2)/2$. With 4 as the base, the change in quantity demanded divided by the base is $4/4 = 1$. The change in price is \$4 − \$6 and the average price is $[\$6 + \$4]2 = \$5$. So the price elasticity is

$$1/(-2/5) = -5/2 = -2.5$$

According to these calculations, demand is elastic over the price range \$4 to \$6.

Using the same information, the point elasticity is the *change* in quantity demanded $(Q_2 - Q_1) = 4$. The change in price is −\$2, from \$6 to \$4. So dividing change in quantity by change in price and multiplying by the price divided by the quantity we get:

$$\text{Elasticity} = (4/2)/(-2/6) = -6$$

According to the calculations, demand is elastic at $P = \$6$.

2.c.3. Income and Cross-Price Elasticities

The calculation of income and cross-price elasticities is virtually identical to that of the price elasticity of demand. We find the change in quantity that results from a change in either income or the price of a related good. We then multiply that by the ratio of the initial levels of the variables.

The definition of income elasticity is: $\Delta Q/\Delta I * I/Q$ where I represents income. So if income changes from 100 to 120 while quantity demanded changes from 4 to 5, then the income elasticity of demand is: $(1/20)(100/4) = 1.25$. The good can be called a normal good.

The definition of the cross-price elasticity of demand is: $\Delta Q/\Delta P_x * P_x/Q$, where P_x is price of a related good. Suppose quantity increases from 4 to 6 when P_x increases from \$20 to \$25. The cross-price elasticity is: $(2/5)(20/4) = 2$. Since the cross-price elasticity is positive, then the goods are substitutes.

2.c.4. Calculating Elasticity from an Equation

Suppose the demand equation is the following and we want to calculate the point elasticity of demand:

$$Q = 10 - 2P + 0.20I + 2P_x$$

Where Q is quantity demanded, P is the product price and P_x is the price of a related good, and I is income. Assume that $P = \$10$, $I = 100$, and $P_x = 20$. Plug the numbers into the demand equation:

$$Q = 10 - 2(10) + 0.2(100) + 2(20) = 50$$

Now find price elasticity of demand: $\Delta Q/\Delta P * P/Q$.

According to the equation, whenever Q changes, P changes by (negative) twice that much. $\Delta Q/\Delta P = -2$. We are given that $P = 10$, and we solved that $Q = 50$ when $P = 10$. So the price elasticity is $-2(10/50) = -2/5$ or $-.40$. Demand is inelastic.

We can calculate income elasticity and cross-price elasticity of demand in essentially the same manner.

Income elasticity is $\Delta Q/\Delta I * I/Q$ where I is income. Since Q changes by 0.2 whenever I changes by 1, and since $I = 100$, the income elasticity is $(0.2)(100/50) = 2$.

Cross-price elasticity is $\Delta Q/\Delta P * P_x/Q$ where P_x is price of a related good. Since Q changes by 2 whenever P_x changes by 1, the cross-price elasticity is $(2)(20/50) = .80$.

Also note that you could calculate the arc elasticity by using two different prices and their associated quantities.

RECAP

1. The cross-price elasticity of demand is the percentage change in the quantity demanded for one product divided by the percentage change in the price of a related product, everything else held constant. If the cross-price elasticity of demand is positive, the goods are substitutes. If the cross-price elasticity of demand is negative, the goods are complements.

2. The income elasticity of demand is the percentage change in the quantity demanded for one product divided by the percentage change in income, everything else held constant. If the income elasticity of a good is greater than zero, the good is called a *normal good*. If the income elasticity of a good is negative, the good is called an *inferior good*. If the income elasticity of a good is a high positive number, the good is called a *luxury good*.

3. Elasticities can be calculated for any determinant of demand. Although income and cross-price elasticities were calculated in the text, other elasticities, such as advertising, international development, service, quality, and expectations elasticities, could have been calculated for any thing that affects demand.

4. Price elasticity of demand: $\Delta Q/\Delta P * P/Q$.

   Cross-price elasticity is $\Delta Q/\Delta P_x * P_x/Q$, where P_x is price of a related good.

   Income elasticity is $\Delta Q/\Delta I * I/Q$, where I is income.

5. The point price elasticity of demand is the elasticity calculated at a single price and quantity. The arc price elasticity of demand is the elasticity calculated over a range of prices and associated quantities.

3. The Price Elasticity of Supply

The price elasticity of supply is a measure of how sellers adjust the quantity of a good or service that they offer for sale when the price of that good changes. The **price elasticity of supply** is the percentage change in the quantity supplied of a good or service divided by the percentage change in the price of that good or service, everything else held constant. The price elasticity of supply is usually a positive number because the quantity supplied typically rises when the price rises. Supply is said to be elastic over a price range if the price elasticity of supply is greater than 1 over that price range. It is said to be inelastic over a price range if the price elasticity of supply is less than 1 over that price range.

3.a. Price Elasticity of Supply and the Shape of the Supply Curve

The price elasticity of supply is either zero or a positive number. A zero price elasticity of supply means that the quantity supplied will not vary as the price varies. A positive price elasticity of supply means that as the price of an item rises, the quantity supplied rises. The price elasticity of supply is zero for goods whose quantities cannot change. This is illustrated in Figure 4(a), where supply is a vertical line. Land surface, Monet paintings, Beethoven symphonies, and the Beatles' songs are all fixed in quantity. Because Monet, Beethoven, and John Lennon are dead, no matter what happens to price, the quantity of their products cannot change.

Figure 4(b) shows a perfectly elastic supply curve, a horizontal line. There are some goods for which the quantity supplied at the current price can be whatever anyone wants given sufficient time. The production of food, for instance, has increased tremendously during the past century, while the price has remained about the same. For most goods, the supply curve lies between the perfectly inelastic and perfectly elastic extremes. In Figure 4(c), two supply curves are drawn illustrating different shapes that the supply curve might have. The steeper curve, S_1, is more inelastic than curve S_2. Just as the elasticity changes along a straight-line demand curve, it also changes along a straight-line supply curve. However, the steeper curve is less elastic at every price compared to the flatter curve.

3.b. The Long and Short Runs

The shape of the supply curve depends primarily on the length of time being considered. Economists view time in terms of two distinct periods, the short run and the long run. The **short run** is a period of time long enough for existing firms to change the quantity of output they produce by changing the quantities of *some* of the resources used to produce their output, but not long enough for the firms to change the quantities of *all* of those resources. In the short run, firms are not able to build new factories or retrain workers, and new firms are unable to open up shop and begin to supply goods and services. The **long run** is a period of time long enough for existing firms to change the quantities of all the resources they use and for new firms to begin producing the product. So the actual or chronological time for the short and the long run varies from industry to industry. The long run for oil refining may be as long as seven to eight years; for personal computers, perhaps a year; for basket making, probably no longer than a day or two.

Usually, the greater the time period allowed, the more readily firms will increase their quantities supplied in response to a price increase. Thus, supply curves applicable to shorter periods of time tend to be more inelastic than supply curves that apply to longer periods of time. A baker who can switch from producing cupcakes to producing muffins within a day has large price elasticities of supply for cupcakes and for muffins; a small increase in the price of muffins relative to that of cupcakes will cause the bakery to significantly increase the quantity of muffins baked and reduce the quantity of cupcakes baked.

4 How do we measure how much sellers respond to a price change?

price elasticity of supply
The percentage change in the quantity supplied divided by the percentage change in price, everything else held constant.

short run
A period of time short enough that the quantities of at least one of the resources used cannot be varied.

long run
A period of time long enough that the quantities of all resources can be varied.

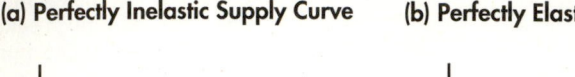

FIGURE 4 The Price Elasticity of Supply

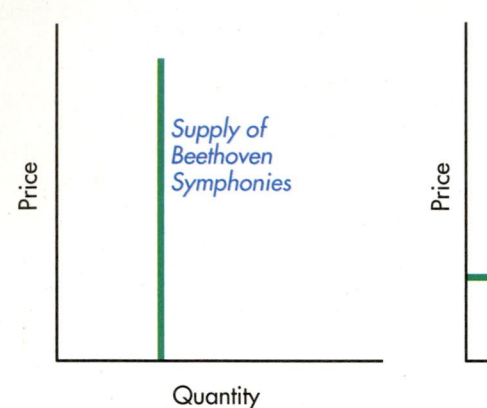

(a) Perfectly Inelastic Supply Curve

Price / Quantity

Supply of Beethoven Symphonies

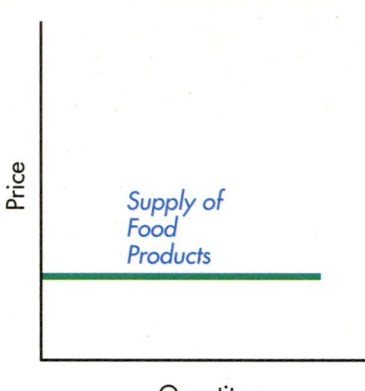

(b) Perfectly Elastic Supply Curve

Price / Quantity

Supply of Food Products

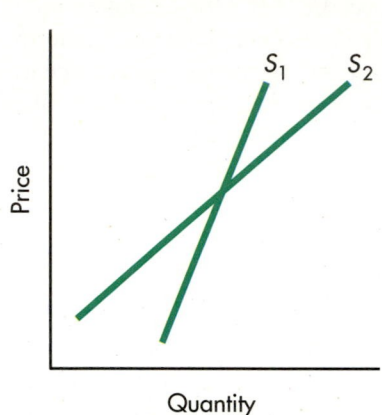

(c) Two Straight-Line Supply Curves

Price / Quantity

S_1 S_2

There are some special types of goods for which supply cannot change no matter what the length of time allowed for change. For such goods, the price elasticity of supply is zero and the supply curve is vertical, as shown in Figure 4(a). Figure 4(b) is a perfectly elastic supply curve, a horizontal line. A perfectly elastic supply curve says that the quantity supplied at the given price is unlimited; a small—infinitesimal—price change would lead to an infinite change in quantity supplied. For most goods, the supply curve lies between the perfectly inelastic and perfectly elastic extremes. In Figure 4(c), two supply curves are drawn. Curve S_1 is less elastic than curve S_2.

© 2013 Cengage Learning

An automobile manufacturing plant that requires several months or years to switch from constructing one type of car to another, however, will have a relatively inelastic supply.

In Figure 4(c), supply curve S_1 represents a shorter-run supply curve. For a given price change, the quantity supplied would change by a small amount, shown by moving along S_1. Curve S_2 represents a longer-run supply curve.

3.c. Calculating Price Elasticity of Supply

The calculation of price elasticity of supply is completely analogous to the calculation of price elasticity of demand. As a result, we will just go over the point elasticity calculation. The definition of the price elasticity of supply is: Percentage change in quantity supplied divided by percentage change in price. This can be written in the familiar form:

$$\Delta Q / \Delta P * P/Q$$

Since $\Delta Q / \Delta P$ is positive, Q goes in the same direction as P, and P/Q is positive, the price elasticity of supply is a positive number. The higher the number, the more elastic is supply.

3.d. Interaction of Price Elasticities of Demand and Supply

It takes both demand and supply to determine the equilibrium price and quantity in a market. Similarly, it takes both the price elasticity of demand and the price elasticity of supply to determine the full effect of a price change. The effect on price and quantity depends on the elasticities of demand and supply. One example of how this works is shown by a supply curve shifting along a single demand curve. If demand is very elastic, then shifts in the supply curve will result in large changes in quantity demanded and small changes in price at the equilibrium point, as in Figure 5(a).

If demand is very inelastic, however, then shifts in the supply curve will result in large changes in price and small changes in quantity at the equilibrium point, as shown in Figure 5(b).

FIGURE 5   Shifts of the Supply Curve

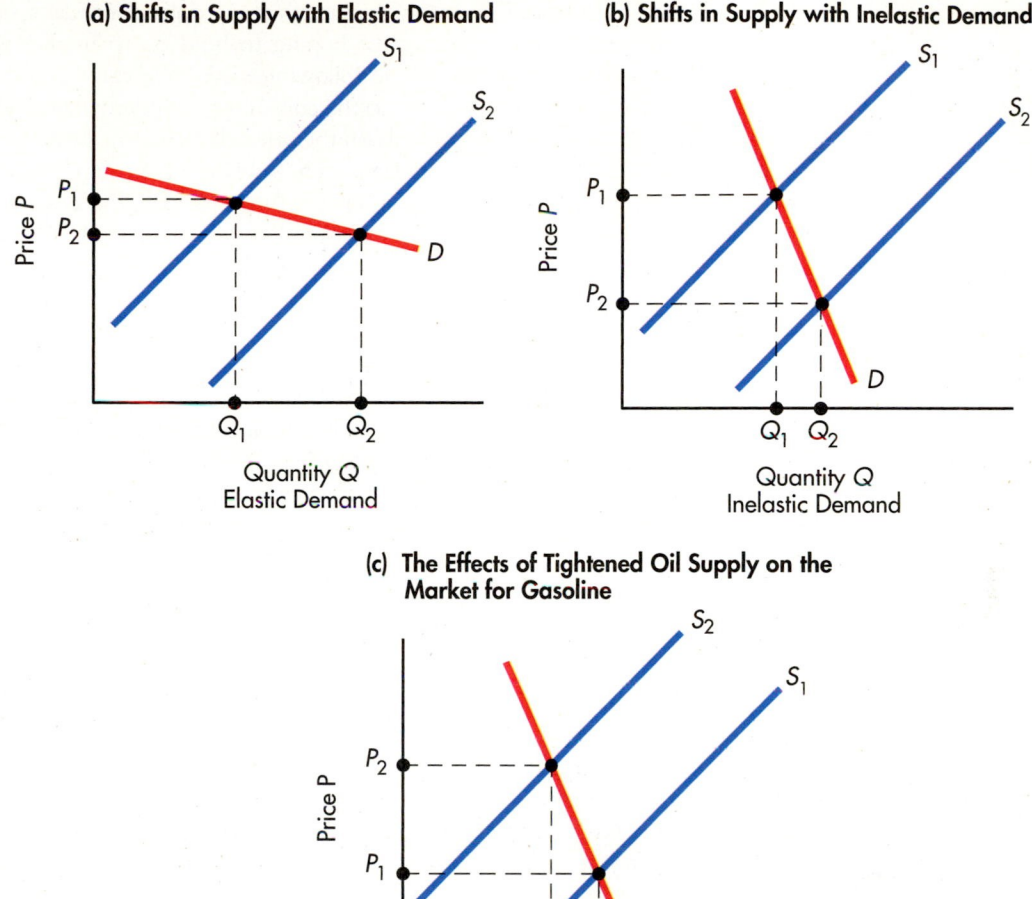

(a) Shifts in Supply with Elastic Demand

(b) Shifts in Supply with Inelastic Demand

(c) The Effects of Tightened Oil Supply on the Market for Gasoline

(a) A shift of supply leads to a small price change and a large quantity change when demand is elastic. (b) A shift of supply, equal horizontal to the shift in Figure 5(a), leads to a much larger change in price and smaller change in quantity if demand is inelastic. (c) A reduction in the supply of gasoline leads to a large price increase without much of a change in the quantity demanded.

Shifts in one curve can have drastically different effects depending on how elastic or inelastic the other curve is. For instance, let's take a look at the market for gasoline. Because demand is relatively inelastic, at least in the short run, when the supply of oil is reduced due to natural disasters or due to the oil cartel, OPEC, the reduction in supply is illustrated by an inward shift of the supply curve and the resulting higher price and lower quantity consumed.

Why? Because consumers do not have good substitutes for driving and thus are not willing to significantly cut their gasoline consumption in the short run (meaning the demand is very inelastic in the short run). In such a case, a shift in the supply curve affects the price much more than the quantity. This means the consumer is paying the bill. If the price changed little or none, but quantity changed a lot, that would indicate that the producer/supplier is paying most of the bill.

Another example of the importance of price elasticity of demand is given by the statement that business simply passes increased costs on to the consumer. In early 2011, prices of steel, wheat, sugar, rice, corn, and other items rose much more rapidly than they had risen during the previous few years. Businesses worried about their profits. Because consumers were still reacting to the 2008 recession, businesses avoided price increases, concerned about driving away price-conscious consumers or hoping to hold on to market share. But more and more businesses were reacting in the following way: "We can't absorb cost increases; we're just going to have to pass them on to the consumer." Under what conditions can costs be passed on to the consumer? It depends on the price elasticities of demand and supply.

Suppose demand is very price-inelastic. Then when the cost to business increases— illustrated by an upward-shifting supply curve (Figure 5[c])—the cost can be shifted to the consumer in terms of higher prices without affecting sales much. Conversely, suppose demand is very price-elastic. Then cost increases (illustrated by Figure 5[a]) cannot be passed on to consumers since a small price increase would reduce sales (Q) significantly.

3.d.1. Who Really Pays a Tax: Tax Incidence
Both the price elasticity of supply and price elasticity of demand come into play when determining which group, buyers or sellers, pay a larger portion of taxes that are imposed on business. Often people claim that any taxes on business will be passed along to the consumer. This is only true under certain conditions, depending on both the price elasticity of demand and the price elasticity of supply. Who actually pays the tax is said to bear the **incidence** of a tax or **tax incidence**.

Inelastic supply, elastic demand If supply is price-inelastic, the supplier will not change the quantity produced very much when the price is changed. The consumer's demand is price-elastic, indicating that the consumer is very sensitive to price. Suppose the market is currently in the situation of S *"without tax"* and D. The price is P *"without tax"* and the quantity is Q *"without tax."* Levying a tax on the producer means the producer's costs are higher at every quantity of production; the S curve shifts up to S *"after tax."* The imposition of the tax causes the market price to increase from P *"without tax"* to P *"with tax."* The consumer reacts by significantly reducing quantity demanded so that the quantity demanded falls from Q *"without tax"* to Q *"with tax"* (Figure 6[a]). Notice that price rises very little, indicating that the producer is unable to pass the tax on to the consumer and the tax ends up being paid by the producer.

Inelastic demand, elastic supply When demand is price-inelastic, a large change in price will cause a smaller change in quantity demanded. With a price-elastic supply, the producer is very sensitive to price. A small drop in price leads to a large drop in the quantity produced. The imposition of the tax causes the market price to increase from P *"without tax"* to P *"with tax"* and the quantity demanded to fall from Q *"without tax"* to Q *"with tax."* So the quantity changes very little and price a great deal following the imposition of the tax. This illustrates that the producer is able to pass almost the entire value of the tax on to the consumer. Even though the tax is being collected from the producer, it is the consumer who ends up paying it.

Similar price elasticities When the price elasticities of demand and supply are about the same, the burden of the tax gets shared between buyer and seller. In Figure 6(c), the tax increase shifts the supply curve upward driving price to P *"with tax"* from P *"without tax."* Quantity adjusts to Q *"with tax"* from Q *"without tax."* The quantity declines more in 6(c) than in 6(b), indicating that consumer demand is more elastic in 6(c) than in 6(b). It declines less in 6(a) than in 6(c), indicating that consumer demand is less elastic in 6(c) than in 6(b). So when price elasticities of supply and demand are about the same, a portion of the tax will be paid by both parties. In other words, the supplier is able to shift a portion of the tax to consumers in terms of the higher price but not as much as in 6(b).

The FICA tax, Social Security and Medicare, is imposed partly on the employer and partly on the employee. (In every year but 2011, the tax was an equal share such as 7.65% paid by employer and 7.65% paid by employee.) However, whether a larger share is actually paid by the employer or the employee will depend on the price elasticities of demand and supply for labor. In addition, how much of the tax is passed on to consumers by the employers will depend on the price elasticities of demand and supply for the good or service offered by the employer.

incidence or **tax incidence** The share of a tax paid by consumers and/or producers. Who pays the larger share is said to bear the incidence of the tax.

FIGURE 6   Incidence of a Tax

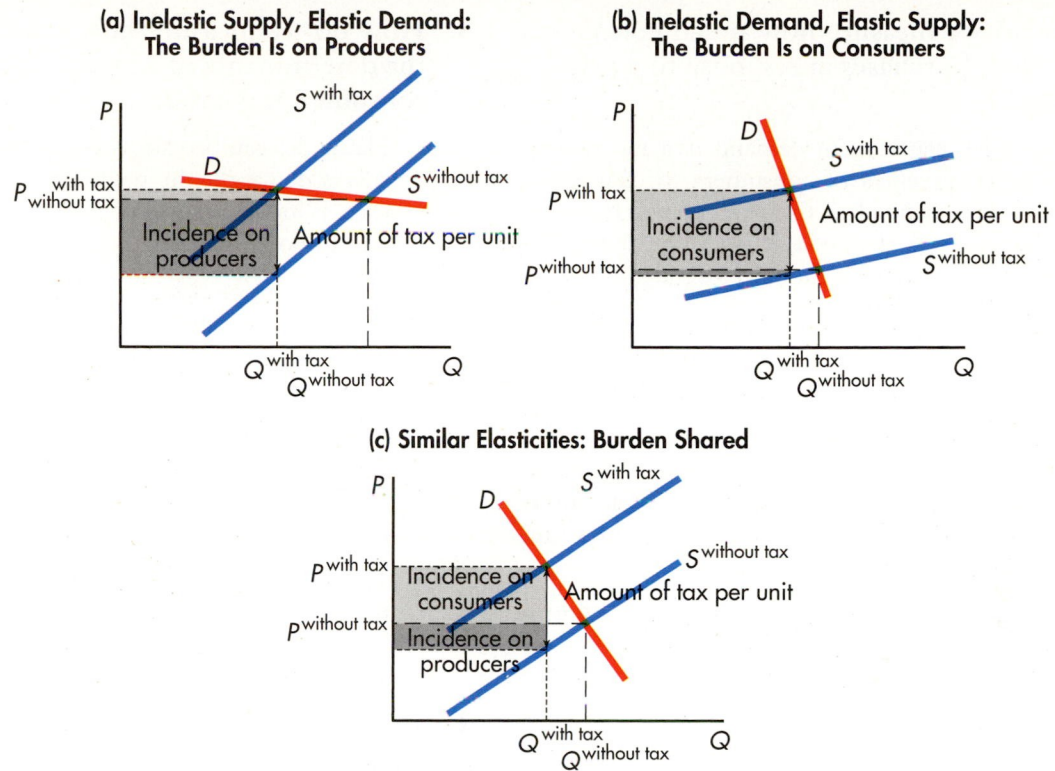

In Figure 6(a), the incidence of a tax is shown when there is an inelastic supply and an elastic demand: the burden is on producers. When supply shifts up, reflecting increased costs, consumers react strongly by reducing the quantity demanded a great deal. As a result, producers are unable to make consumers pay for the higher taxes. In Figure 6(b), demand is inelastic and supply is elastic. Here the firm is able to shift the tax to consumers. Supply shifts up but quantity demanded changes very little. In Figure 6(c), demand and supply have similar elasticities. Here the burden of the tax is about equally shared.

RECAP

1. The price elasticity of supply is the percentage change in the quantity supplied of one product divided by the percentage change in the price of that product, everything else held constant.

2. The price elasticity of supply increases as the time period under consideration increases.

3. The long run is a period of time just long enough that the quantities of all resources used can be varied. The short run is a period of time just short enough that the quantity of at least some of the resources used cannot be varied.

4. The interaction of demand and supply determines the price and quantity produced and sold; the rela-

tive size of demand and supply price elasticities determines how the market reacts to changes.

5. When demand is relatively more elastic than supply, then producers are unable to shift as much of a tax increase to consumers as when demand is relatively less elastic than supply.

6. How much of a tax is paid by producers or consumers is called the incidence of a tax. If producers pay a larger share, it is said that the incidence of a tax falls on producers. Similarly, if consumers pay a larger share, it is said that the incidence falls on consumers.

SUMMARY

1. **How do we measure how much consumers alter their purchases in response to a price change?**

   - The price elasticity of demand is a measure of the responsiveness of consumers to changes in price. It is defined as the percentage change in the quantity demanded of a good divided by the percentage change in the price of the good. *§1.a*

   - The price elasticity of demand is always a negative number because price and quantity demanded are inversely related. *§1.a*

   - A straight-line demand curve is separated into three parts by the price elasticity of demand. Demand is price-elastic at the top of the curve; as you move down the curve, it becomes unit elastic and then price-inelastic. *§1.b.1*

   - Comparing the price elasticity of demand for various products and services allows economists to see how consumers respond to price changes. In other words, it can tell us how big a difference price makes in a particular purchasing decision. *§1.c*

2. **What determines whether consumers alter their purchases a little or a lot in response to a price change?**

   - Everything else held constant, the greater the number of close substitutes, the greater the price elasticity of demand. *§1.d*

   - Everything else held constant, the greater the proportion of a household's budget that a good constitutes, the greater the household's elasticity of demand for that good. *§1.d*

   - Everything else held constant, the longer the time period under consideration, the greater the price elasticity of demand. *§1.d*

3. **How do we measure how much changes in the determinants of demand affect consumer purchases?**

   - Elasticities can be calculated for any variable that affects demand—the determinants of demand—such as income, prices of related goods, advertising, and others. *§2*

   - The cross-price elasticity of demand is defined as the percentage change in the quantity demanded for one good divided by the percentage change in the price of a related good, everything else held constant. *§2.a*

   - When the cross-price elasticity is positive, the goods are substitutes. When it is negative, the goods are complements. *§2.a*

   - The income elasticity of demand is defined as the percentage change in the quantity demanded for a good divided by the percentage change in income, everything else held constant. *§2.b*

4. **How do we measure how much sellers respond to a price change?**

   - The price elasticity of supply is defined as the percentage change in the quantity supplied of a good divided by the percentage change in the price of that good, everything else held constant. *§3*

   - The short run is a period of time short enough that the quantities of at least some of the resources used in production cannot be varied. The long run is a period of time just long enough that the quantities of all resources used can be varied. *§3.b*

KEY TERMS

EXERCISES

Use the following hypothetical demand schedule for movies to do exercises 1–4.

Quantity Demanded	Price	Elasticity
100	$ 5	
80	$10	
60	$15	
40	$20	
20	$25	
10	$30	

1. a. Determine the price elasticity of demand at each quantity demanded using the arc or midpoint formula: Percentage change in quantity demanded $= (Q_2 - Q_1)/Q_1$ divided by percentage change in price $= (P_2 - P_1)/P_1$.
    b. Redo exercise 1a using price changes of $10 rather than $5.

2. Plot the price and quantity data given in the demand schedule of exercise 1. Put price on the vertical axis and quantity on the horizontal axis. Indicate the price elasticity value at each quantity demanded. Explain why the elasticity value gets smaller as you move down the demand curve.

3. What would a 10 percent increase in the price of movie tickets mean for the quantity demanded of a movie theater if the price elasticity of demand was 0.1, 0.5, 1.0, and 5.0?

4. Using the demand curve plotted in exercise 1, illustrate what would occur if the income elasticity of demand was 0.05 and income rose by 10 percent. If the income elasticity of demand was 3.0 and income rose by 10 percent, what would occur?

5. Pick a good whose demand is price elastic. List five substitutes and five complements. Which is easier to come up with, the list of substitutes or the list of complements? Explain.

6. Are the following pairs of goods substitutes or complements? Indicate whether their cross-price elasticities are negative or positive.
    a. Bread and butter
    b. Bread and potatoes
    c. Socks and shoes
    d. Tennis rackets and golf clubs
    e. Bicycles and automobiles
    f. Foreign investments and domestic investments
    g. Cars made in Japan and cars made in the United States

7. Explain how consumers will react to a job loss. What will be the first goods they will do without? What is the income elasticity of demand for those goods?

8. Calculate the income elasticity of demand from the following data (use the arc or average).

Income	Quantity Demanded
$15,000	20,000
$20,000	30,000

   a. Explain why the value is a positive number.
   b. Explain what would happen to a demand curve as income changes if the income elasticity was 2.0. Compare that outcome to the situation that would occur if the income elasticity of demand was 0.2.

9. a. Use the figure to show what occurs to price and quantity when supply decreases and demand is perfectly elastic.
    b. Use the figure to show what occurs to price and quantity when supply increases and demand is perfectly inelastic.

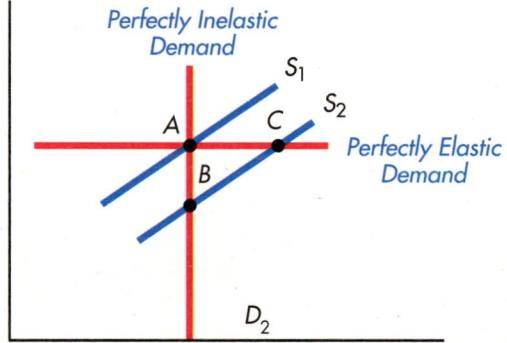

10. Explain why a 40 percent across-the-board tax increase on businesses might harm consumers.

11. The price elasticity of the demand for gasoline is −0.02. The price elasticity of demand for gasoline at Joe's 66 station is −1.2. Explain what might account for the different elasticities.

12. The cross-price elasticity of the demand for cell phones and DVDs is 1.2. Explain. The cross-price elasticity of the demand for the iPod and DVDs is −1.4. Explain.

13. Using the following equation for the demand for a good or service, calculate the price elasticity of

demand (using the point form), cross-price elasticity with good x, and income elasticity.

$$Q = 8 - 2P + 0.10I + P_x$$

Q is quantity demanded, P is the product price, and P_x is the price of a related good, and I is income. Assume that $P = \$10$, $I = 100$, and $P_x = 20$.

14. Plot the following price and quantity. Then calculate price elasticity of demand at $P = 8$, $P = 4$, and $P = 2$.

P	Q
10	0
8	4
7	6
6	8
5	10
4	12
3	14
2	16
1	18

15. The FICA tax is the Social Security tax plus Medicare. It is levied on both the employer and employee. Until 2011, each paid an equal 7.65% of the employee's salary. In 2011 the share levied on the employee was reduced. Illustrate who actually pays the tax when price elasticity of demand is elastic and price elasticity of supply is inelastic.

16. Who would pay a tax imposed on the supplier when the price elasticity of supply is inelastic and the price elasticity of demand is elastic?

You can find further practice tests in the Online Quiz at **www.cengage.com/economics/boyes**.

SUV SALES GET STUCK IN MUD

Ward's Dealer Business, February 1, 2009

Terrible 2008 SUV sales are prompting speculation that the once-popular segment might be permanently stuck in the mud.

Overall light-vehicle sales were down 18% last year to 13.19 million units compared with 16.08 million the year before, according to Ward's data.

But SUV sales took a 39.3% plunge, going from 1.91 million units in 2007 to 1.16 million in 2008.

Middle SUVs was the biggest segment loser, with sales sinking 45% in 2008. By comparison, midsize cross/utility vehicle sales were off 6.8%.

"People are moving out of the midsize SUV market completely and going to CUVs," says Matt Traylen, senior director for Automotive Lease Guide. "What people don't want now is anything with 'SUV' in the name."

Car-based CUVs look like SUVs but offer a smoother ride and nimbler handling than SUVs built on truck platforms.

SUVs had their heyday in the 1990s and into the early years of this decade, when fuel prices were relatively low. What SUVs lacked in fuel economy they made up in bulk and roominess. They also offered off-road capability, even though few owners put them to the test.

When fuel prices spiked in 2008, reaching $4 per gallon, SUVs took a punch, from which they didn't recover. Among the segments hardest hit were the Hummer H3 (down 50.8%), Dodge Durango (off 52.9%), and Nissan Armada (down 50.4%).

Despite SUVs' touted ruggedness, there is an impractical side in their everyday use by most owners, Traylen says. Eighty percent of people who buy SUVs don't use them as SUVs.

"They don't go up mountains or off-roading. They take their kids to school and go to the grocery store," he says. "A lot of people are waking up and asking, 'Why did I buy this vehicle?'"

Ironically, full-size SUVs, the segment's biggest gas guzzlers, suffered its smallest 2008 sales decline, although still it was substantial at 36.2%.

"There will always be a market for big SUVs, just not as large a market as before," Traylen says, noting that the few SUV owners who actually take their vehicles off road and up mountains tend to drive the full-size models.

Because mid-size SUVs are fast becoming unpopular, it is hard to predict what their residuals will be in two to three years, Traylen says. In contrast, "mid-compact and midsize cars are stable."

His residual forecasting centers on what vehicles will be worth when they come off lease. Leasing took a hit of its own last year, particularly when Chrysler Financial and Wells Fargo bank abandoned leasing.

"Chrysler pulling out was a bit of a body blow," Traylen says at a recent Auto Finance Summit. "But Chrysler could return to leasing in a few years, if it sorts things out. When banks leave, they're gone."

"Banks are there to make a profit from leasing, captive finance firms are there to help auto makers sell vehicles. Wells Fargo is not likely to return to leasing."

If leasing penetration gets too high, as it did during the late 1990s, it creates residual problems for auto makers and excess volume for re-marketers faced with waves of vehicles coming off lease.

"Leasing at 30% penetration is too crazy; we saw that," Traylen says. "Twenty percent is pretty healthy. It had been around that until 2008. It will probably drop to the low teens."

Smaller regional banks that know their markets may fill the leasing void created by the likes of Chrysler Financial and Wells Fargo, he says. "If any leasing growth occurs, it will be local and small."

Other predictions from Traylen:

- This year, like 2008, will be difficult, while "2010 and beyond look better."

- Resale values for luxury models will continue to decline.
- Repossessions will "continue to be problematic for high-priced segments," hurting resale performances.

If new-car incentives increase, it will hurt used-car sales and create a false impression of consumer interest. "If people are paying thousands of dollars less, it's not really a demand." But, he adds, "U.S. consumers will not pay high prices for cars right now."

Steve Finlay

Source: Ward's Dealer Business, February 1, 2009.

After September 11, 2001, some of the U.S. public and some of the media started a campaign against the sport utility vehicle, or SUV. American TV ads suggested that owners of gas-guzzling SUVs were indirectly assisting terrorists who obtain financing in oil-exporting Middle East countries, and a group of Christian ministers launched a "What Would Jesus Drive?" campaign, urging SUV owners to consider whether they could switch to more fuel-efficient vehicles to preserve the planet. However, while these campaigns may have changed some consumers' tastes, the real effect on consumers' demand for SUVs has come from the increased gas prices. The article notes that SUV sales took a 39.3% plunge, going from 1.91 million units in 2007 to 1.16 million in 2008. The reason was the rapid increase in fuel prices in 2008, reaching $4 per gallon. SUVs took a punch, from which they didn't recover. Among the segments hardest hit were the Hummer H3 (down 50.8%), Dodge Durango (off 52.9%), and Nissan Armada (down 50.4%).

Why have higher gas prices affected purchases of SUVs? It is the price of gasoline that has risen, not the price of SUVs. The answer is that, in the short run, the demand for gasoline is very inelastic and the cross-price elasticity of gasoline and SUVs is negative. The demand for gasoline is price-inelastic in the short run because there are no close substitutes. When the price increases, people don't have many alternatives to driving; they do not reduce their consumption very much. In the long run, if the price of gasoline should remain high, substitutes for gas would become available. In fact, many people immediately switched purchases from the SUVs to hybrid autos because they use less gas.

The cross-price elasticity is calculated by dividing the percentage change in the demand for SUVs by the percentage change in the price of gasoline. Gasoline prices in the United States rose from $1.30 per gallon in January 2003 to $1.90 per gallon in March 2003, a 46 percent increase. The price rose in 2008 to over $4 per gallon, a more than 200 percent increase from 2003. This increase drove the sales of SUVs down more than 40%. Using these numbers, the percentage change in SUV sales divided by the percentage change in price of gasoline is: $-40\%/200\%$ or -0.20. The cross-price elasticity is negative, indicating that the two products, SUVs and gasoline, are complements.

CHAPTER 20

Consumer Choice

© MACIEJ FROLOW/GETTY IMAGES, INC

ARIEL SKELLEY/GETTY IMAGES; LOGO: © FROXX/SHUTTERSTOCK.COM

FUNDAMENTAL QUESTIONS

1. How do consumers decide what to buy?

2. Why does the demand curve slope down?

3. What are behavioral economics and neuroeconomics?

n previous chapters, we learned that demand measures the quantity of a good or service that people are willing and able to buy at various prices. In the previous chapter, we also learned how the consumer's reaction to price changes and how changes to the consumer's income affect demand. In this chapter, we go behind the scenes of demand. We examine how and why consumers make choices and what factors influence their choices. We even look briefly into their brains—what parts of the brain they use to make decisions and how that makes a difference in their behavior.

1. Decisions

Do we go to college or get a job? Do we get married or remain single? Do we live in the dorm, a house, or an apartment? "Decisions, decisions, decisions! Don't we ever get a break from the pressure of making choices?" Not unless scarcity disappears will we be freed from having to make choices. Although scarcity and choice are pervasive, how people make decisions is a question that has eluded scientific explanation. Some decisions seem to be based on feelings, or to come from the heart, while others seem more calculated. Some are quick and impulsive, while others take months or years of research. Is it the appeal of the book cover that makes you decide to buy one book rather than another? Does a television commercial affect your decision? The answers to these questions depend on your values, on your personality, on where you were raised, on how others might react to your decision, and on many other factors.

Although the important factors in a decision may vary from person to person, everyone makes decisions in much the same way. People tend to compare the perceived costs and benefits of alternatives and select those that they believe will give them the greatest relative benefits.

1.a. Utility

How is success measured in the game of life? It is measured not in the way the bumper sticker says, "The one with the most toys at the end wins," but by happiness. The word *happiness* is used very generally here. It implies that whatever an individual's goals are—peace, serenity, religious devotion, self-esteem, or the well being of others—the more one has of what one desires, the better off one is. **Utility** is the term that economists and philosophers have used to capture this general concept of happiness. You are nourished by a good meal, entertained by a concert, proud of a fine car, and comforted by a nice home and warm clothing. Whatever feelings are described by *nourishment*, *entertainment*, *pride*, and *comfort* are captured in the term *utility*.

People make choices that give them the greatest utility; they maximize their utility. The utility you derive from experiencing some activity or consuming some good depends on your tastes and preferences. You may love opera and intensely dislike country and western music. You may have difficulty understanding how anyone can eat tripe, but you love hot chilies. We shall have little to say about why some people prefer country and western music and others classical music, although the issue is interesting; we simply assume that tastes and preferences are given and use those given tastes and preferences to describe the process of decision making.

utility
A measure of the satisfaction received from possessing or consuming goods and services.

> *Individuals behave so as to maximize their utility.*

1.b. Diminishing Marginal Utility

Utility is used to show why the law of demand is referred to as a law. To illustrate how utility maximization can be useful, we must create a hypothetical world in which we can measure the satisfaction that people receive from consuming goods and services. Suppose that a consumer named Gabrielle can listen to as much country and western music as she wishes during the course of the day. The utility, expressed as *utils*, that Gabrielle associates with each hour of listening is presented in Table 1.

Several important concepts associated with consumer choice can be observed in Table 1. First, each *additional* hour of music yields Gabrielle less satisfaction (fewer utils) than the previous hour. According to Table 1, the first hour yields 200 utils, the second yields another 98, the third another 50, the fourth another 10, and the fifth none. Each additional hour of music, until the fifth hour, adds to total utility, but Gabrielle enjoys each additional hour just a little bit less than she enjoyed the prior hour. This relationship is called **diminishing marginal utility**.

diminishing marginal utility
The principle that the more of a good that one obtains in a specific period of time, the less the additional utility yielded by an additional unit of that good.

TABLE 1	The Utility of Listening to Country and Western Music	
Hours of Listening per Day	Utility of Each Additional Hour of Listening (marginal utility)	Total Utility
1	200	200
2	98	298
3	50	348
4	10	358
5	0	358
6	−70	288
7	−200	88

© 2013 Cengage Learning

marginal utility
The additional utility derived from consuming one more unit of a good or service.

Marginal utility is the change in total utility that occurs because one more unit of the good is consumed or acquired:

$$\text{Marginal utility} = \frac{\text{change in total utility}}{\text{change in quantity}}$$

According to the principle of diminishing marginal utility, the more of a good or service that someone consumes during a particular period of time, the less satisfaction another unit of that good or service provides that individual. Imagine yourself sitting down to a plate piled high with cake. The first piece is delicious, and the second tastes good, but not as good as the first. The fourth piece doesn't taste very good at all, and the sixth piece nearly makes you sick. Instead of satisfaction, the sixth piece of cake yields dissatisfaction, or **disutility**.

disutility
Dissatisfaction.

total utility
A measure of the total satisfaction derived from consuming a quantity of some good or service.

Notice that we are speaking of diminishing *marginal* utility, not diminishing *total* utility. **Total utility**, the measure of the total satisfaction derived from consuming a quantity of some good or service, climbs until dissatisfaction sets in. For Gabrielle, total utility rises from 200 to 298 to 348 and reaches 358 with the fourth hour of music. After the fifth hour, total utility declines. Marginal utility, however, is the additional utility gained from listening to another hour of music, and it declines from the first hour on.

To illustrate the relation between marginal and total utility, we have plotted the total utility data from Table 1 in Figure 1(a). The total utility curve rises as quantity rises until the fifth hour of listening. After five hours, the total utility curve declines. The reason total utility rises at first is that for the first four hours, each additional hour provides a little more utility. The marginal utility of the first hour is 200; the marginal utility of the second hour is 98; that of the third, 50; that of the fourth, 10; and that of the fifth, zero. By the fifth hour, total utility is $200 + 98 + 50 + 10 + 0 = 358$.

We have plotted marginal utility in Figure 1(b), directly below the total utility curve of Figure 1(a). Marginal utility declines with each successive unit, reaches zero, and then turns negative. As long as marginal utility is positive, total utility rises. When marginal utility becomes negative, total utility declines. Marginal utility is zero at the point where total utility is at its maximum (unit 5 in this case). Marginal utility is the slope of the total utility curve.

1.c. Diminishing Marginal Utility and Time

The concept of diminishing marginal utility makes sense only if we define the *period of time* during which consumption is occurring. If Gabrielle listened to the music over a period of several days, we might not observe diminishing marginal utility. But listening to the music in one 24-hour period causes Gabrielle to tire of it rather quickly. Usually, the shorter the time period, the more quickly marginal utility diminishes. Once the time

FIGURE 1   Total and Marginal Utility

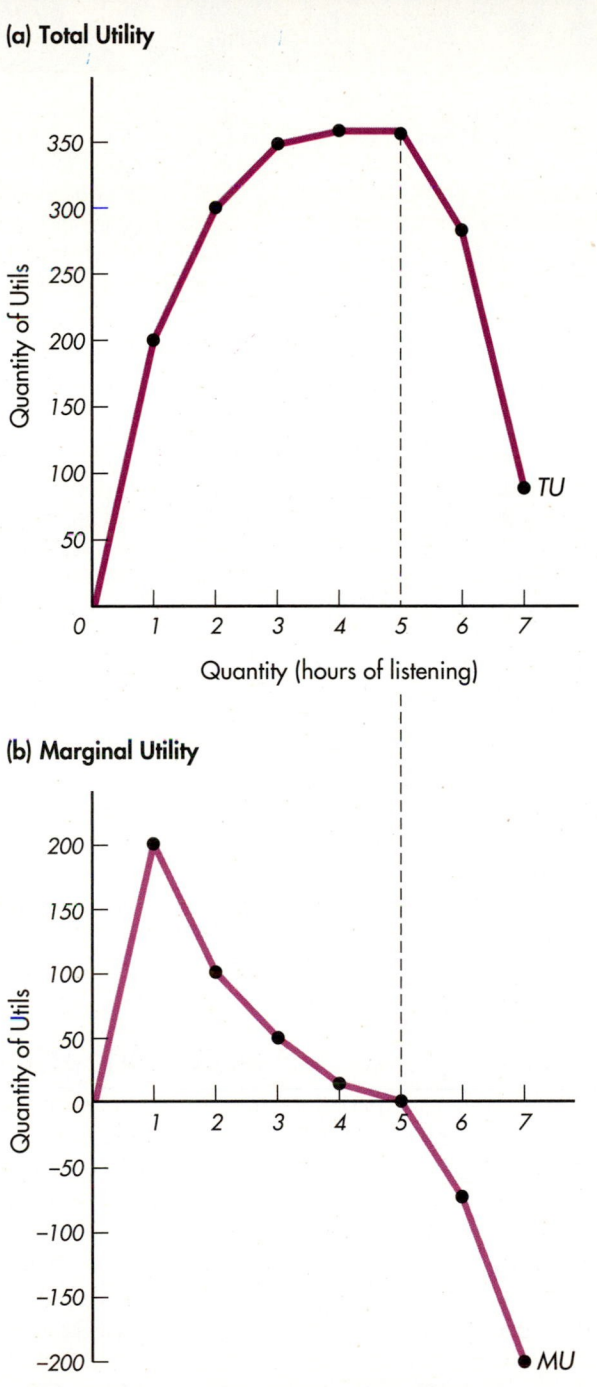

(a) Total Utility

(b) Marginal Utility

Figure 1(a) shows the total utility obtained from listening to country and western music. Total utility reaches a maximum and then declines as additional listening becomes distasteful. For the first hour, the marginal and total utilities are the same. For the second hour, the marginal utility is the additional utility provided by the second unit. The total utility is the sum of the marginal utilities of the first and second units. The second unit provides less utility than the first unit, the third less than the second, and so on, in accordance with the law of diminishing marginal utility. But total utility, the sum of marginal utilities, rises as long as marginal utility is positive. Figure 1(b) shows marginal utility. When marginal utility is zero, total utility is at its maximum. When marginal utility is negative, total utility declines.

ECONOMIC INSIGHT

Does Money Buy Happiness?

Diminishing marginal utility affects consumer purchases of every good. Does diminishing marginal utility affect income as well? This question has been a topic of economic debate for years. The case for progressive taxation—the more income you have, the greater the percentage of each additional dollar that you pay in taxes—is based on the idea that the marginal utility of income diminishes. In theory, if each additional dollar brings a person less utility, the pain associated with giving up a portion of each additional dollar will decline. And as a result of taxing the rich at a higher rate than the poor, the total pain imposed on society from a tax will be less than it would be if the same tax rate were applied to every dollar.

Economists have attempted to confirm or disprove the idea of the diminishing marginal utility of income, but doing so has proved difficult. Experiments have even been carried out on the topic. In one experiment, laboratory rats were trained to work for pay. They had to hit a bar several times to get a piece of food or a drink of water. After a while, after obtaining a certain amount of food and water, the rats reduced their work effort, choosing leisure instead of more food and water. Thus, the rats reacted as if their "income"—food and water—had a diminishing marginal utility.

Economists have also turned to the literature of psychology. Psychologists have carried out many surveys to measure whether people are more or less happy under various circumstances. One survey, from the 1960s, asked people in different income brackets whether they were unhappy, pretty happy, or very happy. The results indicated that the higher income is, the happier people are. Several studies have found that, on average, people in wealthier nations are happier than people in poorer nations, but the wealthiest nation is not the happiest. Among the wealthiest nations, factors other than additional wealth are very important in explaining happiness. For instance, the longer a nation's government has been democratic, the happier are its citizens.

Sources: Bruno S. Frey and Alois Stutzer, *Happiness and Economics* (Princeton, NJ: Princeton University Press, 2002); John Stossel, "The Mystery of Happiness: Who Has It and How to Get It," ABC News, April 15, 1996, and replayed since; David G. Myers, *The Pursuit of Happiness* (New York: William Morrow, 1992); and N. M. Bradburn and D. Caplovitz, *Reports on Happiness* (Chicago: Aldine, 1965), p. 9.

period has been defined, diminishing marginal utility will apply; it applies to everyone and to every good and service, and perhaps even to income itself, as discussed in the Economic Insight "Does Money Buy Happiness?"

1.d. Consumers Are Not Identical

All consumers experience diminishing marginal utility, but the rate at which the marginal utility of any specific good or service declines is not identical for all consumers. The rate at which marginal utility diminishes depends on an individual's tastes and preferences. Gabrielle clearly enjoys country and western music. For a person who dislikes it, the first hour might yield disutility or negative utility. Also, we cannot compare the utility that two people get from something. We can't really say whether Bill likes the first piece of cake twice as much as Gary does. We can't compare their utils. All we can really do is observe whether Bill and Gary eat the cake.

1.e. An Illustration: "All You Can Eat"

When utility is positive, a person is happy; when utility is zero, a person receives no enjoyment. Let's look at an activity such as eating a piece of cake. If the first piece of cake creates 5 utils, then that first piece of cake is enjoyed; if the second piece creates 3 utils, then it is enjoyed less than the first piece. When a piece of cake has 0 utils or has a marginal utility of zero, then that piece is not enjoyed. People stop eating when marginal utility is zero.

Why would a restaurant ever have a policy of "all you can eat"? Won't people run the restaurant into the ground? No. The restaurant understands the concept of diminishing marginal utility. So it charges you a price for entering the restaurant and tells you that you can eat as much as you want—but you cannot have a "doggy bag." All consumers eventually stop eating—their marginal utility falls to zero. This is the point at which one more bite would be distasteful. The restaurant knows that everyone is limited in the amount he or she eats.

RECAP

1. Utility is a concept used to represent the degree to which goods and services satisfy wants.

2. Total utility is the total satisfaction that a consumer obtains from consuming a particular good or service.

3. Marginal utility is the utility that an additional unit of a good or service yields.

4. Total utility increases until dissatisfaction sets in. When another unit of a good would yield disutility, the consumer has been filled up with the good—more of it will not bring greater satisfaction.

5. According to the principle of diminishing marginal utility, marginal utility declines with each additional unit of a good or service that the consumer obtains. When marginal utility is zero, total utility is at its maximum.

2. Utility and Choice

© froox/Shutterstock.com

1 How do consumers decide what to buy?

Can we simply conclude that people will consume goods until the marginal utility of each good is zero? No, we cannot, for if we did so, we would be ignoring scarcity and opportunity costs. No one has enough income to purchase everything until the marginal utility of each item is zero. Because incomes are limited, purchasing one thing means not purchasing other things. Gabrielle, our country and western music fancier, might be able to get more utility by purchasing some other good than by buying more music to listen to.

2.a. Consumer Choice

If you have $10 in your pocket to spend, you will spend it on the item or activity that gives you the most enjoyment—the greatest utility. Moreover, you may not spend all of it on just one thing. Suppose that with that $10 you are considering purchasing a CD, putting some gas in your car, and going to a movie. What will you decide? Well, you will purchase the amount of each that will give you the most enjoyment.

Although we don't go through an elaborate series of calculations when we decide to buy something, we act *as if* we did. We stand in line to purchase a $4 Starbucks latte at 10 A.M. because we need a little kick. We could have spent that $4 on a lot of other things, but at that moment, the latte seemed to give us the greatest satisfaction—the greatest utility. In the following long example, we go through the decision-making process as if the individual were a computer. The goal of this example is to show that people choose what to purchase with their limited budgets or incomes by comparing items to see which gives the most utility. If I am to spend another dollar, I will spend it to make myself as happy as that dollar can.

So let's turn again to Gabrielle. Gabrielle has $10 to spend on CDs, gasoline, and movies. She has found a place that sells used CDs, a gas station with low prices, and a movie theater that sells matinee tickets cheap. We want to know how many units of each she will purchase. The answer is in Table 2.

TABLE 2 The Logic of Consumer Choice

CD (P = $2)			Gas (P = $1)			Movie (P = $3)		
Units	MU	MU/P	Units	MU	MU/P	Units	MU	MU/P
1	200	100	1	200	200	1	150	50
2	98	49	2	150	150	2	90	30
3	50	25	3	50	50	3	60	20
4	10	5	4	30	30	4	30	10
5	0	0	5	0	0	5	9	3
6	−70	−35	6	−300	−300	6	0	0
7	−200	−100	7	−700	−700	7	−6	−2

Steps	Choices		Decision	Remaining
1st purchase	1st CD:	MU/P = 100	Gas	$10 − $1 = $9
	1st movie:	MU/P = 50		
	1st gas:	MU/P = 200		
2nd purchase	1st CD:	MU/P = 100	Gas	$9 − $1 = $8
	2nd gas:	MU/P = 150		
	1st movie:	MU/P = 50		
3rd purchase	1st CD:	MU/P = 100	CD	$8 − $2 = $6
	3rd gas:	MU/P = 50		
	1st movie:	MU/P = 50		
4th purchase	2nd CD:	MU/P = 49	Gas	$6 − $1 = $5
	3rd gas:	MU/P = 50		
	1st movie:	MU/P = 50		
5th purchase	2nd CD:	MU/P = 49	Movie	$5 − $3 = $2
	4th gas:	MU/P = 30		
	1st movie:	MU/P = 50		
6th purchase	2nd CD:	MU/P = 49	CD	$2 − $2 = 0
	4th gas:	MU/P = 30		
	2nd movie:	MU/P = 30		

Note: Purchases made with $10: 2 CDs, 3 gallons of gas, and 1 movie ticket.

© 2013 Cengage Learning

The price (P) of each secondhand CD is $2; the price of each gallon of gas is $1; the price of each movie is $3. The marginal utility (MU) provided by each unit and the ratio of the marginal utility to the price (MU/P) are presented at the top of the table. In the lower part of the table are the steps involved in allocating income among the three goods.

The first purchase involves a choice among the first unit of each of the three goods. The first CD yields a marginal utility (MU) of 200 and costs $2; thus, per dollar of expenditure, the first CD yields 100 utils ($MU/P = 100$). The first gallon of gas yields a marginal utility per dollar of expenditure of 200. The first movie yields a marginal utility per dollar of expenditure of 50; it yields 150 utils and costs $3. Which does Gabrielle choose?

To find the answer, compare the marginal utility per dollar of expenditure (MU/P) for each good, *not* the marginal utility (MU). The ratio of marginal utility to price puts the goods on the same basis (utility per dollar) and allows us to make sense of Gabrielle's decisions. Looking only at marginal utilities would not do this. For instance, another diamond might yield 10,000 utils and another apple might yield only 100 utils; but if the diamond costs $100,000 and the apple costs $1, the marginal utility per dollar of expenditure on the apple is greater than the marginal utility per dollar of expenditure on the diamond, and thus a consumer is better off purchasing the apple.

As indicated in Table 2, Gabrielle's first purchase is the gallon of gas. It yields the greatest marginal utility per dollar of expenditure (she needs gas in her car to be able to go anywhere). Because it costs $1, Gabrielle has $9 left to spend.

The second purchase involves a choice among the first CD, the second gallon of gas, and the first movie. The ratios of marginal utility per dollar of expenditure are 100 for the CD, 150 for the gas, and 50 for a movie. Thus, Gabrielle purchases a second gallon of gas and has $8 left.

For the third purchase, Gabrielle must decide between the first CD, the first movie, and the third gallon of gas. Because the CD yields a ratio of 100 and both the gas and the movie yield ratios of 50, she purchases the CD. The CD costs $2, so she has $6 left to spend.

A utility-maximizing consumer like Gabrielle always chooses the purchase that yields the greatest marginal utility per dollar of expenditure. If two goods offer the same marginal utility per dollar of expenditure, the consumer will be indifferent between the two—that is, the consumer won't care which is chosen. For example, Table 2 indicates that for the fourth purchase, either another gallon of gas or a movie would yield 50 utils per dollar. Gabrielle is completely indifferent between the two and so arbitrarily selects gas. The movie is chosen for the fifth purchase. With the sixth purchase, a second CD, the total budget is spent. For $10, Gabrielle ends up with 2 CDs, 3 gallons of gas, and 1 movie.

In this example, Gabrielle is portrayed as a methodical, robot-like consumer who calculates how to allocate her scarce income among goods and services in a way that ensures that each additional dollar of expenditure yields the greatest marginal utility. This picture is more than a little far-fetched, but it does describe the result, if not the process, of consumer choice. People do have to decide which goods and services to purchase with their limited incomes, and people do select the options that give them the greatest utility.

2.b. Consumer Equilibrium

With $10, Gabrielle purchases 2 CDs, 3 gallons of gas, and 1 movie ticket. For the second CD, the marginal utility per dollar of expenditure is 49; for the third gallon of gas, it is 50; and for the first movie, it is 50. Is it merely a fluke that the marginal utility per dollar of expenditure ratios are nearly equal? No. *In order to maximize utility, consumers must allocate their limited incomes among goods and services in such a way that the marginal utility per dollar of expenditure on the last unit of each good purchased will be as nearly equal as possible.* This is called the **equimarginal principle** and also represents **consumer equilibrium**. It is consumer equilibrium because the consumer will not change from this point unless something changes income, marginal utility, or price.

In our example, the ratios at consumer equilibrium are as close to equal as possible—49, 50, and 50—but they are not identical because Gabrielle (like all consumers) had to purchase whole portions of the goods. Consumers cannot spend a dollar on any good or service and always get the fractional amount that a dollar buys—one-tenth of a tennis lesson or one-third of a bottle of water. Instead, consumers have to purchase

equimarginal principle or **consumer equilibrium**
To maximize utility, consumers must allocate their scarce incomes among goods in such a way as to equate the marginal utility per dollar of expenditure on the last unit of each good purchased.

goods and services in whole units—1 piece or 1 ounce or 1 package—and pay the per unit price.

The equimarginal principle is simply common sense. If consumers have money to spend, they will spend it on those things that give them the most satisfaction. If you have a choice of A or B and A makes you happier, you will take A. At the prices given in Table 2, with an income of $10, and with the marginal utilities given, Gabrielle maximizes her utility by purchasing 2 CDs, 3 gallons of gas, and 1 movie ticket. Everything else held constant, no other allocation of the $10 would yield Gabrielle more utility.

Consumers are in equilibrium when they have no incentive to change what they buy—to reallocate their limited budget or income. With *MU* standing for marginal utility and *P* for price, the general rule for consumer equilibrium is $MU_x/P_x = MU_y/P_y = MU_z/P_z$.

RECAP

1. To maximize utility, consumers must allocate their limited incomes in such a way that the marginal utility per dollar obtained from the last unit consumed is equal for all goods and services; this is the equimarginal principle.

2. As long as the marginal utility per dollar obtained from the last unit of all products consumed is the same, the consumer is in equilibrium and will not reallocate income.

3. Consumer equilibrium, or utility maximization, is summarized by a formula that equates the marginal utility per dollar of expenditure on the last item purchased of all goods: $MU_a/P_a = MU_b/P_b = MU_c/P_c = MU_x/P_x$.

3. The Demand Curve Again

2 Why does the demand curve slope down?

We have shown how consumers make choices—by allocating their scarce incomes among goods in order to maximize their utility. These choices define a demand curve.

3.a. The Downward Slope of the Demand Curve

Recall that as the price of a good falls, the quantity demanded of that good rises. This inverse relation between price and quantity demanded arises from diminishing marginal utility and consumer equilibrium.

The demand curve or schedule can be derived from consumer equilibrium by altering the price of one good or service.

Consumers allocate their income among goods and services in order to maximize their utility. A consumer is in equilibrium (has no reason to change) when the total budget has been spent and the marginal utility per dollar of expenditure on the last unit of each good is the same. A change in the price of one good will disturb the consumer's equilibrium; the marginal utilities per dollar of expenditure for the last unit of each good will no longer be equal. The consumer will then reallocate her income among the goods in order to increase total utility.

In the example presented in Table 2, the price of a CD is $2, the price per gallon of gas is $1, and the price of a movie ticket is $3. Now suppose the price of the CD falls to $1 while the prices of gas and movies and Gabrielle's budget of $10 remain the same. Common sense tells us that Gabrielle will probably alter the quantities purchased by buying more CDs. To find out if she does—and whether the equimarginal principle holds—her purchases can be traced step by step as we did previously.

TABLE 3	A Price Change							
CD (P = $1)			**Gas (P = $1)**			**Movie (P = $3)**		
Units	*MU*	*MU/P*	**Units**	*MU*	*MU/P*	**Units**	*MU*	*MU/P*
1	200	200	1	200	200	1	150	50
2	98	98	2	150	150	2	90	30
3	50	50	3	50	50	3	60	20
4	10	10	4	30	30	4	30	10
5	0	0	5	0	0	5	9	3
6	−71	−70	6	−300	−300	6	0	0
7	−200	−200	7	−700	−700	7	−6	−2

In Table 3, only the *MU/P* ratio for CDs is different from the corresponding figure at the top of Table 2. At the old consumer equilibrium of 2 CDs, 3 gallons of gas, and 1 movie, the marginal utility per dollar of expenditure *(MU/P)* on each good is

$$\text{CD: } 98/\$1 = 98/\$1$$
$$\text{Gas: } 50/\$1 = 50/\$1$$
$$\text{Movie: } 150/\$3 = 50/\$1$$

Clearly, the ratios are no longer equal. In order to maximize utility, Gabrielle must reallocate her budget among the goods. When all $10 is spent, Gabrielle finds that she has purchased 3 CDs, 4 gallons of gas, and 1 movie ticket. The lower price of CDs has induced her to purchase an additional CD. Gabrielle's behavior illustrates what you already know: The quantity demanded of CDs increases as the price of the CD decreases.

If the price of the CD is increased to $3, we find that Gabrielle demands only 1 CD. The three prices and the corresponding quantities of CDs purchased give us Gabrielle's demand for CDs, which is shown in Figure 2. At $3 she is willing and able to buy 1 CD; at $2 she is willing and able to buy 2 CDs; and at $1 she is willing and able to buy 3 CDs.

3.b. Shifts of Demand and the Determination of Market Demand

Individual demand comes from utility maximization. Individuals allocate their scarce incomes among goods in order to get the greatest utility; this occurs when consumer equilibrium is reached, represented in symbols as $MU_x/P_x = MU_y/P_y = MU_z/P_z$. When the price of a good or service is changed, consumer equilibrium is disturbed. In response to the price change, individuals alter their purchases so as to achieve maximum utility.

When the price of one good falls while everything else is held constant, two things occur: (1) other goods become relatively *more* expensive, so consumers buy more of the less expensive good and less of the more expensive goods, and (2) the good purchased prior to the price change now costs less, so the consumer can buy more of all goods.

When a good becomes relatively less expensive, it yields more satisfaction per dollar than before, so consumers buy more of it than before as they decrease their expenditures on other goods. This is the *substitution effect* of a price change.

Figure 2 shows that at the price of $2 per used CD, Gabrielle spends $4 on CDs. When the price falls to $1, she spends only $2 for those two CDs. As a result, Gabrielle can purchase more of all goods, including the good whose price has fallen. This is the *income effect* of a price change. The substitution effect of a price change says that

> *The substitution effect indicates that following a decrease in the price of a good or service, an individual will purchase more of the now less expensive good and less of other goods.*

> *The income effect of a price change indicates that an individual's income can buy more of all goods when the price of one good declines, everything else held constant.*

FIGURE 2   Consumer Surplus and the Demand for Used CDs

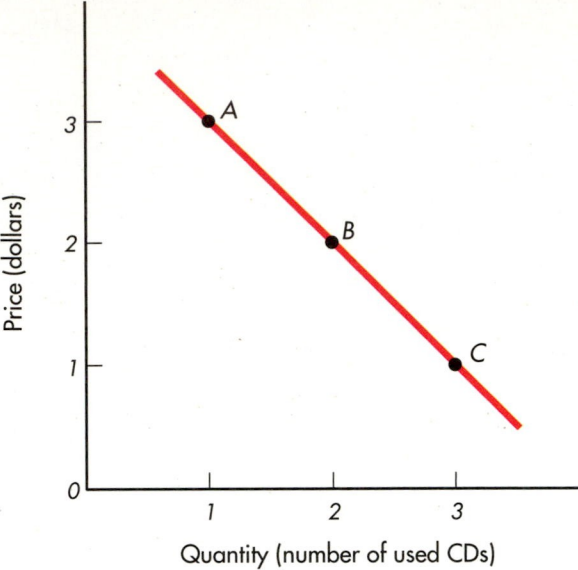

Gabrielle's Demand Curve for Used CDs. The demand curve shows that Gabrielle purchases 1 used CD at a price of $3, 2 used CDs at a price of $2, and 3 used CDs at a price of $1.

consumers will purchase less of more expensive goods and more of less expensive goods. The income effect of a price change says consumers will purchase more of all goods when the price of a good decreases because the consumer's purchasing power has risen. Notice that the substitution and income effects reinforce the relationship between the price of an item and the quantity demanded for that item. Both tell us that when the price of one good or service declines, everything else held constant, the quantity demanded of that item will rise.

Suppose the two effects went in opposite directions; for instance, a lower price led to more purchasing power or income and that this caused the consumer to purchase less of the good. In such a case, whether the quantity demanded would rise or fall would depend on whether the substitution effect was smaller or larger than the income effect. In the Economic Insight "Does Money Buy Happiness?", it is argued that there is some income level at which the income and substitution effects go in opposite directions. As a person's wage/salary rises, the person's opportunity cost of taking more time for family and leisure rises. In other words, saying that wages rise is the same as saying that the price of leisure rises. At some high wage, receiving a slightly higher wage might induce the person to actually work less—taking more personal time. In this case, the income effect leads to less time devoted to working while the substitution effect still leads the person to work more.

The process of changing the price of one good or service while income, tastes and preferences, and the prices of related goods are held constant defines the individual's demand for that good or service. Should income, tastes and preferences, or prices of related goods and services change, then the individual's demand will change. More or less income means that more or less goods and services can be purchased. A change in income affects the ratios of MU/P and disturbs consumer equilibrium. When the price of a related good changes, the ratio of marginal utility to price for that good changes, thus disturbing consumer equilibrium. And changes in tastes and preferences,

Halloween has changed from a child's holiday to the second most popular holiday in the United States. Spending on Halloween supplies exceeds spending for every holiday except Christmas. The increased tastes for Halloween fun have led to an increased demand for costumes. In terms of economic theory, marginal utility for each dollar of spending on Halloween costumes has risen.

represented as changes in the MUs, also alter consumer equilibrium. For each change in a determinant of demand, a new demand curve for a good or service is derived; the demand curve shifts.

The market demand curve is the sum of all the individual demand curves. This means that anything that affects the individual curves also affects the market curve. In addition, when we combine the individual demand curves into a market demand curve, the number of individuals to be combined determines the position of the market demand curve. Changes in the number of consumers alter the market demand curve. We thus say that the determinants of demand are tastes and preferences, income, prices of related goods, international effects, and number of consumers. Also, recall that diminishing marginal utility is defined for consumption during a specific period of time. Since consumer equilibrium and thus the demand curve depend on diminishing marginal utility, the demand curve is also defined for consumption over a specific period of time. Changes in the time period or changes in expectations will therefore also alter demand.

RECAP

1. The principle of diminishing marginal utility and the equimarginal principle account for the inverse relation between the price of a product and the quantity demanded.

2. A price change triggers both the substitution effect and the income effect.

3. The substitution effect occurs because once a good becomes less expensive, it yields more satisfaction per dollar than before and consumers buy more of it than before. They do this by decreasing their purchases of other goods. The income effect of the price change occurs because a lower price raises real income (total utility) and the consumer purchases more of all goods.

4. The market demand curve is the summation of all individual demand curves.

5. Economists derive the market demand curve for a good by assuming that individual incomes are fixed, that the prices of all goods except the one in question are constant, that each individual's tastes remain fixed, that expectations do not change, that the number of consumers is constant, and that the time period under consideration remains unchanged. A change in any one of these determinants causes the demand curve to shift.

---

4. Behavioral Economics and Neuroeconomics

3 What are behavioral economics and neuroeconomics?

Economists generally assume that people are rational—that they compare costs and benefits before undertaking any action. This assumption makes humans seem more like robots than like thinking, feeling beings. In recent years, two fields of study—behavioral economics and neuroeconomics—have attempted to change this assumption.

4.a. Behavioral Economics

bounded rationality

The understanding that perfect information is not likely to be available, and that as a result people make decisions that in hindsight look irrational, but in reality are the rational results of a brain that is economizing.

behavioral economics

The study of decision making assuming that people are rational in a broad sense.

Strict rationality assumes that the decision maker has complete or perfect information. **Bounded rationality** admits that complete and perfect information is not likely to be available, and that as a result, people make decisions that in hindsight look irrational, but in reality are the rational results of a brain that is economizing—finding shortcuts and easier ways to make decisions. **Behavioral economics** attempts to catalogue the biases that result from bounded rationality. Let's look at some well-documented behaviors and explore the interplay of emotions and logic in decision making.

4.a.1. Overconfidence People tend to think that they *are* better and *do things* better than is really the case. For example, 100 percent of drivers say that they are in the top 30 percent of safe drivers; 68 percent of lawyers in civil cases believe that their side will prevail; 81 percent of new business owners think that their own business has at least a 70 percent chance of success, but only 39 percent think that any business like theirs would be likely to succeed. And consider this: Mutual fund managers, analysts, and business executives at a conference were asked to write down how much money they would have at retirement and how much the average person in the room would have. The average figures were $5 million and $2.6 million, respectively.

Making a decision—any decision—requires a certain amount of confidence in our understanding of the risks and benefits. But overconfidence and the illusion of control can add up to bad decisions and big losses. People prefer to drive rather than fly because they feel safer driving, even though the record confirms that flying is significantly safer. Similarly, people start new businesses even when the odds are against them. The U.S. Census Bureau reports that 50 percent of new ventures close within the first four years.

Overconfident chief executive officers (CEOs, or corporate bosses) provide prime examples. The top executives of Enron Corporation seemed to think that they could do and get away with just about anything. The result was the failure of the company. Tyco's former chief executive, Dennis Kozlowski, saw that the company was doing poorly, but denied it, and, rather than readjust to the situation, did things that appeared to be and were fraudulent.

You might think that experience would lead people to become more realistic about their capabilities. But research indicates that overconfidence does not decline over time, perhaps because people generally remember failures very differently from successes. The typical view is that one's successes are due to one's own wisdom and ability, while one's failures are due to forces beyond one's control. Thus, people believe that with a little better luck or fine-tuning, the outcome will be much better next time.

4.a.2. Mental Accounting

A dollar is a dollar is a dollar—at least, that is the way economists tend to view assets. It should not matter whether that dollar comes from the right pocket or the left pocket. The term *mental accounting* refers to the idea that the value people place on money depends on where that money comes from. For instance, people tend to spend money received as gifts or through contests more readily than money they've earned, and people tend to continue gambling with winnings even though they would not continue gambling with money that they earned.

A story about a honeymooning couple in Las Vegas provides an illustration of mental accounting. Knowing that they were headed for Las Vegas, and knowing that they did not have a lot of money, the couple decided that they would spend only a certain amount. Once that was gone, they had to return home. After a few days, the amount had been spent, and the couple was spending their last night in their hotel prior to returning home. The wife was asleep, and the husband, wide awake, noticed a $5 chip that they had saved as a souvenir. Strangely, the number 12 was flashing in the groom's mind. Taking this as an omen, he rushed to the roulette tables, where he placed the $5 chip on the 12; sure enough, the winner was 12, paying 35 to 1. He let the winnings ride and kept on winning until he had won $262 million. He then let it ride once more and lost everything. Broke and dejected, he walked back to his room. "Where were you?" asked his bride. "Playing roulette," he responded. "How did you do?" she asked. "Not bad. I lost five dollars."

This story captures what is referred to as *playing with the house's money*. The idea is that people do not feel that something really belongs to them unless it comes out of their own pocket.

It is more painful to give up something that you possess than it is pleasurable to acquire the exact same thing when you don't already possess it. This means that the price elasticity of demand can be changed—made less elastic—if consumers feel that they own the product. The purchase decision can be influenced by having the buyers assume ownership, even temporarily, prior to purchase. If buyers can be persuaded to take the product home to try it out, they will be reluctant to return it when payment is due, since this will require that they incur a loss. A frequent tactic of home decoration and furniture stores is to encourage customers to take a piece of furniture or a carpet home to "see how it looks." This is also the approach of buy-now, pay-later plans. During holidays, for example, retailers frequently offer installment plans that delay payment for 90 days, so that buyers can integrate the new purchases into their reference points. Health clubs, fitness centers, and weight loss clinics offer an initial trial membership either free or at nominal rates.

Publisher's Clearing House addresses individuals who receive its direct mail promotion as "finalists" and warns them that they are about to lose millions of dollars if they do not return the winning number. Publisher's Clearing House is attempting to give consumers the impression that they possess an asset—the opportunity to win millions of dollars—that they will have to give up if they don't submit the entry form.

4.a.3. Status Quo

In general, people would rather leave things as they are. Once something is the status quo, people don't like to change it; they value the status quo or consider the costs of change too high. For example, if people receive an inheritance of low-risk, low-return bonds, they typically don't change anything. Similarly, if people receive higher-risk securities, they also leave most of the money alone. One explanation for this bias toward the status quo is aversion to loss—people are more concerned about the risk of loss than they are excited by the prospect of gain. If you switch your money from the stock market to housing, you would feel worse if the stock market increases than you would feel good if the housing market increases.

4.a.4. Loss Aversion and Framing

People don't react the same way to equal-sized gains and losses. For instance, if people have come to expect the price of a gallon of gasoline to be $2, a price of $3 is a loss of $1 rather than a loss of $3, and a price of $1 is a gain of $1. The gain and loss are calculated relative to a reference. People tend to create references for most things, not just prices. Moreover, although the gain and loss are the same, $1, people do not react to them in the same way. People dislike losses more than they like gains.

Framing—that is, the context in which a choice is presented—is important to the decision maker. For instance, when a customer calls a hotel for a reservation, the hotel reservationists generally quote their highest room rates, those that they charge during peak demand periods, and then discount those rates. This is an attempt to create a high reference price for the consumer. If the initially stated high price is the buyer's reference, then the buyer looks on the price actually paid as a gain. Similarly, airline reservationists initially quote the highest fare on a route before quoting discounts and associated travel restrictions. In written advertisements or in advertisements on radio, both hotels and airlines provide the lowest price along with a reference to which they want consumers to compare the advertised price. Statements like "this fare is 50 percent below previous fares" and "friends fly free," suggesting a 50 percent discount, are common in advertisements.

Some sense of fairness is important to most people. People will reject something that they perceive as not being fair and will react strongly when they feel that they are being taken advantage of. During a snowstorm, does the local hardware store raise the price of snow shovels? During a hurricane, do grocery stores raise the price of food and water? Not if they want to retain business. The old saying is: "If you gouge them at Christmas, they won't be back in March."

4.a.5. Familiarity

When people must make decisions without having perfect information, they often use things that they are familiar with more than economic theory would seem to suggest. Familiarity leads to decisions that might appear irrational because people are more comfortable with a familiar situation than an unfamiliar one. Consider the following quiz:

1. In four pages of a typical novel (about 2,000 words), how many words would you expect to find that have the form "_ _ _ _ ing" (a seven-letter word that ends in -*ing*)?
2. Now, how many words would you expect to find that have the form "_ _ _ _ n _" (a seven-letter word with an *n* in the sixth position)?

You may have noticed that the second option includes the first—in other words, the answer to the second has to be larger than the answer to the first. Yet, because people are familiar with words that end in -*ing*, they tend to think that these words are likely to appear more often.

This reliance on familiarity also arises in answers to questions such as: "Which is more common in New York City, murder or suicide?" Although suicide is much more prevalent than murder, many people think the answer is murder. The point is that the more familiar people are with something (here, news reports of murders in New York), the more likely they are to choose it.

People generally want more for less, but the framing of "more" and "less" makes a difference. Consider how people respond to the following situation.

Who is happier: Person A, who wins the office football pool for $100 on the same day she ruins the carpet in her apartment and must pay her landlord $75, or Person B, who wins the office football pool for $25?

Most people believe that Person A is happier, even though both A and B end up with the same $25 gain. Consider the same problem with a slight revision.

Who is happier: Person A, who ruins the carpet in her apartment and must pay the landlord $100, or Person B, who wins the office football pool for $25 but also ruins the carpet in his apartment and must pay the landlord $125?

In this case, most people believe that Person B is happier, even though A and B must pay the same amount, $100. If the net result involves a gain, people prefer to have the results of the actions presented separately—a $100 gain and a $25 loss rather than a $75 gain. But if the net result involves losses, people prefer to have the losses integrated or shown just once.

4.a.6. Anchoring

Ask a group of people to write down the last three digits of their phone number, and then ask them to estimate the date of Genghis Khan's death. Time and again, the results show a correlation between the two numbers; people assume that he lived in the first millennium, when in fact he lived from 1162 to 1227. Here is another quiz:

You have five seconds to estimate the value of $1 \times 2 \times 3 \times 4 \times 5 \times 6 \times 7 \times 8$.
Now, take five seconds to do the same for $8 \times 7 \times 6 \times 5 \times 4 \times 3 \times 2 \times 1$.

Typically, most people believe that the results of these two exercises are different—that the result of the first is smaller than the result of the second. The reason is that the guesstimates are "anchored" to the early numbers. In the first exercise, the early numbers are smaller; in the second, the higher numbers are listed first. (Still, few guessed that the product was anywhere near the correct number of 40,320.)

4.a.7. Sunk Costs

You and a friend are on the way to a concert for which you purchased tickets for $100, and the tickets are not refundable. Neither of you is feeling particularly well; both of you think that it would be more fun to simply loaf around in the apartment. Your friend says, "It's too bad we've already purchased the tickets, because if we don't go, we waste $100." You agree. Do you go to the concert, or do you go home?

This problem illustrates the sunk-cost effect, otherwise known as "throwing good money after bad." When we have put effort into something, we are often reluctant to pull out because of the loss that we will suffer, even if continued refusal to jump ship will lead to even more loss. Think about the $100 tickets again and consider the issue another way. The moment you paid $100 for the ticket, your net assets decreased by $100. That decrease occurred several days before the concert. Is the fact that your net assets have decreased by $100 sufficient reason for deciding to spend the night at a place you don't want to be? The $100 *you have already paid* is technically termed a *sunk cost*. Rationally, sunk costs *should not affect decisions about the future*. Sunk means that they are gone—they are not recoverable. The $100 is gone whether you go to the concert or not. So, why choose to do something that you would prefer not to do just because you have already bought tickets? The tendency to do so is the sunk-cost effect.

Executives making strategic investment decisions can also fall into the sunk-cost trap. When large projects overrun their schedules and budgets, the original economic case no longer holds. The project should be abandoned. However, because so much has already been spent, companies keep spending to complete such projects.

Now that we've taken a brief look at how emotions affect economic decisions, let's examine the ways in which biology affects decision making.

4.b. Neuroeconomics

neuroeconomics

The joint study by economists and biologists that attempts to determine how the brain handles economic decisions.

Attempting to delve into the black box known as the consumer, some economists have joined forces with biologists and neurologists to attempt to see how the brain handles economic decisions. This is the study of **neuroeconomics**. It has long been known that different sectors of the human prefrontal cortex are involved in distinctive cognitive and behavioral operations. Figure 3 illustrates the anatomy of the brain. The frontal lobe carries out most decision making. Strategic thinking takes place in the prefrontal cortex, noted as areas 10 and 11. The orbital frontal cortex (CFC), or sections 11 and 12, account for the joy or pain of monetary rewards and punishments. Rewards and punishments are dealt with in different parts of the brain: The right CFC handles punishment, and the bilateral medial handles reward. In addition, pain registers more than an equal reward registers.

4.b.1. The Emotional versus the Logical Brain
Magnetic resonance imaging scans have revealed the two parts of the brain in which most decisions take place. The emotional part is the limbic system (especially the amygdala). The logical part is the prefrontal cortex. Neuroeconomists have found that different kinds of decisions show up as increased electrical activity in either the emotional or the logical part. Often a decision is the result of conflicts between the two brain sections. For instance, decisions about the far-off future involve both the prefrontal cortex and the amygdala. The prefrontal cortex takes a long-term perspective, looking at logical cost-benefit comparisons. The amygdala confuses this logic by bringing in emotions, and in some cases it takes over and demands immediate gratification.

Age-based differences in decision making stem from brain development. Adults have greater activity in their frontal lobes and lower activity in their amygdala than do teenagers. The amygdala is more primitive and deals with emotions; the frontal lobes deal

---

FIGURE 3   Anatomy of the Brain

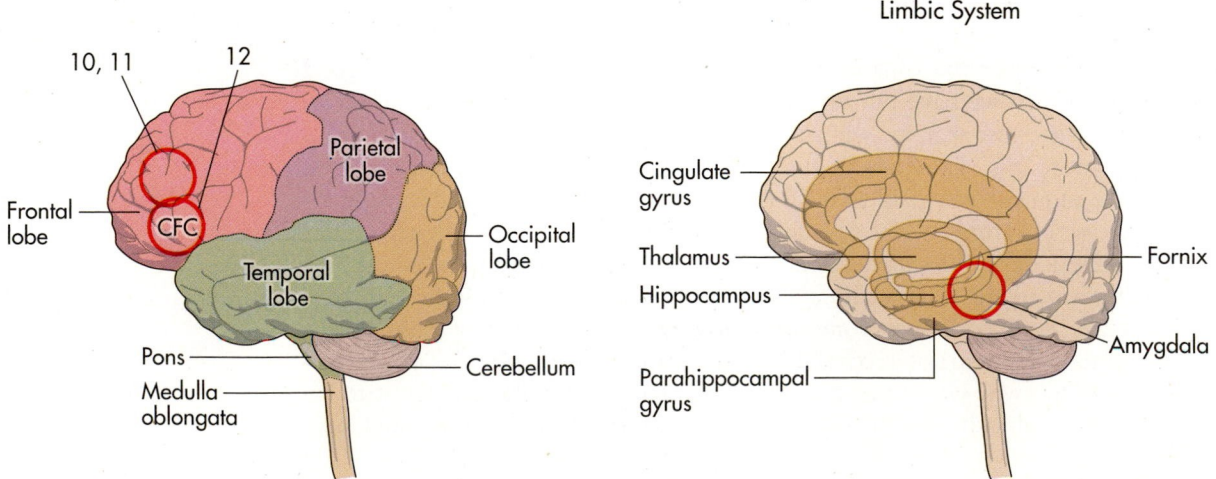

Within the brain, logical decisions take place in the prefrontal cortex. Emotional decisions take place in the limbic system or the amygdala.

© 2013 Cengage Learning

more with reasoning. Another finding is that the limbic system has a hard time imagining the future, even though our prefrontal cortex clearly sees the future consequences of our current actions. Our emotional brain wants to max out the credit card, order dessert, and smoke a cigarette. Our logical brain knows that we should save for retirement, go for a run, and quit smoking. What we actually do depends on which is dominant at that point in time.

RECAP

1. Behavioral economics is the study of decision making assuming that people are rational in a broad sense. The human brain economizes, enabling people to make decisions without having complete and perfect information.

2. Neuroeconomics combines neurology and economics. It attempts to measure brain activity and map where such activity takes place in order to better understand how decisions are made.

SUMMARY

1. **How do consumers decide what to buy?**

   - Utility is a measure of the satisfaction received from possessing or consuming a good. §1.a

   - *Diminishing marginal utility* refers to the decline in marginal utility received from each additional unit of a good that is consumed during a particular period of time. The more of some good a consumer has, the less desirable is another unit of that good. §1.b

   - Even if a good is free, a consumer will eventually reach a point where one more unit of the good would be undesirable or distasteful, and he or she will not consume that additional unit. §1.e

   - Consumer equilibrium refers to the utility-maximizing situation in which the consumer has allocated his or her budget among goods and services in such a way that the marginal utility per dollar of expenditure on the last unit of any good is the same for all goods. It is represented in symbols as $MU_x/P_x = MU_y/P_y = MU_z/P_z$. §2.b

2. **Why does the demand curve slope down?**

   - The demand curve slopes down because of diminishing marginal utility and consumer equilibrium. §3.a

   - The income and substitution effects of a price change occur because of diminishing marginal utility and the equimarginal principle. When the price of one good falls while all other prices remain the same, that good yields more satisfaction per dollar than before, so consumers buy more of it than before. §3.b

   - Market demand is the summation of individual demands. §3.b

3. **What are behavioral economics and neuroeconomics?**

   - The two fields of study are attempts to jump inside the human being, to discover why and how decisions are made. Behavioral economists have focused on observing decisions made by people in various situations; neuroeconomists have focused on measuring brain activity using technologies such as magnetic resonance imaging scans. §4.a, b

KEY TERMS

EXERCISES

1. Using the following information, calculate total utility and marginal utility.
   a. Plot the total utility curve.
   b. Plot marginal utility directly below total utility.
   c. At what marginal utility value does total utility reach a maximum?

Number of utils for the first unit	300
Number of utils for the second unit	250
Number of utils for the third unit	220
Number of utils for the fourth unit	160
Number of utils for the fifth unit	100
Number of utils for the sixth unit	50
Number of utils for the seventh unit	20
Number of utils for the eighth unit	0
Number of utils for the ninth unit	−250

2. Is it possible for marginal utility to be negative and total utility positive? Explain.

3. Suppose Mary is in consumer equilibrium. The marginal utility of good A is 30, and the price of good A is $2.
   a. If the price of good B is $4, the price of good C is $3, the price of good D is $1, and the price of all other goods and services is $5, what is the marginal utility of each of the goods Mary is purchasing?
   b. If Mary has chosen to keep $10 in savings, what is the ratio of MU to P for savings?

4. Using the following utility schedule, derive a demand curve for pizza.
   a. Assume income is $10, the price of each slice of pizza is $1, and the price of each glass of beer is $2. Then change the price of pizza to $2 per slice.
   b. Now change income to $12 and derive a demand curve for pizza.

Slices of Pizza	Total Utility	Glasses of Beer	Total Utility
1	200	1	500
2	380	2	800
3	540	3	900
4	600	4	920
5	630	5	930

5. Using utility, explain the following commonly made statements:
   a. I couldn't eat another bite.
   b. I'll never get tired of your cooking.
   c. The last drop tastes as good as the first.
   d. I wouldn't eat broccoli if you paid me.
   e. My kid would eat nothing but junk food if I allowed her.
   f. Any job worth doing is worth doing well.

6. How would guests' behavior be likely to differ at a BYOB (bring your own bottle) party from one at which the host provides the drinks? Explain your answer.

7. A round of golf on a municipal golf course usually takes about five hours. At a private country club golf course, a round takes less than four hours. What accounts for the difference? Would the time spent playing golf be different if golfers paid only an admission fee (membership fee) and no monthly dues or if they paid only a charge per round and no monthly dues?

8. To increase marginal utility, you must decrease consumption (everything else held constant). This statement is correct, even though it sounds strange. Explain why.

9. Suppose that the marginal utility of good A is 4 times the marginal utility of good B, but the price of good A is only 2 times the price of good B. Is this point consumer equilibrium? If not, what will occur?

10. Last Saturday, you went to a movie and ate a large box of popcorn and two candy bars and drank a medium soda. This Saturday, you went to a movie and ate a medium box of popcorn and one candy bar and drank a large soda. Your tastes and preferences did not change. What could explain the different combinations of goods that you purchased?

11. Peer pressure is an important influence on the behavior of youngsters. For instance, many preteens begin smoking because their friends pressure them into being "cool" by smoking. Using utility theory, how would you explain peer pressure? How would this compare with the explanations provided by behavioral economics and neuroeconomics?

12. Many people who earn incomes below some level receive food stamps from the government. Economists argue that these people would be better off if the government gave them the cash equivalent of the food stamps rather than the food stamps. What is the basis of the economists' argument?

13. What is the purpose of the two fields of study, neuroeconomics and behavioral economics? Why might people tend to be overconfident?

14. What does it mean to say that people like to "play with the house's money"?

15. Can you see a connection between the emotional and logical brain and the action known as loss aversion?

16. Would it make any sense to say that, since a change in tax policy makes Jorge lose utility while Mary and Demitri gain utility, the policy is good if the loss in Jorge's utility is less than the combined gain in Mary and Demitri's utilities? How about the other way around—Jorge's loss of utility is greater than Mary and Demitri's combined gain?

17. As people age, they typically spend more on luxury goods than when they are younger. Does this mean that diminishing marginal utility of money declines as people age?

You can find further practice tests in the Online Quiz at **www.cengage.com/economics/boyes**.

HAPPINESS IS THE MEASURE OF TRUE WEALTH

The Daily Telegraph (London), April 10, 2008

It comes as no surprise to learn from a study published this week that, although Britons are twice as rich as they were in 1987, they are no happier. The lack of relationship between wealth and happiness has long been common knowledge, and the knowledge itself has long been a source of happiness to moralisers who like the fact that money is not life's answer.

There are, though, two confusions involved in the idea that anything significant can be discovered by looking for a correlation between wealth and happiness. One concerns the nature of happiness, the other the nature of wealth.

If you could arrange for Britain's population to make a sudden return to 1987 levels of income and possessions, almost everybody would be unhappy. As wealth increases, so do expectations, and so does being accustomed to the lifestyle that the new level of wealth brings. For most people it is likely that wealth has to improve in order for their happiness level to remain constant; if their wealth were to decline, so would their happiness.

The important point here is that "happiness" is too vague and baggy a notion to be truly helpful. It is like an old pair of knickers that has lost its elastic and become over-capacious and shapeless. Instead of talking about happiness, one should talk about satisfaction, achievement, interest, engagement, enjoyment, growth and the constant opening of fresh possibilities. Very often the activities that yield these things are challenging, even effortful. A person in the midst of doing something objectively worthwhile might not describe himself as happy—usually he will be too absorbed to notice—and only later will realise that what it is to be happy is to be absorbed in something worthwhile.

If mere happiness were the point, we could easily achieve it for everyone by suitably medicating the water supply. But it has often been well said that the surest way to unhappiness is to seek happiness directly. Instead, happiness comes as a sideline of other endeavours that in themselves bring satisfaction and a sense of achievement. It is like the dot of light in a dark room that one cannot see when looking directly at it, but notices out of the corner of one's eye on looking away.

The other confusion concerns wealth. If a person has a million pounds in the bank and never touches a penny of it, or a huge mansion and never occupies it, it is the same as if he had neither the money nor the house. What this shows is that wealth is not so much what one has, but what one does with it. A man who has a thousand pounds and spends it on a wonderful trip to the Galapagos Islands is a rich man indeed: the experiences, the things learnt, the differences wrought in him by both, are true wealth. If you would like to know how rich a person is, you need to ask not how much money he has, but how much he has spent.

This idea is associated with the wise teaching that the philosophers and poets of antiquity never tired of repeating: that a rich person is he who has enough. If his needs are modest and his habits frugal, then so long as his resources provide enough to meet both, he is rich.

But the man is poor who, despite owning millions, restlessly yearns for more because he feels he cannot have enough, and in particular who lacks the things money cannot buy—ah yes, for these unpurchasable treasures can never be left out of the picture: friendship, love, a sound digestion and a reliable, natural ability to sleep at nights, are indispensable to the possibility of happiness, if not directly supplying it.

In thinking about happiness and wealth, one should avoid using the words "happiness" and "wealth," and think instead of more accurate and more substantial words that denote what one truly thinks these things are.

To mention satisfaction and achievement is to suggest activity of some kind—doing and making, helping, learning, changing—which might seem obvious to most, but is chosen by surprisingly few.

Ruskin tellingly remarked "a man wrapped up in himself makes a very small parcel," and this, alas, characterises too many people. The limited surface area of such parcels does not attract much of the golden dust of satisfaction.

The true equation between happiness and wealth is this: that happiness is wealth. Unlike wealth in the form of money and possessions, such happiness can never be quantified, only felt; and if one has it, it does not matter if the level of it always stays the same.

Source: The Daily Telegraph (LONDON), April 10, 2008, A. C. Grayling. © Telegraph Media Group Limited 2008.

Commentary

We all want more—we assume that if we had all the money in the world, we would be happy and fulfilled, don't we? That assumption is wrong; more is not always better than less. More disease, more filth, more garbage, more pollution, more of many things is not better than less. With respect to goods, we do assume that more is better than less as long as there is no problem in storing or keeping the goods and services and as long as our tastes do not change. The cake example used in the text, where our consumer ate so much that he or she nearly got sick, illustrates nicely that more is preferred to less as long as there are no storage costs; it is simply impossible to "store" an infinite amount of cake, that is, to eat it. Eventually, more cake is not desired. This is the law of diminishing marginal utility in operation. It says that during a given period of time, as we get more of an additional good, the marginal amount of that good will provide us less additional happiness than a previous amount did.

In the Economic Insight "Does Money Buy Happiness?" it was shown that up to some income level, money and expressed happiness seem to rise together, but then, as money continues to rise, happiness does not. This article clarifies the issue, indicating that money enables people to purchase time to do those things that make them happier. People want more money—more money enables people to purchase more of everything, and so more money equates to more happiness. This seems to occur, but only up to a point—once someone has a bunch of money, additional amounts do not mean very much.

What does more income do? It enables people to purchase more of everything. The consumer equilibrium formula states that a consumer will purchase additional amounts of items until the consumer's budget is spent and the marginal utility of each dollar of expenditures is nearly equal across all purchases:

$$MU_x/P_x = MU_y/P_y = MU_z/P_z$$

With more income, more of everything can be purchased. The consumer still purchases by spending the budget on each good and service up to the point where the last dollar spent on each item yields the same additional utility. So the question is, do people also experience diminishing marginal utility with money? The answer has to be no as long as there are no costs of storage and tastes do not change.

The theme of the article is that people tend to dislike work, commuting, child care, and housework but enjoy playing, exercising, making love, reading, and walking, and that income enables people to do more of what they like. The study referred to in the article found that those with incomes below $30,000 a year spend about 50 percent more time in an unpleasant state than do people with income above $100,000.

This is not to say that everyone feels the same—many people love their jobs. But, on average, more people like leisure than they do work, house care, and child care. The utility of each individual for the same item (money or any other item) is different; comparing one person's utility (happiness) to another's is not possible. How can you measure whether one person is happier than another? Perhaps some day neuroeconomics will enable such comparisons to be made.

Indifference Analysis

1. Indifference Curves

In Figure 1, four combinations of CDs and gallons of gasoline are listed in the table and plotted in Figure 1(a). Preferring more to less, the consumer will clearly prefer *C* to the other combinations. Combination *C* is preferred to *B* because *C* offers one more gallon of gas than *B* and the same amount of CDs. Combination *C* is preferred to *A* because *C* offers both one more CD and one more gallon of gas than *A*. And Combinations *B* and *D* are preferred to *A*; however, it is not obvious whether *B* is preferred to *D* or *D* is preferred to *B*.

Let's assume that the consumer has no preference between *B* and *D*. We thus say that the consumer is **indifferent** between combination *B* (2 CDs and 1 gallon of gas) and combination *D* (1 CD and 2 gallons of gas). Connecting points *B* and *D*, as in Figure 1(b), produces an indifference curve. An **indifference curve** shows all the combinations of two goods that the consumer is indifferent among, or, in other words, an indifference curve shows all the combinations of goods that will give the consumer the same level of total utility.

indifferent
Lacking any preference.

indifference curve
A curve showing all combinations of two goods that the consumer is indifferent among.

FIGURE 1 Indifference Curve

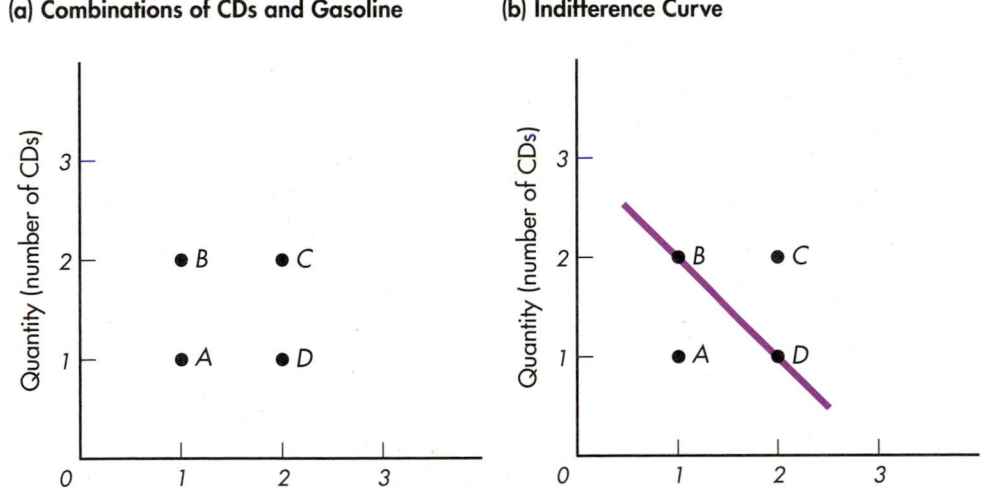

(a) Combinations of CDs and Gasoline

(b) Indifference Curve

Four combinations of two goods, CDs and gasoline, are presented to the consumer in Figure 1(a). Preferring more to less, the consumer will clearly prefer *C* to *A*, *B*, and *D*. Points *B* and *D* are preferred to *A*, but the consumer has no clear preference between *B* and *D*. The consumer is indifferent between *B* and *D*. Figure 1(b) shows that all combinations of goods among which the consumer is indifferent lie along an indifference curve.

The quantity of goods increases as the distance from the origin increases. Thus, any combination lying on the indifference curve (like *B* or *D*) is preferred to any combination falling below the curve, or closer to the origin (like *A*). Any combination appearing above the curve, or farther from the origin (like *C*), is preferred to any combination lying on the curve.

1.a. The Shape of Indifference Curves

The most reasonable shape for an indifference curve is a downward slope from left to right, indicating that as less of one good is consumed, more of another good is consumed. Indifference curves are not likely to be vertical, horizontal, or upward sloping. They do not touch the axes, and they do not touch each other.

An indifference curve that is a vertical line, like the one labeled I_v in Figure 2(a), would mean that the consumer is indifferent to combinations *B* and *A*. For most goods this will not be the case, because combination *B* provides more of one good with no less of the other good.

Similarly, horizontal indifference curves, such as line I_h in Figure 2(b), are ruled out for most goods. People are not likely to be indifferent between combinations *A* and *B* along the horizontal curve, since *B* provides more of one good with no less of the other good than *A*.

An upward-sloping curve, such as I_u in Figure 2(c), would mean that the consumer is indifferent between a combination of goods that provides less of everything and a combination that provides more of everything (compare points *A* and *B*). Rational consumers tend to prefer more to less.

1.b. The Slope of Indifference Curves

The slope, or steepness, of indifference curves is determined by consumer preferences. The amount of one good that a consumer must give up to get an additional unit of the other good and remain equally satisfied changes as the consumer trades off one good for the other. The less a consumer has of a good, the more the consumer values an additional unit of that good. This preference is shown by an indifference curve that bows in toward the origin, like the curve shown in Figure 3. A consumer who has 4 CDs and 1 gallon of gasoline (point *D*) may be willing to give up 2 CDs for 1 more gallon of gasoline, moving from *D* to *E*. But a consumer who has only 2 CDs may be willing to give up only 1 CD to get that additional gallon of gasoline. This preference is shown as the move from *E* to *F*.

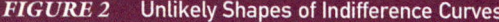

FIGURE 2   Unlikely Shapes of Indifference Curves

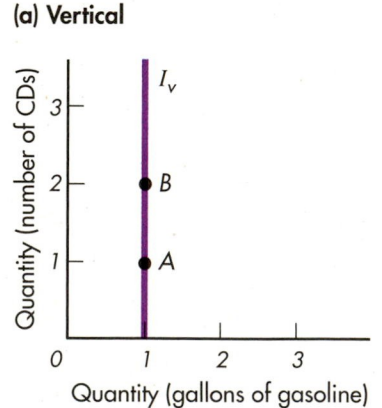
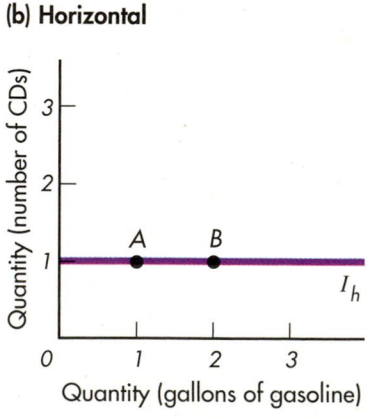
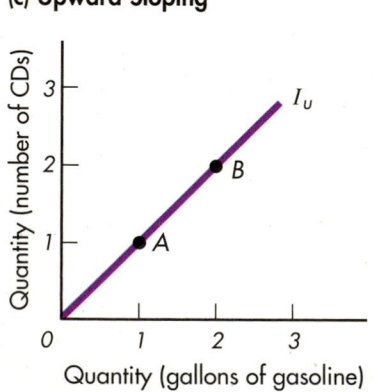

A vertical indifference curve, as in Figure 2(a), would violate the condition that more is preferred to less, as would a horizontal indifference curve, as in Figure 2(b), or an upward-sloping curve, as in Figure 2(c). Thus, indifference curves are not likely to have any of these shapes.

FIGURE 3 Bowed-In Indifference Curve

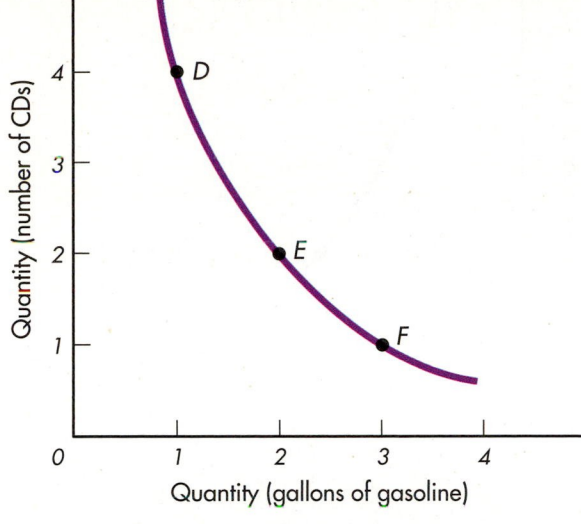

© 2013 Cengage Learning

Indifference curves slope down from left to right and bow in toward the origin. They bow in because consumers value a good relatively more if they have less of it, other things being equal. At the top of the curve, where a little gasoline and many CDs are represented by point *D*, the consumer is willing to give up 2 CDs to get 1 gallon of gasoline. But lower down on the curve, such as at point E, the consumer has more gasoline and fewer CDs than at point *D* and thus is willing to give up fewer CDs to get 1 more gallon of gasoline.

1.c. Indifference Curves Cannot Cross

Indifference curves do not intersect. If the curves crossed, two combinations of goods that clearly are not equally preferred by the consumer would seem to be equally preferred. According to Figure 4, the consumer is indifferent between A and B along indifference curve I_2 and indifferent between B and C along indifference curve I_1. Thus, the consumer appears to be indifferent among A, B, and C. Combination C, however, offers more CDs and no less gasoline than combination A. Clearly, the consumer, preferring more to less, will prefer C to A. Thus, indifference curves are not allowed to cross.

1.d. An Indifference Map

An **indifference map**, located in the positive quadrant of a graph, indicates the consumer's preferences among all combinations of goods and services. The farther from the origin an indifference curve is, the more the combinations of goods along that curve are preferred. The arrow in Figure 5 indicates the ordering of preferences: I_2 is preferred to I_1; I_3 is preferred to I_2 and I_1; I_4 is preferred to I_3, I_2, and I_1; and so on.

indifference map
A complete set of indifference curves.

2. Consumer Equilibrium

The indifference map reveals only the combinations of goods and services that a consumer prefers or is indifferent among—what the consumer is *willing* to buy. It does not tell us what the consumer is *able* to buy. Consumers' income levels or budgets limit the amount that they can purchase.

FIGURE 4   Indifference Curves Do Not Cross

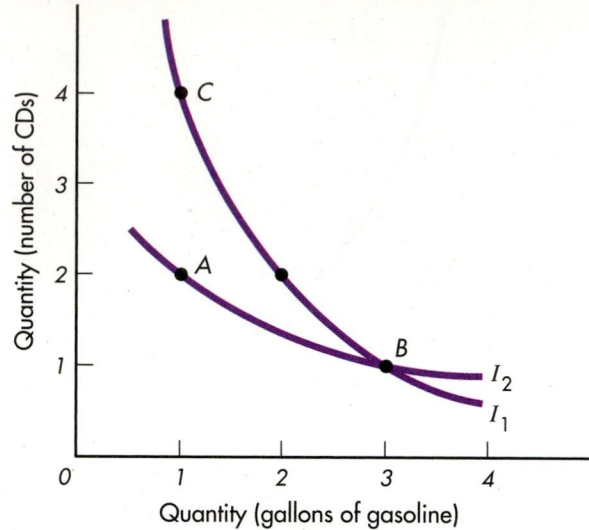

If two indifference curves intersected, such as at point *B*, then the consumer would be indifferent among all points on each curve. But point *C* clearly provides more CDs than point *A* and no less gasoline, so the consumer will prefer *C* to *A*. If the consumer prefers more to less, the indifference curves will not cross.

© 2013 Cengage Learning

FIGURE 5   Indifference Map

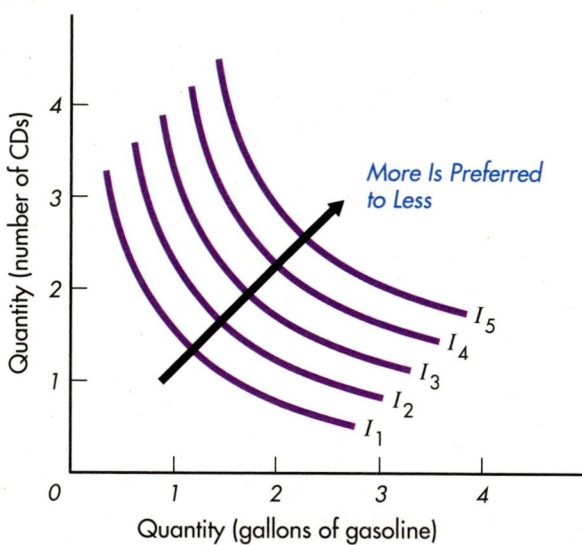

Indifference curves cover the entire positive quadrant. As we move away from the origin, more is preferred to less: I_5 is preferred to I_4, I_4 is preferred to I_3, and so on.

© 2013 Cengage Learning

budget line
A line showing all the combinations of goods that can be purchased with a given level of income.

2.a. Budget Constraint

Let's suppose a consumer has allocated $6 to spend on gas and CDs. Figure 6 shows the **budget line**, a line giving all the combinations of goods that a consumer with a given budget can buy at given prices.

Anywhere along the budget line in Figure 6(a), the consumer is spending $6. When the price of CDs is $1 and the price of gas is $1 per gallon, the consumer can choose among several different combinations of CDs and gas that add up to $6. If only CDs are purchased, 6 CDs can be purchased (point *A*). If only gas is purchased, 6 gallons of gas can be purchased (point *G*). At point *B*, 5 CDs and 1 gallon of gas can be purchased. At point *C*, 4 CDs and 2 gallons of gas can be purchased. At point *F*, 1 CD and 5 gallons of gas can be purchased.

FIGURE 6   The Budget Line

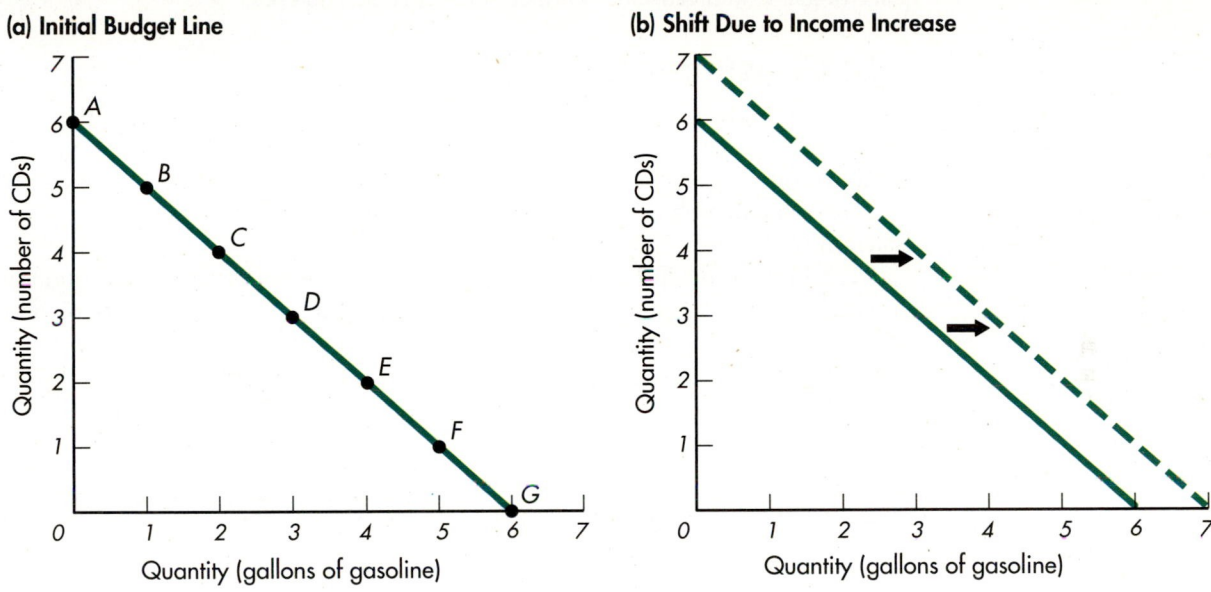

(a) Initial Budget Line

(b) Shift Due to Income Increase

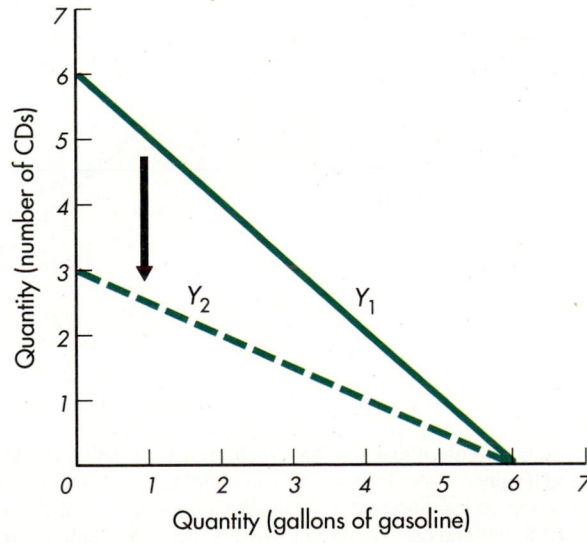

(c) Shift (Rotation) Due to Relative Price Change

In Figure 6(a), a budget line is drawn for a consumer with a $6 budget to be spent on CDs and gallons of gasoline costing $1 each. The consumer can purchase 6 CDs and no gas, 5 CDs and 1 gallon of gas, and so on. In Figure 6(b), the budget line shifts outward because the budget is increased from $6 to $7 and the consumer can purchase more. In Figure 6(c), the initial budget line (Y_1) runs from 6 to 6. When the price of CDs increases from $1 to $2, the budget line ($Y_2$) rotates down along the CD axis. Spending the entire $6 budget on CDs allows the consumer to buy only 3 CDs rather than the 6 that were obtained at the per unit price of $1.

An increase in the consumer's income or budget is shown as an outward shift of the budget line. Figure 6(b) shows an increase in income from $6 to $7. The budget line shifts out to the line running from 7 to 7. A change in income or in the consumer's budget causes a parallel shift of the budget line.

A change in the price of one of the goods causes the budget line to rotate. For example, with a budget of $6 and the prices of both CDs and gas at $1, we have the budget line Y_1 in Figure 6(c). If the price of CDs rises to $2, only 3 CDs can be purchased if the entire budget is spent on CDs. As a result, the budget line Y_2 is flatter, running from 3 on the vertical axis to 6 on the horizontal axis. Conversely, a rise in the price of gas would cause the budget line to become steeper.

2.b. Consumer Equilibrium

Putting the budget line on the indifference map allows us to determine the one combination of goods and services that the consumer is both *willing* and *able* to purchase. Any combination of goods that lies on or below the budget line is within the consumer's budget. Which combination will the consumer choose in order to yield the greatest satisfaction (utility)?

The budget line in Figure 7 indicates that most of the combinations on indifference curve I_1 and point C on indifference curve I_2 are attainable. Combinations on indifference curve I_3 are preferred to combinations on I_2, but the consumer is *not able* to buy combinations on I_3 because they cost more than the consumer's budget. Therefore,

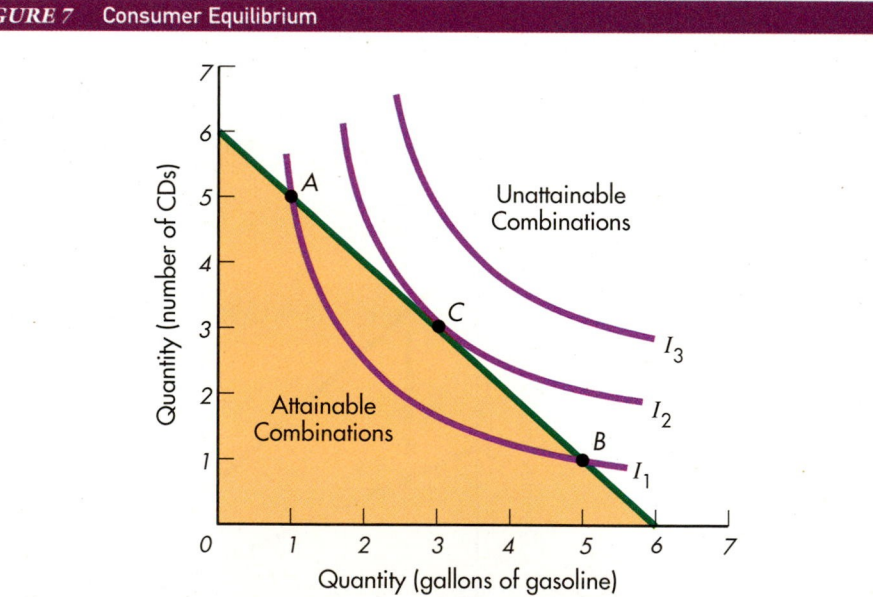

FIGURE 7   Consumer Equilibrium

The consumer maximizes satisfaction by purchasing the combination of goods that is on the indifference curve farthest from the origin but attainable given the consumer's budget. The combinations along I_1 are attainable, but so are some of the combinations that lie above I_1. Combinations beyond the budget line, such as those along I_3, cost more than the consumer's budget. Point C, where the indifference curve I_2 just touches, or is tangent to, the budget line, is the chosen combination and the point of consumer equilibrium.

Source: Adapted from David G. Myers, *The Pursuit of Happiness* (New York: William Morrow, 1992).

point *C* represents the maximum level of satisfaction, or utility, available to the consumer. Point *C* is the point where the budget line is tangent to (just touches) the indifference curve.

SUMMARY

- Indifference curves show all combinations of two goods that give the consumer the same level of total utility. *§1*
- An indifference map is a complete set of indifference curves in the positive quadrant of a graph. *§1.d*
- The indifference curve indicates what the consumer is willing to buy. The budget line indicates what the

consumer is able to buy. Together they determine the combinations of goods that the consumer is both willing and able to buy. *§2.a*
- Consumer equilibrium occurs at the point where the budget line just touches, or is tangent to, an indifference curve. *§2.b*

KEY TERMS

budget line, 464
indifference curve, 461

indifference map, 463

indifferent, 461

EXERCISES

1. Use these combinations for parts a and b:

Combination	Clothes	Food
A	1 basket	1 pound
B	1 basket	2 pounds
C	1 basket	3 pounds
D	2 baskets	1 pound
E	2 baskets	2 pounds
F	2 baskets	3 pounds
G	3 baskets	1 pound
H	3 baskets	2 pounds
I	3 baskets	3 pounds

a. If more is preferred to less, which combinations are clearly preferred to other combinations? Rank the combinations in the order of preference.

b. Some clothes–food combinations cannot be clearly ranked. Why not?

2. Explain why two indifference curves cannot cross.

3. Using the data that follow, plot two demand curves for cake. Then explain what could have led to the shift of the demand curve.

I. Price of Cake	Quantity of Cake Demanded	II. Price of Cake	Quantity of Cake Demanded
$1	10	$1	14
$2	8	$2	10
$3	4	$3	8
$4	3	$4	6
$5	1	$5	5

CHAPTER 21

Supply: The Costs of Doing Business

© MACIEJ FROLOW/GETTY IMAGES, INC

IPANDASTUDIO/ISTOCKPHOTO; LOGO: © FROXX/SHUTTERSTOCK.COM

FUNDAMENTAL QUESTIONS

1 What is the law of diminishing marginal returns?

2 What is the relationship between costs and output in the short run?

3 What is the relationship between costs and output in the long run?

n the previous chapter, we looked closely at demand. We learned that the demand for any one item comes from individuals choosing to allocate their limited income so as to maximize their utility—their happiness or satisfaction. We noted that demand changes when prices of related goods, income, expectations, and tastes and preferences change. In this chapter, we examine supply. We find that supply comes from the profit objectives of firms, and we learn what causes supply to change.

1. Firms and Production

A firm hires labor, purchases materials, rents buildings and land, and spends money on advertising and other selling activities. The quantity of resources used and the amount spent on selling activities depends on how productive these activities are—how much they contribute to the value of the firm. In general, the more the firm wants to supply, the more resources it must have.

1.a. The Relationship between Output and Resources

Supply is the quantities of output that sellers are willing and able to offer for sale at every price, everything else held constant. To determine how much to supply at any given price, sellers must know how much it costs to supply each quantity. The relationship between output and costs depends on the relationship between output and the resources used to create that output. Such a relationship is illustrated in Table 1. A firm has a fixed space—say a 500-square-foot retail space in a mall. The quantity of items offered for sale—supplied—depends on the number of employees. One employee can display 30 items, two employees 65 items, three employees 100 items, and so on in that 500-square-foot space in one day's time. If we look at this in terms of how much each new employee adds, we see that the first employee adds 30, the second adds 35, the third adds another 35, the fourth 30, and so on. In other words, as the shop adds an additional employee, the number of items available for sale rises at an increasing rate, then at a decreasing rate, and finally, adding more employees actually causes output to decline.

Paul Prescott/Shutterstock

Business owners combine quantities of land, labor, and capital to produce goods and services in the most profitable way. Technological improvements help them produce a larger quantity of goods and services at lower cost, thereby increasing profitability. Here, a garment factory in India combines labor with the sewing machines, tables, light, and textiles to produce garments. The sewing machines enable the workers to create many more garments than if they were sewing by hand. With a fixed number of machines and room, employing more people may speed up production; eventually, however, employing more people will not speed up production and could actually retard production as the workers interfere with each other's tasks.

TABLE 1	Diminishing Marginal Returns

As another employee is added to the 500 square feet of space, the number of items that can be displayed and offered for sale rises—initially at an accelerating rate, then at a decreasing rate—and eventually declines. The seventh employee adds no additional output, and the eighth causes output to decline.

Number of Employees	Total Output
0	0
1	30
2	65
3	100
4	130
5	150
6	160
7	160
8	140

© 2013 Cengage Learning

1 What is the law of diminishing marginal returns?

law of diminishing marginal returns
When successive equal amounts of a variable resource are combined with a fixed amount of another resource, marginal increases in output that can be attributed to each additional unit of the variable resource will eventually decline.

1.b. Diminishing Marginal Returns

This relationship between employees and output is called the **law of diminishing marginal returns**. Too many employees on the floor at one time trying to display and sell items makes them inefficient—they get in one another's way.

Diminishing marginal returns are not unique to this small retail shop. In every instance where *increasing* amounts of one resource are combined with *fixed* amounts of other resources, the additional output that can be produced initially increases rapidly, then increases more slowly, and eventually decreases.

Diminishing marginal returns applies anywhere that resources whose quantities can be changed are combined with resources whose quantities are fixed. For instance, consider the effort to improve passenger safety during collisions by installing air bags in cars. The first air bag added to a car increases protection considerably (assuming it is put in the steering wheel). The second adds an element of safety, particularly for the front-seat passenger. But additional air bags provide less and less additional protection and eventually would lessen protection as they interfered with one another. As successive units of the variable resource, air bags, are placed on the fixed resource, the car, the additional amount of protection provided by each air bag declines.

© froox/Shutterstock.com

RECAP

1. According to the law of diminishing marginal returns, as successive units of a variable resource are added to the fixed resources, the additional output produced will initially rise but will eventually decline.

2. Diminishing marginal returns occur because the efficiency of variable resources depends on the quantity of the fixed resources.

2. From Production to Costs

Every firm (and every individual and nation as well) is faced with the law of diminishing marginal returns. The law is, in fact, a physical property, not an economic one, but it is important to economics because it defines the relationship between costs and output in the short run.

2.a. The Calculation of Costs

Suppose, in our example of Table 1, that the cost per employee is $1,000 per month and the rent for the 500 square feet is $6,000 per month. Table 2 shows the costs for the different number of employees used.

We are most interested in the relationship between output and costs because we want to know the costs of supplying output. So we need to convert Table 2 into one that shows the relationship between output and costs. Table 3 shows what happens to costs as output increases in 30-unit increments.

The last column in Table 3, **average total cost (ATC)**, is plotted in Figure 1 with output measured on the horizontal axis and average total cost on the vertical axis. Figure 1 clearly shows that the *ATC* curve is U-shaped. The "U" occurs because of the law of diminishing marginal returns. As the business increases its output, costs rise, but they rise slowly at first and then rapidly. This means that cost per unit declines initially and then rises, creating a U shape.

2.a.1. Marginal Cost
Average total cost is calculated by dividing total cost by output—*ATC* is cost per unit of output, shown in column 5 of Table 3. What does it cost to supply another unit? **Marginal cost (MC)** is the additional cost of supplying another unit of output and is calculated by dividing the change in total cost by the change in output. A change in output, say moving from 0 to 30, causes costs to rise, from $6,000 to $7,000; the change in total cost of $1,000 divided by the change in output of 30 gives the marginal cost of $33. Table 4 presents marginal cost.

In column 5 of Table 4, the relationship between average total cost and marginal cost is noted. When marginal cost is greater than average total cost, average total cost

average total cost (ATC)
The per unit cost, derived by dividing total cost by the quantity of output.

marginal cost (MC)
The change in cost caused by a change in output, derived by dividing the change in total cost by the change in the quantity of output.

TABLE 2	Costs			

As employees are added, costs rise at a rate of $1,000 per employee. The cost of the building space is fixed at $6,000. Adding the cost of employees, variable cost, to the fixed cost gives the total cost, noted in column 5. Column 3 shows total variable costs, the costs of the resources that vary as output changes—employees in our example. Column 4 shows the fixed costs, the costs that do not change as output changes—selling space in the mall in our example. The last column shows total costs, the sum of variable and fixed costs.

1 Employees	2 Total Output	3 Variable Costs (Costs of Employees)	4 Fixed Cost (Cost of 500 Square Feet)	5 Total Cost (Fixed + Variable)
0	0	0	$6,000	$ 6,000
1	30	$1,000	$6,000	$ 7,000
2	65	$2,000	$6,000	$ 8,000
3	100	$3,000	$6,000	$ 9,000
4	130	$4,000	$6,000	$10,000
5	150	$5,000	$6,000	$11,000
6	160	$6,000	$6,000	$12,000
7	160	$7,000	$6,000	$13,000

TABLE 3	Output and Costs			

Column 1 shows output in 30-unit increments. Column 2 shows the cost of employees—variable costs—that are required to increase output by 30 units. Column 3 is the fixed cost—the rent of the 500 square feet. Column 4 is total cost. Column 5 is average total cost (column 4 divided by column 1).

1 Total Output	2 Variable Costs	3 Fixed Costs	4 Total Cost	5 Average Total Cost
0	0	$6,000	$ 6,000	—
30	$1,000	$6,000	$ 7,000	$ 7,000/3 = $233
60	$1,920	$6,000	$ 7,920	$ 7,920/60 = $132
90	$2,820	$6,000	$ 8,820	$ 8,820/90 = $98
120	$3,745	$6,000	$ 9,745	$ 9,745/120 = $81
150	$5,000	$6,000	$11,000	$11,000/150 = $73.33
160*	$6,000	$6,000	$12,000	$12,000/160 = $75
160*	$7,000	$6,000	$13,000	$13,000/160 = $81

*Given 500 square feet, the most that can be produced is 160, according to Table 1.

FIGURE 1	Average Total Cost

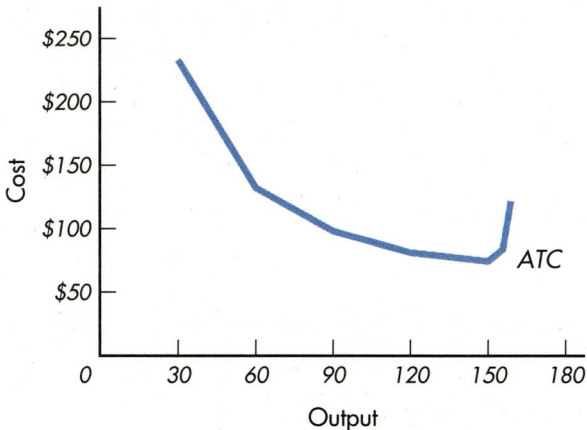

Table 3 plotted. The last column of Table 3 is the average total cost, *ATC*. Plotting the cost on the vertical axis and the quantity of output on the horizontal axis generates the *ATC* curve.

rises—the *ATC* curve slopes up. When marginal cost is below average total cost, then average total cost falls—the *ATC* curve slopes down. Marginal cost equals average total cost when average total cost is at its minimum.

This relationship between marginal and average exists for any average and marginal measurement. Consider your grades, for example. Think of the grade point average (GPA) that you get each semester as your *marginal* GPA, and your cumulative, or overall, GPA as your *average* GPA. You can see the relationship between marginal and average by considering what will happen to your cumulative GPA if this semester's GPA is less than your cumulative GPA. Suppose your GPA this semester is 3.0 for 16 hours of classes and your cumulative GPA, not including this semester, is 3.5 for 48 hours of classes. Your marginal (this semester's) GPA will be less than your average GPA. Thus,

TABLE 4 Marginal Cost

Column 4 is marginal cost, the change in total cost divided by the change in quantity. The change in total cost is the difference between row 1, column 2 and row 2, column 2; then between row 2, column 2 and row 3, column 2, and so on. The change in output is the difference between row 1, column 1 and row 2, column 1; and so on. The last column in the table shows the relationship between MC and ATC. If MC is above ATC, ATC is rising; if MC is below ATC, ATC is declining; $MC = ATC$ at the minimum point of ATC.

1 Total Output, Q	2 Total Costs, TC	3 Average Total Cost, TC/Q	4 Marginal Cost, Change in TC/Change in Q	5 Relationship between Average Total Cost and Marginal Cost
0	$ 6,000	—	—	
30	$ 7,000	$ 7,000/30 = $233	$1,000/30 = $33	$MC < ATC$: ATC falling
60	$ 7,920	$ 7,920/60 = $132	$ 920/30 = $31	$MC < ATC$: ATC falling
90	$ 8,820	$ 8,820/90 = $98	$ 900/30 = $30	$MC < ATC$: ATC falling
120	$ 9,745	$ 9,745/120 = $81	$ 925/30 = $31	$MC < ATC$: ATC falling
150	$11,000	$11,000/150 = $73.33	$1,255/30 = $41.83	$MC < ATC$: ATC falling
160*	$12,000	$12,000/160 = $75	$1,000/10 = $100*	$MC > ATC$: ATC rising

*Notice that we increase output by only 10 units by adding the sixth worker.

when your marginal GPA is added to your average GPA, your average GPA falls, from 3.5 to 3.375. *As long as the marginal is less than the average, the average falls.* If your GPA this semester is 4.0 instead of 3.0, your average GPA will rise from 3.5 to 3.625. *As long as the marginal is greater than the average, the average rises.*

If the average is falling when marginal is below average and rising when marginal is above average, then marginal and average can be the same only when the average is neither rising nor falling. If your GPA this semester is 3.5 and your cumulative GPA up to this semester was 3.5, then your new GPA will be 3.5. Average and marginal are the same when the average is constant. This occurs only when the average curve is at its maximum or minimum point.

We know that if marginal is less than average, average is falling, and if marginal is above average, average is rising. This is illustrated in Figure 2. Note that the MC curve lies below

> *Whenever marginal is less than average, the average is falling, and whenever marginal is greater than average, the average is rising.*

FIGURE 2 Average Total Cost and Marginal Cost

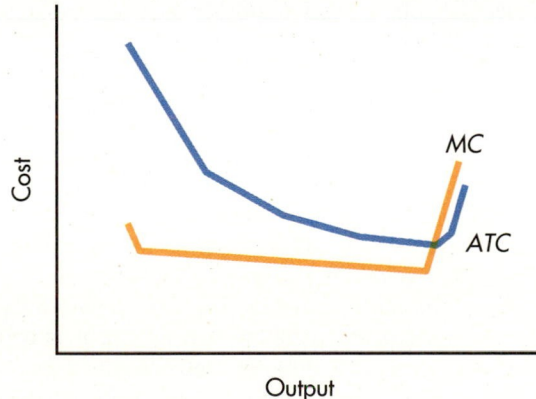

The third and fourth columns of Table 4 are plotted. The relationship between the ATC and the MC is shown in column 5. If MC is less than ATC, ATC is falling; if MC is above ATC, then ATC is rising. $MC = ATC$ at the minimum point of ATC.

total costs (TC)
The expenses that a business has in supplying goods and/or services.

total fixed costs (TFC)
Payments to resources whose quantities cannot be changed during a fixed period of time—the short run.

2 What is the relationship between costs and output in the short run?

total variable costs (TVC)
Payments for additional resources used as output increases.

average fixed cost (AFC)
The total fixed cost divided by total output.

average variable cost (AVC)
Total variable cost divided by total output.

the average-total-cost curve while ATC is declining, and that the marginal-cost curve lies above the average-total-cost curve while ATC is rising. Finally, notice how the marginal-cost curve intersects the average-total cost curve at the minimum point of the average-total-cost curve. This always occurs: The marginal-cost curve intersects the average-total-cost curve at its minimum point. So when MC equals ATC, it is the firm's most efficient point—the firm could not supply at a lower cost per unit of output.

2.b. Definition of Costs

We have mentioned several terms associated with costs—total costs, variable costs, fixed costs, marginal costs, and average total costs. Let us discuss these terms to be sure we understand what they measure. **Total costs (TC)** are the expenses that a business has in supplying goods and/or services. They are the payments to land, labor, and capital. These costs can be divided into variable and fixed costs. **Total fixed costs (TFC)** are payments to resources whose quantities cannot be changed during a fixed period of time—the short run. Typically, fixed costs include rent and some of the payments to workers, suppliers, and others; often there are fixed contracts, such as labor contracts and rental agreements, that cannot be changed for a period of time such as a year. Other costs are variable. **Total variable costs (TVC)** are payments for additional resources used as output increases. For instance, we need more electricity and water when we sell more goods and services. We may need to employ workers for more hours or hire temporary workers. These are variable costs. Average costs are simply the costs per unit of output. **Average fixed cost (AFC)** is the total fixed cost divided by total output. **Average variable cost (AVC)** is total variable cost divided by total

ECONOMIC INSIGHT

Overhead

Economists classify costs as either fixed or variable. Fixed costs do not change as the volume of production changes. Variable costs, on the other hand, depend on the volume of production. In business, costs are often classified into overhead and direct operating costs. Overhead costs are those that are not directly attributable to the production process. They include items such as taxes, insurance premiums, managerial or administrative salaries, paperwork, the cost of electricity not used in the production process (such as electricity used in the administration building), and so on. Overhead costs can be either fixed or variable. Insurance premiums, taxes, and managerial salaries are fixed costs. They must be paid regardless of how much is produced. Electricity used to operate the production process is a variable cost, increasing as the quantity of output produced is increased. The electricity used in a classroom would be a direct cost whereas the electricity used in the administration building would be an indirect cost.

Statements like "we need to spread the overhead" sound somewhat like the concept of declining average

fixed costs—fixed cost per unit of output declines as output rises. But overhead may also include variable costs. Thus, the need to "spread the overhead" refers to reducing the total costs that are not directly attributable to the production process. The more a firm can keep its overhead costs the same and increase its volume of production, the more overhead costs look and act like fixed costs. The higher the percentage of overhead costs that are fixed, the more closely related the economist's and the businessperson's classifications will be. But the two are not—and are not meant to be—the same.

The different classifications provide different information. The economist is interested in the decision to produce—whether to produce at all, and how much to produce. This is the information provided by fixed and variable costs. The businessperson is interested in attributing costs to different activities, that is, in determining whether the business is running as cost-efficiently as it can. The classification of costs into overhead and direct provides this information.

output. **Short-run average total cost (*SRATC*)** is the total cost divided by the total output when the firm is operating in the short run—that is, when at least one resource is fixed. Marginal costs are the changes in costs that occur as output is changed.

short-run average total cost (*SRATC*)
The total cost of production divided by the total quantity of output produced when at least one resource is fixed.

RECAP

1. Costs are the full opportunity costs of resources used to create and sell goods and services.

2. Economists like to discuss costs in terms of fixed and variable costs. Fixed costs are those costs that a firm has in creating and or offering for sale goods and services that do not change as quantities of a good or service offered for sale change. Variable costs are costs that do increase as quantities offered for sale increase.

3. Average costs are total costs divided by the quantity of a good or service being offered for sale—the per unit costs.

4. Marginal costs are the incremental costs, the change in costs that results from a change in the quantity of a good or service offered for sale.

3. The Long Run

The short run refers to any period of time (a day, a month, a year, or whatever) during which at least one resource cannot be changed—its quality or quantity is fixed. In the long run, everything is variable—nothing is fixed. A firm can choose to relocate, build a new plant, rent more floor space, acquire heavy equipment, go out of business, enter a new business, or undertake any other action in the long run.

Perhaps the most important difference between the short run and the long run is that the law of diminishing marginal returns does *not* apply when all resources are variable. Diminishing returns applies only when quantities of variable resources are combined with a fixed resource. In the long run, everything is variable.

If you look at Table 1 and ask, "What could happen if we had more employees and a bigger space in the mall or if we went to a different mall?" you then are thinking about the long run. Table 5 shows the long-run version of Table 1. Recall that in Table 1, the floor space was fixed—our fixed resource. Now, in the long run, nothing is fixed; the owner of the firm is able to choose how many employees to hire, how big a building to rent, and how many other resources to acquire; all combinations are possible in the long run. Table 5 illustrates the difference between the short run and the long run. The short run would be the output combinations available in any one column of the table, such as the first two columns—number of employees and 500 square feet of retail space. In the long run, any size of space can be used by any number of employees to supply output.

The way you read Table 5 is to look at the number of employees and the amount of floor space to find how much output can be supplied. For instance, with 1 employee and 500 square feet of space, 30 units of output can be supplied. Doubling the size of the firm—2 employees and 1,000 square feet—means that 250 units of output can be supplied; doubling both resources again, to 4 employees and 2,000 square feet, means that 640 units of output can be supplied. So, doubling the size of the firm initially allows the firm to supply more than double the output.

If the firm can double its resources (and thus double its costs) but more than double its output, it is experiencing what is called *economies of scale*—getting more efficient as it gets bigger. Conversely, if the firm doubles its resources but does not double its output, then it is experiencing *diseconomies of scale*—it is getting less efficient as it gets bigger.

TABLE 5	Long Run or Planning Period			
	Floor Space (sq ft.)			
Employees	**500**	**1,000**	**1,500**	**2,000**
0	0	0	0	0
1	**30**	100	250	340
2	65	**250**	360	450
3	100	360	480	570
4	130	440	580	**640**
5	150	500	650	710
6	160	540	700	760
7	160	550	720	790
8	140	540	680	800

© 2013 Cengage Learning

3 What is the relationship between costs and output in the long run?

scale
Size; all resources change when scale changes.

long-run average-total-cost curve
The lowest-cost combination of resources with which each level of output is produced when all resources are variable.

3.a. Economies of Scale and Long-Run Cost Curves

If the size of the firm doubles when the quantities of all resources are doubled, this is called doubling the scale of the firm. **Scale** means size. In the long run, a firm has many sizes to choose from—those given in Table 5, for instance. The short run requires that scale be fixed—only one or a few resources can be changed. If we are looking at Table 5 and we decide that column 4 is what we think will be the best, then we sign a lease for 1,500 square feet. At this point, we are in the short run. We can vary the number of employees, but we are stuck with the 1,500 square feet of space until the rental agreement can be revised.

The relationship between the long run and the short run is illustrated in Figure 3. For each size or scale, the firm can vary the quantities of the variable resources and supply different quantities of output. Notice in Figure 3(a) that there are several short-run cost curves. Each curve has a minimum point at a different quantity of output. This quantity of output is the scale or size of the firm in the short run. Whether the firm supplies less or more, its costs are defined by the short-run cost curve. The firm cannot change floor space except in the long run—that is, the firm cannot move from $SRATC_1$ to $SRATC_2$ except in the long run. In the long run, the firm can select any of the short-run curves to operate on. But once it has selected the size, it is in the short run and operates along just one of the short-run average total-cost curves.

Each short-run cost curve is drawn for a particular quantity of building space—that is, a specific column in Table 5. Once the space is selected, the firm brings together combinations of the other resources to supply output. If a small quantity of the building space is selected, the firm might operate along $SRATC_1$. If the firm selects a slightly larger quantity of the fixed resource, then it will be able to operate along $SRATC_2$. With a still larger quantity, the firm can operate along $SRATC_3$, $SRATC_4$, $SRATC_5$, or some other short-run average-total-cost curve.

In the long run, the firm can choose any of the $SRATC$ curves. All it needs to do is choose the level of output it wants to supply and then select the least-cost combination of resources with which to reach that level. All possible least-cost combinations are represented in Figure 3(b) by a curve that just touches each $SRATC$ curve. This curve is the **long-run average-total-cost curve (*LRATC*)**—the lowest cost per unit of output for every level of output when all resources are variable.

The distinction between the short run and the long run is that everything is variable in the long run. In the short run, something is fixed. The long-run average-total-cost

FIGURE 3 The Short-Run and Long-Run Average-Total-Cost Curves

(a) Short-Run Average-Total-Cost Curves

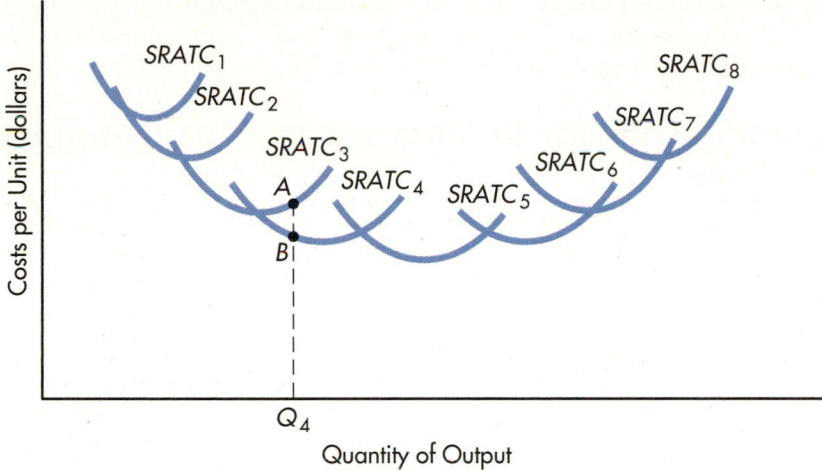

(b) Long-Run Average-Total-Cost Curve

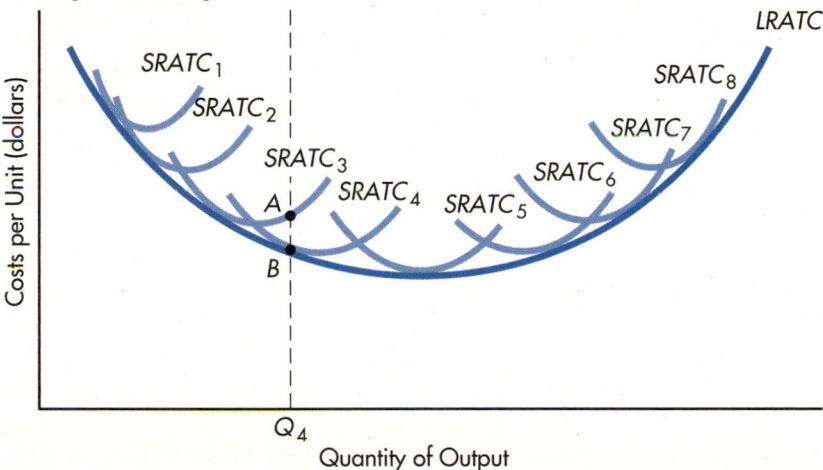

The long-run average-total-cost curve represents the lowest costs of producing any level of output when all resources are variable. Short-run average-total-cost curves represent the lowest costs of producing any level of output in the short run, when at least one of the resources is fixed. Figure 3(a) shows the possible *SRATC* curves facing a firm. Figure 3(b) shows the *LRATC* curve, which connects the minimum cost of producing each level of output. Notice that the *SRATC* curves need not indicate the lowest costs of producing in the long run. If the short run is characterized by $SRATC_3$, then quantity Q_4 can be produced at point *A*. But if some of the fixed resources are allowed to change, managers can shift to $SRATC_4$ and produce at point *B*.

curve gets its shape from **economies of scale** and **diseconomies of scale**. Economies of scale account for the downward-sloping portion of the long-run average-total-cost curve. The firm is able to become more efficient as it gets larger—the cost of supplying each unit of output decreases as the firm gets bigger. Diseconomies of scale account for the upward-sloping portion; the firm becomes less efficient as it gets larger. If the cost per unit of output is constant as output rises, there are **constant returns to scale**.

economies of scale
The decrease in per unit costs as the quantity of production increases and all resources are variable.

diseconomies of scale
The increase in per unit costs as the quantity of production increases and all resources are variable.

constant returns to scale
Unit costs remain constant as the quantity of production is increased and all resources are variable.

Figures 4(a), 4(b), and 4(c) show three possible shapes of a long-run average total-cost curve. Figure 4(a) is the usual U shape, indicating that economies of scale are followed by constant returns to scale and then diseconomies of scale. Figure 4(b) is a curve indicating only economies of scale. Figure 4(c) is a curve indicating only constant returns to scale. Each of these long-run average-total-cost curves would connect several short-run average-total-cost curves, as shown in Figures 4(d), 4(e), and 4(f).

3.b. The Reasons for Economies and Diseconomies of Scale

As a firm gets larger, its employees may be able to specialize based on comparative advantage, making the firm more efficient. Firms that can specialize more as they grow larger may be able to realize economies of scale. Specialization of marketing, sales, pricing, and research, for example, allows some employees to focus on research while others focus on marketing, and still others focus on sales and on pricing. For instance, when Mrs. Fields Cookies was just starting out, it was a one-person operation in northern California. When it moved to Park City, Utah, it was a multiperson operation with cookie outlets throughout most of the western United States. As it grew, the company was able to achieve economies of scale. Its employees could specialize more in just one activity, its advertising did not have to increase as its size increased, and larger machinery enabled it to produce a larger quantity of dough in a shorter period of time.

In 2001 and 2002, oil companies merged—Exxon and Mobil, Chevron and Texaco. The firms resulting from these combinations became two of the largest companies in the world. The reason for merging given by the chief executive officers of these companies was to achieve economies of scale. They believed that having larger oil fields and more refining capability would enable their employees to specialize more and their drilling and refining equipment to be more fully utilized. In 2005 and 2006, Verizon and MCI merged. The executives of these firms claimed that there would be economies of scale. Often the terminology is that there will be synergies that will come with a merger. Overlapping functions can be eliminated—for instance, there is no need for two accounting departments, one from Verizon and one from MCI. Also, MCI might be better at some task than Verizon, so the more efficient can be expanded and the less efficient eliminated. These synergies that arise from being larger, economies of scale, are the most common reason given for mergers.

Economies of scale may also result from the use of larger machines that are more efficient than smaller ones. Large blast furnaces can produce more than twice as much steel per hour as smaller furnaces, but they do not cost twice as much to build or operate. Large electric-power generators are more efficient (more output per quantity of resource) than small ones.

Size, however, does not automatically improve efficiency. The specialization that comes with large size often requires the addition of specialized managers. A 10 percent increase in the number of employees may require an increase of greater than 10 percent in the number of managers. A manager to supervise the other managers is needed. Paperwork increases. Meetings are held more often. The amount of time and labor that are not devoted to producing output grows. In other words, the overhead increases. In addition, it becomes increasingly difficult for the CEO to coordinate the activities of all the division heads and for the division heads to communicate with one another. In this way, size can cause diseconomies of scale. Inefficiencies that come from a larger bureaucracy are most often the reasons for diseconomies of scale.

Again, consider what happened to Mrs. Fields Cookies. As the company continued to add more and more outlets, its CEO could not keep track of everything. Assistant managers, vice presidents, and other executives were hired. The company had achieved economies of scale by utilizing larger equipment in its central location in Park City. But

FIGURE 4 Long-Run and Short-Run Cost Curves

(a) Economies, Constant Returns, and Diseconomies

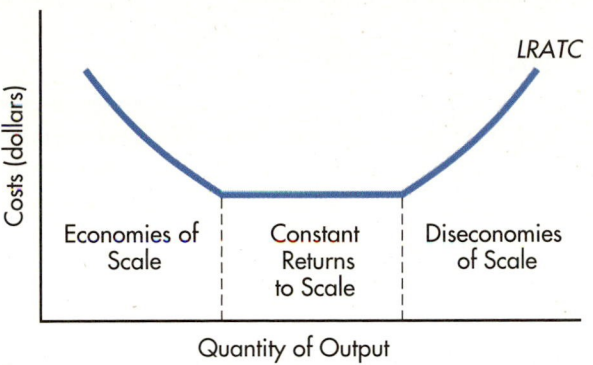

(d) Economies, Constant Returns, and Diseconomies

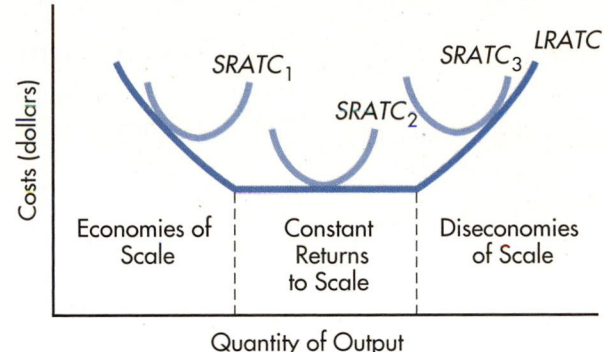

(b) Economies of Scale

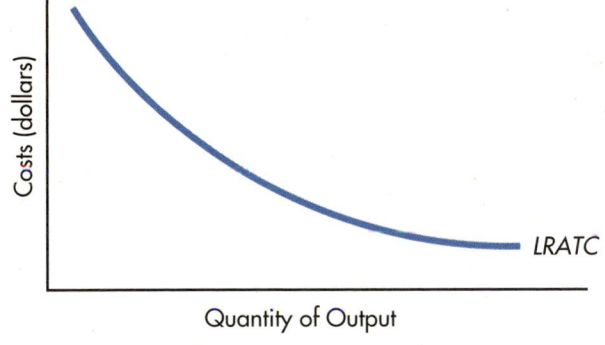

(e) Economies of Scale

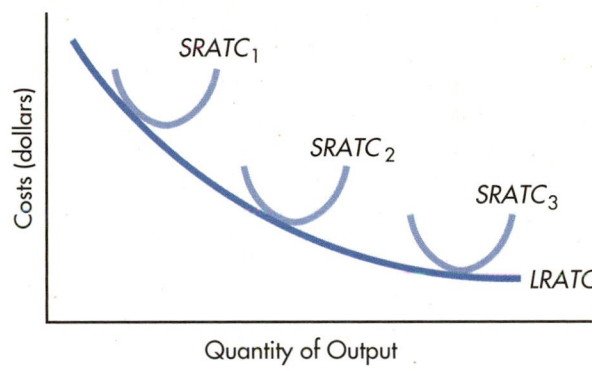

(c) Constant Returns to Scale

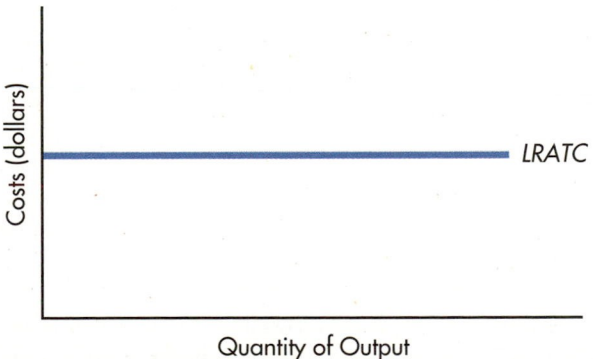

(f) Constant Returns to Scale

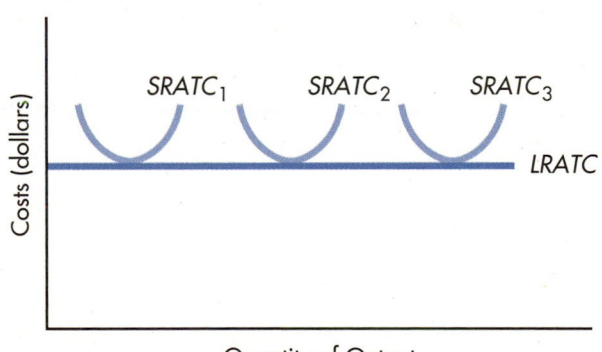

In Figure 4(a), a U-shaped *LRATC* curve is shown. The downward-sloping portion is due to economies of scale, the horizontal portion to constant returns to scale, and the upward-sloping portion to diseconomies of scale. In Figure 4(b), only economies of scale are experienced. In Figure 4(c), only constant returns to scale are experienced. The *LRATC* curve connects the lowest cost for each level of output given by the *SRATC* curves. Three such short-run cost curves for each *LRATC* curve are illustrated in Figures 4(d), 4(e), and 4(f).

as more and more outlets were added at greater distances from Park City, the distribution of the cookie dough became more and more costly. At some size, most companies reach a point where diseconomies of scale set in. Mrs. Fields Cookies went beyond that point and eventually was sold, dismantled, and reorganized.

3.c. The Minimum Efficient Scale

The law of diminishing marginal returns applies to every resource, every firm, and every industry. Whether there are economies of scale, diseconomies of scale, constant returns to scale, or some combination of these depends on the industry under consideration. No law dictates that an industry will have economies of scale, eventually followed by diseconomies of scale, although that seems to be the typical pattern. Theoretically, it is possible for an industry to experience only diseconomies of scale, only economies of scale, or only constant returns to scale.

Most industries experience both economies and diseconomies of scale. As we noted earlier, Mrs. Fields Cookies was able to achieve economies of scale as it grew from one location to 700. But the company then faced diseconomies of scale because the cookie dough was produced at one location and distributed to the outlets in premixed packages. The dough factory was large, but the distribution of dough produced diseconomies of scale that worsened as outlets farther and farther away from the factory were opened.

minimum efficient scale (MES)
The minimum point of the long-run average-total-cost curve; the output level at which the cost per unit of output is the lowest.

If the long-run average-total-cost curve reaches a minimum, the level of output at which the minimum occurs is called the **minimum efficient scale (MES)**. The *MES* varies from industry to industry; it is significantly smaller, for instance, in the production of shoes than it is in the production of cigarettes. A shoe is made by stretching leather around a mold, sewing the leather, and fitting and attaching the soles and insoles. The process requires one worker to operate just two or three machines at a time. Thus, increasing the quantity of shoes made per hour requires more building space, more workers, more leather, and more machines. The cost per shoe declines for the first few shoes made per hour, but rises thereafter. Cigarettes, on the other hand, can be rolled in a machine that can produce several thousand per hour. Producing 100 cigarettes an hour is more costly per cigarette than producing 100,000 per hour.

3.d. The Planning Horizon

The long run is referred to as a planning horizon because the firm has not committed to a specific size. It has all options available to it. In determining the size or scale to select, the manager must look at expected demand and expected costs of production and then select the size that appears to be the most profitable. Once a scale is selected, the firm is operating in the short run, since at least one of the resources is fixed. If you look back at Figure 3(b), you see that the long-run average-total-cost curve does *not* connect the minimum points of each of the short run average-total-cost curves ($SRATC_1$, $SRATC_2$, and so on). The reason is that the minimum point of a short-run average-total-cost curve is not necessarily the lowest-cost method of producing a given level of output. For instance, point A on $SRATC_3$ is much higher than point B on $SRATC_4$, but output level Q_4 could be produced at either A or B. When the quantities of all resources can be varied, the choices open to the manager are much greater than when only one or a few of the resources are variable. The manager can select the lowest cost for a given output level in the long run.

RECAP

1. Many industries are characterized by U-shaped long-run average-total-cost curves, but they need not be. There is no law dictating a U-shaped *LRATC* curve.

The law of diminishing marginal returns dictates the U shape of the short-run cost curves.

2. The long-run average-total-cost curve gets its U shape from economies and diseconomies of scale.

3. The minimum efficient scale (*MES*) is the output of a firm that is at the minimum point of a long-run average-total-cost curve.

4. The *MES* varies from industry to industry. Some industries, like the electric power distribution industry, have large economies of scale and a large *MES*. Other industries, like the fast-food industry, have a relatively small *MES*.

5. Economies of scale may result from specialization and technology. Diseconomies of scale may occur because coordination and communication become more difficult as size increases.

6. The long run is the planning period—the firm can select any size. Once a size is selected, contracts are signed, and resources are acquired, the firm is in the short run.

SUMMARY

1. **What is the law of diminishing marginal returns?**

   - According to the law of diminishing marginal returns, when successive equal amounts of a variable resource are combined with a fixed amount of another resource, there will be a point beyond which the extra or marginal product that can be attributed to each additional unit of the variable resource will decline. *§1.b*

2. **What is the relationship between costs and output in the short run?**

   - Average total cost is the cost per unit of output—total costs divided by the quantity of output produced. *§2.a*

   - The U shape of the short-run average-total-cost curve is due to the law of diminishing marginal returns. *§2.a*

   - Marginal cost is the change in total cost divided by the change in output. *§2.a.1*

   - Average total cost falls when marginal cost is less than average total cost and rise when marginal cost is greater than average total cost. Thus, the marginal-cost curve intersects the average-total-cost curve at the minimum point of the average total cost curve. *§2.a.1*

   - Costs rise as a firm supplies more output. The law of diminishing marginal returns dictates that costs rise at a decreasing and then an increasing rate as output rises. *§2.a, 2.b*

   - Fixed costs are costs that do not vary as the quantity of goods produced varies. *§2.b*

   - Variable costs rise as the quantity of goods produced rises. *§2.b*

   - Total costs are the sum of fixed and variable costs. *§2.b*

   - The short run is a period of time just short enough that the quantity of at least one of the resources cannot be altered. *§2.b*

3. **What is the relationship between costs and output in the long run?**

   - Everything is variable in the long run. *§3*

   - Economies of scale occur when the size of the firm is doubled and the output that the firm can supply more than doubles. *§3.a*

   - Diseconomies of scale occur when the size of the firm is doubled and the output that the firm can supply increases by less than double. *§3.a*

   - The U shape of the long-run average-total-cost curve is due to economies and diseconomies of scale. *§3.a*

   - Constant returns to scale occur when increases in output lead to no changes in unit costs and the quantities of all resources are variable. *§3.a*

   - Specialization can lead to economies of scale—larger size enables people to specialize in the jobs where they use their comparative advantage. *§3.b*

   - The minimum efficient scale (*MES*) occurs at the minimum point of the long-run average-total-cost curve. *§3.c*

   - The long run is the planning horizon, where all resources are variable. Once a size or scale is selected, the firm is operating in the short run. *§3.d*

KEY TERMS

average fixed cost (AFC), 474
average total cost (ATC), 471
average variable cost (AVC), 474
constant returns to scale, 477
diseconomies of scale, 477
economies of scale, 477

law of diminishing marginal
    returns, 470
long-run average-total-cost curve
    ($LRATC$), 476
marginal cost (MC), 471
minimum efficient scale
    (MES), 480

scale, 476
short-run average total cost
    ($SRATC$), 475
total costs (TC), 474
total fixed costs (TFC), 474
total variable costs (TVC), 474

EXERCISES

1. Use the following information to determine the total fixed costs, total variable costs, average fixed costs, average variable costs, average total costs, and marginal costs.

Total Output	Costs	TFC	TVC	AFC	AVC	ATC	MC
0	$100						
1	$150						
2	$225						
3	$230						
4	$300						
5	$400						

2. Use the following table to answer the questions listed below.

Total Output	Cost	TFC	TVC	AFC	AVC	ATC	MC
0	$ 20						
10	$ 40						
20	$ 60						
30	$ 90						
40	$120						
50	$180						
60	$280						

a. Calculate the total fixed costs, total variable costs, average fixed costs, average variable costs, average total costs, and marginal costs.
b. Plot each of the cost curves.
c. At what quantity of output does marginal cost equal average total cost and average variable cost?

3. Using the table in exercise 1, explain what happens to ATC when $MC > ATC$, $MC < ATC$, and $MC = ATC$.

4. Using the table in exercise 2, find the quantity where $MC = ATC$. Find the quantity where ATC is at its minimum. Find the quantity that is the most efficient operating point for the firm.

5. Describe some conditions that might cause large firms to experience inefficiencies that small firms would not experience.

6. What is the minimum efficient scale? Why would different industries have different minimum efficient scales?

7. Describe the relation between marginal and average costs. Describe the relation between marginal and average fixed costs and between marginal and average variable costs.

8. Explain why the ATC and MC curves are U-shaped.

9. Explain why the short-run marginal-cost curve must intersect the short-run average-total-cost curve at the minimum point of the ATC. Does the

marginal-cost curve intersect the average-variable-cost curve at its minimum point? What about the average-fixed-cost curve? Why doesn't the marginal-cost curve also intersect the average-fixed-cost curve at its minimum point?

10. Why does the minimum point of the average-total-cost curve show the quantity at which the firm is most efficiently supplying output in the short run?

11. Consider a firm with a fixed-size production facility as described by its existing cost curves.
    a. Explain what would happen to those cost curves if a mandatory health insurance program is imposed on all firms.
    b. What would happen to the cost curves if the plan required the firm to provide a health insurance program for each employee worth 10 percent of the employee's salary?
    c. How would that plan compare to one that requires each firm to provide a $100,000 group program that would cover all employees in the firm, no matter what the number of employees was?

12. Does the following statement make sense? "You made a real blunder. The $600 you paid for repairs is worth more than the car."

13. Explain the statement, "We had to increase our volume to spread the overhead."

14. Three college students are considering operating a tutoring business in economics. This business would require that they give up their current jobs at the student recreation center, which pay $6,000 per year. A fully equipped facility can be leased at a cost of $8,000 per year. Additional costs are $1,000 a year for insurance and $.50 per person per hour for materials and supplies. Their services would be priced at $10 per hour per person.
    a. What are fixed costs?
    b. What are variable costs?
    c. What is the marginal cost?
    d. How many students would it take to break even?

15. Express Mail offers overnight delivery to customers. It is attempting to come to some conclusion on whether to expand its facilities. Currently its fixed costs are $2 million per month, and its variable costs are $2 per package. It charges $12 per package and has a monthly volume of 2 million packages. If it expands, its fixed costs will rise by $1 million and its variable costs will fall to $1.50 per package. Should it expand?

16. Suppose the cost of starting Business A is very, very high. But once begun, the marginal cost of additional output is near zero. Draw this situation using the marginal cost curve.

17. It requires a large sum of money to produce a musical CD. The band has to be formed, practiced, and so forth. The recording studio has to be rented and the music performed and taped. Once one CD has been created, it costs virtually nothing to produce additional CDs. Draw the average and marginal costs for this business.

You can find further practice tests in the Online Quiz at **www.cengage.com/economics/boyes**.

RUNNING OVER THE SAME OLD GROUND

I enjoy a robust debate. However, I am truly perplexed that the water industry in England appears to want to re-run all the arguments that were aired in Scotland when retail competition was implemented there. Can this really be in the interests of customers or investors? Perhaps this is only initial grandstanding, but it characterised both the recent City Conference and an event at Aston University.

This grandstanding, masquerading as analysis: ignored actual costs in Scotland (one-off and ongoing); asserted that there will be no economies of scale; asserted further that diseconomies of scope are likely; failed to recognise the benefits that are being achieved in Scotland; and claimed that investors will be disadvantaged by any competition. Professor Cave completed a thorough review of competition and innovation. Many of his ideas—customer engagement, refined incentives and encouraging innovation—are being pursued in Scotland. But his review can now be updated with actual costs from Scotland. If we update the Deloitte report referred to in last week's *Utility Week* using those figures, the consultant's scenario that previously showed a negative net present value of £423 million now has a positive value of £225 million. There is still a debate to be had about potential economies of scale and scope. There seems to be overwhelming evidence on economies of scale. The market framework needs adjusting, not reinventing, to work across the whole of Great Britain. Set-up costs per customer will surely be much lower than they were in Scotland, where the two largest ongoing costs are operating the settlement and registration systems, and the regulator's levy for managing the framework. IT systems almost always have economies of scale and so do regulators. Efficient we may be, but our cost per customer is still higher than Ofwat's. Retail separation in the energy industry was followed by a series of mergers to take advantage of economies of scale. Why are the economics of customer service and billing in the water industry different? Economies of scope may be more open to debate. Others assert that separating retail must result in some loss of economies of scope, but present no evidence. I agree they are difficult to measure with any accuracy, but I am not aware of any negative impact in Scotland from separation. Indeed, Scottish Water's retail and wholesale businesses identified redundant activities that neither side wanted at separation. Given that the costs of wholesale and retail activities have fallen, economies of scope, if any, must be limited. Moreover, Bristol and Wessex operate a legally separate billing company; Glas Cymru tendered separately for retail services; Vertex fulfilled this function at United Utilities; and many companies subcontract their call centre operations, meter reading, and other activities. It seems to me that the case that there are necessarily diseconomies of scope would need a lot of proving. As to benefits, the Water Industry Commission for Scotland recently reported on benefits for businesses and public sector organisations in Scotland. Glasgow City Council is saving about £1 million a year through the competitive framework, and households across Glasgow are £3 a year better off as a result. Further tenders are under way from organisations in both public and private sectors. These benefits are greater than anything Professor Cave assumed. We separated retail without adjusting Scottish Water's regulatory capital value or allowed for return, we made retailers responsible for bad debt and required them to pre-pay the wholesaler. The wholesale business becomes less risky, yet can earn the same return. The retail business has a higher return immediately on separation and can flourish by gaining customers or being sold to a rival. As such, it is difficult to see why investors—both debt and equity—would not benefit. By all means let's have a robust debate, but we do a disservice to customers and investors by ignoring the experience gained in Scotland.

Source: Alan Sutherland, *Utility Week*, February 25, 2011.

The article concerns the possible move from a government-controlled water industry to a competitively provided water industry in Great Britain. The crux of the article is captured in the following sentence: "This grandstanding, masquerading as analysis: ignored actual costs in Scotland (one-off and ongoing); asserted that there will be no economies of scale; asserted further that diseconomies of scope are likely; failed to recognise the benefits that are being achieved in Scotland; and claimed that investors will be disadvantaged by any competition." Let's look at each phrase.

The phrase that actual costs in Scotland were ignored. What the author is referring to is that the net present value of water services went from being negative prior to competition to positive after competition. Net present value is the comparison of costs and benefits each year for many years in the future. Then each year is presented in current dollar terms—this is what present value means.

Economies and diseconomies of scale. The advocates of continued government control argue that there are no economies of scale and will surely be diseconomies of scale. Economies of scale are the reduction in per unit costs of producing and supplying water as the size or scale of the water enterprise increases. Diseconomies of scale are the increase in per unit costs of producing and supplying water as the size or scale of the water enterprise increases. The author notes that in Scotland there were large benefits from economies of scale—thus arguing against any future diseconomies of scale. He also notes that there is scant evidence of economies of scope. Economies of scope are the reduction in per unit costs when the enterprise gets large by moving into different activities. In particular, the relationship of retail and wholesale may create economies of scope when combined or may be more efficient if separated. The author believes that there are redundancies when separated that can be reduced if combined—that there are economies of scope—but has no hard evidence.

Allowing competition to prevail in the water industry drives costs down to their lowest possible level. As the author notes, the evidence in Scotland supports that theory—costs have been reduced, providing benefits to both businesses and consumers.

The Mechanics of Going from Production to Costs

1. Output and Resources

The costs of producing and selling output depend on the productivity of resources. The more home runs a baseball player hits in a season, the more valuable he is as a resource. The more welding equipment an employee for Lincoln Electric can make each month, the more valuable he or she is as an employee. They are more valuable because they generate more money for their employers; the baseball team sells more tickets, and Lincoln Electric sells more equipment. The material in this chapter is based on the relationship between resources, output, and costs; in this appendix, we look more closely at this relationship.

The **total physical product (*TPP*)** (also called *total product*) schedule and curve show how the quantity of the variable resource (employees) and the output produced are related for a certain quantity of the fixed resource. In Figure 1(a), with total output measured on the vertical axis and the number of employees measured on the horizontal axis, the combinations of output and employees trace out the *TPP* curve. Both the table and the *TPP* curve in Figure 1(a) show that as additional units of the variable resource are used with a fixed amount of another resource, total output at first rises, initially quite rapidly and then more slowly, and then declines. As the first *MC* units of the variable resource (employees) are used, each additional employee can provide more output. But at some point, there are "too many chefs stirring the broth," and each additional employee adds only a little to total output. Eventually, an additional employee actually detracts from the productivity of the other employees.

The law of diminishing marginal returns shows up more clearly with the average product and marginal-product curves, also called the **average physical product (*APP*)** and **marginal physical product (*MPP*)** curves. The average-product schedule is calculated by dividing total output by the number of employees:

$$APP = \frac{\text{total output}}{\text{number of employees}}$$

Plotting *APP* gives us Figure 1(b), a curve that rises quite rapidly and then slowly declines. The marginal-product schedule is the change in total output divided by the change in the quantity of variable resources (the number of employees):

$$MPP = \frac{\text{change in output}}{\text{change in number of employees}}$$

The *MPP* is shown in Figure 1(c); it is drawn with the *APP* curve so that we can compare *MPP* and *APP*. The *MPP* curve initially rises more rapidly than the *APP* curve, then falls more rapidly than *APP*, and eventually reaches zero. When *MPP* is zero or negative, the additional variable resources are actually detracting from the production of other resources, causing output to decline.

total physical product (*TPP*)
The maximum output that can be produced when successive units of a variable resource are added to fixed amounts of other resources.

average physical-product (*APP*)
Output per unit of resource.

marginal physical product (*MPP*)
The additional quantity that is produced when one additional unit of a resource is used in combination with the same quantities of all other resources.

FIGURE 1 Total, Average, and Marginal Product

(a) The Total Physical Product Curve

Number of Employees	Total Output	Average Physical Product	Marginal Physical Product
0	0	—	—
1	100	100	100
2	250	125	150
3	360	120	110
4	440	110	80
5	500	100	60
6	540	90	40
7	550	78.6	10
8	540	67.5	−10

(b) The Average Physical Product Curve

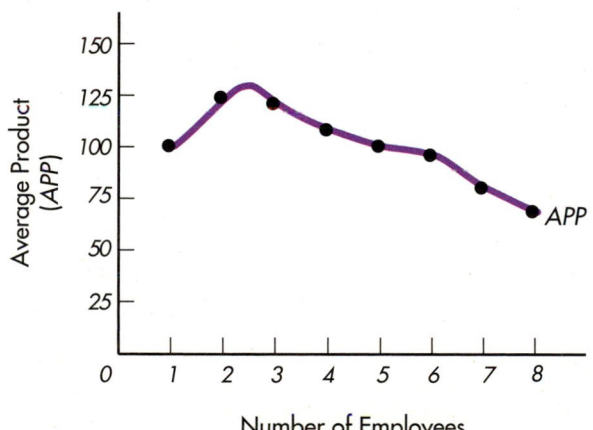

(c) The Marginal Physical Product Curve

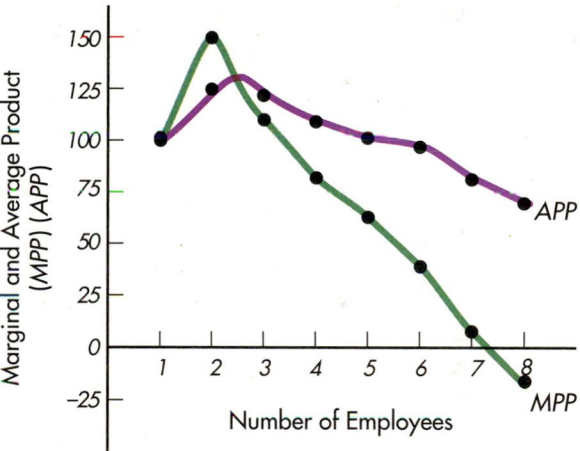

The table provides plotting data for the graphs. Total, average, and marginal product schedules and curves are shown. The total physical product (*TPP*) schedule, shown in Figure 1(a), is derived by fixing one resource. The average physical product (*APP*) and marginal physical product (*MPP*) schedules are calculated from the total physical product schedule. Average is total output divided by number of employees; marginal is the change in the total output divided by the change in the number of employees.

© 2013 Cengage Learning

You can see the relationship between *APP* and *MPP* in Figure 1(c). As long as the *MPP* is greater than the *APP*, the *APP* is rising; whenever the *MPP* is less than the *APP*, the *APP* is falling. Thus, the *MPP* and the *APP* are equal at the peak or top of the *APP* curve. This occurs at between two and three employees.

2. Productivity and Costs

The total-, average-, and marginal-physical-product schedules and curves show the relationship between quantities of resources (inputs) and quantities of output. To examine the costs of doing business rather than the physical production relationships, we must measure the costs of the resources and define how many resources are needed to supply output. This is done in Table 1. The cost per employee is $1,000. We can calculate total costs by multiplying $1,000 times the number of employees.

Notice that as output rises, costs also rise, but output rises by a larger amount at first and then by smaller and smaller amounts, whereas costs rise by a constant $1,000. This means that the cost per unit, or average cost, falls and then rises. In addition, the incremental cost, or cost per additional unit of output, initially declines and then rises. This is shown in Figure 2(b).

In Figure 2(a), the *APP* and *ATC* curves are drawn. In Figure 2(b), the *MPP* and *MC* curves are drawn. Whereas the *MPP* and *APP* curves might be described as hump-shaped, the *MC* and *ATC* curves are described as U-shaped. The shapes are due to the law of diminishing marginal returns and what is measured on the axes. In the case of the *APP* and *MPP* curves, output is on the vertical axis and number of employees is on the horizontal axis. In the case of the *ATC* and *MC* curves, costs are on the vertical axis and output on the horizontal axis. You can see that the relationship between marginal

---

FIGURE 2   Average and Marginal Costs

Quantity of Output	Total Cost	Average Cost	Marginal Cost
100	$1,000	$10	$10
250	$2,000	$8	$6.7
360	$3,000	$8.33	$9.1
440	$4,000	$9	$12.5
500	$5,000	$10	$16.7
540	$6,000	$11.1	$25
550	$7,000	$12.7	$100

(a) Compare *APP* with *ATC*

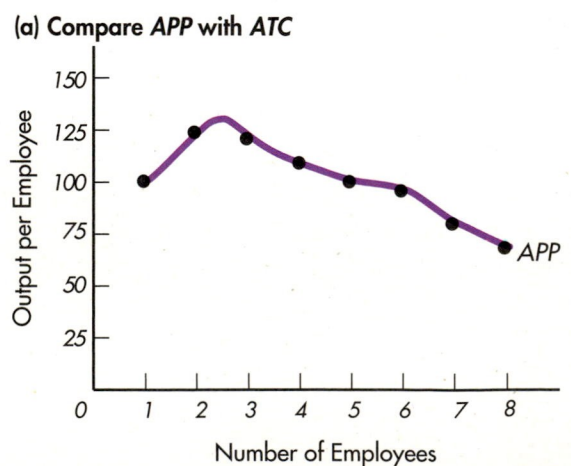

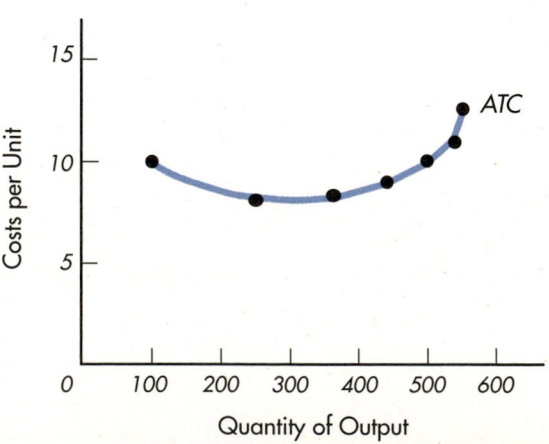

© 2013 Cengage Learning

FIGURE 2   Average and Marginal Costs (Continued)

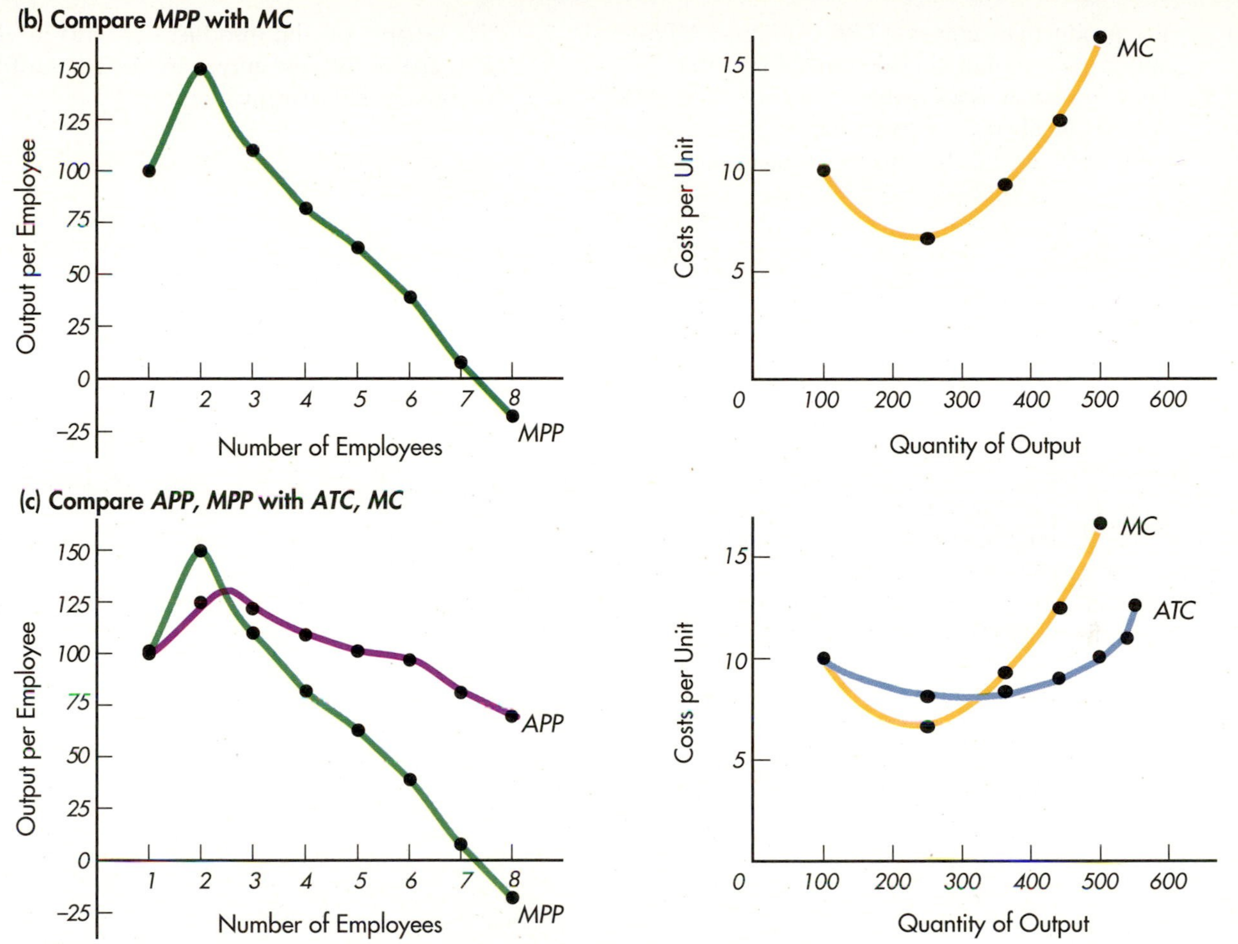

(b) Compare *MPP* with *MC*

(c) Compare *APP*, *MPP* with *ATC*, *MC*

Figure 2(a) shows the *ATC* curve and the *APP* curve. Figure 2(b) shows the *MC* curve and the *MPP* curve. The cost curves are described as U-shaped, and the product curves are described as hump-shaped. The shapes of the curves are due to the law of diminishing marginal returns. Figure 2(c) shows the relationship between average and marginal curves.

and average applies to both the product and the cost curves: Whenever the marginal is above the average, the average is rising, and whenever the marginal is below the average, the average is falling. Note also that $MPP = APP$ at the maximum point of the *APP* curve, while $MC = ATC$ at the minimum point on the *ATC* curve.

Number of Employees	Total Output	Total Cost
0	0	$ 0
1	100	$1,000
2	250	$2,000
3	360	$3,000
4	440	$4,000
5	500	$5,000
6	540	$6,000
7	550	$7,000

SUMMARY

1. The productivity curves—*TPP*, *APP*, and *MPP*—reflect the law of diminishing marginal returns. They show that as a variable resource is increased, output initially rises at an accelerating pace, then at a slower pace, and then may eventually decline. *§1*

2. The shape of the productivity curves and the U shape of the cost curves are the result of the law of diminishing marginal returns. *§2*

KEY TERMS

average physical product (*APP*), 486

marginal physical product (*MPP*), 486

total physical product (*TPP*), 486

EXERCISES

1. Explain the relationship between the shapes of the productivity curves and the shape of the cost curves. Specifically, compare the *APP* curve with the *ATC* curve and the *MPP* curve with the *MC* curve.

CHAPTER 22

Profit Maximization

© MACIEJ FROLOW/GETTY IMAGES, INC

ARIEL SKELLEY/GETTY IMAGES; LOGO: © FROXX/SHUTTERSTOCK.COM

FUNDAMENTAL QUESTIONS

1 How do firms decide how much to supply?

2 What is a market structure?

3 What is the difference between economic profit and accounting profit?

4 What is the role of economic profit in allocating resources?

You start a business. To get it off the ground, you use your own money and perhaps the money of friends and relatives. Then you put in many hours to get the business on a successful footing. If the business provides enough to match what you could have earned working for someone else (taking into account the joy of owning your own business), you consider it a success. Similarly, when you purchase the stock of a publicly traded company, you are expecting that the firm will pay you more than you could have gotten using that money in another way. If it does, then the investment is a success. We measure the success of a business in terms of profit.

1. Profit Maximization

Economists assume that the primary goal of a (for-profit) business is to make a profit. Profit is total revenue less total costs. Total revenue is the quantity of goods and services sold multiplied by the price at which they are sold, PQ. So, profit $= PQ -$ cost of land, labor, and capital.

1 How do firms decide how much to supply?

1.a. Calculation of Total Profit

Consider Table 1, in which column 1 is total output (Q), column 2 is price (P), column 3 is total revenue (TR), and total cost (TC) is listed in column 4. Profit, the difference between total revenue and total cost, is listed in column 5. For each row, column 4 is subtracted from column 3 to get profit. According to Table 1, profit is maximized if the firm supplies either 7 or 8 units of output.

1.a.1. Marginal Revenue and Marginal Cost
Another way to discover the profit-maximizing quantity of output is to compare marginal revenue and marginal cost. Look at columns 6 and 7—the two are equal at quantity 8, the profit-maximizing quantity.

Why would marginal revenue equal marginal cost when profit is maximized? *Marginal cost* is the additional cost of producing one more unit of output. *Marginal revenue* is the additional revenue obtained from selling one more unit of output. If producing and selling one more unit of output increases costs less than it increases revenue—that is, if marginal cost is less than marginal revenue—then producing and selling that unit will increase profit. Conversely, if the production of one more unit costs more than the revenue obtained from the sale of the unit, then producing and selling that unit will decrease profit. When marginal revenue is greater than marginal cost, producing more will increase profit. Conversely, when marginal revenue is less than marginal cost,

TABLE 1	Profit Maximization					
1 **Total Output** **(Q)**	**2** **Price** **(P)**	**3** **Total Revenue** **(TR)**	**4** **Total Cost** **(TC)**	**5** **Profit** **(TR − TC)**	**6** **Marginal Revenue** **(MR)**	**7** **Marginal Cost (MC)**
0	$1,900	$ 0	$1,000	−$1,000	—	—
1	$1,700	$ 1,700	$2,000	−$ 300	$1,700	$1,000
2	$1,650	$ 3,300	$2,800	$ 500	$1,600	$ 800
3	$1,600	$ 4,800	$3,500	$1,300	$1,500	$ 700
4	$1,550	$ 6,200	$4,000	$2,200	$1,400	$ 500
5	$1,500	$ 7,500	$4,500	$3,000	$1,300	$ 500
6	$1,450	$ 8,700	$5,200	$3,500	$1,200	$ 700
7	$1,400	$ 9,800	$6,000	$3,800	$1,100	$ 800
8	$1,350	$10,800	$7,000	$3,800	$1,000	$1,000
9	$1,300	$11,700	$9,000	$2,700	$ 900	$2,000

producing more will lower profit. Thus, *profit is at a maximum when marginal revenue equals marginal cost.*[1]

Consider column 6 of Table 1, where marginal revenue is listed.

Marginal revenue = change in total revenue/change in total output

$$MR = \Delta TR / \Delta Q$$

Marginal revenue (MR) is calculated by subtracting total revenue in column 3, row 1 from total revenue in column 3, row 2 and dividing that by the change in units of output from row 1 to row 2. Do this calculation for each pair of rows, and you derive marginal revenue.

It is important to understand the relationship between demand, price, and marginal revenue. The law of demand says that for a firm to increase the quantity it sells, the price has to be reduced. Consider Table 1 again. Notice that at a price of $1,700, 1 unit of output is sold. Then, when the price is reduced to $1,650, 2 units of output are sold: unit 1 at $1,650 plus unit 2 at $1,650 means total revenue of $3,300. The firm did not sell the first unit at $1,700 and then the second at $1,650; it sold both at the lower price, $1,650 each. Since total revenue changed from $1,700 to $3,300, marginal revenue is $1,600. (Change in total revenue is $3,300 − $1,700 = $1,600, and change in output is 1 unit.) MR = $1,600, but the price is $1,650. Because the firm had to set the price of units 1 and 2 at $1,650 apiece in order to sell 2 units, it lost $50 by reducing the price of the first unit from $1,700 to $1,650 and gained $1,650 by selling the second unit. The marginal revenue is less than the price.

Column 7 of the table lists marginal cost. We know from the previous chapter that

Marginal cost = change in total cost/change in total output

$$MC = \Delta TC / \Delta Q$$

Marginal cost is calculated by subtracting the total cost in row 1 from that in row 2, and dividing that by the change in units of output.

To summarize: Comparing marginal revenue and marginal cost determines whether the firm needs to supply more or less in order to maximize profit. The amount the firm should supply to maximize profit is indicated by the quantity at which marginal revenue equals marginal cost.

1.b. The Graphics of Profit Maximization

We now know that profit is maximized by finding the quantity where $MR = MC$. Let's show how this works graphically. We will use the cost curves derived in the previous chapter and put them together with the demand and marginal-revenue curves derived from Table 1 to illustrate how a firm maximizes profit. In Figure 1 we have drawn the demand and marginal-revenue curves and then added the average-total-cost and marginal-cost curves.

The profit-maximizing quantity of output is given by the quantity at which $MR = MC$. As shown in Figure 1, this occurs at quantity 8. If we then draw a vertical line up from the quantity 8 to the ATC curve, point F, we have identified the cost per unit of output. If we then draw a horizontal line from the ATC curve over to the axis, point E, we will have identified total cost, 08*FE*. This area is total cost, derived by multiplying the cost per unit of output, or ATC, by the number of units of output, 8. Because ATC

---

[1] You might notice that profit is at the maximum level for quantities of 7 and 8 units. This occurs because we are dealing with integers, 1, 2, 3, and so on, when discussing output. There would be a unique quantity for which profit is at its maximum level if we could divide the quantities into very small units instead of having to deal with integers. That unique quantity would be where $MR = MC$. Thus, we always choose the quantity at which marginal revenue and marginal cost are the same as the profit-maximizing quantity.

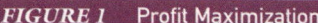

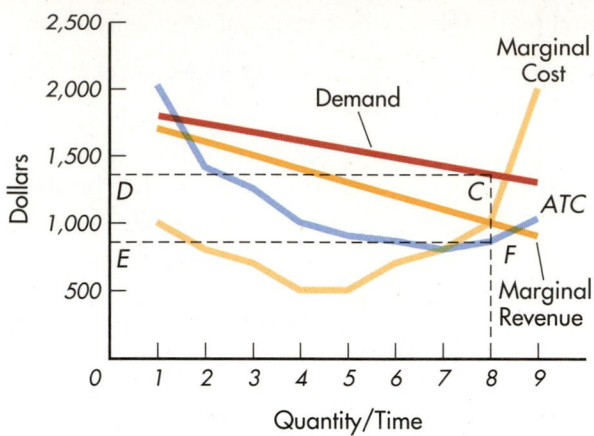

FIGURE 1 Profit Maximization

Demand and marginal revenue from Table 1 are plotted along with the *ATC* and *MC* curves from the previous chapter. The profit-maximizing quantity is given by where *MR = MC*. Profit is found by drawing a vertical line up from quantity 8 to *ATC* and then up to demand. A horizontal line from *ATC* over to the axis shows total cost, 08*FE*. Continuing the horizontal line to demand and then over to the axis shows total revenue, 08*CD*. Subtracting total cost from total revenue yields total profit, *EFCD*.

is total cost divided by Q, multiplying it by Q just leaves total cost [$ATC \times Q =$ (total cost$/Q$) $\times Q =$ total cost].

Back to the quantity of 8 and the vertical line up to the *ATC* curve. Now continue up to the demand curve point C. That identifies the price—it is the price that consumers will pay for that quantity. If we draw a horizontal line from the demand curve over to the axis, point D, we will have identified total revenue, $P \times Q = 08\,CD$. Subtracting total cost $08\,FE$ from total revenue $08\,CD$ leaves the area *EFCD*. This is total profit.

RECAP

1. The profit-maximizing rule is to produce where marginal revenue equals marginal cost.

2. Firms will supply a quantity given by the equality between marginal revenue and marginal cost.

2. Selling Environments or Market Structure

2 What is a market structure?

Profit maximization occurs when marginal revenue equals marginal cost. This means that to identify the output level that a firm will supply, all we need to do is to identify its marginal revenue and marginal cost. This is actually not very difficult, since in the short run every firm, no matter what its size, no matter what its location, and no matter what it does, has a relationship between costs and output dictated by the law of diminishing marginal returns. Thus, the cost curves can have only one shape—the U shape. The marginal-cost curve is a U-shaped curve with output on the horizontal axis and costs on the vertical axis.

The shape of the marginal-revenue curve depends on the shape of the demand curve. The shape of the demand curve, essentially the price elasticity of demand, depends on the number of substitutes, the importance of the good or service in the consumer's budget, and the length of time being considered. These factors are defined by the type of selling environment in which a firm operates. Economists have classified selling environments into four basic models. These are perfect competition, monopolistic competition, oligopoly, and monopoly.

2.a. Characteristics of the Market Structures

The selling environment in which a firm produces and sells its product, called a *market structure*, is defined by three characteristics:

- The number of firms that make up the market. In some industries, such as agriculture, there are hundreds of individual firms. In others, such as the photofinishing supplies industry, there are very few firms.
- The ease with which new firms may enter the market and begin producing the good or service. It is relatively easy and inexpensive to enter the desktop publishing business, but it is much more costly and difficult to start a new airline.
- The degree to which the products produced by the firms are different. Firms may sell identical products—wheat is wheat no matter which farm it comes from—or differentiated products—McDonald's Big Mac is not identical to Jack-in-the-Box's sirloin burger.

Table 2 summarizes the characteristics of the four market structures.

2.a.1. Perfect Competition
Perfect competition is a market structure characterized by the following:

- A very large number of firms, so large that whatever any *one* firm does has no effect on the market
- Firms that produce an identical product (perfect substitutes)
- Easy entry

In perfect competition, a very large number of firms in the market means that consumers have many options when they are deciding where to purchase the good or service, and there is no cost to the consumer of going to a different seller. In this market structure, the product is identical, so consumers do not prefer one seller to another or one brand to another. In fact, there are no brands—only identical, generic products. The large number of sellers also means that any one seller is a very small part of the market, and so its actions will not affect the others. A single firm can sell everything it wants to at the market price, but it cannot try to increase price, and it won't lower price. If a single small firm tried to raise the price even a very small amount, consumers would simply switch to another seller because consumers have a perfectly elastic demand—why pay even a penny more if you can simply turn around and get the identical item for a penny less? This situation is illustrated with a demand curve that is a horizontal line, as shown

TABLE 2	Characteristics of Market Structures		
Market Structure	**Number of Firms**	**Entry Condition**	**Product Type**
Perfect competition	Very large number	Easy	Standardized
Monopoly	One	No entry possible	Only one product
Monopolistic competition	Large number	Easy	Differentiated
Oligopoly	Few	Impeded	Standardized or differentiated

in Figure 2(a). Notice that when price goes above the existing market price, demand disappears—there is no demand except at that one price.

2.a.2. Monopoly Monopoly is a market structure in which:

- There is just one firm.
- Entry by other firms is not possible.

In a monopoly, because there is only one firm, consumers have only one place to buy the good, and there are no close substitutes. The monopolist can do anything it wants, since consumers cannot go to another seller—anything, that is, as long as it earns a profit.

The demand curve facing the single firm in a monopoly is the market demand because the firm is the only supplier in the market. This is shown in Figure 2(b). Being the only producer, the monopolist must carefully consider what price to charge. Unlike a price increase in a perfectly competitive market, a price increase in a monopoly will not drive every customer to another producer. But if the price is too high, consumers will not buy the product. Even if a monopolist had something that was needed—say, insulin or gasoline or electricity—consumers would quit buying it if the price got too high.

2.a.3. Monopolistic Competition A monopolistically competitive market structure is characterized by the following:

- A large number of firms
- Easy entry
- Differentiated products

Product differentiation distinguishes a perfectly competitive market from a monopolistically competitive market. (In both, entry is easy and there are a large number of firms.) Even though there are many firms in a monopolistically competitive market structure, the demand curve faced by *any one firm* slopes downward, as in Figure 2(c). Because each product is slightly different from all other products, each firm is like a mini-monopoly—the only producer of that specific product. The greater the differentiation among products, the less price-elastic the demand.

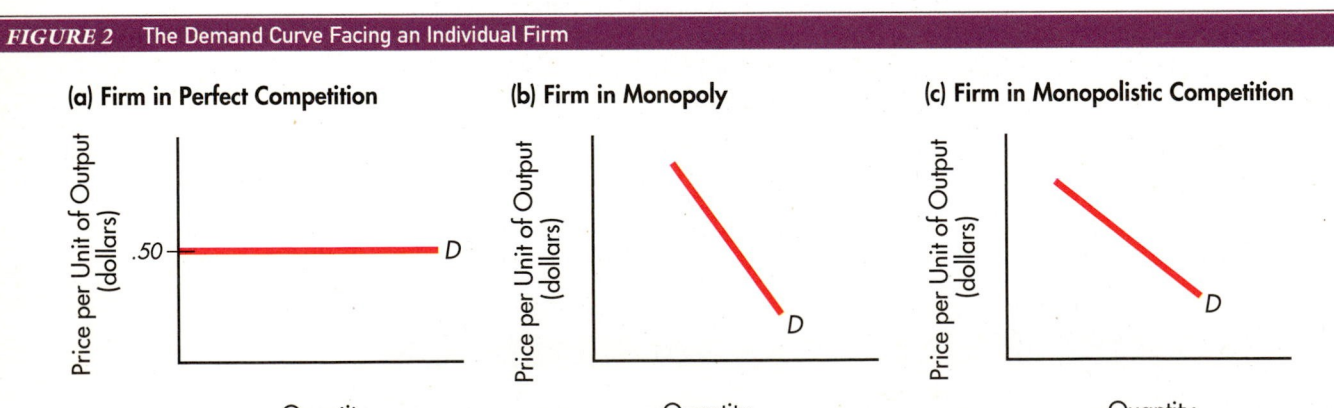

FIGURE 2 The Demand Curve Facing an Individual Firm

(a) Firm in Perfect Competition

(b) Firm in Monopoly

(c) Firm in Monopolistic Competition

The demand curve for an individual firm in perfect competition is a horizontal line at the market price, as shown in Figure 2(a). Figure 2(b) shows the market demand, which is the demand curve faced by a monopoly firm. The firm is the only supplier and thus faces the entire market demand. Figure 2(c) shows the downward-sloping demand curve faced by a firm in monopolistic competition. The curve slopes downward because of the differentiated nature of the products in the industry.

2.a.4. Oligopoly In an oligopoly:

- There are few firms—more than one, but few enough so that each firm alone can affect the market.
- Products can be either differentiated or identical. Automobile producers constitute one oligopoly, steelmakers another.
- Entry is more difficult than entry into a perfectly competitive or monopolistically competitive market, but in contrast to monopoly, entry can occur.
- Firms are *interdependent*, and this interdependence distinguishes oligopoly from the other selling environments.

The oligopolist faces a downward-sloping demand curve, but the shape of the curve depends on the behavior of competitors. Oligopoly is the most complicated of the market structure models to examine because there are so many behaviors that firms might display. Because of its diversity, many economists describe oligopoly as the most realistic of the market structure models.

2.b. Demand and Profit Maximization

Does a perfectly competitive firm maximize profit in a different manner from a monopolist or a monopolistically competitive firm? The answer is not really. Each firm maximizes profit by finding the quantity where marginal revenue equals marginal cost ($MR = MC$) and then setting the price according to demand. The difference is that for a perfectly competitive firm, demand is a horizontal line—it is perfectly elastic. For the perfectly competitive firm, the only decision is what quantity to produce. The output choice of the perfectly competitive firm is shown in Figure 3(a). The perfectly elastic demand, a horizontal line at the market price,

A cab driver in Tokyo dusts the rear seat of his cab prior to picking up passengers. Taxicabs are tightly regulated in Japan, having to serve specific districts and maintain specified quality standards. A particular company may have a government-created monopoly in a certain part of the city. Nevertheless, each cab company attempts to compete with other cab and limousine companies by providing extra service. Cleanliness and order are emphasized. Many cab drivers wear white gloves; others use feather dusters on the seats before each customer enters the cab; still others provide special music and other services.

> *Profit is maximized at the output level where marginal revenue and marginal cost are equal (MR = MC).*

means that marginal revenue, demand, and price are the same. For firms that have a downward-sloping demand curve, marginal revenue lies below demand, as shown in Figure 3(b). Thus, the process of determining the profit-maximizing quantity of output to offer for sale is to find the quantity where $MR = MC$ and then determine what price consumers are willing and able to pay to purchase the quantity of output offered by the firm (tracing a vertical line up to demand, shown in Figure 3[b]). That price is the profit-maximizing price, P^*.

RECAP

1. Economists have identified four market structures: perfect competition, monopoly, monopolistic competition, and oligopoly.

2. Perfect competition is a market structure in which many firms are producing a nondifferentiated product and entry is easy. The demand curve for a perfectly competitive firm is a horizontal line at the market price. $P = MR$.

3. Monopoly is a market structure in which only one firm supplies the product and entry cannot occur. Demand is downward sloping, and the marginal-revenue curve lies below the demand curve. $P > MR$.

4. Monopolistic competition is a market structure in which many firms are producing differentiated products and entry is easy. The demand curve is downward sloping, and marginal revenue is less than demand and less than price. $P > MR$.

5. Oligopoly is a market structure in which a few firms are producing either standardized or differentiated products and entry is possible but not easy. The distinguishing characteristic of oligopoly is that the firms are interdependent. The shape of the demand curve depends on how the firms interact—what form their interdependence takes.

FIGURE 3   Choosing Price and Quantity to Maximize Profit

(a) Perfect Competition—Horizontal Demand

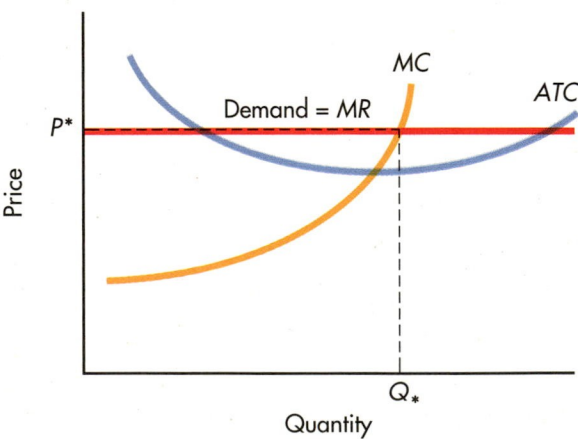

(b) Downward-Sloping Demand

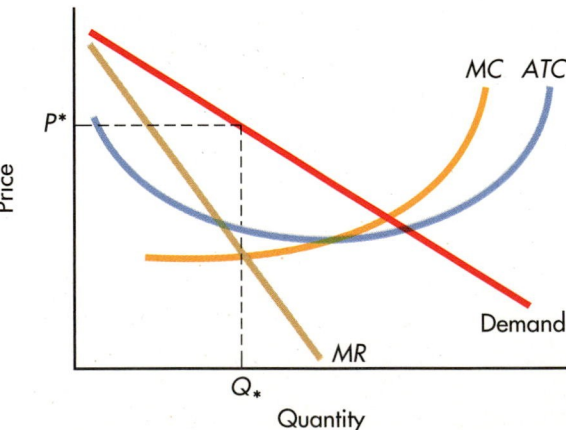

As shown in Figure 3(a), when the firm is perfectly competitive and demand for its goods is perfectly elastic, the demand and marginal revenue are the same. The firm maximizes profit by finding the quantity where $MR = MC$ and the price is the same as MR. As shown in Figure 3(b), when the firm is not perfectly competitive, the demand for its goods slopes down. As a result, marginal revenue is less than demand. The firm maximizes profit by finding the quantity where $MR = MC$ and then setting the price according to demand.

3. Measuring Economic Profit

We now know the mechanics of maximizing profit: Find the quantity where marginal revenue equals marginal cost, determine the price, and then subtract total cost from total revenue. Now let's be sure we understand what profit is. There are two measures of profit: accounting profit and economic profit.

 3 What is the difference between economic profit and accounting profit?

3.a. Calculating Profit

Accounting profit is net operating income, or

$$\text{Accounting profit} = PQ - \text{cost of land} - \text{cost of labor} - \text{cost of capital}$$

The difference between accounting profit and economic profit is the last term, cost of capital. Accounting profit measures the cost of capital as interest expense only. It does not include the cost of ownership, called **equity capital**. **Economic profit** includes all opportunity costs:

$$\text{Economic profit} = \text{accounting profit} - \text{cost of equity capital}$$

To illustrate the difference between accounting profit and economic profit, let's look at a sole proprietorship, a pet grooming business. The owner of the business, Roberto Brawning, left his job at Intel, where he earned $80,000 a year, to start the pet grooming business. He used $50,000 of his own money and a loan of $100,000, which he agreed to pay back with 7 percent interest. His business is bringing in $100,000 a year. Brawning has rent and labor expenses of $30,000. So with the interest expense of $7,000 = (7%)($100,000), Brawning's accounting profit is

$$\$100,000 - \$30,000 - \$7,000 = \$63,000$$

This does not include all of Brawning's opportunity costs, since he gave up the job with Intel and he used $50,000 of his own money. He could have used this $50,000 for anything else—such as buying stock in Microsoft. Suppose Brawning's highest-valued alternative would have returned 8 percent to him last year. It is necessary to account for this $4,000 (8% × $50,000) as well as the $80,000 job he gave up to give a true picture of the success of the grooming business. This is what economic profit does. Brawning's economic profit is

$$\text{Accounting profit} - \text{cost of ownership:}$$
$$\$63,000 - \$4,000 - \$80,000 = -\$21,000$$

Brawning is actually earning a negative economic profit. He is not earning enough to pay all of his opportunity costs. If we changed the example slightly and said that Brawning really enjoys running his own business and puts a value of $28,000 on that enjoyment, then we must add that to the $100,000 the grooming business makes in revenue. In this case, the economic profit would be positive, $7,000.

Accounting profit is always equal to or greater than economic profit. It is possible for economic profit to be negative and accounting profit positive, as in the previous example. Only if there are no equity costs are economic and accounting profit the same; otherwise accounting profit is larger than economic profit.

$$\text{Economic profit} = \text{accounting profit} - (\text{cost of equity})(\text{amount of equity})$$

accounting profit
Net operating income.

equity capital
Ownership; funds investors or owners put into a firm.

economic profit
Accounting profit minus the cost of equity capital.

The calculation of accounting and economic costs is essentially the same for a large, publicly traded company as it is for the pet grooming business. Consider the following data taken from General Motors' annual income statement.

General Motors	Millions of Dollars
Sales	193,518
Expenses	178,813
Interest expense	11,900
Net income	2,805
Cost of equity	44,235

According to the income statement, GM's accounting profit (called net income) is a positive $2,805 million. But to get a true picture of GM's performance, subtract the cost of equity capital:

$$\$2,805 - \$44,835 = -\$42,030$$

Economic profit is negative. So even though GM created a positive accounting profit this year, it did not earn enough to pay the opportunity cost of capital. In 2011, GM was generating a positive accounting profit but a negative economic profit. In 2008, GM was not even generating a positive accounting profit. Obviously, if accounting profit is negative, economic profit is negative. GM went into bankruptcy in 2009.

3.b. The Role of Economic Profit

negative economic profit
Total revenue is less than total costs, including opportunity costs.

Accounting profit is the number reported in financial pages and on financial news. But accounting profit provides very little useful information. Economic profit is a signal indicating whether resources would have a higher value in another use. When economic profit is negative, resources flow elsewhere; when it is positive, resources flow to the activity creating the profit.

4 What is the role of economic profit in allocating resources?

3.b.1. Negative Economic Profit Negative economic profit means that the resources used would have a higher value in another use. If total revenue does not pay for all costs, then owners don't get paid for their time, effort, and investments. When this occurs, the owners take their money and time and go elsewhere. If the economic profit of the pet grooming business is negative, the owner is not earning enough to pay for all of the opportunity costs. He would be better off selling the business or selling pieces of it and going to work for someone else. This is exactly the same as with GM. In fact, GM discontinued the Oldsmobile brand in 2004 and sold assets including stakes in Fiat and Fuji Heavy Industries (Subaru), as well as its locomotive manufacturing business, in 2005. In 2008 and 2009, GM asked for subsidies from the federal government because its economic profit was so negative that its executives were not sure the company could remain in business. In 2009, GM went into bankruptcy.

zero economic profit
Total revenue equal to total costs, including opportunity costs.

normal profit
The accounting profit that corresponds to a zero economic profit.

3.b.2. Zero Economic Profit When total revenue exactly equals total cost, the firm is just breaking even—economic profit is zero. Zero economic profit might sound bad, but it is not. A zero economic profit simply means that the owners could not have expected to have done better elsewhere. The investors have no incentive to sell their business and purchase something else, since they would expect to earn no more than they are currently earning. Remember, accounting profit is greater than economic profit, so even if economic profit is zero, accounting profit is positive. The accounting profit that occurs when economic profit is zero is called **normal profit**.

3.b.3. Positive Economic Profit
When total revenue is greater than total cost, the firm is said to be earning **positive economic profit**. Positive economic profit is a powerful signal in the marketplace. Whenever other investors see the positive economic profit, they want to get in on it as well. As a result, they take their funds from whatever use they are currently in and invest them in existing and new firms that will compete with the profitable firm.

Recall from Chapter 3 the scenario of the bottled water that was carried to the top of a hiking trail and sold to thirsty hikers. As more hikers showed up than there were water bottles available, stand owners were induced to increase supplies to earn greater profits, and new owners were prompted to open their own water stands. With additional firms producing the good or service, the supply increases; this will lower the price of that good or service and reduce the positive economic profit. The entry of new firms will stop once economic profit is zero.

positive economic profit
Total revenue in excess of total costs, including opportunity costs.

RECAP

1. Economic profit refers to the difference between total revenue and the full cost of inputs.

2. Accounting profit is total revenue less total costs but does not include the opportunity cost of the owner's capital.

3. Economic profit is accounting profit less the opportunity cost of the owner's capital.

4. Economic profit can be positive, negative, or zero. A positive economic profit means that the revenue exceeds the full cost of inputs, that is, that inputs are earning more than their opportunity costs. A negative economic profit means that the inputs are not earning their opportunity costs. A zero economic profit means that the inputs are just earning their opportunity costs.

5. Accounting profit is greater than economic profit. Normal profit is the accounting profit when economic profit is zero.

SUMMARY

1. How do firms decide how much to supply?

- The supply rule for all firms is to supply the quantity at which the firm's marginal revenue and marginal cost are equal. §1.a.1

2. What is a market structure?

- A market structure is a model of the producing and selling environments in which firms operate. The three characteristics that define market structure are the number of firms, the ease of entry, and whether the products are differentiated. §2.a

- A perfectly competitive market is a market in which a very large number of firms are producing an identical product and entry is easy. §2.a.1

- The demand curve facing a perfectly competitive firm is a horizontal line at the market price. *Price* = *MR*. §2.a.1

- A monopoly is a market in which there is only one firm and entry by others cannot occur. §2.a.2

- The demand curve facing a monopolist is the market demand, since there is only one firm. The demand curve slopes down. *Price* > *MR*. §2.a.2

- A monopolistically competitive market is a market in which a large number of firms are producing differentiated products and entry is easy. §2.a.3

- The demand curve facing a monopolistically competitive firm is downward sloping because of the differentiated nature of the products offered by the firm. *§2.a.3*

- An oligopoly is a market in which a few firms are producing either differentiated or nondifferentiated products and entry is possible but not easy. *§2.a.4*

- The shape of the demand curve facing a firm in an oligopoly depends on how the firms interact. *§2.a.4*

- The marginal-revenue curve for all firms except those in perfect competition is downward sloping and lies below the demand curve. The marginal-revenue curve for the perfectly competitive firm is the same as the demand curve, a horizontal or perfectly elastic curve. *§2.b*

3. **What is the difference between economic profit and accounting profit?**

   - Accountants measure only the direct costs. Economists measure all opportunity costs. *§3.a*

- Accounting profit is total revenue − cost of land, labor, and capital. Cost of capital is interest expense only. *§3.a*

- Economic profit is accounting profit − cost of ownership. *§3.a*

4. **What is the role of economic profit in allocating resources?**

   - Economic profit indicates whether resources will remain in their current activity or be distributed to a different activity. When economic profit is positive, all resources, including the firm's investors and owners, are getting paid more than they could have expected to get in another activity. Others seeing this will redirect their time and investments to that activity. Conversely, when economic profit is negative, all resources are not getting paid their opportunity costs. Resource owners will take their resources and place them into an activity that promises to pay more. *§3.b.3*

KEY TERMS

accounting profit, 499
economic profit, 499
equity capital, 499

negative economic profit, 500
normal profit, 500
positive economic profit, 501

zero economic profit, 500

EXERCISES

1. Use the following to calculate profit at each quantity of output.

(Total) Output (Q)	Price (P)	Total Revenue (TR)	Total Cost (TC)
0	$1,900	$ 0	$1,000
1	$1,700	$ 1,700	$2,000
2	$1,650	$ 3,300	$2,800
3	$1,600	$ 4,800	$3,500
4	$1,550	$ 6,200	$4,000
5	$1,500	$ 7,500	$4,500
6	$1,450	$ 8,700	$5,200
7	$1,400	$ 9,800	$6,000
8	$1,350	$10,800	$7,000
9	$1,300	$11,700	$9,000

2. Use the table in exercise 1 to calculate marginal revenue and marginal cost.

3. Use the information in exercises 1 and 2 to graphically show maximum profit. Label the profit-maximizing quantity and price, total cost, total revenue, and profit.

4. Can accounting profit be positive and economic profit negative? Can accounting profit be negative and economic profit positive? Explain.

5. Use the following information to calculate accounting profit and economic profit.

   Sales $100
   Employee expenses $40
   Inventory expenses $20
   Value of owner's labor in any other enterprise $40

6. Calculate accounting profit and economic profit for each of the following firms (amounts are in millions of dollars).

	General Motors	Barclays Bank	Microsoft
Sales	$50,091	$5,730	$2,750
Wages and salaries	$29,052	$3,932	$ 400
Cost of capital	$12,100	$ 750	$ 35
Interest on debt	$ 7,585	$ 275	$ 5
Cost of materials	$ 6,500	$ 556	$1,650

7. Which type of market characterizes most businesses operating in the United States today?

8. Given that a firm in a monopoly has no competitors producing close substitutes, does the monopolist set exorbitantly high prices?

9. Give 10 examples of differentiated products. Then list as many nondifferentiated products as you can. Which would have the largest price elasticity of demand, the differentiated or the nondifferentiated goods?

10. Describe profit maximization in terms of marginal revenue and marginal cost.

11. Use the information in the table to calculate total revenue, marginal revenue, and marginal cost. Indicate the profit-maximizing level of output. If the price was $3 and fixed costs were $5, what would variable costs be? At what level of output would the firm produce?

Output	Price	Total Costs
1	$5	$10
2	$5	$12
3	$5	$15
4	$5	$19
5	$5	$24
6	$5	$30
7	$5	$45

12. Try to classify the following firms into one of the four market structure models. Explain your choice.
    a. Rowena's gourmet foods (produces and sells a line of specialty foods)
    b. Shasta Pools & Spas (swimming pool and spa building)
    c. Merck (pharmaceuticals)
    d. US Airways
    e. UDC Homes (builders)
    f. Legal Sea Foods (restaurant chain)

13. Draw a demand curve and the corresponding marginal-revenue curve for a firm selling in a monopoly and another firm selling in perfect competition. Explain which demand curve is the most elastic. What does this mean for the marginal-revenue curve?

14. Explain why accounting profit provides very useful information. Explain why economic profit provides very useful information.

15. GM's net income in 2010 was $4.7 billion. What would its accounting profit be if its cost of equity capital was $5 billion? What would its economic profit be if its cost of equity capital was $5 billion?

You can find further practice tests in the Online Quiz at **www.cengage.com/economics/boyes**.

UBS GETS TIGHT-FISTED ON EXECUTIVE BONUSES

The Daily Telegraph (London), November 18, 2008

UBS has become the first major bank to overhaul executive compensation in an effort to prevent a repeat of past mistakes and ensure its highly paid bankers act in the long-term interests of the group.

In a radical break with tradition and setting the tone for possible changes to executive remuneration in the UK, UBS will in future claw back bonuses under a new "malus"—or negative bonus-system if the Swiss lending giant underperforms.

To ensure funds are recoverable, two-thirds of all cash bonuses will be held in escrow accounts for at least a year after payment. Share-based bonuses will not vest for three years, and executives will be "obliged to hold three quarters of their vested shares (after paying taxes) for several more years," UBS said. The same malus system will apply.

UBS is also stamping out "rewards for failure." Notice periods for executives are being reduced from 12 to six months, and pay-offs calculated against base salary and cash bonus alone— excluding any equity incentives. All bonuses paid on departure will be subject to the malus system.

"This should prevent any payments that prove to be inappropriate in the near future," the bank said. The new structure will filter down to "the so-called risk takers," the bank added.

Bankers' bonuses have been blamed for causing the financial crisis by neglecting long-term stability, and UBS's new model may be used as a template for planned remuneration reforms in the UK.

One key change is a shift to measuring performance against economic profit—a risk-weighted approach that accounts for the cost of risk capital. Economic profit will replace earnings per share targets, which can be flattered by non-trading actions such as share buy-backs. As now, bonuses will also reflect total shareholder return-share price improvement plus dividends paid.

UBS has been under intense scrutiny since requiring a Sfr60bn (pounds 33bn) Swiss state bail-out.

Three former UBS executives blamed for loading the bank with $46bn (pounds 30bn) of "toxic" debt are yet to receive Sfr60.6m they were awarded in pay-offs last year. Chairman Peter Kurer and chief executive Marcel Rohner have pledged to forgo all bonuses this year.

In the 1980s, firms decided to link executive bonuses with profits. The problem was that the linkage was to accounting profits rather than economic profits. Why does this matter? Because while accounting profits may be positive, if the cost of capital is taken into account, economic profits may be negative. The cost of capital is the opportunity cost of the money invested in a firm. If this is not included, then the profits reported for a firm are misleading.

If firms want to incentivize executives to allocate resources efficiently—to their highest valued use—the firms must link economic profit to compensation. According to the article, this is what UBS is doing. It is doing so in response to the huge bonuses paid or promised to executives who performed poorly in terms of economic profit. It is also basing the compensation on a longer time period than just one year. As we noted in the chapter in discussing GM, economic profit one year may be positive and another year negative; it is the long-term generation of economic profits that means success, not the performance of a single year.

CHAPTER 23

Perfect Competition

© MACIEJ FROLOW/GETTY IMAGES, INC

FUNDAMENTAL QUESTIONS

1 What is perfect competition?

2 What does the demand curve facing the individual firm look like, and why?

3 How does the firm maximize profit in the short run?

4 At what point does a firm decide to suspend operations?

5 When will a firm shut down permanently?

6 What is the break-even price?

7 What is the firm's supply curve in the short run?

8 What is the firm's supply curve in the long run?

9 What are the long-run equilibrium results of a perfectly competitive market?

BROCREATIVE/SHUTTERSTOCK.COM; LOGO: © FROXX/SHUTTERSTOCK.COM

The market structure of perfect competition is a model that is intended to capture the behavior of firms when there are a great many competitors offering a virtually identical product. It also captures what is known as a commodity. As we will see, there are many items that have become commoditized or are sold in a market that looks quite a bit like the model of perfect competition.

1. The Perfectly Competitive Firm in the Short Run

We begin our analysis of perfect competition by taking the viewpoint of an individual firm that is currently in business, having already procured the necessary land, tools, equipment, and employees to operate the firm. After we discuss how much the firm produces and at what price it sells its products, we discuss the entry and exit processes. We examine how someone begins a business and how someone leaves or exits a business. We then alter our perspective and look at the market as a whole. Let's start our discussion by reviewing the characteristics of a perfectly competitive market.

1.a. The Definition of Perfect Competition

A market that is perfectly competitive exhibits the following characteristics:

1. **There are many sellers.** No one firm can have an influence on market price. Each firm is such a minute part of the total market that however much the firm produces—nothing at all, as much as it can, or some amount in between—it will have no effect on the market price.
2. **The products sold by all the firms in the industry are identical.** The product sold by one firm can be substituted perfectly for the product sold by any other firm in the industry. Products are not differentiated by packaging, advertising, or quality.
3. **Entry is easy, and there are many potential entrants.** There are no huge economies of scale relative to the size of the market. Laws do not require producers to obtain licenses or pay for the privilege of producing. Other firms cannot take action to keep someone from entering the business. Firms can stop producing and can sell or liquidate the business without difficulty.
4. **Buyers and sellers have perfect information.** Buyers know the price and quantity at each firm. Each firm knows what the other firms are charging and how they are behaving.

1.b. The Demand Curve of the Individual Firm

A firm in a perfectly competitive market structure is said to be a **price taker** because the price of the product is determined by market demand and supply, and the individual firm has to sell at that price or simply not sell. In 2005, the world market price of corn was about $1 per bushel. By 2008 the world market price of corn had been driven up to about $4 per bushel and by 2011 was nearly $7 per bushel because of the use of corn in creating ethanol. Approximately 50 percent of all the corn harvested in the world comes from the United States. Nevertheless, the average farm in the United States produces an extremely small percentage of the total quantity harvested each year.

Just because the numbers are easy to deal with, let's consider the 2005 price of $1 per bushel. What would occur if, in 2005, one U.S. farmer decided to set the price of corn at $1.20 per bushel when the market price was $1 per bushel? According to the model of a perfectly competitive market, no one would purchase the higher-priced corn because the identical product could be obtained without difficulty elsewhere for $1 per bushel. In this instance, what the model predicts is what actually occurs in the real-world corn market. The grain silo owner who buys the farmers' grain would simply pass on that farm's grain and move to the next truckful of grain at $1 per bushel. By setting a price above the market price, the individual farmer may sell nothing.

Is an individual farmer likely to set a price of $.80 per bushel when the market price is $1 per bushel? Not in a perfectly competitive market. All of the produce from a single

1 What is perfect competition?

Perfect competition is a firm behavior that occurs when many firms produce identical products and entry is easy.

2 What does the demand curve facing the individual firm look like, and why?

price taker
A firm in a perfectly competitive market structure.

The individual firm in a perfectly competitive industry is a price taker because it cannot charge more than the market price, and it will not charge less.

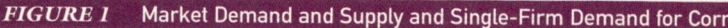

FIGURE 1   Market Demand and Supply and Single-Firm Demand for Corn

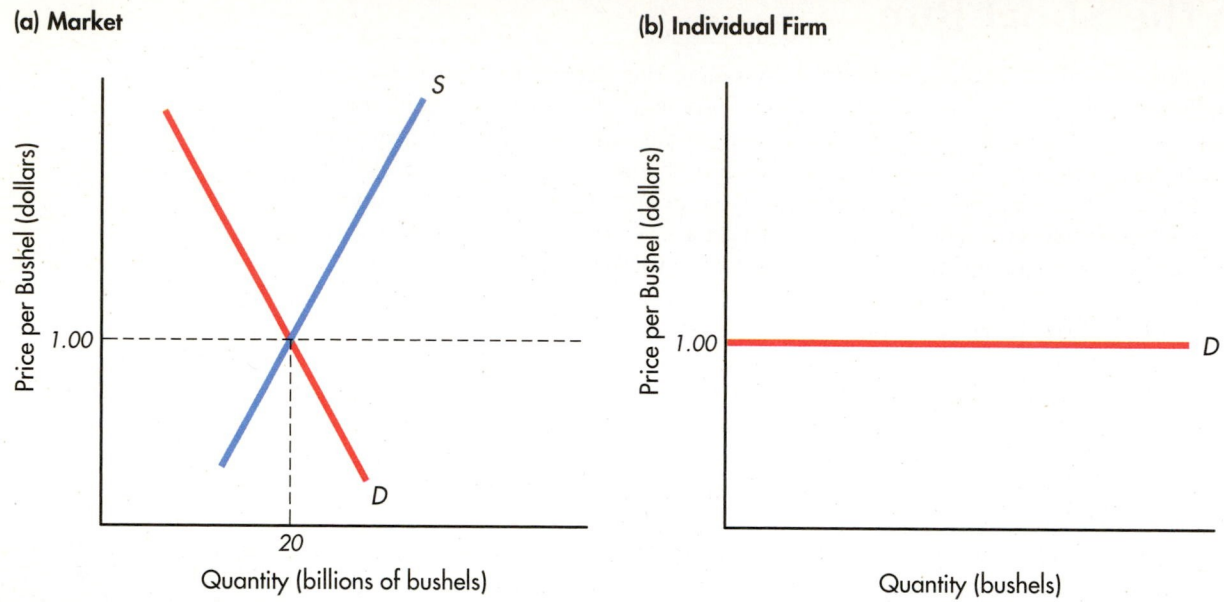

Market demand and supply are shown in Figure 1(a). The equilibrium price is $1 per bushel, and 20 billion bushels are produced and sold. The equilibrium price defines the horizontal or perfectly elastic demand curve faced by the individual perfectly competitive firm in Figure 1(b).

© 2013 Cengage Learning

farm can be sold at the market price. Why would a farmer sell at $.80 per bushel when he or she can get $1 per bushel? The individual farm is a price taker because it cannot charge more than the market price, and it will not charge less.

You could think of price takers as being the sellers in a big auction. The potential buyers bid against each other for the product until a price is determined. The product is then sold at that price. The seller has no control over the price.

Market demand and supply in a perfectly competitive market are shown in Figure 1(a). The demand curve of a single firm is shown in Figure 1(b). The horizontal line at the market price is the demand curve faced by an individual firm in a perfectly competitive market structure. It shows that the individual firm is a price taker—that the demand curve is perfectly elastic. The question facing the individual firm in a perfectly competitive industry is how much to produce, not what price to charge.

  3 How does the firm maximize profit in the short run?

1.c. Profit Maximization

We know that profit is maximized at the quantity where $MR = MC$. Profit rises when the revenue brought in by the sale of one more unit (one more bushel) is greater than the cost of producing that unit. Conversely, if the cost of producing one more unit is greater than the amount of revenue brought in by selling that unit, profit declines with the production of that unit. Only when marginal revenue and marginal cost are the same is profit at a maximum, as illustrated in Figure 2.[1]

© froxx/Shutterstock.com

---

[1] Marginal revenue and marginal cost could be equal at small levels of production and sales, such as with the first bushel, but profit would definitely not be at its greatest level. The reason is that marginal cost is falling with the first unit of production—the marginal cost of the second unit is less than the marginal cost of the first unit. Since marginal revenue is the same for both the first and the second units, profit actually rises as quantity increases. Profit maximization requires both that marginal revenue equal marginal cost and that marginal cost be rising. Since marginal revenue and marginal cost are the same for the ninth bushel and marginal cost is rising, the ninth bushel is the profit-maximizing level of output.

FIGURE 2   Profit Maximization

Total Output (Q)	Price (P)	Total Revenue (TR)	Total Cost (TC)	Total Profit (TR − TC)	Marginal Revenue (MR)	Marginal Cost (MC)	Average Total Cost (ATC)
0	$1	$ 0	$ 1.00	−$1.00	$1	—	—
1	$1	$ 1	$ 2.00	−$1.00	$1	$1.00	$2.00
2	$1	$ 2	$ 2.80	−$ .80	$1	$ .80	$1.40
3	$1	$ 3	$ 3.50	−$ .50	$1	$ .70	$1.1667
4	$1	$ 4	$ 4.00	$ .00	$1	$ .50	$1.00
5	$1	$ 5	$ 4.50	$ .50	$1	$ .50	$ .90
6	$1	$ 6	$ 5.20	$ .80	$1	$ .70	$ .8667
7	$1	$ 7	$ 6.00	$1.00	$1	$ .80	$ .8571
8	$1	$ 8	$ 6.86	$1.14	$1	$ .86	$ .8575
9	$1	$ 9	$ 7.86	$1.14	$1	$1.00	$ .8733
10	$1	$10	$ 9.36	$ .64	$1	$1.50	$ .936
11	$1	$11	$12.00	−$1.00	$1	$2.64	$1.09

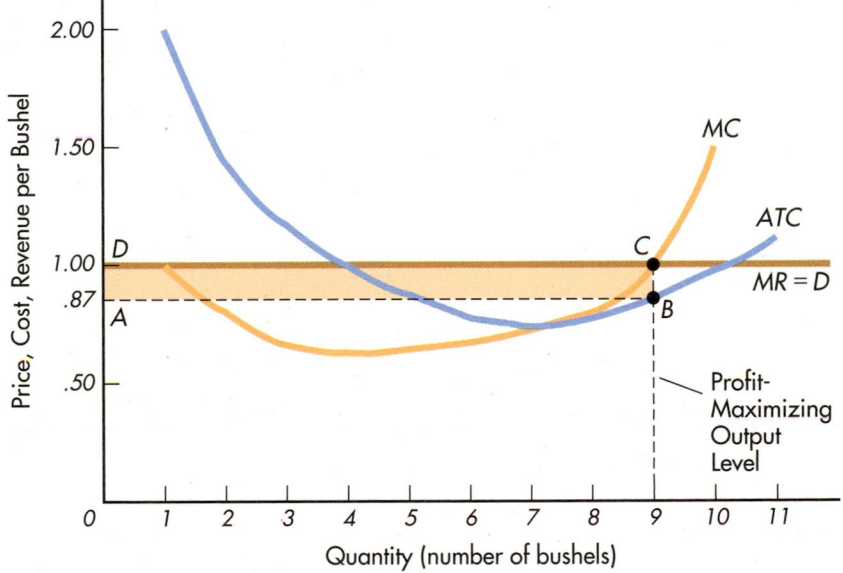

The profit-maximization point for a single firm is shown for a price of $1 per bushel. Marginal revenue and marginal cost are equal at the profit-maximization point, 9 bushels. At quantities less than 9 bushels, marginal revenue exceeds marginal cost, so increased production would raise profits. At quantities greater than 9, marginal revenue is less than marginal cost, so reduced production would increase profits. The point at which profit is maximized is shown by the highlighted row in the table. The profit per unit is the difference between the price line and the average-total-cost curve at the profit-maximizing quantity. Total profit ($1.14) is the rectangle *ABCD*, an area that is equal to the profit per unit times the number of units.

With a price of $1 per bushel, the individual farm maximizes profit by producing 9 bushels. We can illustrate how much profit the individual firm in perfect competition earns, or whether it makes a loss, by calculating total costs at the quantity where $MR = MC$ and comparing that with total revenue.

> *Profit maximization occurs at the output level where MR = MC.*

4 At what point does a firm decide to suspend operations?

MR = MC is the profit-maximizing or loss-minimizing output level.

In Figure 2, the price per bushel of $1 exceeds the cost per bushel (average total cost, $.8733) by the distance BC ($.1267) when 9 bushels are produced. This amount ($.1267) is the profit per bushel. The total profit is the rectangle $ABCD$ (highlighted in the table).

Figure 3 illustrates what happens to the individual firm in a perfectly competitive market as the market price changes. The only curve in Figure 3 that changes as a result of the price change is the perfectly elastic demand curve (which is also the price line and the

---

FIGURE 3 Loss Minimization

Total Output (Q)	Price (P)	Total Revenue (TR)	Total Cost (TC)	Total Profit (TR − TC)	Marginal Revenue (MR)	Marginal Cost (MC)	Average Total Cost (ATC)
0	$.70	$ 0	$ 1.00	−$1.00	—	—	—
1	$.70	$ .70	$ 2.00	−$1.30	$.70	$1.00	$2.00
2	$.70	$1.40	$ 2.80	−$1.40	$.70	$ .80	$1.40
3	$.70	$2.10	$ 3.50	−$1.40	$.70	$ .70	$1.1667
4	$.70	$2.80	$ 4.00	−$1.20	$.70	$ .50	$1.00
5	$.70	$3.50	$ 4.50	−$1.00	$.70	$ .50	$ .90
6	$.70	$4.20	$ 5.20	−$1.00	$.70	$ .70	$ .8667
7	$.70	$4.90	$ 6.00	−$1.10	$.70	$ .80	$ .8571
8	$.70	$5.60	$ 6.86	−$1.26	$.70	$ .86	$ .8575
9	$.70	$6.30	$ 7.86	−$1.56	$.70	$1.00	$ .8733
10	$.70	$7.00	$ 9.36	−$2.36	$.70	$1.50	$ .936
11	$.70	$7.70	$12.00	−$4.30	$.70	$2.64	$1.09

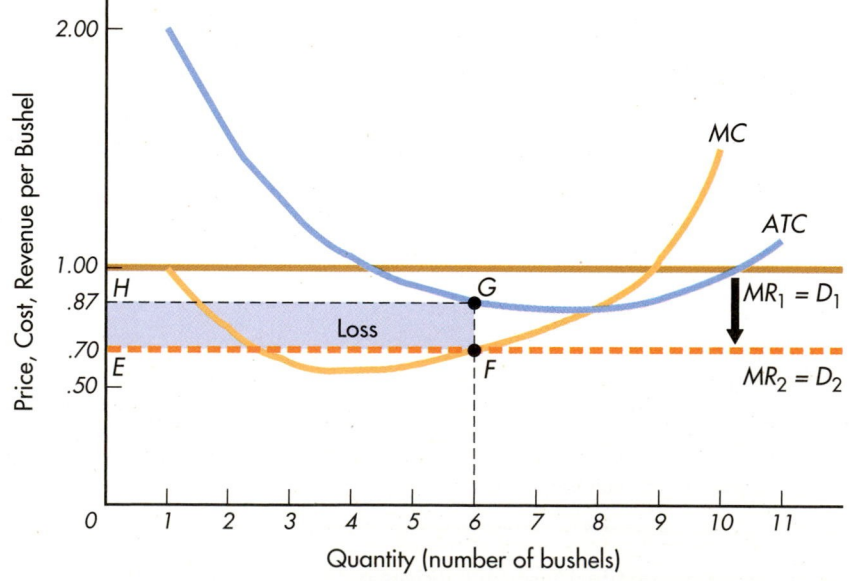

In Figure 3 the price changed from $1 per bushel to $.70 per bushel. The profit-maximization, or loss-minimization, point is the level of output where $MR = MC$. If, at this output level, the price is less than the corresponding average-cost curve, the firm makes a loss. At a price of $.70 per bushel, a loss is incurred—the loss-minimizing level of output is 6 bushels, as shown by the highlighted bar in the table. The total loss is the rectangle $EFGH$.

marginal-revenue curve). Let's assume that the market price changes to $.70 per bushel, so that the individual farm's demand curve shifts down. Whether the firm is making a profit is determined by finding the new quantity at which the new marginal-revenue curve, MR_2, equals the marginal-cost curve, at point F, and then tracing a vertical line from point F to the ATC curve at point G. The distance FG is the profit or loss per unit of output. If the demand curve is above the ATC curve at that point, the firm is making a profit. If the ATC curve exceeds the price line, as is the case in Figure 3, the firm is suffering a loss.

A firm cannot make a profit as long as the price is less than the average-cost curve, because the cost per bushel (ATC) exceeds the revenue per bushel (price). At a price of $.70 per bushel, marginal revenue and marginal cost are equal as the sixth bushel is produced (see Figure 3 and the highlighted bar in the table), but the average total cost is greater than the price. The cost per bushel (ATC) is $.8667, which is higher than the price or revenue per bushel of $.70. Thus, the firm makes a loss, shown as the rectangle $EFGH$ in Figure 3.

Recall that an economic loss means that opportunity costs are not being covered by revenues; that is, the owners could do better in another line of business. An economic loss means that a firm is confronted with the choice of whether to continue producing, shut down temporarily, or shut down permanently. The decision depends on which alternative has the lowest opportunity cost.

1.d. Short-Run Break-Even and Shutdown Prices

5 When will a firm shut down permanently?

In the short run, certain costs, such as rent on land and equipment, must be paid whether or not any output is produced. These are the firm's fixed costs. If a firm has purchased equipment and buildings but does not produce, the firm still has to pay for the equipment and buildings. Thus, the decision about whether to produce or to temporarily suspend operations depends on which option promises the lesser costs. In order to continue producing in the short run, the firm must earn sufficient revenue to pay all of the *variable* costs (the costs that change as output changes), because then the excess of revenue over variable costs will enable the firm to pay some of its fixed costs. If the firm cannot pay all the variable costs out of revenue, then it should suspend operations temporarily because if it continues to produce, it must pay not only its fixed costs but also those variable costs in excess of revenue.

Does suspending operations mean quitting the business altogether—shutting down permanently? It may, but it need not. The decision depends on the long-term outlook. If the long-term outlook indicates that revenue will exceed costs, then production is warranted. However, if the outlook is for continued low prices and inability to cover costs, a firm would be better off quitting the business altogether.

To see how producing at a loss can at times be better than not producing at all, let's return to the individual farm in Figure 4. At a price of $.70 per bushel, the output at which $MR = MC$ is 6 bushels, as shown by the highlighted bar in the table.

At 6 bushels, total revenue is $4.20 and total cost is $5.20. The farm loses $1 by producing 6 bushels. The question is whether to produce at all. If production is stopped, the fixed cost of $1 must still be paid. Thus, the farmer is indifferent between producing 6 bushels and losing $1 or shutting down and losing $1. Should the price be less than the minimum point of the average-variable-cost curve (AVC), as would occur at any price less than $P = $.70 per bushel, the farm is not earning enough to cover its variable costs (see Figure 4 and the accompanying table). By continuing to produce, the farm will lose more than it would lose if it suspended operations or shut down until the outlook improved. The minimum point of the average-variable-cost curve is the **shutdown price**. If the market price is less than the minimum point of the AVC curve, then the firm will incur fewer losses if it does not produce than if it continues to produce in the short run.

shutdown price
The minimum point of the average-variable-cost curve.

FIGURE 4   Shutdown Price

Total Output (Q)	Price (P)	Total Revenue (TR)	Total Cost (TC)	Total Profit (TR − TC)	Marginal Revenue (MR)	Marginal Cost (MC)	Average Total Cost (ATC)	Average Variable Cost (AVC)
0	$.70	$ 0	$ 1.00	−$1.00	—	—	—	—
1	$.70	$ .70	$ 2.00	−$1.30	$.70	$1.00	$2.00	$1.00
2	$.70	$1.40	$ 2.80	−$1.40	$.70	$ .80	$1.40	$ .90
3	$.70	$2.10	$ 3.50	−$1.40	$.70	$ .70	$1.1667	$ .833
4	$.70	$2.80	$ 4.00	−$1.20	$.70	$ .50	$1.00	$ .75
5	$.70	$3.50	$ 4.50	−$1.00	$.70	$ .50	$ .90	$ .70
6	$.70	$4.20	$ 5.20	−$1.00	$.70	$ .70	$ .8667	$ .70
7	$.70	$4.90	$ 6.00	−$1.10	$.70	$ .80	$ .8571	$ .714
8	$.70	$5.60	$ 6.86	−$1.26	$.70	$ .86	$ .8575	$ .7325
9	$.70	$6.30	$ 7.86	−$1.56	$.70	$1.00	$ .8733	$ .7622
10	$.70	$7.00	$ 9.36	−$2.36	$.70	$1.50	$ .936	$ .836
11	$.70	$7.70	$12.00	−$4.30	$.70	$2.64	$1.09	$1.00

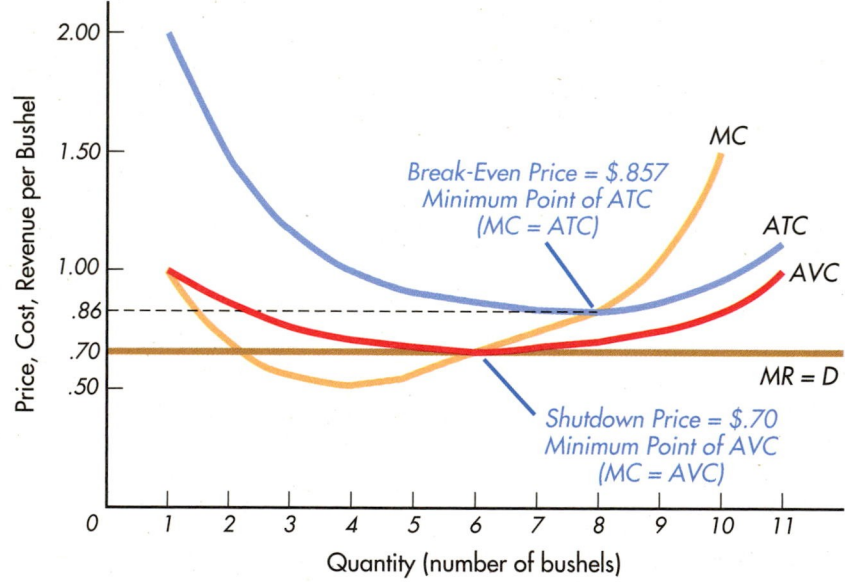

When the firm is making a loss, it must decide whether to continue producing or to suspend operations and not produce. The decision depends on which alternative has higher costs. When the price is equal to or greater than the minimum point of the average-variable-cost curve, $.70, the firm is earning sufficient revenue to pay for all of the variable costs. When the price is less than the minimum point of the average-variable-cost curve, the firm is not covering all of its variable costs. In that case the firm is better off shutting down its operations. For this reason, the minimum point of the *AVC* curve is called the *shutdown price*. The *break-even price* is the minimum point of the *ATC* curve because at that point all costs are being paid.

At prices above the minimum point of the average-variable-cost curve, the excess of revenue over variable costs means that some fixed costs can be paid. A firm is better off producing than shutting down because, by producing, it is able to earn enough revenue to pay all the variable costs and some of the fixed costs. If the firm does not produce, it will still have to pay all of the fixed costs. When the price equals the minimum point of the average-total-cost curve, the firm is earning just enough revenue to pay for all of its costs, fixed and variable. This point is called the **break-even price**. At the break-even price, economic profit is zero—all costs are being covered, including opportunity costs. Because costs include the opportunity costs of the resources already owned by the entrepreneur—his or her own labor and capital—zero economic profit means that the entrepreneur could not do better in another activity. Zero economic profit is normal profit, profit that is just sufficient to keep the entrepreneur in this line of business.

The shutdown price is the price that is equal to the minimum point of the *AVC* curve. The break-even price is the price that is equal to the minimum point of the *ATC* curve. In the examples just discussed, the firm continues to operate at a loss because variable costs are being covered and the long-term outlook is favorable. Many firms decide to operate for a while at a loss, then suspend operations temporarily, and finally shut down permanently. A firm will shut down permanently if it cannot pay all its costs in the long run. In the long run, the minimum point of the *ATC* curve is the permanent shutdown point. Price must exceed the minimum point of the *ATC* curve in the long run if the firm is to remain in business. Of the 80,000 businesses that shut down permanently in 1997, most went through a period in which they continued to operate even though revenue was not large enough to pay variable costs.

break-even price
A price that is equal to the minimum point of the average-total-cost curve.

 6 What is the break-even price?

1.e. The Firm's Supply Curve in the Short Run

As long as revenue equals or exceeds variable costs, an individual firm will produce the quantity at which marginal revenue and marginal cost are equal. This means that the individual firm's supply curve is the portion of the *MC* curve that lies above the *AVC* curve. An individual firm's supply curve shows the quantity that a firm will produce and offer for sale at each price. When the price is less than the minimum point of the *AVC* curve, a firm incurs fewer losses from not producing than from producing. The firm thus produces and supplies nothing, and there is no supply curve. When the price is greater than the minimum point of the *AVC* curve, the firm will produce and offer for sale the quantity yielded at the point where the *MC* curve and the *MR* line intersect for each price. The supply curve is thus the *MC* curve. The portion of the *MC* curve lying above the minimum point of the *AVC* curve is the individual firm's supply curve in the short run.

 7 What is the firm's supply curve in the short run?

In our example of an individual farm illustrated in Figure 4, nothing is produced at a price of $.50 per bushel. At $.70 per bushel, the farm produces 6 bushels in the short run; at $1 per bushel, the farm produces 9 bushels. The higher the price, the greater the quantity produced and offered for sale.

A firm may continue to produce and offer its products for sale even if it is earning a negative economic profit, as long as it earns enough revenue to pay its variable costs and expects revenue to grow enough to pay all costs eventually. If the business does not improve and losses continue to pile up, the firm will shut down permanently. In the long run, the firm must be able to earn enough revenue to pay all of its costs. If it does not, the business will not continue to operate. If the firm does earn enough to pay its costs, the firm will produce and offer for sale the quantity of output yielded at the point where $MR = MC$. This means that the firm's long-run supply curve is the portion of its *MC* curve that lies above the minimum point of the *ATC* curve.

RECAP

1. The firm maximizes profit or minimizes losses by producing at the output level at which *MR* and *MC* are equal.

2. In order to remain in business, the firm must earn sufficient revenue to pay for all of its variable costs. The shutdown price is the price that is just equal to the minimum point of the *AVC* curve.

3. The firm's break-even price is the price that is just equal to the minimum point of the *ATC* curve.

4. The portion of the marginal-cost curve lying above the minimum point of the *AVC* curve is the firm's short-run supply curve.

5. The portion of the marginal-cost curve lying above the minimum point of the *ATC* curve is the firm's long-run supply curve.

2. The Long Run

8 What is the firm's supply curve in the long run?

In the short run, at least one of the resources *cannot* be altered. This means that new firms cannot be organized and begin producing. Thus the supply of firms in an industry is fixed in the short run. In the long run, of course, all quantities of resources can be changed. Buildings can be built or purchased and machinery accumulated and placed into production. New firms may arise as entrepreneurs who are not currently in the industry see that they could earn more than they are currently earning and decide to expand into new businesses.

> Exit and entry are long-run phenomena.

Entry and exit can both occur in the long run. On average, 4.5 percent of the total number of farms in the United States go out of business each year, and more than half of them file for bankruptcy.

How does exit occur? Entrepreneurs may sell their businesses and move to another industry, or they may use the bankruptcy laws to exit the industry. In the United States, a sole proprietor or partnership may file Chapter 13 personal bankruptcy; a corporation may file Chapter 7 bankruptcy or a Chapter 11 reorganization; a farmer may file Chapter 12. The chapters refer to specific sections of the Bankruptcy Law. From the mid-1970s to the present, the average birthrate for all industries (the percent of total businesses that begin during a year) has been just over 11.2 percent, and the average death rate (the percent of total businesses that disappear during a year) has been 9.6 percent.

Bankruptcy laws in the developed nations are similar to those in the United States. Although most nations have some laws regarding going out of business, the laws are not enforced or used in many emerging-market nations. In most less-developed countries, a farmer goes out of business by simply walking away. The farmer does not hold title to the land in the first place, and so when the land no longer provides support for the family, it is left untilled and uncared for.

2.a. The Market Supply Curve and Exit and Entry

> When additional firms enter the industry and begin producing the product, the market supply curve shifts out.

Recall from Chapter 3 that the market supply curve shifts when the number of suppliers changes. The market supply curve is the sum of all the individual firms' supply curves. In the corn-producing business, when new farms enter the market, the total quantity of corn supplied at each price increases. In other words, entry causes the market supply curve to shift out to the right.

> When firms leave the industry, the market supply curve shifts in.

Conversely, exit means that there are fewer producers and lower quantities supplied at each price, and there is a leftward or inward shift of the market supply curve. Suppose some existing firms are not covering their costs and believe that the future is not bright enough to warrant continued production. As a result, they shut down their operations and sell their equipment and land. As the number of farms in the industry declines, everything else held constant, the market supply curve shifts to the left—as long as those remaining in the business produce the same quantity as they did before the farms exited, or less.

2.b. Normal Profit in the Long Run

One of the principal characteristics of the perfectly competitive market structure is that entry and exit can occur easily. Entry and exit occur whenever firms are earning more or less than a *normal profit* (zero economic profit). When a normal profit is being earned, there is no entry or exit. This condition is the long-run equilibrium.

The process of establishing the long-run position is shown in Figure 5. The market demand and supply curves for corn are shown in Figure 5(a), and the cost and revenue curves for a representative firm in the industry are shown in Figure 5(b). Let's assume that the market price is $1. Let's also assume that at $1 per bushel, the demand curve facing the individual farm (the price line) is equal to the minimum point of the *ATC* curve. The quantity produced is 9 bushels. The individual farm and the industry are in equilibrium. There is no reason for entry or exit to occur, and there is no reason for individual farms to change their scale of operation.

To illustrate how the process of reaching the long-run equilibrium occurs in the perfectly competitive market structure, let's begin with the corn market in equilibrium at $S_1 = D_1$. Now, the United States starts using corn in the production of ethanol. As a result of the increased demand, as shown by the rightward shift of the demand curve to D_2 in Figure 5(a), the market price is driven up to $2.50 per bushel, where the new market demand curve intersects the initial market supply curve, S_1. This raises the demand curve for the individual farm to the horizontal line at $2.50 per bushel. In the short run, the individual farms in the industry increase production (by adding variable inputs) from 9 bushels to 10 bushels, the point in Figure 5(b) where $MC = MR_2 = \$2.50$, and earn economic profit of the amount shown by the yellow rectangle.

The above-normal profit attracts others to the farming business. The result of the new entry and expansion is a rightward shift of the market supply curve. How far does the market supply curve shift? It shifts until the market price is low enough that firms in the industry earn normal profit.

As the demand for corn continues to rise, the price continues to rise, and in the long run new acres are used to produce more corn. The process ends when firms are all earning just a normal profit. As a very simple example, let us suppose that the costs of doing business do not rise as the market expands. Then, if the market supply curve shifts to S_2, the new market price, $2.50, is less than the former price of $4 but still high enough for firms to earn above-normal profits. These profits are sufficient inducement for more firms to enter, causing the supply curve to shift farther right. The supply curve continues to shift until there is no incentive for additional firms to enter—that is, until firms are earning the normal profit, where price is equal to the minimum *ATC*, shown as S_3 in Figure 5(a). When the adjustment stops, firms are just earning the normal profit.

2.c. The Predictions of the Model of Perfect Competition

According to the model of perfect competition, whenever *above-normal* profits (positive economic profits) are earned by existing firms, entry occurs until a *normal* profit (zero economic profit) is earned by all firms. Conversely, whenever economic losses occur, exit takes place until a normal profit is made by all remaining firms.

The price taker can do nothing but accept and sell at the market price. When times are bad, the market price may be so low that some firms must exit the market. In this photo, a firm is going out of business, liquidating all its assets, and eventually shutting its doors.

In the long run, perfectly competitive firms earn normal profits.

 9 What are the long-run equilibrium results of a perfectly competitive market?

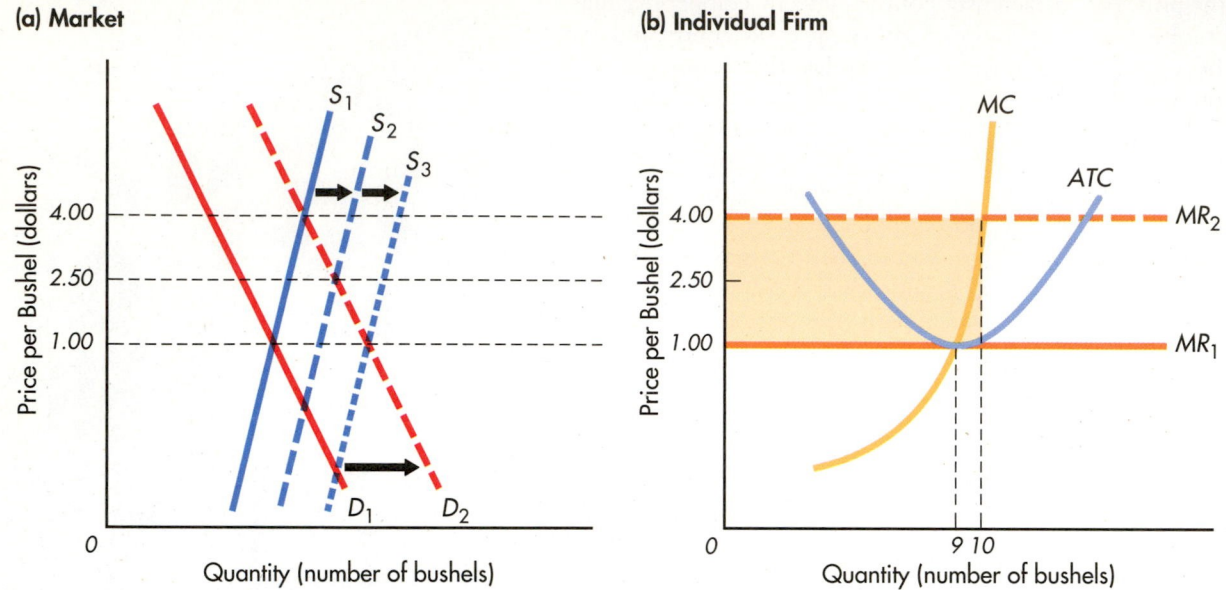

FIGURE 5   Economic Profit in the Long Run

(a) Market

(b) Individual Firm

Market demand and supply determine the price and the demand curve faced by the single perfectly competitive firm. At a price of $1 per bushel, the individual farm is earning normal profit. The demand for corn to use in ethanol production drives the price of corn up to $4 per bushel. At $4 per bushel, the single farm makes a profit equal to the yellow rectangle. Above-normal profits induce new farms to begin raising corn and existing farms to increase their production.

© 2013 Cengage Learning

It is so important to keep in mind the distinctions between economic and accounting terms that we repeatedly remind you of them. A *zero economic profit* is a *normal accounting profit*, or just *normal profit*. It is the profit that is just sufficient to keep a business owner or investors in a particular line of business, the point where revenue exactly equals total opportunity costs. Business owners and investors earning a normal profit are earning enough to cover their opportunity costs—they could not do better by changing—but they are not earning more than their opportunity costs. An *economic loss* refers to a situation in which revenue is not sufficient to pay all of the opportunity costs. A firm can earn a positive accounting profit and yet be experiencing a loss, not earning a normal profit.

> *Perfect competition results in economic efficiency.*

The long-run equilibrium position of the perfectly competitive market structure shows firms producing at the minimum point of their long-run average-total-cost curves. If the price is above the minimum point of the *ATC* curve, then firms are earning above-normal profits, and entry will occur. If the price is less than the minimum of the *ATC* curve, exit will occur. Only when price equals the minimum point of the *ATC* curve will neither entry nor exit take place.

Producing at the minimum of the *ATC* curve means that firms are producing with the lowest possible costs. Changing the way they produce won't allow them to produce less expensively. Altering the resources they use won't allow them to produce less expensively.

economic efficiency
The situation in which the price of a good or service just covers the marginal cost of producing that good or service and people are getting the goods and services that they want.

Firms produce at a level where marginal cost and marginal revenue are the same. Since marginal revenue and price are the same in a perfectly competitive market, firms produce where marginal cost equals price. This means that firms are employing resources until the marginal cost to them of producing the last unit of a good just equals the price of the last unit. Moreover, since price is equal to marginal cost, consumers are paying a price that is as low as it can get; the price just covers the marginal cost of producing that good or service. There is no waste—no one could be made better off without making someone else worse off. Economists refer to this result as **economic efficiency**.

2.c.1. Consumer and Producer Surplus

Efficiency is the term economists give to the situation in which firms are producing with as little cost as they can (at the minimum point of the *ATC* curve) and consumers are getting the products they desire at a price that is equal to the marginal cost of producing those goods. To say that a competitive market is efficient is to say that all market participants get the greatest benefits possible from market exchange.[2]

We measure the benefits from market exchange (the gains from trade) as the sum of the consumer surplus and the producer surplus. Consumer surplus is the difference between what consumers would be willing and able to pay for a product and the price they actually have to pay to buy the product. **Producer surplus** is the difference between the price that firms would have been willing and able to accept for their products and the price they actually receive.

Since the firm is willing to sell the product at the marginal cost, as long as marginal cost is greater than average variable cost, and since the firm receives the market price, the difference between the two is a bonus to the firm, a bonus resulting from market exchange. This bonus is producer surplus.

producer surplus
The difference between the price firms would have been willing to accept for their products and the price they actually receive.

Consumer surplus = area above equilibrium price and below the demand curve

Producer surplus = area below equilibrium price and above the supply curve

Figure 6 illustrates consumer and producer surplus in a competitive market. The sum of producer and consumer surplus represents the total benefits that come from

---

FIGURE 6   Producer and Consumer Surpluses

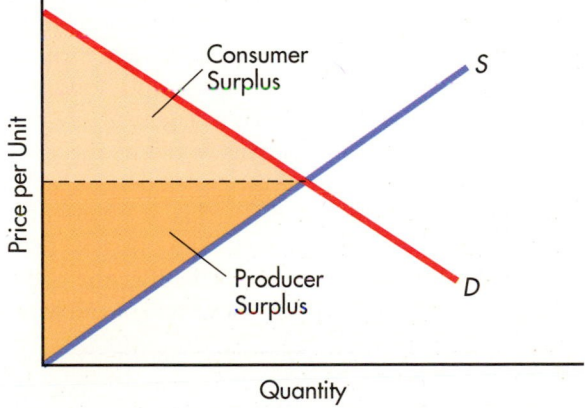

Since the firm is willing to sell the product at the marginal cost and since the firm receives the market price, the difference between the two is a bonus to the firm, a bonus of market exchange. This bonus is producer surplus. The total producer surplus in a competitive market is the sum of the producer surplus received by each firm in the market. Producer surplus is the area below the price line and above the supply curve. Also pictured is total consumer surplus. Recall that consumer surplus is the difference between what the consumer would be willing to pay for a good (the demand curve) and the price actually paid. The sum of producer and consumer surplus represents the total benefits that come from exchange in the market: benefits that accrue to the consumer plus those that accrue to the firm.

---

[2] Economists have classified efficiency into several categories. *Productive efficiency* refers to the firm's use of the least-cost combination of resources to produce any output level. This output level may not be the goods that consumers want, however. *Allocative efficiency* is the term given to the situation in which firms are producing the goods that consumers most want, and consumers are paying a price that is just equal to the marginal cost of producing those goods. Allocative efficiency may occur when firms are not producing at their most efficient level. Economic efficiency exists when both productive and allocative efficiency occur.

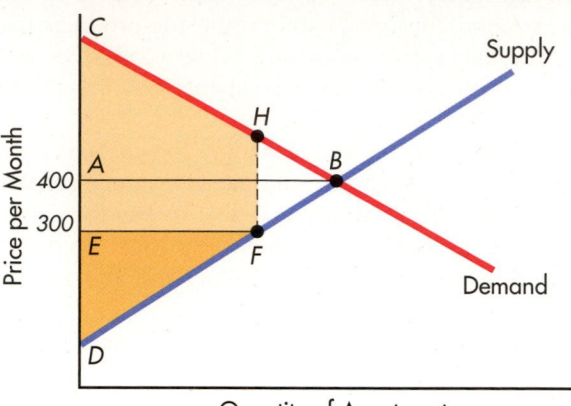

FIGURE 7   Rent Control and Market Efficiency

© 2013 Cengage Learning

The market for rental apartments is pictured in this graph; the market solution would yield a monthly rent of $400. The consumer surplus would be the area *ABC*; the producer surplus would be the area *ABD*. Now, suppose the city imposes rent control at $300 per month. The producer surplus changes to area *EFD* while the consumer surplus changes to *EFHC*. The total surplus has been reduced by the rent control.

exchange in a market (the gains from trade): the benefits that accrue to the consumer plus those that accrue to the firm.

The primary result of perfect competition is that things just do not get any better[3]: Total consumer and producer surplus is at a maximum. Any interference with the market exchange reduces the total surplus. Consider rent control on apartments, for instance. The market for rental apartments is pictured in Figure 7. As shown in Figure 7, the market solution would yield a monthly rent of $400. The consumer surplus would be the area *ABC*; the producer surplus would be the area *ABD*. Now, suppose the city imposes a rent control at $300 per month. The producer surplus changes to area *EFD*, while the consumer surplus changes to *EFHC*. Clearly the total surplus has been reduced. The question that policymakers must decide is whether the additional benefits to consumers offset the additional losses to producers. We will discuss this further in the chapter "Government and Market Failure."

RECAP

1. Entry occurs when firms are earning above-normal profit or positive economic profit.

2. A temporary shutdown occurs when firms are not covering their variable costs in the short run. In the long run, exit occurs when firms are not covering all costs.

3. The short-run market supply curve is the horizontal sum of the supply curves of all individual firms in the industry.

4. In a perfectly competitive market, firms produce goods at the least cost, and consumers purchase the goods that they most desire at a price that is equal to the marginal cost of producing those goods. There is no waste—no one could be made better off without making someone else worse off. Economists refer to this result as economic efficiency.

5. Producer surplus is the benefit that the firm receives for engaging in market exchange; it is the difference between the price the firm would be willing to sell its goods for and the price the firm actually receives.

6. Consumer surplus is the area below the demand curve and above the equilibrium price; producer surplus is the area above the supply curve and below the equilibrium price.

---

[3] As long as everyone wants the identically same generic products.

SUMMARY

1. What is perfect competition?

- Perfect competition is a market structure in which there are many firms that are producing an identical product and where entry and exit are easy. *§1.a*

2. What does the demand curve facing the individual firm look like, and why?

- The demand curve of the individual firm is a horizontal line at the market price. Each firm is a price taker. *§1.b*

3. How does the firm maximize profit in the short run?

- The individual firm maximizes profit by producing at the point where $MR = MC$. *§1.c*

4. At what point does a firm decide to suspend operations?

- A firm will shut down operations temporarily if price does not exceed the minimum point of the average-variable-cost curve. *§1.c*

5. When will a firm shut down permanently?

- A firm will shut down operations permanently if price does not exceed the minimum point of the average-total-cost curve in the long run. *§1.d*

6. What is the break-even price?

- The firm breaks even when revenue and cost are equal—when the demand curve (price) just equals the minimum point of the average-total-cost curve. *§1.d*

7. What is the firm's supply curve in the short run?

- The firm's short-run supply curve is the portion of its marginal-cost curve that lies above the minimum point of the average-variable-cost curve. *§1.e*

8. What is the firm's supply curve in the long run?

- The firm produces at the point where marginal cost equals marginal revenue, as long as marginal revenue exceeds the minimum point of the average-total-cost curve. Thus, the firm's long-run supply curve is the portion of its marginal-cost curve that lies above the minimum point of the average-total-cost curve. *§1.e*

9. What are the long-run equilibrium results of a perfectly competitive market?

- In the long run, all firms operating in perfect competition will earn a normal profit by producing at the lowest possible cost, and all consumers will buy the goods and services that they most want at a price equal to the marginal cost of producing those goods and services. *§2.c*

- Producer surplus is the difference between what a firm would be willing to produce and sell a good for and the price that the firm actually receives for the good. Consumer surplus is the difference between what an individual would be willing to pay for a good and what the individual actually has to pay. Total consumer and producer surpluses (the gains from trade) are at a maximum in a perfectly competitive market. *§2.c.1*

KEY TERMS

break-even price, 513
economic efficiency, 516

price taker, 507
producer surplus, 517

shutdown price, 511

EXERCISES

1. Cost figures for a hypothetical firm are given in the following table. Use them for the exercises below. The firm is selling in a perfectly competitive market.

Output	Fixed Cost	AFC	Variable Cost	AVC	Total Cost	ATC	MC
1	$50		$ 30				
2	$50		$ 50				
3	$50		$ 80				
4	$50		$120				
5	$50		$170				

   a. Fill in the blank columns.
   b. What is the minimum price needed by the firm to break even?
   c. What is the shutdown price?
   d. At a price of $40, what output level would the firm produce? What would its profits be?

2. Label the curves in the following graph.

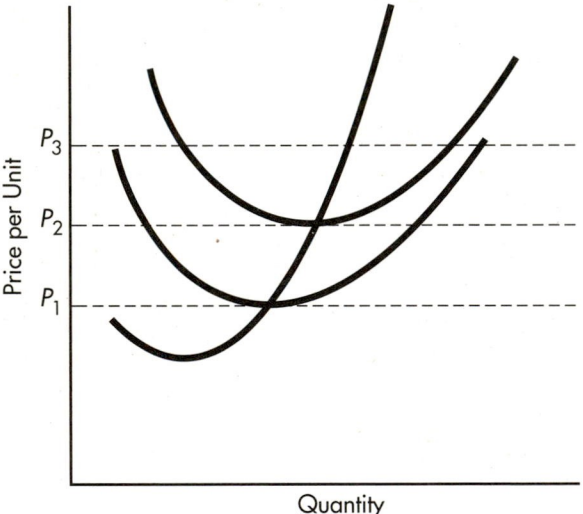

   a. At each market price, P_1, P_2, and P_3, at what output level would the firm produce?
   b. What profit would be earned if the market price was P_1?
   c. What are the shutdown and break-even prices?

3. Why might a firm continue to produce in the short run even though the market price is less than its average total cost?

4. Explain why the demand curve facing the individual firm in a perfectly competitive industry is a horizontal line.

5. Explain what occurs in the long run in a constant-cost industry, an increasing-cost industry, and a decreasing-cost industry when the market demand declines (shifts in).

6. What can you expect from an industry in perfect competition in the long run? What will the price be? What quantity will be produced? What will be the relation between marginal cost, average cost, and price?

7. Assume that the market for illegal drugs is an example of a perfectly competitive market structure. Describe what the perfectly competitive market model predicts for illegal drugs in the long run. What is likely to be the impact of the U.S. government's war on drugs in the short run? In the long run?

8. If no real-life industry meets the conditions of the perfectly competitive model exactly, why do we study perfect competition? What is the relevance of the model to a decision to switch careers? How might it shed some light on pollution, acid rain, and other social problems?

9. Using the model of perfect competition, explain what it means to say, "Too much electricity is generated," or "Too little education is produced." Would the firm be producing at the bottom of the *ATC* curve if too much or too little was being produced?

10. Private swimming pools can be dangerous. There are serious accidents each year in those areas of the United States where backyard pools are common. Should pools be banned? In other words, should the market for swimming pools be eliminated? Answer this in terms of producer and consumer surplus.

11. Discuss whether the following are examples of perfectly competitive industries.
    a. The U.S. stock market
    b. The automobile industry
    c. The consumer electronics market
    d. The market for college students

12. Macy's was making millions of dollars in profits when it declared bankruptcy. Explain Macy's decision.

13. Entry and exit of firms occur in the long run, but not in the short run. Why? What is meant by the long run and the short run? Would you say that entry is more or less difficult than exit?

14. Use the following data for the exercises below.

Price	Quantity Supplied	Quantity Demanded
$20	30	0
$18	25	5
$16	20	10
$14	15	15
$12	10	20
$10	5	25
$ 8	0	30

a. What is the equilibrium price and quantity?
b. Draw the demand and supply curves. If this represents perfect competition, are the curves individual-firm or market curves? How is the quantity supplied derived?

c. Show the consumer surplus. Show the producer surplus.
d. Suppose that a price ceiling of $12 was imposed. How would this change the consumer and producer surplus? Suppose a price floor of $16 was imposed. How would this change the consumer and producer surplus?

15. Use the model of perfect competition to explain the rise in corn prices from $1 per bushel in 2004 to $6 per bushel in 2011.

16. Draw a demand and supply diagram and illustrate what gains from trade are.

17. In exercise 16, explain why this illustrates gains from trade and what the gains mean for consumers and for producers.

You can find further practice tests in the Online Quiz at **www.cengage.com/economics/boyes**.

THE YEAR IN REVIEW AND THE YEARS AHEAD: DEVELOPMENTS IN HOUSING MARKETS

The CoreLogic home price index, a comprehensive and closely watched measure of existing home prices, dropped 32 percent from the peak of the housing market in April 2006 to the trough in March 2009, following the bursting of the housing bubble that built up between 2002 and 2005. The United States had never before suffered such a sharp drop in national house prices. Although house prices fell about 30 percent in nominal terms during the Great Depression, general price levels at that time fell 25 percent. As a result, the real house price decline during the Great Depression was only about 7 percent. During the current episode, the overall inflation rate has slowed but not turned negative, making the recent decline in house prices far larger in real terms than that during the Depression.

House prices have generally stabilized since March 2009, fluctuating around a roughly flat trend line. Nonetheless, house prices have been volatile over the past year, because of unusual market conditions such as the large supply of distressed homes on the market and the short-term impetus to demand from temporary tax credits for homebuyers. Among the factors that continue to keep sales and starts below their long-run trend levels are modest income growth, slower household formation, and tighter mortgage underwriting standards, as well as heightened uncertainty among potential homebuyers and the large "shadow inventory" of foreclosed and other distressed properties on (or soon to be on) the market.

Source: Economic Report of the President, 2011.

Let's illustrate what went on in the housing market during 2002 and 2011, assuming the market can be depicted as perfectly competitive. The demand for houses comes from the need to have a roof over one's head. In addition, some buy a home because they think of it as an investment—its value will increase over time. The number of home buyers depends on how many are willing and able to pay the price for a home. Beginning in the early 2000s, the number of buyers rose because the government made it a requirement that lenders relax their standards and loan to those without perfect credit or lots of assets. As the profits of lenders rose, standards continued to decline and the number of homebuyers continued to rise. Beginning about 2004, the demand for housing began to rise at an accelerating rate. As demand rose, seen as the shift upward of demand to D_2 from D_1 on the left side of the figure below, the price of houses rose, illustrated by the increase from P_1 to P_2. As people experienced the increased value of

their house, they began purchasing more homes, some selling their current home and buying a more expensive one and others buying multiple homes, demand continued shifting up and price continued rising. A bubble was occurring in house prices that popped in 2008. Demand dropped considerably, from D_2 to D_3, which caused the price of houses to decline a great deal, to P_3. What was happening to an individual house developer or seller? On the right side of the figure is an illustration of what occurred to the individual house developer. Initially, at the point of zero economic profit, P_1, the per-unit cost of constructing a house, ATC, is equal to the demand for the house, so that zero economic profit is earned. When demand rose, so did the profit of individual seller. Notice the distance from A to B, the difference between the ATC and price. That is the individual developer's profit. To reap even more profits, the sellers began to construct more houses. But, the bubble popped, driving price down to P_3, where sellers were losing money (price is below ATC).

FIGURE A1 Market for Houses and Individual Housing Developer

Hoursing Market

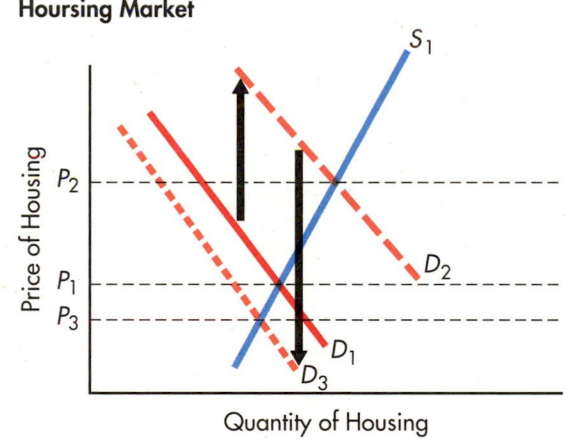

Single Seller

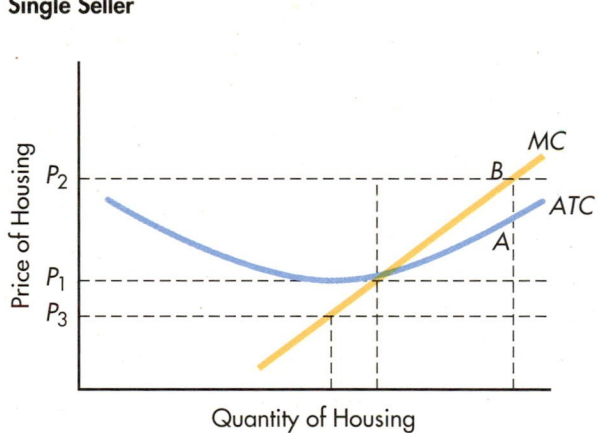

CHAPTER 24

Monopoly

© MACIEJ FROLOW/GETTY IMAGES, INC

RAZVANCOSA/DREAMSTIME.COM; LOGO: © FROXX/SHUTTERSTOCK.COM

FUNDAMENTAL QUESTIONS

1 What is monopoly?

2 How is a monopoly created?

3 What does the demand curve for a monopoly firm look like, and why?

4 Why would someone want to have a monopoly in some business or activity?

5 Under what conditions will a monopolist charge different customers different prices for the same product?

6 How do the predictions of the models of perfect competition and monopoly differ?

Perfect competition captures the behavior of individual firms when there are a great many firms selling an identical product. To find out how a firm's behavior would be different in the opposite situation—that is, when there are no competitors, just one firm selling an item—economists use the model of monopoly. The market structure of monopoly is a model that is intended to be used as a contrast to perfect competition. The comparison enables us to understand the effects of competition and entry into markets.

1. The Market Structure of Monopoly

Does a monopolist earn unseemly profits by charging outrageously high prices? Does a monopolist go its own way no matter what customers want? What is the relation between the Parker Brothers game Monopoly and the economic model of monopoly? We'll discuss these questions in this chapter, and we'll begin by defining what a monopolist is.

1.a. Market Definition

Monopoly is a market structure in which there is a single supplier of a product. A **monopoly firm (monopolist)** may be large or small, but whatever its size, it must be the *only supplier* of the product. In addition, a monopoly firm must sell a product for which there are *no close substitutes*. This means the demand curve for a monopolist's good or service is very inelastic; it need not be perfectly inelastic since consumers may decide to do without the item rather than pay a higher price.

You purchase products from monopoly firms every day, perhaps without realizing it. Congress created the U.S. Postal Service to provide first-class mail service. No other firm is allowed to provide that service. In the United States, the currency you use is issued and its quantity is controlled by the Federal Reserve; in other countries, there is a central bank like the Federal Reserve that controls the money supply. It is illegal for any organization or individual other than the central bank to issue currency.

1.b. The Creation of Monopolies

The pharmaceutical firm GlaxoSmithKline's (formerly GlaxoWellcome) profits doubled in the three years following the introduction of AZT. GlaxoSmithKline was a monopoly supplier of AZT, a drug to slow down AIDS, and it was earning above-normal profits. But if a product is valuable and the owners are getting rich from selling it, won't others develop substitutes and also enjoy the fruits of the market? Yes, unless something gets in the way. The name given to that something is a **barrier to entry**. There are three general classes of barriers to entry:

- Natural barriers, such as economies of scale
- Actions on the part of firms that create barriers to entry
- Governmentally created barriers

1.b.1. Economies of Scale
Economies of scale can be a barrier to entry. For instance, if there are economies of scale in the generation of electricity, then the larger the generating plant, the lower the cost per kilowatt-hour of electricity produced. A large generating plant could produce each unit of electricity much less expensively than several small generating plants. In this case, size would constitute a barrier to entry, since to be able to enter the market and compete with existing large-scale public utilities, a firm would have to be large enough that it could produce each kilowatt-hour as inexpensively as the large-scale plants.

1.b.2. Actions by Firms
Entry is barred when one firm owns an essential resource. The owners of the desiccant clay mine in New Mexico had a monopoly position because they owned the essential resource, clay. No one could produce a close substitute for many years; eventually, a synthetic clay was developed. But until that time, the mine owners had a monopoly. Inventions and discoveries are essential resources, at least until others develop close substitutes. Microsoft owned the important resource known as Windows. Apple introduced the iPod and the iPhone.

1 What is monopoly?

monopoly
A market structure in which there is a single supplier of a product.

monopoly firm (monopolist)
A single supplier of a product for which there are no close substitutes.

2 How is a monopoly created?

barrier to entry
Anything that impedes the ability of firms to begin a new business in an industry in which existing firms are earning positive economic profits.

1.b.3. Government Barriers to entry are often created by governments. The U.S. government issues patents, which provide a firm with a monopoly on certain products, inventions, or discoveries for a period of 20 years. Such was the case with the Glaxo-Wellcome monopoly. The company was granted a patent on AZT and thus was, by law, the only supplier of the drug. Domestic government policy also restricts entry into many industries. The federal government issues broadcast licenses for radio and television and grants airlines landing rights at certain airports. City governments limit the number of taxi companies that can operate, the number of cable television companies that can provide service, and the number of garbage collection firms that can provide service. State and local governments issue liquor licenses, cosmetology licenses (for hair cutters), contractor licenses, and many other licenses to carry on business, and restrict the number of electric utility, cable, satellite, garbage collection, and other companies. These are just a few examples of government-created monopolies in the United States.

1.c. Types of Monopolies

natural monopoly
A monopoly that arises from economies of scale.

The word *monopoly* is often part of another term, such as *natural monopoly, local monopoly, regulated monopoly, monopoly power*, and *monopolization*. A **natural monopoly** is a firm that has become a monopoly because of economies of scale and demand conditions. The adjective *natural* indicates that the monopoly arises from cost and demand conditions, not from government action. If costs decline as the quantity produced rises, only very large producers will be able to stay in business. Their lower costs will enable them to force smaller producers, who have higher costs, out of business. Large producers can underprice smaller producers, as illustrated in Figure 1. The larger firm, operating along ATC_2, can set a price anywhere between P_1 and P_2 that is lower than the smaller firm, operating along ATC_1, can sell its products at and still survive. If the market can support only one producer or if the long-run average-total-cost curve continually slopes downward, the monopoly that results is said to be natural.

Electric utilities are often considered to be natural monopolies because there are large economies of scale in the generation of electricity. One large power plant can generate electricity at a lower cost per kilowatt-hour than can several small power plants. The transmission of electricity is different, however. There are diseconomies of scale in

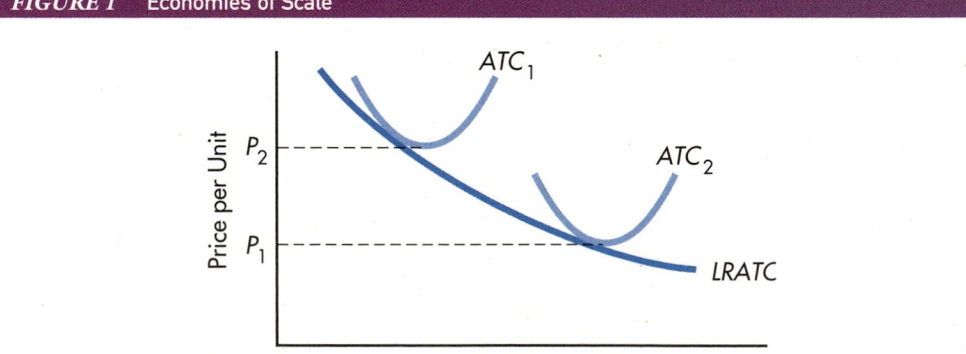

FIGURE 1   Economies of Scale

A large firm producing along ATC_2 can produce output much less expensively per unit than a small firm operating along ATC_1. The large firm, therefore, can set a price that is below the minimum point of the small firm's average-total-cost curve, yet still earn profit. Any price between P_1 and P_2 will provide a profit for the large firm and a loss for the small firm.

© 2013 Cengage Learning

Christopher Morris/VII/Corbis

Most monopolies occur because the government tells the business that it can have an exclusive operation without worrying about entry or competition. In much of the world, the oil monopoly is owned by the government. For instance, in this photo, we see the operations control room at the Aramco Saudi national oil company in Ras Tanura, Dammam, Saudi Arabia. The Aramco Saudi national oil company is the state-run monopoly oil producer in Saudi Arabia.

the transmission of electricity. The farther electricity has to be transmitted, the higher the cost per kilowatt-hour. Together, generation and transmission imply an MES (minimum efficient scale) that is sufficiently large for a local monopoly but not for a national or international monopoly.

A **local monopoly** is a firm that has a monopoly within a specific geographic area. An electric utility may be the sole supplier of electricity in a municipality or local area. A taxicab company may have a monopoly for service to the airport or within a city. Cable TV companies may have monopolies within municipalities. An airline may have a monopoly over some routes.

A **regulated monopoly** is a monopoly whose prices and production rates are controlled by a government entity. Electric utility companies, telephone companies, cable TV companies, and water companies are or have been regulated monopolies. A state corporation or utility commission sets their rates, determines the costs to be allowed in the production of their services, and restricts entry by other firms.

Monopoly power is market power, the ability to set prices rather than just be a price taker. Market power exists whenever the demand curve facing the producer is downward sloping. All firms except those operating in perfectly competitive markets have some monopoly power. A firm that has monopoly power is a **price maker** rather than a price taker. A firm that has to lower prices to sell more is a price maker—it will maximize profit by finding the quantity where $MR = MC$ and then setting price according to demand.

Monopolization refers to the attempt by a firm to take over a market—that is, the attempt to become the only supplier of a good or service. As we'll discuss in the chapter "Antitrust and Regulation," the law forbids monopolization even though it does not always forbid monopolies.

local monopoly
A monopoly that exists in a limited geographic area.

regulated monopoly
A monopoly firm whose behavior is monitored and prescribed by a government entity.

monopoly power
Market power, the ability to set prices.

price maker
A firm that sets the price of the product it sells.

monopolization
An attempt by a firm to dominate a market or become a monopoly.

RECAP

1. A monopoly firm is the sole supplier of a product for which there are no close substitutes.

2. A monopoly firm remains the sole supplier because of barriers to entry.

3. Barriers to entry may be economic, such as economies of scale; they may be due to the exclusive ownership of an essential resource; or they may be created by government policy.

4. A natural monopoly is a monopoly that results from economies of scale. A regulated monopoly is a monopoly whose pricing and production are controlled by the government. A local monopoly is a firm that has a monopoly in a specific geographic region.

5. Monopoly power, or market power, is when a firm can set prices rather than just be a price taker.

2. The Demand Curve Facing a Monopoly Firm

In any market, the market demand curve is a downward-sloping line because of the law of demand. Although the marketing demand curve is downward sloping, the demand curve facing an individual firm in a perfectly competitive market is a horizontal line at the market price. This is not the case for a monopoly. Because a monopolist is the only producer, it *is* the industry, so its demand curve is the market demand curve; it slopes down.

2.a. Marginal Revenue

3 What does the demand curve for a monopoly firm look like, and why?

> The demand curve facing the monopoly firm is the market demand curve.

In 2004, Apple introduced the iPod. Throughout the year, Apple had a monopoly on the iPod. Let's consider the firm's pricing and output decisions, using hypothetical cost and revenue data.

Suppose an iPod sells for $150, and, at that price, the firm is selling 5 iPods per day, as shown in Figure 2. If Apple wants to sell more, it must move down the demand curve. Why? Because of the law of demand. People will do without the iPod rather than pay more than they think it's worth. As the price declines, more people are willing and able to purchase an iPod—sales increase. The table in Figure 2 shows that if the monopoly firm lowers the price to $135 per unit from $140, it will sell 8 iPods per day instead of 7.

What is the firm's marginal revenue? To find marginal revenue, the total revenue earned at $140 per iPod must be compared to the total revenue earned at $135 per iPod—the change in total revenue must be calculated. At $140 apiece, 7 iPods are sold each day, and total revenue each day is

$$\$140 \text{ per iPod} \times 7 \text{ iPods} = \$980$$

At $135 apiece, 8 iPods are sold, and total revenue is

$$\$135 \text{ per iPod} \times 8 \text{ iPods} = \$1,080$$

The difference, change in total revenue, is $100. Thus, marginal revenue is

$$\frac{\Delta TR}{\Delta Q} = \frac{\$100}{1 \text{ iPod}} = \$100$$

The change in revenue is the difference between the increased revenue due to the increased quantity sold, the yellow area in Figure 2, and the decreased revenue due to a lower price, the blue area in Figure 2.

FIGURE 2   Demand Curve for a Monopolist

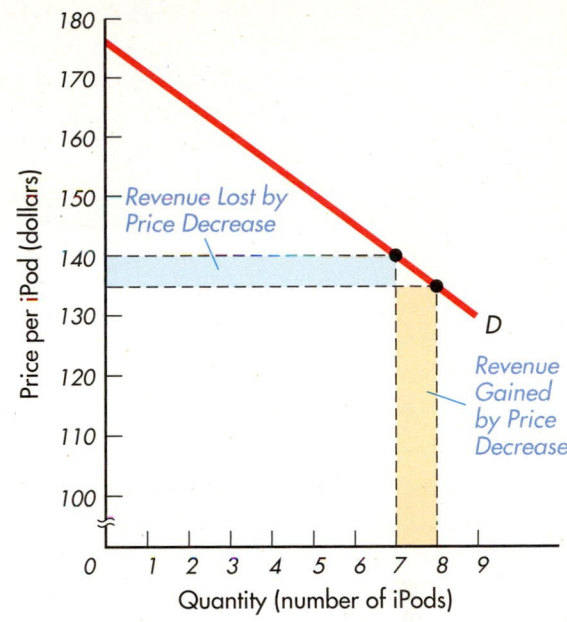

Quantity per Day	Price	Total Revenue	Marginal Revenue
1	$170	$ 170	$170
2	$165	$ 330	$160
3	$160	$ 480	$150
4	$155	$ 620	$140
5	$150	$ 750	$130
6	$145	$ 870	$120
7	$140	$ 980	$110
8	$135	$1,080	$100
9	$130	$1,170	$ 90

As the iPod price is reduced, the quantity demanded increases. But because the price is reduced on all quantities sold, not just on the last unit sold, marginal revenue declines faster than price.

The price is $135 per iPod, but marginal revenue is $100 per iPod. Price and marginal revenue are not the same for a monopoly firm. This is a fundamental difference between a monopolist and a perfect competitor. For a perfect competitor, price and marginal revenue are the same.

Marginal revenue is less than price and declines as output rises because the monopolist must lower the price in order to sell more units. When the price of an iPod is $140, the firm sells 7 iPods. When the price is dropped to $135, the firm sells 8 units. The firm does not sell the first 7 iPods for $140 and the 8th one for $135. It might lose business if it tried to do that. The customer who purchased the iPod at $135 could sell it for $137.50 to a customer who was about to pay $140, and the firm would lose the $140 sale. Customers who would have paid $140 could decide to wait until they too can get the $135 price. As long as customers know about the prices paid by other customers and as long as the firm cannot easily distinguish among customers, the monopoly firm is not able to charge a different price for each additional unit. All units are sold at the same price, and in order to sell additional units, the monopolist must lower the price on all units. As a result, marginal revenue and price are not the same.

> *Marginal revenue is less than price for a monopoly firm.*

2.a.1. Marginal and Average Revenue

Recall from the chapters "Elasticity: Demand and Supply" and "Profit Maximization" that whenever the marginal is greater than the average, the average rises, and whenever the marginal is less than the average, the average falls. Average revenue is calculated by dividing total revenue by the number of units of output sold.

At a price of $150 per iPod, average revenue is $AR = \$750/5 = \$150$. At a price of $145, average revenue is $AR = \$870/6 = \$145$. Average revenue is the same as price; in fact, *the average-revenue curve is the demand curve*. Because of the law of demand, where quantity demanded rises as price falls, average revenue (price) always falls as output rises (the demand curve slopes downward). Because average revenue falls as output rises, marginal revenue must always be less than average revenue. For the monopolist (or any firm facing a downward-sloping demand curve), marginal revenue always declines as output increases, and the marginal revenue curve always lies below the demand curve.

Also recall from previous chapters that the marginal-revenue curve is positive in the elastic region of the demand curve, is zero at the output level where the demand curve is unit-elastic, and is negative in the inelastic portion of the demand curve.[1] This is illustrated in Figure 3.

FIGURE 3   Downward-Sloping Demand Curve and Revenue

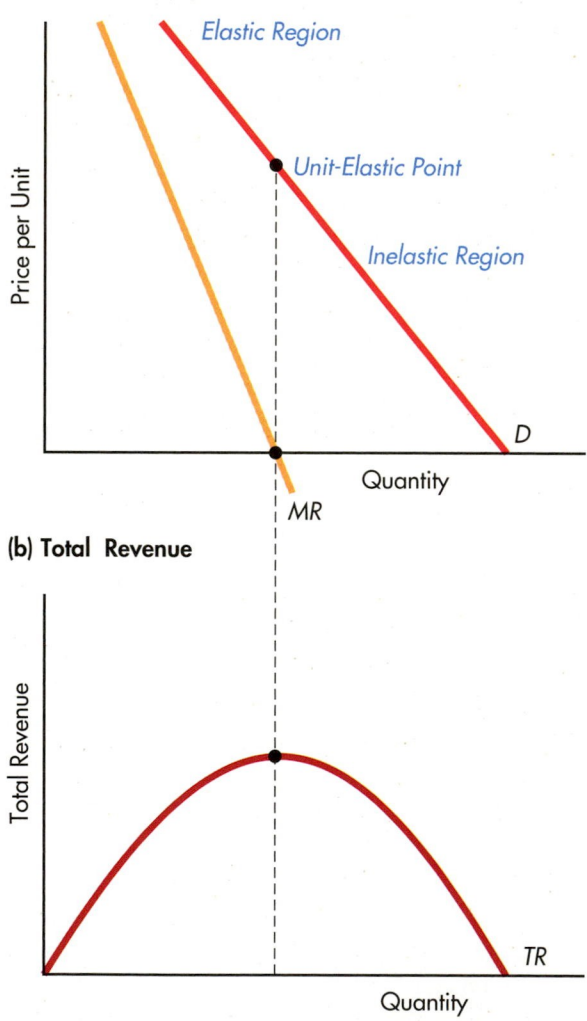

(a) Demand and Price Elasticity

(b) Total Revenue

The straight-line downward-sloping demand curve in Figure 3(a) shows that the price elasticity of demand becomes more inelastic as we move down the curve. At the top of the curve in the elastic region, revenue increases as price is lowered, as shown in Figure 3(b); in the inelastic region, the lower part of the curve, revenue decreases as price is lowered. The revenue-maximizing point, the top of the curve in Figure 3(b), occurs where the demand curve is unit-elastic, shown in Figure 3(a).

---

[1] The slope of the demand curve is one-half the slope of the marginal-revenue curve. Consider the demand formula $P = a - bQ$; total revenue is $PQ - aQ - bQ^2$, so marginal revenue is $MR = a - 2bQ$.

RECAP

1. The demand curve facing a monopoly firm is the market demand curve.

2. For the monopoly firm, price is greater than marginal revenue. For the perfectly competitive firm, price and marginal revenue are equal.

3. As price declines, total revenue increases in the elastic portion of the demand curve, reaches a maximum at the unit-elastic point, and declines in the inelastic portion.

4. The marginal-revenue curve of the monopoly firm lies below the demand curve.

5. For both the perfectly competitive firm and the monopoly firm, price = average revenue = demand.

3. Profit Maximization

The objective of the monopoly firm is to maximize profit. Where does the monopolist choose to produce, and what price does it set? Recall from the chapter "Profit Maximization" that all profit-maximizing firms produce at the point where marginal revenue equals marginal cost.

3.a. What Price to Charge?

A schedule of revenues and costs for the iPod producer accompanies Figure 4. Total revenue (TR) is listed in column 3; total cost (TC), in column 4. Total profit ($TR - TC$), shown in column 5, is the difference between the entries in column 3 and those in column 4. Marginal revenue (MR) is listed in column 6, marginal cost (MC) in column 7, and average total cost (ATC) in column 8.

The quantity of output to be produced is the quantity that corresponds to the point where $MR = MC$. How high a price will the market bear at that quantity? The market is willing and able to purchase the quantity given by $MR = MC$ at the corresponding price on the demand curve. As shown in Figure 4(a), the price is found by drawing a vertical line from the point where $MR = MC$ up to the demand curve and then extending a horizontal line over to the vertical axis. That price is $135 when output is 8.

3.b. Monopoly Profit and Loss

The profit that the monopoly firm generates by selling 8 iPods at a price of $135 is shown in Figure 4(a) as the colored rectangle. The vertical distance between the ATC curve and the demand curve, multiplied by the quantity sold, yields total profit.

Just like any other firm, a monopoly firm could experience a loss. A monopoly supplier of sharpeners for disposable razor blades probably would not be very successful, and the U.S. Postal Service has failed to make a profit in five of the last ten years. Unless price exceeds average total costs, the firm loses money. A monopolist producing at a loss is shown in Figure 4(b)—the price is less than the average total cost.

Like a perfectly competitive firm, a monopolist will suspend operations in the short run if its price does not exceed the average variable cost at the quantity the firm produces. And, like a perfectly competitive firm, a monopolist will shut down permanently if revenue is not likely to equal or exceed all costs in the long run (unless the government subsidizes the firm, as it does in the case of the U.S. Postal Service). In contrast, however, if a monopolist makes a profit, barriers to entry will keep other firms out of the industry. As a result, the monopolist can earn above-normal profits in the long run.

 4 Why would someone want to have a monopoly in some business or activity?

A monopolist can earn above-normal profits in the long run.

FIGURE 4   Profit Maximization for the iPod Seller

(1) Total Output (Q)	(2) Price (P)	(3) Total Revenue (TR)	(4) Total Cost (TC)	(5) Total Profit (TR − TC)	(6) Marginal Revenue (MR)	(7) Marginal Cost (MC)	(8) Average Total Cost (ATC)
0	$175	$ 0	$100	$100			
1	$170	$ 170	$200	$ 30	$170	$100	$200
2	$165	$ 330	$280	$ 50	$160	$ 80	$140
3	$160	$ 480	$350	$130	$150	$ 70	$117
4	$155	$ 620	$400	$220	$140	$ 50	$100
5	$150	$ 750	$450	$300	$130	$ 50	$ 90
6	$145	$ 870	$520	$350	$120	$ 70	$ 87
7	$140	$ 980	$600	$380	$110	$ 80	$ 86
8	$135	$1,080	$700	$380	$100	$100	$ 88
9	$130	$1,170	$900	$270	$ 90	$200	$100

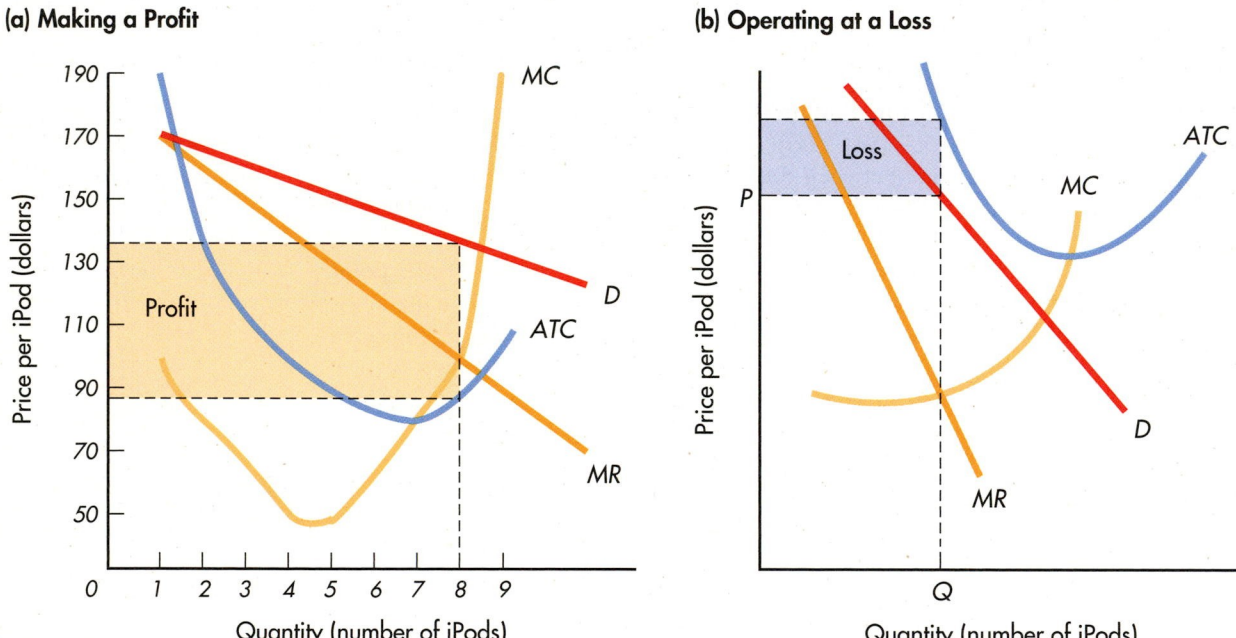

(a) Making a Profit

(b) Operating at a Loss

The data listed in the table are plotted in Figure 4(a). The firm produces where *MR = MC*, 8 units; charges a price given by the demand curve directly above the production of 8 units, a price of $135 per iPod; and earns a profit (yellow rectangle). In Figure 4(b), the firm is shown to be operating at a loss (blue rectangle). It produces output *Q* at price *P*, but the average total cost exceeds the price.

3.c. Supply and the Monopoly Firm

For the firm in perfect competition, the supply curve is that portion of the marginal cost curve that lies above the average-cost curve, and the market-supply curve is the sum of all the individual firms' supply curves. The supply curve for the firm selling in any of the other market structures is not as straightforward to derive, and, therefore, neither is the market supply curve. The reason is that firms selling in market structures other than perfect competition are price makers rather than price takers. This means that the hypothetical experiment of varying the price of a product and seeing how the firm selling that product reacts makes no sense.

In the case of the monopolist, the firm supplies a quantity determined by setting marginal revenue equal to marginal cost, but it also sets the price to go along with this quantity. Varying the price will not change the decision rule, since the firm will choose to produce at its profit-maximizing output level and set the price accordingly. There is, therefore, only one quantity and price at which the monopolist will operate. There is a supply point, not a supply curve. Moreover, because the monopolist is the only firm in the market, its supply curve (or supply point) is also the market supply curve (or point).

The complications of the price makers do not alter the supply rule: A firm will produce and offer for sale a quantity that equates marginal revenue with marginal cost. This supply rule applies to all firms, regardless of the market structure in which the firm operates.

3.d. Monopoly Myths

There are a few myths about monopoly that we have debunked here. The first myth is that a monopolist can charge any price it wants and will reap unseemly profits by continually increasing the price. We know that a monopolist maximizes profit by producing the quantity that equates marginal revenue and marginal cost. We also know that a monopolist can price and sell only the quantities given by the demand curve. If the demand curve is very inelastic, as would be the case for a life-saving pharmaceutical, then the price the monopolist will charge will be high. Conversely, if demand is price elastic, the monopolist will not be able to sell its good or service if it charges exorbitant prices.

A second myth is that a monopolist is not sensitive to customers. The monopolist can stay in business only if it earns at least a normal profit (unless a government entity subsidizes the money-losing monopolist). Ignoring customers, producing a good that no one will purchase, setting prices that all customers think are exorbitant, and providing terrible service or products that customers do not want, will not allow a firm to remain in business for long.

The third myth is that the monopolist cannot make a loss. A monopolist is no different from any other firm in that it has costs of doing business and it must earn sufficient revenues to pay those costs. If the monopolist sets too high a price or provides a product that few people want, revenues may be less than costs and losses may result.

RECAP

1. Profit is maximized at the output level where $MR = MC$.

2. The price charged by the monopoly firm is the point on the demand curve that corresponds to the quantity where $MR = MC$.

3. A monopoly firm can make profits or experience losses. A monopoly firm can earn above-normal profit in the long run.

4. The monopoly firm will shut down in the short run if all variable costs aren't covered. It will shut down in the long run if all costs aren't covered.

5. The amount that a firm is willing and able to supply depends on marginal revenue and marginal cost. A firm will produce and offer for sale a quantity that equates marginal revenue and marginal cost.

4. Market Power and Price Discrimination

Market power is the ability of a firm to determine the price of the good or service it offers for sale. Perfectly competitive firms have no market power; all other firms do. With market power, a firm can choose to charge more and sell less or to charge less and sell more. Under certain conditions, a firm with market power is able to charge different customers different prices. This is called **price discrimination**. Figure 5 shows the demand curve facing a firm with market power. Notice that the demand curve tells us that at price P_1, consumers are willing and able to purchase quantity Q_1. If the price is P_2, they are willing and able to purchase Q_2. If the firm sells to everyone at the same price, say P_2, it does not make as much money as it would if it could charge some customers, those who were willing and able to pay a higher price, P_1, and other customers P_2. It could sell quantity Q_1 at price P_1 and quantity $Q_2 - Q_1$ at price P_2. What would be even better for the firm would be to charge each customer what that customer was willing and able to pay. This is price discrimination; price discrimination enables the firm to capture consumer surplus for itself.

price discrimination
Charging different customers different prices for the same product.

4.a. Necessary Conditions for Price Discrimination

5 Under what conditions will a monopolist charge different customers different prices for the same product?

You read in Section 2.a that the monopoly firm has to sell all of its products at a uniform price; otherwise, one customer could sell to another, thereby reducing the monopoly firm's profit. However, if customers do not come into contact with each other or are somehow separated by the firm, the firm may be able to charge each customer the exact price that he or she is willing to pay.

When different customers are charged different prices for the same product or when customers are charged different prices for different quantities of the same product, price discrimination is occurring. Price discrimination occurs when price changes result not from cost changes but from the firm's attempt to extract more of the consumer surplus. Certain conditions are necessary for price discrimination to occur:

- The firm cannot be a price taker (perfect competitor).
- The firm must be able to separate customers according to price elasticities of demand.
- The firm must be able to prevent resale of the product.

FIGURE 5   Price Discrimination

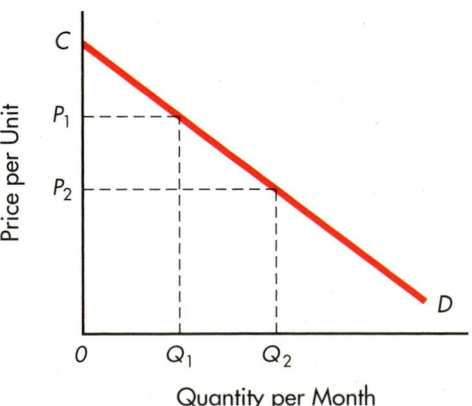

If the firm can charge a price equal to what each person is willing and able to pay, the firm essentially collects the consumer surplus instead of the consumer. In this figure, the firm is charging one set of customers price P_1 and another set of customers price P_2.

4.b. Examples of Price Discrimination

Examples of price discrimination are not hard to find. Senior citizens often pay a lower price than the general population at movie theaters, drugstores, and golf courses. It is relatively easy to identify senior citizens and to ensure that they do not resell their tickets to the general population.

Tuition at state schools is different for in-state and out-of-state residents. It is not difficult to find out where a student resides, and it is very easy to ensure that in-state students do not sell their places to out-of-state students. Airlines discriminate between business passengers and others. Passengers who do not fly at the busiest times, who purchase tickets in advance, and who can stay at their destination longer than a day pay lower fares than business passengers, who cannot make advance reservations and who must travel during rush hours. It is relatively easy for the airlines to separate business from nonbusiness passengers and to ensure that the latter do not sell their tickets to the former.

Electric utilities practice a form of price discrimination by charging different rates for different quantities of electricity used. The rate declines as the quantity purchased increases. A customer might pay $.07 per kilowatt-hour for the first 100 kilowatt-hours, $.06 for the next 100, and so on. Many utility companies have different rate structures for different classes of customers as well. Businesses pay less per kilowatt-hour than households.

Grocery coupons, mail-in rebates, trading stamps, and other discount strategies are also price-discrimination techniques. Shoppers who are willing to spend time cutting out coupons and presenting them receive a lower price than those who are not willing to spend that time. Shoppers are separated by the amount of time they are willing to devote to coupon clipping. Is it possible that the popcorn at the movies is also a price-discrimination tactic? If the excess price of the popcorn and other foodstuffs at the movies was simply added to the price of an admission ticket, the movie theater would lose some of those customers who do not purchase popcorn. By charging a high price for the popcorn, the movie theater is distinguishing those customers who have a lower price elasticity of demand for the entire package of the movie and the popcorn from those with a higher elasticity of demand.

ECONOMIC INSIGHT

Groupon

In 2008, a new form of price discrimination began through a company known as Groupon. Groupon is a website that offers a "deal of the day" to major geographic markets worldwide. The first market for Groupon was Chicago, followed soon thereafter by Boston, New York City, and Toronto. By 2011, Groupon served more than 150 markets in North America and 100 markets in Europe, Asia, and South America, and has amassed 35 million registered users. The company offers one coupon per day in each of the markets it serves. If a certain number of people sign up for the offer, then the deal becomes available to all who have a coupon. If the predetermined minimum is not met, no one gets the deal that day. Groupon makes money by keeping approximately half the money the person pays for the coupon. So, for example, an $80 massage could be purchased by the consumer for $40 and then Groupon and the retailer would split the $40. That is, the retailer gives a massage valued at $80 and gets approximately $20 from Groupon for it. And the consumer gets the massage, in this example, from the retailer for which they have paid $40 to Groupon. Groupon is helping retailers discriminate between those willing to spend the time getting online, signing up for the deal, and waiting until the deal is consummated, from those not willing to spend time and effort dealing with the coupons.

4.c. The Theory of Price Discrimination

How does price discrimination work? Suppose there are two classes of buyers for movie tickets, senior citizens and everybody else, and each class has a different price elasticity of demand. The two classes are shown in Figure 6. Profit is maximized when $MR = MC$. Because the same firm is providing the goods in two submarkets, MC is the same for senior citizens and the general public, but the demand curves differ. Because the demand curves of the two groups differ, there are two MR curves: MR_{sc} for senior citizens, in Figure 6(a), and MR_{gp} for the general population, in Figure 6(b). Profit is maximized when $MR_{sc} = MC$ and when $MR_{gp} = MC$. The price is found by drawing a vertical line from the quantities where $MR = MC$ up to the respective demand curves, D_{sc} and D_{gp}.

Notice that the price to the general population, P_{gp}, is higher than the price to the senior citizens, P_{sc}. The reason is that the senior citizens demand curve is more elastic than the demand curve of the general population. Senior citizens are more sensitive to price than is the general population, so to attract more of their business, the merchant has to offer them a lower price.

By discriminating, a monopoly firm makes greater profits than it would make by charging both groups the same price. If both groups were charged the same price, P_{gp}, the monopoly firm would lose sales to senior citizens who found the price too high, Q_{sc} to Q_2. And if both groups were charged P_{sc}, so few additional sales to the general population would be made that revenues would fall. A firm with market power could collect the entire consumer surplus if it could charge each customer exactly the price that that customer was willing and able to pay. This is called *perfect price discrimination*.

FIGURE 6 Price Discrimination in Action

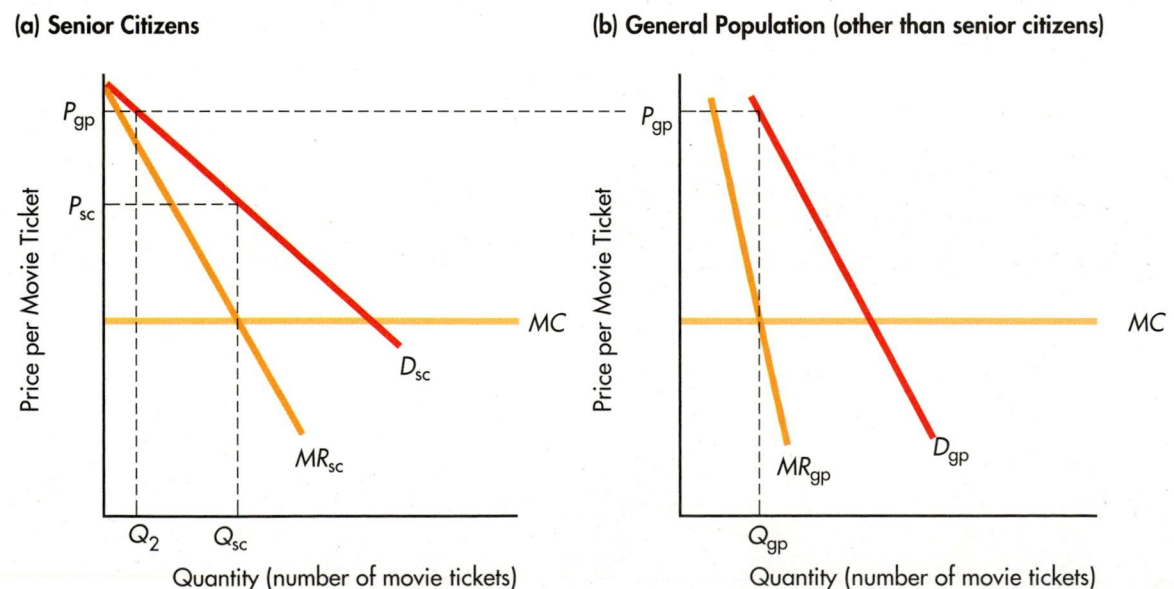

There are two classes of buyers for the same product. Figure 6(a) shows the elasticity of demand for senior citizens. Figure 6(b) shows the elasticity of demand for the general population. The demand of the senior citizens is more elastic than that of the general population. As a result, faced with the same marginal cost, the firm charges senior citizens a lower price than it charges the rest of the population. The quantity sold to senior citizens is Q_{sc}, the intersection between MC and MR_{sc}, and the price charged is P_{sc}. The quantity sold to the general population is Q_{gp}, and the price charged is P_{gp}.

RECAP

1. Price discrimination occurs when a firm charges different customers different prices for the same product or charges different prices for different quantities of the same product.

2. Three conditions are necessary for price discrimination to occur: (a) the firm must have some market power, (b) the firm must be able to separate customers according to price elasticities of demand, and (c) the firm must be able to prevent resale of the product.

5. Comparison of Perfect Competition and Monopoly

Because perfect competition and monopoly are bookends—opposites that are intended to surround all business behavior—it is useful to compare the outcome of the two.

5.a. Costs of Monopoly: Inefficiency

6 How do the predictions of the models of perfect competition and monopoly differ?

In the long run, the perfectly competitive firm operates at the minimum point of the long-run average-total-cost curve, and the firm's price is equal to its marginal cost. Profit is at the normal level. A monopolist does not operate at the minimum point of the average-total-cost curve and does not set price equal to marginal cost. Because entry does not occur, a monopoly firm may earn above-normal profit in the long run.

Figure 7(a) shows a perfectly competitive market. The market demand curve is D; the market supply curve is S. The market price determined by the intersection of D and S is P_{pc}. At P_{pc}, the perfectly competitive market produces Q_{pc}. Consumers are able to enjoy the consumer surplus indicated by the triangle $P_{pc}BA$ by purchasing the quantity Q_{pc} at the price P_{pc}. Firms receive the producer surplus indicated by triangle OBP_{pc} by producing the quantity Q_{pc} and selling that quantity at price P_{pc}.

To compare these results to monopoly, we must assume that all of the firms in a perfectly competitive industry are merged into a single monopoly firm and that the monopolist does not close or alter plants and does not achieve any economies of scale. In other words, what would occur if a perfectly competitive industry were transformed into a monopoly—just one firm that determines price and quantity produced? The market demand curve becomes the monopoly firm's demand curve, and the market supply curve becomes the monopoly firm's marginal-cost curve. Recall that a firm will supply the quantity given by the point where marginal revenue equals marginal-cost curve (above the average-variable-cost curve). This is illustrated in Figure 7(b).

The monopoly firm restricts quantity produced to Q_m, where $MR = MC$, and charges a price P_m, as indicated on the demand curve shown in Figure 7(b). *The monopoly firm thus produces a lower quantity than does the perfectly competitive market, Q_m compared to Q, and sells that smaller quantity at a higher price, P_m compared to P_{pc}.* In addition, the consumer surplus in monopoly is the triangle P_mCA, which is smaller than the consumer surplus under perfect competition, $P_{pc}BA$. The rectangle $P_{pc}ECP_m$ is part of consumer surplus in perfect competition. In monopoly, that part of consumer surplus is transferred to the firm. The total producer surplus is area $0FCP_m$.

Thus, firms are better off (more producer surplus) while consumers are worse off (less consumer surplus) under monopoly compared to perfect competition. Consumers are worse off by area $P_{pc}BCP_m$, and firms are better off by area $P_{pc}ECP_m$ less area EFB.

FIGURE 7   Monopoly and Perfect Competition Compared

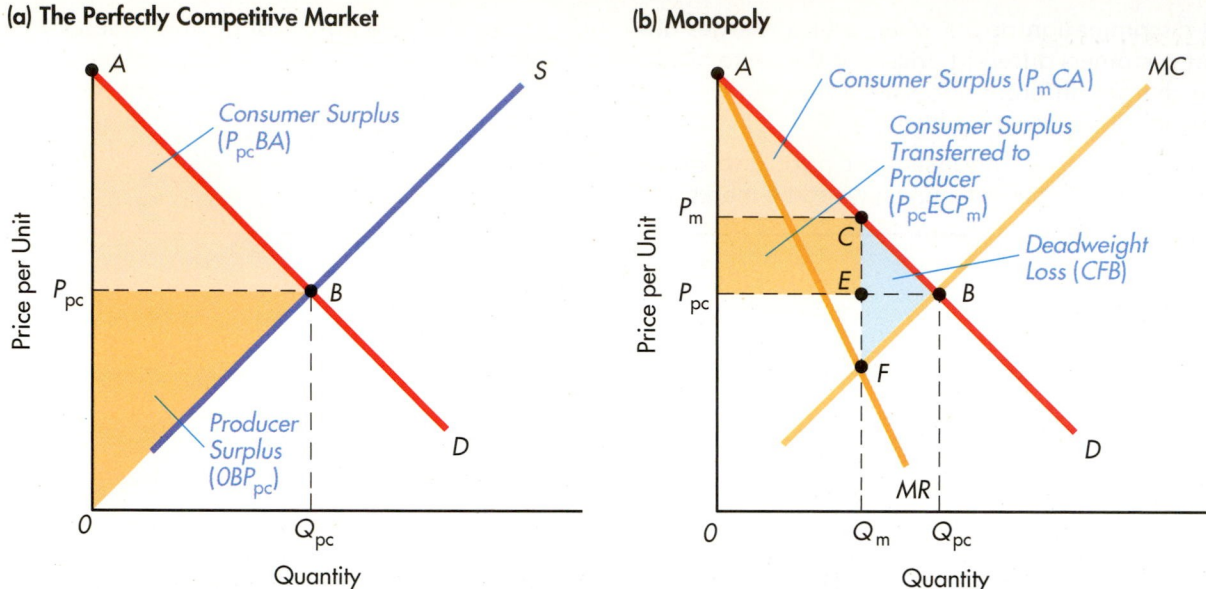

(a) The Perfectly Competitive Market

Consumer Surplus $(P_{pc}BA)$

Producer Surplus (OBP_{pc})

(b) Monopoly

Consumer Surplus (P_mCA)

Consumer Surplus Transferred to Producer $(P_{pc}ECP_m)$

Deadweight Loss (CFB)

© 2013 Cengage Learning

Figure 7(a) shows a perfectly competitive; it produces at the point where demand, *D*, and industry supply, *S*, intersect. The quantity produced by the industry is Q_{pc}; the price charged is P_{pc}. Consumer surplus is the triangle $P_{pc}BA$. Figure 7(b) shows what happens if the industry is monopolized. The single firm faces the industry demand curve, *D*, and has the marginal-revenue curve *MR*. The intersection of the marginal-cost curve and the marginal-revenue curve indicates the quantity that will be produced, Q_m. The price charged for Q_m is P_m. Thus, the monopoly firm produces less and charges more than the perfectly competitive industry. Consumer surplus, shown as the triangle P_mCA, is smaller in the monopoly industry. The area $P_{pc}ECP_m$ is the consumer surplus in perfect competition that is transferred from consumer to producer. The producer surplus is area $0FCP_m$. The deadweight loss is the area *CFB*.

deadweight loss
The reduction of consumer surplus without a corresponding increase in profit when a perfectly competitive firm is monopolized.

The consumer and producer surplus represented by triangle *CFB* is lost by both consumers and firms and goes to no one. This loss is the reduction in consumer surplus and producer surplus that is not transferred to the monopoly firm or to anyone else; it is called a **deadweight loss**.

RECAP

1. A monopoly firm produces a smaller quantity and charges a higher price than a perfectly competitive industry if the two industries have identical costs.

2. The consumer surplus is smaller if an industry is operated by a monopoly firm than it is if an industry is operated by perfectly competitive firms. Profits are larger in the monopoly case.

3. The costs to society that result when a perfectly competitive industry becomes a monopoly are a reduction of consumer surplus and producer surplus that is not transferred to anyone. This loss is called a *deadweight loss.*

SUMMARY

1. What is monopoly?

- Monopoly is a market structure in which there is a single supplier of a product. A monopoly firm, or monopolist, is the only supplier of a product for which there are no close substitutes. *§1.a*

2. How is a monopoly created?

- Natural barriers to entry (such as economies of scale), barriers erected by firms in the industry, and barriers erected by government may create monopolies. *§1.b*

- A natural monopoly refers to a monopoly that exists due to economies of scale. A local monopoly is a monopoly that applies only to a niche of the market or to a small geographical area. A regulated monopoly is a firm whose price and output are controlled by a government entity. Monopoly power refers to market power or the ability a firm has to set prices rather than act as a price taker. *§1.c*

3. What does the demand curve for a monopoly firm look like, and why?

- Because a monopolist is the only producer of a good or service, the demand curve facing a monopoly firm is the industry demand curve. *§2*

- Price and marginal revenue are not the same for a monopoly firm. Marginal revenue is less than price. *§2.a*

- The average-revenue curve is the demand curve. *§2.a.1*

- A monopoly firm maximizes profit by producing the quantity of output yielded at the point where marginal revenue and marginal cost are equal. *§3.a*

- A monopoly firm sets a price that is on the demand curve and that corresponds to the point where marginal revenue and marginal cost are equal. *§3.a*

4. Why would someone want to have a monopoly in some business or activity?

- A monopoly firm can make above-normal or normal profit or even a loss. If it makes above-normal profit, entry by other firms does not occur and the monopoly firm can earn above-normal profit in the long run. Exit occurs if the monopoly firm cannot cover its costs in the long run. *§3.b*

5. Under what conditions will a monopolist charge different customers different prices for the same product?

- Price discrimination occurs when the firm is not a price taker, can separate customers according to their price elasticities of demand for the firm's product, and can prevent resale of the product. *§4.a*

6. How do the predictions of the models of perfect competition and monopoly differ?

- A comparison of monopoly and perfectly competitive firms implies that monopoly imposes costs on society. These costs include less output being produced and that output being sold at a higher price. *§5.a*

KEY TERMS

EXERCISES

1. About 85 percent of the soup sold in the United States is Campbell's brand. Is Campbell Soup Company a monopoly firm?

2. Price discrimination is practiced by movie theaters, motels, golf courses, drugstores, and universities. Are they monopolies? If not, how can they carry out price discrimination?

3. Why is it necessary for the seller to be able to keep customers from reselling the product in order for price discrimination to occur? There are many products for which you get a discount for purchasing large quantities. For instance, most liquor stores will provide a discount on wine if you purchase a case. Is this price discrimination? If so, what is to keep one customer from purchasing cases of wine and then reselling single bottles at a price above the case price but below the liquor store's single-bottle price?

4. Many people have claimed that there is no good for which substitutes are not available. If so, does this mean there is no such thing as monopoly?

5. Suppose that at a price of $6 per unit, quantity demanded is 12 units. Calculate the quantity demanded when the marginal revenue is $6 per unit. (*Hint:* The price elasticity of demand is unity at the midpoint of the demand curve.)

6. In the following figure, if the monopoly firm faces ATC_1, which rectangle measures total profit? If the monopoly firm faces ATC_2, what is total profit? What information would you need in order to know whether the monopoly firm will shut down or continue producing in the short run? In the long run?

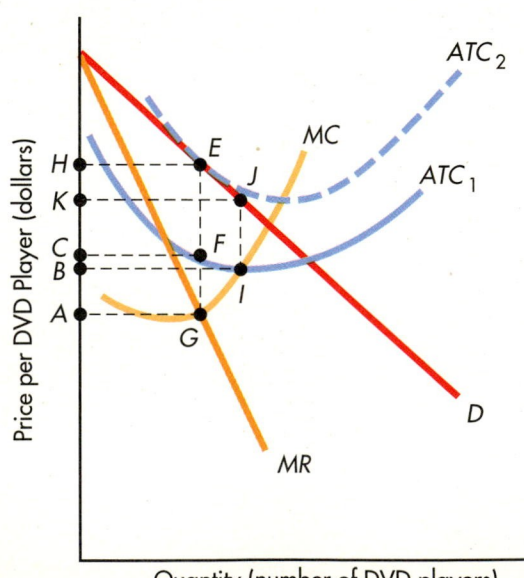

Quantity (number of DVD players)

7. In recent years, U.S. car manufacturers have charged lower prices for cars in western states in an effort to offset the competition from Japanese cars. This two-tier pricing scheme has upset many car dealers in the eastern states. Many have called it discriminatory and illegal. What conditions are necessary for this pricing scheme to be profitable to the U.S. companies?

8. Consider the following demand schedule. Does it apply to a perfectly competitive firm? Compute marginal and average revenue.

Price	Quantity	Price	Quantity
$95	2	$55	5
$88	3	$40	6
$80	4	$22	7

9. Suppose the marginal cost of producing the good in question 8 is a constant $10 per unit of output. What quantity of output will the firm produce?

10. Do you agree or disagree with this statement: "A monopoly firm will charge an exorbitant price for its product"? Explain your answer.

11. Do you agree or disagree with this statement: "A monopoly firm will run a much less safe business than a perfect competitor"? Explain your answer.

12. State colleges and universities have two levels of tuition or fees. The less expensive is for residents of the state; the more expensive is for nonresidents. Assume that the universities are profit-maximizing monopolists and explain their pricing policy. Now, explain why the colleges and universities give student aid and scholarships.

13. Several electric utilities are providing customers with a choice of billing procedures. Customers can select a time-of-day meter that registers electric usage throughout the day, or they can select a regular meter that registers total usage at the end of the day. With the time-of-day meter, the utility is able to charge customers a much higher rate for peak usage than for nonpeak usage. The regular meter users pay the same rate for electric usage no matter when it is used. Why would the electric utility want customers to choose the time-of-day meter?

14. Suppose that a firm has a monopoly on a good with the following demand schedule.

Price	Quantity	Price	Quantity
$10	0	$4	6
$ 9	1	$3	7
$ 8	2	$2	8
$ 7	3	$1	9
$ 6	4	$0	10
$ 5	5		

a. What price and quantity will the monopolist produce at if the marginal cost is a constant $4?

b. Calculate the deadweight loss from having the monopolist produce rather than a perfect competitor.

15. Describe how "quantity discounts" can be price discrimination.

16. Illustrate with a perfectly competitive market (demand and supply) diagram what "gains from trade" are. Now introduce a marginal revenue curve, thereby converting the perfectly competitive market into a monopoly market. Demonstrate how the monopoly reduces gains from trade.

You can find further practice tests in the Online Quiz at **www.cengage.com/economics/boyes**.

PSST! WANNA BUY A DIAMOND?

Toronto Star, December 1, 2005

For almost 100 years, London-based DeBeers and its South African mines had a stranglehold on the diamond industry.

But three major events put an end to the DeBeers cartel: The fall of communism and the Soviet Union in 1989, enabling diamonds to pour out of Russia; the discovery of diamonds in the Northwest Territories in 1991; and the drying up of some of DeBeers' diamond mines in South Africa.

In a nutshell, there is now competition. DeBeers had to rethink its Diamonds are Forever slogan and has given notice to competitors that they are going to have to ante up bucks to push their own gems.

DeBeers' marketing strategy has shifted to branding and the organic nature of diamonds, a change illustrated when the Diamond Trading Company, the marketing arm of DeBeers, brought the world's largest uncut diamond to Toronto last month. The 300-carat treasure, found in South Africa in the 1970s, is the oldest object on the planet, carbon-dated back 3.4 billion years. DeBeers also sponsored Diamonds: Nature's Miracle, an international competition that challenged designers to create an organic piece of jewellery illustrating the "intrinsic value of diamonds and their 3-billion-year struggle to be born."

Canadian Annik Lucier won with a 3-metre long, shimmering diamond strand. She based her design on the ancient belief that diamonds are fallen stars. Her 80-carat strand of 402 diamonds features oval, marquise, princess cut, round brilliant, borealis and rough diamonds and is sold at Birks for $600,000.

DeBeers and its competitors have also realized the marketing potential of branded diamonds and proprietary cuts.

A proprietary cut is exclusive to one supplier and patented so it cannot be copied by other diamond cutters, explains Kim Sutch, director of Toronto's Diamond Information Centre. DeBeers supplies the diamonds for several proprietary cuts, including the Adura and Tycoon. The Adura (Latin for light on fire), a square princess cut with 27 more facets than the traditional 58-facet princess. The extra facets give the diamond much more sparkle.

The Tycoon is rectangular and similar to an emerald cut. It's referred to as "a diamond with a diamond on top" because of its innovative faceting and prominent top.

Exclusive to Birks is the Amorique. Unveiled in October by Birks creative director Holly Brubach, it is a modern version of the classic round cushion cut, says Paul Lombardi, vice-president of gemstone procurement for Birks.

The Amorique's 70 facets surpass the 58 facets that are the norm for round stones. The extra facets give a lot more dazzling light and the cut eliminates shadowing on the diamond. It represents three years of development and a $10 million investment. The Amorique collection includes a solitaire, a three-stone ring, drop earrings and pendants, set in 18k gold or platinum and in sizes ranging from 0.25 to 3 carats. Prices start at $6,500. There is an international waiting list for stones of 2 to 3 carats.

DONNA JEAN MACKINNON

Source: Reprinted with permission-Torstar Syndication Services.

Ask people to name a monopoly and the name that comes up most often is DeBeers. DeBeers never was a true monopolist—the only seller—but it has been the dominant firm in the diamond market for nearly 70 years. The South African company controls over 60 percent of the $7 billion a year global market for uncut diamonds. Over the years, it has used its dominance of the industry to drive up the price of diamonds by buying up surplus diamonds. The policy dates back to 1934, when the Great Depression caused a slump in diamond prices and the chairman of DeBeers at that time, Sir Ernest Oppenheimer, offered to buy all the rough stones on the market. Had prices continued to fall, the move would have probably led to DeBeers's bankruptcy. But the price recovered, and Sir Ernest's gamble laid the foundation for the company's dominance of the diamond industry for the remainder of the century. DeBeers spent billions of dollars to accumulate a large stockpile of diamonds that were never sold. At the end of 1999, DeBeers's diamond mountain, hoarded in its London vaults, was worth around $4 billion. The diamonds were used to maintain or manipulate the price. But that practice is changing. DeBeers has announced that it is giving up its traditional role of buyer of last resort of every stone on the market. The reason given for the change is what are called conflict diamonds, diamonds sold by various forces in Africa to fuel civil wars. DeBeers has announced that it will not purchase or trade in conflict diamonds.

While the policy might have some emotional or ethical appeal, the real reason that DeBeers is ending its buyer of last resort strategy is to reduce its declining economic profits. DeBeers knows that if conflict, or blood, diamonds become an emotional consumer issue, they could trigger a public opinion backlash similar to the one that crippled the fur trade. Moreover, rivals such as BHP, an Australian group, and Rio Tinto of the United Kingdom are gaining more and more market share. DeBeers's strategy is two-pronged: to attempt to reduce the supply of diamonds, and to increase the demand.

DeBeers is attempting to become a monopolist again, but through differentiation—it wants to be the only buyer of rough diamonds that are licensed. It is also differentiating its diamonds by the cut. A proprietary cut is exclusive to one supplier and patented so that it cannot be copied by other diamond cutters, in essence creating a monopoly. The monopoly strategy is illustrated in the figure below. The elastic demand, $Demand_e$, and associated marginal revenue, MR_e, represent the demand for diamonds before successful differentiation. The less elastic demand, $Demand_{ie}$, is the result of successful differentiation. The proprietary cut means that people are willing to pay to have a special cut just as they are willing to pay to own a BMW. Differentiation allows the price to be set higher, P_{ie} as opposed to P_e.

The various cuts also act as a price discrimination strategy. By selling different cuts at different prices, DeBeers is allowing customers to self-select—those choosing one cut pay more than those choosing another. In this way, a buyer choosing the Adura cut pays a different amount than the buyer choosing the Tycoon cut. Even if the costs of the cuts are virtually identical, the buyer is paying significantly different amounts. Thus, demand, $Demand_e$, represents the demand for the Adura while the demand, $Demand_{ie}$, represents the demand for the Tycoon. Due to consumer desires (the price elasticities), the price of the Tycoon is higher than the price of the Adura.

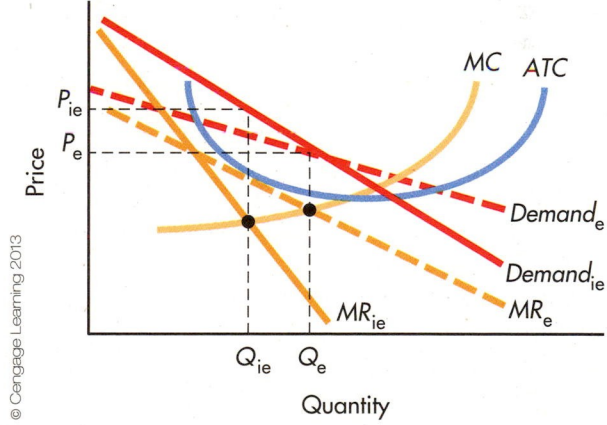

On the demand side, DeBeers spends enormous sums to advertise the gems under its famous slogan, "A diamond is forever."

It is difficult for a monopolist to give up its monopoly power and positive economic profits. DeBeers doesn't plan to do so without a fight.

Monopolistic Competition and Oligopoly

FUNDAMENTAL QUESTIONS

1 What is monopolistic competition?

2 What behavior is most common in monopolistic competition?

3 What is oligopoly?

4 In what form does rivalry occur in an oligopoly?

5 Why does cooperation among rivals occur most often in oligopolies?

6 What are the differences and similarities among the four market structure models?

n 2009, when Saks Fifth Avenue cut prices by 70 percent, smaller boutiques catering to luxury goods customers had to shut their doors. In 2008, Home Depot offered a low price guarantee: If you find the same item at a lower price, Home Depot will give you your money back plus 10 percent. Home Depot is far from alone in the matching of competitors' prices: Best Buy, Staples, Fry's Electronics, and many other firms also claim a price guarantee. The point of these examples is that firms do not often act independently of other firms. In most cases, a firm must take into account the reactions, responses, and strategies of other firms when implementing a policy. The models of perfect competition and monopoly do not capture these competitive actions. In perfect competition, each firm is so small that it has no impact on the market; in monopoly, there is only one firm. Economists look to two other models of selling environments to capture competitive behavior when firms take into account the actions of other firms: monopolistic competition and oligopoly. We discuss these two selling environments in this chapter.

Monopolistic competition is like perfect competition in that there are many firms and new firms may enter easily, but it differs from perfect competition in that each firm produces a slightly different product. It is like monopoly in that each firm in monopolistic competition has some market power—each firm has a unique (slightly differentiated) product. It is unlike monopoly in that there are many close substitutes for the goods and services that each firm produces.

With oligopoly, there are few firms—not one, but not many either. A firm in an oligopoly may sell a product that is identical to that sold by other firms in the oligopoly, or it may sell slightly different products from its competitors. We'll discuss monopolistic competition in the first part of this chapter and oligopoly in the second part.

1. Monopolistic Competition

Monopolistic competition is a market structure in which (1) there are a large number of firms, (2) the products produced by the firms are differentiated, and (3) entry and exit occur easily. The definitions of *monopolistic competition* and *perfect competition* overlap. In both structures, there are a large number of firms. The difference is that each firm in monopolistic competition produces a product that is slightly different from all other products, whereas in perfect competition the products are standardized. The definition of monopolistic competition also overlaps with that of *monopoly*. Because each firm in *monopolistic competition* produces a unique product, each has a "mini" monopoly over its product. Thus, like a monopolist, a firm in a monopolistically competitive market structure has a downward-sloping demand curve, marginal revenue is below the demand curve, and price is greater than marginal cost. What distinguishes monopolistic competition from monopoly is ease of entry. Any time firms in monopolistic competition are earning above-normal profit, new firms enter, and this entry continues until firms are earning normal profit. In a monopoly, a firm can earn above-normal profit in the long run. Table 1 summarizes the differences among perfect competition, monopoly, and monopolistic competition.

1 What is monopolistic competition?

1.a. Profits and Entry

Firms in monopolistic competition tend to use product differentiation more than price to compete. They attempt to provide a product for each market niche. Even though the

TABLE 1	Summary of Perfect Competition, Monopoly, and Monopolistic Competition		
	Perfect Competition	**Monopoly**	**Monopolistic Competition**
Number of firms	Many	One	Many
Type of product	Identical	One	Many
Entry conditions	Easy	Difficult or impossible	Easy
Demand curve for firm	Horizontal (perfectly elastic)	Downward sloping	Downward sloping
Price and marginal cost	$MC = P$	$MC < P$	$MC < P$
Long-run profit	Normal	Yes	Normal

Firms operating in monopolistically competitive environments typically try to differentiate their products from those of their rivals. The more consumers think of a product as being distinctive or unique, the less elastic the demand for the product and the more ability the firm has to raise its price without losing customers. In this photo, we see that Apple is using a highly visible building façade to advertise its iPod.

> **Monopolistically competitive firms produce differentiated products.**

total market may not be expanding, they divide the market into smaller and smaller segments by introducing variations of products. You can think of a market demand curve for clothes, but within that market there are many niches and many demand curves. In fact, there is a separate demand curve for each firm and for each product the firm sells. Each individual demand curve is quite price elastic because of the existence of many close substitutes.

1.a.1. In the Short Run

Figure 1(a) shows the cost and revenue curves of a monopolistically competitive firm providing a single product in the short run. As with all profit-maximizing firms, production occurs at the quantity where $MR = MC$. The price the firm charges, P_1, is given by the demand curve at the quantity where $MR = MC$. Price P_1 is above average total cost, as indicated by the distance AB. Thus, the firm is earning above-normal profit, shown as the rectangle $CBAP_1$.

In Figure 1(b), the firms in a monopolistically competitive market are earning normal profit. The price is the same as the average total cost at Q_1, so a normal profit is obtained. If the firm is earning a loss, then the average-total-cost curve lies above the demand curve at the quantity produced, as shown in Figure 1(c). At Q_1, the firm is earning a loss, the rectangle P_1BAC. The firm must decide whether to temporarily suspend production of that product or to continue producing it because the outlook is favorable. The decision depends on whether revenue exceeds variable costs.

1.a.2. In the Long Run

Whenever existing firms in a market structure without barriers to entry are earning above-normal profit, new firms enter the business and, in some cases, existing firms expand until all firms are earning the normal profit. In a perfectly competitive industry, the new firms supply a product that is identical to the product being supplied by existing firms. *In a monopolistically competitive industry, entering firms produce a close substitute, not an identical or standardized product.*

FIGURE 1   A Monopolistically Competitive Firm

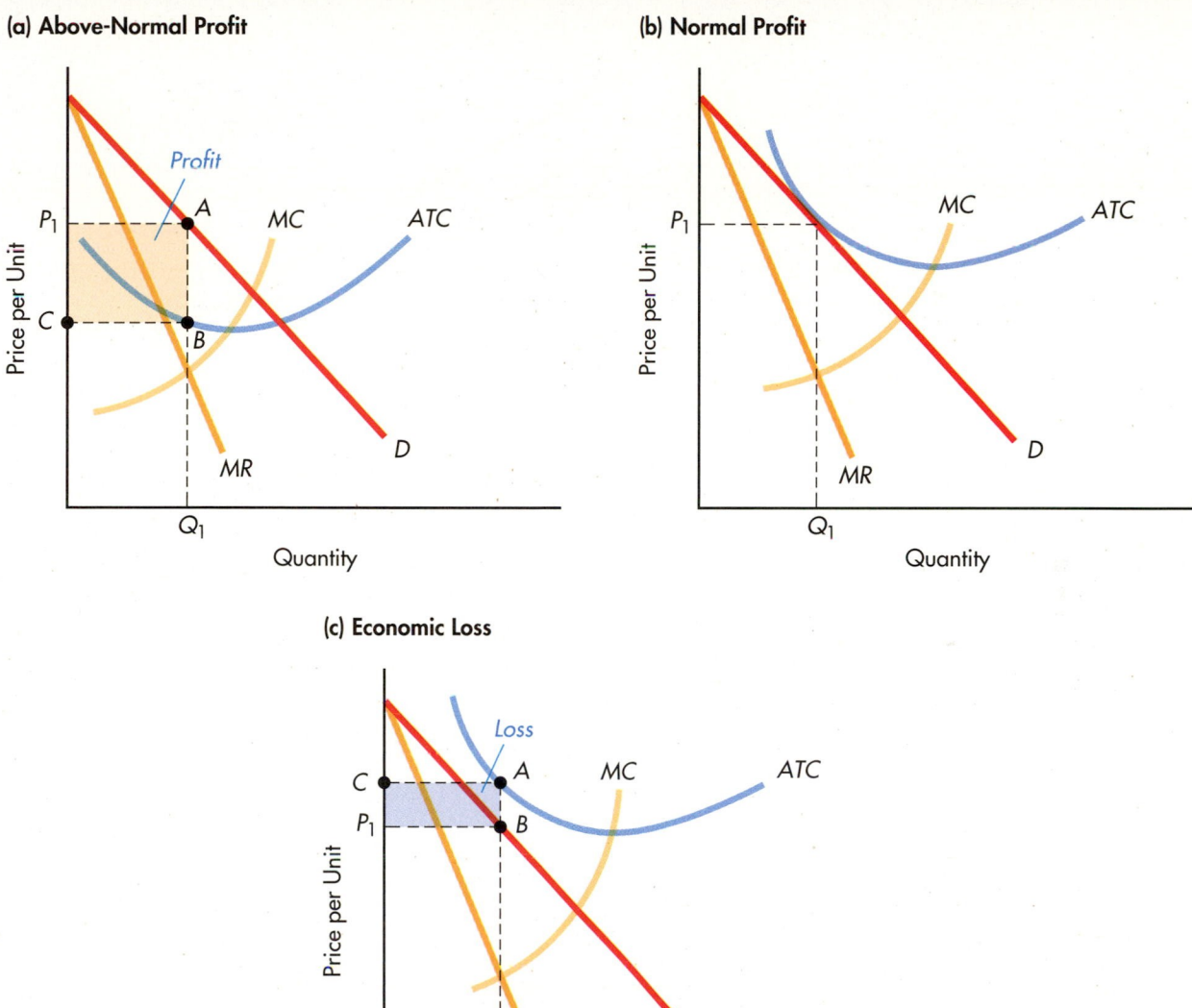

A monopolistically competitive firm faces a downward-sloping demand curve. The firm in Figure 1(a) maximizes profit by producing Q_1, where $MR = MC$, and charging a price, P_1, given by the demand curve above Q_1. Profit is the rectangle $CBAP_1$. In Figure 1(b), the firm is earning a normal profit because where $MR = MC$, price is P_1 on the demand curve above Q_1 and is equal to average total cost. In Figure 1(c), the firm is earning the loss of rectangle P_1BAC. At the profit-maximizing (loss-minimizing) output level, Q_1, average total cost exceeds price.

As the introduction of new products by new or existing firms occurs, the demand curves for existing products shift in until a normal profit is earned. For each firm and each product, the demand curve shifts in, as shown in Figure 2, until it just touches the average-total-cost curve at the price charged and the output produced, P_2 and Q_2. When profit is at the normal level, expansion and entry cease.

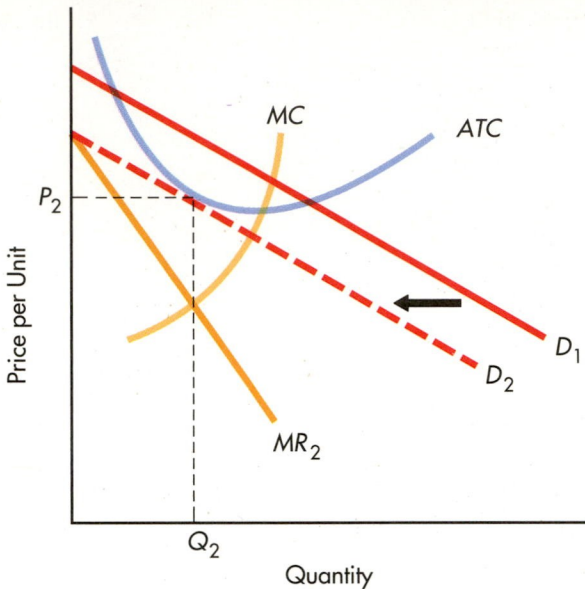

FIGURE 2   Entry and Normal Profit

In the long run, the firm in monopolistic competition earns a normal profit. Entry shifts the firm's demand curve in from D_1 to D_2. Entry, which takes the form of a differentiated product, continues to occur as long as above-normal profits exist. When the demand curve just touches the average-total-cost curve, as at P_2 and Q_2, profit is at the normal level.

When a firm is earning a loss on a product and the long-run outlook is for continued losses, the firm will stop producing that product. Exit means that fewer differentiated products are produced, and the demand curves for the remaining products shift out. This continues until the remaining firms are earning normal profits.

1.b. Monopolistic Competition versus Perfect Competition

Figure 3 shows both a perfectly competitive firm in long-run equilibrium and a monopolistically competitive firm in long-run equilibrium. The perfectly competitive firm, shown as the horizontal demand and marginal-revenue curve, $MR_{pc} = D_{pc}$, produces at the minimum point of the long-run average-total-cost curve at Q_{pc}; the price, marginal cost, marginal revenue, and average total cost are P_{pc}. The long-run equilibrium for a monopolistically competitive firm is shown by the demand curve D_{mc} and the marginal-revenue curve MR_{mc}. The monopolistically competitive firm produces at Q_{mc}, where $MR_{mc} = MC$, and charges a price determined by drawing a vertical line up from the point where $MR_{mc} = MC$ to the demand curve. That price is just equal to the point where the long-run average-total-cost curve touches the demand curve, P_{mc}. In other words, at Q_{mc}, the monopolistically competitive firm is just earning the normal profit.

> *Monopolistically competitive firms produce less and charge a higher price than perfectly competitive firms. Monopolistic competition does not yield economic efficiency because consumers are willing and able to pay for variety.*

The difference between a perfectly competitive firm and a monopolistically competitive firm is clear in Figure 3. Because of the downward-sloping demand curve facing the monopolistically competitive firm, the firm does not produce at the minimum point of the long-run average-total-cost curve, Q_{pc}. Instead, it produces a smaller quantity of output, Q_{mc}, at a higher price, P_{mc}. The difference between P_{mc} and P_{pc} is the

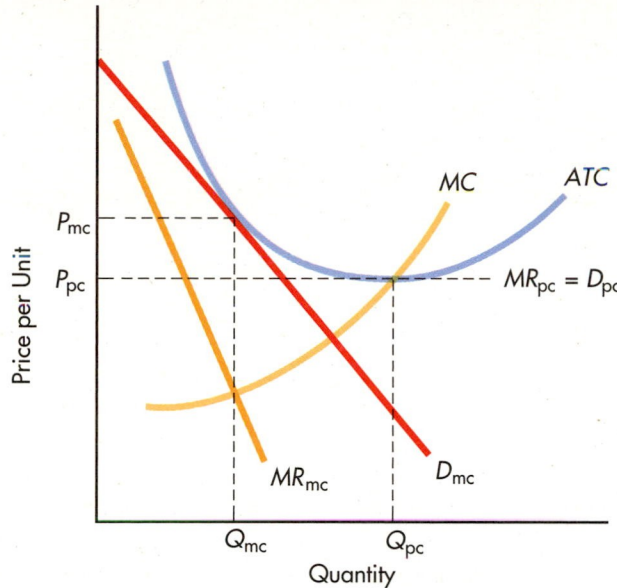

FIGURE 3   Perfect and Monopolistic Competition Compared

The perfectly competitive firm produces at the point where the price line, the horizontal *MR* curve, intersects the *MC* curve. This is the bottom of the *ATC* curve in the long run, quantity Q_{pc} at price P_{pc}. The monopolistically competitive firm also produces where $MR = MC$. The downward-sloping demand curve faced by the monopolistically competitive firm means that the quantity produced, Q_{mc}, is less than the quantity produced by the perfectly competitive firm, Q_{pc}. The price charged by the monopolistically competitive firm is also higher than that charged by the perfectly competitive firm, P_{mc} versus P_{pc}. In both cases, however, the firms earn only a normal profit.

additional amount that consumers pay for the privilege of having differentiated products. If consumers placed no value on product choice—if they desired generic products—they would not pay anything extra for product differentiation, and the monopolistically competitive firm would not exist.

Even though price does not equal marginal cost and the monopolistically competitive firm does not operate at the minimum point of the average-total-cost curve, the firm does earn normal profit in the long run. And although the monopolistically competitive firm does not strictly meet the conditions of economic efficiency (since price is not equal to marginal cost), the inefficiency is not due to the firm's ability to restrict quantity and increase price but instead is a direct result of consumers' desire for variety. It is hard to argue that society is worse off with monopolistic competition than it is with perfect competition, since the difference is due solely to consumer desires. Yet variety is costly, and critics of market economies argue that the cost is not worthwhile. Would the world be a better place if we had a simpler array of products to choose from, if there was a simple generic product—one type of automobile, say—for everyone?

1.c. Nonprice Competition—Product Differentiation

 2   What behavior is most common in monopolistic competition?

A firm in a monopolistically competitive market structure attempts to differentiate its product or itself from its competitors. Successful product differentiation reduces the price elasticity of demand. The demand curve, shown as the rotation from D_1 to D_2 in Figure 4, becomes steeper.

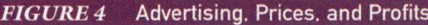

FIGURE 4   Advertising, Prices, and Profits

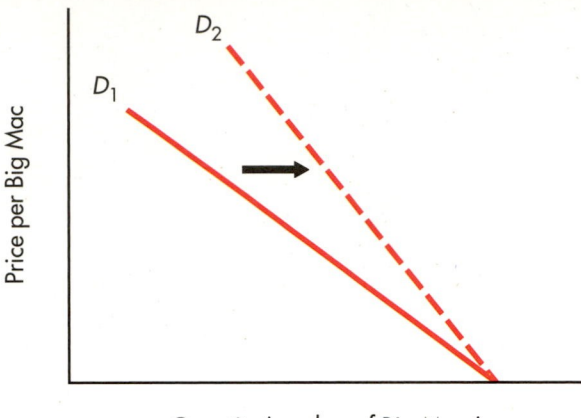

A successful differentiation program will reduce the price elasticity of demand, shown as a steeper demand curve, D_2, as compared with D_1. The successful differentiation enables the firm to charge a higher price.

Numerous characteristics may serve to differentiate products: quality, color, style, safety features, taste, packaging, purchasing terms, warranties, and guarantees. All it takes is for the consumer to think there is a difference for there to be a difference. A firm might change its hours of operation—for example, a supermarket might offer service 24 hours a day—to call attention to itself. Firms can also use location to differentiate their products. A firm may locate where traffic is heavy and the cost to the consumer of making a trip to the firm is minimal. If location is used for differentiation, however, why do fast-food restaurants tend to be clustered together? Where you find a McDonald's, you usually find a Taco Bell or a Wendy's nearby. The model of monopolistic competition explains this behavior. Suppose that five identical consumers—A, B, C, D, and E—are spread out along a line as shown in Figure 5. Consumer C is the median consumer, residing equidistantly from consumers B and D and equidistantly from consumers A and E. Assume that the five consumers care about the costs incurred in getting to a fast-food restaurant and are indifferent about the food offered. McDonald's is the first fast-food provider to open near these five consumers. Where does it locate? It locates as close to consumer C as possible because that location minimizes the total distance of all five consumers from McDonald's.

Taco Bell wants to open in the same area. If it locates near consumer D, it will pull customers D and E from McDonald's but will have no chance to attract A, B, or C. Similarly, if it locates near consumer A, only A will go to Taco Bell. Only if Taco Bell locates next door to McDonald's will it have a chance to gather a larger market share than McDonald's. As other fast-food firms enter, they too will locate close to McDonald's.

Being able to earn positive economic profits is what drives firms to differentiate their goods and services. Every firm—producer, fabricator, seller, broker, agent, or merchant—tries to distinguish its offering from all others. The reason that firms try to differentiate themselves or their products is to make it more difficult for competitors to take away business.

Successful differentiation reduces the price elasticity of demand and gives the firm more market power. What does this mean for a firm? It means that the firm can raise the price of the good or service that it sells without incurring the loss of revenue that would

---

FIGURE 5   Location under Monopolistic Competition

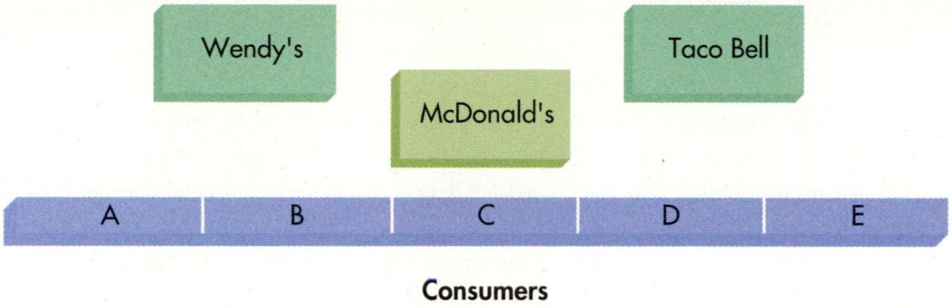

Consumers

Five consumers—A, B, C, D, and E—reside along a straight line. Consumer C is in the middle, equidistant from B and D and from A and E. McDonald's decides to locate a restaurant at the spot that is closest to all five consumers. This is the median position, where consumer C resides. Other fast-food firms locate nearby because any other location will increase the total distance of some consumers from the fast-food restaurant, thereby causing some consumers to go elsewhere.

---

result if the elasticity were higher. For years, Intel was able to charge more for its microchips than competitors could charge for essentially the same microchip. Intel was able to do that because of its successful campaign to differentiate itself—"Intel Inside." Intel was able to shift the demand curve for its products out and make it more inelastic.

1.c.1. Brand Name
Starbucks has created a powerful brand name. People know that a Starbucks store will provide an identical product, whether that Starbucks is in Seattle or Beijing. The Starbucks brand name provides value to consumers, so they are willing to pay a higher price for Starbucks products than for similar products without the Starbucks name. A brand name is valuable to a firm; it makes the demand less elastic and can enable the firm to earn higher profits. How is a brand name created, and why does it have value?

Most goods and services have many different attributes—look, feel, taste, sensation, reliability, performance, and so on. You learn about many products by trying them, but this learning may be costly. For example, you may go into a coffee shop and pay for a crummy cup of coffee that you throw away. Or perhaps you buy a new TV that you later find does not have the picture quality you hoped for. A brand name can provide reliability and save you from these costly mistakes.

If you see someone selling neckties from a table set up on the street corner, you have less confidence in that "firm" than you would have in the Nordstrom store across the street, so you might be willing to pay more for the same tie at Nordstrom than at the street vendor. The reason is at least partly that Nordstrom has devoted huge resources to that large building. You see many types of firms trying to assure customers of their reliability by locating in large buildings or beautiful offices or by spending lavishly on advertisements. For some products, a guarantee or warranty is an important signal that the product is of high quality.

Reliability is the important differentiator for some goods and services, such as Starbucks, McDonald's, and so on. But for customers to know that the product is reliable, they must first try the product. A firm may advertise that its product "tastes great" or "refreshes you." Goods may be advertised by showing groups of people having fun on a beach or in the mountains—such as with Coors beer, for example. The goods may be placed in a setting of upper class or wealth—Grey Poupon being requested by a passenger in a limousine, for instance. These advertisements are intended to get people to try the good or service.

Reliability may be represented by the consistent flavor of a McDonald's hamburger, the infrequency with which a machine breaks down, or the soundness of the opinions of a professional adviser. The consumer has to experience these products and services over a relatively long period of time before reliability is established. Once a consumer has had a positive experience with a good, the price elasticity of demand for that good typically decreases—the consumer becomes loyal to the product. For instance, Coke and Pepsi drinkers are usually loyal to one of the two brands, even though the products are similar. Prudential Insurance shows "the rock" and Allstate shows the "good hands" to illustrate their reliability. Although these symbols have nothing to do with the actual service, they promote an aspect of the service that consumers find valuable—the idea that the service will continue to be offered in the future, so that an experience now can be used to evaluate the service in the future. Lawyers and financial advisers need to present an image of success. Who wants to use an unsuccessful attorney or financial adviser? Thus, attorneys and financial advisers typically have richly appointed offices located in large central-city buildings. They dress in expensive clothes and carry expensive briefcases.

Many people claim that marketing and advertising create phony or artificial distinctions among products and that the benefits conferred by brand names are illusory. These critics note that there may be no difference between Tide laundry detergent and the generic detergent sold under the grocery store's label, that Ralph Lauren's Polo brand shirts may be constructed of exactly the same fabric and knit design as several less-expensive brands, and that aspirin is aspirin whether or not it is Bayer. Nonetheless, consumers are often willing to pay a higher price for a brand name product than for a similar product without a brand name. Why? Because the brand name signals something valuable—reliability, confidence, assurance.

The objective of creating a brand name is to reduce the price elasticity of demand. The greater the consumer's reluctance to shift brands, the lower the price elasticity of demand. Consumers who are loyal to a brand or to a firm will purchase that brand or purchase from that firm even if the prices are above those of competing brands.

Because it takes a long time to establish a reputation and a brand name, some firms attempt to rent a reputation that has been established in one market and use it in a new market. Endorsement of products by famous personalities is a clear example. Everyone knows that when celebrities endorse a product, it is not because the celebrities have scoured the market for the best product, but rather because they have canvassed potential sponsors to see who will offer the highest fee. So why are consumers influenced by the endorsement? Because the endorser is, to some degree, putting his or her reputation at risk. If the product is of low quality, the celebrity's reputation and value to other sponsors can be damaged. For the manufacturer, payment of the endorsement fee is a demonstration of its commitment to the market. Willingness to pay the endorsement fee is therefore actually a measure of product quality.

Firms will sometimes use their established reputation in one market to enter a new market. BMW's reputation for producing cars reinforces its reputation for producing motor bikes, and vice versa. BMW also endorses a range of "Active Line" sportswear. Caterpillar has a line of clothing, CAT, that portrays the image of its tough, no-nonsense equipment. There is little reason to believe that the capabilities that distinguish BMW cars or CAT equipment are applicable to the manufacture of clothes. But it would clearly be foolish for the companies to attach their name to poor-quality clothes.

Guarantees and warranties can also be ways to get people to experience a good or service. When Japanese automobile companies first entered the U.S. market in the 1960s, they faced the problem of convincing consumers of the quality of the cars. Although the manufacturers knew that their products were of high quality, their potential consumers did not. In fact, many potential consumers believed that Japanese goods were shoddy imitations of Western products. "Made in Japan" had become synonymous with cheap and crummy. Accordingly, Japanese manufacturers offered more extensive warranties than had been usual in the market. Guarantees are difficult to fake. A low-quality product will break down frequently, making the guarantee quite costly for the firm. Thus, the higher the quality of the product, the better the guarantee that the firm can offer.

If a firm establishes a warranty policy, then other firms have to either follow or admit to having a lower-quality product. If another firm is unable to imitate its rivals' existing warranties, it may decide not to enter the market in the first place. This is what the Japanese auto producers did to the U.S. auto producers in the 1970s. U.S. auto producers did not offer as extensive warranties as the Japanese auto producers. As a result, customers soon came to see that "Made in Japan" meant quality. A similar strategy was employed in the late 1990s and early 2000s with respect to the Korean-manufactured Hyundai. Hyundai offered a 100,000-mile full warranty at a time when other manufacturers were offering 36,000-mile warranties.

The key aspect of firms in monopolistic competition is that they devote considerable resources to differentiating their goods and services. But since entry is easy, does that differentiation do the firm any good?

An innovation or successful differentiation in any area—style, quality, location, service—leads initially to above-normal profit, but it eventually brings in copycats that drive profit back down to the normal level. In a monopolistically competitive market structure, innovation and above-normal profit for one firm are followed by entry of other firms and normal profit. Differentiation and above-normal profit then occur again. They induce entry, which again drives profit back to the normal level. The cycle continues until product differentiation no longer brings above-normal profit.

Although an above-normal profit attracts competitors, even a short-lived period of above-normal profit is better than no positive economic profit. That is why firms in monopolistic competition devote so many resources to differentiating their products.

RECAP

1. The market structure called *monopolistic competition* describes an industry in which many sellers produce a differentiated product and entry is easy.

2. In the short run, a firm in monopolistic competition can earn above-normal profit.

3. In the long run, a firm in a monopolistically competitive market structure will produce a lower output at a higher cost than a firm in a perfectly competitive market structure will. In both market structures, firms earn only a normal profit.

4. Monopolistic competitors may engage more in nonprice competition than in price differentiation.

5. The key aspect of monopolistic competition is differentiation.

6. As a firm successfully differentiates its product and earns a positive economic profit, other firms will mimic the successful firm and reduce the differentiation. As a result, the positive economic profit will be competed down toward a normal economic profit.

2. Oligopoly and Interdependence

 3 What is oligopoly?

In Mexico, only two or three companies provide goods and services in areas such as finance, telecommunications, broadcasting, and retailing. And in Poland, a candidate for finance minister argued that the country's current economic problems are due to the dominance of just one or a few firms in the fuel sectors and the financial markets. When a few firms dominate a market, an oligopoly is said to exist. *Oligopoly* is a market structure characterized by (1) few firms, (2) either standardized or differentiated products, and (3) difficult entry. Oligopoly may take many forms. It may consist of one dominant firm coexisting with many smaller firms or a group of giant firms that dominate the industry. The characteristic that describes oligopoly is *interdependence*; an individual firm in an oligopoly does not decide what to do without considering what the other firms in the industry will do. When a large firm in an oligopoly changes its behavior, the demand curves of the other firms are affected significantly.

In perfectly competitive markets, what one firm does affects each of the other firms so slightly that each firm essentially ignores the others. Each firm in an oligopoly, however, must watch the actions of the other firms closely because the actions of one can dramatically affect the others. This interdependence among firms leads to actions not found in the other market structures.

2.a. The Creation of Oligopolies

In the chapter titled "Monopoly," it was noted that a monopoly could, theoretically, arise as a result of natural barriers to entry such as economies of scale, actions on the part of firms that create barriers to entry, or governmentally created barriers. Oligopolies can arise for similar reasons. Many exist because of government regulations. The roots of Mexico's oligopolies, for example, reach back to the 1950s and 1960s, when the government funded private businesses and closed the domestic market to international competition. During that era, the government created a culture in which the state supported companies—government officials forced mergers to create larger companies, and later helped their friends who headed those companies. Large companies owned by powerful dynasties such as the mining company Grupo Mexico, the transportation company TMM, and Bancomer, the country's biggest bank, date from this period. Nowadays, this policy is known as "crony capitalism." In Russia, crony capitalism dominated after the fall of the Soviet Empire. Former government officials, red directors, and oligarchs grabbed assets and took control of former state-owned enterprises such as mining, oil, and utilities.

It is not just developing nations whose governments create oligopolies. In Japan, businesses require government approval for many actions, including entering a new business. For instance, from the early 1990s through 2005, the government allowed only three phone companies—NTT DoCoMo Inc., KDDI Corp., and Vodafone KK—to offer services, although it is now widening the market to allow six new firms to enter the business. In the European Union, the large monopolies and oligopolies created by national governments must now restructure as union-wide companies.

Oligopoly can arise as the result of economies of scale. Since the cost per unit of output declines as a firm gets larger, only the larger firms can remain in business. A small business cannot offer goods and services at as low a price as a larger business can. Thus, the number of companies is determined by the size of the market—where the market-demand curve intersects the long-run average-total-cost curve. Whereas in a monopoly or a government-created oligopoly, competition may be very limited or nonexistent; in an oligopoly that is not supported by the government, the firms must constantly innovate and seek other barriers to entry. Cutthroat competition—competition through innovation, patents, and other means—is often the companion of oligopoly.

Walmart is the dominant retail firm in the United States and Microsoft is the dominant software company, but neither is the only firm in its industry. Both firms dominate because of the efficiencies they have experienced as they have grown and because of the strategies they undertake to maintain their dominance.

4 In what form does rivalry occur in an oligopoly?

2.b. Oligopoly and Competition

Competition does not just mean that firms lower their prices. In the real world, we observe as much competition through innovation as we do through price. In computer hardware and software, for example, firms race to see which will be the first to come out with a new product or which can obtain the patent on an innovation. Consumers are constantly being presented with upgrades and improvements to existing products as well as with brand-new products. Pharmaceutical companies race to create new drugs. They don't compete on price, but rather on innovation.

Firms earning economic profits must attempt to sustain the profit—to keep others from entering and eroding the profit. Firms looking to enter must figure out how best to do that, by lowering price, offering better quality, mimicry, or innovation. Strategy is the process of making decisions—choosing what to do and what to forgo. **Strategic behavior** occurs when what is best for A depends on what B does, and what is best for B depends on what A does. It is much like a card game—bridge, say—where strategies are designed depending on the cards the players are dealt. Underbidding, overbidding, bluffing, deceit, and other strategies are used. In fact, the analogy between games and firm behavior is so strong that economists and mathematicians developed the field of **game theory** to apply to strategic behavior. Game theory emerged in the 1940s and 1950s with the publication of *The Theory of Games and Economic Behavior* and the invention of the prisoners' dilemma.[1]

Oligopoly is the general market structure economists refer to when they mean that one firm's actions affect other firms and one firm is affected by the actions of others. So it seems a perfect fit for the use of game theory to describe the behavior of firms in an oligopoly. If one firm chooses to do something, what is to prevent others from doing the same or countering the direction of the first firm? Walmart created a competitive advantage with its inventory system that essentially reduced the ratio of cost of goods sold (COGS) to sales. The choice to focus on low prices followed from that competitive advantage. The strategy was dependent on what Walmart thought other firms could do. If Walmart executives had anticipated that a rival could immediately do the same thing, they might have selected a different strategy. But they expected to be able to enjoy economic profit for a few years before other firms caught up.

Managers of each firm must make decisions in the context of existing rivals and must even take into account the possible actions of potential rivals. There is no doubt that all managers are absorbed in their own firm's situations, but putting themselves in the shoes of competitors and focusing on the competitors' probable responses to actions they might undertake can be a useful exercise.

2.c. The Dilemma: Noncooperative Games

Consider the situation in which firms must decide whether to devote more resources to advertising. When a firm in any given industry advertises its product, its demand increases for two reasons. First, people who had not used that type of product before learn about it, and some will buy it. Second, other people who already consume a different brand of the same product may switch brands. The first effect boosts sales for the industry as a whole, whereas the second redistributes existing sales within the industry.

Assume that Figure 6 illustrates the possible actions that two firms might take and the results of those actions. The top left rectangle represents the payoffs, or results, if both A and B advertise; the bottom left is the payoffs when A advertises but B does not; the top right is the payoffs when B advertises but A does not; and the bottom right is the payoffs if neither advertises. If firm A can earn higher profits by advertising than by not advertising, whether or not firm B advertises, then firm A will surely advertise. This

strategic behavior
The behavior that occurs when what is best for A depends on what B does, and what is best for B depends on what A does.

game theory
A description of oligopolistic behavior as a series of strategic moves and countermoves.

---

[1] *Theory of Games and Economic Behavior*, by mathematician John von Neumann and economist Oskar Morgenstern, published in 1944 by Princeton University Press. In 1950, while addressing an audience of psychologists at Stanford University, A. W. Tucker created the prisoners' dilemma to illustrate the difficulty of analyzing certain kinds of games. His simple explanation has since given rise to a vast body of literature in subjects as diverse as philosophy, ethics, biology, sociology, political science, and economics.

FIGURE 6 Dilemma: Dominant Strategy Game

Figure 6 illustrates the dominant strategy game. The dominant strategy for firm A is to advertise. No matter what firm B does, firm A is better off advertising. If firm B does not advertise, firm A earns 80 not advertising and 100 advertising. If firm B does advertise, firm A earns 40 not advertising and 70 advertising. Similarly, firm B is better off advertising no matter what firm A does. Both A and B have dominant strategies—advertise.

© 2013 Cengage Learning

dominant strategy

A strategy that produces better results no matter what strategy the opposing firm follows.

is referred to as a **dominant strategy**—a strategy that produces the best results no matter what strategy the opposing player follows.

Firm A compares the left side of the matrix to the right side and sees that it earns more by advertising, no matter what firm B does. If B advertises and A advertises, then A earns 70, but if B advertises and A does not advertise, it earns 40. If B does not advertise, then A earns 100 by advertising and only 80 by not advertising. The dominant strategy for firm A is to advertise. And according to Figure 6, the dominant strategy for firm B is also to advertise. Firm B will earn 80 by advertising and 50 by not advertising if A advertises, and will earn 100 by advertising but only 90 by not advertising if A does not advertise. But notice that both firms would be better off if neither advertised; firm A would earn 80 instead of 70, and firm B would earn 90 instead of 80. Yet the firms cannot afford to *not* advertise because they would lose more if the other firm advertised and they didn't. This situation is known as the prisoners' dilemma; see the Economic Insight "The Prisoners' Dilemma" for a more complete description of why it has this name.

This is exactly the situation cigarette producers were facing in the 1960s. None of the cigarette manufacturers wanted to do much advertising. Yet strategic behavior suggested that they must. Firm A advertises, so firm B must also do so. Each firm ups the advertising ante. How can this expensive advertising competition be controlled? Each firm alone has no incentive to do it, since unilateral action will mean a significant loss of market share. The two parties have fallen into a dilemma, something called a dominant strategy equilibrium. This remarkable result—that individually rational action results in both persons being made worse off in terms of their own self-interested purposes—is what has made the wide impact in modern social science. There are many interactions in the modern world that seem very much like this dominant strategy equilibrium: for example, arms races, road congestion, and the depletion of fisheries.

Let's consider a many-person version of this game. Assume people have two choices of transportation: cars or buses. The basic idea here is that car commuting increases congestion and slows down traffic. The more commuters drive their cars to work, the longer it takes to get to work, and the lower the payoffs are for both car commuters and bus commuters.

ECONOMIC INSIGHT

The Prisoners' Dilemma

Strategic behavior characterizes oligopoly. Perhaps the best-known example of strategic behavior occurs in what is called the prisoners' dilemma. Two people have been arrested for a crime, but the evidence against them is weak. The sheriff keeps the prisoners separated and offers each of them a special deal: If the prisoner confesses, that prisoner can go free as long as only he confesses, and the other prisoner will get ten or more years in prison. However, if both prisoners confess, each will receive a reduced sentence of two years in jail. The prisoners know that if neither confesses, they will be cleared of all but a minor charge and will serve only two days in jail. The problem is that they do not know what deal the other is being offered, or whether the other will take the deal.

The options available to the two prisoners are shown in the four cells of the figure. Prisoner B's options are shown in the horizontal direction, and prisoner A's are shown in the vertical direction. In the upper left cell is the result if both prisoners confess. In the lower left cell is the result if prisoner A does not confess but prisoner B does; in the upper right cell is the result of prisoner A's confessing but prisoner B's not confessing; and in the lower right cell is the result when neither prisoner confesses. The dominant strategy for both prisoners is to confess and receive two years of jail time.

If the prisoners had been loyal to each other, each would have received a much smaller penalty. Because both chose to confess, each is worse off than he or she would have been if he or she had known what the other was doing. Yet in the context of the interdependence of the decisions, each made the best choice.

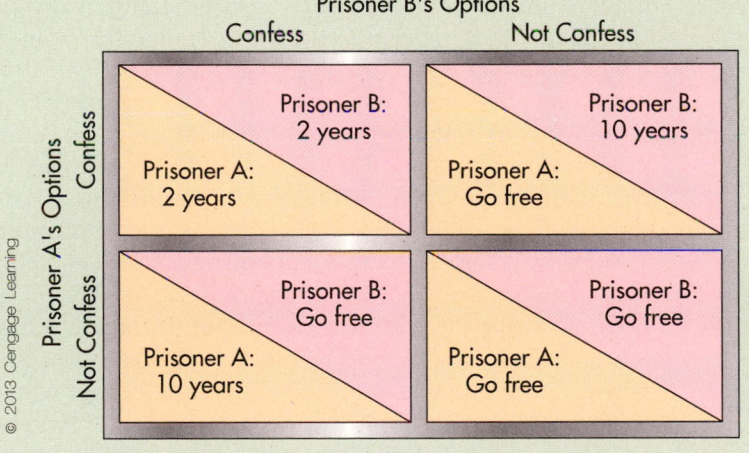

Figure 7 illustrates this. In the figure, the horizontal axis measures the proportion of commuters who drive their cars. Accordingly, the horizontal axis varies from a lower limit of zero to a maximum of 100 percent. The vertical axis shows the payoffs for this game. The upper (green) line shows the payoffs for car commuters. We see that it declines as the proportion of commuters in their cars increases. The lower (red) line shows the payoffs to bus commuters. We see that, regardless of the proportion of commuters in cars, cars have a higher payoff than buses. In other words, commuting by car

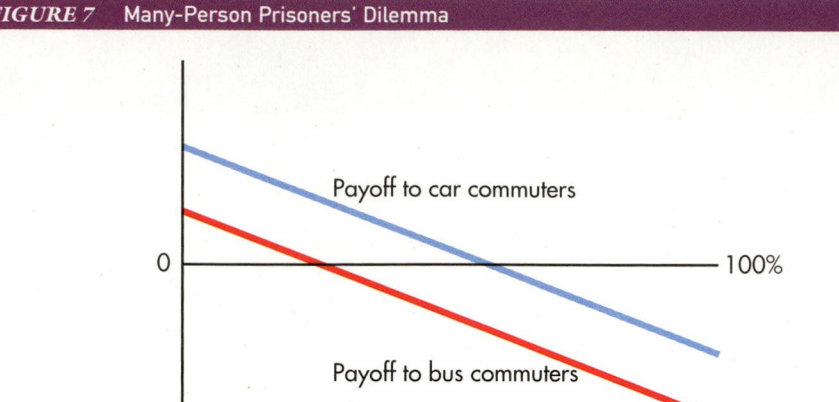

FIGURE 7   Many-Person Prisoners' Dilemma

The horizontal axis measures the proportion of commuters who drive their cars, from zero to 100 percent. The vertical axis shows the payoffs for this game. The upper (blue) line shows the payoffs for car commuters. The lower (red) line is the payoff to bus commuters. The choice of the dominant strategies makes everyone worse off.

© 2013 Cengage Learning

is a dominant strategy in this game. In a dominant strategy equilibrium, all drive their cars. The result is that they all have negative payoffs, whereas, if all rode buses, all would have positive payoffs.

This is an extension of the prisoners' dilemma in that there is a dominant strategy equilibrium, and the choice of dominant strategies makes everyone worse off. To make the game a little more realistic, let us assume that some people do ride buses and that congestion does slow buses but slows cars even more.

Congestion slows the buses down, but because of a few special lanes for buses, the payoff for car commuters drops faster than for bus commuters. In Figure 8, when the proportion of people in their cars reaches q, the payoff for car commuters overtakes the payoff for bus riders, and for larger proportions of car commuters (to the right of q), the payoff for commuting is worse than that for bus commuters.[2]

The game no longer has a dominant strategy equilibrium, but it has what is called a **Nash equilibrium**.[3] A Nash equilibrium occurs when a unilateral move by a participant does not make the participant better off. In Figure 8, starting from q, if one bus commuter shifts to commuting by car, that person moves into the region to the right of q, where car commuters are worse off, so the person who switched is worse off. On the other hand, starting from q, if one car commuter switches to the bus, that moves into the region to the left of q, where bus commuters are worse off, so, again, the switcher is worse off. No one can be better off individually by switching from q. When no one can move from the equilibrium and improve the outcome, the result is a Nash equilibrium.

Nash equilibrium
No player can be made better off by changing unilaterally.

2.c.1. Repeated Games
Notice that in these games, the two parties interacted only once. Repetition of the interactions leads to quite different results. In fact, what occurred with the cigarette companies and their advertising dilemma is that the companies, along with consumers, lobbied to have the government pass a law banning cigarette advertising. A ban on cigarette advertising on television has been in effect since

---

[2] This example was provided by Roger McCain's *Game Theory: A Nontechnical Introduction to the Analysis of Strategy*, which is available at: http://william-king. www.drexel.edu/top/eco/game/game.html.

[3] Named after Nobel Laureate John Nash. Nash's life is featured in the movie *A Beautiful Mind*.

FIGURE 8   Nash Equilibrium

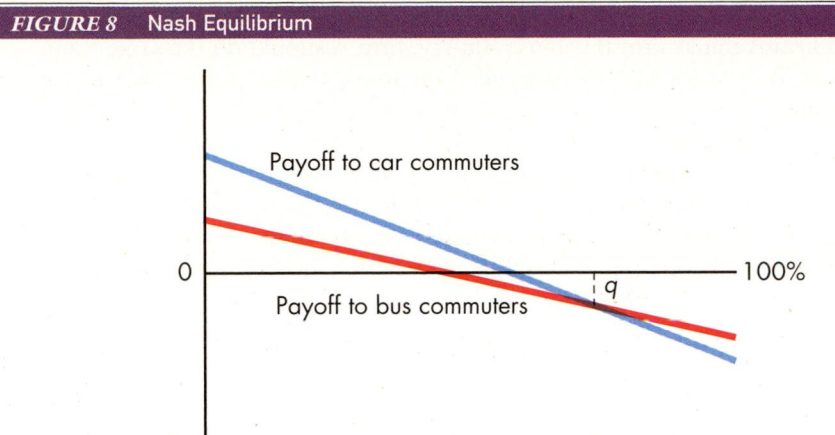

Congestion slows the buses down, so that the payoff for bus commuters declines as congestion increases; but the payoff for car commuters declines even faster. When the proportion of people in their cars reaches *q*, the payoff for car commuters overtakes the payoff for bus riders, and for larger proportions of car commuters (to the right of *q*), the payoff to for commuting is worse than that for bus commuters.

January 1, 1971. The ban was intended by the government as a means to reduce cigarette smoking—of helping the consumer. Yet who did this ban really benefit?

2.d. Cooperation

Notice that in these dilemma games there has been no communication between the parties. If they could communicate and commit themselves to coordinated strategies, a different outcome would result. Consider the decision to go with HD (high definition) or Blu-ray video technology.

Many households were holding off buying HD televisions and associated equipment because they were not sure which standard would prevail. Similarly, until February 2008, many manufacturers were debating whether to use HD or Blu-ray technology. Toshiba, the maker of HD, conceded defeat and left the market to Blu-ray. Suppose there are two firms considering whether to introduce new equipment but do not know which technology to use. This is represented in Table 2.

If each firm produces equipment using HD, each firm will earn profits of $100. Similarly, if each firm produces equipment using Blu-ray, each firm will earn $100. However, if the two firms produce equipment using different technologies, each firm will

 5 Why does cooperation among rivals occur most often in oligopolies?

TABLE 2	The Cooperation Game		
		Firm B	
	Strategy	**HD**	**Blu-ray**
Firm A	HD	$100, $100	$0, $0
	Blu-ray	$0, $0	$100, $100

The two players are better off agreeing to a standard or a similar technology. Without that, the solution is the possibility of selecting a result that is not a Nash equilibrium.

earn zero. What will each firm do? If firm A thinks firm B will use HD, it should use HD as well. If firm A thinks firm B will use Blu-ray, firm A should do the same thing.

Although it looks a lot like the prisoners' dilemma at first glance, this is a more complicated game. The best strategy for each participant depends on the strategy chosen by the other participant; there are no dominant strategies. When there are no dominant strategies, the equilibrium is a Nash equilibrium. This game has two Nash equilibria; the firms do the same thing—both use HD or both use Blu-ray. How do they get to a Nash equilibrium? The firms might compete, they might communicate and agree to provide just one type of equipment, or they might lobby the government to create a standard for the protection of the consumer: Everyone must use HD or everyone must use Blu-ray. What actually occurred is that Sony (Blu-ray) was able to enlist more market participants than Toshiba (HD), including movie producers and studios.

The lack of communication in the prisoners' dilemma games is an artificial situation. The firms don't have to simply wait to see what the other does—they can sit down and talk it out. Acting jointly allows firms to earn more profits than they would if they acted independently or against each other. To avoid the destructiveness of strategic behavior, the few firms in an oligopoly may collude or come to some agreement about price and output levels. Typically these agreements provide the members of the oligopoly with higher profits and thus raise prices to consumers. A constraint facing firms is that it is illegal to collude. They cannot agree to fix prices or restrict competition. So how do they cooperate without breaking the law?

2.d.1. Conventions
How do firms cooperate to avoid being in a prisoners' dilemma and also avoid colluding? Suppose you are talking on the telephone with a business associate and the connection is broken. Do you call your associate or do you wait for her to call you? If you call, you might get only a busy signal because she is also calling. If you wait, neither of you might call. What is best for you depends on what your associate does, and vice versa. There are two Nash equilibria to this problem. In one, you call and she does not; in the other, she calls and you do not. Even though there are two Nash equilibria, the problem is that without some rule of behavior, you may end up with a busy signal or no call. You could prevent this problem by announcing at the beginning of each phone conversation who will call if the connection is broken. Of course, this is very inefficient. No one wants to make such an announcement at the beginning of each call. What arises, then, is an efficient way to move toward the Nash equilibrium—called a **convention**. A typical convention is that the person who called originally calls again.

convention
An institution or procedure increasing efficiency.

2.d.2. Price-Leadership Oligopoly
One way for firms to communicate without illegally colluding is to allow one firm to be the leader in changes in price or advertising activities. When the leader makes a change, the others duplicate what the leader has done. This enables all firms to know exactly what their rivals will do. It avoids the prisoners' dilemma situation where excessive expenditures are made on advertising or other activities. This type of oligopoly is called a *price-leadership oligopoly*.

The steel industry in the 1960s is an example of a dominant-firm price-leadership oligopoly. For many years, steel producers allowed U.S. Steel to set prices for the entire industry. The cooperation of the steel companies probably led to higher profits than would have occurred with rivalry. However, the absence of rivalry is said to be one reason for the decline of the steel industry in the United States. Price leadership removed the need for the steel companies to compete by maintaining and upgrading their equipment and materials and by developing new technologies. As a result, foreign firms that chose not to behave as price followers emerged as more sophisticated producers of steel than U.S. firms.

For many years, airlines also relied on a price leader. In many cases, the price leader was not the dominant airline, but instead was one of the weaker or new airlines. In recent years, however, airlines have communicated less through a price leader and more through their computerized reservation systems, according to the Justice Department.

2.d.3. Cartels and Other Cooperative Mechanisms
A **cartel** is an organization of independent firms whose purpose is to control and limit production and maintain or increase prices and profits. A cartel can result from either formal or informal agreement among members. Like collusion, cartels are illegal in the United States. The cartel most people are familiar with is the Organization of Petroleum Exporting Countries (OPEC), a group of nations rather than a group of independent firms. During the 1970s, OPEC was able to coordinate oil production in such a way that it drove the market price of crude oil from $1.10 a barrel to $32 a barrel. For nearly eight years, each member of OPEC agreed to produce a certain, limited amount of crude oil as designated by the OPEC production committee. Then in the early 1980s, the cartel began to fall apart as individual members began to cheat on the agreement. Members began to produce more than their allocation in an attempt to increase profit. As each member of the cartel did this, the price of oil fell, reaching $12 per barrel in 1988.

Production quotas for different firms or different nations are not easy to maintain. Most cartels do not last very long because their members cheat on the agreements. If each producer thinks that it can increase its own production, and thus its profits, without affecting what the other producers do, all producers end up producing more than their assigned amounts; the price of the product declines, and the cartel falls apart.

Economists have identified certain conditions that make it likely that a cartel will be stable. The conditions under which a cartel is likely to remain in force are as follows.

- There are few firms in the industry.
- There are significant barriers to entry.
- An identical product is produced.
- There are few opportunities to keep actions secret.
- There are no legal barriers to sharing agreements.

To illustrate, consider just two firms fixing prices. Figure 9 shows the market demand curve, *D*, with the simplifying assumption that marginal and average costs are constant. If the two firms were a monopolist rather than being two firms, the monopolist's marginal-revenue curve would be as shown in Figure 9(a), intersecting the marginal-cost curve at a quantity of 130 and a price of $40. If the two companies act as one, they will select the monopoly price of $40 and quantity of 130 and then split the market, with each having 65. The average cost is $20, so each firm earns a profit of $1,300 ($20 × 65).

If instead the two firms compete with each other, then their demand curves will lie inside the market or monopoly demand curve. Figure 9(b) shows the demand and marginal revenue for firm 1. Firm 2 is identical to firm 1. As a result of competition, each firm sets a lower price and serves more customers. The profit each firm makes is $700 ($10 × 70). When the two firms compete, their combined profits are $1,400; when they collude by fixing the price and setting the quantities each will produce, their profits are $1,300 each, or $2,600 combined.

The extra profits from collusion create an incentive for firms to cheat on their agreements. Suppose that one of the firms decides to sell more than its allotted quantity of 65. It will be able to sell the higher quantity only if the price is lower or if the other firm serves fewer customers. Either case hurts at least one of the colluding firms, and the cartel breaks apart.

Because there is a strong incentive for firms that are members of a cartel or that are colluding to cheat on their agreements, a way to stop cheaters, to penalize them, must

cartel
An organization of independent firms whose purpose is to control and limit production and maintain or increase prices and profits.

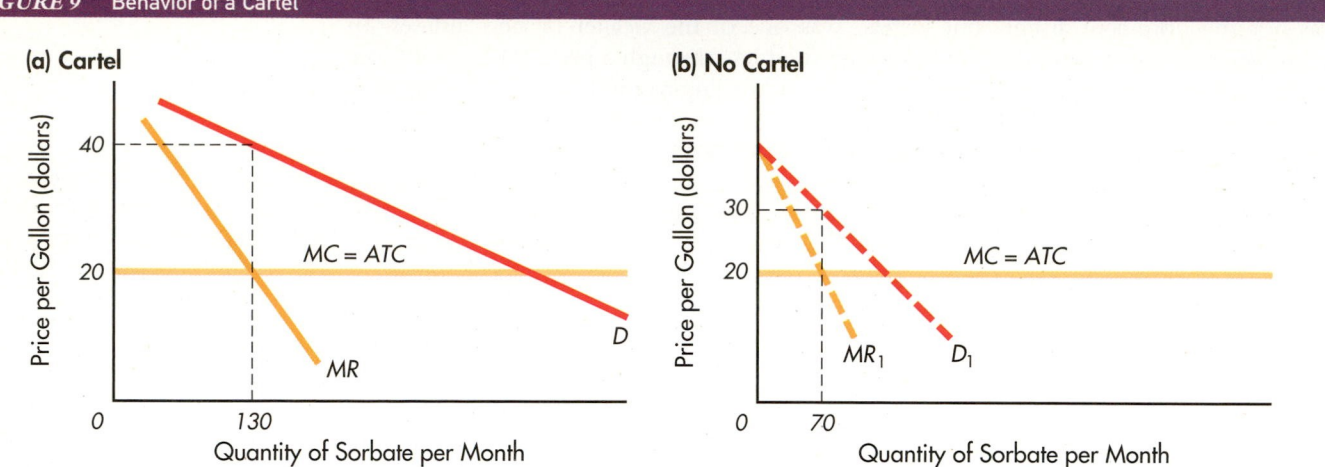

FIGURE 9   Behavior of a Cartel

(a) Cartel

(b) No Cartel

© 2013 Cengage Learning

In Figure 9(a), the firms agree to act as a monopolist, setting the price where the monopolist would maximize profit and then sharing the resulting profits. When the cartel members act alone, as shown in Figure 9(b), they maximize profit by setting a lower price and selling to fewer customers than was the case when they acted as monopolists. The result is a lower profit.

be found if the cartel is to remain in place. In most cartels, the strongest member takes over and polices it. In OPEC, it is Saudi Arabia that serves as police. When a member does not adhere to the prescribed quantity, Saudi Arabia opens its valves and floods the market with petroleum. Saudi Arabia can do this because it is the nation with the largest supply of petroleum. The flooded market means a lower price and thus lower profits for all countries. With the drug cartels of Colombia and Mexico, one family polices the agreement; cheaters typically end up dead. Without a policing authority, the cartel will fall apart.

Even though cartels are generally illegal in the United States, a few have been sanctioned by the government. The National Collegiate Athletic Association (NCAA) is a cartel of colleges and universities. It sets rules of behavior and enforces those rules through a governing board. Member schools are placed on probation or their programs are dismantled if they violate the agreement. The citrus cartel, composed of citrus growers in California and Arizona, enforces its actions through its governing board. Sunkist Growers Inc., a cooperative of many growers, represents more than half of the California and Arizona citrus producers and also plays an important role in enforcing the rules of the cartel. Major professional sports leagues are government-sanctioned cartels.

2.d.4. Facilitating Practices

facilitating practices
Actions by oligopolistic firms that can contribute to cooperation and collusion even though the firms do not formally agree to cooperate.

cost-plus/markup pricing
A pricing policy whereby a firm computes its average cost of producing a product and then sets the price at some percentage above this cost.

2.d.4. Facilitating Practices Actions by firms can contribute to cooperation and collusion even though the firms do not formally agree to cooperate. Such actions are called **facilitating practices**. Pricing policies can give the impression that firms are explicitly fixing prices, or cooperating, when in fact they are merely following the same strategies. For instance, the use of **cost-plus/markup pricing** tends to lead to similar or identical pricing behavior among rival firms. If firms set prices by determining the average cost of an item and adding a fixed markup to the cost, they are engaging in cost-plus pricing. If all firms face the same cost curves, then all firms will set the same prices. If costs decrease, then all firms will lower prices the same amount and at virtually the same time. Such pricing behavior is common in the grocery business.

Another practice that leads to implicit cooperation is the most-favored-customer policy. Often, the time between purchase and delivery of a product is quite long. To avoid the possibility that customer A purchases a product at one price and then learns that customer B purchased the product at a lower price or benefited from product features that were unavailable to customer A, a producer will guarantee that customer A will receive the lowest price and all features for a certain period of time. Customer A is thus a **most-favored customer (MFC)**.

most-favored customer (MFC)
A customer who receives a guarantee of the lowest price and all product features for a certain period of time.

The most-favored-customer policy actually gives firms an incentive not to lower prices, even in the face of reduced demand. A firm that lowers the price of its product must then give rebates to all most-favored customers, which forces all other firms with most-favored-customer policies to do the same. In addition, the MFC policy allows a firm to collect information on what its rivals are doing. Customers will return products for a refund when another firm offers the same product for a lower price.

A most-favored-customer policy discourages price decreases because it requires producers to lower prices retroactively with rebates. If all rivals provide all buyers with most-favored-customer clauses, a high price is likely to be stabilized in the industry.

RECAP

1. Oligopoly is a market structure in which there are so few firms that each must take into account what the others do, entry is difficult, and either undifferentiated or differentiated products are produced.

2. An oligopoly may come into being because government allows only a few firms to control or dominate an industry, or it may arise as a result of economies of scale.

3. Interdependence and strategic behavior characterize oligopoly.

4. The shape of the demand curve and the marginal-revenue curve facing an oligopolist depend on how rival firms react to changes in price and product.

5. The prisoners' dilemma is an example of how competition among firms that are interdependent can result in an outcome that is not the best for the competing firms.

6. Oligopolistic firms have incentives to cooperate. In a price-leadership oligopoly, one firm determines the price and quantity, knowing that all other firms will follow suit. The price leader is usually the dominant firm in the industry.

7. Collusion, or making a secret cooperative agreement, is illegal in the United States. Cartels, also illegal in the United States, rest on explicit cooperation achieved through formal agreement.

8. The incentive for cartel members to cheat typically leads to the collapse of the cartel. To minimize cheating, one member must police the others.

9. Facilitating practices implicitly encourage cooperation in an industry.

---

3. Summary of Market Structures

 6 What are the differences and similarities among the four market structure models?

We have now discussed each of the four market structures in some detail. Table 3 summarizes the characteristics of each model and the main predictions yielded by that model. The model of perfect competition predicts that firms will produce at a point where price and marginal cost are the same (at the bottom of the average-total-cost curve) and profit will be zero in the long run. The model characterizes competition as an ideal—consumers get what they want at the lowest possible prices, and the efficiency for society is maximized. The model of monopoly predicts that price will exceed marginal cost and that the firm can earn positive economic profit in the long run. This model is the opposite of the ideal of perfect competition—the seller obtains the largest producer surplus and creates a deadweight loss. With monopolistic competition and oligopoly, we turn from the theoretical bookends of perfect competition and monopoly to

TABLE 3	Summary of Perfect Competition, Monopoly, Monopolistic Competition, and Oligopoly			
	Perfect Competition	**Monopoly**	**Monopolistic Competition**	**Oligopoly**
Number of firms	Many	One	Many	Few
Type of product	Identical	One	Differentiated	Identical or differentiated
Entry conditions	Easy	Difficult or impossible	Easy	Difficult
Demand curve	Horizontal (perfectly elastic)	Downward sloping	Downward sloping	Downward sloping
Price and marginal cost	$MC = P$	$MC < P$	$MC < P$	$MC < P$
Long-run profit	Normal	Yes	Normal	Depends on whether entry occurs

more real-life behaviors. With monopolistic competition, price will exceed marginal cost and the firm will not produce at the bottom point of the average-total-cost curve, but this is due to consumers' desire for product differentiation. In the long run, the firm in monopolistic competition will earn a normal profit. In oligopoly, a firm may be able to earn above-normal profit for a long time—as long as entry can be restricted. In oligopoly, price exceeds marginal cost, and the firm does not operate at the bottom of the average-total-cost curve.

Under perfect competition, consumers purchase products at the lowest possible price; there is no advertising, no excessive overhead, and no warranties or guarantees. Under monopoly, people purchase a single product and advertising is virtually nonexistent. With monopolistic competition and oligopoly, advertising commonly plays an important role.

SUMMARY

1. What is monopolistic competition?

- Monopolistic competition is a market structure in which many firms are producing a slightly different product and entry is easy. *§1*

- Monopolistically competitive firms will earn a normal profit in the long run. *§1.a.2*

2. What behavior is most common in monopolistic competition?

- Entry occurs in monopolistically competitive industries through the introduction of a slightly different product. *§1.a*

- A monopolistically competitive firm will produce less output and charge a higher price than an identical perfectly competitive firm if demand and costs are assumed to be the same. *§1.a*

3. What is oligopoly?

- Oligopoly is a market structure in which a few large firms produce identical or slightly different

products and entry is difficult but not impossible. The firms are interdependent. *§2*

- Oligopolies may arise from government restrictions or from natural economic factors such as economies of scale. *§2.a*

4. In what form does rivalry occur in an oligopoly?

- Strategic behavior characterizes oligopoly. The firms are interdependent. The actions of each oligopolist will affect its competitors, and each will be affected by the actions of its rivals. *§2.b*

- Game theory is a description of behavior when players' decisions depend on the decisions of the other players. *§2.b*

- The prisoners' dilemma illustrates an outcome in which competition among interdependent firms results in an outcome that is less than the best for each firm. *§2.c*

- The prisoners' dilemma is a noncooperative game also called a dominant strategy game, one in which the parties select the dominant strategy. By doing so they do not select the best outcome for the parties as a whole. *§2.c*

- A dominant strategy is one a player will select no matter what strategy other players choose. *§2.c*

- Nash equilibrium is an equilibrium when unilateral action by one party will make the party worse off. *§2.c*

5. **Why does cooperation among rivals occur most often in oligopolies?**

- The small number of firms in an oligopoly and the interdependence of these firms creates the situation in which the firms are better off if they cooperate. *§2.d*

- Cooperation games indicate that by agreeing to a solution, the parties in a game will be better off than if they do not agree to a solution. *§2.d*

- Price leadership is another type of strategic behavior. One firm determines prices for the entire industry. All other firms follow the leader in increasing and decreasing prices. The dominant firm in the industry is most likely to be the price leader. *§2.d.1*

- Practices like collusion and cartels minimize profit, reduce rivalry, and ensure cooperation. *§2.d.3*

- Cartels are illegal in the United States and in many other nations but are acceptable in a few nations. *§2.d.2, 2.d.3*

- The incentive for members of a cartel to cheat on the other members often leads to a breakdown of the cartel. *§2.d.3*

- Cost-plus pricing ensures that firms with the same costs will charge the same prices. The most-favored-customer policy guarantees a customer that the price he or she paid for a product will not be lowered for another customer. Cost-plus pricing and the most-favored-customer policy are facilitating practices. *§2.d.4*

6. **What are the differences and similarities among the four market structure models?**

- Perfect competition and monopolistic competition involve many firms and easy entry and exit. Economic profit is zero in the long run. *§3*

- Monopoly means there is no entry and that competition will not drive profits to zero. *§3*

- Oligopoly refers to interdependence, or strategic behavior on the part of firms. Because entry is often difficult, an oligopolist can maintain profit until competition from entry does occur. If successful with cartels, collusion, or other practices of cooperation, the oligopolies may be able to maintain above-normal profits for a long period of time. *§3*

KEY TERMS

EXERCISES

1. Disney, Universal, and MGM, among others, have movie studios in Hollywood. Each of these major studios also has one or several subsidiary studios. Disney, for example, has Touchstone. What market structure best describes these movie production companies? Why would each studio have subsidiary studios? Consider the movies that have come out under the Disney name and those that have come out under Touchstone. Are they different?

2. Suppose that Disney was experiencing above-normal profits. If Disney is a member of a monopolistically competitive industry, what would you predict would happen to the demand curve for Disney movies over time? Suppose that Disney is a member of an oligopoly. How would this change your answer?

3. Why is monopolistic competition said to be inefficient? Suppose that you counted the higher price the consumer pays for the monopolistically

competitive firm's product as part of consumer surplus. Would that change the conclusion regarding the efficiency of monopolistic competition?

4. Why might some people claim that the breakfast cereal industry is monopolistically competitive but that the automobile industry is an oligopoly? In both cases, about eight to ten firms dominate the industry.

5. The graph that follows shows an individual firm in long-run equilibrium. In which market structure is this firm operating? Explain. Compare the long-run quantity and price to those of a perfectly competitive firm. What accounts for the difference? Is the equilibrium price greater than, equal to, or less than marginal cost? Why or why not?

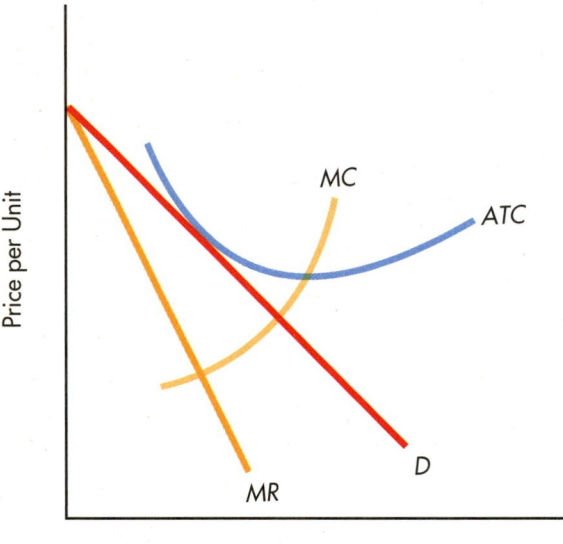

6. Explain what is meant by strategic behavior.

7. The NCAA is described as a cartel. In what way is it a cartel? What is the product being produced? How does the cartel stay together?

8. Almost every town has at least one funeral home, even if the number of deaths could not possibly keep the funeral home busy. What market structure does the funeral home industry best exemplify? Use the firm's demand and cost curves and long-run equilibrium position to explain the fact that the funeral home can handle more business than it has. (*Hint:* Is the firm operating at the bottom of the average-total-cost curve?)

9. What is the cost to a firm in an oligopoly that fails to take rivals' actions into account?

10. Suppose a firm in monopolistic competition has the demand schedule shown in the following table. Suppose the marginal cost is a constant $70. How much will the firm produce? Is this a long-or short-run situation? If the firm is earning above-normal profit, what will happen to this demand schedule?

Price	Quantity	Price	Quantity
$100	1	$70	5
$ 95	2	$55	6
$ 88	3	$40	7
$ 80	4	$22	8

11. The cement industry is an example of an undifferentiated oligopoly. The automobile industry is a differentiated oligopoly. Which of these two is more likely to advertise? Why?

12. The South American cocaine industry consists of several "families" that obtain the raw material, refine it, and distribute it in the United States. There are only about three large families, but there are several small families. What market structure does the industry most closely resemble? What predictions based on the market structure models can be made about the cocaine business? How do you explain the lack of wars among the families?

13. Use the payoff matrix below for the following exercises. The payoff matrix indicates the profit outcome that corresponds to each firm's pricing strategy.

		Firm A's Price	
		$20	$15
Firm B's Price	$20	Firm A earns $40 profit Firm B earns $37 profit	Firm A earns $35 profit Firm B earns $39 profit
	$15	Firm A earns $49 profit Firm B earns $30 profit	Firm A earns $38 profit Firm B earns $35 profit

a. Firms A and B are members of an oligopoly. Explain the interdependence that exists in oligopolies using the payoff matrix facing the two firms.

b. Assuming that the firms cooperate, what is the solution to the problem facing the firms?

c. Given your answer to part (b), explain why cooperation would be mutually beneficial and then explain why one of the firms might cheat.

14. What is the purpose of a brand name? What would occur if any maker of aspirin could put a Bayer Aspirin label on its product?

15. Explain the difference between a dominant strategy and a Nash equilibrium.

16. Explain why repeated interactions tends to break down the solution of a prisoners' dilemma. Why does the dilemma go away?

You can find further practice tests in the Online Quiz at **www.cengage.com/economics/boyes**.

MEXICAN AUTHORITIES WORK TO BREAK UP DRUG CARTEL

Houston Chronicle, September 3, 2005

MEXICO CITY—Federal authorities have charged 15 police officers from the violent border city of Nuevo Laredo with organized crime and kidnapping, alleging they worked for the Gulf Cartel, officials said Friday.

The federal Attorney General's Office said in a statement that witnesses linked to a rival drug organization, the Sinaloa Cartel, allege the officers abducted them and handed them over to the Zetas, the Gulf Cartel's army of enforcers.

The witnesses were part of a group of 44 people found bound and gagged in a Nuevo Laredo house raided by federal agents and soldiers in June, the Attorney General's Office said.

The Gulf Cartel, led by the imprisoned Osiel Cardenas, and the Sinaloa Cartel, led by escaped convict Joaquin "Shorty" Guzman, are fighting a bloody turf war to control Nuevo Laredo and its billion-dollar drug-smuggling routes into Texas, investigators say. The Gulf Cartel, authorities allege, had a number of local policemen on its payroll.

"The police used their position as municipal officers to detain people they thought were linked to the Shorty Guzman organization," the Attorney General's Office said. "They gave (the detainees) to the Zetas, who tortured them and used them to get information, get a ransom, or kill them."

Since Jan. 1, drug-related violence has left more than 100 people dead, including 15 police officers, in Nuevo Laredo, a city of 500,000 across the Rio Grande from Laredo. One of the victims, Police Chief Alejandro Dominguez, was gunned down just hours after taking office.

The 15 accused policemen were part of a group of 41 Nuevo Laredo officers arrested in June after a shootout with federal agents. The fate of the other 26 detained officers will be decided soon, authorities said.

President Vicente Fox has declared the "mother of all battles" against drug traffickers and has promised to crack down on any corrupt police officer working for the cartels.

Since Jan. 1, there have been more than 830 drug-related killings in Mexico, mostly in states near the U.S. border.

IOAN GRILLO

Nuevo Laredo is a battleground. Warring drug organizations there are fighting for control of the billion-dollar drug-smuggling routes into the United States. In recent years, the drug trade, once the province of Colombian drug families, has been taken over by Mexican cartels. In particular, the Gulf Cartel and the Sinaloa Cartel have taken over drug smuggling. But now the two cartels are battling with each other. Let's use the material of this chapter to consider some of the cartels' actions.

Let's begin with the fact that the two factions are battling. Wouldn't cooperation seem to be preferred by each of them? We can present the alternatives in the matrix below.

		Sinaloa	
		Share Market	**Take Market**
Gulf	**Share Market**	Sinaloa = $75* Gulf = $75*	Sinaloa = $150* Gulf = 0
	Take Market	Sinaloa = 0 Gulf = $150*	Sinaloa = $50* Gulf = $50*

*Amounts given are in hundreds of millions of dollars.

If the Sinaloa Cartel shares the market with the Gulf Cartel, each earns $75 hundred million. If Sinaloa tries to take the market while Gulf tries to share, Sinaloa gets $150 hundred million and Gulf gets nothing. Conversely, if Gulf tries to take the market while Sinaloa tries to share, Gulf gets $150 hundred million and Sinaloa gets nothing. If both cartels try to take the market, then they both end up with $50 hundred million, since the costs of battle take away from their profits. Notice from the matrix that the two will choose to fight—to take the market. Although each would be better off sharing the market than fighting for it, each has an incentive to try to take the market. This prisoners' dilemma points to the situation in which the two cartels find themselves.

The prisoners' dilemma points out that if the cartels could cooperate and share, they would be better off. We can show this on a standard demand and supply diagram as well. Consider the following diagram with the market-demand curve, *D*. If the cartels cooperated and acted as a single monopolist, they would have the marginal-revenue curve, *MR*, associated with demand, *D*, which would intersect the supply or *MC* at a quantity of 150 units and

a price of $30. So by cooperating or colluding, the result would be greater profits for each—each must agree to sell 75 units at a price of $30.

However, if they are colluding and have increased the price to $30, the drug suppliers will each think to themselves, "Why don't I sell 100 units at a price of $30?" The problem is that when the cartels begin selling more than their quota, the market price declines. The only way that the price can be kept high while one of the drug groups increases quantity is for the other group to reduce quantity. This means that one group gains while the other loses—something that neither group will accept. As a result, both groups begin selling more, and the price declines.

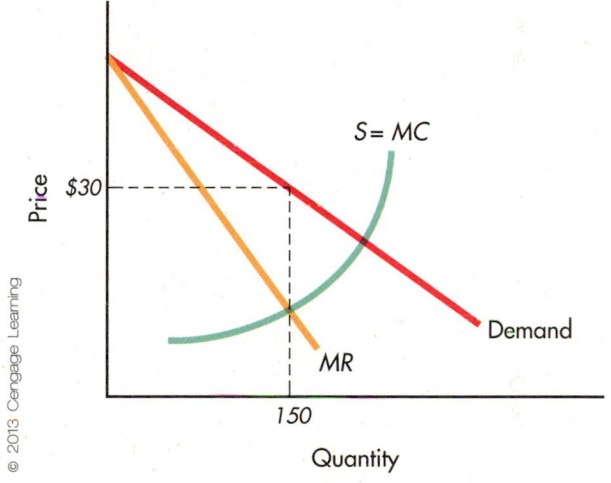

This is a common problem with cartels—the members have a huge incentive to cheat. Because there is a strong incentive for firms that are members of the drug cartel to cheat on agreements, a way to stop cheaters must be found, or else the cartel falls apart. In the illegal drug trade, cheaters are dealt with through violence and drug wars. When one drug cartel moves into the territory of another, drug wars break out. When one cartel expands its business without dealing with another cartel, violence erupts. According to the article, between January 1, 2005, and September 3, 2005, over 830 drug-related killings occurred in Mexico, and more than 100 people were killed in Nuevo Laredo.

CHAPTER 26

Antitrust, Regulation, and Public Finance

© MACIEJ FROLOW/GETTY IMAGES, INC

JOE GOUGH/SHUTTERSTOCK.COM; LOGO: © FROXX/SHUTTERSTOCK.COM

FUNDAMENTAL QUESTIONS

1 What is antitrust policy?

2 What is the difference between economic regulation and social regulation?

3 What international agencies regulate business behavior?

4 How does government pay for its activities?

Government is involved in the economy by the laws it makes and regulations it prescribes, by the taxes it imposes and the expenditures it makes. Those laws and regulations are enforced though a multitude of government agencies and departments. Table 1 provides a simple list of U.S. federal government agencies. There are a lot of agencies, but these numbers are only from the federal government. State and local governments also have many agencies and departments. In other words, government is a large player in the economy. In this chapter, we focus on government involvement in the private sector. We discuss government's policies toward business as well as government's role in defining rules and regulations for the private sector. We begin with a look at antitrust, the government's policies directed toward competition. We then turn to regulations—both those directed to business and those directed to the entire populace. Finally, we discuss how the government finances all its activities.

1. Antitrust

Antitrust means against trusts. Trusts are combinations of businesses that allegedly reduce competition. Thus **antitrust policy** prohibits agreements or practices that restrict free trade and competition among business entities. It also restricts abusive behavior by a firm dominating a market, or anticompetitive practices that tend to lead to such a dominant position. Antitrust enforcement at the U.S. federal government level takes place through the Department of Justice and the Federal Trade Commission, an "independent agency."

antitrust policy
Government policies and programs designed to control the growth of monopoly and enhance competition.

1.a. Antitrust Policy

Three laws define the U.S. government's approach to antitrust—the Sherman, Clayton, and Federal Trade Commission Acts. You can see in Table 2 that the laws were enacted in the period between 1890 and 1914, a period in which the railroads, steel, oil, mining, and finance were becoming large and dominant businesses. The story at the time involved large, successful companies and their domination over smaller competitors—not too much unlike Microsoft and Walmart and their competitors today.

 1   What is antitrust policy?

1.b. Procedures

Any one of four different entities may sue a firm for alleged antitrust behavior: the U.S. Department of Justice, the Federal Trade Commission (FTC), state attorneys general,

TABLE 1	A Simple List of the Numbers of U.S. Federal Government Departments and Agencies
Department or Office	**Number of Agencies**
Executive Office of the President	22
Department of Agriculture	18
Department of Commerce	21
Department of Defense	50
Department of Education	43
Department of Energy	37
Department of Health and Human Services	28
Department of Homeland Security	14
Department of Housing and Urban Development	6
Department of the Interior	9
Department of Justice	45
Department of Labor	17
Department of State	37
Department of Transportation	11
Department of the Treasury	23
Department of Veterans Affairs	4
Independent Agencies (under no specific department)	61
Legislative Branch	9
Judicial Branch	10

© froxx/Shutterstock.com

© 2013 Cengage Learning

TABLE 2	Antitrust Acts

Sherman Antitrust Act (1890)

Section 1 outlaws contracts and conspiracies in restraint of trade.

Section 2 forbids monopolization and any attempts to monopolize.

Clayton Antitrust Act (1914)

Section 2, as amended by the Robinson-Patman Act (1936), bans price discrimination that substantially lessens competition or injures particular competitors.

Section 3 prohibits certain practices that might keep other firms from entering an industry or competing with an existing firm.

Section 7, as amended by the Celler-Kefauver Act (1950), outlaws mergers that substantially lessen competition.

Federal Trade Commission Act (1914)

Section 5, as amended by the Wheeler-Lea Act (1938), prohibits unfair methods of competition and unfair or deceptive acts.

© 2013 Cengage Learning

and private individuals or firms. Since 1941, the FTC and the Justice Department together have filed nearly 2,800 cases, but private suits have far outnumbered those filed by the Justice Department and the FTC combined. One reason is that if the private plaintiffs are able to win in court, they can receive compensation of up to three times the amount of the damages caused by the action. The Justice Department and the FTC do not obtain treble damages but can impose substantial penalties. They can force firms to break up through dissolution or divestiture, and the Justice Department can file criminal actions for violations of the Sherman Act. A guilty finding can result in fines and prison sentences.

1.c. Violations—Proof

Price fixing is by definition illegal—there is no justification for it. An executive of one firm can not call up an executive at a competitor and the two decide to set prices. Other aspects of the antitrust statutes are not as clear-cut and are, therefore, difficult to prove. For instance, Section 1 of the Sherman Act outlaws "every contract, combination … or conspiracy" that is "in restraint of trade," but it defines none of these terms. Similarly, Section 2 of the Sherman Act outlaws "monopolization" but does not forbid monopolies and does not define "to monopolize." As a result of these ambiguities, the application of antitrust law has often depended on politics—the views of the judges appointed to the various courts, particularly the Supreme Court, and what party was in power—as much as or more than economics.

There have been several distinct phases of antitrust policy in the United States, as illustrated in Figure 1. The first began with passage of the Sherman Antitrust Act in 1890 and lasted until about 1914. In this period, litigation was infrequent. The courts used a *rule of reason* to judge firms' actions: Being a monopoly or attempting to monopolize was not in itself illegal; to be illegal, an action had to be shown to have negative economic effects. The second phase of antitrust policy began in 1914 with the passage of the Clayton Antitrust Act and the Federal Trade Commission Act. Operating under these two acts, the courts used the *per se rule* to judge firms' actions. Activities that were potentially monopolizing tactics were illegal; the mere existence of these activities was sufficient evidence to lead to a guilty verdict. The per se approach was strengthened during the 36 years that Justice William O. Douglas served on the Supreme Court.

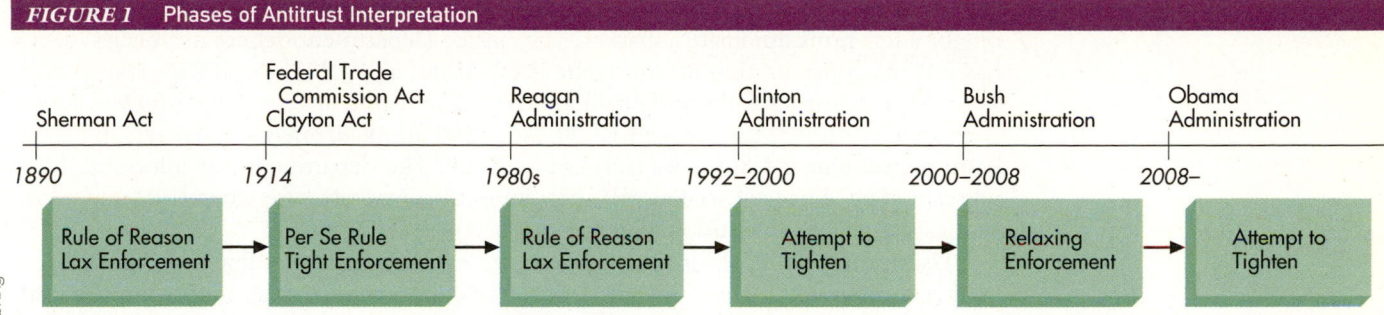

FIGURE 1   Phases of Antitrust Interpretation

The degree to which antitrust law has been enforced has varied over the years. With the Sherman Act of 1890, the government formally began antitrust policy. But enforcement was lax, based on a rule of reason, until about 1914. Between 1914 and the early 1980s, strict enforcement based on a per se rule was used. With the Reagan administration, enforcement was relaxed again to the rule of reason standard. The Clinton administration tightened enforcement, Bush relaxed it, and Obama tightened it again, but the rule of reason still prevails.

Appointed by President Franklin Roosevelt in 1939, Douglas maintained a strong antitrust stance until his departure from the Supreme Court in 1975. Following Douglas's departure, the court made a gradual move back to rule of reason. Justice Sandra Day O'Connor argued in 1984 that it was time to abandon the per se label and refocus the inquiry on the adverse economic effects and potential economic benefits. In general, this is how U.S. antitrust cases have been tried and decided since 1990. Nevertheless, the Democratic Clinton and Obama administrations have devoted more resources to antitrust than did the Republican Bush administrations.

Antitrust cases are complex and often confusing. The typical approach is to demonstrate that a firm is a dominant firm and thus can raise or lower prices and quantities and carry out other practices at will. A dominant firm is one that has sufficient market share to be able to control prices and quantities. When a firm or a few firms are able to dictate the competitive conditions in a market, the market is called *concentrated*. Several ways to measure how concentrated a market is have been developed. The measure that is most relied on is called the *Herfindahl index* and is defined as the sum of the squared market shares of each firm in the industry:[1]

$$\text{Herfindahl index} = (S_1)^2 + (S_2)^2 + \cdots + (S_n)^2$$

where S refers to the market share of the firm, the subscripts refer to the firms, and there are n firms. The higher the Herfindahl index number, the more concentrated the industry.

A monopoly would have one firm with 100 percent of the market share, so the Herfindahl index would be $(100)^2 = 10,000$. An industry in which each of five firms has 20 percent of the market would have a Herfindahl index value of 2,000:

$$(20)^2 + (20)^2 + (20)^2 + (20)^2 + (20)^2 = 2,000$$

An industry in which there are five firms, but the largest firm has 88 percent of the market and each of the others has 3 percent, would have a Herfindahl index of 7,780:

$$(88)^2 + (3)^2 + (3)^2 + (3)^2 + (3)^2 = 7,780$$

[1] The four-firm concentration ratio is another commonly used measure of concentration, but it has come under criticism because it does not account for the size distribution of firms. It merely divides the total output of the four largest firms by the total market output.

The higher number indicates a much more concentrated market—an indication that one or a few firms dominate a market. The Justice Department defines its policies on the basis of the concentration measures. In 1982, 1984, and 1992, the Justice Department stated that industries with Herfindahl indexes below 1,000 are considered *highly competitive*; those with indexes between 1,000 and 1,800 are *moderately competitive*; and those with indexes above 1,800 are *highly concentrated*. The department was informing businesses that they needed to consider their impact on market share when they undertook actions; reducing competition could bring government lawsuits.

Using the Herfindahl index to gauge the extent to which a few firms dominate a market sounds simple, but it is not. Before the concentration of an industry can be calculated, there must be some definition of the market. In a $100 billion market, an $80 billion firm would have an 80 percent market share. But in a $1,000 billion market, an $80 billion firm would have only an 8 percent market share. The Herfindahl index in the former case would exceed 2,000, but in the latter case it would be less than 1,000. Obviously, those accusing a firm of attempting to monopolize a market would want the market defined narrowly, making it small. Conversely, those that are accused of monopolization would argue for broadly defined markets in order to give the appearance that they possess a very small market share.

For example, Coca-Cola, Dr Pepper, PepsiCo, and Seven-Up are usually identified as producers of carbonated soft drinks (CSD). These firms provide bottlers with the syrup that is used to make the drinks. Is this the appropriate market in which to assess the competitive consequences of the CSD behavior, or should the market be more widely defined—perhaps to encompass all potable liquids (fruit juices, milk, coffee, tea, etc.)?

In the Microsoft antitrust case, the Justice Department defined the market very narrowly. All of Microsoft's rivals were defined as not being in the same market—the market of single-user desktop PCs that run on an Intel chip. Thus, Apple's market share did not count because Apple ran on a Motorola chip. Nor did Sun Microsystems' share count because Sun was not Intel-based. Linux did not count because it came into being after the government's complaints against Microsoft. And the 15 percent of the PC market that consisted of machines offered without any operating system were not counted. Thus, the very narrow market as defined by the Justice Department led to a Herfindahl index of 10,000, whereas in a broader market, where Microsoft's market share was 65 percent or less, the Herfindahl index was about 5,000.

Defining the market and the degree of concentration is just the beginning. Perhaps the most difficult part of any antitrust lawsuit is establishing intent—did the firm intend the actions that it took to reduce competition? Did a firm set prices below costs in an attempt to run competitors out of business, or was it simply matching competitors' prices? Did a firm unfairly restrict access to customers by bundling products together or requiring exclusive deals with suppliers, or were these policies beneficial for the consumer? Did the combined efforts of companies benefit consumers, or were they attempts to create cartels? Questions like these are at the center of antitrust lawsuits.

1.d. Business Policy from a Global Perspective

A firm doing business in the United States must be wary of its actions once it gets large. The impact of its behavior on the Herfindahl index is carefully scrutinized when it wants to purchase other companies or merge with other firms. Moreover, the executives of the company must always be aware of how its actions might be viewed by the antitrust authorities. But if a business might be confused about what to do in the United States, consider a company that carries on business in many different nations. Each nation has a different set of laws. Approximately 70 jurisdictions have enacted merger review laws and merger notification regimes.

In an attempt to make the national antitrust laws more consistent with one another, the International Competition Network (ICN) was formed in October 2001. This is an informal network of antitrust agencies from developed and developing countries around the world. It began with antitrust officials from 14 jurisdictions—Australia, Canada, the European Union, France, Germany, Israel, Italy, Japan, Korea, Mexico, South America, the United Kingdom, the United States, and Zambia—but today, 90 member competition agencies from 80 jurisdictions participate. In addition to the ICN, the United States and the European Union have been attempting to encourage close cooperation between the agencies and to see the laws converge to become essentially the same. Right now, the laws are not the same and are applied in very different ways. Typically, the United States relies more on economic theory and the rule of reason approach (what the impact is), whereas the European Union relies more on the per se approach (guilty if it exists, without consideration of impact); it specifies particular actions as simply being prohibited irrespective of economic arguments. Other nations often attempt to simply be different from or more restrictive than the United States, not wanting to appear to be merely a puppet of U.S. antitrust authorities. Recently, more governments have been attacking cartels, using antitrust action to limit the actions of international cartels.

Microsoft illustrates the problems of globalization and national antitrust laws. The first antitrust case against Microsoft was filed in the United States in 1998 by the Justice Department and 20 state attorneys general as well as several private firms competing with Microsoft. The case was completed in 2002 with the finding that Microsoft had illegally maintained its Windows monopoly. Microsoft was required to allow PC makers and consumers to install competing products on their computers instead of the Internet Explorer browser and Media Player. Microsoft also had to reveal parts of its software code to other companies so that these companies could create products that would work with the Windows-based PCs.

The cases against Microsoft were far from over, however. In the European Union, EU regulators ruled that Microsoft had abused its near-monopoly in desktop computer systems to illegally dominate the media software market and threaten the position of competitors selling office networking software. It fined Microsoft and ordered it to both share code with rivals and offer an unbundled version of Windows without the Media Player software. In South Korea, antitrust regulators ruled that Microsoft had abused its market dominance, fined the company, and ordered it to offer alternative versions of Windows. Other countries have also looked at Microsoft from the perspective of their antitrust laws.

RECAP

1. Antitrust policy in the United States is based on the Sherman, Clayton, and Federal Trade Commission Acts.

2. Antitrust lawsuits may be brought by private firms or individuals, the Justice Department, and the Federal Trade Commission. When a firm's actions are proven to be damaging to competition, the penalties imposed depend on who brought suit. If private concerns are involved, then penalties of up to three times the damages created by the actions may be imposed.

3. The Herfindahl index is a measure of concentration, attempting to provide an indication of how one or a few firms might control a market. It is the sum of the squares of the market shares of the firms in an industry. The higher the number, the more concentrated the market.

4. Currently, the United States tends to take a rule of reason approach, as do some other nations, but still others rely more on a per se rule.

2 What is the difference between economic regulation and social regulation?

2. Regulation

There are two categories of regulation: economic regulation and social regulation. **Economic regulation** refers to the prescribing of prices and output levels for entire industries. **Social regulation** refers to the prescribing of performance standards, work-place health and safety standards, emission levels, and a variety of output and job standards that apply across most if not all industries.

2.a. Economic Regulation

A natural monopoly exists when economies of scale make it efficient for a single firm to supply the entire market. Regulation of monopolies is based on the idea that certain industries—utilities, railroads, communication, and others—are natural monopolies. Most economic regulation of natural monopolies began during the Great Depression of the 1930s. The idea was to make the natural monopolist's price and supply much like what a perfectly competitive industry would provide.

Figure 2 shows the demand, marginal-revenue, long-run average-total-cost, and long-run marginal-cost curves for a natural monopoly. The huge economies of scale mean that it would be inefficient to have many small firms supply the product. Yet

FIGURE 2   Natural Monopoly and Regulation

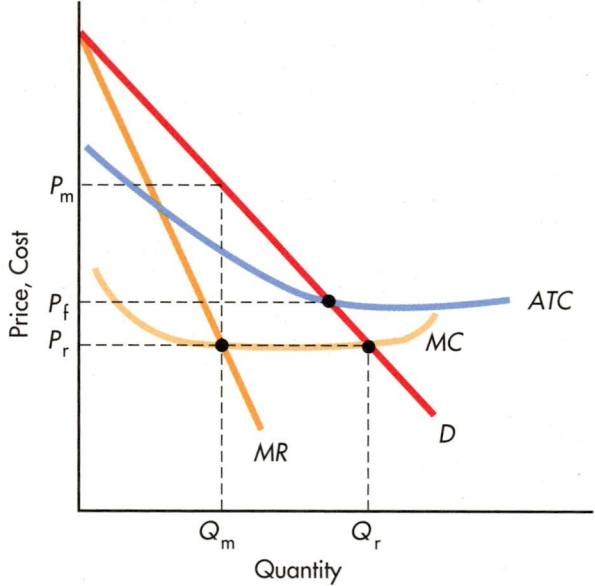

The demand, marginal-revenue, long-run average-total-cost, and marginal-cost curves for a natural monopoly are shown. The huge economies of scale mean that it would be inefficient to have many small firms supply the product. Yet producing at $MR = MC$ and setting a price of P_m from the demand curve yields too small an output and too much profit for the firm, in comparison to the perfectly competitive result. Too few resources are devoted to this product—too few because if more were produced, MC would equal price. To achieve allocative efficiency (giving consumers the goods they most want), the regulatory agency must attempt to have the monopolist set a price equal to marginal cost. This price would be P_r. The monopolist would then produce at quantity Q_r. The problem with the regulated price P_r is that the revenues do not cover average costs. The fair-rate-of-return price is set to allow the monopolist a normal profit. The price corresponding to the normal profit is the one where demand and average total costs are equal, P_f.

allowing the natural monopoly to produce at $MR = MC$ and set a price of P_m from the demand curve yields too little output and too much profit for the firm, in comparison to the perfectly competitive result. In addition, since price is greater than marginal cost, resources are not being allocated efficiently. In fact, too few resources are devoted to this product—too few because if MC were equal to price, more output would be produced. Can regulation solve this problem?

If the natural monopolist is to look like a perfectly competitive industry, then its price should be set equal to its marginal cost. At P_r in Figure 2, $P = MC$, and the monopolist would then produce at quantity Q_r. The problem with the regulated price P_r is that the regulated firm could actually make a loss. You can see in Figure 2 that demand lies below ATC, which means that revenues are less than total costs. Figure 2 illustrates a fairly common situation with public utility companies. Most public utilities acquire enough capacity to be able to provide the services needed during the *peak periods*. For instance, air conditioning is used most heavily during the 5 p.m. to 9 p.m. time period during the summer months. The demand during this period may be twice as great as the highest demand in any other time period. To be able to supply enough electricity for the peak period, the electric company has to have nearly double the generating capacity it would need in order to satisfy demand in other time periods. And this generating capacity simply sits idle most of the time. To avoid the problem of forcing utilities into bankruptcy, regulatory commissions allow for a **fair rate of return**. The fair-rate-of-return price is set to allow the monopolist a normal profit—that is, a zero economic profit. The price corresponding to the normal profit is one at which demand and average total cost curves intersect, P_f. Remember, a perfectly competitive firm in the long run would have price equal to marginal cost and equal to the minimum of the average total cost.

The fair rate of return avoids driving a regulated firm into bankruptcy, but it creates a different problem. When the firm is allowed to set the price as a percentage of average costs, it has an incentive to increase costs. The regulated firm thus ends up with "too much" capital—it builds too much capacity or more office space than is needed because these capital costs can be included in the rate base.

fair rate of return
A price that allows a monopoly firm to earn a normal profit.

2.b. Deregulation and Privatization in the United States

Regulation alters incentives and forces firms to change the way they do business. For instance, if firms are not allowed to compete using price, then they compete using other things. When airlines were unable to compete with prices, they competed instead with schedules, movies, food, and size of aircraft. The result was a much larger number of flights and expansion of aircraft capacity than was demanded by passengers. The load factor (the average percentage of seats filled) fell to less than 50 percent in the early 1970s.

Price competition among truckers was also stifled by regulation. The Interstate Commerce Commission (ICC) had a complex rate schedule and restrictions affecting whether trucks could be full or less than full and the routes that trucks could take. As a result, by the mid-1970s, 36 percent of all truck-miles were logged by empty trucks.

These problems and the higher costs that resulted finally led to a change. Trucking was deregulated in 1980 and air flight in 1982. Trucks were allowed to haul what they wanted, where they wanted, at rates set by the trucking companies. In air transportation, deregulation of route authority and fares was completed by 1982. But the government did not free up the airports and the air traffic control system. These remain government controlled and typically government owned. Much of the telecommunications industry was deregulated in 1984. Long-distance communication became free of restraint immediately, but local markets still retain some restrictions.

stranded assets
Assets acquired by a firm when it was regulated that have little value when the firm is deregulated.

The deregulation of electricity generation and other utilities has not been uniform. Some states have lessened regulation more than others, but most continue to regulate utilities. Deregulation is a politically difficult thing to accomplish. The regulated companies argue that competition will cost too much because of their **stranded assets**. Electric and cable companies argue that if regulation is eliminated, they need to be compensated for the cable they have laid, the lines they have built, and the power plants they have created. Fair-rate-of-return regulation induced these companies to purchase a great deal of capital that they would not otherwise have purchased. The companies argue that they invested for the public good on the assumption that their monopolies would be preserved, and that to tell them that they aren't guaranteed a return on these assets is not right; exposing them to competition without compensating them for their previous investments amounts to an unconstitutional "taking" of their property.

privatization
Transferring a publicly owned enterprise to private ownership.

contracting out
The process of enlisting a private firm to provide a product or service for a government entity.

Privatization is the term for changing from a government-run business to a privately owned and run business. Cities and local governments in the United States have **contracted out** (privatized) many services in recent years. Many local governments are now allowing private firms to provide garbage services, water services, and even road building and maintenance. Rural/Metro Company in Scottsdale, Arizona, has been running a private fire department for several decades. It is now purchasing contracts to run fire departments and emergency medical services throughout Arizona and in other states. Corrections Corporation of America in Nashville, Tennessee, is building prisons. Many members of Congress are looking at the U.S. Postal Service and arguing that private firms could deliver mail better and less expensively. Even highways are subjects for privatization. Arguing that the first good highways in the United States were privately built and operated in the late 1700s, some economists argue that congestion and air pollution today could be reduced if highways were privatized. And in a few locations, such as between Los Angeles and San Diego, highways have been privately built and maintained. As will be discussed in the chapter "Aging, Social Security, and Health Care," proposals for improving the Social Security system include privatization.

2.c. Social Regulation

Social regulation is concerned with the conditions under which goods and services are produced and the impact of these conditions on the public. Social regulation is often applied across all industries. For instance, the Environmental Protection Agency (EPA) enforces emission standards that apply to all businesses, and the Occupational Safety and Health Administration (OSHA) imposes workplace requirements on all businesses.

Who decides whether a regulation is necessary? How is the regulation to be implemented? According to economists, a cost–benefit calculation is necessary to determine whether a regulation should be implemented.

2.c.1. Cost–Benefit Calculations
There have been several studies that focused on estimating the costs of regulations on the economy. These range from about $400 billion to over $800 billion, depending on what is included as a cost.[2] Who pays these costs? It may be the business, it may be the consumer, or both may end up paying, depending on the elasticities of demand and supply. The impact of social regulation on a business is illustrated in Figure 3. The firm is producing quantity Q_1 at a cost of C_1 and selling at a price of P_1. The firm, an automobile company, is told that it must increase the fuel efficiency of its fleet of cars. This requirement means that the company must modify its manufacturing plants and alter the parts it uses in its autos. The result is an increase in the company's fixed and variable costs, shown as an upward shift of the ATC

[2] Clyde Wayne Crews Jr., "Ten Thousand Commandments: An Annual Snapshot of the Federal Regulatory State," Cato Institute, 2003.

and MC curves. The regulation leads to less output being produced (Q_2 rather than Q_1) at higher costs (C_2 rather than C_1), and the output being sold at higher prices (P_2 rather than P_1). In virtually every case of regulation, consumers pay higher prices for the goods and services sold by the regulated firm. How much more does the consumer pay? The answer depends on the price elasticities of demand and supply.

If demand is inelastic, then the consumer will not be very likely to switch to a substitute good or service as the price rises. In such a case, the firm will be able to pass along a larger portion of the increased costs to the consumer in the form of higher prices than it will if demand is elastic, everything else the same. On the other hand, the firm is likely to have to bear a greater portion of the increased costs if supply is inelastic. An inelastic supply means that the firm is not able to easily switch its production and sales from the now more regulated and more costly good or service to a less regulated and less costly good or service.

Since both prices and costs are higher as a result of regulation, both producers and consumers lose benefits—consumer and producer surplus is reduced. Consider Figure 4(a), in which the demand and supply curves for the market for automobiles are illustrated. Consumer surplus is shown as triangle ABP_1, and producer surplus is shown as triangle ACP_1. Total societal surplus is thus the area outlined as ABC.

Autos pollute, and the cost of the pollution to society is shown as the area FGQ_1H. So suppose that a regulation is imposed on auto producers that requires them to produce cleaner-burning engines. The regulation causes the supply curve (the sum of the MC curves of each of the automobile firms) to shift up or in, as shown in Figure 4(b). This reduces consumer surplus to the area EBP_2 and producer surplus to EJP_2. The area $CAEJ$ is the cost of the regulation. What are the benefits? The benefits are the cost of the pollution that is no longer created by the automobiles. This is shown as the rectangle GIQ_2Q_1.

When a business is required to pay for environmental protection or cleanup, its costs of supplying goods and services rise. This can lead to higher prices for the consumer. Who pays the higher proportion of the costs, the consumers or the owners of the firm, depends on the price elasticities of demand for and supply of the firm's goods and services. In this photo, a group is cleaning up after an oil tanker accident caused a 2.7-million-gallon spill on the shore of South Korea. You can see the black oil on the rocks.

The cost–benefit calculation indicates whether a regulation benefits society or not. If the costs exceed the benefits, then, according to economic theory, the regulation should not be imposed. If a regulation is to be imposed, the amount or restrictiveness of the regulation should be at a level where marginal benefits equal marginal costs. Carrying out cost–benefit analyses on regulations is an approach that has been agreed to in principle by the U.S. federal government's Office of Management and Budget and by the main financial agencies of most industrial countries.

In many instances, the cost–benefit calculation is done in terms of lives saved and lives lost. For example, a program to detect and treat breast cancer among women over the age of 50 has been estimated to cost less than \$15,000 per life-year saved, whereas the cost per life-year saved of a regulation to reduce airborne exposure to benzene is approximately \$17.5 million. According to the federal government, the cost of some environmental regulations is high, as shown in Table 3.

Regulations may not be costly just in terms of dollars; they can also cost lives. The argument, according to economists, is that regulations are costly to implement and conform to, and so reduce income. When people are poorer, they spend less on health care and safety measures and engage in riskier behavior. For example, they buy smaller cars and visit the doctor less often. Hence, regulations that reduce people's incomes can increase fatalities from other causes. A cost–benefit calculation for a regulation that is intended to save lives should compare the number of lives saved with the number of lives lost as a result of the regulation.

FIGURE 3   Regulatory Costs

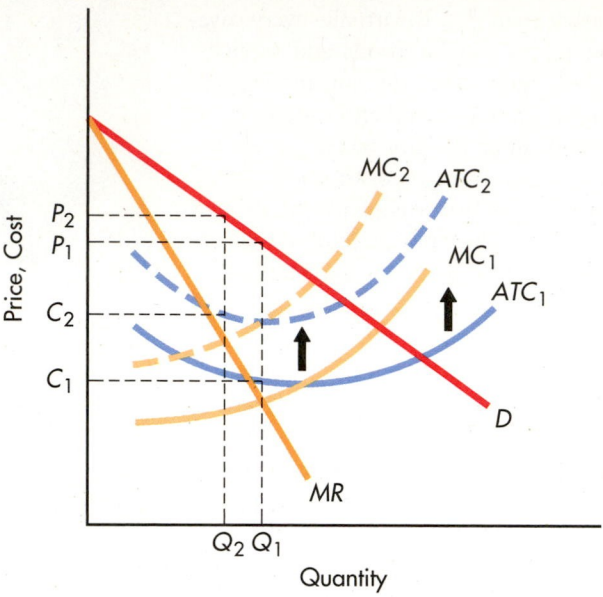

The firm producing at Q_1 with costs of C_1 and selling at price P_1 is required to implement changes in production in order to meet pollution requirements. The increased costs of the regulation are illustrated as upward shifts of the *ATC* and *MC* curves, leading to less output being produced (Q_2 rather than Q_1) at higher costs (C_2 rather than C_1) and thus being sold at higher prices (P_2 rather than P_1).

FIGURE 4   Costs and Benefits of Regulation

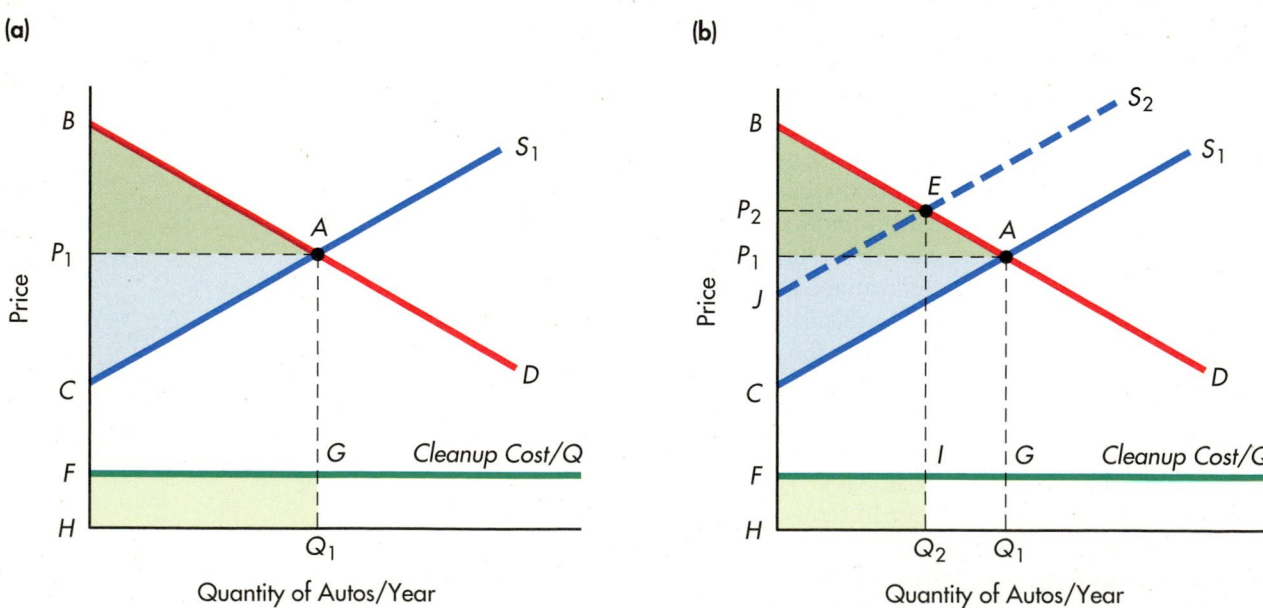

Figure 4(a) shows the market prior to regulation, and Figure 4(b) shows the effects of regulation. The regulation causes the supply curve (the sum of the *MC* curves of each of the automobile firms) to shift up. This reduces consumer surplus to the area *EBP_2* and producer surplus to *EJP_2*. The area *CAEJ* is the cost of the regulation. The benefits of the regulation are the costs of the pollution that is no longer created by the automobiles (area GIQ_2Q_1).

TABLE 3	The Cost of Regulation	
Regulation of	**Saves**	**At a Cost per Life of**
Grain dust	4.00 lives/year	$5.3 million
Uranium mines	1.10 lives/year	6.9 million
Benzene	3.80 lives/year	17.1 million
Glass plants	0.11 life/year	19.2 million
Ethylene oxide	2.80 lives/year	25.6 million
Copper smelters	0.06 life/year	26.5 million
Uranium mill tailings, active	2.10 lives/year	53 million
Low-arsenic copper	0.08 life/year	764 million
Land disposal	2.52 lives/year	3,500 million
Formaldehyde	0.01 life/year	72,000 million

Source: U.S. Office of Management and Budget, Office of Information and Regulatory Affairs, *Report to Congress on the Costs and Benefits of Federal Regulations, 1998.* Each year the OMB provides cost–benefit calculations for rules implemented during the year; see www.whitehouse.gov/omb.

Studies have shown that any regulation costing more than about $8.4 million for each life saved is likely to cause overall fatalities to rise. Looking at the cost of regulations suggests that many do the opposite of their intended objective. Most of the Federal Aviation Administration's regulations cost less than $8.4 million per life saved, and thus arguably yield a net saving of lives. The same is true for most of the National Highway Traffic Safety Administration's rules. The record of the Occupational Safety and Health Administration (OSHA) is not so good. OSHA regulations are about evenly divided between those that are cheap enough to save lives on balance and those (e.g., OSHA's ethylene dibromide and formaldehyde rules) that are so costly that they have no doubt killed far more people than would have died in the absence of the regulations. The Environmental Protection Agency's (EPA) regulations are almost all more costly in terms of lives lost than they are beneficial in terms of lives saved. The arsenic standard, for example, costs almost $27 million per life saved, according to the official numbers. This income loss leads to about three added fatalities from other causes for each life saved. Similarly, the EPA asbestos standard was supposed to save 10 lives each year. However, its cost per life saved (about $144 million) suggests that 18 people will die each year to save those 10.[3]

A cost-benefit test would limit regulations to those that create benefits greater than their cost. But as shown by the examples presented in Table 2, many regulations do not pass a cost-benefit test but are implemented anyway. Why? We will discuss this issue further in the next chapter, "Market Failure, Government Failure, and Rent Seeking."

2.d. Multinationals, International Regulation, GATT, and the WTO

International regulation occurs at two levels, one in which a specific government regulates the activities of individual firms operating within the country, and another in which several nations are involved. The General Agreement on Tariffs and Trade (GATT) is a

3 What international agencies regulate business behavior?

[3] Ulf-G. Gerdtham and Magnus Johannesson, "Do Life-Saving Regulations Save Lives?" *Journal of Risk and Uncertainty*, Vol. 24, pp. 231–249, 2002. John F. Morrall III, "A Review of the Record," *Regulation*, November/December 1986, pp. 25–34. Daniel K. Benjamin, "Killing Us with Kindness," *PERC Reports*, Vol. 20, No. 3, September 2002, perc@perc.org.

ECONOMIC INSIGHT

Economic Freedom

How big of a player is the government in the private sector in countries? The Heritage Foundation and *The Wall Street Journal* created the Index of Economic Freedom in 1994 and have published the index each year since, as a response to this question.[4] Economic freedom is the degree to which individuals are able to carry out voluntary transactions independent of government. "Individuals are economically free if they can fully control their own labor and property."[5]

According to the Index of Economic Freedom, the United States is not the freest economy in the world. In 2009, nations such as Australia, Ireland, New Zealand, and Singapore are rated as being economically freer than the United States. Hong Kong, being controlled by communist China, is rated as one of the most economically free areas in the world. What this means is that government is more involved in the economy in the United States than it is in these other nations. Higher taxes mean less economic freedom, more rules and regulations mean less economic freedom, restrictions on travel mean less economic freedom, restrictions on international trade mean less economic freedom, the paperwork necessary to comply with government rules and regulations means less economic freedom, and so on. The index is composed of 10 components:

1. *Business freedom* is the ability to create, operate, and close an enterprise quickly and easily. Burdensome, redundant regulatory rules are the most harmful barriers to business freedom.
2. *Trade freedom* is a composite measure of the absence of tariff and non-tariff barriers that affect imports and exports of goods and services.
3. *Fiscal freedom* is a measure of the burden of government from the revenue side. It includes both the tax burden in terms of the top tax rate on income (individual and corporate separately) and the overall amount of tax revenue as a portion of gross domestic product (GDP).
4. *Government size* is defined to include all government expenditures, including consumption and transfers.
5. *Monetary freedom* combines a measure of price stability with an assessment of price controls. Both inflation and price controls distort market activity.
6. *Investment freedom* is an assessment of the free flow of capital, especially foreign capital.
7. *Financial freedom* is a measure of banking security as well as independence from government control.
8. *Property rights* is an assessment of the ability of individuals to accumulate private property, secured by clear laws that are fully enforced by the state.

9. *Freedom from corruption* is based on quantitative data that assess the perception of corruption in the business environment.

TABLE 4	The Ten Most Free Economies and Ten Least Free Economies	
RANK	**COUNTRY**	**OVERALL**
	Ten Most Free Economies	
1	Hong Kong	89.7
2	Singapore	87.2
3	Australia	82.5
4	New Zealand	82.3
5	Switzerland	81.9
6	Canada	80.8
7	Ireland	78.7
8	Denmark	78.6
9	United States	77.8
10	Bahrain	77.7
	Ten Least Free Economies	
170	Timor-Leste	42.8
171	Iran	42.1
172	Democratic Republic of Congo	40.7
173	Libya	38.6
174	Burma	37.8
175	Venezuela	37.6
176	Eritrea	36.7
177	Cuba	27.7
178	Zimbabwe	22.1
179	North Korea	1.0

Source: Data adapted from the *2011 Index of Economic Freedom;* http://www.heritage.org/index/ranking.aspx.

---

[4] The Frasier Institute introduced the Economic Freedom of the World Index a year earlier. The measures are very similar.

[5] The index is available at http://www.heritage.org. Methodology used in calculating the Index of Economic Freedom is available at http://www.heritage.org/index/PDF/2011/Index2008_Chap4.pdf.

10.   *Labor freedom* is a measure of the ability of workers and businesses to interact without restriction by the state.

A measure of the amount of freedom in each component is calculated, and the components are equally weighted to create the index. The top 10 and bottom 10 nations in terms of economic freedom are listed in Table 4. Index values for each country are shown in page 582.

Economic freedom had generally increased until 2007. The economic recession that began in 2007 altered the momentum toward economic freedom in most parts of the world. In North America and Europe, banks were nationalized, large companies were provided with government handouts, and economic regulations in financial and other sectors increased. (See the Economic Insight "U.S. History of Bailouts.") Throughout Asia, Eastern Europe, and Latin America, governments increased spending and control over industries.

form of the latter. In April 1947, delegates from the United States, Asia, Europe, and Latin America traveled to Geneva, Switzerland. Aware of the effects of trade restrictions on economic health that had been experienced during the Great Depression, they all sought to liberalize trade, reduce barriers, and create an environment in which economies would prosper. The first global trade agreement resulted, called GATT. Today the successor to GATT is called the World Trade Organization (WTO). Its 149 member nations have agreed to settle trade disputes in the WTO courts rather than raise barriers, impose tariffs, or otherwise restrict trade. The WTO was created on January 1, 1995, by the Uruguay Round of the GATT. It is located in Geneva.

Although trade was increasingly globalized between 1990 and 2007, the recession beginning in 2007 led many governments to begin restricting trade. Bills introduced in the United States in 2009 included some restrictions to "buy American," which required entities receiving government subsidies or government spending programs to ensure that they purchased resources from American suppliers. Other nations reacted to such restrictions by imposing tariffs and taxes on U.S. goods. Overall, trade was reduced as a result.

RECAP

1. Economic regulation means that the government dictates the price that a firm may charge and/or the quantity that a firm must supply.

2. Economic regulation typically applies to an entire industry.

3. Since the mid-1970s, deregulation has occurred in airlines, trucking, railroads, and communications in the United States.

4. Social regulation deals with workplace safety, product safety, the environment, and other aspects of doing business; it applies to all industries. Social regulation accounts for most of the growth of regulations in the United States.

5. A cost–benefit calculation measures whether the benefits of a rule or regulation exceed the costs. Economists assert that only those regulations that create more benefits than costs should be implemented.

6. The costs of a rule or regulation include the reduction in output produced, higher costs of production, and higher prices. They also include the lost consumer and producer surplus. The benefits of the rule or regulation are the reductions in the costs of cleaning up wastes and reductions in the risk to human life.

7. In other countries, nationalization occurred instead of regulation. In those countries, deregulation means privatization, the transferring of ownership from the government to private individuals.

8. Attempts to increase trade among nations have led to the creation of GATT and then the WTO.

3. Public Finances

With antitrust and regulation, government has lots of activities. These and other government activities have expanded since the founding of the United States. In 1789 when the U.S. Constitution was adopted, there were only two departments that were specified as necessary, the State Department and the Defense Department. Today there are 15 departments. In addition, there are agencies that are not part of any department, but report directly to the Executive Office of the President. These include:

- Environmental Protection Agency (EPA)
- National Aeronautics and Space Administration (NASA)
- Office of Management and Budget (OMB)
- Office of National Drug Control Policy (ONDCP)
- Office of the United States Trade Representative (USTR)

The Constitution grants the president a very limited set of duties, including representing the United States in foreign affairs, commanding the armed forces, and nominating Supreme Court justices, executive officials, ambassadors, and other public officers. The Constitution and Bill of Rights enumerate the duties of Congress to be:

> to lay and collect Taxes, to pay the Debts and provide for the common Defence and general Welfare of the United States, to borrow money on the credit of the United States, to regulate Commerce with foreign Nations, and among the several States, and with the Indian Tribes, to declare war, to raise and support Armies, but not for any longer than two years, and to provide and maintain a Navy.

U.S. Constitution, Article I, Section 8

As you can readily observe by simply looking around, these limited powers of the federal government bear no resemblance to government today. There is virtually nothing the government does not do and virtually nothing that many scholars claim the government can do. This means that spending by the government has risen over the years.

3.a. Government Spending

4 How does government pay for its activities?

In Figure 5, Government expenditures as a percentage of gross domestic product (GDP) is plotted. GDP is the total value of output produced in a country over one year; it is a measure of the size of the total economy. So if GDP is increasing, and the ratio of government expenditures to GDP is rising, then government expenditures are rising faster than the total value of output created each year. The spending shown in Figure 5 includes federal, state, and local levels of government.

Where does the government get the money to spend? The federal government can collect taxes and borrow; some state and local governments can also raise taxes and borrow while others can only collect taxes—they are required to have a balanced budget.

3.b. Taxes

Most government spending is financed with tax revenues. Taxation in the United States includes payments to federal, state, and local governments as well as municipal, township, district, and county governments, and regional entities such as school, utility, and transit districts.

The federal government collects most of its revenue from individual income taxes, although the money collected from the payroll taxes is growing rapidly, as illustrated in Figure 6.

The current breakdown of federal revenues is shown in Figure 7. Figure 8 shows the growth of federal government revenues since 1965. The revenues have tripled over that time period even though federal government spending has increased even more.

FIGURE 5 Total Government Spending as a Percent of GDP 1910 to 2015

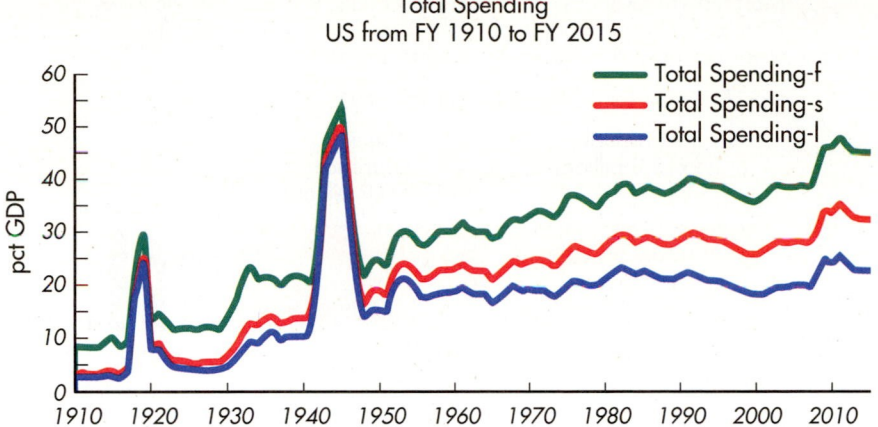

Total Spending
US from FY 1910 to FY 2015

Government spending has risen faster than the economy (GDP) since 1910. The blue is federal spending, red is state spending, and the green is local spending.

Blue = total spending by federal government as % of GDP

Red = total spending by state government as % of GDP

Green = total spending by local governments as % of GDP

Source: http://www.usgovernmentspending.com/downchart_gs.php?year=1910_2015

FIGURE 6 Sources of Government Revenues from 1934–the Present

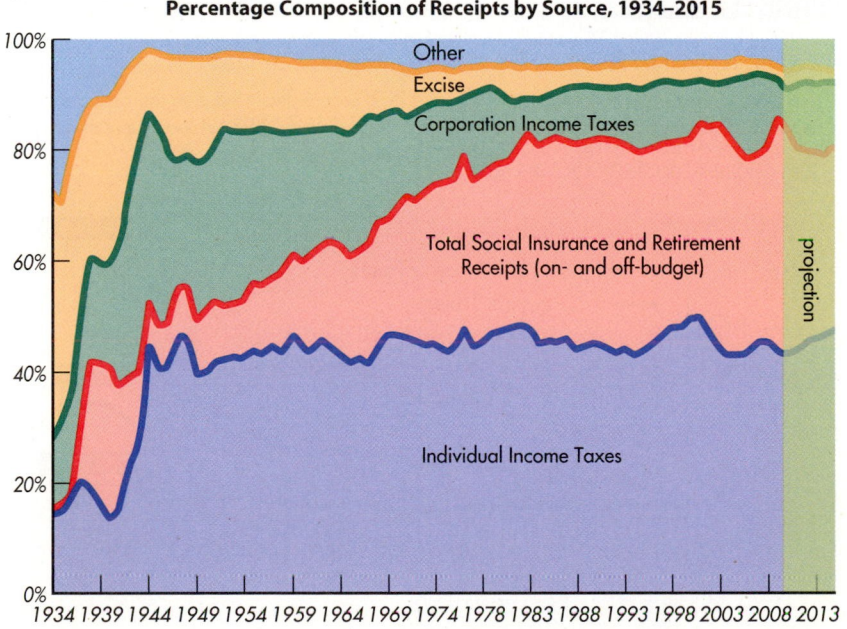

Percentage Composition of Receipts by Source, 1934–2015

In 1944, the source of government revenues was the individual income tax. Since then, the share of total revenues coming from the individual income tax has remained fairly constant. The fastest-growing revenues have come from payroll taxes, Social Security, and Medicare.

Source: Heritage Foundation; www.heritage.org/charts; 2011.

FIGURE 7   Federal Revenues by Source

Most federal revenues come from individuals. Personal income taxes provide the largest portion of total tax revenues. Social Security and Medicare payroll taxes are the second-largest source.

PERCENTAGE OF TOTAL FEDERAL REVENUE (2009)

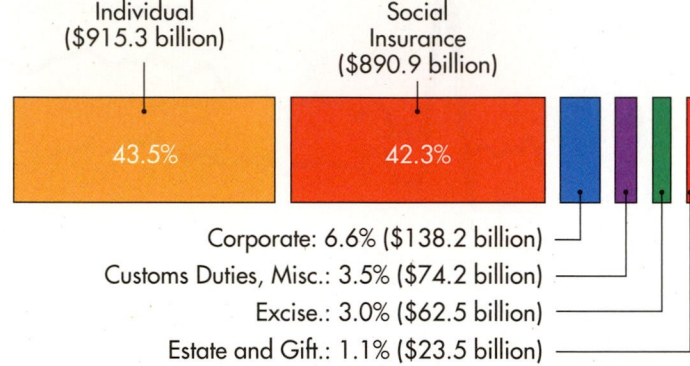

Individual income taxes provided 43.5% of total government revenues and social insurance (payroll taxes) 42.3%. All other sources are relatively small.

Source: Heritage Foundation; www.Heritage.org/budgetchartbook; accessed October 21, 2011.

FIGURE 8   The Growth of Federal Government Revenues

Federal Government Revenues Have More Than Tripled Since 1965

Tax revenue have been rising historically despite a recent decline due to the recession. Income, Capital gains, and corporate tax cuts in 2001 and 2003 helped revenues surge.

INFLATION-ADJUSTED DOLLARS (2009)

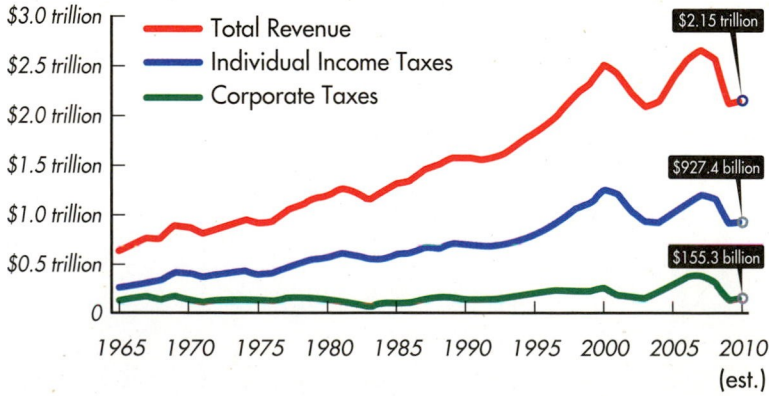

Revenues have more than tripled since 1965. FICA has been the source of most of the increase. Individual income taxes have increased, but corporate taxes have remained about the same.

Source: Heritage Foundation; www.Heritage.org/budgetchartbook; accessed October 21, 2011.

The largest source of government revenue is the individual income tax. Taxes can be progressive, proportional, or regressive. **Progressive** means the higher the income, the higher is the tax rate; **proportional** is when the same tax rate applies to all income levels; **regressive** is when the higher the income, the lower is the tax rate. The income tax is a progressive tax, meaning that the higher the income, the higher is the tax rate.

The next largest tax is the Social Security tax, formally known as the Federal Insurance and Contributions Act (FICA). This tax is 6.2% of an employee's income paid by the employer, and 6.2% paid by the employee (12.4% total, employee's share reduced to 4% in 2011). Self-employed workers must pay both halves of the Social Security tax because they are their own employers. The Social Security tax is a proportional tax up to the income level at which the tax is no longer levied. Currently, the tax is levied on incomes below $106,800. Income above $106,800 is not taxed. Thus considering all income levels, the FICA tax is a regressive tax. A proportional tax maintains a constant tax rate as income rises. A regressive tax means that the higher is your income, the lower is the tax rate. Together, Social Security and Medicare taxes compose the payroll tax.

The government's revenues have mostly increased over the years. There are a few years where revenues declined, mostly years of recession.

3.c. Deficits and Debt

The difference between revenue collected and expenditures is the deficit. The deficit is financed using debt. The federal government deficit as a percent of GDP is shown in Figure 9.

The government borrows by having the Treasury Department sell IOUs or bonds. This is government debt. It is no different than if you took out student loans. The loans are your debt; they enable you to spend more than your revenue, but at some point you have to pay them back.

In Figure 9 is the ratio of total government debt to GDP. The total federal government debt was about $14 trillion in 2011 and will rise to about $16 trillion in 2012. (See debt clock in real time at www.usdebtclock.org.)

progressive tax
A tax where the rate increases as the base increases; for example, the tax rate rises as income rises income rises.

proportional tax
A tax where the tax rate is constant as the base increases; for example, the tax rate is 20% no matter the level of income.

regressive tax
A tax where the rate decreases as the base increases; for example, a smaller rate applies to higher income levels than lower income levels.

| FIGURE 9 | Federal Deficit as a Percent of the Total Economy |

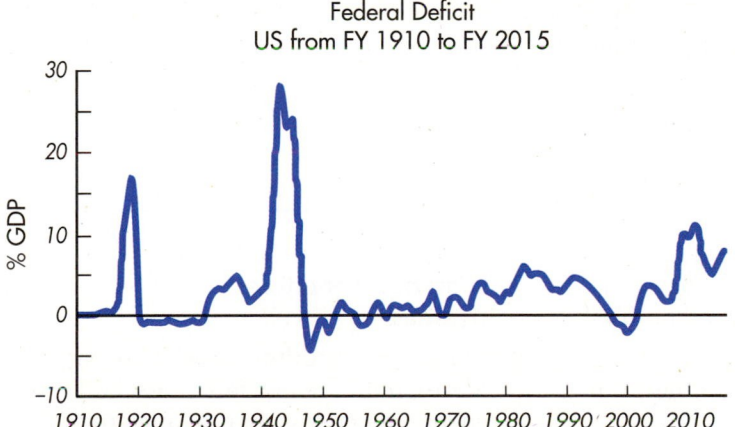

When the government spends more than its revenue, it runs a deficit. Deficits were large in war years, smaller but positive in the 1980s and 1990s, and high in 2010 and 2011.

Source: *Economic Report of the President.*

FIGURE 10   Total Debt as a Percentage of the Economy

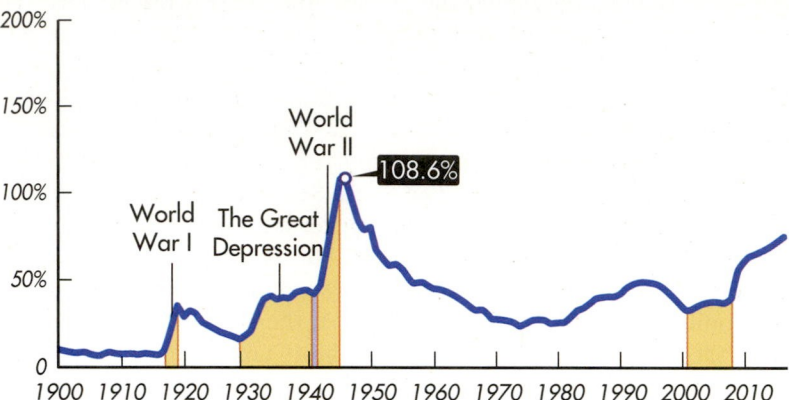

Debt rose to pay for World War I, then the Great Depression, and World War II. It declined until 1980 and then rose until the late 1990s; since 2000 it has risen rapidly.

Source: Heritage Foundation compilations of data from U.S. Department of the Treasury, Institute for the Measurement of Worth (Alternative Fiscal Scenario), Congressional Budget Office, and White House Office of Management and Budget.

Figure 10 shows the amount of federal government debt to GDP since 1900. Other than during World War II, the amount of debt relative to GDP is the highest it has ever been.

3.d. International Comparisons

Government spending as a percentage of GDP from 1995 to 2010 for the OECD (Organization for Economic Cooperation and Development) is listed in Table 5. The OECD countries are mainly the developed nations of the world.

Total government spending as a percent of GDP for the OECD nations is shown in Table 5. You can see that the United States' government spending as a share of the economy is smaller than just a few countries.

The total government debt as a percentage of GDP in these nations is shown in Table 6. Those nations with higher debt than GDP are noted with yellow shading: Japan, Greece and Italy. Other countries with very large debt are Belgium, Hungary, Iceland, Israel, United Kingdom, and Portugal.

RECAP

1. Government in the United States has only grown in size and number of activities since the founding of the United States.

2. Government spending in the United States has risen at all levels, municipal, state, and federal.

3. Except for World War II, U.S. government revenues basically matched U.S. government expenditures until the 1980s. Government revenues have fallen short of expenditures in most years of the last three decades.

4. Compared to other developed nations, the United States, until the last few years, had less government spending and less debt relative to GDP. Since 2008, the U.S. government debt relative to GDP has risen significantly.

TABLE 5	Government Spending as a Percentage of GDP													
	1996	**1997**	**1998**	**1999**	**2000**	**2001**	**2002**	**2003**	**2004**	**2005**	**2006**	**2007**	**2008**	**2009**
Australia	35.55	34.42	34.84	34.41	35.52	35.00	34.35	34.41	34.48	33.74	33.47	33.39	35.30	..
Austria	55.95	53.69	53.96	53.67	52.13	51.60	50.95	51.50	54.01	50.16	49.39	48.48	48.78	52.32
Belgium	52.49	51.23	50.43	50.18	49.14	49.18	49.84	51.12	49.44	52.27	48.64	48.45	50.20	54.22
Canada	46.59	44.28	44.80	42.68	41.11	41.99	41.23	41.18	39.86	39.30	39.45	39.35	39.82	44.05
Chile	..	..	..	..	..	..	..	..	..	..	..	..	..	..
Czech Republic	42.57	43.20	43.16	42.27	41.82	44.35	46.31	47.32	45.14	44.98	43.75	42.50	42.89	45.93
Denmark	58.91	56.68	56.33	55.50	53.68	54.19	54.57	55.07	54.55	52.79	51.59	50.92	51.83	58.55
Finland	60.03	56.51	52.89	51.68	48.29	47.83	48.85	50.15	50.04	50.18	49.03	47.25	49.35	56.01
France	54.47	54.09	52.68	52.57	51.64	51.57	52.64	53.27	53.19	53.38	52.71	52.31	52.80	55.99
Germany	49.31	48.35	48.03	48.06	45.11	47.56	48.10	48.49	47.09	46.84	45.31	43.56	43.75	47.50
Greece	44.08	44.87	44.33	44.39	46.69	45.29	45.09	44.74	45.52	43.95	45.07	46.71	49.11	53.56
Hungary	50.61	49.25	50.36	48.39	46.76	47.20	51.18	49.40	48.69	50.21	52.01	49.98	48.82	50.46
Iceland	42.21	40.69	41.30	42.05	41.87	42.60	44.25	45.62	44.05	42.21	41.64	42.27	57.76	50.86
Ireland	39.09	36.65	34.53	34.10	31.27	33.14	33.40	33.20	33.60	33.95	34.44	36.79	42.72	48.90
Israel	53.11	52.59	51.47	50.45	48.50	51.08	52.21	51.59	48.59	46.59	45.89	44.94	44.30	44.27
Italy	52.45	50.25	49.24	48.18	46.18	48.02	47.38	48.32	47.74	48.16	48.71	47.86	48.85	51.87
Japan	36.71	35.72	42.46	38.60	39.05	38.55	38.82	38.41	37.02	38.44	36.17	35.90	37.08	..
Korea	21.21	21.82	24.14	23.19	22.43	23.92	23.58	28.90	26.08	26.59	27.73	28.65	30.45	..
Luxembourg	41.13	40.65	41.06	39.19	37.59	38.13	41.53	41.78	42.55	41.52	38.58	36.17	36.88	42.17
Mexico	..	..	..	..	..	..	..	19.11	18.27	18.47	19.13	19.32	24.16	..
Netherlands	49.43	47.54	46.67	46.02	44.17	45.35	46.21	47.10	46.09	44.79	45.54	45.27	46.04	51.35
New Zealand	40.38	40.92	40.65	39.96	38.32	37.59	36.90	37.03	37.13	38.02	39.27	39.38	41.91	..
Norway	48.50	46.83	49.08	47.69	42.30	44.11	47.06	48.18	45.43	42.11	40.47	41.13	40.62	46.33
Poland	51.01	46.44	44.34	42.72	41.08	43.80	44.26	44.68	42.62	43.44	43.86	42.19	43.19	44.40
Portugal	42.07	41.14	40.82	41.00	41.13	42.48	42.31	43.78	44.67	45.77	44.53	43.78	43.65	48.29
Slovak Republic	53.78	48.96	45.82	48.14	52.18	44.50	45.09	40.16	37.70	38.01	36.64	34.33	34.85	41.32
Slovenia	44.45	44.83	45.71	46.49	46.73	47.56	46.34	46.38	45.84	45.20	44.51	42.43	44.13	49.02
Spain	43.21	41.63	41.06	39.87	39.12	38.64	38.89	38.40	38.88	38.44	38.39	39.18	41.29	45.80
Sweden	62.92	60.66	58.78	58.11	55.09	54.52	55.60	55.67	54.18	53.85	52.71	50.97	51.51	54.90
Switzerland	35.29	35.52	35.77	34.30	35.10	34.78	36.16	36.39	35.95	35.27	33.48	32.32	32.23	33.74
Turkey	..	..	..	..	..	..	..	..	..	..	..	..	..	..
United Kingdom	42.27	40.51	39.47	38.88	39.05	40.16	41.09	42.11	42.94	44.10	44.19	43.97	47.42	51.63
United States	36.59	35.46	34.62	34.17	33.88	34.98	35.89	36.27	36.02	36.28	35.96	36.76	38.94	42.18
Euro area	50.63	49.37	48.53	48.13	46.31	47.32	47.66	48.12	47.58	47.43	46.72	46.04	46.93	50.83

TABLE 6	Total Government Debt as a Percentage of GDP												
	1997	**1998**	**1999**	**2000**	**2001**	**2002**	**2003**	**2004**	**2005**	**2006**	**2007**	**2008**	**2009**
Australia	18.5	15.6	13.8	11.4	9.6	8.6	7.5	6.7	6.3	5.8	5.2	4.9	8.1
Austria	59.2	59.9	62.0	61.2	60.7	60.4	60.9	62.2	62.1	60.6	58.1	59.6	64.3
Belgium	109.9	105.3	103.4	99.5	99.1	97.9	95.4	92.8	91.8	87.6	85.3	90.2	95.3
Canada	52.7	50.1	46.7	40.9	39.7	38.1	35.9	32.1	30.2	28.0	25.1	28.6	35.7
Chile	13.2	12.5	13.7	13.6	14.9	15.7	13.0	10.7	7.3	5.3	4.1	5.2	6.1
Czech Republic	9.6	9.8	11.0	13.2	14.7	16.1	19.1	21.1	23.2	24.9	25.2	27.1	32.5
Denmark	69.1	64.0	60.9	54.8	52.0	51.6	49.6	47.0	39.3	32.7	27.8	32.4	37.8
Finland	65.0	59.9	55.7	48.0	44.4	41.3	43.5	41.9	38.2	35.6	31.2	29.5	37.6
France	45.6	46.3	47.8	47.4	48.3	49.9	51.9	52.6	53.3	52.1	52.1	54.2	60.8
Germany	24.3	26.1	34.1	34.1	34.6	36.1	37.7	39.2	40.4	40.9	39.4	38.8	43.8
Greece	105.2	103.7	103.6	108.9	109.7	109.2	105.8	108.3	110.3	107.5	105.8	109.6	125.7
Hungary	60.9	59.0	59.1	54.1	50.5	53.6	56.3	55.7	58.1	61.9	61.3	68.2	72.7
Iceland	46.2	40.7	35.3	33.8	39.2	35.3	33.3	28.2	19.4	24.8	23.2	44.3	87.2
Ireland	57.4	47.8	44.1	34.8	30.9	27.9	26.9	25.4	23.6	20.3	19.8	27.7	46.0
Israel	103.0	103.8	93.1	83.3	87.8	95.3	97.7	96.7	92.1	82.9	76.4	75.4	78.3
Italy	111.0	108.7	106.7	103.6	102.7	99.5	96.8	96.2	97.5	96.7	95.2	98.0	106.6
Japan	76.7	87.7	97.0	106.1	123.5	137.6	140.9	156.7	164.3	161.4	164.2	178.0	..
Korea	10.0	14.3	16.3	16.7	17.4	17.6	20.7	23.7	27.6	30.1	29.7	29.0	32.6
Luxembourg	3.7	4.1	3.5	3.2	3.1	2.7	1.7	1.4	0.8	1.4	1.4	8.2	8.6
Mexico	23.5	25.4	23.3	21.2	20.5	21.9	22.1	20.7	20.2	20.5	21.0	24.5	28.2
Netherlands	53.9	52.0	49.2	44.1	41.3	41.5	43.0	43.8	43.0	39.2	37.8	50.1	49.9
New Zealand	36.3	37.9	35.1	32.2	30.2	28.5	26.4	23.8	22.1	21.6	20.4	20.6	27.5
Norway	24.7	22.2	20.9	19.3	18.1	19.0	21.3	18.4	17.2	12.5	11.7	13.8	26.1
Poland	43.0	39.5	39.7	35.8	36.4	40.6	44.9	43.6	44.8	45.1	42.6	44.8	47.1
Portugal	58.0	54.8	55.1	54.1	56.0	58.7	60.2	63.0	68.2	69.8	69.2	71.2	81.1
Slovak Republic	20.8	22.5	22.7	23.9	36.0	35.1	35.1	38.4	33.1	29.2	28.1	26.3	33.6
Slovenia	..	..	..	..	..	..	26.9	27.1	26.9	25.8	23.2	21.3	34.1
Spain	55.3	53.6	52.3	49.9	46.3	43.9	40.7	39.3	36.4	33.0	30.0	33.7	46.1
Sweden	74.1	72.0	64.0	56.9	48.6	46.8	47.7	46.6	46.2	42.3	36.4	35.5	37.8
Switzerland	25.3	27.7	25.4	25.6	24.8	28.2	28.3	28.1	28.1	25.2	23.2	22.5	20.7
Turkey	32.9	31.0	39.8	38.2	74.1	69.2	62.2	56.6	51.1	45.5	39.6	40.0	46.3
United Kingdom	..	49.7	44.1	42.2	38.8	39.1	38.7	40.0	43.4	43.3	42.6	61.3	75.1
United States	45.4	42.5	39.0	33.9	32.4	33.2	34.9	36.0	36.1	36.0	35.6	40.0	53.1

SUMMARY

1. **What is antitrust policy?**

   - Antitrust policy is an attempt to enhance competition by restricting certain activities that could be anticompetitive. *§1*

   - The antitrust statutes include Sections 1 and 2 of the Sherman Antitrust Act, which forbid conspiracies and monopolization; Sections 2, 3, and 7 of the Clayton Antitrust Act, which prohibit anticompetitive pricing and nonprice restraints; and Section 5 of the Federal Trade Commission Act, which prohibits deceptive and unfair acts. *§1.a, Table 1*

   - Interpretation of the antitrust statutes has gone through several phases. In the early years, a rule of reason prevailed; acts had to be unreasonable to be a violation of the statutes. Between 1914 and 1980, a per se rule was applied more often. Under this policy, the mere existence of actions that could be used anticompetitively was a violation. In the early 1980s, the interpretations returned to the rule-of-reason standard. *§1.c*

   - The Herfindahl index is used to measure size and influence; industries with a Herfindahl index above 1,800 are considered highly concentrated. *§1.c*

   - Although each country has its own antitrust laws, the International Competition Network, an organization of about 90 nations, has attempted to create more similar laws. *§1.d*

2. **What is the difference between economic regulation and social regulation?**

   - Economic regulation refers to the prescription of price and output for a particular industry. Social regulation refers to the setting of health and safety standards for products and the workplace, and environmental and operating procedures for all industries. *§2*

   - Because monopoly is inefficient and perfect competition is efficient, governments have attempted to regulate natural monopolies to make them more like perfect competitors. The huge economies of scale involved rule out breaking up the natural monopolies into small firms. Instead, price has been set at a fair rate of return, $P = ATC$. *§2.a*

   - Social regulation has increased even as economic regulation has decreased. *§2.c*

   - Regulations create costs and provide benefits. The economist's view is that a regulation should be implemented only if its benefits exceed its costs. *§2.c.1*

   - Deregulation in other developed countries took the form of privatization: the selling, auctioning, or contracting out of a government enterprise to private interests. *§2.d*

3. **What international agencies regulate business behavior?**

   - The World Trade Organization (WTO) is intended to lower tariffs and increase trade. *§2.d*

   - The WTO was created on January 1, 1995, by the Uruguay Round of the GATT. It is located in Geneva. *§2.d*

4. **How does government pay for its activities?**

   - Governments at all levels—federal, state, and local—collect taxes to pay for their activities. When governments do not collect enough taxes to pay expenses, then governments borrow. *§3.a, 3.b, 3.c*

   - Government spending has risen as a percentage of GDP since about 1910. *§3.a*

   - In the United States the largest tax is the income tax. At the federal government level, the next largest tax is the payroll or FICA—Social Security and Medicare—tax. *§3.b*

   - Debt as a percentage of GDP has risen in recent years. *§3.c*

   - Governments in developed nations around the world spend, tax, and run debts. Some governments are much bigger as a percentage of GDP than is the case in the United States. *§3.d*

KEY TERMS

antitrust policy, 571
contracting out, 578
economic regulation, 576
fair rate of return, 577

privatization, 578
progressive tax, 587
proportional tax, 587
regressive tax, 587

social regulation, 576
stranded assets, 578

EXERCISES

1. Using the average-total-cost and marginal-cost curves, demonstrate what huge fixed costs and near-zero marginal costs mean for the average-total-cost curve.

2. Using the demand and cost curves of an individual firm in oligopoly, demonstrate the effects of each of the following:
   a. The Clean Air Act
   b. The Nutrition and Labeling Act
   c. A ban on smoking inside the workplace
   d. A sales tax

3. Kodak has developed an important brand name through its advertising, innovation, and product quality and service. Suppose Kodak sets up a network of exclusive dealerships, and one of the dealers decides to carry Fuji and Mitsubishi as well as Kodak products. If Kodak terminates the dealership, is it acting in a pro- or anticompetitive manner?

4. Explain why a market in which broadcast licenses can be purchased might be more efficient than having the FCC assign licenses on some basis designed by the FCC.

5. Which of the three types of government policies—antitrust, social regulation, and economic regulation—is the basis for each of the following?
   a. Beautician education standards
   b. Certified Public Accounting requirements
   c. Liquor licensing
   d. Justice Department guidelines
   e. The Clean Air Act
   f. The Nutrition and Labeling Act

6. Some airline executives have called for reregulation. Why might an executive of an airline prefer to operate in a regulated environment?

7. Suppose the Herfindahl index for domestic production of televisions is 5,000. Does this imply a very competitive or a noncompetitive environment?

8. Suppose a monopolist is practicing price discrimination and a lawsuit against the monopolist forces an end to the practice. Is it possible that the result is a loss in efficiency? Explain.

9. The Justice Department sued several universities for collectively setting the size of scholarships offered. Explain why the alleged price fixing on the part of universities might be harmful to students.

10. The FDA is considering the adoption of a higher standard of success in clinical trials for any pharmaceutical that the agency will permit to be sold in the United States. Explain how a cost–benefit calculation would be carried out.

11. Suppose that in exercise 10, the benefits of the regulation were 1,000 lives saved per year. Would you support adoption of the regulation? Explain.

12. Explain what the costs of the regulation are in the scenario in exercises 10 and 11.

13. What does a loss of consumer surplus mean? In the case of exercises 10–12, exactly how do the losses of consumer surplus occur?

14. Go to http://www.heritage.org and find the Economic Freedom map. Use the map to determine the most economically free continent and the least economically free continent. Then do a search to find out the real GDP per capita of people in representative countries of those continents.

15. What is the pattern of U.S. government as a share of the total economy since the 1900s?

16. What is government debt? Why has it increased or decreased?

17. Is the United States the nation with the most government debt? If not, who is?

You can find further practice tests in the Online Quiz at
www.cengage.com/economics/boyes.

AN UNBOUND INDIA FLOURISHES, BUT THE JOB'S NOT YET DONE

The Globe and Mail (Canada), July 18, 2007

One day in the 1980s, Gurcharan Das found himself arguing with the finance minister of India about the value of face creams for women. Mr. Das, then an executive with Procter & Gamble, was pleading with the minister to lower India's 120-percent excise duty on toiletries, which were making it hard for P&G to sell its Oil of Olay cream to Indian women.

"A face cream won't do anything for an ugly face," said the minister impatiently. "These are luxuries of the rich."

When Mr. Das protested that even a young woman from the village used traditional beauty pastes, the minister said, "No, it's best to leave a face to nature."

"Sir," Mr. Das objected, "how can you decide what she wants? After all, it is her hard-earned money."

"Yes, and I don't want her wasting it. Let her buy food," said the minister, ending the meeting with an imperious wave of his hand.

Those were the bad old days. Like many Indian executives, Mr. Das spent hours in the stale corridors of Delhi's government offices, suffering the disdain of countless time-serving officials as he tried to negotiate a web of taxes, regulations, and restrictions.

Under the Licence Raj, as India's stifling business rules were called, "you could actually go to jail for producing more than your approved limit. A farmer could not sell his produce beyond state borders. A young entrepreneur faced up to 37 functionaries and inspectors, each of them wanting his cut. It was a crime to invite your customer to lunch abroad while travelling because it exceeded your foreign exchange allowance."

These were more than just minor annoyances for Indian businessmen. The Licence Raj held India back for decades, curbing its economic growth as first Japan, then South Korea, Taiwan, and Hong Kong, and then China leapt from poverty to prosperity. "By suppressing economic liberty for 40 years, we destroyed growth and the futures of two generations," he writes in his 2000 book *India Unbound*.

That made Mr. Das mad, and he wasn't afraid to say so. A government official's son educated at Harvard on a scholarship, he had no patience for the petty tyranny of Indian officialdom. He once even had the nerve to challenge the regal Indira Gandhi. "Does the market always make the right decisions?" she demanded when he questioned the Licence Raj after a speech she gave to a business audience.

"Not always, madam, but always better than bureaucrats," Mr. Das replied.

"Ah," she said with a condescending smile, "we have a market-wallah, do we?"

He doesn't have to suffer that kind of sneering any more. Since finance minister (now Prime Minister) Manmohan Singh introduced market-oriented reforms in 1991, the Licence Raj has crumbled. India is, indeed, unbound. With its natural entrepreneurial talent liberated, the country has registered steadily accelerating economic growth, which touched 9 per cent last year, close to booming China's.

Unlike China's government-directed, top-down formula, India's miracle has been "a people's success—a success from below," Mr. Das says.

"It has happened in spite of the state, not because of the state," he said in a recent conversation as he walked his dog in Delhi's sprawling Lodhi Garden.

The Italian saying, he says, applies equally to India: "The economy grows at night when the government sleeps."

In every sector where the government has stopped meddling, from telecoms to airlines, private industry has grabbed the ball and run with it. But the job isn't done yet. While socialist follies like central planning and import substitution have largely been done away with, India still limits foreign investment, still restricts companies' ability to let unneeded employees go, and still operates too many companies itself.

India's government, says Mr. Das, needs to stop doing what it should not be doing: mucking with the market.

Just as important, it needs to start doing what it should be doing.

Government's role in enabling economic development is to make sure that basic health care is provided to its citizens; to direct the building of roads, airports, and sea ports to carry the nation's products; and to regulate the market with clear and legally enforceable rules; and, most important, to educate young people so that they can do the work of a modern economy.

As it stands, primary education is a wreck. One-quarter of Indian school teachers don't even show up for work. One in four men and one in two women cannot read or write. "The Indian state's biggest failure has been in building human capabilities," Mr. Das writes in *India Unbound*.

India's economy may grow while government sleeps, but India won't truly prosper until government wakes up and does its job.

Making India His Business

Gurcharan Das grew up in modest circumstances as the son of a public works official for irrigation and canals.

The family moved to Washington, D.C., in the 1950s when his father was posted there to negotiate with newly created Pakistan over the sharing of rivers. When they returned to India, Mr. Gurcharan stayed on to finish high school and then take a scholarship at Harvard, where he graduated with honours and attended the business school.

Homesick, he returned to India to work as a minor executive for Vicks, travelling around the country promoting its famous Vaporub. He worked his way up to chief executive officer of Procter & Gamble India and then director of strategic planning for Proctor & Gamble Worldwide. Since taking early retirement, he has been a consultant to industry and government. He writes a column for the *Times of India* and has written several plays and a novel, *A Fine Family*.

Marcus Gee

Source: Marcus Gee.

This article contains quite a few important points. First, notice the attitude of the finance minister. He knows best. He knows better what the woman should do with her money than does the woman. This attitude is common among people who do not like the market outcome. They know better than the market. Second, the bad old days—the days of the License Raj—were days when economic freedom in India was extremely low. Things have improved, as the article notes, but have a long way to go. The Economic Freedom Index in 2009 ranked India the 123rd freest in the 2009 index. Its score is only 0.3 point higher than last year because improvements in financial freedom, government size, and business freedom were offset by significant decreases in investment freedom and labor freedom. India is ranked 25th out of 41 countries in the Asia-Pacific region, and its overall score is below the world average.

Although it has given up central planning, India continues to move forward only slowly with market-oriented economic reforms. The average tariff rate is high, and nontariff barriers further impede trade. Foreign investment is overly regulated, and the judicial system remains clogged by a large case backlog. Public debt is high, and the general government fiscal deficit continues to grow. The following table compares India with the average of all countries in each element of economic freedom.

Ten Economic Freedoms of India*		
Economic Freedom	**India**	**Avg**
Business freedom	54.4	64.3
Investment freedom	30.0	48.8
Trade freedom	51.0	51.0
Financial freedom	40.0	49.1
Fiscal freedom	73.8	74.9
Property rights	50.0	44.0
Government size	77.8	65.0
Freedom from corruption	35.0	40.3
Monetary freedom	69.3	74.0
Labor freedom	62.3	61.3

*Economic Freedom Index 2009, http://www.heritage.org/index/ Country/India.

Regulations and red tape increase the cost of doing business. Consider the following graph of a non-perfectly competitive firm. The marginal cost MC represents what business costs would be with a much better business freedom. The marginal cost MC_{lr} represents the higher costs due to the regulations under the License Raj.[6] Notice that output is lower and prices higher.

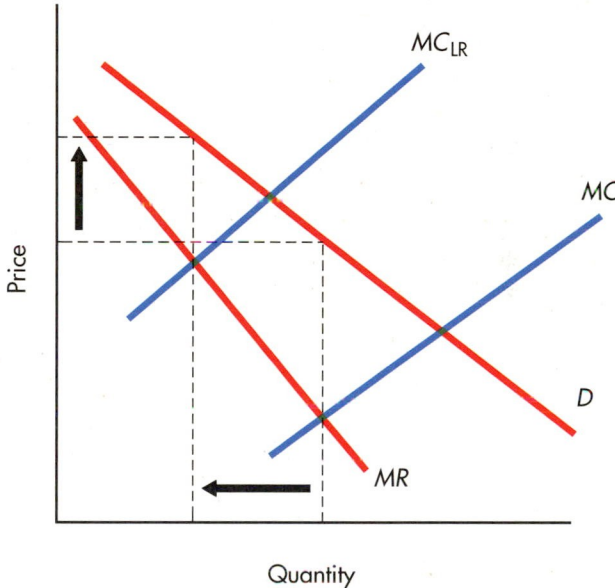

Indira Gandhi, whose father began India's independence with a centrally planned economy, asked whether the market always makes the right decision. After reading this and the next chapter, we might respond to Gandhi as follows: There are times when markets fail due to lack of private property rights or imperfect information, but generally private actions and markets can solve the difficulties. There are times, perhaps, when certain limited government actions are useful, but central planning, where everything is controlled by a central authority, creates many more failures.

[6] *Permit Raj* (or *License Raj*) refers to the licenses, regulations, and the accompanying red tape that were required to set up and run business in India between 1947 and 1990. The License Raj was a result of India's decision to have a centrally planned economy. For more on the permit raj and the Prime Minister Manmohan Singh's attitude toward it see: http://www .andhranews.net/India/2011/Govt-wont-allow-return-permit-raj-6587.htm.

Although both China and India are moving toward private property rights and market economies, they are taking very different routes, as the article says. India is attempting to reduce regulations and red tape and just let the people go at it. China is attempting to control each step and to move incrementally toward some private property rights and markets. Which approach will be more successful will require some time to determine. Nevertheless, as the article notes, in those sectors of India where government has stopped meddling, the sectors have done very well.

CHAPTER 27

Market Failures, Government Failures, and Rent Seeking

© MACIEJ FROLOW/GETTY IMAGES, INC

© WANG JIANGANG/XINHUA/LANDOV; LOGO: © FROXX/SHUTTERSTOCK.COM

FUNDAMENTAL QUESTIONS

1. What are the benefits of free markets?

2. How are private property rights defined?

3. Why does a lack of private property rights lead to market failures?

4. What are externalities?

5. What are free rider problems?

6. How does the government solve externality and free rider problems?

7. What are moral hazard and adverse selection problems?

8. What are network externalities?

9. Is government intervention necessary or justified to solve market failures?

As we noted in the last chapter, economic freedom is a measure of the degree to which government gets involved in private transactions. In general, the greater a nation's economic freedom, the higher its standard of living, as shown in Figure 1. Economies rated "free" or "mostly free" in the 2009 Economic Freedom Index have per-capita incomes that are more than double the average levels in all other countries and more than eight times higher than the "repressed" economies. The prosperity that flows from economic freedom results in greater access to education, reduced illiteracy, increased access to higher quality health care and food supplies, and longer life expectancy. In other words, economic freedom leads to a higher quality of living. As shown in Figure 2, the United Nations

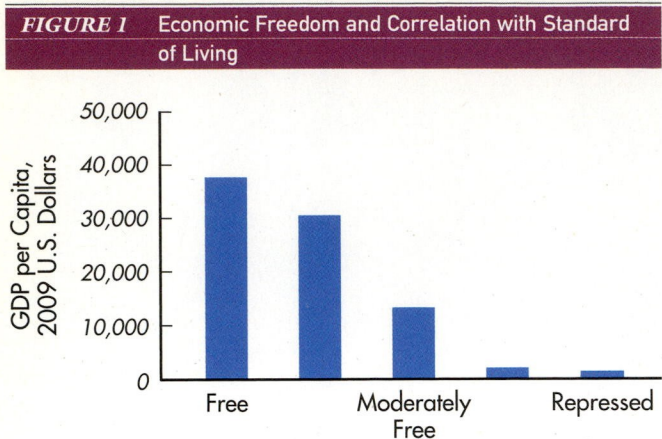

FIGURE 1   Economic Freedom and Correlation with Standard of Living

Measured as GDP per capita, Purchasing Power Parity Method.

Sources: 2009 Index of Economic Freedom (Washington, D.C.: The Heritage Foundation and Dow Jones & Company, Inc., 2009) at http://www.heritage.org/index. International Monetary Fund, World Economic Outlook database, April 2007, at http://www.imf.org.

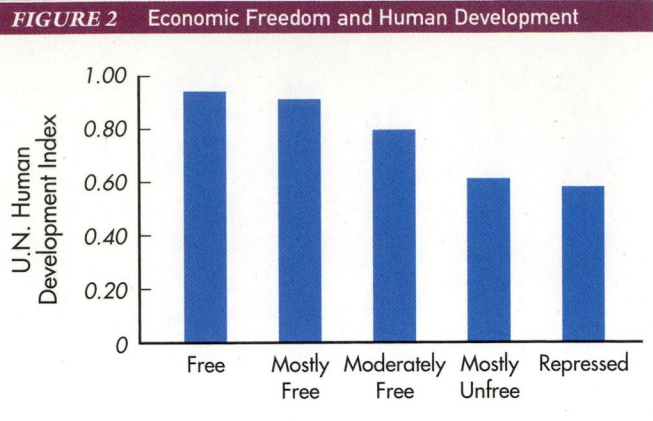

FIGURE 2   Economic Freedom and Human Development

Sources: 2009 Index of Economic Freedom (Washington, D.C.: The Heritage Foundation and Dow Jones & Company, Inc., 2009) at http://www.heritage.org/index. Human Development Reports 2007/2008, U.N. Human Development Programme, at http://hdr.undp.org.

Human Development Index, which measures life expectancy, literacy, education, and the standard of living in countries worldwide, is strongly correlated with economic freedom.

If free markets and economic freedom lead to higher standards of living and a better quality of living, why does the government play such a large role in the economy? There are two arguments against unfettered free markets. First, the markets do not always work to allocate resources to their highest-valued uses. In other words, markets sometimes fail. A **market failure** occurs when the market outcome is not the socially efficient outcome—that is, when resources are not allocated to their highest-valued use and people don't get what they are willing and able to buy at the lowest possible price. So when a market failure occurs, it is argued that

market failure
A situation in which resources are not allocated to their highest-valued use.

the government must intervene to solve the failure. Second, even though the unfettered market may lead to higher standards of living, it also causes some businesses to fail and some people to do without. It is sad to see people lose jobs, for people to do without homes or cars or other goods; it is sad to see people in poverty. Also, governments may provide monopolies to specific businesses or provide aid to other businesses for a variety of reasons. So, speaking very generally, a second reason that government intervenes in free markets is because people do not like the outcome of a free market; they want to change the result of the market. In this chapter, we discuss the market failure arguments.

In this chapter we also discuss the economic theory of market failures, as well as the normative economics of what should be done about potential market failures.[1]

[1] What we discuss is the broad consensus among economists. If you want to read more contrarian views on the failures of governments to increase efficiency and on what some refer to as the myth of market failures, see the Internet chapter "Government Failures and Markets."

1. Private Property Rights

In 1978 in Xiaogang, Anhui province—the heart of China's rice-growing region—20 families held a secret meeting to find ways to combat starvation. This was just after Mao's death when communist rule was very strict. The system that the communists had in place was generating less and less food. Under this system, everybody was collectively responsible for tilling the land and everybody had a share in the land's output. You got your rice share whether you worked hard or not and, as a result, people hardly worked.

The villagers of Xiaogang decided they would divide up the land and farm it individually with each person keeping the output of his own land. They had to keep this arrangement secret out of fear of the communist authorities. But as rice production in Xiaogang continued to rise, the secret became known. Neighboring villages discovered the secret and implemented their own arrangements. It was not long until the communist authorities found out. In 1982 the Communist Party decided to allow some individual farming.[2]

Private property rights mean that when you own something, that something is yours to do with as you want—at least as long as you do not harm others. This seems like such a simple idea. Think about renting a house or renting a car. You don't take care of it in the same way you do when you own the house or own the car. You have no incentive, other than avoiding a fee for damages, because if you spend the time, effort, and money to maintain the house or car or improve it, you get nothing in return.

When private property rights are secure, others, including governments and organizations, are not allowed to steal or damage your private property. When private property rights are not secure, people are unlikely to be able to sell the things they own or to use them for collateral on a loan or pass them along to family. And they have much less incentive to improve the property because they are not assured of keeping their property.

The farmers in Xiaogang who agreed to divide up the land for cultivation could not sell their land or even pass it along to family. Although their produce was privately owned, the land on which it was grown belonged to the state. The amount of rice raised on the so-called private plots was significantly greater than when everything was communal, but there was a limit on what could be done with the property and thus a limit to possible returns on that land.

Private property rights are crucial to a market; without ownership of a good or resource, no one can voluntarily exchange that good or resource and the value of that good or resource cannot be determined. So what happens when private property rights do not exist or are not well defined and secure?

1.a. Private, Public, Common, and Club Goods

The **principle of mutual excludability** refers to a well-defined private property right. It says that if you own a good, I cannot use it or consume it without your permission; and if I own a good, you cannot use it or consume it unless I grant permission. When I purchase a pizza, it is mine to do with as I wish. You have no right to the pizza unless I provide that right. The **principle of rivalry** says that when I consume or use a good or service, that reduces the amount available to anyone else. When I eat a piece of pizza, less of the pizza remains; this is what is meant by rivalry. When excludability and rivalry exist, private property rights are easy to define.

Table 1 illustrates the role of excludability and rivalry in defining private property rights. If a good is both excludable and rivalrous, then the good is a **private good**. Property rights to private goods are easily established. If a good is excludable but nonrivalrous, such as cable television, then the good is called a **club good**. The name, club,

1 What are the benefits of free markets?

2 How are private property rights defined?

private property rights
The right of individuals to own property.

principle of mutual excludability
The rule that an owner of private property is entitled to enjoy the consumption of that property privately.

principle of rivalry
When one consumes or uses a good or service, less remains for others.

private good
A good that is both excludable and rivalrous.

club good
A good that is excludable but nonrivalrous.

---

[2] William Easterly, *The White Man's Burden*, New York: Penguin Press, 2006, p. 108.

TABLE 1	Classification of Goods	
	Excludable	**Nonexcludable**
Rivalrous	Private Goods *Food, clothing, toys, furniture, pizza*	Commons Goods *Fish, water, air*
Nonrivalrous	Club Goods *Cable television, private golf courses*	Public Goods *National defense, free-to-air television, MP3 files*

© Cengage Learning 2013

makes sense since people have to belong to the "club" to be able to enjoy the good or service. People can be excluded from its use so that private ownership can occur. Rivalry may occur in the case of a club good when the club good becomes congested—for example, too many people trying to play golf on the private golf course makes the potential players compete for playing time. In most cases, private property rights to the club can be established—membership can be purchased.

In the case where neither the principle of mutual exclusivity nor the principle of rivalry apply, the good is called a **public good**. The exchange of MP3 music files on the Internet is nonrivalrous and nonexcludable: The use of these files by any one person does not restrict the use by anyone else, and there is little effective control over the exchange of these music files.

If a good is rivalrous but nonexcludable, such as fish in oceans and parks, then the good is called a **commons good**. The establishment of ownership over commons goods is difficult.

Without well-defined and secure private property rights, such as with commons and public goods, market failure may occur. If something is available for you to use and you don't have to pay for it, why would you pay? That's a problem with both common and public goods: People can get these goods without paying for them. When goods are nonexcludable, an individual has an incentive to be a **free rider**—a consumer or producer who enjoys the benefits of a good or service without paying for that good or service. Examples of public goods that are often given are national defense, lighthouses, fire protection, and police protection. If one rich person established a missile defense system on her property, all her neighbors would enjoy the protection without paying anything. A problem would arise because you would be protected whether or not you paid for the national defense as long as others, your neighbors, paid. Of course, because each person has an incentive not to pay for it, few will voluntarily do so. As a result, the good may not be provided, or, if it is provided, the quantity produced will be "too small" from society's viewpoint.

Lighthouses warn passing ships about rocks and land masses. Because any ship can see the light and heed the warning, none of them has an incentive to pay for the service. So no one provides a lighthouse. These are *market failures*: **too few resources are devoted to the production of the public good.**

1.b. Externalities

In 2011 the price of a gallon of gasoline in the U.S. exceeded $4 per gallon. This caused a few people to abandon their SUVs, purchasing smaller, gasoline-efficient or hybrid cars. Nevertheless, many people continued to drive those larger SUVs that got perhaps eight or nine miles per gallon. The decision to purchase and drive the SUV affects people other than just the owner and driver. The emissions are larger than those of a small

public good
A good that is nonexcludable and nonrivalrous.

commons good
A good that is rivalrous but nonexcludable.

free rider
A consumer or producer who enjoys the benefits of a good or service without paying for that good or service.

 3 Why does a lack of private property rights lead to market failures?

© froxx/Shutterstock.com

car or a hybrid car. In addition, if a collision between an SUV and a small car occurs, the inhabitants of the SUV are much less likely to be injured. Yet the SUV owners don't have to compensate the small car owners for putting their lives at risk. Nor do they compensate people with breathing problems that are made worse by the emissions created as the SUVs cruise around town. But since these are the costs of driving the less fuel-efficient car, someone has to pay. The problem is that it is people who are not voluntarily part of the transaction to purchase the SUV who have to pay.

Because costs are imposed on people who are external to the decision to purchase and drive the SUV, these costs are called **externalities**. The problem created by externalities is that the price does not reflect all the costs. If it did, the price of the SUVs would be higher and fewer would be purchased. This means that *too many* SUVs are driven, *too much* pollution is created, and *too much* risk is created for drivers of smaller vehicles. The *too many* and *too much* refer to the quantities that would occur if there were no external costs.[3]

The price someone pays for the SUV is the **private cost** of that SUV. But the SUV comes with the external costs. The cost to society is the sum of private costs and external costs. When you buy a Big Mac, the price you pay for the Big Mac is the private cost of that food item. But the Big Mac comes in a cardboard wrapper. When you throw the wrapper into a garbage can two blocks away, you are creating a cost that you are not paying. You did not voluntarily transfer ownership of that wrapper; you simply dumped it. As a result, people who had nothing to do with that Big Mac must pay the cost of picking up the garbage.

Externalities may be negative or positive. The examples just given are *negative externalities*. A *positive externality* may result when the benefits of an activity are received by consumers or firms that are not directly involved in the activity. For instance, inoculations for mumps, measles, flu, and other communicable diseases provide benefits to all of society. If some people get a flu shot, you may have less chance of getting the flu even though you did not get a flu shot. You receive a positive externality from those who were vaccinated.

The total cost of a transaction, the private cost plus the external cost, is called the **social cost**. If all the costs and benefits of a transaction are borne by the participants in that transaction, the private costs and the social costs are the same. When private costs differ from social costs, the full opportunity cost of using a scarce resource is borne not by the producer or the consumer, but by others. When you don't have to pay the full cost of a good or service, you will consume more than you would if you had to pay the full cost. In this sense, "too much" of the good or service is consumed. If the owners of SUVs were directly responsible for the social costs borne by those in smaller cars and for the extra pollution emitted by the SUV, then fewer consumers would have an incentive to purchase SUVs. Similarly, if you bought ownership of the wrapper each time you purchased a Big Mac and had to pay for each wrapper you threw away, you would have had an incentive to consume or produce less of the product and thus pollute less.

When not all aspects of a transaction are privately owned—that is, whenever there is a divergence between social costs and private costs—the result is either *too much* or *too little* production and consumption. In either case, resources are not being used in their highest-valued activity. For instance, those who pollute do not bear the entire costs of the pollution; therefore, they pollute more than they otherwise would. Those who smoke do not pay a cost for secondhand smoke; therefore, they tend to smoke more than they otherwise would. Those who get flu shots provide some protection for those

externality
The cost or benefit of a transaction that is borne by someone not directly involved in the transaction.

 4 What are externalities?

private cost
Cost that is borne solely by the individuals involved in the transaction that created the costs.

social cost
The total cost of a transaction, the private cost plus the external cost.

© froxx/Shutterstock.com

---

[3] You may have noticed that we have moved from positive to normative. "Too much," "too many," and "too few" are normative statements, comparing outcomes with those derived under perfect competition.

who do not get the shots, but those who benefit from others getting the inoculations don't pay for the benefit. If they did, it would lower the price for those who purchase the shots, and more people would get the inoculations.

$$\text{Social cost} = \text{private cost} + \text{value of externality}$$

To illustrate an externality using a typical market diagram, consider a gas station selling gasoline with pumps that have no emission-control equipment. Each time a consumer pumps gas, a certain quantity of pollutants is released into the air. Consumers are willing and able to purchase gasoline at various prices, as shown by the demand curve, D, in Figure 3. Gas is supplied according to the supply curve S_p. The equilibrium price and quantity are P_p and Q_p. The pollution imposes costs on society, but neither those selling the gas nor those buying the gas pay these costs. If the gas station did have to account for the pollution costs, its costs of supplying the gas would rise. The supply of gas would be given by the supply curve S_s, because with higher costs, firms are willing and able to supply less at each price. The (social) equilibrium, the equilibrium taking into account all costs and benefits, is the intersection of demand and supply at price P_s and quantity Q_s.

In contrast to negative externalities, private costs exceed social costs when external benefits are created. Figure 4 represents the market for inoculations against some communicable disease. People would be willing and able to purchase the inoculations according to D_s if there were no externalities. However, because some people in society can benefit from the inoculations without purchasing them, the demand for the inoculations is less (D_p instead of D_s). This means that fewer people receive the inoculations than would be the case if the price took all the benefits into account. The social

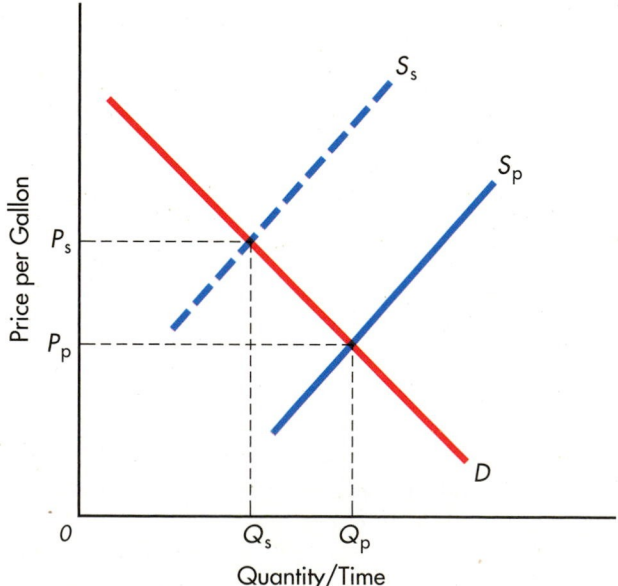

FIGURE 3   **Negative Externalities**

When a private transaction imposes costs on society that are not paid by the private transactors, a negative externality exists. With a negative externality, the supply of a product that is provided, S_p, is greater than it would be if the suppliers had to pay the externality, as shown by S_s.

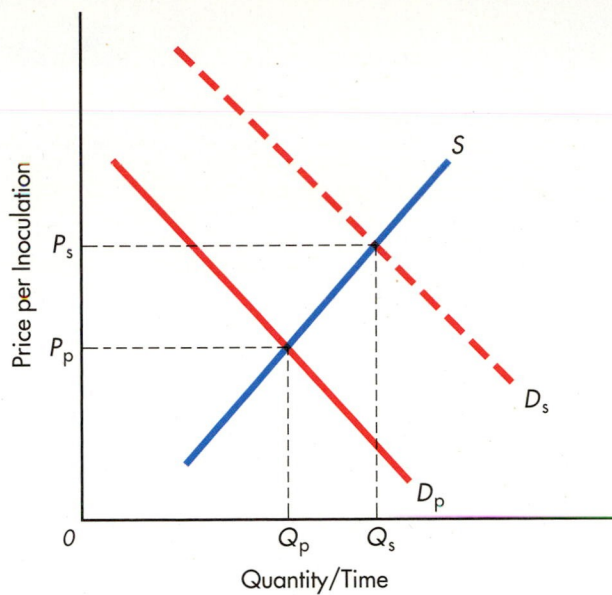

FIGURE 4   Positive Externalities

When a private transaction creates benefits for society that exceed those involved in the private transaction, positive externalities exist. D_p represents the demand for inoculations against a communicable disease when there is no externality. D_s represents the demand with an externality. Fewer people get the inoculations than would be desired by society.

© 2013 Cengage Learning

equilibrium would have Q_s getting the inoculations, but the smaller number Q_p actually do—"too little" of the good is purchased.

1.c. Public Goods

An externality exists when some aspects of a transaction are not privately owned but instead spill over to others. When none of a transaction is privately owned—that is, when an item is communally owned—additional problems arise. Again, suppose you have purchased a pizza to be delivered to your house. If you have a well-defined private property right in that pizza, only you can decide who can enjoy the pizza. However, if you do not have a well-defined private property right in the pizza, anyone can simply run over and begin eating the pizza. You can see that if there were no private property rights, no one would spend the money to buy a pizza.

To illustrate why common ownership is a problem, let's consider a situation in which a small village has communal property—everyone owns everything. There are five villagers, and each has $100. Each villager could use the $100 to buy a lamb or could deposit it in a bank account and earn $10 over one year. Lambs are allowed to graze for free on a small grass field called the commons. The free commons means that everyone free rides—everyone uses the commons without paying. The price the lamb will sell for after one year depends on the amount of weight it gains during the year, which, in turn, depends on the number of lambs sent onto the commons, as shown in Table 2.

If just one lamb grazes on the field, it will sell for $130, a gain of $30, or 30 percent for the year. This is three times the interest rate earned on the savings. Clearly, one lamb will be purchased and sent out to graze. With two lambs, the sale price is $120 each, so the total income for each owner is $20, for a return of 20 percent. With three lambs, the

5 What are free rider problems?

© frox/Shutterstock.com

GLOBAL BUSINESS
INSIGHT

Why Aren't Cows and Chickens on the Endangered Species List?

There are plenty of cows and chickens—and although they are consumed in huge numbers, their populations are not declining. Other species are experiencing declining numbers. *The Red List of Threatened Species*, compiled by the World Conservation Union, gives details of 11,167 species of animals and plants that are known to be at risk of extinction. Among the 10 animals that are of most concern because of their commercial value is the Hawksbill sea turtle, which is threatened because of the demand for its beautiful shell; the species is the sole source of "tortoise-shell" used to make curios and jewelry. Among the three species of Asian rhinos, the Sumatran rhino is the most threatened, as a result of both habitat loss and poaching for rhino horn, which is used in traditional Chinese medicine. A keystone species for Amazon rain forests, big leaf mahogany, is highly prized for furniture in the United States, which is the world's leading importer of the wood. Marketed under the more appealing name of "Chilean sea bass," the toothfish has suffered from its popularity among seafood lovers in the United States and Japan. Yellow-headed Amazon parrots are in demand as pets. There are 32 known species of seahorses, and at least 20 are threatened by the unregulated trade in both live seahorses for aquariums and dried seahorses, which are sold as curios and as treatments in traditional Chinese medicine. Whale sharks are the world's largest fish—growing as long as 50 feet—and are found in tropical and warm temperate seas. They have been overfished for their meat, fins, liver, cartilage, and skin. The Malayan giant turtle, along with dozens of other Asian tortoises and freshwater turtles, is threatened largely by unsustainable collection for food, primarily in China.

What is the difference between cows and chickens and these endangered species? Private ownership. When a species is privately owned, it will flourish because its owner will ensure that its numbers remain at the level that will earn the owner the most income. When a species is commonly owned—or not owned—no one has an incentive to ensure that the species endures. The command approach defines the endangered species list. Once a species is placed on the list, there are bans on hunting it, fishing for it, or otherwise endangering it. But unless the bans carry huge penalties and are easily enforced, the hunting and fishing will continue.

sale price is $112 each, so each owner receives a 12 percent return. With four lambs, the return to each owner is the same as the return from putting the money in the bank, 10 percent. And with five lambs, the owners of the lambs are worse off than they would have been if they had simply put the money in the bank. So four lambs use the commons. Each lamb returns $10 profit at the end of the year. Thus, with $40 from the lambs and $10 from interest, the total income of the village is $50, exactly what it would be if no lambs had been raised and the money had just been put in the bank.

Would things turn out differently if the village charged a fee for using the commons? What is the most that one person would pay to enable her lamb to graze on the commons? The opportunity cost of the $100 used to purchase the lamb was $10 (what could have been earned from the bank), so the economic profit from the single lamb is $20—$30 from the sale of the lamb minus the $10 opportunity cost. But with a cost to grazing on the commons, the situation changes. A single commune member would pay no more than $10 to rent the land, since with that rent the total return is just

$$\$10 = \$30 \text{ from the sale of the lamb} - \$10 \text{ opportunity cost} - \$10 \text{ rent.}$$

At a rent of $10, just one lamb would use the commons. In this case, total village income would be $10 from the rent, $40 from bank interest, and $10 from sale of the one lamb, or $60. The benefits to the village have risen from $50 to $60 as a result of privatizing the commons.

TABLE 2	Lambs on the Commons	
Number of Lambs	**Price after One Year**	**Income/Year**
1	$130	$30
2	$120	$20
3	$112	$12
4	$110	$10
5	$109	$ 9

© Cengage Learning 2013

When the "commons" are owned—when there are private property rights—utilization is reduced, and the benefits to society rise. The problem with communal property is that everyone free rides; no one takes into account the costs that each additional user imposes on others. When no one owns the fish in the sea, or no one owns the elephants that roam the African plains, or no one owns the American buffalo or bald eagle, or when no one owns the forests, a "too rapid" rate of use or harvest occurs; the "commons" is overutilized.

Common ownership fails to create an incentive for people to produce and consume the amount that is best for society. This is why communism failed. Under communism, no one has a private property right to anything, including his or her own labor. As a result, no one has an incentive to improve his or her human capital—to increase the value of personal skills and training—and no one has an incentive to ensure that companies are run efficiently. In China prior to 1990, people could not own the apartments in

The tragedy of the commons is the name given to the problem created when something is owned commonly rather than privately. Fish, for instance, are overfished because no one owns them. Because there are no private property rights, everyone can catch the fish and no one has an incentive to ensure that enough fish are left to propagate. If the beach is a commons, then anyone can use it and abuse it.

© Damian Herde/Shutterstock.com

which they lived. All urban living took place in government-owned buildings. Since no one had a private property right to a home, no one had an incentive to take care of it. The buildings were dilapidated, the hallways were filthy, and the landscaping was non-existent. When the Chinese leaders allowed some private ownership of apartments, those that were privately owned immediately became much improved. The hallways became clean, the landscaping reappeared, and the apparent quality of the buildings changed virtually overnight.

RECAP

1. An externality occurs when the costs and/or benefits of a private transaction are borne by those who are not involved in that private transaction.

2. A positive externality is a situation in which a private transaction creates benefits for members of society who are not involved in the transaction. In the case of positive externalities, not enough of the good or service is produced and consumed.

3. A negative externality is a situation in which a private transaction creates costs for members of society who are not involved in the transaction. In the case of a negative externality, too much of the good or service is produced and consumed.

4. Private property rights enable someone to own an item, that is, to dispose of, destroy, share, give away, or do anything that the person wants with the item.

5. When there are no private property rights to an item, that item cannot be bought or sold. No one has an incentive to produce the item or to purchase it.

6. When something is commonly owned, that something is overutilized.

7. A public good is one for which the principle of mutual excludability does not hold; when one person uses the item, that use does not reduce the quantity available for others.

8. Since a public good can be used without paying for it, people have no incentive to purchase it. A free rider problem arises.

9. A free rider problem occurs when someone can contribute less to an activity than that person can get back in return because that person relies on others to make up the difference. The problem is that if many people free ride, the item or activity is not produced.

2. Solutions to Market Failure

The solution to the lack of private property rights seems pretty straightforward: Create and enforce private property rights. For instance, in many nations in which elephants reside, no one owns the elephants. The result is that they are *overutilized*—they are becoming extinct. In most nations with elephants, large national parks have been created in which hunting is forbidden. But even in the face of these bans on hunting, the reduction in the number of elephants has continued. A decade ago, Africa's elephant population was more than a million; it has now fallen to less than half of that. In contrast to the common ownership strategy, the governments of Botswana, Zimbabwe, and South Africa created private property rights by allowing individuals to own elephants. These elephant farmers ensure that the elephants breed and reproduce so that they can be sold for their tusks, for hunting in special hunting parks, or to zoos in developed nations. This has led to a revival of the elephant population in these nations.

Sweden and Finland have more standing forest today than at any time in the past. Unlike the situation in Canada, where the forest is dwindling, most of the forest land in Sweden is privately owned. Private owners do not cut at a loss and do not cut to maintain employment levels or other political reasons. They cut at the rate that yields them the greatest return. If they simply razed their forests, they would have no income in coming years. So they cut or harvest at rates that ensure viable populations.

2.a. Government's Role

If all the costs or benefits of a private transaction belonged to the people creating them, then externalities would be no problem. When the people causing externalities pay for them, we say the externality has been **internalized**. Many people argue that it is the government's responsibility to reduce the externality problem: Just as it is the government that must assign and enforce private property rights in many cases, it is the government that must force the internalization of externalities. If so, how can the government get the externalities to be internalized?

internalized
When external costs or benefits are borne by the transactors creating them.

2.a.1. Tax or Subsidize the Externality
Suppose a firm pollutes as it creates its good. If the government imposed a tax on that company based on the amount of pollution the firm created, the firm would have to consider the extra cost when deciding whether to increase its output (and thereby pollution). This is shown in Figure 5 as the supply curve $S + t$, the supply curve plus the tax. The tax reduces the amount produced from Q to Q_s, and thereby reduces the amount of pollution created by the firm. The tax is a way in which the government can force the polluter to *internalize* the externality—that is, to pay for it rather than have society pay for it.

 6 How does the government solve externality and free rider problems?

The firm could avoid the tax by either reducing the amount it produces or purchasing pollution abatement equipment—equipment that will reduce the amount of pollution created. With less pollution, the firm will pay fewer taxes. Either choice, paying the tax or buying the equipment, means that the externality is internalized by the firm.

FIGURE 5   Pollution Tax

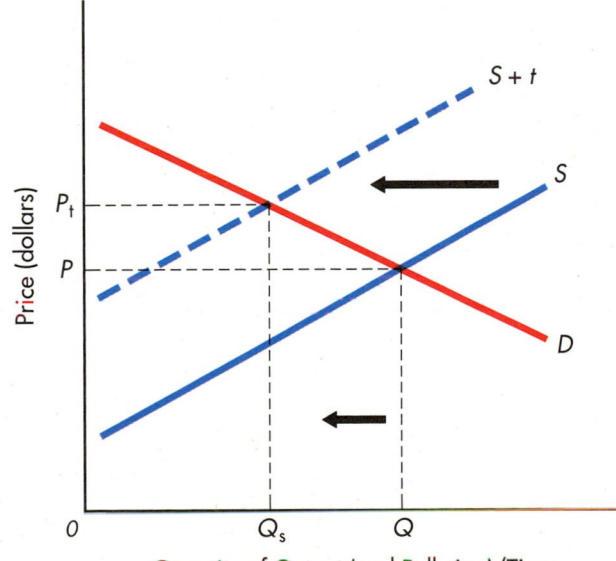

A tax on a firm that creates a negative externality reduces the quantity supplied and thus forces the firm to internalize the externality. Q_s is produced rather than Q.

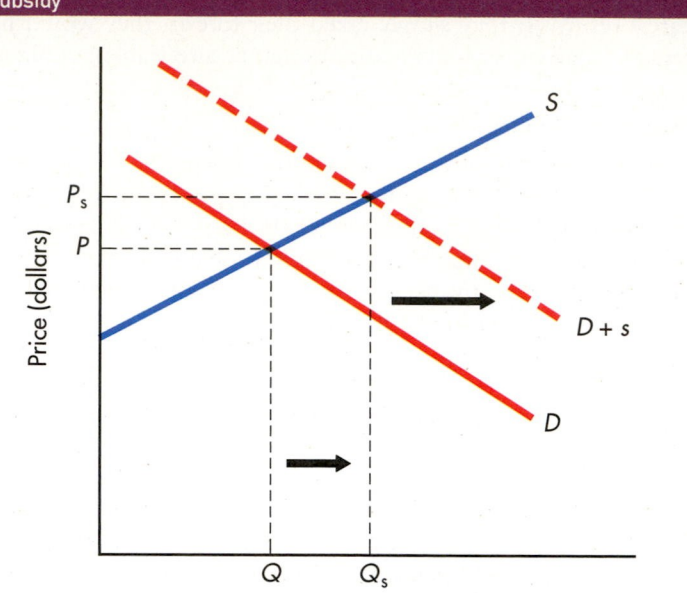

FIGURE 6 Subsidy

A subsidy to people getting inoculated increases the demand for inoculations, leading to more inoculations being obtained, Q_s.

© 2013 Cengage Learning

In the case of a positive externality, the government might provide a subsidy rather than impose a tax. Suppose each person getting an inoculation is given some money. More people would be willing to be inoculated, as shown in Figure 6. The subsidy, s, induces buyers to increase the quantities that they are willing and able to buy at each price. The total amount produced and consumed rises from Q to Q_s.

2.a.2. Command and Control
Rather than imposing a tax, the government could simply require or command that the company not create waste. For instance, the government could tell a copper mining operation to produce no more than three gallons of waste per ton of copper. The firm will then have no choice; it will have to either reduce the amount of waste it produces or go out of business. However, the command approach provides no incentive for the firm to utilize any new technology that might reduce waste beyond the mandated amount.

With a positive externality, the government might dictate who must use or consume the beneficial activity. For instance, by mandating that all children under the age of six be inoculated, the government is using a command approach: It is forcing the children to be inoculated. But by forcing everyone to be inoculated, the government is not selecting the socially optimal amount of inoculations. As a result, more than the socially optimal number of people get inoculations, and the costs of the inoculations are higher than would be necessary.

2.a.3. Marketable Pollution Permits: Cap and Trade
Governments have attempted to establish a market for the right to create some externalities, such as air pollution. The government specifies that a certain quantity of pollutants will be permitted in a particular area. It then issues permits that enable the owners of the permits to pollute. For example, if the target pollution level in the Los Angeles basin is 400 billion

particulates per day, the government could issue a total of 400 permits, each allowing the emission of 1 billion particulates per day. Then the government could sell the permits. Demanders, typically firms, would purchase the permits, allowing them to pollute up to the amount specified by the permits they own. If a firm purchased 20 permits, it could emit up to 20 billion particulates per day. If that firm implemented a cleaner technology or for some other reason did not use all of its permits, it could sell them to other firms.

The marketable permit idea is illustrated in Figure 7. The pollution target or cap set by the EPA is indicated by the vertical supply curve for pollution rights in Figure 7 labeled "1." The demand for permits to pollute is shown by the downward-sloping demand curve, D. With a price, P_1, for pollution rights determined, firms choose whether to pollute the amount they have purchased, to not produce as much and sell the excess permits, or to adopt cleaner technology and thus be able to sell the permits they don't use.

If the government decides to reduce pollutants more than it has in the past, it will reduce its pollution target. This is shown in Figure 7 as an inward shift of the total pollution permitted line. Demanders will bid for the now fewer pollution permits, driving the price of the permits up. As the price rises, some firms will decide not to purchase the permits, but instead to purchase new pollution abatement equipment or to reduce the amount they produce. The higher price gives firms an incentive to adopt more efficient pollution abatement equipment.

The permit market also enables others to influence the total amount of pollution created. Anyone can purchase permits. Some environmental groups, such as the Nature

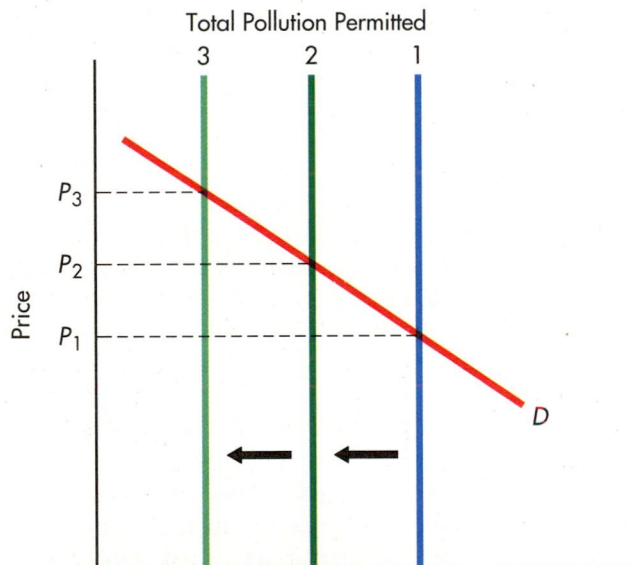

FIGURE 7   The Market for Pollution Permits

The government establishes the amount of pollution to be permitted. It then issues permits, each allowing a certain amount of pollution. To be able to pollute, a firm, individual, or group must have a permit. Holders of permits and those wanting permits then trade. The price of permits is determined by demand and supply. As the government reduces the amount of pollution allowed, the price of the permits increases.

Conservancy and the Sierra Club, have purchased permits simply to reduce the total amount of pollution that can occur in a specific area or industry. By purchasing the permits and taking them out of circulation, they essentially reduce the total number of permits and the total amount of pollution permitted.

RECAP

1. Government intervention to resolve the lack of private property rights include tax and subsidy, command and control, trade and cap, and assignment of ownership.

3. New Market Failure Arguments

Until the latter part of the twentieth century, market failure arguments were based on the lack of private property rights as exemplified by public goods, commons goods, and externalities. A general consensus developed in the economics profession that governments should intervene in a few markets to solve market failures, but that in most markets failures did not occur. This consensus began changing in the 1970s and 1980s as economists developed new market failure arguments based on the idea that there were information imperfections in markets. It was argued that these imperfections led to market failures as people made decisions on faulty or limited information. With this new approach, it seemed market failures occurred everywhere.

7 What are moral hazard and adverse selection problems?

asymmetric information
When the parties to a transaction do not have the same information about the transaction.

3.a. Asymmetric Information

When one party to an exchange knows a lot more about the good or service than the other party, the knowledgeable party may take advantage of the less-informed party. This is the problem of **asymmetric information**. When you purchase a used car, you are probably unsure of the car's quality. Most people assume that cars offered for sale by private individuals are defective in some way, and they are not willing to pay top dollar for such a car. In Figure 8, the market for high-quality used cars and that for low-quality used cars is shown. People offer their cars for sale as shown along the supply curve. Although demand for high-quality used cars would be D_{hq} if demanders could differentiate high-from low-quality used cars, the actual demand is D_a. Thus, people who do have high-quality used cars for sale cannot obtain the high price that they deserve. The result is that low-quality cars continue to be sold in the secondhand market, but high-quality cars do not. This result of the good being driven out of a market by the bad is called **adverse selection**. A market in which adverse selection occurs is often referred to as a **lemons market**, based on the idea of the used car being a lemon.

adverse selection
The situation in which higher-quality goods, consumers, or producers are driven out of the market by lower-quality examples because of limited information about the quality.

Adverse selection can occur in many different markets. For instance, banks do not always know which people who are applying for loans will default and which will pay on time. What happens if a bank increases the interest rate it charges on loans in an attempt to drive high-risk applicants out of the market? High-risk applicants continue to apply for loans because they don't have other alternatives that are less expensive. But low-risk applicants have other sources for loans, and so they stop applying to this bank. As a result, only high-risk applicants remain in the market.

lemons market
Market in which adverse selection occurs.

People purchase automobile or health insurance even if they are excellent drivers and enjoy good health. However, as the cost of insurance rises, the good drivers and healthy people may reduce their coverage, while the poor drivers and unhealthy people maintain their coverage. As a result, high-risk applicants take the place of more desirable low-risk applicants in the market for insurance.

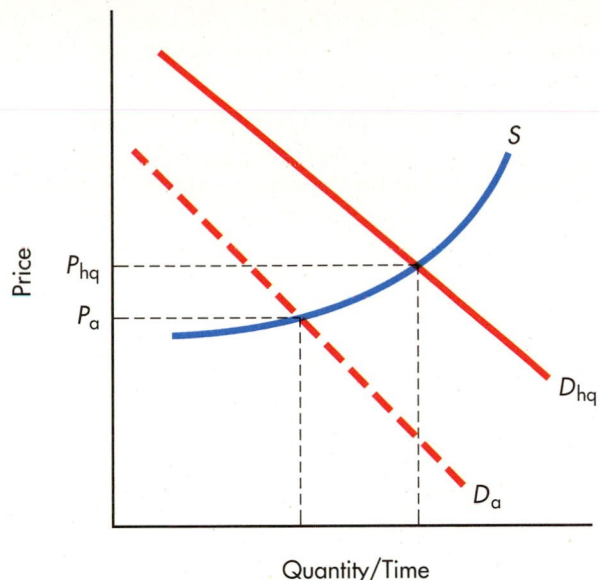

FIGURE 8   Adverse Selection

Quantity/Time

High-quality cars should be priced at *Phq*. Because potential buyers cannot distinguish between high- and low-quality cars, the actual price of high-quality cars is P_a. The result is that only low-quality cars remain in the used car market.

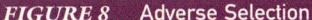

Another problem that can arise in markets when information is imperfect is called **moral hazard**. When you enter into an agreement you can have secure private property rights to the agreement only if the other parties do not change their behavior. A person who drives much less carefully after obtaining car insurance is creating a moral hazard. A person who takes less care to be healthy after obtaining health insurance is creating a moral hazard. The incentive for creating a moral hazard arises because the person buying the insurance knows more about his behavior than the insurance company does. These information imperfections lead to market failure.

moral hazard
The problem that arises when people change their behavior from what was expected of them when they engaged in a trade or contract.

3.b. Solutions to Adverse Selection and Moral Hazard

How can you be assured that the used car you are buying is high quality? How can you be sure the food and drugs you purchase are high quality? Many argue that you cannot, and that this is why government rules and regulations are necessary. The Federal Trade Commission restricts advertising, requiring that claims be demonstrable. Many governments require a time period after an exchange has occurred during which the buyer can change her mind; if before two days are up I decide that I don't want the product, I can return it and get my money back. In the case of insurance and loans, government rules and regulations indicate who is eligible for loans and whether different customers can be charged different rates. Governments ban certain ingredients in foods, such as trans fats, or regulate the quality of food and products, because consumers have less information about these foods than do the producers. The Food and Drug Administration inspects foods and drugs because producers have much more information about the foods and drugs than do consumers. Ingredients have to be listed on the packaging for foods and drugs. Government rules and regulations are used to minimize averse selection and moral hazard.

4. Increasing Returns and Network Externalities

Another market failure argument based on information imperfections claims that the economy is a "winner takes all" world. The first firm to gain market share drives all others out; the richest person gets richer and others do not; inefficient technologies keep efficient ones out of the market.

4.a. Diminishing and Increasing Returns

When a firm has a building and equipment and alters short-run supplies by increasing or decreasing the number of employees, the first few employees each generate increasing amounts of additional output. Eventually, however, another employee adds to output but less than previous employees did. As additional employees continue to be added, the additional output added continues declining. As we know from the chapter on "Supply: The Costs of Doing Business," this is called diminishing marginal returns. You can't keep adding more and more labor to a fixed amount of capital and land and expect that the labor will continue to be more productive.

increasing returns
Each additional resource adds increasing additional output.

Suppose, however, that new technology enables more employees to work out of the office without any loss in productivity. The new knowledge alters the fixity of capital and land, which in turn alters diminishing marginal returns. If the knowledge factor changes each period, then each additional worker is adding increasing amounts of additional output rather than decreasing amounts. This is called **increasing returns**.

The comparison of increasing returns and diminishing returns is illustrated in Figure 9. The point at which diminishing returns would set in if capital remains fixed doesn't occur when capital is embellished by new knowledge. The implication of increasing returns is that the bigger a firm becomes, the larger it is still likely to become. The more of something there is, the more valuable each additional one becomes. So if the world is one of increasing returns, a monopoly is likely to control each market. This has been called a "winner takes all" world.

8 What are network externalities?

network externalities
Each additional user increases value of entire network.

4.b. Network Externalities and Lock-In

A related aspect of the knowledge economy leading to potential market failures is **network externalities**.

The idea of a network can be illustrated by comparing fax machines to refrigerators. The first refrigerator provided great value to the owner. The second refrigerator provided value to the owner but had no effect on the owner of the first refrigerator. On the other hand, the first fax machine was worth little because there was no one to send a fax to. The second fax machine made the first one more valuable. Each additional

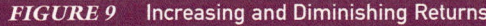

FIGURE 9   Increasing and Diminishing Returns

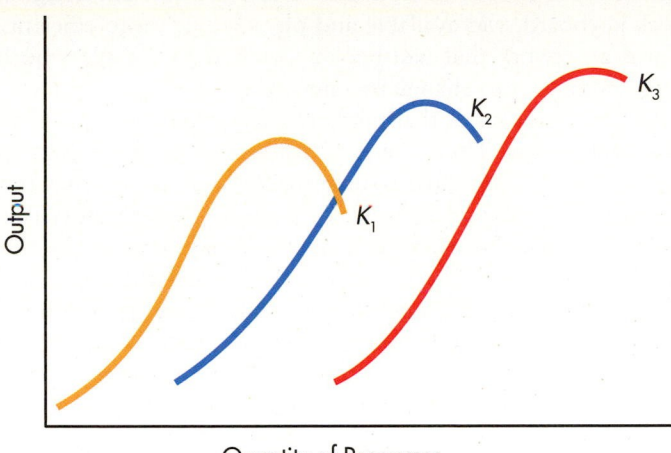

Combining additional resources with a fixed amount of capital eventually leads to a decline in the productivity of the resources. This is diminishing returns and is shown as the curve labeled K_1. If that capital is increased as well, then adding more resources with that capital need not cause diminishing returns. It could cause productivity to rise. This is increasing returns, shown as the shifts to curves labeled K_2 and K_3.

fax machine sold added value to every fax machine sold before it, because it increased the network of fax machines. An externality is provided to all other machine owners when someone purchases a machine. And, therefore, like a snowball rolling down a snow-covered hill, the bigger the snowball is, the bigger it gets. As more of us bought fax machines, more of us wanted fax machines—to communicate with those who already had them.

Suppose that the value of a network to each individual member rises as the number of members rises. Specifically, suppose that value is proportional to the number of users that can interconnect, so that if there are n users, the value of the membership is proportional to $n(n - 1) = n^2 - n$. If the value of a network to a single user is $1 for each other user on the network, then a network of size 20 has a value of $(20 \times \$20) - 20 = \$380$, whereas a network of size 200 has a value of $(200 \times \$200) - \$200 = \$40,000 - \$200 = \$39,800$.

In this numerical example, the value of the network increases exponentially as users increase linearly. If this situation does characterize a network, it implies that it would be difficult for a small network to survive. For the same cost of connection, would a user choose the smaller, 20-person network or the larger, 200-person network? Clearly, a new member would choose the larger network. Another aspect of a network is that it is difficult (costly) for a member to switch to another network. The cost for any one individual user to switch to another network (the opportunity cost of not being connected to the large network) increases the larger the network. As a result, it would seem that one network would dominate—that there would be a winner takes all.

One example widely used to support the winner takes all argument is the typewriter keyboard, presented in shorthand as QWERTY. The first letter line on a computer keyboard is QWERTYUIOP, or QWERTY for short. According to many economists, it is not the most efficient layout in terms of finger movement. Manufacturers designed a layout that forced typists to work more slowly because of the tendency of keys to jam on

locked in
The cost of changing to a more efficient technology is higher than the benefit.

early typewriters.[4] But several decades ago, jamming keys was no longer a problem, and it would have made sense to shift to an alternative, more efficient design. A rival layout, called the Dvorak keyboard, was available and purportedly more efficient. But the standard keyboard was a network that had become **locked in**. People who learned on the old keyboard were not about to change to a new one.

The QWERTY story shows us that markets are not likely to lead to the adoption of the most efficient technology. There is a *path dependence* to technology; once some historical accident or random event favors some technology, it becomes the standard and used thereafter *even if it is not the most efficient*. The QWERTY story is used to explain why VHS is used rather than the *superior* Beta; why Windows is used rather than the *better* Mac system; why gas-powered automobiles are used rather than the *better* steam-powered ones; and why light-water nuclear power plants are used rather than the *better* inert gas nuclear power plants. All these examples are used to support the general view that free markets cannot be relied on to select the best technology. "In a QWERTY world, markets cannot be trusted," says Paul Krugman, 2008 Nobel Laureate.[5]

The argument is that market winners will only by the sheerest of coincidences be the best of the available alternatives.[6] The first technology that attracts development, the first standard that attracts adopters, or the first product that attracts consumers will tend to have an insurmountable advantage, even over superior rivals that happen to come along later. According to this argument, if DOS is the first operating system, then improvements such as the Macintosh will fail because consumers are so locked in to DOS that they will not make the switch to the better system. The success of Windows-based computers, in this view, is a tragic piece of bad luck.

It is argued that to avoid the winner-takes-all result, the government must ensure new entry and limit the size of networks. Government has to offset increasing returns. Some economists have argued that confiscating taxes on the "winners" is necessary to ensure people don't keep running on a treadmill trying to "keep up with the Joneses" when it is impossible to do so.[7]

RECAP

1. Diminishing returns occur when each additional worker added to a fixed capital and land stock adds diminishing marginal output. Increasing returns occur when each additional worker is adding increasing amounts of additional output. New knowledge may create increasing returns.

2. Network externalities occur when each additional user or member of a network increases the value of entire network.

3. As a result of increasing returns and/or network externalities, it would seem that one network or one technology would dominate—that there would be a winner takes all.

4. There is a *path dependence* to technology; once some historical accident or random event favors some technology, it becomes the standard and is used thereafter *even if it is not the most efficient*.

---

[4] This question was first asked by Paul David (1986) "Understanding the Economics of QWERTY: The Necessity of History," in W. N. Parker (ed.), *Economic History and the Modern Economist*, Basil Blackwell.

[5] Stan Liebowitz and Stephen E. Margolis, "The Fable of the Keys," *Journal of Law and Economics*, Vol. 33, April 1990, p. 1; *Reason*, June 1996, Vol. 28, No. 2, p. 28.

[6] See *The Winner-Take-All Society: Why the Few at the Top Get So Much More Than the Rest of Us*, by Robert H. Frank and Philip Smith, New York: Penguin (September 1, 1996).

[7] Ibid.

5. The Market Does Not Fail

The market fails when there is a lack of well-defined private property rights. Many economists argue that when the market fails, the government must step in. Some economists argue that the market does not fail, that private individuals and free markets can solve problems that appear to be market failures.

9 Is government intervention necessary or justified to solve market failures?

5.a. There Are Externalities Everywhere

The externalities argument is based upon a distinction between private goods and services (the use of which benefits only the consumer in question) and public or collective goods (consumption of which necessarily affects the "external" parties). The distinction is often made in terms of excludability. In the case of private goods, the consumer is able to exclude all others from the benefits. In the case of public goods, everyone cannot be excluded, so some of the benefits spill over onto third parties.

One argument against government intervention to resolve externalities is that it is impossible to find cases in which externalities do not appear. Take, for example, socks. They are a private good. Yet people who do not wear socks are liable to get colds, sore feet, blisters, and possibly pneumonia, and sickness means lost days of work and lost production; it means possible contagion; it may result in rising doctor bills and increased health insurance premiums for other policyholders. Increased demand for doctors' time and energy will result in reduced medical attention for others. There is, in addition, the problem that many people are offended by socklessness—that is why we see "no shoes no service" signs.

Or consider a private garden. Suppose you love gardening and have created a magnificent garden in the front of your house. People walking by can enjoy the garden for free; conversely, a few might be allergic to the flowers and bear the cost of sneezing, for which they will not be compensated. You do not own either their enjoyment or their disutility; it is an externality you create with the garden.

When you go to the supermarket to buy groceries, you run across all kinds of externalities. You are able to purchase your favorite cereal because others have purchased it, inducing the store to stock it for your benefit. When you get in line at the checkout counter, you impose a waiting cost on everyone behind you. Why don't you turn around and offer to compensate those behind you? Why don't those enjoying your garden offer to compensate you for creating it? It is not worth the costs.

5.a.1. Coase

If every transaction creates externalities, there is no basis for government intervention in selective cases. When a problem is important to people, they will solve it. Nobel Laureate Ronald Coase was the first to point out that if people can negotiate with one another over the right to perform activities that cause externalities, they will arrive at an efficient solution.

To illustrate Coase's intuition, consider the following situation. Suppose that a city has a noise ordinance forbidding the operation of lawnmowers and leaf blowers prior to 8 a.m. on Sunday mornings. Neighbor Ralph ignores the ordinance and mows and blows his lawn every Sunday morning, which neighbor Louis finds increasingly irritating. The noise ordinance gives Louis the right to demand that Ralph be quiet. So Louis could call the cops and require Ralph to obey the ordinance. If Ralph has no other time when he can mow the lawn, he might try to pay Louis to allow him to mow on Sunday morning.

Suppose there was no city noise ordinance. Then Louis could not demand that Ralph be quiet. Instead, Louis might pay Ralph not to start mowing until after 10 a.m. This is the point that Coase made: If ownership is established—that is, if private property

transactions costs
The cost of carrying out a transaction.

rights are well defined and enforced—private parties can negotiate a solution to the externality problem. The solution will make both parties happy—one receives money, and the other receives the right to make noise or to obtain quiet. If negotiation is possible, then resources will be allocated to their highest-valued use even if an externality should occur.

A motorist with a polluting automobile imposes costs on everyone who breathes the air, but as a practical matter, all these people can't stop the motorist and offer him money to fix his car, and the motorist surely cannot contact everyone touched by the pollution. The **transactions costs** are too high for negotiation to occur. But this does not necessarily call for government action. If transactions costs are too high, perhaps they can be reduced by forming smaller groups and through voluntary actions. People could agree to binding pledges to contribute to building a public good as long as enough others do also. If not enough people contribute, the money is refunded. This could be done by a profit-seeking entrepreneur who could provide the good for a profit by selling shares in the public good. He could create a contract to provide the good with a promise to refund the initial pledge plus an additional sum of money if not enough people sign up. A similar alternative for public goods is to produce the public good but refuse to release it into the public until some form of payment to cover costs is met. Stephen King wrote several chapters of a novel and made them downloadable for free on his website; but he would not complete the story unless a certain amount of money was raised.

It is possible that voluntarism could overcome transactions costs. A free rider might litter in a public park, but a more public-spirited individual would not do so, getting an inherent pleasure from helping the community. People might voluntarily pick up some of the existing litter. Isn't this arguing that people will act against their self interest? It is not, because people often get enjoyment out of volunteering. In some cases, a social stigma develops regarding some action, such as littering. If you throw trash out of your car, others might honk at you, give you obscene gestures, or even collect your litter and send it in the mail to you. If enough people begin doing something, that behavior becomes the expected, socially correct way of behaving. Think, for instance, why people leave a tip at a restaurant when they do not plan on ever returning to that restaurant. It is not simply to provide income to poorly paid servers or to reward good service, but instead, it is to avoid feeling guilty, a reaction to going against a social stigma.

Contributions to online collaborative media, such as Wikipedia and other projects utilizing wiki technology, represent an example of voluntary contributions, because they provide a public good freely to all readers.[8] Wikipedia has millions of contributors with billions of contributions. Something so large would seem to require managers, budgets, hierarchy, and so on. However, Wikipedia is able to aggregate hundreds of millions of contributions without the traditional business infrastructure. The contributors are not employees and do not get paid. Their incentive is to interact with others and to see their work spread. Each contribution does not need to be competent, because other readers will improve the initial work until the end result is high quality. A bad article will be rewritten and essentially disappear as improvement on it takes place. With current and future technologies, the ability to attract voluntary action to a public good seems to be more likely. Thus, according to many economists, although free riding does identify situations that involve the potential for further gains, it does not follow that government provision of goods or other coercive arrangements will improve the situation.

5.b. Imperfect Information

The idea that information was important to markets was not new to the economists of the 1970s and 1980s. The Austrian school—economists working in Austria in the 1930s—stressed that imperfect information and dispersed knowledge were fundamental

[8] Clay Shirky, *Here Comes Everybody*, New York: Penguin Press, 2008.

arguments for the necessity of free markets. They noted that the market process—countless individuals pursuing their own interests by trading with one another—is a path of discovery. Through the price system and free competition, the tradeoffs of scarce resources are clarified, the lowest-cost solutions are reached, and feedback about success and failure are provided through profit and loss. When people buy something, they are showing they value the item they purchase more than anything else a comparable amount of money could buy. Similarly, when people sell something, they are showing they would rather have the money price of that item than they would the item. They value something else more than what they are selling. So when buyers and sellers agree to exchange some item, the price of the item is the result of the buyer saying that the item has more value to him than the money price while the seller simultaneously says the item has less value than the money price.

The market price incorporates all the information—the trillions and trillions of bits of information—involved in buyers' and sellers' tastes, preferences, beliefs, and expectations. If the buyer learns something new about the item—say, that it has more uses than was previously known—the buyer will immediately be willing to pay a higher price. The new price incorporates the buyer's newfound information. Similarly, if the seller learns that the costs of an important resource are going to increase, the seller will cut supply or require a higher price to supply. The market price rises to reflect the increased costs of resources. The market does this without anyone dictating what buyers and sellers do or defining the price at which trade will occur.

Nobel Laureate Friedrich A. Hayek attacked central planning and socialism because of the information gathering power of the free market. Central planning didn't and doesn't work for nations. The central planners could not possibly know what price to set on items to be traded. It would be impossible for the central planners to collect all of the information that the anonymous buyers and sellers in a market have. As a result, the price set by the planners is either too high or too low, resulting in shortages of some items and surpluses of others. Simply stated, there is too much information for a central planner or government to determine price and quantity. It takes the invisible hand of the market to determine the price and quantity necessary for efficient resource allocation.

The economists emphasizing information imperfections in the 1970s and 1980s argued that the imperfections caused markets to fail, as opposed to Hayek's view that imperfect information is what makes markets necessary. In essence, the new market failure arguments turned Hayek's insight on its head. Information problems were a cause of market failure rather than a reason for praising markets. Although the *new* market failure arguments introduced new aspects to the economic debate, not all economists were swayed.

5.b.1. Market Solutions to Moral Hazard

Moral hazard is a form of externality. Moral hazard arises because an individual or institution does not bear the full consequences of its actions, and therefore has a tendency to act less carefully than it otherwise would, leaving another party to bear some responsibility for the consequences of those actions. Sometimes a moral hazard problem can be reduced by having the person or firm creating the hazard and the person or firm being taken advantage of share in the costs. This does not require government interference, but instead will arise because the companies subject to moral hazard want to minimize the cost. Insurance companies require a **deductible**, and banks and other lending institutions require a down payment to ensure that the company and the customer share in the expenses and risks. You are more likely to drive carefully and safeguard your health if you have to pay some of the costs of an accident or illness. Similarly, if you must make a **copayment**, you are less likely to behave in a way that causes you to bear a large number of such copayments.

deductible
The amount of expenses that must be paid out of pocket before an insurer will cover any expenses.

copayment
Paid by an insured person each time the insured service is accessed.

5.b.2. Market Solutions to Adverse Selection

Why can't someone with a high-quality used car simply tell the buyer about the car's condition? The reason is that the seller has an incentive to exaggerate the condition of the car, and the buyer has an incentive to believe that it is of lower quality than it is, which leads to adverse selection. The problem can be resolved privately if the seller can credibly demonstrate the high quality of the car. A seller must provide credible information about the quality of the good. When moral hazard or adverse selection exists, there may be an opportunity for someone to profit from providing information. CARFAX provides the history of a car for a fee. Equifax provides individual credit histories for a fee. These firms illustrate that the market can often solve what is called a market failure problem. When the missing information can be privately provided, the market failure problem disappears.

5.b.3. Market Solutions to Path Dependence and Lock-In

Many economists argue that if the government does not intervene when increasing returns and network externalities exist, an inefficient technology is likely to dominate markets. Other economists oppose this view, arguing that as long as there is a profit opportunity, people will find a way to offset the increasing returns. Remember QWERTY, the keyboard configuration that many people called inefficient? According to some economists, the QWERTY story is wrong.[9] QWERTY was not an inferior structure designed to slow down typing; there were many competitive systems offered on typewriters in the 1880s and 1890s, but none could perform better than the QWERTY system.

So it is not correct to claim that QWERTY illustrated a case of inefficient lock-in. Similarly, to accept the idea of inefficient lock-in regarding DOS and Windows, we need to ignore the fact that DOS was not the first operating system, that consumers did switch away from DOS when they moved to Windows, that the DOS system was an appropriate choice for many users given the hardware of the time, and that the Mac was far more expensive. Many people are switching from Windows to Mac, and the two systems are becoming compatible.

RECAP

1. Adverse selection and moral hazard problems are often resolved privately through copayments, deductibles, and other arrangements that reduce the incentives to change behavior or not reveal information.

2. If there is a profit opportunity to provide information, it will be provided. There is no reason to think that imperfect information necessarily leads to a market failure.

---

6. Government Failure and Rent Seeking

Economists have pointed to several possible types of market failure. For each, there are usually two types of solutions proposed—government intervention or a private solution. Whereas it is one thing to argue that a market failure cannot be resolved privately, it is quite another to argue that the inefficiency created by the failure is worse than the inefficiency of having the government try to solve the problem. At least, this is what James Buchanan, who received the 1986 Nobel Prize in economics, argued. Inefficiencies often arise not because legislators are incompetent or ignorant, but because of problems with individual incentives.

[9] See Stan Liebowitz and Stephen E. Margolis, "The Fable of the Keys," *Journal of Law and Economics*, Vol. 33, April 1990, p. 1; *Reason*, June 1996, Vol. 28, No. 2, p. 28.

6.a. Logrolling and Pork

Consider a group of diners who are going to split the bill for the dinner equally. Herb and nine friends are having dinner at Chimichanga in Phoenix. To simplify the task of paying for their meal, they have agreed in advance to split the cost of the meal equally, with each paying one-tenth of the total check. Herb recognizes that if he orders more expensive items than the others, he will be gaining at the expense of his nine friends. So he orders appetizers, the most expensive entrée, and the most exorbitant dessert and drinks. The problem is that each of his nine friends recognizes the same thing. Each orders far more than he would if he were dining alone. As a result, the total bill rises.

This is the way democratic government works. Legislators will support one another's special earmarks, or so-called pork barrel programs, causing total government spending to rise significantly. Why would legislator A support such a project in legislator B's home district? After all, B's project will cause A's constituents' taxes to rise by a small amount, while they get absolutely no benefit. The answer is that if A does not support B's project, then B will not support A's. The practice of legislators supporting one another's projects is called **logrolling**.

Beyond the fact that the legislative process often results in pork barrel programs, we must worry that government employees may not have incentives to get the most for what the government spends. Since the government is not a profit-maximizing entity, it has no incentive to minimize costs. Instead, what often occurs is bureaucracy building. An agency director will have more say in policy if her agency is large than if it is small. So she may have an incentive to increase the spending, and therefore the size, of her agency. And whereas an appointed government official might engage in bureaucracy building, an elected official wants to get reelected. That might mean supporting special-interest projects in order to secure votes, even if those projects are inefficient.

logrolling
An inefficiency in the political process in which legislators support one another's projects in order to ensure support for their own.

6.b. Rent Seeking and the Power of Organized Interests

Consider a voter in a congressional district that contains one one-hundredth of the country's taxpayers. Suppose that district's representative is able to deliver a public project that generates benefits of $100 million for the district, but costs the government $150 million. Because the district's share of the tax bill for the project will be only $150 million/100 = $1.5 million, residents of the district are $98.5 million better off with the project than without it. And that explains why so many voters favor legislators who have a successful record of "bringing home the bacon."

When a new government project is financed, a very few people get large benefits, while the taxpayers pay an only slightly larger amount in taxes. This means that individual taxpayers have little at stake and therefore have little incentive to incur the cost of mobilizing themselves in opposition. **Rent seeking** is the process of devoting resources to taking wealth away from one group in order to benefit another group. Resources devoted to getting the government to provide benefits to special interest groups are called *rent*, and the special interest group is said to be *rent seeking*.

Rent seeking is a very rewarding activity in many cases. Rent seeking does not create new products or income; it merely transfers wealth from one group to another. Typically the transfer takes resources from large, diverse groups, like taxpayers, and gives them to small, organized groups. This means that the beneficiaries have an incentive to organize and lobby in favor of their projects. For example, in the 1990s, the Cosmetology Association in many states lobbied the state legislators to require more stringent licensing requirements for manicurists. The reason for the lobbying was the number of new spas and salons that were being established by immigrants. These spas were driving prices down; some of them were offering manicures for $10 rather than the $25 charged at

rent seeking
The use of resources simply to transfer wealth from one group to another without increasing production or total wealth.

the established spas. If manicurists were required to go to school for six months, the number of new spas that would open for business would decline, and prices at established spas could be upheld. The new requirements benefited the existing cosmetologists at the expense of new manicurists.

SUMMARY

1. What are the benefits of free markets?

- The index of economic freedom is highly correlated with standards of living. The greater the economic freedom, the higher the nation's standard of living. *Preview*

- The index of economic freedom is correlated with the United Nations index of human development. Prosperity of economic freedom enables people to purchase a higher quality of living. *Preview*

2. How are private property rights defined?

- A property right is the right to ownership, to do what you want with what you have as long as you don't harm others or interfere with the private property rights. *§1.a*

- A market failure occurs when the market is not able to reach the equilibrium that is most efficient, when resources are not allocated to their highest-valued use. *§1.a*

- Private property rights provide ownership. In order to buy or sell something, one must be able to decide how that something is to be used. *§1.a*

- Without private property rights, anyone can claim partial ownership of an item and thereby consume that item. Without private ownership, no one would be willing to purchase an item, because others could consume that item. *§1.a*

3. Why does a lack of private property rights lead to market failures?

- A freely functioning market results in resources being allocated to their highest-valued use. When something occurs that leads resources not to be so allocated, we say that a market failure has resulted. *§1.a*

- A market failure problem occurs when no one owns something or when everyone owns something. *§1.a*

4. What are externalities?

- Private benefits of a transaction are the gains from trade that the individuals involved in the transaction achieve. Private costs are the opportunity costs that the individuals involved in the transaction must bear. *§1.b*

- Social costs and benefits are the total costs and benefits created by a transaction. When some costs are borne by those who are not involved in the private transaction, so that social costs exceed private costs, a negative externality occurs. When some benefits are received by those who are not involved in the private transaction, so that social benefits exceed private benefits, a positive externality occurs. *§1.b*

- When social costs and benefits are not equal to private costs and benefits, the market outcome is either overutilization or underutilization: Resources are not allocated to their highest-valued use. *§1.b*

5. What are free rider problems?

- Common ownership results in a market failure. Too much of the commonly owned good is consumed, and not enough is produced. *§1.c*

- Free riding means that one person will contribute less than that person expects to get in return because the person expects others to make up the difference. *§1.c*

- People free ride because they can—their self-interest tells them to get the most for the least. *§1.c*

- The problem with free riding is that if many people or everyone free rides, nothing gets done. *§1.c*

6. How does the government solve externality and free rider problems?

- Solutions to public good problems include private provision of the public good with government financing and government provision of the good. *§2.a*

- There are several approaches to reducing the inefficiencies created by externalities. One approach is to impose a tax on the individual or institutions creating the externality. In another approach, the government requires or commands that those creating negative externalities reduce the amount created or that more production of positive externalities occur. In yet another, the government creates a market for the negative externalities by establishing ownership of the right to create the negative externality and allowing that ownership to be exchanged. *§2.a.1, 2.a.2, 2.a.3*

7. **What are moral hazard and adverse selection problems?**

- When buyers have less information than sellers, a situation can arise in which high-quality products are driven out of the market, leaving just low-quality products. This is called *adverse selection*. *§3.a*

- When buyers have more information than sellers about a particular item, buyers may alter their behavior with regard to that item once they have purchased it. For instance, once someone is insured, that person may act differently, taking on more risk. This is called *moral hazard*. *§3.b*

8. **What are network externalities?**

- Diminishing returns occur when each additional worker added to a fixed capital and land stock contributes to diminishing marginal output. Increasing returns occurs when each additional worker adds increasing amounts of additional output. New knowledge may create increasing returns. *§4.a*

- Network externalities occur when each additional user or member of a network increases the value of entire network. *§4.b*

- As a result of increasing returns and/or network externalities, it would seem that one network or one technology would dominate—that there would be a winner takes all. *§4.b*

- There is a *path dependence* to technology; once some historical accident or random event favors some technology, it becomes the standard and is used thereafter *even if it is not the most efficient*. *§4.b*

9. **Is government intervention necessary or justified to solve market failures?**

- One argument against government intervention to resolve externalities is that it is impossible to find cases where externalities do not appear. *§5.a*

- Coase stated that private parties can negotiate solutions to externalities when transactions costs are not too high. *§5.a.1*

- Voluntary contributions and actions can offset the problems of commons and public goods. *§5.a.1*

- According to Hayek, there is too much information for a central planner or government to determine price and quantity. It takes the invisible hand of the market to determine the price and quantity necessary for efficient resource allocation. *§5.b*

- An adverse selection or moral hazard problem can be reduced by having the person or firm creating the hazard and the person or firm being taken advantage of share in the costs. This is done through copayments and deductibles. *§5.b.1*

- The inefficiency of having the government try to solve a market failure problem is worse than the inefficiency of the market failure itself. *§6.a*

- Logrolling, pork barrel spending, and earmarks are all the result of legislators in a democracy appealing to constituents. *§6.a*

- The incentive of people working in government is not to provide a good or service in the most efficient manner. *§6.a*

- Rent seeking is the process of devoting resources to taking wealth away from one group in order to benefit another group. *§6.b*

- Small organized interests are able to secure rents from large disorganized groups. *§6.b*

KEY TERMS

adverse selection, 610	internalized, 607	principle of rivalry, 599
asymmetric information, 610	lemons market, 610	private cost, 601
club good, 599	locked in, 614	private good, 599
commons good, 600	logrolling, 619	private property rights, 599
copayment, 617	market failure, 598	public good, 600
deductible, 617	moral hazard, 611	rent seeking, 619
externality, 601	network externalities, 612	social cost, 601
free rider, 600	principle of mutual	transactions costs, 616
increasing returns, 612	excludability, 599	

EXERCISES

1. How would you derive the demand for milk at the local grocery store? How would you derive the demand for tuna? How would you derive the demand for national defense?

2. Explain why an externality might be a market failure. What does market failure mean?

3. Use the accompanying table to answer the following questions.

Quantity	Private Cost	Social Cost	Benefit
1	$ 2	$ 4	$12
2	$ 6	$ 10	$22
3	$ 12	$ 18	$30
4	$ 20	$ 28	$36
5	$ 30	$ 40	$40

   a. What is the external cost per unit of output?
   b. What level of output will be produced?
   c. What level of output should be produced to achieve economic efficiency?
   d. What is the value to society of correcting the externality?

4. What level of tax would be appropriate to internalize the externality in exercise 3?

5. If the private cost and social cost columns were reversed in exercise 3, what would be the result? Would too much or too little of the good be produced? How would the market failure be resolved, by a tax or by a subsidy?

6. What is meant by the term *overfishing*? What is the fundamental problem associated with overfishing of the oceans? What might lead to *underfishing*?

7. How much pollution would exist if all externalities were internalized? Why would it not be zero? Use the same explanation to discuss the amount of health and safety that the government should require in the workplace.

8. Suppose the following table describes the marginal costs and marginal benefits of waste (garbage) reduction. What is the optimal amount of garbage? What is the situation if no garbage is allowed to be produced?

Percentage of Waste Eliminated	Marginal Costs (millions of dollars)	Marginal Benefits (millions of dollars)
10%	10	1,000
20%	15	500
30%	25	100
40%	40	50
50%	70	20
60%	110	5
70%	200	3
80%	500	2
90%	900	1
100%	2,000	0

9. Elephants eat 300 pounds of food per day. They flourished in Africa when they could roam over huge areas of land, eating the vegetation in one area and then moving on so that the vegetation could renew itself. Now the area over which elephants can roam is declining. Without some action, elephants will become extinct. What actions might save elephants? What are the costs and benefits of such actions?

10. Explain why the value of pollution permits in one area of the country rose 20 percent per year, while in another remained unchanged from year to year?

What would you expect to occur as a result of this differential?

11. Smokers impose negative externalities on nonsmokers. Suppose the air in a restaurant is a resource owned by the restaurant owner.
    a. How would the owner respond to the negative externalities of smokers?
    b. Suppose the smokers owned the air. How would that change matters?
    c. How about if the nonsmokers owned the air?
    d. Finally, consider what would occur if the government passed a law banning all smoking. How would the outcome compare with the outcomes described above?

12. Discuss the argument that education should be subsidized because it creates a positive externality.

13. If the best solution to solving the positive externality problem of education is to provide a subsidy, explain why educational systems in all countries are government entities.

14. Amazon.com was the first mover in online book sales. It patented the one-click purchasing system. Barnes & Noble was a later entrant with bn.com. Is this a battle with a "winner takes all" outcome? Why or why not?

15. Which of the three types of government policies—antitrust, social regulation, or economic regulation—is the basis for each of the following? Which market failure would provide a theoretical basis for the government policy?
    a. Beautician education standards
    b. Certified Public Accounting requirements
    c. Liquor licensing
    d. The Clean Air Act
    e. The Nutrition and Labeling Act

16. Some airline executives have called for "re-reregulation." Why might an executive of an airline prefer to operate in a regulated environment?

17. Discuss the claim that social regulation is unnecessary. Does the claim depend on whether the structure of a market is primarily one of perfect competition or of oligopoly?

18. Explain why the government's bailout of some banks in 2008 caused a moral hazard.

19. Describe what a lemons market is and give two examples.

You can find further practice tests in the Online Quiz at **www.cengage.com/economics/boyes**.

DO ECONOMISTS DISAGREE ABOUT ANYTHING? NOBEL SAVAGES

National Post (Canada), August 20, 2008

Joseph Stiglitz is a Nobel Prize winner in economics who doesn't like capitalism or markets very much. This does not make him that unusual. The very first economics Nobel, Jan Tinbergen, admitted without embarrassment that he had always seen his academic task as making the case for socialism. The roster of laureates is filled with skeptics about Adam Smith's invisible hand. Mr. Stiglitz has claimed, for example, that the hand "is invisible, at least in part, because it is not there."

Throughout the twentieth century, much of the economics profession drifted towards "Welfare Economics," which emphasized not how markets worked, but how they "failed." Their creed was that governments, guided by smart economists like themselves, might—nay, had to—prevent, or compensate for, market shortcomings.

One of the founding members of the school was Arthur C. Pigou, whose hatching of market-correcting "Pigovian taxes" is bemoaned in the *Post*'s Nopigou Club. In an age when it is claimed that markets have to be "greened," and that all that this requires is a little judicious fiddling with taxes and prices, Mr. Pigou is much in fashion. After all, catastrophic man-made climate change is "the greatest market failure the world has ever seen," even if the world hasn't actually seen it yet.

Welfare economists suffer from twin delusions. One—as pointed out by the "Public Choice" school championed by another Nobel laureate, James Buchanan—is that politicians are selflessly interested in making effective policy rather than winning elections. The second delusion is that the market actually can be "fine tuned." Traditionally, welfare-oriented interventions—from minimum wage laws through rent controls to the promotion of biofuels—have ended both in taxpayer tears and damage to those who are meant to be "helped."

The very fact that Messrs. Stiglitz and Buchanan are Nobel economics laureates with diametrically opposed views was one of the reasons Alfred Nobel never set up a prize for economics in the first place (it was added later by Swedish bankers). Economics is not a science in which there is a broad body of knowledge on which all economists agree. Rather—when it is not mathematically abstruse and irrelevant—it is a field of ideological conflict which many economists enter intent on "improving" markets without understanding them in the first place.

Many such economists, including Messrs. Tinbergen and Stiglitz, not to mention the late John Kenneth Galbraith, are primarily moralists, who reject the market as a messy affair based on greed and exploitation, and swell with pride at their role in "redistributing" other people's money. They are always on the lookout for evidence of market failure or government success. Since this coincides with naive public perceptions, they are often "popular economists" (which is thus a contradiction in terms).

They are also inclined—as does Joseph Stiglitz—to write off promoters of markets as "fundamentalists," as if their conclusions were based not on studying the counter-intuitive workings of the economic order, but on some form of wacky religious faith-cum-mental disorder. To the extent that such blinkered fundamentalists might exist, as opposed to being merely straw men, they certainly have little or no voice in current policy-making.

In a recent piece in the *Globe and Mail*, Mr. Stiglitz suggested that free-market "rhetoric" is only ever used selectively; "embraced when it serves special interests, discarded when it does not." While this may certainly be true, it is no argument against markets any more than the Nazi doctor Joseph Mengele invalidated the case for medical science. No sensible economist suggests that markets are perfect, but those on the supposed "right" point out that they are much more efficient than most people imagine, while government meddling seldom if ever has the intended results.

The Invisible Hand may not be perfect, but it beats governments' Visible Bull in the China Shop every time.

Certainly, governments are needed to maintain property and contract rights, and to protect us against the threats posed by other governments, but expansive government tends to be both ineffective and oppressive. For men such as Mr. Stiglitz, however, it is sufficient to point out the theoretical shortcomings of the market and leave the question of the practical shortcomings of politics unaddressed. Thus, he is quick to point to the current financial crisis as "market failure," but to downplay the role of inflationary government policies, or de facto government-backed institutions such as Fannie Mae and Freddie Mac, in the debacle.

Mr. Stiglitz points out that, among their other failures, free markets produce "too much" pollution and "too little" research and development. Both these claims are dubious. The problems of pollution spring from inadequate property rights, and sometimes need correcting by governments, but it is surely worth reflecting that pollution laws tend to be much stricter in mature capitalist democracies. That's because capitalism gives rise to demands for democracy, and democratic governments derive much of their power from exploiting exaggerated fears of market failure!

As for markets promoting "too little" R&D, fans of governments claim that they have the responsibility, and ability, to promote society-wide innovation and investment. According to Professor Stiglitz, for example, the U.S. government "invented" the Internet. I plan to examine that claim, and its broader implications, in my next column.

PETER FOSTER

Source: National Post, Aug 20, 2008, Peter Foster. Material reprinted with the express permission of: "National Post Inc."

Commentary

This article is a terrific one in pointing out how much economists disagree. But it fails to show that it is actually just one aspect of the field of economics in which disagreements occur. Intellectual disagreement among economists occurs on a vital aspect of the field: Do markets work to provide people what they want and are willing to pay for at the lowest possible prices? Do resources get allocated to where they have the greatest value? Notice that it is not disagreement on what markets are, on demand, on supply, on the determination of prices and quantities; it is disagreement on the determination of whether the outcome provided by markets is better than the outcome that comes from government. This is the area of welfare economics.

Most economists would agree with the proposition that there are problems with markets when there is a lack of well-defined private property rights. But the consensus breaks down at this point. Some economists find such market failures everywhere, whereas others see such market failures as being few and far between. Some economists see a need for government intervention while others argue that government intervention makes matters worse rather than better.

The "public choice" school argues that politicians are self-interested individuals who cannot be seen as benevolent leaders selflessly interested in making effective policy. They want to get elected or reelected, they want power and prestige or fame and money. These desires lead them to make decisions that are not necessarily in the best interests of the public. As the article notes, traditionally, welfare-oriented interventions—from minimum wage laws through rent controls to the promotion of biofuels—have ended both in taxpayer tears and damage to those who are meant to be "helped."

This aspect of economics is indeed a "field of ideological conflict." The economists mentioned by the author, including Tinbergen, Stiglitz, and the late John Kenneth Galbraith, do not like the outcome of the market—as the author said, these economists are primarily moralists who reject the market as a messy affair based on greed. They are always on the lookout for evidence of market failure. These economists, and many others, looked on the financial crisis that began in 2007 as a giant market failure, perhaps even the end of free-market capitalism. But they failed to look at the role of the government in creating the financial mess. Some economists would argue that rather than market failure, the problem was one of government failure.

CHAPTER 28

Resource Markets

© MACIEJ FROLOW/GETTY IMAGES, INC

FUNDAMENTAL QUESTIONS

1. Who are the buyers and sellers of resources?

2. How are resource prices determined?

3. How does a firm allocate its expenditures among the various resources?

Do you recycle? Are you concerned with global warming, saving the rain forest, and reducing pollution? Perhaps you've noticed the number of homeless people on the streets and wondered why they are homeless and what can be done about homelessness. Have you ever been discriminated against because of your age, race, or sex? Have you been touched by illegal drugs—gang wars, drive-by shootings, crime? Do you or do your parents have health insurance and medical coverage, or is it simply too expensive? Has anyone in your family been unemployed? In the following chapters we discuss some aspects of these issues as we examine the resource markets. Remember that resource markets provide the resources, or ingredients, for producing goods and services. They include the markets for labor, capital, and land in general terms, but more specifically they involve people and their jobs, physical and financial capital, and natural resources. In this chapter, we'll look at how firms choose their resources and how firms draw on economic theory to help them decide which resources and how much of a given resource to use. In the chapters that follow, we'll look at each market more closely, examining some of the societal questions and issues that arise in the process.

1. Buyers and Sellers of Resources

1 Who are the buyers and sellers of resources?

resource market

A market that provides one of the resources for producing goods and services: labor, capital, and land.

There are three general types of resource markets: those for land, labor, and capital. The price and quantity of each resource are determined in its **resource market**. Rent and the quantity of land used are determined in the land market. The wage rate and the number of people employed are determined in the labor market. The cost of capital (the interest rate) and the quantity of capital used are determined in the capital market. Although each of these markets is somewhat unique, they are all markets, and thus they simply involve the demand for and supply of that particular resource.

1.a. The Resource Markets

To understand the resource markets, you need to realize that the roles of firms and households are reversed from what they are in the product markets. Figure 1 is the simplest circular flow diagram that you saw in Chapter 4. It illustrates the roles of firms and households in the product and resource markets. The market for goods and services is represented by the top lines in the figure. Households buy goods and services from firms, as shown by the line going from firms to households; and firms sell goods and services and receive revenue, as shown by the line going from households to firms. The resource market is represented by the bottom half of the diagram in Figure 1.

FIGURE 1 The Market for Resources

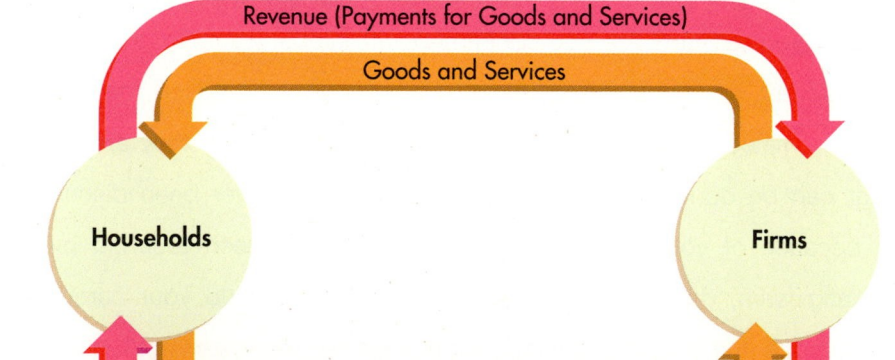

The buyers of resources are firms that purchase resources in order to produce goods and services. The sellers of resources are households that supply resources in order to obtain income with which to purchase goods and services.

Households are the sellers of resources, and firms are the buyers of resources. Households sell resources, as shown by the line going from households to firms; and firms pay households income, as shown by the line going from firms to households.

Households supply resources in order to earn income. By offering to work, individuals supply their labor; by saving, households supply firms with the funds used to purchase machines, equipment, and buildings; by offering their land and the minerals, trees, and other natural resources associated with it, households supply land. The supply of a resource consists of the sum of the quantities supplied by every resource owner. The supply of unskilled workers consists of the sum of the quantities that each and every unskilled worker is willing to work at each wage rate. The supply of office space in Phoenix, Arizona, offered for rent consists of the supplies offered by every owner of office space in Phoenix.

Resources are wanted not for themselves, but for what they produce. A firm uses resources in order to produce goods and services. Thus, the demand for a resource by a firm depends on the demand for the goods and services that the firm produces. For this reason, the demand for resources is often called a **derived demand**: An automobile manufacturer uses land, labor, and capital to produce cars; a retail T-shirt store uses land, labor, and capital to sell T-shirts; a farmer uses land, labor, and capital to produce agricultural products. The market demand for a resource consists of the demands of each firm that is willing and able to pay for that resource. An electric utility firm in Iowa demands engineers, as does a construction firm in Minnesota. The market demand for engineers consists of the demands of the Iowa utility and the Minnesota construction firm. Each firm's demand depends on separate and distinct factors, however. The electric utility firm hires more engineers to modernize its plant; the construction firm hires more engineers to fulfill its contracts with the state government to build bridges. Yet all firms have the same decision-making process for hiring or acquiring resources.

In resource markets, the sellers are the owners of land, labor, or capital, whereas the buyers are firms. In this particular situation, a chef is purchasing fresh lemons. The seller is the farmer who has grown the lemons.

derived demand
Demand stemming from what a resource can produce, not demand for the resource itself.

RECAP

1. Resource markets are classified into three types: those for land, labor, and capital.

2. The buyers of resources are firms; the suppliers are households.

2. Demand for and Supply of Resources

How do you decide how much you are willing to pay for something? Don't you decide how much it is worth to you? This is what businesses do when they decide how much to pay a worker or how much to pay for a machine. A firm uses the quantity of each resource that will enable the firm to maximize profit.

2.a. The Firm's Demand

We know from previous chapters that firms maximize profit when they operate at the level where marginal revenue (MR) equals marginal cost (MC). The same thing occurs

 2 How are resource prices determined?

in the resource markets. *MR* is called the marginal revenue product (*MRP*), and *MC* is called the marginal factor cost (*MFC*).

The additional value that an additional resource creates for a firm is called the **marginal revenue product (*MRP*)**. If Jennifer Aniston can bring in $30 million in additional revenue to the movie studio for performing in one movie, then we can say that Jennifer Aniston's marginal revenue product for that movie is $30 million. If an additional server at Applebee's can bring in $30 an hour to the restaurant, we say that the server's *MRP* is $30 an hour.

The marginal-revenue-product curve for a resource that is not unique is drawn in Figure 2. It slopes down because the additional revenue that an additional resource can generate for a firm declines as more resources are acquired. This is the law of diminishing marginal product we encountered in the chapter "Supply: The Costs of Doing Business." As Applebee's adds more and more servers, the additional revenue that each additional server can create for the restaurant declines. The *MRP* for a unique resource also declines as that resource is used more and more during a specific time period. If Jennifer Aniston performed in several movies during a year's time, it is likely that the additional revenue she could bring into the movie studio for each additional movie would decline.

2.b. Marginal Factor Costs

The cost of an additional unit of a resource, called the **marginal factor cost**, depends on whether the firm is purchasing resources in a market with many suppliers or in a

marginal revenue product (*MRP*)
The additional revenue that an additional resource can create for a firm.

> The MRP of a resource is a measure of how much the additional output generated by the last unit of that resource is worth to the firm.

marginal factor cost (*MFC*)
The additional cost of an additional unit of a resource.

FIGURE 2   Resource Market Demand and Market Supply

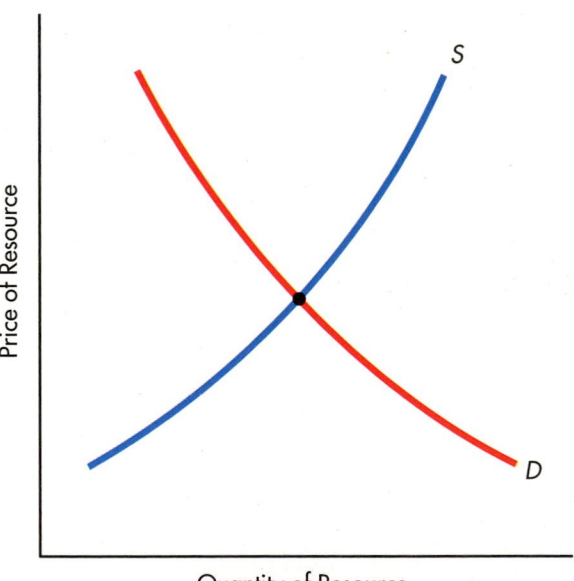

The demand curve for a resource slopes down, reflecting the inverse relation between the price of the resource and the quantity demanded. The supply curve for a resource slopes up, reflecting the direct relation between the price of the resource and the quantity supplied. Equilibrium occurs where the two curves intersect; the quantities demanded and supplied are the same at the equilibrium price. If the resource price is greater than the equilibrium price, a surplus of the resource arises and drives the price back down to equilibrium. If the resource price is less than the equilibrium price, a shortage occurs and forces the price back up to equilibrium.

market with one or only a few suppliers. The marginal factor cost is the actual cost to the firm of acquiring an additional resource.

2.b.1. Hiring Resources in a Perfectly Competitive Market

If the firm is purchasing resources in a market in which there is a very large number of suppliers of an identical resource—a perfectly competitive resource market—the price to the firm of each additional unit of the resource is constant. Why? Because no seller is large enough to individually change the price. Servers at Applebee's would be an example. There are many people who are willing and able to work for Applebee's, and the firm can hire as much of the resource as it wants without affecting either the quantity available or the price of that resource.

Let's use the information in the table and graph of Figure 3 to determine how many servers an Applebee's restaurant would hire. The firm can employ as many servers as it wants at $15 per day—the *MFC* is a straight horizontal line at $15. The first server hired has a marginal revenue product of $130 per day and costs $15 per day. It is profitable to hire her. A second brings in an additional $60 per day and costs $15 per day, and so is also profitable. The third server brings in $40 per day, the fourth $20 per day, the fifth $10 per day, and the sixth nothing. Thus, the third and fourth servers are profitable, but the fifth, sixth, and seventh are not. The firm hires four servers. You can see in the graph that the marginal revenue product lies above the wage rate until after the fourth server is hired.

The firm hires additional servers until the *MRP* of one more server is equal to the marginal factor cost of that server ($MRP = MFC$). This is a general rule; it holds whether the firms sells its output in a perfectly competitive, monopoly, monopolistically competitive, or oligopoly market; and it holds for all resources, land and capital as well as labor.

> *Resources will be employed up to the point at which MRP = MFC.*

FIGURE 3   The Employment of Resources

Number of Servers	MRP	MFC
1	$130	$15
2	$ 60	$15
3	$ 40	$15
4	$ 20	$15
5	$ 10	$15
6	$ 0	$15

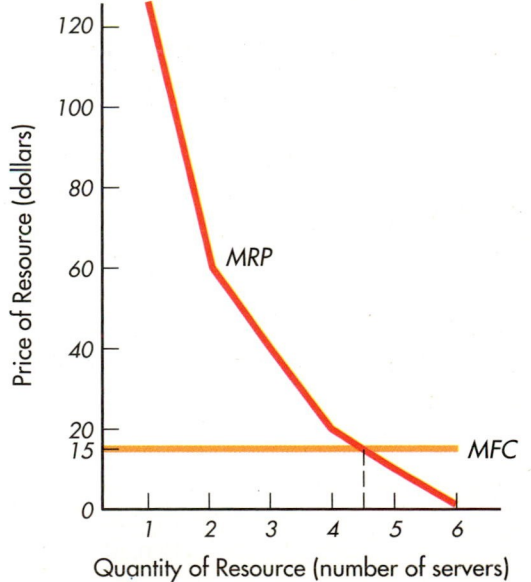

The marginal revenue product and the marginal factor cost together indicate the number of servers the restaurant would hire. The *MRP* and the *MFC* for a restaurant are listed in the table. The *MRP* curve and the *MFC* curve are shown in the graph. The marginal revenue product exceeds the marginal factor cost (wage rate) until after the fourth server is hired. The firm will not hire more than four servers, for then the costs would exceed the additional revenue produced by the last server hired.

monopsonist

A firm that is the only buyer of a resource.

A firm buying in a perfectly competitive resource market will pay the marginal revenue product; a monopsonistic firm will pay less than the marginal revenue product.

2.b.2. Hiring Resources as a Monopoly Buyer When just one firm is acquiring a resource, that firm is called a **monopsonist**. A monopsonist is a monopoly buyer. In the early days of mining in the United States, it was not uncommon for firms to create entire towns in order to attract a readily available supply of labor. The sole provider of jobs in the town was the mining company. Thus, when the company hired labor, it affected the prices of all workers, not just the worker it recently hired. In the 1970s along the Alaskan pipeline, and in the 1980s in foreign countries where U.S. firms were hired to carry out specialized engineering projects or massive construction jobs, small towns dependent on a single U.S. firm were created. There are cases in which a monopsony exists even though a company town was not created. For instance, many universities in small communities are monopsonistic employers—they are the primary employer in the town. When these universities hire a mechanic, they affect the wage rates of all mechanics in the town. Walmart is often called a monopsony because it locates a store in a small town and quickly becomes the major, if not almost the only, employer in the town.

A monopsony firm is able to pay resources less than their marginal revenue products because the resource owners have no choice. They can't rent their land to someone else or go work for someone else.

 3 How does a firm allocate its expenditures among the various resources?

2.c. Hiring When There Is More Than One Resource

To this point we've examined the firm's hiring decision for one resource, with everything else, including the quantities of all other resources, held constant. However, a firm uses several resources and makes hiring decisions regarding most of them all the time. How does the firm decide what combinations of resources to use? Like the consumer deciding what combinations of goods and services to purchase, the firm will ensure that the benefits of spending one more dollar are the same no matter which resource the firm chooses to spend that dollar on.

You may recall that the consumer maximizes utility when the marginal utility per dollar of expenditure is the same for all goods and services purchased:

$$MU_{coffee}/P_{coffee} = MU_{gas}/P_{gas} = \cdots = MU_n/P_n$$

A similar rule holds for the firm that is attempting to purchase resource services in order to maximize profit and minimize costs. The firm will be maximizing profit when its marginal revenue product per dollar of expenditure on all resources is the same:

$$MRP_{land}/MFC_{land} = MRP_{labor}/MFC_{labor} = \cdots = MRP_n/MFC_n$$

In equilibrium, the last dollar spent on resources must yield the same marginal revenue product no matter which resource the dollar is spent on.

As long as the marginal factor cost of a resource is less than its marginal revenue product, the firm will increase profit by hiring more of the resource. If a dollar spent on labor yields less marginal revenue product than a dollar spent on capital, the firm will increase profit more by purchasing the capital than by purchasing the labor.

If a resource is very expensive relative to other resources, then the expensive resource must generate a significantly larger marginal revenue product than the other resources. For instance, for a firm to remain in Manhattan (New York City), it must generate a significantly larger marginal revenue product than it could obtain in Dallas or elsewhere because rents are so much higher in Manhattan. A professional athlete who gets paid $30 million a year has to bring in more revenue for the team than another who earns $2 million a year.

A firm that is in equilibrium in terms of allocating its expenditures among resources will alter the allocation only if the cost of one of the resources rises relative to the others. For instance, if government-mandated medical or other benefits mean that labor costs rise while everything else remains constant, then firms will tend to hire less labor and use more capital and land if they can. Everything else the same, if the costs of doing business in the United States rise, firms will locate offices or plants in other countries.

2.d. Product Market Structures and Resource Demand

Firms purchase the types and quantities of resource services that allow them to maximize profit; each firm equates the MRP per dollar of expenditure on all resource services used. The MRP depends on the market structure in which the firm sells its output. A perfectly competitive firm produces more output and sells that output at a lower price than a firm operating in any other type of market, everything else the same. Since the perfectly competitive firm produces more output, it must use more resources.

For the perfectly competitive firm, price and marginal revenue are the same, $P = MR$. Thus, the marginal revenue product is often called the value of the marginal product, VMP, to distinguish it from the marginal revenue product.

The demand for a resource by a single firm is the MRP of that resource, no matter whether it sells its goods and services as a monopolist or as a perfect competitor (for the perfectly competitive firm, $VMP = MRP$, so that MRP is its resource demand as well). However, since price is greater than marginal revenue for the firms that are not selling in a perfectly competitive market, VMP would be greater than MRP, which indicates that the perfectly competitive firm's demand curve for a resource lies above (or is greater than) the demand curve for a resource by a monopoly firm, an oligopoly firm, or a monopolistically competitive firm.

RECAP

1. The MRP of a resource is a measure of how much the additional output generated by the last unit of the resource is worth to the firm.

2. Resources are hired up to the point at which $MRP = MFC$.

3. In a perfectly competitive resource market, resources are paid an amount equal to their marginal revenue product. In a monopsonistic resource market, resources are paid less than their marginal revenue product.

4. A firm will allocate its budget on resources up to the point where the last dollar spent yields an equal marginal revenue product no matter on which resource the dollar is spent.

5. A perfectly competitive firm will hire and acquire more resources than firms selling in monopoly, oligopoly, or monopolistically competitive product markets, everything else the same.

3. Resource Supplies

The owners of land, labor, and capital are households or individuals. Individuals act so as to maximize their utility. They receive utility when they consume goods and services, but they need income to purchase these goods and services. To acquire income, households must sell the services of their resources. They must give up some of their leisure time and go to work or offer the services of the other resources they own in order to acquire income. The quantity of resources that are supplied depends on the wages, rents, interest, and profits offered for those resources. If, while everything else is held constant, people can get higher wages, they will offer to work more hours; if they can obtain more rent for their land, they will offer more of their land for use, and so on. The quantity supplied of a resource rises as the price of the resource rises.

3.a. Economic Rent

economic rent
The portion of earnings above transfer earnings.

transfer earnings
The amount that must be paid to a resource owner to get him or her to allocate the resource to another use.

When a resource has a perfectly inelastic supply (vertical supply curve), its pay or earnings is called **economic rent**. If a resource has a perfectly elastic supply curve, its pay or earnings is called **transfer earnings**. For upward-sloping supply curves, resource earnings consist of both transfer earnings and economic rent. Transfer earnings is what a resource could earn in its best alternative use (its opportunity cost). It is the amount that must be paid to get the resource to "transfer" to another use. Economic rent is earnings in excess of transfer earnings. It is the portion of a resource's earnings that is not necessary to keep the resource in its current use. A movie star can earn more than $20 million per movie but probably could not earn that kind of income in another occupation. Thus, the greatest part of the movie star's earnings is economic rent.

There are two different meanings for the term *rent* in economics. The most common meaning refers to the payment for the use of something, as distinguished from payment for ownership. In this sense, you purchase a house but rent an apartment; you buy a car from Chrysler but rent cars from Avis. The second use of the term *rent* is to mean payment for the use of something that is in fixed—that is, perfectly inelastic—supply. The total quantity of land is fixed; therefore, payment for land is economic rent. When something is in fixed supply, even a higher rent cannot increase its quantity. Because the term *economic rent* is associated with payments for something that don't increase the quantity supplied, it is often applied to politics. For instance, a payment for favors from a government official is called economic rent; it is a payment that does not create anything or increase the quantity supplied of anything. The government official uses tax money to provide you benefits; thus, the payment merely transfers wealth from one person to another. It does not increase the quantity of something.

RECAP

1. Firms purchase resources in such a way that they maximize profits. Households sell resources in order to maximize income.

2. Transfer earnings is the portion of total earnings required to keep a resource in its current use.

3. Economic rent is earnings in excess of transfer earnings.

---

4. A Look Ahead

In the next few chapters, we will examine some interesting features of resource markets. We'll look at labor markets and discuss why different people receive different wages, why firms treat employees the way they do, the impact of labor laws, and the causes and results of discrimination. We'll discuss financial markets, physical and financial capital, and explore why firms carry out research and development. We'll look at the markets for land and natural resources. Selling resource services creates income, so we'll examine who has income and why. And we'll look at how the government gets involved in providing needed human services such as health care and social security.

Often we will discuss resource markets at the level of the individual firm or individual household, but typically we will refer to the market as a whole. For instance, if we talk about the "labor market," we are talking about the demand for every worker by every firm and the supply of every possible employee by every individual. The market demand curve slopes downward, indicating that as the price of a resource falls, the quantity demanded rises, everything else held constant. The market supply curve slopes upward, indicating that as the price of a resource falls, the quantity supplied falls, everything else held constant.

SUMMARY

1. Who are the buyers and sellers of resources?

- The term *resource markets* refers to the buyers and sellers of three classes of resources: land, labor, and capital. *§1*

- The buyers of resources are firms that purchase resources in order to produce goods and services. *§1.a*

- The sellers of resources are households that supply resources in order to obtain income with which to purchase goods and services. *§1.a*

2. How are resource prices determined?

- A single firm's demand for a resource is the marginal-revenue-product (*MRP*) curve for that resource. *§2.a*

- A firm purchasing resources in a perfectly competitive resource market will hire resources up to the point where *MRP* = *MFC*. A firm that is one of only a few buyers or the only buyer of a particular resource (a monopsonist) will face a

marginal-factor-cost (*MFC*) curve that is above the supply curve for that resource. As a result, the resource is paid less than its marginal revenue product. *§2.b.1, 2.b.2*

3. How does a firm allocate its expenditures among the various resources?

- A firm will allocate its budget on resources in such a way that the last dollar spent will yield the same marginal revenue product no matter on which resource the dollar is spent. *§2.c*

- Households own resources and decide how much of the resource services to offer for use. The supply of a resource depends on the income received by the owners of that resource. *§3*

- Payments for the use of resources consist of two parts: transfer earnings and economic rent. Transfer earnings are the rate of pay necessary to keep a resource in its current use. Economic rent is the excess of pay above transfer earnings. *§3.a*

KEY TERMS

derived demand, 629
economic rent, 634
marginal factor cost
  (*MFC*), 630

marginal revenue product
  (*MRP*), 630
monopsonist, 632

resource market, 628
transfer earnings, 634

EXERCISES

1. What does it mean to say that the demand for resources is a derived demand? Is the demand for all goods and services a derived demand?
2. Using the information in the following table, calculate the marginal revenue product ($MRP = MPP \times MR$).

Unit of Resources	Total Output	Price	Resource Price
1	10	$5	$10
2	25	$5	$10
3	35	$5	$10
4	40	$5	$10
5	40	$5	$10

3. Using the data in exercise 2, determine how many units of resources the firm will want to acquire.
4. Suppose the output price falls from $5 to $4 to $3 to $1 in exercise 2. How would that change your answers to exercises 2 and 3?
5. Using the data in exercise 2, calculate the marginal factor cost.
6. Suppose the resource price rises from $10 to $12 to $14 to $18 to $20 as resource units go from 1 to 5. How would that change your answer to exercise 5? How would it change your answer to exercise 3?
7. Using exercise 6, calculate the transfer earnings and economic rent of the third unit of the resource when four units of the resource are employed.

Do the same calculations when only three units of the resource are employed. How do you account for the different answers?

8. Can you explain why Jennifer Aniston earns $30 million a year and a schoolteacher $40,000 a year?

9. What is a monopsonist? How does a monopsonist differ from a monopolist?

10. Supposedly Larry Bird once said that he would play basketball for $10,000 per year. Yet he was paid over $1 million per year. If the quote is correct, how much were Bird's transfer earnings? How much was his economic rent?

11. Walmart is vilified by many people as being evil, destroying jobs and cities. Others note that it has the lowest prices and is the largest employer in the country. What is the difference? Is Walmart a monopsonist?

12. Early in her journalistic career, Gloria Steinem posed as a Playboy Bunny to examine the inside of a Playboy Club. Steinem discovered that the Bunnies had to purchase their costumes from the club, pay for cleaning them, purchase their food from the club, and so on. This "company store" exploited the employees (the Bunnies), according to Steinem. Explain what Steinem meant by exploitation.

13. Explain the idea behind the lyrics "You load 16 tons, and what do you get? You get another day older and deeper in debt. Saint Peter, don't you call me, 'cause I can't go. I owe my soul to the company store."

14. In some small cities, Walmart is the only firm offering many types of goods. Suppose the demand for those goods is very price-inelastic. How does that affect how Walmart treats its employees? What is the marginal factor cost and the wage rate?

15. The National Economic Council recently sent an e-mail to each of its state affiliates requesting that they send a letter to their Congressperson and Senators asking them to support the bill to provide government funds to the Council. Explain whether this is rent seeking or not.

16. Small, well-organized groups are often more successful at rent seeking than other organizations. Why?

You can find further practice tests in the Online Quiz at **www.cengage.com/economics/boyes**.

JAZZ WON'T BITE ON "OUTLANDISH" OFFERS

Deseret Morning News, June 27, 2004

The Jazz will not match crazy offers, and will not overpay, even for one of their own.

Fair warning has been issued.

Or so has suggested Jazz owner Larry H. Miller, who made it clear when the 2003–04 NBA season ended that any or all who intend to be back next season must be realistic—even if Utah does have roughly $26 million in under-the-cap money to spend on NBA free agents this summer.

"Everybody has to fit into our salary structure," Miller said. "If someone has an outlandish offer, that's something we're trying to stay away from."

All four of the Jazz's restricted free agents, however, are expected to test the open market when the league's summer negotiating period opens Thursday.

The Jazz seem quite intent on re-signing shooting guard Gordan Giricek, though Portland and possibly New Jersey may pursue him as well. They like big man Jarron Collins, too—so much so he was not exposed for last Tuesday's NBA Expansion Draft.

Guards Carlos Arroyo and Mo Williams could both be back, though Miami may show interest in Arroyo, and the Charlotte Observer reported Saturday that the expansion Charlotte Bobcats might consider extending an offer sheet to Williams.

As for unrestricted free agent center Greg Ostertag, it remains possible he will be back for a 10th season in Utah.

Miller, though, has made it known the price tag on 'Tag—who made $8.67 million last season—would have to drastically come down.

"We know, pretty much, who Greg is," the Jazz owner said. "So, what we'd have to do is make our expectations on what we think he'll give us match up with what he's earning."

Source: Tim Buckley, June 27, 2004, Deseret Morning News. Reprinted with permission.

Commentary

People are paid an amount that depends on how much their work contributes to the profits of the firm. This is measured by the marginal revenue product (*MRP*), the additional revenue of one more unit of work times the productivity of that one unit of work. If a person has skills that enable him or her to be more productive, then he or she will be paid more.

According to the article, "The Jazz will not match crazy offers, and will not overpay, even for one of their own." The Salt Lake City basketball franchise and its owner, Larry Miller, says it will not overpay. What does the term "overpay" mean? If Greg Ostertag or any basketball player is offered a large salary to play basketball it is because the team making the offer believes Ostertag will bring in enough fans to the basketball games that revenues will offset Ostertag's pay. Now if another team, say the Phoenix Suns, offers him more than the Jazz offers Ostertag, then the Suns franchise must believe Ostertag will bring in more revenues to the Suns than he brings in to the Jazz. This is not overpaying. This is simply paying the market price. But, should the Suns offer Ostertag more than the Suns franchise thinks Ostertag will bring in in revenue, then the Suns would be "overpaying."

Why would a team "overpay" some player? It wouldn't. If a player is expected to perform at a high level but then does not, that is not overpaying—it is paying on the expectation of future revenues brought in by that player. In hindsight the player is being paid more than he contributes to the franchise, but not in foresight. It makes no sense for a firm to overpay. A firm that overpays employees, just like a team that overpays players, will lose profits. Why would a firm do that? Why would a basketball franchise do that? They wouldn't. So perhaps Larry Miller is trying to bluff his players into not attempting to get more pay; but this bluff will be called if a player is worth more than the Jazz are paying him.

CHAPTER 29

The Labor Market

© MACIEJ FROLOW/GETTY IMAGES, INC

© STEPHEN COBURN/SHUTTERSTOCK.COM; LOGO: © FROXX/SHUTTERSTOCK.COM

I s something out of balance when teachers, firefighters, and police officers earn salaries that are just 1 percent of the salary of the average professional basketball player? Why are some jobs that could be done by Americans being sent to other countries? Why are unskilled people from less-developed countries flooding into the developed countries to do menial or unskilled jobs? Are these events things to worry about? In this chapter we examine these issues.

 FUNDAMENTAL QUESTIONS

1 Are people willing to work more hours for higher wages?

2 What are compensating wage differentials?

3 What is the impact of technological change on workers?

4 What is offshoring?

5 What is the impact of a minimum wage law on unskilled labor?

6 What is the effect of income taxes on workers?

7 What is the effect of illegal immigration on the economy?

8 Are discrimination and freely functioning markets compatible?

ECONOMIC INSIGHT

Labor Leisure Trade-off and Indifference Curves

The income-leisure trade-off is typically illustrated using indifference curves and income constraints discussed in the Appendix to the chapter "Consumer Choice." In the following figure we plot income on the vertical axis and leisure on the horizontal axis. The assumption here is that to get more income a person has to put more time into working and thus has less time for leisure. So as leisure increases (we move out the horizontal axis), we can earn less income. The indifference curves labeled I_1 through I_4 represent all combinations of income and leisure between which the individual is indifferent. All combinations of income and leisure along I_1, such as points A and B, generate the same utility for the individual. All combinations of income and leisure along I_2 are preferred to those along I_1 under the assumption that more is preferred to less. Similarly, I_3 is more preferred than I_2 and I_4 over I_3. The indifference curves illustrate the trade-off between income and leisure.

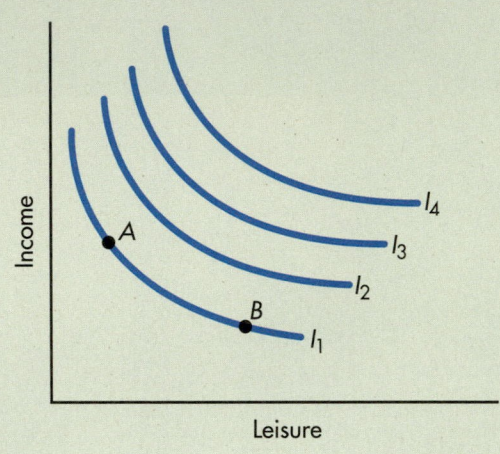

1. The Supply of Labor

The supply of labor comes from individual households. Each member of a household must determine whether to give up a certain number of hours each day to work. That decision is the individual's labor supply decision and is called the *labor-leisure trade-off*.

1 Are people willing to work more hours for higher wages?

> People have 24 hours a day during which they can either work or do something other than work (leisure).

1.a. Individual Labor Supply: Labor-Leisure Trade-off

There are only 24 hours in a day, and there are only two things that people can do during this time: (1) work for pay or (2) not work for pay. *Any* time spent not working is called *leisure time*. Leisure time includes being a "couch potato," going to clubs, volunteering to serve food at a homeless shelter, or participating in any other activity except working at a paying job. People want leisure time, but they also want food, housing, cars, fun, and many other things. To be able to buy goods and services, people usually have to work.

It is important to recognize that the cost of leisure time is the money that could be earned working. A person's wage or salary is his or her opportunity cost of leisure. This creates an interesting dilemma—you want to earn more money so you can purchase goods and services, yet you want to have time to enjoy the things you buy. So you have to trade off work and leisure time: If you take more leisure, you work less, and vice versa. So how many hours do people spend working and how many hours do they devote to other activities?

In addition to going to school, do you work? Let's say that you earn \$10 per hour and work 10 hours a week. What would you do if the wage rate for your job increased to \$15 per hour? You might ask to work *more* hours each week. What would you do if the wage rate increased to \$50 per hour? You might drop your classes and work 40 or more hours a week. The higher wage means that an hour of leisure costs more—\$50 rather than \$10. As the price of a normal good goes up, people purchase less of it. As the price of leisure goes up, people work more.

Leisure is a little different from other normal goods—such as books, gasoline, and Starbucks coffee—because of the limited number of hours in a day. You can't work 24 hours a day—at least, not for very long. What happens with most people is that as they earn more money, they want more time to enjoy what the money can buy. This becomes a problem: If I work more, I have more money, but I have less time to enjoy what the money can buy; if I work less so that I can have more time to enjoy what I purchase, I have less income.

When the wage rate increases, people choose to work more (or work harder or better), but since they now have more money, they can purchase more and may decide that they would rather take a little more leisure time. Thus, a wage increase creates two opposing effects; one leads to increased hours of work, and one leads to decreased hours of work. This means that the quantity of labor supplied may rise or fall as the wage rate rises.

The labor supply curve shown in Figure 1 is what the labor supply curve for an individual usually looks like. It rises as the wage rate rises until the wage is sufficiently high that people begin to choose more leisure; then the curve begins to turn backward. This is called the **backward-bending labor supply curve**.

1.a.1. Do People Really Trade Off Labor and Leisure?
About one-half of the workers in the United States report being paid an hourly wage. Although it might seem that people who work a set number of hours a week at a particular hourly wage do not have the luxury of deciding at each minute whether to work or to take leisure time, it is not inappropriate to examine the labor market as if they do. This is because there is flexibility in that some people might be able to choose between part-time and full-time work, and because over a month, a year, or several years, people do choose to put in more or less time on the job. Some people choose occupations that enable them to have

backward-bending labor supply curve
A labor supply curve indicating that a person is willing and able to work more hours as the wage rate increases until, at some sufficiently high wage rate, the person chooses to work fewer hours.

FIGURE 1   The Backward-Bending Labor Supply Curve

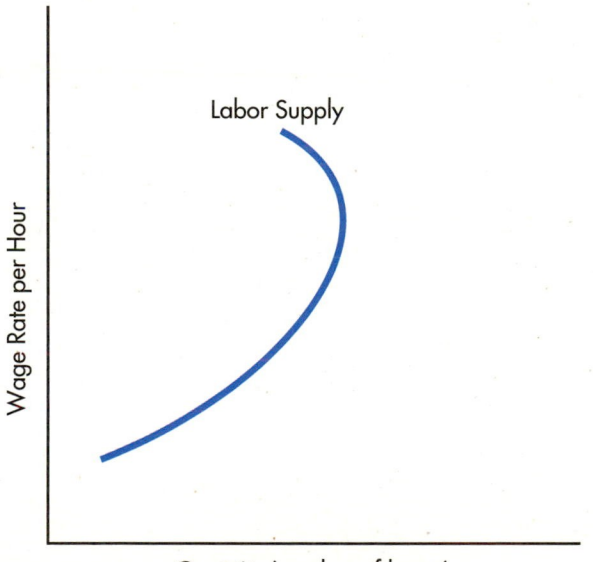

Labor Supply

Wage Rate per Hour

Quantity (number of hours)

As the wage rate rises, people are willing and able to supply more labor, at least up to some high wage rate. A higher wage rate means that the opportunity cost of leisure time increases, so that people will purchase less leisure (will work more). Conversely, as the wage rate rises and people's incomes rise, more of all goods are purchased, including leisure time. As a result, fewer hours of work are supplied. Which of these opposing effects is larger determines whether the labor supply curve slopes upward or downward. The most commonly shaped labor supply curve is one that slopes upward until the wage rate reaches some high level and then, as people choose more leisure time, begins to bend backward.

more flexibility; many prefer to be self-employed in order to be able to choose whether to put in more or less time on the job. People can also *moonlight*—that is, work an additional job or put in extra hours after their full-time job is completed.

1.b. From Individual to Market Supply

If the labor supply curve for each individual slopes upward, then the market supply curve (the sum of all individual supply curves) also slopes upward. Even if each individual labor supply curve bends backward at some high wage, it is unlikely that all of the curves will bend backward at the same wage. Not everyone has the same trade-offs between labor and leisure; not all offer to work at the same wage rate; not all want the same kind of job. As the wage rate rises, some people who choose not to participate in the labor market at lower wages are induced to offer their services for employment at a higher wage. The labor market supply curve slopes up because the number of people who are both willing and able to work rises as the wage rate rises and because the number of hours that each person is willing and able to work rises as the wage rate rises, at least up to some high wage rate.

1.c. Equilibrium

The labor market consists of the labor demand and labor supply curves. We've just discussed labor supply. Labor demand is based on the firm's marginal-revenue-product curves, as discussed in the previous chapter. The marginal revenue product is the value that the individual employee contributes to the firm. The term *productivity* typically refers to all workers together and means the output per worker or average product. If we talk about the productivity of an individual person, then we are referring to the marginal product, the additional product provided by that individual worker. The intersection of the labor demand and labor supply curves determines the equilibrium wage, W_e, and the quantity of hours people work at this equilibrium wage, Q_e, as shown in Figure 2.

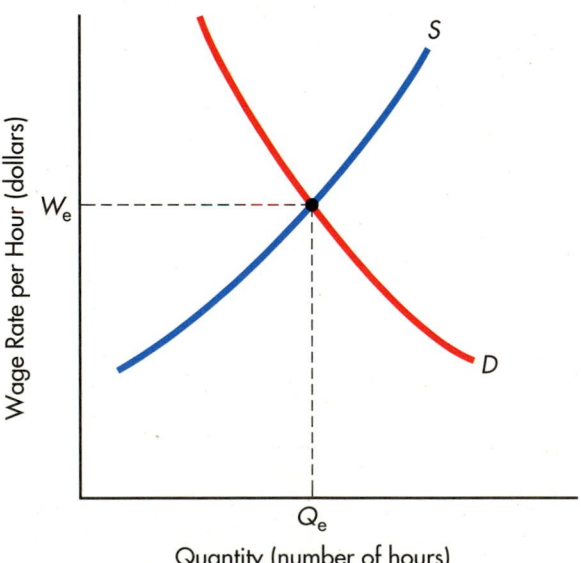

FIGURE 2   Labor Market Equilibrium

If all workers are the same to all firms—that is, if a firm doesn't care whether it hires Roberto, Renee, or Ryan—and if all firms and jobs are the same to workers—that is, if a worker doesn't care whether a job is with IBM or Ted's Hot Dog Stand—then one demand curve and one supply curve define the labor market. The intersection of the two curves is the labor market equilibrium at which the wage rate is determined.

© 2013 Cengage Learning

GLOBAL BUSINESS INSIGHT

Hours Spent Working

The average employed person in the United States is now on the job 1,824 hours a year, but the average employed person in seven other nations puts in more time. The nation in which the average annual number of hours worked is largest is Korea, followed by the former Communist bloc countries of Poland, Hungary, and the Czech Republic, and then Greece, Mexico, and New Zealand. The Netherlands, Norway, Germany, Denmark, and France remain the nations with the lowest average annual hours of work, just slightly more than 26 hours a week. In the United States, the average workweek is 35 hours. If you consider that the average vacation time is less than two weeks in the United States and around four weeks in the European countries, the number of hours spent working when not on vacation is 37 in the United States and 29 in Europe.

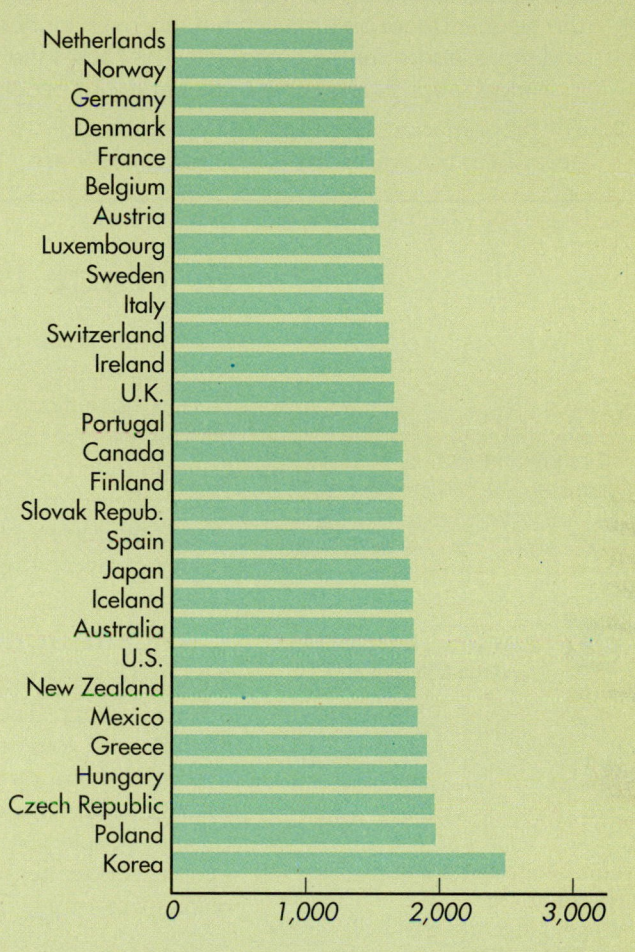

Source: OECD Statistics Portal, February 2011; http://www.oecd.org/topicstatsportal.

The labor market pictured in Figure 2 suggests that as long as all workers are the same and all jobs are the same, there will be one equilibrium wage. But workers are not all the same, jobs are not all the same, and wages are definitely not all the same. College-educated people earn more than people with only a high school education, and people with a high school education earn more than those with only a grammar school education. Older workers earn more than younger workers. Men earn more than women. Whites earn more than nonwhites.

In general, workers will be paid their marginal revenue products—that is, they are paid according to how much they contribute to the profits of their employers. The more productive a worker is, the higher his or her compensation will be, and vice versa. However, in reality, there are large salary differences for people with similar levels of productivity, and people who are vastly different in terms of productivity are paid the same. This occurs because, even though two people generate about the same output, the value that one provides exceeds the value provided by the other. We'll discuss a few cases in the remainder of this chapter.

RECAP

1. An increase in the wage rate causes workers to increase the hours they are willing and able to work and reduce their hours of leisure; at the same time, the wage increase also means that income is higher and more leisure can be purchased. This causes the individual labor supply curve to be backward bending.

2. The labor market supply curve slopes upward because as the wage rate rises, more people are willing and able to work, and people are willing and able to work more hours.

3. Equilibrium in the labor market defines the wage rate and the quantity of hours that people work at that wage.

2. Wage Differentials

If all workers are the same to a firm—that is, if a firm doesn't care whether it hires Roberto, Renee, or Ryan—and if all firms and jobs are the same to workers—that is, if IBM is no different from Ted's Hot Dog Stand to individual workers—then the one demand for labor and the one supply of labor define the one equilibrium wage. However, firms do differentiate among workers and workers do differentiate among firms and jobs, and so there is more than one labor market and more than one equilibrium wage level. Wages differ from job to job and from person to person. The reasons for wage differences include compensating wage differentials and differences in individual levels of productivity.

> If people were identical, if jobs were identical, and if information were perfect, there would be no wage differentials.

 2 What are compensating wage differentials?

2.a. Compensating Wage Differentials

Some jobs are dangerous or unhealthy. Table 1 shows which jobs have people missing the most work. Table 2 lists the jobs with the greatest chance of dying on the job. For instance, loggers and pilots of small planes used as crop dusters have the greatest chance of dying on the job, according to Table 2. Other jobs, such as coal mining or garbage collecting, might be considered quite unpleasant. In most market economies, enough people voluntarily choose to work in unpleasant jobs that the jobs get filled. People choose to work in unpleasant occupations because of **compensating wage differentials**—wage differences that make up for the high risk or poor working conditions

compensating wage differentials
Wage differences that make up for the higher risk or poorer working conditions of one job over another.

TABLE 1	Days Away from Work
Occupational injuries and illnesses involving days away from work for selected occupations, 2007 (thousands)	
Occupation	**Thousands**
Registered nurses	20.02
Maintenance and repair workers, general	23.46
Carpenters	23.80
Janitors and cleaners, except maids and housekeeping cleaners	30.06
Retail salespersons	32.92
Truck drivers, light or delivery services	32.93
Construction laborers	34.18
Nursing aides, orderlies, and attendants	44.93
Truck drivers, heavy and tractor-trailer	57.05
Laborers and freight, stock, and material movers	79.00

Source: U.S. Department of Labor, Bureau of Statistics, *Census of Fatal Occupational Injuries, 2004, 2009.*

© froxx/Shutterstock.com

Job	Fatality Rate (per 100,000 employees)	Number of Deaths
TABLE 2 Most Dangerous Jobs		
Logging workers	92.4	85
Aircraft pilots	92.4	109
Fishers	86.4	38
Iron and steel workers	47.0	31
Garbage collectors	43.2	35
Farmers and ranchers	37.5	307
Roofers	34.9	94
Power line workers	30.0	36
Truckers and driver/sales workers (e.g., pizza and newspaper delivery)	27.6	905
Taxi drivers, chauffeurs	24.2	67

Source: U.S. Department of Labor, Bureau of Labor Statistics, *Census of Fatal Occupational Injuries, 2004, 2009.*

of a job. Workers mine coal, clean sewers, and weld steel beams 50 stories off the ground because, compared to alternative jobs for which they qualify, these jobs pay well.

Figure 3 illustrates the concept of compensating wage differentials. There are two labor markets, one for a risky occupation and one for a less risky occupation. At each

FIGURE 3   Compensating Wage Differentials

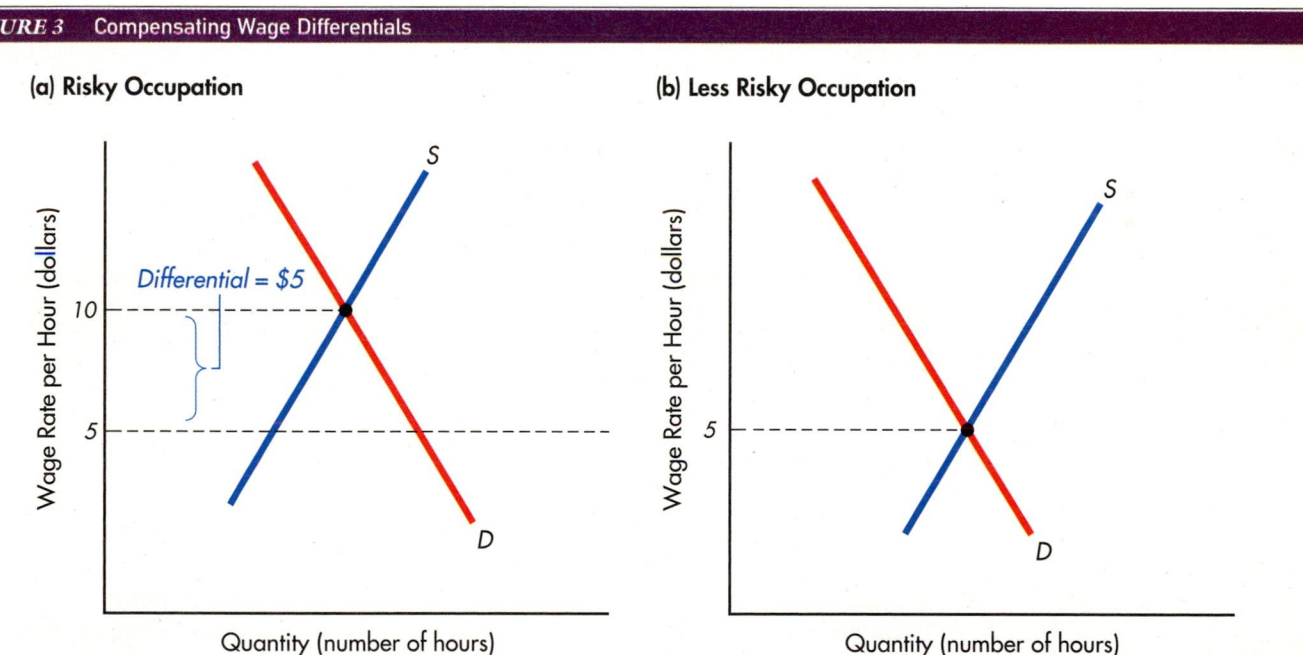

Figure 3(a) shows the market for a risky occupation. Figure 3(b) shows the market for a less risky occupation. At each wage rate, fewer people are willing and able to work in the risky occupation than in the less risky occupation. Thus, the supply curve of the risky occupation is higher (supply is less) than the supply curve of the less risky occupation. As a result, the wage in the risky occupation ($10 per hour) is higher than the wage in the less risky occupation ($5 per hour). The differential ($10 − $5 = $5) is an equilibrium differential—the amount necessary to induce enough people to fill the jobs. If the differential were any higher, more people would flow to the risky occupation, driving wages there down and wages in the less risky occupation up. If the differential were any lower, shortages would prevail in the risky occupation, driving wages there up.

Commercial deep-sea divers are exposed to the dangers of drowning and several physiological disorders that result from compression and decompression. Even though it is risky, the divers choose the job because they are paid well.

wage rate, fewer people are willing and able to work in the risky occupation than in the less risky occupation. Thus, if the demand curves are identical, the supply curve of the risky occupation will be to the left of the supply curve of the less risky occupation. As a result, the equilibrium wage rate is higher in the risky occupation ($10) than in the less risky occupation ($5). The difference between the wage in the risky occupation ($10 per hour) and the wage in the less risky occupation ($5 per hour) is an *equilibrium differential*—the compensation that a worker receives for undertaking the greater risk.

Commercial deep-sea divers are exposed to the dangers of drowning and severe physiological disorders that result from compression and decompression. They choose this job because they earn about 90 percent more than the average high school graduate. Coal miners in West Virginia and in the United Kingdom are exposed to coal dust, black lung disease, and cave-ins. They choose to work in the mines because the pay is twice what they could earn elsewhere. Wage differentials ensure that deep-sea diving jobs, coal-mining jobs, and jobs in other risky occupations are filled.

Any characteristic that distinguishes one job from another may result in a compensating wage differential. A job that requires a great deal of travel and time away from home usually pays more than a comparable job without the travel requirements because most people find extensive travel and time away from home to be costly. If people were indifferent to extensive travel, there would be no compensating wage differential.

2.b. Human Capital

People differ with respect to their training and abilities. These differences influence the level of wages for two reasons: (1) Skilled workers have higher marginal revenue products than unskilled workers, and (2) the supply of skilled workers relative to the demand

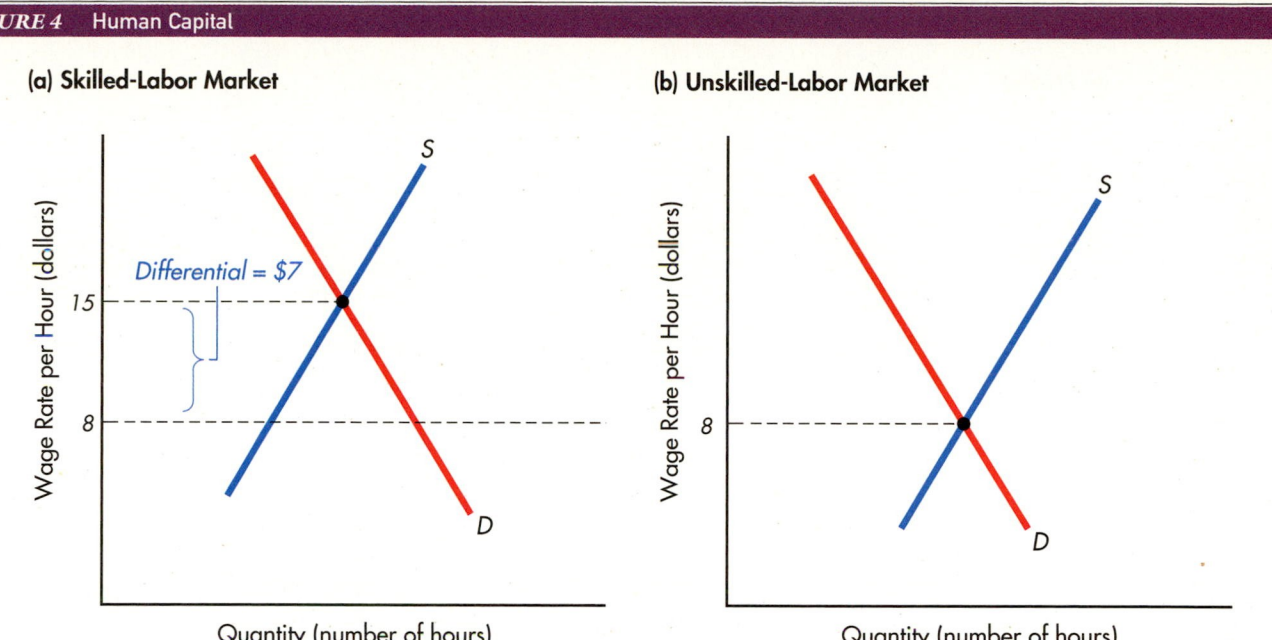

FIGURE 4   Human Capital

(a) Skilled-Labor Market

Wage Rate per Hour (dollars)

Differential = $7

15

8

D

S

Quantity (number of hours)

(b) Unskilled-Labor Market

Wage Rate per Hour (dollars)

8

S

D

Quantity (number of hours)

Two labor markets are pictured. Figure 4(a) shows the market for skilled labor. Figure 4(b) shows the market for unskilled labor. The smaller supply in the skilled-labor market results in a higher wage there. The equilibrium differential between the wages in the two markets is the return to human capital.

for skilled workers is smaller than the supply of unskilled workers relative to the demand for unskilled workers. As a result, skilled labor generates higher wages than less skilled labor. In Figure 4, we illustrate the differences between the skilled and unskilled labor markets; the skilled labor market is shown to generate a wage of $15 per hour, and the unskilled labor market a wage of $8 per hour. The difference exists because the demand for skilled labor relative to the supply of skilled labor is greater than the demand for unskilled labor relative to the supply of unskilled labor.

The expectation of higher income induces people to acquire **human capital**—skills and training acquired through education and job experience. People go to college or vocational school or enter training programs because they expect the training to increase their future income. These activities are *investments in human capital*. Like investments in real capital (machines and equipment), education and training are purchased in order to generate output and income in the future.

human capital
Skills and training acquired through education and on-the-job training.

2.b.1. Investment in Human Capital
Individuals who go to college or obtain special training expect the costs of going to college or obtaining the training to be more than offset by the income and other benefits they will obtain in the future. Individuals who acquire human capital reap the rewards of that human capital over time. Figure 5(a) is an illustration of what the income profiles of a worker with a college degree and a worker without a college degree might look like. We might expect the income of the worker without the degree to increase rapidly from the early working years until the worker gets to be about 50; then income might rise more slowly until the worker reaches retirement age. Until around age 30, the worker without the college degree clearly enjoys more income than the college-educated worker. The shaded areas represent estimated income lost to the college-educated worker while he or she is attending classes and then

FIGURE 5   Income Profiles and Educational Level

(a) Profiles

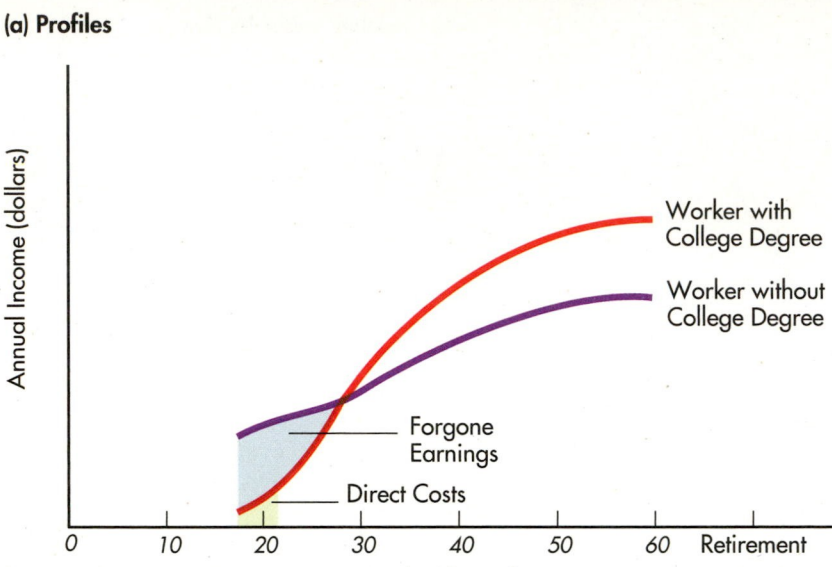

(b) College Income Premium

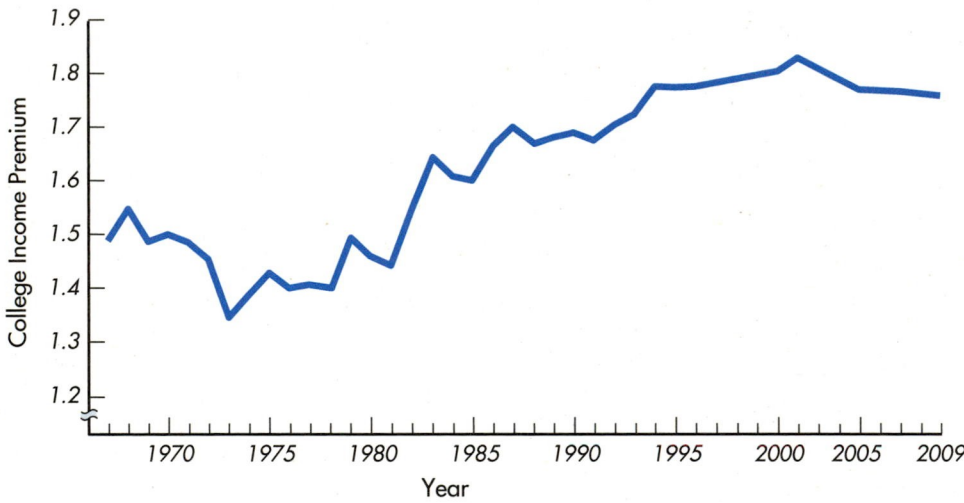

Income rises rapidly until age 50, then rises more slowly until retirement. Figure 5 compares the income earned by a worker without a degree with the income earned by a college graduate. Figure 5(a) suggests what the actual pattern looks like. Initially, the college graduate gives up substantial income in the form of direct costs and forgone earnings to go to college. Eventually, however, the income of the college graduate exceeds that of the high school-educated worker. Figure 5(b) illustrates the college income premium, the ratio of median income of college-educated to median income of non-college-educated individuals.

Source: Statistical Abstract of the United States, 2009; Economic Report of the President, 2009.

gaining work experience. It may take several years after entering the labor market for a college-degree recipient to achieve and then surpass the income level of a worker without a degree, but on average a college-educated person does earn more than someone without a college education. Figure 5(b) shows the ratios of the median income of college-to-high school–educated workers. This is called the college income premium. As mentioned in the chapter "Economics: The World around You", college-educated people earn more over their lifetimes than people without a college degree. This is their earnings, not their after-tax earnings or their after-debt-payment earnings. In some cases, the debt required to obtain a college degree may offset the college income premium.

The economic model of labor suggests that the reason that so many young adults go to college is that college-educated people have better-paying jobs and jobs with greater benefits and security than non-college-educated people.

2.b.2. Choice of a Major
If you decide to attend college, you must then decide what field to major in. Your decision depends in part on the opportunity costs that you face. If your opportunity costs of devoting a great deal of time to a job are high, you may choose to major in a field that is not overly time-consuming. For instance, for several years after college, men and women who have studied to become medical doctors, lawyers, and accountants face long training periods and very long workdays, and they have to devote significant amounts of time each year to staying abreast of new developments in their profession. If you think that you are not likely to be willing to undertake and complete a four-or five-year apprenticeship after college in order to reap the rewards from your expenditure of time and money, then it would be very costly for you to be a premed student or to major in accounting or law. The greater the opportunity costs of any particular occupation, the smaller the number of people who will select that occupation, everything else the same. For instance, it takes more time, money, and effort to become a medical doctor than to become a teacher in the K–12 schools. For this reason, many more people choose to become teachers than choose to become doctors. As a result, there is a wage differential between the two fields that is sufficient to compensate those who become doctors for the extra opportunity costs of a medical career.

2.b.3. Changing Careers
Today it is estimated that one in three people in the U.S. labor force will change careers at least once during their work lives. People choose a major and thus a career on the basis of the information they have at their disposal, family influences, and other related factors. People acquire additional information once they are involved in their occupation, and sometimes their tastes change. They decide to embark on another career path. Who will make such a change? What types of occupations might see more changes?

Relying on the labor market model, we can suggest some answers to these questions. There might be a temptation to say that those who devoted the most effort, time, and money to their first occupation would be the least likely to change. But it is the marginal cost that matters; the effort, time, and money that have been devoted to that first career are gone, whether one remains in the first occupation or moves to another. In the words of the chapter on monopolistic competition and oligopoly, these are sunk, or unrecoverable, costs. Thus, we would expect people who have the greatest expected net gains from a change to make that change. Those who see that they are in dead-end positions or in occupations whose outlook for future income increases is not as good as the outlook in other occupations are more likely to move to a new career. We might expect people not to remain in or enter those professions where the marginal costs of remaining in the profession are high. For instance, those occupations that require continuous time and/or financial commitments if their members are to remain productive, such as the high-tech occupations, the hard sciences, engineering, accounting, or law, might lose relatively more people to areas that do not require similar time and money expenditures, such as management and administration.

3 What is the impact of technological change on workers?

4 What is offshoring?

outsourcing
The process in which one firm purchases services from another firm (rather than having the services performed in-house).

offshoring
The process in which one firm purchases services from another firm in another country (rather than having the services performed in-house).

> *Outsourcing is the process of purchasing services from another firm rather than employing someone to perform those services inside the firm. Outsourcing is called offshoring when the jobs are purchased from a firm in another country.*

5 What is the impact of a minimum wage law on unskilled labor?

2.b.4. Outsourcing The labor market adjusts to technological changes. New markets are created for highly skilled workers, and old markets are eliminated. The economy makes it possible for many jobs—ranging from routine clerical jobs like processing insurance claims and handling customer calls to positions in highly skilled occupations like software development and radiology—to be performed anywhere in the world, with the results being transmitted electronically to wherever they are demanded. So if the work can be done as well by another firm at a lower cost, companies will purchase the work from that firm. If firms in India or China can perform the work at a much lower price, companies in the United States and other developed nations will purchase the work from these countries. This is why an increasing number of IT jobs are being done offshore. This process is called **outsourcing** if the firm is located in the same country and **offshoring** if the firm is located in another country. For instance, rather than have a telephone receptionist sitting outside the main office of a firm's headquarters, a firm could pay to have the service provided by an Indian company that could do it at a fourth of the cost. Offshoring eliminates domestic jobs, but it also enables companies to reduce the prices of goods and services.

Outsourcing is not just something that U.S. firms do. Every developed country sends jobs to low-wage nations—India, Mexico, Latin America, and much of Asia. Studies have found that for each dollar a U.S. company spends offshore, it saves 58 cents; this translates into lower prices for the goods it produces. The lower prices enable customers to demand other goods and services and thus create jobs in other areas.

Figure 6 illustrates the dynamic process of offshoring jobs and its impact on prices of goods and services. Initially, the firm is hiring U.S. labor to produce its goods and/or services. The wage rate is indicated as W_{US} in the labor market. In the output market, the firm maximizes profit with its costs ATC_{US} and MC_{US} at the point where $MR = MC_{US}$. The resulting price that the firm charges is P_{US}. If the firm can obtain the same labor services from India at a much lower cost, its cost curves shift down to ATC_{India} and MC_{India}, and it prices its product at the point where $MR = MC_{India}$, or P_{India}, which is much lower than P_{US}. The demand for U.S. workers declines or disappears and is replaced by the demand for Indian workers. The lower prices for the goods and services in the United States enable customers to purchase other goods and services and increase the demand for workers in these other areas.

2.c. The Minimum Wage

Because the demand for highly skilled workers has increased and the demand for unskilled workers has not kept pace, the inequality of income has become greater. In the 1970s, a high school dropout was 3.5 times more likely to be unemployed than a college graduate; this is now more than 4.5 times. Those with a college degree now make about 74 percent more than those who have only a high school education, a figure that has nearly doubled since 1979. The unemployment rate for those who hold at least a bachelor's degree is 2.7 percent, compared with 8.3 percent for those without a high school diploma. Several politicians and others have argued that the minimum wage (the government-set price floor on wages) should be raised in order to ensure that unskilled workers can make a decent living. A minimum wage has existed in the United States since 1938, when it was set at $.25 per hour. In 2009, the federal government minimum wage was set at $7.25 per hour. Today, about 80 percent of all jobs that are not in agriculture are required to pay at least the minimum wage, although some are granted exemptions. States may have their own minimum wage if that wage exceeds the federal level. In 2009, the state of Washington's minimum wage was the highest at $8.55 per hour. If cities are not happy with the level of either the federal or the state minimum wage, they may set their own. More than 100 cities have their own minimum wage

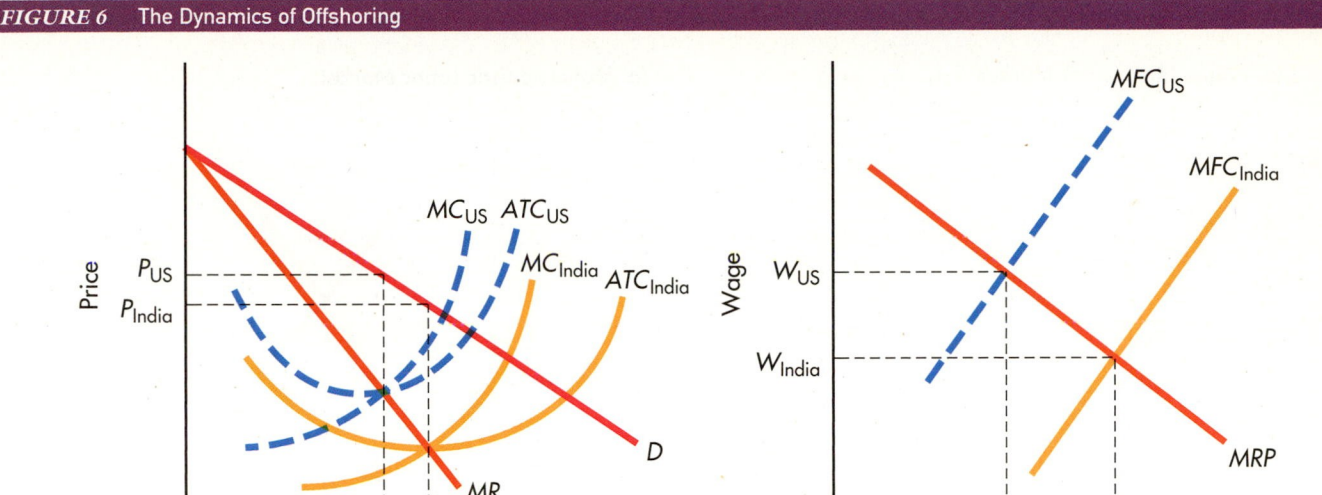

FIGURE 6   The Dynamics of Offshoring

The U.S. firm has costs given by MC_{US} and ATC_{US} when using U.S. workers. These costs come from the cost of labor, W_{US}. The firm maximizes profit at $MR = MC_{US}$ and sells the good at P_{US}. If the firm can obtain the same labor services from India, the firm's cost curves shift down to MC_{India} and ATC_{India}, and the firm maximizes profit at the point where $MR = MC_{India}$, or a price of P_{India}.

ordinances. In 2009, the highest effective rates were \$9.79 in San Francisco and \$9.49 in Santa Fe, New Mexico.[1]

The intention of a minimum wage is to raise the wage rate above the equilibrium level. Let's suppose that government wants a family to earn at least \$20,000 per year. This requires an hourly wage of \$10 per hour if it is assumed that a worker will spend 40 hours a week for 50 weeks a year at the job. So in Figure 7(a) the minimum wage (W_m) is set at \$10, above the equilibrium wage (W) of \$4. In markets such as the unskilled labor markets for agricultural workers, construction workers, and restaurant busboys, the minimum wage would create a labor surplus, as the quantity of jobs offered would be reduced and the quantity of people wanting jobs would increase.

While the minimum wage drives wages up for those who have a job, it hurts the chances of employment for others. Studies show that the minimum wage adversely affects teenagers the most and then affects those with the least skills or value to a firm. An increase in the minimum wage of 1 to 3 percent results in a 10 percent increase in teenage unemployment.

Notice that the market we discuss in Figure 7(a) is a perfectly competitive one. The MRP of all firms constitutes the demand for labor, and the MFC for all workers is the supply of labor. The minimum wage could have a different effect if just one employer, a monopsony, was hiring unskilled labor. If an employer is a monopsonist, a worker's wage (W) is less than MRP. The imposition of a minimum wage set at a level that is less than MRP but greater than the wage rate that the monopsonistic firm wants to pay may actually increase the level of employment. Recall from the previous chapter that a monopsonist drives up the costs of all other workers when it hires one more—it does

[1] http://www.paywizard.org/main/Minimumwageandovertime/

FIGURE 7   The Effect of Minimum Wage

(a) Competitive Labor Market

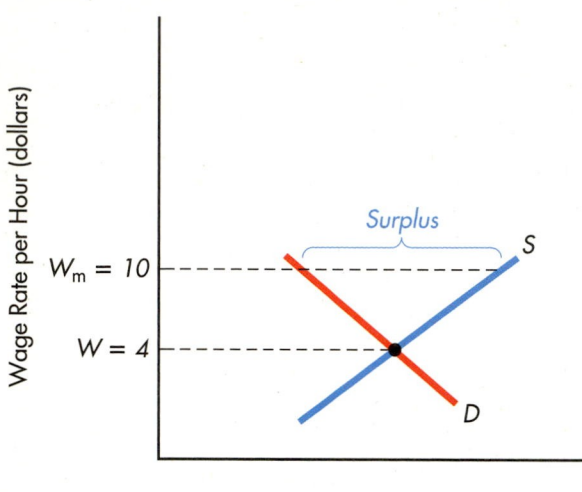

(b) Monopsonistic Labor Market

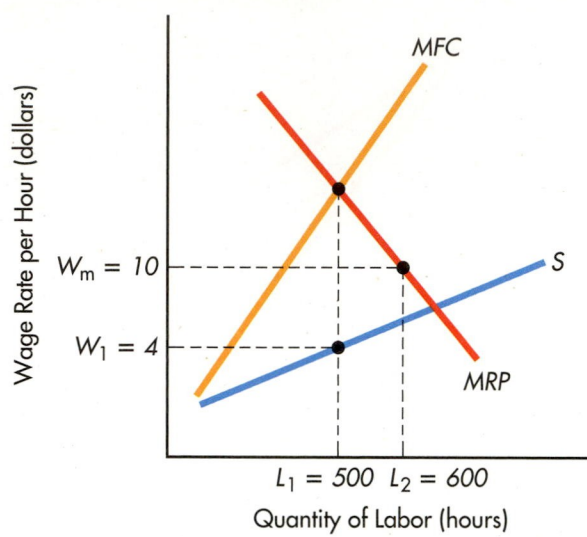

In a competitive labor market, a minimum wage above equilibrium causes a surplus—that is, increases unemployment. This is shown in Figure 7(a). In a monopsonistic market, a minimum wage can increase both the wage and the employment rate, as shown in Figure 7(b). The wage rises from $W_1 = \$4$ (the wage rate that the monopsonistic firm wants to pay) to $W_m = \$10$, the legal minimum wage; and the quantity of labor employed rises from L_1 to L_2.

not hire a worker at one wage and another identical worker at a different wage. The minimum wage limits the increase in marginal costs, and, as shown in Figure 7(b), at a W_m of $10, employment actually rises. How important is this in the unskilled labor market? If labor is not mobile, and a single firm, such as a large agricultural firm, controls a particular region—say, the Yuma valley in Arizona—then could we think of the unskilled labor market in that region as being monopsonistic?

6   What is the effect of income taxes on workers?

2.d. Income Taxes

Does a tax on income affect the supply of labor? The main types of taxes on individuals are income taxes, levied on a person's salary or wages, and consumption taxes, levied on consumer spending. These include sales taxes, used by many U.S. states, and the value-added tax, or VAT, widely used in Europe.

The simple rule of taxes is that when you tax something you get less of it. All taxes distort market decisions, affecting the buying and selling of goods and services. A tax on a good, for example, raises the price of the product, making it more expensive to purchase that good. However, if consumers buy less, forcing the market price down, then the tax affects sellers, who receive a lower price for their products. Whether buyers or sellers bear the greatest share of a tax burden is based on the concepts of supply and demand elasticity. As discussed in the chapter "Elasticity: Demand and Supply," the most inelastic side of a market (supply or demand) will bear the greatest share of the tax burden. The demand for cigarettes, for example, is price-inelastic. A tax on cigarettes, then, will likely be borne mostly by smokers themselves, because they do not alter their smoking habits very much after the tax.

ECONOMIC INSIGHT

Labor-Leisure and Income Taxes

In the Figure below, the income leisure choices are shown. This is the same diagram as in the first Economic Insight in this chapter, except that we added the income lines. The income that can be earned for each hour spent on leisure is shown by what is called the "Income Constraint," Y. As we move down Y, income is foregone in order to have more leisure time. Point "$Y_1 24$" would represent 24 hours spent working; Point "$L_1 24$" would represent 24 hours spent on leisure (zero income). As shown in the Appendix to the chapter "Consumer Choice," utility is maximized where the budget line is just touching or is tangent to an indifference curve. In the figure, the individual chooses income Y_1 and leisure L_1. What happens when an income tax is levied? The income line rotates down from "$Y_1 24$" to "$Y_2 24$." It rotates because 24 hours devoted to leisure still generates zero income, but 24 hours devoted to work generates income "$Y_1 24$" less the income tax, or "$Y_2 24$." Under the income tax, the individual maximizes utility by choosing more leisure and less work.

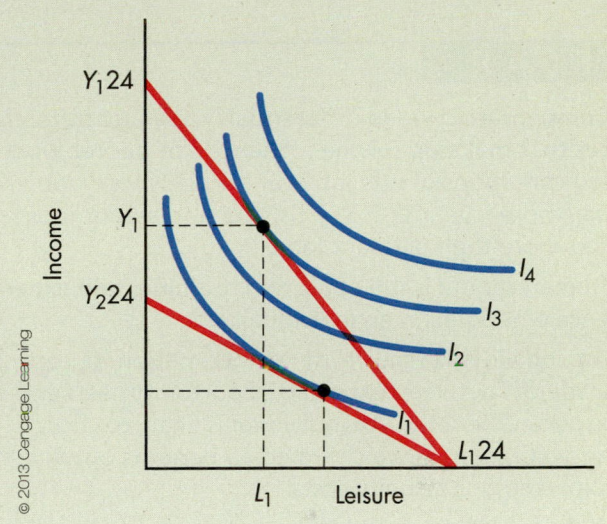

Taxes also affect incentives to work, earn, and invest, and this is what is of most concern in this chapter. For example, suppose a tax rate of 20 percent applies to all income up to $50,000 a year, and income between $50,000 and $60,000 a year is taxed at a rate of 30 percent, and then income above $60,000 is taxed at 40 percent. A person earning $50,000 a year would pay $10,000 in taxes; however, if that person earns an additional $10,000 ($60,000 a year total), that additional $10,000 would be taxed at 30 percent, or $3,000. Another $10,000 in income would result in $4,000 more additional taxes, a total of $10,000 + $3,000 + $4,000 = $17,000. This means that the cost of working becomes higher (and the cost of leisure lower) as income rises. At some point people might decide that it is not worthwhile to work more or perhaps they might decide to quit working altogether.

The example in the previous paragraph is a progressive tax. An income tax is progressive if the tax rate increases as income increases; the opposite of a progressive tax is a regressive tax—the tax rate decreases as income rises; a proportional income tax is one where the tax rate is constant, taking the same proportion of each income level.

A flat tax is a proportional tax where lower incomes are not taxed. For instance, the flat tax rate might be 20 percent. If the exempt income is $50,000, no one earning less than $50,000 is taxed. The distortions created by income taxes could be minimized by changing the progressive system to a flat tax. A flat tax would eliminate all deductions and exemptions and apply a fixed tax rate to income. In the case of the flat tax, as your income rises, you would pay the same tax rate. While many people support the idea of a flat tax, many think that a consumption-based tax would work better because it penalizes consumption rather than work. A tax based on consumption rather than income would be collected at the cash register when people purchase goods and services, just like a national sales tax. The difference between a flat tax and a consumption tax is where the tax is collected. A flat tax is levied on income—but only once and at one low rate—as it is earned. A sales tax is levied on income—but only once and at one low rate—as it is spent.

RECAP

1. Compensating wage differentials are wage differences that make up for the higher risk or poorer working conditions of one job over another. Risky jobs pay more than risk-free jobs, and unpleasant jobs pay more than pleasant jobs.

2. Human capital is the education, training, and experience embodied in an individual.

3. An individual's choice of an occupation reflects a trade-off between expected opportunity costs and expected benefits. An individual is likely to choose an occupation in which expected benefits outweigh expected opportunity costs.

4. A firm that used to have an accountant but then eliminated the accounting position and purchased its accounting services from another firm would be said to be outsourcing. Outsourcing refers to firm A purchasing from firm B something firm A used to do itself. If firm B is a foreign firm, outsourcing is called offshoring.

5. If the market is competitive, increasing the minimum wage benefits those who have and can retain jobs and harms those who are least skilled and have the least value to the firm.

6. If the employer is a monopsonist, a minimum wage set between supply and marginal factor cost can increase employment while increasing wages.

7. Income taxes distort the decision to work or take leisure time. A progressive tax tends to discourage additional work as income rises. A progressive income tax is one where the rate increases as income increases.

8. A regressive income tax is one where the tax rate decreases as income increases. A proportional income tax is one where the tax rate is constant as income rises.

3. Immigration

Approximately 700,000 people cross legally into the United States from Mexico every day to shop and work, returning afterward to their homes in Mexico. About 3,500 people cross the border *illegally* every day, and many of them don't return to Mexico. In the United States, the illegal population from Mexico is estimated to be between 6 and 7 million. Another 3 to 4 million undocumented aliens living in the United States are from other Latin American countries and Asia. Why do so many people leave their home countries and migrate to the United States?

3.a. The United States Is a Nation of Immigrants

In Figure 8, you can see the pattern of legal immigration to the United States from about 1850. Immigration has not taken place at a steady pace, but instead has been cyclical, with peaks in the number of people coming to the United States from other countries occurring in 1870, 1920, and 2004–2005.

The amount of immigration relative to the existing population is also shown in Figure 8. The total foreign-born population as a percentage of the total U.S. population

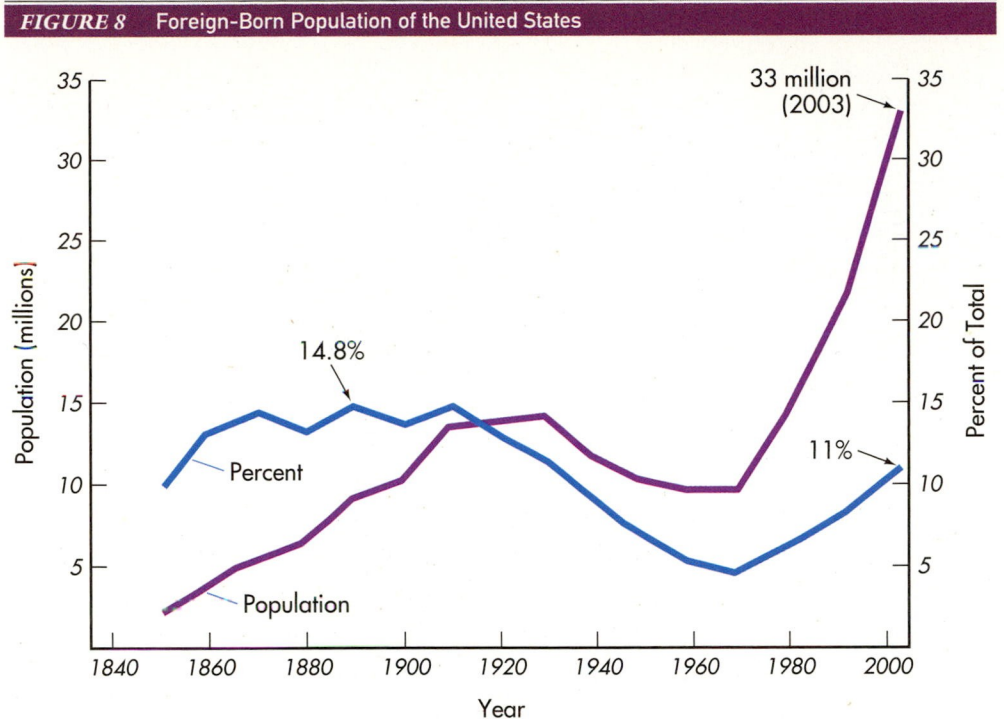

FIGURE 8 Foreign-Born Population of the United States

The foreign-born population of the United States in numbers and percentages is shown for the period from 1860 to 2000. The amounts (total numbers and percentages) rose until the early 1900s, then declined until the late 1960s and have risen since.

Sources: "Foreign-Born Population of the United States," *Current Population Survey*, March 2009, and previous years; http://www.census.gov/population/www/socdemo/foreign/ppl-176.html.

declined from a peak in 1880 and 1910 of about 15 percent to a low of 5 percent around 1970 and has risen since.

3.b. Why Immigrate?

People leave their home country and go to another country to live primarily because they seek a higher quality of life. Their own country may be politically repressive or economically stagnant, or there may be no upward mobility among income classes in their home country. For instance, most immigrants to the United States in the 1800s and 1900s were from northern and western Europe. Economic events like the potato famine in Ireland, recessions in the United Kingdom and western Europe, and religious persecution led to migrant flows to the United States. Beginning about 1950, immigration to the United States switched from being primarily from Europe to being mostly from Latin America and Asia. This was caused by changes in U.S. immigration policy and the relatively more severe political and economic problems in the Asian and Latin American countries.

For example, the greatest number of recent immigrants to the United States comes from Mexico. The reason: proximity and wage differentials. Compare incomes in Mexico with those in the United States—the per capita income in the United States is more than four times higher than that in Mexico.

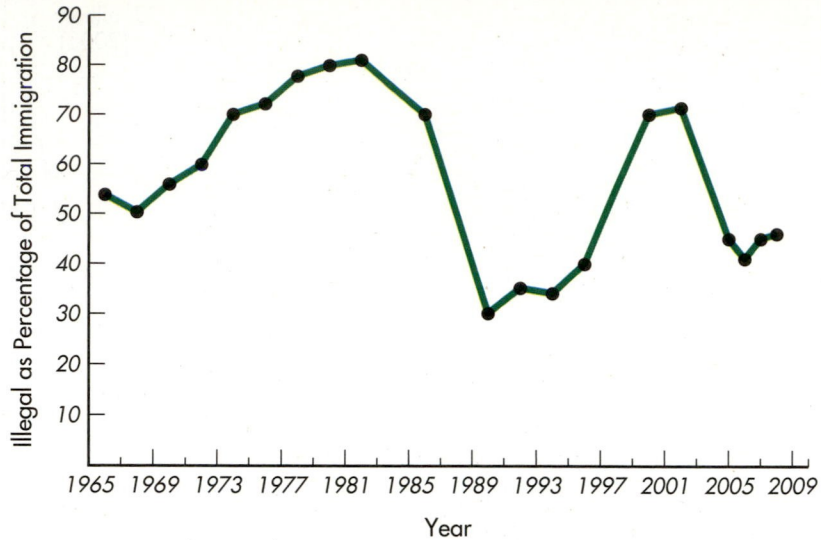

FIGURE 9   Illegal Immigration in the United States as a Percentage of Total Immigration

The number of illegal immigrants as a percentage of total immigrants is shown for the period 1965–2004. The percentage rose until the early 1980s, then declined until the mid-1990s and rose until the current period.

Source: http://www.migrationinformation.org/Feature.

7 What is the effect of illegal immigration on the economy?

3.b.1. Why Immigrate Illegally? As Figure 9 shows, illegal immigration is a significant percentage of immigration and has been growing rapidly in the past few years. However, fewer than half of illegal immigrants cross the nation's borders clandestinely; most illegal immigrants enter legally and overstay their visas.

For much of U.S. history, there were few restrictions on immigration, so illegal immigration was not an issue. The first restriction was the Chinese Exclusion Act of 1882. Chinese immigrants had been brought in to work during the labor shortages of the 1840s, but they became increasingly disliked by the native unskilled laborers. The Chinese Exclusion Act suspended immigration of Chinese laborers for 10 years, removed the right of Chinese entrants to be naturalized, and provided for the deportation of Chinese who were in the United States illegally. It was not until 1943 that the Chinese exclusion laws were repealed. In 1924, the United States established a quota system specifying how many people from each country could immigrate to the United States each year. The law placed a ceiling of 150,000 per year on immigrants from Europe, completely barred immigrants from Japan, and based the admission of immigrants from other countries on the proportion of people of that national origin that were present in the United States as measured by the 1890 census. In 1965, the national origins quota system was replaced with a uniform limit of 20,000 immigrants per country for all countries outside the Western Hemisphere and a limit on immigration from the Western Hemisphere (most notably from Mexico). The Immigration Reform and Control Act of 1986 (IRCA) was the first to address the issue of illegal immigration. It introduced penalties for employers who knowingly hire illegal immigrants.

The United States currently admits about 700,000 immigrants annually as legal ("green card") residents who will be eligible to apply for citizenship after living in the

United States for five years. Only about 110,000 of those receiving green cards do not have family members who are U.S. citizens. Of these, about 65,000 are highly skilled workers on H1-B visas, and about 44,000 are low-skilled workers.

To understand what these developments mean, we need to look at the unskilled labor market as depicted in Figure 10. In Figure 10, the equilibrium wage is $15 per hour if only legal immigrants and natives are considered. What happens when illegal immigration takes place? The supply of low-skilled labor rises—the supply curve shifts out—and the equilibrium wage drops to $9 per hour. At $9, fewer natives choose to work—the quantity supplied of native workers declines from *A* to *B*. The shortage of native workers, *B* to *C*, is made up by illegal immigrants.

Have you heard the claim that illegal immigrants take jobs that Americans won't take? Those making this claim are focusing on the distance from *B* to *C* in Figure 10. What they are not including in their discussion is the distance from *A* to *B* caused by the lower wage. What the claim actually should say is that illegal immigrants take jobs that Americans won't take at the wage rate for these jobs. If the wage rate was $15, then enough native workers would be willing to work to match the quantity demanded. Yet that higher cost has economic effects on the goods and services produced by this unskilled labor.

Labor is a resource—it is used to produce goods and services, and the wages and salaries provided to workers are part of the costs of doing business. So when the cost of labor declines, the costs of doing business also decline. A typical firm will produce more and earn greater profits when its costs decline. As firms increase their output and new firms enter the business, the market supply of the products being produced by the unskilled labor will rise, and the market price of the good or service will decline. This is what happens with illegal immigration. Illegal immigration has reduced costs in certain businesses—construction, restaurants, agriculture, meatpacking, textiles, and poultry

---

FIGURE 10 Unskilled Labor Market and Illegal Immigration

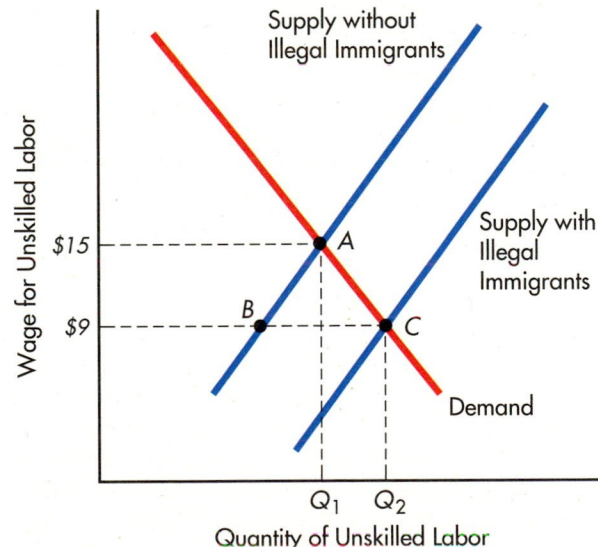

Without illegal immigrants, the equilibrium wage is $15, and the equilibrium quantity is quantity Q_1. With illegal immigration, the supply increases and the wage rate declines to $9. At $9, there would be a shortage of *B − C* if no illegal immigrants supplied labor.

production in particular. The lower costs lead to lower prices for houses and buildings, child care, housekeeping, gardening, produce, poultry, meats, and restaurants.

3.c. Immigration Policy

Illegal immigration in the United States is one of the topics of greatest concern to the American public. The costs and benefits of illegal immigration have been examined in a number of studies. The costs include the effects of illegal immigration on unskilled workers; the property damage caused by immigrants sneaking into the United States; the expenditures on health care for immigrants at emergency clinics and hospitals, which are legally unable to deny care to anyone or to inquire whether someone is a legal resident; expenditures on public education for the children of immigrants who attend public schools; and burglaries and other crimes committed by illegal immigrants.

Benefits created by the illegal immigrants include the lower wages and thus the lower costs in the occupations they work as well as the taxes they pay. It is estimated that about three-fourths of illegal immigrants pay Social Security and other withholding taxes, but since an illegal immigrant must have fake identification and Social Security numbers, any payments made to Social Security will not be assigned to a potential recipient. Instead, when the Social Security number does not match the SSA's records, the payments go into a slush fund called the "suspense file." Since 2002, the suspense file has been growing by more than $60 billion a year. The net effect of these costs and benefits varies according to the study, but most studies conclude that the first generation of illegal immigrants imposes costs that exceed the benefits they create, but every generation thereafter creates more benefits than it costs.

Those most affected by the benefits want immigrants to have a way to take a job, whereas those most affected by the costs want immigrants kept out of the country. Views on illegal immigration range from using the military to guard the borders and the construction of a fence along the border to amnesty for illegal aliens already in the United States.

3.c.1. Enforcement of Borders
As illegal immigration has increased, so have government expenditures on border enforcement. Between 1986 and 2005, the U.S. Border Patrol more than tripled in size, and the hours spent patrolling increased more than eight times. In addition to the Border Patrol, the U.S. Customs Service and the Immigration and Naturalization Service have intensified their inspections, and the Drug Enforcement Agency (DEA) and the Bureau of Alcohol, Tobacco, and Firearms (BATF) have increased their presence. Border apprehensions increased from 200,000 in 1970 to more than 2 million in 2004, and yet the apprehension rate—apprehensions per total illegal crossings—declined because the number of crossings had increased more quickly. With the economic downturn in 2007–2009, the number of people illegally entering the United States declined.

What would be the effects of more intense border enforcement? In Figure 10, the supply curve would shift in to the supply without illegal immigrants curve as a result of the border enforcement. With fewer illegal immigrants, in order to hire people to work in restaurants and agricultural fields and other unskilled areas, firms would have to pay more. Suppose the wage is driven up to $15. The firms that before the increased enforcement had employed the illegal unskilled workers would now have to pay more; their costs of doing business would rise and profits would decline. Those businesses that survive after the wage hike would not produce as much, and fewer firms would be in business. The market supply of the products created by unskilled labor would decline, and the prices of these products would rise.

RECAP

1. Immigration has occurred throughout U.S. history. The highest annual rates of immigration were in the 1880s, the 1920s, and currently.

2. Immigration law began with the Chinese Exclusion Act of 1882; before that there were no restrictions. The current system has quotas assigned to countries—a certain number of people from each country can obtain visas.

3. The total number of legal immigrants each year is about 700,000. Most of them have family members who live in the United States. About 110,000 visas are given to people applying to work in the United States who don't have family members here. H1-B visas for highly skilled workers each year total about 65,000. Less than 45,000 visas are granted to unskilled workers.

4. The number of illegal immigrants entering each year has been growing since 1990; in 2004, the number of illegal immigrants exceeded the number of legal immigrants.

5. The impact of illegal immigrants on the labor market is to increase the supply of unskilled workers, which reduces the wage rate. The lower wage induces many native workers to leave the market—to refuse to work at the low wage. The lower wage is also a reduced cost for businesses employing illegal immigrants, and the lower cost means lower prices for the goods and services produced by the illegals.

6. Border enforcement, if effective, would reduce the number of unskilled workers and thereby drive up wages and the cost of business for firms that had been employing illegal immigrants. Consumers would be paying higher prices for the goods and services produced by the illegals.

4. Discrimination

What would you think if you found out that women earn only about 75 percent of what men earn, that African Americans earn only about 60 percent of what whites earn, or that there are pay differentials among Hispanics, Asians, African Americans, and whites? Would you think that this result was evidence of discrimination? Could the differentials be explained in any other way? We'll provide some answers in this section.

4.a. Definition of Discrimination

Is **discrimination** present when there is prejudice, or just when prejudice has harmful results? Consider a firm with two branch offices. One office employs only African Americans, and the other employs only whites. Workers in both branches are paid the same wages and have the same opportunities for advancement. Is discrimination occurring?

Is a firm that provides extensive training to employees discriminating when it prefers to hire young workers who are likely to stay with the firm long enough for it to recoup the training costs? Is a university economics department that has no African American faculty members guilty of discrimination if African American economists constitute only 1 percent of the profession? Would your answer change if the department could show that it advertised job openings widely and made the same offers to African Americans and whites? Clearly, discrimination is a difficult subject to define and measure.

From an economist's viewpoint, a worker's value in the labor market depends on the factors affecting the marginal revenue product. When a factor that is unrelated to marginal revenue product acquires a positive or negative value in the labor market, discrimination is occurring. In Figure 11, if D_m is the demand for males and D_f is the

8 Are discrimination and freely functioning markets compatible?

discrimination
Prejudice that occurs when factors unrelated to marginal revenue product affect the wages or jobs that are obtained.

© froxx/Shutterstock.com

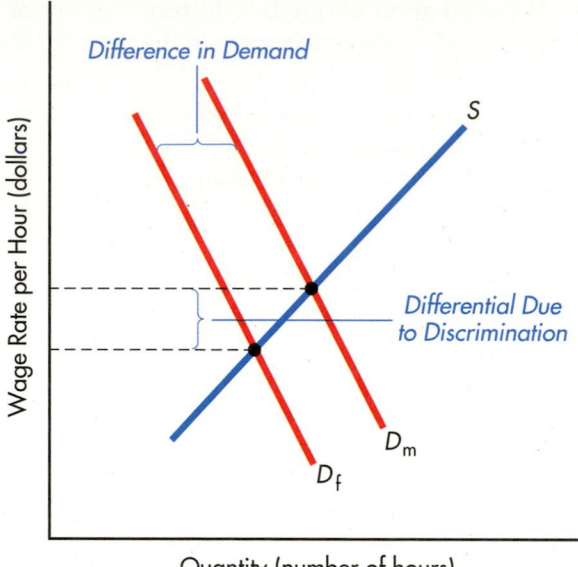

FIGURE 11   Discrimination

The curve D_m is the demand for males, and D_f is the demand for females. The two groups of workers are identical except in gender. The greater demand and the higher wage rate for males, even though males and females are equally productive, are due to discrimination.

demand for females, and if males and females have identical marginal revenue products, then the resulting wage differences can be attributed to discrimination. Race, gender, age, physical handicaps, religion, sexual preference, and ethnic heritage are factors that can take on positive or negative values in the labor market and yet are unrelated to marginal revenue products.

4.b. Theories of Discrimination

Wage differentials based on race or gender pose a theoretical problem for economists because the labor market model attributes differences in wages to demand and supply differences that depend on productivity and the labor-leisure trade-off. How can economists account for different pay scales for men and women, or for one race versus another, in the absence of differences in marginal productivity between sexes or races? They identify discrimination as the cause of the differences, even though they find discrimination difficult to rationalize because it is costly to those who discriminate.

In the freely functioning labor market, there is a profit to be made from *not* discriminating; therefore, discrimination should not exist. But because discrimination *does* exist, economists have attempted to find plausible explanations for it. They have identified two sources of labor market discrimination. The first is *personal prejudice*: Employers, fellow employees, or customers dislike associating with workers of a given race or sex. The second is *statistical discrimination*: Employers project certain perceived group characteristics onto individuals. Economists tend to argue that personal prejudice is not consistent with a market economy but have acknowledged that statistical discrimination can coexist with a market economy.

4.b.1. Personal Prejudice
Certain groups in a society could be precluded from higher-paying jobs or from jobs that provide valuable human capital by personal prejudice on the part of employers, fellow workers, or customers.

Employer Prejudice If two workers have identical marginal revenue products and one worker is less expensive than the other, firms will want to hire the lower cost worker. If they do otherwise, profits will be lower than they need to be. Suppose white males and others are identically productive, but managers prefer white males. Then white males will be more expensive than women and minorities, and hiring white males will lower profits.

Under what conditions will lower profits as a result of personal prejudice be acceptable? Perhaps a monopoly firm can forgo some of its monopoly profit in order to satisfy the manager's personal prejudices, or perhaps firms that do not maximize profits can indulge in personal preferences. However, for profit-maximizing firms selling their goods in the market structures of perfect competition, monopolistic competition, or oligopoly, personal prejudice will mean a loss of profit unless all rivals also discriminate. Could firms form a cartel to discriminate? Recall from the discussion of oligopoly that cartels do not last long—there is an incentive to cheat—unless an entity like the government sanctions and enforces the cartel.

In the United States, well-meaning legislation intended to protect women actually created a situation in which women were denied access to training and education and thus were not able to gain the human capital necessary to compete for highly skilled, high-paying jobs. Until the 1960s, women were barred from jobs by legislation that attempted to protect them from heavy labor or injury. In reality, this legislation precluded women from obtaining certain kinds of human capital. Without this human capital, a generation or more of women were unable to obtain many high-paying jobs.

Worker Prejudice Workers may not want to associate with other workers of different races or sexes. White males may resist taking orders from females or sharing responsibility with a member of a minority group. White male workers who have these discriminatory preferences will tend to quit employers who employ women or minorities on a nondiscriminatory basis.

The worker prejudice explanation of discrimination assumes that white males are willing to accept lower-paying positions in order to avoid working with anyone other than a white male. Such discrimination is costly to those who discriminate.

Consumer Prejudice Customers may prefer to be served by white males in some situations and by minorities or women in others. If their preferences for white males extend to high-paying jobs such as physicians and lawyers, and their preferences for women and minorities are confined to lower-paying jobs like maids, nurses, and flight attendants, then women and minorities will be forced into occupations that work to their disadvantage.

This explanation of discrimination assumes that consumers are willing to pay higher prices in order to be served by a person of a specific race or gender. In certain circumstances and during certain periods of time, this may be true; but over wide geographic areas or across different nations and over long periods of time, consumer prejudice does not appear to be a very likely explanation of discrimination.

Be sure you recognize that economists are not saying that discrimination based on personal prejudice never occurs. They are saying that when it does occur, it costs the person doing the discriminating.

4.b.2. Statistical Discrimination
Discrimination that is not related to personal prejudices can occur because of a lack of information. Employers must try to predict the potential productivity of job applicants, but rarely do they know what a worker's actual productivity will be. Often, the only information that is available when they hire

> *Discrimination might occur if employers attempt to hire only certain kinds of workers, employees attempt to work only with certain kinds of coworkers, or customers attempt to purchase goods and services only from certain kinds of workers. Discrimination is costly in that either less productive employees are used or more expensive but not more productive employees are used.*

someone is information that may be imperfectly related to productivity in general and may not apply to a particular person at all. Reliance on indicators of productivity such as education, experience, age, and test scores may keep some very good people from getting a job and may result in the hiring of some unproductive people. This is called **statistical discrimination**.

statistical discrimination
Discrimination that results when an indicator of group performance is incorrectly applied to an individual member of the group.

Suppose two types of workers apply for a word-processing job: those who can process 80 words per minute and those who can process only 40 words per minute. The problem is that these actual productivities are unknown to the employer. The employer can observe only the results of a five-minute word-processing test that is given to all applicants. How can the employer decide who is lucky or unlucky on the test and who can actually process 80 words per minute? Suppose the employer discovers that applicants from a particular vocational college, the DeVat School, are taught to perform well on preemployment tests, but that their overall performance as employees is the same as that of the rest of the applicants—some do well and some do not. The employer might decide to reject all applicants from DeVat because the good and bad ones can't be differentiated. Is the employer discriminating against DeVat? The answer is yes. The employer is using statistical discrimination.

Let's extend this example to gender.

4.c. Occupational Segregation

crowding
Forcing members of a group into certain kinds of occupations.

Statistical discrimination and imperfect information can lead to **crowding**—forcing women and members of minority groups into occupations where they are unable to obtain the human capital necessary to compete for high-paying jobs. Today, even in the United States and other industrialized nations, some occupations are considered women's jobs and other occupations are considered men's jobs. This separation of jobs by sex is called **occupational segregation**.

occupational segregation
The separation of jobs by sex.

One reason for occupational segregation is differences in the human capital acquired by males and females. Much of the human capital portion of the discrepancy between men and women is due to childbearing. Data suggest that marriage and children handicap women's efforts to earn as much as men. Many women leave the labor market during pregnancy, at childbirth, or when their children are young. These child-related interruptions are damaging to subsequent earnings because three out of four births occur to women before the age of thirty, the period in which men are gaining the training and experience that lead to higher earnings later in life. Second, even when mothers stay in the labor force, responsibility for children frequently constrains their choice of job: They accept lower wages in exchange for shorter or more flexible hours, a location near home, limited out-of-town travel, and the like. Third, women have a disproportionate responsibility for child care and often have to make sacrifices that men do not have to make. For instance, when a couple has a young child, the woman is more likely than the man to be absent from work, even when the man and woman have equal levels of education and wages.

Perhaps most important of all, because most female children are expected to become mothers, they have been less likely than male children to acquire marketable human capital while in school. In the past, this difference was reflected in the choice of a curriculum in primary and secondary schools, in a college major, and in the reluctance of females to pursue graduate school training or to undergo the long hours and other rigors characteristic of apprenticeships in medicine, law, business, and other financially rewarding occupations. Females were channeled into languages, typing, and home economics, while males were channeled into mechanical drawing, shop, chemistry, and physics. This situation is changing, but the remnants of the past continue to influence the market.

ECONOMIC INSIGHT

Pay and Performance

In 2010, Tiger Woods earned over $100 million. Although he was the highest-paid athlete that year, most professional athletes earn pretty good incomes; the 10 highest-paid athletes earned more than $15 million each. This seems small compared to the income of some celebrities: Oprah Winfrey pulled in $275 million; and many others exceeded $90 million. Why do these people make so much money? One explanation is called the superstar effect.

If you own a firm and an employee generates a huge income for you, you'd be willing to pay that employee a high salary. Similarly, if an athlete is bringing in fans or a performer is increasing the numbers of viewers, the owners of the firm that employs that person will willingly pay him or her a high salary. So athletes, celebrities, and TV performers are paid a lot because they make their employers lots of money. Yet some athletes make a lot more money than other athletes, and a few celebrities make a lot more money than others, even though their appeal to the public is not much different. The reason is that the public has limited time to devote to watching sports or television shows. As a result, they watch the best, even if the best is only slightly better than others.

Sometimes small differences in ability translate into huge differences in compensation. The playing ability of the top tennis players or golfers is not much better than the playing ability of the players ranked between 40 and 50. Nonetheless, the differences in compensation and in the demand for the top performers are incredibly large. If you watch golf tournaments, you will notice that huge throngs surround Tiger Woods, while lesser-known players play the game without the attention of adoring fans. In a similar manner, people choosing among television shows must select one over others, so if Oprah Winfrey is just slightly preferred to other personalities, she will draw thousands more viewers than a competing personality. The demand for the superstars is huge relative to the demand for the lesser-ranked players or personalities.

This effect may also explain big pay differences among attorneys, physicians, and even economists. Two lawyers of relatively equal ability may earn significantly different fees, or two economic consultants with apparently similar abilities may earn vastly different consulting fees. Consider the economist who offers advice to lawyers in cases involving firm behavior. The outcome of a lawsuit filed against a firm might involve billions of dollars. Even if the differences between economists are very small, if hiring the better economist means a win, then the better economist will receive huge compensation relative to the lesser economist. A $40 billion victory means that the value of the better economist is significantly greater than the value of the lesser economist.

If new female entrants into the labor force have human capital equal to the human capital of new male entrants and thus greater than the human capital of females who are already in the labor force, then the average human capital and wages of females will rise. But even though the wage gap between males and females is decreasing, a gap will continue to exist because the average male in the labor force has more marketable human capital than the average female. The average rate of pay of males will continue to exceed that of females.

Since the late 1970s, about half of all law school classes and about one-half of medical school classes have been female. Nonetheless, mostly females major in languages, literature, education, and home economics, while mostly males major in physics, mathematics, chemistry, and engineering.

4.d. Wage Differentials and Government Policies

Not until the 1960s did wage disparities and employment practices become a major public policy issue in the United States. In 1963, the Equal Pay Act outlawed separate pay scales for men and women performing similar jobs, and Title VII of the 1964 Civil Rights Act prohibited all forms of discrimination in employment.

Prior to the 1960s, sex discrimination was officially sanctioned by so-called protective labor laws, which limited the total hours that women were allowed to work and prohibited them from working at night, lifting heavy objects, and working during pregnancy. The argument was that women were not strong enough to do certain jobs. Interestingly, if you look at the supporters of these laws, they were the people who worked in the jobs that women were being kept out of. With the Civil Rights Act of 1964, it became unlawful for any employer to discriminate on the basis of race, color, religion, sex, or national origin. Unions also were forbidden from excluding anyone on the basis of those five categories. Historically, it had been very difficult for members of racial minorities to obtain admission into unions representing workers in the skilled trades. This exclusion prevented members of racial minorities from obtaining the human capital necessary to compete for higher-paying jobs.

The Civil Rights Act applied only to actions after its effective date, July 1, 1965. It also permitted exceptions in cases where religion, sex, or national origin is a bona fide occupational qualification reasonably necessary to the normal operation of a business. This qualification might apply to certain jobs in religious organizations, for example. In addition, the act permits an employer to differentiate wages and other employment conditions on the basis of a bona fide seniority system, provided that such differences are not the result of an intention to discriminate. As a result of these exceptions, the Civil Rights Act has had neither as large nor as quick an impact on wage and job differentials as many had anticipated. It has, however, led to a clearer definition of discrimination.

disparate treatment
Different treatment of individuals because of their race, sex, color, religion, or national origin.

Two standards, or tests, of discrimination have evolved from court cases: disparate treatment and disparate impact. **Disparate treatment** means treating individuals differently because of their race, sex, color, religion, or national origin. The difficulty created by this standard is that personnel policies that appear to be neutral because they ignore race, gender, and so on may nevertheless continue the effects of past discrimination. For instance, a seniority system that fires first the last person hired will protect those who were historically favored in hiring and training practices. Similarly, a practice of hiring by word of mouth will perpetuate past discrimination if current employees are primarily of one race or sex.

disparate impact
An impact that differs according to race, sex, color, religion, or national origin, regardless of the motivation.

This concern with perpetuating past discrimination led to the second standard, **disparate impact**. Under this standard, it is the result of different treatment, not the motivation, that matters. Thus, statistical discrimination is illegal under the impact standard even though it is not illegal under the treatment standard.

4.d.1. Comparable Worth

comparable worth
The idea that pay ought to be determined by job characteristics rather than by supply and demand, and that people in jobs with comparable requirements should receive comparable wages.

The persistent wage gap between men and women in particular, but also between white males and minorities, has prompted well-meaning reformers to seek a new remedy for eliminating the gap—laws requiring companies to offer equal pay for jobs of comparable worth. **Comparable worth** is a catchword for the idea that pay ought to be determined by job characteristics rather than by supply and demand, and that people in jobs with comparable requirements should receive comparable wages.

To identify jobs of comparable worth, employers would be required to evaluate all of the different jobs in their firms, answering questions such as these: What level of formal education is needed? How much training is necessary? Is previous experience needed? What skills are required? How much supervision is required? Is the work dangerous? Are working conditions unpleasant? By assigning point values to the answers, employers could create job classifications based on job characteristics and could pay comparable wages for jobs with comparable "scores." A firm employing both secretaries and steelworkers, for example, would determine the wages for these jobs by assessing job characteristics. If the assessment showed that secretaries' work was comparable to that of steelworkers, then the firm would pay secretaries and steelworkers comparable wages.

Proponents of comparable worth claim that market-determined wages are inappropriate because, as a result of statistical discrimination, team production, and personal prejudice, the market is unable to assess marginal products. They argue that mandating a comparable worth system would minimize wage differentials resulting from statistical discrimination and occupational segregation, and they charge that a freely functioning market will continue to misallocate pay.

Opponents of comparable worth argue that interfering with the functioning of the labor market will lead to shortages in some occupations and excess supplies in others. For instance, Figure 12 shows two markets for university professors, a market for computer science professors and a market for English professors. The supply and demand conditions in the two markets determine a wage for English professors that is less than the wage for computer science professors. The wage differential exists even though professors in both disciplines are required to have a PhD and have essentially the same responsibilities.

Advocates of comparable worth would say that the two groups of professors should earn the same wage, the wage of the computer science professors, W_{cs}. But at this wage there would be a surplus of English professors, $QE_2 - QE_1$. The higher wage would cause the university to reduce the number of English professors it employs, from QE to QE_1. The net effect of comparable worth would be to reduce the number of English professors employed, but to increase the wages of those who were employed. The policy would also have a detrimental effect in the future. The wage would send an incorrect signal to current college students. It would tell them to remain in English instead of forgoing English for computer science.

FIGURE 12 Comparable Worth

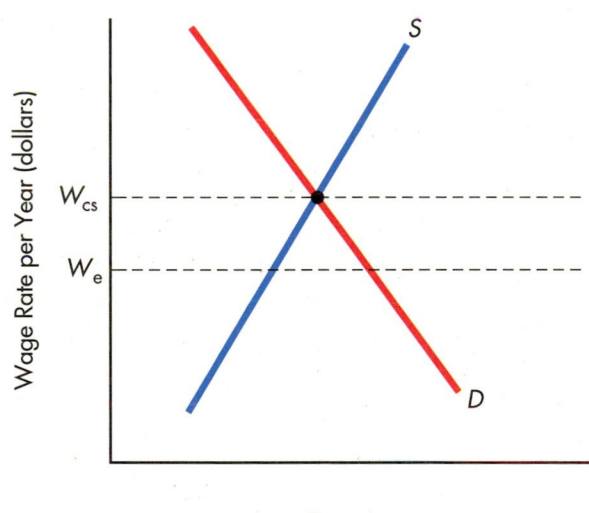

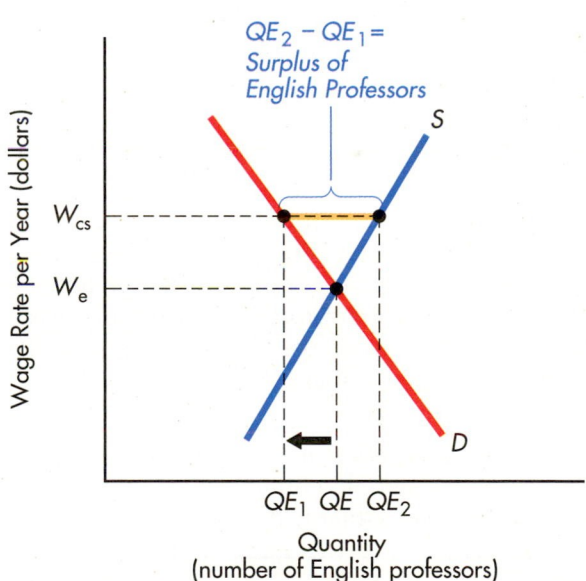

(a) Market for Computer Science Professors

(b) Market for English Professors

Two markets are shown, a market for computer science professors and a market for English professors. Demand and supply conditions determine that the wages for computer science professors are higher than the wages for English professors. Proponents of comparable worth might argue that the wages of both groups of professors should be equal to the higher wages of computer science professors, since the requirements and responsibilities of the two jobs are virtually identical. However, the effect of imposing a higher wage in the market for English professors, W_{cs}, is to create a surplus of English professors, $QE_2 - QE_1$. In addition, the higher wage sends the signal to current college students that majoring in English will generate the same expected income as majoring in computer science. Students who might have studied computer science turn to English. In the future, an excess of English professors remains and even grows, while the number of computer science professors shrinks.

Comparable worth has not fared well in U.S. courtrooms. On the whole, U.S. federal courts have not accepted the notion that unequal pay for comparable jobs violates existing employment discrimination law. Perhaps not surprisingly, therefore, the concept has made little headway in the private sector. It has had greater success in the public sector at the local and state levels. In Colorado Springs, San Jose, and Los Angeles, and in Iowa, Michigan, New York, and Minnesota, pay adjustments have been made on the basis of comparable worth. More than two-thirds of the state governments have begun studies to determine whether the compensation of state workers reflects the worth of their jobs. Why has comparable worth had more success in the government sector? State governments suffer from the problem of team production, and if personal prejudice is to occur, it is more likely to occur in nonprofit organizations such as government, where firms do not employ to the profit-maximizing point where $MFC = MRP$. Thus, it is in the state, local, and federal governments that comparable worth can be an effective policy. Comparable worth was adopted nationwide in Australia in the early 1970s, and aspects of it have arisen in parts of the United Kingdom.

RECAP

1. Discrimination occurs when factors unrelated to marginal physical product acquire a positive or negative value in the labor market.

2. Earnings disparities may exist for a number of reasons, including personal prejudice, statistical discrimination, and human capital differentials. Human capital differentials may exist because of occupational choice, statistical discrimination, or unequal opportunities to acquire human capital.

3. There are two general classes of discrimination theories: prejudice theory and statistical theory. Prejudice theory claims that employers, workers, and consumers express their personal prejudices by, respectively, earning lower profits, accepting lower wages, and paying higher prices. Statistical discrimination theory asserts that firms have imperfect information and must rely on general indicators of marginal physical product when they pay wages and hire people, and that reliance on these general indicators may create a pattern of discrimination.

4. Occupational segregation is the separation of jobs by sex. Some jobs are filled primarily by women, and other jobs are filled primarily by men.

5. The first national antidiscrimination law was the Civil Rights Act of 1964. It forbade firms from discriminating on the basis of sex, race, color, religion, or national origin.

6. Two tests of discrimination have evolved from court cases. According to the disparate treatment standard, it is illegal to intentionally treat individuals differently because of their race, sex, color, religion, or national origin. According to the disparate impact standard, it is the result, not the intention, of actions that is illegal.

7. Comparable worth is the idea that jobs should be evaluated on the basis of a number of characteristics, and that all jobs receiving the same evaluation should receive the same pay, regardless of demand and supply conditions. Proponents argue that comparable worth is a solution to a market failure problem. Opponents argue that it will create surpluses and shortages in labor markets.

SUMMARY

1. **Are people willing to work more hours for higher wages?**

   - The individual labor supply curve is backward bending because at some high wage, people choose to enjoy more leisure rather than to earn additional income. §1.a

2. **What are compensating wage differentials?**

   - Equilibrium in the labor market defines the wage and quantity of hours worked. If all workers and all jobs were identical, then one wage would prevail. However, because jobs and workers differ, there are different wages. §1.c

- A compensating wage differential exists in situations where a higher wage is determined in one labor market than in another because of differences in job characteristics. *§2.a*

- Human capital is the training, education, and skills that people acquire. Human capital increases productivity. Because acquiring human capital takes time and money, the necessity of obtaining human capital for some jobs reduces the supply of labor to those jobs. *§2.b*

3. What is the impact of technological change on workers?

- Technological changes occurring in information and knowledge transmission and development increases the demand for skilled workers and reduces that for unskilled workers. *§2.b.4*

4. What is offshoring?

- The ability to transmit information quickly almost anywhere in the world enables firms to seek out the least costly resources wherever they are located, and thus to have many jobs performed at a lower price in a less developed country, with the output being transmitted back to the firm in a developed country. This is called offshoring. *§2.b.4*

- The ability to use offshoring to produce goods and services at lower prices enables firms to reduce prices on these goods and services. *§2.b.4*

5. What is the impact of a minimum wage law on unskilled labor?

- The minimum wage in the United States is currently more than $7 per hour. States and individual cities can set a higher wage. *§2.c*

- The objective of a minimum wage law is to ensure that the poor are able to earn a decent living. *§2.c*

- The effect of a minimum wage is to create a labor surplus because it reduces the quantity of jobs offered and increases the number of people who want a job. A minimum wage has an effect only if it is higher than the equilibrium wage, thereby acting as a wage floor. *§2.c*

- Should a labor market be monopsonistic, a minimum wage could increase employment because it reduces the marginal cost of hiring another worker. *§2.c*

6. What is the effect of income taxes on workers?

- A simple rule of thumb is that when you tax something you get less of it. When you tax work, you get less of it. *§2.d*

- Income taxes can be progressive, proportional, or regressive. A progressive income tax is one where the tax rate increases as income increases; a regressive income tax is the opposite of a progressive income tax; and a proportional income tax is one where the tax rate is constant as income rises. *§2.d*

- A flat tax is a proportional tax on income except that the lower income levels are exempted from paying the tax. *§2.d*

- A consumption tax is a tax imposed on consumption rather than income. *§2.d*

7. What is the effect of illegal immigration on the economy?

- It is primarily those without skills who immigrate illegally. U.S. immigration policy allows only about 65,000 skilled workers to obtain visas each year. Only about 45,000 unskilled workers can obtain legal entry. All other workers must enter the United States illegally. *§3.b.1*

- An increase in unskilled labor causes the wage rate of unskilled labor to decline. This reduces the willingness to work for many native workers who would have earned more had there been no illegal immigration. *§3.b.1*

- The lower costs that result from illegal immigration carry over into the prices of the goods and services produced by illegal immigrants. Without illegal immigration, prices of agricultural products, poultry, meat, textiles, and home services would be as much as 25 percent higher. *§3.b.1*

8. Are discrimination and freely functioning markets compatible?

- Earnings disparities may result from discrimination, occupational choice, human capital differences, educational opportunity differences, age, and immigration. *§4.a, 4.c*

- Discrimination occurs when some factor that is not related to marginal revenue product affects the wage rate someone receives. *§4.a*

- There are two general types of discrimination—personal prejudice and statistical discrimination. *§4.b*

- Personal prejudice is costly to those who demonstrate the prejudice and should not last in a market economy. For it to last, some restrictions on the functioning of markets must exist. §4.b.1

- Statistical discrimination is the result of imperfect information and can occur as long as information is imperfect. §4.b.2

- Occupational segregation exists when some jobs are held mainly by one group in society and other jobs are held by other groups. A great deal of occupational segregation exists between males and females in the United States. §4.c

KEY TERMS

backward-bending labor
 supply curve, 641
comparable worth, 664
compensating wage
 differentials, 644

crowding, 662
discrimination, 659
disparate impact, 664
disparate treatment, 664
human capital, 647

occupational segregation, 662
offshoring, 650
outsourcing, 650
statistical discrimination, 662

EXERCISES

1. What could account for a backward-bending labor supply curve?

2. What is human capital? Is a college degree considered to be human capital?

3. Define equilibrium in the labor market. Illustrate equilibrium on a graph. Illustrate the situation in which there are two types of labor, skilled and unskilled.

4. Describe how people choose a major in college. If someone majors in English literature knowing that the starting salary for English literature graduates is much lower than the starting salary for accountants, is the English literature major irrational?

5. What is the difference between legal and illegal immigration?

6. What is the effect of immigration laws restricting the number of immigrants?

7. Explain what is meant by discrimination, and explain the difference between personal prejudice and statistical discrimination.

8. How does technological change benefit firms? Does it benefit workers?

9. Explain what outsourcing is. Explain what offshoring is. Do you believe that unemployment is being created by CEOs who send jobs to less-developed nations such as India and China?

10. Explain why occupational segregation by sex might occur. Can you imagine a society in which you would not expect to find occupational segregation by sex? Explain. Would you expect to find occupational segregation by race in most societies?

11. Why are women's wages only 60 to 80 percent of men's wages, and why has this situation existed for several decades? Now that women are entering college and professional schools in increasing numbers, why doesn't the wage differential disappear?

12. Why do economists say that discrimination is inherently inefficient and therefore will not occur in general?

13. Demonstrate, using two labor markets, what is meant by comparable worth. What problems are created by comparable worth? Under what conditions might comparable worth make economic sense? Explain.

14. Consider a working woman or man who has young children or elderly relatives to take care of. Explain in terms of the labor supply curve how this person's decision to work is affected by the presence of dependents. What happens to the opportunity cost of working? How is the labor supply curve affected?

15. Demonstrate how a minimum wage affects the unskilled labor market. Is the labor market perfectly competitive? Can you find any examples of monopsonistic hiring? What would a minimum wage do in a monopsonistic market?

16. If a progressive income tax discourages additional work as income rises, what would a regressive tax do?

17. Use the indifference curves and income constraints discussed in the Economic Insights to illustrate the effect on work when income taxes are reduced.

You can find further practice tests in the Online Quiz at **www.cengage.com/economics/boyes**.

OBESE WORKERS GETTING SMALLER PAY; STANFORD STUDY TIES LOWER WAGES TO HIGHER HEALTH CARE COSTS

San Francisco Chronicle, May 12, 2005

Employers may be compensating for the expected higher health costs of obese workers by giving them slimmer paychecks, according to a just released study.

Previous studies have shown that severely overweight workers get paid less than other employees. But in the latest look at the issue, researchers at Stanford University have found that the pay gap exists only in workplaces with employer-paid health insurance.

"We view this as evidence that the higher expected expense of obese people is being passed along in the form of lower wages," said study coauthor Kate Bundorf, assistant professor of health research and policy at Stanford.

The study was published online as a working paper on the Web site of the National Bureau of Economic Research, a nonprofit Massachusetts research organization.

Nearly 59 million Americans are classified as obese. Medical spending attributed to excess weight was estimated at about $92.6 billion in 2002 dollars, according to research published in 2003. That study found yearly medical expenses are $732 higher on average for obese people than for people of normal weight.

Many assume that normal-weight workers are sharing the medical costs of such obesity-related conditions as diabetes and hypertension, Bundorf said. Her research suggests that obese workers are paying these costs themselves by collecting smaller paychecks.

According to the Stanford survey, obese people with health coverage were paid an adjusted average of $1.20 less per hour than non-obese workers during the study period of 1989 through 1998, with the amount rising incrementally to $2.58 in 1998. That suggests the gap widened as workers aged, the authors said.

The study used older data from a Bureau of Labor Statistics youth survey because it contained detailed information about employees' height, weight and health, as well as their jobs, wages and education.

Researchers compared hourly wages of obese and non-obese workers, factoring in experience and job type. They found no significant difference when comparing the wages, retirement and life insurance benefits of obese and non-obese workers whose employers did not provide health insurance. But there was a discrepancy among workers whose employers offered health insurance.

The study did not address whether employers intentionally adjusted wages for obese workers to account for health costs.

San Francisco resident Marilyn Wann, a board member of the National Association to Advance Fat Acceptance, said the study shows that obese people face bias on the job.

"For anyone to act like there isn't that discrimination, which is pervasive and unchallenged … is completely ridiculous," Wann said.

But Paul Fronstin of the Employee Benefit Research Institute in Washington said he doubts that employers would risk litigation by deliberately paying obese workers less.

"They are very hesitant about any type of discrimination, be it weight, age or racial discrimination," he said.

An increasing number of employers are battling fat in the workplace by offering programs to promote weight loss, noted Lisa Horn with the Society for Human Resource Management in Alexandria, Va.

Compensating wage differentials refers to the differences in pay that result from differences in the characteristics of jobs or job conditions. For instance, an identical person working at a risky job would earn more than one working at a less risky job. The reason is that the worker has to be compensated for taking the risk. As shown in the first figure, it is the marginal factor cost (*MFC*) that is higher.

The other factor that enters into wage differentials is productivity. People are paid according to their contribution to the firm's profits, the marginal revenue product (*MRP*). If a person has skills that enable him or her to be more productive, then he or she will be paid more, as shown in the second figure.

So how could one's weight be a factor in pay? What does the finding that *the pay gap exists only in workplaces with employer-paid health insurance* have to do with pay differentials? It has to do with the marginal factor cost. In addition to salaries, many firms also pay for workers' health insurance, retirement benefits, disability insurance, and other benefits. Firms are choosing to allocate their per employee expenditure for wages and benefits so that total pay per individual is the same. Suppose that the salary for a normal-weight person is $10 per hour and benefits are $9 per hour, including $4 for health insurance, for a total expenditure of $19 per hour. To maintain the same $19 total expenditure per employee and yet pay $5 for health insurance, the firm would have to pay $9 salary and $10 benefits.

Yet Marilyn Wann, a board member of the National Association to Advance Fat Acceptance, said that the study shows that obese people face bias on the job. She stated, "For anyone to act like there isn't that discrimination, which is pervasive and unchallenged ... is completely ridiculous." Is this discrimination?

Discrimination occurs when marginal revenue product is the same and pay is not for any given marginal factor cost. Pay is not different here if total pay includes salary and benefits and the firm has merely shifted categories and not changed the total. However, the study also said that the pay differential exceeds the marginal cost of insuring the obese individual. If that is the case and the *MRP* is the same, we could say that there does appear to be discrimination against obese people. On the other hand, if it is found that the *MRP* differs or if there are other costs that should be included in the *MFC*, then the differential may be merely a compensating wage differential. For instance, perhaps obese people have to spend more time away from the job, so that the *MRP* is different. Or perhaps the firm must provide special equipment or services for the obese, so that the *MFC* is higher. To know the answer, more information is required.

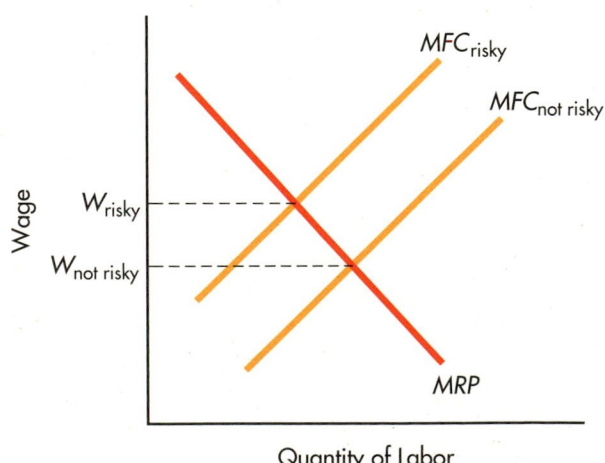

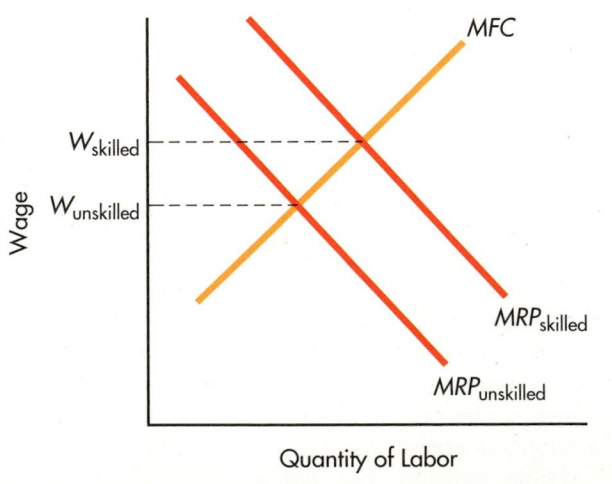

CHAPTER 30

Capital Markets

© MACIEJ FROLOW/GETTY IMAGES, INC

© LOSEVSKY PAVEL/SHUTTERSTOCK.COM; LOGO: © FROXX/SHUTTERSTOCK.COM

The three broad categories of resources are land, labor, and capital. Capital refers to the equipment, machinery, structures, and buildings necessary to produce goods and services. How do businesses acquire capital, and how much do they acquire? In this chapter, we examine the decision to acquire capital and the role that financial capital plays in this decision.

 FUNDAMENTAL QUESTIONS

1 What is the capital market?

2 What is the impact of technological change on the capital market?

3 What are stocks? How are stocks bought and sold?

4 What does a stock index represent?

5 What causes stock prices to rise and fall?

6 What causes bond prices to rise and fall?

7 What are bubbles and panics?

1. The Capital Market

1 What is the capital market?

A firm will hire another worker when the marginal revenue product of that additional worker exceeds the marginal factor cost of the worker. In exactly the same way, a firm will decide to rent more building space or more equipment if the marginal revenue product of the additional capital exceeds its marginal factor cost. If a firm is going to own the building or the equipment, it is planning on using that capital for a few years and thus can think of it as renting it to itself. It is just like the case when people purchase a house; they are using the house for a few years instead of renting, so it is as if they were renting to themselves.

1.a. The Demand for Capital

The demand for capital is shown in Figure 1(a) as a downward-sloping curve with the quantity of capital measured on the horizontal axis and the price of capital measured on the vertical axis. Just as the price of labor is a rental price, the price of capital is also a rental price. An increase in the price of capital, say from $80,000 to $100,000 per machine in Figure 1(a), decreases the quantity of capital demanded, from 350,000 to 300,000 machines. For instance, a farmer will postpone getting a new tractor if the price increases, or an airline will postpone purchasing a new airplane when the price of airplanes increases.

2 What is the impact of technological change on the capital market?

The demand curve for capital shifts when one of the nonprice determinants of demand changes. Perhaps the most important nonprice determinant of demand for capital is the interest rate. A firm has a choice of where to put its money. If it rents capital,

---

FIGURE 1 The Market Demand for Capital

(a) Change in Quantity Demanded

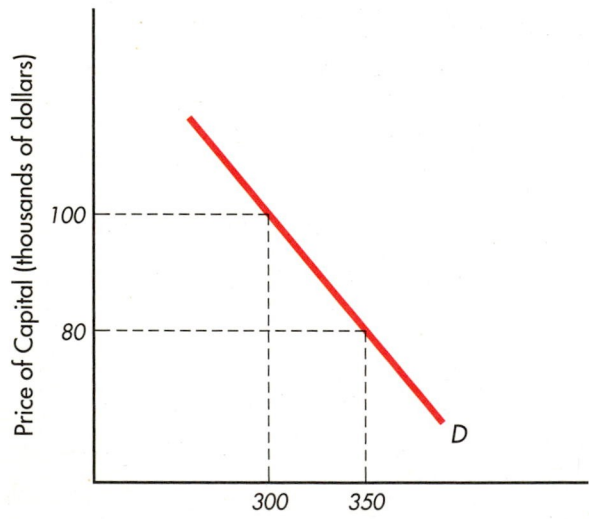

(b) Change in Demand

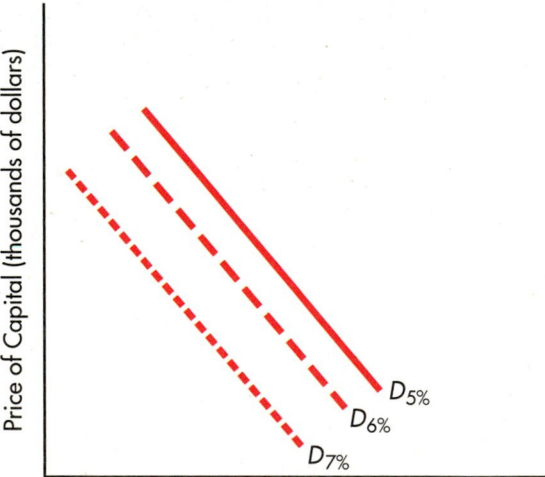

In Figure 1(a), the demand for capital is shown as a downward-sloping line, with the quantity of capital measured on the horizontal axis and the price of capital measured on the vertical axis. As the price of capital changes, say from $80,000 to $100,000 per unit of capital (per machine), the quantity of capital demanded changes, from 350,000 to 300,000 machines. In Figure 1(b), the relationship between the demand for capital and the interest rate is illustrated. As the rate of interest rises, the demand for capital declines—the demand curve shifts in. The interest rate associated with each demand curve is given as a subscript.

then it cannot deposit the money into an interest-earning account. So if the interest rate rises, the opportunity cost of renting capital rises, and less capital will be rented. Because this occurs at every rental price, the demand curve shifts when the interest rate changes. Each time the interest rate increases, from 5 to 6 to 7 percent, the demand curve for capital shifts in, as shown in Figure 1(b) by the move from $D_{5\%}$ to $D_{6\%}$ to $D_{7\%}$.

The demand curve also shifts when any other determinant of demand changes. For instance, technological change will affect the demand for capital. Technological change is an increase in the amount that resources are able to produce, everything else the same. For instance, each generation of computers is faster and more powerful than previous generation. Many firms need the latest and most advanced technology to be able to compete, so when technological change occurs rapidly, firms demand more capital.

Expectations will also alter the demand for capital. A business that expects strong demand for its goods will want more capital, causing the demand curve for capital to shift out. Conversely, if a business expects increased regulations or taxes and reduced profits, it will not want more capital; in fact, it will want less capital, driving the demand curve for capital to shift in.

In sum, a change in the interest rate, a change in technology, a change in expectations, or a change in any other nonprice determinant of demand will change the demand for capital.

1.b. The Supply of Capital

The suppliers of capital are firms like John Deere, which supplies farm equipment; Boeing, which supplies airplanes; Dell, IBM, and Gateway, which supply computers; Intel and AMD, which supply computer chips; Lincoln Electric, which supplies arc welding equipment; and so on. The quantity of capital supplied by these firms depends on the price of the capital. As the price of capital rises, the quantity that producers are willing and able to offer rises, as shown in Figure 2 by the upward-sloping curve, S.

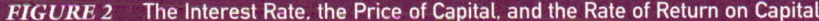

FIGURE 2 The Interest Rate, the Price of Capital, and the Rate of Return on Capital

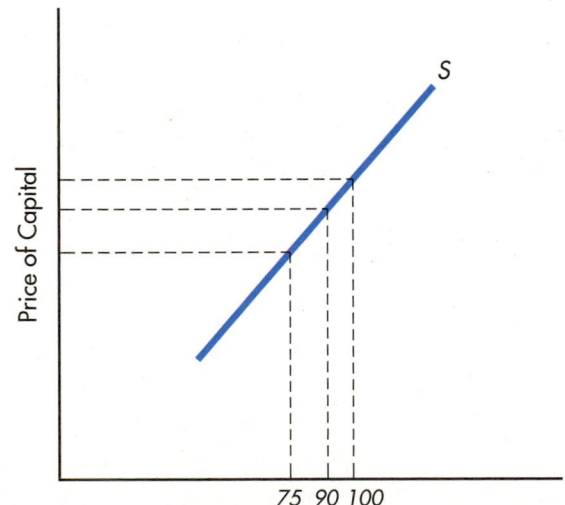

The supply of capital is an upward-sloping curve, indicating that the quantity of capital supplied rises as the price of capital rises, everything else the same. As the price of airplanes rises, the quantity of airplanes supplied by Boeing, Airbus, or the smaller firms rises.

FIGURE 3   The Interest Rate, the Price of Capital, and the Rate of Return on Capital

(a) Interest Rate and Rate of Return

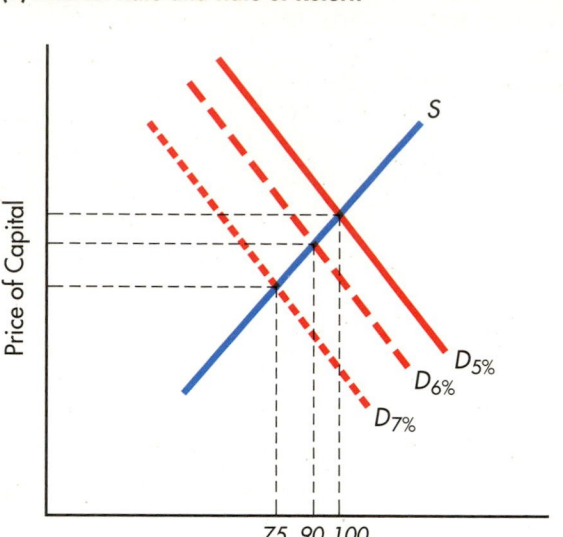

(b) Cost and Supply

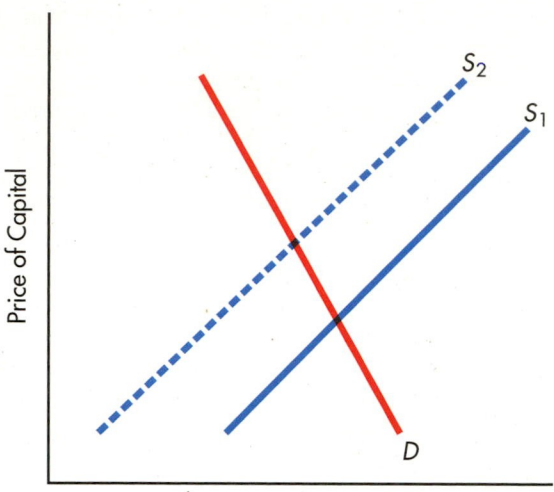

The demand for and the supply of capital determine both the price of capital and the quantity of capital produced and purchased. The rate of return on capital is the additional annual revenue generated by additional capital, divided by the purchase price of the capital. As shown in Figure 3(a), as the interest rate rises, the demand for capital declines (the demand curve shifts in), and the price of capital declines. As a result of the lower price, the rate of return rises. As shown in Figure 3(b), if the costs of supplying capital rise, everything else the same, the supply curve shifts in. This increases the price of capital and lowers the equilibrium quantity.

1.c. Equilibrium

The demand for and supply of capital determine the price of capital and the quantity supplied. Changes in demand or supply change the equilibrium price and quantity. For example, if the interest rate rises, the demand for capital decreases and the price of capital falls, as shown by the move from $D_{5\%}$ to $D_{6\%}$ to $D_{7\%}$ in Figure 3(a). Similarly, if the costs of supplying capital rise, the equilibrium price and quantity are affected. As an example, suppose that a law is enacted requiring all farm equipment to have costly safety equipment. The costs to John Deere rise and the quantity of farm equipment supplied decreases, everything else held constant. The supply curve shifts in, as illustrated in Figure 3(b) by the move from S_1 to S_2.

RECAP

1. The capital market is the market in which physical capital is acquired.

2. The demand for capital is represented by a downward-sloping curve, illustrating that the quantity of capital demanded rises as the price of capital falls.

3. The demand for capital shifts when the interest rate rises, when technological change occurs, when

expectations change, or in general when any non-price determinant of demand changes.

4. The supply of capital is represented by an upward-sloping curve, illustrating that the quantity of capital supplied rises as the rental price of capital rises.

5. The demand for and supply of capital determine the rental price of capital.

2. Equity

Stocks and bonds are called *financial capital* because they provide the funds with which capital can be purchased.

2.a. Stocks

Whether you say shares, equity, or stock doesn't matter; these terms all mean the same thing—ownership of a piece of a company. Technically, owning a share of stock means that you own a share of everything the firm owns—every item of furniture, every piece of equipment, every building. In actuality, you are entitled only to a share of the company's earnings; you can't walk into the company's headquarters and walk out with a chair. There are two main types of stock: common and preferred stock. When people talk about stocks in general, they are referring to common stock. Preferred shares usually guarantee a fixed annual payment, or **dividend**. Common stock may or may not provide such a payment; that choice is at the discretion of the company.

2.a.1. Stock Exchanges Stocks are bought and sold on stock exchanges.

The New York Stock Exchange (NYSE), founded in 1792, is located on Wall Street in Manhattan and is the largest stock exchange in the world. Until 2006, trading on the NYSE could occur only on the trading floor. Beginning in 2006, customers have been able to choose between the floor-based auction market and sub-second electronic trading. The NASDAQ is a virtual market—for example, there is no central location and no floor brokers. Trading takes place only through computers. Buyers and sellers submit orders electronically, and there are no specialists like there are on the NYSE.

The third largest exchange in the United States is the American Stock Exchange (AMEX). Almost all the firms listed on the AMEX are small firms.

In addition to the various U.S. stock exchanges, many other countries have stock exchanges. In fact, trading is taking place somewhere in the world 24 hours a day.

3 What are stocks? How are stocks bought and sold?

dividend
The amount paid to shareholders on each share of stock owned.

Stock markets exist in all capitalist countries. They are the mechanism through which ownership in companies is bought and sold. Most stock market results are printed each day in newspapers, magazines, or online. Here we see the heading for the Hong Kong stock market called the Hang Seng Index.

GLOBAL BUSINESS INSIGHT

ADRs, or American Depositary Receipts

Suppose you want to purchase the stock of a foreign company, one that is listed on the London Stock Exchange. You need to convert your dollars to pounds and then get a broker to purchase that stock for you. When you have the broker sell the stock, you have to pay whatever taxes are required in the United Kingdom and then convert the pounds back to dollars. Or suppose you run a Scottish firm that needs a large sum of money in order to enter Asian markets. You know that the United States provides more funds to businesses than any other country, so you want to sell stock in the United States. To do so, you would have to go through the process of meeting all U.S. requirements and then finding an exchange on which you could list your company, translating your currency to dollars, and converting all your accounting statements to dollars. In addition to these difficulties, certain countries have regulations limiting foreign ownership (e.g., China, South Korea, Taiwan, and India) or controls on the movement of financial capital that make owning stock in a company in these nations difficult for U.S. investors. In the past, these transactions were very difficult, which meant that few U.S. investors owned stock in foreign companies and few foreign businesses raised money in the United States. American Depositary Receipts (ADRs) allow easy access to non-U.S. stocks for U.S. investors.

An ADR is a stock that trades in the United States but represents a specified number of shares in a foreign corporation. ADRs are bought and sold on American markets just like regular stocks, and are issued or sponsored in the United States by a bank or brokerage. A U.S. bank purchases shares of a company, say Sainsbury's in England. The bank then issues ADRs representing ownership of the shares of Sainsbury's stock and sells them in the United States as a Sainsbury's ADR. Each ADR is backed by a specific number of the issuer's local shares; for instance, 1 Sainsbury's ADR = 1.5 Sainsbury's shares in the United Kingdom.

ADRs offer U.S. investors a convenient, easy-to-use avenue for owning international stocks. And for foreign companies, ADRs are an easy way to raise money from U.S. investors. Today, ADRs are used by approximately 2,200 non-U.S. issuers from more than 80 countries. Of the 2,200 ADRs, approximately 600 are listed on U.S. stock exchanges. The remainder are sold "over the counter." (A stock that is not traded on an exchange is said to trade over the counter.)

Figure 4 shows how trading begins each day and continuously moves west to London and then on to New York. Not only can you trade in different exchanges around the world, but trading for a stock listed on one exchange may occur "off hours." Although the NYSE might close at 4:00 p.m. Eastern Time, trading on some stocks may occur through computer-based exchanges throughout the night.

2.a.2. How to Read a Stock Table/Quote Most newspapers report stock prices. The reports look something like Figure 5 and include the columns listed here.

Columns 1 and 2: 52-week high and low. These are the highest and lowest prices at which the stock has traded over the previous 52 weeks (one year).

Column 3: Company name and type of stock. This column gives the name of the company. If there are no special symbols or letters following the name, the stock is common stock. Different symbols identify different classes of shares. For example, "pf" means that the shares are preferred stock.

Column 4: Ticker symbol. This is the unique alphabetic name that identifies the stock. If you are looking for stock quotes online, you use the ticker symbol.

Column 5: Dividend per share. This indicates the annual dividend payment per share. If this space is blank, the company does not currently pay dividends.

FIGURE 4   Stock Exchanges Around the World

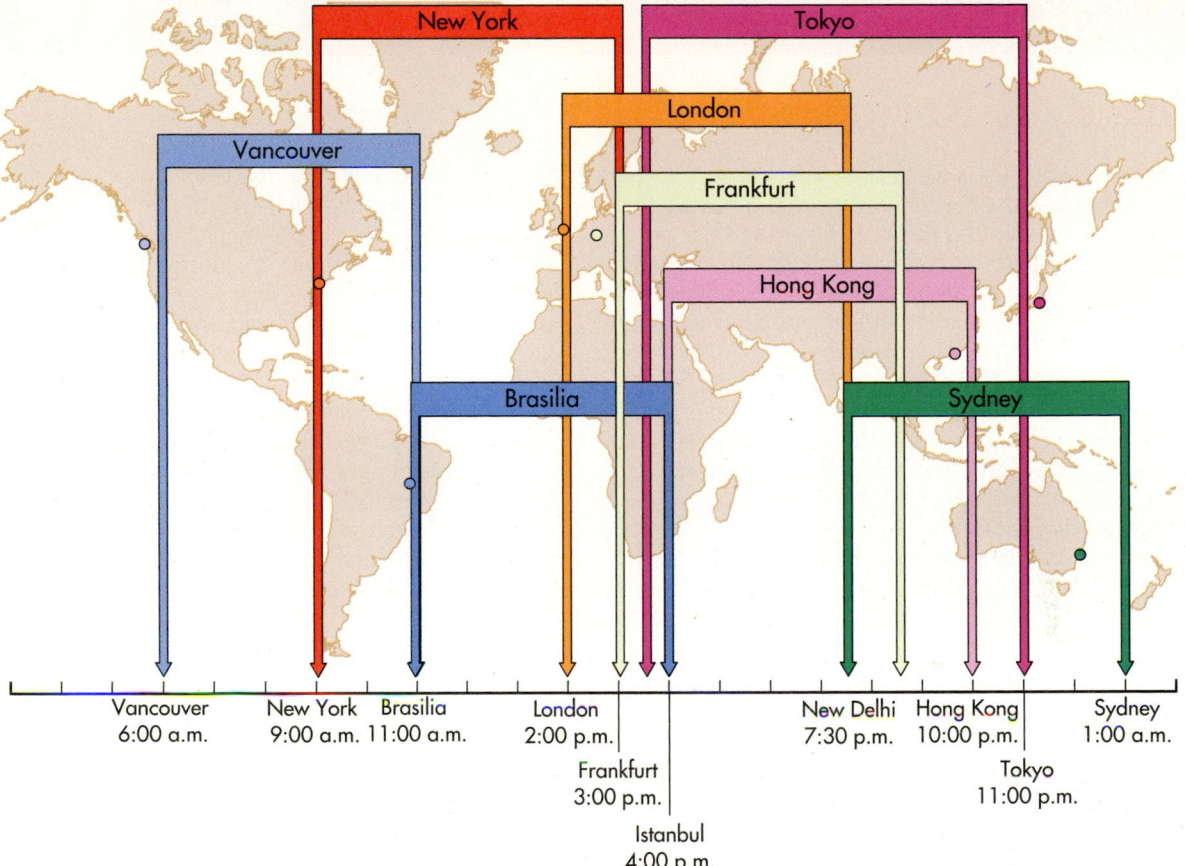

Hours of Trading
(9:00 a.m. Eastern Time)

Stocks can be traded literally 24 hours a day. The day begins in one location and continues to move West. When Hong Kong is ready to shut down, London opens up, followed later by New York.

FIGURE 5   Stock Market Listing

52W high	52W low	Stock	Ticker	Yield Div	%	P/E	Vol 00s	High	Low	Close	Net chg
45.39	19.75	ResMed	RMD			52.5	3831	42.00	39.51	41.50	−1.90
11.63	3.55	RevlonA	REV				162	6.09	5.90	6.09	+0.12
77.25	55.13	RioTinto	RTP	2.30	3.2		168	72.75	71.84	72.74	+0.03
31.31	16.63	RitchieBr	RBA			20.9	15	24.49	24.29	24.49	−0.01
8.44	1.75	RiteAid	RAD				31028	4.50	4.20	4.31	+0.21
38.63	18.81	RobtHalf	RHI			26.5	6517	27.15	26.50	26.50	+0.14
51.25	27.69	Rockwell	ROK	1.02	2.1	14.5	6412	47.99	47.08	47.54	+0.24

Column 1 Column 2 Column 3 Column 4 Column 5 Column 6 Column 7 Column 8 Column 9 Column 10 Column 11 Column 12

Stocks are listed in newspapers in a standard form, showing annual highs and lows, dividends, P/E ratios, and daily volume and activity.

ECONOMIC INSIGHT

The P/E Ratio

How does a potential buyer decide which stocks to purchase? How does the buyer know when is a good time to buy? One method used is to see whether the stock price is appropriately related to the firm's earnings. The P/E ratio is an indicator of this relationship. The P/E ratio is the ratio of a company's share price (P) to its earnings per share (E). To calculate the P/E, you divide a company's current stock price by its earnings per share (EPS). Most of the time the P/E is calculated using the EPS from the last four quarters (known as the trailing P/E). Occasionally, however, you will see earnings expected over the next four quarters (known as the leading P/E) used as EPS.

Theoretically, a stock's P/E tells us how much investors are willing to pay for each dollar of earnings. For this reason, the P/E is also called the *multiple* of a stock. In other

words, a P/E ratio of 20 suggests that investors in the stock are willing to pay $20 for every $1 of earnings that the company generates during the period. If a company has a P/E higher than the market or industry average, this is interpreted as meaning that the market is expecting that the company will have better performance than the average firm in the market or industry over the next few months or years. But you can't just compare the P/Es of two different companies to determine which is a better value because the companies may have very different growth rates. If two companies both have a P/E of 20, but one is growing twice as fast as the other, then the faster-growing firm is undervalued relative to the slower-growing one. Finally, a low P/E ratio could mean that the market believes that the company is headed for trouble in the near future.

Column 6: Dividend yield. This gives the percentage return provided by the dividend. It is calculated as annual dividends per share divided by price per share.

Column 7: Price/earnings ratio. This is calculated by dividing the current stock price by the earnings per share for the last four quarters.

Column 8: Trading volume. This figure gives the total number of shares traded for the day, in hundreds. To get the actual number traded, add "00" to the end of the number given.

Columns 9 and 10: High and low for the day. This indicates the price range within which the stock has traded that day.

Column 11: Close. The close is the last trading price recorded when the market closed for the day. If the closing price is up or down more than 5 percent from the previous day's close, the entire listing for that stock is given in bold type.

Column 12: Net change. This is the dollar value change in the stock price from the previous day's closing price.

Stock quotes are also available on the Internet and are reported in the same way that the newspapers report them.

4   **What does a stock index represent?**

market capitalization (market cap)

The stock price multiplied by the number of shares of stock that are outstanding.

2.a.3. Stock Indexes A stock index is a measure of the price movements of a group of stocks. The number of stocks in the group may vary; for example, there are 30 stocks in the Dow Jones Industrial Average (DJIA) and 6,500 in the Wilshire Index. Since the prices of individual stocks do not necessarily go up or down at the same time, the importance or weight of a single stock in an index will vary. Most indexes weight companies based on their **market capitalization (market cap)**, which is the stock price multiplied by the number of shares of that stock that are outstanding. If a company's market cap is $1,000,000 and the value of all stocks in the index is $100,000,000, then that company has a weight of 1 percent of the index. An exception to weighting stocks by market cap is the DJIA, which uses the stock price relative to the sum of the prices of all the stocks in the index.

The most popular indexes are the DJIA, the Standard & Poor's 500 (S&P 500), the Wilshire 5000, and the Nasdaq Composite Index. The DJIA contains 30 companies, the S&P 500 includes 500 companies, the Nasdaq Composite includes all companies listed on the Nasdaq stock exchange, and the Wilshire 5000 contains more than 6,500 stocks (the 5000 in the name is misleading). The S&P 500 tries to represent all major areas of the U.S. economy. It does not use the 500 largest companies, but rather includes 500 companies that are widely owned and that represent all sectors of the economy. The stocks in the index are chosen by the S&P Index Committee, which typically makes between 25 and 50 changes every year. Non-U.S. companies were included in the past, but today, and in the future, only U.S. companies are included. The Nasdaq Composite Index includes all the stocks that are traded on the NASDAQ stock market. Most are technology- and Internet-related, although there are financial, consumer, biotech, and industrial companies as well. The Wilshire 5000 Index contains more than 6,500 stocks that trade in the United States. It includes all of the stocks on the New York Stock Exchange and most of the NASDAQ and AMEX issues. Another index, the Russell 2000, measures the performance of smaller stocks (small-cap stocks), which are often excluded from the big indexes. The average market capitalization in the Russell 2000 is approximately $530 million. To put that into perspective, Walmart alone had a market capitalization of over $225 billion in 2006.

These well-known indexes are only a few among many indexes; every major country has an index that represents its stock exchange.

2.b. Mutual Funds

More than 80 million people, or half of the households in the United States, invest in mutual funds. A **mutual fund** is a group of stocks or bonds of individual firms that are placed into a single investment pool by an investment company. For instance, one of the larger mutual fund investment companies is the Vanguard Group, which has many different mutual funds. One of its mutual funds is focused on high-tech firms, another on manufacturing firms, another on international firms, and so on. Individual investors are thus able to purchase a large set of stocks by simply purchasing shares in a mutual fund. There are more than 10,000 mutual funds offered to investors in the United States.

There are three general types of mutual funds: equity funds (made up of stocks), fixed-income funds (composed of corporate and government bonds), and money market funds (made up mostly of short-term U.S. government securities, but also including some corporate bonds).

If a fund includes international investments, it is called a **global fund** or an international fund. Some mutual funds focus on a specific sector of the economy, such as financial, technology, or health care stocks, whereas others focus on a specific area of the world, such as Latin America, or an individual country, such as Mexico. These are called **specific funds**. **Socially responsible funds** invest only in companies that meet certain criteria. Most socially responsible funds don't invest in companies producing such things as tobacco, alcoholic beverages, weapons, or nuclear power. An **index fund** attempts to mimic the performance of a broad market index, such as the S&P 500 or the Dow Jones Industrial Average. These mutual funds purchase shares of stock in those companies that are included in the index and weight them so as to create as close a copy of the index as possible.

Funds may be load or no-load. **Load** refers to fees paid to a fund manager. With a **front-end load**, you pay a fee when you purchase the fund. If you invest $1,000 in a mutual fund with a 5 percent front-end load, $50 will be used to pay for the sales

mutual fund
An investment tool that aggregates many different individual stocks or bonds into one entity.

global fund
A mutual fund that includes international investments.

specific fund
A mutual fund that focuses on a particular industry or a particular part of the world.

socially responsible fund
A group of stocks or bonds of companies that meet specified requirements for ethical behavior or environmental behavior.

index fund
A mutual fund that tries to match the performance of a broad market index.

load
The fees paid to the manager of a mutual fund.

front-end load
A fee that you pay when you purchase a mutual fund.

charge, and \$950 will be invested in the fund. With a **back-end load**, you pay a fee if you sell the fund within a certain time frame. For example, a fund may have a 5 percent back-end load that decreases to 0 percent in the sixth year. The load is 5 percent if you sell in the first year, 4 percent if you sell in the second year, and so on. If you don't sell the mutual fund until the sixth year, you don't have to pay the back-end load at all. A **no-load fund** sells its shares without a commission or sales charge (fees are typically paid by clients on a prearranged basis).

2.b.1. How to Read a Mutual Fund Table

A typical newspaper report on mutual funds looks like Figure 6. The columns in the mutual fund table provide the following information:

Columns 1 and 2: 52-week high and low. These columns show the highest and lowest asset values that the mutual fund has experienced over the previous 52 weeks (one year). They typically do not include the previous day's price.

Column 3: Fund name. This column gives the name of the mutual fund. The name of the company that manages the fund is written above the funds that the company manages in bold type.

Column 4: Fund specifics. Different letters and symbols have various meanings. For example, N means no load, FR means front-end load, and B means that the fund has both front-and back-end fees. X refers to an index fund.

Column 5: Dollar change. This states the dollar change in the asset value of the mutual fund from the close of the previous day's trading. NAVPS stands for net asset value per share, the value of the mutual fund divided by the number of shares of the fund.

Column 6: Percentage change. This states the percentage change in the asset value of the mutual fund from the close of the previous day's trading.

FIGURE 6　The Reporting of Mutual Funds

52W high	52W low	Fund	Spec.	Fri. NAVPS $chg	Fri. NAVPS %chg	Wkly NAVPS high	Wkly NAVPS low	Wkly NAVPS cls	Wkly NAVPS $chg	Wkly NAVPS %chg
Montrusco Bolton Funds										
11.71	10.12	Bal Plus	*N	−0.08	−0.76	10.58	10.50	10.50	0.02	0.15
12.50	10.25	Growth Plus	*N	−0.10	−0.96	10.89	10.78	10.78	0.02	0.22
31.39	24.78	Quebec Growth	*FR	0.05	0.17	26.97	26.75	26.97	0.43	1.61
13.78	7.24	RSP Intl Growth	*N	−0.08	−1.01	7.45	7.36	7.36	−0.03	−0.41
11.16	9.09	Value Plus	*N	−0.07	−0.75	9.39	9.32	9.32	0.01	0.14
9.65	8.90	World Inc	*N	−0.04	−0.40	9.52	9.39	9.48	0.04	0.43
Montrusco Select Funds CS(a)										
12.87	10.49	Balanced	*N	−0.04	−0.37	10.85	10.80	10.81	0.05	0.45
16.32	12.11	Balanced+	*N	−0.05	−0.43	12.57	12.52	12.52	0.06	0.45
10.36	9.86	Bond Index+	X*N	−0.03	−0.32	10.35	10.30	10.30	0.04	0.37

Column 1　Column 2　Column 3　Column 4　Column 5　Column 6　Column 7　Column 8　Column 9　Column 10　Column 11

Financial newspapers report on mutual fund performance in a standard manner, showing annual and weekly activity.

Column 7: Week high. This is the highest asset value at which the fund was sold during the past week.

Column 8: Week low. This is the lowest asset value at which the fund was sold during the past week.

Column 9: Close. The asset value of the fund at the end of the trading day is shown in this column.

Column 10: Week's dollar change. This represents the dollar change in the asset value of the mutual fund from the previous week.

Column 11: Week's percentage change. This shows the percentage change in the asset value of the mutual fund from the previous week.

R E C A P

1. Shares, equity, and stock mean the same thing—ownership of a piece of a company.

2. There are two main types of stock: common and preferred stock.

3. A stock index is a measure of the price movements of a group of stocks.

4. A mutual fund is an entity that invests money in stocks, bonds, and other securities for groups of people.

3. The Stock Market

The prices of stocks vary from day to day, and even from minute to minute. What causes stock prices to rise or fall? The answer is the same things that affect prices in any other market—demand and supply. The demand for stocks comes from investors—individuals, mutual funds, and other institutions like insurance companies—who are looking for the highest return on their funds. The return to a shareholder is the dividend the stock pays and the appreciation in the price of the stock. Suppose, for instance, that you purchased Microsoft at $5 per share in 1996 and then sold it for $100 per share in 2006. Your appreciation would have been $95 per share over the 10-year period. Since Microsoft paid no dividends during this period, your total return would have been that appreciation.

The demand curve for the shares of a company's stock slopes downward, since the higher the price of the stock, everything else the same, the lower the quantity of stock demanded. Nonprice determinants of demand are the prices of other companies' stocks and other possible investments, expectations regarding stock price movements, income, and tastes and preferences. When one of the nonprice determinants of demand for a firm's stock changes, the demand curve shifts. For instance, if people expect the price of the stock to increase, demand will increase, as shown in Figure 7.

The supply of a stock comes from current shareholders who want to sell their shares of stock and from firms issuing new shares.[1] The supply curve for a company's stock slopes upward, indicating that the higher the price, the greater the quantity offered for sale, everything else the same. The nonprice determinants of supply are the prices of related stocks and other investments and the expectations of shareholders. When one of

---

[1] The primary market refers to the market in which a firm issues stock for the very first time (an IPO, or the initial public offering of stocks by a firm) or issues additional stock. The secondary market is what we are typically referring to when we speak of the stock market. This is the market in which outstanding shares are bought and sold.

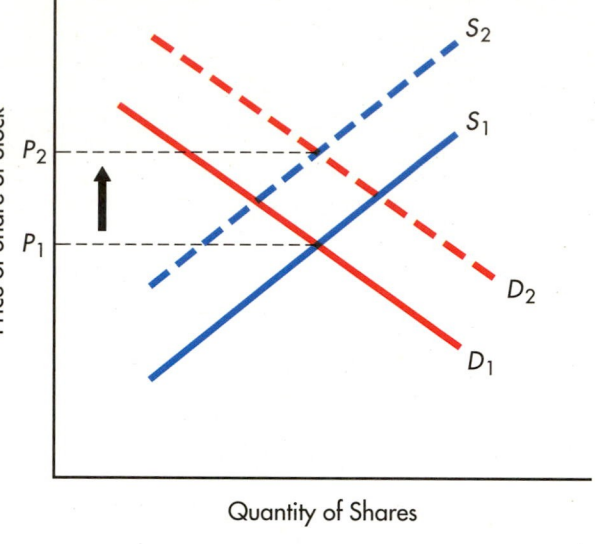

FIGURE 7   The Equity Market

Demand for stocks comes from investors looking to acquire wealth; the quantity demanded of a stock rises when the price of the stock declines. Supply of stocks comes from investors wanting to obtain money. The quantity supplied rises as the price of the stock rises. Demand shifts when the determinants of demand change; supply shifts when the determinants of supply shift.

© 2013 Cengage Learning

the nonprice determinants of supply changes, the supply curve shifts. For instance, if current shareholders begin to believe that the future price of the stock will be higher than they had previously believed, then they will tend to hold on to their shares—that is, to offer less for sale—and the supply curve will shift to the left, as illustrated in Figure 7.

You can see in Figure 7 that the effect of expectations that the price of a stock will rise in the future is an increase in the price of the stock today from P_1 to P_2. Buyers want to purchase more shares now, so demand increases from D_1 to D_2, and sellers are offering less for sale, so supply decreases from S_1 to S_2. The result is a higher price today, P_2.

For one investor to sell a share of a particular company's stock to another investor, the buyer has to expect that the purchase of this stock will return more than any other comparable purchase, and the seller has to expect that the purchase of other financial assets, goods, or services with the money obtained from the sale of this stock will generate more satisfaction than holding onto the shares of this stock. An important point here is that buyers and sellers are comparing all possible investments and seeking the one that they think will give them the best return. Buyers and sellers evaluate the firm's stock on the basis of a comparison with all other comparable investments. A **comparable investment** is an investment that has the same features, such as risk and ease of selling (called liquidity), as the one being considered.

comparable investment
A stock that has the same features, such as risk and liquidity, as the one that buyers and sellers are evaluating.

5 What causes stock prices to rise and fall?

3.a. Risk

Risk and return are related—if you take more risk, you expect more return. What is risk? It is the possibility that some unexpected event will occur. Most people are risk averse, meaning that they will pay to have less risk. Suppose you are given the opportunity to win some money, and there are two ways of doing it. With choice A, you get $1,000,

© froxx/Shutterstock.com

and with choice B, you have a 50 percent chance of getting 0 and a 50 percent chance of getting $2,000. Which do you prefer?

Choice A = $1,000

Choice B = $0 × 50% = $0 or $2,000 × 50% = $1,000

The average outcome of the choices is the same. Therefore, risk-averse people will choose A. To get risk-averse people to select B, we would have to offer them more, say $100 × 50% or $2,100 × 50% = $1,100. This extra $100 is called the risk premium—the amount that a risk-averse person requires in order to take on risk. A purchase of a firm's stock will include a risk premium, and the more risky the firm, the higher the premium. So if you have a choice of investing in Microsoft or a brand-new biotech company, you would need to have the possibility of earning a great deal more on the new company to get you to invest in it.

Rather than investing in the risky biotech firm or the less risky Microsoft, investors could decide not to take any risk at all. By not taking any risk, investors would expect to receive a return that is even lower than the return that an established firm like Microsoft would provide and much lower than the return that the high-risk firm would provide. Risk-averse people must be paid to take on more risk, and the more risk they take on, the more they must be paid.

3.b. Stock Price Changes

Stock prices change every day because of supply and demand. If more people want to buy a stock (demand) than want to sell it (supply), the price moves up. Conversely, if more people want to sell a stock than want to buy it, the price will fall. What causes demand and supply to change? When investors change their expectations so that they now expect the price of the stock to rise more than they previously did, more investors will want to buy. At the same time, fewer will want to sell. As illustrated in Figure 8,

---

FIGURE 8   Revisions of Expectations

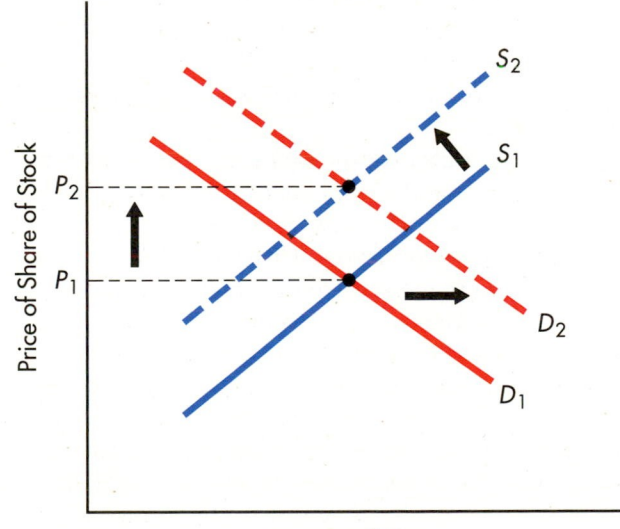

When a firm earns more than it had been expected to earn, investors in that firm's stock are likely to change their expectations of what the future may bring. This will induce investors to purchase more shares of the stock and sell fewer—an increase in demand and a decrease in supply.

when expectations are revised upward, demand will increase, supply will decrease, and price will rise from P_1 to P_2. When expectations are revised downward, fewer investors will want to buy and more will want to sell. In this case, supply will increase (shift right), demand will decrease (shift down), and price will fall from P_2 to P_1.

Firms are required to report their earnings (accounting profit) at the end of each quarter (for most companies, the end of March, June, September, and December). These quarterly reports are used by stock market analysts and investors to evaluate how well their previous forecasts of the firm's performance match what has actually been happening. When the quarterly results are not consistent with the investors' forecasts or expectations, the investors will revise their expectations of the firm's future performance up or down. If the earnings reports indicate lower earnings than had been expected, the forecasts will be revised downward, and the stock price will decline. When a firm does better than it had been expected to do, the forecasts will be revised upward, and the stock price will rise. As an illustration, consider the following report: "Google stock soared Friday, continuing Wall Street's love affair with the company, after its earnings easily topped estimates." The report states that investors realized that the revenues they had expected Google to earn were less than what Google actually earned, and so they began to think that the value of the company was higher than they had previously thought, and as a result they wanted to own more of it. The greater demand drove the price up.

3.c. Market Efficiency

There are hundreds of millions of people who own shares of stock. Some of these people analyze all available information about companies, and some don't even know which stocks they own. It would seem that those people who study the stock markets would be so much better informed than the average investor that they would be able to reap large returns relative to the average investor. But this is not necessarily so. To see why, suppose that a particular investor gains a reputation as a stock market guru—a very successful investor—and that the investor's activities are easily observed by others. What will happen? As with any market that does not have significant barriers to entry, when some firm (some person) begins making positive economic profits, others will mimic that firm (that person) and compete with it. As others copy the initial investor's strategy and mimic every move, the initial investor's returns drop—economic profit is driven down to zero. This view of the behavior of the stock markets suggests that no investor can continually outperform the market.

Another way in which this idea is expressed is by saying that one can do as well at picking stocks by throwing darts at the stock tables as by picking them in any other way.[2] If there was one best way to pick stocks, then everyone would focus on that method, and the price would reflect all such information. There would be no way to do better than everyone else. This is what people mean when they say that the market is *efficient*.

Prices are the result of demand and supply, and demand and supply take into account all relevant or important information. Stock prices reflect or incorporate all relevant information about a company, expectations concerning the company's performance and the economy's performance, and any other event that could affect the firm. The point is that stock prices will incorporate and reflect all relevant information once that information appears. Thus, even though investors possess widely differing amounts of information, there is no way in which one investor can continually make above-normal profits or "beat the market." Of course there are some investors who seem to do better than others, but in few cases does a single investor continually do better than others.

---

[2] This statement was made in a 1973 book by Burton Malkiel, *A Random Walk down Wall Street* (W. W. Norton and Company).

The basic idea of efficient markets is that there are no sure profits. Investing is a risky business, as prices continually adjust to new information and circumstances.

If the market is efficient, how can stock market bubbles and panics be explained? A bubble or panic is a sudden increase or decrease in prices that occurs simply because people are jumping on the bandwagon without an underlying economic basis. In the tech bubble of the 1990s, the price of Amazon.com stock was very high even though the company had never made a profit. Perhaps some of that stock price was based on expectations of future profits, but a great deal of it was the result of investors gambling or speculating on the basis of wishful thinking. In that period, people heard about "the secretary in a start-up company who became a millionaire," and so they purchased stocks in start-up companies in order to become rich also. The problem is that wishful thinking by itself cannot drive stock prices up for very long. Eventually a firm must earn positive economic profits. The stock market collapsed in 2000 partly because it became evident that firms were not earning economic profits that were high enough to support the inflated stock prices. In the short run, psychological aspects may drive stock prices, but over the long run, stock prices will reflect profit.

RECAP

1. The equity market is the market in which stocks are bought and sold.

2. The demand for equities comes from investors who are seeking the greatest return on their savings.

3. The supply of equities comes from stock owners who want to sell their stock and purchase something else.

4. Demand depends on expectations, income, and the prices of and returns on other investments. Supply depends on expectations and the prices of and returns on other investments. A change in one of these determinants of demand and/or supply will cause the curve to shift. If buyers want to buy more stock (demand) than sellers want to sell (supply), then the price will move up. Conversely, if sellers want to sell more of a stock than buyers want to buy, the price will fall.

5. The equity market is said to be an efficient market in the sense that it is difficult for an investor to continually earn above-normal profits. If there were a secret formula for becoming rich in the stock market, everyone would soon learn that formula, and it would no longer be an effective strategy.

4. Bonds

Firms can raise cash by selling ownership rights (shares of stock—equity—in the case of a public company), by retaining earnings in the firm (not distributing profits to owners in the form of dividends), and by selling bonds or taking out loans (debt). A **bond** (sometimes called a fixed-income security or debt security) is an IOU issued by a borrower to a lender. When you buy a newly issued bond, you are lending money to the borrower. When you purchase a bond that is not a new issue, you are buying that bond not from the issuing firm but from an investor or lender that initially provided the loan. You are choosing to own a portion of the debt obligation of a company because you think that the return on that bond exceeds the return on whatever else you might have done with the money used to purchase the bond. The seller of the bond has decided that he is better off selling that debt and thus receiving money now than waiting for the debtor (the issuing firm) to pay off the loan.

There is a specified time at which the borrower will repay your loan; this is the **maturity date**. In most cases, the bond's **face** or **par value** is $1,000; this is the amount that the lender will be repaid once the bond matures. The borrower pays the lender a

bond
An IOU issued by a borrower to a lender.

maturity date
The specified time at which the issuer of a bond will repay the loan.

face or **par value**
The amount that the lender will be repaid when a bond matures.

GLOBAL BUSINESS INSIGHT

Country Bond Ratings

Governments issue bonds in order to raise money, and government bonds are rated in terms of risk much like corporate bonds are. During the financial crisis of 2008–2010, many governments increased their debt so much that their bonds become very risky. Greece was the first to experience serious problems. On April 27, 2010, the Greek debt rating was decreased because of fears of default by the Greek government. When the risk is higher, then the borrowing entity must offer higher interest rates or yields on the debt

to entice lenders to lend. The following figure shows how fast the interest rate offered on Greek bonds rose; the rise was necessary to try to induce people to take the risk and purchase Greek bonds. Then just below the Greek picture is the United States. While the U.S. debt also has soared, it remains Aaa rated—low risk by Moody's and Fitch rating firms but was downgraded by S&P rating firm to AA+ in the summer of 2011.

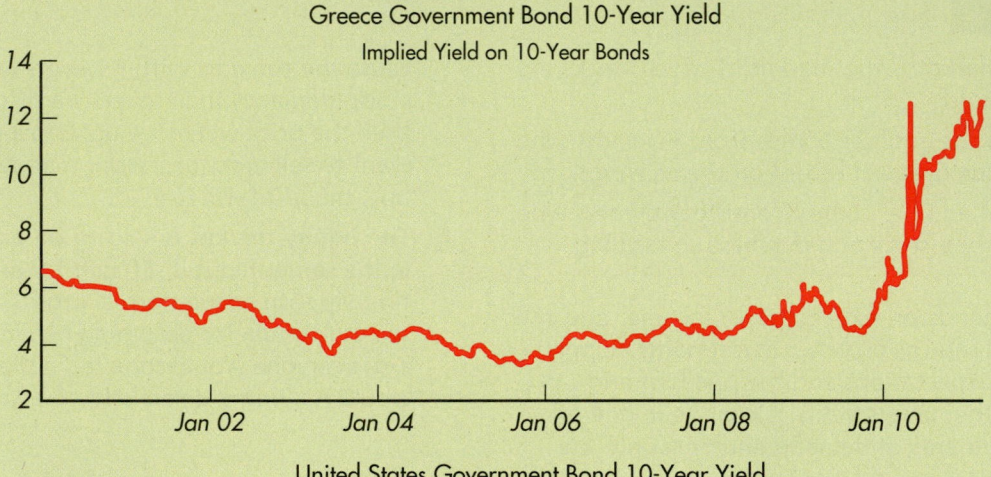

Greece Government Bond 10-Year Yield
Implied Yield on 10-Year Bonds

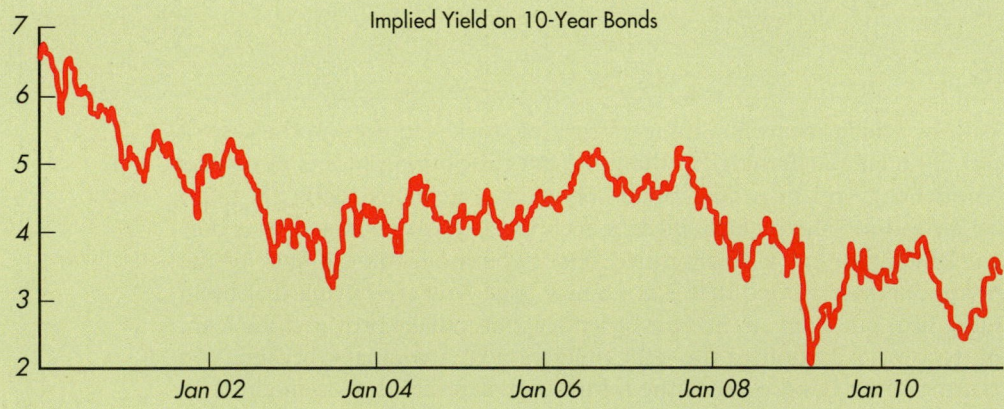

United States Government Bond 10-Year Yield
Implied Yield on 10-Year Bonds

Sources: TradingEconomics.com, Reuters, Bloomberg.

FIGURE 9   Bond Ratings

Bond Rating		Grade	Risk
Moody's	**Standard & Poor's**		
Aaa	AAA	Investment	Lowest risk
Aa	AA	Investment	Low risk
A	A	Investment	Low risk
Baa	BBB	Investment	Medium risk
Ba, B	BB, B	Junk	High risk
Caa/Ca/C	CCC/CC/C	Junk	Highest risk
C	D	Junk	In default

Rating agencies provide measures of the amount of risk associated with particular bonds.

© 2013 Cengage Learning

fixed amount, called a **coupon**, each year. These interest payments are usually made every six months until the bond matures. The rate of interest that must be paid—that is, the *coupon rate*—depends on how risky the borrower is. The chart in Figure 9 illustrates the different bond rating scales from the two major rating agencies, Moody's and Standard & Poor's, their associated grades, and the risk levels that the ratings indicate.

4.a. Bond Ratings

U.S. government bonds are considered no-risk investments because it is so unlikely that the United States will default on its obligations. Corporations must offer a higher yield than the government in order to entice lenders to purchase corporate bonds because corporate bonds are more risky. AAA corporate bonds—often referred to as blue chip bonds—are the lowest-risk corporate bonds. The highest-risk corporate bonds are called junk bonds. Junk bonds are typically rated at BB/Ba or lower. On average, a bond carries less risk than a share of stock because in the event of the firm's collapse, the shareholders cannot get anything until all debtholders have been paid.

4.b. Reading a Bond Table

In every financial newspaper there are bond tables similar to the one shown in Figure 10. The columns in the bond table provide the following information:

coupon
The fixed amount that the issuer of a bond agrees to pay the bondholder each year.

FIGURE 10   Reading a Bond Table

	Coupon	Mat. Date	Bid $	Yld%
Corporate				
GTE Florida Inc	6.860	Feb 01/28	102.562	6.635
General Motors Corp	8.375	Jul 15/33	76.000	11.205
General Mtrs Acep Corp	8.000	Nov 01/31	98.358	8.152
General Elec Co	5.000	Feb 01/13	100.112	4.979
Ford Mtr Co Del	7.450	Jul 16/31	74.437	10.306
Column 1	Column 2	Column 3	Column 4	Column 5

Bonds are reported in financial newspapers and on the Internet in a standard manner.

© 2013 Cengage Learning

Column 1: Issuer. This is the company, state (or province), or country that issued the bond.

Column 2: Coupon. The coupon refers to the fixed interest rate that the issuer pays to the lender. The coupon rate varies by bond.

Column 3: Maturity date. This is the date when the borrower will pay the lenders (investors) their principal back. Typically only the last two digits of the year are quoted: 25 means 2025, 04 is 2004, and so on.

Column 4: Bid price. This is the price that someone is willing to pay for the bond. It is quoted in relation to 100, no matter what the par value is. Think of the bond price as a percentage: A bid of $93 means that the bond is trading at 93 percent of its par value.

Column 5: Yield. The yield indicates the annual return until the bond matures. Yield is calculated as the amount of interest paid on a bond divided by the price; it is a measure of the income generated by a bond. If the bond is callable, the yield will be given as "c—," where the "—" is the year in which the bond can be called. For example c10 means that the bond can be called as early as 2010.

You will hear some bonds referred to as bills or notes. The name indicates the length of time until the bond matures. *Bills* are debt securities maturing in less than one year. *Notes* are debt securities maturing in one to ten years. *Bonds* are debt securities maturing in more than ten years. A bond that provides no interest payments but instead is issued at a value that is lower than its face value is called a **zero-coupon bond**.

zero-coupon bond
A bond that provides no interest payments but is issued at a value lower than its face value.

6   What causes bond prices to rise and fall?

4.c. The Bond Market

The market for bonds is not very different from the stock market, and the two are closely linked. Demanders of bonds are investors who are looking for the best return on their savings. They will purchase a bond when the return on the bond is expected to be greater than the return on other comparable investments—for instance, better than the return on stocks adjusted for risk. Consider a $100 bond maturing in one year that pays a 5 percent rate of interest, or coupon rate. The bondholder receives $5 per year in interest until the bond matures. If the price of the bond is $100, the same as the face value, then the yield is 5 percent ($5/$100). But if the price of the bond is lower than the face value, say $95, the yield is $10/$95 = 10.52 percent. Thus, for a bond paying a 5 percent coupon, as the price rises, everything else the same, the quantity demanded will decline, so the demand curve slopes down. The demand for bonds depends on the coupon, the prices of and interest rates on other bonds and other investments, expectations of investors, income, and other factors. When one of the determinants of demand other than the bond's own price changes, the demand curve shifts. For instance, in Figure 11, an increase in interest rates on other investments will cause the demand for a bond offering a 5 percent coupon to decline—the demand curve shifts down from D_1 to D_2.

The suppliers of bonds are companies, governments, and other institutions offering new issues of IOUs and investors who own previously issued bonds and want to sell them. The supply curve slopes upward, illustrating the idea that as the price of an IOU rises, everything else the same, the quantity offered for sale rises. The supply depends on the prices of other bonds and investments, interest rates on other bonds and investments, and expectations of bond sellers. If interest rates on other investments rise, the quantity of bonds offering a 5 percent coupon that suppliers are willing and able to sell will rise—the supply curve shifts out, and the bond price falls.

As illustrated in Figure 11, the result of an increase in interest rates, everything else the same, is to cause the price on a 5 percent coupon bond to fall. This illustrates the fact that bond prices and interest rates are inversely related. Everything else the same, when interest rates rise, bond prices fall.

FIGURE 11 The Bond Market

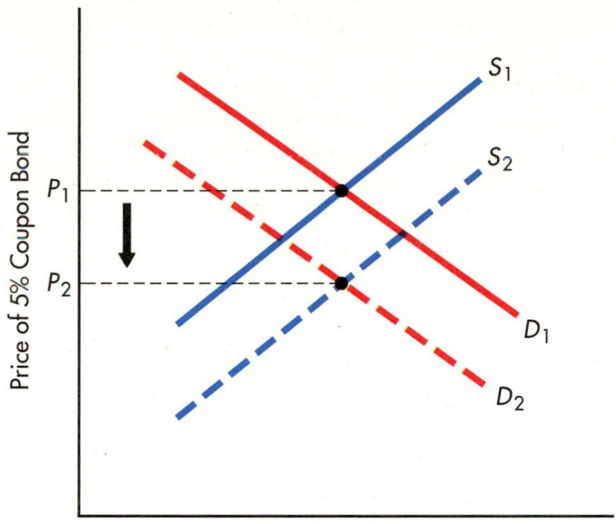

The demand for bonds comes from lenders—investors who want to earn interest on their savings. The supply of bonds comes from the holders of bonds—firms and governments that are attempting to borrow and bond owners that are offering to sell. The quantity demanded of a bond paying a fixed coupon declines as the price of the bond rises; the quantity supplied of a bond paying a fixed coupon rises as the price of the bond rises. Demand and supply together determine the price of the bond. If expectations, interest rates on other investments, or something else other than the price of the bond changes, the demand for the bond and/or the supply of the bond will change—the curves will shift.

© 2013 Cengage Learning

Bonds and stocks are often substitute goods, meaning that as the price of stocks rise, the demand for bonds rises. The reason for this is that investors sell their shares of stock and purchase bonds when interest rates are higher than the expected return on stocks. Suppose that investors are expecting stock prices to decline in the future. Then current shareholders will offer to sell more stock. The supply of shares of stock increases and demand drops, forcing stock prices down. Expecting stock prices to drop, investors purchase bonds and other assets, driving the price of bonds up. As the price of bonds rises, the interest rate declines (remember the inverse relationship between interest rate and bond price).

In some cases, bonds and stocks are complementary goods. An investor will purchase both stocks and bonds when both are expected to yield better returns than other investments and when the investor wants to diversify his or her portfolio—to not put all of his or her eggs in one basket. Thus, we can't always say that when stock prices rise, bond prices will fall, and vice versa. In some circumstances, bond and stock prices will rise and fall together.

RECAP

1. Bonds are IOUs provided by the lender or issuer of the bond to the purchaser of the bond.

2. The demanders of bonds are individuals and mutual funds seeking the highest return given a certain amount of risk.

3. The suppliers of bonds are the original issuers or borrowers—corporations and governments—and bond owners who choose to sell bonds that they own.

4. The market for a bond consists of the demand for and supply of that bond. The price of the bond is determined by demand and supply.

7 What are bubbles and panics?

bubble

A situation in which the price of an asset is being bid up through speculation or gambling rather than because of the value of the services the asset returns.

5. Asset Prices and Bubbles

The term **bubble** means that the price of an asset is being bid up through gambling rather than because of the value of the services the asset returns. In other words, the price of an asset is *not* based on its fundamentals. Economists value an asset as the discounted sum of the revenues it will yield. When the price of a stock rises significantly higher than can be justified by the dividends the firm can be expected to pay in the future, a stock bubble is said to have occurred. The frenetic rise in stock prices that occurred from 1995 until 2000 is called the dot-com bubble. The same applies to any asset—when the price of the asset rises significantly above the value of the services the asset provides, a bubble occurs.

5.a. Bubbles and Panics

What defines a bubble or panic? It starts as a development with far-reaching, perhaps unknowable, implications, such as the collapse of mortgage-backed securities or a government grant of a monopoly. People leverage or buy on margins—borrowing for most of their purchase. The buying drives prices up further and induces even more buying. Eventually, some event triggers a downturn. Margin buyers (optimists) get squeezed and are forced to pay their debts. Pessimism takes over and the decline in prices leads to mass selling. Eventually, pessimism runs its course, prices turn up, and people step in to buy.

Do bubbles in asset prices exist? That is, is it possible for the prices of stocks and other assets to rise well above the values justified by economic fundamentals? Those who experienced the rise in stock prices in the late 1990s, the rise in housing prices in the 2000s, and the great boom and bust in Tokyo commercial real estate in the 1980s will no doubt wonder how anyone could ask the question. Yet many financial economists are skeptical that bubbles are possible. They ask: Why would people knowingly pay a price for an asset that is out of line with any reasonable estimate of its value in the near future?

Some of the more famous bubbles and panics are listed in Table 1. The three most famous are the Tulipomania, the Mississippi Company, and the South Sea Company bubbles. According to one study, in all three cases, the prices of the assets—whether bulbs or shares—were apparently based on economic fundamentals.[3] Since economists value an asset as the discounted sum of the revenues the asset will yield, the future value of a tulip bulb could justify high prices. For instance, bulbs that yield tulips with beautiful patterns can themselves be propagated, so they yield many more bulbs. Hence, high prices for the original rare bulbs that fall as the supply rises should be no more surprising than high prices for corn.

So what differentiates a bubble and a price rise based on fundamentals? You have to know when the price of an asset is not linked to the fundamentals. If you can know that only with hindsight, then the original price increase does not constitute a classic bubble.[4]

5.b. Housing Bubble

Between 2001 and 2006, house prices in the United States rose more than 45 percent after adjusting for inflation. People want housing for the services it provides—a roof over their heads, among others—and people can obtain these services either by renting or by purchasing. The choice most people face is whether to purchase a house and give up part

---

[3] *Famous First Bubbles*, Peter M. Garber, MIT Press, 2001.

[4] Discussion of *Famous First Bubbles* at http://www.davidrhenderson.com/articles/0900_famousfirst-bubbles.html; http://people.few.eur.nl/smant/m-economics/bubbles.htm.

TABLE 1	Famous Bubbles and Panics

Tulipomania, Holland, 1636–1637

Prices of tulip bulbs rose twelve-fold from January 1, 1637, to a peak on February 3, 1637, of 1,500 guilders a pound (about four years' income for a master carpenter). Later in February 1637, prices fell by about 90 percent.

Mississippi Company Bubble, France, 1717–1720

In August 1717, the Companie des Indes (commonly known as the Mississippi Company) was incorporated. The French regent gave it a monopoly on trading rights with French colonies, including what was then known as French Louisiana. In August 1719, a scheme was devised by consultant John Law in which the Mississippi Company subsumed the entire French national debt, and launched a plan whereby portions of the debt would be exchanged for shares in the company. The bubble burst in May 1720 when a run on the Banque Royale forced the government to acknowledge that the amount of metallic currency in the country was not quite equal to half the total amount of paper currency in circulation.

South Sea Company Bubble, England, 1720–1721

Shares of stock in South Sea Company rose dramatically: At one point the company was more highly valued than the entire island of England. During the same period that French speculators were driving up the price of shares in the Mississippi Company, English speculators were purchasing stock in the South Sea Company. Formed in 1711 by Robert Harley, the South Sea Company was created to convert £10 million of government war debt (incurred during the War of Spanish Succession) into its own shares. In 1720, following John Law's example in France, the company proposed to take over the entire British national debt. As soon as the plan was announced to Parliament, the company's share prices began to rise as speculators gambled on the conversion plan.

Stock Market Crash, United States, 1920s–1930s

The driving factor behind both the inflation (during the 1920s) and the burst (in 1929) of the stock market bubble was the expanding use of leverage (i.e., debt) by individuals as well as corporations. On October 24, 1929, Black Thursday, stock prices plummeted, and a record 12,894,650 shares were traded on the New York Stock Exchange. Five days later, on October 29, 1929 (Black Tuesday), 16,410,030 shares were traded on the New York Stock Exchange, and prices collapsed from a peak reached in August 1929.

The Bubble Economy, Japan, 1984–1989

The stock market bubble was fueled by a Japanese corporate invention, known as "zaitech," or "financial engineering," by which speculation became an integral part of corporate earnings statements. After obtaining low-interest loans, corporations were easily able to raise funds on the markets.

Dot-Com Bubble, United States, 1995–2001

Stock prices rose rapidly, driving price-to-earnings ratios in high-tech companies far above normal ranges. In March 2000, the stock market crashed. The collapse of the dot-com bubble wiped out $5 trillion in market value of technology companies from March 2000 to October 2002.

of their disposable personal income (DPI) in order to purchase it, or to rent a house and use the DPI that is not used on the house to purchase stocks or other assets. People will purchase housing when it is relatively less costly than renting.

When people purchase an asset, any asset, they expect that asset to provide benefits or payments in the future. For a stock, the payoff is the future earnings of the firm. People buy a stock thinking they will be paid each year through dividends or appreciation, so the price they are willing to pay depends on how long they think it will take for the firm to pay them back. The P/E ratio gives an indication of this.[5] If you pay $40 for a share of stock, and the earnings per share is $2, then the P/E ratio is 20/1, which tells us that if the performance of the firm stays the same, it will take 20 years for the firm's earnings to add up to the purchase price. If the P/E ratio rises to 40, then you are essentially waiting 40 years for the return. During the stock market bubble, P/E ratios hit levels of 80 for many companies and even higher for start-up high-tech companies. This is illustrated in Figure 12.

If you think about a house in the same way as other assets, then you want to find how long it will take for the value of the housing services you receive each year to add up to the price of the house; this should be about the same as adding up all rents to be paid in the future. A ratio of the prices of houses to the rents on houses (P/R) between 1980 and 2009 is shown in Figure 13. The figure suggests that in 2004, prices were

---

[5] The P/E ratio is price per share divided by earnings per share of a given stock.

FIGURE 12   A Plot of the S&P 500 Composite Index Price to Earnings (P/E) Ratio

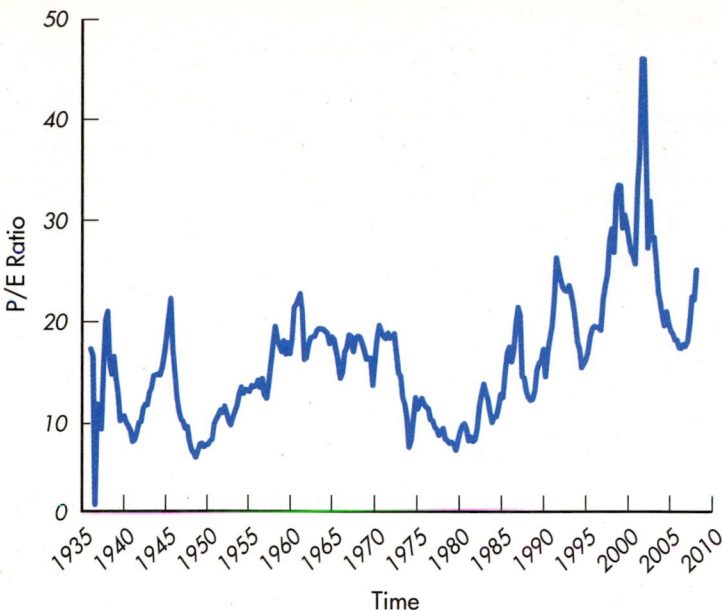

Source: http://www2.standardandpoors.com.

FIGURE 13   The Price-Rent (P/R) Ratio, Q1 1997 = 1.0, National Case-Shiller Home Price Index and Owner Equivalent Rent

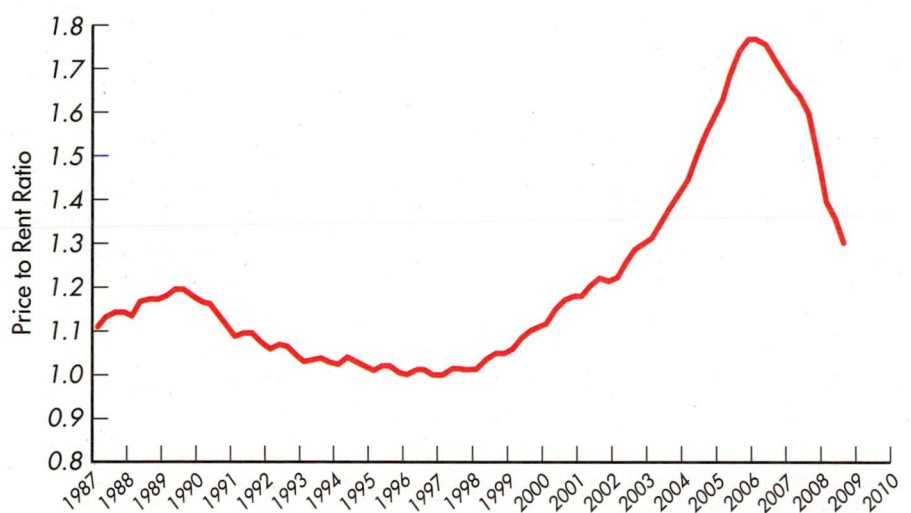

The annual value of housing services should be approximately equal to the discounted cost of rents. In this diagram the house price index created by economists Case and Shiller is divided by the rental price. The two are equal to 1 in 1997, but rise to nearly 1.8 in 2006. This means that housing prices were significantly greater than the rental value of the house.

Source: Used by kind permission of Bill McBride, who shared this information through his blog, "Calculated Risk." http://calculatedrisk.blogspot.com.

high relative to rents. Could you say that this indicates a housing bubble? In fact, it was; the bubble burst in 2006. House prices fell from 2006 to 2009 by around 30 percent.

Several factors are necessary for an asset's value to rise in such a way that it looks like a bubble. First, demand must rise relative to supply. In order for demand to rise, it must be financed by increased liquidity—that is, buyers must be willing and able to purchase more. In both the dot-com boom and the housing bubble, the liquidity was provided by the Federal Reserve as it kept interest rates low by increasing the rate of growth of the money supply. Adding to the demand were the actions of government in increasing the amount of lending provided to what are called subprime or low-quality borrowers.

The second part of an apparent bubble is that the demand rises due to the expectation that prices will continue rising. Many house purchases were made by investors hoping to resell the house in the future at higher prices. So the expectations of gains induced an increase in demand. When the Federal Reserve began raising interest rates, the housing market slowed and eventually crashed. Was it a bubble or did housing prices reflect fundamentals?

RECAP

1. A bubble refers to a situation where an asset price is being bid up not by the fundamental value of that asset, but by gambling.

2. The fundamentals refer to the value of services an asset provides over its life or the discounted value of the sum of revenues the asset will provide.

3. The housing bubble of 2002–2006 is called a bubble because, in hindsight, it is clear that the price of housing far exceeded the discounted value of rents the houses would have provided.

SUMMARY

1. **What is the capital market?**

   - Capital includes the machines, equipment, structures, and buildings that firms use to produce goods and services. *Preview*

   - The demand for capital comes from firms that want to use capital in order to supply goods and services. The supply of capital comes from firms that provide the machines or buildings to other firms. *§1.a, 1.b*

   - The demand for and supply of capital determine the rental price of capital and the quantities supplied and demanded. Nonprice determinants of demand include interest rates—the higher the interest rate, everything else the same, the lower is the quantity demanded. *§1.a, 1.c*

2. **What is the impact of technological change on the capital market?**

   - Technological change refers to improvements that allow more output to be produced for each unit of input. *§1.a*

   - Firms demand more capital when technological change occurs. Thus, technological change is a nonprice determinant of demand. *§1.a*

3. **What are stocks? How are stocks bought and sold?**

   - The supply of funds with which firms acquire capital comes from selling stocks and bonds and taking out loans from financial institutions. *§1.b, 1.c*

   - Shares, equity, and stock mean the same thing—ownership of a piece of a company. *§2.a*

   - There are two main types of stocks: common stock and preferred stock. *§2.a*

   - Stocks are bought and sold on stock exchanges. A company will complete specified requirements and pay fees to have its stock listed on a particular exchange. Typically, the NYSE lists larger, well-known companies; NASDAQ lists high-tech and biotech companies; and the AMEX lists small-cap stocks. Non-U.S. companies are listed on stock exchanges in their own countries. §2.a.1

4. What does a stock index represent?

- A stock index is a measure of the price movements of a group of stocks. The best-known indexes are the Dow Jones Industrial Average, the S&P 500, the NASDAQ Composite, and the Wilshire 5000, but there are other indexes for U.S. companies and indexes for every stock exchange in the world. §2.a.3

- A mutual fund is an investment tool that aggregates many different individual stocks or bonds into a single investment pool. §2.b

5. What causes stock prices to rise and fall?

- The equity market is the market in which stocks are bought and sold. §3

- The demand for equities comes from investors who are seeking the greatest return on their savings—individuals, mutual funds, and institutions like insurance companies. §3

- The supply of equities comes from stock owners who want to sell their stock and purchase something else. This is known as the secondary market. The primary market is the market for new issues—stocks that have not previously been sold by the firms. It is the secondary market that people are referring to when they speak of the stock market. §3

- Demand depends on expectations, income, and prices of and returns on other investments. Supply depends on expectations and on prices of and returns on other investments. A change in one of these determinants of demand and/or supply will cause demand and/or supply to change. §3.b

- If buyers want to buy more of a stock (demand) than sellers want to sell (supply), then the price will move up. Conversely, if sellers want to sell more of a stock than buyers want to buy, the price will fall. §3.b

- The equity market is said to be an efficient market in the sense that it is difficult for an investor to continually earn above-normal profits. If there were a secret formula for becoming rich in the stock market, everyone would soon learn that

formula, and it would no longer be an effective strategy. §3.c

- Bubbles and panics occur because people are simply jumping on the bandwagon without an underlying economic basis. Although these tendencies can affect the prices of stocks in the short run, it is the performance of the firm that determines the stock price in the long run. §3.c

6. What causes bond prices to rise and fall?

- Bonds are IOUs provided by a lender or issuer of the bond to the purchaser of the bond. §4

- The demanders of bonds are individuals and mutual funds that are seeking the highest return given a certain amount of risk. §4.c

- The suppliers of bonds are corporations and governments attempting to borrow money and the owners of previously issued bonds who choose to sell their bonds. §4.c

- The market for a bond consists of the demand for and supply of that bond. As with the stock market, demand depends on the prices of and expected returns on other investments, income, and investor expectations; supply depends on the prices of and expected returns on other investments and supplier (bond issuer) expectations. §4.c

- The price of a bond is determined by demand and supply. §4.c

- There is an inverse relationship between bond prices and interest rates. As the interest rate rises, bond prices fall, and vice versa. §4.c

7. What are bubbles and panics?

- A bubble refers to a rise in the price of an asset that is not related to the future value of services provided by the asset. §5

- It is very difficult to know at the time whether a price rise is due to fundamentals or is a bubble. §5.a

- The value of an asset is the discounted value of the future earnings or value of services provided by the asset. §5.a

- The housing price appreciation during 2001–2006 is called the housing bubble. The price of purchasing a house relative to renting one rose to above-normal levels. §5.b

KEY TERMS

back-end load, 680	front-end load, 679	mutual fund, 679
bond, 685	global fund, 679	no-load fund, 680
bubble, 690	index fund, 679	socially responsible fund, 679
comparable investment, 682	load, 679	specific fund, 679
coupon, 687	market capitalization (market	zero-coupon bond, 688
dividend, 675	cap), 678	
face or *par value*, 685	maturity date, 685	

EXERCISES

1. What is saving? What role does it play in financial markets?

2. Investors know for sure that the CEO of firm A will undertake an investment that will yield $100 million profit next year and then $2 million each year after that for 10 years. They also know for sure that the CEO of firm B will undertake an investment that will yield nothing for two years and then a profit of $20 million per year for 10 years. Which company will have the higher stock price today, next year, the second year, and the third year?

3. The investors in exercise 2 are surprised by firm B's performance in year 5. Instead of being $20 million, the firm's profits are $40 million. What happens to firm B's stock price in years 6 and 7?

4. Nova Corporation just announced that it had a record year. Its earnings have increased nearly 10 percent. Explain how this announcement can lead to a decline in the price of Nova Corporation's stock.

5. The Benly Company needs to raise funds for a major expansion. The company is debating whether to issue stock or to issue bonds. If the company issues bonds, then its debt will increase and it will be under additional stress to ensure that its revenues can cover the costs of its debt. If it issues stock, the current owners will lose power and influence. What should the company do? Explain your answer.

6. The Federal Reserve just lowered interest rates. Explain the effect on bond prices.

7. In exercise 6, not only bond prices but also stock prices are affected. Explain why.

8. Suppose the price elasticity of demand for stocks is 1.5. This means that for every 10 percent increase in stock prices, the quantity demanded will decline by 15 percent. Does this price elasticity make sense? Explain.

9. Suppose the cross-price elasticity of demand between stocks and bonds is −1.2. If stock prices are expected to rise by 10 percent, what is expected to happen to bond prices? Does this make sense? Explain.

10. Which would you expect bonds and stocks to be, substitutes or complements? Explain.

11. From 2000 to 2003, stock prices declined by about 33 percent. Explain why this occurred. If stock prices have been falling for a period of time, what would cause them to rise again?

12. The price of a stock is determined by the demand for and supply of that stock. Both demand and supply depend on investors' expectations of the future performance—future economic profits—of the firm. Explain what happens to a firm's stock when the company earns less than investors expect.

13. During the second quarter of 2003, both bond prices and stock prices fell. Explain why this occurred.

14. Explain why stock prices fall when a company is found to be carrying out unethical and illegal activities.

15. What led to the rise in housing prices after 2001? Was this a housing bubble? If so, what event(s) popped the bubble?

16. The rental value of a domicile is the "fundamental value" of the domicile. The price of a house includes both the fundamental value and any expected appreciation of the property. Explain why the Price/Rent ratio is essentially the same for a domicile as the P/E ratio is for a stock.

17. What happens to an asset bubble when the amount of liquidity or money in circulation is reduced? Explain.

You can find further practice tests in the Online Quiz at **www.cengage.com/economics/boyes**.

BETTING ON BOB.
THE NEXT THING IN STUDENT LOANS: INVESTORS PAY YOUR BILLS, YOU GIVE THEM A SHARE OF YOUR FUTURE

Boston Globe, November 30, 2008

In 1997, David Bowie applied his well-known penchant for experimentation to finance: He offered to sell shares of his albums' future revenues. If you had faith in the enduring popularity of "Ziggy Stardust" and "Space Oddity," you could purchase Bowie Bonds and receive a percentage of the royalties for 10 years. In return, the aging rock star got an immediate infusion of cash.

When Miguel Palacios, a young Colombian financial analyst, heard the news of this arrangement, he had an epiphany. As a college student, he'd witnessed classmates reluctantly drop out of school because they couldn't afford to continue. Had they been able to offer their own version of Bowie Bonds, perhaps they could have earned their degrees.

"If he could do it," Palacios thought, "why couldn't all those bright, talented students do it as well?"

Other thinkers have begun to ask the same basic question. The result is an innovative way to think about paying for higher education. The idea, sometimes called human capital contracts, is that investors agree to cover the costs of college or graduate school in return for a percentage of the students' future earnings over a fixed period of time. Since payments are scaled to wages, the odds of default—and of financial hardship for the graduate—are greatly reduced. This scheme transfers much of the risk from students to investors. But if the students earn handsomely, the investors stand to gain more than they would under a traditional loan.

Over the last few years, several companies have begun brokering these agreements in Europe and Latin America. One of these, Lumni, which Palacios cofounded, is laying the groundwork for operations in the United States, and its first few clients here plan to sign contracts by the year's end.

The contracts could offer a new way for students and their families to handle the burden of postsecondary education bills. In recent years, rising tuition costs, combined with limits on federal loans, have increasingly forced students to resort to private loans, which have markedly higher interest rates. The challenges of paying for college promise to intensify during the economic downturn. Disruptions in the credit market have caused turmoil for student borrowers, while diminished endowments may force many colleges to jack up tuition rates even higher. Constraints on the federal budget will limit the options of President-elect Obama and the next Congress, regardless of their plans to aid students.

The system is straining, and both students and schools are looking for creative solutions. These contracts, proponents say, would allow more kids to finish college. They would free graduates from crushing debt. And they could liberate youngsters to pursue socially valuable but low-paying work such as teaching.

"We are putting all of the risk burden on students," says Kevin Carey, research and policy manager at Education Sector, a think tank, and coauthor of a recent article promoting this concept in *The American*, a magazine published by the American Enterprise Institute. "Our idea was to change that and allow students to pledge the most valuable thing they have—their intellectual capital."

The movement for human capital contracts is still small, with only a handful of companies offering them worldwide. And several aspects of this invention could hinder its success in the United States. To function on a large scale, it requires a broad pool of students to spread the risk—tomorrow's doctors and lawyers, not just future artists and non-profit staffers. The former group, however, has less incentive to participate. The legal details also remain murky, as some advocates admit, prompting worries that graduates could wriggle out of their obligations, among other concerns.

What's more, the core idea strikes some critics as akin to indentured servitude. While they acknowledge that the analogy is in some ways inapt—graduates are free to pursue the careers of their choice, and debt, after all, imposes similar burdens—the notion that investors have a stake in a graduate's income can evoke uncomfortable associations for some.

"The whole thing makes me very nervous," wrote Sandy Baum, a professor of economics at Skidmore College and a policy analyst for the College Board, in an e-mail. "I don't like the idea of someone owning a piece of someone else."

The concept of human capital contracts was originally the brainchild of economist Milton Friedman. In 1955, he wrote a paper, later reprinted in *Capitalism and Freedom*, proposing that equity-like instruments, rather than debt, should finance higher education.

For Friedman, equity financing was a way to keep government out of the business of paying for higher education, and even today some supporters see it as an idea that could ultimately lift the taxpayer burden of subsidizing grants and loans. Realistically, however, the current proposals would supplement, rather than replace, federal aid.

The chief benefit, as proponents see it, is that human capital contracts remove the risk of overwhelming debt for students, and mitigate the social costs of trying to repay it. Today, especially as more students take out private loans with high interest rates, many graduates struggle to make their monthly payments. Some of these graduates default, causing long-term credit problems for themselves, and costing lenders money. Others shape their career choices around the need to pay back their loans—for instance, law school students who aspire to do public interest work, but feel pressured by debt into taking corporate law jobs.

By gearing repayment to income, human capital contracts reduce those burdens sharply—a student who earns less money is obligated to pay less back. Of course, there is still a risk of default, and the system all but guarantees that investors would lose money on lower-income graduates—the ones who do take nonprofit jobs, or who fail to land lucrative positions. But investors would temper the risk by diversifying, funding a group of students with a range of future prospects.

"The best analogy is insurance," says Palacios. A car wreck, for example, would ruin an uninsured driver. "But not everybody crashes. If you pool everybody together, you are in a much better position."

In fits and starts, the theory of human capital contracts has begun to be realized in practice. In the spring of 2001, a company called My Rich Uncle launched, offering such contracts to more than 100 students. But the business was located on the 78th floor of the World Trade Center, so the attacks of Sept. 11 dealt it a severe blow. And in the recession that followed, says Raza Khan, one of the cofounders, investors were wary of gambling on unfamiliar ideas. The company has shifted to a more conventional private lending model, although Khan says they hope to resume the income-based contracts someday.

Also in 2001, Palacios and his partner, Felipe Vergara, founded Lumni, which has financed a total of about 150 students in Chile, Colombia, and Mexico. Students pay no more than 15 percent of their income, and in some cases as little as 1 percent, for up to seven years. The company's U.S. branch, based in San Francisco, is working with investors, foundations, and institutions to start offering contracts here. Next semester, Lumni's first clients in the United States—several MBA candidates—will begin to receive funding.

A far larger company following this model is Career Concept, based in Germany. Started in 2002 by three business school graduates, the company now finances about 2,000 students at 180 universities in more than 20 countries, mostly in the EU. Typically, students are obliged to repay between 3 percent and 10 percent of their income over a period of between four and six years.

"We've proven that the model is working," says Rolf Zipf, one of the board members. Last year, a new company, Deutsche Bildung, started up in Germany to offer similar contracts.

The U.S. government has recently enacted policies to tackle some of the problems caused by student loan debt. Legislation passed last year introduces a cap on debt repayment for federal loans—students who opt for income-based repayment will not be required to pay more than 15 percent of their discretionary income—and forgives federal loans for graduates who spend 10 years in public service. These measures, which take effect next year, will surely help graduates, but they do not offer a comprehensive solution. There are still limits on federal loans, which means many students still need to turn to the private lending market.

The potentially lower payments explain why human capital contracts would draw students, but there are attractions for investors as well.

Human capital companies would essentially be creating a new type of asset, based on the wages of college graduates, offering investors another way to diversify their portfolios. An "educational fund offers you as an investor a very steady flow," said Zipf. "There is a protection against inflation. If inflation goes up, the income will go up."

The contracts could also provide a more targeted hedge for large employers. For example, a hospital could invest in medical students, thereby protecting itself against a rise in salaries for doctors; if salaries grew, the rising cost to the hospital would be partly offset by the higher returns on the investment. In the same vein, Google might invest in computer science students, and Boeing in engineering majors.

Other investors could be motivated by philanthropic goals. Wealthy alumni might see this as a way to help students attend their high-priced alma maters. Certain foundations, which are working with Lumni in Latin America, see these contracts as a more sustainable alternative to scholarships.

Instead of doling out money with no strings attached, as in a conventional scholarship, foundations could require students to sign contracts. These would state that nothing is owed up to a certain point, but high-earning graduates would repay a percentage of their income, allowing the foundation to recycle that money into later classes. Schools themselves could also incorporate this strategy into their financial aid packages.

For all the potential benefits of human capital contracts, however, they pose multiple challenges in practice. They create an incentive for graduates to hide their income; they also make it easier for graduates to loaf on their couches instead of working, since no fixed payment is required. Lumni, Career Concept, and My Rich Uncle all say that they have addressed this risk with intensive evaluations— Lumni even employs psychologists—and rigorously designed contracts.

The other danger is what economists call "adverse selection." Why, after all, would students who anticipate fabulous success sign up to subsidize their less go-getting peers? A student who intends to be a high-flying investment analyst might calculate that the payments on a traditional private loan are likely to take a smaller bite out of her salary than those for a human capital contract would.

Companies have dealt with this problem by offering more favorable terms to likely high earners. A Harvard student majoring in economics, for example, would repay a lower percentage of future income than would an art major at a community college. Ultimately, the graduates who prosper still must subsidize the graduates who flounder, or who choose unprofitable careers. But proponents point out that all insurance works this way. Life insurance, for example, requires contributions from the healthy and the lucky in order to operate. "You don't say, I just wasted my premium because I just subsidized someone who died," says Ian Ayres, an economist and Yale law professor who supports the idea of human capital contracts.

Another worry is that the companies would discriminate against students from low-income backgrounds, either by offering them unfavorable terms or no contract at all, since they are less likely to enroll at prestigious institutions and excel academically. Proponents acknowledge that the contracts are not a panacea for higher-education financing, and that government financial aid would still play an important role. But if contracts help some students, they say, government funds can be diverted to others. Altruistic investors may also target low-income students.

There are legal questions, too. It's not clear how the contracts would be enforced, how the IRS would treat them, and what would happen in the case of bankruptcy. My Rich Uncle declined to discuss the details of their contracts, but said that, having meticulously consulted lawyers, they did not encounter legal obstacles. If more companies begin to offer the contracts, these issues will no doubt be tested in court.

In addition to the benefits for students and investors, proponents believe that if human capital contracts became widespread, they could actually influence higher education itself, by pushing schools to better prepare students for professional success. As investors became more sophisticated, they would offer better terms to students at schools that offer good value—measured in terms of the boost to earning power per dollar of tuition invested. Today, information about the economic worth of an education—about the jobs, promotions, and salaries of graduates—is surprisingly inaccessible for applicants. But companies would have the incentive, and the resources, to find those data, which would be reflected in the contracts they offered for different institutions. In theory, this could eventually pressure schools that are low-performing, at least in this economic sense, to tackle their failings or lower their tuition.

"If college is doing a really bad job at all these things, students would start to see that," says Carey, author of the recent article in *The American*. "That will force colleges to pay more attention."

REBECCA TUHUS-DUBROW

Source: Rebecca Tuhus-Dubrow.

Commentary

The capital markets are innovative, move at almost instantaneous speed, and are global. Money flows at the touch of a button from anywhere to anywhere. When the Basel agreement required that developed countries use the same risk definitions for lending, the capital markets responded by creating new financial instruments that spread the risk around the globe. These new instruments—derivatives, credit default obligations, mortgage-backed securities, and others—were at the center of the 2007 housing and stock market collapses. Many politicians argue that these collapses should not have developed, that additional controls and regulations are needed. Some have even called for banning the development of such instruments.

If financial instruments and contracts such as the developments that led to the recession that began in 2007 are risky, what does that mean for financial instruments based on human capital? Capital markets considering new instruments called human capital contracts, or BOB (betting on Bob). How would they work? Could a market in such contracts be developed; could investors buy and sell shares of different people or bundles of human capital contracts? Capital refers to products such as machinery and equipment that are used in production. Human capital refers to the skills and attributes of a person that enables him to produce labor services. If capital can be financed through the capital markets, then why not human capital?

One reason that capital can obtain financing quite readily is that the value of that capital is easily determined. If the financial capital is not repaid, the capital might have value alone or in another use. Human capital is part and parcel of the individual. It cannot be separated from the individual. So if the borrower defaults or the person does not provide returns to investors, the capital cannot be taken and used elsewhere. Can the person be thrown into debtors' prison or subjected to indentured servitude? No, those types of penalties are not legal.

If investors are willing to bet on Bob, then they have to take into account the risk of not collecting. Thus, the return required on the investment would be higher than the return required on a less risky investment. It does make sense that investors would predict the likelihood of high returns based on the majors and specialties of the individuals and offer different rates to different individuals. But this creates the possibility of moral hazard. Bob declares a major in economics and obtains an investment or loan based on his future expected earnings. Then Bob changes his major to sociology, which promises to return much less than majoring in economics. What can the investor do about it? Nothing, if the investor owns only the Bob contract. In the case of a stock market in human capital contracts, the investor would take a loss by selling the stock in Bob after Bob changed majors. Of course, there are also other problems, such as Bob becoming an alcoholic or a drug addict, or getting in an accident and destroying his chance of earning a living. These risks would tend to raise the rate of return the investor would require to make an investment in Bob.

If enough human capital contracts could be bundled together, such as in a mutual fund, the risk that Bob might default would be spread across all the individuals bundled in the fund. This is the way insurance works; high-risk and low-risk individuals are bundled together to spread the risk.

The capital markets are innovative, but can the problems in human capital contracts be overcome? Insurance firms are able to minimize moral hazard and adverse selection. Could mutual funds in human capital contracts do the same thing? Some firms are already trying it out. It will be interesting to observe how well they do.

The Land Market and Natural Resources

FUNDAMENTAL QUESTIONS

1. What is the difference between the land market and the markets for uses of land?

2. What is the difference between renewable and nonrenewable natural resources?

3. What is the optimal rate of use of natural resources?

Global warming, the destruction of the rain forests, the depletion of the ozone layer, the extinction of animal species, and other environmental issues are of great concern to many people. So are the costs that people have to pay in the name of the environment: higher prices for cars as a result of emission controls, annual fees to test for emissions from cars, higher gas prices because of refining requirements, higher taxes to pay for cleaning up the environment, and so on. All of these issues occur in the "land market." In this chapter we examine the market for land and natural resources.

1. Land

The category of resources that we call "land" refers not just to the land surface, but to everything associated with the land—the natural resources. Natural resources are the nonproduced resources with which a society is endowed. A market exists for each type of natural resource and for each use of land.

1.a. Fixed Supply of Land: Economic Rent

The market for land is, in the most general terms, a market with a fixed supply. There is only so much land available. Obviously land is used in many different ways—for cities and housing, parks, wilderness areas, agricultural areas, and on and on. For each use of land, there is a market in which the typical demand and supply curves apply. For instance, the market for land on which to put housing has a demand curve that slopes down and a supply curve that slopes up. As the price of land available for housing rises, the quantity of land demanded for housing declines and the quantity of land available increases. However, in the general market for land, where there is a fixed supply of land, we have a downward-sloping demand curve but a perfectly inelastic supply curve.

Recall from the discussion of resource markets that when a resource has a perfectly inelastic supply curve, its earnings are called **economic rent**. If a resource has a perfectly elastic supply curve, its earnings are called **transfer earnings**. For resources with upward-sloping supply curves, earnings consist of both transfer earnings and economic rent. Transfer earnings are what a resource could earn in its best alternative use. This is the amount that must be paid to get the resource owner to "transfer" the resource to

economic rent
The portion of earnings above transfer earnings.

transfer earnings
The amount that must be paid to a resource owner to get him or her to allocate the resource to another use.

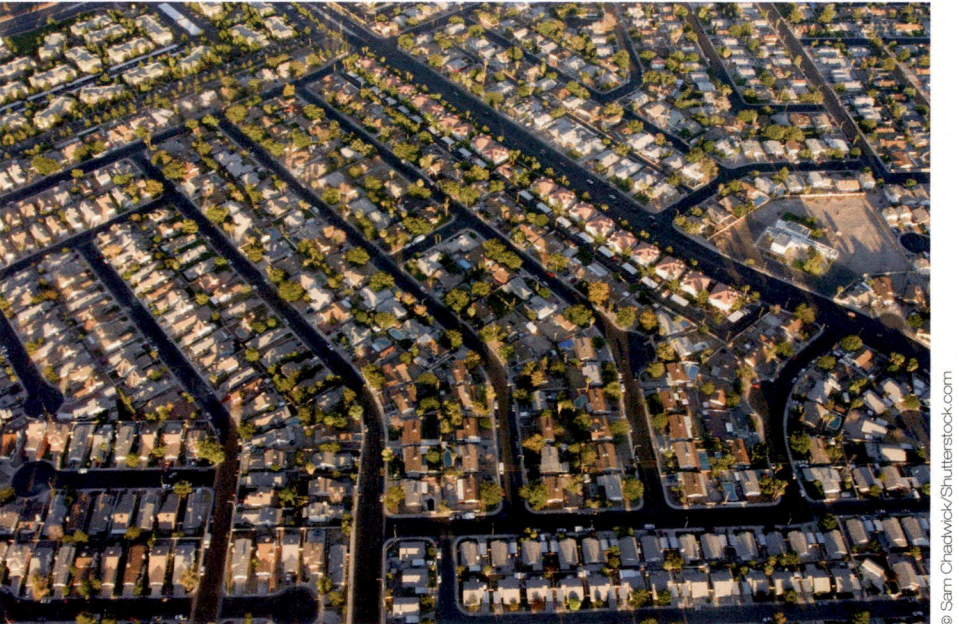

This sea of roofs is the result of new homes built in Las Vegas, Nevada, the fastest-growing city in the United States until 2006. It then became the largest loser in the housing markets in major metropolitan areas. The demand for new housing means a demand for land on which to put new housing. Because the use of land for housing is more valuable than the use of the land as open desert, the land is reallocated. Water is a different matter. Las Vegas has no natural supply of water; instead, water is brought in from the Colorado River. Yet there is a huge demand for water to be used in swimming pools. As the population of Las Vegas continues to grow, the demand for water will continue to rise. Eventually, water prices will begin rising to match demand and supply.

another use. Economic rent is earnings in excess of transfer earnings. It is the portion of a resource's earnings that is not necessary to keep the resource in its current use.

You've seen that there are two different meanings for the term *rent* in economics. The more common meaning refers to the payment for the use of something—the rent on an apartment, for instance. The second use of the term *rent* is to mean payment for something whose quantity is fixed—that is, something that has a perfectly inelastic supply. The total quantity of land is fixed, so payment for land is economic rent.

The reason that the earnings of a good, service, or resource whose supply is fixed are called economic rent is to distinguish the result of changes in rent from that of changes in the price of a good, service, or resource that is not fixed in quantity. When the price of a good increases, everything else the same, the quantity supplied will increase. But when economic rent increases, quantity supplied cannot increase. Therefore, an increase in economic rent is simply a transfer from the buyer to the seller without any change in quantity.

As we saw in the chapter "Market Failure, Government Failure, and Rent Seeking," the term *rent seeking* is used to distinguish the result of actions designed to gain additional income or wealth by seeking profits from the result of actions designed to do so by seeking rents. An increase in profits will bring on additional production and increased quantities supplied; an increase in rents simply transfers income from buyers to sellers. Rent seeking is not a productive activity; profit seeking is. Thus, economists refer to lobbying by individuals or groups to gain favors from the government as rent seeking. The resources devoted to the lobbying will not increase productive activities and quantities supplied; they merely transfer income and wealth from one individual or group to another. Rent seeking does not increase an economy's growth and improve its standards of living; profit seeking does.

1.b. Uses of Land

When we break the market for land into markets for uses of land, then the supplies are not fixed, and prices and profits function as they do in any other market: They allocate land to alternative uses. For instance, an increase in the demand for housing will drive the price of land used for housing up, inducing landowners to offer more of their land in the housing market. The land has to come from somewhere, so an increase in land devoted to housing means less land devoted to parks or agriculture or wilderness. The use of land is shifted to where the land has the highest value.

RECAP

1. The total supply of land is fixed.

2. The payment to landowners is economic rent because there are no transfer payments that serve to allocate resources.

3. The amount of land devoted to any given use is not fixed. The use of land depends on the demand for and supply of that use.

2. Nonrenewable Resources

2 What is the difference between renewable and nonrenewable natural resources?

nonrenewable (exhaustible) natural resources
Natural resources whose supply is fixed.

Nonrenewable (exhaustible) natural resources can be used only once and cannot be replaced. Examples include coal, natural gas, and oil. The market for nonrenewable natural resources consists of the demand for and supply of these resources. Supply depends on the amount of the resource, and the supply curve is perfectly inelastic. Only a fixed amount of oil or coal exists, so the more that is used in any given year, the less remains for future use. (This assumes that all sources of oil or coal are known.) But for any particular period of time, such as a year, the quantity that resource owners are willing to extract and offer for sale depends on the price of the resource. The supply curve in Figure 1(a) is upward sloping to reflect the relationship between the price of the resource today and the amount extracted and offered to users today. Resource owners are willing to extract more of a resource from its natural state and offer it for sale as the price of the resource increases.

When some of the resource is used today, less is available next year. The supply curve of the resource in the future shifts in, as shown in Figure 1(b) by the move from S_1 to S_2. The shift occurs because the cost of extracting any quantity of the resource rises as the amount of the resource in existence falls. The first amounts extracted come from the most accessible sources, and each additional quantity then comes from a less-accessible source. For instance, in the late 1800s, oil became an important resource. At first, it was extracted with small pumps that gathered oil seeping out of the ground. Once that extremely accessible source was gone, wells had to be dug. Over time, wells had to be deeper and had to be placed in progressively more difficult terrain. From land, to the ocean off California, to the rugged waters off Alaska, to the wicked North Sea, the search for oil has progressed. New drilling technology has led to the collection of oil by the process of fracking or fracturing. Fracking is the process of drilling wells 10,000 feet below the surface and then hundreds of feet sideways, and then water and chemicals are used to blast into the rock to force natural gas and oil out of it.

As more and more resources are extracted, the marginal cost of extracting any given amount increases, and the supply curve shifts up. If 200 billion barrels of crude oil are

---

FIGURE 1   The Market for Nonrenewable Resources

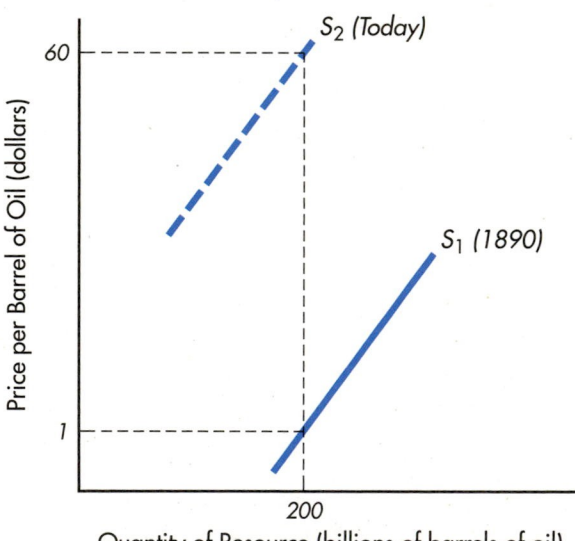

(a) Demand and Supply

(b) Costs of Extraction Rise over Time

The demand curve slopes down, and the supply curve slopes up. The intersection of demand and supply determines the quantity used today and the price at which the quantity was sold, as shown in Figure 1(a). As quantities are used today, less remains for the future. Because the available quantities come from increasingly more expensive sources, the supply curve shifts in over time, as shown in Figure 1(b). The curve S_1 represents the supply in 1890 and S_2 represents the supply today. For the quantity supplied at 200 billion barrels, the price was $1 per barrel in 1890, and today the price is $60.

extracted this year, then the extraction of another 200 billion barrels in the future will be more difficult—more expensive—than the extraction of the 200 billion barrels was this year. This increase is illustrated by an upward shift of the supply curve in Figure 1(b).

The demand for a nonrenewable natural resource is determined in the same way as the demand for any other resource. It is the marginal revenue product of the resource. Thus, anything that affects the *MRP* of the nonrenewable resource will affect the demand for that resource.

Equilibrium occurs in the market for a nonrenewable natural resource when the demand and supply curves intersect, as shown in Figure 2. The equilibrium price, $75, and quantity, 200 billion barrels, represent the price and quantity today. Extracting and selling the equilibrium quantity of 200 billion barrels today reduces the quantity available tomorrow by 200 billion barrels. This means that extracting the resource tomorrow is probably going to be more costly than extracting it today. Thus, the supply curve for the resource in the future lies above the supply curve for today—S_2 rather than S_1, if any of the resource is being consumed today. With a higher supply curve and the same demand, the price is higher, $100 rather than $75. Thus, the price in the future is likely to be higher than the price today if some of the resource is extracted and sold today.

The resource owner must decide whether to extract and sell the resource today or leave it in the ground for future use. Suppose that by extracting and selling the oil that lies below the land today, a landowner can make a profit of $10 per barrel after all costs

---

FIGURE 2   Price Today and in the Future

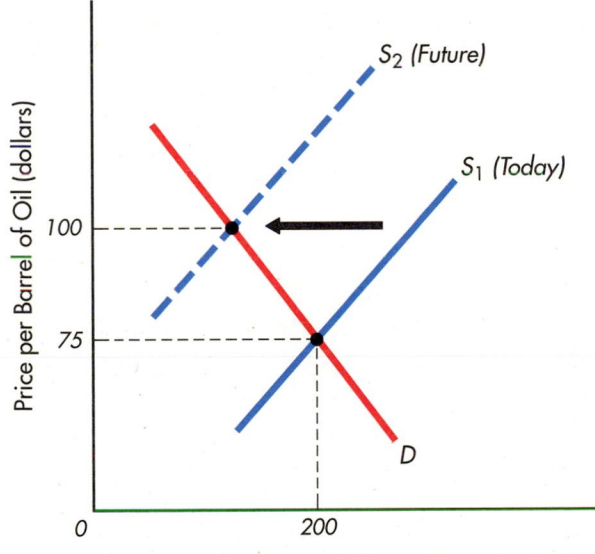

Equilibrium occurs in the market for an exhaustible natural resource when the demand and supply curves intersect. The equilibrium price, $75, and quantity, 200 billion barrels, represent the price and quantity of the resource used today. Selling the equilibrium quantity of 200 billion barrels today reduces the quantity available tomorrow by 200 billion barrels. With a smaller and probably less-accessible quantity available, extracting the resource tomorrow is probably going to be more costly than extracting it today. Thus, the supply curve for the resource in the future lies above the supply curve for today, S_2 rather than S_1, if any of the resource is being consumed today. With a higher supply curve, the price is higher, $100 rather than $75. Thus, the price in the future is likely to be higher than the price today.

of extraction have been paid. The owner could buy stocks or bonds with that $10, put the money into a savings account, or use it to acquire education or marketable skills. If the interest rate is 10 percent, the owner could realize $11 one year from now from the $10 profit obtained today. Should the oil be extracted today? The answer depends on how much profit the resource owner expects to earn on the oil one year from now, and this depends on what the price of oil and the cost of extraction will be one year from now.

If the owner expects to obtain a profit of $13 a barrel one year from now, the oil should be left in the ground. If the profit on the oil one year from now is expected to be only $10.50, the oil should be extracted and the proceeds used to buy stocks or bonds or put in a savings account. The more that a simple bank account or interest-bearing investment yields, the more oil is extracted and sold. As the interest rate rises, more is extracted and sold today, and less is left for the future.

> **3** What is the optimal rate of use of natural resources?

Because suppliers and potential suppliers continually calculate whether to extract now or in the future and how much to extract, an equilibrium arises in which the year-to-year rate of return for the resource equals the rate of interest on alternative uses of the funds. If the rate of interest is 10 percent a year, everything else held constant, the resource price will rise at a rate of about 10 percent a year (the rate of return must be 10 percent).

Suppose the interest rate rises above the current rate of return on the nonrenewable resource, oil. The higher interest rate means that producers will pump more oil out of the ground today and purchase stocks, bonds, or savings accounts with the money they get from selling the oil. More extraction means that the supply curve today shifts out and today's price falls. At the same time, the supply curve in the future shifts in (since less will be available in the future) and the future price rises. This will occur until the rate of return on leaving the oil in the ground equals the interest rate—that is, until the value of pumping the oil and selling it is the same as the value of the oil left in the ground. A higher interest rate implies the use of more resources today. Conversely, a lower interest rate implies the use of fewer resources today.

RECAP

1. Nonrenewable natural resources are natural resources whose supply is fixed.

2. The market's role is to ensure that resources are allocated across time to where they are most highly valued. If more is used today, the return on saving the resource for future use rises.

3. The higher the interest-earning potential on financial investments, the more of the nonrenewable resource is extracted today.

4. The more a nonrenewable resource is consumed today, the less it is available in the future and the higher its price is in the future.

3. Renewable Resources

renewable (nonexhaustible) natural resources
Natural resources whose supply can be replenished.

Renewable (nonexhaustible) natural resources can be used repeatedly without depleting the amount available for future use. Plants and animals are classified as non-exhaustible natural resources because it is possible for them to renew themselves and thus replace those used in production and consumption activities. The prices of renewable resources and the quantities used are determined in the markets for renewable resources. The role of the market is to determine a price at which the quantity of the resource used is just sufficient to enable the resource to renew itself at a rate that best satisfies society's wants.

Owners of forest lands could harvest all their trees in one year and reap a huge profit. But if they did so, several years would pass before the trees grew enough to be cut again. The rate at which the trees are harvested depends on the interest rate. A large harvest one year means fewer trees available in the future and a longer time for renewal to occur. This would suggest a lower price today and a higher price in the future. If the interest rate rises, everything else held constant, owners will want to increase harvesting in order to get more money with which to purchase stocks and bonds. This means harvesting more trees now and having fewer available in the future, thereby driving up the price of the trees that are not cut today. If the interest rate falls, owners will want to harvest fewer trees today. This means that today's price will rise and the future price will fall. As was the case with the nonrenewable resources, the market adjusts so that the resources are allocated to their highest-valued use now and in the future. The timing of the use of resources depends on the rate of interest.

Suppose you raise beef cattle and you want to remain in that business for most of your lifetime and eventually to pass it along to your children. You will sell only part of your herd each year to ensure that you will have a herd to raise next year, the year after, and so on. If you sell more in any one year, the size of your herd the next year will be smaller. If you sell the entire herd, you will have nothing in the future. What you want to do is to maximize your economic profit over the time periods during which you and your family remain in the business of cattle raising. Thus, you allocate the sale of your cattle over the various time periods. If the price of beef cattle increases rapidly one year because of mad cow disease in Britain, then you would sell more of your herd that year. Conversely, if the price of beef cattle falls substantially one year because of reports that eating beef causes heart disease, then you would sell fewer cattle that year. But even though the size of your herd varies with the price of cattle and the interest-earning potential of other financial investments, you don't sell off your entire herd unless you plan to get out of the cattle business. You retain enough cattle so they can propagate and replenish the herd.

The same principle applies to any renewable resource that is privately owned. The owner has the incentive to ensure that sufficient supplies exist in the future to maximize profits over all time periods. Some people argue that forests should not be privately owned because logging firms would raze or clear-cut the forests, leaving nothing for the future. But this makes no sense. No logging company that owns and logs its own forests would sell off all its trees unless it planned to get out of the logging business. When renewable resources are privately owned, the market ensures that resources are allocated between the current period and the future so those resources are used in the most valuable manner. The private owners want to maximize their profit over the current and future periods.

A problem arises with the current use of a resource, whether renewable or nonrenewable, when the resource is not privately owned. Recall from the chapter "Market Failures, Government Failures, and Rent Seeking" that private property rights are necessary if markets are to work. When common ownership exists, the common property is overused. Many natural resources are overused because they are not privately owned. For instance, many fish are overfished; some are nearly extinct. Many animals are over-hunted; some are nearly extinct. Many forests are razed; these are owned commonly (by a government). Air, lakes, streams, and oceans are often overused or polluted because they are not privately owned.

In summary, the markets for nonrenewable and renewable resources operate to ensure that current and future wants are satisfied in the least costly manner and that resources are used in their highest-valued alternative now and in the future. When a nonrenewable resource is being rapidly depleted, its future price rises and the value of using the resource in the future rises, so that less of the resource is used today. When a renewable resource is being used at a rate that does not allow it to replenish itself, the future price rises and the value of the future use rises, so that less of the resource is used today.

RECAP

1. Renewable natural resources are natural resources that can be replenished.

2. The rate of use of renewable resources in a functioning market system is one that equalizes the rate of return on the resource and the return on comparable investments.

3. A problem arises with the current use of resources, whether they are renewable or nonrenewable, when the resource is not privately owned. When common ownership exists, the common property is overused. Many natural resources are overused because they are not privately owned.

SUMMARY

1. **What is the difference between the land market and the markets for uses of land?**

   • The total amount of land is fixed. *§1.a*

   • Changes in the price of land do not change the quantity supplied. *§1.a*

   • There are many uses of land, and how much land is allocated to each use depends on the demand for and supply of land for each use. *§1.b*

2. **What is the difference between renewable and nonrenewable natural resources?**

   • Nonrenewable natural resources are inert resources—coal, oil, and so on—that are fixed in supply. *§2*

   • Renewable natural resources are resources that can regenerate, such as wildlife, flora, and fauna. *§3*

3. **What is the optimal rate of use of natural resources?**

   • The optimal rate of use of renewable resources is the rate that equates the expected return from using the resources and the expected return from not using them. *§2*

   • The optimal rate of use of nonrenewable resources is not zero. It is the rate at which the nonrenewable resource can satisfy society's wants now and in the future. *§3*

KEY TERMS

economic rent, 702
nonrenewable (exhaustible)
 natural resources, 703

renewable (nonexhaustible)
 natural resources, 706

transfer earnings, 702

EXERCISES

1. The market for some good or service is shown by the demand and supply curves below.
   a. Illustrate what transfer earnings and economic rent are.
   b. Explain what would occur if the demand for the good or service were to increase.

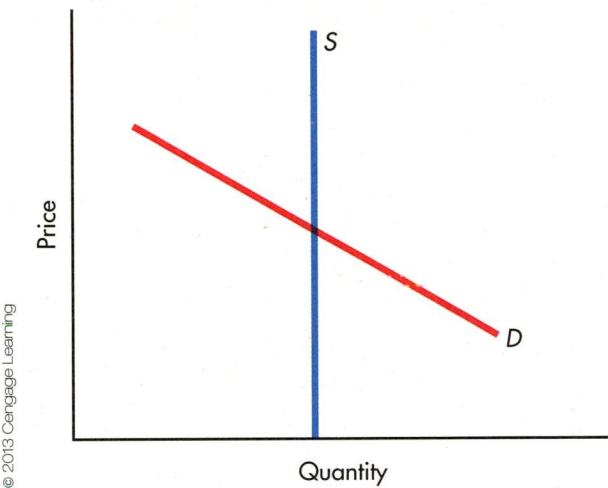

2. The market for some good or service is shown by the demand and supply curves below.
   a. Illustrate what transfer earnings and economic rent are.
   b. Explain what would occur if the demand for the good or service were to increase.

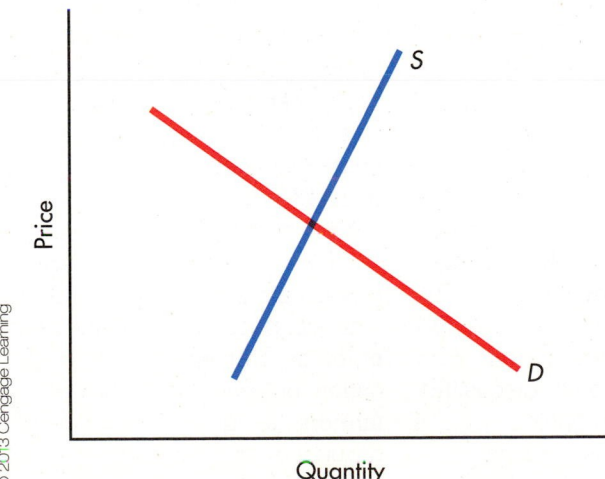

3. It is often stated that an artist is not famous until after he or she dies. Why do artists' works rise in price much more rapidly after the artist is dead than during the artist's life? How does this relate to the land market?

4. How would you describe economic rent in the case of a movie star earning millions of dollars each year?

5. If the world's population is rising and the quantity of land is not changing, won't the world eventually run out of room? Explain, using the market for land.

6. Will the world ever run out of a nonrenewable resource? Explain.

7. Suppose the supply of oil that had not yet been used was suddenly lost as a result of a rupture in the earth. What would occur?

8. The difference between a renewable and a nonrenewable resource is that the renewable resource can be replenished. Is there a difference between the markets for the two types of resources? What is the "optimal" rate of use of either renewable or nonrenewable resources?

9. In 2003, Alan Greenspan, chairman of the Federal Reserve, convinced the Open Market Committee to reduce the interest rate to near zero percent in an attempt to stimulate spending in the economy and increase the growth of income and employment. What might this policy do to the use of natural resources? Explain.

10. Urban sprawl is described as the establishment of housing and commercial development increasingly far from the city center. What might be the effect on sprawl if it was the policy of a city to build the infrastructure—sewers, power, and other essential services—to these developments at the average cost to the city? If it built the infrastructure at the marginal cost to the city?

11. If a city's political leaders decided to limit sprawl by restricting residential and commercial development to an area within a prescribed distance from the city center, what would be the effect on land prices in the areas inside the development boundary and outside the development boundary?

12. Illustrate the effect of the destruction of the oil fields of Saudi Arabia on the oil market. Explain what then happens to the market for gasoline.

13. Why are environmental problems often said to be simply a problem of common ownership?

You can find further practice tests in the Online Quiz at **www.cengage.com/economics/boyes**.

FAIR-TRADE COFFEE FIX; SMALL-SCALE PRODUCERS OFTEN END UP POORER, THANKS TO OUR GOOD INTENTIONS

National Post, May 14, 2011

Coffee is one of our guilty pleasures, and not only because of the calories that can be packed into a double latte. Many of us feel guilty that our pleasure is coming at the expense of the Third World coffee farmer, so much so that we gladly pay more for "fair-trade" coffee, which certifies that farmers receive more revenue for their crop.

Today, on World Fair Trade Day, we have something else to feel guilty about. That fair-trade cup of coffee we savour may not only fail to ease the lot of poor farmers, it may actually help to impoverish them, according to a study out recently from Germany's University of Hohenheim.

The study, which followed hundreds of Nicaraguan coffee farmers over a decade, concluded that farmers producing for the fair-trade market "are more often found below the absolute poverty line than conventional producers."

"Over a period of 10 years, our analysis shows that organic and organic fair-trade farmers have become poorer relative to conventional producers."

These findings do not surprise me. I speak as someone who has had contact with various Third World producers in my capacity as president of Green Beanery, a company I founded seven years ago to raise funds for Energy Probe Research Foundation, a federally registered charity that I manage. Green Beanery sells more varieties of coffee, including fair-trade and organic coffees, than any other company in Canada, giving me occasion to witness the nature of the fair-trade business, and hear first-hand of its impact on small producers that supply us.

The fair-trade business is filled with contradictions.

For starters, it discriminates against the very poorest of the world's coffee farmers, most of whom are African, by requiring them to pay high certification fees. These fees—one of the factors that the German study cites as contributing to the farmers' impoverishment—are especially perverse, given that the majority of Third World farmers are not only too poor to pay the certification fees, they're also too poor to pay for the fertilizers and the pesticides that would disqualify coffee as certified organic.

Their coffee is organic by default, but because the farmers can't provide the fees that certification agencies demand to fly down and check on their opera-tions, the farmers lose out on the premium prices that can be fetched by certified coffee.

To add to the perversity, it's an open secret that the certification process is lax and almost impossible to police, making it little more than a high-priced honour system. Although the certification associations have done their best to tighten flaws in the system, farmers and middlemen who want to get around the system inevitably do, bagging unearned profits. Those who remain scrupulous and follow the onerous and costly regulations—another source of inefficiency the German study notes in its analysis—lose out.

The study, published in the journal *Ecological Economics*, recommends that policy "move from certification schemes to investments in the farm and business management skills of producers"—in other words, phase out the certification fees.

Most merchants of certified coffees are aware of these contradictions, but most won't be aware of other problems in the certification business. For Third World farmers to qualify as fair-trade producers, and thus obtain higher prices for their coffee, farmers must join co-operatives. In some Third World societies, farmers readily accept the compromises of communal enterprise. In others, they balk. In patriarchal African societies, for example, the small coffee farm is the family business, its management a source of pride to the male head of the household. Joining a co-operative, and being told when and what and how to plant, entails loss of dignity.

The contradictions are acknowledged even by many fair-trade merchants, who often refer instead to anecdotal reports of less quantifiable benefits such as better health care or schooling in a village or even, most tangentially, improved habitat for birds or wildlife.

The contradictions extend to consumers of coffee in the West. Several years ago, I received a call from a church in Kingston, inquiring whether Green Beanery could supply it with freshly roasted fair-trade coffee on a weekly basis.

Along the way, the church officer mentioned that the parishioners wanted to do what they could to help poor farmers in the Third World. I replied that I'd be happy to supply the church, but I also advised him that fair-trade coffee would not help the poorest of farmers—these smallholders are actually hurt when Western consumers forsake them for coffee produced by better-off farmers who can afford the certification fees.

I also mentioned that various coffees produced by small farmers in some of the neediest parts of Africa would taste superb while costing the church less, allowing it to spend the difference on some other worthwhile cause.

After a long pause, the church official replied something like: "I still think the parishioners would feel better knowing that they were drinking fair-trade coffee."

Some believe that certified coffee is superior in some way. But it is not always so. The small-scale farms whose local ecologies produce distinctive, niche coffee beans can't operate on a scale that would justify official certification. As the German study notes, "Certified coffees have distinct production and marketing systems with different associated costs than the conventional system."

Neither is certified coffee different at all. In fact, at Green Beanery we have received bags of coffee, some labelled fair trade, some not, grown on the very same farm and identical in every respect. The fair-trade certified farmer himself can't tell which beans will be sold as fair trade and which not—that decision is made by the higher-ups.

Because the fair-trade associations are intent on keeping the price of fair-trade coffee up, they limit the supply of coffee that can be labelled as certified. To the certified farmer's chagrin, most of his fair-trade certified crop could end up being sold as uncertified conventional coffee.

And in this well-intentioned price-fixing game, the fair-trade farmer is the pawn and the joke is on the customer.

LAWRENCE SOLOMON

Source: National Post, May 14, 2011, Lawrence Solomon. Material reprinted with the express permission of: "National Post Inc."

Commentary

Is it foolish to hope that consumers are willing and able to pay a premium to ensure poor country laborers are paid more? If every coffee consumer purchased only fair trade coffee, would the world be better off? In essence, fair-trade schemes ask us to pay more for things we are told have been farmed in a sustainable way by workers protected by International Labor Organisation conventions. If every consumer agreed to this, paying, say, 25 percent more for coffee, would the laborer end up with 25 percent more pay? How much additional pay, if any, the laborer would receive depends on the price elasticities of demand for and supply of coffee, and the demand for and supply of laborers. If consumers are willing to pay more for the coffee and purchase nearly as much, their demand is price inelastic. But if there is a very elastic supply of laborers, it is unlikely that the price premium that consumers pay would go to the laborers. Owners would have every incentive to keep the premium. Only if some monitoring and regulations were enforced, which would take some portion of the 25 percent premium, would the laborers be better off with the fair-trade regulations.

When people spend more of their incomes on coffee in order to ensure fair-trade practices, they are spending less on other goods and services. What happens to the laborers producing the goods and services on which consumers now spend less? Yes, their pay goes down. So the fair-trade policy has transferred wealth from non-coffee-related laborers to the coffee laborers. Is this "fair"?

According to the article, the unregulated market ends up with "... gross disparities of wealth, corruption, child labor, and sweatshops." Do free markets create wealth inequalities? Yes, because in a free market resources are paid the value of their productivity; different skills and other characteristics will yield different pay. The amazing thing about the market is that this pay disparity has no inclination to stay in place; people have incentives to upgrade skills and increase productivity. People move up in income classes over time.*

Child labor and sweatshops go hand in hand in the minds of the citizens of many developed countries. Sweatshops refer to manufacturing facilities in less-developed countries that have lesser working conditions and much lower pay than the workers in developed countries are used to. But a job in a sweatshop is often the best job a poor, unskilled person in a less-developed country can get. As long as people work voluntarily in the sweatshop, we know they are better off than they would be in the next best occupation. Child labor existed in the agrarian United States and even in the beginning of the U.S. industrial revolution. Again, as long as the labor was provided voluntarily, the children benefited. If forced into child labor, then the child is worse off and that is not consistent with a free market. People do not engage in voluntary trade unless they expect to be better off.

Although on the surface it seems that fair-trade regulations would help the poor in the poor nations, the logic of economics suggests otherwise.

---

* Edward Browning, in *Stealing from Each Other* (Westport, CT: Praeger Publishers, 2008), notes that, when adjusted for government transfers and other issues, incomes in the United States have not become more unequal.

CHAPTER 32

Aging, Social Security, and Health Care

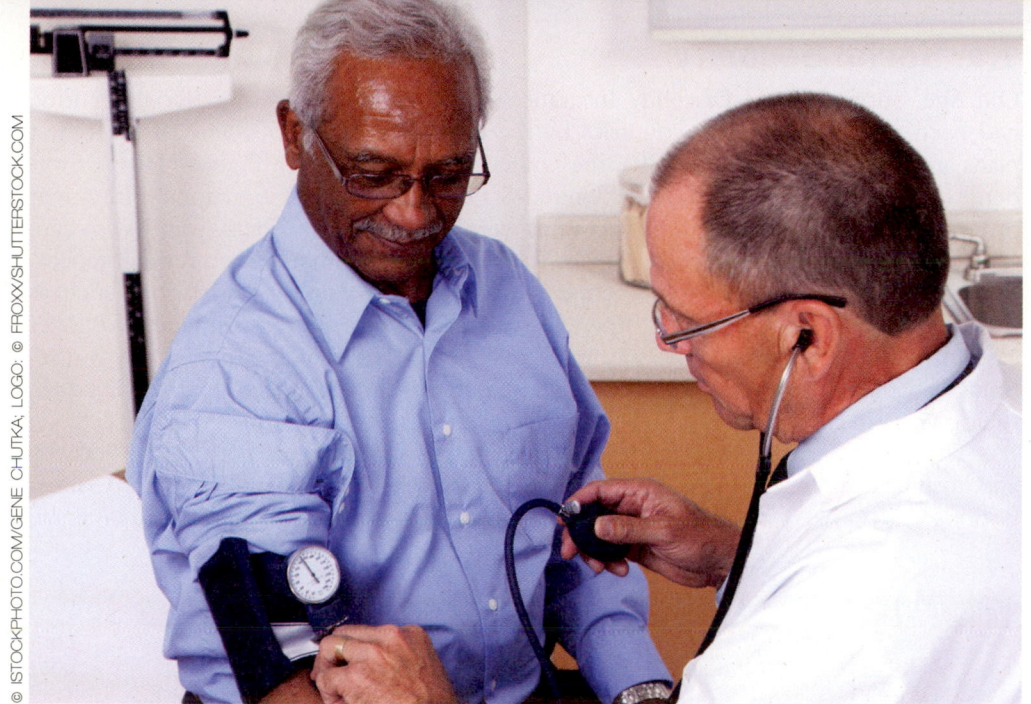

© MACIEJ FROLOW/GETTY IMAGES, INC

 FUNDAMENTAL QUESTIONS

1 Why worry about Social Security?

2 Why is health care heading the list of U.S. citizens' concerns?

The population of the United States is aging rapidly. Currently, more than 12 percent of the population is retired—living off pensions, savings, and Social Security. By the year 2030, 21 percent of the population will be older than 65. The aging of the population is likely to have a dramatic effect on living standards. For instance, the elderly will increasingly influence the types of goods and services produced. In particular, expenditures on health care will continue to rise. The aging of the population also means that an increasing percentage of people will be retired and a smaller percentage will be producing goods and services and paying taxes. What are the implications for Social Security and for productivity? In this chapter, we look at the impact of an aging population on medical care and Social Security.

1. Aging and Social Security

In the United States, persons 65 years or older represent more than 13 percent of the total population, about one in every eight Americans, and the oldest group of Americans is getting older. In 2009, the 65 to 74 age group was more than 8 times larger than in 1900, but the 75 to 84 age group was more than 12 times larger, and the 85-plus age group was more than 22 times larger. The median age in 1850 was 18.9. It is now approaching 40.

The pattern of aging is clearly visible in Figure 1, which shows the percentage of total U.S. population that is 65 years old or more than 65 years old.

1 Why worry about Social Security?

1.a. Social Security

Old-Age, Survivors, and Disability Insurance (OASDI), also known as Social Security, had been established in 108 countries by the beginning of 1975. Some of the oldest plans are those of Germany (1889), the United Kingdom (1908), France (1910), Sweden (1913), and Italy (1919). The United States did not enact a national retirement program until 1935. Before these programs were instituted, the elderly were taken care of by family, organizations, and religions. It was not uncommon to see several generations living in one house or for people to belong to voluntary associations such as Moose, Elk, and other so-called "friendly societies." Once the government took over care for the elderly, the membership in friendly societies declined and very few households had more than parent and child. Grandparents and great grandparents lived on their own or in care facilities.

The Social Security system in the United States, which covers both Social Security and hospital insurance (Medicare), is financed by a payroll tax, Federal Insurance Contributions Act (FICA), which is levied on the employer and the employee in equal

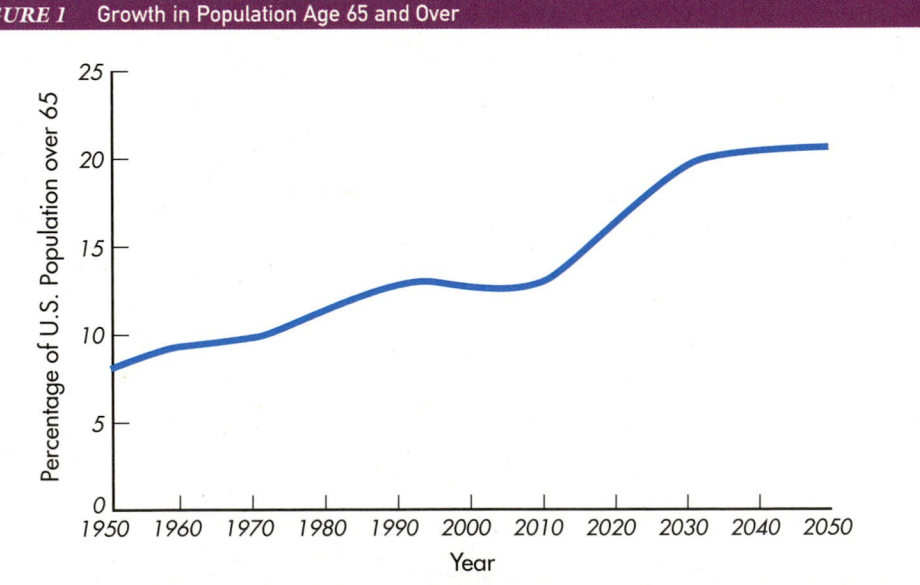

| FIGURE 1 | Growth in Population Age 65 and Over |

It is clear that the United States population is aging. The growth of people 65 or over is currently about 13 percent of the total population but will rise to 20 percent by 2030.

Source: http://www.whitehouse.gov/omb/budget/fy2009/outlook.html.

portions, although in 2011 the portion levied on the employee was decreased (4.2% for employees, 6.2% for employers in 2011). The initial FICA tax rate was 1 percent of the first $3,000 of wage income paid by both parties. In 2011, the tax rate for employers was 6.2 percent on the first $106,800 of earnings on both parties (although the rate on employees was temporarily reduced to 4.2%) for the Social Security contribution and 1.45 percent on all earnings for the Medicare contribution. For a self-employed person, the tax rate is 12.4 percent for Social Security and 2.9 percent for Medicare.

1.b. The Viability of Social Security

The Social Security taxes that the working population pays today are used to provide benefits for current retirees. The Social Security system is called a pay-as-you-go system. Taxes collected are paid to current retirees and any surplus is given to the Treasury. As a result, the financial viability of the system depends on the ratio of those working to those retired. The age distribution of the U.S. population has affected this viability. As illustrated in Figure 2, the ratio has declined from 16.5 in 1950 to about 3 today and is expected to decline to 2 by 2030. The situation in the United States is no different from that in many other parts of the world, as noted in the Global Business Insight "The World Is Aging."

In the past two decades, the Social Security tax has risen more rapidly than any other tax. Social Security tax revenues were less than 5 percent of personal income in 1960 and currently exceed 11 percent of personal income. The revenues from the personal income tax were 3.4 percent of personal income in 1940 and rose to more than 15 percent in the early 1980s. Social Security expenditures also have risen more rapidly than expenditures for any other government program. Social Security, Medicare, and

> *Social Security was intended to supplement the retirement funds of individuals.*

FIGURE 2 Social Security Viability

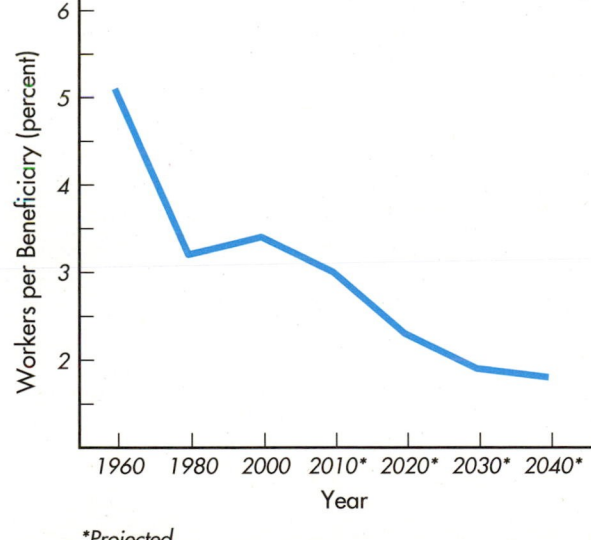

*Projected

The ratio of workers to Social Security beneficiaries is shown. The ratio has declined from 16.5 in 1950 to about 3 today and is expected to decline to 2 or less by 2030. This trend means that the source of Social Security benefits is getting relatively smaller. The viability of the system depends on whether the trends of recent years continue.

Source: Social Security Administration.

GLOBAL BUSINESS
INSIGHT

The World Is Aging

The United States is not the only country whose population is growing older. Most of the developed nations in the world are experiencing the same aging of their populations. As seen in the accompanying figure, in 1985 the elderly population constituted about 12 percent in the United States but nearly 17 percent in Sweden. Although three-quarters of the world's population resides in developing areas, these areas contain only about 50 percent of the world's elderly. The developed countries are aging because the birthrates in these countries have decreased and life expectancy has increased. Japan's life expectancy of 77 years is the highest among the major countries, but life expectancies in most developed nations approach 75 years. In contrast, Bangladesh and some African nations south of the Sahara have life expectancies of 49 years.

As longevity has increased and families have had fewer children, the ratio of persons 65 and older to persons age 20 to 64 has risen in most of the developed countries. These elderly support ratios will rise modestly over the next 15 years because the large number of people born between 1946 and 1961 will still be in the labor force. But as the large working-age population begins to retire after 2005, the elderly support ratio will rise sharply.

Source: U.S. Department of Commerce, U.S. Bureau of the Census, *International Population Reports.*

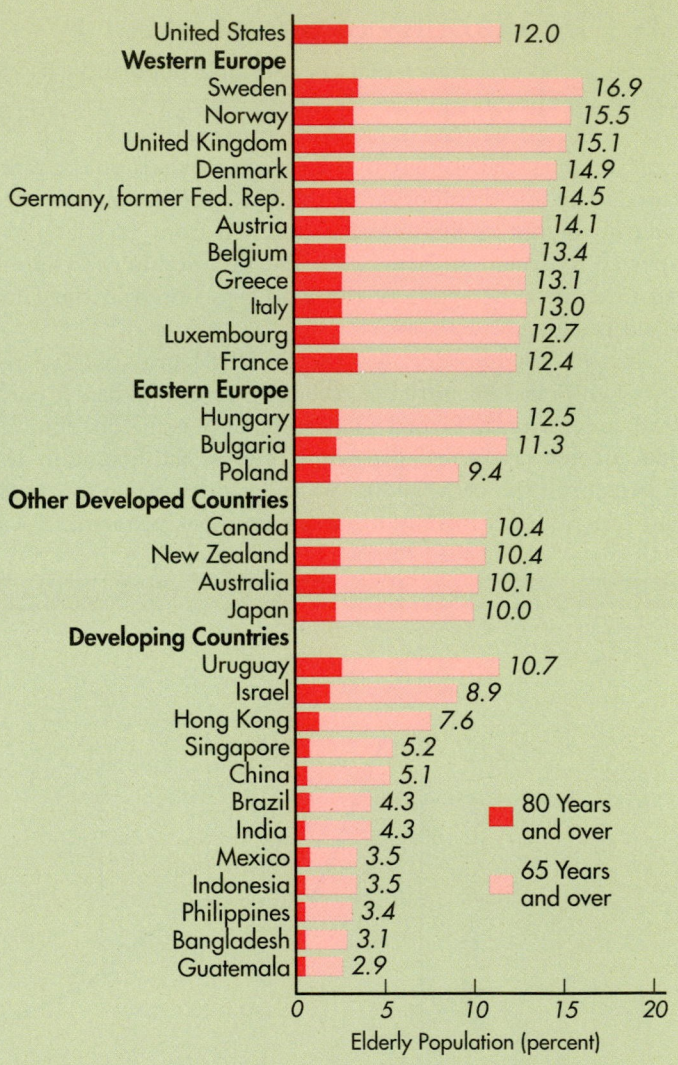

Medicaid outlays currently constitute 8.7 percent of GDP, whereas national defense is less than 4 percent, and education and training expenditures are less than 1 percent.

One of the concerns about Social Security is that Social Security taxes are not put into a place that is touched only when benefits are paid, that is, a trust fund. Instead, the money raised from the Social Security tax is used to purchase government

ECONOMIC INSIGHT

Myths about Social Security

There are several myths about Social Security. Here we examine just a few.

We've contributed to that fund all our lives! It's our money! It's not the government's money!

This is one of the most strongly and widely held myths about the Social Security system. In fact, the typical retiree in the 1980s and 1990s collected more than twice the amount represented by employer and employee contributions plus interest. Between 2000 and 2011, retirees collected more than they contributed by about 75 percent.

The benefits of the system are determined by a scientific formula designed to ensure that the fund remains viable.

Actually, the system of adjusting Social Security benefits annually as the cost of living increases dates only from 1975, and it came about as the result of political machinations, not foresight. In 1975, the annual benefits were about $7,000. Attempting to hold the line on federal spending, President Nixon proposed a 5 percent increase in Social Security benefits and threatened a veto of anything

higher. Democrats saw an opportunity to embarrass the president. They decided to pass a 10 percent increase and force Nixon to make an unpopular veto. The 10 percent increase was introduced in the Senate, but then rumors that Nixon would double-cross them and sign the bill anyway began circulating. So Congress increased the benefits by 20 percent, knowing that this huge increase would be vetoed. Nixon, however, signed the bill and proudly boasted of how well he had taken care of the elderly. Congress, irritated at being outflanked, passed the cost-of-living adjustment program to show that it, too, cared about the elderly.

Social Security ensures that only the elderly poor are cared for.

In fact, there are at least a million individuals currently collecting Social Security benefits who have incomes exceeding $100,000 per year.

There is a surplus in the Social Security Trust Fund.

There is no trust fund in which money is invested. The taxes collected are used to purchase Treasury bonds. It is these government bonds that make up the Social Security fund.

bonds—essentially giving the government a loan. The money the government gets from the loan is used to pay for general government expenditures. When the time comes for Social Security to cash in its IOUs to pay benefits, the federal government, which holds no assets earmarked for that contingency, pays the bill by issuing additional debt or raising taxes.

Another concern is that the amount paid into the Social Security system by an individual is far less, on average, than the amount received by that individual in retirement benefits. For example, people who retired in the 1980s, after working since the age of 21 at the minimum wage level, recovered all Social Security taxes paid—both employer and employee shares—in less than four years; an individual who earned the maximum taxable amount each year would recover the total contributions in only five years. Retirees in the 1990s recovered their total contributions and interest earnings in seven years. At the age of 82, the average worker who retired at age 65 will have received more than twice his and his employer's contributions to Social Security. Other Social Security issues are noted in the Economic Insight "Myths about Social Security."

So what's the alternative? There have been many proposals—increasing taxes, increasing the eligibility age, means testing, and holding down cost-of-living increases. The eligibility age—the age at which individuals can start collecting Social Security—was increased from 59 to 67 for those born in 1960 or later. Means testing—not paying Social Security benefits to anyone earning above a certain level of income—has been resisted but is under serious consideration. One of the more controversial proposals has been to privatize the system. This is what Chile, Australia, Turkey, Sweden, Italy, Argentina, Mexico, the Philippines, Great Britain, and several other nations have done.

Privatization allows individuals to choose among an approved list of possible investments rather than give the money to the government. What the individual earns on those investments will be the individual's retirement funds. Unlike the government program, which is a pay-as-you-go system and provides defined benefits to contributors, the private system will pay what individual investments earn. Some systems, like Chile's, are fully privatized: Workers are required to save a portion of their own salary for retirement, but they give no money directly to the government. Others, like Great Britain's, are partially privatized: Workers still pay taxes, but only part of this money is used to support a government-run system; the rest may be used for a private plan chosen by the worker. In Australia, workers are required to contribute 9 percent of their income to a fund of their choice.

The difference between what $1 put into the Social Security system earns and what that $1 would earn if it were invested in the stock market, for example, is very large. If individuals born in 1970 were allowed to invest in stocks the amount that they currently pay in Social Security taxes, those individuals could receive nearly six times the benefits that they are scheduled to receive under Social Security. Even low-wage earners would receive nearly three times what they would receive from Social Security.

But as good as this looks, people are critical of private investment because of the fear that many people will invest badly and end up with nothing. They look at what happened to the stock market in 2008 and wonder what would have happened to people who were planning to retire in 2009. Social Security, in contrast, seems to be a sure thing. Most of the privatization plans have met this criticism by ensuring that no one contributing to the new plan will receive less than he or she would have received under the former government-run plan.

The form of privatization differs from country to country, but the results have been uniformly positive. In every case, the returns that individuals have received have exceeded those of the government system. In addition, national savings rates have increased and government borrowing and debt creation have decreased.

RECAP

1. The U.S. population is aging as a result of lower birthrates, higher life expectancy, and the impact of the baby boom generation.

2. Social Security, otherwise known as Old-Age, Survivors, and Disability Insurance, is financed by a tax imposed on employers and employees.

3. Social Security uses the current working population's contributions to provide benefits to the current retirees. As the population ages, the ratio of contributors to beneficiaries declines.

4. Solutions to the Social Security problem include means testing, increasing the eligibility age, and privatization.

2. Health Economics

2 Why is health care heading the list of U.S. citizens' concerns?

Figure 3 shows that health care expenditures were only 5.9 percent of GDP in 1965 but exceeded 16 percent of GDP in 2010. (How this compares with other countries is shown in the Global Business Insight "Health Care Spending in OECD Countries.") What are the reasons that health care expenditures have risen so dramatically over that time?

2.a. Overview

Expenditures for hospital services constitute 31 percent of the nation's health care bill; nursing home expenditures, 8 percent; spending for physicians' services, 21 percent;

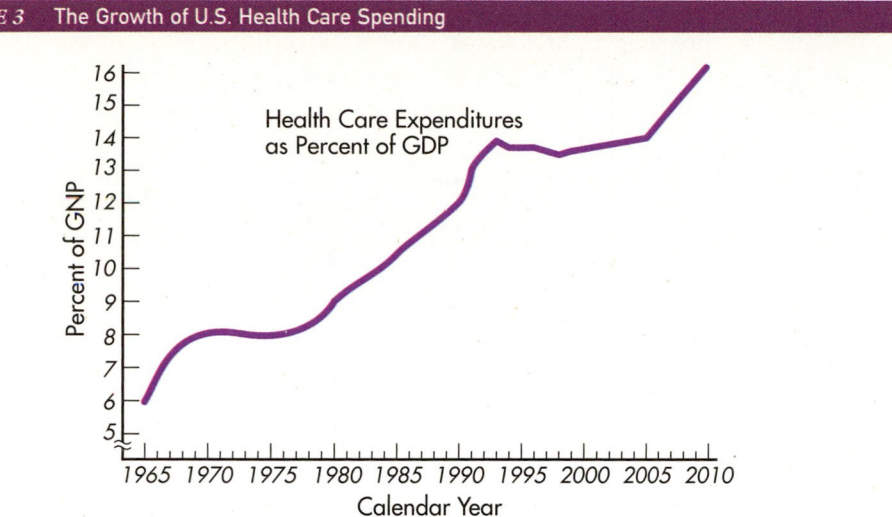

FIGURE 3 The Growth of U.S. Health Care Spending

As a percentage of gross domestic product, health care expenditures have risen from about 6 percent in 1965 to over 17 percent in 2009.

Source: *Health Care Financing Review*, May 2009; Office of National Health Statistics, Office of the Actuary; www.hcfa.gov/; http://www.nchc.org/facts/cost.shtml.

spending for other personal health care services, 11 percent; spending on prescription drugs, 10 percent; and spending on medical equipment at retail stores, 13 percent.

Of the $2 trillion spent on health care, private health insurance, the single largest payer for health care, accounts for 40 percent. Private direct payments account for 15 percent. Direct payments consist of out-of-pocket payments made by individuals, including copayments and deductibles required by many third-party payers (third-party payers are insurance companies and government).

Government spending on health care constitutes 45 percent of the total; the federal government pays about 70 percent of this. **Medicare**, the largest publicly sponsored health care program, funds health care services for about 40 million aged and disabled enrollees. The Medicare program pays for 20 percent of all national health expenditures and is rising due to part D, the drug benefit plan enacted in 2006. **Medicaid**, a jointly funded federal and state program, finances 16 percent of all health care, covering the costs of medical care for poor families, the neediest elderly, and disabled persons who are eligible for Social Security disability benefits. Other government programs pay for 9 percent.

Health care spending varies tremendously among various groups in the U.S. population. The top 1 percent of persons ranked by health care expenditures account for almost 30 percent of total health care expenditures, and the top 5 percent incur 55 percent of all health care expenditures. The bottom 50 percent of the population account for only 4 percent of these expenditures, and the bottom 70 percent account for only 10 percent of costs.

2.b. The Market for Medical Care

Rising costs or expenditures mean that the demand for medical care has risen relative to the supply (Figure 4). The initial demand for medical care is D_1, and the supply of medical care is S_1. The intersection determines the price of medical care, P_1, and the total

Medicare
A federal health care program for the elderly and the disabled.

Medicaid
A joint federal-state program that pays for health care for poor families, the neediest elderly, and disabled persons.

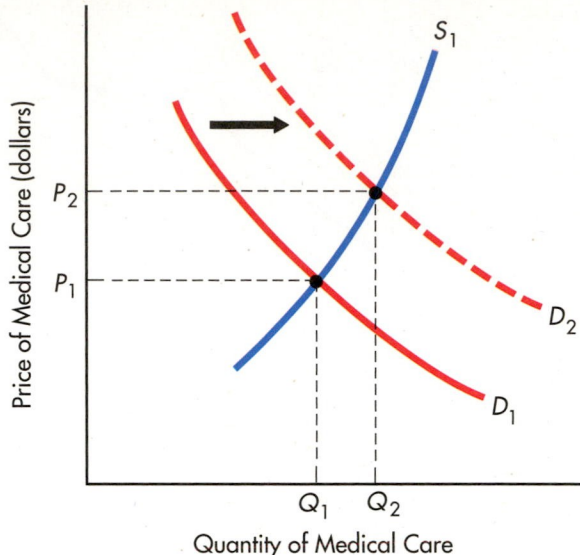

FIGURE 4   The Market for Medical Care: A Demand Shift

The demand for and supply of health care determine the price of medical care, P_1, and the total expenditures, P_1 times Q_1. Rising health care expenditures may be due to increased demand. A larger demand, D_2 means a higher price and a greater total quantity of expenditures, P_2 times Q_2.

© 2013 Cengage Learning

expenditures, P_1 times Q_1. An increase in demand relative to supply is shown as an outward shift of the demand curve, from D_1 to D_2. As a result, the price of medical care rises, from P_1 to P_2, as do the total expenditures on medical care, from P_1 times Q_1 to P_2 times Q_2. What accounts for the rising demand relative to supply?

> *Health care costs have risen because the demand for health care has risen relative to supply.*

2.b.1. Demand Increase: The Aging Population

The aging of the population stimulates the demand for health care. The elderly consume four times as much health care per capita as the rest of the population. About 90 percent of the expenditures for nursing home care are for persons 65 or over, a group that constitutes only 12 percent of the population. The aged (those 65 or older) currently account for 35 percent of hospital expenditures. In contrast, the young, although they constitute 29 percent of the population, consume only 11 percent of hospital care. Per capita spending on personal health care for those 85 years of age or over is 2.5 times that for people age 65 to 69 years. For hospital care, per capita consumption is twice as great for those age 85 or over as for those age 65 to 69; for nursing home care, it is 23 times as great.

2.b.2. Demand Increase: The Financing Mechanism

For demand to increase, the aged must be both *willing* to buy medical care and *able* to pay for it. The emergence of Medicare and Medicaid in 1966 gave many elderly the ability to buy more health care. Medicare covers the cost of the first 100 days of hospital or nursing home care for the elderly and disabled, providing benefits to over 32 million people. Medicare also, since 2006, provides prescription drug benefits. Like Social Security, Medicare is funded by payroll taxes and is available on the basis of age (or disability), *not* need. By contrast, Medicaid helps only the neediest people, including many elderly people whose Medicare benefits have run out.

The effect of the Medicare and Medicaid programs has been to increase the demand for services and to decrease the price elasticity of demand because individuals do not pay for much of their health care. Private sources pay for about 55 percent of personal health care for the population as a whole, and Medicare and Medicaid pick up most of the remainder. Private sources, however, pay for 74 percent of care for people under age 65. For the elderly, the private share of spending is only 15 percent for hospital care, 36 percent for physicians' services, and 58 percent for nursing home care.[1] Medicaid spending for those 85 or over is seven times the spending for people age 65 to 69 and three times greater than the spending for people age 75 to 79. This difference is attributable to the heavy concentration of Medicaid money in nursing home care, which those 85 or over use much more than others. Medicare spending for the oldest group is double that for the 65 to 69 age group.

2.b.3. Demand Increase: New Technologies
New medical technologies provide the very sick with increased opportunities for treatment. Everyone wants the latest technology to be used when their life or the lives of their loved ones are at stake. But because these technologies are cost-increasing innovations and because costs are not paid by the users, the increased technology increases demand.

2.b.4. Supply
Even if the demand curve for medical care was not shifting out, the cost of medical care could be forced up by a leftward shift of the supply curve, as shown in Figure 5. The supply curve, composed of the marginal-cost curves of individual suppliers of medical care, shifts up, from S_1 to S_2, if the cost of producing medical care is rising—that is, if resource prices are rising or if diseconomies of scale are being experienced.

Hospitals The original function of hospitals was to provide the poor with a place to die. Not until the twentieth century could wealthy individuals who were sick find more comfort, cleanliness, and service in a hospital than in their own homes. As technological

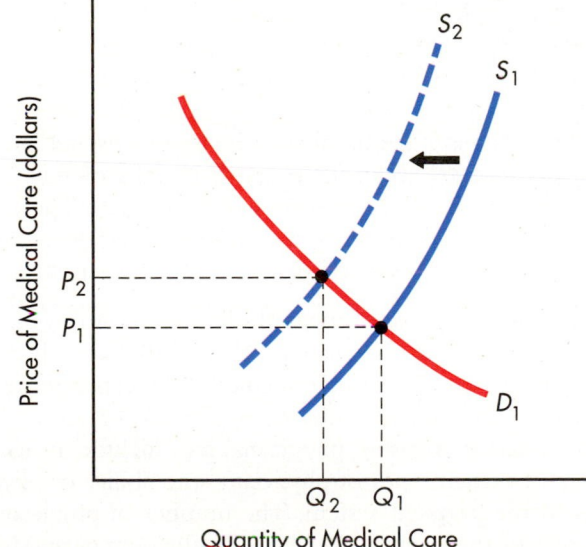

FIGURE 5   The Market for Medical Care: A Supply Shift

The rising cost of medical care may be caused by an increase in the costs of supplying medical care. The supply curve shifts up, from S_1 to S_2, and the price of medical care rises, from P_1 to P_2.

[1] *Health Care Financing Review,* various issues.

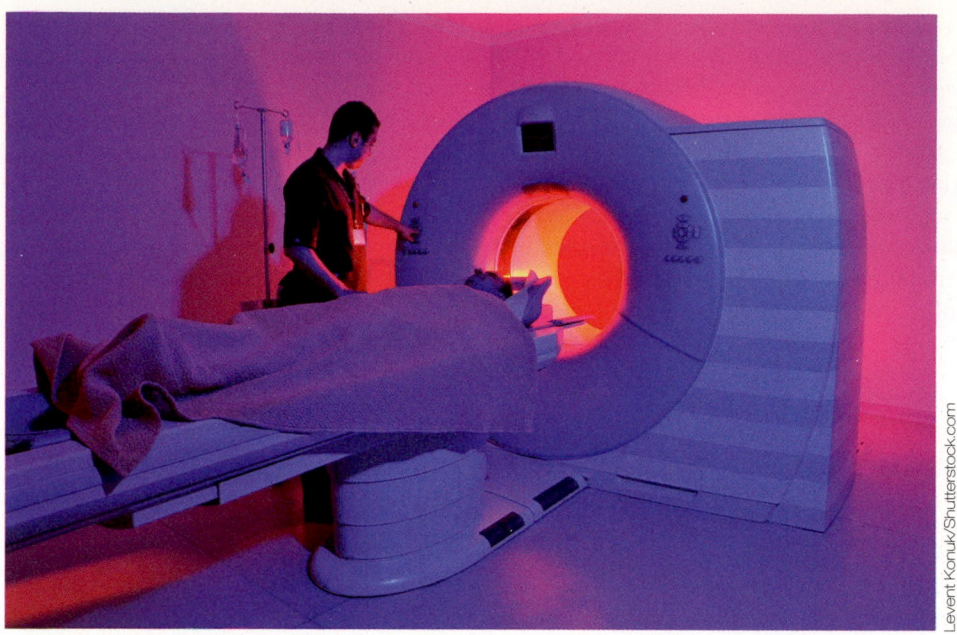

Medical care in the United States is expensive, but it is technologically superior to that in other nations. If patients do not have to pay the higher costs of the higher-quality care and instead insurance or government pays it, then patients will want the highest-quality care. As long as they get paid, doctors and care facilities will provide the high-quality care.

changes in medicine occurred, the function of the hospital changed: The hospital became the doctor's workshop.

The cost of hospital care is attributable in large part to the way in which current operations and capital purchases are financed. Only a small fraction of the cost of hospital care is paid directly by patients; the bulk comes from *third parties*, of which the government is the most important. The term *third-party payers* refers to insurance companies and government programs: Neither the user (the patient) nor the supplier (the physician or hospital) pays.

In the past 20 years, the average number of beds per hospital increased by 50 percent, inpatient days declined by about 10 percent, lengths of stay declined by about 10 percent, and occupancy rates declined by nearly 20 percent. The problem that more beds per hospital and shorter stays create for the hospital is that the occupancy rate is only about 66 percent, whereas the efficient occupancy rate is between 80 and 88 percent.

Physicians Physicians affect the cost of medical care not only through their impact on the operation of the hospital, but also through their fees. Expenditures on physicians' services rose more rapidly than any other medical care expenditure category in the 1980s and 1990s.

The factors that have led to rising physicians' fees include an increase in demand relative to the supply of certain types of physicians, the ability of physicians to restrict price competition, and the payment system. The number of physicians per population has risen in many areas of the country. Yet because the American Medical Association restricts advertising by physicians, consumers are unable to obtain complete information about prices or professional quality, and physicians are less likely to compete through advertising or lower prices. Moreover, the restrictions on advertising enable established physicians to keep new, entering physicians from competing for their customers.

The payment system influences both physicians' fees and the supply of physicians. Over 31 percent of all physicians' fees are set by the government. Physicians are reimbursed on the basis of procedures and according to specialty. A gynecologist would have to examine 275 women a week to achieve the income earned by a cardiac surgeon doing two operations per week. More than 60 percent of all physicians in the United States are specialists. The payment system has induced more physicians to specialize in certain areas than would have occurred otherwise.

The costs of doing business have risen for physicians. For instance, the cost of malpractice insurance has increased about 25 percent a year during the past two decades. Although only about 1 percent of health care expenditures can be directly attributed to malpractice suits, there are some implicit costs associated with the fear of such suits. This fear has caused an increase in both the number of tests ordered by physicians and the quantity of medical equipment purchased by them.

Prescription Drugs The fastest-growing health expenditure category since 1995 has been prescription medicines. Prescription drug expenditures grew by an annual average of 15 percent during this period. Again, looking at the demand for and supply of prescription drugs explains the increase. Medicare has increased the ability to buy drugs. In addition, the existence of new drugs raises the demand for drugs as people seek better medicines and previously unavailable cures for diseases. On the supply side, the cost of producing a new drug has risen dramatically; on average it exceeds one billion dollars. Part of the production cost is caused by government restrictions regarding which drugs can be placed on the market in the United States. The only way a company can sell a new drug or medical device in the United States is to get permission from the Food and Drug Administration (FDA), and the FDA is increasingly reluctant to give this permission. It has a very strong incentive to keep unsafe products off the market, even if in doing so it may block beneficial new products. As a result, the FDA has made it increasingly difficult to bring a new drug to market. The time required to bring a new drug to market, including preclinical testing, clinical development, and regulatory review, has increased from a low of 6.3 years in 1963–1965 to 16.1 years. This delay means that the percentage of drugs that are available first in the United States is low. Although more than 60 percent of biopharmaceutical products approved in the United States, Europe, or Japan originated in the United States, less than 18 percent were first marketed in the United States. The latest estimate of the cost to develop a new drug and bring it to market exceeds $800 million; in 1987 the cost was $231 million.[2]

2.c. Do the Laws of Economics Apply to Health Care?

Many people claim that the laws of economics do not apply to health care and that is why the government must be responsible for health care. People tend to look at health care as a right, something that everyone is entitled to regardless of costs. You may recall our survey and discussion about allocation mechanisms in the chapter "Markets, Demand and Supply, and the Price System"; most people look at health care as something different from other goods and services. They do not want the market system to determine who gets health care and who doesn't.

Is health care a scarce good? The answer is a clear yes; at a zero price, more people want health care than there is health care available, the definition of a scarce good. Scarcity means that choices must be made, that there is an opportunity cost for choosing to purchase the scarce good. The choice is made on the basis of rational self interest. These principles of economics suggest that health care is an economic good and is subject to the laws of economics.

[2] Denise Myshko, "Pricing—The Cost of Doing Business," *PharmaVOICE*, March 1, 2002 (www.websterconsultinggroup. com/pharmapricing_030102.html#head1). Tufts Center for the Study of Drug Development, 2004; http://csdd.tufts.edu/ NewsEvents/RecentNews.asp?newsid=6.

The demand curve for medical care looks like any other demand curve; it slopes down because the higher the price, the lower the quantity demanded. The demand curve is probably quite inelastic. There also is a standard-looking supply curve. Physicians, hospitals, and medical firms offer an increasing quantity of medical care for sale as the price rises. As shown in Figures 4 and 5 and repeated in Figure 6, the demand and supply curves look no different from the curves representing a market for any other economic good.

In Figure 6, the price for medical care is the level at which the demand and supply curves intersect, the point of equilibrium. At price P_1, the quantity of medical care demanded is equal to the quantity supplied. Those people who are willing and able to pay price P_1 (all those lying along the demand curve from A to B) get the medical care. Those who are not willing and able to pay the price (all those lying along the demand curve from B to C) do not get the care.

The problems that arise in the health care market are due not to a repeal of the laws of economics, but instead to the nature of the product. People believe that they and others have an inalienable right to medical care—that it is not right to ignore those people making up the demand curve from B to C on D_1. As a result, government programs such as Medicare and Medicaid have been created. These programs, along with private insurance programs, mean that most of the payments for medical care are made by third parties, as described earlier in this chapter. The third-party payment system allows many of those who would not otherwise be willing and able to purchase health care, those lying along the demand curve from B to C, to be able to purchase the care. This shifts the demand curve out, which drives health care costs up, as shown by the shift from D_1 to D_2 in Figure 6.

> "Repealing the laws of economics" in the case of health care means that the demand for and supply of health care do not determine the price or quantity and that it is not just those who are willing and able to pay who get the care.

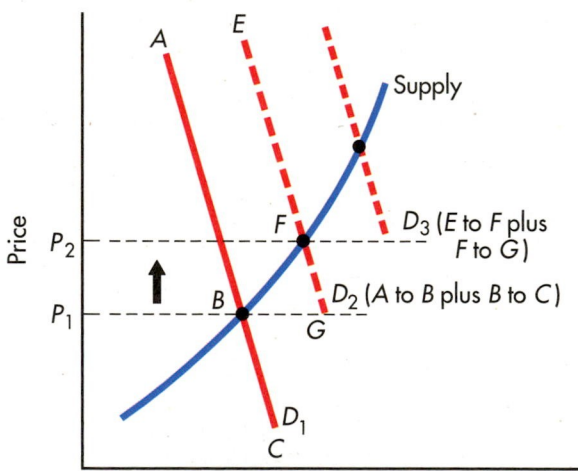

FIGURE 6   Do Laws of Economics Apply to Health Care?

Quantity of Medical Care

The price of medical care is the level at which the demand and supply curves intersect, the point of equilibrium. At price P_1, the quantity of medical care demanded is equal to the quantity supplied. Those people who are willing and able to pay price P_1 (all those lying along demand curve D_1 from A to B) get the medical care. Those who are not willing and able to pay the price (all those lying along the demand curve from B to C) do not get the medical care. The third-party payment system allows many who would not otherwise be willing and able to purchase health care (those lying along the demand curve from B to C) to be able to purchase the care. This shifts the demand curve out and drives health care costs up, as shown by the shift in the demand curve from D_1 to D_2.

The government and private insurance programs thus face ever-rising health care costs. Each new equilibrium means that some are unable to afford the care; if their demand is covered, the demand curve shifts out again, to D_3. This continues as long as someone is willing and able to pay the price. That someone has been the government, principally through Medicare, and private employers through employee benefit plans. The result has been double-digit price increases for health care for over a decade.

2.c.1. The Market for Human Organs

Many respected doctors, lawyers, economists, and ethicists argue that a legal and open market in organs, such as kidneys, hearts, and livers, could help cure the chronic organ shortage that is gripping transplant medicine. If the price is right and the seller is willing, why should someone not be allowed to sell a kidney? The debate over the issue is intense. Many who are against an open and free market in organs argue that it will result in exploitation of the poor. They point to cases in which black market activity has occurred, such as in India's poorest sectors, where, for about $1,500, poor Indians have sold a kidney and in just a few years are back in poverty, with huge debts and with one less kidney. But how people choose to spend the money gained from selling an organ has nothing to do with the market for the organs. People may fritter away money, but that has nothing to do with where they earned the money. The debate over the market for organs must focus on the supply of organs and the lives saved or lost because of the existence of a market in organs or due to the fact that a market is not allowed.

Supporters of a free and open market argue that it would increase supplies of transplant organs and save many lives. In the United States alone, there are 50,000 people on dialysis waiting for a donor kidney. About 3,000 people die each year while waiting for a kidney transplant. Thousands also die while waiting for livers, hearts, and other vital organs, and the number of people dying is increasing each year.

How would a legal market work? One part of the market would be the purchase of organs from living individuals. A person would offer a kidney or a part of a liver (since only pieces of livers, not whole livers, are needed for transplant) for a price. The price would be set by demand and supply. A second part of the market would be organs harvested from people who die suddenly, such as those killed in accidents. These people would have sold their organs, such as lungs, hearts, and kidneys, in what can be called a "futures" market. The rights to harvest these organs after death could be purchased from donors while they were still living, at prices set by supply and demand. Donors would be paid for future rights to their organs. So you could sell the rights to your kidneys once you die and receive the payment today.

What would be the outcome of such a market be? Let's use Figure 7 to illustrate the market for organs. The demand for organs would be price inelastic, since those who need the organs would be willing to pay just about anything they were able to pay to get them. The supply of organs is expected to be price elastic, at least once the price reaches some threshold level. For instance, a 10 percent increase in the price, say from $100,000 to $110,000, would induce more than a 10 percent increase in the number of organs offered for sale. And if a futures market developed, the supply would be price elastic, since everyone who now volunteers to donate organs would continue to do so, and many others would also do so because they would receive some income for almost no cost. The market for human organs would look something like Figure 7, where the equilibrium price would be P_1 and the equilibrium quantity Q_1. What would the price be? In the United States in 2000, a kidney was auctioned on eBay. The government terminated the auction after only a few hours, but when it was stopped, the price had reached $5 million. At the other end of the price range, the black market (illegal market) price of a kidney in India was about three times the average annual income, or $1,500. Some studies predict that the supply of organs and the alternatives to organs created by

FIGURE 7   The Market for Human Organs

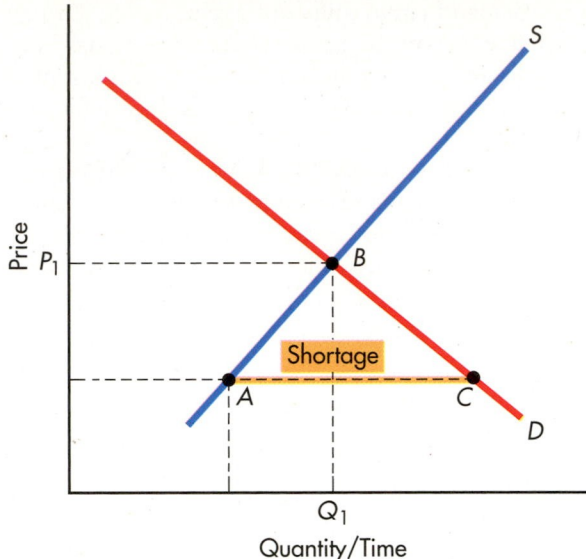

Quantity/Time

The demand for transplant organs would be quite price inelastic, since people awaiting a donor organ would be willing and able to pay nearly any price to save their lives. The demand and supply would determine the equilibrium price and quantity.

© 2013 Cengage Learning

technological changes spurred by the profits possible would drive prices to a very low level, perhaps $200, in just a matter of years.[3]

A black market arises when an item that some people are willing and able to buy and others are willing and able to supply cannot be legally traded. Black markets are less efficient or more costly than legal markets simply because traders have to be discreet, cannot meet buyers and sellers openly, and have no means to enforce agreements. As a result, the number of traders in the market is less than it would be in a legal market. Most of the evidence available regarding human organs shows that the market would be immensely larger if it were legal than the black market in human organs currently is.

The problem that most people have with the idea of a market in human organs is the potential for what they call exploitation. They point out that the organs would be going one way—from poor people to rich people, from the Third World to the First World or to rich people in the Third World. This is the way markets work—from those who are willing and able to sell to those who are willing and able to buy. Arguing that this result is bad is a normative argument, not a positive one. Similarly, the counterargument that a father who is desperate to provide a plate of rice for his starving family should be entitled to sell one of his kidneys on the open market is a normative argument. No matter what the normative viewpoints, there is a market for human organs; transplant surgery is a business driven by the simple market principle of supply and demand. The positive aspect of the issue is not who would gain and who would lose in a free, open market, because both buyers and sellers gain as measured by consumer and producer surplus, but instead, how does the current black market situation compare with a free, open, legal market?

[3] David L. Kaserman and A. H. Barnett, *The U.S. Organ Procurement System: A Prescription for Reform* (Washington D.C., The AEI Press, 2002).

2.c.2. Why Does Competition Not Drive Price Down? When the Mazda Miata

was first introduced in the United States, the price in Southern California exceeded the price in Detroit by about 25 percent, with the result being that the supply of cars in Southern California rose as cars in Detroit were shipped out. When housing prices rose faster than inflation or prices of other assets, the quantity of houses on the market rose. In general, when the price in one sector rises relative to other sectors, resources flow to where they are more highly valued. In the case of medical care, demand and supply have caused prices to rise significantly faster than inflation or prices in other sectors of the economy. We should expect resources to flow into health care and reduce the differential between its prices and prices elsewhere. Why has this not happened?

We have mentioned a few reasons—restrictions on entry, for instance. The American Medical Association restricts the supply of physicians. The AMA limits who can give prescriptions to only its members; a few years ago, pharmacists were responsible for dispensing drugs. The government restricts entry of drugs to the U.S. marketplace. The Medicare system restricts the movement of resources from one area in the health care market to another. In sum, restrictions do not allow the market to work to allocate goods and services and resources to where they have the highest value.

The market for medical care is far from a free, unregulated market. The restrictions and regulations inhibit the entry and exit of firms and inhibit the effect of competition on prices. In fact, most of the problems of the health care area in the United States could be minimized by turning the health care markets into more freely functioning markets. For instance, eliminating the incentive for people to purchase much more health care than they would if they were using their own money would lower the demand for health care. This could be done with the use of Health Savings Accounts (HSAs), wherein an individual would receive a sum of money, say $8,000 per year to spend on health care. If they do not spend it all they get to retain what is left. Some private companies are doing this with great success—such as grocers Whole Foods and Safeway. Currently, HSAs allow people to put a sum of money away tax free that they can then use to purchase health care. If Medicare and Medicaid were eliminated and those who would have been enrolled in those programs would be given HSAs instead, many malincentives of the current system would be eliminated.

Eliminating the reimbursement of physicians according to procedures would reduce the incentive of physicians to specialize in areas that are procedure-based. With HSAs, people would be much more discriminating in their purchases than when using Medicare or Medicaid. People would purchase only the care they feel they need. The resulting competition among providers would lower costs. The fact that this would occur is evident in two areas of health care where insurance has not played a role, laser eye surgery and cosmetic surgery. In both cases competition has lowered prices and increased quality.

Rather than moving the U.S. health care market toward more individual responsibility and free exchange, recent legislative actions have moved it toward increased government intervention and control. In 2010 the Democrats in the House and Senate, without any support from Republicans, enacted a law to enhance the role of government in the U.S. health care market.

2.c.3. The Patient Protection and Affordable Care Act of 2010 (Obamacare)

At more than 2,500 pages and 500,000 words long, the 2010 health care law is the most significant transformation of the American health care system since Medicare and Medicaid. The Act requires that every American purchase a government-designed insurance package. It alters the insurance market and essentially turns insurers into something like public utilities where the companies are privately owned but rates, profits, and other aspects of business are regulated by the federal government. The legislation was and remains highly unpopular. Several states have passed acts that prohibit mandatory health insurance, and numerous court challenges have been filed. As of this writing, the constitutionality of the Act is headed for determination by the U.S. Supreme Court.

The most controversial aspect of the law is its individual mandate, a legal requirement that everyone purchase health insurance that meets the government's "minimum care" specifications. Until the new law is implemented, people who believe they are healthy and/or don't otherwise want to purchase insurance do not have to. But, if the government plan is going to extend coverage, it has to include more low-risk individuals to offset the cost of the high-risk individuals that will be covered.

Other aspects of the law are that it takes the regulation of health insurance away from states and gives it to the federal government. It imposes many new regulations on insurance companies. One important restriction is to ban insurers denying coverage because of preexisting conditions. While this particular restriction is popular, many critics argue that people will not purchase insurance until they get sick. This is an "adverse selection" issue because insurance will only cover people who are sick.

The primary effect of the Act is to shift responsibility even more away from individuals to determine their health insurance and health care and give it to government. It moves health care away from market-based allocation and more toward government-based allocation.

RECAP

1. Health care is the fastest-growing portion of total national expenditures.

2. The demand for medical care has risen at a very rapid rate. One reason for the increase is the introduction of Medicare and Medicaid and private insurance plans that make demand relatively inelastic. The aging of the population has also increased the demand for medical care.

3. The cost of providing medical care has risen because of increases in hospital costs and physicians' fees. Rising hospital costs are partly a result of the reimbursement plans of third-party providers and partly a result of the control of the operation of hospitals by physicians.

4. Physicians' fees have risen even though the supply of physicians has risen. The demand for medical services does not match the supply; reimbursement methods have led to higher rates of return in certain specialties and thus have drawn an increasing number of physicians to those specialties.

5. The laws of economics do apply to the medical arena. They apply even in the case of markets for human organs.

6. The Patient Protection and Affordable Care Act of 2010 (referred to as Obamacare) alters the market for health care by shifting decision making away from individuals and giving it to government.

SUMMARY

1. **Why worry about Social Security?**

   - Social Security is a government-mandated pension fund. In the United States it is funded by a tax on employer and employee. The current tax collections are used to provide benefits to current retirees. *§1.a*

2. **Why is health care heading the list of U.S. citizens' concerns?**

   - The rapidly rising costs of medical care result from increases in demand relative to supply. *§2.b*

   - The increasing demand results from the aging of the population and from payment systems that decrease the price elasticity of demand. *§2.b.1, 2.b.2*

   - The reduced supply (higher costs of producing medical care) results from inefficiencies in the allocation of physicians among specialties and inefficiencies in the operation and organization of hospitals. *§2.b.4*

KEY TERMS

medicaid, 719   medicare, 719

EXERCISES

1. What is Social Security? What is Medicare? What is the economic role of these government programs?
2. Why have expenditures on medical care risen more rapidly than expenditures on any other goods and services?
3. Explain how both the supply of physicians and physicians' fees can increase at the same time.
4. Why are there more medical specialists and fewer general practitioners in the United States now than was the case 50 years ago?
5. What is the economic logic of increasing Social Security benefits?
6. What does it mean to say that people have a right to a specific good or service? Why do people believe that they have a right to medical care but do not believe that they have a right to a 3,000-square-foot house?
7. Suppose the objective of government policy is to increase an economy's growth and raise citizens' standards of living. Explain in this context the roles of retirement, Social Security, and Medicare.
8. Explain why the U.S. system of payment for medical procedures leads to higher health care costs than a system of payment for physicians' services.
9. Analyze the following solutions to the problem of Social Security.
   a. The retirement age is increased to 70.
   b. The FICA tax is increased.
   c. Income plus Social Security payments cannot exceed the poverty level.
   d. The total amount of Social Security benefits received cannot exceed the amount paid in by employer and employee plus the interest earnings on those amounts.
10. Oregon proposed a solution to the health care costs problem that was widely criticized. Under this solution, the state paid only for common medical problems. Special and expensive problems would not be covered. Using the market for medical care, analyze the Oregon plan.
11. What would be the impact of a policy that did away with Medicare and Medicaid and instead provided each individual with the amount that he or she had contributed to the Medicare program during his or her working life?
12. Why is a third-party payer a problem? Private insurance companies are third-party payers, and yet they want to maximize profit. So wouldn't they ensure that the allocation of dollars was efficient?
13. "We must recognize that health care is not a commodity. Those with more resources should not be able to purchase services while those with less do without. Health care is a social good that should be available to every person without regard to his or her resources." Evaluate this statement.
14. Explain and illustrate how a market for human organs could increase the amount of organs available and save lives. Explain and illustrate what would have to occur in order for the lives saved to decline as a result of a legal market for human organs.
15. Suppose firms provide health care coverage and drug benefits as part of their competition for employees. Suppose the government enacts a law that provides drug benefits to everyone, whether employed or not. What is the effect on employment and wages?
16. Why would the Patient Protection and Affordable Care Act of 2010 require everyone to purchase health insurance?
17. What is the moral hazard problem in banning insurance companies from denying coverage due to preexisting conditions?

You can find further practice tests in the Online Quiz at **www.cengage.com/economics/boyes**.

WHY SELLING A KIDNEY IS SUCH A DISTASTEFUL TRADE

© 2008 EXPRESS SYNDICATION

Whose life is it anyway? asked a famous play about euthanasia. Now there's a similar question over the sale of human organs for transplant: Whose body is it anyway?

A BBC Scotland investigation broadcast last night found evidence of an illegal black market in transplant organs—not the well-documented "organ tourism" by wretched Third World donors, but people here in the UK exploiting the despair of the sick by offering up healthy kidneys at fancy prices.

Many, I expect, will find it hard to imagine anything more grasping, twisted or callous. Yet it prompted a distinguished former president of the International College of Surgeons, Nadey Hakim, to argue that the unmet need for organs is now so acute that those prepared to donate a kidney to help someone else survive should get paid.

Hakim's argument is that, since the illegal trade is going on, it would be better if people who exercised their right under the Human Tissue Act to offer strangers a kidney for transplant were paid a set state fee.

That way, donor profiteering would be eradicated, and recipients could be judged by clinical need, not personal wealth.

Others would go still further. Why rely on the altruism of the few? In this age of eBay, every commodity has its price. Why should a healthy kidney, brought to market, be any different? What business is it of the state's if I choose to get by with one kidney rather than two? Whose body is it anyway?

Well, it may sound seductive as an argument, but it couldn't be more wrong. Trade in human organs is like trade in human lives or human souls: some things are just morally beyond the reach of the laws of supply and demand. As Billy Bragg once remarked, a market is a fine place to shop but a rotten place to be ill. The legislation was drafted to make room for those few fine folk whose compassion extends to sacrificing a kidney to save a stranger. It wasn't about creating a new industry for hucksters.

Charging to give a kidney is as wrong as charging to give blood.

Transplant entitlement is for the doctor, not the bank manager, to determine. Even Hakim's proposal, while better than an open market, fails the test. The principle of payment is no more acceptable for the bill being charged to the taxpayer. There's no reason to think it would prevent illegal trading while there's a profit to make.

Worse, it would tempt the poor to self-mutilate for money. I suspect some politicians would be only too ready to add a kidney count to the means test for benefits. We do need, urgently, to address the acute shortage of organs available for transplant. Britain has one of the lowest donor rates in Europe. But the right way to improve it is by "presumed consent" (an opt-out, rather than an opt-in regime) where fatalities occur, not by turning the clock back to the survival of the richest.

KEITH AITKEN

Source: Keith Aitken, Copyright 2008 EXPRESS SYNDICATION.

No one denies that an organ-shortage problem exists. Nearly 90,000 people are on waiting lists to get transplants. Every year, about 7,000 patients who need organ transplants die without getting them. The only legal way to get a transplant now is through voluntary donation. No country subscribes to an open, free market in human organs. But given the huge demand and the large shortage, people seek other ways to obtain what they need. The Internet allows a look at both sides of the issue: Advertisements placed by those seeking organs and those willing to sell organs abound. One ad from Korea provided information about health, blood type, and other crucial information regarding a man's kidney and liver. Another offered to sell at a price significantly lower than what was being mentioned in other ads.

Ignore for a moment what item we are talking about here. Look at a simple demand and supply diagram where the price is below the equilibrium. The shortage created is quickly erased as the price increases and the quantity supplied rises while the quantity demanded declines. If the price is not allowed to rise—if, in fact, the market is not allowed to legally exist—then the shortage will continue. Allocation of the scarce human organs will take place first come, first served or as government dictates. There will be no incentive for more human organs to be supplied or for anyone to come up with a technological innovation that might substitute for the human organs.

But if a market in the organs were made legal, the equilibrium would be reached as the quantity of organs supplied rose. So why does the public see it as such a terrible thing for a market in human organs to be made legal?

One fear often voiced on this subject is that you will be attacked and your organs stolen from you. There are two counterarguments against this. First, for a market to exist, private property rights must exist, and these rights must be enforced. You own a car. Do you constantly fear that someone will throw you out of the car and steal it? Do you constantly fear that someone will break down the door to your house and take all your property? You do not fear these things because you know that the police and the courts will enforce the laws that give you the right of ownership. Do these terrible things happen? Yes, but they are not very common relative to the number of cars and houses owned. In the case of human organs, you own your body—it is your private property. No one will be able to steal your organs—there are serious penalties for doing so, just as there are for murder. The market would provide the incentive for people to offer their organs—perhaps not right away, but instead through a futures market, in which they agree to sell their organs when they die.

A legal market in human organs would help the poor; it is one means by which parents can support their families. If a legal market existed, the poor could sell organs—get money now and give up organs in the future as well as sell a kidney or liver now—and use the money to send their kids to school or simply to feed the family. A market for human organs would work in the developed as well as the developing world. In the United States today, there is a thriving market to induce women to furnish ova for infertile couples.

CHAPTER 33

Income Distribution, Poverty, and Government Policy

FUNDAMENTAL QUESTIONS

1 Are incomes distributed equally in the United States?

2 How is poverty measured, and does poverty exist in the United States?

3 Who are the poor?

4 What are the determinants of poverty?

5 Do government programs intended to reduce poverty benefit the poor?

6 Why are incomes unequally distributed among nations?

ncome is what resource owners receive as payment for the use of their resources. Resource owners have incentives to increase the value of their resources—that is, to increase their income. They will innovate and adopt the latest technology in order to enhance the value of capital. They will acquire additional skills and education in order to increase their wages and salaries. They will redirect their land from agricultural uses to commercial uses when they gain from so doing, and they will make improvements to their land to enhance its value. Resource owners want to ensure that they get the highest value for the use of their resources, now and in the future.

In every society, different people own different resources and differently valued resources. This means that incomes vary from person to person. The United States is a wealthy society. Yet many Americans today are living on city streets, in parks, under bridges, or in temporary shelters. Income is unequally distributed in the United States. However, even the poor in the United States are better off than the entire populations of other nations. In Bolivia, the average life expectancy is only 53 years, whereas in the United States it is over 78. In Burma, only about one-fourth of the population has access to safe water. In Burundi, less than one-fourth of the urban houses have electricity. In Chad, less than one-third of the children reach the sixth grade. In Ethiopia, average income is just $120 a year. That is less than $1 per day.

Why is Ethiopia so poor and the United States so rich? Would the poor in the United States be rich in Ethiopia? Who are the poor and the rich? Is the inequality of incomes something that can or should be corrected? These questions are the topic of this chapter. Previous chapters have discussed how the market system works to ensure that resources flow to their highest-valued uses, that output is produced in the least-cost manner, and that people get what they want at the lowest possible price. But the market does not produce equal incomes. Markets ensure that goods and services are allocated to those with the ability to pay, not necessarily to those with needs, and definitely not in equal amounts to everyone.

One of the major controversies in economics over the last 100 years has been which system makes people better off—capitalism and free markets or socialism and government-controlled markets? In general, the answer is that capitalism and free markets lead to higher standards of living than government-run economies. The poorest nations in the world are the most repressive, and the wealthiest are the freest. Yet some wealthy nations attempt to ensure that incomes do not differ much from one individual to another. Sweden and Denmark, for instance, are wealthy societies in which government has a large role and family incomes do not differ much from one family to another. Hong Kong, on the other hand, has risen from a destitute little outcropping of China 50 years ago to one of the wealthiest societies in the world, and it has very little government involvement and wide differences in income from one family to another. In this chapter we discuss income distribution and how economic well-being is measured.

1. Income Distribution and Poverty

In March of each year, the U.S. Census Bureau conducts a survey of about 60,000 American families carefully selected to be representative of the whole population. Families are ranked in order of income from highest to lowest. Then they are separated into five equal-sized groups each containing a fifth of all families. The highest income fifth contains the 20 percent of families who have the highest incomes, the second fifth contains families with incomes between the 60th and 80th percentiles, and so on. Then the total income of the families within each fifth is summed and that sum is expressed as a percentage of the total income of all families. The result is five percentages that give the share of total income received by each fifth of families. Table 1 shows the results for 2005–2009. In 2009, the lowest fifth, containing the 20 percent of families with the lowest incomes, received 4.1 percent of total income, while the highest fifth received 47.3 percent.

 1 Are incomes distributed equally in the United States?

TABLE 1	Income Distributions, 2005–2009					
Year	Lowest Fifth	Second Fifth	Third Fifth	Fourth Fifth	Highest Fifth	Top 5 Percent
Share of Aggregate Income*						
2009	3.9	9.4	15.3	23.2	48.2	20.7
2008	4.0	9.6	15.5	23.1	47.8	20.5
2007	4.1	9.7	15.6	23.3	47.3	20.1
2006	4.0	9.5	15.1	22.9	48.5	21.5
2005	4.0	9.7	15.3	22.9	48.1	21.1
Mean Income*†						
2009	15,289	37,045	59,907	90,962	189,486	325,023
2008	15,906	38,125	61,582	92,160	190,400	294,709
2007	11,551	29,442	49,968	79,111	167,991	287,191
2006	15,539	36,769	58,485	88,394	187,389	297,405

*Families as of March of the following year.
†Income in 2009 dollars.
Source: http://www.census.gov/hhes/www/income/histinc/f03AR.html.

Clearly, incomes are not equal among families. This is to be expected in a market-based economy. People have different skills and abilities and earn different incomes as a result. But how much inequality is there, and can too much inequality be a bad thing? It is not easy to measure income inequality. We have to decide what should be counted as income and whether income is a better measure of people's standards of living than some other measure, such as their expenditures. Then, once these choices have been made, a way to present the degree of inequality has to be chosen.

1.a. Income Inequality

The most common way to present income inequality is using a graph known as the Lorenz Curve. Equal incomes among members of a population can be plotted as a 45-degree line that is equidistant from the axes (see Figure 1). The horizontal axis measures the total population in cumulative percentages. Cumulative means that as we move along the horizontal axis, we are adding up the percentages. The numbers end at 100, which designates 100 percent of the population. The vertical axis measures total income in cumulative percentages. As we move up the vertical axis, the percentage of total income being counted rises to 100 percent. A point half way up and half way out to 100 percent would be 50 percent of families and 50 percent of income. The 45-degree line splitting the distance between the axes is called the *line of income equality*. At each point on the line, the percentage of total population and the percentage of total income are equal. The line of income equality indicates that 10 percent of the population earns 10 percent of the income, 20 percent of the population earns 20 percent of the income, and so on, until we see that 90 percent of the population earns 90 percent of the income and 100 percent of the population earns 100 percent of the income.

Points off the line of income equality indicate an income distribution that is unequal. Figure 1 shows the line of income equality and a curve that bows down below the income-equality line. The bowed curve is a **Lorenz curve**. The Lorenz curve in Figure 1 is for the United States in 2009. It shows that the bottom 20 percent of the population received 3.9 percent of income, seen at point *A*. The second

Lorenz curve
A curve measuring the degree of inequality of income distribution within a society.

FIGURE 1   The U.S. Lorenz Curve

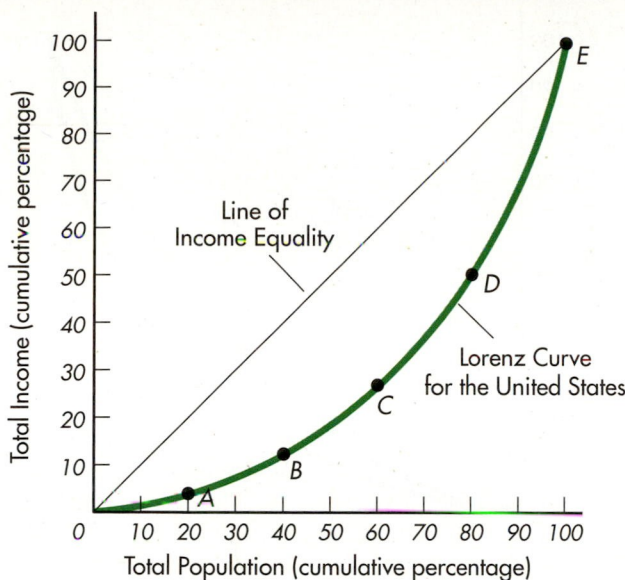

The farther a Lorenz curve lies from the line of income equality, the greater the inequality of the income distribution. The bottom 20 percent of the U.S. population receives 3.9 percent of total income, seen at point A. The Lorenz curve is plotted by successively adding 10 percent of the population and each group's percentage of total income.

Source: http://www.census.gov/hhes/www/income/data/historical/inequality/index.html.

---

20 percent accounts for another 8.6 percent of income, shown as point *B*. The third 20 percent accounts for another 14.5 percent of income, so point *C* is plotted at a population of 60 percent and an income of 26.5 (3.4 + 8.6 + 14.5) percent. The fourth 20 percent accounts for another 23.2 percent of income, shown as point *D*. The richest 20 percent accounts for the remaining 50.3 percent of income, shown as point *E*. With the last 20 percent of the population and the last 50.3 percent of income, 100 percent of the population and 100 percent of income are accounted for. Point *E*, therefore, is plotted where both income and population are 100 percent.[1] Notice that the more bowed out the Lorenz curve, the greater the income inequality. For instance, in Figure 2 a comparison of income distribution in the United States and Mexico in 2009 is illustrated. You can see at a glance that incomes are more unequally distributed in Mexico than in the United States because the Lorenz curve for Mexico bows out farther than the U.S. curve does.

Another way you will see income distributions reported is with the **Gini coefficient**. The Gini coefficient is the area between the Lorenz curve and the line of perfect equality divided by the total area under the line of income equality. A Gini of 0 would occur if every family had the exact same amount of income, since there would be no difference between the line of income equality and the Lorenz curve. A Gini of 1 would occur if one family had all the income, since the Lorenz curve would be the rectangle going from 0 to 100 on the horizontal axis and from 100 on the horizontal axis up to the line

Gini coefficient
A measure of income inequality ranging between 0 and 1; 0 means that all families have the same income; 1 means that one family has all of the income.

---

[1] A Lorenz curve for wealth could also be shown. It would bow down below the Lorenz curve for income, indicating that wealth is more unequally distributed than income. Wealth and income are different and should be kept distinct. Wealth is the stock of assets. Income is the flow of earnings that results from the stock of assets.

FIGURE 2   Lorenz Curves for Mexico and the United States

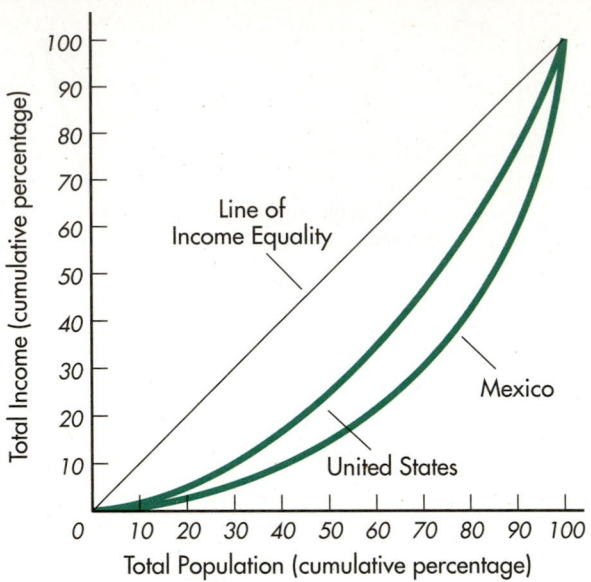

Based on data for the United States and Mexico, the two Lorenz curves show that total income in Mexico is distributed among Mexican citizens much more unequally than total income in the United States is distributed among citizens of the United States.

Source: Data are from *World Development Report, 2009.*

FIGURE 3   The Gini Coefficient

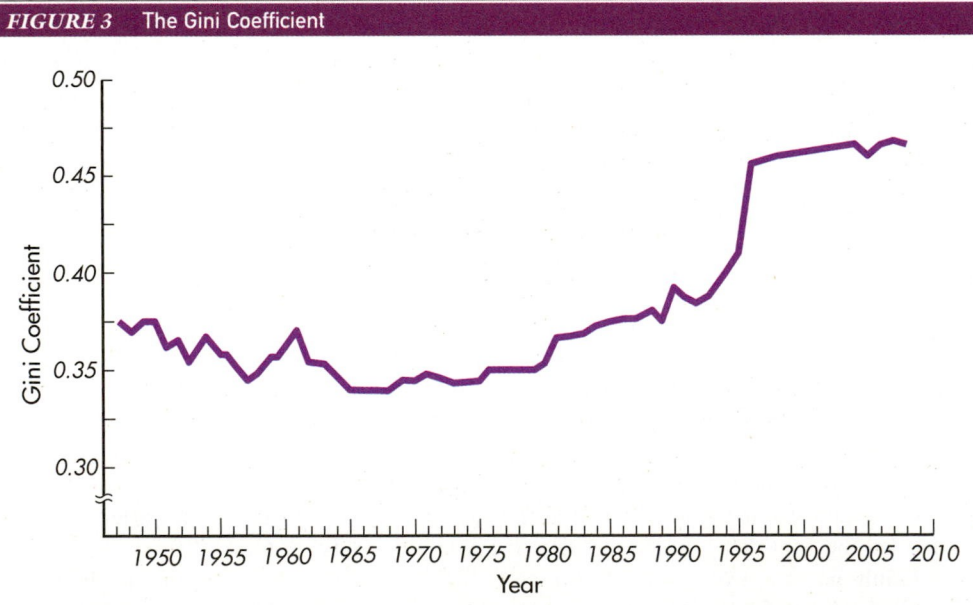

The Gini coefficient is a measure of the dispersion of income that ranges between 0 and 1. A lower value indicates less dispersion in the income distribution: A Gini of 0 would occur if every family had the exact same amount of income, whereas a Gini of 1 would occur if all income accrued to only one family. Figure 3 shows that from 1947 to 1968, the dispersion of income fell gradually. Since then the dispersion has risen slowly.

Source: Economic Report of the President, 2000 and *2006.*

of income equality—the entire area. According to Figure 3, the Gini coefficient was between .35 and .37 until the 1990s; it then increased and reached 469 in 2009. This means that the distribution of income in the United States has become more unequally distributed since 1968.

A simpler measure of income inequality is the ratio of the average income in the top fifth to average income in the bottom fifth, or the ratio of shares of the top fifth to the bottom fifth. This is called the HiLo ratio.[2] In 2009, as noted in Table 1, the ratio was $189,486/15,289 = 12.39$.

Notice that all of these measures are just indicators of inequality. They do not tell us what is too much or too little, whether an amount is good or harmful, or even whether absolute incomes are high or low. For instance, if all incomes double, the shares are unchanged even though everyone is better off. Thus, the shares are only indicative of relative inequality, how families stand relative to one another.

1.a.1. Families or Households
The Census Bureau also provides income shares for households. The primary difference is that a household can be a single person living alone, whereas a family must be composed of at least two people. The family data that we have been discussing do not contain single persons living on their own. As a result, the family data contain about 80 million families, whereas the household data contain about 120 million households. The household distribution also has a problem: The number of persons per household varies widely among the five fifths. The number of households is the same in each fifth but the number of persons is not. In fact, the top fifth of households contains 72 percent more people than the lowest fifth. Thus income per person in the top fifth is only 8.6 times income per person in the bottom fifth. If we have to choose between the family data and the household data, the family income data is preferable because family size varies less among the quintiles.

1.a.2. In-Kind Transfers
The census data overstate inequality because of what they do and do not measure. The census figures are for before-tax incomes, but isn't it the after-tax incomes that count? After all, much real income received by people is in nonmonetary form and so is not counted at all. Particularly important are government in-kind transfers that add to people's incomes but are not counted as income. **In-kind transfers**, or noncash transfers, are services or products provided to certain sectors of society. For example, food stamps, Medicaid, and housing assistance are not counted as income. Even the Earned Income Tax Credit is not counted even though it is a cash transfer and contributed about $380 billion in income in 2008.

in-kind transfers
The allocations of goods and services from one group in society to another.

1.a.3. Size of Family or Household Units
The census data do not account for differences in the number of persons per family/household. Thus, as mentioned already, the distribution of income by families does not present a true picture because higher income families/households have more persons to support. There are about twice as many persons in the highest quintile group as in the lowest quintile.

1.a.4. Consumer Expenditures
Income inequality might not be the best measure of how well off people are. People's standards of living are better evaluated by how much they consume, not their income. Many economists believe we would get a better picture of how rich or poor people are by looking at their consumption: what they have versus what they earn. The distribution of consumer expenditures is quite a bit more equal than is the distribution of income. According to the Bureau of Labor Statistics, the distribution of consumer expenditures had a HiLo ratio of 3.8 in 2008 in contrast to the income ratio of 11.97. The reason is that low-income households have substantially greater consumer expenditures than their income. In 2009, the poorest fifth consumed almost twice as much as their before-tax incomes.

[2] Edgar Browning, *Stealing from Each Other*, Westport, Conn.: Praeger, 2008, Chapter 2.

Incomes are unequally distributed in every nation. In developing countries, the distinction between rich and poor is greater than in the industrial nations, although the per capita income is significantly less in the developing countries. For instance, although the per capita income in Nigeria is only 7 percent of the per capita income in the United States, the wealthy in Lagos, Nigeria, live very well, with large houses, servants, expensive clothes, and other accoutrements of wealth. During the 1970s, many Nigerians became very wealthy as the price of oil surged and Nigerian oil production rose. Economic crisis and the collapse of oil prices since the late 1970s have led to a decline in Nigeria that has wiped out the gains of the previous 20 years.

1.a.5. Mobility

mobility
The extent to which people move from one income quintile to another over time.

When assessing the degree of inequality in a nation, it is important to know what happens over time. Do the poor stay poor and wealthy stay wealthy? When people see the history of the income shares, such as shown by the Gini coefficient of Figure 3, it seems to suggest that the rich got richer and the poor got poorer. These implications or suggestions are misleading because the same people are not in the same income quintiles over time. Economists use the term **mobility** to refer to the extent of movement within the income distribution over time. The lowest income quintile, for instance, tends to be largely the young and old. But as time passes, the young go from being in the lowest quintile to being in a higher quintile as they move into prime earning years, and new young move into the lowest quintile. In fact, of all workers in the lowest quintile in 2001, 32 percent had moved to a higher quintile just one year later. Similarly, those in peak earning years tend to be in the top quintile of income but drop into lower ones as they age and retire. Among those in the top quintile in 2001, 25 percent had fallen to a lower quintile one year later. The longer the time period considered, the greater the mobility. Of those in the lowest quintile in 2001, two-thirds were in a higher quintile in 2007. Of those in the highest quintile in 2001, 61 percent were in a lower quintile in 2007.[3] About 55 percent of taxpayers move to a different income quintile within 10 years.

1.a.6. Income Distribution in Other Nations

Income is much more equally distributed in industrial nations than it is in developing countries. In developing countries, the richest 20 percent of the population have more than 50 percent of total household income while the poorest 20 percent have less than 4 percent. Interestingly, the income distribution in the former and current communist countries of Russia and China is more

[3] http://blog.american.com/?p=29147.

unequal than that in the United States. Although the inequality of incomes within a nation compares the relative status of residents in that nation, it does not tell us anything about their absolute levels. It tells us very little about the quality of life of the people in different nations. Per capita income in the United States exceeds $47,000, whereas in China it is near $6,000, and in Cameroon it is about $400.

1.b. Measuring Poverty

Defining poverty is difficult. We can, without too much trouble, say which groups have higher or lower income levels and how incomes are distributed in a society, but this does not provide much information about a person's quality of life. All the income inequality measures can tell us is what one's income is relative to that of others; they are relative measures. Per capita income—income per person—is an absolute measure. It doesn't compare incomes, but simply states the level. Per capita income does not indicate how people feel about their income status or whether they enjoy good health and a decent standard of living. Those who are comfortable in one country could be impoverished in another. The poverty level in the United States would represent a substantial increase in living standards for people in many other nations. Yet members of a poor family in the United States would probably not feel less poor if they knew that their income level exceeded the median income in other countries.

1.b.1. What Is Income? In the United States, data related to poverty are collected and published annually by the Department of Health and Human Services. Table 2 lists

2 How is poverty measured, and does poverty exist in the United States?

TABLE 2	Average Income Poverty Cutoffs for a Nonfarm Family of Four in the United States, 1959–2010		
Year	**Poverty Level**	**Year**	**Poverty Level**
1959	$ 2,973	1990	$ 13,359
1960	$ 3,022	1991	$ 13,924
1966	$ 3,317	1992	$ 13,950
1969	$ 3,743	1993	$ 14,764
1970	$ 3,968	1994	$ 15,200
1975	$ 5,500	1995	$ 15,600
1976	$ 5,815	1996	$ 16,036
1977	$ 6,191	1997	$ 16,400
1978	$ 6,662	1998	$ 16,660
1979	$ 7,412	1999	$ 16,895
1980	$ 8,414	2000	$ 17,463
1981	$ 9,287	2001	$ 17,463
1982	$ 9,862	2002	$ 18,244
1983	$10,178	2003	$ 18,900
1984	$10,609	2004	$ 19,424
1985	$10,989	2005	$ 19,874
1986	$11,203	2006	$ 20,516
1987	$11,611	2007	$ 21,100
1988	$12,090	2008	$ 21,834
1989	$12,675	2009	$ 22,050
		2010	**$22,162**

Source: www.census.gov/hhes/www/poverty.html.

the poverty thresholds of income for a nonfarm family of four since 1959. Families with incomes above the cutoffs would be above the poverty level, in the eyes of the federal government. These cutoffs are arbitrary numbers selected by the government to provide an indication of how many people are in poverty.

Where does the poverty income threshold come from? A 1955 study found that the average family in the United States spent about one-third of its income on food, so when the government decided to begin measuring poverty in the 1960s, it calculated the cost to purchase meals that met a predetermined nutritional standard for a year and multiplied that cost by 3. That is where it drew the poverty line. Since then, the official poverty-line income has been adjusted for inflation each year.

cash transfers
Money allocated away from one group in society to another.

The poverty thresholds count earnings from cash transfers (except earned income tax credit) but not in-kind transfers. **Cash transfers** are unearned funds given to certain sectors of the population. They include some Social Security benefits and disability pensions, as well as unemployment compensation to those who are temporarily out of work.

How many Americans fall below the poverty line? Figure 4 compares the number of people living in poverty and the percentage of the total population living in poverty (the incidence of poverty) for each year.

FIGURE 4   The Trends of Poverty Incidence

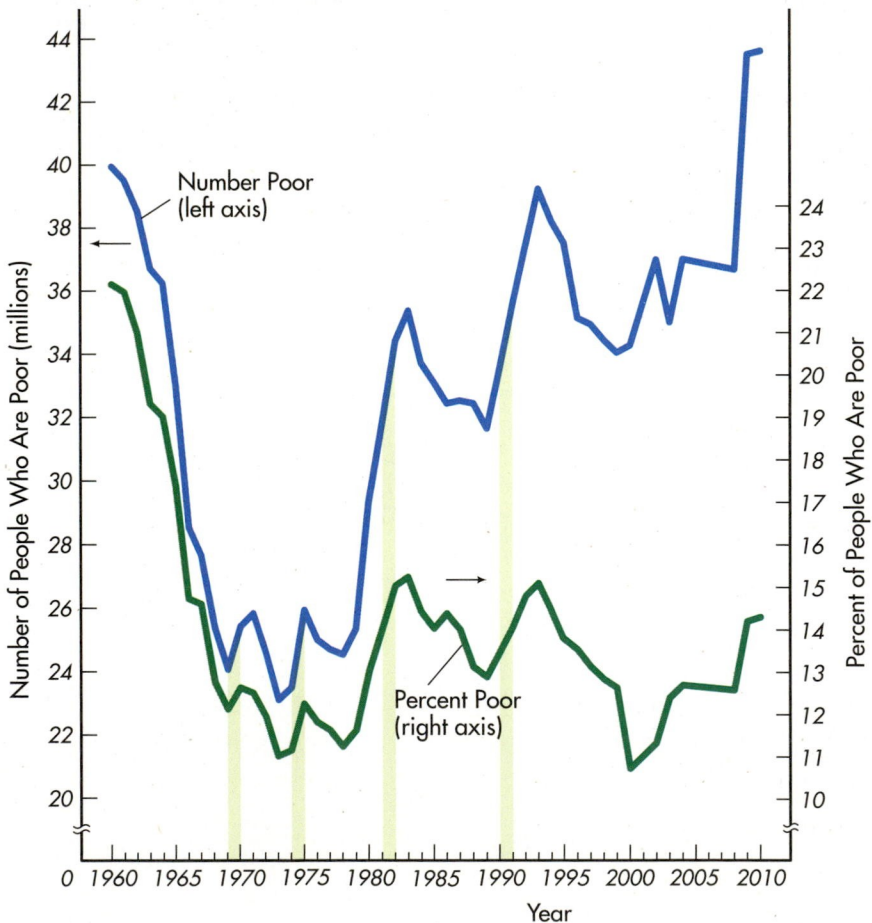

The number of people classified as living in poverty is measured on the left vertical axis. The percentage of the population classified as living in poverty is measured on the right vertical axis.

Sources: www.census.gov/hhes/www/poverty.html; http://aspe.hhs.gov/POVERTY/09poverty.shtml.

There are many controversies over how poverty should be measured. Some argue that the poverty rate is really not nearly as high as Figure 4 indicates—that government transfers and other programs are not properly taken into account. Also, the poverty measure makes no distinction between the needs of a 3-month-old and those of a 14-year-old or between a rural family in a cold climate and an urban family in the sub-tropics. It draws no distinction between income and purchasing power. A welfare mom living on $400 a month is treated in a manner identical to that of a graduate student who earns $400 a month at a part-time job and borrows an additional $1,500 from her parents. Nor does it consider the problem of income from the underground economy—the income that is not reported or measured in income statistics.

RECAP

1. The Lorenz curve shows the degree to which incomes are distributed equally in a society. The more the Lorenz curve bows out, the more unequal is the income distribution.

2. The Gini coefficient is a measure of the degree to which the Lorenz curve bows down away from the line of income equality. The higher the Gini coefficient, the greater the income inequality.

3. The HiLo ratio is the ratio of the average income of the top quintile divided by the average income of the bottom quintile.

4. Income inequality measured on the basis of before-tax income is considerably reduced by adjusting for taxes and transfers as well as the number of people in the family or household, and by relying on expenditures rather than income.

5. Inequality is a measure of relative status in a country. It does not tell us the absolute level of income or consumption nor the standard of living.

6. The income level selected as the poverty threshold is arbitrary, based on an attempt to measure the income people would need to purchase three meals of a certain nutritious value.

7. The incidence of poverty is the percentage of the population whose income falls below the poverty threshold.

2. The Poor

A higher percentage of women fall into poverty than do men; a higher percentage of African Americans and Hispanics fall into poverty than do others; a higher percentage of those without high school education fall into poverty than do those with high school educations.

3 Who are the poor?

> The health of the economy is a primary determinant of the incidence of poverty.

2.a. Temporary and Permanent Poverty

If those who are poor at any one time are poor only temporarily, then their plight is only temporary. If people in poverty are able to improve their situation even while others slip into poverty temporarily, the problem of poverty for society is not as serious as it is if poverty is a permanent condition once a person has fallen into it. Approximately 25 percent of all Americans fall below the poverty line at some time in their lives. Many of these spells of poverty are relatively short; nearly 45 percent last less than a year.

2.a.1. The Economy and Poverty
The major factor accounting for the incidence of poverty is the health of the economy. People are generally made better off by economic growth. Economic stagnation and recession throw the relatively poor out of their jobs

4 What are the determinants of poverty?

and into poverty. Economic growth increases the number of jobs and draws people out of poverty and into the mainstream of economic progress. Recessions increase poverty and economic booms reduce poverty.

The recession of 1969–1970 was relatively mild. Between 1969 and 1971, the unemployment rate rose from 3.4 to 5.8 percent, and the total number of people unemployed rose from 2,832,000 to 5,016,000. This recession halted the decline in poverty rates for two years. When the economy once again began to expand, the poverty rates dropped. The 1974 recession brought on another bout of unemployment that threw people into poverty. This recession was relatively serious, causing the unemployment rate to rise to 8.3 percent by 1975 and the number of unemployed to rise to 7,929,000. Once again, however, the poverty rate declined as the economy picked up after 1975. The recession of 1980–1982 threw the economy off track again. In 1979, the total number of people unemployed was 6,137,000; by 1982, 10,717,000 were without jobs. As the economy came out of this recession, the poverty rate began to decline, and it continued to decline as the economy grew throughout the 1980s. The poverty rate then rose as the economy fell into recession in 1990 and struggled into 1992. The poverty rate of 14.2 percent in 1991 was the highest level in nearly three decades; the number of people living in poverty grew to 35.7 million. Somewhat surprisingly, the number of people in poverty and the incidence of poverty both grew in 1993 and 1994, years of economic growth. Throughout the rest of the 1990s, however, both the poverty rate and the number of people in poverty declined. As the economy again entered a recession in 2000, the number of people in poverty began to rise. But as the economy grew following 2001, the number in poverty fell. The 2008–2010 recession saw the number of poor rise to 43.5 million and the percent of poor rise to 14.2 percent. This compares to about 38 million and 13 percent in 2008.

Common sense says that the primary reason people might have no or little income is that they don't have jobs or don't have jobs that pay well. Why don't people have jobs or good jobs? The primary reason is that their skills and education don't offer value to employers. People who do not have a high school education are many more times likely to have an income at the poverty level than people with a high school diploma. And a technical school or college degree offers even more likelihood that one won't fall into poverty. Because it is primarily the very young who don't have skills or education, they are the primary population group with poverty-level incomes. In 2010, 21 percent of the U.S. population under the age of 18 had incomes below the poverty threshold, whereas less than 14 percent of the rest of the population had poverty-level incomes.

African Americans and Hispanics carry a much heavier burden of poverty relative to the size of their populations than do whites. Families headed by a female are much more likely to be in poverty than families headed by a male. Why? At least part of the answer is skills and education: White males have higher levels of education than do African American or Hispanic males or females of all ethnic groups.

A significant percentage of those in poverty have less than eight years of education. Fully 22 percent of the people with less than eight years of education fall below the poverty level of income. Less than 4 percent of those with a college degree fell below the poverty cutoff.[4] Lack of education prevents people from securing well-paying jobs. Without the human capital obtained from education or training programs, finding a job that is stable and will not disappear during a recession is very difficult. Even someone who has the desire to work but has no exceptional abilities and has not acquired the skills necessary for a well-paying job is unlikely to escape poverty completely. Minorities, women, the young, and the disabled have disproportionately less education than the rest of the population, and as a result have a higher likelihood of falling into poverty.

> *The primary characteristic of those who fall below the poverty line is the lack of a job.*

> *The less education a person has, the greater his or her chance of experiencing poverty.*

[4] http://www.census.gov/hhes/www/macro/032008/pov/toc.htm.

1. Many people experience poverty only temporarily. Nearly 45 percent of the spells of poverty last less than a year.

2. The health of the economy is a primary determinant of the incidence of poverty.

3. The incidence of poverty is much higher among African Americans and Hispanics than it is among whites, and higher among females than males.

3. Government Antipoverty Policies

3.a. Tax Policy

If people are provided with enough income to bring them above the poverty level, the number of people in poverty will be reduced. Funds used to supplement the incomes of the poor must come from somewhere. Many societies adopt a Robin Hood approach, taxing the rich to give to the poor.

A **progressive tax** is a tax that rises as income rises—the marginal tax rate increases as income increases. If someone with an annual income of $20,000 pays $5,000 in taxes while someone else with an annual income of $40,000 pays $12,000 in taxes, the tax is progressive. The first person is paying a 25 percent rate, and the second is paying a 30 percent rate.

A **proportional tax** is a tax whose rate does not change as the tax base changes. The rate of a proportional income tax remains the same at every level of income. If the tax rate is 20 percent, then all individuals pay 20 percent, whether they earn $10,000 or $100,000.

A **regressive tax** is one whose rate decreases as the tax base increases. The Social Security tax is regressive; a specified rate is paid on income up to a specified level, but no Social Security taxes are paid on income beyond that level. In 2009, the cutoff level of income was $106,000 and the tax rate was 6.2 percent. A person earning $300,000 paid no more in Social Security taxes than someone earning $106,000, and therefore had a lower Social Security tax rate.

> There are two general approaches the government uses to provide benefits to the poor: tax policies and welfare programs.

progressive tax
A tax whose rate increases as income increases.

proportional tax
A tax whose rate does not change as the tax base changes.

regressive tax
A tax whose rate decreases as the tax base increases.

3.b. Welfare Programs

The U.S. welfare program consists of Temporary Assistance for Needy Families (TANF), formerly known as Aid to Families with Dependent Children (AFDC). The Green Book provided by the U.S. House of Representatives identifies 85 separate programs that provide cash and noncash aid that is directed primarily to persons with limited income. These programs, together with Social Security, Medicare, and public schools, constitute the welfare system in the United States.[5] According to the government's own accounting, there are 85 welfare programs on which expenditures were $620 billion. Of this, about 70 percent was financed by the federal government.

Since about 37 million people were considered to be in poverty and expenditures were $620 billion, over $16,750 was spent on each person in poverty. This

---

[5] The House Ways and Means Committee Green Book provides program descriptions and historical data on a wide variety of social and economic topics, including social security, employment, earnings, welfare, child support, health insurance, the elderly, families with children, poverty, and taxation. It has become a standard reference work for those interested in the direction of social policy in the United States. It is compiled by the staff of the Committee on Ways and Means of the U.S. House of Representatives. GPO Access contains the Green Book for 1996, 1998, 2000, and 2004.

means that for a family of three persons, welfare expenditures were over $50,000, well above the poverty threshold. How can so much be spent and still have 37 million people in poverty? Some of the money covers administrative costs. Some of the money goes to poor persons who are not in poverty. More importantly, some of the money is used to provide benefits that are not counted as income when the government counts the poor.

The main transfer programs are social insurance, cash welfare or public assistance, in-kind transfers, and employment programs. Social Security—officially known as Old-Age, Survivors, and Disability Insurance (OASDI) and listed as FICA on paycheck stubs—is the largest social insurance program. Coverage is nearly universal, so the total amount of money involved is immense—more than $200 billion annually. Two-thirds of the aged rely on Social Security for more than half of their income.

Unemployment insurance provides temporary benefits to regularly employed people who become temporarily unemployed. Funded by a national tax on payrolls levied on firms with eight or more workers, the system is run by state governments. Benefits normally amount to about 50 percent of a worker's usual wage.

Supplemental security income (SSI) ranks first among cash welfare programs. Most of the SSI population is blind or otherwise disabled (65 percent), and the rest are over age 65. Unlike Social Security recipients, who are *entitled* to receive benefits because they are a certain age or otherwise qualify, recipients of SSI must meet certain disability requirements or be of a certain age and must have incomes below about $4,500 per year.

About 60 percent of all poor households receive in-kind transfers. The largest of these programs is Medicaid (for a discussion of Medicaid and the medical care industry, see the chapter "Aging, Social Security, and Health Care"). Medicaid provides federal funds to states to help them cover the costs of long-term medical and nursing home care. Second in magnitude is the food stamp program, which gives households coupons that are redeemable at grocery stores. The amounts vary with income and household size. Other programs include jobs and training directed toward disadvantaged workers and the Head Start program, an education program available to poor children. Total government outlays for social service (welfare) programs run more than $700 billion annually.

5 Do government programs intended to reduce poverty benefit the poor?

3.c. The Effectiveness of Welfare Programs

In 1964, President Lyndon Johnson declared "unconditional war on poverty." In 1967, total transfers were about $10 billion. Now they run nearly $1 trillion. Is the war being won? Unfortunately, there is no easy or straightforward answer to that question. In fact, there is disagreement about whether antipoverty programs have reduced or increased poverty. Some people maintain that without these programs, income inequality and poverty would have been much more severe. Others argue that welfare has been a drag on the economy and may have made poverty and inequality worse than they otherwise would have been. It is impossible to compare what did happen with what would have happened in the absence of the government's programs. All economists can do is look at the incentives created by the programs and observe what actually occurred.

3.c.1. Incentives and Government Income Transfer Programs

Taxes are one method of collecting revenues with which antipoverty or welfare programs can be paid for. Taxes affect those who pay the taxes; they may lead to less labor being supplied. As we discussed in the chapter "The Labor Market," the supply of labor comes from the decisions that individuals make regarding the number of hours of work they are willing and able to perform at each wage. The individual trades off labor and leisure, essentially buying leisure time—giving up the income gained by working. Thus, when the cost of

FIGURE 5 Taxes and Jobs

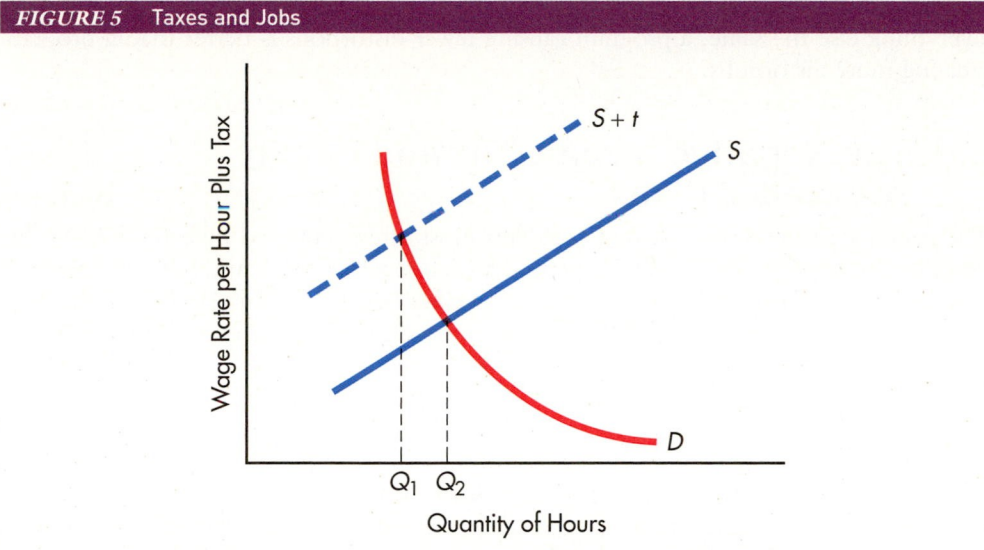

If a tax is imposed on the worker, the individual will choose to supply less labor at each wage rate. The supply curve shifts in, and the number of hours worked decreases.

© 2013 Cengage Learning

leisure to an individual is decreased, individuals will buy more leisure; that is, they will work less. A tax increases the cost of working or, conversely, decreases the cost of leisure. It should be expected that people will choose the now less expensive leisure time over the now more costly work time when taxes increase. This will affect the cost of labor to firms. In Figure 5, suppose the equilibrium in the labor market prior to a tax on labor is Q_2. Now, suppose a tax of rate t is imposed on each dollar of income. As a result of the tax, the worker decides to supply less labor at every wage rate, shown as an inward shift of supply, to $S + t$. The number of hours worked declines to Q_1. The tax has led to fewer hours worked and thus less income earned.

When funds are distributed to the unemployed or to those who are employed at low-paying jobs, it affects the incentives of these individuals to work. When a low-income individual receives a transfer payment, that individual has less of an incentive to forgo leisure time for work time. This raises the question about whether welfare leads to a permanent dependency on welfare and an unwillingness to work.

3.c.2. Disincentives Created by the Welfare System Those who argue that welfare programs are a drag on the economy and may make poverty and income inequality worse typically focus on the disincentives created by the transfers. Incentives to work hard and increase productivity may be reduced for both the rich and the poor by programs that take from the rich and give to the poor. Those who are paying taxes may ask themselves, "Why should I work an extra hour every day if all the extra income does is pay additional taxes?" Someone who gets to keep only 60 cents of the next dollar earned has less incentive to earn that dollar than someone who gets to keep it all.

In addition, those who receive benefits may lose the incentive to change their status. Why should someone take a job paying $6,000 per year when he or she can remain unemployed and receive $8,000? Someone who is out of work might wonder, "Why should I spend eight hours a day in miserable working conditions when I can relax every day and bring home nearly the same amount of income?" If incentives to work are weak, then the total income created in the economy is less than it otherwise would be. Less income and lower economic growth mean more people in poverty.

Antipoverty programs must pay special attention to the incentives they create. Everything else the same, a program causing fewer distortions is better than a program creating more distortions.

3.d. The Negative Income Tax and Family Allowance Plans

negative income tax (NIT)
A tax system that transfers increasing amounts of income to households earning incomes below some specified level as their income declines.

The solution to the welfare system problems most often proposed by economists is the **negative income tax (NIT)**—a tax system that transfers increasing amounts of income to households earning incomes below some specified level. The lower the income, the more that is transferred. As income rises above the specified level, a tax is applied. Economists like the NIT because, at least in theory, it reduces poverty without causing too many distortions in the economy.

The NIT would work like this. Suppose policymakers determine that a family of four is to be guaranteed an income of $10,000. If the family earns nothing, then it will get a transfer of $10,000. If the family earns some income, it will receive $10,000 less a tax on the earned income. If the tax rate is 50 percent, then for each dollar earned, $.50 will be taken out of the $10,000 transfer.

With a 50 percent tax rate, there would be some incentive to work because each additional dollar of earnings would bring the recipient of the transfer $.50 in additional income. At some income level, the tax taken would be equal to the transfer of $10,000. This level of income is referred to as the *break-even income level*. In the case of a $10,000 guaranteed income and a 50 percent tax rate, the break-even income level is $20,000. Once a family of four earns more than $20,000, its taxes exceed the transfer of $10,000.

The break-even level of income is determined by the income floor and the tax rate:

$$\text{Break-even income level} = \frac{\text{income floor}}{\text{negative income tax rate}}$$

If the guaranteed income floor is $13,000 and the tax rate is 50 percent, then the break-even income level would be $26,000. If the guaranteed income floor is $13,000 but the tax rate is 33 percent, then the break-even income level would be $39,000.

For the negative income tax to eradicate poverty, the guaranteed level of income has to be equal to the poverty threshold. But if the tax rate is less than 100 percent, the break-even income level will be above the poverty level, and families who are not officially considered "poor" will also receive benefits. At a guaranteed income level of $19,874 and a 33 percent tax rate, the break-even income level is $60,224. All families of four earning less than $60,224 would receive some income benefits.

For people who are now covered by welfare programs, the negative income tax would increase the incentive to work, and that is what proponents of the negative income tax like. However, for people who are too well off to receive welfare but who would become eligible for NIT payments, the negative income tax might create work disincentives. It would provide these families with more income, and they might choose to buy more leisure.

The possibility of disincentive effects has worried both social reformers and legislators, so in the late 1960s the government carried out a number of experiments to estimate the effect of the negative income tax on the supply of labor. Families from a number of U.S. cities were offered negative income tax payments in return for allowing social scientists to monitor their behavior. A matched set of families who were not given NIT payments was also observed. The idea was to compare the behavior of the families receiving NIT payments with that of the families who did not receive them. The experiments lasted about a decade and showed pretty clearly that the net effects of the negative income tax on labor supply were quite small.

Even though disincentive effects did not seem to occur to any great extent, the negative income tax has not gained political acceptability. One reason is the high break-even income level. Politicians are not very supportive of programs that may provide income transfers to a family earning significantly more than the poverty income level. Another reason is the transfer of dollars rather than in-kind benefits (food and medical care). Policymakers do not look favorably on the idea of giving a family cash that it can use as it pleases, even though it would make economic sense to do so.

While politicians focus on poverty and government expenditures on programs and support for the poor rise, the poor remain. In a market system, there will always be some people with higher incomes and others with lower incomes. So if those with low incomes are considered poor, there will always be people who are poor in a market economy. Eliminating the difference affects incentives to work, innovate, take risks, acquire education, and so on. Is there an optimal level of income inequality, and can programs be used to minimize some of the negative effects of low income without negatively affecting incentives? These are questions economists attempt to answer. One of the findings with which economists generally agree is that economic growth is a necessary component for reducing poverty. So economists must determine what leads to economic growth. We will discuss this briefly in the next section.

RECAP

1. Government policies designed to change the distribution of income to one that is more equal involve taking from the rich and giving to the poor—a Robin Hood approach.

2. A tax may be progressive, proportional, or regressive. A progressive tax is one with a marginal tax rate that increases as income rises. A proportional tax is one that rises as income rises, but with the marginal tax rate remaining constant. A regressive tax is one whose marginal tax rate decreases as income increases.

3. Transfer mechanisms include Social Security, welfare, and unemployment programs.

4. The incentives created by transfer programs may make the problem of poverty worse rather than better.

5. The negative income tax is a proposal to provide transfers, but in a way that minimizes disincentives.

4. Income Distribution among Nations

Incomes differ greatly from one nation to another as well as within nations. There are "haves" and "have-nots" throughout the world—the lowest 90 percent of the population in terms of income has less than 20 percent of the total world income, shown as point *A* in Figure 6. The richest 10 percent of the world's population has more than 80 percent of total world income, the difference between *A* and *B*.

4.a. World Income Distribution

There is a huge gap in income and wealth between the "haves" and "have-nots" in the world. About 80 percent of the world's population lives in what countries in North America and Europe consider to be poverty. The poorest 10 percent of Americans are better off than two-thirds of the world's population. (The Global Business Insight

6 Why are incomes unequally distributed among nations?

FIGURE 6   World Lorenz Curve

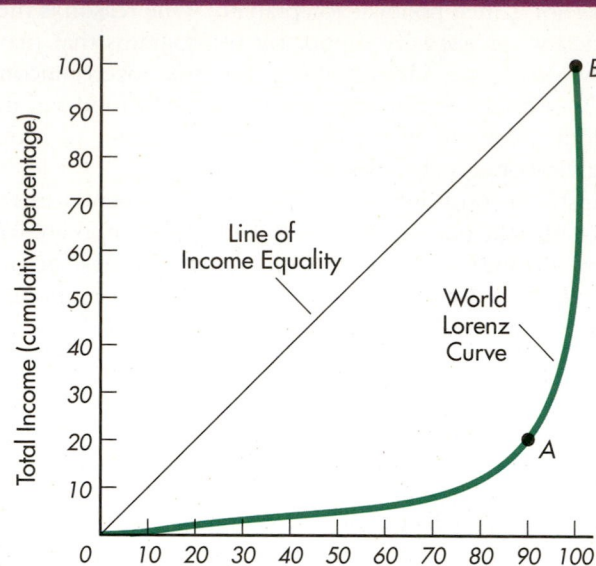

The Lorenz curve is typically used to illustrate the income distribution within countries. In this figure, a Lorenz curve is drawn to compare how world income is distributed across countries. The bottom 90 percent of the world's population, residing in the less-developed countries, accounts for 20 percent of the world's income, shown as point *A*. The richest 10 percent of the population, residing in the developed countries, accounts for 80 percent of total income, shown as point *B*.

Source: Data are from *World Development Report, 1999* and *2000*.

"Economic Development and Happiness" suggests that the feeling of well-being of a population depends on the level of per capita income and also on freedom.)

Why are some nations rich and others poor? If two countries were equal today, but one's economy was growing faster than the other's, would the two remain equal? Suppose one nation was growing at a rate of 4 percent per year and another nation was growing at a rate of 2 percent per year. How long would it take each of the two countries to double its income? Using the rule of 72, where dividing the growth rate into 72 yields the number of time periods until the item that is growing doubles, we find that an economy with a 4 percent growth rate doubles every 18 years, whereas one with a 2 percent growth rate doubles every 36 years. Thus, if all nations started out with the same level of income and some grew faster than others, it would not take long before the incomes of different nations were widely unequal.

The answer to why nations have different levels of income is that their economies have grown at different rates. Why have their economies grown at different rates? One reason is that economic growth depends on economic and political systems—the freer the economic and political system, the greater is the rate of economic growth.

4.b. Foreign Aid

How should the unequal distribution among nations that exists today be dealt with? One approach is welfare—transferring income from the rich countries to the poor countries. Another is to try to increase the growth rates of the poor countries. *Foreign aid* is

GLOBAL BUSINESS INSIGHT

Economic Development and Happiness

A nation's standard of living influences the attitudes of the nation's population toward life in general, although it is not the only factor. Using subjective measures of happiness or satisfaction with life, researchers find that year after year, the Danes, Swiss, Irish, and Dutch feel happier and more satisfied with life than do the French, Greeks, Italians, and Germans. Whether they are German-, French-, or Italian-speaking, the Swiss rank very high in life satisfaction—much higher than their German, French, and Italian neighbors. People in the Scandinavian countries generally are both prosperous and happy. However, the link between national affluence and well-being isn't consistent. Although the developed nations all had higher per capita incomes than the Mexicans, the Mexicans had a higher satisfaction with life than the populations of many of the developed nations. The overall pattern does show that wealthier nations tend to have higher levels of life satisfaction than poorer ones, but income and wealth are not the only factors influencing happiness.

Related to wealth is the type of government under which citizens live. The most prosperous nations have enjoyed stable democratic governments, and there is a link between a history of stable democracy and national well-being. The 13 nations that have maintained democratic institutions continuously since 1920 all enjoy higher life satisfaction levels than do the 11 nations whose democracies developed after World War II.

Source: Bruno Frey and Alois Stutzer, *Happiness and Economics* (Princeton, NJ: Princeton University Press, 2002).

the name given to programs that transfer income from rich nations to poor nations. The questions about foreign aid include all the questions regarding welfare within the United States: What are the effects on incentives for recipients and for donors, and how much of the aid reaches those who are needy? But foreign aid also involves issues such as whether the aid will spur economic growth. It is possible that the aid will actually hinder growth, because it creates the wrong incentives.

Another approach to the inequality issue that creates positive incentives for economic growth lies in private property rights and title to property. Hernando de Soto, a Peruvian economist, has received a lot of publicity with his study of developing nations. He has suggested that if the institutions of private property in the poorer nations were comparable to those in the industrial nations, rapid economic growth would take place. Poor countries have to reform their political and legal systems to allow poor people to establish clear title to assets, so they can more easily borrow money against those assets. In Mexico, for instance, the assets for which there are no legal property rights include over 11 million houses, 137 million hectares of land (338.4 million acres), and 6 million unregistered micro-, small-, and medium-sized businesses. About 78 percent of the population of Mexico is involved in that side of the economy. These assets are worth about $315 billion, which is equivalent to 31 times all foreign direct investment in Mexico for all time. No one has title to this property. Thus no one can get a loan using the property as collateral, and no one has the right to sell the property.

Even when legal title is established, it is often difficult to use that title because of the failure of countries to enforce people's ownership of property. In poor nations, the legal system exists for a privileged elite, but it is cumbersome and costly for most of the population. For example, creating a mortgage in Mexico takes a buyer 24 months, working eight hours a day. Foreclosing on a mortgage takes 43 months. Selling a house, if you're among the 78 percent of Mexicans who are poor and you want to do it legally, takes

24 months working eight hours a day. Obtaining legal access for a business—that is to say, setting up a limited liability corporation, or whatever other form allows you to have shareholders—takes 17 months working eight hours a day and 126 contacts with government.

The creation and enforcement of private property rights is a necessary prelude to the functioning of markets, and an economy without markets does not grow very rapidly. Markets do not work when there are no private property rights or when private property rights are not widely available and enforced. As we'll discover in the next chapter, other approaches to enhancing economic growth have been tried. But these policies as a whole have not worked. Poor nations that have not established private property rights remain poor.

RECAP

1. Income is not distributed equally within individual nations, and different nations do not have the same income.

2. The poor nations are poor at least partly because of their lack of provision and enforcement of private property rights.

3. One approach used to improve the conditions of people in poor nations is foreign aid—a transfer of income from rich nations to poor nations.

4. The incentives created by foreign aid are analogous to the incentives created by welfare systems and so might not be conducive to economic growth.

5. An approach to stimulate economic growth is to provide the population of a country, particularly its poor, with the legal means to establish and maintain private property.

SUMMARY

1. **Are incomes distributed equally in the United States?**

   - The Lorenz curve, the Gini coefficient, and the HiLo ratio provide measures of the degree of income inequality. *§1.a*

   - If the Lorenz curve corresponds with the line of income equality, then incomes are distributed equally. If the Lorenz curve bows down below the line of income equality, then income is distributed in such a way that more people earn low incomes than earn high incomes. *§1.a*

   - The Gini coefficient is a measure of the area between the Lorenz curve and the line of equality. The higher the Gini coefficient, the greater is income inequality. *§1.a*

   - The HiLo ratio is the ratio of the share of income earned by the top quintile of families to the share of income earned by the bottom quintile of families. *§1.a*

2. **How is poverty measured, and does poverty exist in the United States?**

   - The poverty threshold is based on a 1955 study of how much the average family in the United States spent on food. *§1.b*

   - The income counted in the calculation of poverty statistics is resource earnings and cash transfers. *§1.b.1*

3. **Who are the poor?**

   - Many people fall below the poverty line for a short time only. *§2.a*

   - The incidence of poverty decreases as the economy grows and increases as the economy falls into recession. *§2.a.1*

4. **What are the determinants of poverty?**

   - A lack of education and thus a lack of a full-time or well-paying job, as well as the health of the economy, are the primary determinants of poverty. *§2.a.1*

5. **Do government programs intended to reduce poverty benefit the poor?**

- Tax policies that are progressive can reduce the incentives to acquire more income. §3.c.1, 3.c.2

- Government programs can reduce individuals' incentives to climb out of poverty. §3.c.2

6. **Why are incomes unequally distributed among nations?**

- As a rule, incomes are distributed more unequally in developing countries than in developed countries. §4

- A fundamental reason that standards of living differ among nations is the different growth rates that the economies of these nations have experienced over time. §4.a

- Free markets and political freedom lead to economic growth. §4.a

- The creation and enforcement of private property rights is a necessity if a nation's economy is to grow. §4.b

KEY TERMS

cash transfers, 740
Gini coefficient, 735
in-kind transfers, 737

Lorenz curve, 734
mobility, 738
negative income tax (NIT), 746

progressive tax, 743
proportional tax, 743
regressive tax, 743

EXERCISES

1. What is a Lorenz curve? What would the curve look like if income were equally distributed? Could the curve ever bow upward above the line of income equality?
2. Why does the health of the economy affect the number of people living in poverty?
3. What would it mean if the poverty income threshold level of the United States were applied to Mexico?
4. What positive arguments can be made for reducing income inequality? What normative arguments are made for reducing income inequality?
5. If one country is growing at a rate of 3 percent per year and another at a rate of 8 percent per year, how long will it take for each to double? What factors might account for the rate at which nations' standards of living grow?
6. Are people who are poor today in the United States likely to be poor for the rest of their lives? Under what conditions is generational poverty likely to exist?

7. Use the following information to plot a Lorenz curve.

Percent of Population	Percent of Income
20	5
40	15
60	35
80	65
100	100

8. If the incidence of poverty decreases during periods when the economy is growing and increases during periods when the economy is in recession, what policies might be used to reduce poverty most effectively?
9. If the arguments for reducing income inequality and poverty are normative, why rely on the government to reduce the inequality? Why doesn't the private market resolve the problem?
10. How could transfer programs (welfare programs) actually increase the number of people in poverty?

11. What is the difference between in-kind and cash transfers? Which might increase the utility of the recipients the most? Why is there political resistance to the negative income tax?

12. The Gini coefficient for a nation indicates the degree of income inequality within that nation; the Gini coefficient among nations indicates the degree of income inequality among nations. Would you ever expect to see the following scenarios?

    a. A case in which the Gini coefficient for a nation is smaller than the average of the Gini coefficients for all nations

    b. A case in which the Gini coefficient for income distribution among nations is larger than the average of all nations' Gini coefficients

    c. A case in which the Gini coefficient is zero

13. Consider the following three solutions offered to get rid of homelessness and discuss whether any of them would solve the problem.

    a. Provide permanent housing for all who are homeless.

    b. Provide free hospital care for the one-third of the homeless who are mentally ill.

    c. Provide subsidies for the homeless to purchase homes.

14. What is the relationship between the Gini coefficient and the Lorenz curve? Illustrate your answer using exercise 7.

15. Why would Hernando de Soto's suggestions, if implemented, stimulate economic growth?

16. Why do countries need a system of well-defined and enforced private property rights to succeed and grow?

17. Explain how foreign aid and welfare programs create disincentives to work, produce, and generally improve economic conditions.

You can find further practice tests in the Online Quiz at **www.cengage.com/economics/boyes**.

AMERICAN GAINS IN EDUCATIONAL ATTAINMENT ARE SLOWING

Economic Report of the President, 2011

The rapid technological changes of the 20th century not only enhanced productivity and created new industries but also increased demand for skilled labor (Goldin and Katz 2007). Higher education is the key to many modern occupations, and over the years Americans have correspondingly raised their educational attainment, with average years of schooling at age 30 rising 6.2 years between 1900 and 2000. But American gains in educational attainment are slowing. Average schooling duration in the final quarter of the 20th century increased at only about one-third of its previous pace.

Compared with other countries, American educational attainment also appears to be falling behind.

While growth in educational attainment has slowed, the demand for skilled workers continues to increase. According to the Bureau of Labor Statistics, 14 of the 30 fastest-growing occupations in the United States require at least a bachelor's degree, with 7 others requiring either an associate's degree or a postsecondary vocational certificate or award. Moreover, over the past 30 years, the return to a college education has also risen, further suggesting that increasing demand for high-skilled workers is outstripping their supply. . . . In 2009, workers with a bachelor's degree or more earned more than twice as much as those with only a high school diploma, while those with some college or an associate's degree earned 25 percent more. These wage premiums have risen 72 percentage points and 10 percentage points, respectively, since 1963. Although not shown in the figure, the returns to postgraduate education have risen even more steeply. In the mid-1960s, those with postgraduate degrees earned about 50 percent more than high school graduates; by 2009, this wage premium had more than tripled to 159 percent.

While earnings of workers who have attended college have risen, the annual income of those with only a high school degree or less has fallen since the 1970s, even before the declines during the recent recession. High school dropouts have fared the worst among all workers, with earnings falling 12 percent, in real terms, since 1963. These workers currently earn 30 percent less than high school graduates. This trend mirrors a broader pattern of rising wage and income inequality in the United States, with gains from economic growth concentrated in some segments of the population. In the past 20 years, real income for the top 20 percent of all households has grown by 20 percent, while incomes for households in the bottom half of the distribution have been essentially flat. By contrast, in other periods of economic growth, such as that from World War II to the mid-1970s, advances in labor income were spread roughly evenly throughout the wage distribution. A leading hypothesis about the causes of rising income inequality over the past 30 years points to technological advances that have increased the demand for high-skilled workers, while the supply of these workers has not accelerated to meet the demand.

Further, the overall data on educational attainment mask large disparities by race and socioeconomic status. Whereas 49 percent of non-Hispanic whites aged 25 to 34 hold a postsecondary degree, only 29 percent of African Americans and 19 percent of Hispanics do. In addition, children from high income households are almost four times as likely to obtain a postsecondary degree by age 24 as those from low-income families. Finally, achievement lags in science, technology, engineering, and mathematics (SteM) fields, all areas that show high wage returns to training and underpin future innovation. Recent test results in primary and secondary education suggest that American schoolchildren are lagging behind in math and science. The 2009 Programme for International Student Assessment survey, for example, showed that American students placed 17th of 34 developed countries in science and 25th in math. President Obama recognizes that education is not only a driver of growth but also the surest way for individuals to share in the gains from growth. The challenge in developing a world-leading workforce involves both increasing educational attainment and enhancing the quality of education in this country. That is why

the President has established a goal for the United States to resume world leadership in college degree attainment by 2020. to reach this goal, the Nation must raise its college completion rate from 40 percent to 60 percent. That requires 8 million additional young people to graduate from America's colleges and universities over the next 10 years. The Administration has put forward a

two-pronged strategy that, first, seeks to ensure that higher education is accessible and affordable to all individuals and, second, promotes innovative reform to ensure educational quality.

Source: Economic Report of the President, 2011 U.S. Government Printing Office, pp. 63–72.

In "The Spirit Level," British academics Richard Wilkinson and Kate Pickett argue that the social costs of inequality are huge. They assert something like if the United Kingdom were to cut income inequality in half, murder rates would halve, mental illness would reduce by two-thirds, obesity would halve, imprisonment would reduce by 80 percent, teen births would reduce by 80 percent, and levels of trust would increase by 85 percent. While these purported effects of reducing inequality are unlikely and there are severe criticisms of the study, there are many people who, like Wilkinson and Pickett, worry a great deal about income inequality.

What does income inequality mean? Clearly, it means that few have much and many have little. But is this a problem? Measures of inequality tell us nothing about the living conditions of the poor, their health and their access to economic opportunity. Income inequality in a rich country could mean that the poorest members of that society are wealthier or better off than the wealthiest members of a poor country. Under a free-market system, those who are most productive receive the highest income. When the economy is growing, it is likely that a few have been so much more productive that they receive much higher incomes than others—but almost all incomes are rising. Consider the founders of Microsoft, Google, Facebook and others; while their wealth rose astronomically because they created new companies, they also created thousands of well paying jobs that would not have existed had the founders not introduced their companies.

While income inequality in the United States has risen over the past 100 years, would the poorest today choose to live in 1900? Life expectancy was only about 40 years, and life was tough. Very long workdays without vacations existed; common appliances today such as refrigerators, air conditioners, televisions, cable, the internet, computers and many other items that make life better and easier did not exist. Very few people in a rich country would prefer to live as a wealthy person in that country 100 years ago.

According to the 2011 Economic Report of the President, different skill levels have led to much of the income inequality we observe. Jobs require much higher skills than a few years ago, but, according to the Report, not enough people have gone to college to acquire these skills. The Administration proposes to spend more to increase college graduation rates and enhance educational attainment. But is this necessary? Why won't a free market in labor lead people to select careers that pay more? And, as more people move into those occupations, won't wages slow their growth relative to wages in other sectors of the economy? The Report suggests that the demand for skilled workers has grown far faster than the supply of such workers. Again, if this has occurred and continues to occur, and those with skills earn increasingly more than those without skills, won't many without skills choose to acquire those skills? If higher skills generate increasingly higher incomes, won't that induce a lot more people to embark on a journey where they acquire these skills?

What would be the effects of a government-subsidized program for more people to be able to afford to attend college? More people would attend college, which would increase the demand for college and drive up the price of college. If the government subsidizes college, then many people who would not otherwise have chosen to attend college will attend. What effect might this have? Could it lead to increased drop-out rates as people who were not able to complete the requirements chose to attend college because it was subsidized by the government. Might it cause classes to lower requirements and quality of courses so that failure rates don't rise?

CHAPTER 34

World Trade Equilibrium

© MACIEJ FROLOW/GETTY IMAGES, INC

© DAVID PEARSON/ALAMY; LOGO: © FROXX/SHUTTERSTOCK.COM

 **FUNDAMENTAL QUESTIONS**

1 What are the prevailing patterns of trade between countries? What goods are traded?

2 What determines the goods that a nation will export?

3 How are the equilibrium price and the quantity of goods traded determined?

4 What are the sources of comparative advantage?

The United States' once-dominant position as an exporter of color television sets has since been claimed by nations like Japan and Taiwan. What caused this change? Is it because Japan specializes in the export of high-tech equipment? If countries tend to specialize in the export of particular kinds of goods, why does the United States import Heineken beer at the same time it exports Budweiser? This chapter will examine the volume of world trade and the nature of trade linkages between countries. As you saw in Chapter 2, trade occurs because of specialization in production. No single individual or country can produce everything better than anyone else can. The result is specialization of production based on comparative advantage. Remember that comparative advantage is in turn based on relative opportunity costs: A country will specialize in the production of those goods for which its opportunity costs of production are lower than the costs in other countries. Nations then trade what they produce in excess of their own consumption to acquire other things that they want to consume. In this chapter, we will go a step further and discuss the sources of comparative advantage. We will look at why one country has a comparative advantage in, say, automobile production, while another country has a comparative advantage in wheat production.

The world equilibrium price and quantity traded are derived from individual countries' demand and supply curves. This relationship between the world trade equilibrium and individual country markets will be utilized in the chapter "International Trade Restrictions" to discuss the ways in which countries can interfere with free international trade to achieve their own economic or political goals.

1. An Overview of World Trade

Trade occurs because it makes people better off. International trade occurs because it makes people better off than they would be if they could consume only domestically produced products. In what sense are they better off? Goods are available at lower prices and with more variety in a world with trade than in a world in which every country consumes only what it produces. Who trades with whom, and what sorts of goods are traded? These are the questions we consider first, before investigating the underlying reasons for trade.

 1 What are the prevailing patterns of trade between countries? What goods are traded?

1.a. The Direction of Trade

Table 1 shows patterns of trade between two large groups of countries: the industrial countries and the developing countries. The industrial countries include all of Western Europe, Japan, Australia, New Zealand, Canada, and the United States. The developing countries are, essentially, the rest of the world. Table 1 shows the dollar values and percentages of total trade between these groups of countries. The column at the left lists the origin of exports, and the row at the top lists the destination of imports.

As Table 1 shows, trade between industrial countries accounts for the bulk of international trade. Trade between industrial countries is a little more than $5.2 trillion in value and amounts to 42 percent of world trade. Exports from industrial countries to developing countries represent 19 percent of total world trade. Exports from developing countries to industrial countries account for 25 percent of total trade, while exports from developing countries to other developing countries currently represent only 14 percent of international trade.

	Destination	
Origin	**Industrial Countries**	**Developing Countries**
Industrial countries	$5,243	$2,413
	42%	19%
Developing countries	$3,098	$1,811
	25%	14%

TABLE 1 The Direction of Trade (in billions of dollars and percentages of world trade)

Source: *IMF, Direction of Trade Statistics Quarterly,* February 2011.

TABLE 2 Major Trading Partners of Selected Countries

United States				**Canada**			
Exports		**Imports**		**Exports**		**Imports**	
Canada	19%	China	19%	U.S.	75%	U.S.	51%
Mexico	12%	Canada	14%	Japan	3%	China	10%
Japan	5%	Mexico	10%	U.K.	3%	Japan	4%
China	7%	Japan	7%	China	2%	Mexico	4%
U.K.	4%	Germany	5%	Mexico	1%	Germany	3%
Germany				**Mexico**			
Exports		**Imports**		**Exports**		**Imports**	
France	10%	Netherlands	12%	U.S.	81%	U.S.	48%
U.S.	7%	France	8%	Canada	6%	China	14%
U.K.	7%	Belgium	7%	Spain	2%	Japan	6%
Netherlands	7%	Italy	6%	Germany	2%	Germany	4%
Italy	6%	U.K.	5%	Japan	1%	Canada	2%
Japan				**United Kingdom**			
Exports		**Imports**		**Exports**		**Imports**	
U.S.	16%	China	22%	U.S.	15%	Germany	13%
China	19%	U.S.	11%	Germany	11%	U.S.	10%
Korea	8%	Australia	6%	France	8%	China	8%
Hong Kong	5%	Korea	4%	Netherlands	8%	Netherlands	7%
Singapore	3%	Indonesia	4%	Ireland	7%	Belgium	5%

Source: *IMF, Direction of Trade Statistics Quarterly*, February 2011.

Trade between industrial countries accounts for the bulk of international trade.

Table 2 lists the major trading partners of selected countries and the percentage of total exports and imports accounted for by each country's top ten trading partners. For instance, 19 percent of U.S. exports went to Canada, and 7 percent of U.S. imports came from Japan. From a glance at the other countries listed in Table 2, it is clear that the United States is a major trading partner for many nations. This is true because of both the size of the U.S. economy and the nation's relatively high level of income. It is also apparent that Canada and Mexico are very dependent on trade with the United States: 75 percent of Canada's exports and 51 percent of its imports involve the United States, as do 81 percent of Mexico's exports and 48 percent of its imports. The dollar value of trade among the three North American nations is shown in Figure 1.

The volume of trade in fuels exceeds that of any other category of goods.

1.b. What Goods Are Traded?

Because countries differ in their comparative advantages, they will tend to export different goods. Countries also have different tastes and technological needs, and thus tend to differ in what they will import. Some goods are more widely traded than others, as Table 3 shows. Fuels like crude petroleum are the most heavily traded category of goods in the world, accounting for 15 percent of the total volume of world trade. Office and telecom equipment and chemicals are essentially tied for second place in share of world trade. The importance of a few major categories in international trade should not obscure the fact that international trade involves all sorts of products from all over the world.

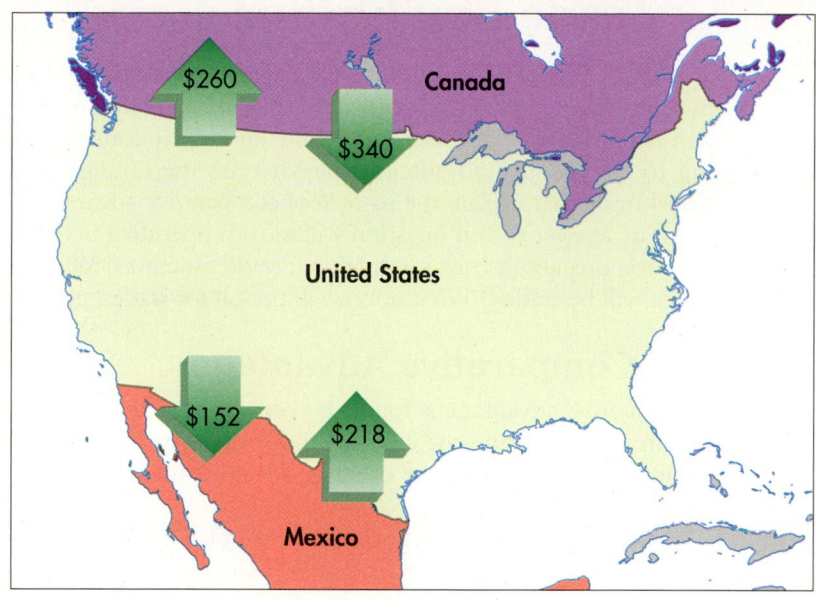

FIGURE 1   Merchandise Trade Flows in North America (billions of dollars)

$260
Canada
$340
United States
$152
$218
Mexico

In 2008, the United States exported $260 billion worth of goods to Canada and imported $340 billion of goods from Canada. The same year, U.S. merchandise exports to Mexico were $152 billion, while merchandise imports from Mexico were $218 billion.

TABLE 3   World Merchandise Exports by Major Product Groups

Product Category	Value (billion dollars)	Percentage of World Merchandise Trade
Agricultural products	**1,169**	**9.6**
Fuels & mining products	**2,263**	**19.5**
Fuels	**1,608**	**14.8**
Manufactures (total)	**8,355**	**69.8**
Iron & steel	481	4.0
Chemicals	1,447	10.9
Office & telecom equipment	1,323	11.1
Automotive products	847	7.0
Textiles	211	2.5
Clothing	316	3.5

Note: Values in this table may not total 100 due to rounding.
Source: World Trade Organization, *International Trade Statistics 2010*; http://www.wto.org/english/res_e/statis_e/its2010_e/its2010_e.pdf.

RECAP

1. Trade between industrial countries accounts for the bulk of international trade.

2. The most important trading partners of the United States are Canada, Mexico, China, and Japan.

3. Fuels are the most heavily traded category of goods in the world, in terms of value of exports.

4. World trade is distributed across a great variety of products.

2. An Example of International Trade Equilibrium

2 What determines the goods that a nation will export?

The international economy is very complex. Each country has a unique pattern of trade, in terms both of trading partners and of goods traded. Some countries trade a great deal, and others trade very little. We already know that countries specialize and trade according to comparative advantage, but what are the fundamental determinants of international trade that explain the pattern of comparative advantage?

The answer to this question will in turn provide a better understanding of some basic questions about how international trade functions: What goods will be traded? How much will be traded? What prices will prevail for traded goods?

2.a. Comparative Advantage

Comparative advantage is found by comparing the relative costs of production in each country. We measure the cost of producing a particular good in two countries in terms of opportunity costs—what other goods must be given up in order to produce more of the good in question.

Table 4 presents a hypothetical example of two countries, the United States and India, that both produce two goods, wheat and cloth. The table lists the amounts of each good that can be produced by each worker. This example assumes that labor productivity differences alone determine comparative advantage. In the United States, a worker can produce either 8 units of wheat or 4 units of cloth. In India, a worker can produce 4 units of wheat or 3 units of cloth.

The United States has an **absolute advantage**—greater productivity—in producing both wheat and cloth. Absolute advantage is determined by comparing the absolute productivity of workers producing each good in different countries. Since one worker can

absolute advantage
An advantage derived from one country having a lower absolute input cost of producing a particular good than another country.

Comparative advantage is based on what a country can do relatively better than other countries. This photo shows a sheep in Canterbury, New Zealand. New Zealand has a comparative advantage in sheep raising and wool production.

TABLE 4	An Example of Comparative Advantage	
	Output per Worker per Day in Either Wheat or Cloth	
	U.S.	**India**
Wheat	8	4
Cloth	4	3

produce more of either good in the United States than in India, the United States is the more efficient producer of both goods.

It might seem that, since the United States is the more efficient producer of both goods, there would be no need for it to trade with India. But absolute advantage is not the critical consideration. What matters in determining the benefits of international trade is comparative advantage, as originally discussed in Chapter 2. To find the **comparative advantage**—the lower opportunity cost—we must compare the opportunity cost of producing each good in each country.

The opportunity cost of producing wheat is what must be given up in cloth using the same resources, like one worker per day. Look again at Table 4 to see the production of wheat and cloth in the two countries. Since one U.S. worker can produce 8 units of wheat or 4 units of cloth, if we take a worker from cloth production and move him to wheat production, we gain 8 units of wheat and lose 4 units of cloth.

The opportunity cost of producing wheat equals $^4/_8$, or $^1/_2$, unit of cloth:

$$\frac{\text{Output of cloth given up}}{\text{Output of wheat gained}} = \frac{\text{opportunity cost of producing 1 unit of}}{\text{wheat (in terms of cloth given up)}}$$

$$\frac{4}{8} = \frac{1}{2}$$

Applying the same thinking to India, we find that one worker can produce 4 units of wheat or 3 units of cloth. The opportunity cost of producing 1 unit of wheat in India is $^3/_4$ unit of cloth.

A comparison of the domestic opportunity costs in each country will reveal which one has the comparative advantage in producing each good. The U.S. opportunity cost of producing 1 unit of wheat is $^1/_2$ unit of cloth; the Indian opportunity cost is $^3/_4$ unit of cloth. Because the United States has a lower domestic opportunity cost, it has the comparative advantage in wheat production and will export wheat. Since wheat production costs are lower in the United States, India is better off trading for wheat rather than trying to produce it domestically.

The comparative advantage in cloth is found the same way. Taking a worker in the United States from wheat production and putting her in cloth production, we gain 4 units of cloth but lose 8 units of wheat per day. So the opportunity cost is

$$\frac{\text{Output of wheat given up}}{\text{Output of cloth gained}} = \frac{\text{opportunity cost of producing 1 unit of}}{\text{cloth (in terms of wheat given up)}}$$

$$\frac{8}{4} = 2$$

In India, moving a worker from wheat to cloth production means that we gain 3 units of cloth but lose 4 units of wheat, so the opportunity cost is $^4/_3$, or $1^1/_3$ units of wheat for 1 unit of cloth. Comparing the U.S. opportunity cost of 2 units of wheat with the Indian opportunity cost of $1^1/_3$ units, we see that India has the comparative advantage in cloth production and will therefore export cloth. In this case, the United States is better off trading for cloth rather than producing it, since India's costs of production are lower.

comparative advantage
An advantage derived from comparing the opportunity costs of production in two countries.

In international trade, as in other areas of economic decision making, it is opportunity cost that matters—and opportunity costs are reflected in comparative advantage. Absolute advantage is irrelevant, because knowing the absolute number of labor hours required to produce a good does not tell us if we can benefit from trade.

We benefit from trade if we are able to obtain a good from a foreign country by giving up less than we would have to give up to obtain the good at home. Because only opportunity cost can allow us to make such comparisons, international trade proceeds on the basis of comparative advantage.

2.b. Terms of Trade

Countries export goods in which they have a comparative advantage.

On the basis of comparative advantage, India will specialize in cloth production, and the United States will specialize in wheat production. The two countries will then trade with each other to satisfy the domestic demand for both goods. International trade permits greater consumption than would be possible from domestic production alone. Since countries trade when they can obtain a good more cheaply from a foreign producer than they can obtain it at home, international trade allows all traders to consume more. This is evident when we examine the terms of trade.

terms of trade
The amount of an exported good that must be given up to obtain an imported good.

The **terms of trade** are the amount of an exported good that must be given up to obtain one unit of an imported good. The Global Business Insight "The Dutch Disease" provides a popular example of a dramatic shift in the terms of trade. As you saw earlier, comparative advantage dictates that the United States will specialize in wheat production and export wheat to India in exchange for Indian cloth. But the amount of wheat that the United States will exchange for a unit of cloth is limited by the domestic tradeoffs. If a unit of cloth can be obtained domestically for 2 units of wheat, the United States will be willing to trade with India only if the terms of trade are less than 2 units of wheat for a unit of cloth. India, in turn, will be willing to trade its cloth for U.S. wheat only if it can receive a better price than its domestic opportunity costs. Since a unit of cloth in India costs $1\frac{1}{3}$ units of wheat, India will gain from trade if it can obtain more than $1\frac{1}{3}$ units of wheat for its cloth.

The limits of the terms of trade are determined by the opportunity costs in each country:

1 unit of cloth for more than $1\frac{1}{3}$ but less than 2 units of wheat

Within this range, the actual terms of trade will be decided by the bargaining power of the two countries. The closer the United States can come to giving up only $1\frac{1}{3}$ units of wheat for cloth, the better the terms of trade for the United States. The closer India can come to receiving 2 units of wheat for its cloth, the better the terms of trade for India.

Though each country would like to push the other as close to the limits of the terms of trade as possible, any terms within the limits set by domestic opportunity costs will be mutually beneficial. Both countries benefit because they are able to consume goods at a cost that is less than their domestic opportunity costs. To illustrate the *gains from trade*, let us assume that the actual terms of trade are 1 unit of cloth for $1\frac{1}{2}$ units of wheat.

Suppose the United States has 2 workers, one of whom goes to wheat production and the other to cloth production. This would result in U.S. production of 8 units of wheat and 4 units of cloth. Without international trade, the United States can produce and consume 8 units of wheat and 4 units of cloth. If the United States, with its comparative advantage in wheat production, chooses to produce only wheat, it can use both workers in wheat production and produce 16 units. If the terms of trade are $1\frac{1}{2}$ units of wheat per unit of cloth, the United States can keep 8 units of wheat and trade the other 8 for $5\frac{1}{3}$ units of cloth (8 divided by $1\frac{1}{2}$). By trading U.S. wheat for Indian cloth, the United States is able to consume more than it could without trade. With no trade and

GLOBAL BUSINESS INSIGHT

The Dutch Disease

The terms of trade are the amount of an export that must be given up to obtain a certain quantity of an import. The price of an import will be equal to its price in the foreign country of origin multiplied by the exchange rate (the domestic-currency price of foreign currency). As the exchange rate changes, the terms of trade will change. This can have important consequences for international trade.

A problem can arise when one export industry in an economy is booming relative to others. In the 1970s, for instance, the Netherlands experienced a boom in its natural gas industry. The dramatic energy price increases of the 1970s resulted in large Dutch exports of natural gas. Increased demand for exports from the Netherlands caused the Dutch currency to appreciate, making Dutch goods more expensive for foreign buyers. This situation caused the terms of trade to worsen for the Netherlands. Although the natural gas sector was booming, Dutch manufacturers were finding it difficult to compete in the world market.

This phenomenon of a boom in one industry causing declines in the rest of the economy is popularly called the Dutch Disease. It is usually associated with dramatic increases in the demand for a primary commodity, and it can afflict any nation experiencing such a boom. For instance, a rapid rise in the demand for coffee could lead to a Dutch Disease problem for Colombia, where a coffee boom would be accompanied by a decline in other sectors of the economy.

---

half its labor devoted to each good, the United States could consume 8 units of wheat and 4 units of cloth. After trade, the United States consumes 8 units of wheat and $5\frac{1}{3}$ units of cloth. By devoting all its labor hours to wheat production and trading wheat for cloth, the United States gains $1\frac{1}{3}$ units of cloth. This is the gain from trade—an increase in consumption, as summarized in Table 5.

> The gain from trade is increased consumption.

2.c. Export Supply and Import Demand

The preceding example suggests that countries benefit from specialization and trade. Realistically, however, countries do not completely specialize. Typically, domestic industries satisfy part of the domestic demand for goods that are also imported. To understand how the quantity of goods traded is determined, we must construct demand and supply curves for each country and use them to create export supply and import demand curves.

The proportion of domestic demand for a good that is satisfied by domestic production and the proportion that will be satisfied by imports are determined by the domestic supply and demand curves and the international equilibrium price of a good. The international equilibrium price and quantity may be determined once we know the export supply and import demand curves for each country. These curves are derived from the

---

TABLE 5   Hypothetical Example of U.S. Gains from Specialization and Trade

Without International Trade

1 worker in wheat production: produce and consume 8 wheat

1 worker in cloth production: produce and consume 4 cloth

With Specialization and Trade

2 workers in wheat production: produce 16 wheat and consume 8; trade 8 wheat for $5\frac{1}{3}$ cloth

Before Trade: consume 8 wheat and 4 cloth

After Trade: consume 8 wheat and $5\frac{1}{3}$ cloth; gain $1\frac{1}{3}$ cloth by specialization and trade

© 2013 Cengage Learning

© matthagraphics/Shutterstock.com

domestic supply and demand in each country. Figure 2 illustrates the derivation of the export supply and import demand curves.

Figure 2(a) shows the domestic supply and demand curves for the U.S. wheat market. The domestic equilibrium price is $6, and the domestic equilibrium quantity is 200 million bushels. (The domestic no-trade equilibrium price is the price that exists prior to international trade.) A price above $6 will yield a U.S. wheat surplus. For instance, at a price of $9, the U.S. surplus will be 200 million bushels. A price below equilibrium will produce a wheat shortage: At a price of $3, the shortage will be 200 million bushels. The key point here is that the world price of a good may be quite different from the domestic no-trade equilibrium price. And once international trade occurs, the world price will prevail in the domestic economy.

If the world price of wheat is different from a country's domestic no-trade equilibrium price, the country will become an exporter or an importer. For instance, if the world price is above the domestic no-trade equilibrium price, the domestic surplus can be exported to the rest of the world. Figure 2(b) shows the U.S. **export supply curve**. This curve illustrates the U.S. domestic surplus of wheat for prices above the domestic no-trade equilibrium price of $6. At a world price of $9, the United States would supply 200 million bushels of wheat to the rest of the world. The export supply is equal to the domestic surplus. The higher the world price above the domestic no-trade equilibrium, the greater the quantity of wheat exported by the United States.

If the world price of wheat is below the domestic no-trade equilibrium price, the United States will import wheat. The **import demand curve** is the amount of the U.S. shortage at various prices below the no-trade equilibrium. In Figure 2(b), the import demand curve is a downward-sloping line, indicating that the lower the price below the domestic no-trade equilibrium of $6, the greater the quantity of wheat imported by the United States. At a price of $3, the United States will import 200 million bushels.

The domestic supply and demand curves and the export supply and import demand curves for India appear in Figures 2(c) and (d). The domestic no-trade equilibrium price in India is $12. At this price, India would neither import nor export any wheat because the domestic demand would be satisfied by the domestic supply. The export supply curve for India is shown in Figure 2(d) as an upward-sloping line that measures the amount of the domestic surplus as the price level rises above the domestic no-trade equilibrium price of $12. According to Figure 2(c), if the world price of wheat is $15, the domestic surplus in India is equal to 200 million bushels. The corresponding point on the export supply curve indicates that at a price of $15, 200 million bushels will be exported. The import demand curve for India reflects the domestic shortage at a price below the domestic no-trade equilibrium price. At $9, the domestic shortage is equal to 200 million bushels; the import demand curve indicates that at $9, 200 million bushels will be imported.

2.d. The World Equilibrium Price and Quantity Traded

The international equilibrium price of wheat and the quantity of wheat traded are found by combining the import demand and export supply curves for the United States and India, as in Figure 3. International equilibrium occurs if the quantity of imports demanded by one country is equal to the quantity of exports supplied by the other country. In Figure 3, this equilibrium occurs at the point labeled *e*. At this point, the import demand curve for India indicates that India wants to import 200 million bushels at a price of $9. The export supply curve for the United States indicates that the United States wants to export 200 million bushels at a price of $9. Only at $9 will the quantity of wheat demanded by the importing nation equal the quantity of wheat supplied by the exporting nation. So the equilibrium world price of wheat is $9, and the equilibrium quantity of wheat traded is 200 million bushels.

export supply curve
A curve showing the relationship between the world price of a good and the amount that a country will export.

import demand curve
A curve showing the relationship between the world price of a good and the amount that a country will import.

3 How are the equilibrium price and the quantity of goods traded determined?

International equilibrium occurs at the point where the quantity of imports demanded by one country is equal to the quantity of exports supplied by the other country.

FIGURE 2 The Import Demand and Export Supply Curves

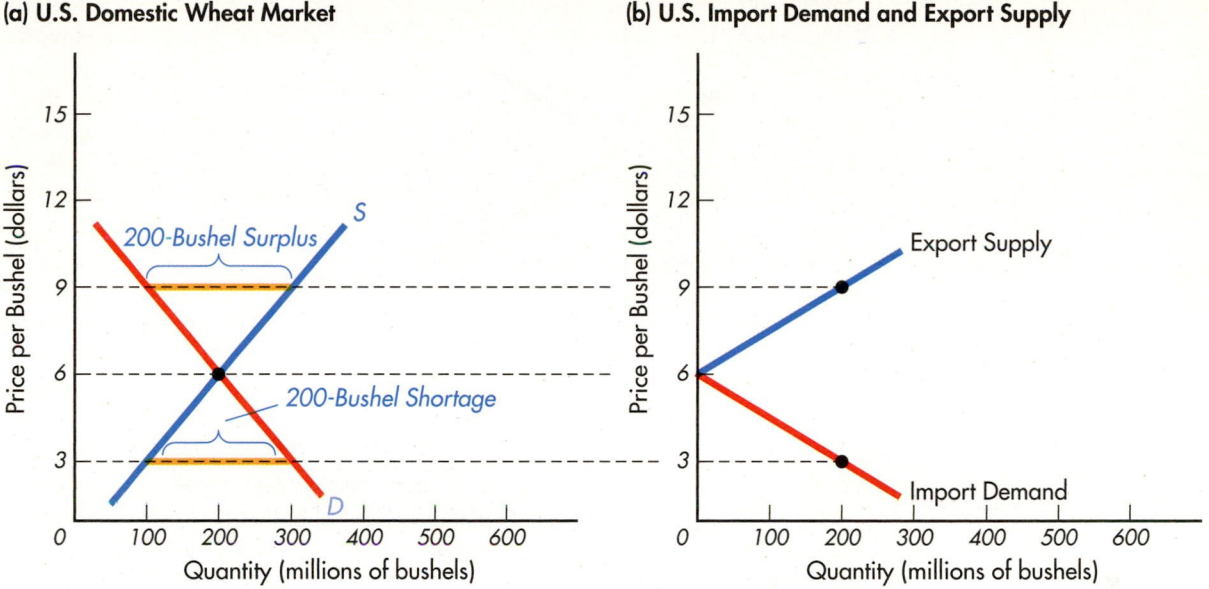

(a) U.S. Domestic Wheat Market

(b) U.S. Import Demand and Export Supply

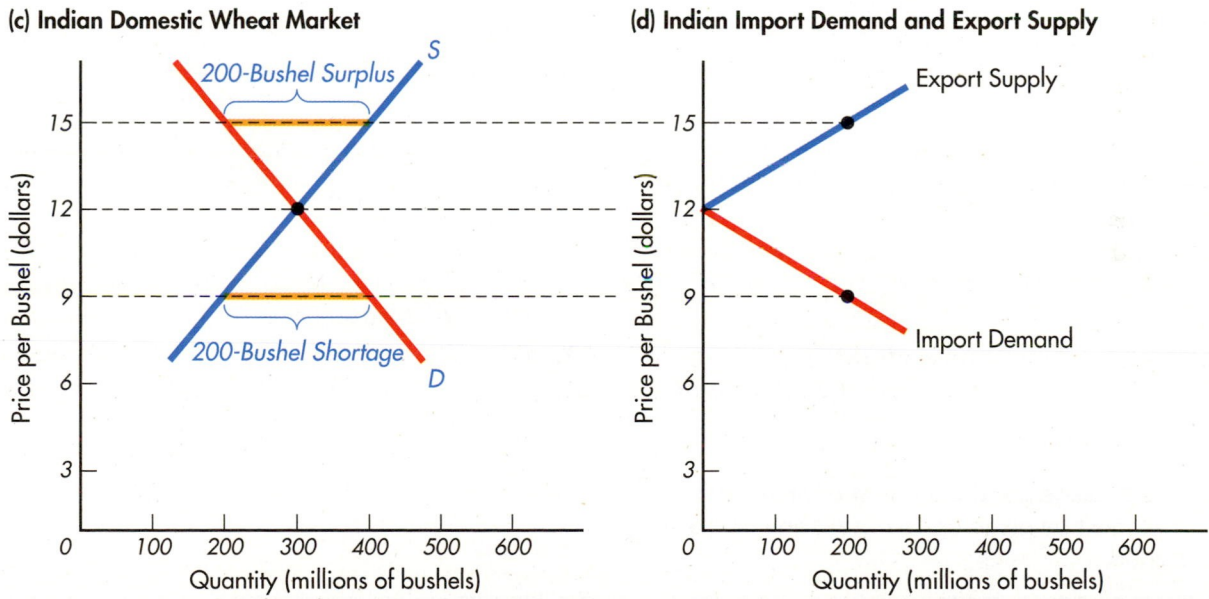

(c) Indian Domestic Wheat Market

(d) Indian Import Demand and Export Supply

Figures 2(a) and 2(c) show the domestic demand and supply curves for wheat in the United States and India, respectively. The domestic no-trade equilibrium price is $6 in the United States and $12 in India. Any price above the domestic no-trade equilibrium prices will create domestic surpluses, which are reflected in the export supply curves in Figures 2(b) and 2(d). Any price below the domestic no-trade equilibrium prices will create domestic shortages, which are reflected in the import demand curves in Figures 2(b) and 2(d).

| FIGURE 3 | International Equilibrium Price and Quantity |

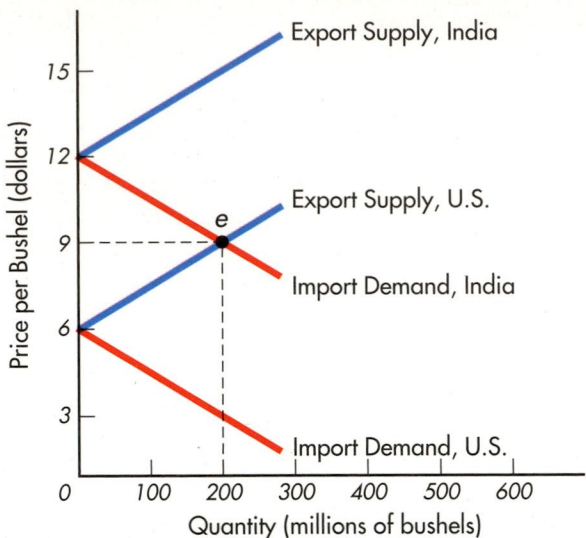

The international equilibrium price is the price at which the export supply curve of the United States intersects the import demand curve of India. At the equilibrium price of $9, the United States will export 200 million bushels to India.

RECAP

1. Comparative advantage is based on the relative opportunity costs of producing goods in different countries.

2. A country has an absolute advantage when it can produce a good more efficiently than can other nations.

3. A country has a comparative advantage when the opportunity cost of producing a good, in terms of forgone output of other goods, is lower than that of other nations.

4. The terms of trade are the amount of an export good that must be given up to obtain one unit of an import good.

5. The limits of the terms of trade are determined by the domestic opportunity costs of production in each country.

6. The export supply and import demand curves measure the domestic surplus and shortage, respectively, at different world prices.

7. International equilibrium occurs at the point where one country's import demand curve intersects with the export supply curve of another country.

3. Sources of Comparative Advantage

4 What are the sources of comparative advantage?

We know that countries specialize and trade in accordance with comparative advantage, but what gives a country a comparative advantage? Economists have suggested several theories of the source of comparative advantage. Let us review these theories.

3.a. Productivity Differences

The example of comparative advantage given earlier in this chapter showed the United States to have a comparative advantage in wheat production and India to have a comparative advantage in cloth production. Comparative advantage was determined by differences in the number of labor hours required to produce each good. In this example, differences in the *productivity* of labor accounted for comparative advantage.

For over two hundred years, economists have argued that productivity differences account for comparative advantage. In fact, this theory of comparative advantage is often called the *Ricardian model*, after David Ricardo, a nineteenth-century English economist who explained and analyzed the idea of productivity-based comparative advantage. Variations in the productivity of labor can explain many observed trade patterns in the world.

Although we know that labor productivity differs across countries, and that this can help explain why countries produce the goods they do, there are factors other than labor productivity that determine comparative advantage. Furthermore, even if labor productivity were all that mattered, we would still want to know why some countries have more productive workers than others. The standard interpretation of the Ricardian model is that technological differences between countries account for differences in labor productivity. The countries with the most advanced technology would have a comparative advantage with regard to those goods that can be produced most efficiently with modern technology.

> *Comparative advantage due to productivity differences between countries is often called the Ricardian model of comparative advantage.*

3.b. Factor Abundance

Goods differ in terms of the resources, or factors of production, required for their production. Countries differ in terms of the abundance of different factors of production: land, labor, capital, and entrepreneurial ability. It seems self-evident that countries would have an advantage in producing those goods that use relatively large amounts of their most abundant factor of production. Certainly countries with a relatively large amount of farmland would have a comparative advantage in agriculture, and countries with a relatively large amount of capital would tend to specialize in the production of manufactured goods.

The idea that comparative advantage is based on the relative abundance of factors of production is sometimes called the *Heckscher-Ohlin model*, after the two Swedish economists, Eli Heckscher and Bertil Ohlin, who developed the original argument. The original model assumed that countries possess only two factors of production: labor and capital. Thus, researchers have examined the labor and capital requirements of various industries to see whether labor-abundant countries export goods whose production is relatively labor intensive, and capital-abundant countries export goods that are relatively capital intensive. In many cases, factor abundance has served well as an explanation of observed trade patterns. However, there are cases in which comparative advantage seems to run counter to the predictions of the factor-abundance theory. In response, economists have suggested other explanations for comparative advantage.

> *Comparative advantage based on differences in the abundance of factors of production across countries is described in the Heckscher-Ohlin model.*

3.c. Other Theories of Comparative Advantage

New theories of comparative advantage have typically been developed in an effort to explain the trade pattern in some narrow category of products. They are not intended to serve as general explanations of comparative advantage, as do factor abundance and productivity. These supplementary theories emphasize human skills, product life cycles, and preferences.

Human Skills This approach emphasizes differences across countries in the availability of skilled and unskilled labor. The basic idea is that countries with a relatively abundant stock of highly skilled labor will have a comparative advantage in producing goods that require relatively large amounts of skilled labor. This theory is similar to the factor-abundance theory, except that here the analysis rests on two segments (skilled and unskilled) of the labor factor.

The human skills argument is consistent with the observation that most U.S. exports are produced in high-wage (skilled labor) industries and most U.S. imports are products produced in relatively low-wage industries. Since the United States has a well-educated labor force, relative to many other countries, we would expect the United States to have a comparative advantage in industries requiring a large amount of skilled labor. Developing countries would be expected to have a comparative advantage in industries requiring a relatively large amount of unskilled labor.

Product Life Cycles This theory explains how comparative advantage in a specific good can shift from one country to another over time. This occurs because goods experience a *product life cycle*. At the outset, development and testing are required to conceptualize and design the product. For this reason, the early production will be undertaken by an innovative firm. Over time, however, a successful product tends to become standardized, in the sense that many manufacturers can produce it. The mature product may be produced by firms that do little or no research and development, specializing instead in copying successful products that were invented and developed by others.

> Manufactured goods have life cycles. At first they are produced by the firm that invented them. Later, they may be produced by firms in other countries that copy the technology of the innovator.

The product life cycle theory is related to international comparative advantage in that a new product will first be produced and exported by the nation in which it was invented. As the product is exported elsewhere and foreign firms become familiar with it, the technology is copied in other countries by foreign firms seeking to produce a competing version. As the product matures, comparative advantage shifts away from the country of origin if other countries have lower manufacturing costs using the now-standardized technology.

The history of color television production shows how comparative advantage can shift over the product life cycle. Color television was invented in the United States, and U.S. firms initially produced and exported color TVs. Over time, as the technology of color television manufacturing became well known, countries like Japan and Taiwan came to dominate the business. Firms in these countries had a comparative advantage over U.S. firms in the manufacture of color televisions. Once the technology is widely available, countries with lower production costs, due to lower wages, can compete effectively against the higher-wage nation that developed the technology.

Preferences The theories of comparative advantage that we have looked at so far have all been based on supply factors. It may be, though, that the demand side of the market can explain some of the patterns observed in international trade. Different producers' goods are seldom exactly identical. Consumers may prefer the goods of one firm to those of another firm. Domestic firms usually produce goods to satisfy domestic consumers. But since different consumers have different preferences, some consumers will prefer goods produced by foreign firms. International trade allows consumers to expand their consumption opportunities.

Consumers who live in countries with similar levels of development can be expected to have similar consumption patterns. The consumption patterns of consumers in countries at quite different levels of development are much less similar. This would suggest that firms in industrial countries will find a larger market for their goods in other industrial countries than in developing countries.

As you saw earlier in this chapter, industrial countries tend to trade with other industrial countries. This pattern runs counter to the factor-abundance theory of comparative advantage, which would suggest that countries with the most dissimilar endowments of resources would find trade most beneficial. Yet rich countries, with large supplies of capital and skilled labor forces, trade more actively with other rich countries than they do with poor countries. Firms in industrial countries tend to produce goods that relatively wealthy consumers will buy. The key point here is that we do not live in a world based on simple comparative advantage, in which all cloth is identical, regardless of the producer. We inhabit a world of differentiated products, and consumers want choices between different brands or styles of a seemingly similar good.

Another feature of international trade that may be explained by consumer preference is **intraindustry trade**, a circumstance in which a country both exports and imports goods in the same industry. The fact that the United States exports Budweiser beer and imports Heineken beer is not surprising when preferences are taken into account. Supply-side theories of comparative advantage rarely provide an explanation of intraindustry trade, since they would expect each country to export only those goods produced by industries in which a comparative advantage exists. Yet the real world is characterized by a great deal of intraindustry trade.

We have discussed several potential sources of comparative advantage: labor productivity, factor abundance, human skills, product life cycles, and preferences. Each of these theories, which are summarized in Figure 4, has proven useful in understanding certain trade patterns. Each has also been shown to have limitations as a general theory that is applicable to all cases. Once again we are reminded that the world is a very complicated place. Theories are simpler than reality. Nevertheless, they help us to understand how comparative advantage arises.

intraindustry trade
The simultaneous import and export of goods in the same industry by a particular country.

RECAP

1. Comparative advantage can arise because of differences in labor productivity.

2. Countries differ in their resource endowments, and a given country may enjoy a comparative advantage in products that use its most abundant factor of production intensively.

3. Industrial countries may have a comparative advantage in products requiring a large amount of skilled labor. Developing countries may have a comparative advantage in products requiring a large amount of unskilled labor.

4. Comparative advantage in a new good initially resides in the country that invented the good. Over time, other nations learn the technology and may gain a comparative advantage in producing the good.

5. In some industries, consumer preferences for differentiated goods may explain international trade flows, including industry trade.

FIGURE 4   Theories of Comparative Advantage

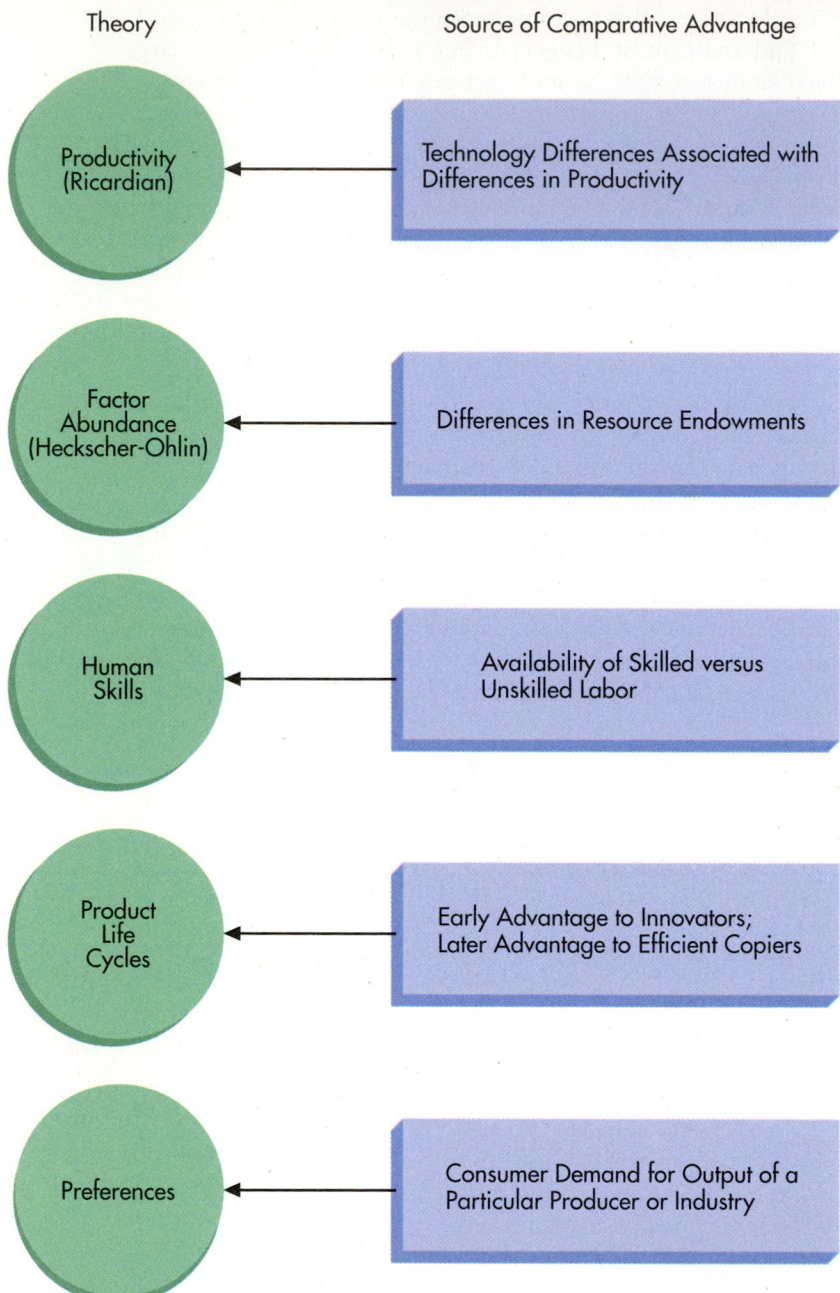

Several theories exist that explain comparative advantage: labor productivity, factor abundance, human skills, product life cycles, and preferences.

SUMMARY

1. **What are the prevailing patterns of trade between countries? What goods are traded?**

   • International trade flows largely between industrial countries. *§1.a*

   • International trade involves many diverse products. *§1.b*

2. **What determines the goods that a nation will export?**

   • Comparative advantage is based on the opportunity costs of production. *§2.a*

   • Domestic opportunity costs determine the limits of the terms of trade between two countries—that is, the amount of exports that must be given up to obtain imports. *§2.b*

   • The export supply curve shows the domestic surplus and amount of exports available at alternative world prices. *§2.c*

   • The import demand curve shows the domestic shortage and amount of imports demanded at alternative world prices. *§2.c*

3. **How are the equilibrium price and the quantity of goods traded determined?**

   • The international equilibrium price and quantity of a good traded are determined by the intersection of the export supply curve of one country with the import demand curve of another country. *§2.d*

4. **What are the sources of comparative advantage?**

   • The productivity-differences and factor-abundance theories of comparative advantage are general theories that seek to explain patterns of international trade flow. *§3.a, 3.b*

   • Other theories of comparative advantage aimed at explaining trade in particular kinds of goods focus on human skills, product life cycles, and consumer preferences. *§3.c*

KEY TERMS

absolute advantage, 760
comparative advantage, 761

export supply curve, 764
import demand curve, 764

intraindustry trade, 769
terms of trade, 762

EXERCISES

1. Why must voluntary trade between two countries be mutually beneficial?

   Use the following table for exercises 2–6.

Amount of Beef or Computers Produced by One Worker in a Day

	Canada	Japan
Beef	8	5
Computers	3	4

2. Which country has the absolute advantage in beef production?

3. Which country has the absolute advantage in computer production?

4. Which country has the comparative advantage in beef production?

5. Which country has the comparative advantage in computer production?

6. What are the limits of the terms of trade? Specifically, when is Canada willing to trade with Japan, and when is Japan willing to trade with Canada?

7. Use the following supply and demand schedule for two countries to determine the international equilibrium price of shoes. How many shoes will be traded?

Demand and Supply of Shoes (in thousands)

| Price | Mexico | | Chile | |
	Qty. Demanded	Qty. Supplied	Qty. Demanded	Qty. Supplied
$10	40	0	55	0
$20	35	20	44	10
$30	30	40	33	20
$40	25	60	22	30
$50	20	80	11	40

8. How would each of the following theories of comparative advantage explain the fact that the United States exports computers?
   a. Productivity differences
   b. Factor abundance
   c. Human skills
   d. Product life cycle
   e. Preferences

9. Which of the theories of comparative advantage could explain why the United States exports computers to Japan at the same time that it imports computers from Japan? Explain.

10. Developing countries have complained that the terms of trade they face are unfavorable. If they voluntarily engage in international trade, what do you suppose they mean by "unfavorable terms of trade"?

11. If two countries reach equilibrium in their domestic markets at the same price, what can be said about their export supply and import demand curves and about the international trade equilibrium?

You can find further practice tests in the Online Quiz at **www.cengage.com/economics/boyes**.

LETTER TO SENATE MAJORITY LEADER HARRY REID

January 30, 2008

The Honorable Harry Reid
Majority Leader
United States Senate
U.S. Senate, S-221
Washington, DC 20515
Dear Majority Leader Reid:

We would like to offer our support for prioritizing trade legislation addressing China. We face a host of difficult trade issues with China that require strong action, ranging from currency manipulation and unfair subsidies, to trade law and counterfeit enforcement problems, to imported food and product safety. These issues are hurting American competiveness and expose American consumers to unsafe goods.

The problems facing workers and manufacturers due to unfair trading practices in China and other countries are growing more severe each day. The U.S. trade deficit with China hit $237.5 billion through November 2007, eclipsing the previous year's record of $232.6 billion. This is the highest annual imbalance ever recorded with a single country—and December's figures have yet to be calculated. The deficit with China now accounts for 32.5 percent of the U.S. total trade deficit in goods—and more than half of the U.S. non-petroleum goods deficit.

China is by far the leading violator of international trade rules and its actions continue to harm American workers, industry, and manufacturing. China has done little to address the fundamental misalignment of its currency, a practice that continues to take jobs and wealth from the United States. There is also strong evidence that the massive subsidies the Chinese government provides its producers gives them an unfair advantage in international trade. These factors, in addition to low wages, unsafe working conditions, and the absence of worker rights, have contributed to the loss of millions of manufacturing jobs and our country's reliance on imports.

The American people are demanding action to stop our trading partners from rigging the game. It is time for Congress to meet that demand and take strong action.

It is our belief that any such measure taken to correct this imbalance should ensure that China and other nations float their currencies against the dollar and the other currencies of the world. Should China and other nations fail to do so, an appropriate remedy would treat currency misalignment as a subsidy that is countervailable under U.S. trade law.

We also support provisions that would apply countervailing duties to non-market economies.

Current anti-subsidies rules allow the world's largest trade subsidizer, China, to continue its unfair practices without penalty.

Further, we believe it is necessary to ensure that World Trade Organization decisions do not undermine trade law enforcement. We must ensure that U.S. anti-dumping law will work effectively and fairly against China and other trade law violators.

Since Congress granted permanent normal trade relations status to China, intellectual property theft and illegal counterfeiting have increased, costing American businesses billions of dollars annually. We believe a comprehensive approach to China trade issues must include attention to intellectual property enforcement.

Finally, the recent recalls of unsafe toys, food, and other products from China emphasize the need to ensure that our trading system protects public health and safety. While the President's Interagency Working Group on Import Safety has developed recommendations for the federal government and industry to follow, we believe that memoranda of understanding with China alone cannot ensure the safety of products for American consumers. We would like to ensure that increased Customs and Border Patrol surveillance of imported food and products and market-based principles be considered to ensure that importers of products from all countries are liable for their safety and quality.

The challenges facing our nation's manufacturers, farmers, and workers increase with each passing week. We support efforts to address these issues in a comprehensive manner before the consideration of proposed free trade agreements, and we share the view that now is the time to move legislation forward.

Source: Senator Sherrod Brown website listing letter sent by eight senators to Senate Majority Leader Reid: http://brown.senate.gov/news room/press_releases/release/?id=45ebb90f-c 7be-4e54-815b-eaab5a57a533.

There is no lack of stories in the U.S. media on the threat of foreign economic domination. As this letter indicates, officials within the U.S. government were concerned about U.S. trade with China. The United States had experienced a growing trade deficit with China, and some senators wanted action to address what they saw as unfair international trade practices by China.

However, the bilateral trade accounts provide little, if any, information on such issues. Indeed, it is easy to think of an example in which a country has a persistent trade deficit with one of its trading partners but has its overall trade account in balance. Suppose there are three countries that trade among themselves, which we will call countries A, B, and C. The people of each country produce only one type of good and consume only one other type of good. The people of country A produce apples and consume bananas, the people of country B produce bananas and consume cucumbers, and the people of country C produce cucumbers and consume apples. Even when the trade account of each country is balanced, each has a deficit with one of its trading partners and a surplus with the other. Furthermore, a larger trade deficit between countries A and B (with each country retaining balanced trade) implies that the people of country A are better off, since they are consuming more. If the government of country A tried to impose a law forcing bilateral trade balance with country B, citizens of country A could not consume as many bananas as before and would be forced to attempt to sell apples to the uninterested citizens of country B.

This simple example demonstrates that the U.S. trade deficit with China should not in itself be a cause for concern. The United States could have a persistent trade deficit with China and yet maintain an overall balanced trade account. In fact, any country would be expected to have a trade deficit with some countries and a trade surplus with others. This reflects comparative advantage. Trade between countries makes both the exporting and the importing countries better off.

This is not to say that there may not be problems in terms of China failing to allow U.S. exporters access to its consumers, or problems with pirating of intellectual property, or problems in exchange rate management. Also, concern about the overall trade deficit may be well founded. An overall trade deficit indicates that a country is consuming more than it is producing. At any particular time, a country may want to run a trade deficit or a trade surplus, depending on the circumstances it faces. But regardless of the overall trade account of a country, we should expect bilateral trade imbalances among trading partners.

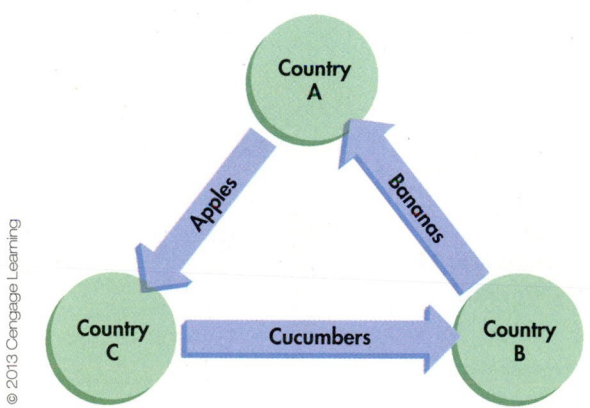

International Trade Restrictions

 **FUNDAMENTAL QUESTIONS**

1 Why do countries restrict international trade?

2 How do countries restrict the entry of foreign goods and promote the export of domestic goods?

3 What sorts of agreements do countries enter into to reduce barriers to international trade?

The Japanese government once announced that foreign-made skis would not be allowed into Japan because they were unsafe. Japanese ski manufacturers were active supporters of the ban. The U.S. government once imposed a tax of almost 50 percent on imports of motorcycles with engines larger than 700 cc. The only U.S.-owned motorcycle manufacturer, Harley-Davidson, produced no motorcycles with engines smaller than 1,000 cc and so did not care about the small-engine market. In the mid-1980s, Britain began replacing the distinctive red steel telephone booths that were used all through the country with new booths. Many U.S. residents were interested in buying an old British phone booth to use as a decorative novelty, so the phone booths were exported to the United States. However, when the phone booths arrived, the U.S. Customs Service impounded them because there was a limit on the amount of iron and steel products that could be exported from Britain to the United States. The phone booths would be allowed to enter the country only if British exports of some other iron and steel products were reduced. The British exporters protested the classification of the phone booths as iron and steel products and argued that they should be considered antiques (which have no import restrictions). The phone booths were not reclassified; as a result, few have entered the United States, and prices of old British phone booths have been in the thousands of dollars. There are many examples of government policy influencing the prices and quantities of goods that are traded internationally.

International trade is rarely determined solely by comparative advantage and the free market forces of supply and demand. Governments often find that political pressures favor policies that at least partially offset the prevailing comparative advantages. Government policy aimed at influencing international trade flows is called **commercial policy**. This chapter first examines the arguments in support of commercial policy and then discusses the various tools of commercial policy employed by governments.

commercial policy
Government policy that influences international trade flows.

1. Arguments for Protection

Governments restrict foreign trade to protect domestic producers from foreign competition. In some cases the protection may be justified; in most cases it harms consumers. Of the arguments used to promote such protection, only a few are valid. We will look first at arguments that are widely considered to have little or no merit, and then at those that may sometimes be valid.

International trade on the basis of comparative advantage maximizes world output and allows consumers access to better-quality products at lower prices than would be available in the domestic market alone. If trade is restricted, consumers pay higher prices for lower-quality goods, and world output declines. Protection from foreign competition imposes costs on the domestic economy as well as on foreign producers. When production does not proceed on the basis of comparative advantage, resources are not expended on their most efficient uses. Whenever government restrictions alter the pattern of trade, we should expect someone to benefit and someone else to suffer. Generally speaking, protection from foreign competition benefits domestic producers at the expense of domestic consumers.

 1 Why do countries restrict international trade?

Protection from foreign competition generally benefits domestic producers at the expense of domestic consumers.

1.a. Creation of Domestic Jobs

If foreign goods are kept out of the domestic economy, it is often argued, jobs will be created at home. This argument holds that domestic firms will produce the goods that otherwise would have been produced abroad, thus employing domestic workers instead of foreign workers. The weakness of this argument is that only the protected industry will benefit in terms of employment. Since domestic consumers will pay higher prices to buy the output of the protected industry, they will have less to spend on other goods and services, which could cause employment in other industries to drop. In addition, if other countries retaliate by restricting the entry of U.S. exports, the output of U.S. firms that produce for export will fall as well. Typically, restrictions to "save domestic jobs" simply redistribute jobs by creating employment in the protected industry and reducing employment elsewhere.

TABLE 1	The Cost of Protecting U.S. Jobs from Foreign Competition		
Protected Industry	**Jobs Saved**	**Total Cost (in millions)**	**Annual Cost per Job Saved**
Benzenoid chemicals	216	$ 297	$1,376,435
Luggage	226	290	1,285,078
Softwood lumber	605	632	1,044,271
Sugar	2,261	1,868	826,104
Polyethylene resins	298	242	812,928
Dairy products	2,378	1,630	685,323
Frozen concentrated orange juice	609	387	635,103
Ball bearings	146	88	603,368
Maritime services	4,411	2,522	571,668
Ceramic tiles	347	191	551,367
Machine tools	1,556	746	479,452
Ceramic articles	418	140	335,876
Women's handbags	773	204	263,535
Canned tuna	390	100	257,640
Glassware	1,477	366	247,889
Apparel and textiles	168,786	33,629	199,241
Peanuts	397	74	187,223
Rubber footwear	1,701	286	168,312
Women's nonathletic footwear	3,702	518	139,800
Costume jewelry	1,067	142	132,870
Total	191,764	$44,252	
Average (weighted)			$ 231,289

Source: Federal Reserve Bank of Dallas 2002 Annual Report, "The Fruits of Free Trade," by W. Michael Cox and Richard Alm, http://dallasfed.org/fed/annual/2002/ar02f.cfm.

Table 1 shows estimates of the cost of saving U.S. jobs from foreign competition. For instance, the cost of saving 226 jobs in the U.S. luggage industry is $290 million, or $1,285,078 per worker. Studies have consistently shown that the costs of protecting domestic jobs typically outweigh the benefits. So while it is possible to erect barriers to foreign competition and save domestic jobs, restricting international trade may impose large costs on an economy. Consumers end up paying much more for the goods they buy in order to subsidize the relatively inefficient domestic producer.

Table 2 shows the annual cost to the United States of import restrictions in terms of reduced GDP as estimated by an agency of the U.S. government. The total estimated amount of $4,622 million means that U.S. GDP would be over $4.6 billion higher without import restrictions. This estimate by the U.S. International Trade Commission incorporates estimates of all gains and losses from labor and capital income, tax revenue changes, and effects on consumption of changes in prices of goods and services. The amount of $4.6 billion is a very small fraction of U.S. GDP but would involve substantial changes for a few industries. For instance, in fabric mills, employment would fall by 11 percent and output by about 10 percent, and in the ball bearings sector, employment and output would both fall about 4.3 percent.

Saving domestic jobs from foreign competition may cost domestic consumers more than it benefits the protected industries.

TABLE 2	Annual Gain in U.S. GDP if U.S. Import Restrictions Were Eliminated
Sector	**GDP Gain (millions of dollars)**
Simultaneous liberalization of all significant restraints	4,622
Individual liberalization	
Textiles and apparel	2,254
Dairy	733
Sugar	514
Ethyl alcohol	356
Footwear and leather products	325
Tobacco	99
Tuna	23
Costume jewelry	21
Ball and roller bearings	14
Pens, mechanical pencils, and parts	13
Cutlery and hand tools	13
Table and kitchenware	10
Watches, clocks, watch cases, and parts	7
Dehydrated fruit	4
Ceramic wall and floor tile	1
Glass and glass products	1

Source: *The Economic Effects of Significant U.S. Imports Restraints, Sixth Update* (U.S. International Trade Commission, Washington, D.C., 2009), http://www.usitc.gov/publications/332/pub4094.pdf.

Tables 1 and 2 demonstrate the very high cost per job saved by protection. If the costs to consumers are greater than the benefits to the protected industries, you may wonder why government provides any protection aimed at saving jobs. The answer, in a word, is politics. Protection of the U.S. textile and sugar industries means that all consumers pay a higher price for clothing and sugar. But individual consumers do not know how much of the price they pay for clothes and sugar is due to protection, and consumers rarely lobby their political representatives to eliminate protection and reduce prices. Meanwhile, there is a great deal of pressure for protection. Employers and workers in the protected industries know the benefits of protection: higher prices for their output, higher profits for owners, and higher wages for workers. As a result, there will be active lobbying for protection against foreign competition.

1.b. Creation of a "Level Playing Field"

Special interest groups sometimes claim that other nations that export successfully to the home market have unfair advantages over domestic producers. Fairness, however, is often in the eye of the beholder. People who call for creating a "level playing field" believe that the domestic government should take steps to offset the perceived advantage of the foreign firm. They often claim that foreign firms have an unfair advantage because foreign workers are willing to work for very low wages. "Fair trade, not free trade" is the cry that this claim generates. But advocates of fair trade are really claiming that production in accordance with comparative advantage is unfair. This is clearly wrong. A country with relatively low wages is typically a country with an abundance of low-skilled labor. Such a country will have a comparative advantage in products that use low-skilled labor most intensively. To create a "level playing field" by imposing restrictions that eliminate the comparative advantage of foreign firms will make domestic consumers worse off and undermine the basis for specialization and economic efficiency.

Some calls for "fair trade" are based on the notion of reciprocity. If a country imposes import restrictions on goods from a country that does not have similar restrictions, reciprocal tariffs and quotas may be called for in the latter country in order to stimulate a reduction of trade restrictions in the former country. For instance, it has been claimed that U.S. construction firms are discriminated against in Japan, because Japanese construction firms do billions of dollars' worth of business in the United States each year, but U.S. construction companies rarely are seen in Japan. Advocates of fair trade could argue that U.S. restrictions should be imposed on Japanese construction firms.

One danger of calls for fairness based on reciprocity is that calls for fair trade may be invoked in cases where, in fact, foreign restrictions on U.S. imports do not exist. For instance, suppose the U.S. auto industry wanted to restrict the entry of imported autos to help stimulate sales of domestically produced cars. One strategy might be to point out that U.S. auto sales abroad had fallen and to claim that this was due to unfair treatment of U.S. auto exports in other countries. Of course, there are many other possible reasons why foreign sales of U.S. autos might have fallen. But blaming foreign trade restrictions might win political support for restricting imports of foreign cars into the United States.

1.c. Government Revenue Creation

Tariffs on trade generate government revenue. Industrial countries, which find income taxes easy to collect, rarely justify tariffs on the basis of the revenue they generate for government spending. But many developing countries find income taxes difficult to levy and collect, whereas tariffs are easy to collect. Customs agents can be positioned at ports of entry to examine all goods that enter and leave the country. The observability of trade flows makes tariffs a popular tax in developing countries, whose revenue requirements may provide a valid justification for their existence. Table 3 shows that tariffs account for a relatively large fraction of government revenue in many developing countries, and only a small fraction in industrial countries.

1.d. National Defense

It has long been argued that industries that are crucial to the national defense, such as shipbuilding, should be protected from foreign competition. Even though the United States does not have a comparative advantage in shipbuilding, the argument goes, a domestic shipbuilding industry is necessary, since foreign-made ships may not be available during war. This is a valid argument as long as the protected industry is genuinely critical to the national defense. In some industries, such as copper or other basic metals, it might make more sense to import the crucial products during peacetime and store them for use in the event of war; these products do not require domestic production in order to be useful. Care must be taken to ensure that the national defense argument is not used to protect industries other than those that are truly crucial to the nation's defense.

1.e. Infant Industries

Nations are often inclined to protect new industries on the basis that the protection will give those industries adequate time to develop. New industries need time to establish themselves and to become efficient enough that their costs are no higher than those of

Calls for "fair trade" are typically aimed at imposing restrictions to match those imposed by other nations.

Developing countries often justify tariffs as an important source of government revenue.

Industries that are truly critical to the national defense should be protected from foreign competition if that is the only way to ensure their existence.

TABLE 3	Tariffs as a Percentage of Total Government Revenue
Country	**Tariffs as Percentage of Government Revenue**
European Union	14.12%
United States	1.7%
Canada	1.7%
Mexico	2.0%
China	5.8%
Korea	4.6%
India	18.0%
Jordan	10.4%
Lesotho	64.0%

Source: World Customs Organization, "Annual Survey to Determine Percentage of National Revenues Represented by Customs Duties, 2010," http://www.wcoomd.org/files/1.%20Public%20files/PDFandDocuments/HarmonizedSystem/HS%20Overview/Duty%20Survey%20Jan2010_E.pdf.

their foreign rivals. An alternative to protecting young and/or critical domestic industries with tariffs and quotas is to subsidize them. Subsidies allow such firms to charge lower prices and to compete with more-efficient foreign producers, while permitting consumers to pay the world price rather than the higher prices associated with tariffs or quotas on foreign goods.

Protecting an infant industry from foreign competition may make sense, but only until the industry matures. Once the industry achieves sufficient size, protection should be withdrawn, and the industry should be made to compete with its foreign counterparts. Unfortunately, such protection is rarely withdrawn, because the larger and more successful the industry becomes, the more political power it wields. In fact, if an infant industry truly has a good chance to become competitive and produce profitably once it is well established, it is not at all clear that government should even offer protection to reduce short-run losses. New firms typically incur losses, but they are only temporary if the firm is successful.

> *Countries sometimes justify protecting new industries that need time to become competitive with the rest of the world.*

1.f. Strategic Trade Policy

There is another view of international trade that regards the description of comparative advantage presented in the previous chapter as misleading. According to this outlook, called **strategic trade policy**, international trade largely involves firms that pursue economies of scale—that is, firms that achieve lower costs per unit of production the more they produce. In contrast to the constant opportunity costs illustrated in the example of wheat and cloth in the chapter "World Trade Equilibrium," opportunity costs in some industries may fall with the level of output. Such **increasing-returns-to-scale industries** will tend to concentrate production in the hands of a few very large firms, rather than many competitive firms. Proponents of strategic trade policy contend that government can use tariffs or subsidies to give domestic firms with decreasing costs an advantage over their foreign rivals.

A monopoly exists when there is only one producer in an industry and no close substitutes for the product exist. If the average costs of production decline with increases in output, then the larger a firm is, the lower its per unit costs will be. One large producer will be more efficient than many small ones. A simple example of a natural-monopoly industry

strategic trade policy
The use of trade restrictions or subsidies to allow domestic firms with decreasing costs to gain a greater share of the world market.

increasing-returns-to-scale industry
An industry in which the costs of producing a unit of output fall as more output is produced.

Government can use trade policy as a strategy to stimulate production by a domestic industry that is capable of achieving increasing returns to scale.

will indicate how strategic trade policy can make a country better off. Suppose that the production of buses is an industry characterized by increasing returns to scale and that there are only two firms capable of producing buses: Volkswagen in Germany and Ford in the United States. If both firms produce buses, their costs will be so high that both will experience losses. If only one of the two produces buses, however, it will be able to sell buses both at home and abroad, creating a level of output that allows the firm to earn a profit.

Assume further that a monopoly producer will earn $100 million and that if both firms produce, they will each lose $5 million. Obviously, a firm that doesn't produce earns nothing. Which firm will produce? Because of the decreasing-cost nature of the industry, the firm that is the first to produce will realize lower costs and be able to prevent the other firm from entering the market. But strategic trade policy can alter the market in favor of the domestic firm.

Suppose Volkswagen is the world's only producer of buses. Ford does not produce them. The U.S. government could offer Ford an $8 million subsidy to produce buses. Ford would then enter the bus market, since the $8 million subsidy would more than offset the $5 million loss it would suffer by entering the market. Volkswagen would sustain losses of $5 million once Ford entered. Ultimately, Volkswagen would stop producing buses to avoid the loss, and Ford would have the entire market and earn $100 million plus the subsidy.

Strategic trade policy is aimed at offsetting the increasing-returns-to-scale advantage enjoyed by foreign producers and at stimulating production in domestic industries that are capable of realizing decreasing costs. One practical problem for government is the need to understand the technology of different industries and to forecast accurately the subsidy needed to induce domestic firms to produce new products. A second problem is the likelihood of retaliation by the foreign government. If the U.S. government subsidizes Ford in its attack on the bus market, the German government is likely to subsidize Volkswagen rather than lose the entire bus market to a U.S. producer. As a result, taxpayers in both nations will be subsidizing two firms, each producing too few buses to earn a profit.

RECAP

1. Government restrictions on foreign trade are usually aimed at protecting domestic producers from foreign competition.

2. Import restrictions may save domestic jobs, but the costs to consumers may be greater than the benefits to those who retain their jobs.

3. Advocates of "fair trade," or the creation of a "level playing field," call for import restrictions as a means of lowering foreign restrictions on markets for domestic exports.

4. Tariffs are an important source of revenue in many developing countries.

5. The national-defense argument in favor of trade restrictions is that protection from foreign competition is necessary to ensure that certain key defense-related industries continue to produce.

6. The infant-industries argument in favor of trade restriction is to allow a new industry a period of time in which to become competitive with its foreign counterparts.

7. Strategic trade policy is intended to provide domestic increasing-returns-to-scale industries with an advantage over their foreign competitors.

2. Tools of Commercial Policy

2 How do countries restrict the entry of foreign goods and promote the export of domestic goods?

Commercial policy makes use of several tools, including tariffs, quotas, subsidies, and nontariff barriers like health and safety regulations that restrict the entry of foreign products. Since 1945, barriers to trade have been reduced. Much of the progress toward free trade may be linked to the *General Agreement on Tariffs and Trade*, or *GATT*, which

GLOBAL BUSINESS *INSIGHT*

Smoot-Hawley Tariff

Many economists believe that the Great Depression of the 1930s was at least partly due to the Smoot-Hawley Tariff Act, signed into law by President Herbert Hoover in 1930. Hoover had promised that, if elected, he would increase tariffs on agricultural products to raise U.S. farm income. Congress began work on the tariff increases in 1928. Congressman Willis Hawley and Senator Reed Smoot conducted the hearings.

In testimony before Congress, manufacturers and other special interest groups also sought protection from foreign competition. The resulting bill increased tariffs on over 12,000 products. Tariffs reached their highest levels ever, about 60 percent of average import values. Only twice before in U.S. history had tariffs approached the levels of the Smoot-Hawley era.

Before President Hoover signed the bill, 38 foreign governments made formal protests, warning that they would retaliate with high tariffs on U.S. products. A petition signed by 1,028 economists warned of the harmful effects of the bill. Nevertheless, Hoover signed the bill into law.

World trade collapsed as other countries raised their tariffs in response. Between 1930 and 1931, U.S. imports fell 29 percent, but U.S. exports fell 33 percent. By 1933, world trade was about one-third of its 1929 level. As the level of trade fell, so did income and prices. In 1934, in an effort to correct the mistakes of Smoot-Hawley, Congress passed the Reciprocal Trade Agreements Act, which allowed the president to lower U.S. tariffs in return for reductions in foreign tariffs on U.S. goods. This act ushered in the modern era of relatively low tariffs. In the United States today, tariffs are about 5 percent of the average value of imports.

Many economists believe that the collapse of world trade and the Depression were linked by a decrease in real income caused by abandoning production based on comparative advantage. Few economists argue that the Great Depression was caused solely by the Smoot-Hawley tariff, but the experience serves as a lesson to those who support higher tariffs to protect domestic producers.

---

began in 1947. In 1995, the *World Trade Organization (WTO)* was formed to incorporate the agreements under GATT into a formal permanent international organization to oversee world trade. The WTO has three objectives: to help global trade flow as freely as possible, to achieve reductions in trade restrictions gradually through negotiation, and to provide an impartial means of settling disputes. Nevertheless, restrictions on trade still exist, and this section will review the most commonly used restrictions.

2.a. Tariffs

A **tariff** is a tax on imports or exports. Every country imposes tariffs on at least some imports. Some countries also impose tariffs on selected exports as a means of raising government revenue. Brazil, for instance, taxes coffee exports. The United States does not employ export tariffs, which are forbidden by the U.S. Constitution.

Tariffs are frequently imposed in order to protect domestic producers from foreign competition. The dangers of imposing tariffs are well illustrated in the Global Business Insight "Smoot-Hawley Tariff." The effect of a tariff is illustrated in Figure 1, which shows the domestic market for oranges. Without international trade, the domestic equilibrium price, P_d, and the quantity demanded, Q_d, are determined by the intersection of the domestic demand and supply curves. If the world price of oranges, P_w, is lower than the domestic equilibrium price, this country will import oranges. The quantity imported will be the difference between the quantity Q_1 produced domestically at a price of P_w and the quantity Q_2 demanded domestically at the world price of oranges.

When the world price of the traded good is lower than the domestic equilibrium price without international trade, free trade causes domestic production to fall and domestic

tariff
A tax on imports or exports.

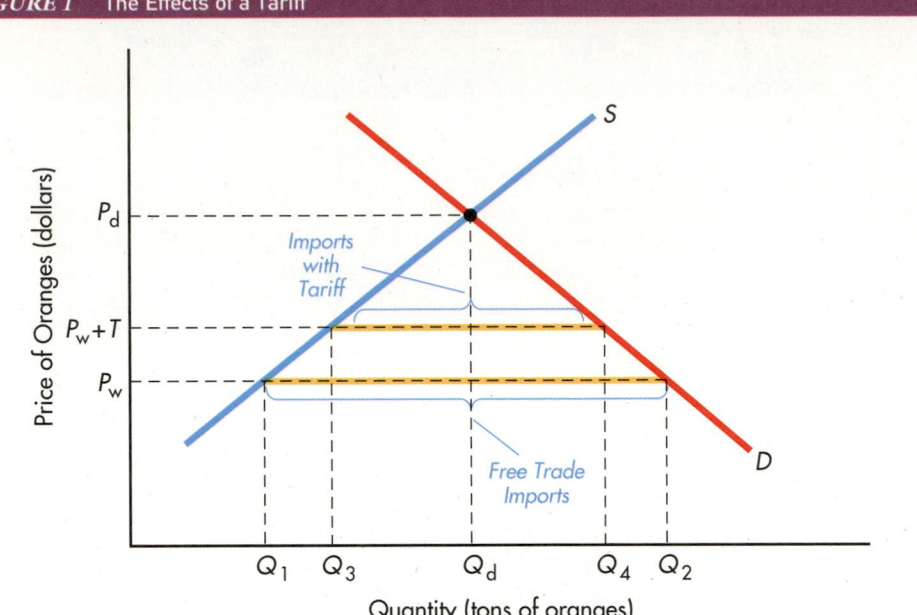

FIGURE 1   The Effects of a Tariff

The domestic equilibrium price and quantity with no trade are P_d and Q_d, respectively. The world price is P_w. With free trade, therefore, imports will equal $Q_2 - Q_1$. A tariff added to the world price reduces imports to $Q_4 - Q_3$.

© 2013 Cengage Learning

consumption to rise. The domestic shortage at the world price is met by imports. Domestic consumers are better off, since they can buy more at a lower price. But domestic producers are worse off, since they now sell fewer oranges and receive a lower price.

Suppose a tariff of T (the dollar value of the tariff) is imposed on orange imports. The price paid by consumers is now $P_w + T$, rather than P_w. At this higher price, domestic producers will produce Q_3 and domestic consumers will purchase Q_4. The tariff has the effect of increasing domestic production and reducing domestic consumption, relative to the free trade equilibrium. Imports fall accordingly, from $Q_2 - Q_1$ to $Q_4 - Q_3$.

Domestic producers are better off, since the tariff has increased their sales of oranges and raised the price they receive. Domestic consumers pay higher prices for fewer oranges than they would with free trade, but they are still better off than they would be without trade. If the tariff had raised the price paid by consumers to P_d, there would be no trade, and the domestic equilibrium quantity, Q_d, would prevail.

The government earns revenue from imports of oranges. If each ton of oranges generates tariff revenue of T, the total tariff revenue to the government is found by multiplying the tariff by the quantity of oranges imported. In Figure 1, this amount is $T \times (Q_4 - Q_3)$. As the tariff changes, so do the quantity of imports and the government revenue.

2.b. Quotas

quantity quota
A limit on the amount of a good that may be imported.

Quotas are limits on the quantity or value of goods imported and exported. A **quantity quota** restricts the physical amount of a good. For instance, for 2009, the United States allowed only 1.1 million tons of sugar to be imported. Even though the United States is not a competitive sugar producer compared to other nations like the Dominican Republic or Cuba, the quota allows U.S. firms to produce about 80 percent of the sugar consumed in the United States. A **value quota** restricts the monetary value of a good that may be traded. Instead of a physical quota on sugar, the United States could have limited the dollar value of sugar imports.

Quotas are used to protect domestic producers from foreign competition. By restricting the amount of a good that may be imported, they increase the price of that good and allow domestic producers to sell more at a higher price than they would with free trade. For example, one effect of the U.S. sugar quota is a higher sugar price for U.S. consumers. In the fourth quarter of 2010, the world price of sugar was $0.2952 per pound, but the U.S. price was about 32 percent higher at $0.3883 per pound. Beyond the obvious effect on sugar production and consumption in the United States, there are spillover effects in related industries, such as candy manufacturing. The high price of sugar in the United States has resulted in candy manufacturers moving jobs to other countries, like Canada, where the price of sugar is about half the U.S. price. The lesson is that one must think about the total effects of trade restrictions on the economy when evaluating costs and benefits.

Figure 2 illustrates the effect of a quota on the domestic orange market. The domestic equilibrium supply and demand curves determine that the equilibrium price and quantity without trade are P_d and 250 tons, respectively. The world price of oranges is P_w. Since P_w lies below P_d, this country will import oranges. The quantity of imports is equal to the amount of the domestic shortage at P_w. The quantity demanded at P_w is 400 tons, and the quantity supplied domestically at P_w is 100 tons, so imports will equal 300 tons of oranges. With free trade, domestic producers sell 100 tons at a price of P_w.

But suppose domestic orange growers convince the government to restrict orange imports. The government then imposes a quota of 100 tons on imported oranges. The effect of the quota on consumers is to shift the supply curve to the right by the amount

value quota
A limit on the monetary value of a good that may be imported.

FIGURE 2   The Effects of a Quota

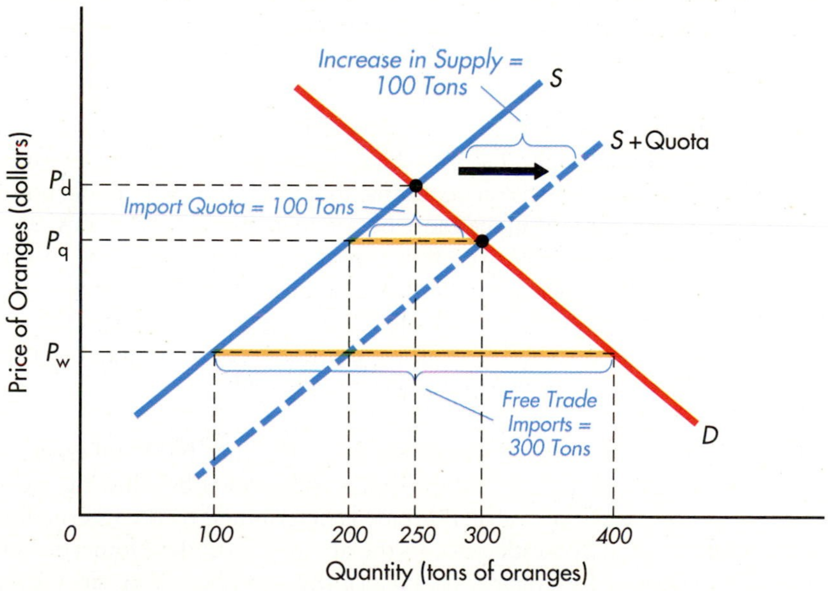

The domestic equilibrium price with no international trade is P_d. At this price, 250 tons of oranges would be produced and consumed at home. With free trade, the price is P_w, and 300 tons will be imported. An import quota of 100 tons will cause the price to be P_q, where the domestic shortage equals the 100 tons allowed by the quota.

© 2013 Cengage Learning

of the quota, 100 tons. Since the quota is less than the quantity of imports with free trade, the quantity of imports will equal the quota. The domestic equilibrium price with the quota occurs at the point where the domestic shortage equals the quota. At price P_q, the domestic quantity demanded (300 tons) is 100 tons more than the domestic quantity supplied (200 tons).

Quotas benefit domestic producers in the same way that tariffs do. Domestic producers receive a higher price (P_q instead of P_w) for a greater quantity (200 instead of 100) than they do under free trade. The effect on domestic consumers is also similar to that of a tariff: They pay a higher price for a smaller quantity than they would with free trade. A tariff generates government tax revenue; a quota does not (unless the government auctions off the right to import under the quota). Furthermore, a tariff raises the price of the product only in the domestic market. Foreign producers receive the world price, P_w. With a quota, both domestic and foreign producers receive the higher price, P_q, for the goods sold in the domestic market. So foreign producers are hurt by the reduction in the quantity of imports permitted, but they receive a higher price for the amount that they do sell.

2.c. Other Barriers to Trade

Tariffs and quotas are not the only barriers to the free flow of goods across international borders. There are three additional sources of restrictions on free trade: subsidies, government procurement, and health and safety standards. Though these practices are often entered into for reasons other than protection from foreign competition, a careful analysis reveals their import-reducing effect.

Before discussing these three types of barriers, let us note the cultural or institutional barriers to trade that also exist in many countries. Such barriers may exist independently of any conscious government policy. For instance, Japan has frequently been criticized by U.S. officials for informal business practices that discriminate against foreigners. Under the Japanese distribution system, goods typically pass through several layers of middlemen before appearing in a retail store. A foreign firm faces the difficult task of gaining entry to this system to supply goods to the retailer. Furthermore, a foreigner cannot easily open a retail store. Japanese law requires a new retail firm to receive permission from other retailers in the area in order to open a business. A firm that lacks contacts and knowledge of the system cannot penetrate the Japanese market.

The economic stimulus bill that the U.S. Congress passed in February 2009 included a "buy American" provision requiring that any steel or manufactured goods bought with federal government funds must be made in the United States. Many U.S. trade partners expressed concerns over the protectionist aspects of this policy. Such inward-looking policies in response to the financial crisis were not confined just to the United States. The level of international trade fell during the crisis and there was a fear that if many countries tried to stimulate their domestic economies at the expense of other nations, trade would not recover once the crisis passed.

export subsidies
Payments made by a government to domestic firms to encourage exports.

2.c.1. Export Subsidies Export subsidies are payments by a government to an exporter. These subsidies are paid in order to stimulate exports by allowing the exporter to charge a lower price. The amount of a subsidy is determined by the international price of a product relative to the domestic price in the absence of trade. Domestic consumers are harmed by subsidies in that their taxes finance the subsidies. Also, since the subsidy diverts resources from the domestic market toward export production, the increase in the supply of export goods could be associated with a decrease in the supply of domestic goods, causing domestic prices to rise.

Subsidies may take forms other than direct cash payments. These include tax reductions, low-interest loans, low-cost insurance, government-sponsored research funding, and other devices. The U.S. government subsidizes export activity through the U.S. Export-Import Bank, which provides loans and insurance to help U.S. exporters sell their goods to foreign buyers. Subsidies are more common in Europe than in Japan or the United States.

2.c.2. Government Procurement
Governments are often required by law to buy only from local producers. In the United States, a "buy American" act passed in 1933 required U.S. government agencies to buy U.S. goods and services unless the domestic price was more than 12 percent above the foreign price. This kind of policy allows domestic firms to charge the government a higher price for their products than they charge consumers; the taxpayers bear the burden. The United States is by no means alone in the use of such policies. Many other nations also use such policies to create larger markets for domestic goods. The World Trade Organization has a standing committee working to reduce discrimination against foreign producers and open government procurement practices to global competition.

2.c.3. Health and Safety Standards
Government serves as a guardian of the public health and welfare by requiring that products offered to the public be safe and fulfill the use for which they are intended. Government standards for products sold in the domestic marketplace can have the effect (intentional or not) of protecting domestic producers from foreign competition. These effects should be considered in evaluating the full impact of such standards.

As mentioned in the Preview, the government of Japan once threatened to prohibit foreign-made snow skis from entering the country for reasons of safety. Only Japanese-made skis were determined to be suitable for Japanese snow. The government of Japan certifies auto parts that are safe for use by repair shops. U.S.-manufactured parts are not certified for use, so U.S. parts manufacturers are excluded from the Japanese market. Several western European nations once announced that U.S. beef would not be allowed into Europe because the U.S. government had approved the feeding of hormones to U.S. beef cattle. In the late 1960s, France required tractors sold there to have a maximum speed of 17 miles per hour; in Germany, the permissible speed was 13 miles per hour, and in the Netherlands, it was 10 miles per hour. Tractors produced in one country had to be modified to meet the requirements of the other countries. Such modifications raise the price of goods and discourage international trade.

Product standards may not eliminate foreign competition, but standards different from those of the rest of the world do provide an element of protection to domestic firms.

RECAP

1. The World Trade Organization works to achieve reductions in trade barriers.

2. A tariff is a tax on imports or exports. Tariffs protect domestic firms by raising the prices of foreign goods.

3. Quotas are government-imposed limits on the quantity or value of an imported good. Quotas protect domestic firms by restricting the entry of foreign products to a level less than the quantity demanded.

4. Subsidies are payments by the government to domestic producers. Subsidies lower the price of domestic goods to foreign buyers.

5. Governments are often required by law to buy only domestic products.

6. Health and safety standards can also be used to protect domestic firms.

3. Preferential Trade Agreements

3 What sorts of agreements do countries enter into to reduce barriers to international trade?

In an effort to stimulate international trade, groups of countries sometimes enter into agreements to abolish most barriers to trade among themselves. Such arrangements between countries are known as preferential trading agreements. The European Union and the North American Free Trade Agreement (NAFTA) are examples of preferential trading agreements.

3.a. Free Trade Areas and Customs Unions

free trade area
An organization of nations whose members have no trade barriers among themselves but are free to fashion their own trade policies toward nonmembers.

customs union
An organization of nations whose members have no trade barriers among themselves but impose common trade barriers on nonmembers.

Two common forms of preferential trade agreements are **free trade areas** (FTAs) and **customs unions** (CUs). These two approaches differ with regard to the treatment of countries outside the agreement. In an FTA, member countries eliminate trade barriers among themselves, but each member country chooses its own trade policies toward non-member countries. Members of a CU agree to both eliminate trade barriers among themselves and maintain common trade barriers against nonmembers.

The best-known CU is the European Union (EU), formerly known as the European Community and still earlier as the European Economic Community (EEC), created in 1957 by France, West Germany, Italy, Belgium, the Netherlands, and Luxembourg. The United Kingdom, Ireland, and Denmark joined in 1973, followed by Greece in 1981 and Spain and Portugal in 1986. In 1992 the EEC was replaced by the EU with an agreement to create a single market for goods and services in western Europe. On May 1, 2004, 10 new members were admitted to the EU: Cyprus, Czech Republic, Estonia, Hungary, Latvia, Lithuania, Malta, Poland, Slovakia, and Slovenia. In 2007, Bulgaria and Romania were admitted to the EU. Turkey is negotiating to be included in future enlargements of the EU. In addition to free trade in goods, European financial markets and institutions will eventually be able to operate across national boundaries. For instance, a bank in any EU country will be permitted to operate in any or all other EU countries.

The North American Free Trade Agreement stimulates trade among Mexico, Canada, and the United States. The act results in more container ships from Mexico unloading their cargo at U.S. docks. Similarly, freight from Canada and the United States will increase in volume at Mexican ports.

In 1989, the United States and Canada negotiated a free trade area. The United States, Canada, and Mexico negotiated a free trade area in 1992 that became effective on January 1, 1994. The North American Free Trade Agreement (NAFTA) lowered tariffs on 8,000 different items and opened each nation's financial market to competition from institutions in the other two nations. NAFTA does not eliminate all barriers to trade among the three nations, but it is a significant step in that direction.

3.b. Trade Creation and Diversion

Free trade agreements provide for free trade among a group of countries, not worldwide. As a result, a customs union or free trade area may make a nation better off or worse off compared to the free trade equilibrium.

Figure 3 illustrates the effect of a free trade area. With no international trade, the U.S. supply and demand curves for oranges would result in an equilibrium price of $500 per ton and an equilibrium quantity of 425 tons. Suppose there are two other orange-producing countries, Israel and Brazil. Israel, the low-cost producer of oranges, is willing to sell all the oranges the United States can buy for $150 per ton, as represented by the horizontal supply curve S_I. Brazil will supply oranges for a price of $200 per ton, as represented by the horizontal supply curve S_B.

With free trade, the United States would import oranges from Israel. The quantity demanded at $150 is 750 tons, and the domestic quantity supplied at this price is 100 tons. The shortage of 650 tons is met by imports from Israel.

Now suppose a 100 percent tariff is imposed on orange imports. The price that domestic consumers pay for foreign oranges is twice as high as before. For oranges

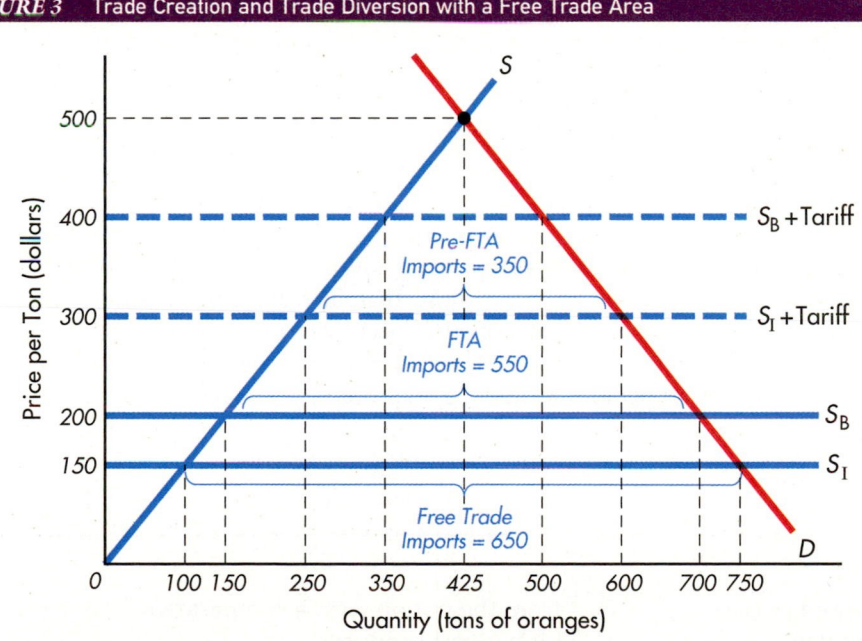

FIGURE 3 Trade Creation and Trade Diversion with a Free Trade Area

With no trade, the domestic equilibrium price is $500, and the equilibrium quantity is 425 tons. With free trade, the price is $150, and 650 tons would be imported, as indicated by the supply curve for Israel, S_I. A 100 percent tariff on imports would result in imports of 350 tons from Israel, according to the supply curve S_I + Tariff. A free trade agreement that eliminates tariffs on Brazilian oranges only would result in a new equilibrium price of $200 and imports of 550 tons from Brazil, according to supply curve S_B.

from Israel, the new price is $300, twice the old price of $150. The new supply curve for Israel is represented as S_I + Tariff. Oranges from Brazil now sell for $400, twice the old price of $200; the new supply curve for Brazil is shown as S_B + Tariff. After the 100 percent tariff is imposed, oranges are still imported from Israel. But at the new price of $300, the domestic quantity demanded is 600 tons, and the domestic quantity supplied is 250 tons. Thus, only 350 tons will be imported. The tariff reduces the volume of trade relative to the free trade equilibrium, at which 650 tons were imported.

Now suppose that the United States negotiates a free trade agreement with Brazil, eliminating tariffs on imports from Brazil. Israel is not a member of the free trade agreement, so imports from Israel are still covered by the 100 percent tariff. The relevant supply curve for Brazil is now S_B, so oranges may be imported from Brazil for $200, a lower price than Israel's price including the tariff. At a price of $200, the domestic quantity demanded is 700 tons and the domestic quantity supplied is 150 tons; 550 tons will be imported.

The effects of the free trade agreement are twofold. First, trade is diverted away from the lowest-cost producer, Israel, to the FTA partner, Brazil. This **trade-diversion** effect of an FTA reduces worldwide economic efficiency, since production is diverted from the country with the comparative advantage. Oranges are not being produced as efficiently as possible. The other effect of the FTA is that the quantity of imports increases relative to the effect of a tariff applicable to all imports. Imports rise from 350 tons (the quantity imported from Israel with the tariff) to 550 tons. The FTA thus has a **trade-creation** effect as a result of the lower price that is available after the tariff reduction. Trade creation is a beneficial aspect of the FTA: The expansion of international trade allows this country to realize greater benefits from trade than would be possible without trade.

Countries form preferential trade agreements because they believe that FTAs will make each member country better off. The member countries view the trade creation effects of such agreements as benefiting their exporters by increasing exports to other member countries and as benefiting consumers by making a wider variety of goods available at a lower price. From the point of view of the world as a whole, preferential trade agreements are more desirable the more they stimulate trade creation to allow the benefits of trade to be realized and the less they emphasize trade diversion, so that production occurs on the basis of comparative advantage. This principle suggests that the most successful FTAs or CUs are those that increase trade volume but do not change the patterns of trade in terms of who specializes and exports each good. In the case of Figure 3, a more successful FTA would reduce tariffs on Israeli as well as Brazilian oranges, so that oranges would be imported from the lowest-cost producer, Israel.

trade diversion
An effect of a preferential trade agreement that reduces economic efficiency by shifting production to a higher cost producer.

trade creation
An effect of a preferential trade agreement that allows a country to obtain goods at a lower cost than is available at home.

RECAP

1. Countries form preferential trade agreements in order to stimulate trade among themselves.

2. The most common forms of preferential trade agreement are free trade areas (FTAs) and customs unions (CUs).

3. Preferential trade agreements have a harmful trade-diversion effect when they cause production to shift from the nation with a comparative advantage to a higher-cost producer.

4. Preferential trade agreements have a beneficial trade-creation effect when they reduce prices for traded goods and stimulate the volume of international trade.

SUMMARY

1. **Why do countries restrict international trade?**

   - Commercial policy is government policy that influences the direction and volume of international trade. *Preview*

   - Protecting domestic producers from foreign competition usually imposes costs on domestic consumers. *§1*

   - Rationales for commercial policy include saving domestic jobs, creating a fair-trade relationship with other countries, raising tariff revenue, ensuring a domestic supply of key defense goods, allowing new industries a chance to become internationally competitive, and giving domestic industries with increasing returns to scale an advantage over foreign competitors. *§1.a–1.f*

2. **How do countries restrict the entry of foreign goods and promote the export of domestic goods?**

   - Tariffs protect domestic industry by increasing the price of foreign goods. *§2.a*

   - Quotas protect domestic industry by limiting the quantity of foreign goods allowed into the country. *§2.b*

   - Subsidies allow relatively inefficient domestic producers to compete with foreign firms. *§2.c.1*

   - Government procurement practices and health and safety regulations can protect domestic industry from foreign competition. *§2.c.2, 2.c.3*

3. **What sorts of agreements do countries enter into to reduce barriers to international trade?**

   - Free trade areas and customs unions are two types of preferential trade agreements that reduce trade restrictions among member countries. *§3.a*

   - Preferential trade agreements have harmful trade-diversion effects and beneficial trade-creation effects. *§3.b*

KEY TERMS

commercial policy, 777
customs union, 788
export subsidies, 786
free trade area, 788
increasing-returns-to-scale industries, 781
quantity quota, 784
strategic trade policy, 781
tariff, 783
trade creation, 790
trade diversion, 790
value quota, 785

EXERCISES

1. What are the potential benefits and costs of a commercial policy designed to pursue each of the following goals?
   a. Save domestic jobs
   b. Create a level playing field
   c. Increase government revenue
   d. Provide a strong national defense
   e. Protect an infant industry
   f. Stimulate exports of an industry with increasing returns to scale

2. For each of the goals listed in exercise 1, discuss what the appropriate commercial policy is likely to be (in terms of tariffs, quotas, subsidies, etc.).
3. Tariffs and quotas both raise the price of foreign goods to domestic consumers. What is the difference between the effects of a tariff and the effects of a quota on the following?
   a. The domestic government
   b. Foreign producers
   c. Domestic producers

4. Would trade-diversion and trade-creation effects occur if the whole world became a free trade area? Explain.

5. What is the difference between a customs union and a free trade area?

6. Draw a graph of the U.S. automobile market in which the domestic equilibrium price without trade is P_d and the equilibrium quantity is Q_d. Use this graph to illustrate and explain the effects of a tariff if the United States were an auto importer with free trade. Then use the graph to illustrate and explain the effects of a quota.

7. If commercial policy can benefit U.S. industry, why would any U.S. resident oppose such policies? Find two newspaper articles illustrating opposition to commercial policies and summarize their arguments.

8. Suppose you were asked to assess U.S. commercial policy to determine whether the benefits of protection for U.S. industries are worth the costs. Do Tables 1 and 2 provide all the information you need? If not, what else would you want to know?

9. How would the effects of international trade on the domestic orange market change if the world price of oranges were above the domestic equilibrium price? Draw a graph to help explain your answer.

10. Suppose the world price of kiwi fruit is $25 per case and the U.S. equilibrium price with no international trade is $40 per case. If the U.S. government had previously banned the import of kiwi fruit but then imposed a tariff of $5 per case and allowed kiwi imports, what would happen to the equilibrium price and quantity of kiwi fruit consumed in the United States?

11. Think of an industry in your country (if you currently have a job, use that industry). What kind of nontariff barrier could you design that would keep out foreign competitors to the domestic industry? This should be something like a health or safety standard or some other criterion that a government could use as an excuse to protect the domestic industry from foreign competition.

You can find further practice tests in the Online Quiz at **www.cengage.com/economics/boyes**.

USDA INCREASES FY11 RAW SUGAR TARIFF-RATE QUOTA, DOMESTIC SUGAR OVERALL ALLOTMENT QUANTITY AND REASSIGNS DOMESTIC SUGAR ALLOTMENTS AND ALLOCATIONS

United States Department of Agriculture News Release No. 0265.11, June 21, 2011

The U.S. Department of Agriculture today increased the fiscal year 2011 raw sugar tariff-rate quota (TRQ) by 120,000 short tons raw value (STRV*). . . . In a separate action, USDA increased the overall allotment quantity (OAQ) for domestic sugar marketing by 164,750 STRV to provide U.S. producers with the statutory minimum market share of 85 percent. This OAQ action increased both cane and beet sugar allotments given the sector proportions specified in statute. The increased cane sugar allotment was greater than the domestic cane sugar supply. Thus, the surplus cane sugar allotment was reassigned from domestic sugarcane processors to raw sugar imports. This reassignment, as well as the enlarged beet sugar allotment, is effective June 21.

The individual company allocations that reflect the change in the OAQ are below. The Office of the U.S. Trade Representative will announce country allocations for the TRQ increase separately.

FY 2011 Raw Sugar TRQ Increase

On August 5, 2010, USDA established the FY 2011 TRQ for raw cane sugar at 1,231,497 STRV, the minimum to which the United States is committed under the World Trade Organization (WTO) Uruguay Round Agreement on Agriculture.

On April 12, 2011, USDA increased the raw cane sugar TRQ by 325,000 STRV to a total of 1,556,497 STRV. Pursuant to Additional U.S. Note 5 to Chapter 17 of the U.S. Harmonized Tariff Schedule (HTS) and Section 359k of the Agricultural Adjustment Act of 1938, as amended, USDA today announced in the Federal Register an increase in the raw sugar TRQ of 120,000 STRV, which brings the overall FY 2011 raw sugar TRQ to 1,676,497 STRV . . .

FY 2011 Reassignment of Sugar Marketing Allotments

USDA's Commodity Credit Corporation (CCC) latest review of domestic demand indicated that the OAQ had to be increased to provide domestic processors with the minimum 85 percent domestic market share, as required by the 2008 farm bill. This increase helps some beet sugar processors, who had inadequate allocations, to market all their supplies. Thus, the beet sector allotment was increased by 89,542 STRV to 5,108,900 STRV and redistributed from beet processors with surplus allocation to those with deficit allocation to release all blocked beet sugar stocks for sale. . . .

The 2008 farm bill requires that any OAQ increase be implemented in fixed proportions between the beet and cane sectors. Thus, the OAQ increase resulted in a 75,208 STRV increase in the cane sugar allotment, which was distributed among the sugar cane states and processors. The resulting CCC estimate of a 600,000 STRV cane sugar allotment surplus must be reassigned to raw sugar imports. Here, 480,000 STRV is reassigned to Mexico raw sugar imports already anticipated, while 120,000 STRV is reassigned to the TRQ increase announced above.

All sugarcane states' sugar marketing allotments are reduced, with the total cane sector allotment decreased from 3,890,892 STRV to 3,366,100 STRV. The new cane state allotments are: Florida, 1,464,666 STRV; Louisiana, 1,526,050 STRV; Texas, 147,138 STRV; and Hawaii, 228,246 STRV. The FY 2011 sugar marketing allotment program will allow all domestic supply to be marketed.

*Conversion factor: 1 metric ton = 1.10231125 short tons.

Source: Article online at http://www.usda.gov/wps/portal/usda/usdahome?contentid=2011/06/0265.xml&contentidonly=true

This article illustrates some important differences between free and restricted trade. In certain markets, such as the sugar market, domestic firms may seek protection, in the form of quotas or tariffs, from international competition. This is not a unique situation; it is a familiar story worldwide as firms that are threatened with foreign competition seek government protection from that competition. The protectionist measure of imposing quotas or tariffs on imports saves jobs in the domestic import-competing industries, but at a great cost to consumers and, sometimes, to other producers.

Recall that in our supply and demand models, the market clears at a price for which quantity supplied is equal to quantity demanded. Did you notice phrases in the press release like "allow all domestic supply to be marketed" or "redistributed from beet processors with surplus allocation to those with deficit allocation"? These and other mentions of reassignment and reallocation illustrate how trade restrictions complicate the market-equilibrating mechanisms and introduce a need for outside planning that is unnecessary in a free market. Even trade restrictions that are imposed for the sake of "fairness," like the requirement that allotment increases be implemented in fixed proportions between the beet and cane sectors, introduce distortions.

The effect of reducing domestic competition with quotas can be understood using supply and demand analysis. Let's analyze the case of quotas on textile imports into the United States. In the diagram, S_1 is the domestic supply of textiles, S_2 is the sum of the domestic supply and the foreign supply allowed in by the quotas, and D is the demand for textiles. Under the quota system, the price of textiles in the United States is represented by P_q, and the quantity of textiles consumed is Q_q. If the quotas were removed, the price of textiles in the United States would equal the world price of P_w, and this lower price would be associated with an increase in the consumption of textiles to Q_w. The quota represents a cost to society in terms of both a loss of

consumer welfare and a loss from the inefficient use of resources in an industry in which this country has no comparative advantage, just as Maine has no comparative advantage in the production of pineapples.

Given the costs to society of these quotas, why is there such strong support for them in Congress? An important political aspect of protectionist policies is that their benefits are concentrated among a relatively small number of people—in the case of the article, sugar beet and sugar cane growers—while their costs are diffused and spread across all consumers. Each individual import-competing producer faces very large losses from free trade, whereas the cost of a protectionist policy for each consumer is less dramatic. It is also easier to organize a relatively small number of manufacturers than to mobilize a vast population of consumers. These factors explain the strong lobby for the protection of industries like textiles and the absence of a legislative lobby that operates specifically in the interest of textile consumers.

Industrial arguments for trade protection should be seen for what they are: an attempt by an industry to increase its profits at the expense of the general public.

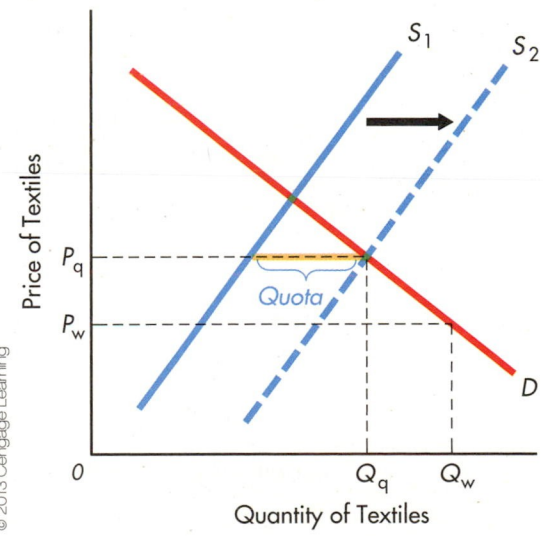

CHAPTER 36

Exchange Rates and Financial Links between Countries

FUNDAMENTAL QUESTIONS

1 How does a commodity standard fix exchange rates between countries?

2 What kinds of exchange-rate arrangements exist today?

3 How is equilibrium determined in the foreign exchange market?

4 How do fixed and floating exchange rates differ in their adjustment to shifts in supply and demand for currencies?

5 What are the advantages and disadvantages of fixed and floating exchange rates?

6 How does a change in the exchange rate affect the prices of goods traded between countries?

7 Why don't similar goods sell for the same price all over the world?

8 How do we find the domestic currency return on a foreign bond?

9 What is the relationship between domestic and foreign interest rates and changes in the exchange rate?

An exchange rate is the link between two nations' monies. The value of a U.S. dollar in terms of Japanese yen or European euros determines how many dollars a U.S. resident will need in order to buy goods that are priced in yen or euros. Thus, changes in exchange rates can have far-reaching implications. Exchange rates may be determined in free markets, through government intervention in the foreign exchange market, or even by law.

In June 2007, one U.S. dollar was worth about 122 Japanese yen. By June 2011, the dollar was worth 81 yen, a 33 percent depreciation of the dollar against the yen. Why does the dollar fluctuate in value relative to the yen? What are the effects of such changes? Should governments permit exchange rates to change? What can governments do to discourage changes in exchange rates? These are all important questions, and this chapter will help answer them.

The chapter begins with a review of the history of exchange-rate systems. It follows with an overview of exchange-rate practices in the world today, and how exchange rates provide a link between prices and interest rates across countries. Along the way, it introduces terminology and institutions that play a major role in the evolution of exchange rates.

1. Past and Current Exchange-Rate Arrangements

1.a. The Gold Standard

In ancient times, government-produced monies were made of precious metals such as gold. Later, when governments began to issue paper money, that money was usually convertible into a fixed amount of gold. Ensuring the convertibility of paper money into gold was a way to maintain confidence in the currency's value, both at home and abroad. If a unit of currency was worth a fixed amount of gold, its value could be stated in terms of its gold value. The countries that maintained a constant gold value for their currencies were said to be on a **gold standard**.

Some countries had backed their currencies with gold long before 1880; however, the practice became widespread around 1880, so economists typically date the beginning of the gold standard to this period. From roughly 1880 to 1914, currencies had fixed values in terms of gold. For instance, the U.S. dollar's value was fixed at $20.67 per ounce of gold. Any other currency that was fixed in terms of gold also had a fixed exchange rate against the dollar. A simple example will illustrate how this works.

Suppose the price of an ounce of gold is $20 in the United States and £4 in the United Kingdom. The pound is worth five times the value of a dollar, since it takes five times as many dollars as pounds to buy one ounce of gold. Because 1 pound buys five times as much gold as 1 dollar, the exchange rate is £1 = $5. Since currency values are linked by gold values, as the supply of gold fluctuates, there will be pressure to alter the prices of goods and services. The gold standard fixes only the current price of gold. As the stock of gold increases, everything else held constant, the gold and currency prices of goods and services will tend to rise (as would occur when the money supply increases).

A gold standard is only one possible *commodity money standard*. Any other highly valued commodity (silver, for instance) could serve as a standard linking monies in a fixed-exchange-rate system.

The gold standard ended with the outbreak of World War I. The war was partially funded by increases in the money supplies of the hostile nations. A gold standard would not permit such a rapid increase in the money supply unless the stock of gold increased dramatically, which it did not. As money supplies grew faster than gold supplies, the link between money and gold had to be broken. During the war years and the Great Depression of the 1930s, and on through World War II, there was no organized system for setting exchange rates. Foreign trade and investment shrank as a result of the war, obviating the need for a well-functioning method of determining exchange rates.

 1 How does a commodity standard fix exchange rates between countries?

gold standard
A system whereby national currencies are fixed in terms of their value in gold, thus creating fixed exchange rates between currencies.

A commodity money standard exists when exchange rates are fixed based on the values of different currencies in terms of some commodity.

1.b. The Bretton Woods System

At the end of World War II, there was widespread political support for an exchange rate system linking all monies in much the same way as the gold standard had done. It was believed that a system of fixed exchange rates would promote the growth of world trade. In 1944, delegates from 44 nations met in Bretton Woods, New Hampshire, to discuss the creation of such a system. The agreement reached at this conference has had a profound impact on the world.

The exchange-rate arrangement that emerged from the Bretton Woods conference is often called a **gold exchange standard**. Each country was to fix the value of its currency in terms of gold, just as it had under the gold standard. The U.S. dollar price of gold, for instance, was $35 an ounce. However, there were fundamental differences between this system and the old gold standard. The U.S. dollar, rather than gold, served as the focal point of the system. Instead of buying and selling gold, countries bought and sold U.S. dollars to maintain a fixed exchange rate with the dollar. Since the United States had the world's largest financial market and the strongest economy, its currency was the dominant world currency. The United States had the productive capacity to supply much-needed goods to the rest of the world, and these goods were priced in dollars.

The U.S. dollar was the **reserve currency** of the system. International debts were settled with dollars, and international trade contracts were often denominated in dollars. In effect, the world was on a dollar standard following World War II.

1.c. The International Monetary Fund and the World Bank

Two new organizations also emerged from the Bretton Woods conference: the International Monetary Fund and the World Bank. The **International Monetary Fund (IMF)** was created to supervise the exchange-rate practices of member countries and to encourage the free convertibility of any national money into the monies of other countries. The IMF also lends money to countries that are experiencing problems meeting their international payment obligations. The funds available to the IMF come from the annual membership fees (called *quotas*) of the 185 member countries of the IMF. The U.S. quota, for instance, is about $57 billion, or about 17 percent of the total quotas of all member countries. (The term *quota* has a different meaning in this context from the one it has in international trade.)

The **World Bank** was created to help finance economic development in poor countries. It provides loans to developing countries at more favorable terms than are available from commercial lenders, and it also offers technical expertise. The World Bank obtains the funds it lends by selling bonds. It is one of the world's major borrowers. See the Global Business Insight "The IMF and the World Bank" for an explanation of how these institutions work.

1.d. The Transition Years

The Bretton Woods system of fixed exchange rates required countries to actively buy and sell dollars in order to maintain fixed exchange rates when the *free market equilibrium* in the foreign exchange market differed from the fixed rate. The free market equilibrium exchange rate is the rate that would be established in the absence of government intervention. Governmental buying and selling of currencies to achieve a target exchange rate is called **foreign exchange market intervention**. The effectiveness of such intervention is limited to situations in which free market pressure to deviate from the fixed exchange rate is temporary. For instance, suppose a country has a bad harvest and earns less foreign exchange than usual. This may be only a temporary situation if the

---

gold exchange standard
An exchange-rate system in which each nation fixes the value of its currency in terms of gold, but buys and sells the U.S. dollar rather than gold to maintain fixed exchange rates.

reserve currency
A currency that is used to settle international debts and is held by governments to use in foreign exchange market interventions.

International Monetary Fund (IMF)
An international organization that supervises exchange-rate arrangements and lends money to member countries that are experiencing problems meeting their external financial obligations.

World Bank
An international organization that makes loans and provides technical expertise to developing countries.

foreign exchange market intervention
The buying and selling of currencies by a central bank to achieve a specified exchange rate.

GLOBAL BUSINESS
INSIGHT

The IMF and the World Bank

The International Monetary Fund (IMF) and the World Bank were both created at the Bretton Woods conference in 1944. The IMF oversees the international monetary system, promoting stable exchange rates and macroeconomic policies. The World Bank promotes the economic development of the poor nations. Both organizations are owned and directed by their 182 member countries.

The IMF provides loans to nations that are having trouble repaying their foreign debts. Before the IMF lends any money, however, the borrower must agree to certain conditions. The IMF *conditionality* usually requires that the country meet targets for key macroeconomic variables like money-supply growth, inflation, tax collections, and subsidies. The conditions attached to IMF loans are aimed at promoting stable economic growth.

The World Bank assists developing countries by providing long-term financing for development projects and programs. The bank also provides expertise in many areas in which poor nations lack expert knowledge: agriculture, medicine, construction, and education, as well as economics. The IMF primarily employs economists to carry out its mission.

The diversity of World Bank activities results in the employment of about 10,000 people. The IMF has a staff of approximately 2,400. Both organizations post employees around the world, but most work at the organizations' headquarters in Washington, D.C.

World Bank funds are largely acquired by borrowing on the international bond market. The IMF receives its funding from member-country subscription fees, called quotas. A member's quota determines its voting power in setting IMF policies. The United States, whose quota accounts for the largest fraction of the total, has the most votes.

next harvest is plentiful and the country resumes its typical export sales. During the period of reduced exports, it will be necessary for the government of this country to intervene to avoid a depreciation of its domestic currency. In the 1960s, however, there were several situations in which permanent rather than temporary changes called for changes in exchange rates rather than government foreign exchange market intervention.

The Bretton Woods system was officially dissolved in 1971, at a meeting of the finance ministers of the leading world powers at the Smithsonian Institution in Washington, D.C. The Smithsonian agreement changed the exchange rates set during the Bretton Woods era. One result was a **devaluation** of the U.S. dollar. (A currency is said to be devalued when its value is officially lowered.)

Under the Smithsonian agreement, countries were to maintain fixed exchange rates at newly defined values. It soon became clear, however, that the new exchange rates were not **equilibrium exchange rates** that could be maintained without government intervention and that government intervention could not maintain the disequilibrium fixed exchange rates forever. The U.S. dollar was devalued again in February 1973, when the dollar price of gold was raised to $42.22. This new exchange rate was still not an equilibrium rate, and in March 1973 the major industrial countries abandoned fixed exchange rates.

1.e. Today

When the major industrial countries abandoned fixed exchange rates in March 1973, the world did not move to purely free-market–determined floating exchange rates. Under the system that has been in existence since that time, the major industrial countries intervene to keep their currencies within acceptable ranges, while many smaller countries maintain fixed exchange rates.

devaluation
A deliberate decrease in the official value of a currency.

equilibrium exchange rates
The exchange rates that are established in the absence of government foreign exchange market intervention.

> In March 1973, the major industrial countries abandoned fixed exchange rates for floating rates.

 2 What kinds of exchange-rate arrangements exist today?

© mathagraphics/Shutterstock.com

© froxx/Shutterstock.com

The world today consists of some countries with fixed exchange rates, whose governments keep the exchange rates between two or more currencies constant over time; other countries with floating exchange rates, which shift on a daily basis according to the forces of supply and demand; and still others whose exchange-rate systems lie somewhere in between. Table 1, which lists the exchange-rate arrangements of over 180 countries, illustrates the diversity of exchange-rate arrangements currently in effect.

TABLE 1   Exchange Rate Arrangements

Exchange Rate Arrangement (number of countries)	Monetary Policy Framework						
	Exchange Rate Anchor				Monetary Aggregate Target	Inflation Targeting Framework	Other[1]
	U.S. dollar (66)	Euro (27)	Composite (15)	Other (7)	(22)	(44)	(11)
Exchange arrangement with no separate legal tender (10)	Ecuador El Salvador Marshall Islands Micronesia, Fed. States of	Palau Panama Timor-Leste Zimbabwe	Kosovo Montenegro San Marino	Kiribati			
Currency board arrangement (13)	Antigua and Barbuda[2] Djibouti Dominica[2] Grenada[2] ECCU Hong Kong SAR St. Kitts and Nevis[2]	St. Lucia[2] St. Vincent and the Grenadines[2]	Bosnia and Herzegovina Bulgaria Estonia[3] Lithuania[3]	Brunei Darussalam			
Other conventional fixed peg arrangement (68)	Aruba Bahamas Bahrain Bangladesh Barbados Belize Eritrea Guyana Honduras Jordan Kazakhstan Lebanon Malawi Maldives Mongolia Netherlands Antilles Oman Qatar Rwanda Saudi Arabia	Seychelles Sierra Leone Solomon Islands Sri Lanka Suriname Tajikistan Trinidad and Tobago Turkmenistan United Arab Emirates Venezuela, Rep. Bolivariana de Vietnam Yemen, Rep. of	Cameroon[5] Cape Verde Central African Rep.[5] Chad[5] Comoros Congo, Rep. of[5] Côte d'Ivoire[4] Croatia Denmark[3] Equatorial Guinea[5] Gabon[5] Guinea-Bissau[4] Latvia[3] Macedonia, FYR Mali[4] Niger[4] Senegal[4] Togo[4]	Fiji Kuwait Libya Morocco Russian Federation Samoa Tunisia	Bhutan Lesotho Namibia Nepal Swaziland	Argentina Malawi Rwanda Sierra Leone	
Pegged exchange rate within horizontal bands (3)			Slovak Rep.[3]	Syria Tonga Belarus			

TABLE 1   Exchange Rate Arrangements (Continued)

Exchange Rate Arrangement (number of countries)	Monetary Policy Framework						
	Exchange Rate Anchor				Monetary Aggregate Target	Inflation Targeting Framework	Other[1]
	U.S. dollar (66)	Euro (27)	Composite (15)	Other (7)	(22)	(44)	(11)
Crawling peg (8)	Bolivia China Ethiopia Nicaragua Uzbekistan		Botswana Iran, I.R. of				
Crawling band (2)	Costa Rica		Afghanistan, I.R. of Burundi Gambia Georgia Guinea Haiti Jamaica Kenya Madagascar	Azerbaijan			
Managed floating with no predetermined path for the exchange rate (44)	Cambodia Kyrgyz Rep. Lao P.D.R. Liberia Mauritania Mauritius Myanmar Ukraine	Algeria Singapore Vanuatu	Moldova Mozambique Nigeria Papua New Guinea São Tomé and Príncipe Sudan Tanzania Uganda	Colombia Ghana Guatemala Indonesia Peru Romania Serbia[6] Thailand Uruguay	Dominican Rep. Egypt India Malaysia Pakistan Paraguay		Armenia[6]
Independently floating (40)		Zambia	Albania Australia Austria[7] Belgium Brazil Canada Chile Cyprus[7] Czech Rep. Finland[7] France[7] Germany[7] Greece[7] Hungary Iceland Ireland[7] Israel Italy[7] Korea, Rep. of	Luxembourg[7] Malta[7] Mexico Netherlands[7] New Zealand Norway Philippines Poland Portugal[7] Slovenia[7] South Africa Spain[7] Sweden Turkey United Kingdom	Congo, Dem. Rep. of Japan Somalia[8] Switzerland United States		

[1]Includes countries that have no explicitly stated nominal anchor, but rather monitor various indicators in conducting monetary policy.
[2]The member participates in the Eastern Caribbean Currency Union.
[3]The member participates in the Exchange Rate Mechanism II arrangement to maintain a fixed exchange rate with the euro with the eurozone.
[4]The member participates in the Central African Economic and Monetary Community.
[5]The member participates in the West African Economic and Monetary Union.
[6]The central bank has taken preliminary step toward inflation targeting and is preparing for the transition to full-fledged inflation targeting.
[7]The member participates in the European Economic and Monetary Union.
[8]As of end-December 1989.

Source: IMF, "De Facto Classification of Exchange Rate Arrangements and Monetary Frameworks," 2010, http://www.imf.org/external/pubs/ft/ar/2010/eng/pdf/a2.pdf.

We provide a brief description of each:

Crawling pegs The exchange rate is adjusted periodically by small amounts at a fixed, preannounced rate or in response to certain indicators (such as inflation differentials against major trading partners).

Crawling bands The exchange rate is maintained within certain fluctuation margins around a central rate that is periodically adjusted at a fixed, preannounced rate or in response to certain indicators.

Managed floating The monetary authority (usually the central bank) influences the exchange rate through active foreign exchange market intervention with no preannounced path for the exchange rate.

Independently floating The exchange rate is market determined, and any intervention is aimed at moderating fluctuations rather than at determining the level of the exchange rate.

No separate legal tender Either another country's currency circulates as the legal tender or the country belongs to a monetary union where the legal tender is shared by the members (like the euro).

Currency board A fixed exchange rate is established by a legislative commitment to exchange domestic currency for a specified foreign currency at a fixed exchange rate. New issues of domestic currency are typically backed in some fixed ratio (like 1-to-1) by additional holdings of the key foreign currency.

Fixed peg The exchange rate is fixed against a major currency or some basket of currencies. Active intervention may be required to maintain the target pegged rate.

Horizontal bands The exchange rate fluctuates around a fixed central target rate. Such target zones allow for a moderate amount of exchange-rate fluctuation while tying the currency to the target central rate.

Note that the countries that use the euro as their currency are listed as "Independently floating." The euro floats against other currencies, but each of the member nations of the euro has no separate national money.

Table 2 lists the end-of-year exchange rates for several currencies versus the U.S. dollar beginning in 1950. For most of the currencies, there was little movement in the

TABLE 2	Exchange Rates of Selected Countries (currency units per U.S. dollar)						
Year	**Canadian Dollar**	**Japanese Yen**	**French Franc**	**German Mark**	**Italian Lira**	**British Pound**	**Euro**
1950	1.06	361	3.5	4.2	625	0.36	—
1955	1	361	3.5	4.22	625	0.36	—
1960	1	358	4.9	4.17	621	0.36	—
1965	1.08	361	4.9	4.01	625	0.36	—
1970	1.01	358	5.52	3.65	623	0.42	—
1975	1.02	305	4.49	2.62	684	0.5	—
1980	1.19	203	4.52	1.96	931	0.42	—
1985	1.4	201	7.56	2.46	1,679	0.69	—
1990	1.16	134	5.13	1.49	1,130	0.52	—
1995	1.36	103	4.9	1.43	1,584	0.65	—
2000	1.49	114	—	—	—	0.67	1.06
2005	1.16	118	—	—	—	0.58	0.84
2010	0.99	81	—	—	—	0.64	0.75

Source: End-of-year exchange rates from International Monetary Fund, *International Financial Statistics*, Washington, D.C., various issues, and Pacific Exchange Rate Service, http://fx.sauder.ubc.ca/cgi/fxdata.

1950s and 1960s, the era of the Bretton Woods agreement. In the early 1970s, exchange rates began to fluctuate. More recently, there has been considerable change in the foreign exchange value of a dollar, as Table 2 illustrates.

RECAP

1. Under a gold standard, each currency has a fixed value in terms of gold. This arrangement provides for fixed exchange rates between countries.

2. At the end of World War II, the Bretton Woods agreement established a new system of fixed exchange rates. Two new organizations—the International Monetary Fund (IMF) and the World Bank—also emerged from the Bretton Woods conference.

3. Fixed exchange rates are maintained by government intervention in the foreign exchange market; governments or central banks buy and sell currencies to keep the equilibrium exchange rate steady.

4. The governments of the major industrial countries adopted floating exchange rates in 1973. In fact, the prevailing system is characterized by managed floating—that is, by occasional government intervention—rather than being a pure free-market–determined exchange-rate system.

5. Some countries choose floating exchange rates; others peg their currencies to a single currency or a composite.

2. Fixed or Floating Exchange Rates

Is the United States better off today with floating exchange rates than it was with the fixed exchange rates of the post–World War II period? The choice of an exchange-rate system has multiple implications for the performance of a nation's economy and, therefore, for the conduct of macroeconomic policy. As with many policy issues in economics, economists often disagree about the merits of fixed versus flexible exchange rates. Let us look at the characteristics of the different exchange-rate systems.

 3 How is equilibrium determined in the foreign exchange market?

2.a. Equilibrium in the Foreign Exchange Market

An exchange rate is the price of one money in terms of another. Equilibrium is determined by the supply of and demand for the two currencies in the foreign exchange market. Figure 1 contains two supply and demand diagrams for the U.S. dollar–euro foreign exchange market. The downward-sloping demand curve indicates that the higher the dollar price of the euro, the fewer euros will be demanded. The upward-sloping supply curve indicates that the higher the dollar price of the euro, the more euros will be supplied.

In Figure 1(a), the initial equilibrium occurs at the point where the demand curve D_1 intersects the supply curve. At this point, the equilibrium exchange rate is $1.00 (1 euro costs $1.00), and the quantity of euros bought and sold is Q_1.

Suppose U.S. residents increase their demand for French wine. Because euros are needed to pay for the wine, the greater U.S. demand for French wine generates a greater demand for euros by U.S. citizens who hold dollars. The demand curve in Figure 1(a) thus shifts from D_1 to D_2. This increased demand for euros causes the euro to appreciate relative to the dollar. The new exchange rate is $1.03, and a greater quantity of euros, Q_2, is bought and sold.

If the U.S. demand for French wine falls, the demand for euros also falls, as illustrated by the shift from D_1 to D_3 in Figure 1(a). The decreased demand for euros causes the euro to depreciate relative to the dollar, so the exchange rate falls to $.97.

So far, we have considered how shifts in the U.S. demand for French goods affect the dollar-euro exchange rate. We can also use the same supply and demand diagram to analyze how

Equilibrium in the foreign exchange market occurs at the point where the foreign exchange demand and supply curves intersect.

FIGURE 1   The Supply of and Demand for Foreign Exchange

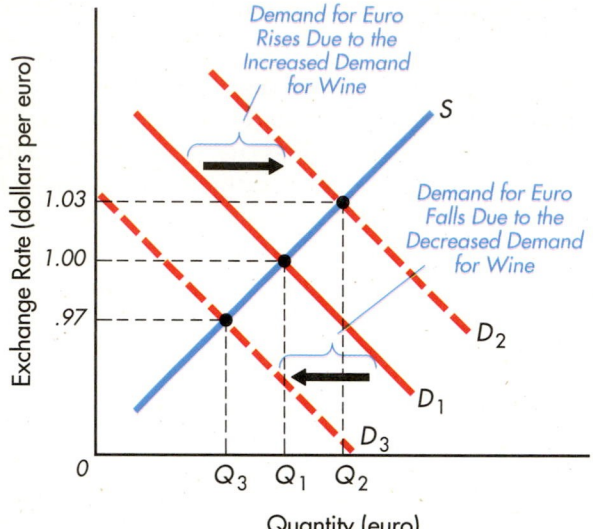
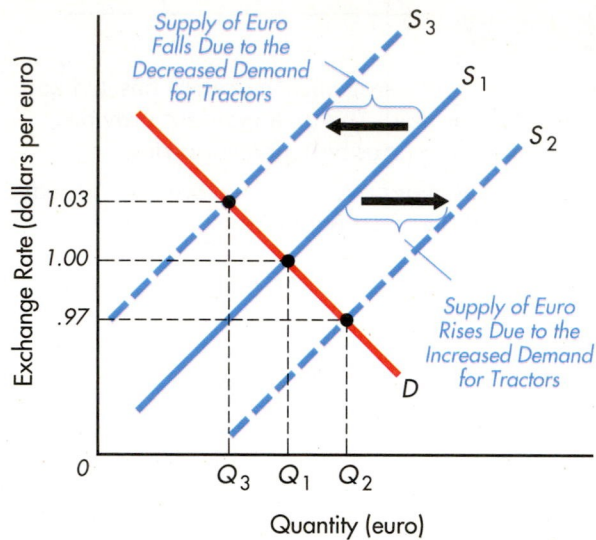

This figure represents the foreign exchange market for euros traded for dollars. The demand curve for euros is based partly on the U.S. demand for French products, and the supply curve of euros is based partly on the French demand for U.S. products. An increase in demand for French wine causes demand for euros to increase from D_1 to D_2. This shift causes an increase from Q_1 to Q_2 in the equilibrium quantity of euros traded and causes the euro to appreciate to $1.03 from the initial equilibrium exchange rate of $1.00. A decrease in demand for French wine causes the demand for euros to fall from D_1 to D_2. This shift leads to a fall in the equilibrium quantity traded to Q_2 and a depreciation of the euro to $.97. If the French demand for U.S. tractors falls, fewer euros are supplied for exchange for dollars, as illustrated by the fall in supply from S_1 to S_3. This shift causes the euro to appreciate to $1.03 and the equilibrium quantity of euros traded to fall to Q_3. If the French demand for U.S. tractors rises, then more euros are supplied for dollars and the supply curve increases from S_1 to S_2. This causes the euro to depreciate and the equilibrium quantity of euros traded to rise to Q_2.

changes in the French demand for U.S. goods affect the equilibrium exchange rate. The supply of euros to the foreign exchange market partly originates with French residents who buy goods from the rest of the world. If a French importer buys a tractor from a U.S. firm, the importer must exchange euros for dollars to pay for the tractor. As French residents' demand for foreign goods and services rises and falls, the supply of euros to the foreign exchange market changes.

Suppose the French demand for U.S. tractors increases. This brings about a shift of the supply curve: As euros are exchanged for dollars to buy the U.S. tractors, the supply of euros increases. In Figure 1(b), the supply of euros curve shifts from S_1 to S_2. The greater supply of euros causes the euro to depreciate relative to the dollar, and the exchange rate falls from $1.00 to $.97. If the French demand for U.S. tractors decreases, the supply of euros decreases from S_1 to S_3, and the euro appreciates to $1.03.

Foreign exchange supply and demand curves are affected by changes in tastes and technology and by changing government policy. As demand and supply change, the equilibrium exchange rate changes. In fact, continuous shifts in supply and demand cause the exchange rate to change as often as every day, on the basis of free-market forces. Now let us consider how fixed exchange rates differ from floating exchange rates.

4 How do fixed and floating exchange rates differ in their adjustment to shifts in supply and demand for currencies?

2.b. Adjustment Mechanisms under Fixed and Flexible Exchange Rates

Figure 2 shows the dollar-euro foreign exchange market. The exchange rate is the number of dollars required to buy 1 euro; the quantity is the quantity of euros bought and

---

FIGURE 2   Foreign Exchange Market Equilibrium under Fixed and Flexible Exchange Rates

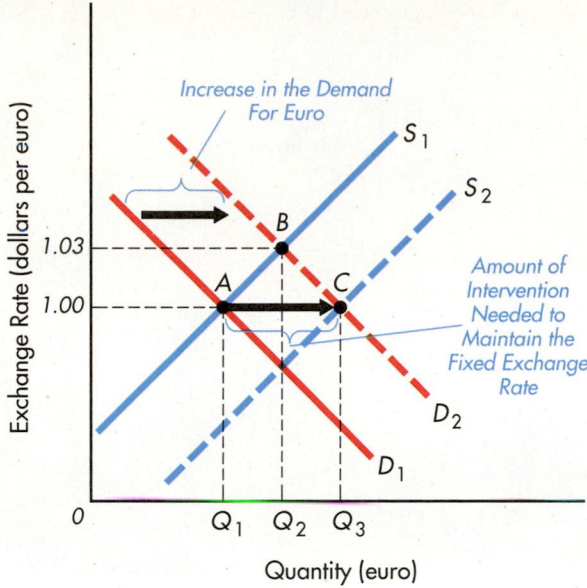

Initially, equilibrium is at point *A*; the exchange rate is $1.00 and Q_1 euros are traded. An increase in demand for French wine causes the demand for euros to increase from D_1 to D_2. With flexible exchange rates, the euro appreciates in value to $1.03 and Q_2 euros are traded; equilibrium is at point *B*. If the government is committed to maintaining a fixed exchange rate of $1.00, the supply of euros must be increased to S_2 so that a new equilibrium can occur at point *C*. The government must intervene in the foreign exchange market and sell euros to shift the supply curve to S_2.

---

sold. Suppose that, initially, the equilibrium is at point A, with quantity Q_1 euros traded at $1.00 per euro.

Suppose French wine becomes more popular in the United States, and the demand for euros increases from D_1 to D_2. With flexible exchange rates (as in Figure 1), a new equilibrium is established at point B. The exchange rate rises to $1.03 per euro, and the quantity of euros bought and sold is Q_2. The increased demand for euros has caused the euro to **appreciate** (rise in value against the dollar) and the dollar to **depreciate** (fall in value against the euro). This is an example of a freely floating exchange rate, determined by the free-market forces of supply and demand.

Now suppose the Federal Reserve is committed to maintaining a fixed exchange rate of $1.00 per euro. The increase in demand for euros causes a shortage of euros at the exchange rate of $1.00. According to the new demand curve, D_2, the quantity of euros demanded at $1.00 is Q_3. The quantity supplied is found on the original supply curve S_1, at Q_1. The only way to maintain the exchange rate of $1.00 is for the Federal Reserve to supply euros to meet the shortage of $Q_3 - Q_1$. In other words, the Fed must sell $Q_3 - Q_1$ euros to shift the supply curve to S_2 and thus maintain the fixed exchange rate.

If the increased demand for euros is temporary, the Fed can continue to supply euros for the short time necessary. However, if the increased demand for euros is permanent, the Fed's intervention will eventually end when it runs out of euros. This situation—a permanent change in supply or demand—is referred to as a **fundamental disequilibrium**. The fixed exchange rate is no longer an equilibrium rate. Under the Bretton Woods agreement, a country was supposed to devalue its currency in such cases.

appreciate
When the value of a currency increases under floating exchange rates—that is, exchange rates determined by supply and demand.

depreciate
When the value of a currency decreases under floating exchange rates.

fundamental disequilibrium
A permanent shift in the foreign exchange market supply and demand curves such that the fixed exchange rate is no longer an equilibrium rate.

Speculators buy and sell currencies in anticipation of future changes in exchange rates.

Suppose that the shift to D_2 in Figure 2 is permanent. In this case, the dollar should be devalued. A devaluation to $1.03 per euro would restore equilibrium in the foreign exchange market without requiring further intervention by the government. Sometimes, however, governments try to maintain the old exchange rate ($1.00 per euro, in this case), even though most people believe the shift in demand to be permanent. When this happens, **speculators** buy the currency that is in greater demand (euros, in our example) in anticipation of the eventual devaluation of the other currency (dollars, in Figure 2). A speculator who purchases the euro for $1.00 prior to the devaluation and sells them for $1.03 after the devaluation earns $.03 per euro purchased.

Speculation puts greater devaluation pressure on the dollar: The speculators sell dollars and buy euros, causing the demand for euros to increase even further. Such speculative activity contributed to the breakdown of the Bretton Woods system of fixed exchange rates. Several countries intervened to support exchange rates that were far out of line with free-market forces. The longer a devaluation was put off, the more obvious it became that the devaluation was forthcoming and the more speculators entered the market. In 1971 and 1973, speculators sold dollars for yen and German marks. They were betting that the dollar would be devalued; both times they were correct. The speculative activity of the early 1970s drew attention to the folly of efforts to maintain fixed exchange rates in the face of a change in the fundamental equilibrium exchange rate.

2.c. Constraints on Economic Policy

Fixed exchange rates can be maintained over time only between countries with similar economic policies and similar underlying economic conditions. As prices rise within a country, the domestic value of a unit of that country's currency falls, since the currency buys fewer goods and services. In the foreign exchange market too, the value of a unit of domestic currency falls, since it buys relatively fewer goods and services than the foreign currency does. A fixed exchange rate thus requires that the purchasing power of the

speculators
People who seek to profit from an expected shift in an exchange rate by selling the currency that is expected to depreciate and buying the currency that is expected to appreciate, then exchanging the appreciated currency for the depreciated currency after the exchange-rate adjustment.

5 What are the advantages and disadvantages of fixed and floating exchange rates?

two currencies change at roughly the same rate over time. Only if two nations have approximately the same inflation experience will they be able to maintain a fixed exchange rate. This condition was a frequent source of problems in the Bretton Woods era of fixed exchange rates. In the late 1960s, for instance, the U.S. government was following a more expansionary macroeconomic policy than was Germany. U.S. government expenditures on the war in Vietnam and domestic antipoverty initiatives led to inflationary pressures that were not matched in Germany. Between 1965 and 1970, price levels rose by 23.2 percent in the United States but by only 12.8 percent in Germany. Since the purchasing power of the dollar was falling faster than that of the mark, the fixed exchange rate could not be maintained. The dollar had to be devalued.

One of the advantages of floating exchange rates is that countries are free to pursue their own macroeconomic policies without worrying about maintaining an exchange-rate commitment. If U.S. policy produces a higher inflation rate than Japanese policy, the dollar will automatically depreciate in value against the yen. The United States can choose the macroeconomic policy it wants, independently of other nations, and let the exchange rate adjust if its inflation rate differs markedly from that of other nations. If the dollar were fixed in value relative to the yen, the two nations couldn't follow independent policies and expect to maintain the exchange rate.

It became obvious in the late 1960s that many governments considered other issues more important than maintenance of a fixed exchange rate. A nation that puts a high priority on reducing unemployment will typically stimulate the economy to try to increase income and create jobs. This initiative may cause the domestic inflation rate to rise and the domestic currency to depreciate relative to other currencies. If one goal or the other—lower unemployment or a fixed exchange rate—must be given up, it is likely that the exchange-rate goal will be sacrificed.

Floating exchange rates allow countries to formulate their domestic economic policy solely in response to domestic issues; they need not pay attention to the economic policies of the rest of the world. For residents of some countries, this freedom may be more of a problem than a benefit. The freedom to choose a rate of inflation and let the exchange rate adjust itself can have undesirable consequences in countries whose politicians, for whatever reason, follow highly inflationary policies. In these countries, a fixed-exchange-rate system would impose discipline, since maintenance of the exchange rate would not permit policies that diverged sharply from those of its trading partner.

RECAP

1. Under a fixed-exchange-rate system, governments must sometimes intervene in the foreign exchange market to maintain the exchange rate. A fundamental disequilibrium requires a currency devaluation.

2. Fixed exchange rates can be maintained only between countries with similar macroeconomic policies and similar underlying economic conditions.

3. Fixed exchange rates serve as an anchor to constrain inflationary government policies.

3. Prices and Exchange Rates

An exchange rate, as you learned in earlier chapters, is the price of one money in terms of another. The exchange rate doesn't enter into the purchase and sale of Fords in Michigan and California because each state uses the U.S. dollar. But for goods and services that are traded across national borders, the exchange rate is an important part of the

 6 How does a change in the exchange rate affect the prices of goods traded between countries?

total price. We will assume that currencies are traded freely for each other and that foreign exchange markets respond to supply and demand without government intervention.

Let's look at an example. A U.S. wine importer purchases 1,000,000 euros (€1,000,000) worth of wine from France. The importer demands euros in order to pay the French wine seller. Suppose the initial equilibrium exchange rate is $1 = €1. At this rate, the U.S. importer needs 1,000,000 euros at $1 apiece, or $1,000,000.

3.a. Appreciation and Depreciation

When the exchange rate between two currencies changes, we say that one currency *depreciates* while the other *appreciates*. Suppose the exchange rate goes from $1 = €1 to $1.10 = €1. The euro is now worth $1.10 instead of $1. The dollar has depreciated in value in relation to the euro; dollars are worth less in terms of euros. At the new equilibrium exchange rate, the U.S. importer needs $1,100,000 ($1.10 × 1,000,000) to buy €1,000,000 worth of wine.

Instead of saying that the dollar has depreciated against the euro, we can say that the euro has *appreciated* against the dollar. If the dollar is depreciating against the euro, the euro must be appreciating against the dollar. Whichever way we describe the change in the exchange rate, the result is that euros are now worth more in terms of dollars. The price of a euro has gone from $1 to $1.10.

As exchange rates change, the prices of goods and services traded in international markets also change. Suppose the dollar appreciates against the euro. This means that a euro costs fewer dollars; it also means that French goods cost U.S. buyers less. If the exchange rate falls to $.90 = €1, then €1,000,000 costs $900,000 ($.90 × 1,000,000). The French wine has become less expensive to the U.S. importer.

- When the domestic (home) currency *depreciates*, foreign goods become *more expensive* to domestic buyers.
- When the domestic currency *appreciates*, foreign goods become *less expensive* to domestic buyers.

Let's look at the problem from the French side. When the dollar price of the euro rises, the euro price of the dollar falls; and when the dollar price of the euro falls, the euro price of the dollar rises. If the dollar price of the euro ($/€) is originally $1, the euro price of the dollar (€/$) is the reciprocal (1/1), or €1. If the dollar depreciates against the euro to $1.10, then the euro appreciates against the dollar to 1/1.10, or €.91. As the euro appreciates, U.S. goods become less expensive to French buyers. If the dollar appreciates against the euro to $.90, then the euro depreciates against the dollar to 1/.90, or €1.11. As the euro depreciates, U.S. goods become more expensive to French buyers.

- When the domestic currency *depreciates*, domestic goods become *less expensive* to foreign buyers.
- When the domestic currency *appreciates*, domestic goods become *more expensive* to foreign buyers.

The exchange rate is just one determinant of the demand for goods and services. Income, tastes, the prices of substitutes and complements, expectations, and the exchange rate all determine the demand for U.S. wheat, for example. As the dollar depreciates in relation to other currencies, the demand for U.S. wheat increases (along with foreign demand for all other U.S. goods), even if all the other determinants do not change. Conversely, as the dollar appreciates, the demand for U.S. wheat falls (along with foreign demand for all other U.S. goods), even if all the other determinants do not change.

3.b. Purchasing Power Parity

Within a country, where prices are quoted in terms of a single currency, all we need to know is the price in the domestic currency of an item in two different locations to determine where our money buys more. If Joe's bookstore charges $20 for a book and Pete's bookstore charges $30 for the same book, the purchasing power of our money is greater at Joe's than it is at Pete's.

International comparisons of prices must be made using exchange rates because different countries use different monies. Once we cross national borders, prices are quoted in different currencies. Suppose Joe's bookstore in New York City charges $20 for a book and Pierre's bookstore in Paris charges €30. To compare the prices, we must know the exchange rate between dollars and euros.

If we find that goods sell for the same price in different markets, our money has the same purchasing power in those markets, which means that we have **purchasing power parity (PPP)**. The PPP reflects a relationship among the domestic price level, the exchange rate, and the foreign price level:

$$P = EP^F$$

where

P = the domestic price

E = the exchange rage (units of domestic currency per unit of foreign currency)

P^F = the foreign price

If the dollar-euro exchange rate is .67 ($.67 = €1), then a book priced at €30 in Pierre's store in Paris costs the same as a book priced at $20 in Joe's New York store:

$$P = EP^F$$
$$= \$.67 \times 30$$
$$= \$20$$

The domestic price (we are assuming that the U.S. dollar is the domestic currency) equals the exchange rate times the foreign price. Because the dollar price of the book in Paris is $20 and the price in the United States is $20, PPP holds. The purchasing power (value) of the dollar is the same in both places.

Realistically, similar goods don't always sell for the same price everywhere. Actually, they don't even sell for the same price within a country. If the same textbook is priced differently at different bookstores, it is unrealistic to expect the price of the book to be identical worldwide. There are several reasons why PPP does not hold. The most important are that goods are not identical, that information is costly, that shipping costs affect prices, and that tariffs and legal restrictions on trade affect prices. If these factors did not exist, we would expect that anytime a price was lower in one market than in another, people would buy in the low-price market (pushing prices up) and simultaneously sell in the high-price market (pushing prices down). This activity, known as *arbitrage*, would ensure that PPP holds.

purchasing power parity (PPP)
The condition under which monies have the same purchasing power in different markets.

 7 Why don't similar goods sell for the same price all over the world?

© froxx/Shutterstock.com

RECAP

1. When the exchange rate between two currencies changes, one currency depreciates while the other appreciates.

2. Purchasing power parity means that money has the same purchasing power in different markets.

3. Similar goods do not sell for the same price all over the world because goods are not identical, information is costly, shipping costs affect prices, and tariffs and legal restrictions on international trade affect prices.

4. Interest Rates and Exchange Rates

Exchange rates are used to compare international prices of goods and services. They are also used to compare the return on foreign currency–denominated stocks and bonds to the return on domestic assets. For example, suppose you have a choice of buying a U.S. bond or a U.K. bond. The U.S. bond is denominated in dollars and pays 15 percent interest; the U.K. bond is denominated in British pounds and pays 10 percent interest. Because you are a U.S. resident and you ultimately want dollars for household spending, you must compare the dollar return from holding each bond.

4.a. The Domestic Currency Return from Foreign Bonds

The U.S. bond is denominated in dollars, so the 15 percent interest is a dollar return. The U.K. bond, on the other hand, promises to pay 10 percent in terms of British pounds. If you buy the U.K. bond, you exchange dollars for pounds at the time the bond is purchased. When the bond matures, you exchange the principal and interest (the proceeds), trading pounds for dollars. If the exchange rate remains the same, the return on the U.K. bond is 10 percent. But if the exchange rate changes between the time you buy the bond and the time it matures, your return in dollars may be more or less than 10 percent.

Figure 3 shows what happens when a U.S. resident buys a one-year U.K. bond. Suppose the exchange rate is $2 = £1$ when the bond is purchased, and the bond sells

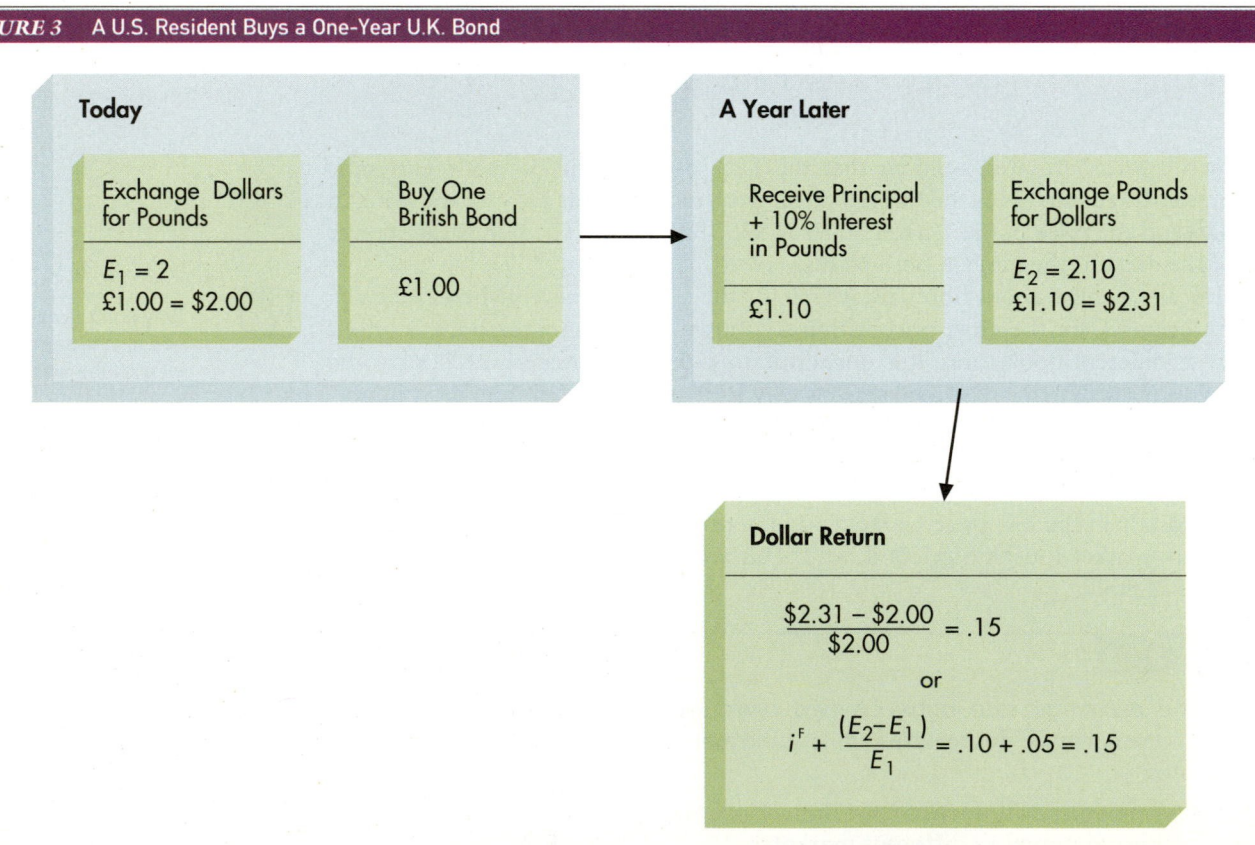

FIGURE 3   A U.S. Resident Buys a One-Year U.K. Bond

Today

Exchange Dollars for Pounds	Buy One British Bond
$E_1 = 2$ £1.00 = $2.00	£1.00

A Year Later

Receive Principal + 10% Interest in Pounds	Exchange Pounds for Dollars
£1.10	$E_2 = 2.10$ £1.10 = $2.31

Dollar Return

$$\frac{\$2.31 - \$2.00}{\$2.00} = .15$$

or

$$i^F + \frac{(E_2 - E_1)}{E_1} = .10 + .05 = .15$$

for £1. The U.S. resident needs $2 to buy the bond. A year later, the bond matures. The bondholder receives the principal of £1 plus 10 percent interest (£.10). Now the U.S. resident wants to convert the pounds into dollars. If the exchange rate has gone up from $2 = £1 to $2.10 = £1, the £1.10 proceeds from the bond are converted into dollars at the rate of 2.10 dollars per pound. The *dollar value* of the proceeds is $2.31 (the exchange rate [2.10] multiplied by the pound proceeds [£1.10]). The *dollar return* from the U.K. bond is the percentage difference between the dollar proceeds received after one year and the initial dollar amount invested, or approximately 15 percent:

$$\text{Dollar return} = \frac{\$2.31 - \$2}{\$2}$$
$$= \frac{\$.31}{\$2}$$
$$= .15$$

We can also determine the dollar return from the U.K. bond by adding the U.K. interest rate to the percentage change in the exchange rate. The percentage change in the exchange rate is 5 percent:

$$\text{Percentage change in exchange rate} = \frac{\$2.10 - \$2}{\$2}$$
$$= \frac{\$.10}{\$2}$$
$$= .05$$

The dollar return from the U.K. bond equals the 10 percent interest paid in British pounds plus the 5 percent change in the exchange rate, or 15 percent.

In our example, the pound appreciates against the dollar. When the pound increases in value, foreign residents holding pound-denominated bonds earn a higher return on those bonds than the pound interest rate. If the pound depreciates against the dollar, so that the pounds received at maturity are worth less than the pounds originally purchased, then the dollar return from the U.K. bond is lower than the interest rate on the bond. If the pound depreciates 5 percent, the dollar return is just 5 percent (the interest rate [10 percent] *minus* the exchange rate change [5 percent]).

We calculate the domestic currency return on a foreign bond by adding the foreign interest rate (i^F) plus the percentage change in the exchange rate $[(E_2 - E_1)/E_1]$, where E_2 is the dollar price of a unit of foreign currency in the next period, when the bond matures, and E_1 is the exchange rate in the current period, when the bond is purchased:

$$\text{Domestic currency return} = \text{foreign interest rate} + \text{percentage change in}$$
$$\text{exchange rate}$$
$$= i^F + \frac{E_2 - E_1}{E_1}$$

4.b. Interest Rate Parity

Because U.S. residents can hold U.S. bonds, U.K. bonds, or the bonds or other securities of any country they choose, they compare the returns from the alternatives when deciding what assets to buy. Foreign investors do the same thing. One product of this process is a close relationship among international interest rates. Specifically, the return, or interest rate, on similar bonds tends to be the same when returns are measured in terms of the domestic currency. This is called **interest rate parity (IRP)**.

Interest rate parity is the financial asset version of purchasing power parity. Similar financial assets have the same percentage return when that return is computed in terms

 8 How do we find the domestic currency return on a foreign bond?

 9 What is the relationship between domestic and foreign interest rates and changes in the exchange rate?

interest rate parity (IRP)
The condition under which similar financial assets have the same interest rate when measured in the same currency.

of one currency. Interest rate parity defines a relationship among the domestic interest rate, the foreign interest rate, and the expected change in the exchange rate:

Domestic interest rate = foreign interest rate + expected change in exchange rate

In our example, the U.S. bond pays 15 percent interest; the U.K. bond offers 10 percent interest in pounds. If the pound is expected to appreciate 5 percent, the U.K. bond offers U.S. residents an expected dollar return of 15 percent. Interest rate parity holds in this case. The domestic interest rate is 15 percent, which equals the foreign interest rate (10 percent) plus the expected change in the exchange rate (5 percent).

Interest rate parity is the product of arbitrage in financial markets. If U.S. bonds and U.K. bonds are similar in every respect except for the currency used to pay the principal and interest, then they should yield similar returns to bondholders. If U.S. investors can earn a higher return by buying U.K. bonds, they are going to buy more U.K. bonds and fewer U.S. bonds. This tends to raise the price of U.K. bonds, pushing U.K. interest rates down. At the same time, the price of U.S. bonds drops, raising U.S. interest rates. The initial higher return on U.K. bonds and resulting greater demand for U.K. bonds increases the demand for pounds, increasing the value of the pound versus the dollar today. As the pound appreciates today, if investors expect the same future exchange rate as they did before the current appreciation, the expected appreciation in the future falls. The change in the exchange rate and interest rates equalizes the expected dollar return from holding a U.S. bond or a U.K. bond. U.K. bonds originally offered a higher return than U.S. bonds, but the increase in demand for U.K. bonds relative to U.S. bonds lowers both U.K. interest rates and the expected appreciation of the pound, so that the bond returns are equalized.

RECAP

1. The domestic currency return from a foreign bond equals the foreign interest rate plus the percentage change in the exchange rate.

2. Interest rate parity exists when similar financial assets have the same interest rate when measured in the same currency or when the domestic interest rate equals the foreign interest rate plus the expected change in the exchange rate.

SUMMARY

1. How does a commodity standard fix exchange rates between countries?

- Between 1880 and 1914, a gold standard provided for fixed exchange rates among countries. *§1.a*

- The gold standard ended with World War I, and no established international monetary system replaced it until after World War II, when the Bretton Woods agreement created a fixed-exchange-rate system. *§1.b*

2. What kinds of exchange-rate arrangements exist today?

- Today some countries have fixed exchange rates, others have floating exchange rates, and still others have managed floats or other types of systems. *§1.e*

3. How is equilibrium determined in the foreign exchange market?

- Foreign exchange market equilibrium is determined by the intersection of the demand and supply curves for foreign exchange. *§2.a*

4. **How do fixed and floating exchange rates differ in their adjustment to shifts in supply and demand for currencies?**

   - Under fixed exchange rates, central banks must intervene in the foreign exchange market to keep the exchange rate from shifting. *§2.b*

5. **What are the advantages and disadvantages of fixed and floating exchange rates?**

   - Floating exchange rates permit countries to pursue independent economic policies. A fixed exchange rate requires a country to adopt policies similar to those of the country whose currency it is pegged to. A fixed exchange rate may serve to prevent a country from pursuing inflationary policies. *§2.c*

6. **How does a change in the exchange rate affect the prices of goods traded between countries?**

   - When the domestic currency depreciates against other currencies, foreign goods become more expensive to domestic buyers and domestic goods become less expensive to foreign buyers. *§3.a*

   - When the domestic currency appreciates against other currencies, foreign goods become less expensive to domestic buyers and domestic goods become more expensive to foreign buyers. *§3.a*

   - Purchasing power parity exists when monies have the same value in different markets. *§3.b*

7. **Why don't similar goods sell for the same price all over the world?**

   - Deviations from PPP arise because goods are not identical in different countries, information is costly, shipping costs affect prices, and tariffs and restrictions on trade affect prices. *§3.b*

8. **How do we find the domestic currency return on a foreign bond?**

   - The domestic currency return from holding a foreign bond equals the foreign interest rate plus the percentage change in the exchange rate. *§4.a*

9. **What is the relationship between domestic and foreign interest rates and changes in the exchange rate?**

   - Interest rate parity exists when the domestic interest rate equals the foreign interest rate plus the expected change in the exchange rate, so that similar financial assets yield the same return when measured in the same currency. *§4.b*

KEY TERMS

appreciate, 805	fundamental disequilibrium, 805	purchasing power parity
depreciate, 805	gold exchange standard, 798	(PPP), 809
devaluation, 799	gold standard, 797	reserve currency, 798
equilibrium exchange rates, 799	interest rate parity (IRP), 811	speculators, 806
foreign exchange market	International Monetary Fund	World Bank, 798
intervention, 798	(IMF), 798	

EXERCISES

1. Under a gold standard, if the price of an ounce of gold is 1,400 U.S. dollars and 1,300 Canadian dollars, what is the exchange rate between U.S. and Canadian dollars?

2. What were the three major results of the Bretton Woods conference?

3. What is the difference between the IMF and the World Bank?

4. How can Mexico fix the value of the peso relative to the dollar when the demand for and supply of dollars and pesos changes continuously? Illustrate your explanation with a graph.

5. Draw a foreign exchange market supply and demand diagram to show how the yen-dollar exchange rate is determined. Set the initial equilibrium at a rate of 100 yen per dollar.

6. Using the diagram in exercise 5, illustrate the effect of a change in tastes that prompts Japanese residents to buy more goods from the United States. If the exchange rate is floating, what will happen to the foreign exchange market equilibrium?

7. Using the diagram in exercise 5, illustrate the effect of the change in Japanese tastes if exchange rates are fixed. What will happen to the foreign exchange market equilibrium?

8. When and why should exchange rates change under a fixed-exchange-rate system?

9. Suppose you just returned home from a vacation in Mazatlán, Mexico, where you exchanged U.S. dollars for Mexican pesos. How did your trip to Mexico affect the supply and demand for dollars and the exchange rate (assume that all other things are equal)?

10. What does it mean to say that a currency appreciates or depreciates in value? Give an example of each and briefly mention what might cause such a change.

11. How does a currency speculator profit from exchange-rate changes? Give an example of a profitable speculation.

12. Find the U.S. dollar value of each of the following currencies at the given exchange rates:
   a. $1 = C$.96 (Canadian dollars)
   b. $1 = ¥81 (Japanese yen)
   c. $1 = A$.95 (Australian dollars)
   d. $1 = SKr6 (Swedish kronor)
   e. $1 = SF.90 (Swiss francs)

13. You are a U.S. importer who buys goods from many different countries. How many U.S. dollars do you need to settle each of the following invoices?

   a. 1,000,000 Australian dollars for wool blankets (exchange rate: A$1 = $.769)
   b. 500,000 British pounds for dishes (exchange rate: £1 = $1.5855)
   c. 100,000 Indian rupees for baskets (exchange rate: Rs1 = $.0602)
   d. 350 million Japanese yen for stereo components (exchange rate: ¥1 = $.0069)
   e. 825,000 euros for German wine (exchange rate: €1 = $1.05)

14. What is the dollar value of the invoices in exercise 13 if the dollar:
   a. depreciates 10 percent against the Australian dollar
   b. appreciates 10 percent against the British pound
   c. depreciates 10 percent against the Indian rupee
   d. appreciates 20 percent against the Japanese yen
   e. depreciates 100 percent against the euro

15. Explain purchasing power parity and why it does not hold perfectly in the real world.

16. Write an equation that describes purchasing power parity and explain the equation.

17. Write an equation that describes interest rate parity and explain the equation.

18. If the interest rate on one-year government bonds is 5 percent in Germany and 8 percent in the United States, what do you think is expected to happen to the dollar value of the euro? Explain your answer.

19. In 1960 a U.S. dollar sold for 620 Italian lire. If PPP held in 1960, what would the PPP value of the exchange rate have been in 1987 if Italian prices rose 12 times and U.S. prices rose 4 times between 1960 and 1987?

You can find further practice tests in the Online Quiz at **www.cengage.com/economics/boyes**.

FREQUENTLY ASKED QUESTIONS: EU ENLARGEMENT AND ECONOMIC AND MONETARY UNION (EMU)

1. Which countries have joined the EU since the ECB was established in 1998?
The Czech Republic, Estonia, Cyprus, Latvia, Lithuania, Hungary, Malta, Poland, Slovenia, and Slovakia became members of the EU on May 1, 2004. Two other countries, Bulgaria and Romania, joined the EU on January 1, 2007. Croatia, the Former Yugoslav Republic of Macedonia, and Turkey are official candidates for accession to the EU.

2. Will the new Member States automatically adopt the euro after joining the EU?
No, they won't. However, they are expected to do so when they fulfill the Maastricht convergence criteria (see question 4 below). Unlike Denmark and the United Kingdom, the new EU Member States do not have a right to opt out of the single currency.

3. When are the new Member States expected to adopt the euro?
There is no preset timetable for the adoption of the euro by these countries as the Governing Council of the ECB noted in its "Policy position of the Governing Council of the ECB on exchange rate issues relating to the acceding countries," published on December 18, 2003. In order to adopt the euro, they have to achieve a high degree of sustainable economic convergence. This is assessed by the EU Council on the basis of reports produced by the Commission and the ECB on the degree of these countries' fulfillment of the Maastricht convergence criteria. These reports are prepared at least once every two years, or at the request of a Member State wishing to adopt the euro.

4. What are the convergence criteria?
In order to adopt the euro, Member States have to achieve a high degree of sustainable economic convergence. This is assessed on the basis of the fulfillment of the Maastricht convergence criteria set out in Article 121 of the Treaty establishing the European Community and further detailed in a Protocol attached to the Treaty. The criteria entail:

- "the achievement of a high degree of price stability." This means that "a Member State has a price performance that is sustainable and an average rate of inflation, observed over a period of one year before the examination, that does not exceed by more than 1½ percentage points that of, at most, the three best performing Member States in terms of price stability";
- "the sustainability of the government financial position." This means that, at the time of the examination, the Member State should not be deemed by the Council to have an excessive deficit. The Council decides whether or not an excessive deficit exists by referring to:

  1. the ratio of the planned or actual government deficit to GDP at market prices, which should not exceed 3 percent,
  2. the ratio of government debt to GDP at market prices, which should not exceed 60 percent.

However, the assessment of compliance with the fiscal discipline requirement will also take into account other factors, such as past progress in reducing budgetary imbalances and/or the existence of exceptional and temporary factors contributing to

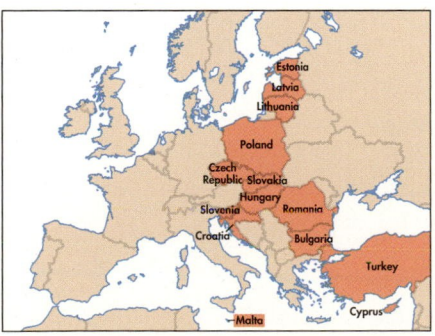

such imbalances. At the same time, Member States with government debt ratios to GDP in excess of 60 percent are expected to bring them down toward the reference level at a satisfactory pace.

- "the observance of the normal fluctuation margins provided for by the exchange rate mechanism of the European Monetary System, for at least two years, without devaluing against the currency of any other Member State."

Source: European Central Bank, http://www.ecb.int/ecb/history/enlargement/html/faqenlarge.en.html#l4.

The expansion of the European Union to include the countries from eastern Europe holds much promise for the economic development of these countries. Once in the EU, these countries can trade freely with the other EU countries, just as the states of the United States trade freely with one another. Just as the U.S. states all share a common money to help facilitate interstate trade, it is likely that the Eastern European countries will also welcome the adoption of the euro as their money to further solidify the links between their economies and those of the rest of the EU. The article discusses the criteria that the new accession countries must meet before joining the euro. In general, their macroeconomic policy must converge to that of the current euro-area countries as defined by the "Maastricht convergence criteria" (Maastricht is a town in the Netherlands where the convergence treaty was agreed upon). The criteria include such things as convergence of inflation rates, budget deficits, and government debt to levels near the average existing in the euro area.

A fixed-exchange-rate system represents an agreement among countries to convert their individual currencies from one to another at a given rate. The adoption of one money for Europe is the strongest possible commitment to fixed exchange rates among the EU countries. If every nation uses the same currency, the euro, then all will be linked to the same inflation rate and there will be no fluctuation of the value of the currency across the EU nations using the currency—just as each state in the United States uses the same money, the U.S. dollar. The adoption of a single currency requires that economic policies across EU countries be similar. This means that individual countries must subjugate their monetary policies to the goals of the European Central Bank. If each nation insists on exercising its own monetary and fiscal policies and chooses different interest and inflation rates, there can never be one money. A crisis in the eurozone arose in 2010–2011 due to the divergence of fiscal policy in

Greece, Portugal, Ireland, and Spain. This experience just underscores the difficulty of having different nations with different policies sharing one money.

A convergence in inflation rates is necessary for the smooth operation of any fixed exchange rate. Persistent inflation differentials across the members of a fixed-exchange-rate system affect the competitiveness of each member's exports in the world market. Though a fixed-exchange-rate system maintains stable *nominal exchange rates* (the rate observed in the foreign exchange market), the competitiveness of a currency is represented by the *real exchange rate*. The real exchange rate is the nominal exchange rate adjusted for the price level at home compared to the price level abroad:

Real exchange rate =

$$\frac{\text{nominal exchange rate} \times \text{foreign price level}}{\text{domestic price level}}$$

The disruptive changes in competitiveness caused by persistent inflation differentials require a realignment of a fixed-exchange-rate system that adjusts nominal exchange rates to keep real exchange rates from drifting too far from their correct value. For instance, if the Italian price level starts to rise faster than the German price level, Italian goods will be priced out of the German market unless there is an Italian currency that depreciates on the foreign exchange market. According to the equation just presented, if Italy is the domestic country and its price level rises, the real exchange rate falls and Italian goods are, therefore, relatively more expensive unless the nominal exchange rate rises to offset the higher domestic price level. The need for similar inflation rates within a fixed-exchange-rate system indicates that a country can successfully join a fixed-exchange-rate system or a region with one money only when its inflation rate falls to a level close to that of other European countries.

Any countries seeking to join the euro area must align their economic policies with those of the other member countries.

glossary

A

absolute advantage - an advantage derived from one country having a lower absolute input cost of producing a particular good than another country.

accounting profit - net operating income.

adaptive expectation - an expectation formed on the basis of information collected in the past.

adverse selection - the situation in which higher-quality goods, consumers, or producers are driven out of the market by lower-quality examples because of limited information about the quality.

aggregate demand curve - a curve that shows the different equilibrium levels of expenditures on domestic output at different levels of prices.

aggregate supply curve - a curve that shows the amount of real GDP produced at different price levels.

antitrust policy - government policies and programs designed to control the growth of monopoly and enhance competition.

appreciate - when the value of a currency increases under floating exchange rates—that is, exchange rates determined by supply and demand.

arc elasticity - price elasticity of demand measured over a range of prices and quantities along the demand curve.

Asian tigers - Hong Kong, Korea, Singapore, and Taiwan, countries that globalized in the 1960s and 1970s and experienced fast economic growth.

association as causation - the mistaken assumption that because two events seem to occur together, one causes the other.

asymmetric information - when the parties to a transaction do not have the same information about the transaction.

automatic stabilizer - an element of fiscal policy that changes automatically as national income changes.

autonomous consumption - consumption that is independent of income.

average fixed cost (AFC) - the total fixed cost divided by total output.

average physical-product (APP) - output per unit of resource.

average propensity to consume (APC) - the proportion of disposable income spent for consumption.

average propensity to save (APS) - the proportion of disposable income saved.

average total cost (ATC) - the per unit cost, derived by dividing total cost by the quantity of output.

average variable cost (AVC) - total variable cost divided by total output.

B

back-end load - a fee that you pay if you sell a mutual fund within a certain time frame.

backward-bending labor supply curve - a labor supply curve indicating that a person is willing and able to work more hours as the wage rate increases until, at some sufficiently high wage rate, the person chooses to work fewer hours.

balance of payments - a record of a country's trade in goods, services, and financial assets with the rest of the world.

balance of trade - the balance in the merchandise account in a nation's balance of payments.

barrier to entry - anything that impedes the ability of firms to begin a new business in an industry in which existing firms are earning positive economic profits.

barter - the direct exchange of goods and services without the use of money.

base year - the year against which other years are measured.

behavioral economics - the study of decision making assuming that people are rational in a broad sense.

bilateral aid - foreign aid that flows from one country to another.

bond - an IOU issued by a borrower to a lender.

bounded rationality - the understanding that perfect information is not likely to be available, and that as a result people make decisions that in hindsight look irrational, but in reality are the rational results of a brain that is economizing.

break-even price - a price that is equal to the minimum point of the average-total-cost curve.

bubble - a situation in which the price of an asset is being bid up through speculation or gambling rather than because of the value of the services the asset returns.

budget deficit - the shortage that results when government spending is greater than tax revenue.

budget line - a line showing all the combinations of goods that can be purchased with a given level of income.

budget surplus - the excess that results when government spending is less than tax revenue.

business cycle - fluctuations in the economy between growth (expressed in rising real GDP) and stagnation (expressed in falling real GDP).

business firm - a business organization controlled by a single management.

C

capital - products such as machinery and equipment that are used in production.

capital consumption allowance - the estimated value of depreciation plus the value of accidental damage to capital stock.

cartel - an organization of independent firms whose purpose is to control and limit production and maintain or increase prices and profits.

cash transfers - money allocated away from one group in society to another.

circular flow diagram - a model showing the flow of output and income from one sector of the economy to another.

classical economics - a school of thought that assumes that real GDP is determined by aggregate supply, while the equilibrium price level is determined by aggregate demand.

club good - a good that is excludable but nonrivalrous.

coincident indicator - a variable that changes as the as real output changes.

commercial bank loan - a bank loan at market rates of interest, often involving a bank syndicate.

commercial policy - government policy that influences international trade flows.

commons good - a good that is rivalrous but nonexcludable.

comparable investment - a stock that has the same features, such as risk and liquidity, as the one that buyers and sellers are evaluating.

comparable worth - the idea that pay ought to be determined by job characteristics rather than by supply and demand, and that people in jobs with comparable requirements should receive comparable wages.

comparative advantage - an advantage derived from comparing he opportunity costs of production in two countries; the ability to produce a good or service at a lower opportunity cost than someone else.

compensating wage differentials - wage differences that make up for the higher risk or poorer working conditions of one job over another.

complementary goods - goods that are used together; as the price of one rises, the demand for the other falls.

composite currency - an artificial unit of account that is an average of the values of several national currencies.

constant returns to scale - unit costs remain constant as the quantity of production is increased and all resources are variable.

consumer price index (CPI) - a measure of the average price of goods and services purchased by the typical household.

consumer sovereignty - the authority of consumers to determine what is produced through their purchases of goods and services.

consumption - household spending.

consumption function - the relationship between disposable income and consumption.

contracting out - the process of enlisting a private firm to provide a product or service for a government entity.

convention - an institution or procedure increasing efficiency.

copayment - paid by an insured person each time the insured service is accessed.

corporation - a legal entity owned by shareholders whose liability for the firm's losses is limited to the value of the stock they own.

cost-of-living adjustment (COLA) - an increase in wages that is designed to match increases in the prices of items purchased by the typical household.

cost-plus/markup pricing - a pricing policy whereby a firm computes its average cost of producing a product and then sets the price at some percentage above this cost.

cost-push inflation - inflation caused by rising costs of production.

coupon - the fixed amount that the issuer of a bond agrees to pay the bondholder each year.

credit - available savings that are lent to borrowers to spend.

cross-price elasticity of demand - the percentage change in the quantity demanded for one good divided by the percentage change in the price of a related good, everything else held constant.

crowding - forcing members of a group into certain kinds of occupations.

crowding out - a drop in consumption or investment spending caused by government spending.

currency substitution - the use of foreign money as a substitute for domestic money when the domestic economy has a high rate of inflation.

current account - the sum of the merchandise, services, income, and unilateral transfers accounts in the balance of payments.

customs union - an organization of nations whose members have no trade barriers among themselves but impose common trade barriers on nonmembers.

D

deadweight loss - the reduction of consumer surplus without a corresponding increase in profit when a perfectly competitive firm is monopolized.

deductible - the amount of expenses that must be paid out of pocket before an insurer will cover any expenses.

deficit - in a balance of payments account, the amount by which debits exceed credits.

demand - the amount of a product that people are willing and able to purchase at each possible price during a given period of time, everything else held constant.

demand curve - a graph of a demand schedule that measures price on the vertical axis and quantity demanded on the horizontal axis.

demand-pull inflation - inflation caused by increasing demand for output.

demand schedule - a table or list of prices and the corresponding quantities demanded for a particular good or service.

dependent variable - a variable whose value depends on the value of the independent variable.

deposit expansion multiplier - the reciprocal of the reserve requirement.

depreciate - when the value of a currency decreases under floating exchange rates.

depreciation - a reduction in the value of capital goods over time as a result of their use in production.

depression - a severe, prolonged economic contraction.

derived demand - demand stemming from what a resource can produce, not demand for the resource itself.

determinants of demand - factors other than the price of the good that influence demand—income, tastes, prices of related goods and services, expectations, and number of buyers.

determinants of supply - factors other than the price of the good that influence supply—prices of resources, technology and productivity, expectations of producers, number of producers, and the prices of related goods and services.

devaluation - a deliberate decrease in the official value of a currency.

diminishing marginal utility - the principle that the more of a good that one obtains in a specific period of time, the less the additional utility yielded by an additional unit of that good.

direct, or positive, relationship - the relationship that exists when the values of related variables move in the same direction.

discount rate - the interest rate that the Fed charges commercial banks when they borrow from it.

discouraged workers - workers who have stopped looking for work because they believe that no one will offer them a job.

discretionary fiscal policy - changes in government spending and taxation that are aimed at achieving a policy goal.

discrimination - prejudice that occurs when factors unrelated to marginal revenue product affect the wages or jobs that are obtained.

diseconomies of scale - the increase in per unit costs as the quantity of production increases and all resources are variable.

disequilibrium - prices at which quantity demanded and quantity supplied are not equal at a particular price.

disparate impact - an impact that differs according to race, sex, color, religion, or national origin, regardless of the motivation.

disparate treatment - different treatment of individuals because of their race, sex, color, religion, or national origin.

disposable personal income (DPI) - personal income minus personal taxes.

dissaving - spending financed by borrowing or using savings.

disutility - dissatisfaction.

dividend - the amount paid to shareholders on each share of stock owned.

dominant strategy - a strategy that produces better results no matter what strategy the opposing firm follows.

double coincidence of wants - the situation that exists when A has what B wants and B has what A wants.

double-entry bookkeeping - a system of accounting in which every transaction is recorded in at least two accounts.

dual economy - an economy in which two sectors (typically manufacturing and agriculture) show very different levels of development.

E

economic bad - any item for which we would pay to have less.

economic efficiency - the situation in which the price of a good or service just covers the marginal cost of producing that good or service and people are getting the goods and services that they want.

economic good - any item that is scarce.

economic growth - an increase in real GDP.

economic profit - accounting profit minus the cost of equity capital.

economic regulation - the prescription of price and output for a specific industry.

economic rent - the portion of earnings above transfer earnings.

economies of scale - the decrease in per unit costs as the quantity of production increases and all resources are variable.

elasticity - the responsiveness of quantity demanded or quantity supplied to a change in one of the determinants of demand and/or supply.

equation of exchange - an equation that relates the quantity of money to nominal GDP.

equilibrium - the price and quantity at which quantity demanded and quantity supplied are equal.

equilibrium exchange rates - the exchange rates that are established in the absence of government foreign exchange market intervention.

equimarginal principle or consumer equilibrium - to maximize utility, consumers must allocate their scarce incomes among goods in such a way as to equate the marginal utility per dollar of expenditure on the last unit of each good purchased.

equity capital - ownership; funds investors or owners put into a firm.

Eurocurrency market or offshore banking - the market for deposits and loans generally denominated in a currency other than the currency of the country in which the transaction occurs.

European currency unit (ECU) - a unit of account formerly used by Western European nations as their official reserve asset.

excess reserves - the cash reserves beyond those required, which can be loaned.

exchange rate - the price of one country's money in terms of another country's money.

export subsidies - payments made by a government to domestic firms to encourage exports.

export substitution - the use of resources to produce manufactured products for export rather than agricultural products for the domestic market.

export supply curve - a curve showing the relationship between the world price of a good and the amount that a country will export.

exports - products that a country sells to other countries.

expropriation - the government seizure of assets, typically without adequate compensation to the owners.

externality - the cost or benefit of a transaction that is borne by someone not directly involved in the transaction.

F

face or *par value* - the amount that the lender will be repaid when a bond matures.

facilitating practices - actions by oligopolistic firms that can contribute to cooperation and collusion even though the firms do not formally agree to cooperate.

fair rate of return - a price that allows a monopoly firm to earn a normal profit.

fallacy of composition - the mistaken assumption that what applies in the case of one applies to the case of many.

Federal Deposit Insurance Corporation (FDIC) - a federal agency that insures deposits in commercial banks.

federal funds rate - the interest rate that a bank charges when it lends excess reserves to another bank.

Federal Open Market Committee (FOMC) - the official policy-making body of the Federal Reserve System.

financial account - the record in the balance of payments of the flow of financial assets into and out of a country.

financial intermediaries - institutions that accept deposits from savers and make loans to borrowers.

FOMC directive - instructions issued by the FOMC to the Federal Reserve Bank of New York to implement monetary policy.

foreign aid - gifts or low-cost loans made to developing countries from official sources.

foreign direct investment - the purchase of a physical operating unit or more than 10 percent ownership of a firm in a foreign country.

foreign exchange - currency and bank deposits that are denominated in foreign money.

foreign exchange market - a global market in which people trade one currency for another.

foreign exchange market intervention - the buying and selling of currencies by a central bank to achieve a specified exchange rate.

fractional reserve banking system - a system in which banks keep less than 100 percent of their deposits available for withdrawal.

free good - a good for which there is no scarcity.

free rider - a consumer or producer who enjoys the benefits of a good or service without paying for that good or service.

free trade area - an organization of nations whose members have no trade barriers among themselves but are free to fashion their own trade policies toward nonmembers.

front-end load - a fee that you pay when you purchase a mutual fund.

fundamental disequilibrium - a permanent shift in the foreign exchange market supply and demand curves such that the fixed exchange rate is no longer an equilibrium rate.

G

gains from trade - the difference between what can be produced and consumed without specialization and trade and with specialization and trade.

game theory - a description of oligopolistic behavior as a series of strategic moves and countermoves.

GDP price index (GDPPI) - a broad measure of the prices of goods and services included in the gross domestic product.

Gini coefficient - a measure of income inequality ranging between 0 and 1; 0 means that all families have the same income; 1 means that one family has all of the income.

global fund - a mutual fund that includes international investments.

gold exchange standard - an exchange-rate system in which each nation fixes the value of its currency in terms of gold, but buys and sells the U.S. dollar rather than gold to maintain fixed exchange rates.

gold standard - a system whereby national currencies are fixed in terms of their value in gold, thus creating fixed exchange rates between currencies.

gross domestic product (GDP) - the market value of all final goods and services produced in a year within a country.

gross investment - total investment, including investment expenditures required to replace capital goods consumed in current production.

gross national product (GNP) - gross domestic product plus receipts of factor income from the rest of the world minus payments of factor income to the rest of the world.

H

hawala - an international informal financial market used by Muslims.

household - one or more persons who occupy a unit of housing.

human capital - skills and training acquired through education and on-the-job training.

hyperinflation - an extremely high rate of inflation.

I

import demand curve - a curve showing the relationship between the world price of a good and the amount that a country will import.

import substitution - the substitution of domestically produced manufactured goods for imported manufactured goods.

imports - products that a country buys from other countries.

in-kind transfers - the allocations of goods and services from one group in society to another.

incidence or tax incidence - the share of a tax paid by consumers and/or producers; determining who pays the larger share is said to bear the incidence of the tax.

income elasticity of demand - the percentage change in the demand for a good divided by the percentage change in income, everything else held constant.

increasing returns - each additional resource adds increasing additional output.

increasing-returns-to-scale industry - an industry in which the costs of producing a unit of output fall as more output is produced.

independent variable - a variable whose value does not depend on the values of other variables.

index fund - a mutual fund that tries to match the performance of a broad market index.

indifference curve - a curve showing all combinations of two goods that the consumer is indifferent among.

indifference map - a complete set of indifference curves.

indifferent - lacking any preference.

indirect business tax - a tax that is collected by businesses for a government agency.

inferior goods - goods for which demand decreases as income increases; goods for which the income elasticity of demand is negative.

inflation - a sustained rise in the average level of prices.

interest rate effect - a change in interest rates that causes investment and therefore aggregate expenditures to change as the level of prices changes.

interest rate parity (IRP) - the condition under which similar financial assets have the same interest rate when measured in the same currency.

intermediate good - a good that is used as an input in the production of final goods and services.

intermediate target - an objective used to achieve some ultimate policy goal.

internalized - when external costs or benefits are borne by the transactors creating them.

international banking facility (IBF) - a division of a U.S. bank that is allowed to receive deposits from and make loans to nonresidents of the United States without the restrictions that apply to domestic U.S. banks.

International Monetary Fund (IMF) - an international organization that supervises exchange-rate arrangements and lends money to member countries that are experiencing problems meeting their external financial obligations.

international reserve asset - an asset used to settle debts between governments.

international reserve currency - a currency held by a government to settle international debts.

international trade effect - a change in aggregate expenditures resulting from a change in the domestic price level that changes the price of domestic goods relative to that of foreign goods.

intraindustry trade - the simultaneous import and export of goods in the same industry by a particular country.

inventory - the stock of unsold goods held by a firm.

inverse, or negative, relationship - the relationship that exists when the values of related variables move in opposite directions.

investment - spending on capital goods to be used in producing goods and services.

K

Keynesian economics - a school of thought that emphasizes the role government plays in stabilizing the economy by managing aggregate demand.

L

labor - the physical and intellectual services of people, including the training, education, and abilities of the individuals in a society.

lagging indicator - a variable that changes after real output changes.

land - all natural resources, such as minerals, timber, and water, as well as the land itself.

law of demand - the quantity of a well-defined good or service that people are willing and able to purchase during a particular period of time decreases as the price of that good or service rises and increases as the price falls, everything else held constant.

law of diminishing marginal returns - when successive equal amounts of a variable resource are combined with a fixed amount of another resource, marginal increases in output that can be attributed to each additional unit of the variable resource will eventually decline.

law of supply - the quantity of a well-defined good or service that producers are willing and able to offer for sale during a particular period of time increases as the price of the good or service increases and decreases as the price decreases, everything else held constant.

leading indicator - a variable that changes real output changes.

legal reserves - the cash a bank holds in its vault plus its deposit in the Fed.

lemons market - market in which adverse selection occurs.

liquid asset - an asset that can easily be exchanged for goods and services.

load - the fees paid to the manager of a mutual fund.

local monopoly - a monopoly that exists in a limited geographic area.

locked in - the cost of changing to a more efficient technology is higher than the benefit.

logrolling - an inefficiency in the political process in which legislators support one another's projects in order to ensure support for their own.

long run - a period of time long enough that the quantities of all resources can be varied.

long-run aggregate supply curve (LRAS) - a vertical line at the potential level of real GDP.

long-run average-total-cost curve - the lowest-cost combination of resources with which each level of output is produced when all resources are variable.

Lorenz curve - a curve measuring the degree of inequality of income distribution within a society.

luxury goods - goods for which the income elasticity of demand is a large positive number.

M

M1 money supply - the financial assets that are the most liquid.

M2 money supply - M1 plus less liquid assets.

macroeconomics - the study of the economy as a whole.

marginal cost (MC) - the change in cost caused by a change in output, derived by dividing the change in total cost by the change in the quantity of output.

marginal cost or marginal opportunity cost - the amount of one good or service that must be given up to obtain one additional unit of another good or service, no matter how many units are being produced.

marginal factor cost (MFC) - the additional cost of an additional unit of a resource.

marginal physical product (MPP) - the additional quantity that is produced when one additional unit of a resource is used in combination with the same quantities of all other resources.

marginal propensity to consume (MPC) - the change in consumption as a proportion of the change in disposable income.

marginal propensity to import (MPI) - the change in imports as a proportion of the change in income.

marginal propensity to save (MPS) - the change in saving as a proportion of the change in disposable income.

marginal revenue product (MRP) - the additional revenue that an additional resource can create for a firm.

marginal utility - the additional utility derived from consuming one more unit of a good or service.

market - a place or service that enables buyers and sellers to exchange goods and services.

market capitalization (market cap) - the stock price multiplied by the number of shares of stock that are outstanding.

market failure - a situation in which resources are not allocated to their highest-valued use.

maturity date - the specified time at which the issuer of a bond will repay the loan.

Medicaid - a joint federal-state program that pays for health care for poor families, the neediest elderly, and disabled persons.

Medicare - a federal health care program for the elderly and the disabled.

microeconomics - the study of economics at the level of the individual.

minimum efficient scale (MES) - the minimum point of the long-run average-total-cost curve; the output level at which the cost per unit of output is the lowest.

mobility - the extent to which people move from one income quintile to another over time.

monetarist economics - a school of thought that emphasizes the role changes in the money supply play in determining equilibrium real GDP and price level.

monetary reform - a new monetary policy that includes the introduction of a new monetary unit.

money - anything that is generally acceptable to sellers in exchange for goods and services.

monopolization - an attempt by a firm to dominate a market or become a monopoly.

monopoly - a market structure in which there is a single supplier of a product.

monopoly firm (monopolist) - a single supplier of a product for which there are no close substitutes.

monopoly power - market power, the ability to set prices.

monopsonist - a firm that is the only buyer of a resource.

moral hazard - the problem that arises when people change their behavior from what was expected of them when they engaged in a trade or contract.

most-favored customer (MFC) - a customer who receives a guarantee of the lowest price and all product features for a certain period of time.

multilateral aid - aid provided by international organizations that are supported by many nations.

multinational business - a firm that owns and operates producing units in foreign countries.

mutual fund - an investment tool that aggregates many different individual stocks or bonds into one entity.

N

Nash equilibrium - no player can be made better off by changing unilaterally.

national income (NI) - net national product plus or minus statistical discrepancy.

national income accounting - the framework that summarizes and categorizes productive activity in an economy over a specific period of time, typically a year.

natural monopoly - a monopoly that arises from economies of scale.

natural rate of unemployment - the unemployment rate that would exist in the absence of cyclical unemployment.

negative economic profit - total revenue is less than total costs, including opportunity costs.

negative income tax (NIT) - a tax system that transfers increasing amounts of income to households earning incomes below some specified level as their income declines.

net exports - the difference between the value of exports and the value of imports.

net investment - gross investment minus capital consumption allowance.

net national product (NNP) - gross national product minus capital consumption allowance.

network externalities - each additional user increases value of entire network.

neuroeconomics - the joint study by economists and biologists that attempts to determine how the brain handles economic decisions.

new classical economics - a school of thought that holds that changes in real GDP are a product of unexpected changes in the level of prices.

NICs - newly industrialized countries.

no-load fund - a mutual fund that sells its shares without a commission or sales charge.

nominal GDP - a measure of national output based on the current prices of goods and services.

nominal interest rate - the observed interest rate in the market.

nonrenewable (exhaustible) natural resources - natural resources whose supply is fixed.

normal goods - goods for which demand increases as income increases; goods for which the income elasticity of demand is positive.

normal profit - the accounting profit that corresponds to a zero economic profit.

normative analysis - analysis of what ought to be.

O

occupational segregation - the separation of jobs by sex.

offshoring - the process in which one firm purchases services from another firm in another country (rather than having the services performed in-house).

open market operations - the buying and selling of government and federal agency bonds by the Fed to control bank reserves, the federal funds rate, and the money supply.

opportunity cost - the highest-valued alternative that must be forgone when a choice is made.

outsourcing - the process in which one firm purchases services from another firm (rather than having the services performed in-house).

P

partnership - a business with two or more owners who share the firm's profits and losses.

per capita real GDP - real GDP divided by the population.

perfectly elastic demand curve - a horizontal demand curve indicating that consumers can and will purchase all they want at one price.

perfectly inelastic demand curve - a vertical demand curve indicating that there is no change in the quantity demanded as the price changes.

personal income (PI) - national income plus income currently received but not earned, minus income currently earned but not received.

Phillips curve - a graph that illustrates the relationship between inflation and the unemployment rate.

point elasticity - price elasticity of demand measured at a single point on the demand curve.

portfolio investment - the purchase of securities.

positive analysis - analysis of what is.

positive economic profit - total revenue in excess of total costs, including opportunity costs.

potential real GDP - the output produced at the natural rate of unemployment.

precautionary demand for money - the demand for money to cover unplanned transactions or emergencies.

price ceiling - a situation in which the price is not allowed to rise above a certain level.

price discrimination - charging different customers different prices for the same product.

price elasticity of demand - the percentage change in the quantity demanded of a product divided by the percentage change in the price of that product.

price elasticity of supply - the percentage change in the quantity supplied divided by the percentage change in price, everything else held constant.

price floor - a situation in which the price is not allowed to decrease below a certain level.

price index - a measure of the average price level in an economy.

price maker - a firm that sets the price of the product it sells.

price taker - a firm in a perfectly competitive market structure.

primary product - a product in the first stage of production, which often serves as an input in the production of another product.

principle of mutual excludability - the rule that an owner of private property is entitled to enjoy the consumption of that property privately.

principle of rivalry - when one consumes or uses a good or service, less remains for others.

private cost - cost that is borne solely by the individuals involved in the transaction that created the costs.

private good - a good that is both excludable and rivalrous.

private property right(s) - the right of ownership; the right of individuals to own property.

private sector - households, businesses, and the international sector.

privatization - transferring a publicly owned enterprise to private ownership.

producer price index (PPI) - a measure of average prices received by producers.

producer surplus - the difference between the price firms would have been willing to accept for their products and the price they actually receive.

production possibilities curve (PPC) - a graphical representation showing all possible combinations of quantities of goods and services that can be produced using the existing resources fully and efficiently.

productivity - the quantity of output produced per unit of resource.

progressive tax - a tax where the rate increases as the base increases; for example, the tax rate rises as income rises income rises.

proportional tax - a tax where the tax rate is constant as the base increases; for example, the tax rate is 20% no matter the level of income; a tax whose rate does not change as the tax base changes.

public good - a good that is nonexcludable and nonrivalrous.

public sector - the government.

purchasing power parity (PPP) - the condition under which monies have the same purchasing power in different markets.

Q

quantitative easing - buying financial assets to stimulate the economy when the central bank target interest rate is near or at zero and the interest rate cannot be lowered further.

quantity demanded - the amount of a product that people are willing and able to purchase at a specific price.

quantity quota - a limit on the amount of a good that may be imported.

quantity supplied - the amount that sellers are willing and able to offer at a given price during a particular period of time, everything else held constant.

quantity theory of money - the theory that, with constant velocity, changes in the quantity of money change nominal GDP.

R

"race to the bottom" - the argument that, with globalization, countries compete for international investment by offering low or no environmental regulations or labor standards.

rational expectation - an expectation that is formed using all available relevant information.

rational self-interest - the means by which people choose the options that give them the greatest amount of satisfaction.

real GDP - a measure of the quantity of final goods and services produced, obtained by eliminating the influence of price changes from the nominal GDP statistics.

real interest rate - the nominal interest rate minus the rate of inflation.

recession - a period in which real GDP falls.

recessionary gap - the increase in expenditures required to reach potential GDP.

regressive tax - a tax where the rate decreases as the base increases; for example, a smaller rate applies to higher income levels than lower income levels.

regulated monopoly - a monopoly firm whose behavior is monitored and prescribed by a government entity.

renewable (nonexhaustible) natural resources - natural resources whose supply can be replenished.

rent seeking - the use of resources simply to transfer wealth from one group to another without increasing production or total wealth.

required reserves - the cash reserves (a percentage of deposits) that a bank must keep on hand or on deposit with the Federal Reserve.

reservation wage - the minimum wage that a worker is willing to accept.

reserve currency - a currency that is used to settle international debts and is held by governments to use in foreign exchange market interventions.

resource market - a market that provides one of the resources for producing goods and services: labor, capital, and land.

resources, factors of production or inputs - goods used to produce other goods, i.e., land, labor, and capital.

ROSCA - a rotating savings and credit association popular in developing countries.

rule of 72 - the number of years required for an amount to double in value is 72 divided by the annual rate of growth.

S

saving function - the relationship between disposable income and saving.

scale - size; all resources change when scale changes.

scarcity - the shortage that exists when less of something is available than is wanted at a zero price.

shock - an unexpected change in a variable.

short run - a period of time short enough that the quantities of at least one of the resources used cannot be varied.

short-run average total cost (*SRATC*) - the total cost of production divided by the total quantity of output produced when at least one resource is fixed.

shortage - a quantity supplied that is smaller than the quantity demanded at a given price; it occurs whenever the price is less than the equilibrium price.

shutdown price - the minimum point of the average-variable-cost curve.

slope - the steepness of a curve, measured as the ratio of the rise to the run.

social cost - the total cost of a transaction, the private cost plus the external cost.

social regulation - the prescription of health, safety, performance, and environmental standards that apply across several industries.

socially responsible fund - a group of stocks or bonds of companies that meet specified requirements for ethical behavior or environmental behavior.

sole proprietorship - a business owned by one person who receives all the profits and is responsible for all the debts incurred by the business.

special drawing right (SDR) - a composite currency whose value is the average of the values of the U.S. dollar, the euro, the Japanese yen, and the U.K. pound.

specific fund - a mutual fund that focuses on a particular industry or a particular part of the world.

speculative attack - a situation in which private investors sell domestic currency and buy foreign currency, betting that the domestic currency will be devalued.

speculative demand for money - the demand for money created by uncertainty about the value of other assets.

speculators - people who seek to profit from an expected shift in an exchange rate by selling the currency that is expected to depreciate and buying the currency that is expected to appreciate, then exchanging the appreciated currency for the depreciated currency after the exchange-rate adjustment.

spending multiplier - a measure of the change in equilibrium income or real GDP produced by a change in autonomous expenditures.

statistical discrimination - discrimination that results when an indicator of group performance is incorrectly applied to an individual member of the group.

sterilization - the use of domestic open market operations to offset the effects of a foreign exchange market intervention on the domestic money supply.

stranded assets - assets acquired by a firm when it was regulated that have little value when the firm is deregulated.

strategic behavior - the behavior that occurs when what is best for A depends on what B does, and what is best for B depends on what A does.

strategic trade policy - the use of trade restrictions or subsidies to allow domestic firms with decreasing costs to gain a greater share of the world market.

substitute goods - goods that can be used in place of each other; as the price of one rises, the demand for the other rises.

supply - the amount of a good or service that producers are willing and able to offer for sale at each possible price during a period of time, everything else held constant.

supply curve - a graph of a supply schedule that measures price on the vertical axis and quantity supplied on the horizontal axis.

supply schedule - a table or list of prices and the corresponding quantities supplied of a particular good or service.

surplus - a quantity supplied that is larger than the quantity demanded at a given price; it occurs whenever the price is greater than the equilibrium price; in a balance of payments account, the amount by which credits exceed debits.

T

tariff - a tax on imports or exports.

technology - ways of combining resources to produce output.

terms of trade - the amount of an exported good that must be given up to obtain an imported good.

time inconsistent - a characteristic of a policy or plan that changes over time in response to changing conditions.

total costs (*TC*) - the expenses that a business has in supplying goods and/or services.

total factor productivity (*TFP*) - the ratio of the economy's output to its stock of labor and capital.

total fixed costs (*TFC*) - payments to resources whose quantities cannot be changed during a fixed period of time—the short run.

total physical product (*TPP*) - the maximum output that can be produced when successive units of a variable resource are added to fixed amounts of other resources.

total utility - a measure of the total satisfaction derived from consuming a quantity of some good or service.

total variable costs (*TVC*) - payments for additional resources used as output increases.

trade creation - an effect of a preferential trade agreement that allows a country to obtain goods at a lower cost than is available at home.

trade credit - allowing an importer a period of time before it must pay for goods or services purchased.

trade deficit - the situation that exists when imports exceed exports.

trade diversion - an effect of a preferential trade agreement that reduces economic efficiency by shifting production to a higher cost producer.

trade surplus - the situation that exists when imports are less than exports.

trade-off - the giving up of one good or activity in order to obtain some other good or activity.

transactions account - a checking account at a bank or other financial institution that can be drawn on to make payments.

transactions costs - the cost of carrying out a transaction.

transactions demand for money - the demand to hold money to buy goods and services.

transfer earnings - the amount that must be paid to a resource owner to get him or her to allocate the resource to another use.

transfer payment(s) - income transferred by the government from a citizen who is earning income to another citizen; a payment to one person that is funded by taxing others.

U

underemployment - the employment of workers in jobs that do not utilize their productive potential.

unemployment rate - the percentage of the labor force that is not working.

utility - a measure of the satisfaction received from possessing or consuming goods and services.

V

value added - the difference between the value of output and the value of the intermediate goods used in the production of that output.

value quota - a limit on the monetary value of a good that may be imported.

value-added tax (VAT) - a general sales tax collected at each stage of production.

velocity of money - the average number of times each dollar is spent on final goods and services in a year.

W

wealth - the value of all assets owned by a household.

wealth effect - a change in the real value of wealth that causes spending to change when the level of prices changes.

World Bank - an international organization that makes loans and provides technical expertise to developing countries.

Z

zero economic profit - total revenue equal to total costs, including opportunity costs.

zero-coupon bond - a bond that provides no interest payments but is issued at a value lower than its face value.

index

U.S. Macroeconomic Data for Selected Years, 1965–2011

Year	Real GDP	Consumption	Investment	Government Spending	Net Exports	GDP Growth Rate
			$ billions			%
1965	3,392.3	2,241.8	437.3	1,086.4	−18.9	6.4
1970	4,269.9	2,740.2	475.1	1,212.4	−52.0	0.2
1975	4,879.5	3,214.1	504.1	1,268.4	−2.4	−0.2
1976	5,141.3	3,393.1	605.9	1,249.7	−37.0	5.3
1977	5,377.7	3,535.9	697.4	1,272.3	−61.1	4.6
1978	5,677.6	3,691.8	781.5	1,331.2	−61.9	5.6
1979	5,855.0	3,779.5	806.4	1,343.8	−41.0	3.2
1980	5,839.0	3,766.2	717.9	1,349.4	12.6	−0.2
1981	5,987.2	3,823.3	782.4	1,379.9	8.3	2.5
1982	5,870.9	3,876.7	672.8	1,420.1	−12.6	−1.9
1983	6,136.2	4,098.3	735.5	1,443.2	−60.2	4.5
1984	6,577.1	4,315.6	952.1	1,532.3	−122.4	7.2
1985	6,849.3	4,540.4	943.3	1,635.5	−141.5	4.1
1986	7,086.5	4,724.5	936.9	1,716.6	−156.3	3.5
1987	7,313.3	4,870.3	965.7	1,755.6	−148.4	3.4
1988	7,613.9	5,066.6	988.5	1,786.2	−106.8	4.1
1989	7,885.9	5,209.9	1,028.1	1,829.4	−79.2	3.5
1990	8,033.9	5,316.2	993.5	1,859.8	−54.7	1.9
1991	8,015.1	5,324.2	912.7	1,875.6	−14.6	−0.2
1992	8,287.1	5,505.7	986.7	1,897.9	−15.9	3.3
1993	8,523.4	5,701.2	1,074.8	1,883.9	−52.1	2.7
1994	8,870.7	5,918.9	1,220.9	1,884.1	−79.4	4.0
1995	9,093.7	6,079.0	1,258.9	1,872.5	−81.53	2.5
1996	9,433.9	6,291.2	1,370.3	1,925.9	−101.61	3.7
1997	9,854.3	6,523.4	1,540.8	1,951.5	−169.26	4.5
1998	10,283.5	6,865.5	1,659.1	2,018.1	−276.28	4.2
1999	10,779.8	7,240.9	1,844.3	2,095.9	−381.98	4.5
2000	11,226.0	7,608.1	1,970.3	2,099.8	−475.28	3.7
2001	11,347.2	7,813.9	1,831.9	2,216.4	−488.39	0.8
2002	11,553.0	8,021.9	1,807.0	2,305.7	−595.20	1.6
2003	11,840.7	8,247.6	1,871.6	2,343.7	−614.30	2.7
2004	12,263.8	8,532.7	2,058.2	2,357.6	−726.63	4.2
2005	12,638.4	8,819.0	2,172.2	2,283.9	−745.44	3.5
2006	12,976.4	9,073.50	2,230.4	2,409.4	−694.70	2.70
2007	13,228.9	9,289.50	2,161.6	2,455.3	−564.60	1.90
2008	13,228.2	9,265.00	1,957.3	2,520.5	−478.00	0.00
2009	12,880.6	9,153.90	1,515.7	2,548.5	−346.86	−2.60
2010	13,248.7	9,315.70	1,708.0	2,570.1	−414.20	2.80
2011*	12,260.3	9,430.00	1,769.0	2,570.1	−414.20	2.80

*Values are estimates